Lecture Notes in Computer Science 13434

More information about this series at https://link.springer.com/bookseries/558

Linwei Wang · Qi Dou · P. Thomas Fletcher ·
Stefanie Speidel · Shuo Li (Eds.)

Medical Image Computing and Computer Assisted Intervention – MICCAI 2022

25th International Conference
Singapore, September 18–22, 2022
Proceedings, Part IV

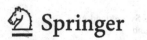

Springer

Editors
Linwei Wang
Rochester Institute of Technology
Rochester, NY, USA

Qi Dou (ID)
Chinese University of Hong Kong
Hong Kong, Hong Kong

P. Thomas Fletcher (ID)
University of Virginia
Charlottesville, VA, USA

Stefanie Speidel (ID)
National Center for Tumor Diseases
(NCT/UCC)
Dresden, Germany

Shuo Li (ID)
Case Western Reserve University
Cleveland, OH, USA

ISSN 0302-9743   ISSN 1611-3349 (electronic)
Lecture Notes in Computer Science
ISBN 978-3-031-16439-2   ISBN 978-3-031-16440-8 (eBook)
https://doi.org/10.1007/978-3-031-16440-8

This Springer imprint is published by the registered company Springer Nature Switzerland AG
The registered company address is: Gewerbestrasse 11, 6330 Cham, Switzerland

in the acceptance of a total of 574 papers, reaching an overall acceptance rate of 31% for MICCAI 2022.

In our additional effort to ensure review quality, two Reviewer Tutorials and two Area Chair Orientations were held in early March, virtually in different time zones, to introduce the reviewers and area chairs to the MICCAI 2022 review process and the best practice for high-quality reviews. Two additional Area Chair meetings were held virtually in July to inform the area chairs of the outcome of the review process and to collect feedback for future conferences.

For the MICCAI 2022 proceedings, 574 accepted papers were organized in eight volumes as follows:

- Part I, LNCS Volume 13431: Brain Development and Atlases, DWI and Tractography, Functional Brain Networks, Neuroimaging, Heart and Lung Imaging, and Dermatology
- Part II, LNCS Volume 13432: Computational (Integrative) Pathology, Computational Anatomy and Physiology, Ophthalmology, and Fetal Imaging
- Part III, LNCS Volume 13433: Breast Imaging, Colonoscopy, and Computer Aided Diagnosis
- Part IV, LNCS Volume 13434: Microscopic Image Analysis, Positron Emission Tomography, Ultrasound Imaging, Video Data Analysis, and Image Segmentation I
- Part V, LNCS Volume 13435: Image Segmentation II and Integration of Imaging with Non-imaging Biomarkers
- Part VI, LNCS Volume 13436: Image Registration and Image Reconstruction
- Part VII, LNCS Volume 13437: Image-Guided Interventions and Surgery, Outcome and Disease Prediction, Surgical Data Science, Surgical Planning and Simulation, and Machine Learning – Domain Adaptation and Generalization
- Part VIII, LNCS Volume 13438: Machine Learning – Weakly-supervised Learning, Machine Learning – Model Interpretation, Machine Learning – Uncertainty, and Machine Learning Theory and Methodologies

We would like to thank everyone who contributed to the success of MICCAI 2022 and the quality of its proceedings. These include the MICCAI Society for support and feedback, and our sponsors for their financial support and presence onsite. We especially express our gratitude to the MICCAI Submission System Manager Kitty Wong for her thorough support throughout the paper submission, review, program planning, and proceeding preparation process – the Program Committee simply would not have be able to function without her. We are also grateful for the dedication and support of all of the organizers of the workshops, tutorials, and challenges, Jianming Liang, Wufeng Xue, Jun Cheng, Qian Tao, Xi Chen, Islem Rekik, Sophia Bano, Andrea Lara, Yunliang Cai, Pingkun Yan, Pallavi Tiwari, Ingerid Reinertsen, Gongning Luo, without whom the exciting peripheral events would have not been feasible. Behind the scenes, the MICCAI secretariat personnel, Janette Wallace and Johanne Langford, kept a close eye on logistics and budgets, while Mehmet Eldegez and his team from Dekon Congress & Tourism, MICCAI 2022's Professional Conference Organization, managed the website and local organization. We are especially grateful to all members of the Program Committee for

Preface

We are pleased to present the proceedings of the 25th International Conference on Medical Image Computing and Computer-Assisted Intervention (MICCAI) which – after two difficult years of virtual conferences – was held in a hybrid fashion at the Resort World Convention Centre in Singapore, September 18–22, 2022. The conference also featured 36 workshops, 11 tutorials, and 38 challenges held on September 18 and September 22. The conference was also co-located with the 2nd Conference on Clinical Translation on Medical Image Computing and Computer-Assisted Intervention (CLINICCAI) on September 20.

MICCAI 2022 had an approximately 14% increase in submissions and accepted papers compared with MICCAI 2021. These papers, which comprise eight volumes of Lecture Notes in Computer Science (LNCS) proceedings, were selected after a thorough double-blind peer-review process. Following the example set by the previous program chairs of past MICCAI conferences, we employed Microsoft's Conference Managing Toolkit (CMT) for paper submissions and double-blind peer-reviews, and the Toronto Paper Matching System (TPMS) to assist with automatic paper assignment to area chairs and reviewers.

From 2811 original intentions to submit, 1865 full submissions were received and 1831 submissions reviewed. Of these, 67% were considered as pure Medical Image Computing (MIC), 7% as pure Computer-Assisted Interventions (CAI), and 26% as both MIC and CAI. The MICCAI 2022 Program Committee (PC) comprised 107 area chairs, with 52 from the Americas, 33 from Europe, and 22 from the Asia-Pacific or Middle East regions. We maintained gender balance with 37% women scientists on the PC.

Each area chair was assigned 16–18 manuscripts, for each of which they were asked to suggest up to 15 suggested potential reviewers. Subsequently, over 1320 invited reviewers were asked to bid for the papers for which they had been suggested. Final reviewer allocations via CMT took account of PC suggestions, reviewer bidding, and TPMS scores, finally allocating 4–6 papers per reviewer. Based on the double-blinded reviews, area chairs' recommendations, and program chairs' global adjustments, 249 papers (14%) were provisionally accepted, 901 papers (49%) were provisionally rejected, and 675 papers (37%) proceeded into the rebuttal stage.

During the rebuttal phase, two additional area chairs were assigned to each rebuttal paper using CMT and TPMS scores. After the authors' rebuttals were submitted, all reviewers of the rebuttal papers were invited to assess the rebuttal, participate in a double-blinded discussion with fellow reviewers and area chairs, and finalize their rating (with the opportunity to revise their rating as appropriate). The three area chairs then independently provided their recommendations to accept or reject the paper, considering the manuscript, the reviews, and the rebuttal. The final decision of acceptance was based on majority voting of the area chair recommendations. The program chairs reviewed all decisions and provided their inputs in extreme cases where a large divergence existed between the area chairs and reviewers in their recommendations. This process resulted their diligent work in the reviewer assignments and final paper selection, as well as the reviewers for their support during the entire process. Finally, and most importantly, we thank all authors, co-authors, students/postdocs, and supervisors, for submitting and presenting their high-quality work which made MICCAI 2022 a successful event.

We look forward to seeing you in Vancouver, Canada at MICCAI 2023!

September 2022

Linwei Wang
Qi Dou
P. Thomas Fletcher
Stefanie Speidel
Shuo Li

Organization

General Chair

Shuo Li   Case Western Reserve University, USA

Program Committee Chairs

Linwei Wang   Rochester Institute of Technology, USA
Qi Dou   The Chinese University of Hong Kong, China
P. Thomas Fletcher   University of Virginia, USA
Stefanie Speidel   National Center for Tumor Diseases Dresden,
                                    Germany

Workshop Team

Wufeng Xue   Shenzhen University, China
Jun Cheng   Agency for Science, Technology and Research,
                                    Singapore
Qian Tao   Delft University of Technology, the Netherlands
Xi Chen   Stern School of Business, NYU, USA

Challenges Team

Pingkun Yan   Rensselaer Polytechnic Institute, USA
Pallavi Tiwari   Case Western Reserve University, USA
Ingerid Reinertsen   SINTEF Digital and NTNU, Trondheim, Norway
Gongning Luo   Harbin Institute of Technology, China

Tutorial Team

Islem Rekik   Istanbul Technical University, Turkey
Sophia Bano   University College London, UK
Andrea Lara   Universidad Industrial de Santander, Colombia
Yunliang Cai   Humana, USA

Clinical Day Chairs

Jason Chan   The Chinese University of Hong Kong, China
Heike I. Grabsch   University of Leeds, UK and Maastricht
                                University, the Netherlands
Nicolas Padoy   University of Strasbourg & Institute of
                                Image-Guided Surgery, IHU Strasbourg,
                                France

Young Investigators and Early Career Development Program Chairs

Marius Linguraru   Children's National Institute, USA
Antonio Porras   University of Colorado Anschutz Medical
                               Campus, USA
Nicole Rieke   NVIDIA, Deutschland
Daniel Racoceanu   Sorbonne University, France

Social Media Chairs

Chenchu Xu   Anhui University, China
Dong Zhang   University of British Columbia, Canada

Student Board Liaison

Camila Bustillo   Technische Universität Darmstadt, Germany
Vanessa Gonzalez Duque   Ecole centrale de Nantes, France

Submission Platform Manager

Kitty Wong   The MICCAI Society, Canada

Virtual Platform Manager

John Baxter   INSERM, Université de Rennes 1, France

Program Committee

Ehsan Adeli   Stanford University, USA
Pablo Arbelaez   Universidad de los Andes, Colombia
John Ashburner   University College London, UK
Ulas Bagci   Northwestern University, USA
Sophia Bano   University College London, UK
Adrien Bartoli   Université Clermont Auvergne, France
Kayhan Batmanghelich   University of Pittsburgh, USA

Hrvoje Bogunovic   Medical University of Vienna, Austria
Ester Bonmati   University College London, UK
Esther Bron   Erasmus MC, the Netherlands
Gustavo Carneiro   University of Adelaide, Australia
Hao Chen   Hong Kong University of Science and
                               Technology, China
Jun Cheng   Agency for Science, Technology and Research,
                               Singapore
Li Cheng   University of Alberta, Canada
Adrian Dalca   Massachusetts Institute of Technology, USA
Jose Dolz   ETS Montreal, Canada
Shireen Elhabian   University of Utah, USA
Sandy Engelhardt   University Hospital Heidelberg, Germany
Ruogu Fang   University of Florida, USA
Aasa Feragen   Technical University of Denmark, Denmark
Moti Freiman   Technion - Israel Institute of Technology, Israel
Huazhu Fu   Agency for Science, Technology and Research,
                               Singapore
Mingchen Gao   University at Buffalo, SUNY, USA
Zhifan Gao   Sun Yat-sen University, China
Stamatia Giannarou   Imperial College London, UK
Alberto Gomez   King's College London, UK
Ilker Hacihaliloglu   University of British Columbia, Canada
Adam Harrison   PAII Inc., USA
Mattias Heinrich   University of Lübeck, Germany
Yipeng Hu   University College London, UK
Junzhou Huang   University of Texas at Arlington, USA
Sharon Xiaolei Huang   Pennsylvania State University, USA
Yuankai Huo   Vanderbilt University, USA
Jayender Jagadeesan   Brigham and Women's Hospital, USA
Won-Ki Jeong   Korea University, Korea
Xi Jiang   University of Electronic Science and Technology
                               of China, China
Anand Joshi   University of Southern California, USA
Shantanu Joshi   University of California, Los Angeles, USA
Bernhard Kainz   Imperial College London, UK
Marta Kersten-Oertel   Concordia University, Canada
Fahmi Khalifa   Mansoura University, Egypt
Seong Tae Kim   Kyung Hee University, Korea
Minjeong Kim   University of North Carolina at Greensboro, USA
Baiying Lei   Shenzhen University, China
Gang Li   University of North Carolina at Chapel Hill, USA

Xiaoxiao Li	University of British Columbia, Canada
Jianming Liang	Arizona State University, USA
Herve Lombaert	ETS Montreal, Canada
Marco Lorenzi	Inria Sophia Antipolis, France
Le Lu	Alibaba USA Inc., USA
Klaus Maier-Hein	German Cancer Research Center (DKFZ), Germany
Anne Martel	Sunnybrook Research Institute, Canada
Diana Mateus	Centrale Nantes, France
Mehdi Moradi	IBM Research, USA
Hien Nguyen	University of Houston, USA
Mads Nielsen	University of Copenhagen, Denmark
Ilkay Oksuz	Istanbul Technical University, Turkey
Tingying Peng	Helmholtz Zentrum Muenchen, Germany
Caroline Petitjean	Université de Rouen, France
Gemma Piella	Universitat Pompeu Fabra, Spain
Chen Qin	University of Edinburgh, UK
Hedyeh Rafii-Tari	Auris Health Inc., USA
Tammy Riklin Raviv	Ben-Gurion University of the Negev, Israel
Hassan Rivaz	Concordia University, Canada
Michal Rosen-Zvi	IBM Research, Israel
Su Ruan	University of Rouen, France
Thomas Schultz	University of Bonn, Germany
Sharmishtaa Seshamani	Allen Institute, USA
Feng Shi	United Imaging Intelligence, China
Yonggang Shi	University of Southern California, USA
Yang Song	University of New South Wales, Australia
Rachel Sparks	King's College London, UK
Carole Sudre	University College London, UK
Tanveer Syeda-Mahmood	IBM Research, USA
Qian Tao	Delft University of Technology, the Netherlands
Tolga Tasdizen	University of Utah, USA
Pallavi Tiwari	Case Western Reserve University, USA
Mathias Unberath	Johns Hopkins University, USA
Martin Urschler	University of Auckland, New Zealand
Maria Vakalopoulou	University of Paris Saclay, France
Harini Veeraraghavan	Memorial Sloan Kettering Cancer Center, USA
Satish Viswanath	Case Western Reserve University, USA
Christian Wachinger	Technical University of Munich, Germany
Hua Wang	Colorado School of Mines, USA
Hongzhi Wang	IBM Research, USA
Ken C. L. Wong	IBM Almaden Research Center, USA

Fuyong Xing   University of Colorado Denver, USA
Ziyue Xu   NVIDIA, USA
Yanwu Xu   Baidu Inc., China
Pingkun Yan   Rensselaer Polytechnic Institute, USA
Guang Yang   Imperial College London, UK
Jianhua Yao   Tencent, China
Zhaozheng Yin   Stony Brook University, USA
Lequan Yu   University of Hong Kong, China
Yixuan Yuan   City University of Hong Kong, China
Ling Zhang   Alibaba Group, USA
Miaomiao Zhang   University of Virginia, USA
Ya Zhang   Shanghai Jiao Tong University, China
Rongchang Zhao   Central South University, China
Yitian Zhao   Chinese Academy of Sciences, China
Yefeng Zheng   Tencent Jarvis Lab, China
Guoyan Zheng   Shanghai Jiao Tong University, China
Luping Zhou   University of Sydney, Australia
Yuyin Zhou   Stanford University, USA
Dajiang Zhu   University of Texas at Arlington, USA
Lilla Zöllei   Massachusetts General Hospital, USA
Maria A. Zuluaga   EURECOM, France

Reviewers

Alireza Akhondi-asl   Manas Nag
Fernando Arambula   Tianye Niu
Nicolas Boutry   Seokhwan Oh
Qilei Chen   Theodoros Pissas
Zhihao Chen   Harish RaviPrakash
Javid Dadashkarimi   Maria Sainz de Cea
Marleen De Bruijne   Hai Su
Mohammad Eslami   Wenjun Tan
Sayan Ghosal   Fatmatulzehra Uslu
Estibaliz Gómez-de-Mariscal   Fons van der Sommen
Charles Hatt   Gijs van Tulder
Yongxiang Huang   Dong Wei
Samra Irshad   Pengcheng Xi
Anithapriya Krishnan   Chen Yang
Rodney LaLonde   Kun Yuan
Jie Liu   Hang Zhang
Jinyang Liu   Wei Zhang
Qing Lyu   Yuyao Zhang
Hassan Mohy-ud-Din   Tengda Zhao

Yingying Zhu
Yuemin Zhu
Alaa Eldin Abdelaal
Amir Abdi
Mazdak Abulnaga
Burak Acar
Iman Aganj
Priya Aggarwal
Ola Ahmad
Seyed-Ahmad Ahmadi
Euijoon Ahn
Faranak Akbarifar
Cem Akbaş
Saad Ullah Akram
Tajwar Aleef
Daniel Alexander
Hazrat Ali
Sharib Ali
Max Allan
Pablo Alvarez
Vincent Andrearczyk
Elsa Angelini
Sameer Antani
Michela Antonelli
Ignacio Arganda-Carreras
Mohammad Ali Armin
Josep Arnal
Md Ashikuzzaman
Mehdi Astaraki
Marc Aubreville
Chloé Audigier
Angelica Aviles-Rivero
Ruqayya Awan
Suyash Awate
Qinle Ba
Morteza Babaie
Meritxell Bach Cuadra
Hyeon-Min Bae
Junjie Bai
Wenjia Bai
Ujjwal Baid
Pradeep Bajracharya
Yaël Balbastre
Abhirup Banerjee
Sreya Banerjee

Shunxing Bao
Adrian Barbu
Sumana Basu
Deepti Bathula
Christian Baumgartner
John Baxter
Sharareh Bayat
Bahareh Behboodi
Hamid Behnam
Sutanu Bera
Christos Bergeles
Jose Bernal
Gabriel Bernardino
Alaa Bessadok
Riddhish Bhalodia
Indrani Bhattacharya
Chitresh Bhushan
Lei Bi
Qi Bi
Gui-Bin Bian
Alexander Bigalke
Ricardo Bigolin Lanfredi
Benjamin Billot
Ryoma Bise
Sangeeta Biswas
Stefano B. Blumberg
Sebastian Bodenstedt
Bhushan Borotikar
Ilaria Boscolo Galazzo
Behzad Bozorgtabar
Nadia Brancati
Katharina Breininger
Rupert Brooks
Tom Brosch
Mikael Brudfors
Qirong Bu
Ninon Burgos
Nikolay Burlutskiy
Michał Byra
Ryan Cabeen
Mariano Cabezas
Hongmin Cai
Jinzheng Cai
Weidong Cai
Sema Candemir

Qing Cao
Weiguo Cao
Yankun Cao
Aaron Carass
Ruben Cardenes
M. Jorge Cardoso
Owen Carmichael
Alessandro Casella
Matthieu Chabanas
Ahmad Chaddad
Jayasree Chakraborty
Sylvie Chambon
Yi Hao Chan
Ming-Ching Chang
Peng Chang
Violeta Chang
Sudhanya Chatterjee
Christos Chatzichristos
Antong Chen
Chao Chen
Chen Chen
Cheng Chen
Dongdong Chen
Fang Chen
Geng Chen
Hanbo Chen
Jianan Chen
Jianxu Chen
Jie Chen
Junxiang Chen
Junying Chen
Junyu Chen
Lei Chen
Li Chen
Liangjun Chen
Liyun Chen
Min Chen
Pingjun Chen
Qiang Chen
Runnan Chen
Shuai Chen
Xi Chen
Xiaoran Chen
Xin Chen
Xinjian Chen

Xuejin Chen
Yuanyuan Chen
Zhaolin Chen
Zhen Chen
Zhineng Chen
Zhixiang Chen
Erkang Cheng
Jianhong Cheng
Jun Cheng
Philip Chikontwe
Min-Kook Choi
Gary Christensen
Argyrios Christodoulidis
Stergios Christodoulidis
Albert Chung
Özgün Çiçek
Matthew Clarkson
Dana Cobzas
Jaume Coll-Font
Toby Collins
Olivier Commowick
Runmin Cong
Yulai Cong
Pierre-Henri Conze
Timothy Cootes
Teresa Correia
Pierrick Coupé
Hadrien Courtecuisse
Jeffrey Craley
Alessandro Crimi
Can Cui
Hejie Cui
Hui Cui
Zhiming Cui
Kathleen Curran
Claire Cury
Tobias Czempiel
Vedrana Dahl
Tareen Dawood
Laura Daza
Charles Delahunt
Herve Delingette
Ugur Demir
Liang-Jian Deng
Ruining Deng

Rongjun Ge
Sairam Geethanath
Shiv Gehlot
Yasmeen George
Nils Gessert
Olivier Gevaert
Ramtin Gharleghi
Sandesh Ghimire
Andrea Giovannini
Gabriel Girard
Rémi Giraud
Ben Glocker
Ehsan Golkar
Arnold Gomez
Ricardo Gonzales
Camila Gonzalez
Cristina González
German Gonzalez
Sharath Gopal
Karthik Gopinath
Pietro Gori
Michael Götz
Shuiping Gou
Maged Goubran
Sobhan Goudarzi
Alejandro Granados
Mara Graziani
Yun Gu
Zaiwang Gu
Hao Guan
Dazhou Guo
Hengtao Guo
Jixiang Guo
Jun Guo
Pengfei Guo
Xiaoqing Guo
Yi Guo
Yuyu Guo
Vikash Gupta
Prashnna Gyawali
Stathis Hadjidemetriou
Fatemeh Haghighi
Justin Haldar
Mohammad Hamghalam
Kamal Hammouda

Bing Han
Liang Han
Seungjae Han
Xiaoguang Han
Zhongyi Han
Jonny Hancox
Lasse Hansen
Huaying Hao
Jinkui Hao
Xiaoke Hao
Mohammad Minhazul Haq
Nandinee Haq
Rabia Haq
Michael Hardisty
Nobuhiko Hata
Ali Hatamizadeh
Andreas Hauptmann
Huiguang He
Nanjun He
Shenghua He
Yuting He
Tobias Heimann
Stefan Heldmann
Sobhan Hemati
Alessa Hering
Monica Hernandez
Estefania Hernandez-Martin
Carlos Hernandez-Matas
Javier Herrera-Vega
Kilian Hett
David Ho
Yi Hong
Yoonmi Hong
Mohammad Reza Hosseinzadeh Taher
Benjamin Hou
Wentai Hou
William Hsu
Dan Hu
Rongyao Hu
Xiaoling Hu
Xintao Hu
Yan Hu
Ling Huang
Sharon Xiaolei Huang
Xiaoyang Huang

Yangsibo Huang
Yi-Jie Huang
Yijin Huang
Yixing Huang
Yue Huang
Zhi Huang
Ziyi Huang
Arnaud Huaulmé
Jiayu Huo
Raabid Hussain
Sarfaraz Hussein
Khoi Huynh
Seong Jae Hwang
Ilknur Icke
Kay Igwe
Abdullah Al Zubaer Imran
Ismail Irmakci
Benjamin Irving
Mohammad Shafkat Islam
Koichi Ito
Hayato Itoh
Yuji Iwahori
Mohammad Jafari
Andras Jakab
Amir Jamaludin
Mirek Janatka
Vincent Jaouen
Uditha Jarayathne
Ronnachai Jaroensri
Golara Javadi
Rohit Jena
Rachid Jennane
Todd Jensen
Debesh Jha
Ge-Peng Ji
Yuanfeng Ji
Zhanghexuan Ji
Haozhe Jia
Meirui Jiang
Tingting Jiang
Xiajun Jiang
Xiang Jiang
Zekun Jiang
Jianbo Jiao
Jieqing Jiao

Zhicheng Jiao
Chen Jin
Dakai Jin
Qiangguo Jin
Taisong Jin
Yueming Jin
Baoyu Jing
Bin Jing
Yaqub Jonmohamadi
Lie Ju
Yohan Jun
Alain Jungo
Manjunath K N
Abdolrahim Kadkhodamohammadi
Ali Kafaei Zad Tehrani
Dagmar Kainmueller
Siva Teja Kakileti
John Kalafut
Konstantinos Kamnitsas
Michael C. Kampffmeyer
Qingbo Kang
Neerav Karani
Turkay Kart
Satyananda Kashyap
Alexander Katzmann
Anees Kazi
Hengjin Ke
Hamza Kebiri
Erwan Kerrien
Hoel Kervadec
Farzad Khalvati
Bishesh Khanal
Pulkit Khandelwal
Maksim Kholiavchenko
Ron Kikinis
Daeseung Kim
Jae-Hun Kim
Jaeil Kim
Jinman Kim
Won Hwa Kim
Andrew King
Atilla Kiraly
Yoshiro Kitamura
Stefan Klein
Tobias Klinder

Lisa Koch
Satoshi Kondo
Bin Kong
Fanwei Kong
Ender Konukoglu
Aishik Konwer
Bongjin Koo
Ivica Kopriva
Kivanc Kose
Anna Kreshuk
Frithjof Kruggel
Thomas Kuestner
David Kügler
Hugo Kuijf
Arjan Kuijper
Kuldeep Kumar
Manuela Kunz
Holger Kunze
Tahsin Kurc
Anvar Kurmukov
Yoshihiro Kuroda
Jin Tae Kwak
Francesco La Rosa
Aymen Laadhari
Dmitrii Lachinov
Alain Lalande
Bennett Landman
Axel Largent
Carole Lartizien
Max-Heinrich Laves
Ho Hin Lee
Hyekyoung Lee
Jong Taek Lee
Jong-Hwan Lee
Soochahn Lee
Wen Hui Lei
Yiming Lei
Rogers Jeffrey Leo John
Juan Leon
Bo Li
Bowen Li
Chen Li
Hongming Li
Hongwei Li
Jian Li

Jianning Li
Jiayun Li
Jieyu Li
Junhua Li
Kang Li
Lei Li
Mengzhang Li
Qing Li
Quanzheng Li
Shaohua Li
Shulong Li
Weijian Li
Weikai Li
Wenyuan Li
Xiang Li
Xingyu Li
Xiu Li
Yang Li
Yuexiang Li
Yunxiang Li
Zeju Li
Zhang Li
Zhiyuan Li
Zhjin Li
Zi Li
Chunfeng Lian
Sheng Lian
Libin Liang
Peixian Liang
Yuan Liang
Haofu Liao
Hongen Liao
Ruizhi Liao
Wei Liao
Xiangyun Liao
Gilbert Lim
Hongxiang Lin
Jianyu Lin
Li Lin
Tiancheng Lin
Yiqun Lin
Zudi Lin
Claudia Lindner
Bin Liu
Bo Liu

Chuanbin Liu
Daochang Liu
Dong Liu
Dongnan Liu
Fenglin Liu
Han Liu
Hao Liu
Haozhe Liu
Hong Liu
Huafeng Liu
Huiye Liu
Jianfei Liu
Jiang Liu
Jingya Liu
Kefei Liu
Lihao Liu
Mengting Liu
Peirong Liu
Peng Liu
Qin Liu
Qun Liu
Shenghua Liu
Shuangjun Liu
Sidong Liu
Tianrui Liu
Xiao Liu
Xingtong Liu
Xinwen Liu
Xinyang Liu
Xinyu Liu
Yan Liu
Yanbei Liu
Yi Liu
Yikang Liu
Yong Liu
Yue Liu
Yuhang Liu
Zewen Liu
Zhe Liu
Andrea Loddo
Nicolas Loménie
Yonghao Long
Zhongjie Long
Daniel Lopes
Bin Lou

Nicolas Loy Rodas
Charles Lu
Huanxiang Lu
Xing Lu
Yao Lu
Yuhang Lu
Gongning Luo
Jie Luo
Jiebo Luo
Luyang Luo
Ma Luo
Xiangde Luo
Cuong Ly
Ilwoo Lyu
Yanjun Lyu
Yuanyuan Lyu
Sharath M S
Chunwei Ma
Hehuan Ma
Junbo Ma
Wenao Ma
Yuhui Ma
Anderson Maciel
S. Sara Mahdavi
Mohammed Mahmoud
Andreas Maier
Michail Mamalakis
Ilja Manakov
Brett Marinelli
Yassine Marrakchi
Fabio Martinez
Martin Maška
Tejas Sudharshan Mathai
Dimitrios Mavroeidis
Pau Medrano-Gracia
Raghav Mehta
Felix Meissen
Qingjie Meng
Yanda Meng
Martin Menten
Alexandre Merasli
Stijn Michielse
Leo Milecki
Fausto Milletari
Zhe Min

Jorg Peters
Terry Peters
Eike Petersen
Jens Petersen
Micha Pfeiffer
Dzung Pham
Hieu Pham
Ashish Phophalia
Tomasz Pieciak
Antonio Pinheiro
Kilian Pohl
Sebastian Pölsterl
Iulia A. Popescu
Alison Pouch
Prateek Prasanna
Raphael Prevost
Juan Prieto
Federica Proietto Salanitri
Sergi Pujades
Kumaradevan Punithakumar
Haikun Qi
Huan Qi
Buyue Qian
Yan Qiang
Yuchuan Qiao
Zhi Qiao
Fangbo Qin
Wenjian Qin
Yanguo Qin
Yulei Qin
Hui Qu
Kha Gia Quach
Tran Minh Quan
Sandro Queirós
Prashanth R.
Mehdi Rahim
Jagath Rajapakse
Kashif Rajpoot
Dhanesh Ramachandram
Xuming Ran
Hatem Rashwan
Daniele Ravì
Keerthi Sravan Ravi
Surreerat Reaungamornrat
Samuel Remedios

Yudan Ren
Mauricio Reyes
Constantino Reyes-Aldasoro
Hadrien Reynaud
David Richmond
Anne-Marie Rickmann
Laurent Risser
Leticia Rittner
Dominik Rivoir
Emma Robinson
Jessica Rodgers
Rafael Rodrigues
Robert Rohling
Lukasz Roszkowiak
Holger Roth
Karsten Roth
José Rouco
Daniel Rueckert
Danny Ruijters
Mirabela Rusu
Ario Sadafi
Shaheer Ullah Saeed
Monjoy Saha
Pranjal Sahu
Olivier Salvado
Ricardo Sanchez-Matilla
Robin Sandkuehler
Gianmarco Santini
Anil Kumar Sao
Duygu Sarikaya
Olivier Saut
Fabio Scarpa
Nico Scherf
Markus Schirmer
Alexander Schlaefer
Jerome Schmid
Julia Schnabel
Andreas Schuh
Christina Schwarz-Gsaxner
Martin Schweiger
Michaël Sdika
Suman Sedai
Matthias Seibold
Raghavendra Selvan
Sourya Sengupta

Carmen Serrano
Ahmed Shaffie
Keyur Shah
Rutwik Shah
Ahmed Shahin
Mohammad Abuzar Shaikh
S. Shailja
Shayan Shams
Hongming Shan
Xinxin Shan
Mostafa Sharifzadeh
Anuja Sharma
Harshita Sharma
Gregory Sharp
Li Shen
Liyue Shen
Mali Shen
Mingren Shen
Yiqing Shen
Ziyi Shen
Luyao Shi
Xiaoshuang Shi
Yiyu Shi
Hoo-Chang Shin
Boris Shirokikh
Suprosanna Shit
Suzanne Shontz
Yucheng Shu
Alberto Signoroni
Carlos Silva
Wilson Silva
Margarida Silveira
Vivek Singh
Sumedha Singla
Ayushi Sinha
Elena Sizikova
Rajath Soans
Hessam Sokooti
Hong Song
Weinan Song
Youyi Song
Aristeidis Sotiras
Bella Specktor
William Speier
Ziga Spiclin

Jon Sporring
Anuroop Sriram
Vinkle Srivastav
Lawrence Staib
Johannes Stegmaier
Joshua Stough
Danail Stoyanov
Justin Strait
Iain Styles
Ruisheng Su
Vaishnavi Subramanian
Gérard Subsol
Yao Sui
Heung-Il Suk
Shipra Suman
Jian Sun
Li Sun
Liyan Sun
Wenqing Sun
Yue Sun
Vaanathi Sundaresan
Kyung Sung
Yannick Suter
Raphael Sznitman
Eleonora Tagliabue
Roger Tam
Chaowei Tan
Hao Tang
Sheng Tang
Thomas Tang
Youbao Tang
Yucheng Tang
Zihao Tang
Rong Tao
Elias Tappeiner
Mickael Tardy
Giacomo Tarroni
Paul Thienphrapa
Stephen Thompson
Yu Tian
Aleksei Tiulpin
Tal Tlusty
Maryam Toloubidokhti
Jocelyne Troccaz
Roger Trullo

Chialing Tsai
Sudhakar Tummala
Régis Vaillant
Jeya Maria Jose Valanarasu
Juan Miguel Valverde
Thomas Varsavsky
Francisco Vasconcelos
Serge Vasylechko
S. Swaroop Vedula
Roberto Vega
Gonzalo Vegas Sanchez-Ferrero
Gopalkrishna Veni
Archana Venkataraman
Athanasios Vlontzos
Ingmar Voigt
Eugene Vorontsov
Xiaohua Wan
Bo Wang
Changmiao Wang
Chunliang Wang
Clinton Wang
Dadong Wang
Fan Wang
Guotai Wang
Haifeng Wang
Hong Wang
Hongkai Wang
Hongyu Wang
Hu Wang
Juan Wang
Junyan Wang
Ke Wang
Li Wang
Liansheng Wang
Manning Wang
Nizhuan Wang
Qiuli Wang
Renzhen Wang
Rongguang Wang
Ruixuan Wang
Runze Wang
Shujun Wang
Shuo Wang
Shuqiang Wang
Tianchen Wang

Tongxin Wang
Wenzhe Wang
Xi Wang
Xiangdong Wang
Xiaosong Wang
Yalin Wang
Yan Wang
Yi Wang
Yixin Wang
Zeyi Wang
Zuhui Wang
Jonathan Weber
Donglai Wei
Dongming Wei
Lifang Wei
Wolfgang Wein
Michael Wels
Cédric Wemmert
Matthias Wilms
Adam Wittek
Marek Wodzinski
Julia Wolleb
Jonghye Woo
Chongruo Wu
Chunpeng Wu
Ji Wu
Jianfeng Wu
Jie Ying Wu
Jiong Wu
Junde Wu
Pengxiang Wu
Xia Wu
Xiyin Wu
Yawen Wu
Ye Wu
Yicheng Wu
Zhengwang Wu
Tobias Wuerfl
James Xia
Siyu Xia
Yingda Xia
Lei Xiang
Tiange Xiang
Deqiang Xiao
Yiming Xiao

Hongtao Xie
Jianyang Xie
Lingxi Xie
Long Xie
Weidi Xie
Yiting Xie
Yutong Xie
Fangxu Xing
Jiarui Xing
Xiaohan Xing
Chenchu Xu
Hai Xu
Hongming Xu
Jiaqi Xu
Junshen Xu
Kele Xu
Min Xu
Minfeng Xu
Moucheng Xu
Qinwei Xu
Rui Xu
Xiaowei Xu
Xinxing Xu
Xuanang Xu
Yanwu Xu
Yanyu Xu
Yongchao Xu
Zhe Xu
Zhenghua Xu
Zhoubing Xu
Kai Xuan
Cheng Xue
Jie Xue
Wufeng Xue
Yuan Xue
Faridah Yahya
Chaochao Yan
Jiangpeng Yan
Ke Yan
Ming Yan
Qingsen Yan
Yuguang Yan
Zengqiang Yan
Baoyao Yang
Changchun Yang

Chao-Han Huck Yang
Dong Yang
Fan Yang
Feng Yang
Fengting Yang
Ge Yang
Guanyu Yang
Hao-Hsiang Yang
Heran Yang
Hongxu Yang
Huijuan Yang
Jiawei Yang
Jinyu Yang
Lin Yang
Peng Yang
Pengshuai Yang
Xiaohui Yang
Xin Yang
Yan Yang
Yifan Yang
Yujiu Yang
Zhicheng Yang
Jiangchao Yao
Jiawen Yao
Li Yao
Linlin Yao
Qingsong Yao
Chuyang Ye
Dong Hye Ye
Huihui Ye
Menglong Ye
Youngjin Yoo
Chenyu You
Haichao Yu
Hanchao Yu
Jinhua Yu
Ke Yu
Qi Yu
Renping Yu
Thomas Yu
Xiaowei Yu
Zhen Yu
Pengyu Yuan
Paul Yushkevich
Ghada Zamzmi

Ramy Zeineldin
Dong Zeng
Rui Zeng
Zhiwei Zhai
Kun Zhan
Bokai Zhang
Chaoyi Zhang
Daoqiang Zhang
Fa Zhang
Fan Zhang
Hao Zhang
Jianpeng Zhang
Jiawei Zhang
Jingqing Zhang
Jingyang Zhang
Jiong Zhang
Jun Zhang
Ke Zhang
Lefei Zhang
Lei Zhang
Lichi Zhang
Lu Zhang
Ning Zhang
Pengfei Zhang
Qiang Zhang
Rongzhao Zhang
Ruipeng Zhang
Ruisi Zhang
Shengping Zhang
Shihao Zhang
Tianyang Zhang
Tong Zhang
Tuo Zhang
Wen Zhang
Xiaoran Zhang
Xin Zhang
Yanfu Zhang
Yao Zhang
Yi Zhang
Yongqin Zhang
You Zhang
Youshan Zhang
Yu Zhang
Yubo Zhang
Yue Zhang

Yulun Zhang
Yundong Zhang
Yunyan Zhang
Yuxin Zhang
Zheng Zhang
Zhicheng Zhang
Can Zhao
Changchen Zhao
Fenqiang Zhao
He Zhao
Jianfeng Zhao
Jun Zhao
Li Zhao
Liang Zhao
Lin Zhao
Qingyu Zhao
Shen Zhao
Shijie Zhao
Tianyi Zhao
Wei Zhao
Xiaole Zhao
Xuandong Zhao
Yang Zhao
Yue Zhao
Zixu Zhao
Ziyuan Zhao
Xingjian Zhen
Haiyong Zheng
Hao Zheng
Kang Zheng
Qinghe Zheng
Shenhai Zheng
Yalin Zheng
Yinqiang Zheng
Yushan Zheng
Tao Zhong
Zichun Zhong
Bo Zhou
Haoyin Zhou
Hong-Yu Zhou
Huiyu Zhou
Kang Zhou
Qin Zhou
S. Kevin Zhou
Sihang Zhou

Tao Zhou
Tianfei Zhou
Wei Zhou
Xiao-Hu Zhou
Xiao-Yun Zhou
Yanning Zhou
Yaxuan Zhou
Youjia Zhou
Yukun Zhou
Zhiguo Zhou
Zongwei Zhou
Dongxiao Zhu
Haidong Zhu
Hancan Zhu

Lei Zhu
Qikui Zhu
Xiaofeng Zhu
Xinliang Zhu
Zhonghang Zhu
Zhuotun Zhu
Veronika Zimmer
David Zimmerer
Weiwei Zong
Yukai Zou
Lianrui Zuo
Gerald Zwettler
Reyer Zwiggelaar

Outstanding Area Chairs

Ester Bonmati   University College London, UK
Tolga Tasdizen   University of Utah, USA
Yanwu Xu   Baidu Inc., China

Outstanding Reviewers

Seyed-Ahmad Ahmadi   NVIDIA, Germany
Katharina Breininger   Friedrich-Alexander-Universität
                         Erlangen-Nürnberg, Germany
Mariano Cabezas   University of Sydney, Australia
Nicha Dvornek   Yale University, USA
Adrian Galdran   Universitat Pompeu Fabra, Spain
Alexander Katzmann   Siemens Healthineers, Germany
Tony C. W. Mok   Hong Kong University of Science and
                         Technology, China
Sérgio Pereira   Lunit Inc., Korea
David Richmond   Genentech, USA
Dominik Rivoir   National Center for Tumor Diseases (NCT)
                         Dresden, Germany
Fons van der Sommen   Eindhoven University of Technology,
                         the Netherlands
Yushan Zheng   Beihang University, China

Honorable Mentions (Reviewers)

Chloé Audigier   Siemens Healthineers, Switzerland
Qinle Ba   Roche, USA

Meritxell Bach Cuadra	University of Lausanne, Switzerland
Gabriel Bernardino	CREATIS, Université Lyon 1, France
Benjamin Billot	University College London, UK
Tom Brosch	Philips Research Hamburg, Germany
Ruben Cardenes	Ultivue, Germany
Owen Carmichael	Pennington Biomedical Research Center, USA
Li Chen	University of Washington, USA
Xinjian Chen	Soochow University, Taiwan
Philip Chikontwe	Daegu Gyeongbuk Institute of Science and Technology, Korea
Argyrios Christodoulidis	Centre for Research and Technology Hellas/Information Technologies Institute, Greece
Albert Chung	Hong Kong University of Science and Technology, China
Pierre-Henri Conze	IMT Atlantique, France
Jeffrey Craley	Johns Hopkins University, USA
Felix Denzinger	Friedrich-Alexander University Erlangen-Nürnberg, Germany
Adrien Depeursinge	HES-SO Valais-Wallis, Switzerland
Neel Dey	New York University, USA
Guodong Du	Xiamen University, China
Nicolas Duchateau	CREATIS, Université Lyon 1, France
Dmitry V. Dylov	Skolkovo Institute of Science and Technology, Russia
Hooman Esfandiari	University of Zurich, Switzerland
Deng-Ping Fan	ETH Zurich, Switzerland
Chaowei Fang	Xidian University, China
Nils Daniel Forkert	Department of Radiology & Hotchkiss Brain Institute, University of Calgary, Canada
Nils Gessert	Hamburg University of Technology, Germany
Karthik Gopinath	ETS Montreal, Canada
Mara Graziani	IBM Research, Switzerland
Liang Han	Stony Brook University, USA
Nandinee Haq	Hitachi, Canada
Ali Hatamizadeh	NVIDIA Corporation, USA
Samra Irshad	Swinburne University of Technology, Australia
Hayato Itoh	Nagoya University, Japan
Meirui Jiang	The Chinese University of Hong Kong, China
Baoyu Jing	University of Illinois at Urbana-Champaign, USA
Manjunath K N	Manipal Institute of Technology, India
Ali Kafaei Zad Tehrani	Concordia University, Canada
Konstantinos Kamnitsas	Imperial College London, UK

Ruisheng Su	Erasmus MC, the Netherlands
Liyan Sun	Xiamen University, China
Raphael Sznitman	University of Bern, Switzerland
Elias Tappeiner	UMIT - Private University for Health Sciences, Medical Informatics and Technology, Austria
Mickael Tardy	Hera-MI, France
Juan Miguel Valverde	University of Eastern Finland, Finland
Eugene Vorontsov	Polytechnique Montreal, Canada
Bo Wang	CtrsVision, USA
Tongxin Wang	Meta Platforms, Inc., USA
Yan Wang	Sichuan University, China
Yixin Wang	University of Chinese Academy of Sciences, China
Jie Ying Wu	Johns Hopkins University, USA
Lei Xiang	Subtle Medical Inc, USA
Jiaqi Xu	The Chinese University of Hong Kong, China
Zhoubing Xu	Siemens Healthineers, USA
Ke Yan	Alibaba DAMO Academy, China
Baoyao Yang	School of Computers, Guangdong University of Technology, China
Changchun Yang	Delft University of Technology, the Netherlands
Yujiu Yang	Tsinghua University, China
Youngjin Yoo	Siemens Healthineers, USA
Ning Zhang	Bloomberg, USA
Jianfeng Zhao	Western University, Canada
Tao Zhou	Nanjing University of Science and Technology, China
Veronika Zimmer	Technical University Munich, Germany

Mentorship Program (Mentors)

Ulas Bagci	Northwestern University, USA
Kayhan Batmanghelich	University of Pittsburgh, USA
Hrvoje Bogunovic	Medical University of Vienna, Austria
Ninon Burgos	CNRS - Paris Brain Institute, France
Hao Chen	Hong Kong University of Science and Technology, China
Jun Cheng	Institute for Infocomm Research, Singapore
Li Cheng	University of Alberta, Canada
Aasa Feragen	Technical University of Denmark, Denmark
Zhifan Gao	Sun Yat-sen University, China
Stamatia Giannarou	Imperial College London, UK
Sharon Huang	Pennsylvania State University, USA

Anand Joshi	University of Southern California, USA
Bernhard Kainz	Friedrich-Alexander-Universität Erlangen-Nürnberg, Germany and Imperial College London, UK
Baiying Lei	Shenzhen University, China
Karim Lekadir	Universitat de Barcelona, Spain
Xiaoxiao Li	University of British Columbia, Canada
Jianming Liang	Arizona State University, USA
Marius George Linguraru	Children's National Hospital, George Washington University, USA
Anne Martel	University of Toronto, Canada
Antonio Porras	University of Colorado Anschutz Medical Campus, USA
Chen Qin	University of Edinburgh, UK
Julia Schnabel	Helmholtz Munich, TU Munich, Germany and King's College London, UK
Yang Song	University of New South Wales, Australia
Tanveer Syeda-Mahmood	IBM Research - Almaden Labs, USA
Pallavi Tiwari	University of Wisconsin Madison, USA
Mathias Unberath	Johns Hopkins University, USA
Maria Vakalopoulou	CentraleSupelec, France
Harini Veeraraghavan	Memorial Sloan Kettering Cancer Center, USA
Satish Viswanath	Case Western Reserve University, USA
Guang Yang	Imperial College London, UK
Lequan Yu	University of Hong Kong, China
Miaomiao Zhang	University of Virginia, USA
Rongchang Zhao	Central South University, China
Luping Zhou	University of Sydney, Australia
Lilla Zollei	Massachusetts General Hospital, Harvard Medical School, USA
Maria A. Zuluaga	EURECOM, France

Contents – Part IV

Positron Emission Tomography

Ultrasound Imaging

Video Data Analysis

Image Segmentation I

Microscopic Image Analysis

An End-to-End Combinatorial Optimization Method for R-band Chromosome Recognition with Grouping Guided Attention

Chao Xia[1,2], Jiyue Wang[3], Yulei Qin[1,2], Yun Gu[1,2], Bing Chen[3], and Jie Yang[1,2(✉)]

[1] Institute of Image Processing and Pattern Recognition,
Shanghai Jiao Tong University, Shanghai, China
{qinyulei,geron762,jieyang}@sjtu.edu.cn
[2] Institute of Medical Robotics, Shanghai Jiao Tong University, Shanghai, China
[3] Shanghai Institute of Hematology, Ruijin Hospital,
Shanghai Jiao Tong University School of Medicine, Shanghai, China
wangjiyue@sjtu.edu.cn

Abstract. Chromosome recognition is a critical and time-consuming process in karyotyping, especially for R-band chromosomes with poor visualization quality. Existing computer-aided chromosome recognition methods mainly focus on better feature representation of individual chromosomes while neglecting the fact that chromosomes from the same karyotype share some common distribution and are more related compared to chromosomes across different patients. In the light of such observation, we start from a global perspective and propose an end-to-end differential combinatorial optimization method for R-band chromosome recognition. To achieve this, a grouping guided feature interaction module (GFIM) is built for feature aggregation between similar chromosome instances. Specially, a mask matrix is built for self-attention computation according to chromosome length grouping information. Furthermore, a deep assignment module (DAM) is designed for flexible and differentiable label assignment. It exploits the aggregated features to infer class probability distributions between all chromosomes in a cell. Experimental results on both normal and numerically abnormal karyotypes confirmed that our method outperforms state-of-the-art chromosome recognition and label assignment methods. The code is available at: https://github.com/xiabc612/R-band-chromosome-recognition.

Keywords: R-band chromosome · Label assignment · Transformer

The first two authors contributed equally to this work.

Supplementary Information The online version contains supplementary material available at https://doi.org/10.1007/978-3-031-16440-8_1.

1 Introduction

Chromosome identification is a critical step in karyotyping, which is a powerful tool for the diagnosis of various hematological malignancies and genetic diseases [3]. Abnormalities in chromosome number and structure directly correlate with diseases like leukemia and Down syndrome [16,17]. In clinical, the commonly used staining techniques for chromosome banding are Giemsa (G)-, Reverse (R)-, and Centromere (C)- banding [6]. Specifically, the R-band chromosome of bone marrow cells can help to identify the abnormalities occurring at the end of chromosomes [2]. A typical microscopic image of R-band chromosome and the corresponding karyotyping result are shown in Fig. 1.

Manual chromosome karyotyping is a time-consuming work that highly depends on expert knowledge. To reduce the burden of manual karyotyping, many computer-aided methods have been recently developed, including traditional morphology-based methods [1,14] and deep learning-based methods [10,12,18,19,21-23,26-28]. The majority of these work only focused on the G-band chromosome by hand-crafted features or deep neural networks. Compared with G-band images, R-band chromosomes of bone marrow cells are poorly visualized with more blurred bands and thus are more challenging for recognition. Only [23] proposed an R-band metaphase chromosome classification method based on the human-computer interaction.

A normal karyotype contains 23 pairs of chromosomes, with two instances of each autosomal category (for allosome, male XY female XX), which can be classified into 24 categories in total. Considering this prior knowledge, [19] designed dispatch rules to re-assign the predicted labels within a karyotype using the probability distribution of 24 categories over all chromosomes.

This dispatch process can be formulated as a bipartite graph matching problem and solved by Hungarian algorithm (HA) [13]. However, there are two weaknesses to directly apply classical HA on chromosome classes assignment: 1) it has a strict hypothesis on classes distribution, which is only feasible to normal karyotypes. For karyotypes with numerical abnormalities, the chromosomes may be assigned incorrectly; 2) it is not differentiable and not friendly to neural networks. In recent years, some differentiable matching methods have been designed for the task of multi-object tracking [7,29] and graph matching [20,25] with more flexible ways.

Motivated by the aforementioned progress in chromosome classification and graph matching, we propose an end-to-end combinatorial optimization method for R-band chromosome recognition in this work. It has a flexible assignment manner and can deal with both normal and numerically abnormal karyotypes. Considering that the self-attention mechanism of Transformer [24], after feature extraction by a deep convolutional neural network (CNN), a grouping guided feature interaction module (GFIM) with three Transformer encoder layers is built to explore relative information between chromosome instances. Specially, due to the definition of chromosome categories is related to chromosome length, we take the chromosome length as prior knowledge to generate mask matrix in the encoder layers. Such masking operation aims to avoid attention on chromosomes

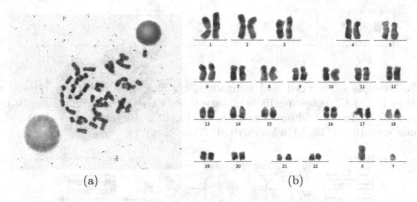

(a)   (b)

Fig. 1. (a). A microscopic image of R-band chromosome metaphase (male). (b). Karyotyping result of (a).

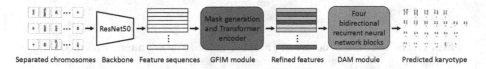

Separated chromosomes   Backbone   Feature sequences   GFIM module   Refined features   DAM module   Predicted karyotype

Fig. 2. The overall architecture of the proposed end-to-end combinatorial optimization R-band chromosome recognition method. GFIM and DAM are the grouping guided feature interaction module and deep assignment module respectively.

with large variance in length. Furthermore, a differentiable deep assignment module (DAM) with four bidirectional recurrent neural network (Bi-RNN) blocks is constructed to redistribute the initial classification results w.r.t. the class probability distribution, which simulates the process of HA in a differentiable way. The schematic representation of the proposed method is illustrated in Fig. 2.

Our contributions can be summarized as: (1). An end-to-end differentiable method is introduced to recognize both normal and abnormal karyotypes. It is not specific to any feature extraction backbone and can improve chromosome classification performance in a plug-and-play manner. (2). GFIM provides an effective way for feature aggregation to reduce confusion between chromosomes with similar lengths. (3). DAM is proposed to provide a learnable and flexible soft assignment manner. (4). We demonstrate the merit of the proposed method on a large-scale bone marrow R-band chromosome dataset collected and labeled by clinical cytogeneticists. The proposed method surpass Hungarian algorithm with 0.81% and 2.29% on normal and numerically abnormal karyotypes respectively.

2 Method

2.1 Overview

We consider chromosome recognition task from a global perspective and predict labels of all chromosomes in a karyotype simultaneously. Note that the

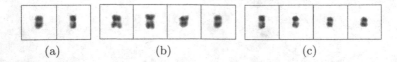

(a)   (b)   (c)

Fig. 3. Example of cropped and normalized chromosomes from karyotype-A and karyotype-B. (a) Chromosome 19 from karyotype-A (left) and chromosome 16 from karyotype-B (right). (b) Chromosomes 16, 16, 19, 19 in karyotype-A respectively. (c) Chromosomes 16, 16, 19, 19 in karyotype-B respectively.

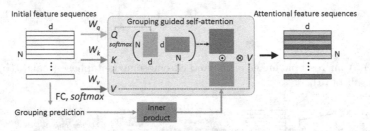

Fig. 4. The detailed structure of grouping guided feature interaction module.

classification of chromosomes can be difficult if each chromosome is inferred individually. This is because the greyscale distribution of R-banding and the morphology of chromosomes vary greatly from cell to cell and from patient to patient. However, this process will be easier if we compare and recognize it with similar chromosomes in the same karyotype to discover discriminative features and distribution characteristics. For example, one can hardly identify and distinguish these two chromosomes in Fig. 3(a) independently, but much easier when comparing them with similar chromosomes in the same karyotype (See Fig. 3(b) and Fig. 3(c)).

The proposed method contains three parts, which are: 1). batch feature extraction backbone; 2). grouping guided feature interaction module; and 3). deep assignment module. We take all N chromosomes in a karyotype ($N = 46$ for normal karyotype) as a batch for feature extraction with CNN. Then, each chromosome image is represented by a feature vector with the dimension of d. The extracted $N \times d$ features can be viewed as a feature sequence with the length of N. To build a long-range connection between chromosome instances, a grouping guided feature interaction module is designed based on the Transformer encoder [4]. Inspired by the mask strategies used in Natural Language Processing (NLP) [8], a masked self-attention encoder is proposed w.r.t. the predicted chromosome length grouping information to avoid illogical attention. To make the label assignment process more flexible and differentiable, a deep assignment module with four Bi-RNN blocks is proposed to infer the predicted distribution among chromosomes and output final predictions in parallel.

2.2 Grouping Guided Feature Interaction Module

Transformer was firstly designed for sequence-to-sequence prediction in NLP field [8,24] and recently in vision tasks [4,9]. To construct the self-attention and long-range interactions between chromosome sequences in the feature level, we propose Grouping Guided Feature Interaction Module (GFIM), as shown in Fig. 4. Specially, we generate attention mask in the multi-head attention layer by the prediction of chromosome length grouping information.

The extracted features with the size of $N \times d$ are used for two purposes: one is input to the encoder for self-attention, and the other is fed to the fully-connected layer (FC) for group prediction. We classify all types of chromosomes into seven length groups according to [15] and guide the generation of attention mask M. Due to the input sequences of Transformer may being a variable length, the module can handle karyotypes with numerical abnormalities.

We adopt a standard architecture of Transformer encoder. The N input feature sequences $X \in \mathbb{R}^{N \times d}$ are embedded into queries Q, keys K and values V with the embedding matrices W_q, W_k and W_v respectively. In general, attention mask matrix M is added to the calculated weights as Eq. 1.

$$\text{Attention}(Q, K, V) = softmax(\frac{QK^T}{\sqrt{d}} + M)V \tag{1}$$

The mask matrix M is used to filter information that does not require attention, which has a binary value of $-\infty$ and 0. We change this binary mask to soft mask to improve the stability. To achieve this, we firstly compute attention weights W_a as Eq. 2, where W_a is an $N \times N$ matrix.

$$W_a = softmax(\frac{QK^T}{\sqrt{d}}) \tag{2}$$

Then, the inner product of the grouping probability distributions of each two samples p_i and p_j is used to generate the mask as $M(i, j) = \sum_{g=1}^{G} p_{ig}p_{jg}$, where p_{ig} means the gth class probability in vector p_i, G is the group number, here $G = 7$. In the ideal situation, $M(i, j)$ tends to be zero if sample i and sample j belong to a different group, otherwise $M(i, j)$ tends to be one. We conduct element-wise product to compute the masked attention weights W_{ma} and then row normalization as Eqs. 3 and 4.

$$W_{ma} = W_a \odot M \tag{3}$$

$$W_{ma}(i, j) = \frac{W_{ma}(i, j)}{\sum_{j=1}^{N} W_{ma}(i, j)} \tag{4}$$

Finally, the attention output in Eq.(1) can be represented as Eq.(5).

$$\text{Attention}(Q, K, V) = W_{ma}V \tag{5}$$

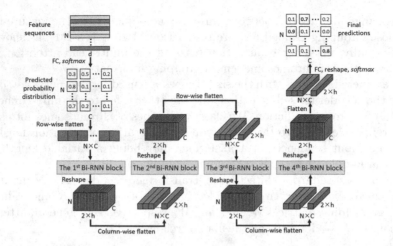

Fig. 5. Detailed structure of deep assignment module. N means the number of chromosomes, C means chromosome classes, h means the hidden dimension of RNN layers.

2.3   Deep Assignment Module

The assignment process of chromosome recognition results can be formulated as a bipartite graph matching problem between the predicted probability distribution and normal karyotype templates. This can be generally solved by HA. However, this operation is based on a strict hypothesis that each type of chromosome meets a normal karyotype distribution, which is not suitable for the karyotypes with numerical abnormalities. Besides, this process is not differentiable and solely relies on the predicted probability distribution, so that the global constraint information cannot be used to optimize the preceding feature extraction process.

To address these problems, we propose DAM, a differentiable module to approximates HA, which learns label structures from the training sample combinations automatically. We choose Bi-RNN to fit the input data with various sizes and let each output neuron have a receptive field equal to the entire input.

The detailed structure of DAM is shown in Fig. 5. DAM includes four Bi-RNN blocks sequentially with different weights and the same hidden dimension of h. Each Bi-RNN block consists of two Bi-RNN layers, and the basic unit of all Bi-RNN layers is gated recurrent unit (GRU) [5]. To simulate the alternating operations on the rows and columns in HA, the category probability distribution matrix P with the size of $N \times C$ (C is the chromosome classes number) is firstly flattened in row-wise order and input into the first Bi-RNN block. The output is $N \times C$ elements and each element with a size of $2 \times h$ (h set as 64 here). Then the output of the first Bi-RNN block is flattened column-wise and input into the second Bi-RNN block to give an output of the same size as the input. The latter two Bi-RNN blocks conduct the same operations as the first two Bi-RNN blocks but with different weights. Finally, fully-connected layers and softmax function are used to output the final result with the size of $N \times C$. Different

Table 1. Statistics of the datasets.

	Patient			Karyotype			Chromosome
	Male	Female	All	Male	Female	All	
Normal	714	559	1273	1795	1326	3121	143566
Abnormal	16	16	32	95	83	178	8234

from the method mentioned in [29], we employ four Bi-RNN blocks to simulate the alternating and repetitive operations on rows and columns in HA and output final predictions directly.

3 Experiments

3.1 Datasets and Implementation Details

We collected 3299 bone marrow R-band chromosome metaphase microscopic images from Shanghai Institute of Hematology, Ruijin Hospital. Which containing 3121 normal karyotypes and 178 karyotypes with numerical abnormalities (including the acute myeloid leukemia related $+8$, -7, $+11$, $+12$, $+21$, $-Y$). For normal karyotypes, we split the collected dataset into training set, test set and validation set with the ratio of 3:1:1 and conduct five-fold cross validation. All abnormal karyotypes are kept for test only. All chromosomes were separated and labeled by cytogeneticists manually (See Table 1 for details).

To preserve chromosome length information better, we normalize each chromosome's image size within the corresponding karyotype. Specifically, we pad each cropped individual chromosome into a square image with the side length of the longest chromosome in each karyotype (See Fig. 3 for example). During training, we randomly select chromosomes from the entire training set and construct batch samples based on the combinations of normal (including 46, XX and 46, XY) or abnormal karyotypes. Models are implemented with PyTorch and trained for 40000 iterations with the initial learning rate of 0.0001. Pre-trained weights of ResNet50 [11] and DETR [4] are used for initialization. The loss function is a weighted combination of chromosome grouping loss and chromosome classification loss based on cross-entropy.

3.2 Results on Normal Karyotypes

The results are evaluated by three metrics: accuracy of testing images (Acc_{Image}), the average F_1-score over all classes of testing images (F_1), and average accuracy of the complete karyotyping per patient case ($Acc_{Patient}$). Here, $F_1 = \frac{1}{C} \sum_{j=1}^{C} \frac{2 \cdot Precision_j \cdot Recall_j}{Precision_j + Recall_j}$, where C is 24, $Precision_j = \frac{TP_j}{TP_j + FP_j}$, $Recall_j = \frac{TP_j}{TP_j + FN_j}$, TP_j, TN_j, FP_j, FN_j are true positives, true negatives, false positives, false negatives samples of class j respectively.

Table 2. Comparative results and ablation studies of recognition accuracy per image Acc_{Image}, accuracy per patient case $Acc_{Patient}$ and F_1-score on normal karyotypes.

Method	GFIM	DAM	Backbone	Acc_{Image} (%)	$Acc_{Patient}$ (%)	F_1 (%)
Baseline [11]			ResNet-50	96.24	96.22	95.84
Varifocal-Net [19]			Varifocal-Net	97.35	97.37	97.02
Hungarian [13]			ResNet-50	97.96	97.93	97.66
DeepMOT [29]			ResNet-50	97.02	97.05	96.90
Proposed	✓		ResNet-50	97.55	97.57	97.23
		✓		98.63	98.64	98.55
	✓	✓		**98.77**	**98.76**	**98.68**

Table 3. Comparative results and ablation studies on numerically abnormal karyotypes.

Method	GFIM	DAM	Backbone	Acc_{Image} (%)	$Acc_{Patient}$ (%)	F_1 (%)
Baseline [11]			ResNet-50	91.04	90.15	90.30
Varifocal-Net [19]			Varifocal-Net	93.95	93.02	93.10
Hungarian [13]			ResNet-50	94.04	93.23	93.04
DeepMOT [29]			ResNet-50	92.57	91.81	92.05
Proposed	✓		ResNet-50	93.50	92.77	92.83
		✓		95.40	94.94	94.98
	✓	✓		**96.33**	**95.85**	**96.17**

.We choose ResNet50 [11] as baseline for all experiments. Testing results are compared with state-of-the-art chromosome recognition method [19] and bipartite graph matching based methods [13,29]. Specially, [19] proposed a rule-based dispatch strategy, which can improve the classification results given directly by the network. Besides, due to the diverse combination of allosomes, we only use HA to re-assign the predicted labels of 22 autosomal categories. As shown in Table 2, our proposed method achieves the best performance in both accuracy and F_1-score, which demonstrates that the end-to-end feature interaction and assignment method can utilize more global information to make decisions. Besides, ablation studies confirm that single GFIM or DAM module can also improve the classification accuracy from different perspectives. The confusion matrix and the performance of our method on each type of chromosome are available in supplementary material.

3.3   Results on Karyotypes with Numerical Abnormalities

Clinically, chromosome number and structural abnormalities are directly related to disease diagnosis. A clinically valuable method requires the ability to identify abnormal samples. We provide the evaluation results of abnormal karyotypes in Table 3 to test the robustness of different methods. Due to the poor quality of karyotype images in patients like leukemia, the performances have a relative decline in both individual chromosomes and patient cases accuracy. However, our end-to-end combinatorial optimization method with both GFIM and DAM still achieve the best performance. Our method surpasses HA by 2.29%, 2.62% and 3.13% in Acc_{Image}, $Acc_{Patient}$ and F_1-score respectively, which indicates that it has learned the intrinsic combinatorial features of chromosome karyotypes and thus is more robust to handle diverse numerically abnormal karyotypes. See supplementary materials for the confusion matrix and the detailed performance.

4   Conclusion

This paper proposes an end-to-end combinatorial optimization method for R-band chromosome recognition with feature aggregation and soft label assignment among individual chromosomes within a cell. Label structures of normal and numerically abnormal karyotypes are automatically learned in both features and classes distribution levels. The proposed method can be easily adopted with any feature extraction backbone in a plug-and-play manner, significantly outperforming the state-of-the-art chromosome recognition and label assignment baselines in both normal and numerically abnormal karyotypes. Our method has been deployed as a powerful clinical tool to help cytogeneticists conduct chromosome karyotyping.

References

1. Abid, F., Hamami, L.: A survey of neural network based automated systems for human chromosome classification. Artif. Intell. Rev. **49**(1), 41–56 (2016). https://doi.org/10.1007/s10462-016-9515-5
2. Bernheim, A.: Cytogenomics of cancers: from chromosome to sequence. Mol. Oncol. **4**(4), 309–322 (2010)
3. Campbell, L.J.: Cancer cytogenetics: Methods and Protocols. Springer, New York (2011). https://doi.org/10.1007/978-1-4939-6703-2
4. Carion, N., Massa, F., Synnaeve, G., Usunier, N., Kirillov, A., Zagoruyko, S.: End-to-end object detection with transformers. In: Vedaldi, A., Bischof, H., Brox, T., Frahm, J.-M. (eds.) ECCV 2020. LNCS, vol. 12346, pp. 213–229. Springer, Cham (2020). https://doi.org/10.1007/978-3-030-58452-8_13
5. Cho, K., van Merrienboer, B., Gulcehre, C., Bougares, F., Schwenk, H., Bengio, Y.: Learning phrase representations using RNN encoder-decoder for statistical machine translation. In: Conference on Empirical Methods in Natural Language Processing (EMNLP 2014) (2014)
6. Craig, J.M., Bickmore, W.A.: Genes and genomes: chromosome bands-flavours to savour. Bioessays **15**(5), 349–354 (1993)
7. Dai, P., Weng, R., Choi, W., Zhang, C., He, Z., Ding, W.: Learning a proposal classifier for multiple object tracking. In: Proceedings of the IEEE/CVF Conference on Computer Vision and Pattern Recognition, pp. 2443–2452 (2021)
8. Devlin, J., Chang, M.-W., Lee, K., Toutanova, K.: BERT: pre-training of deep bidirectional transformers for language understanding. arXiv preprint arXiv:1810.04805, 2018

9. Dosovitskiy, A., et al.: An image is worth 16x16 words: transformers for image recognition at scale. arXiv preprint arXiv:2010.11929 (2020)
10. Haferlach, C., et al.: Artificial intelligence substantially supports chromosome banding analysis maintaining its strengths in hematologic diagnostics even in the era of newer technologies. Blood **136**, 47–48 (2020)
11. He, K., Zhang, X., Ren, S., Sun, J.: Deep residual learning for image recognition. In: Proceedings of the IEEE Conference on Computer Vision and Pattern Recognition, pp. 770–778 (2016)
12. Jindal, S., Gupta, G., Yadav, M., Sharma, M., Vig, L.: Siamese networks for chromosome classification. In: Proceedings of the IEEE International Conference on Computer Vision Workshops, pp. 72–81 (2017)
13. Kuhn, H.W.: The Hungarian method for the assignment problem. Naval Res. Logist. Q. **2**(1–2), 83–97 (1955)
14. Lerner, B., Guterman, H., Dinstein, I., Romem, Y.: Medial axis transform-based features and a neural network for human chromosome classification. Pattern Recogn. **28**(11), 1673–1683 (1995)
15. McGowan-Jordan, J.: ISCN 2016: an international system for human cytogenomic nomenclature (2016); recommendations of the international standing human committee on human cytogenomic nomenclature including new sequence-based cytogenomic. Karger (2016)
16. Natarajan, A.T.: Chromosome aberrations: past, present and future. Mutation Res./Fundam. Mol. Mech. Mutagenesis **504**(1–2), 3–16 (2002)
17. Patterson, D.: Molecular genetic analysis of down syndrome. Hum. Genet. **126**(1), 195–214 (2009)
18. Peng, J., et al.: Identification of incorrect karyotypes using deep learning. In: Farkaš, I., Masulli, P., Otte, S., Wermter, S. (eds.) ICANN 2021. LNCS, vol. 12891, pp. 453–464. Springer, Cham (2021). https://doi.org/10.1007/978-3-030-86362-3_37
19. Qin, Y., et al.: Varifocal-net: a chromosome classification approach using deep convolutional networks. IEEE Trans. Med. Imaging **38**(11), 2569–2581 (2019)
20. Sarlin, P.-E., DeTone, D., Malisiewicz, T., Rabinovich, A.: Superglue: learning feature matching with graph neural networks. In: Proceedings of the IEEE/CVF Conference on Computer Vision and Pattern Recognition, pp. 4938–4947 (2020)
21. Sharma, M., Saha, O., Sriraman, A., Hebbalaguppe, R., Vig, L., Karande, S.: Crowdsourcing for chromosome segmentation and deep classification. In: Proceedings of the IEEE Conference on Computer Vision and Pattern Recognition Workshops, pp. 34–41 (2017)
22. Sharma, M., Vig, L., et al.: Automatic chromosome classification using deep attention based sequence learning of chromosome bands. In: 2018 International Joint Conference on Neural Networks (IJCNN), pp. 1–8. IEEE (2018)
23. Vajen, B., et al.: Classification of fluorescent r-band metaphase chromosomes using a convolutional neural network is precise and fast in generating Karyograms of hematologic neoplastic cells. Cancer Genet. **260**, 23–29 (2022)
24. Vaswani, A., et al.: Attention is all you need. In: Advances in Neural Information Processing Systems, pp. 5998–6008 (2017)
25. Wang, R., Yan, J., Yang, X.: Neural graph matching network: learning Lawler's quadratic assignment problem with extension to hypergraph and multiple-graph matching. IEEE Trans. Pattern Anal. Mach. Intell. (2021)
26. Wei, H., Gao, W., Nie, H., Sun, J., Zhu, M.: Classification of Giemsa staining chromosome using input-aware deep convolutional neural network with integrated uncertainty estimates. Biomed. Sig. Process. Control **71**, 103120 (2022)

27. Wu, Y., Yue, Y., Tan, X., Wang, W., Lu, T.: End-to-end chromosome karyotyping with data augmentation using GAN. In: 2018 25th IEEE International Conference on Image Processing (ICIP), pp. 2456–2460. IEEE (2018)
28. Xiao, L., Luo, C.: DeepACC: automate chromosome classification based on metaphase images using deep learning framework fused with priori knowledge. In: 2021 IEEE 18th International Symposium on Biomedical Imaging (ISBI), pp. 607–610. IEEE (2021)
29. Xu, Y., Osep, A., Ban, Y., Horaud, R., Leal-Taixé, L., Alameda-Pineda, X.: How to train your deep multi-object tracker. In: Proceedings of the IEEE/CVF Conference on Computer Vision and Pattern Recognition, pp. 6787–6796 (2020)

Efficient Biomedical Instance Segmentation via Knowledge Distillation

Xiaoyu Liu[1], Bo Hu[1], Wei Huang[1], Yueyi Zhang[1,2(✉)], and Zhiwei Xiong[1,2]

[1] University of Science and Technology of China, Hefei, China
zhyuey@ustc.edu.cn
[2] Institute of Artificial Intelligence, Hefei Comprehensive National Science Center,
Hefei, China

Abstract. Biomedical instance segmentation is vulnerable to complicated instance morphology, resulting in over-merge and over-segmentation. Recent advanced methods apply convolutional neural networks to predict pixel embeddings to overcome this problem. However, these methods suffer from heavy computational burdens and massive storage. In this paper, we present the first knowledge distillation method tailored for biomedical instance segmentation to transfer the knowledge from a cumbersome teacher network to a lightweight student one. Different from existing distillation methods on other tasks, we consider three kinds of essential knowledge of the instance segmentation task, *i.e.*, instance-level features, instance relationships in the feature space and pixel-level instance boundaries. Specifically, we devise two distillation schemes: (i) instance graph distillation that transfers the knowledge of instance-level features and instance relationships by the instance graphs built from embeddings of the teacher-student pair, respectively, and (ii) pixel affinity distillation that converts pixel embeddings into pixel affinities and explicitly transfers the structured knowledge of instance boundaries encoded in affinities. Experimental results on a 3D electron microscopy dataset (CREMI) and a 2D plant phenotype dataset (CVPPP) demonstrate that the student models trained through our distillation method use fewer than 1% parameters and less than 10% inference time while achieving promising performance compared with corresponding teacher models. Code is available at https://github.com/liuxy1103/BISKD.

Keywords: Biomedical instance segmentation · Pixel embeddings · Instance graph distillation · Pixel affinity distillation

1 Introduction

Biomedical instance segmentation is a crucial and challenging task for biomedical image analysis, aiming to assign each pixel of an image to an instance. The

Supplementary Information The online version contains supplementary material available at https://doi.org/10.1007/978-3-031-16440-8_2.

prevalent methods are either based on the semantic segmentation of instance contours [4,19] or by means of object detection [8,10]. Since they are sensitive to the instance morphology [5], these methods are unreliable in the cases of dense distribution and severe occlusions of the instances, resulting in over-merge and over-segmentation. Recent advanced methods [5,14,17,18,20,24] tackle the problem by applying a convolutional neural network (CNN) to predict pixel-level instance-aware embeddings. These embeddings are not affected by instance morphology and can be clustered into the final instance segmentation results by different post-processing algorithms. However, these methods heavily rely on cumbersome network models for the dense estimation of the pixel-level features, which leads to heavy computational burdens and massive storage. Especially for 3D CNNs, the simplified network is imperative for faster inference speed.

Knowledge distillation [11,12,27,31] has been one of the most popular solutions to achieve satisfactory performance while reducing computational burdens and storage by transferring effective knowledge from a cumbersome teacher network to a lightweight student one. Existing distillation methods are mainly devised for image-level classification and semantic segmentation tasks. For example, Zagoruyko et al. [32] and Tung et al. [29] transfer the knowledge distilled from feature maps in intermediate layers of the teacher model to the student model. Qin et al. [25] utilize semantic region information and the output logits of the teacher model to guide the learning of the student model. However, it is not suitable to directly apply these knowledge distillation methods to biomedical instance segmentation. Firstly, existing distillation methods neglect instance-level features and instance relationships in the feature space, which are indispensable knowledge to distinguish different instances. Secondly, the logits distillation in the semantic segmentation [25] cannot be applied to pixel embeddings, and more complicated pixel-level instance boundary information contained in embeddings is supposed to be distilled by special designs. Although Chen et al. [6] propose a distillation method by a review mechanism of multiple feature maps which can be applied to biomedical instance segmentation, the distilled knowledge is difficult to be learned since the lightweight network cannot pay enough attention to the features at each pixel location.

In this paper, we address the above-mentioned problems by a knowledge distillation method that distills three kinds of knowledge from multi-level feature maps, i.e., instance-level features, instance relationships in the feature space, and pixel-level instance boundaries, by two distillation schemes. To the best of our knowledge, it is the first distillation method tailored for biomedical instance segmentation. Firstly, we devise an instance graph distillation (IGD) scheme to transfer the knowledge of instance features and instance relationships by nodes and edges of an instance graph, respectively. The IGD scheme constructs instance graphs from embeddings of the teacher-student pair, and enforces the consistency of graphs constructed from the teacher and student networks. Secondly, we introduce a pixel affinity distillation (PAD) scheme to transfer the knowledge of precise instance boundaries extracted from multi-level feature maps. The PAD scheme converts the pixel embeddings into pixel affinities that encode structured information of instance boundaries, and then enforces the student model to generate affinities similar to its teacher model.

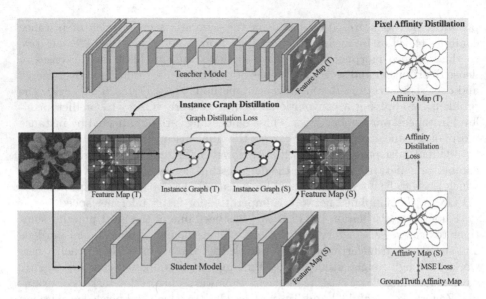

Fig. 1. Workflow of our proposed distillation method. The Instance Graph Distillation (IGD) scheme forces the student model to mimic its teacher's instance-level features and instance relationships by an instance graph. The Pixel Affinity Distillation (PAD) scheme converts pixel embeddings into pixel affinities, and transfers the knowledge of instance boundaries to the student model.

We conduct extensive experiments to demonstrate the superiority of our knowledge distillation method over existing distillation methods on a 3D electron microscopy dataset (CREMI) and a 2D plant phenotype dataset (CVPPP) dataset. The student models trained through our distillation method use fewer than 1% parameters and less than 10% inference time while achieving promising performance compared with corresponding teacher models.

2   Methodology

The workflow of our proposed distillation method is shown in Fig. 1, which can be applied to both the 2D network for images and the 3D network for volumes. We construct a cumbersome teacher model T and a lightweight student model S, as shown in the top and bottom blue rectangles of the figure. For an input image of size $H \times W$, both T and S predict a group of feature maps $E \in \mathbb{R}^{D \times H \times W}$, where D is the number of channels of the last layer of the network. The embedding vector of the pixel p is $e_p \in \mathbb{R}^D$, which is unique to different instances in the feature space and can be clustered into instances by post-processing algorithms. The two schemes, IGD and PAD, take charge of the knowledge distillation mechanism to transfer the effective knowledge from multi-level feature maps generated by networks. Details of the proposed method are decomposed below.

Instance Graph Distillation. Embeddings of pixels $p \in \mathbb{S}^i$ belonging to the same instance i and locating in the corresponding area $\mathbb{S}^i$ are similar, while embeddings of pixels belonging to different instances are dissimilar. It ensures that different instances $i \in \mathbb{I}$ can be distinguished by the distance in the feature space. Therefore, the distribution of embeddings in the feature space contains effective knowledge related to the instance-level features and instance relationships.

To effectively distill this knowledge, we construct an instance graph that encodes the knowledge of instance-level features and instance relationships by nodes and edges, respectively. The nodes are extracted from pixel embeddings of a group of feature maps with the guidance of labeled instance masks which provide precise areas to calculate instance central features: $v_i = \frac{1}{|\mathbb{S}^i|} \sum_{p \in \mathbb{S}^i} e_p$. The edges are defined as the cosine distance between two nodes: $\varepsilon_{ij} = \frac{v_i^T \cdot v_j}{\|v_i\| \|v_j\|}$, where instances $i, j \in \mathbb{I}$ and $i \neq j$.

Given the computational complexity of the construction of the instance graph, we accelerate it through matrix operations [2] so that the training time of the student model by the distillation method is slightly longer than that of the standard training method.

Then we force the instance graph of the student model to be consistent with the instance graph of the teacher model. The distillation loss of this scheme L_{IGD} can be divided into two parts, respectively related to nodes and edges:

$$L_{IGD} = \lambda_1 L_{Node} + \lambda_2 L_{Edge}$$
$$= \lambda_1 \frac{1}{|\mathbb{I}|} \sum_{i \in \mathbb{I}} \left\| v_i^T - v_i^S \right\|_2 + \lambda_2 \frac{1}{|\mathbb{I}|^2} \sum_{i \in \mathbb{I}} \sum_{j \in \mathbb{I}} \left\| \varepsilon_{ij}^T - \varepsilon_{ij}^S \right\|_2, \qquad (1)$$

where λ_1 and λ_2 are weighting coefficients to balance the two terms, and the superscripts indicate the teacher and student models.

Pixel Affinity Distillation. To efficiently transfer the structured information of instance boundaries, we adopt a PAD scheme to convert pixel embeddings into pixel affinities [15] and force the consistency of affinities from the teacher-student pair by the mean square error loss. The pixel affinity describes the relationship between pixels by their pixel embeddings: $a_{n,p} = \frac{e_p^T \cdot e_{p+n}}{\|e_p\| \|e_{p+n}\|}$, where pixel p and pixel $p+n$ are constrained to be locally adjacent within n pixel strides to ensure efficient use of the embedding space, as demonstrated in [5]. Accordingly, the group of feature maps E is converted into the affinity map $A \in \mathbb{R}^{N \times H \times W}$, where N denotes the adjacent relations within different pixel strides.

Let A^T and A^S denote affinity maps respectively generated from the teacher and student models, and the distillation loss of the PAD scheme is given as

$$L_{PAD} = \left\| A^T - A^S \right\|_2$$
$$= \frac{1}{N \times H \times W} \sum_{n=1}^{N} \sum_{p=1}^{H \times W} \left\| a_{n,p}^T - a_{n,p}^S \right\|_2. \qquad (2)$$

Table 1. Model complexity and inference time for different teacher-student pairs.

Method	#Params (M)	FLOPs (GMAC)	#Infer time (s)
3D U-Net MALA (T)	84.02	367.04	53.5 ± 2.0
3D U-Net MALA (S)	0.37	22.01	2.7 ± 0.2
2D Residual U-Net (T)	33.61	98.79	2.0 ± 0.1
2D Residual U-Net (S)	0.30	0.97	0.2 ± 0.03

The affinity map converted from the feature map of the last layer of the student model is also supervised by the affinity label $\hat{A}$ from the groundtruth segmentation, we formulate the loss as

$$L_{aff} = ||\hat{A} - A^S||_2. \tag{3}$$

Overall Optimization. Given a well pre-trained teacher network, the overall object function for the student network training terms

$$L_{total} = L_{aff} + \lambda_1 L_{Node} + \lambda_2 L_{Edge} + \lambda_3 L_{PAD}, \tag{4}$$

where λ_1, λ_2, and λ_3 are empirically set to make these loss value ranges comparable. In practice, we use a 'bottleneck' layer [32] (1×1 convolution) to make the student's feature maps match the number of channels of the teacher's one in the intermediate layers.

3   Experiments

3.1   Datasets and Metrics

Electron Microscopy Volumes. The CREMI [7] dataset is imaged from the adult drosophila brain at $4 \times 4 \times 40$ nm resolution. This dataset has been widely used in electron microscopy image segmentation algorithm evaluation [9,13,21]. It is composed of three sub-volumes (CREMI-A/B/C) corresponding to different neuron types, each of which contains 125 images with a size of 1250×1250. We use the middle 50 slices for training, the bottom 25 slices for validation, and the top 50 slices for testing. Two widely used metrics in the field of EM image segmentation are adopted for quantitative evaluation, *i.e.*, Variation of Information (VOI) [22] and Adapted Rand Error (ARAND) [26]. Note that smaller values of these two metrics indicate better segmentation performance.

Plant Phenotype Images. The CVPPP A1 dataset [28] contains leaves with more complex shapes and more severe occlusions than instances commonly found in biomedical images. We randomly sampled 108 images for training and 20 images for testing, where each image is with a resolution of 530×500. The quality of the segmentation result is measured by symmetric best dice (SBD) and absolute difference in counting ($|DiC|$) metrics [23].

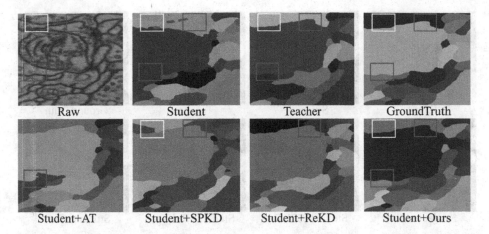

Fig. 2. Visualization of an example for the segmentation results of different knowledge distillation methods on the CREMI-C dataset. Over-merge and over-segmentation in the results of the student model are highlighted by red and white boxes, respectively. (Color figure online)

Table 2. Quantitative comparison of different knowledge distillation methods on three CREMI datasets. VOI/ARAND are adopted as metrics.

U-Net MALA	CREMI-A		CREMI-B		CREMI-C	
	Waterz ↓	LMC ↓	Waterz ↓	LMC ↓	Waterz ↓	LMC ↓
Teacher	0.85/0.13	0.85/0.13	1.65/0.13	1.50/0.09	1.52/0.12	1.62/0.20
Student	1.10/0.18	0.96/0.15	2.04/0.24	1.78/0.12	2.09/0.24	1.73/0.20
AT [32]	1.07/0.18	0.90/**0.13**	1.96/0.16	1.77/0.15	1.81/0.15	1.69/0.23
SPKD [29]	0.96/0.15	0.89/0.14	1.79/0.15	1.72/0.12	1.75/0.16	1.67/0.23
ReKD [6]	0.93/0.15	0.88/0.14	1.88/0.15	1.65/0.12	1.65/0.13	1.68/0.19
Ours	**0.89/0.14**	**0.86**/0.14	**1.74/0.14**	**1.60/0.11**	**1.60/0.12**	**1.57/0.16**

3.2 Implementation Details

We adopt two state-of-the-art models as cumbersome teacher networks to demonstrate the superiority of our knowledge distillation method, *i.e.*, 3D U-Net MALA [9] and 2D Residual U-Net (ResUnet) [1]. We reduce the number of channels in each layer of the two teacher networks by approximately 90% to obtain their corresponding lightweight student networks. We illustrate the model complexity and inference time on test datasets for different teacher and student networks in Table 1. The student networks for 3D U-Net MALA and 2D Residual U-Net use 0.4% and 0.9% parameters and 5.0% and 10.0% inference time, compared with corresponding teacher networks. We compare our method with three state-of-the-art knowledge distillation methods commonly applied for multi-level feature maps, *i.e.*, attention transferring (AT) [32], Similarity Preserving knowledge distillation (SPKD) [29] and review knowledge distillation (ReKD) [6].

We train all models using Adam optimizer [16] with $\beta_1 = 0.9$ and $\beta_2 = 0.99$, a learning rate of 10^{-4}, and a batch size of 2 on one NVIDIA TitanXP

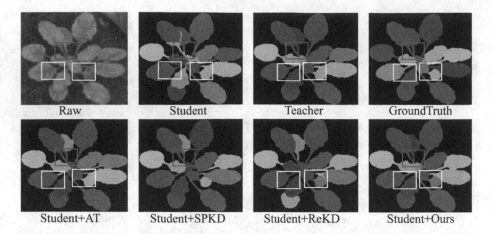

Fig. 3. Visualization of an example for the segmentation results of different knowledge distillation methods on the CVPPP dataset.

Table 3. Quantitative comparison of different methods on the CVPPP dataset.

Residual U-Net	SBD ↑	|DiC| ↓
Teacher	88.6	1.15
Student	81.9	2.15
AT [32]	83.9	1.60
SPKD [29]	85.2	1.30
ReKD [6]	85.6	1.25
Ours	**86.4**	**1.15**

GPU for 30,0000 iterations. The environment of all experiments is based on Pytorch 1.0.1, CUDA 9.0, Python 3.7.4 and Ubuntu 16.04. Given the limited GPU memories, the embedding dimension of the last layer is set to 16, and the affinity is calculated by adjacent pixel embeddings within one voxel stride for the 3D network and within 27-pixel strides for the 2D network. The final segmentation results of the 3D network are generated by two common post-processing algorithms, *i.e.*, waterz [9] and LMC [3]. The 2D results are generated by Mutex [30].

3.3   Experimental Results

Electron Microscopy Volumes. We list an extensive quantitative comparison of different knowledge distillation methods for the 3D U-Net MALA teacher-student pair on three CREMI subvolumes in Table 2. Our method outperforms the competing methods almost on all metrics. Our proposed method significantly alleviates the performance gap between the student and teacher networks by more than 65% for the key VOI metric on all experimental results.

Table 4. Ablation study for our distillation method on the CREMI-C dataset.

Method	Waterz ↓	LMC ↓
Student	2.09/0.24	1.73/0.20
Student + Node	1.75/0.14	1.66/0.19
Student + Node + Edge	1.62/0.13	1.65/0.19
Student + Node + Edge + PAD	**1.60/0.12**	**1.57/0.16**

The corresponding visual comparison is given in Fig. 2. Our method helps the student model to better distinguish different instances with accurate instance boundaries and solve the severe over-segmentation and over-merge problems in the results of the student model. The baseline methods only force the student to mimic the pixel embeddings predicted by the teacher, which is difficult for a lightweight network to pay enough attention to the features at each pixel location. Due to a lack of knowledge of instance-level features and instance relationships, these methods cannot guide the student to enlarge the difference of adjacent instances and reduce the feature variance of pixels belonging to the same instance, leading to severe over-merge and over-segmentation. Moreover, these baseline methods ignore the structure knowledge of instance boundaries, which causes segmentation errors and coarse boundaries.

Plant Phenotype Images. We demonstrate the effectiveness of our knowledge distillation method for the 2D Residual U-Net teacher-student pair on the CVPPP dataset. As listed in Table 3, our method outperforms the existing methods and significantly reduces the performance gap of the teacher-student pair by 68% for the key SBD metric. Visual results also demonstrate the superior segmentation performance of our distillation method in dealing with challenging cases, as shown in Fig. 3.

Ablation Study. To verify the effectiveness of the distillation components of our method, we conduct the ablation study about the proposed IGD and PAD schemes, where the IGD scheme is divided into edge and node parts that are separately validated. As listed in Table 4, we can observe that every component has a positive effect on the performance of the student model. The node part of the IGD scheme improves the undistilled student model by 10.7% on the average VOI metric of the two post-processing algorithms. The gain increases to 14.4% when the edge part of the IGD scheme is also adopted. Further introducing the PAD scheme boosts the improvement to 17.0%. The IGD scheme and the PAD scheme are complementary to each other.

4   Conclusion

In this paper, we propose the first knowledge distillation method tailored for biomedical instance segmentation. The proposed method transfers the knowledge of instance-level features, instance relationships and pixel-level instance boundaries from cumbersome teacher networks to corresponding lightweight student networks, by the specially designed graph distillation scheme and pixel affinity distillation scheme. Experimental results on the 3D and 2D datasets demonstrate that our method outperforms existing distillation methods and significantly fills the performance gap between the cumbersome teacher networks and the corresponding lightweight student networks.

Acknowledgement. This work was supported in part by the National Key R&D Program of China under Grant 2017YFA0700800, the National Natural Science Foundation of China under Grant 62021001, the University Synergy Innovation Program of Anhui Province No. GXXT-2019-025, and Anhui Provincial Natural Science Foundation under grant No. 1908085QF256.

References

1. Anas, E.M.A., et al.: Clinical target-volume delineation in prostate brachytherapy using residual neural networks. In: Descoteaux, M., Maier-Hein, L., Franz, A., Jannin, P., Collins, D.L., Duchesne, S. (eds.) MICCAI 2017. LNCS, vol. 10435, pp. 365–373. Springer, Cham (2017). https://doi.org/10.1007/978-3-319-66179-7_42
2. Avelar, P.H., Tavares, A.R., da Silveira, T.L., Jung, C.R., Lamb, L.C.: Superpixel image classification with graph attention networks. In: 2020 33rd SIBGRAPI Conference on Graphics, Patterns and Images (SIBGRAPI), pp. 203–209. IEEE (2020)
3. Beier, T., et al.: Multicut brings automated neurite segmentation closer to human performance. Nat. Methods **14**(2), 101–102 (2017)
4. Chen, H., Qi, X., Yu, L., Heng, P.A.: DCAN: deep contour-aware networks for accurate gland segmentation. In: Proceedings of the IEEE Conference on Computer Vision and Pattern Recognition, pp. 2487–2496 (2016)
5. Chen, L., Strauch, M., Merhof, D.: Instance segmentation of biomedical images with an object-aware embedding learned with local constraints. In: Shen, D., et al. (eds.) MICCAI 2019. LNCS, vol. 11764, pp. 451–459. Springer, Cham (2019). https://doi.org/10.1007/978-3-030-32239-7_50
6. Chen, P., Liu, S., Zhao, H., Jia, J.: Distilling knowledge via knowledge review. In: Proceedings of the IEEE/CVF Conference on Computer Vision and Pattern Recognition, pp. 5008–5017 (2021)
7. CREMI: Miccal challenge on circuit reconstruction from electron microscopy images (2016). https://cremi.org/
8. Dong, M., et al.: Instance segmentation from volumetric biomedical images without voxel-wise labeling. In: Shen, D., et al. (eds.) MICCAI 2019. LNCS, vol. 11765, pp. 83–91. Springer, Cham (2019). https://doi.org/10.1007/978-3-030-32245-8_10
9. Funke, J., et al.: Large scale image segmentation with structured loss based deep learning for connectome reconstruction. IEEE Trans. Pattern Anal. Mach. Intell. **41**(7), 1669–1680 (2018)
10. He, K., Gkioxari, G., Dollár, P., Girshick, R.: Mask R-CNN. In: Proceedings of the IEEE International Conference on Computer Vision, pp. 2961–2969 (2017)
11. Hinton, G., Vinyals, O., Dean, J., et al.: Distilling the knowledge in a neural network. arXiv preprint arXiv:1503.02531 2(7) (2015)
12. Hu, B., Zhou, S., Xiong, Z., Wu, F.: Cross-resolution distillation for efficient 3D medical image registration. IEEE Trans. Circuits Syst. Video Technol. (2022)

13. Huang, W., et al.: Semi-supervised neuron segmentation via reinforced consistency learning. IEEE Trans. Med. Imaging (2022)
14. Huang, W., Deng, S., Chen, C., Fu, X., Xiong, Z.: Learning to model pixel-embedded affinity for homogeneous instance segmentation. In: Proceedings of AAAI Conference on Artificial Intelligence (2022)
15. Ke, T.W., Hwang, J.J., Liu, Z., Yu, S.X.: Adaptive affinity fields for semantic segmentation. In: Proceedings of the European Conference on Computer Vision (ECCV), pp. 587–602 (2018)
16. Kingma, D.P., Ba, J.: Adam: a method for stochastic optimization. arXiv preprint arXiv:1412.6980 (2014)
17. Kulikov, V., Lempitsky, V.: Instance segmentation of biological images using harmonic embeddings. In: Proceedings of the IEEE/CVF Conference on Computer Vision and Pattern Recognition, pp. 3843–3851 (2020)
18. Lee, K., Lu, R., Luther, K., Seung, H.S.: Learning and segmenting dense voxel embeddings for 3D neuron reconstruction. IEEE Trans. Med. Imaging **40**(12), 3801–3811 (2021)
19. Li, M., Chen, C., Liu, X., Huang, W., Zhang, Y., Xiong, Z.: Advanced deep networks for 3D mitochondria instance segmentation. In: 2022 IEEE 19th International Symposium on Biomedical Imaging (ISBI), pp. 1–5. IEEE (2022)
20. Liu, X., Huang, W., Zhang, Y., Xiong, Z.: Biological instance segmentation with a superpixel-guided graph. In: IJCAI (2022)
21. Liu, X., et al.: Learning neuron stitching for connectomics. In: de Bruijne, M., et al. (eds.) MICCAI 2021. LNCS, vol. 12908, pp. 435–444. Springer, Cham (2021). https://doi.org/10.1007/978-3-030-87237-3_42
22. Meilă, M.: Comparing clusterings by the variation of information. In: Schölkopf, B., Warmuth, M.K. (eds.) COLT-Kernel 2003. LNCS (LNAI), vol. 2777, pp. 173–187. Springer, Heidelberg (2003). https://doi.org/10.1007/978-3-540-45167-9_14
23. Minervini, M., Fischbach, A., Scharr, H., Tsaftaris, S.A.: Finely-grained annotated datasets for image-based plant phenotyping. Pattern Recogn. Lett. **81**, 80–89 (2016)
24. Payer, C., Štern, D., Neff, T., Bischof, H., Urschler, M.: Instance segmentation and tracking with cosine embeddings and recurrent hourglass networks. In: Frangi, A.F., Schnabel, J.A., Davatzikos, C., Alberola-López, C., Fichtinger, G. (eds.) MICCAI 2018. LNCS, vol. 11071, pp. 3–11. Springer, Cham (2018). https://doi.org/10.1007/978-3-030-00934-2_1
25. Qin, D., et al.: Efficient medical image segmentation based on knowledge distillation. IEEE Trans. Med. Imaging **40**(12), 3820–3831 (2021)
26. Rand, W.M.: Objective criteria for the evaluation of clustering methods. J. Am. Stat. Assoc. **66**(336), 846–850 (1971)
27. Romero, A., Ballas, N., Kahou, S.E., Chassang, A., Gatta, C., Bengio, Y.: Fitnets: hints for thin deep nets. arXiv preprint arXiv:1412.6550 (2014)
28. Scharr, H., Minervini, M., Fischbach, A., Tsaftaris, S.A.: Annotated image datasets of rosette plants. In: ECCV (2014)
29. Tung, F., Mori, G.: Similarity-preserving knowledge distillation. In: Proceedings of the IEEE/CVF International Conference on Computer Vision, pp. 1365–1374 (2019)
30. Wolf, S., et al.: The mutex watershed and its objective: efficient, parameter-free graph partitioning. IEEE Trans. Pattern Anal. Mach. Intell. (2020)

31. Xiao, Z., Fu, X., Huang, J., Cheng, Z., Xiong, Z.: Space-time distillation for video super-resolution. In: Proceedings of the IEEE/CVF Conference on Computer Vision and Pattern Recognition, pp. 2113–2122 (2021)
32. Zagoruyko, S., Komodakis, N.: Paying more attention to attention: improving the performance of convolutional neural networks via attention transfer. arXiv preprint arXiv:1612.03928 (2016)

Tracking by Weakly-Supervised Learning and Graph Optimization for Whole-Embryo *C. elegans* lineages

Peter Hirsch[1,2]([envelope]) [ID], Caroline Malin-Mayor[4] [ID], Anthony Santella[3],
Stephan Preibisch[4] [ID], Dagmar Kainmueller[1,2] [ID], and Jan Funke[4] [ID]

[1] Max-Delbrueck-Center for Molecular Medicine in the Helmholtz Association,
Berlin, Germany
{peter.hirsch,dagmar.kainmueller}@mdc-berlin.de
[2] Faculty of Mathematics and Natural Sciences, Humboldt-Universität zu Berlin,
Berlin, Germany
[3] Sloan Kettering Cancer Center, Molecular Cytology Core, Developmental Biology,
New York, USA
[4] HHMI Janelia Research Campus, Ashburn, USA

Abstract. Tracking all nuclei of an embryo in noisy and dense fluorescence microscopy data is a challenging task. We build upon a recent method for nuclei tracking that combines weakly-supervised learning from a small set of nuclei center point annotations with an integer linear program (ILP) for optimal cell lineage extraction. Our work specifically addresses the following challenging properties of *C. elegans* embryo recordings: (1) Many cell divisions as compared to benchmark recordings of other organisms, and (2) the presence of polar bodies that are easily mistaken as cell nuclei. To cope with (1), we devise and incorporate a learnt cell division detector. To cope with (2), we employ a learnt polar body detector. We further propose automated ILP weights tuning via a structured SVM, alleviating the need for tedious manual set-up of a respective grid search.

Our method outperforms the previous leader of the cell tracking challenge on the *Fluo-N3DH-CE* embryo dataset. We report a further extensive quantitative evaluation on two more *C. elegans* datasets. We will make these datasets public to serve as an extended benchmark for future method development. Our results suggest considerable improvements yielded by our method, especially in terms of the correctness of division event detection and the number and length of fully correct track segments. Code: https://github.com/funkelab/linajea.

Keywords: Detection · Tracking · Deep learning · Optimization

D. Kainmueller and J. Funke—Equal contribution.

Supplementary Information The online version contains supplementary material available at https://doi.org/10.1007/978-3-031-16440-8_3.

1   Introduction

Advances in microscopy have made the recording of whole embryo development possible [10,11]. However there is an inherent trade-off between frame rate, resolution and the prevention of phototoxicity [26]. While it is possible to capture high signal-to-noise images with high resolution, this can damage the organism, especially during early embryonic development. Consequently, embryonic development is commonly captured at low frame rate and with low signal-to-noise ratio (SNR). Together with cell-cycle inherent signal fluctuation, low SNR renders automated cell detection challenging. Furthermore, low frame rate renders automated tracking challenging as overlap-based tracking approaches are not applicable. Last but not least, the similar shape and appearance of distinct cell nuclei also renders similarity-based tracking approaches ineffective.

A number of automated cell tracking approaches have been developed to tackle reduced SNR as well as frame rates on the order of minutes. Such methods have enabled a range of studies on a variety of organisms, where it wouldn't have been feasible to do tracking manually [2,5,12,16,18,27]. The *Cell Tracking Challenge* (CTC) [25], an extensive benchmark that contains 2d+time and 3d+time datasets of different organisms recorded with a variety of microscopes, allows for a quantitative comparison of automated cell tracking methods.

Current methods for cell tracking in *C. elegans* follow the *tracking-by-detection* paradigm, which first computes (candidate) cell detections in all frames, and in a second step links matching cell detections across frames. To this end, Starrynite [1], which is widely used by practitioners, uses classical computer vision to detect locations of maximum signal in each frame, nearest neighbor matching for link detection, and local post-processing to resolve ambiguities that occur in case of cell divisions. Linkage can also be achieved in a globally optimal manner by means of combinatorial optimization, as in the competitive method Baxter [13] (former rank 2 on the CTC *C. elegans* benchmark), which employs the Viterbi algorithm in the linkage step. Related methods can also directly yield an optimal feasible cell lineage tree, in the face of over- and underdetections [22], as well as for an overcomplete set of candidate detections [9,14]. To modernize the detection step, Cao et al. [2] replaced the classical detection step of Starrynite by neural network-based cell segmentation. Similarly, the recently proposed active learning framework Elephant [23] (former rank 1 on the CTC *C. elegans* benchmark) uses modern deep learning for segmentation and detection. However, both perform local linkage via nearest neighbor search (in case of Elephant optionally supported via a learned optical flow estimate).

We propose a method that unifies the individual advantages of Baxter [13] and Elephant [23]. To this end we build upon Linajea [14], a recent method that combines deep learning and combinatorial optimization for cell tracking. We propose extensions of Linajea to capture properties specific to recordings of the model organism *C. elegans*, namely relatively many cell divisions, and the presence of *polar bodies* which look similar to nuclei. Our extended method yields state of the art accuracy on benchmark *C. elegans* data. Besides accuracy, we also address efficiency. We propose to use a structured SVM (sSVM) to facilitate

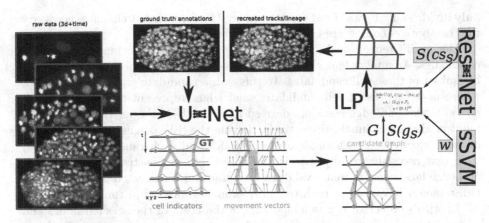

Fig. 1. Method overview: We use a 4d U-Net to predict cell candidates and movement vectors. These are used to construct a candidate graph G with node and edge scores g_s as in [14]. We propose to integrate learnt cell state scores cs_s. Graph G, feature matrix S, weights w and a set of feasibility constraints form an ILP that yields the cell lineage. We propose to find w via a structured SVM (sSVM); proposed changes highlighted in magenta; figure adapted from [14].

the tuning of the weights of the ILP objective which alleviates the need for manual configuration of a grid search. This is particularly useful in light of our extensions as they introduce additional weights and thereby would increase the dimensionality of the search. In summary our contributions are:

- A learnt cell state and polar body detector, integrated into an existing approach that combines deep learning and an ILP for nuclei tracking.
- Fully automated tuning of the weights of the ILP objective via a sSVM.
- The new state-of-the-art for *C. elegans* in the Cell Tracking Challenge.
- Two new datasets made publicly available as benchmark data, namely three confocal and three lightsheet recordings of *C. elegans*, all fully annotated.

2   Method

Our method extends the tracking-by-detection approach Linajea [14]. We briefly review Linajea, and then describe our extensions in detail. For more details on Linajea, please refer to [14]. For an overview of our extended method, see Fig. 1.

Linajea. Linajea [14] implements a 4d U-Net [3,4,20] to predict the position and movement of each nucleus. Position is encoded as a single-channel image of Gaussian-shaped blobs, one per nucleus, as in [7]. The locations of the respective intensity maxima correspond to nuclei center points. Movement is encoded as 3d vectors per pixel within a nucleus. Each vector points to the spatial location (center point) of the same (or parent) nucleus in the previous time frame. Note, the backwards direction of the movement vectors simplifies tracking as cells can only divide going forward but cannot merge. The four output channels necessary for the above encoding are trained jointly via L2 loss.

During inference, local maxima of the predicted position map serve as cell candidates. An integer linear program (ILP) is employed to select and link a feasible subset of these cell candidates. To this end, a candidate graph is established, where nodes represent cell candidates, and edges represent cell linkage candidates. Node- and edge costs are derived from the U-Net's position- and movement prediction channels, respectively. Solving the ILP assigns a label "selected" or "not selected" to each candidate cell (node) and each candidate link (edge) such that a cost-based objective is minimized. Linear constraints on the node- and edge labels ensure that a valid tracking solution is extracted from the graph, i.e., a binary forest where each tree only branches forward in time.

Linajea's objective is a weighted sum of the costs of the selected nodes and edges. There are four tunable weights: A constant cost $w_{\text{node-sel}}$ for selecting a node, a factor $w_{\text{node-cost}}$ to scale the position prediction, a factor $w_{\text{edge-cost}}$ to scale the distance between predicted movement vector target and linked cell position, and a constant cost $w_{\text{track-cost}}$ for each track. The track cost is incorporated via an additional binary node label "track start", with appropriate constraints to ensure consistency with the selection labels. Linajea performs grid-search within a manually defined range to find a set of suitable weights.

We propose two extensions to Linajea: (1) An additional network to classify cell state, and respective additional costs and feasibility constraints in the ILP, and (2) the use of a structured SVM (sSVM) to automatically find the optimal weights for the ILP objective, as described in the following.

Cell State Classifier. We propose to incorporate a classifier to determine the cell state of each cell candidate similarly to [21]. We assign to each candidate one of four classes: parent cell (i.e., a cell that is about to undergo cell division), daughter cell (cell that just divided), continuation cell (cell track that continues without division) and polar body. We train a 3d ResNet18 [6] with 3d convolutions for this task. The parent/daughter/continuation classes are incorporated into the ILP as a separate set of node labels, with their weighted prediction scores as costs. In addition to Linajea's feasibility constraints on node and edge selection [14], we impose novel constraints that ensure that (1) selection- and cell state labels are consistent, and (2) a parent at time t can only be linked to a daughter at time $t+1$ and vice versa.

Formally, for each edge $e = (u, v)$ between nodes u and v in the graph (directed forward in time), let $y_{\text{edge},e}$, $y_{\text{node},u} \in \{0,1\}$ denote binary variables that represent edge- and node selection as in Linajea. We introduce novel binary variables $y_{\text{daughter},u}, y_{\text{parent},u}, y_{\text{continue},u} \in \{0,1\}$ that represent daughter-, parent- and continuation cell state labels per node. To ensure that a selected node is assigned exactly one cell state, for each node, we introduce the linear equality constraint $y_{\text{parent},u} + y_{\text{daughter},u} + y_{\text{continue},u} - y_{\text{node},u} = 0$ to be included in the ILP. To ensure that selected edges constitute feasible parent-daughter links, for each edge, we introduce novel inequality constraints $y_{\text{parent},u} + y_{\text{edge},e} - y_{\text{daughter},v} \leq 1$ and $y_{\text{daughter},v} + y_{\text{edge},e} - y_{\text{parent},u} \leq 1$ to be included in the ILP. Thus, e.g., if node u is labelled parent ($y_{\text{parent},u} = 1$), and edge e is selected ($y_{\text{edge},e} = 1$), node v has to be labelled daughter ($y_{\text{daughter},v} = 1$).

We add the cell state predictions to Linajea's objective. This entails new weights $w_{\text{parent}}, w_{\text{daughter}}, w_{\text{continue}}$ that serve to scale the prediction scores of respectively selected and labelled nodes. A further weight w_{division} serves as constant division cost, contributed by each selected parent.

By default, we do not perform any postprocessing on the tracks (such as removal of short tracks). We propose one exception regarding the polar bodies: Depending on the specific study they might not be of interest, and even if they are often not contained in the ground truth tracks as they are not considered "proper" cells. That is why we add them as an additional class to our cell state classifier. The score for the polar body class can be used to optionally detect and remove them from the tracks. Suppl. Fig. 2 shows an exemplary polar body.

Structured SVM-Based Weights Search. Manually configured grid search for optimal weights as in [14] can be costly and generally a dataset specific search range has to be found for each new dataset. To alleviate the need for this manual step, we propose the use of a structured SVM (sSVM) for automatic weight selection [8,24]. Following [14], our extended objective can be phrased as

$$\min_{\mathbf{y}}\langle S\mathbf{w}, \mathbf{y}\rangle \quad s.t. \quad G(\mathbf{y}) \in \mathcal{F}_2, \tag{1}$$

where $\mathbf{y}$ is a vector of all binary indicator variables, including our new ones

$$\mathbf{y} = \left[\mathbf{y}_{\text{node}}^T, \mathbf{y}_{\text{track}}^T, \mathbf{y}_{\text{parent}}^T, \mathbf{y}_{\text{daughter}}^T, \mathbf{y}_{\text{continue}}^T, \mathbf{y}_{\text{edge}}^T\right]^T \in \{0,1\}^{5|V|+|E|}.$$

$G(\mathbf{y})$ denotes the graph formed by the selected nodes and edges in $\mathbf{y}$. $\mathcal{F}_2$ denotes the set of all feasible binary forests. $S^{\dim(y)\times\dim(w)}$ is a sparse feature matrix that contains all node- and edge features. It has the following columns: (1) 1 for *node* indicators (i.e., in the first $|V|$ rows), and 0 otherwise. (2) Candidate cell prediction for *node* indicators, and 0 otherwise. (3) 1 for *track start* indicators, 0 otherwise. (4) 1 for *parent class* indicators, 0 otherwise. (5-7) Parent/daughter/continue class predictions for *parent/daughter/continue* indicators, 0 otherwise. (8) Edge cost for *edge* indicators, and 0 otherwise. $\mathbf{w}$ is the vector of weights

$$\mathbf{w} = \left[w_{\text{node-sel}}, w_{\text{node-score}}, w_{\text{track}}, w_{\text{div}}, w_{\text{parent}}, w_{\text{daughter}}, w_{\text{continue}}, w_{\text{edge}}\right]^T.$$

Solving the ILP (1) yields the best feasible $\mathbf{y}$ given some $\mathbf{w}$. However, appropriate values for $\mathbf{w}$ are unknown a priori. With the help of the ground truth annotations, what we can determine though is a "best effort" indicator vector $\mathbf{y}'$. This equates to the best possible feasible solution given the set of predicted cell candidates and movement vectors. We thus want to find the weights $\mathbf{w}$ such that solving (1) yields $\mathbf{y} = \mathbf{y}'$, or as close as possible to it.

To find such weights, given $\mathbf{y}'$, we derive a modified objective from Eq. 1 which we then minimize w.r.t. the weights. We thus follow the sSVM approach with a loss-augmented objective [8,24]. Formally, we seek a $\mathbf{w}$ that minimizes

$$L(\mathbf{w}) = \langle S\mathbf{w}, \mathbf{y}'\rangle - \min_{\mathbf{y}:\, G(\mathbf{y})\in\mathcal{F}_2} \left(\langle S\mathbf{w}, \mathbf{y}\rangle - \Delta(\mathbf{y}', \mathbf{y})\right) + \lambda|\mathbf{w}|^2, \tag{2}$$

with Hamming cost function Δ to measure the deviation of the optimal $\mathbf{y}$ for a given $\mathbf{w}$ and the best effort $\mathbf{y}'$, and a hyperparameter $\lambda \geq 0$ for weighing L2 regularization on the weights (we use $\lambda = 0.001$).

To give a brief intuition why optimizing this loss yields the desired parameters (for which we neglect the L2 regularizer for the moment): It is easy to see that $L(\mathbf{w}) \geq 0$ because $\Delta \geq 0$ and $\min_{\mathbf{y}:\ G(\mathbf{y}) \in \mathcal{F}_2} \langle S\mathbf{w}, \mathbf{y} \rangle \leq \langle S\mathbf{w}, \mathbf{y}' \rangle$. Furthermore, if $\mathbf{w}$ yields $\mathbf{y}'$ as minimum of the ILP, $\operatorname{argmin}_{\mathbf{y}:\ G(\mathbf{y}) \in \mathcal{F}_2} \langle S\mathbf{w}, \mathbf{y} \rangle = \mathbf{y}'$, then $L(\mathbf{w}) = 0$, i.e., the loss is minimized. Last but not least, if a $\mathbf{w}$ with zero loss does not exist, the loss seeks a $\mathbf{w}$ that yields an ILP-minimizing $\mathbf{y}$ that is at least "close" to $\mathbf{y}'$ both in terms of the Hamming loss and in terms of its objective value $\langle S\mathbf{w}, \mathbf{y} \rangle$. For details on the sSVM optimization procedure, please refer to [8,24].

3   Results

To measure the performance of our method we evaluate it on three different datasets of developing *C. elegans* embryos, the **Fluo-N3DH-CE** dataset of the Cell Tracking Challenge benchmark (CTC) [25], three confocal recordings (**mskcc-confocal**) and three lightsheet recordings (**nih-ls**). See Suppl. Table 5 for information on implementation and computational details.

*The **Fluo-N3DH-CE** dataset* [18] consists of four 3d+time anisotropic confocal recordings until the 350 cell stage; 2 public ones for training and 2 private ones for the official evaluation. All tracks are annotated. The polar body filter is not used for this dataset. Our method (named JAN-US) achieves a detection score (DET) of 0.981, and a tracking score (TRA) of 0.979, thereby outperforming the previous state of the art from Elephant [23] (DET 0.979, TRA 0.975) at the time of submission. These results, which are listed on the challenge website, were generated using our cell state classifier (*linajea+csc*). See Suppl. Table 4 for a short description of the metrics. For details on the dataset, the challenge format and the metrics, please refer to [15,25].

Discussion. As the labels for CTC test data are not public, a qualitative assessment of the improvement over the previous state of the art is not possible. However, the challenge scores are defined to be interpretable in terms of reduction of manual labor necessary for fixing an automated tracking solution. In this regard, our improvement in TRA over Elephant should mean that our method entails a 16% reduction in manual curation effort as compared to Elephant ($\frac{(1-0.975)-(1-0.979)}{(1-0.975)} = 0.16$).

Our improvement in DET and TRA scores on the challenge test data can further be put into perspective by comparison with the improvements in DET and TRA that we obtain and analyze on our other datasets (as described in the following, summarized in Table 1). We take this comparison as further indication that in terms of DET and TRA, an improvement in the 3rd decimal place as achieved on the CTC data can mean a considerable difference in performance.

*The **mskcc-confocal** dataset* consists of three fully annotated 3d+time anisotropic confocal recordings (data: https://doi.org/10.5281/zenodo.6460303).

Table 1. Quantitative results on **mskcc-confocal** and **nih-ls** data. For description of error metrics see Suppl. Table 4; absolute number of errors normalized per 1000 GT edges; best value bold, value with insignificant difference to best value underlined (significance assessed with Wilcoxon's signed-rank test and $p < 0.01$).

	FP	FN	IS	FPdiv	FNdiv	div	sum	DET	TRA
mskcc-confocal 270 frames									
Starrynite	7.9	13	0.62	0.58	1.2	1.8	24	0.97875	0.97495
linajea	**3.6**	**5.5**	<u>0.062</u>	0.89	**0.26**	1.2	10.3	0.99514	0.99418
lin.+csc+sSVM	<u>3.7</u>	<u>5.6</u>	**0.046**	**0.053**	0.40	**0.46**	**9.6**	**0.99570**	**0.99480**
nih-ls 270 frames									
Starrynite	22	18	2.4	0.66	1.6	2.2	45	0.81850	0.81114
linajea	**12**	<u>6.5</u>	**0.46**	1.5	**0.40**	1.86	<u>21</u>	0.99367	0.99279
lin.+csc+sSVM	<u>13</u>	**5.3**	<u>0.59</u>	**0.20**	<u>0.49</u>	**0.69**	**20**	**0.99511**	**0.99433**

The ground truth has been created using Starrynite [1,21], followed by manual curation (supported and verified by using the fixed *C. elegans* lineage). The annotations include the polar bodies (marked separately). We report the uncurated Starrynite results as a baseline. As we perform weakly-supervised training on point annotations yet Elephant requires segmentation masks we cannot compare to it on this data. We train and evaluate all models on the first 270 frames (approximately 570 cells in the last frame and 52k in total per sample).

Per experiment we use one recording each as training, validation and test set. We do this for all six possible combinations. For each combination, we perform three experimental runs, starting from different random weight initializations, leading to a total of 18 experimental runs (all numbers averaged). Divisions that are off by one frame compared to the annotations are not counted as errors as the limited frame rate leads to inherent inaccuracies in the data and annotations.

Both Linajea and our extended method considerably outperform Starrynite (see Table 1, and Suppl. Fig. 3 for the respective box plots). We conducted an ablation study on the **mskcc-confocal** dataset to measure the effect of the individual extensions we propose (see Table 2): We report results without the ILP, and without the cell state classifier in the ILP (this matches [14]). Both strongly suffer from false positive (FP)-type errors. We compare results with and without sSVM for weights tuning, and find that sSVM-determined weights yield competitive results. The sSVM finds similar weights for all experimental runs (see Suppl. Fig. 5). Finally we employ the polar body filter (we remove them from the ground truth, too). This reduces FP errors. Due to the strong tree structure of the tracks the notion of "how many tracks are correct" is not well defined. To still try to quantify the intention behind it we evaluate the fraction of error-free tracklets of varying lengths [14], see Suppl. Fig. 4.

Table 2. Ablation study on the **mskcc-confocal** data. We ablate solving an ILP altogether (ILP), incorporating the cell state classifier (csc), employing an sSVM for weights search (ssvm), and incorporating the polar body filter (pbf).

ILP	csc	ssvm	pbf	FP	FN	IS	FPdiv	FNdiv	div	sum	DET	TRA
mskcc-confocal 270 frames												
✗	✗	✗	✗	5.0	**4.6**	<u>0.048</u>	1.6	**0.25**	1.9	11.6	<u>0.99567</u>	0.99464
✓	✗	✗	✗	<u>3.6</u>	5.5	0.062	0.89	<u>0.26</u>	1.2	10.3	0.99514	0.99418
✓	✓	✗	✗	<u>3.4</u>	5.7	**0.028**	0.11	<u>0.27</u>	**0.38**	<u>9.5</u>	0.99526	0.99437
✓	✓	✓	✗	<u>3.7</u>	5.6	<u>0.046</u>	<u>0.053</u>	0.40	0.46	<u>9.6</u>	**0.99570**	**0.99480**
✓	✓	✓	✓	**2.5**	5.5	<u>0.047</u>	**0.048**	0.39	0.44	**8.5**	<u>0.99533</u>	<u>0.99441</u>

Discussion. We did not expect to see large differences between the results for the sSVM-determined weights and for the manually configured grid search as we have gathered experience in choosing appropriate parameters for the weights grid search for this data. Thus the explicit search is often faster as it can be parallelized trivially. However, for other data, where this information is not at hand, the targeted sSVM is very convenient and is computationally more efficient. Interestingly, depending on the weights, the system appears to be able to exchange FP and FN errors. The sSVM-determined weights seem to prioritize FP errors. By adapting the cost function Δ one can modulate this depending on respective application-specific needs (see Suppl. Table 3).

*The **nih-ls** dataset* contains three fully annotated 3d+time isotropic lightsheet recordings [17] (data: https://doi.org/10.5281/zenodo.6460375). Our experimental setup is similar to **mskcc-confocal**.

Discussion. It is interesting to compare our results on **nih-ls** and **mskcc-confocal**: Due to the isotropic resolution of **nih-ls** we expected the results to be superior, yet the error metrics we observe do not support this intuition. A closer look at qualitative results reveals some clues that may explain part of it: Apoptotic cells are more distinct and visible earlier in **nih-ls** (see e.g. Suppl. Fig. 2) and thus have not been annotated in the ground truth. Yet in the current state our model does not handle this transition explicitly and thus continues to track them temporarily, leading to a larger number of false positives, as indicated by the quantitative results. As we already have a cell state classifier as part of our model, it will be straightforward to add apoptotic cells as a remedy.

4   Conclusion

We presented extensions to the tracking method Linajea [14] to improve tracking of all cells during embryonic development. In addition to combining deep learning to learn position and movement vectors of each cell and integer linear programming to extract tracks over time and ensure long term consistency, we integrate cell state information into the ILP, together with a method to automatically determine the weights of the ILP objective, alleviating the need for potentially suboptimal manually configured grid-search.

At the time of submission our method headed the leaderboard of the CTC for the DET and TRA scores for the **Fluo-N3DH-CE** dataset. On two other datasets of both confocal and lightsheet recordings of *C. elegans* our method outperforms the tool Starrynite, which is often used by practitioners for studies of *C. elegans*, by a wide margin. Furthermore, an ablation study reveals that each of our proposed methodological advances improves upon baseline Linajea.

The low error rate achieved by our method will further push down the required time for manual curation This will facilitate studies that require a large number of samples. More effort is still necessary in the later stages of development. In future work we will extend the tracking all the way to the end of the embryonic development. This poses additional challenges as the whole embryo starts to twitch, causing abrupt movements. A second avenue of future work is to combine the two stages of the method. Recent work [19] has proposed a method to incorporate black box solvers into a gradient-based end-to-end neural network learning process. This shows great promise to increase the performance of our method even further.

Acknowledgments. We would like to thank Anthony Santella, Ismar Kovacevic and Zhirong Bao and Ryan Christensen, Mark W. Moyle and Hari Shroff for providing us with their data and annotations, for generously allowing us to make the data public and for valuable information and feedback. P.H. was funded by the MDC-NYU exchange program and HFSP grant RGP0021/2018-102. P.H. and D.K. were supported by the HHMI Janelia Visiting Scientist Program. A.S. was supported by grant 2019-198110 (5022) from the Chan Zuckerberg Initiative and the Silicon Valley Community Foundation.

References

1. Bao, Z., Murray, J.I., Boyle, T., Ooi, S.L., Sandel, M.J., Waterston, R.H.: Automated cell lineage tracing in caenorhabditis elegans. Proc. Natl. Acad. Sci. **103**(8), 2707–2712 (2006). https://doi.org/10.1073/pnas.0511111103

2. Cao, J., et al.: Establishment of a morphological atlas of the caenorhabditis elegans embryo using deep-learning-based 4d segmentation. Nat. Commun. **11**(1) (2020)

3. Cicek, O., Abdulkadir, A., Lienkamp, S.S., Brox, T., Ronneberger, O.: 3D U-net: learning dense volumetric segmentation from sparse annotation. CoRR (2016). https://arxiv.org/abs/1606.06650v1

4. Funke, J.: 4D convolution implementation (2018)

5. Guignard, L., et al.: Contact area–dependent cell communication and the morphological invariance of ascidian embryogenesis. Science **369**(6500) (2020). https://doi.org/10.1126/science.aar5663

6. He, K., Zhang, X., Ren, S., Sun, J.: Deep residual learning for image recognition. CoRR (2015). https://arxiv.org/abs/1512.03385v1

7. Höfener, H., Homeyer, A., Weiss, N., Molin, J., Lundström, C.F., Hahn, H.K.: Deep learning nuclei detection: a simple approach can deliver state-of-the-art results. Comput. Med. Imaging Graph. **70**, 43–52 (2018)

8. Joachims, T., Hofmann, T., Yue, Y., Yu, C.N.: Predicting structured objects with support vector machines. Commun. ACM **52**(11), 97–104 (2009). https://doi.org/10.1145/1592761.1592783

9. Jug, F., et al.: Optimal joint segmentation and tracking of *Escherichia Coli* in the mother machine. In: Cardoso, M.J., Simpson, I., Arbel, T., Precup, D., Ribbens, A. (eds.) BAMBI 2014. LNCS, vol. 8677, pp. 25–36. Springer, Cham (2014). https://doi.org/10.1007/978-3-319-12289-2_3

10. Keller, P.J., et al.: Fast, high-contrast imaging of animal development with scanned light sheet-based structured-illumination microscopy. Nat. Methods **7**(8), 637–642 (2010)

11. Krzic, U., Gunther, S., Saunders, T.E., Streichan, S.J., Hufnagel, L.: Multiview light-sheet microscope for rapid in toto imaging. Nat. Methods **9**(7) (2012)

12. Li, X., et al.: Systems properties and spatiotemporal regulation of cell position variability during embryogenesis. Cell Rep. **26**(2), 313-321.e7 (2019). https://doi.org/10.1016/j.celrep.2018.12.052

13. Magnusson, K.E.G., Jalden, J., Gilbert, P.M., Blau, H.M.: Global linking of cell tracks using the Viterbi algorithm. IEEE Trans. Med. Imaging **34**(4), 911–929 (2015). https://doi.org/10.1109/tmi.2014.2370951

14. Malin-Mayor, C., et al.: Automated reconstruction of whole-embryo cell lineages by learning from sparse annotations. bioRxiv (2021). https://doi.org/10.1101/2021.07.28.454016

15. Matula, P., Maška, M., Sorokin, D.V., Matula, P., de Solórzano, C.O., Kozubek, M.: Cell tracking accuracy measurement based on comparison of acyclic oriented graphs. PLoS ONE **10**(12), e0144959 (2015). https://doi.org/10.1371/journal.pone.0144959

16. de Medeiros, G., Ortiz, R., Strnad, P., Boni, A., Maurer, F., Liberali, P.: Multiscale light-sheet organoid imaging framework. bioRxiv (2021). https://doi.org/10.1101/2021.05.12.443427

17. Moyle, M.W., et al.: Structural and developmental principles of neuropil assembly in C. elegans. Nature **591**(7848) (2021). https://doi.org/10.1038/s41586-020-03169-5

18. Murray, J.I., et al.: Automated analysis of embryonic gene expression with cellular resolution in C. elegans. Nat. Methods **5**(8) (2008). https://doi.org/10.1038/nmeth.1228

19. Pogančić, M.V., Paulus, A., Musil, V., Martius, G., Rolinek, M.: Differentiation of blackbox combinatorial solvers. In: International Conference on Learning Representations (2020). https://openreview.net/forum?id=BkevoJSYPB

20. Ronneberger, O., Fischer, P., Brox, T.: U-net: convolutional networks for biomedical image segmentation. CoRR (2015). https://arxiv.org/abs/1505.04597v1

21. Santella, A., Du, Z., Bao, Z.: A semi-local neighborhood-based framework for probabilistic cell lineage tracing. BMC Bioinform. **15**(1) (2014). https://doi.org/10.1186/1471-2105-15-217

22. Schiegg, M., Hanslovsky, P., Kausler, B.X., Hufnagel, L., Hamprecht, F.A.: Conservation tracking. In: Proceedings of the IEEE International Conference on Computer Vision (2013)

23. Sugawara, K., Cevrim, C., Averof, M.: Tracking cell lineages in 3D by incremental deep learning. bioRxiv (2021). https://doi.org/10.1101/2021.02.26.432552

24. Teo, C.H., Vishwanthan, S., Smola, A.J., Le, Q.V.: Bundle methods for regularized risk minimization. J. Mach. Learn. Res. **11**(10), 311–365 (2010). https://jmlr.org/papers/v11/teo10a.html

25. Ulman, V., et al.: An objective comparison of cell-tracking algorithms. Nat. Methods **14**(12), 1141–1152 (2017). https://doi.org/10.1038/nmeth.4473
26. Weigert, M., et al.: Content-aware image restoration: pushing the limits of fluorescence microscopy. Nat. Methods **15**(12), 1090–1097 (2018). https://doi.org/10.1038/s41592-018-0216-7
27. Wolff, C., et al.: Multi-view light-sheet imaging and tracking with the Mamut software reveals the cell lineage of a direct developing arthropod limb. eLife **7**, e34410 (2018). https://doi.org/10.7554/eLife.34410

Mask Rearranging Data Augmentation
for 3D Mitochondria Segmentation

Qi Chen[1], Mingxing Li[1], Jiacheng Li[1], Bo Hu[1], and Zhiwei Xiong[1,2](✉)

[1] University of Science and Technology of China, Hefei, China
zwxiong@ustc.edu.cn
[2] Institute of Artificial Intelligence, Hefei Comprehensive National Science Center,
Hefei, China

Abstract. 3D mitochondria segmentation in electron microscopy (EM) images has achieved significant progress. However, existing learning-based methods with high performance typically rely on extensive training data with high-quality manual annotations, which is time-consuming and labor-intensive. To address this challenge, we propose a novel data augmentation method tailored for 3D mitochondria segmentation. First, we train a Mask2EM network for learning the mapping from the ground-truth instance masks to real 3D EM images in an adversarial manner. Based on the Mask2EM network, we can obtain synthetic 3D EM images from arbitrary instance masks to form a sufficient amount of paired training data for segmentation. Second, we design a 3D mask layout generator to generate diverse instance layouts by rearranging volumetric instance masks according to mitochondrial distance distribution. Experiments demonstrate that, as a plug-and-play module, the proposed method boosts existing 3D mitochondria segmentation networks to achieve state-of-the-art performance. Especially, the proposed method brings significant improvements when training data is extremely limited. Code will be available at: https://github.com/qic999/MRDA_MitoSeg.

Keywords: Mitochondria segmentation · Data augmentation · 3D convolution · Generative adversarial networks · Electron microscopy

1 Introduction

Electron microscopy (EM) imaging reveals biological information at a nanometer scale, facilitating the exploration of finer scales in cell biology and biomedical research. The diameter of mitochondria is in the range of 0.5 to 5 microns, which can be observed more clearly under the EM. As one of the most common organelles in biomedical images, the mitochondria are the energy powerhouse of the cell and mitochondrial dysfunction has emerged as a critical factor

Supplementary Information The online version contains supplementary material available at https://doi.org/10.1007/978-3-031-16440-8_4.

in many diseases, including neurodegenerative and metabolic disorders [19,23]. Accurate mitochondria segmentation in EM images is the prerequisite for quantitatively analyzing its morphology and distributions [14,28]. However, existing deep learning-based mitochondria segmentation methods with high performance typically rely on extensive training data with high-quality manual annotations, which is time-consuming and labor-intensive. In addition, the lack of diversity of the training data leads to overfitting of the segmentation networks on the training set, resulting in poor segmentation performance on the testing set.

Data augmentation is a widely used and effective technique to increase the amount and diversity of available labeled data. Traditional data augmentation methods for biomedical images (e.g., crops, translation, rotation, elastic transformations) mainly apply simple random transformations to labeled images. While these data augmentation techniques can expand the diversity of training data to a certain extent, the produced data still remain highly correlated, which limits the improvement of segmentation performance. In order to solve this problem, many attempts have been made for biomedical image segmentation with specifically designed data augmentation for CT, MRI, and fluorescence microscopy images [1–3,21,26]. However, none of them can be directly applied for 3D mitochondria segmentation in EM images.

In this paper, we propose a mask rearranging data augmentation method for 3D mitochondria segmentation in EM images, which aims to synthesize enough diverse mitochondria EM training data to reduce the burden of obtaining considerable accurate segmentation annotations. The proposed method includes two components: a 3D EM image generator and a 3D mask layout generator. For the 3D EM image generator, we train a Mask2EM network by adopting paired ground-truth instance masks with random noise and real EM volumes as training data. This network is then used to generate perceptual realistic 3D EM images from arbitrary instance masks to form paired training data for segmentation. The 3D mask layout generator operates with an exemplar mask database and mask rearranging strategies. The exemplar mask database comprises all mitochondrial instance masks from the available ground-truth labels. The mask rearranging strategies determine the sampling order and the spatial location of sampled mitochondria. Therefore, the 3D mask layout generator can efficiently produce varied synthetic instance layouts with realistic mitochondrial distribution.

This paper has the following contributions: 1) We propose a data augmentation method tailored for mitochondria segmentation in EM images. To the best of our knowledge, this is the first work to study the synthesis of 3D EM images from ground-truth instance masks. 2) Experiments demonstrate that, as a plug-and-play module, our method boosts existing 3D mitochondria segmentation networks to achieve state-of-the-art performance. 3) Our method brings significant improvements when training data is extremely limited.

2   Method

The workflow of 3D mitochondria segmentation with our method is shown in Fig. 1. We first train a 3D EM image generator to learn the mapping from

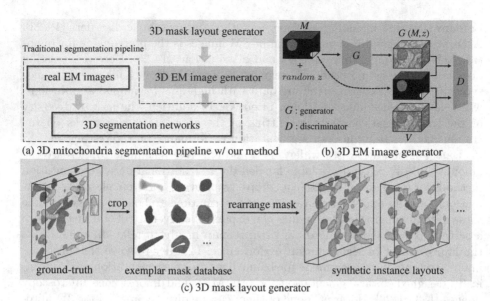

(a) 3D mitochondria segmentation pipeline w/ our method

(b) 3D EM image generator

(c) 3D mask layout generator

Fig. 1. Workflow of 3D mitochondria segmentation with our method. Our method adds two modules to the traditional segmentation pipeline in (a). Note that during training the segmentation networks, the parameters of the 3D EM image generator are fixed.

instance masks to real EM images. Then we construct a 3D mask layout generator and utilize this to produce more diverse instance layouts. Finally, we feed our produced instance layouts into the 3D EM image generator to synthesize perceptual realistic 3D EM images as augmented training data for segmentation. The details of the proposed method are as follows.

2.1   3D EM Image Generator

Generative adversarial networks (GANs) have been widely used for image translation in applications that need pixel-to-pixel mapping. Pix2pix [9] provides an effective strategy to learn such translation mapping with a conditional setting to capture structure information. Inspired by it, we utilize its pix2pix framework and introduce 3D convolution to train a Mask2EM network using paired instance masks and real EM volumes in Fig. 1 (b). In our setting, the Mask2EM network learns a mapping from a set of instance masks M and random noise vector z to EM volume V, $G : \{M, z\} \rightarrow V$. The generator G is trained to produce synthetic EM images that are difficult to identify as real or fake for an adversarially trained discriminator D. For the generator G, we formulate the objective as

$$L_G = -\mathbb{E}_{M,z} \left[log D \left(M, G \left(M, z \right) \right) \right] - \mathbb{E}_{M,V,z} \left[\| V - G \left(M, z \right) \|_1 \right]. \qquad (1)$$

For the discriminator D, we have

$$L_D = \mathbb{E}_{M,V} \left[log D \left(M, V \right) \right] + \mathbb{E}_{M,V,z} \left[log \left(1 - D \left(M, G \left(M, z \right) \right) \right) \right]. \qquad (2)$$

The generator G uses U-Net [25] with skip connections as the backbone structure. We apply 5 times downsampling with $3 \times 3 \times 3$ convolution of stride 2, so the maximum downsampling rate is 32. The upsampling part is symmetric. Two sequential convolutions are used for each resolution, as it performs better than using one. We replace transposed convolutions with nearest upsampling of stride 2 followed by a $3 \times 3 \times 3$ convolution to realize upsampling as well as channel changes, avoiding checkerboard artifacts [24]. For the discriminator D, we adopt the architecture of PatchGAN following [31]. This discriminator aims to classify whether each $P \times P \times P$ patch is real or fake. We perform this discriminator convolutionally across the volume, averaging all responses as the ultimate output. Here we empirically set P to 32.

2.2 3D Mask Layout Generator

As can be seen in Fig. 1 (a), to make the EM images generator synthesize more diverse EM images for segmentation networks, we need to produce more synthetic instance layouts. Thus, as illustrated in Fig. 1 (c), we design a 3D mask layout generator that utilizes an exemplar mask database and mask rearranging strategies.

Exemplar Mask Database. We denote the size of the training volume as (D, H, W) and the number of labeled mitochondria in this volume as N. For the i_{th} mitochondrion, we formulate its instance mask as a tuple (m_i, s_i), where m_i denotes the morphology of this mitochondrion and s_i denotes the number of pixels occupied by this mitochondrion. So the instance layout of ground-truth can be formulated as a set of masks that are located at corresponding locations l_i on the background B:

$$\{(m_1, s_1, l_1), (m_2, s_2, l_2), ..., (m_N, s_N, l_N), B\}. \tag{3}$$

We build the exemplar mask database by collecting all mitochondrial instance masks cropped from the ground-truth labels. Once obtaining the database, we can sample any mitochondria mask from it into a background volume of size (D, H, W) and generate a synthetic instance layout:

$$\{(m_1, s_1, l_1'), (m_2, s_2, l_2'), ..., (m_N, s_N, l_N'), B\}. \tag{4}$$

where l_i' denotes the new location for the i_{th} mitochondria. Moreover, whenever we sample the instance mask from the database, a set of probabilistic augmentations formulated as $\Phi(\cdot)$ can be applied to diversify the appearance to create unseen cases. We adopt the augmentation includes flipping along z-, y- and x-axes as well as swap y- and x-axes from [12]. So the synthetic instance layout can be formulated:

$$\{(\Phi(m_1), s_1, l_1'), (\Phi(m_2), s_2, l_2'), ..., (\Phi(m_N), s_N, l_N'), B\}. \tag{5}$$

Mask Rearranging Strategies. When generating synthetic instance layouts, the process of mitochondrial placement can be regarded as a space search problem in a 3D volume. To solve this problem efficiently and prevents mitochondrial distribution from being unreal, we adopt two strategies: 1) the larger first strategy and 2) the distance sampling strategy. These strategies respectively determine the sampling sequence and spatial location of mitochondria.

1) In general, the numbers of pixels occupied by mitochondria present a long-tail distribution and vary significantly in the EM data. For example, the numbers of pixels of some mitochondria differ by 10^3 of magnitude. Motivated from the greedy algorithm in the 0–1 knapsack problem [6], object placement priority is essential for search efficiency, especially when the size of the objects varies greatly. We adopt the larger first strategy, which means that if a mitochondrion occupies more pixels, its priority to place is higher. Since there should not overlap between mitochondria, mitochondria placed first will impose additional spatial constraints on the subsequent placement. If first placing small mitochondria, it will result in much invalid spatial search for the follow-up large mitochondria location and burden search time. Therefore, the larger first strategy can effectively avoid this problem and save the search time.

2) The most intuitive way to put the mask into a 3D volume is iteratively sampling the coordinates at random and placing the mask at the sampled location if there is no overlapping with previous ones. However, such an approach results in a uniform random distribution of mitochondria over the volume, which is unrealistic. Therefore, we turn to the distance sampling strategy. In other words, we calculate the distance between mitochondria to each other in the training data and estimate the probability density of the distance as priors. In practice, we randomly select one of the already placed masks as a reference and sample the appropriate distance according to the probability density, restricting the newly placed mask and the reference mask to satisfy the distance condition.

3 Experiments

3.1 Dataset and Experiment Settings

Dataset and Metrics. We evaluate our method on Lucchi [17] dataset. Lucchi dataset involves two stacks with voxel-wise annotations for training and testing mitochondria segmentation. Each stack consists of 165 consecutive slices of size 768×1024 with an isotropic resolution. The segmentation quality is measured by the Dice similarity coefficient (DSC), Jaccard-index coefficient (JAC), Aggregated Jaccard Index (AJI) [11] and Panoptic Quality (PQ) [10].

Implementation Details for the Mask2EM Network. To optimize the Mask2EM network, we follow the standard approach [8], alternating between one gradient descent step on D, then one step on G. We adopt Adam to optimize the network parameters and set the batch size as 1. The initial learning rate is set as 0.0001 for the first half of the total training iterations and linearly decays to 0 for the other half.

Table 1. Performance comparison between baselines and the networks with mask rearranging data augmentation.

Methods	Class-level		Instance-level	
	DSC	JAC	AJI	PQ
Lucchi [16]	86.0	75.5	74.0	63.5
2D U-Net [25]	91.5	84.4	83.0	75.5
Franco-Barranco [5]	94.3	89.2	88.9	84.3
Xiao [29]	94.7	90.0	88.6	83.1
HED-Net [18]	94.7	89.9	89.7	85.0
HIVE-Net [30]	94.8	90.1	89.0	83.9
3D U-Net [4]	93.5	87.8	86.9	80.6
3D V-Net [20]	93.7	88.2	87.6	83.4
3D UNet++ [32]	93.9	88.5	88.1	82.8
3D Res-UNet-R [13]	93.9	88.6	88.3	85.0
3D U-Net (w/ ours)	$94.3_{(+0.8)}$	$89.2_{(+1.4)}$	$89.0_{(+2.1)}$	$85.1_{(+4.5)}$
3D V-Net (w/ ours)	$94.0_{(+0.3)}$	$88.7_{(+0.5)}$	$88.1_{(+0.5)}$	$85.3_{(+1.9)}$
3D UNet++ (w/ ours)	$94.4_{(+0.5)}$	$89.4_{(+0.9)}$	$89.2_{(+1.1)}$	$85.9_{(+3.1)}$
3D Res-UNet-R (w/ ours)	$94.6_{(+0.7)}$	$89.7_{(+1.1)}$	$89.4_{(+1.1)}$	$86.4_{(+1.4)}$

Implementation Details for 3D Mitochondria Segmentation Networks.
Four types of representative segmentation networks are used in our experiments, including 3D U-Net [4], 3D V-Net [20], 3D UNet++ [32], 3D Res-UNet-R [13]. We adopt the networks implementation following [13, 15, 22]. During training, all volumes are online randomly cropped into the size of $d \times h \times w$. We use the same random data augmentation as in [13], including random affine transformation, random horizontal and vertical flipping, random global intensity transformation and elastic transformation. All segmentation networks are trained with a batch size of 2 and each batch contains two volumes, one from the real and the other from the synthesis. We adopt Adam optimizer. The initial learning rate is 0.0001, with linear warming up in the first 1000 iterations. Our experiments are conducted with Pytorch1.1 on two TITAN XP GPUs. Through segmentation networks, we can obtain the semantic mask $\boldsymbol{X}_M \in \mathbb{R}^{d \times h \times w}$ and the instance boundary $\boldsymbol{X}_B \in \mathbb{R}^{d \times h \times w}$. Furthermore, based on the following post-processing, we can get the seed map $\boldsymbol{S} \in \mathbb{R}^{d \times h \times w}$, which can be computed by:

$$S^j = \begin{cases} 1 & \boldsymbol{X}_M^j > t_1, \boldsymbol{X}_B^j < t_2 \\ 0 & else \end{cases} \tag{6}$$

where $j \in [1, d \times w \times h]$, t_1 and t_2 are two thresholds. In our experiments, we set $t_1 = 0.94$, $t_2 = 0.76$, $d = 32$ and $w = h = 256$. Then we convert the seed map to an affinity graph and adopt the watershed and agglomerate method [7] to obtain the final instance segmentation results. All experiments in the testing stage use the same post-processing and hyperparameter configuration.

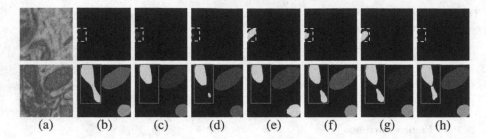

(a)   (b)   (c)   (d)   (e)   (f)   (g)   (h)

Fig. 2. Visualization results for the comparison experiments. From left to right: (a) testing data, (b) ground-truth, (c) V-Net, (d) V-Net w/ ours, (e) UNet++, (f) UNet++ w/ ours, (g) Res-UNet-R, (h) Res-UNet-R w/ ours. The white and red rectangles are drawn for clear comparison. (Color figure online)

Table 2. 3D mitochondria segmentation performance across different amounts of training data. The last line represents the limiting case with our method.

Data rate	Without our method				With our method			
	Class-level		Instance-level		Class-level		Instance-level	
	DSC	JAC	AJI	PQ	DSC	JAC	AJI	PQ
1	93.9	88.6	88.3	85.0	94.6(+0.7)	89.7(+1.1)	89.4(+1.1)	86.4(+1.4)
$\frac{1}{8}$	90.1	82.1	81.6	77.5	91.2(+1.1)	83.9(+1.8)	83.7(+2.1)	78.5(+1.0)
$\frac{1}{12}$	88.9	80.1	79.4	75.7	91.0(+2.1)	83.6(+3.5)	82.5(+3.1)	78.3(+2.6)
$\frac{1}{16}$	86.9	77.0	75.1	74.4	90.7(+3.8)	83.2(+6.2)	82.8(+7.7)	78.2(+3.8)
$\frac{1}{20}$	86.8	76.8	75.3	73.5	90.3(+3.5)	82.4(+5.6)	81.4(+6.1)	75.2(+1.7)
$\frac{1}{42}$	80.5	67.6	65.5	66.3	84.2(+3.7)	72.9(+5.3)	70.6(+5.1)	68.9(+3.6)

We train Mask2EM networks for 20 epochs and crop 4000 patches online every epoch, which costs about 24–25 h with 1 TITAN XP GPU. We train 300K iterations for segmentation networks with our method, which costs about 7–8 days with 2 TITAN XP GPUs. As for the other training hyperparameters, we follow pix2pix [9] and Res-UNet-R [13], which are consistent across all experiments. We use a 24 GB memory footprint for both synthesis and segmentation. More details can be found in our code.

3.2   Experiments and Results

Application to Existing Segmentation Networks. To validate the universality and effectiveness of our method, we apply it to several existing 3D mitochondria segmentation networks and compare the results with state-of-the-art methods. The comparison results on the Lucchi dataset are summarized in Table 1. These results clearly show that our method obviously improves the baseline networks. Taking 3D Res-UNet-R as an example, our method increases 0.7% DSC, 1.1% JAC, 1.1% AJI, and 1.4% PQ. We visualize the segmentation results for comparison in Fig. 2. Our approach can improve the segmentation performance by alleviating the false and missed detection cases, respectively. The

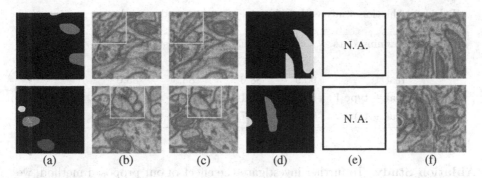

Fig. 3. Visualization results for ablation study. From left to right: (a) ground-truth, (b) real EM images (real), (c) synthesized EM images from ground-truth (type 1), (d) synthetic instance layouts by mask rearrangement, (e) no real EM images corresponding to (d), (f) synthesized EM images from synthetic instance layouts (type 2). (Color figure online)

corresponding statistical significance analysis can be found in supplementary materials.

Learning from Limited Training Data. To demonstrate the effectiveness of our method in a data scarcity condition, we adopt the 3D Res-UNet-R as the segmentation network backbone and train the network using limited available training data. We first crop the training volume of the Lucchi dataset by half in the x, y, z directions, respectively. Then we keep the size constant on the x, y axes and simulate the situation where the amount of data is getting scarcer and scarcer by decreasing the training volume on the z-axis, which are one-half, one-third, one-fourth, and one-fifth, respectively. As shown in Table 2, without our method, the performance of the segmentation networks significantly degrades as the size of training data decreases. Our method can help the segmentation networks attain evident improvement and yield competitive results compared to 2D U-Net, which uses all available training data. The last row of Table 2 shows the limiting case of our method. When using 1/42 of training data whose size is $33 \times 306 \times 306$, we can train an acceptable EM image generator that still synthesizes realistic-looking EM data. If we further reduce the data, the synthesis quality will become very poor. Besides, the volume contains two mitochondria and satisfies the usage conditions of the distance sampling strategy.

We also conduct a test on the mitoEM-rat [27] dataset. Using Res-UNet-R as the backbone and under the data scarcity condition, i.e., 1/64 ($100 \times 1024 \times 1024$) and 1/640 ($40 \times 512 \times 512$) real data for training, the results are shown in supplementary materials, which confirm the effectiveness of our method again. Overall, our method can boost 3D mitochondria segmentation performance using all or only a small amount of the available training data.

Table 3. Ablation study with EM image generator and mask layout generator.

Training data	Class-level		Instance-level	
	DSC	JAC	AJI	PQ
real	93.9	88.6	88.3	85.0
real + type 1	$94.2_{(+0.3)}$	$89.1_{(+0.5)}$	88.3	$85.6_{(+0.6)}$
real + type 2	$94.6_{(+0.7)}$	$89.7_{(+1.1)}$	$89.4_{(+1.1)}$	$86.4_{(+1.4)}$

Ablation Study. To further investigate the effect of our proposed method, we perform 3D Res-UNet-R to compare the results of three cases during training the segmentation networks in Table 3. We respectively use i) real data (real), ii) real data with synthesized EM images from ground-truth (real + type 1), iii) real data with synthesized EM images from synthetic instance layouts (real + type 2). The results clearly show that the synthesized EM images (type 1 and type 2) are beneficial to mitochondria segmentation. We also visualize several synthesized example images in Fig. 3. Type 1 generate different texture while remaining correlated compared with real EM images. Type 2 synthesized from synthetic instance layouts produce totally unseen cases.

4   Conclusions

In this work, we propose a mask rearranging data augmentation method to improve 3D mitochondria segmentation in EM images, which can generate diverse synthetic EM images. Experiments demonstrate that our method as a plug-and-play module can boost existing 3D mitochondria segmentation networks to state-of-the-art performance. In particular, it can bring significant improvements when training data is extremely limited.

Acknowledgement. This work was supported in part by the National Key R&D Program of China under Grant 2017YFA0700800, the National Natural Science Foundation of China under Grant 62021001, and the University Synergy Innovation Program of Anhui Province No. GXXT-2019-025.

References

1. Bailo, O., Ham, D., Min Shin, Y.: Red blood cell image generation for data augmentation using conditional generative adversarial networks. In: CVPRW (2019)
2. Calimeri, F., Marzullo, A., Stamile, C., Terracina, G.: Biomedical data augmentation using generative adversarial neural networks. In: Lintas, A., Rovetta, S., Verschure, P.F.M.J., Villa, A.E.P. (eds.) ICANN 2017. LNCS, vol. 10614, pp. 626–634. Springer, Cham (2017). https://doi.org/10.1007/978-3-319-68612-7_71
3. Chen, C., et al.: Realistic adversarial data augmentation for MR image segmentation. In: Martel, A.L., et al. (eds.) MICCAI 2020. LNCS, vol. 12261, pp. 667–677. Springer, Cham (2020). https://doi.org/10.1007/978-3-030-59710-8_65

4. Çiçek, Ö., Abdulkadir, A., Lienkamp, S.S., Brox, T., Ronneberger, O.: 3D U-net: learning dense volumetric segmentation from sparse annotation. In: Ourselin, S., Joskowicz, L., Sabuncu, M.R., Unal, G., Wells, W. (eds.) MICCAI 2016. LNCS, vol. 9901, pp. 424–432. Springer, Cham (2016). https://doi.org/10.1007/978-3-319-46723-8_49

5. Franco-Barranco, D., Muñoz-Barrutia, A., Arganda-Carreras, I.: Stable deep neural network architectures for mitochondria segmentation on electron microscopy volumes. Neuroinformatics, pp. 1–14 (2021)

6. Fréville, A.: The multidimensional 0–1 knapsack problem: an overview. Eur. J. Oper. Res. **155**(1), 1–21 (2004)

7. Funke, J., et al.: Large scale image segmentation with structured loss based deep learning for connectome reconstruction. IEEE Trans. Pattern Anal. Mach. Intell. **41**(7), 1669–1680 (2018)

8. Goodfellow, I., Pouget-Abadie, J., Mirza, M., Xu, B., Warde-Farley, D., Ozair, S., Courville, A., Bengio, Y.: Generative adversarial nets. In: Advances in Neural Information Processing Systems, vol. 27 (2014)

9. Isola, P., Zhu, J.Y., Zhou, T., Efros, A.A.: Image-to-image translation with conditional adversarial networks. In: CVPR, pp. 1125–1134 (2017)

10. Kirillov, A., He, K., Girshick, R., Rother, C., Dollár, P.: Panoptic segmentation. In: Proceedings of the IEEE/CVF Conference on Computer Vision and Pattern Recognition, pp. 9404–9413 (2019)

11. Kumar, N., Verma, R., Sharma, S., Bhargava, S., Vahadane, A., Sethi, A.: A dataset and a technique for generalized nuclear segmentation for computational pathology. IEEE Trans. Med. Imaging **36**(7), 1550–1560 (2017)

12. Lee, K., Zung, J., Li, P., Jain, V., Seung, H.S.: Superhuman accuracy on the SNEMI3D connectomics challenge. arXiv preprint arXiv:1706.00120 (2017)

13. Li, M., Chen, C., Liu, X., Huang, W., Zhang, Y., Xiong, Z.: Advanced deep networks for 3D mitochondria instance segmentation. In: 2022 IEEE 19th International Symposium on Biomedical Imaging (ISBI), pp. 1–5. IEEE (2022)

14. Li, Z., Chen, X., Zhao, J., Xiong, Z.: Contrastive learning for mitochondria segmentation. In: 2021 43rd Annual International Conference of the IEEE Engineering in Medicine and Biology Society (EMBC), pp. 3496–3500. IEEE (2021)

15. Lin, Z., Wei, D., Lichtman, J., Pfister, H.: Pytorch connectomics: a scalable and flexible segmentation framework for EM connectomics. arXiv preprint arXiv:2112.05754 (2021)

16. Lucchi, A., Li, Y., Fua, P.: Learning for structured prediction using approximate subgradient descent with working sets. In: CVPR, pp. 1987–1994 (2013)

17. Lucchi, A., Smith, K., Achanta, R., Knott, G., Fua, P.: Supervoxel-based segmentation of mitochondria in EM image stacks with learned shape features. IEEE Trans. Med. Imaging **31**(2), 474–486 (2011)

18. Luo, Z., Wang, Y., Liu, S., Peng, J.: Hierarchical encoder-decoder with soft label-decomposition for mitochondria segmentation in EM images. Front. Neurosci. **15** (2021)

19. McBride, H.M., Neuspiel, M., Wasiak, S.: Mitochondria: more than just a powerhouse. Curr. Biol. **16**(14), R551–R560 (2006)

20. Milletari, F., Navab, N., Ahmadi, S.A.: V-net: fully convolutional neural networks for volumetric medical image segmentation. In: 2016 fourth International Conference on 3D Vision (3DV), pp. 565–571. IEEE (2016)

21. Naghizadeh, A., Xu, H., Mohamed, M., Metaxas, D.N., Liu, D.: Semantic aware data augmentation for cell nuclei microscopical images with artificial neural networks. In: ICCV, pp. 3952–3961 (2021)

22. Nikolaos, A.: Deep learning in medical image analysis: a comparative analysis of multi-modal brain-MRI segmentation with 3D deep neural networks. Master's thesis, University of Patras (2019). https://github.com/black0017/MedicalZooPytorch

23. Nunnari, J., Suomalainen, A.: Mitochondria: in sickness and in health. Cell **148**(6), 1145–1159 (2012)

24. Odena, A., Dumoulin, V., Olah, C.: Deconvolution and checkerboard artifacts. Distill **1**(10), e3 (2016)

25. Ronneberger, O., Fischer, P., Brox, T.: U-net: convolutional networks for biomedical image segmentation. In: Navab, N., Hornegger, J., Wells, W.M., Frangi, A.F. (eds.) MICCAI 2015. LNCS, vol. 9351, pp. 234–241. Springer, Cham (2015). https://doi.org/10.1007/978-3-319-24574-4_28

26. Shin, H.-C., et al.: Medical image synthesis for data augmentation and anonymization using generative adversarial networks. In: Gooya, A., Goksel, O., Oguz, I., Burgos, N. (eds.) SASHIMI 2018. LNCS, vol. 11037, pp. 1–11. Springer, Cham (2018). https://doi.org/10.1007/978-3-030-00536-8_1

27. Wei, D., et al.: MitoEM dataset: large-scale 3D mitochondria instance segmentation from EM images. In: Martel, A.L., et al. (eds.) MICCAI 2020. LNCS, vol. 12265, pp. 66–76. Springer, Cham (2020). https://doi.org/10.1007/978-3-030-59722-1_7

28. Wu, S., Chen, C., Xiong, Z., Chen, X., Sun, X.: Uncertainty-aware label rectification for domain adaptive mitochondria segmentation. In: de Bruijne, M., et al. (eds.) MICCAI 2021. LNCS, vol. 12903, pp. 191–200. Springer, Cham (2021). https://doi.org/10.1007/978-3-030-87199-4_18

29. Xiao, C., et al.: Automatic mitochondria segmentation for Em data using a 3D supervised convolutional network. Front. Neuroanat. **12**, 92 (2018)

30. Yuan, Z., Ma, X., Yi, J., Luo, Z., Peng, J.: Hive-net: centerline-aware hierarchical view-ensemble convolutional network for mitochondria segmentation in Em images. Comput. Methods Programs Biomed. **200**, 105925 (2021)

31. Zhang, Z., Yang, L., Zheng, Y.: Translating and segmenting multimodal medical volumes with cycle-and shape-consistency generative adversarial network. In: CVPR, pp. 9242–9251 (2018)

32. Zhou, Z., Rahman Siddiquee, M.M., Tajbakhsh, N., Liang, J.: UNet++: a nested U-net architecture for medical image segmentation. In: Stoyanov, D., et al. (eds.) DLMIA/ML-CDS -2018. LNCS, vol. 11045, pp. 3–11. Springer, Cham (2018). https://doi.org/10.1007/978-3-030-00889-5_1

Semi-supervised Learning for Nerve Segmentation in Corneal Confocal Microscope Photography

Jun Wu[1], Bo Shen[1], Hanwen Zhang[1], Jianing Wang[2,4], Qi Pan[3,4(✉)],
Jianfeng Huang[2,4], Lixin Guo[3,4], Jianchun Zhao[5], Gang Yang[6], Xirong Li[6],
and Dayong Ding[5]

[1] School of Electronics and Information, Northwestern Polytechnical University,
Xi'an 710072, China
junwu@nwpu.edu.cn, {shenbo123,zhanghanwen}@mail.nwpu.edu.cn
[2] Department of Ophthalmology, Beijing Hospital, Beijing 100730, China
huangjianfeng4434@bjhmoh.cn
[3] Department of Endocrinology, Beijing Hospital, Beijing 100730, China
panqi621@126.com
[4] National Center of Gerontology, Institute of Geriatric Medicine,
Chinese Academy of Medical Sciences, Beijing 100730, China
[5] Vistel AI Lab, Visionary Intelligence Ltd., Beijing 100080, China
{jianchun.zhao,dayong.ding}@vistel.cn
[6] Key Lab of DEKE, Renmin University of China, Beijing 100872, China
{yanggang,xirong}@ruc.edu.cn

Abstract. Corneal nerve fiber medical indicators are promising metrics for diagnosis of diabetic peripheral neuropathy. However, automatic nerve segmentation still faces the issues of insufficient data and expensive annotations. We propose a semi-supervised learning framework for CCM image segmentation. It includes self-supervised pre-training, supervised fine-tuning and self-training. The contrastive learning for pre-training pays more attention to global features and ignores local semantics, which is not friendly to the downstream segmentation task. Consequently, we adopt pre-training using masked image modeling as a proxy task on unlabeled images. After supervised fine-tuning, self-training is employed to make full use of unlabeled data. Experimental results show that our proposed method is effective and better than the supervised learning using nerve annotations with three-pixel-width dilation.

Keywords: Semi-supervised learning · Deep learning · Corneal confocal microscopy · Diabetic peripheral neuropathy

1 Introduction

Diabetic peripheral neuropathy (DPN) is one of the most common chronic complications of diabetes [6,23]. At present, the diagnosis of DPN mostly depends on

L. Wang et al. (Eds.): MICCAI 2022, LNCS 13434, pp. 47–57, 2022.
https://doi.org/10.1007/978-3-031-16440-8_5

clinical symptoms and signs and electrophysiological examination [5,6], and these traditional examination methods are mostly used to diagnose large nerve fiber disease. However, small nerve fibers are the first to be damaged in the pathogenesis of DPN [25,40], and the examination technology of small nerve fibers can be used for early diagnosis of DPN. Corneal confocal microscope (CCM) is a high-resolution microscope that can non-invasively observe the intravital cornea at the cellular level. Based on CCM images, DPN can be quantitatively evaluated, and has the potential to become an ideal substitute metric.

There already have been some preliminary works on the CCM image segmentation, such as dual model filter (DMF) [26], morphological filter [10]. With the development of artificial intelligence, supervised deep learning model is also applied to this field. Salahuddin et al. [20] evaluated the loss functions of three different parameters in the U-net deep learning network on the CCM images. Kucharski et al. [11] proposed a marker-driven segmentation method of corneal endothelial cells based on watershed algorithm and a encoder-and-decoder convolutional neural network based on sliding window training to predict the probability of cell center (marker) and cell boundary. Wei et al. [27] used convolution neural network to establish sub-corneal neural segmentation network (CNS net). ·Mou et al. [15] proposed a curve structure segmentation network (CS-net), which introduces a self attention mechanism in the encoder and decoder to learn the rich hierarchical representation of curve structure. Bryan et al. [28] independently trained five deep learning segmentation models for CCM image nerve fibers, and adopted the mechanism of multiple models combined with voting for the same location segmentation structure, which effectively improved the accuracy of the segmentation results of the deep learning model.

Yildiz et al. [33] proposed a deep learning algorithm based on generative adversarial network (GAN) to realize nerve segmentation of CCM images. Yang et al. [32] proposed a multi-discriminator adversarial convolutional network, in which the generator and two discriminators emphasize multi-scale feature representation. The generator is a U-shaped fully convolution network, using the multi-scale split and concatenate block (MSc). These two discriminators have different receptive fields and are sensitive to the characteristics of different scales. In order to solve the problems of inaccurate pixel-wise annotation, uneven illumination and contrast change in most CCM data sets, Lin et al. [14] proposed a generative adversarial network (GAN) framework based on multi-layer and patch-wise contrastive learning to synthesize and enhance the CCM images.

However, the supervised learning relies on sufficient training images with high-quality complete annotations. Due to the expensive manual annotation and unavoidable noisy labels for corneal nerves by the ophthalmologists, especially for pixel-wise annotation, current methods still have space to improve.

Self-supervised learning is practical to further improve the model performance [41]. However, image-level self-supervised learning [2,7,8] is unfriendly to pixel-level downstream tasks. Inspired by image reconstruction [12,16,17,36], masked image modeling (MIM) [1,9,31,39], as a pre-training method, has been proved to be able to learn more local semantic features rather than global features by the contrastive learning method [3], which is more adaptable to downstream segmentation task. It masks some parts of the input image, and utilizes an auto-encoder to predict these masked pixels, resulting in a new similar image. Using this as data augmentation to pre-train neural network can make it learn more detailed semantics from unlabeled data, so we can use only a few labeled data to achieve better performance in pixel-wise image segmentation.

Semi-supervised learning utilizes both labeled and unlabeled data during training. Consistent regularization [21,24,30] is based on a simple concept that adding a small disturbance to the data should not affect prediction results significantly. It can restrict the boundary of classification model to the area with low data density. Pseudo labels [13,18,29] utilize prediction model to generate proxy labels (might with noises) on the unlabeled data, and mixes them with the completely labeled data to provide additional information.

The low-quality CCM images with noises and low contrast are prone to disconnect the nerve fibers or make wrong predictions, especially for small nerve fibers. It results in poor coherence of nerve fiber segmentation results. How to solve the disconnection and improve the pixel-wise accuracy, we still need a method which can sufficiently explore the corneal nerve characteristics of CCM images. In this paper we propose a novel semi-supervised learning framework to segment and analyze nerve fibers to further aid for DPN diagnosis.

2   The Proposed Method

As illustrated in Fig. 1, we propose a semi-supervised learning framework for nerve fibers segmentation in CCM images. It can achieve better performance when there are only a few labeled data samples. During the training stage, a three-step procedure is applied. First, a Segmentation Network will be pre-trained on a large-scale unlabelled data set using masked image modeling, followed with fine-tuning on a small-scale labelled data set. Then, this Segmentation Network will be applied to predict the unlabelled data set to generate the pseudo-labels for corneal nerve fibers. Finally, both two date sets, including small-scale labelled one and large-scale unlabelled one with pseudo-labels, will be gathered for re-training a student segmentation network.

2.1   Pre-training

Masked image modeling (MIM) works well on Transformer, however CNN is still the mainstream in the field of medical image processing. Therefore, there is an urgent need for a kind of CNN model that can pre-train with MIM. As CNN has more spatial priors, it is possible for pre-training to obtain an initial network with satisfactory visual representation. In addition, this pre-training needs a few thousand of unlabeled CCM images plus only dozens of images with pixel-wise nerve labels, which is easy to access and friendly to computing resources.

However, there still have two problems that keep masked image modeling from being applied to CNN. 1) Neural network cannot distinguish between

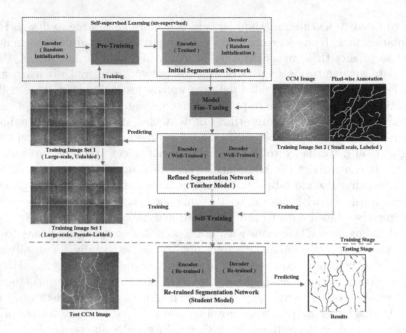

Fig. 1. The semi-supervised learning framework to segment the nerve fibers.

masked and non-masked regions within a convolution kernel window, so it does not know to predict which pixel. 2) If a specific color is used to mask pixels, the network is prone to learn the characteristics about this color, which is actually invalid and helpless for downstream tasks. To solve these, we propose a CNN model for masked image modeling. As shown in Fig. 2, it is divided into three parts: coarse repairing network, fine repairing network and discriminator.

First, certain pixels from an input image are masked in a random position and shape. **Coarse Repairing Network** will be trained to predict the low-frequency information of masked pixels, such as the background color and texture. Next, **Refine Repairing Network** is further trained to reconstruct more detailed information of missing pixels, especially the nerve fibers, based on the coarse repairing network. Finally, **Discriminator**, where SN-PatchGAN [34] is applied, judges whether predicted image is reasonable, where predicted pixels conforms with semantic context. The Discriminator takes the result of refine repairing network as the input and judges whether it is true or false (i.e., whether it is a natural or normal CCM image). It propagates back the GAN loss, as in Eq. (1). As shown in Eq. (3), our final loss function L for refine repairing network is the composition of the reconstruction loss L_{rec} and the GAN loss L_{GAN}.

$$L_{GAN} = -E_{x \sim P_x(x)}[D^{sn}(R(C((1 - M) \odot x)))] \tag{1}$$

$$L_{rec} = -|M \odot (x - R(C((1 - M) \odot x)))| \tag{2}$$

$$L = \lambda_{rec}L_{rec} + \lambda_{GAN}L_{GAN} \tag{3}$$

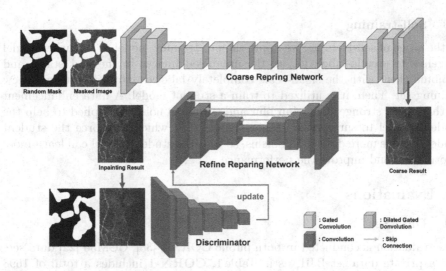

Fig. 2. The network structure of pre-training, using masked image modeling(MIM).

where D^{sn} represents spectral-normalized discriminator, x represents the input, M represents a binary mask, R represents refine repairing network, C represents coarse repairing network. λ_{rec} and λ_{GAN} are their weights.

Discriminator guides neural network to locate the repair position. As each pixel combines the context information, it is able to judge pixel category and generate a reasonable image. During this process, the neural network can learn more about the semantic information. At the same time, it also reduces the requirement for recovering the original image result, and makes the neural network emphasize on high-level semantics, instead of exactly the same as the original.

It should be noted that with the gated convolution which can eliminate the influence of masked areas, coarse repairing network preliminarily repairs masked pixels to smooth the whole image, so that the input of refine repairing network for convolution kernel is smooth, continuous and in a normal color, rather than a special color region or a highly-variable boundary. Therefore, refine repairing network is not prone to mislead its normal optimization direction, and we only use refine repairing network in the following step.

2.2 Model Fine-Tuning

During the fine tuning, we only extract the encoder part which extract future and encodes it of the refine repairing network and combine it with a randomly initialized decoder to fine-tune the segmented network into a final version. Because in the pre-training model, the coarse repairing network only provides a smoother input for the refine repairing network, which is not necessary for downstream tasks. At the same time, the discriminator only provides semantic constraints at the original image level for the refine repairing network.

2.3   Self-training

In the stage of self-training, we apply the pre-training model as a teacher model to generate pseudo-labels for all the unlabeled images in the first stage, and combine them with the small-scale completely labeled data set to form a new training set. Then, it is utilized to train a student model. A data enhancement method (e.g., stronger Gaussian blur and Gaussian noise) is applied to help the student model to surpass the teacher model [29], which will force the student model to solve more difficult problems, so that the student model can learn more information and improve the performance.

3   Evaluations

3.1   Data Set

The evaluation is conducted in both public CORN-1 [38], CCM30 [22] data sets and a private data set BJH, as in Table 1. **CORN-1** includes a total of 1698 images of corneal subbasal epithelium. **CCM30** is a small data set consisting of 30 images. **BJH** includes 82 CCM images (25 subjects) using the Heidelberg Retina Tomograph-2 (HRT-2), collected by Beijing Hospital. The pixel-wise nerve fiber annotations were traced by an ophthalmologist.

Table 1. An overview of the data sets: CORN-1, CCM30, BJH. Each image has a resolution of 384×384 pixels covering a FOV of $400 \times 400 \,\mu m^2$. Annotation *center-line3* means 3-pixel-width dilation of the original center-line nerve annotations.

Code	Type	Function	Name	#image	Annotation	Comments
S0	Public	Training	Corn-1	1426	Center-line3	3-pixel-width dilation, for S4
S1	Public	Training	Corn-1	1426	N/A	Pre-training
S2	Private	Training	BJH	57	Pixel-wise	U-net; Fine-tuning
S3	Mixup	Training	S1+S2	57	Pixel-wise	Self-training
S4	Mixup	Training	S0+S2	57	Mixup	3pixel-dilation-supervised
T1	Public	Testing	CCM30	30	Center-line	For ALL
T2	Private	Testing	BJH	25	Pixel-wise	For ALL

3.2   Experimental Setup

Our framework is implemented using PyTorch and it runs on NVIDIA RTX1080Ti. The coarse repairing network uses the gated convolution [34]. The refine repairing network is flexible, where U-net or Unet++ is applied respectively. When training segmentation network, the weighted sum of Dice loss and binary cross entropy loss $L = \alpha L_{Dice} + (1 - \alpha)L_{BCE}$ is taken as final loss function, where $\alpha = 0.5$. During the pre-training process, the batch size is 4 (while the batch size of SimCLR [3] is 4096), and it takes about 15 h in 200 epochs. During the training process, the SGD optimizer is employed, and the batch size is 4. The maximum training epoch is 1000, where it takes about 30 h.

3.3 Ablation Study

Pretrain. Pre-trained model can reach the higher IoU and lower loss at the beginning of fine-tuning, which indicates that the refine repairing network has learned semantic information of CCM image and has better initial values than the randomly initialized model. And this may lead to better results, from Table 2, it can be concluded that the pre-training module can improve the baseline (U-net) significantly in terms of most of evaluation metrics.

Table 2. Experimental results taking U-net as backbone. It includes ablation study and comparing our method with supervised learning with three-pixel-width dilation (training on Corn-1 and **BJH**) and other semi-supervised methods. UAMT: uncertainty aware mean teacher. 3PD-Supervised: three-pixel-dilation-supervised. PRE: Precision, SEN: Sensitivity, SPE: Specificity, ACC: Accuracy.

TestSet	Method	PRE	SEN	SPE	ACC	F1	AUC	IoU
CCM30	U-net [19]	0.7101	0.8516	0.9767	0.9682	0.7715	0.8813	0.6298
CCM30	U-net(pretrain)	0.7369	0.8732	0.9790	0.9722	0.7974	0.8975	0.6647
CCM30	Self-train(ours)	0.7377	**0.8772**	0.9791	0.9724	0.7996	**0.8999**	0.6676
CCM30	3PD-Supervised	0.5665	0.6788	0.8215	0.8162	0.5838	0.6983	0.4394
CCM30	Mean Teacher [24]	0.7942	0.8230	0.9860	**0.9753**	8064	0.8703	**0.6771**
CCM30	Cross Pseudo [4]	**0.7992**	0.7419	**0.9879**	0.9723	0.7652	0.8260	0.6219
CCM30	UAMT [35]	0.7525	0.8024	0.9832	0.9714	0.7743	0.8574	0.6335
CCM30	Adversarial [37]	0.7521	0.8343	0.9823	0.9722	0.7886	0.8754	0.6526
BJH	U-net [19]	0.8560	0.7392	0.9930	0.9789	0.7913	0.8400	0.6591
BJH	U-net(pretrain)	0.8578	**0.7706**	0.9931	0.9808	**0.8123**	0.8578	**0.6875**
BJH	Self-train(ours)	0.8758	0.7596	0.9939	0.9812	0.8116	0.8528	0.6863
BJH	3PD-Supervised	0.6266	0.6124	0.7976	0.7937	0.5587	0.6654	0.4185
BJH	Mean Teacher [24]	**0.8800**	0.7059	0.9946	0.9787	0.7802	0.8237	0.6437
BJH	Cross Pseudo [4]	0.8779	0.5802	**0.9957**	0.9736	0.6922	0.7609	0.5352
BJH	UAMT [35]	0.8365	0.6927	0.9932	0.9765	0.7545	0.8175	0.6095
BJH	Adversarial [37]	0.8650	0.6947	0.9943	0.9777	0.7679	0.8190	0.6277

Self-training. After fine-tuning the segmentation network, it is considered as the teacher model to generate pseudo labels on the training set of CORN-1 (ignore its annotation, taken as unlabeled data set). A supervised learning strategy is compared, which is trained from the CORN-1 training set (use the 3-pixel-wide nerve annotation which is derived from its original centerline annotation).

As illustrated in Fig. 3, compared to the supervised learning with annotations from CORN-1, our method has higher performance, better continuity and smoothness. Our method can also distinguish large and small nerve fibers, especially for some tiny unclear nerves as marked within red boxes.

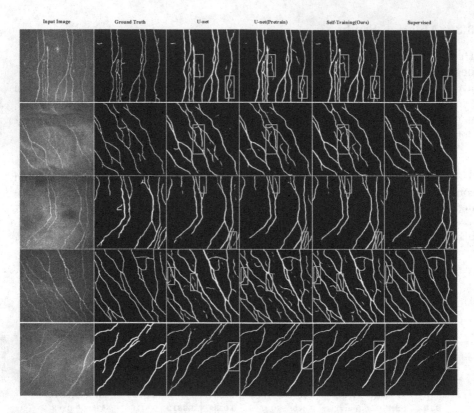

Fig. 3. Typical examples of method comparison, the backbone is U-net. (Color figure online)

3.4   Comparisons with Semi-supervised Methods

Further, we compare our method with other semi-supervised methods [4, 24, 35, 37]. From Table 2, in terms of representative sensitivity and AUC, these existing methods are worse than our methods. And it is even worse than the model trained with only a small amount of data, which means these methods mistakenly marking many nerve pixels as background pixels. On the contrary, our method generates pseudo labels after training of teacher model and use pre-training to improve teacher's ability to generate more accurate pseudo labels. As a result, it can achieve better performance.

4   Conclusions

In this paper, we have proposed a semi-supervised learning framework for corneal nerve segmentation in CCM images. First, masked image modeling is applied to pre-training for an initial segmentation network, using a large-scale or middle-scale unlabeled data set. Then, model fine-tuning is conducted on a small-scale completely labeled data set to make the segmentation network adapt to segmentation task (i.e., a teacher model). Next, this teacher model is employed to predict pseudo labels on the large-scale unlabeled data set in the first stage. Finally, this data set with pseudo labels is combined with the small-scale labeled data set to train a student model as the final segmentation network. Experimental results shows that the un-supervised pre-training stage is effective and can speedup the convergence of training procedure. Further, our proposed framework with less labeled training data is better than three-pixel-width dilation supervised learning method with more labeled training data. Current results are promising, and this is an interesting practical solution to sufficiently utilize limited training data with expensive pixel-wise annotations, together with large amount of unlabeled data which is tremendous and cheap.

Acknowledgements. This work is supported by China National Key R&D Program (No. 2020YFC2009006 and 2020YFC2009000), and Natural Science Basic Research Plan in Shaanxi Province of China (2020JM-129).

References

1. Bao, H., et al.: BEIT: BERT pre-training of image transformers. arXiv preprint arXiv:2106.08254 (2021)
2. Chen, T., et al.: A simple framework for contrastive learning of visual representations. In: ICML, pp. 1597–1607 (2020)
3. Chen, X., et al.: Context autoencoder for self-supervised representation learning. arXiv preprint arXiv:2202.03026 (2022)
4. Chen, X., et al.: Semi-supervised semantic segmentation with cross pseudo supervision. In: CVPR, pp. 2613–2622 (2021)
5. Chen, X., et al.: Small nerve fiber quantification in the diagnosis of diabetic sensorimotor polyneuropathy: comparing corneal confocal microscopy with intraepidermal nerve fiber density. Diabetes Care **38**(6), 1138–1144 (2015)
6. Ferdousi, M., et al.: Diagnosis of neuropathy and risk factors for corneal nerve loss in type 1 and type 2 diabetes: a corneal confocal microscopy study. Diabetes Care **44**(1), 150–156 (2021)
7. Grill, J.B., et al.: Bootstrap your own latent - a new approach to self-supervised learning. In: NIPS, vol. 33, pp. 21271–21284 (2020)
8. He, K., et al.: Momentum contrast for unsupervised visual representation learning. In: CVPR, pp. 9729–9738 (2020)
9. He, K., et al.: Masked autoencoders are scalable vision learners. arXiv preprint arXiv:2111.06377 (2021)
10. Kim, J., et al.: Automatic analysis of corneal nerves imaged using in vivo confocal microscopy. Clin. Exp. Optom. **101**(2), 147–161 (2018)
11. Kucharski, A., et al.: CNN-watershed: a watershed transform with predicted markers for corneal endothelium image segmentation. Biomed. Sign. Process. Control **68**, 102805 (2021)
12. Ledig, C., et al.: Photo-realistic single image super-resolution using a generative adversarial network. In: CVPR, pp. 4681–4690 (2017)
13. Lee, D.H.: Pseudo-label: the simple and efficient semi-supervised learning method for deep neural networks. In: ICML, p. 896 (2013)

14. Lin, L., et al.: Automated segmentation of corneal nerves in confocal microscopy via contrastive learning based synthesis and quality enhancement. In: ISBI, pp. 1314–1318 (2021)
15. Mou, L., et al.: CS2-net: deep learning segmentation of curvilinear structures in medical imaging. Med. Image Anal. **67**, 101874 (2021)
16. Noroozi, M., Favaro, P.: Unsupervised learning of visual representations by solving Jigsaw puzzles. In: Leibe, B., Matas, J., Sebe, N., Welling, M. (eds.) ECCV 2016. LNCS, vol. 9910, pp. 69–84. Springer, Cham (2016). https://doi.org/10.1007/978-3-319-46466-4_5
17. Pathak, D., et al.: Context encoders: Feature learning by inpainting. In: CVPR, pp. 2536–2544 (2016)
18. Pham, H., et al.: Meta pseudo labels. In: CVPR, pp. 11557–11568 (2021)
19. Ronneberger, O., Fischer, P., Brox, T.: U-net: convolutional networks for biomedical image segmentation. In: Navab, N., Hornegger, J., Wells, W.M., Frangi, A.F. (eds.) MICCAI 2015. LNCS, vol. 9351, pp. 234–241. Springer, Cham (2015). https://doi.org/10.1007/978-3-319-24574-4_28
20. Salahuddin, T., et al.: Evaluation of loss functions for segmentation of corneal nerves. In: IECBES, pp. 533–537 (2021)
21. Samuli, L., et al.: Temporal ensembling for semi-supervised learning. In: ICLR, pp. 6–17 (2017)
22. Scarpa, F., et al.: Automatic evaluation of corneal nerve tortuosity in images from in vivo confocal microscopy. Invest. Opthalmol. Visual Sci. **52**(9), 6404–6408 (2011)
23. Shtein, R.M., et al.: Corneal confocal microscopy as a measure of diabetic neuropathy. Diabetes **62**(1), 25–26 (2013)
24. Tarvainen, A., et al.: Mean teachers are better role models: weight-averaged consistency targets improve semi-supervised deep learning results. In: NIPS, vol. 30, pp. 1195–1204 (2017)
25. Tavakoli, M., et al.: Corneal confocal microscopy: a novel noninvasive test to diagnose and stratify the severity of human diabetic neuropathy. Diabetes Care **33**(8), 1792–1797 (2010)
26. Tavakoli, M., et al.: Dual-model automatic detection of nerve-fibres in corneal confocal microscopy images. In: ICLR, 13, no. 1, pp. 300–307 (2010)
27. Wei, S., et al.: A deep learning model for automated sub-basal corneal nerve segmentation and evaluation using in vivo confocal microscopy. Transl. Vis. Sci. Technol. **9**(2), 32–32 (2020)
28. Williams, B.M., et al.: An artificial intelligence-based deep learning algorithm for the diagnosis of diabetic neuropathy using corneal confocal microscopy: a development and validation study. Diabetologia **63**(2), 419–430 (2019). https://doi.org/10.1007/s00125-019-05023-4
29. Xie, Q., et al.: Self-training with noisy student improves imagenet classification. In: CVPR, pp. 10687–10698 (2020)
30. Xie, Q., et al.: Unsupervised data augmentation for consistency training. In: NIPS, vol. 33, pp. 6256–6268 (2020)
31. Xie, Z., et al.: SimMIM: a simple framework for masked image modeling. arXiv preprint arXiv:2111.09886 (2021)
32. Yang, C., et al.: Multi-discriminator adversarial convolutional network for nerve fiber segmentation in confocal corneal microscopy images. IEEE J. Biomed. Health Inform. **26**(2), 648–659 (2022)
33. Yildiz, E., et al.: Generative adversarial network based automatic segmentation of corneal subbasal nerves on in vivo confocal microscopy images. Transl. Vis. Sci. Technol. **10**(6), 33–33 (2021)

34. Yu, J., et al.: Free-form image inpainting with gated convolution. In: ICCV (2019)
35. Yu, L., Wang, S., Li, X., Fu, C.-W., Heng, P.-A.: Uncertainty-aware self-ensembling model for semi-supervised 3D left atrium segmentation. In: Shen, D., et al. (eds.) MICCAI 2019. LNCS, vol. 11765, pp. 605–613. Springer, Cham (2019). https://doi.org/10.1007/978-3-030-32245-8_67
36. Zhang, R., Isola, P., Efros, A.A.: Colorful image colorization. In: Leibe, B., Matas, J., Sebe, N., Welling, M. (eds.) ECCV 2016. LNCS, vol. 9907, pp. 649–666. Springer, Cham (2016). https://doi.org/10.1007/978-3-319-46487-9_40
37. Zhang, Y., Yang, L., Chen, J., Fredericksen, M., Hughes, D.P., Chen, D.Z.: Deep adversarial networks for biomedical image segmentation utilizing unannotated images. In: Descoteaux, M., Maier-Hein, L., Franz, A., Jannin, P., Collins, D.L., Duchesne, S. (eds.) MICCAI 2017. LNCS, vol. 10435, pp. 408–416. Springer, Cham (2017). https://doi.org/10.1007/978-3-319-66179-7_47
38. Zhao, Y., et al.: Automated tortuosity analysis of nerve fibers in corneal confocal microscopy. IEEE Trans. Med. Imaging **39**(9), 2725–2737 (2020)
39. Zhou, J., et al.: iBot: image BERT pre-training with online tokenizer. arXiv preprint arXiv:2111.07832 (2021)
40. Ziegler, D., et al.: Early detection of nerve fiber loss by corneal confocal microscopy and skin biopsy in recently diagnosed type 2 diabetes. Diabetes **63**(7), 2454–2463 (2014)
41. Zoph, B., et al.: Rethinking pre-training and self-training. In: NIPS, vol. 33, pp. 3833–3845 (2020)

Implicit Neural Representations for Generative Modeling of Living Cell Shapes

David Wiesner[1]([⊠])[iD], Julian Suk[2][iD], Sven Dummer[2][iD], David Svoboda[1][iD], and Jelmer M. Wolterink[2][iD]

[1] Centre for Biomedical Image Analysis, Masaryk University, Brno, Czech Republic
`wiesner@fi.muni.cz`
[2] Department of Applied Mathematics and Technical Medical Centre, University of Twente, Enschede, The Netherlands

Abstract. Methods allowing the synthesis of realistic cell shapes could help generate training data sets to improve cell tracking and segmentation in biomedical images. Deep generative models for cell shape synthesis require a light-weight and flexible representation of the cell shape. However, commonly used voxel-based representations are unsuitable for high-resolution shape synthesis, and polygon meshes have limitations when modeling topology changes such as cell growth or mitosis. In this work, we propose to use level sets of signed distance functions (SDFs) to represent cell shapes. We optimize a neural network as an implicit neural representation of the SDF value at any point in a 3D+time domain. The model is conditioned on a latent code, thus allowing the synthesis of new and unseen shape sequences. We validate our approach quantitatively and qualitatively on *C. elegans* cells that grow and divide, and lung cancer cells with growing complex filopodial protrusions. Our results show that shape descriptors of synthetic cells resemble those of real cells, and that our model is able to generate topologically plausible sequences of complex cell shapes in 3D+time.

Keywords: Cell shape modeling · Neural networks · Implicit neural representations · Signed distance function · Generative model · Interpolation

1 Introduction

Deep learning has led to tremendous advances in segmentation and tracking of cells in high-resolution 2D and 3D spatiotemporal microscopy images [1]. To a large extent, this development has been driven by community projects like the Broad Bioimage Benchmark Collection [2] and Cell Tracking Challenge [3] that provide easily accessible biomedical image datasets. Nevertheless, the performance of deep learning methods is heavily dependent on the amount, quality, and diversity of the provided training data, and there is still a lack of diverse annotated datasets [4]. This fuels an interest in methods for synthesis of microscopy images and accompanying ground truth masks.

© The Author(s), under exclusive license to Springer Nature Switzerland AG 2022
L. Wang et al. (Eds.): MICCAI 2022, LNCS 13434, pp. 58–67, 2022.
https://doi.org/10.1007/978-3-031-16440-8_6

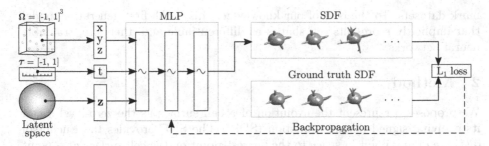

Fig. 1. Conceptual diagram of the proposed method. The multilayer perceptron (MLP) with *sine* activation functions is given a latent code z sampled from a multivariate normal distribution, coordinates x, y, z from a spatial domain Ω, and a temporal coordinate t from temporal domain τ. The network is optimized to output the values of given spatio-temporal SDFs, whereas each latent code is optimized to describe a particular spatio-temporal SDF. The trained network is able to output SDF values based on a given latent code and space-time coordinates, where the optimized latent codes represent existing spatio-temporal SDFs from the training set. When given new latent codes, the trained network is able to infer new spatio-temporal SDFs and thus produce new evolving shapes.

The synthesis of microscopy images from ground truth masks has been widely studied [5], and has taken a major leap with the advent of generative adversarial networks [6–12]. In this work, we focus on the synthesis of ground truth masks. Here, a key question is how cell shapes should be represented. A range of parametric models have been proposed that use ellipses [6] or elliptical Fourier descriptors [13] in 2D, statistical shape models [8] in 2D+time, ellipsoids [11,12] (3D) and spherical harmonics [14] in 3D, or ellipsoids deformed using active contours in 3D+time [5]. Deep learning has led to the popularization of volumetric voxel-based representations in 3D due to their natural integration with CNN architectures [9,10,15]. However, the size of a 3D voxel mask, and thus its memory footprint, grows cubically with the shape resolution, making them unsuitable for complex cell shapes. Alternatives like polygonal meshes have limitations when modeling growth or mitosis in living cells [16].

Here, we propose to model the cell surface as the zero level-set of a continuous signed distance function (SDF) in space and time. We represent this function via a multilayer perceptron (MLP) that takes as input spatial coordinates, a time point, and a latent code. Following the DeepSDF model proposed by Park et al. [17], we jointly optimize this MLP and its latent space using a large set of 3D+time cell shape sequences. Once trained, the DeepSDF can synthesize completely new cell shape sequences at any spatial or temporal resolution (see Fig. 1). We demonstrate on shapes of *C. elegans* [18] and lung cancer cells [19] that this single MLP provides topologically plausible cell shape, growth, and mitotic division. We show how periodic activations [20] substantially improve the model's ability to represent highly complex shapes. Moreover, we show how the artificially generated shapes can be used as ground truth masks in benchmark datasets. To the best of our knowledge, this is the first generative model that implicitly represents cell shapes as differentiable and, therefore, trainable neural networks.

2 Method

We propose to represent the evolution of a cell surface as the zero-level set of its evolving signed distance function (SDF). The SDF provides the Euclidean distance of any point in space to the nearest point on the cell surface at a point in time, where negative values are inside the surface and positive values outside. More precisely, let $\Omega = [-1,1]^3$ be a spatial domain, $\tau = [-1,1]$ a temporal domain, and $\mathcal{M}_t$ be a 2D manifold embedded in Ω at time $t \in \tau$. For any point $\boldsymbol{x} = (x,y,z) \in \Omega$, the $SDF_{\mathcal{M}_t} : \Omega \to \mathbb{R}$ is defined as

$$SDF_{\mathcal{M}_t}(\boldsymbol{x}) = \begin{cases} \min_{u \in \mathcal{M}_t} \|\boldsymbol{x} - \boldsymbol{u}\|_2, & \boldsymbol{x} \text{ outside } \mathcal{M}_t \\ 0, & \boldsymbol{x} \text{ belonging to } \mathcal{M}_t \\ -\min_{u \in \mathcal{M}_t} \|\boldsymbol{x} - \boldsymbol{u}\|_2, & \boldsymbol{x} \text{ inside } \mathcal{M}_t \end{cases}$$

The zero-level set, and thus the surface of the cell at time t, is represented by all points where $SDF_{\mathcal{M}_t}(\cdot) = 0$.

2.1 Learning a Latent Space of Shapes

Recent works have shown that the function $SDF_{\mathcal{M}_t}(\boldsymbol{x})$ can be approximated using a multi-layer perceptron (MLP) f_θ with trainable parameters θ [17,20]. Such an MLP takes a coordinate vector $\boldsymbol{x}$ as input, and provides an approximation of $SDF_{\mathcal{M}_t}(\boldsymbol{x})$ as output. We here propose to condition the MLP on a time parameter $t \in \tau$ to provide an approximation of the SDF of $\mathcal{M}_t$ for arbitrary $t \in \tau$. In addition, the MLP can be conditioned on a latent space vector $\boldsymbol{z}$ drawn from a multivariate Gaussian distribution with a spherical covariance $\sigma^2 I$ (see Fig. 1). Combining these terms results in an MLP $f_\theta(\boldsymbol{x},t,\boldsymbol{z})$ that approximates the SDF of the manifold $\mathcal{M}_t$ for arbitrary $t \in \tau$, given latent space vector $\boldsymbol{z}$. Here, we describe how we optimize such a model, or *auto-decoder* [17], for cell shape sequences $\mathcal{M}_t$.

We optimize the auto-decoder given a training set consisting of N cell shape sequences. For each cell shape sequence, reference values of its SDF are known at a discrete set of points in Ω and τ. An important aspect of the auto-decoder model is that not only the parameters θ are optimized during training, but also the latent code $\boldsymbol{z}$ for each sequence. The loss function therefore consists of two components. The first component is the reconstruction loss that computes the L_1 distance between reference SDF values and their approximation by the MLP, i.e.

$$\mathcal{L}_{recon}(f_\theta(\boldsymbol{x},t,\boldsymbol{z}), SDF_{\mathcal{M}_t}(\boldsymbol{x})) = \|f_\theta(\boldsymbol{x},t,\boldsymbol{z}) - SDF_{\mathcal{M}_t}(\boldsymbol{x})\|_1,$$

The second component is given by

$$\mathcal{L}_{code}(\boldsymbol{z},\sigma) = \frac{1}{\sigma^2}\|\boldsymbol{z}\|_2^2.$$

This term, with regularization constant $\frac{1}{\sigma^2}$, ensures that a compact latent space is learned and improves the speed of convergence [17]. Note that σ in this term corresponds to the Gaussian distribution of the latent vectors, and that latent vector z is fixed for one cell shape sequence. During training of the auto-decoder we have access to a training set of N cell shape sequences from which we extract mini-batches of points, and thus the full loss function becomes

$$\mathcal{L}(\theta, \{z_i\}_{i=1}^N, \sigma) = \mathbb{E}_{(\boldsymbol{x},t)} \left(\sum_{i=1}^N \mathcal{L}_{recon}(f_\theta(\boldsymbol{x}, t, z_i), SDF_{\mathcal{M}_t^i}(\boldsymbol{x})) + \mathcal{L}_{code}(z_i, \sigma) \right),$$

where each sequence $\{\mathcal{M}_t^i\}_{i=1}^N$ is assigned a latent code z_i.

2.2 Neural Network Architecture

The function $f_\theta(\boldsymbol{x}, t, z_i)$ is represented by an MLP. In all experiments, we used a network with 9 hidden layers, each containing 128 units. We present experiments with two activation functions. First, the commonly employed rectified linear unit (ReLU) $\sigma(x) = \max(0, x)$. While this activation function produces good results on low-frequency signals, an accurate representation of high-frequency information is not possible due to its inherent low frequency bias [21]. Therefore, we also present results with periodic activation functions $\sigma(x) = \sin(x)$ (*sine*). The weights of layers using *sine* activations have to be initialized by setting a parameter ω to ensure a good convergence [20]. The value of ω directly affects the range of frequencies that the model is able to represent, where low values of ω encourage low frequencies and smooth surfaces, and high values favor high-frequencies and finely detailed surfaces. Initial latent code vectors z_i of size 192 were sampled from $\mathcal{N}(0, 0.1^2)$ and inserted in the first, fifth, and eight layer of the network to improve reconstruction accuracy [17]. Inserting this information into more layers did not yield measurable improvement. Moreover, the coordinates $\boldsymbol{x}$ and t were given to all hidden layers. In this case, we found out that the model would not converge on long spatio-temporal sequences without this additional inserted information.

2.3 Data

To demonstrate modeling of different phenomena occurring during the cell cycle, we selected two existing annotated datasets for our experiments. First, a population of real *C. elegans* developing embryo cells that grow and divide [18] ($\mathcal{D}_{cel}$). Second, synthetic actin-stained A549 lung adenocarcinoma cancer cells with growing filopodial protrusions [19] ($\mathcal{D}_{fil}$). Both datasets are produced in fluorescence microscopy modality and contain full 3D time-lapse annotations, i.e., they consist of pairs of microscopy images and corresponding segmentation masks. The *C. elegans* dataset has a resolution of $708 \times 512 \times 35$ voxels (voxel size: $90 \times 90 \times 1000$ nanometers) and was acquired with a one-minute time step, whereas the filopodial cell dataset has a resolution of $300 \times 300 \times 300$ voxels

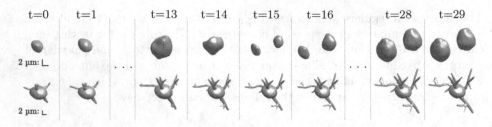

Fig. 2. New spatio-temporal sequences produced using the proposed method. The figure shows 3D renderings of cell surface meshes of *C. elegans* (top row) and lung cancer cell with filopodial protrusions (bottom row) at selected time points. Each sequence has 30 frames, with mesh surfaces obtained from the inferred 3D+t SDFs having $30 \times 256 \times 256 \times 256$ samples.

(voxel size: $125 \times 125 \times 125$ nanometers) and was simulated with a 20-second time step.

The data preparation and visualization algorithms were implemented in Matlab R2021a[1]. Using the segmentation masks of evolving shapes from $\mathcal{D}_{\text{cel}}$ and $\mathcal{D}_{\text{fil}}$, we prepared 66 diverse 3D+time SDF sequences, 33 for *C. elegans* and 33 for filopodial cells, with each sequence having shapes at 30 time points. As the cell surfaces occupy only a fraction of the considered 3D space, we sampled 70% of SDF points around the cell surface and remaining 30% in the rest of the space [17]. This allowed us to save memory in comparison to uniform sampling that would use considerable amount of data points to represent empty space around the object. We will refer to these SDF datasets as $\mathcal{D}_{\text{cel}}^{SDF}$ and $\mathcal{D}_{\text{fil}}^{SDF}$.

3   Experiments and Results

The auto-decoder network was implemented in Python using PyTorch (see footnote 1). We trained separate models on $\mathcal{D}_{\text{cel}}^{SDF}$ and $\mathcal{D}_{\text{fil}}^{SDF}$ for 1250 epochs. The weights were optimized using Adam with a learning rate 10^{-4} that decreases every 100 epochs by multiplication with a factor 0.5. Models were trained both with ReLU activation functions and periodic activation functions. For model utilizing the *sine* activation functions, the ω parameter for weight initialization was set to 30. Because the trained model is continuous, it can be used to generate point clouds, meshes, or voxel volumes [17]. In this work, we use voxel volumes for quantitative evaluation and meshes obtained using marching cubes [22] for visualization. With a trained model, generating one 30-frame 3D+t SDF sequence with $30 \times 256 \times 256 \times 256$ uniform samples took 40 s on an NVIDIA A100 and required 3 GB of GPU memory. We used these models to perform a series of experiments.

---

[1] Source codes, trained models, and produced datasets are made publicly available at: https://cbia.fi.muni.cz/research/simulations/implicit_shapes.html.

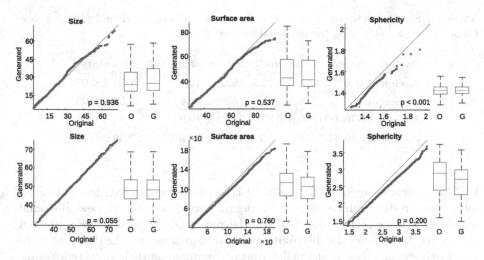

Fig. 3. Quantile-quantile (QQ) plots and boxplots for the shape descriptor distributions of original (O) and new generated (G) shapes of C. elegans (top row) and filopodial cells (bottom row). The QQ plots show the ideal identical distribution as a straight line and include the p-values of the Kolmogorov-Smirnov test. The whiskers of the boxplots correspond to the min and max values, the boxes represent the interquartile ranges, and the thin marks show the median values.

3.1   Reconstruction of Cell Sequences

In our first experiment, we evaluated the ability of the trained model to reconstruct a cell shape sequence in the training set, given its latent code z. To evaluate the reconstruction accuracy, we compute the Jaccard index (JI) on $256 \times 256 \times 256$ voxel volumes obtained from training ($\mathcal{D}_{cel}^{SDF}$ and $\mathcal{D}_{fil}^{SDF}$) and reconstructed SDF sequences. JI is computed on individual frames, i.e., we obtain one value for each pair of training and reconstructed frame. We computed mean and standard deviation to quantify the similarity of the reconstructed datasets. For *C. elegans*, we obtained JI: 0.782 ± 0.033 (ReLU model) and 0.821 ± 0.029 (*sine* model), for filopodial cells: 0.833 ± 0.051 (ReLU model) and 0.880 ± 0.022 (*sine* model). The JI values show that the reconstruction accuracy of the auto-decoder using *sine* activation functions is measurably higher. Visually, the thin protrusions of the filopodial cells lost their sharp edges and occasionally merged together with the ReLU model. In the remainder of this work, we present results for models using *sine* activation functions.

3.2   Generating New Cell Sequences

In our second experiment, we used the trained auto-decoders to produce new cell shape sequences (see Fig. 2). For the *C. elegans* cells, we randomly generated 33 new latent codes z by sampling from $\mathcal{N}(0, 0.1^2)$. For filopodial cells, a noise vector sampled from $\mathcal{N}(0, 0.01^2)$ was added to the 33 learned latent vectors

Table 1. Shape descriptors (mean ± standard deviation) of original (O) and new shapes generated (G) using the proposed method.

Dataset	Size $[\mu m^3]$	Surface area $[\mu m^2]$	Sphericity
C. elegans (O)	34.7 ± 12.5	62.8 ± 16.1	1.54 ± 0.09
C. elegans (G)	36.5 ± 11.5	65.2 ± 14.6	1.54 ± 0.06
Filopodial cells (O)	50.8 ± 3.1	117.8 ± 19.9	2.64 ± 0.51
Filopodial cells (G)	51.7 ± 3.2	115.0 ± 19.5	2.50 ± 0.49

for $\mathcal{D}_{fil}^{SDF}$ reconstruction. The produced latent codes were given to the trained auto-decoders to produce 33 new *C. elegans* sequences and 33 new filopodial sequences. To investigate how realistic the produced shapes are, we evaluated the similarity between the distribution of real sequences and the distribution of generated sequences using shape descriptors computed on their voxel representations, i.e., cell size (volume) in μm^3, surface area in μm^2, and sphericity [23]. We compared the descriptor distributions using quantile-quantile plots, box plots, and the Kolmogorov-Smirnov (KS) test (see Fig. 3). The plots show that the new shapes exhibit high similarity to the ones from the training sets. The KS test retained the null hypothesis ($p > 0.05$) that the descriptors are from the same distribution at 5% significance level for all tests except for the sphericity of the generated *C. elegans* cells, which exhibits a modest shift to lower values. For the mean and standard deviation values of each descriptor, see Table 1.

3.3   Temporal Interpolation

Because the 3D+t SDF representation is continuous, we can use the trained auto-decoder to produce sequences in arbitrary spatial and temporal resolution without the need of additional training. In particular, the temporal interpolation can be used to improve segmentation results [24]. To evaluate the interpolation accuracy, we trained the auto-decoder on 33 filopodial sequences, but with half the number of frames (15) in each sequence. We then used this model to reconstruct the sequences with a double framerate (30). Similarly to Sect. 3.1, we compared the reconstruction accuracy using JI with respect to the $\mathcal{D}_{fil}^{SDF}$ dataset. We obtained a JI of 0.868 ± 0.044, which is very close to the accuracy of the model trained on the "full" $\mathcal{D}_{fil}^{SDF}$ dataset (0.880 ± 0.022).

3.4   Generating Benchmarking Datasets

To demonstrate the application of the method, we produced a new 2D+time benchmarking dataset of *C. elegans* cells that grow and divide. Furthermore, we produced a new 2D+time dataset of cells with growing filopodial protrusions. Both datasets contain pairs of textured cell images and ground truth segmentations. The segmentation masks are maximum intensity projections of the voxel volumes of SDFs produced using the proposed method. The texture was generated using a conditional GAN, more specifically pix2pixHD [25], which was

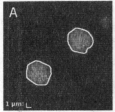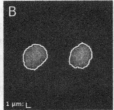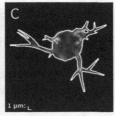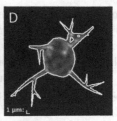

Fig. 4. Comparison of original (A, C) and generated (B, D) images of *C. elegans* (A, B) and filopodial cells (C, D). The images are maximum intensity projections of one frame from the respective time-lapse datasets. The respective segmentation masks are represented as white contours. The masks were obtained using the proposed method and the texture was produced using a conditional GAN.

trained on maximum intensity projections of textures and corresponding masks from the $\mathcal{D}_{cel}$ and $\mathcal{D}_{fil}$ datasets. For a visual comparison, see Fig. 4.

4   Discussion and Conclusion

We have presented a deep learning-based framework that can be used for accurate spatio-temporal representation and synthesis of highly-detailed evolving shapes and structures in microscopy imaging. To achieve this, we use a fully connected neural network to learn implicit neural representations of spatio-temporal SDFs. Owing to the employed periodic activation functions and SDF data representation, the method allows for shape synthesis with virtually unlimited spatial and temporal resolution at an unprecedented level of detail that would not have been possible with existing voxel-based methods [5,9,10] and models utilizing ReLU activations [17,26]. The produced SDFs can be converted to mesh-based, voxel-based, or point cloud representations, depending on the desired application. The proposed model is simple and can be easily trained on a common workstation to produce a desired class of shapes without the need for laborious customization or an expensive computational platform.

We presented the results and quantitative evaluation on two diverse datasets, the *C. elegans* embryo cells and the actin-stained A549 lung adenocarcinoma cancer cells with protrusions. The modeling of cell growth and mitosis facilitates gaining better understanding of cell development and can be used for deriving accurate quantitative models, e.g., for embryogenesis. Specifically, the A549 lung cancer cells are subject to an active research because filopodia and their relationship to cell migration is of great importance to understanding of wound healing, embryonic development, or the formation of cancer metastases. For these two cell classes, we produced benchmarking datasets for training and evaluation of image analysis algorithms.

The framework can be used for increasing spatial and temporal resolution of existing datasets, for data augmentation, or for generating brand-new benchmarking datasets. We have here presented the application of this generative model for cell shape synthesis, but organisms present many spatiotemporal dynamics at micro- and macro scales. The model could, for example, be extended to synthesize brain atrophy in patients with Alzheimer's disease, or the progression of abdominal aortic aneurysms.

In conclusion, conditional implicit neural representations or auto-decoders are a feasible representation for generative modeling of living cells.

Acknowledgements. This work was partially funded by the 4TU Precision Medicine programme supported by High Tech for a Sustainable Future, a framework commissioned by the four Universities of Technology of the Netherlands. Jelmer M. Wolterink was supported by the NWO domain Applied and Engineering Sciences VENI grant (18192). David Wiesner was supported by the Grant Agency of Masaryk University under the grant number MUNI/G/1446/2018. David Svoboda was supported by the MEYS CR (Projects LM2018129 and CZ.02.1.01/0.0/0.0/18_046/0016045 Czech-BioImaging).

References

1. Meijering, E.: A bird's-eye view of deep learning in bioimage analysis. Comput. Struct. Biotechnol. J. **18**, 2312–2325 (2020)
2. Ljosa, V., Sokolnicki, K.L., Carpenter, A.E.: Annotated high-throughput microscopy image sets for validation. Nat. Methods **9**(7), 637–637 (2012)
3. Ulman, V., Maška, M., et al.: An objective comparison of cell-tracking algorithms. Nat. Methods **14**(12), 1141–1152 (2017)
4. Kozubek, M.: Challenges and benchmarks in bioimage analysis. In: De Vos, W.H., Munck, S., Timmermans, J.-P. (eds.) Focus on Bio-Image Informatics. AAECB, vol. 219, pp. 231–262. Springer, Cham (2016). https://doi.org/10.1007/978-3-319-28549-8_9
5. Svoboda, D., Ulman, V.: MitoGen: a framework for generating 3D synthetic time-lapse sequences of cell populations in fluorescence microscopy. IEEE Trans. Med. Imaging **36**(1), 310–321 (2017)
6. Böhland, M., Scherr, T., et al.: Influence of synthetic label image object properties on GAN supported segmentation pipelines. In: Proceedings 29th Workshop Computational Intelligence, pp. 289–305 (2019)
7. Bailo, O., Ham, D., Min Shin, Y.: Red blood cell image generation for data augmentation using conditional generative adversarial networks. In: 2019 IEEE/CVF Conference on Computer Vision and Pattern Recognition Workshops (CVPRW), pp. 1039–1048 (2019)
8. Bähr, D., Eschweiler, D., et al.: CellCycleGAN: spatiotemporal microscopy image synthesis of cell populations using statistical shape models and conditional GANs. In: 18th International Symposium on Biomedical Imaging (ISBI), pp. 15–19. IEEE (2021)
9. Fu, C., Lee, S., et al.: Three dimensional fluorescence microscopy image synthesis and segmentation. In: Proceedings of the IEEE Conference on Computer Vision and Pattern Recognition Workshops, pp. 2221–2229 (2018)
10. P Baniukiewicz, EJ Lutton, et al. Generative adversarial networks for augmenting training data of microscopic cell images. Front. Comput. Sci. **1** (2019). ISSN 2624-9898

11. Dunn, K.W., Fu, C., et al.: DeepSynth: three-dimensional nuclear segmentation of biological images using neural networks trained with synthetic data. Sci. Rep. **9**(1), 1–15 (2019)
12. Han, S., Lee, S., et al.: Nuclei counting in microscopy images with three dimensional generative adversarial networks. In: Medical Imaging 2019: Image Processing, vol. 10949. International Society for Optics and Photonics, pp. 753–763. SPIE (2019)
13. Scalbert, M., Couzinie-Devy, F., Fezzani, R.: Generic isolated cell image generator. Cytometry Part A **95**(11), 1198–1206 (2019)
14. Ducroz, C., Olivo-Marin, J.C., Dufour, A.: Characterization of cell shape and deformation in 3D using spherical harmonics. In: 9th International Symposium on Biomedical Imaging (ISBI), pp. 848–851. IEEE (2012)
15. Wiesner, D., Nečasová, T., Svoboda, D.: On generative modeling of cell shape using 3D GANs. In: Ricci, E., Rota Bulò, S., Snoek, C., Lanz, O., Messelodi, S., Sebe, N. (eds.) ICIAP 2019. LNCS, vol. 11752, pp. 672–682. Springer, Cham (2019). https://doi.org/10.1007/978-3-030-30645-8_61
16. Li, Y., Kim, J.: Three-dimensional simulations of the cell growth and cytokinesis using the immersed boundary method. Math. Biosci. **271**, 118–127 (2016)
17. Park, J.J., Florence, P., et al.: DeepSDF: learning continuous signed distance functions for shape representation. In: Proceedings of the IEEE/CVF Conference on Computer Vision and Pattern Recognition, pp. 165–174 (2019)
18. Murray, J.I., Bao, Z., et al.: Automated analysis of embryonic gene expression with cellular resolution in C. elegans. Nat. Methods **5**(8), 703–709 (2008)
19. Sorokin, D.V., Peterlík, I., et al.: FiloGen: a model-based generator of synthetic 3-D time-lapse sequences of single motile cells with growing and branching filopodia. IEEE Trans. Med. Imaging **37**(12), 2630–2641 (2018)
20. Sitzmann, V., Martel, J., et al.: Implicit neural representations with periodic activation functions. Adv. Neural. Inf. Process. Syst. **33**, 7462–7473 (2020)
21. Mildenhall, B., Srinivasan, P.P., Tancik, M., Barron, J.T., Ramamoorthi, R., Ng, R.: NeRF: representing scenes as neural radiance fields for view synthesis. In: Vedaldi, A., Bischof, H., Brox, T., Frahm, J.-M. (eds.) ECCV 2020. LNCS, vol. 12346, pp. 405–421. Springer, Cham (2020). https://doi.org/10.1007/978-3-030-58452-8_24
22. Lorensen, W.E., Cline, H.E.: Marching cubes: a high resolution 3D surface construction algorithm. ACM SIGGRAPH Comput. Graph. **21**(4), 163–169 (1987)
23. Luengo, C., Caarls, W., et al.: DIPlib: a library for quantitative image analysis (2022). https://diplib.org. Accessed 02 Jan 2022
24. Coca-Rodríguez, A., Lorenzo-Ginori, J.V.: Effects of interpolation on segmentation in cell imaging. Computación y Sistemas **18**(1), 97–109 (2014)
25. Wang, T.-C., Liu, M.-Y., et al.: High-resolution image synthesis and semantic manipulation with conditional GANs. In: Proceedings of the IEEE Conference on Computer Vision and Pattern Recognition, pp. 8798–8807 (2018)
26. Remelli, E., Lukoianov, A., et al.: MeshSDF: differentiable isosurface extraction. Adv. Neural. Inf. Process. Syst. **33**, 22468–22478 (2020)

Trichomonas Vaginalis Segmentation in Microscope Images

Lin Li[1,2], Jingyi Liu[3], Shuo Wang[4], Xunkun Wang[1(✉)],
and Tian-Zhu Xiang[5(✉)]

[1] Qingdao Huajing Biotechnology Co., LTD, Qingdao, China
maksimljc@163.com
[2] Ocean University of China, Qingdao, China
[3] Qingdao University of Science and Technology, Qingdao, China
[4] ETH Zürich, Zürich, Switzerland
[5] Inception Institute of Artificial Intelligence, Abu Dhabi, UAE
tianzhu.xiang19@gmail.com

Abstract. Trichomoniasis is a common infectious disease with high incidence caused by the parasite Trichomonas vaginalis, increasing the risk of getting HIV in humans if left untreated. Automated detection of Trichomonas vaginalis from microscopic images can provide vital information for diagnosis of trichomoniasis. However, accurate Trichomonas vaginalis segmentation (TVS) is a challenging task due to the high appearance similarity between the Trichomonas and other cells (*e.g.*, leukocyte), the large appearance variation caused by their motility, and, most importantly, the lack of large-scale annotated data for deep model training. To address these challenges, we elaborately collected the first large-scale Microscopic Image dataset of Trichomonas Vaginalis, named *TVMI3K*, which consists of 3,158 images covering Trichomonas of various appearances in diverse backgrounds, with high-quality annotations including object-level mask labels, object boundaries, and challenging attributes. Besides, we propose a simple yet effective baseline, termed *TVNet*, to automatically segment Trichomonas from microscopic images, including high-resolution fusion and foreground-background attention modules. Extensive experiments demonstrate that our model achieves superior segmentation performance and outperforms various cutting-edge object detection models both quantitatively and qualitatively, making it a promising framework to promote future research in TVS tasks.

Keywords: Segmentation · Microscope images · Trichomoniasis

1 Introduction

Trichomoniasis (or "trich"), caused by infection with a motile, flagellated protozoan parasite called Trichomonas vaginalis (TV), is likely the most common,

---

Supplementary Information The online version contains supplementary material available at https://doi.org/10.1007/978-3-031-16440-8_7.

L. Wang et al. (Eds.): MICCAI 2022, LNCS 13434, pp. 68–78, 2022.
https://doi.org/10.1007/978-3-031-16440-8_7

non-viral sexually transmitted infection (STI) worldwide. According to statistics, there are more than 160 million new cases of trichomoniasis in the world each year, with a similar probability of males and females [10,27]. A number of studies have shown that Trichomonas vaginalis infection is associated with an increased risk of infection with several other STIs, including human papillomavirus (HPV) and human immunodeficiency virus (HIV) [32]. The high prevalence of Trichomonas vaginalis infection globally and the frequency of co-infection with other STIs make trichomoniasis a compelling public health concern.

Automatic Trichomonas vaginalis segmentation (TVS) is crucial to the diagnosis of Trichomoniasis. Recently, deep learning methods have been widely used for medical image segmentation [12] and made significant progress, such as brain region and tumor segmentation [11,36], liver and tumor segmentation [26,38], polyp segmentation [1,7,14], lung infection segmentation [8,19] and cell segmentation [18,23,35]. Most of these methods are based on the encoder-decoder framework, such as U-Net [23] and its variants [24] (e.g., U-Net++ [38], Unet 3+ [13]), and PraNet [7], or are inspired by some commonly-used natural image segmentation models, e.g., fully convolutional networks (FCN) [36] and DeepLab [26]. These works have shown great potentials in the segmentation of various organs and lesions from different medical imaging modalities. To our knowledge, however, deep learning techniques have not yet been well-studied and applied for TVS in microscope images, due to three key factors: 1) The large variation in morphology (e.g., size, appearance and shape) of the Trichomonas is challenging for detection. Besides, Trichomonas are often captured out of focus (blurred appearance) or under occlusion due to their motility, which aggregates the difficulty of accurate segmentation. 2) The high appearance similarity between Trichomonas and other cells (e.g., leukocyte) makes them easily confused with complex surroundings. Most importantly, 3) the lack of large-scale annotated data restricts the performance of deep models that rely on sufficient training data, thereby hindering further research in this field. It is worth noting that the above factors also reflect the clear differences in object segmentation between the microscope images of Trichomonas in our work and conventional cells (e.g., HeLa cells [23] and blood cells [16]). Furthermore, we noted that recently Wang et al. [28] proposed a two-stage model for video-based Trichomonas vaginalis detection, which utilizes video motion cues (e.g., optical flow) to greatly reduce the detection difficulty. The difference is that this work focuses on image-based Trichomonas vaginalis detection, without motion information, which increases the difficulty of detection. As we know, no one has set foot on this field so far. Hence, accurate TV segmentation remains a challenging and under-explored task.

To address above issues, we first elaborately construct a novel large-scale microscope images dataset exclusively designed for Trichomonas Vaginalis segmentation, named *TVMI3K*. Moreover, we develop a simple but effective deep neural network, termed *TVNet*, for TVS. In a nutshell, our main contributions are threefold: (1) We carefully collect **TVMI3K, a large-scale dataset for TVS**, which consists of 3,158 microscopic images covering Trichomonas of

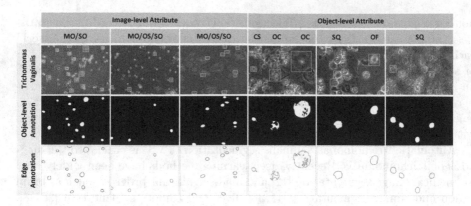

Fig. 1. Various examples of our proposed *TVMI3K*. We provide different annotations, including object-level masks, object edges and challenging attributes. We use red boxes to mark Trichomonas and green boxes to mark leukocyte on images for better visualization. Leukocyte shows high similarity with Trichomonas.

various appearances in diverse backgrounds, with high-quality annotations of object-level labels, object boundaries and challenging attributes. To our knowledge, this is the first large-scale dataset for TVS that can serve as a catalyst for promoting further research in this field in the deep learning era. (2) We proposed **a novel deep neural network, termed** *TVNet*, which enhances high-level feature representations with edge cues in a high-resolution fusion (HRF) module and then excavates object-critical semantics based on foreground-background attention (FBA) module under the guidance of coarse location map for accurate prediction. (3) Extensive experiments show that our method achieves superior performance and outperforms various cutting-edge segmentation models both quantitatively and qualitatively, making it a promising solution to the TVS task. The dataset, results and models will be publicly available at: https://github.com/CellRecog/cellRecog.

2   Proposed Dataset

To facilitate the research of TVS in deep learning era, we develop the *TVMI3K* dataset, which is carefully collected to cover TV of various appearances in diverse challenging surroundings, *e.g.*, large morphological variation, occlusion and background distractions. Examples can be seen in Fig. 1.

2.1   Data Collection

To construct the dataset, we first collect 80 videos of Trichomonas samples with resolution 3088×2064 from more than 20 cases over seven months. The phase-contrast microscopy is adopted for video collection, which captures samples clearly, even unstained cells, making it more suitable for sample imaging and

Table 1. Attribute descriptions of Our *TVMI3K* dataset

	Attr	Descriptions
Image-level	**MO**	*Multiple Objects*. Number of objects in each image ≥ 2
	SO	*Small Objects*. The ratio of object area to image area ≤ 0.1
	OV	*Out of view*. Incomplete objects clipped by image boundary
Object-level	**CS**	*Complex Shape*. In diverse shapes with tiny parts (*e.g.*, flagella)
	OC	*Occlusions*. Object is partially obscured by surroundings
	OF	*Out-of-focus*. Ghosting due to poor focus
	SQ	*Squeeze*. The object appearance changes when squeezed

microscopy evaluation than ordinary light microscopy. We then extract images from these videos to build our *TVMI3K* dataset, which finally contains 3,158 microscopic images (2,524 Trichomonas and 634 background images). We find that videos are more beneficial for data annotation, because objects can be identified and annotated accurately according to the motion of Trichomonas. Thus, even unfocused objects can also be labeled accurately. Besides, to avoid data selection bias, we collect 634 background images to enhance generalization ability of models. It should be noted that images are collected by the microscope devices independently, and we do not collect any patient information, thus the dataset is free from copyright and loyalties.

High-quality annotations are critical for deep model training [17]. During the labeling process, 5 professional annotators are divided into two groups for annotation and cross-validation is conducted between each group to guarantee the quality of annotation. We label each image with accurately object-level masks, object edges and challenging attributes, *e.g.*, occlusions and complex shapes. Attribute descriptions are shown in Table 1.

2.2 Dataset Features

- *Image-level Attributes*. As listed in Table 1, our data is collected with several image-level attributes, *i.e.*, multiple objects (MO), small object (SO) and out-of-view (OV), which are mostly caused by Trichomonas size, shooting distance and range. According to statistics, each image contains 3 objects averagely, up to 17 objects. The size distribution ranges from 0.029% to 1.179%, with an average of 0.188%, indicating that it belongs to a dataset for tiny object detection.
- *Object-level Attributes*. Trichomonas objects show various attributes, including complex shapes (CS), occlusions (OC), out-of-focus (OF) and squeeze (SQ), which are mainly caused by the growth and motion of trichomonas, highly background distraction (*e.g.*. other cells) and the shaking of acquisition devices. These attributes lead to large morphological differences in Trichomonas, which increase the difficulty of detection. In addition, there is a high similarity in appearance between Trichomonas and leukocyte, which can easily confuse the detectors to make false detections. Examples and the details of object-level attributes are shown in Fig. 1 and Table 1 respectively.

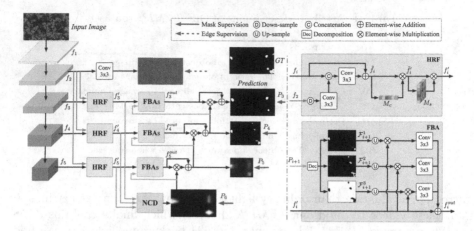

Fig. 2. Overview of our proposed *TVNet*, which consists of high-resolution fusion (HRF) module and foreground-background attention (FBA) module. See § 3 for details.

- *Dataset Splits.* To provide a large amount of training data for deep models, we select 60% of videos as training set and 40% as test set. In order to be consistent with practical applications, we select data according to the chronological order of the sample videos from each case instead of random selection, that is, the data collected first for each case is used as the training set, and the data collected later is used as the test set. Thus, the dataset is finally split into 2,305 images for training and 853 images for testing respectively. Note that 290 background images in the test set are not included in our test experiments.

3   Method

3.1   Overview

Figure 2 illustrates the overall architecture of the proposed *TVNet*. Specifically, for an input Trichomonas image I, the backbone network Res2Net [9] is adopted to extract five levels of features $\{f_i\}_{i=1}^5$. Then we further explore the high-level features (*i.e.*, $f_3 \sim f_5$ in our model) to effectively learn object feature representation and produce object prediction. As shown in Fig. 2, we first design a high-resolution fusion (HRF) module to enhance feature representation by integrating high-resolution edge features and get three refined features ($\{f_i'\}_{i=3}^5$). Next, we introduce the neighbor connection decoder (NCD) [5], a new cutting-edge decoder component which improves the partial decoder component [33] with neighbor connection, to aggregate these three refined features and generate the initial prediction map P_6. It can capture the relatively coarse location of objects so as to guide the following object prediction. Specially, $\{P_i\}_{i=3}^5$ represents the prediction map of the i layer, which corresponds to the i-layer in

$\{f_i^{'}\}_{i=3}^5$. Finally, we propose a foreground-background attention (FBA) module to excavate object critical cues by exploring semantic differences between foreground and background and then accurately predict object masks in a progressive manner.

3.2 High-Resolution Fusion Module

With the deepening of the neural network, local features, such as textures and edges, are gradually diluted, which may reduce the model's capability to learn the object structure and boundaries. Considering too small receptive field and too much redundant information of f_1 feature, in this paper, we design a high-resolution fusion (HRF) module which adopts the low-level f_2 feature to supplement local details for high-level semantic features and boost feature extraction for segmentation. To force the model to focus more on the object edge information, we first feed feature f_2 into a 3×3 convolutional layer to explicitly model object boundaries with the ground-truth edge supervision. Then we integrate the low-level feature f_2 with the high-level features ($f_3 \sim f_5$) to enhance representation with channel and spatial attention operations [2,31], denoted as:

$$\begin{cases} \tilde{f}_i = f_i + \mathcal{G}\left(Cat(f_i;\ \mathcal{G}(\delta_\downarrow^2(f_2)))\right), i \in \{3, ..., 5\}, \\ \tilde{f}_i^{'} = M_c(\tilde{f}_i) \otimes \tilde{f}_i, \\ f_i^{'} = M_s(\tilde{f}_i^{'}) \otimes \tilde{f}_i^{'}, \end{cases} \tag{1}$$

where $\delta_\downarrow^2(\cdot)$ denotes $\times 2$ down-sampling operation. $\mathcal{G}(\cdot)$ is a 3×3 convolution layer, and Cat is concatenation operation. $M_c(\cdot)$ and $M_s(\cdot)$ represent channel attention and spatial attention respectively. $\otimes$ is the element-wise multiplication operation. After that, a 1×1 convolution is used to adjust the number of channels to ensure the consistent output of each HRF.

3.3 Foreground-Background Attention Module

To produce accurate prediction from the fused feature ($f_3^{'} \sim f_5^{'}$) progressively in the decoder, we devise a foreground-background attention (FBA) module to filtrate and enhance object related features using region sensitive map derived from the coarse prediction of the previous layer. For the fused feature $\{f_i^{'}\}_{i=3}^5$, we first decompose the previous initial prediction P_{i+1} into three regions, i.e., strong foreground region ($\mathcal{F}_{i+1}^1$), weak foreground region ($\mathcal{F}_{i+1}^2$) and background region ($\mathcal{F}_{i+1}^3$). The decomposition process can refer to [25]. Then each region is normalized into [0,1] as a region sensitive map to extract the corresponding features from $f_i^{'}$. Noted that $\mathcal{F}^1$ provides the location information, and $\mathcal{F}^2$ contains the object edge/boundary information. The $\mathcal{F}^3$ denotes the remaining region.

After that, the region sensitive features can be extracted from the fused feature by an element-wise multiplication operation with up-sampled region sensitive maps followed by a 3×3 convolution layer. Next, these features are aggregated by an element-wise summation operation with a residual connection. It

Table 2. Quantitative comparison on our *TVMI3K* dataset. "↑" indicates the higher the score the better. "↓" denotes the lower the score the better.

Methods	Pub.	S_α ↑	E_ϕ^{max} ↑	F_β^w ↑	F_β^{mean} ↑	$\mathcal{M}$ ↓	mDice↑	mIoU↑
UNet++ [39]	TMI19	0.524	0.731	0.069	0.053	0.006	0.004	0.003
SCRN [34]	ICCV19	0.567	0.789	0.145	0.254	0.011	0.201	0.135
U^2Net [22]	PR20	0.607	0.845	0.209	0.332	0.013	0.301	0.209
F^3Net [30]	AAAI20	**0.637**	0.809	0.320	0.377	0.005	0.369	0.265
PraNet [7]	MICCAI20	0.623	0.792	0.300	0.369	0.006	0.328	0.230
SINet [6]	CVPR20	0.492	0.752	0.010	0.113	0.104	0.095	0.061
MSNet [37]	MICCAI21	0.626	0.786	0.321	0.378	0.005	0.366	0.268
SANet [29]	MICCAI21	0.612	0.800	0.289	0.361	0.006	0.338	0.225
SINet-v2 [5]	PAMI21	0.621	0.842	0.309	0.375	0.005	0.348	0.245
Ours	-	0.635	**0.851**	**0.343**	**0.401**	**0.004**	**0.376**	**0.276**

can be denoted as:

$$f_i^{out} = \sum\nolimits_{k=1}^{3} \mathcal{G}(\delta_\uparrow^2(\mathcal{F}_{i+1}^k) \otimes f_i') + f_i' \tag{2}$$

where $\delta_\uparrow^2(\cdot)$ denotes ×2 up-sampling operation. Inspired by [5], FBA can also be cascaded multiple times to gradually refine the prediction. For more details please refer to the *Supp.* In this way, FBA can differentially handle regions with different properties and explore region-sensitive features, thereby strengthening foreground features and reducing background distractions.

4 Experiments and Results

4.1 Experimental Settings

Baselines and Metrics. We compare our *TVNet* with 9 state-of-the-art medical/natural image segmentation methods, including U-Net++ [39], SCRN [34], U^2Net [22], F^3Net [30], PraNet [7], SINet [6], MSNet [37], SANet [29] and SINet-v2 [5]. We collect the source codes of these models and re-train them on our proposed dataset. We adopt 7 metrics for quantitative evaluation using the toolboxes provided by [7] and [29], including structural similarity measure (S_α, $\alpha = 0.5$) [3], enhanced alignment measure (E_ϕ^{max}) [4], F_β measure (F_β^w and F_β^{mean}) [20], mean absolute error (MAE, $\mathcal{M}$) [21], Sorensen-Dice coefficient (mean Dice, mDice) and intersection-over-union (mean IoU, mIoU) [7].

Training Protocols. We adopt the standard binary cross entropy (BCE) loss for edge supervision, and the weighted IoU loss [30] and the weighted BCE loss [30] for object mask supervision. During the training stage, the batch size is set to 20. The network parameters are optimized by Adam optimizer [15] with an initial learning rate of 0.05, a momentum of 0.9 and a weight decay of 5e-4. Each image is resized to 352×352 for network input. The whole training time is about 2 h for 50 epochs on a NVIDIA GeForce RTX 2080Ti GPU.

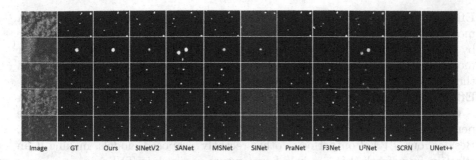

Image   GT   Ours   SINetV2   SANet   MSNet   SINet   PraNet   F3Net   U²Net   SCRN   UNet++

Fig. 3. Visual comparison of different methods. Obviously, our method provides more accurate predictions than other competitors in various challenging scenarios.

Table 3. Ablation study for TVNet on the proposed *TVMI3K* datasets.

No.	Backbone	HRF	FBA	$S_\alpha \uparrow$	$F_\beta^w \uparrow$	$F_\beta^{mean} \uparrow$	$\mathcal{M} \downarrow$	mDice	mIoU
a	✓			0.593	0.234	0.302	0.005	0.251	0.163
b	✓	✓		0.619	0.291	0.357	0.005	0.328	0.228
c	✓		✓	0.623	0.258	0.330	**0.004**	0.271	0.185
d	✓	✓	✓	**0.635**	**0.343**	**0.401**	**0.004**	**0.376**	**0.276**

4.2 Comparison with State-of-the-Art

Quantitative Comparison. Table 2 shows the quantitative comparison between our proposed model and other competitors on our *TVMI3K* dataset. It can be seen that our TVNet significantly outperforms all other competing methods on all metrics except S_α which is also on par with the best one. Particularly, our method achieves a performance gain of 2.2% and 2.3% in terms of F_β^w and F_β^{mean}, respectively. This suggests that our model is a strong baseline for TVS.

Qualitative Comparison. Figure 3 shows some representative visual results of different methods. From those results, we can observe that TVNet can accurately locate and segment Trichomonas objects under various challenging scenarios, including cluttered distraction objects, occlusion, varied shape and similarity with other cells. In contrast, other methods often provide results with a considerable number of missed or false detection, or even failed detection.

4.3 Ablation Study

Effectiveness of HRF. From Table 3, we observe that the HRF module outperforms the baseline model with significant improvement, *e.g.*, 2.6%, 5.7%, 5.7%, 7.7% and 6.5% performance improvement in S_α, F_β^w F_β^{mean}, *mDice* and *mIoU* metrics, respectively. This shows the fusion of local features is beneficial for object boundary localization and segmentation. Note that the adopted explicit edge supervision facilitates the model to focus more on object boundaries and enhance the details of predictions.

Effectiveness of FBA. We further investigate the contribution of the FBA module. As can be seen in Table 3, FBA improves the segmentation performance by 3%, 2.4% and 2.8% in S_α, F_β^w and F_β^{mean}, respectively. FBA enables our model to excavate object-critical features and reduce background distractions, thus distinguishing TV objects accurately.

Effectiveness of HRF & FBA. From Table 3, the integration of HRF and FBA is generally better than other settings (a~c). Compared with the baseline, the performance gains are 1.2%, 5.2% and 4.4% in S_α, F_β^w and F_β^{mean} respectively. Besides, our *TVNet* outperforms other recently proposed models, making it an effective framework that can help boost future research in TVS.

Model Complexity. We observe that the number of parameters and FLOPs of the proposed model are ~155M and ~98GMac, respectively, indicating that there is room for further improvement, which is the focus of our future work.

5   Conclusion

This paper provides the first investigation for the segmentation of Trichomonas vaginalis in microscope images based on deep neural networks. To this end, we collect a novel large-scale, challenging microscope image dataset of TV called *TVMI3K*. Then, we propose a simple but effective baseline, *TVNet*, for accurately segmenting Trichomonas from microscope images. Extensive experiments demonstrate that our *TVNet* outperforms other approaches. We hope our study will offer the community an opportunity to explore more in this field.

References

1. Brandao, P., Mazomenos, E., Ciuti, G., Caliò, R., Bianchi, F., Menciassi, A., et al.: Fully convolutional neural networks for polyp segmentation in colonoscopy. In: Medical Imaging: Computer-Aided Diagnosis. vol. 10134, pp. 101–107 (2017)
2. Chen, L., et al.: SCA-CNN: spatial and channel-wise attention in convolutional networks for image captioning. In: IEEE CVPR, pp. 5659–5667 (2017)
3. Fan, D.P., Cheng, M.M., Liu, Y., Li, T., Borji, A.: Structure-measure: a new way to evaluate foreground maps. In: IEEE ICCV, pp. 4548–4557 (2017)
4. Fan, D.P., Gong, C., Cao, Y., Ren, B., Cheng, M.M., Borji, A.: Enhanced-alignment measure for binary foreground map evaluation. In: IJCAI. pp. 698–704 (2018)
5. Fan, D.P., Ji, G.P., Cheng, M.M., Shao, L.: Concealed object detection. IEEE TPAMI, pp. 1 (2021)
6. Fan, D.P., Ji, G.P., Sun, G., Cheng, M.M., Shen, J., Shao, L.: Camouflaged object detection. In: IEEE CVPR, pp. 2777–2787 (2020)
7. Fan, D.P., et al.: Pranet: parallel reverse attention network for polyp segmentation. In: MICCAI, pp. 263–273 (2020)
8. Fan, D.P., Zhou, T., Ji, G.P., Zhou, Y., Chen, G., Fu, H., Shen, J., Shao, L.: INF-NET: Automatic covid-19 lung infection segmentation from CT images. IEEE TMI **39**(8), 2626–2637 (2020)
9. Gao, S.H., Cheng, M.M., Zhao, K., Zhang, X.Y., Yang, M.H., Torr, P.: Res2net: A new multi-scale backbone architecture. IEEE TPAMI **43**(2), 652–662 (2019)

10. Harp, D.F., Chowdhury, I.: Trichomoniasis: evaluation to execution. Eur. J. Obstet. Gynecol. Reprod. Biol. **157**(1), 3–9 (2011)
11. Havaei, M., Davy, A., Warde-Farley, D., Biard, A., et al.: Brain tumor segmentation with deep neural networks. Med. Image Anal. **35**, 18–31 (2017)
12. Hesamian, M.H., Jia, W., He, X., Kennedy, P.: Deep learning techniques for medical image segmentation: achievements and challenges. J. Digit. Imaging **32**(4), 582–596 (2019)
13. Huang, H., Lin, L., Tong, R., Hu, H., Zhang, Q., Iwamoto, Y., Han, X., Chen, Y.W., Wu, J.: Unet 3+: A full-scale connected unet for medical image segmentation. In: ICASSP. pp. 1055–1059 (2020)
14. Ji, G.-P., Chou, Y.-C., Fan, D.-P., Chen, G., Fu, H., Jha, D., Shao, L.: Progressively normalized self-attention network for video polyp segmentation. In: de Bruijne, M., Cattin, P.C., Cotin, S., Padoy, N., Speidel, S., Zheng, Y., Essert, C. (eds.) MICCAI 2021. Progressively normalized self-attention network for video polyp segmentation, vol. 12901, pp. 142–152. Springer, Cham (2021). https://doi.org/10.1007/978-3-030-87193-2_14
15. Kingma, D.P., Ba, J.: Adam: a method for stochastic optimization. In: ICLR (2015)
16. Li, D., et al.: Robust blood cell image segmentation method based on neural ordinary differential equations. In: Computational and Mathematical Methods in Medicine 2021 (2021)
17. Li, J., et al.: A systematic collection of medical image datasets for deep learning. arXiv preprint arXiv:2106.12864 (2021)
18. Li, L., Liu, J., Yu, F., Wang, X., Xiang, T.Z.: Mvdi25k: A large-scale dataset of microscopic vaginal discharge images. BenchCouncil Transactions on Benchmarks, Standards and Evaluations **1**(1), 100008 (2021)
19. Liu, J., Dong, B., Wang, S., Cui, H., Fan, D.P., Ma, J., Chen, G.: Covid-19 lung infection segmentation with a novel two-stage cross-domain transfer learning framework. Med. Image Anal. **74**, 102205 (2021)
20. Margolin, R., Zelnik-Manor, L., Tal, A.: How to evaluate foreground maps? In: IEEE CVPR. pp. 248–255 (2014)
21. Perazzi, F., Krähenbühl, P., Pritch, Y., Hornung, A.: Saliency filters: contrast based filtering for salient region detection. In: IEEE CVPR, pp. 733–740. IEEE (2012)
22. Qin, X., Zhang, Z., Huang, C., Dehghan, M., et al.: U2-net: going deeper with nested u-structure for salient object detection. Pattern Recogn. **106**, 107404 (2020)
23. Ronneberger, O., Fischer, P., Brox, T.: U-Net: convolutional networks for biomedical image segmentation. In: Navab, N., Hornegger, J., Wells, W.M., Frangi, A.F. (eds.) MICCAI 2015. U-net: Convolutional networks for biomedical image segmentation, vol. 9351, pp. 234–241. Springer, Cham (2015). https://doi.org/10.1007/978-3-319-24574-4_28
24. Siddique, N., Paheding, S., Elkin, C.P., Devabhaktuni, V.: U-net and its variants for medical image segmentation: a review of theory and applications. IEEE Access, pp. 82031–82057 (2021)
25. Sun, P., Zhang, W., Wang, H., Li, S., Li, X.: Deep RGB-D saliency detection with depth-sensitive attention and automatic multi-modal fusion. In: IEEE CVPR, pp. 1407–1417 (2021)
26. Tang, W., Zou, D., Yang, S., Shi, J., Dan, J., Song, G.: A two-stage approach for automatic liver segmentation with faster R-CNN and deeplab. Neural Comput. Appl. **32**(11), 6769–6778 (2020)

27. Vos, T., Allen, C., Arora, M., Barber, R.M., Bhutta, Z.A., Brown, A., et al.: Global, regional, and national incidence, prevalence, and years lived with disability for 310 diseases and injuries, 1990–2015: a systematic analysis for the global burden of disease study 2015. The Lancet **388**(10053), 1545–1602 (2016)

28. Wang, X., Du, X., Liu, L., Ni, G., Zhang, J., Liu, J., Liu, Y.: Trichomonas vaginalis detection using two convolutional neural networks with encoder-decoder architecture. Appl. Sci. **11**(6), 2738 (2021)

29. Wei, J., Hu, Y., Zhang, R., Li, Z., Zhou, S.K., Cui, S.: Shallow attention network for polyp segmentation. In: MICCAI. pp. 699–708 (2021)

30. Wei, J., Wang, S., Huang, Q.: F^3net: fusion, feedback and focus for salient object detection. In: AAAI, pp. 12321–12328 (2020)

31. Woo, S., Park, J., Lee, J.Y., Kweon, I.S.: Cbam: Convolutional block attention module. In: ECCV. pp. 3–19 (2018)

32. Workowski, K.A.: Sexually transmitted infections and HIV: diagnosis and treatment. Topics Antiviral Med. **20**(1), 11 (2012)

33. Wu, Z., Su, L., Huang, Q.: Cascaded partial decoder for fast and accurate salient object detection. In: IEEE CVPR, pp. 3907–3916 (2019)

34. Wu, Z., Su, L., Huang, Q.: Stacked cross refinement network for edge-aware salient object detection. In: IEEE ICCV, pp. 7263–7272 (2019)

35. Zhang, Y., et al.: A multi-branch hybrid transformer network for corneal endothelial cell segmentation. In: de Bruijne, M., Cattin, P.C., Cotin, S., Padoy, N., Speidel, S., Zheng, Y., Essert, C. (eds.) MICCAI 2021. LNCS, vol. 12901, pp. 99–108. Springer, Cham (2021). https://doi.org/10.1007/978-3-030-87193-2_10

36. Zhao, X., Wu, Y., Song, G., Li, Z., et al.: A deep learning model integrating FCNNs and CRFs for brain tumor segmentation. Med. Image Anal. **43**, 98–111 (2018)

37. Zhao, X., Zhang, L., Lu, H.: Automatic polyp segmentation via multi-scale subtraction network. In: de Bruijne, M., Cattin, P.C., Cotin, S., Padoy, N., Speidel, S., Zheng, Y., Essert, C. (eds.) MICCAI 2021. LNCS, vol. 12901, pp. 120–130. Springer, Cham (2021). https://doi.org/10.1007/978-3-030-87193-2_12

38. Zhou, Z., Rahman Siddiquee, M.M., Tajbakhsh, N., Liang, J.: Unet++: a nested u-net architecture for medical image segmentation. In: DLMIA, pp. 3–11 (2018)

39. Zhou, Z., Siddiquee, M.M.R., Tajbakhsh, N., Liang, J.: Unet++: redesigning skip connections to exploit multiscale features in image segmentation. IEEE TMI, pp. 1856–1867 (2019)

NerveFormer: A Cross-Sample Aggregation Network for Corneal Nerve Segmentation

Jiayu Chen[1,2], Lei Mou[2], Shaodong Ma[2], Huazhu Fu[4], Lijun Guo[1],
Yalin Zheng[5], Jiong Zhang[2,3(✉)], and Yitian Zhao[2,3(✉)]

[1] Faculty of Electrical Engineering and Computer Science, Ningbo University,
Ningbo, China
[2] Cixi Institute of Biomedical Engineering, Ningbo Institute of Materials Technology
and Engineering, Chinese Academy of Sciences, Ningbo, China
{zhangjiong,yitian.zhao}@nimte.ac.cn
[3] Affiliated Ningbo Eye Hospital of Wenzhou Medical University, Ningbo, China
[4] Institute of High Performance Computing, A*STAR, Singapore, Singapore
[5] Department of Eye and Vision Science, University of Liverpool, Liverpool, UK

Abstract. The segmentation of corneal nerves in corneal confocal microscopy (CCM) is of great to the quantification of clinical parameters in the diagnosis of eye-related diseases and systematic diseases. Existing works mainly use convolutional neural networks to improve the segmentation accuracy, while further improvement is needed to mitigate the nerve discontinuity and noise interference. In this paper, we propose a novel corneal nerve segmentation network, named NerveFormer, to resolve the above-mentioned limitations. The proposed NerveFormer includes a Deformable and External Attention Module (DEAM), which exploits the Transformer-based Deformable Attention (TDA) and External Attention (TEA) mechanisms. TDA is introduced to explore the local internal nerve features in a single CCM, while TEA is proposed to model global external nerve features across different CCM images. Specifically, to efficiently fuse the internal and external nerve features, TDA obtains the *query* set required by TEA, thereby strengthening the characterization ability of TEA. Therefore, the proposed model aggregates the learned features from both single-sample and cross-sample, allowing for better extraction of corneal nerve features across the whole dataset. Experimental results on two public CCM datasets show that our proposed method achieves state-of-the-art performance, especially in terms of segmentation continuity and noise discrimination.

Keywords: Corneal nerve segmentation · Transformer · Cross-sample

1 Introduction

The morphological characteristics of the corneal subbasal nerves, such as length, density, tortuosity [13,17,20], are closely related to many ocular or systemic

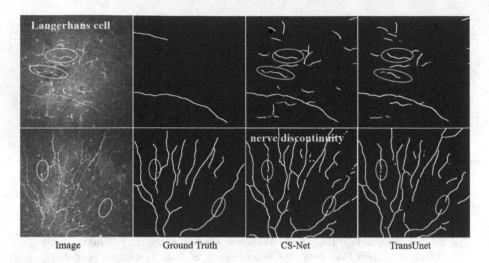

Fig. 1. Typical corneal nerves segmentation issues in CCM images. Top row: interference of Langerhans cells; Bottom row: nerve discontinuity. The automated results were obtained by two recent methods (CS-Net [10] and TransUnet [2]).

diseases. In clinical practice, corneal nerve images acquired by corneal confocal microscopy (CCM), are commonly used to assist ophthalmologists with rich pathological information, for studying disease-related alternations. Manual annotation of nerve fiber is able to support the quantitative analysis, however, it is time-consuming and subjective. Moreover, the inter- and intra-observer variations introduced by manual labeling greatly diminish the accuracy of quantitative assessment of corneal nerves [21]. Therefore, a fully automated and accurate corneal nerve segmentation method is essentially needed.

Many studies [1,3,4,10,16,18,19] have been conducted to automatically segment the corneal nerve fibers. Early works mainly focus on designing various enhancement filters, such as Gabor filters [4] and Gaussian filters [1] to obtain geometric features for better nerve fiber extraction. However, these methods rely heavily on low-level features and require parameter tuning by hand, and thus segmentation performance is limited. Deep learning-based models have recently been established to improve segmentation accuracy, by exploring high-level features rather than relying on low-level ones. For example, Colonna et al. [3] utilized U-Net [12] for end-to-end corneal nerve fibres tracking. Mou et al. [11] introduced a channel and spatial dual attention network (CS^2-Net) to improve the segmentation performance of nerve fibers.

Although the above-mentioned deep learning methods have achieved promising segmentation performances, they are still deficient in tackling the interference of background artifacts, e.g., Langerhans cells (LC) [14,18], as shown in the top row of Fig. 1 - the LCs are often falsely identified as nerve fibers. In addition, many methods [2,10] failed to preserve continuities of the nerve fibers especially in low-quality CCM images, as shown in the bottom row of Fig. 1. Recently,

Transformer [15] has been widely applied in medical image, with its powerful global modeling capabilities. For example, the ability of the network to extract local and global information can be enhanced by embedding the transformer module in the CNN framework [2,5]. MCTrans [9] proposed to use transformer-self-attention and transformer-cross-attention to enhance feature representation of the network.

Inspired by the above approaches, we consider to establish a transformer-based network by incorporating potentially valuable attention modules to learn more informative corneal nerve features for better segmentation performance. In this paper, a novel corneal nerve segmentation model named NerveFormer is introduced. It specifically targets at reducing the interferences caused by background artifacts in CCM images, and enhancing the continuity of nerve fiber segmentation. The main contributions are summarized as follows:

- A new corneal nerve segmentation method is proposed with a transformer-based deformable and external attention module (DEAM), which not only learns internal nerve features from single CCM image, but also learns shared nerve properties across multi-CCM images.
- A transformer-based external attention (TEA) is introduced to further fuse the internal features extracted by transformer-based deformable attention (TDA) with the shared properties of the external CCM images, allowing our method to obtain the most discriminative nerve features to alleviate the background artifacts interferences, and thus improves the ability to preserve the nerve continuity.

2   Proposed Method

The proposed method consists of a pre-trained feature extractor (i.e. encoder), a deformable and external attention module (DEAM), and a decoder. The architecture is shown in Fig. 2. We employed a ResNet34 model pre-trained on ImageNet as encoder. DEAM is a fusion of transformer-based deformable attention (TDA) and external attention (TEA), Where N represents the number of DEAM modules. The decoder is designed to recover the dimensions of the feature map layer by layer.

2.1   CNN Encoder

Given an input CCM image with height H and width W. We can obtain feature maps $\mathbf{F}_l \in \mathbb{R}^{C \times \frac{H}{2^{l+1}} \times \frac{W}{2^{l+1}}}$ of the lth layer by the encoder, where C represents the number of channels and $l \in \{1, 2, 3, 4\}$. To feed the extracted features into DEAM, we first flatten the features in the last three layers of the encoder into one-dimensional (1D) sequences and map them to the same channel dimension, respectively. Later, all these three sequences were concatenated into one sequence to extract the multi-scale information of the corneal nerves. To recover the lost spatial information caused by the flattening operation, we compute the position coordinates of each dimension using a sine and cosine functions of different frequencies [15], which is subsequently summed pixel-by-pixel with the multi-scale features to construct the input of the DEAM.

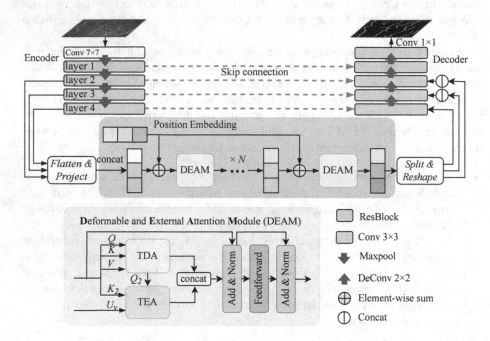

Fig. 2. Diagram of the proposed NerveFormer. It contains three main components: a pre-trained encoder, a deformable and external attention module (DEAM), and a CNN decoder, where the fused attention of transformer-based deformable attention (TDA) and external attention (TEA) constitute the key components of DEAM.

2.2   Deformable and External Attention Module (DEAM)

The proposed DEAM consists of two major components: TDA and TEA.

TDA: Inspired by deformable attention [22], we motivate our model to focus only on a small fraction of key sampling points around the reference point, without considering the spatial size of the feature map, thus alleviating the challenge of large feature resolution.

The TDA can be formulated as:

$$D\left(z_q, p_q, x\right) = \sum_{h=1}^{H} W_h \left[\sum_{k=1}^{K} A_{hqk} \cdot W_h' x\left(p_q + \Delta p_{hqk}\right)\right],   \tag{1}$$

where $x \in \mathbb{R}^{C \times H \times W}$ is the input feature map, z_q and p_q are the content feature and reference point of the qth query element, respectively. W_h is the encoding of the key element and A_{hqk} is the weight of the kth key element. K is the number of sampled key elements, and Δp_{hqk} is the sampling offset of the kth sampling point in the hth head. The TDA enables the proposed DEAM to learn more crucial information in a single CCM image.

TEA: Self-attention in a typical transformer is a linear combination of self-values to refine the input features. However, self-attention in this style only considers the relationship between elements (i.e., nerve fiber pixels) in a single CCM image, failing to explore the shared characteristics of the same elements across different CCM images. For a small number of CCM images containing Langerhans cells, we can further explore the shared characteristics of nerve fibers in different CCM images to better discriminate corneal nerves from Langerhans cells and background artifacts. Therefore, we introduce an external attention (EA) mechanism [8] to address the limitation of self-attention. The EA is defined by $EA = (\alpha)_{i,j} = \text{Norm}(QU_k^{\mathbf{T}}))U_v$, where U_k and U_v are two learnable external memory units. $(\alpha)_{i,j}$ is the similarity between i^{th} pixel and j^{th} row of U_k, U_v. $Q \in \mathbb{R}^{S \times d}$ indicates the set of *query*, where S is the number of elements, d is the number of feature dimensions. The EA is specifically designed to learn shared characteristics across images, while in our case, we aim to establish a more complete representation module by embedding both of the internal and external feature information of corneal nerves. Thus, we propose a transformer-based external attention (TEA) module by taking TDA as its query input. Comparing with original external attention, our TEA can learn the fused features from a single CCM image itself and external CCM images, which are beneficial to our model for learning the shared characteristics of multiple corneal nerves and also the discriminative features against background artifacts (e.g., Langerhans cells). In addition, multi-head attention [15] is employed to improve the capacity of single head attention by capturing different relations between tokens. Finally, we build up a multi-head transformer-based external attention (TEA) in our model, which can be written as:

$$TEA_{multi\_head} = \sum_{h}^{H} \text{Norm}\left(Q_{2h}K_{2h}^{\mathbf{T}}\right)U_v, \tag{2}$$

where H is the number of heads, Q_2 and K_2 are the output features of TDA and output features of encoder, respectively.

2.3 CNN Decoder

The 1D feature map output from DEAM is split and reshaped into three two-dimensional (2D) feature maps, based on the dimensions of the lth ($l = 2, 3, 4$) layer in the encoder. In the decoder, we gradually upsample the feature maps to the input resolution using a five-layer CNN module, where each layer consists of a deconvolutional layer and a 3×3 convolutional layer. In addition, a skip connection is added to the corresponding layer between the encoder and the decoder, to retain more low-level and spatial information. Finally, a 1×1 convolutional layer is applied to the features to generate the segmentation map. Mean square error (MSE) loss and Dice coefficient (DC) loss are employed to compute the error between segmentation map and ground truth in a 4:6 ratio.

Table 1. Comparisons of results between different methods.

Methods	CCM-1				CCM-2			
	SEN	FDR	DICE	AUC	SEN	FDR	DICE	AUC
U-Net [12]	0.8425	0.2444	0.7943	0.9165	0.8100	0.2071	0.7965	0.9012
CE-Net [6]	0.8584	0.2114	0.8174	0.9225	0.8390	0.1993	0.8171	0.9159
CS-Net [10]	0.8532	0.1869	0.8294	0.9210	0.8363	0.1940	0.8183	0.9147
MDACN [18]	0.8486	0.1847	0.8282	0.9188	0.8144	0.2061	0.7952	0.9033
TransUnet [2]	0.8578	0.1878	0.8317	0.9232	0.8278	0.1929	0.8148	0.9103
MCTrans [9]	0.8600	0.1860	0.8325	0.9242	0.8395	0.1891	0.8230	0.9164
UTNet [5]	0.8559	0.1827	0.8325	0.9224	0.8263	0.1889	0.8162	0.9098
NerveFormer	**0.8738**	**0.1813**	**0.8432**	**0.9314**	**0.8541**	**0.1864**	**0.8317**	**0.9236**

3 Experiments

3.1 Datasets and Implementation Details

CCM-1 and **CCM-2** are two subsets of a public dataset CORN-1 [10]. CORN-1 includes a total of 1698 CCM images of the corneal basal nerves, of which 1578 are available for CCM-1 and 120 for CCM-2. These images were acquired by using Heidelberg Retina Tomography equipment with a Rostock Cornea Module (HRT-III) microscope. Each image has a resolution of 384×384 pixels, and with 1×1 pixel centerline annotation, which was traced by an ophthalmologist using the open source software ImageJ[1]. In the CCM-1 and CCM-2 datasets, the ratio of training set, validation set, and test set is set as 3:1:1. Our method was implemented in PyTorch framework and all the experiments are run with two NVIDIA GPUs (Tesla V100). The adaptive moment estimation (Adam) with an initial learning rate of 0.0003 served as the optimizer, and the cosine annealing strategy is introduced to update the learning rate. The batch sizes were set as 32 and 8 for training models on CCM-1 and CCM-2, respectively. Random rotations in the range of $[-30°, 30°]$ and random horizontal and vertical flips were set with a probability of 0.5 for data augmentation.

3.2 Comparison with the State-of-the-Art Methods

To demonstrate the superiority of the proposed NerveFormer, we employed several state-of-the-art methods for the comparison. CNN-based methods: U-Net [12], CE-Net [6], CS-Net [10], MDACN [18]; Transformer-based methods:

---

[1] https://imagej.nih.gov/ij/.

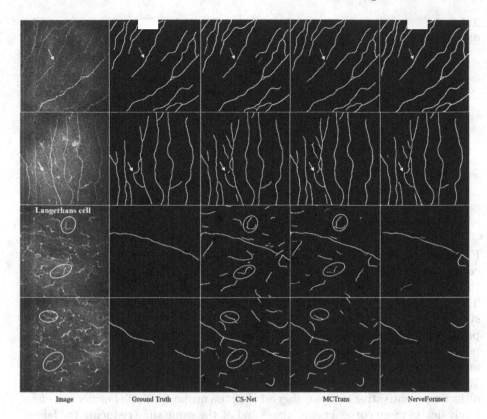

Fig. 3. Automated nerve segmentation results in CCM images with low-contrast, and heavy background artifacts (e.g. Langerhans cells).

TransUnet [2], MCTrans [9] and UTNet [5]. For fair comparison, all these methods are trained and validated on CCM-1 and CCM-2 with the same data split as ours. Figure 3 qualitatively illustrates corneal nerve segmentation results from challenging cases. By observing the results in the first two rows, we can conclude that the proposed method obtains more complete segmentations with better nerve fiber continuity than CS-Net [10] and TransUnet [2], as indicated by the red arrows. Moreover, we can see that our method presents better immunization against background artifacts, as demonstrated in the last two rows in Fig. 3. Specifically, as illustrated in the third row, we can observe that both CS-Net and TransUNet incorrectly identify the curve-like Langerhans cells as corneal nerves, while the proposed NerveFormer effectively distinguishes between them. The proposed method also enables better extraction of corneal nerves in regions covered by background noise, especially in the case of tiny corneal nerves. The above analyses indicate that the proposed network effectively explores the internal and external features in different CCM images, and thus can improve the performance of the corneal nerve segmentation in challenging CCM images.

Table 2. Ablation study results of the proposed model on the CCM-1 and CCM-2 datasets.

Methods	CCM-1				CCM-2			
	SEN	FDR	DICE	AUC	SEN	FDR	DICE	AUC
Backbone	0.8446	0.2127	0.8128	0.9158	0.8359	0.2008	0.8151	0.9142
Backbone+TDA	0.8598	0.1895	0.8325	0.9243	0.8509	0.1960	0.8252	0.9219
Backbone+TEA	0.8534	0.1844	0.8315	0.9211	0.8487	0.1928	0.8256	0.9209
Backbone+DEAM	**0.8738**	**0.1813**	**0.8432**	**0.9314**	**0.8541**	**0.1864**	**0.8317**	**0.9236**

To facilitate better objective performance evaluation of our NerveFormer, we calculated the following metrics: *sensitivity* (SEN) = $TP/(TP + FN)$, *false discovery rate* (FDR) = $FP/(FP + TP)$, *dice* coefficent (DICE) = $2 \times TP/(2 \times TP + FP + FN)$, where TP denotes true positive, FN denotes false negative, and FP denotes false positive and area under the ROC curve (AUC). We follow [7] to compute the evaluation metrics in terms of a three-pixel tolerance region around the ground truth centerline. Based on quantitative segmentation comparisons in Table 1, we can clearly observe that the proposed method outperforms the other state-of-the-art methods on both CCM-1 and CCM-2 datasets. Specifically, the proposed NerveFormer achieves the highest sensitivity and lowest FDR compared with the other methods. In detail, for CCM-1, our method is 1.6% higher and 2.59% lower than MCTrans [9] in terms of SEN and FDR, respectively, and 1.73% higher and 1.44% lower than MCTrans [9] for CCM-2, respectively. These objective quantitative analyses suggest that the proposed NerveFormer can effectively detect more corneal nerve pixels and at the same time reducing the falsely detected background artifacts, which is consistent with the observation in Fig. 3 that our method is more capable of discriminating between corneal nerves and Langerhans cells.

3.3   Ablation Study

In order to investigate the contributions of TDA and TEA in the proposed Nerve-Former, we conduct the following ablation studies. The encoder-decoder architecture with the pre-trained ResNet34 are taken as the Backbone. The TDA and TEA modules are gradually added into the Backbone, namely Backbone+TDA, Backbone+TEA and Backbone+DEAM, to assess their contributions to corneal nerve segmentation. Table 2 illustrates the contributions of different modules to the segmentation performance on CCM-1 and CCM-2. Compared to the Backbone, the network with only TDA achieves better performance, with an increase of approximate 1.80%, 10.91%, 2.42% and 0.93% in SEN, FDR, DICE and AUC on CCM-1, respectively, and an increase of approximate 2.40%, 2.4%, 1.24%, 0.84% on CCM-2, respectively. By integrating TEA into the Backbone, we can observe an improvement of approximate 1.04%, 13.31%, 2.30% and 0.58% in SEN, FDR, DICE and AUC on CCM-1, respectively, and an improvement of approximate 1.53%, 4.00%, 1.29%, 0.73% on CCM-2, respectively. Furthermore, we found that the Backbone+TEA obtains a lower FDR than Backbone+TDA, indicating that TEA with constraints of external samples can be more robust to the interference of background cells. Finally, the proposed NerveFormer that incorporates both TDA and TEA (Backbone+DEAM) achieves the best performance on all the metrics.

3.4 Conclusion

In this paper, we have proposed a cross-sample aggregation network, i.e., NerveFormer, for corneal nerve segmentation. The proposed NerveFormer can effectively learn the internal and external corneal nerve features by integrating a proposed deformable and external attention module. Experimental results on the two publicly available corneal nerve datasets demonstrate that our method achieves state-of-the-art performance by enhancing segmentation continuity and suppressing background artifacts interference.

Acknowledgement. This work was supported in part by the National Science Foundation Program of China (62103398 and 61906181), Zhejiang Provincial Natural Science Foundation of China (LR22F020008), in part by the Youth Innovation Promotion Association CAS (2021298), in part by the Ningbo major science and technology task project (2021Z054) and in part by the AME Programmatic Fund (A20H4b0141).

References

1. Annunziata, R., Kheirkhah, A., Hamrah, P., Trucco, E.: Scale and curvature invariant ridge detector for tortuous and fragmented structures. In: Navab, N., Hornegger, J., Wells, W.M., Frangi, A.F. (eds.) MICCAI 2015. LNCS, vol. 9351, pp. 588–595. Springer, Cham (2015). https://doi.org/10.1007/978-3-319-24574-4_70
2. Chen, J., et al.: Transunet: transformers make strong encoders for medical image segmentation. arXiv preprint arXiv:2102.04306 (2021)
3. Colonna, A., Scarpa, F., Ruggeri, A.: Segmentation of corneal nerves using a U-Net-based convolutional neural network. In: Stoyanov, D., et al. (eds.) OMIA/COMPAY -2018. LNCS, vol. 11039, pp. 185–192. Springer, Cham (2018). https://doi.org/10.1007/978-3-030-00949-6_22
4. Dabbah, M.A., Graham, J., Petropoulos, I., Tavakoli, M., Malik, R.A.: Dual-model automatic detection of nerve-fibres in corneal confocal microscopy images. In: Jiang, T., Navab, N., Pluim, J.P.W., Viergever, M.A. (eds.) MICCAI 2010. LNCS, vol. 6361, pp. 300–307. Springer, Heidelberg (2010). https://doi.org/10.1007/978-3-642-15705-9_37
5. Gao, Y., Zhou, M., Metaxas, D.N.: UTNet: a hybrid transformer architecture for medical image segmentation. In: de Bruijne, M., Cattin, P.C., Cotin, S., Padoy, N., Speidel, S., Zheng, Y., Essert, C. (eds.) MICCAI 2021. LNCS, vol. 12903, pp. 61–71. Springer, Cham (2021). https://doi.org/10.1007/978-3-030-87199-4_6
6. Gu, Z., et al.: Ce-net: Context encoder network for 2d medical image segmentation. IEEE Trans. Med. Imaging 38(10), 2281–2292 (2019)
7. Guimarães, P., Wigdahl, J., Poletti, E., Ruggeri, A.: A fully-automatic fast segmentation of the sub-basal layer nerves in corneal images. In: 2014 36th Annual International Conference of the IEEE Engineering in Medicine and Biology Society, pp. 5422–5425. IEEE (2014)

8. Guo, M.H., Liu, Z.N., Mu, T.J., Hu, S.M.: Beyond self-attention: External attention using two linear layers for visual tasks. arXiv preprint arXiv:2105.02358 (2021)

9. Ji, Y., Zhang, R., Wang, H., Li, Z., Wu, L., Zhang, S., Luo, P.: Multi-compound transformer for accurate biomedical image segmentation. In: de Bruijne, M., et al. (eds.) MICCAI 2021. LNCS, vol. 12901, pp. 326–336. Springer, Cham (2021). https://doi.org/10.1007/978-3-030-87193-2_31

10. Mou, L., et al.: CS-net: channel and spatial attention network for curvilinear structure segmentation. In: Shen, D., et al. (eds.) MICCAI 2019. LNCS, vol. 11764, pp. 721–730. Springer, Cham (2019). https://doi.org/10.1007/978-3-030-32239-7_80

11. Mou, L., et al.: Cs2-net: deep learning segmentation of curvilinear structures in medical imaging. Med.l Image Anal. **67**, 101874 (2021)

12. Ronneberger, O., Fischer, P., Brox, T.: U-Net: convolutional networks for biomedical image segmentation. In: Navab, N., Hornegger, J., Wells, W.M., Frangi, A.F. (eds.) MICCAI 2015. LNCS, vol. 9351, pp. 234–241. Springer, Cham (2015). https://doi.org/10.1007/978-3-319-24574-4_28

13. Su, P., et al.: Corneal nerve tortuosity grading via ordered weighted averaging-based feature extraction. Med. Phys. **47**(10), 4983–4996 (2020)

14. Su, P.Y., Hu, F.R., Chen, Y.M., Han, J.H., Chen, W.L.: Dendritiform cells found in central cornea by in-vivo confocal microscopy in a patient with mixed bacterial keratitis. Ocular Immunology Inflammation **14**(4), 241–244 (2006)

15. Vaswani, A., et al.: Attention is all you need. Advances in Neural Information Processing Systems 30 (2017)

16. Wei, S., Shi, F., Wang, Y., Chou, Y., Li, X.: A deep learning model for automated sub-basal corneal nerve segmentation and evaluation using in vivo confocal microscopy. Trans. Visi. Sci. Technol. **9**(2), 32–32 (2020)

17. Williams, B.M., et al.: An artificial intelligence-based deep learning algorithm for the diagnosis of diabetic neuropathy using corneal confocal microscopy: a development and validation study. Diabetologia **63**(2), 419–430 (2019). https://doi.org/10.1007/s00125-019-05023-4

18. Yang, C., et al.: Multi-discriminator adversarial convolutional network for nerve fiber segmentation in confocal corneal microscopy images. IEEE J. Biomed. Health Inf. (2021)

19. Zhang, D., et al.: Automatic corneal nerve fiber segmentation and geometric biomarker quantification. Europ. Phys. J. Plus **135**(2), 1–16 (2020). https://doi.org/10.1140/epjp/s13360-020-00127-y

20. Zhao, Y., et al.: Automated tortuosity analysis of nerve fibers in corneal confocal microscopy. IEEE Trans. Med. Imaging **39**(9), 2725–2737 (2020)

21. Zhao, Y., et al.: Uniqueness-driven saliency analysis for automated lesion detection with applications to retinal diseases. In: Frangi, A.F., Schnabel, J.A., Davatzikos, C., Alberola-López, C., Fichtinger, G. (eds.) MICCAI 2018. LNCS, vol. 11071, pp. 109–118. Springer, Cham (2018). https://doi.org/10.1007/978-3-030-00934-2_13

22. Zhu, X., Su, W., Lu, L., Li, B., Wang, X., Dai, J.: Deformable DETR: deformable transformers for end-to-end object detection. arXiv preprint arXiv:2010.04159 (2020)

Domain Adaptive Mitochondria Segmentation via Enforcing Inter-Section Consistency

Wei Huang[1], Xiaoyu Liu[1], Zhen Cheng[1], Yueyi Zhang[1,2],
and Zhiwei Xiong[1,2(✉)]

[1] University of Science and Technology of China, Hefei, China
`zwxiong@ustc.edu.cn`
[2] Institute of Artificial Intelligence, Hefei Comprehensive National Science Center,
Hefei, China

Abstract. Deep learning-based methods for mitochondria segmentation require sufficient annotations on Electron Microscopy (EM) volumes, which are often expensive and time-consuming to collect. Recently, Unsupervised Domain Adaptation (UDA) has been proposed to avoid annotating on target EM volumes by exploiting annotated source EM volumes. However, existing UDA methods for mitochondria segmentation only address the intra-section gap between source and target volumes but ignore the inter-section gap between them, which restricts the generalization capability of the learned model on target volumes. In this paper, for the first time, we propose a domain adaptive mitochondria segmentation method via enforcing inter-section consistency. The key idea is to learn an inter-section residual on the segmentation results of adjacent sections using a CNN. The inter-section residuals predicted from source and target volumes are then aligned via adversarial learning. Meanwhile, guided by the learned inter-section residual, we can generate pseudo labels to supervise the segmentation of adjacent sections inside the target volume, which further enforces inter-section consistency. Extensive experiments demonstrate the superiority of our proposed method on four representative and diverse EM datasets. Code is available at https://github.com/weih527/DA-ISC.

Keywords: Mitochondria segmentation · Unsupervised domain adaptation · Inter-section consistency · Electron microscopy images

1 Introduction

Automated mitochondria segmentation from Electron Microscopy (EM) volumes, *i.e.*, sequential EM sections, is a critical step for neuroscience researches

---

Supplementary Information The online version contains supplementary material available at https://doi.org/10.1007/978-3-031-16440-8_9.

L. Wang et al. (Eds.): MICCAI 2022, LNCS 13434, pp. 89–98, 2022.
https://doi.org/10.1007/978-3-031-16440-8_9

and clinical studies [7,21,27]. Existing deep learning-based methods have enabled great progress in mitochondria segmentation on large-scale EM volumes [9,11,15]. However, the success of these methods is heavily reliant upon a large number of annotations. Due to dense distributions and complex 3D structures of mitochondria, collecting these annotations for each target volume is often expensive and time-consuming.

On the other hand, since different EM volumes are often acquired by different EM devices from different organisms and tissues, there is severe domain gap between source and target EM volumes in two aspects: i) Intra-section gap, *i.e.*, different shapes and distributions of mitochondria within an individual section. ii) Inter-section gap, *i.e.*, the shape and distribution variation of mitochondria across sections. These two kinds of gap pose great challenges for the generalization capability of the learned model on the target domain. As a rescue, Unsupervised Domain Adaptation (UDA) methods have been proposed to learn domain-invariant features to reduce the domain gap [12,18,19,25]. They often align the distribution of segmentation results on an individual section between source and target volumes via adversarial learning to make the distribution of mitochondria predictions on the target volume similar to that on the source volume. However, these solutions only consider the intra-section gap but ignore the inter-section gap, which restricts the generalization capability of the learned model on the target domain.

In this paper, we propose a domain adaptive mitochondria segmentation method via enforcing inter-section consistency, which addresses the inter-section gap within EM volumes for the first time. Specifically, we introduce the inter-section residual to describe the variation of mitochondria across sections, which is learned by a Convolutional Neural Network (CNN) along with segmentation results of adjacent sections. Then, we align both segmentation results and inter-section residuals predicted from source and target volumes via adversarial learning to reduce the intra-section and inter-section gap within EM volumes. Meanwhile, to further enforce the inter-section consistency inside the target volume, we generate a pseudo label by the exclusive-OR (XOR) logical operation between the inter-section residual and the segmentation result of one section to supervise the segmentation of the other section. As demonstrated by comprehensive experimental results, our proposed method significantly outperforms existing UDA methods for mitochondria segmentation on four representative and diverse EM datasets acquired by different EM devices from different organisms and tissues.

2   Related Works

Since the pixel-wise label collection for microscopy images is often expensive, domain adaptation attracts increasing attention for the segmentation of microscopy images, especially for mitochondria segmentation [1,2,12,18,19,24,25] and neuron segmentation [6]. They aim to learn domain-invariant features to minimize the distribution discrepancy between source and target domains by statistical distance metrics [1,2], denoising auto-encoder [19], or domain-adversarial

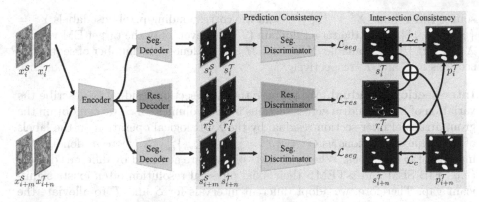

Fig. 1. The framework of our inter-section consistency-based UDA method for mito-chondria segmentation. Given two adjacent sections with a certain interval $(x_i^S/x_i^T$ and $x_{i+m}^S/x_{i+n}^T)$ from source domain $(\mathcal{S})$ and target domain $(\mathcal{T})$, the U-Net variant with two decoders outputs corresponding segmentation results $(s_i^S/s_i^T$ and $s_{i+m}^S/s_{i+n}^T)$ and the inter-section residual (r_i^S/r_i^T) simultaneously. Then, for the prediction consistency, two discriminators minimize the distribution discrepancy on s_i^S/s_i^T, s_{i+m}^S/s_{i+n}^T and r_i^S/r_i^T, respectively. For the inter-section consistency in $\mathcal{T}$, a pseudo label (p_i^T) is generated by the XOR logical operation $(\oplus)$ between s_{i+n}^T and r_i^T to supervise the segmentation of the current section (s_i^T), and vice versa. Details of network structure can be found in the supplementary material.

learning [12,25]. Recently, Wu *et al.* [24] introduce the pseudo label rectification strategy for EM images for the first time, which utilizes the estimated uncertainty to rectify noisy target labels predicted by the model trained on the source domain. Peng *et al.* [18] combine the denoising auto-encoder and the domain-adversarial learning to align source and target domains on both visual and geometrical features, which achieves the state-of-the-art performance on the task of domain adaptive mitochondria segmentation. Different from these UDA methods, our proposed method not only considers the intra-section gap but also addresses the inter-section gap between source and target domains.

The inter-section consistency in EM volumes is similar to temporal consistency in videos. They both aim to maintain the segmentation consistency between adjacent images. Recently, Guan *et al.* [5] propose a temporal consistency-based UDA method for video segmentation, which adopts the optical flows estimated from raw images to guide the temporal consistency of segmentation results. In contrast, we introduce the inter-section residual to avoid the requirement of optical flows which are often difficult to estimate and suffer from severe noise.

3 Method

Problem Formulation. Given the labeled source domain and the unlabeled target domain, we aim to learn a model which can produce accurate segmentation results in the target domain. In the source domain $(\mathcal{S})$, we have access to the source EM volume $X^S = \{x_i^S\}_{i=1}^M$ and the corresponding pixel-wise labels $Y^S = \{y_i^S \in \{0,1\}\}_{i=1}^M$. In the target domain $(\mathcal{T})$, however, only the target EM volume $X^T = \{x_i^T\}_{i=1}^N$ is available. Note that M and N denote the number of sequential sections in S and $\mathcal{T}$, respectively.

Inter-section Residual. We propose the inter-section residual to describe the variation of mitochondria across sections in EM volumes. In S, we can obtain the groundtruth of inter-section residual by the XOR logical operation on the labels of two adjacent sections as $G^S = \{g_i^S = y_i^S \oplus y_{i+m}^S\}_{i=1}^{M-m}$, where m denotes the interval of two sections. When two EM volumes are acquired by different devices (*e.g.*, FIB-SEM and ssTEM), their axial physical resolution often exists significant gap. Therefore, we adopt different intervals for S and $\mathcal{T}$ to alleviate the inter-section distribution discrepancy caused by different physical resolutions. In this paper, we term two sections with a certain interval as adjacent sections for convenience.

As shown in Fig. 1, to predict the segmentation results and the inter-section residual simultaneously, we adopt a U-Net [20] variant with one encoder and two decoders, namely, segmentation decoder and residual decoder. The encoder adopts two adjacent sections from S and $\mathcal{T}$ as input, *i.e.* x_i^S/x_i^T and x_{i+m}^S/x_{i+n}^T. The segmentation decoder predicts their corresponding segmentation results, *i.e.*, s_i^S/s_i^T and s_{i+m}^S/s_{i+n}^T, while the residual decoder predicts the inter-section residual r_i^S/r_i^T within these two adjacent sections. In S, we have the corresponding segmentation labels y_i^S, y_{i+m}^S, and the inter-section residual groundtruth g_i^S. Therefore, we adopt standard Cross-Entropy (CE) as supervised loss $\mathcal{L}_s$ as

$$\mathcal{L}_s = CE(s_i^S, y_i^S) + CE(s_{i+m}^S, y_{i+m}^S) + CE(r_i^S, g_i^S). \tag{1}$$

Prediction Consistency. To address the intra-section and inter-section gap between S and $\mathcal{T}$, we enforce the distribution of target predictions to be similar to that of source predictions on both segmentation results and the inter-section residual through adversarial learning. As shown in Fig. 1, we adopt two discriminators to align these two terms respectively, namely, segmentation discriminator and residual discriminator. The segmentation discriminator $\mathbb{D}_{seg}$ focus on the alignment of segmentation results between S and $\mathcal{T}$, while the residual discriminator $\mathbb{D}_{res}$ focus on the alignment of inter-section residuals.

For the alignment of segmentation results, $\mathbb{D}_{seg}$ takes s_i^S (s_{i+m}^S) and s_i^T (s_{i+n}^T) as input to address the intra-section gap between S and $\mathcal{T}$. Note that we utilize $\mathbb{D}_{seg}$ twice to input these two adjacent segmentation results independently. Therefore, the adversarial segmentation loss $\mathcal{L}_{seg}$ can be formulated as

$$\mathcal{L}_{seg} = log(\mathbb{D}_{seg}(s_i^S)) + log(1 - \mathbb{D}_{seg}(s_i^T))$$
$$+ log(\mathbb{D}_{seg}(s_{i+m}^S)) + log(1 - \mathbb{D}_{seg}(s_{i+n}^T)). \tag{2}$$

For the alignment of inter-section residuals, $\mathbb{D}_{res}$ takes r_i^S and r_i^T as input to address the inter-section gap between S and $\mathcal{T}$. Similar to $\mathcal{L}_{seg}$, the adversarial residual loss $\mathcal{L}_{res}$ can be formulated as

$$\mathcal{L}_{res} = log(\mathbb{D}_{res}(r_i^S)) + log(1 - \mathbb{D}_{res}(r_i^T)). \tag{3}$$

Table 1. Four representative and diverse EM datasets are used in our experiments, which are acquired by different EM devices from different organisms and tissues.

Name	VNC III [4]	Lucchi [13]	MitoEM-R [23]	MitoEM-H [23]
Organism	Drosophila	Mouse	Rat	Human
Tissue	Ventral nerve cord	Hippocampus	Cortex	Cortex
Device	ssTEM	FIB-SEM	mbSEM	mbSEM
Resolution	$50 \times 5 \times 5$ nm	$5 \times 5 \times 5$ nm	$30 \times 8 \times 8$ nm	$30 \times 8 \times 8$ nm
Training set	$20 \times 1024 \times 1024$	$165 \times 768 \times 1024$	$400 \times 4096 \times 4096$	$400 \times 4096 \times 4096$
Test set	-	$165 \times 768 \times 1024$	$100 \times 4096 \times 4096$	$100 \times 4096 \times 4096$

Inter-section Consistency. To further enforce the inter-section consistency inside $\mathcal{T}$, we propose a cross loss $\mathcal{L}_c$ which utilizes the predicted inter-section residual $r_i^{\mathcal{T}}$ as guidance to supervise the segmentation of adjacent sections in $\mathcal{T}$. Specifically, we adopt the XOR logical operation between $r_i^{\mathcal{T}}$ and the segmentation result of the adjacent section $s_{i+n}^{\mathcal{T}}$ to obtain the pseudo label of the current section as $p_i^{\mathcal{T}} = s_{i+n}^{\mathcal{T}} \oplus r_i^{\mathcal{T}}$. Analogously, the pseudo label of the adjacent section also can be obtained as $p_{i+n}^{\mathcal{T}} = s_i^{\mathcal{T}} \oplus r_i^{\mathcal{T}}$. Through these pseudo labels, we can further supervise the segmentation of these two sections in $\mathcal{T}$ as

$$\mathcal{L}_c = CE(s_i^{\mathcal{T}}, p_i^{\mathcal{T}}) + CE(s_{i+n}^{\mathcal{T}}, p_{i+n}^{\mathcal{T}}). \qquad (4)$$

Training and Inference Details. Our used U-Net variant and discriminator are based on [16] and [5] respectively. Note that the last two convolution layers in the segmentation (Seg.) decoder are not shared, which is designed to decode separate features for each input image and output two segmentation maps simultaneously. Their detailed network specifications can be found in the supplementary material. In the training phase, the above four loss terms are combined for the end-to-end training as

$$\mathcal{L}_{total} = \alpha \mathcal{L}_s + \beta(\mathcal{L}_{seg} + \mathcal{L}_{res}) + \gamma \mathcal{L}_c, \qquad (5)$$

where α, β, and γ are weighting coefficients to balance these four loss terms. In the inference phase, we remove the residual decoder and only adopt the trained encoder and segmentation decoder to obtain the final segmentation results. Note that we don't adopt any post-processing operations and test time augmentations to modify the predicted segmentation results.

4 Experiments

Datasets and Metrics. We adopt four representative and diverse EM datasets to demonstrate the effectiveness of our UDA method, as listed in Table 1. In this paper, they are divided into two groups to fully demonstrate the superiority of our method. In the first group, we use the VNC III dataset [4] as the source

Table 2. Quantitative comparisons on the Lucchi and MitoEM datasets. 'Oracle' denotes using the labels of the target domain to train the model, while 'NoAdapt' denotes directly applying the model trained on the source domain to the target domain without any domain adaptation strategy. Their values are directly obtained from [18] and [24].

Methods	VNC III → Lucchi (Subset1)				VNC III → Lucchi (Subset2)			
	mAP (%)	F1 (%)	MCC (%)	IoU (%)	mAP (%)	F1 (%)	MCC (%)	IoU (%)
Oracle	–	92.7	–	86.5	–	93.9	–	88.6
NoAdapt	–	57.3	–	40.3	–	61.3	–	44.3
Y-Net [19]	–	68.2	–	52.1	–	71.8	–	56.4
DANN [3]	–	68.2	–	51.9	–	74.9	–	60.1
AdaptSegNet [22]	–	69.9	–	54.0	–	79.0	–	65.5
UALR [24]	80.2	72.5	71.2	57.0	87.2	78.8	77.7	65.2
DAMT-Net [18]	–	74.7	–	60.0	–	81.3	–	68.7
DA-VSN [5]	82.8	75.2	73.9	60.3	91.3	83.1	82.2	71.1
Ours	**89.5**	**81.3**	**80.5**	**68.7**	**92.4**	**85.2**	**84.5**	**74.3**
Methods	MitoEM-R → MitoEM-H				MitoEM-H → MitoEM-R			
	mAP (%)	F1 (%)	MCC (%)	IoU (%)	mAP (%)	F1 (%)	MCC (%)	IoU (%)
Oracle	97.0	91.6	91.2	84.5	98.2	93.2	92.9	87.3
NoAdapt	74.6	56.8	59.2	39.6	88.5	76.5	76.8	61.9
UALR [24]	90.7	83.8	83.2	72.2	92.6	86.3	85.5	75.9
DAMT-Net [18]	92.1	84.4	83.7	73.0	94.8	86.0	85.7	75.4
DA-VSN [5]	91.6	83.3	82.6	71.4	94.5	86.7	86.3	76.5
Ours	**92.6**	**85.6**	**84.9**	**74.8**	**96.8**	**88.5**	**88.3**	**79.4**

domain and the Lucchi dataset [13] as the target domain. Note that the Lucchi dataset contains two subsets with the same size. Following [18], we adopt two-fold cross validation, where one subset is used as unlabeled target images while the other is used as the testing set. In the second group, following [24], we transfer the model from rat to human and from human to rat respectively on the MitoEM dataset [23].

Following [24], we adopt four popular metrics for evaluation, *i.e.*, mean Average Precision (mAP), F1 score, Mattews Correlation Coefficient (MCC) [14], and Intersection over Union (IoU, also referred as Jaccard index in [18]). Note that the network predictions, *i.e.*, probabilities, are directly measured by the mAP metric, while the binarization results generated from the predictions with a fixed threshold of 0.5 are measured by the other three metrics.

Implementation Details. Our experiments are implemented on PyTorch [17], using an NVIDIA TITAN Xp GPU with 12 GB memory. All models are trained using the Adam optimizer [8] with $\beta_1 = 0.9$, $\beta_2 = 0.999$. The learning rate is set at 10^{-4} and has a polynomial decay with a power of 0.9. We totally train 200,000 iterations with a batch size of 2, containing a pair of adjacent source images and a pair of adjacent target images with the size of 512×512. Since the axial resolution of VNC III is ten times that of Lucchi, we set the section intervals m and n as 1 and 10 respectively, while we set $m = n = 1$ on the MitoEM dataset due to the same axial resolutions on human and rat volumes.

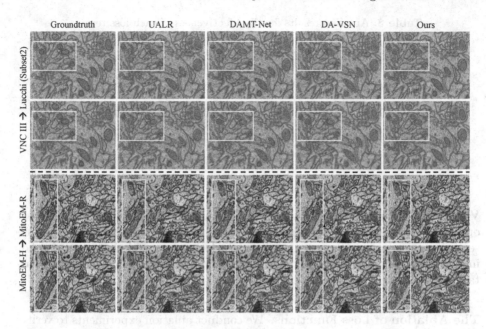

Fig. 2. Qualitative comparisons on Lucchi and MitoEM datasets. We show the segmentation results of two adjacent sections to compare the inter-section consistency of different methods, where red and green markers denote the ground truth and segmentation results, respectively. Compared with existing UDA methods, our method generates better segmentation results and maintains better inter-section consistency on the target volume (highlighted by orange boxes). (Color figure online)

The balancing weights α and β are set as 1 and 0.001, respectively. Note that the value of γ for the cross loss $\mathcal{L}_c$ is not fixed. Following [10, 26], we set γ as a time-dependent Gaussian warming-up function $\gamma(t) = 0.1 * exp(-5(1-t/t_{max})^2)$, where t and t_{max} denote the current training step and the maximum training step, respectively. Such design can ensure that at the beginning, the objective loss is dominated by the supervised loss and the adversarial losses to avoid the network get stuck in a degenerate solution [26].

Comparison with Baselines. We quantitatively compare our method with multiple UDA baselines [5, 18, 24] under different datasets [13, 23] to demonstrate the superiority of our method. UALR [24] and DAMT-Net [18] are the two most representative and competitive methods for domain adaptive mitochondria segmentation, while DA-VSN [5] is proposed for domain adaptive video segmentation by temporal consistency, where we directly migrate it to our task to make a comparison. As listed in Table 2, our proposed method outperforms these three methods consistently by a large margin, which demonstrates that our method can improve the generalization capacity of the learned model on the target domain by exploiting the inter-section information between EM images. We further qualitatively compare our method with UALR, DAMT-Net, and DA-

Table 3. Ablation results for the effectiveness of each loss term.

VNC III → Lucchi (Subset1)

Settings	$\mathcal{L}_s$	$\mathcal{L}_{seg}$	$\mathcal{L}_{res}$	$\mathcal{L}_c$	mAP(%)	F1(%)	MCC(%)	IoU(%)
i	✓				76.0	68.0	66.7	51.9
ii	✓	✓			80.9	72.5	71.2	57.1
iii	✓		✓		81.1	73.6	72.4	58.8
iv	✓	✓	✓		84.4	74.5	73.3	59.6
v	✓	✓	✓	✓	**89.5**	**81.3**	**80.5**	**68.7**

VSN in two different experimental settings, as shown in Fig. 2. We can find that our method generates better segmentation results and maintains better inter-section consistency on the target domain, which demonstrates that our proposed inter-section consistency can better address the domain gap between source and target domains.

The Ablation of Loss Functions. We conduct ablation experiments to verify the effectiveness of each loss term used in our proposed framework. As listed in Table 3, our proposed method achieves the best performance when all loss terms are adopted at the same time. Specifically, we can draw three observations as follows: a) According to the ablation experiments i, ii, and iii, we can find that adopting adversarial segmentation loss $\mathcal{L}_{seg}$ and adversarial residual loss $\mathcal{L}_{res}$ independently can both improve the generalizability of the learned model on the target domain (+4.9% and +5.1% on the mAP metric). b) According to ii and iv, adding $\mathcal{L}_{res}$ can further improve the segmentation performance (+3.5% on the mAP metric), which demonstrates that the alignment of the inter-section residual is beneficial to reduce the domain gap between source and target domains. c) According to iv and v, adding the cross loss $\mathcal{L}_c$ can significantly improve the segmentation performance (+5.1% on the mAP metric), which demonstrates that maintaining the inter-section consistency by the generated pseudo labels plays an important role in enhancing the generalization capability of the learned model on the target domain. Note that the ablation of key hyper-parameters can be found in the supplementary material, *i.e.*, the weights of loss terms β, γ, and the section interval n.

5   Conclusion

In this paper, for the first time, we propose a domain adaptive mitochondria segmentation method via enforcing inter-section consistency. We introduce the inter-section residual to address both the intra-section and inter-section gap between source and target domains. Meanwhile, we utilize the predicted inter-section residual to further enforce the inter-section consistency on the target domain. Extensive and diverse experiments demonstrate the superiority of our proposed method for the domain adaptive mitochondria segmentation.

Acknowledgement. This work was supported in part by the National Key R&D Program of China under Grant 2017YFA0700800, the National Natural Science Foundation of China under Grant 62021001, the University Synergy Innovation Program of Anhui Province No. GXXT-2019-025, and Anhui Provincial Natural Science Foundation under grant No. 1908085QF256.

References

1. Bermúdez-Chacón, R., Altingövde, O., Becker, C., Salzmann, M., Fua, P.: Visual correspondences for unsupervised domain adaptation on electron microscopy images. IEEE Trans. Med. Imaging **39**(4), 1256–1267 (2019)
2. Bermúdez-Chacón, R., Márquez-Neila, P., Salzmann, M., Fua, P.: A domain-adaptive two-stream u-net for electron microscopy image segmentation. In: ISBI (2018)
3. Ganin, Y., et al.: Domain-adversarial training of neural networks. J. Mach. Learn. Res. **17**(1), 2096–2030 (2016)
4. Gerhard, S., Funke, J., Martel, J., Cardona, A., Fetter, R.: Segmented anisotropic sstem dataset of neural tissue. Figshare (2013)
5. Guan, D., Huang, J., Xiao, A., Lu, S.: Domain adaptive video segmentation via temporal consistency regularization. In: ICCV (2021)
6. Januszewski, M., Jain, V.: Segmentation-enhanced cyclegan. bioRxiv (2019)
7. Kasahara, T., et al.: Depression-like episodes in mice harboring mtdna deletions in paraventricular thalamus. Mol. Psychiatry **21**(1), 39–48 (2016)
8. Kingma, D.P., Ba, J.: Adam: a method for stochastic optimization. arXiv preprint arXiv:1412.6980 (2014)
9. Li, M., Chen, C., Liu, X., Huang, W., Zhang, Y., Xiong, Z.: Advanced deep networks for 3D mitochondria instance segmentation. In: ISBI (2022)
10. Li, S., Zhang, C., He, X.: Shape-aware semi-supervised 3d semantic segmentation for medical images. In: Martel, A.L., et al. (eds.) MICCAI 2020. LNCS, vol. 12261, pp. 552–561. Springer, Cham (2020). https://doi.org/10.1007/978-3-030-59710-8_54
11. Li, Z., Chen, X., Zhao, J., Xiong, Z.: Contrastive learning for mitochondria segmentation. In: EMBC (2021)
12. Liu, D., et al.: Pdam: a panoptic-level feature alignment framework for unsupervised domain adaptive instance segmentation in microscopy images. IEEE Trans. Med. Imaging **40**(1), 154–165 (2020)
13. Lucchi, A., Li, Y., Fua, P.: Learning for structured prediction using approximate subgradient descent with working sets. In: CVPR (2013)
14. Matthews, B.W.: Comparison of the predicted and observed secondary structure of t4 phage lysozyme. Biochimica et Biophysica Acta (BBA)-Protein Struct. **405**(2), 442–451 (1975)
15. Nightingale, L., de Folter, J., Spiers, H., Strange, A., Collinson, L.M., Jones, M.L.: Automatic instance segmentation of mitochondria in electron microscopy data. bioRxiv (2021)

16. Nishimura, K., Hayashida, J., Wang, C., Ker, D.F.E., Bise, R.: Weakly-supervised cell tracking via backward-and-forward propagation. In: Vedaldi, A., Bischof, H., Brox, T., Frahm, J.-M. (eds.) ECCV 2020. LNCS, vol. 12357, pp. 104–121. Springer, Cham (2020). https://doi.org/10.1007/978-3-030-58610-2_7
17. Paszke, A., et al.: Automatic differentiation in pytorch (2017)
18. Peng, J., Yi, J., Yuan, Z.: Unsupervised mitochondria segmentation in EM images via domain adaptive multi-task learning. IEEE J. Sel. Topics Sig. Process. **14**(6), 1199–1209 (2020)
19. Roels, J., Hennies, J., Saeys, Y., Philips, W., Kreshuk, A.: Domain adaptive segmentation in volume electron microscopy imaging. In: ISBI (2019)
20. Ronneberger, O., Fischer, P., Brox, T.: U-Net: convolutional networks for biomedical image segmentation. In: Navab, N., Hornegger, J., Wells, W.M., Frangi, A.F. (eds.) MICCAI 2015. LNCS, vol. 9351, pp. 234–241. Springer, Cham (2015). https://doi.org/10.1007/978-3-319-24574-4_28
21. Schubert, P.J., Dorkenwald, S., Januszewski, M., Jain, V., Kornfeld, J.: Learning cellular morphology with neural networks. Nat. Commun. **10**(1), 1–12 (2019)
22. Tsai, Y.H., Hung, W.C., Schulter, S., Sohn, K., Yang, M.H., Chandraker, M.: Learning to adapt structured output space for semantic segmentation. In: CVPR (2018)
23. Wei, D., et al.: MitoEM dataset: large-scale 3D mitochondria instance segmentation from EM images. In: Martel, A.L., et al. (eds.) MICCAI 2020. LNCS, vol. 12265, pp. 66–76. Springer, Cham (2020). https://doi.org/10.1007/978-3-030-59722-1_7
24. Wu, S., Chen, C., Xiong, Z., Chen, X., Sun, X.: Uncertainty-aware label rectification for domain adaptive mitochondria segmentation. In: de Bruijne, M., Cattin, P.C., Cotin, S., Padoy, N., Speidel, S., Zheng, Y., Essert, C. (eds.) MICCAI 2021. LNCS, vol. 12903, pp. 191–200. Springer, Cham (2021). https://doi.org/10.1007/978-3-030-87199-4_18
25. Yi, J., Yuan, Z., Peng, J.: Adversarial-prediction guided multi-task adaptation for semantic segmentation of electron microscopy images. In: ISBI (2020)
26. Yu, L., Wang, S., Li, X., Fu, C.-W., Heng, P.-A.: Uncertainty-aware self-ensembling model for semi-supervised 3D left atrium segmentation. In: Shen, D., et al. (eds.) MICCAI 2019. LNCS, vol. 11765, pp. 605–613. Springer, Cham (2019). https://doi.org/10.1007/978-3-030-32245-8_67
27. Zeviani, M., Di Donato, S.: Mitochondrial disorders. Brain **127**(10), 2153–2172 (2004)

DeStripe: A Self2Self Spatio-Spectral Graph Neural Network with Unfolded Hessian for Stripe Artifact Removal in Light-Sheet Microscopy

Yu Liu[1], Kurt Weiss[2], Nassir Navab[1,3], Carsten Marr[4], Jan Huisken[2], and Tingying Peng[5(✉)]

[1] Technical University of Munich, Munich, Germany
[2] Georg-August-University Goettingen, Goettingen, Germany
[3] Johns Hopkins University, Baltimore, USA
[4] Institute of AI for Health, Helmholtz Munich - German Research Center for Environmental Health, Neuherberg, Germany
[5] Helmholtz AI, Helmholtz Munich - German Research Center for Environmental Health, Neuherberg, Germany
tingying.peng@helmholtz-muenchen.de

Abstract. Light-sheet fluorescence microscopy (LSFM) is a cutting-edge volumetric imaging technique that allows for three-dimensional imaging of mesoscopic samples with decoupled illumination and detection paths. Although the selective excitation scheme of such a microscope provides intrinsic optical sectioning that minimizes out-of-focus fluorescence background and sample photodamage, it is prone to light absorption and scattering effects, which results in uneven illumination and striping artifacts in the images adversely. To tackle this issue, in this paper, we propose a blind stripe artifact removal algorithm in LSFM, called DeStripe, which combines a self-supervised spatio-spectral graph neural network with unfolded Hessian prior. Specifically, inspired by the desirable properties of Fourier transform in condensing striping information into isolated values in the frequency domain, DeStripe firstly localizes the potentially corrupted Fourier coefficients by exploiting the structural difference between unidirectional stripe artifacts and more isotropic foreground images. Affected Fourier coefficients can then be fed into a graph neural network for recovery, with a Hessian regularization unrolled to further ensure structures in the standard image space are well preserved. Since in realistic, stripe-free LSFM barely exists with a standard image acquisition protocol, DeStripe is equipped with a Self2Self denoising loss term, enabling artifact elimination without access to stripe-free ground truth images. Competitive experimental results demonstrate the efficacy of DeStripe in recovering corrupted biomarkers in LSFM with both synthetic and real stripe artifacts.

Keywords: Light-sheet fluorescence microscopy · Deep unfolding · Graph neural network · Hessian

L. Wang et al. (Eds.): MICCAI 2022, LNCS 13434, pp. 99–108, 2022.
https://doi.org/10.1007/978-3-031-16440-8_10

1   Introduction

Light-sheet Fluorescence Microscopy (LSFM) is a planar illumination technique that is revolutionizing biology by enabling rapid *in toto* imaging of entire embryos or organs at subcellular resolution [14,16]. By illuminating the specimen perpendicular to the detection direction, LSFM excites fluorescence only in a thin slice (Fig. 1a), which allows for a higher signal-to-noise ratio and better imaging contrast [12]. However, a drawback of such a lateral illumination scheme is the presence of striped artifacts along the illumination direction in the resulting image, caused by the absorption of coherent light within the sample [12,17] (Fig. 1b). Although several optical solutions, multi-view LSFM for instance [7], can remove stripes in the source, they are limited by low acquisition rate and increased photobleaching, rendering them unsuitable for rapid *in toto* imaging [12,17,22]. Therefore, computational strategies, which attempt to remove stripe artifacts after acquisition, are highly attractive.

Inspired by the desirable properties of Fourier transform in condensing stripings into isolated values on x-axis in Fourier space (for vertical stripes in Fig. 1b), one line of model-based destriping studies [11,13] suppresses stripe noises by constructing a Fourier filter on a transformed domain, e.g., wavelet [13]. However, filtering-based methods risk removing structural information of the sample which falls within the same filter band, resulting in image blurring negatively [3,18]. On the contrary, another line of works treats the destriping issue as an ill-posed inverse problem in the standard image space, where regularizations, such as stationary prior on the stripes [5], are commonly adopted to find the optimal solution [3,4]. However, despite their promising abilities to preserve structural information such as sharp edges, some strict spatial constraints, e.g., low-rank assumption for the noise [4], only hold true when the stripes cover the entire field of view, which is not the case in LSFM imaging [8].

With recent advances in deep learning, emerging structural noise removal studies put image denoising tasks into a more general framework, where a mapping from a corrupted image to its noise-free counterpart is directly learned by training a generative network on a large dataset of clean/noisy images, e.g., pix2pix GAN with paired images [10], or cycleGAN on non-paired images [26]. However, neither clean ground truth images [23], nor an extensive training dataset [15], is easily accessible in LSFM [17]. Encouragingly, recent developments in learning self-supervised denoising from single images, Self2Self [1] and Self2Void [9] for instance, circumvent the acquisition of clean/noisy image pairs by using the same noisy image as both input and target. For example, Self2Void proposed to randomly exclude pixels of a noise-corrupted image and optimize the denoising network only on these blind spots to prevent the model from simply learning an identical mapping [9]. Unfortunately, their assumption of a limited size of artifacts, which cannot span more than several connected pixels, is intrinsically not applicable to our case of striping artifacts with arbitrary shapes.

To address the aforementioned issues, in this paper, we propose a blind stripe artifact remover in LSFM, called DeStripe, by using a self-supervised spatio-spectral graph neural network with unfolded Hessian prior. The main contributions of this paper are summarized as follows:

- DeStripe is a unified stripe artifact remover that operates in both spatial and spectral domains, enabling a complete stripe elimination by using a deep learning-parameterized Fourier filtering, while also preserving sample biological structures with an unfolded Hessian-based spatial constraint.
- Unlike previous convolutional image denoising networks, which adopt a U-net architecture directly in the image space to deal with artifacts spanning across multiple pixels, we formulate a graph neural network (GNN) in the spectral domain to recover stripe-affected Fourier coefficients, which is more efficient due to the isolation of stripes in Fourier space.
- Aided by a Self2Self denoising loss formulation, DeStripe is trained completely in a self-supervised fashion, allowing blind stripe artifact removal in LSFM without the need for stripe-free LSFM images.

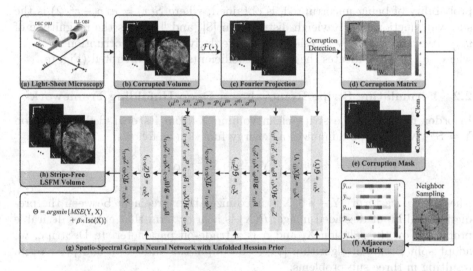

Fig. 1. An overview of DeStripe (see text for explanation)

2   Methods

We illustrate DeStripe for blind stripe artifact removal in LSFM as a schematic plot in Fig. 1. First, by assuming that the Fourier projection of structured stripes is more directional than the sample itself, we locate corrupted Fourier coefficients within a wedge region in the Fourier space (Fig. 1b–e). We then feed the affected Fourier projection into a GNN for recovery, in which the network reconstructs every noise-related Fourier coefficient based on its uncorrupted neighbors on a polar coordinate (Fig. 1f). In addition, we unfold a Hessian minimization process into our graph-based Fourier recovery network via the split Bregman algorithm (Fig. 1g), to ensure local continuity and preserve sample structure.

2.1 Detecting of Corruption in Fourier Space

Given a LSFM volume $Y \in \mathbb{R}^{N_d \times N_h \times N_v}$ with total N_d slices of $N_h \times N_v$ images, DeStripe is to recover the underlying stripe-clean volume X from its degraded observation $Y = S \odot X$, where S is the distortion caused by stripes. In Fourier space, the spectral energy of unidirectional stripes S, which is assumed to be perpendicular to the edge in LSFM images, is highly condensed in a narrow wedge-shape frequency band perpendicular to the direction of the stripes [18], whereas the underlying stripe-clean sample X has no strong direction preference in its edges (see Fig. 1c). Therefore, for every slice $Y_k \in \mathbb{R}^{N_h \times N_v}$, its Fourier coefficients $\tilde{y}_{kij} \in \mathbb{C}$, which fall within the same thin concentric annulus $\mathbb{A}_k^r$, mathematically follow a two-dimensional Gaussian distribution and in turn lead to the Rayleigh distribution as the amplitude distribution model [8], except those stripe-corrupted ones. Therefore, a corruption matrix $W \in \mathbb{R}^{N_d \times N_h \times N_v}$ (Fig. 1d), whose (k, i, j)-th element $w_{kij} = S(\|\tilde{y}_{kij}\|) \in [0, 1]$ indicates the degree of corresponding Fourier coefficient fulfilling the Gaussian distribution, i.e., the probability of being uncorrupted, is obtained, where $S(x) = exp(-x^2/2)$ is the survival function of a Rayleigh distribution [8], and $\|\tilde{y}_{kij}\|$ is the magnitude of $\tilde{y}_{kij}$ after whitening. By thresholding W, we derive a binary corruption mask M, where $m_{i,j,k} = 1$ indicates the Fourier coefficients being corrupted (Fig. 1e).

2.2 Formulating Stripe Removal as a Deep Unfolding Framework

In order to recover the stripe-clean volume X from its degraded observation $Y = S \odot X$, DeStripe minimizes an energy function as follows:

$$X = \underset{X}{argmin} \left\{ \|Y - S \odot X\|^2 + \alpha R(X)) \right\} \tag{1}$$

where the data term $\|Y - S \odot X\|^2$ maximizes the agreement between the prediction and input degraded image, $R(X)$ is a prior term that enforces desirable properties on the solution X, and α is a trade-off parameter. In DeStripe, we adopt split Bregman algorithm [24] to decouple the data term and prior term, resulting in three sub-problems:

$$\begin{cases} X^{k+1} = \underset{X}{argmin} \left\{ \|Y - S \odot X\|^2 + \frac{\mu}{2} \|Z^k - X - B^k\|^2 \right\} & (2a) \\[2mm] Z^{k+1} = \underset{Z}{argmin} \left\{ \alpha R(Z) + \frac{\mu}{2} \|Z - X^{k+1} - B^k\|^2 \right\} & (2b) \\[2mm] B^{k+1} = B^k + X^{k+1} - Z^{k+1} & (2c) \end{cases}$$

where $k = 1, 2, \ldots, K$ denotes the k-th iteration, Z is introduced for splitting, B is the Bregman variable, and μ is the Lagrange multiplier. Next, in contrast to traditional model-based destriping approaches [3,8,18], which derive handcrafted solutions for each sub-problem in Eq. (2), we propose to:

- formulate a GNN-parameterized Fourier filtering to solve the data sub-problem in Eq. (2a), denoted as $\mathcal{G}(\bullet)$ yellow bar in Fig. 1g;

- solve the prior sub-problem in Eq. (2b) with the regularizer specified as Hessian in the image space [24], denoted as $\mathcal{H}(\bullet)$ green bar in Fig. 1g;
- adapt Bregman variable in every iteration based on Eq. (2c), denoted as $\mathcal{B}(\bullet)$ purple par in Fig. 1g;
- inherit the hyper-parameter generator in [25] as $\mathcal{P}(\bullet)$ to avoid manual parameter tuning, shown as peach bar in Fig. 1g.

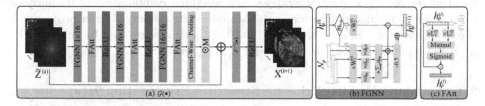

Fig. 2. Structure of (a) k-th $\mathcal{G}(\bullet)$, (b) l-th FGNN, and (c) FAtt. (Color figure online)

2.3   Graph-Based Fourier Recovery Network $\mathcal{G}(\bullet)$

Inspired by the homogeneous Fourier projection of the sample against directional one for stripings, sample-only spectral response within the corruption mask M is modeled as a combination of their uncorrupted neighbors on a polar coordinate. To this end, we adopt a GNN, which is able to vary the neighborhood size by constructing the receptive field and is shown in Fig. 2a. Specifically, we firstly reformulate Fourier projection $\tilde{Y} \in \mathbb{C}^{N_d \times N_h \times N_v}$ as a graph $\mathcal{G} = \{\mathcal{V}, H, A\}$, where $\mathcal{V}$ is the vertex set with $|\mathcal{V}| = N_d \times N_h \times N_v$ nodes, $H \in \mathbb{C}^{|\mathcal{V}| \times 1}$ is the node attributes, whose p-th row is the Fourier component $\tilde{y}_{k_p i_p j_p}$ indexed by node p, and $A \in \mathbb{R}^{|\mathcal{V}| \times |\mathcal{V}|}$ is the adjacency matrix, whose (p, q)-th entry indicates connection from node q to p. According with the isotropic hypothesis that we assume on the stripe-free X, we define neighboring connections on a polar coordinate:

$$a_{pq} = 1_{q \in \mathcal{N}_p} \times w_{k_q i_q j_q}, \ \mathcal{N}_p = \left\{ q \,\middle|\, q \in \mathbb{A}_{k_p}^{r_p}, m_{k_q i_q j_q} = 0, |\mathcal{N}_p| = N \right\} \quad (3)$$

where $\mathcal{N}_p$ is the neighboring set of node p, consisting of total N uncorrupted nodes that are randomly selected from $\mathbb{A}_{k_p}^{r_p}$ of node p. We define the proposed stripe filtering process, FGNN (Fig. 2b), as a message passing scheme on $\mathcal{G}$:

$$h_p^{(l+1)} = \begin{cases} 0.5 \left(h_p^{(l)} W_1^{(l)} + (\sum_{q \in \mathcal{N}(p)} a_{pq} \times h_q^{(l)} W_1^{(l)} / \sum_q a_{pq} \right), & m_{k_p i_p j_p} = 0 \\ h_p^{(l)} W_2^{(l)} - (\sum_{q \in \mathcal{N}(p)} a_{pq} \times h_q^{(l)} W_1^{(l)}) / \sum_q a_{pq}, & m_{k_p i_p j_p} = 1 \end{cases} \quad (4)$$

where $l = 1 \ldots, L$ is the number of layers, $h_p^{(l)} \in \mathbb{C}^{1 \times N_l}$ is the activation of node p at the l-th layer. Since corrupted Fourier coefficients are an accumulation of components belonging to both stripes and underlying sample, we project sample-only

$h_p^{(l)}$ $(m_{k_p i_p j_p} = 0)$ and stripe-related $h_p^{(l)}$ $(m_{k_p i_p j_p} = 1)$ by $W_1^{(l)} \in \mathbb{C}^{N_l \times N_{(l+1)}}$ and $W_2^{(l)} \in \mathbb{C}^{N_l \times N_{(l+1)}}$ separately. Note that we borrow the design of complex-valued building blocks from [20] for $W_1^{(l)}$ and $W_2^{(l)}$, which simulates complex arithmetic using two real-valued entities. Additionally, we insert a frequency-aware self-attention unit [21], called FAtt (Fig. 2c), between every two successive FGNN, which encodes recovery importance by taking not only the Fourier coefficients but also corresponding frequencies into account. As a result, the sample-only spectral response is explicitly modeled as a weighted combination of its uncorrupted neighbors on a polar coordinate. Moreover, stripe-only Fourier projection is exclusively reserved as activation $M \odot H^{(L+1)}$, which can then be subtracted from the input stripe-sample mixture for striping removal.

2.4 Unfolded Hessian Prior for Structure Preservation $\mathcal{H}(\bullet)$

By specifying regularizer $R(X)$ in Eq. (2b) as a Hessian prior in the image space:

$$
\begin{aligned}
R_{Hessian}(X) &= \lambda_x \|X_{xx}\|_1 + \lambda_y \|X_{yy}\|_1 + \lambda_z \|X_{zz}\|_1 \\
&+ 2\sqrt{\lambda_x \lambda_y} \|X_{xy}\|_1 + 2\sqrt{\lambda_x \lambda_z} \|X_{xz}\|_1 + 2\sqrt{\lambda_y \lambda_z} \|X_{yz}\|_1
\end{aligned}
\tag{5}
$$

where λ_x, λ_y and λ_z are the penalty parameters of continuity along x, y and z axes, respectively, X_i denotes the second-order partial derivative of X in different directions. Equation (5) then has solution as:

$$
Z_i^{k+1} = shrink(\lambda_i X_i^{k+1} + B_i^k, \frac{\alpha}{\mu})
\tag{6}
$$

where $\lambda_i = \lambda_x, \lambda_y, \lambda_z, 2\sqrt{\lambda_x \lambda_y}, 2\sqrt{\lambda_x \lambda_z}, 2\sqrt{\lambda_y \lambda_z}$ for $i = xx, yy, zz, xy, xz, yz$, and $shrink(\bullet)$ is the scalar shrinkage operator [24].

2.5 Self2Self Denoising Loss Formulation

We propose to train learnable parameters Θ in DeStripe via a self-supervised denoising scheme, where training targets are still stripe-corrupted volume Y:

$$
\Theta = \underset{\Theta}{argmin} \left\{ \|Y - X\|^2 + \beta \sum_{k=1}^{N_d} \sum_r \sum_{\tilde{x} \in \mathbb{P}_k^r} \left\| \|\tilde{x}\| - \frac{1}{|\mathbb{Q}_k^r|} \sum_{\tilde{z} \in \mathbb{Q}_k^r} \|\tilde{z}\| \right\|^2 \right\}
\tag{7}
$$

where mean square error $\|Y - X\|^2$ is adopted to encourage the agreement between prediction X and input image Y in the image space. Particularly, the second term in Eq. (7) is to prevent the model from learning an identical mapping by quantifying isotropic properties of recovered $\tilde{X}$ in Fourier space, where $\mathbb{P}_k^r$ is the corrupted subset of $\mathbb{A}_k^r$, and $\mathbb{Q}_k^r = \{\tilde{x} \,|\, \tilde{x} \in \mathbb{A}_k^r, \tilde{x} \notin \mathbb{P}_k^r\}$.

2.6   Competitive Methods

We compare DeStripe to five baseline methods: (i) wavelet-FFT [13]: a Fourier filter-based destriping method in wavelet space; (ii) variational stationary noise remover (VSNR) [5]: a Bayesian-based restoration framework in image space; (iii) filling the wedge [18]: a total variation model-based Fourier recovery approach for stripe artifacts removal; (iv) strip the stripes [8]: a Fourier reconstruction method using sparsity of the image gradient and longitudinal smoothness of the stripes for spatial constraint; (v) SN2V [2]: a self-supervised deep learning network, which enables removal of structured noise by using a structured blind spots scheme; and two DeStripe variations: (vi) DeStripe $\mathcal{G}(\bullet)$ only: constructed by removing the Hessian prior $\mathcal{H}(\bullet)$ to disable spatial constraints; (vii) DeStripe $\mathcal{H}(\bullet)$ only: formulated by replacing $\mathcal{G}(\bullet)$ with a plain U-Net in the image space, regardless of the isolation of stripes in Fourier domain.

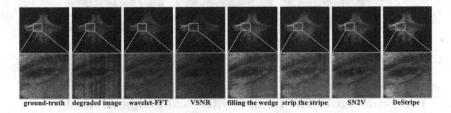

Fig. 3. Visualization of stripe-removal quality with respect to ground-truth.

3   Results and Discussion

3.1   Evaluation on LSFM Images with Synthetic Stripe Artifact

We firstly evaluate DeStripe in removing synthetic stripes. As stated in the Introduction, there is no stripe-free LSFM with the conventional parallel light illumination. Yet special image acquisition protocol, such as diffused light-sheet microscopy, could illuminate the blind spots and alleviate stripe artifacts in the source [19]. Here we take a diffused LSFM volume collected in [19], add simulated stripes following [8] for thirty times, perform DeStripe and other stripe removal methods, and compare the restored images to the original artifact-free ground truth. DeStripe's reconstruction achieves the best peak signal-to-noise ratio (PSNR) and structural similarity index (SSIM), far surpassing other approaches (Table.1, p < 0.001 using Wilcoxon signed-rank test). Only DeStripe resolves stripes without affecting original image details with a SSIM of 0.98. In comparison, wavelet-FFT, VSNR, and strip the stripes could distort the original signal gradient when removing the stripe artifacts (Fig. 3). Filling the wedge and SN2V, on the other hand, has residual stripes after correction (see enlarged image details). Additionally, we perform an ablation study to assess individual components of DeStripe, $\mathcal{H}(\bullet)$ and $\mathcal{G}(\bullet)$. We discover that they complement one another and contribute to the overall outstanding performance.

Table 1. DeStripe achieves best quantitative results on synthetic stripes.

	wavelet-FFT [13]	VSNR [5]	filling the wedge [18]	strip the stripes [8]	SN2V [2]	DeStripe $\mathcal{H}(\bullet)$ only	DeStripe $\mathcal{G}(\bullet)$ only	**DeStripe**
PSNR	24.25 ±0.77	19.23 ±0.76	31.74 ±1.74	26.13 ±1.56	20.22 ±0.83	24.24 ±0.78	31.18 ±2.08	**36.34 ±1.19**
SSIM	0.87 ±0.02	0.74 ±0.03	0.93 ±0.01	0.87 ±0.01	0.73 ±0.03	0.89 ±0.02	0.92 ±0.02	**0.98 ±0.01**

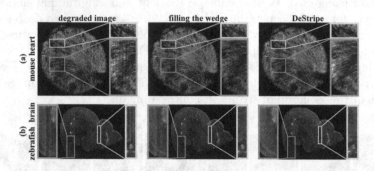

Fig. 4. Visualization of stripe-removal quality in real scenario. (Color figure online)

3.2 Evaluation on LSFM Images with Real Stripe Artifact

DeStripe is further evaluated on real stripes in LSFM against filling the wedge [18], the baseline that achieves the best performance on synthetic data. Two large sample volumes, mouse heart ($100 \times 1484 \times 1136$) and zebrafish brain ($50 \times 2169 \times 1926$), both with a resolution of 1.06 um in x, y and 10 um in z axially, were optically cleared and imaged using a light sheet microscope. A multichannel coherent laser source (Omicron Sole-6) was collimated and expanded to achieve the required light sheet size for the ca. 3 mm × 5 mm field of view and 15 um sheet waist for optical sectioning (see [6] for detailed image acquisition protocol). As shown in Fig. 4a, although filling the wedge can erase most of the quasi-periodic stripes, it also distorts the original image, e.g., causing a fake signal to appear in the formerly dark region (red box). Moreover, filling the wedge cannot resolve aperiodic thick stripes (residual stripes remain after correction, Fig. 4b). DeStripe, on the other hand, resolves both types of stripe while preserving the original image details.

4   Conclusion

In this paper, we propose DeStripe, a self-supervised spatio-spectral graph neural network with unfolded Hessian prior, to remove stripe artifacts in lightsheet fluorescence microscopy images. DeStripe is trained completely in a self-supervised manner, with the stripe-corrupted image serving both network input and target, obviating the need for a stripe-free LSFM for network training. Furthermore, by combing data-driven Fourier filtering in soectral domain with a

Hessian-based spatial constraint, DeStripe can localize and filter isolated stripe-corrupted Fourier coefficients while better preserving sample biological structures. Both qualitative and quantitative evaluations show that DeStripe surpasses other state-of-the-art LSFM stripe removal methods by a large margin. DeStripe code will be made accessible for biologists for academic usage.

Acknowledgements. C.M. has received funding from the European Research Council (ERC) under the European Union's Horizon 2020 research and innovation programme (Grant agreement No. 866411). Y.L. is supported by the China Scholarship Council (No. 202106020050).

References

1. Batson, J., Royer, L.: Noise2self: blind denoising by self-supervision. In: International Conference on Machine Learning, pp. 524–533. PMLR (2019)
2. Broaddus, C., Krull, A., Weigert, M., Schmidt, U., Myers, G.: Removing structured noise with self-supervised blind-spot networks. In: 2020 IEEE 17th International Symposium on Biomedical Imaging (ISBI), pp. 159–163. IEEE (2020). https://doi.org/10.1109/ISBI45749.2020.9098336
3. Chang, Y., Fang, H., Yan, L., Liu, H.: Robust destriping method with unidirectional total variation and framelet regularization. Opt. Express **21**(20), 23307–23323 (2013). https://doi.org/10.1364/OE.21.023307
4. Chang, Y., Yan, L., Wu, T., Zhong, S.: Remote sensing image stripe noise removal: From image decomposition perspective. IEEE Trans. Geosci. Remote Sens. **54**(12), 7018–7031 (2016). https://doi.org/10.1109/TGRS.2016.2594080
5. Fehrenbach, J., Weiss, P., Lorenzo, C.: Variational algorithms to remove stationary noise: applications to microscopy imaging. IEEE Trans. Image Process. **21**(10), 4420–4430 (2012). https://doi.org/10.1109/TIP.2012.2206037
6. Huisken, J., Stainier, D.Y.R.: Even fluorescence excitation by multidirectional selective plane illumination microscopy (mspim). Opt. Lett. **32**(17), 2608–2610 (2007). https://doi.org/10.1364/OL.32.002608. http://opg.optica.org/ol/abstract.cfm?URI=ol-32-17-2608
7. Huisken, J., Swoger, J., Del Bene, F., Wittbrodt, J., Stelzer, E.H.: Optical sectioning deep inside live embryos by selective plane illumination microscopy. Science **305**(5686), 1007–1009 (2004). https://doi.org/10.1126/science.1100035
8. Khalilian-Gourtani, A., Tepper, M., Minden, V., Chklovskii, D.B.: Strip the stripes: artifact detection and removal for scanning electron microscopy imaging. In: ICASSP 2019–2019 IEEE International Conference on Acoustics, Speech and Signal Processing (ICASSP), pp. 1060–1064. IEEE (2019). https://doi.org/10.1109/ICASSP.2019.8683119
9. Krull, A., Buchholz, T.O., Jug, F.: Noise2void - learning denoising from single noisy images. In: 2019 IEEE/CVF Conference on Computer Vision and Pattern Recognition (CVPR), pp. 2124–2132 (2019). https://doi.org/10.1109/CVPR.2019.00223
10. Lata, K., Dave, M., Nishanth, K.N.: Image-to-image translation using generative adversarial network. In: 2019 3rd International conference on Electronics, Communication and Aerospace Technology (ICECA), pp. 186–189 (2019). https://doi.org/10.1109/ICECA.2019.8822195

11. Liang, X., et al.: Stripe artifact elimination based on nonsubsampled contourlet transform for light sheet fluorescence microscopy. J. Biomed. Opt. **21**(10), 106005 (2016). https://doi.org/10.1117/1.JBO.21.10.106005

12. Mayer, J., Robert-Moreno, A., Sharpe, J., Swoger, J.: Attenuation artifacts in light sheet fluorescence microscopy corrected by optispim. Light Sci. Appl. **7**(1), 1–13 (2018). https://doi.org/10.1038/s41377-018-0068-z

13. Münch, B., Trtik, P., Marone, F., Stampanoni, M.: Stripe and ring artifact removal with combined wavelet — fourier filtering. Opt. Express **17**(10), 8567–8591 (2009). https://doi.org/10.1364/OE.17.008567, http://opg.optica.org/oe/abstract.cfm?URI=oe-17-10-8567

14. Power, R.M., Huisken, J.: A guide to light-sheet fluorescence microscopy for multiscale imaging. Nat. Methods **14**(4), 360–373 (2017). https://doi.org/10.1038/nmeth.4224

15. Prakash, M., Krull, A., Jug, F.: Fully unsupervised diversity denoising with convolutional variational autoencoders. arXiv preprint arXiv:2006.06072 (2020)

16. Reynaud, E.G., Peychl, J., Huisken, J., Tomancak, P.: Guide to light-sheet microscopy for adventurous biologists. Nat. Methods **12**(1), 30–34 (2015). https://doi.org/10.1038/nmeth.3222

17. Ricci, P., Gavryusev, V., Müllenbroich, C., Turrini, L., de Vito, G., Silvestri, L., Sancataldo, G., Pavone, F.S.: Removing striping artifacts in light-sheet fluorescence microscopy: a review. Prog. Biophys. Mol. Biol. (2021). https://doi.org/10.1016/j.pbiomolbio.2021.07.003

18. Schwartz, J., et al.: Removing stripes, scratches, and curtaining with nonrecoverable compressed sensing. Microsc. Microanal. **25**(3), 705–710 (2019). https://doi.org/10.1017/S1431927619000254

19. Taylor, M.A., Vanwalleghem, G.C., Favre-Bulle, I.A., Scott, E.K.: Diffuse light-sheet microscopy for stripe-free calcium imaging of neural populations. J. Biophotonics **11**(12), e201800088 (2018). https://doi.org/10.1002/jbio.201800088

20. Trabelsi, C., et al.: Deep complex networks (2018)

21. Vaswani, A., et al.: Attention is all you need. In: Advances in Neural Information Processing Systems. vol. 30. Curran Associates, Inc. (2017). https://proceedings.neurips.cc/paper/2017/file/3f5ee243547dee91fbd053c1c4a845aa-Paper.pdf

22. Wei, Z., et al.: Elimination of stripe artifacts in light sheet fluorescence microscopy using an attention-based residual neural network. Biomed. Opt. Express **13**(3), 1292–1311 (2022). https://doi.org/10.1364/BOE.448838

23. Weigert, M., et al.: Content-aware image restoration: pushing the limits of fluorescence microscopy. Nat. Methods **15**(12), 1090–1097 (2018). https://doi.org/10.1038/s41592-018-0216-7

24. Zhao, W., et al.: Sparse deconvolution improves the resolution of live-cell super-resolution fluorescence microscopy. Nature Biotechnol., 1–12 (2021). https://doi.org/10.1038/s41587-021-01092-2

25. Zheng, C., Shi, D., Shi, W.: Adaptive unfolding total variation network for low-light image enhancement. In: 2021 IEEE/CVF International Conference on Computer Vision (ICCV), pp. 4419–4428 (2021). https://doi.org/10.1109/ICCV48922.2021.00440

26. Zhu, J.Y., Park, T., Isola, P., Efros, A.A.: Unpaired image-to-image translation using cycle-consistent adversarial networks. In: 2017 IEEE International Conference on Computer Vision (ICCV), pp. 2242–2251 (2017). https://doi.org/10.1109/ICCV.2017.244

End-to-End Cell Recognition by Point Annotation

Zhongyi Shui[1,2], Shichuan Zhang[1,2], Chenglu Zhu[1,2], Bingchuan Wang[3], Pingyi Chen[1,2], Sunyi Zheng[1,2], and Lin Yang[2(✉)]

[1] College of Computer Science and Technology, Zhejiang University, Hangzhou, China
[2] School of Engineering, Westlake University, Hangzhou, China
yanglin@westlake.edu.cn
[3] School of Automation, Central South University, Changsha, China

Abstract. Reliable quantitative analysis of immunohistochemical staining images requires accurate and robust cell detection and classification. Recent weakly-supervised methods usually estimate probability density maps for cell recognition. However, in dense cell scenarios, their performance can be limited by pre- and post-processing as it is impossible to find a universal parameter setting. In this paper, we introduce an end-to-end framework that applies direct regression and classification for preset anchor points. Specifically, we propose a pyramidal feature aggregation strategy to combine low-level features and high-level semantics simultaneously, which provides accurate cell recognition for our purely point-based model. In addition, an optimized cost function is designed to adapt our multi-task learning framework by matching ground truth and predicted points. The experimental results demonstrate the superior accuracy and efficiency of the proposed method, which reveals the high potentiality in assisting pathologist assessments.

Keywords: Cell recognition · Point annotation · Proposal matching

1 Introduction

Quantitative immunohistochemistry image analysis is of great importance for treatment selection and prognosis in clinical practice. Assessing PD-L1 expression on tumor cells by the Tumor Proportion Score (TPS) [5] is a typical example. However, large inter-reader variability may lead to a lack of consistency in the assessment, and the labor-intensive manual observation cannot guarantee the accuracy of clinical diagnosis. Hence, there is a strong demand to develop an AI tool that provides high-quality quantification results through accurate cell detection and classification.

Z. Shui and S. Zhang—These authors contributed equally to this work.

L. Wang et al. (Eds.): MICCAI 2022, LNCS 13434, pp. 109–118, 2022.
https://doi.org/10.1007/978-3-031-16440-8_11

With the advances in computing power and increased data volume in recent years, deep learning-based cell recognition methods [2,12,20] have shown more advantages over conventional methods. However, deep learning models usually require a massive amount of labeled data. To improve the labeling efficiency, pixel-wise annotations are gradually replaced with point annotations in cell recognition. Recent studies usually build a regression model to predict probability density maps (PDMs) of cells. In this case, pre-processing is required to convert point annotations into reference density maps (RDMs) for model training. Many studies on RDMs generation have been conducted to improve the cell recognition performance of the regression models. For instance, Zhou *et al.* [20] convolved raw point labels with a customized Gaussian kernel to generate circle-shape masks. Qu *et al.* [12] utilized Voronoi transformation and local pixel clustering methods to generate pseudo labels. Liang *et al.* [9] proposed a repel coding method to suppress the responses between two cell centers. Conversely, the post-processing is required to obtain the final recognition results from the predicted PDMs of cells, which is also a challenge for the identification of adjacent cells. The local maximum searching algorithm [7] is typically adopted to locate cells. However, it is difficult to find an appropriate set of hyper-parameters to deal with the scale variations between tissues and cells in the immunohistochemical (IHC) membrane-stained image.

To address the aforementioned issues, we develop an end-to-end model that regresses and classifies preset anchor points to recognize cells directly. In this point-based model, we combine the high-level semantic features with low-level local details, which benefit cell localization and classification [4,10,14] in large-scale histopathological scenes. Moreover, an improved cost function is proposed towards multi-task learning to determine which ground truth point should the current proposal point be responsible for in the one-to-one matching procedure [13]. In addition, to prevent the model from overfitting to noisy labels, we extend the classification loss with an L2 normalization term to penalize sharp softmax predictions. The experimental results demonstrate the superior performance and efficiency of the proposed method for dense cell recognition over previous studies.

2   Methods

The overall framework of the proposed model is depicted in Fig. 1, which includes a feature extraction module, a multi-task prediction module, and a proposal matching module. Initially, the feature extraction module generates multi-level representation from the encoding layers by pyramidal feature aggregation. Subsequently, the generated representation is performed separately in three branches of regression, detection, and classification, which can further improve the cell recognition performance by multi-task learning. Finally, the proposal matching module matches the proposal points to the ground truth targets.

Pyramidal Feature Aggregation. The high-dimensional semantic representation can usually be obtained by the encoding of a deep network model. Specifically, the semantic information of an image is gradually extracted from low-level

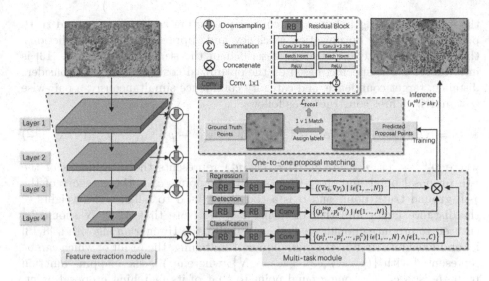

Fig. 1. Framework of our model

to high-level by a series of layers and then used for downstream tasks to complete the model training. However, it may not be sufficient to recognize each cell with the high-level semantic generalization in a large-scale histopathological scene. The low-level regional descriptions (color, edge, etc.) are also considered to promote cell recognition [4,14]. Consequently, pyramidal features extracted from all layers are aggregated with a unified shape to generate adequate representation.

Multi-task Learning. The success of some previous studies [2,17] of cell recognition shows the advantage of the multi-task strategy in weakly supervised learning. Thus a similar structure is introduced in our recognition framework. Instead of general recognition models which need to recover the prediction to the original image size, the high-dimensional features are directly fed into three separate task modules (regression, detection, and classification) in our method. Specifically, two residual blocks followed by a 1×1 convolutional layer comprise each task module. The outputs of the regression head are the offsets $(\nabla x_i, \nabla y_i)$ of each proposal point p_i, which refines the cell location prediction as follows:

$$\hat{x}_i = x_i + \nabla x_i, \quad \hat{y}_i = y_i + \nabla y_i \tag{1}$$

in which (x_i, y_i) is the initial coordinate of p_i and $(\hat{x}_i, \hat{y}_i)$ represents its refined coordinate. The detection head outputs the scores (p_i^{bkg}, p_i^{obj}), where p_i^{obj} indicates its confidence of being a cell center. Lastly, the classification head outputs the category scores $\boldsymbol{p}_i = (p_i^1, \cdots, p_i^C)$, in which p_i^j indicates its probability of being the j-th cell category and C is the number of cell categories. All output information will be combined for training and inference.

Proposal Matching. Generally, cell recognition aims at predicting point sets of indeterminate size is inherently an open set problem [16]. The key is to determine the unique matching between the current prediction and various ground truth points. To improve optimization efficiency and suppress duplicate predictions, the one-to-one matching strategy described in the study of Song et $al.$ [13] is introduced. To be specific, based on the optimized cost function that considers distance, target confidence, and category confidence simultaneously, a pair-wise cost matrix is first constructed as follows:

$$\mathcal{E} = \alpha\mathcal{D} - \mathcal{F}_t - \mathcal{F}_c = (\alpha \left\| \boldsymbol{p}_i^{loc} - \boldsymbol{p}_j^{loc*} \right\|_2 - p_i^{obj} - p_i^{c_j^*})_{i=1,\cdots,M,\, j=1,\cdots,N} \quad (2)$$

where $\boldsymbol{p}_i^{loc} = (\hat{x}_i, \hat{y}_i)$ and $\boldsymbol{p}_j^{loc*} = (x_i^*, y_i^*)$ represents the coordinates of the i-th proposal point and the j-th ground truth point, c_j^* is the category of the j-th ground truth point and α is a coefficient used to balance the weights of the distance factor and the confidence factors. Note that $M \geq N$ should be ensured to produce enough predictions. Finally, the Hungarian algorithm [8,13] is conducted on $\mathcal{E}$ to find the minimum-cost matching, the result of which can be represented with $\{(p_{\delta(j)}, p_j^*), j = 1, \cdots, N\}$, where $\delta(\cdot)$ is the mapping function from the subscript of one ground point to that of its matching proposal point. The predicted points that fail to match any ground truth point are treated as negative proposals.

Loss Function. We adopt the mean square error (MSE) loss for the regression training [13].

$$\mathcal{L}_{reg} = \frac{1}{N} \sum_{j=1}^{N} \| p_{\delta(j)}^{loc} - p_j^{loc*} \|_2 \quad (3)$$

in which β is a balance factor.

For the cell detection task, the labels are noise-free because there is a high probability that cells exist at the annotated points. Therefore, the cross entropy (CE) loss is adopted to prompt the model to focus on the samples whose softmax predictions are less consistent with provided labels [19].

$$\mathcal{L}_{det} = -\frac{1}{M} \left(\sum_{i \in \mathcal{P}} \log(p_i^{obj}) + \beta \sum_{i \in \mathcal{N}} \log(p_i^{bkg}) \right) \quad (4)$$

where $\mathcal{P} = \{\delta(j) \mid j = 1, \cdots, N\}$ is the set of positive proposals and $\mathcal{N} = \{1, \cdots, M\} \setminus \mathcal{P}$ is the set of negative proposals.

For the cell classification task, the categorical labels are noisy due to intra-reader variability. Therefore, to improve the robustness of our model to label noise during training, we extend the generalized cross entropy (GCE) loss [19] with an L2 regularization term as follows:

$$\widetilde{\mathcal{L}}_q(\boldsymbol{p}_{\delta(j)}, c_j^*) = \frac{1 - (p_{\delta(j)}^{c_j^*})^q}{q} + \gamma \|\boldsymbol{p}_{\delta(j)}\|_2 \quad (5)$$

where q is a parameter to balance convergence and noise robustness of the GCE loss. The additional term prevents the model from being overconfident and improves its generalization ability. The total classification loss is:

$$\mathcal{L}_{cls} = \sum_{j=1}^{N} \tilde{\mathcal{L}}_q(\boldsymbol{p}_{\delta(j)}, c_j^*) \tag{6}$$

Finally, the total loss is as follows:

$$\mathcal{L}_{total} = \lambda \mathcal{L}_{reg} + \mathcal{L}_{det} + \mathcal{L}_{cls} \tag{7}$$

where λ adjusts the weight of the regression loss.

3   Experiments

3.1   Dataset Description and Experimental Settings

Dataset. To evaluate the proposed method, we performed experiments on PD-L1 IHC stained images of tumor tissues, which are utilized to analyze the PD-L1 expression in non-small cell lung cancer samples. We first collected 485 patches with the resolution of 1920 × 1080 from the desensitized data obtained at 40× magnification of whole slide images. Subsequently, three pathologists labeled all cells in the patches by point annotation method with four categories including PD-L1 positive tumor cells, PD-L1 negative tumor cells, PD-L1 positive non-tumor cells, and PD-L1 negative non-tumor cells. Finally, the patches are randomly split into the training set and test set at a ratio of 4:1. Notably, to guarantee the quality of the test set, a senior pathologist further verified the annotations of test images.

Implementation Details. We compared our method with seven competitors under the same training and test environment. To be specific, for the training of regression models, we applied a 2D Gaussian filter on the point annotations to generate RDMs, which ensures the highest response at the center point of each cell. The optimal parameters (kernel size 7×7, *sigma* = 6) were selected through experiments. Note that all regression models are trained using the binary cross entropy (BCE) loss and intersection over union (IOU) loss, whose weights are set to 0.8 and 0.2, respectively.

Since cells are highly dense in the constructed dataset, we preset 5 anchor points in each 32 × 32 pixel region on the original image. One is in the center and the other four are generated by shifting the center point with $(-8, -8)$, $(-8, 8)$, $(8, 8)$ and $(8, -8)$ pixels respectively. The other hyper-parameters of our method are set as follows, $\alpha = 0.05, \beta = 0.6, \gamma = 0.1, q = 0.4$ and $\lambda = 2 \times 10^{-3}$. Data augmentation including random resized cropping and flipping are used in the training stage.

We trained all networks on a single NVIDIA A100-SXM4 GPU. The AdamW optimizer [11] was used for minimizing the loss function with an initial learning rate of 10^{-4} and weight decay of 10^{-4}.

Evaluation Metric. To evaluate the performance of different methods, we use precision (P), recall (R) and F1 scores that are calculated as follows:

$$P = \frac{TP}{TP + FP}, R = \frac{TP}{TP + FN}, F1 = \frac{2 * P * R}{P + R} \qquad (8)$$

where TP, FN and FP represent the number of true positives, false negatives and false positives, which are counted through the quantitative evaluation strategy adopted by Cai *et al.* [1]. Note that the radius of the valid matching area was set to 12 pixels in this work. In addition, the average inference time on test patches was introduced as an additional indicator for evaluating the analysis efficiency, the unit of which is seconds.

3.2 Experimental Results

The quantitative comparison results are listed by cell detection and classification as Table 1 shows.

Table 1. Comparison of cell recognition with different methods

Type	Model	Detection			Classification			Time (seconds)
		P	R	F1	P	R	F1	
Single task	FCRN-A [15]	79.67	70.67	74.90	55.76	47.68	50.91	2.31
	FCRN-B [15]	68.29	78.27	72.94	47.46	52.04	49.30	3.04
	UNet [6]	82.90	71.70	76.89	63.76	49.98	54.60	2.46
	ResUNet [18]	83.49	70.02	76.17	56.66	42.99	46.59	2.56
	DeepLab v3+ [3]	77.64	78.70	78.17	64.45	60.70	61.75	2.51
Multi-task	Zhang [17]	75.89	79.10	77.46	63.48	64.80	63.86	2.52
	P2PNet [13]	80.34	82.91	81.61	67.33	67.85	67.30	0.12
	Ours	**81.21**	**85.17**	**83.14**	**68.13**	**70.36**	**69.09**	**0.11**

In comparison with the model proposed by Zhang *et al.* [17] that performs best among previous cell recognition studies, our model improves the F1 score by 5.68% point in cell detection and 5.23% point in cell classification, respectively. In addition, the average inference time of the proposed model is nearly 23 times shorter than that of [17], which demonstrates its higher practicality as quantitative TPS calculation requires a wide range of cell recognition with hundreds of patches cropped from a whole-slide image. The superiority of our method is intuitively reflected in the visualization results shown in Fig. 2, where the black dashed area indicates the inadequacy of competitors.

The regression models, which recognize cells by predicting the PDMs, may yield missed detections due to required post-processing. Specifically, if the minimum distance between peaks is set to a small value in the local maximum searching algorithm, overlapping cells are easily mistaken as a connected whole. On the contrary, if a larger value is set, missed detections may be caused by

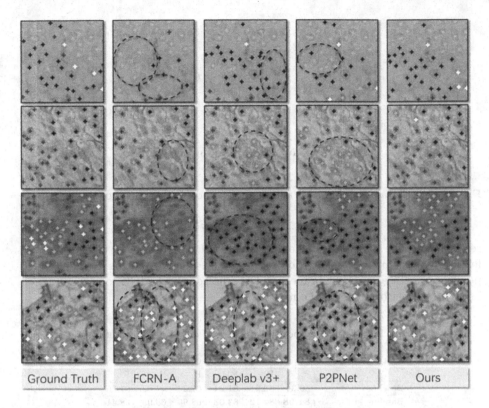

Fig. 2. Visualization results of different methods. We mark positive tumor cells, negative tumor cells, positive non-tumor cells, and negative non-tumor cells in red, green, yellow, and pink, respectively. (Color figure online)

filtering out cells with weaker intensity. Therefore, predicting points directly can avoid the performance degradation brought by post-processing.

We also recorded the average F1 score of cell classification with q ranging from 0.1 to 0.9 to clarify the impact of label noise on the cell recognition performance of our model in Fig. 3. To be specific, the GCE loss can be considered as the CE loss when $q \to 0$ and the MAE loss when $q \to 1$. The CE loss is sensitive to label noise but has good convergence characteristics. On the contrary, the MAE loss is robust to label noise while challenging to optimize. As shown in Fig. 3, the average F1 score of classification is the lowest when $q = 0.1$. With the increase of q in the GCE loss, our model becomes more robust to noisy labels, and its performance gradually improves. The highest F1 score is obtained when $q = 0.4$. As q increases further, the performance of our model degrades because the convergence of the GCE loss gets worse.

Ablation Study. Ablation experiments are built to assess the improvement for the baseline (P2PNet) as Table 2 shows. It is worth noticing that PFA improves the F1 score by 1.42% point in detection and 1.11% point in classification,

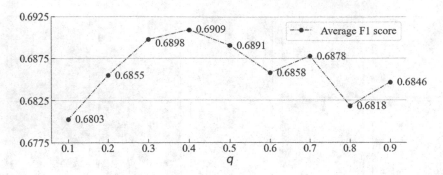

Fig. 3. The cell classification performance of our model with q ranging from 0.1 to 0.9

respectively. The improvement demonstrates the effectiveness of using low-level features to promote cell recognition performance. In addition, the designed independent classification (IC) branch and the noise-robust GCE loss can further improve the performance of the model.

Table 2. Pipeline component analysis of our proposed method

Method	Detection			Classification		
	P	R	F1	P	R	F1
Baseline	80.34	82.91	81.61	67.33	67.85	67.30
Baseline+PFA	**81.98**	84.12	83.03	68.95	68.93	68.41
Baseline+PFA+IC	81.21	**85.17**	**83.14**	**68.13**	**70.36**	**69.09**

4   Conclusion

In this paper, we propose a purely point-based cell recognition model that can recognize cells in an end-to-end manner. Unlike the mainstream regression-based methods that require pre-processing to generate reference density maps and post-processing of local maximum searching to locate cells, the proposed model can directly recognize cells by preset anchor points. Specifically, we propose a pyramidal feature aggregation strategy to combine semantic features with detailed information, which helps the model distinguish the boundaries and categories of cells. In addition, an optimized cost function is proposed to adapt our multi-task learning framework by matching ground truth and proposal points. An extended loss function is also proposed to improve the robustness of our model to noisy labels. Finally, the experimental results demonstrate the superior performance and efficiency of our proposed method, and the results of the ablation study show the effectiveness of our designed modules. Such a model can reduce the workload of pathologists in the quantitative analysis of IHC stained images.

Acknowledgements. This work was funded by China Postdoctoral Science Foundation (2021M702922).

References

1. Cai, J., et al.: Generalizing nucleus recognition model in multi-source ki67 immuno-histochemistry stained images via domain-specific pruning. In: de Bruijne, M., et al. (eds.) MICCAI 2021. LNCS, vol. 12908, pp. 277–287. Springer, Cham (2021). https://doi.org/10.1007/978-3-030-87237-3_27

2. Chamanzar, A., Nie, Y.: Weakly supervised multi-task learning for cell detection and segmentation. In: 2020 IEEE 17th International Symposium on Biomedical Imaging (ISBI), pp. 513–516. IEEE (2020)

3. Chen, L.C., Zhu, Y., Papandreou, G., Schroff, F., Adam, H.: Encoder-decoder with atrous separable convolution for semantic image segmentation. In: Proceedings of the European Conference on Computer Vision (ECCV), pp. 801–818 (2018)

4. Cosatto, E., Miller, M., Graf, H.P., Meyer, J.S.: Grading nuclear pleomorphism on histological micrographs. In: 2008 19th International Conference on Pattern Recognition, pp. 1–4. IEEE (2008)

5. Doroshow, D.B., et al.: Pd-l1 as a biomarker of response to immune-checkpoint inhibitors. Nat. Rev. Clin. Oncol. **18**(6), 345–362 (2021)

6. Falk, T., et al.: U-net: deep learning for cell counting, detection, and morphometry. Nat. Methods **16**(1), 67–70 (2019)

7. Huang, Z., et al.: BCData: a large-scale dataset and benchmark for cell detection and counting. In: Martel, A.L., et al. (eds.) MICCAI 2020. LNCS, vol. 12265, pp. 289–298. Springer, Cham (2020). https://doi.org/10.1007/978-3-030-59722-1_28

8. Kuhn, H.W.: The Hungarian method for the assignment problem. Naval Res. Logist. Quart. **2**(1–2), 83–97 (1955)

9. Liang, H., Naik, A., Williams, C.L., Kapur, J., Weller, D.S.: Enhanced center coding for cell detection with convolutional neural networks. arXiv preprint arXiv:1904.08864 (2019)

10. Lin, T.Y., Dollár, P., Girshick, R., He, K., Hariharan, B., Belongie, S.: Feature pyramid networks for object detection. In: Proceedings of the IEEE Conference on Computer Vision and Pattern Recognition, pp. 2117–2125 (2017)

11. Loshchilov, I., Hutter, F.: Decoupled weight decay regularization. arXiv preprint arXiv:1711.05101 (2017)

12. Qu, H., et al.: Weakly supervised deep nuclei segmentation using points annotation in histopathology images. In: International Conference on Medical Imaging with Deep Learning, pp. 390–400. PMLR (2019)

13. Song, Q., et al.: Rethinking counting and localization in crowds: a purely point-based framework. In: Proceedings of the IEEE/CVF International Conference on Computer Vision, pp. 3365–3374 (2021)

14. Veta, M., Van Diest, P.J., Kornegoor, R., Huisman, A., Viergever, M.A., Pluim, J.P.: Automatic nuclei segmentation in h&e stained breast cancer histopathology images. PLoS ONE **8**(7), e70221 (2013)

15. Xie, W., Noble, J.A., Zisserman, A.: Microscopy cell counting and detection with fully convolutional regression networks. Comput. Meth. Biomech. Biomed. Eng. Imaging Visual. **6**(3), 283–292 (2018)

16. Xiong, H., Lu, H., Liu, C., Liu, L., Cao, Z., Shen, C.: From open set to closed set: counting objects by spatial divide-and-conquer. In: Proceedings of the IEEE/CVF International Conference on Computer Vision, pp. 8362–8371 (2019)

17. Zhang, S., Zhu, C., Li, H., Cai, J., Yang, L.: Weakly supervised learning for cell recognition in immunohistochemical cytoplasm staining images. In: 2022 IEEE 19th International Symposium on Biomedical Imaging (ISBI), pp. 1–5. IEEE (2022)

18. Zhang, Z., Liu, Q., Wang, Y.: Road extraction by deep residual u-net. IEEE Geosci. Remote Sens. Lett. **15**(5), 749–753 (2018)
19. Zhang, Z., Sabuncu, M.R.: Generalized cross entropy loss for training deep neural networks with noisy labels. In: 32nd Conference on Neural Information Processing Systems (NeurIPS) (2018)
20. Zhou, Y., Dou, Q., Chen, H., Qin, J., Heng, P.A.: SFCN-OPI: detection and fine-grained classification of nuclei using sibling FCN with objectness prior interaction. In: Proceedings of the AAAI Conference on Artificial Intelligence, vol. 32 (2018)

ChrSNet: Chromosome Straightening Using Self-attention Guided Networks

Sunyi Zheng[1,2], Jingxiong Li[1,2,3], Zhongyi Shui[1,2], Chenglu Zhu[1,2], Yunlong Zhang[1,2,3], Pingyi Chen[1,2,3], and Lin Yang[1,2(✉)]

[1] Artificial Intelligence and Biomedical Image Analysis Lab, School of Engineering, Westlake University, Hangzhou, China
yanglin@westlake.edu.cn
[2] Institute of Advanced Technology, Westlake Institute for Advanced Study, Hangzhou, China
[3] College of Computer Science and Technology, Zhejiang University, Hangzhou, China

Abstract. Karyotyping is an important procedure to assess the possible existence of chromosomal abnormalities. However, because of the non-rigid nature, chromosomes are usually heavily curved in microscopic images and such deformed shapes hinder the chromosome analysis for cytogeneticists. In this paper, we present a self-attention guided framework to erase the curvature of chromosomes. The proposed framework extracts spatial information and local textures to preserve banding patterns in a regression module. With complementary information from the bent chromosome, a refinement module is designed to further improve fine details. In addition, we propose two dedicated geometric constraints to maintain the length and restore the distortion of chromosomes. To train our framework, we create a synthetic dataset where curved chromosomes are generated from the real-world straight chromosomes by grid-deformation. Quantitative and qualitative experiments are conducted on synthetic and real-world data. Experimental results show that our proposed method can effectively straighten bent chromosomes while keeping banding details and length.

Keywords: Karyotyping · Chromosome straightening · Self-attention · Microscopy

1 Introduction

Metaphase chromosome analysis is a fundamental step in the investigation of genetic diseases such as Turner syndrome, Down syndrome, and Cridu chat syndrome [6,16]. Chromosomes tend to be curved in random degrees in the stained micro-photographs because of their non-rigid nature [14]. Such a morphological deformation pose difficulties for chromosome analysis. Straightening

---

S. Zheng and J. Li—These authors contributed equally to this work.

L. Wang et al. (Eds.): MICCAI 2022, LNCS 13434, pp. 119–128, 2022.
https://doi.org/10.1007/978-3-031-16440-8_12

of chromosomes could alleviate this problem and, therefore, has the potential to boost the efficiency of karyotyping for cytogeneticists.

Prior works designed for chromosome straightening are mainly based on geometry. These geometric methods can be divided into two directions: medial axis extraction and bending point detection. For the first direction, Somasundaram et al. [13] employed the Stentiford thinning algorithm to select the medial axis and the projective straightening algorithm for axis correction. The axis was then considered as a reference to reconstruct straight chromosomes by projection. Similarly, Arora et al. [3] acquired the medial axis via morphological operations, and details were interpolated iteratively along the medial axis to produce straight chromosomes. Although the straightening methods using medial axis extraction can erase the curvature of bent chromosomes, some banding patterns can be distorted. Another type of method took the advantage of bending points to straighten chromosomes. For example, Roshtkhari et al. [11] and Sharma et al. [12] utilized bending points to separate a chromosome into parts. Rotation and stitching were applied to these parts for the reconstruction of straight chromosomes. However, these methods can cause discontinued banding patterns and inconsistent length after straightening. Besides, this method relied on bending points and inaccurately located points can severely harm the straightening performance.

Deep learning techniques have reached great achievements in the classification of chromosome types [9,18,21], image translation [1,2,5] and portrait correction [15,22], but rare studies have successfully applied deep learning in chromosome straightening. One of the challenges is that it is difficult to collect images of the same chromosome with both straight and curved shapes in the real-world to build a deep learning based mapping model for chromosome straightening. Recently, Song et al. [14] developed a model utilizing conditional generative adversarial networks to erase curvatures in chromosomes. Their model created mappings between bent chromosomes and synthetic bent backbones. After model training, the model inversely transformed synthetic straight backbones to straightened chromosomes. Although banding patterns can be effectively restored by this method, the length of the straightened chromosome is inconsistent with the curved one's. Furthermore, the customized model was required to be implemented every time for each new chromosome. The feasibility of applying such a model in clinical practice needs to be further considered. To date, while many methods have been developed for chromosome straightening, challenges including limited model generalizability, lack of paired images for training, inconsistent length and inaccurate patterns after straightening remain in this task.

To this end, we propose a novel chromosome straightening approach using self-attention guided networks. The developed method combines low-level details and global contexts to recover banding patterns. A refinement module is applied to further recover fine details using the input bent chromosome as complementary information. Moreover, we design dedicated geometric constraints in terms of length and straightness to optimize the straightening process. In order to train our model, we propose a non-rigid transformation strategy that synthesizes curved chromosomes from the real-world straight ones. Note that we are the first study that creates mappings between straight and curved chromosomes for chromosome straightening. Our experiments show that the developed framework can effectively straighten various types of chromosomes with preserved banding details and length on both synthetic and real-world data.

2 Methods

The proposed approach for chromosome straightening mainly consists of two major steps. We first create a chromosome synthesizer that produces curved chromosomes from straight ones which exist in the real-world. With the use of curved and straight chromosome pairs, a framework is then trained for the removal of chromosome distortions. Methods are described in detail as follows:

2.1 Curved Chromosome Synthesizer

To build up a framework for chromosome straightening, our intuition is to create mappings between bent and straight chromosome pairs. However, acquiring such pairs from the same chromosome is challenging under a microscope. Moreover, chromosomes can be deformed randomly and it is nearly impossible to collect sufficient data that covers all possible situations in the real-world.

Studies show that synthetic data generation could provide a solution for the lack of data in training deep learning methods [7,19]. Inspired by this idea, we create a chromosome synthesizer that uses straight samples selected from a public chromosome dataset [8] to emulate their corresponding curved chromosomes. In the real-world, distortions of chromosomes can be a mixture of curvatures. To mimic real-world situations as closely as possible, two common types of distortions, slight curves and strong curves, are carefully defined on distortion meshes which are employed to convert straight chromosomes to bent ones. Detailed procedures for the generation of bent chromosome are composed as follows.

Deformation Modeling. When wrapping a chromosome image, a mesh M with size $H \times W$ is given with a control point p that is randomly selected from points on the skeleton of a straight chromosome. A random vector v, representing the deformation direction, is then generated to be perpendicular to the skeleton. The deformation function is defined as:

$$p' = p + \omega v \tag{1}$$

where p' stands for the vertex after deformation. The factor ω controls the strength of deformation and it attenuates with the increasing distance d between p and the straight line defined by p and v. The definition of ω for slight and strong curves could be expressed as:

$$\omega_{sli} = 1 - d^\alpha \tag{2}$$

$$\omega_{str} = \frac{\alpha}{d + \alpha} \tag{3}$$

where distance d is normalized and constant α controls the propagation of deformation. A small α leads to a limited deformation only affecting in a local area around p, whereas a large α causes a global deformation.

2.2   ChrSNet: Chromosome Straightening Networks

Chromosome straightening could be treated as a regression task that aims to provide pixel-to-pixel predictions from an image x with size $H \times W \times C$ to a target $y \in \mathbf{R}^{H \times W \times C}$. This inspires us to follow the classic encoder-decoder architecture using a convolutional neural network (CNN). In spite of CNN's superiority on the extraction of local textures, it might not be able to recover spatial features in the straightening task due to CNN's drawback on modeling explicit long-range relationships [4]. In contrast, by evaluating image through tokenized patches globally, transformer learns spatial information which can be used to reduce regression uncertainty. Hence, we build up a straightening model by importing self-attention via transformer layers which are implemented in a CNN-based encoder-decoder architecture. To produce straightened chromosomes with consistent morphological features and structure details, customized loss functions are also designed.

Network Architecture. The overview of our proposed framework ChrSNet is illustrated in Fig. 1. The framework could be divided into a regression module and a refinement module. Specifically, in the regression module, a curved chromosome image x is first down-sampled by a CNN encoder to create a feature map f_M with size $h \times w \times c$. Then we divide f_M into patches with the same size and flatten them into a one-dimensional sequence. These patches are denoted as $\{f_t^i \in \mathbf{R}^{p \times p \times c} \mid i = 1, 2, 3 ... N_k\}$, where $p \times p$ is the size of one patch and $N_k = \frac{hw}{p^2}$ is the number of tokenized patches. Afterwards, patches are mapped into a latent embedding space via a linear projection. To encode the spatial information, patch embeddings and specific position embeddings are merged to generate the encoded image representation z that is forwarded into multiple transformer layers. These embeddings are combined with low-level features by skip-connections to construct the preliminary mesh M_1. Since M_1 can be unsatisfactory, UNet [10] is employed as a refinement module to further improve the detailed information. In this module, we apply the input x here to provide the complementary information. The input is concatenated with M_1 to generate M_2 which is refined again to acquire M_3. The final result y can be acquired by applying M_3 on x.

Loss Function. A hybrid loss function is designed with constraints in the aspects of structure and texture to ensure the quality of the straightening process.

Regarding the structure loss, length and straightness are considered. In the real-world, chromosomes are normally curved rather than stretched because of their non-rigid nature. The straightened chromosome y should have the same length as the deformed case x. To estimate the length of a chromosome, we

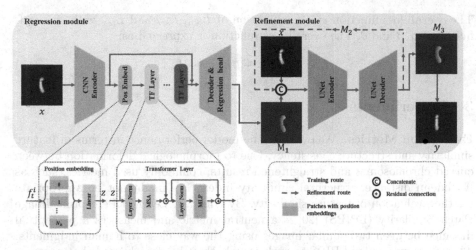

Fig. 1. Overview of the proposed architecture. The architecture consists of a regression module using self-attention and a refinement module to improve fine details. A curved chromosome image x is first fed into the regression module to obtain a rough mapping mesh M_1. Then the combination of M_1 and x is fed into the refinement module to produce M_2 that is refined again for the generation of M_3. At last, the chromosome is straightened by applying M_3 on x.

count the number of pixels in the skeletonized chromosome I_s. As a result, the length preserving loss L_{len} can be written as:

$$L_{len} = \frac{|l - l'|}{l'} \tag{4}$$

where l is the predicted length and l' is the target length.

In addition to the consistent length after straightening, the skeleton of the chromosome should be straight. For this purpose, we propose a straightness loss L_{str} for chromosome straightening. It is calculated by the overall slope (OS) and slope variations with uniformly sampled n points $s_0, s_1, ..., s_n$. The straightness loss function can be presented as:

$$OS = \frac{y_{s_0} - y_{s_n}}{x_{s_0} - x_{s_n}} \tag{5}$$

$$L_{str} = \frac{1}{n} \sum_{i=1,...,n} \left[\frac{y_{s_i} - y_{s_{i-1}}}{x_{s_i} - x_{s_{i-1}}} - OS \right] \tag{6}$$

where the coordinates of the point s_i are (x_{s_i}, y_{s_i}) and the total number of sample points n is set to 6.

Preservation of banding textures is also important for later analysis including chromosome classification and abnormality identification. To keep texture features consistent after straightening, we use the $L1$ loss as the texture loss:

$$L_{tex} = |y - y'| \tag{7}$$

The overall loss function is a combination of L_{len}, L_{str} and L_{tex} with the coefficient of α, β and θ. The overall loss function is expressed as:

$$L_{all} = \alpha L_{tex} + \beta L_{len} + \theta L_{str} \tag{8}$$

3　Experiments

Evaluation Metrics. We evaluate the model performance in terms of feature similarity and structure consistency. Due to morphological deformation between curved chromosomes and straightened results, commonly used metrics, such as Euclidean distance, structural similarity index [17], might not be appropriate for the evaluation of feature similarity. By contrast, Learned Perceptual Image Patch Similarity (LPIPS) [20] is a neutral metric and measures a perceptual distance between two similar images using the way close to human judgments. Therefore, we employ LPIPS to evaluate whether the straightened chromosomes contain image features consistent with their corresponding curved chromosomes.

In the clinic, length can determine types of autosomes and curvature reflects deformation levels which affects difficulties for pattern analysis. Both of them are critical factors for later analysis, such as autosome classification. Hence, we assess the structure consistency by a length score (L score) and a straightness score (S score), where L score $= 1 - L_{len}$, S score $= 1 - L_{str}$. An increasing L score means the length is more consistent after straightening, while a larger S score represents the corrected chromosome has a more straight shape.

Dataset Settings. Every human cell normally has 46 chromosomes and curvatures are often observed on chromosomes with long arms. Therefore, this study focuses on the straightening of chromosomes 1–12. We select 1310 human chromosome images (704 straight and 606 curved individuals) from a public dataset [8] for experiments. To create curved and straight chromosome pairs for training the straightening model, our proposed data generator produces 100 synthetic curved chromosomes with 1–3 control points randomly selected on each straight chromosome. Slight curving and strong curving distortions are applied in a ratio of 1:1 for the generation of synthetic chromosomes with different curvatures. Before training or test, chromosome images are centered and unified to the size of $256 * 256$ with zero-padding.

Implementation Details. Experiments are implemented based on PyTorch using a NVIDIA A100 GPU. The synthetic dataset is randomly separated into a training, validation and test set in a ratio of $10 : 1 : 1$ for modelling. The straightening model is trained with an initial learning rate of 5×10^{-4} gradually decreased to 1×10^{-5}. The optimizer is Adam and the batch size is 24. The training stops if the performance on the validation set does not improve for 20 epochs. Our code is available at https://github.com/lijx1996/ChrSNet.

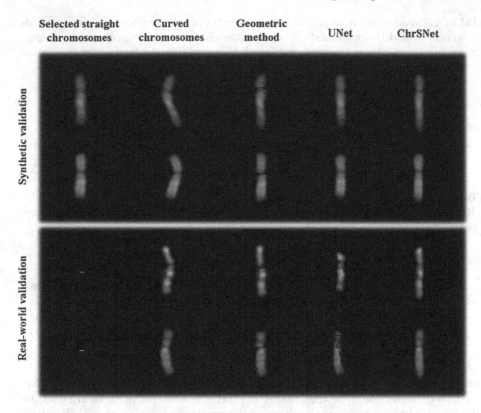

Fig. 2. Examples of chromosomes straightened from the curved chromosomes by a geometric method [11], UNet and ChrSNet on synthetic and real-world datasets. In the synthetic validation, straight chromosomes are selected from the real-world to generate curved chromosomes, whereas there is no corresponding straight chromosome for the curved chromosomes in the real-world validation.

Results and Discussions. We perform comparisons among a geometric method [11], UNet and our proposed method ChrSNet for chromosome straightening on synthetic and real-world data. Image examples of straightened chromosomes generated by each method on both sets are illustrated in Fig. 2. The results of different methods are presented in Table 1. From the table, if straightness and length are considered, we can find that our designed method shows the best straightening performance on both datasets. This fact shows the superior performance of our method in the restoration of chromosome structures. When we only take the straightness into account, ChrSNet and UNet have competitive scores on both two datasets, but outperform the geometric method. In terms of length, although UNet performs much better than the geometry method on synthetic data, it fails to recover the length information on real data. Regarding the restoration of banding details, UNet has the highest LPIPS score of 89.29, similar to the score of ChrSNet on synthetic data, but its performance degrades

Table 1. Quantitative comparisons between our proposed ChrSNet and other methods on synthetic and real-world data. We assess the chromosome structure after straightening from straightness (S score) and length (L score). The learned perceptual image patch similarity (LPIPS) is applied to evaluate preserved banding details.

Models	Synthetic validation			Real-world validation		
	S score	L score	LPIPS	S sore	L score	LPIPS
Geometry	76.94 ± 20.4	82.32 ± 18.8	85.20 ± 5.33	81.07 ± 10.4	86.25 ± 12.3	85.38 ± 6.48
UNet	86.01 ± 10.3	92.70 ± 5.36	89.29 ± 4.00	88.46 ± 6.81	74.90 ± 11.4	80.56 ± 5.50
ChrSNet	87.68 ± 7.95	96.22 ± 4.49	88.75 ± 4.17	88.56 ± 5.98	94.87 ± 5.05	87.18 ± 5.36

Table 2. Ablation study of our proposed network on two datasets. "RG", "RT", "SL", "RR" refer to the regression module, refinement module in the training route, structure loss and refinement process in the refinement route.

Components				Synthetic validation			Real-world validation		
RG	RT	SL	RR	S score	L score	LPIPS	S sore	L score	LPIPS
✓				85.90 ± 9.30	93.90 ± 5.81	90.01 ± 4.07	85.59 ± 6.90	93.13 ± 5.38	89.02 ± 5.96
✓	✓			85.78 ± 8.89	94.22 ± 5.19	89.70 ± 4.05	87.05 ± 6.50	93.62 ± 6.41	88.43 ± 5.34
✓	✓	✓		86.14 ± 9.32	95.35 ± 4.58	89.10 ± 4.01	87.44 ± 6.57	94.66 ± 5.59	87.50 ± 5.33
✓	✓	✓	✓	87.68 ± 7.95	96.22 ± 4.49	88.75 ± 4.17	88.56 ± 5.98	94.87 ± 5.05	87.18 ± 5.36

in the real-world validation. The reason for the performance difference of UNet on two datasets could be that real-world data is more complex than synthetic data and generalizability of Unet is poor without self-attention on complex data. Conversely, ChrSNet achieves a much higher LPIPS value of 87.18 compared to UNet in real cases, which shows the model generalizability and effectiveness of ChrSNet in preserving banding patterns.

We also assess the effect of four components in ChrSNet on both synthetic and real-world datasets (Table 2). First, baseline results are produced using the regression module with the texture loss only. Based on this, we verified the functionality of the refinement module in the training route, structure loss and refinement process in the refinement route. From Table 2, we can observe that S and L scores always show an increasing trend on both two sets after adding extra components. Based on a relatively high baseline, the S score improves by 2.3 at most, while the L score increases by 3.0 at most. Of note, standard deviations are smaller with more added components, which suggests the results become more stable. Therefore, adding extra architectures is helpful to improve model performance and robustness. Besides, the use of the regression module alone results in a LPIPS score of 90.01 (RG in Table 2) that is higher than the score of UNet (89.29 in Table 1) on synthetic data. In addition, as shown in Fig. 2, UNet without self-attention fails to recover correlated patterns at the bottom and top on real-world data, while ChrSNet using self-attention restores long-range patterns. These findings show that the use of self-attention is effective to keep pattern details in chromosome straightening. Although the LPIPS score slightly decreases when all components are combined, it is still comparable to the baseline result and therefore, will not significantly affect later analysis.

4   Conclusion

In this study, we proposed a novel framework that utilized attention mechanism and convolutional neural networks to obtain global textures and local details for chromosome straightening. We also attempted to solve the limitations regarding length consistency and generalizability of the existing framework. Our method generated deformed chromosomes using two basic curving distortions and created direct mappings between straight and deformed chromosomes for straightening. The experimental results on synthetic and real-world data showed the effectiveness and robustness of our proposed approach in preserving banding details and structures on various types of chromosomes.

References

1. Armanious, K., Jiang, C., Abdulatif, S., Küstner, T., Gatidis, S., Yang, B.: Unsupervised medical image translation using cycle-medgan. In: 2019 27th European Signal Processing Conference (EUSIPCO), pp. 1–5. IEEE (2019)
2. Armanious, K., et al.: MEDGAN: medical image translation using GANs. Comput. Med. Imaging Graph. **79**, 101684 (2020)
3. Arora, T., Dhir, R., Mahajan, M.: An algorithm to straighten the bent human chromosomes. In: 2017 Fourth International Conference on Image Information Processing (ICIIP), pp. 1–6. IEEE (2017)
4. Chen, J., et al.: Transunet: transformers make strong encoders for medical image segmentation. arXiv preprint arXiv:2102.04306 (2021)
5. Eslami, M., Tabarestani, S., Albarqouni, S., Adeli, E., Navab, N., Adjouadi, M.: Image-to-images translation for multi-task organ segmentation and bone suppression in chest x-ray radiography. IEEE Trans. Med. Imaging **39**(7), 2553–2565 (2020)
6. Jørgensen, I.F., et al.: Comorbidity landscape of the Danish patient population affected by chromosome abnormalities. Genet. Med. **21**(11), 2485–2495 (2019)
7. Pan, Y., Chen, Y., Shen, D., Xia, Y.: Collaborative image synthesis and disease diagnosis for classification of neurodegenerative disorders with incomplete multimodal neuroimages. In: de Bruijne, M., et al. (eds.) MICCAI 2021. LNCS, vol. 12905, pp. 480–489. Springer, Cham (2021). https://doi.org/10.1007/978-3-030-87240-3_46
8. Poletti, E., Grisan, E., Ruggeri, A.: Automatic classification of chromosomes in q-band images. In: 2008 30th Annual International Conference of the IEEE Engineering in Medicine and Biology Society, pp. 1911–1914. IEEE (2008)
9. Qin, Y., et al.: Varifocal-net: a chromosome classification approach using deep convolutional networks. IEEE Trans. Med. Imaging **38**(11), 2569–2581 (2019)
10. Ronneberger, O., Fischer, P., Brox, T.: U-Net: convolutional networks for biomedical image segmentation. In: Navab, N., Hornegger, J., Wells, W.M., Frangi, A.F. (eds.) MICCAI 2015. LNCS, vol. 9351, pp. 234–241. Springer, Cham (2015). https://doi.org/10.1007/978-3-319-24574-4_28

11. Roshtkhari, M.J., Setarehdan, S.K.: A novel algorithm for straightening highly curved images of human chromosome. Pattern Recogn. Lett. **29**(9), 1208–1217 (2008)
12. Sharma, M., Saha, O., Sriraman, A., Hebbalaguppe, R., Vig, L., Karande, S.: Crowdsourcing for chromosome segmentation and deep classification. In: Proceedings of the IEEE conference on Computer Vision and Pattern Recognition Workshops, pp. 34–41 (2017)
13. Somasundaram, D., Kumar, V.V.: Straightening of highly curved human chromosome for cytogenetic analysis. Measurement **47**, 880–892 (2014)
14. Song, S., et al.: A novel application of image-to-image translation: chromosome straightening framework by learning from a single image. In: 2021 14th International Congress on Image and Signal Processing, BioMedical Engineering and Informatics (CISP-BMEI), pp. 1–9. IEEE (2021)
15. Tan, J., Zhao, S., Xiong, P., Liu, J., Fan, H., Liu, S.: Practical wide-angle portraits correction with deep structured models. In: Proceedings of the IEEE/CVF Conference on Computer Vision and Pattern Recognition, pp. 3498–3506 (2021)
16. Theisen, A., Shaffer, L.G.: Disorders caused by chromosome abnormalities. Appl. Clin. Genet. **3**, 159 (2010)
17. Wang, Z., Bovik, A.C., Sheikh, H.R., Simoncelli, E.P.: Image quality assessment: from error visibility to structural similarity. IEEE Trans. Image Process. **13**(4), 600–612 (2004)
18. Xiao, L., Luo, C.: Deepacc: automate chromosome classification based on metaphase images using deep learning framework fused with priori knowledge. In: 2021 IEEE 18th International Symposium on Biomedical Imaging (ISBI), pp. 607–610. IEEE (2021)
19. Ye, J., Xue, Y., Liu, P., Zaino, R., Cheng, K.C., Huang, X.: A multi-attribute controllable generative model for histopathology image synthesis. In: de Bruijne, M., et al. (eds.) MICCAI 2021. LNCS, vol. 12908, pp. 613–623. Springer, Cham (2021). https://doi.org/10.1007/978-3-030-87237-3_59
20. Zhang, R., Isola, P., Efros, A.A., Shechtman, E., Wang, O.: The unreasonable effectiveness of deep features as a perceptual metric. In: CVPR (2018)
21. Zhang, W., et al.: Chromosome classification with convolutional neural network based deep learning. In: 2018 11th International Congress on Image and Signal Processing, BioMedical Engineering and Informatics (CISP-BMEI). pp. 1–5. IEEE (2018)
22. Zhu, F., Zhao, S., Wang, P., Wang, H., Yan, H., Liu, S.: Semi-supervised wide-angle portraits correction by multi-scale transformer. arXiv preprint arXiv:2109.08024 (2021)

Region Proposal Rectification Towards Robust Instance Segmentation of Biological Images

Qilong Zhangli[1], Jingru Yi[1], Di Liu[1], Xiaoxiao He[1], Zhaoyang Xia[1],
Qi Chang[1], Ligong Han[1], Yunhe Gao[1], Song Wen[1], Haiming Tang[2], He Wang[2],
Mu Zhou[3], and Dimitris Metaxas[1(✉)]

[1] Department of Computer Science, Rutgers University, New Brunswick, NJ, USA
dnm@cs.rutgers.edu
[2] School of Medicine, Yale University, New Haven, CT, USA
[3] SenseBrain Research, San Jose, CA, USA

Abstract. Top-down instance segmentation framework has shown its superiority in object detection compared to the bottom-up framework. While it is efficient in addressing over-segmentation, top-down instance segmentation suffers from over-crop problem. However, a complete segmentation mask is crucial for biological image analysis as it delivers important morphological properties such as shapes and volumes. In this paper, we propose a region proposal rectification (RPR) module to address this challenging incomplete segmentation problem. In particular, we offer a progressive ROIAlign module to introduce neighbor information into a series of ROIs gradually. The ROI features are fed into an attentive feed-forward network (FFN) for proposal box regression. With additional neighbor information, the proposed RPR module shows significant improvement in correction of region proposal locations and thereby exhibits favorable instance segmentation performances on three biological image datasets compared to state-of-the-art baseline methods. Experimental results demonstrate that the proposed RPR module is effective in both anchor-based and anchor-free top-down instance segmentation approaches, suggesting the proposed method can be applied to general top-down instance segmentation of biological images. Code is available (https://github.com/qzhangli/RPR).

Keywords: Instance segmentation · Detection · Pathology · Cell

1 Introduction

Instance segmentation of biological images is challenging due to the uneven texture, unclear boundary, and touching problem of the biological objects, as widely seen in plant phenotyping [18] and computational pathology [1,10,14,16,20]. Current research efforts mainly rely on two strategies including bottom-up [2,19] and top-down [6,9,11,27,28] frameworks. Bottom-up approach performs semantic segmentation first on the whole input images. Instance masks are obtained

© The Author(s), under exclusive license to Springer Nature Switzerland AG 2022
L. Wang et al. (Eds.): MICCAI 2022, LNCS 13434, pp. 129–139, 2022.
https://doi.org/10.1007/978-3-031-16440-8_13

subsequently according to features such as contours [2,19,29], morphological shapes [15,23,30], and pixel similarities [3,4,8,13,17,21]. This framework suffers from careful feature designs to avoid over-/under-segmentation. Meanwhile, top-down framework utilizes global objectness features and generates region proposals as a crucial initialization step [6,11,26,28]. A region proposal is represented as a bounding box around each object. Semantic segmentation is performed subsequently on region of interest (ROI) features inside each region proposal. The ROI features are usually cropped through ROIAlign [6,11].

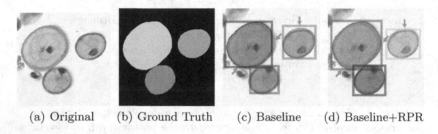

(a) Original   (b) Ground Truth   (c) Baseline   (d) Baseline+RPR

Fig. 1. Illustration of incomplete segmentation problem for top-down instance segmentation on urothelial cell images. (a) and (b) are the original image and ground truth annotation. In (c), a top-down baseline method (i.e., CenterMask [11]) outputs incomplete segmentation masks due to inaccurate region proposals (i.e., bounding boxes). In (d), with the proposed region proposal rectification (RPR) module, the box boundaries are corrected and the segmentation masks are intact.

Top-down framework highlights its superiority in object detection while it brings significant challenges. First, an ROI region could contain noisy pixels from neighbor objects, which is difficult to be suppressed by network. Second, a region proposal restricts the ROI space for intact and high-quality segmentation. A slight variation in region proposal location can cut off object boundary and result in incomplete mask (see Fig. 1). As a segmentation mask carries object's morphological properties (e.g., shape, volume) for biological image analysis, generating a complete segmentation mask is of great importance.

In this paper, to address the challenging incomplete segmentation problem in top-down instance segmentation, we propose a region proposal rectification (RPR) module which involves two components: a progressive ROIAlign and an attentive feed-forward network (FFN). Progressive ROIAlign incorporates neighbor information into a series of ROI features and attentive FFN studies spatial relationships of features and delivers rectified region proposals. Segmentation masks are generated subsequently with the rectified proposals. On three biological image datasets, RPR shows significant improvement in region proposal location rectification and achieves favorable performances in instance segmentation for both anchor-based and anchor-free approaches (e.g., Mask R-CNN [6] and CenterMask [11]). Results suggest that the proposed method is able to serve for general top-down instance segmentation of biological images. To the best of our knowledge, we are the first work that adopts this Transformer-based architecture on the refinement of region proposals in biological instance segmentation.

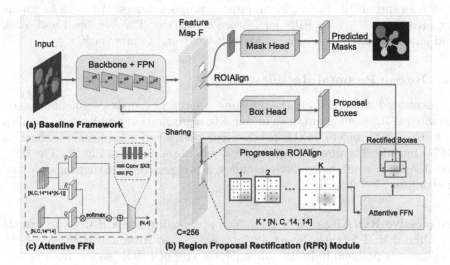

Fig. 2. Diagram of top-down instance segmentation method with (a) a representative baseline framework; (b) region proposal rectification (RPR) module; (c) attentive FFN. Input image resolution is resized to 800×800. We use ResNet50 [7] as backbone network. Box head generates region proposal boxes based on output features from backbone+FPN. For each region proposal box, progressive ROIAlign module extracts a series of ROIs and feeds them to attentive FFN for box rectification. Mask head makes segmentation on ROI features cropped by ROIAlign based on rectified boxes.

2   Method

The overview of the proposed approach is shown in Fig. 2, which contains three main components: the baseline framework (Fig. 2a), the region proposal rectification (RPR) module (Fig. 2b), and the attentive feed-forward network (FFN) (Fig. 2c). Component details are illustrated in the following sections.

2.1   Baseline Framework

Figure 2a shows a representative top-down instance segmentation framework that involves three steps: (1) feature extraction; (2) region proposal generation; and (3) mask prediction. Feature extraction employs a backbone network (i.e. deep neural network) to extract multi-scale features from input image. Feature pyramid network (FPN) [12] is usually adopted to build high-level semantic features at all scales. Based on the learned feature maps F, region proposal boxes are generated through a box head (see Fig. 2a). With proposal boxes, ROIAlign [6] extracts ROIs from F and a mask head performs segmentation on ROIs subsequently. In this paper, we adopt two representative top-down instance segmentation methods as our baseline: Mask R-CNN [6] and CenterMask [11]. Mask R-CNN employs anchor-based region proposal network (RPN) [22] while CenterMask uses anchor-free FCOS [24] to provide proposal boxes. We use a backbone (e.g., ResNet50 [7]) with FPN for feature extraction. The box head and mask head share the same structures as Mask R-CNN and CenterMask.

2.2   Region Proposal Rectification

As mentioned above, since the baseline approaches make segmentation on extracted ROIs, it suffers from an incomplete segmentation problem (see Fig. 1c). To address this problem, in this paper, we propose a region proposal rectification (RPR) module. The flowchart of the RPR module is shown in Fig. 2b. The RPR module mainly contains two sub-modules: a progressive ROIAlign module and an attentive FFN module.

Progressive ROIAlign. ROIAlign [6] is proposed in Mask R-CNN to extract well-aligned ROI features based on proposal boxes. Although it improves the misalignment problem in ROI Pooling [5], the cropped ROIs suffers from incomplete segmentation problem (see Fig. 1c). To relieve this problem, Mask R-CNN [6] attempts a second-stage box regression based on cropped ROI features. However, the limited view of ROIs lacks global knowledge and therefore brings difficulty for the network to correct proposal boxes. In this study, we propose to rectify the region proposal locations from features with an expanded view. In particular, a progressive ROIAlign module is employed to expand proposal regions progressively and a batch of ROIs features are obtained for the following proposal rectification. We show that by introducing neighbor features, the network gains more related knowledge and is able to rectify the proposal locations.

As shown in Fig. 2b, progressive ROIAlign extracts ROIs features ($\text{ROIs}^{\text{rec}} = \{\text{ROI}_i^{\text{rec}} \in \mathbb{R}^{N \times C \times 14 \times 14}\}_{i=1}^{K}$) from proposal boxes $\mathcal{B} \in \mathbb{R}^{N \times 4}$, where C indicate feature channels, K represents the number of extracted ROIs from each proposal box, N is the total number of proposal boxes. Given input feature map F and proposal boxes $\mathcal{B}$, the extracted ROI features can be expressed as:

$$\text{ROIs}^{\text{rec}} = \text{progressive ROIAlign}(F, \mathcal{B}). \tag{1}$$

For each proposal box $B = (x_1, y_1, x_2, y_2) \in \mathcal{B}$, where (x_1, y_1) and (x_2, y_2) represent the top-left and bottom-right corner points of B, the progressive ROIAlign expands B in K iterations with a dilation rate ρ and generates expanded proposal boxes $B^{\text{expand}} = \{B_i^{\text{expand}}\}_{i=1}^{K}$. Each $B_i^{\text{expand}} = (\hat{x}_{i_1}, \hat{y}_{i_1}, \hat{x}_{i_2}, \hat{y}_{i_2})$ is formulated as:

$$\hat{x}_{i_1} = \max(x_1 \times (1 - r_i),\ 0),\ \hat{y}_{i_1} = \max(y_1 \times (1 - r_i),\ 0)$$
$$\hat{x}_{i_2} = \min(x_2 \times (1 + r_i),\ \hat{W}),\ \hat{y}_{i_2} = \min(y_2 \times (1 + r_i),\ \hat{H}) \tag{2}$$
$$r_i = r_{i-1} + \frac{\rho}{K},\ r_0 = 0,$$

where r represents expansion ratio, $\hat{W}$ and $\hat{H}$ represent input image width and height. We find that different hyperparameter K values only caused minor differences in performance across three datasets. For consistency, we use $\rho = 0.4, K = 5$ in this paper. In this scenario, the RPR module brings negligible extra memory consumption during inference (about $0.01\,$s per iteration per device). Next, ROIAlign [6] extracts $\text{ROI}_i^{\text{rec}}$ from feature map F based on each expanded proposal box B_i^{expand}:

$$\text{ROI}_i^{\text{rec}} = \text{ROIAlign}(F, B_i^{\text{expand}}), \ i = 1, \ldots, K. \tag{3}$$

Attentive FFN. The ROI features (ROIs^{rec}) extracted from progressive ROIAlign module are then fed into the proposed attentive feed-forward network (FFN) for region proposal box rectification. As shown in Fig. 2c, the attentive FFN module employs a self-attention mechanism [25] to help build pixel relationships in spatial space of ROIs^{rec}.

Before self-attention module, we separate the ROIs^{rec} into two sets: ROI^{ori} and $\text{ROIs}^{\text{expand}}$. $\text{ROI}^{\text{ori}} \in \mathbb{R}^{N \times C \times D}$ where $D = 14 \times 14$ represents the ROI feature extracted using original region proposal box. $\text{ROIs}^{\text{expand}} \in \mathbb{R}^{N \times C \times (K-1)D}$ involves the ROI features from expanded proposal boxes, note that we stack the ROIs in the spatial dimension. We use ROI^{ori} as query features, and $\text{ROIs}^{\text{expand}}$ as value and key features. To perform self-attention, we first project channel dimension $C = 256$ of query, key, value features to $\hat{C} = 64$ with 1×1 convolutional layers. We use $\mathcal{Q} \in \mathbb{R}^{N \times \hat{C} \times D}, \mathcal{K} \in \mathbb{R}^{N \times \hat{C} \times (K-1)D}$ and $\mathcal{V} \in \mathbb{R}^{N \times \hat{C} \times (K-1)D}$ to represent the projected query, key and value features. The attentive ROI features ($\text{ROI}^{att} \in \mathbb{R}^{N \times \hat{C} \times D}$) from the self-attention module is then obtained as:

$$\text{ROI}^{att} = \mathcal{Q} + \mathcal{V} \cdot \text{softmax}(\frac{(\mathcal{Q}^T \mathcal{K})^T}{\sqrt{\hat{C}}}). \tag{4}$$

Finally, convolutional layers and fully connected (FC) layers are utilized to linearly transform the ROI^{att} to rectified proposal boxes $\mathcal{B}^{\text{rec}} \in \mathbb{R}^{N \times 4}$. We use smooth L_1 loss [5] for box regression, we term the loss as L_{RPR}.

3   Experiment

3.1   Datasets

We evaluate the performance of proposed method on three datasets: urothelial cell, plant phenotyping and DSB2018. Plant phenotyping and DSB2018 are public datasets. For each dataset, we use 70%, 15%, 15% of images for training, validation, and testing. (1) **Urothelial Cell**. Instance segmentation of urothelial cells is of great importance in urine cytology for urothelial carcinoma detection. The urothelial cell dataset contains 336 pathological images with a resolution of 1024×1024. The images are cropped from ThinPrep slide images and are annotated by three experts. (2) **Plant Phenotyping**. The plant phenotyping dataset [18] contains 535 top-down view plant leave images with various resolutions. (3) **DSB2018**. The Data Science Bowl 2018 (DSB2018[1]) dataset consists of 670 annotated cell nuclei images with different sizes.

Table 1. Quantitative evaluation results of baseline methods with and without proposed region proposal rectification (RPR) module on three biological datasets.

Methods	Datasets	AP^{bbox} (%)			AP^{mask} (%)		
		AP^{bbox}	$AP^{bbox}_{0.5}$	$AP^{bbox}_{0.75}$	AP^{mask}	$AP^{mask}_{0.5}$	$AP^{mask}_{0.75}$
Mask R-CNN [6]	Plant	58.10	88.14	65.85	56.15	84.39	65.29
Mask R-CNN+RPR		**60.69**	**88.23**	**67.32**	**57.56**	**84.49**	**65.93**
CenterMask [11]		55.15	87.76	60.33	50.39	**83.43**	56.45
CenterMask+RPR		**59.78**	**87.79**	**66.94**	**51.52**	83.15	**58.44**
Mask R-CNN [6]	DSB2018	53.36	78.82	60.84	50.46	**77.63**	57.08
Mask R-CNN+RPR		**54.02**	**78.88**	**61.10**	**50.75**	77.62	**57.25**
CenterMask [11]		55.30	79.71	62.82	51.84	**78.51**	59.62
CenterMask+RPR		**55.82**	**79.75**	**63.56**	**52.09**	78.46	**59.63**
Mask R-CNN [6]	Urothelial Cell	76.56	91.16	87.65	77.35	91.16	**89.02**
Mask R-CNN+RPR		**77.98**	**91.16**	**88.49**	**77.65**	**91.16**	88.99
CenterMask [11]		76.11	94.52	88.03	76.87	94.55	88.51
CenterMask+RPR		**80.76**	**94.66**	**91.00**	**78.81**	**94.66**	**91.05**

3.2 Experimental Details

We follow the same training skills and hyper-parameter settings as Mask R-CNN [6] and CenterMask [11]. In particular, we use stochastic gradient descent (SGD) algorithm as optimizer with an initial learning rate of 0.001. We use random flipping as data augmentation and train the network for 10k iterations with a batch size of 16. The weights of the backbone network are pre-trained on ImageNet dataset. We use 8 Quadro RTX 8000 GPUs for training. The overall object loss function is $L = L_{box} + L_{mask} + L_{RPR}$, where L_{box} and L_{mask} represent the proposal box loss and mask prediction loss. We use the same L_{box} and L_{mask} losses as Mask R-CNN [6] and CenterMask [11].

3.3 Evaluation Metric

We report the average precision (AP) [6] averaged over IoU threshold ranges from 0.5 to 0.95 at an interval of 0.05 as evaluation metric:

$$AP = \frac{1}{10} \sum_{t=0.5:0.05:0.95} AP_t, \tag{5}$$

where t indicates the IoU threshold between predicted bbox/mask and ground truth bbox/mask. We use AP^{bbox} and AP^{mask} to represent the box- and mask-level AP. We additionally report AP at IoU threshold of 0.5 and 0.75 in Table 1.

---

[1] https://www.kaggle.com/c/data-science-bowl-2018.

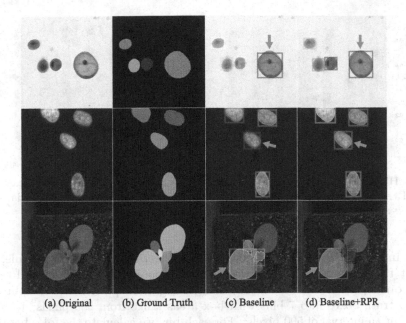

(a) Original   (b) Ground Truth   (c) Baseline   (d) Baseline+RPR

Fig. 3. The qualitative results of baseline methods (i.e., Mask R-CNN [6] and Center-Mask [11]) with and without region proposal rectification (RPR) module. From left to right, we show the original image, the ground-truth annotation, results by either Mask R-CNN or CenterMask without RPR, and results with RPR. From top to bottom, we illustrate the images from urothelial cell, DSB2018, and plant datasets respectively.

4   Results and Discussion

The qualitative and quantitative instance segmentation results are shown in Fig. 3 and Table 1 respectively. In particular, we have compared the results of baseline methods (i.e., Mask R-CNN [6] and CenterMask [11]) with and without the proposed region proposal rectification (RPR) on Urothelial Cell, Plant Phenotyping and DSB2018 datasets.

As shown in Table 1, with region proposal rectification, the performances of object detection (AP^{bbox}) and instance segmentation (AP^{mask}) are consistently improved for baseline methods on three biological datasets. Specifically, Mask R-CNN with RPR improves AP^{bbox} by 2.59, 0.66, 1.42 points and AP^{mask} by 1.41, 0.29, 0.3 points on Plant, DSB2018, and Urothelial Cell datasets, respectively. CenterMask with RPR improves AP^{bbox} by 4.63, 0.52, 4.65 points and AP^{mask} by 1.13, 0.25, 1.94 points on the three biological datasets. From qualitative results in Fig. 3, we observe that the incomplete segmentation mask problem is remarkably relieved with the proposed region proposal rectification.

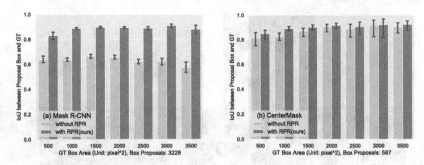

Fig. 4. Histogram of intersection-over-union (IoU) between region proposal boxes and ground truth (GT) boxes along with GT box areas on urothelial cell testing dataset. The box area unit is pixel^2. Error bars (mean $\pm$ std) are added.

To investigate the effect of region proposal rectification (RPR) module, we exhibit the histogram of IoU between region proposal boxes and ground truth boxes on urothelial cell testing datasets in Fig. 4. In particular, we split the ground truth boxes into 7 bins with box areas range from 500 pixels^2 to 3500 pixels^2 at an interval of 500 pixels^2. For each bin, we calculate the IoUs between the ground truth boxes and corresponding proposal boxes. We add error bars (means $\pm$ std) on histograms. As shown in Fig. 4a, Mask R-CNN with RPR shows significant improvement over Mask R-CNN without RPR in box IoU, suggesting that the RPR module corrects region proposal boxes significantly.

The results demonstrate that introduction of neighbor spatial knowledge to ROI features is effective for box rectification. Note that this improvement does not relate with the AP^{bbox} in Table 1 as we do not employ non-maximum-suppression (NMS) here since it helps us better observe the rectification results of the RPR module. In Fig. 4b, CenterMask with RPR also shows superiority in box IoU especially on cells with smaller box areas. The improvement is not as significant as Mask R-CNN, one possible reason would be that Mask R-CNN uses anchor-based object detector and provides a large number of proposal boxes (e.g., 3228 boxes). On the contrary, CenterMask employs anchor-free FCOS to provide a small number of precise proposal boxes (e.g., 587 boxes). Before NMS

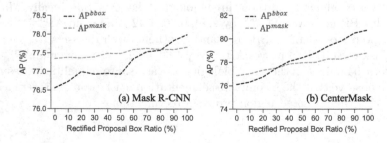

Fig. 5. AP^{bbox} and AP^{mask} along with various fractions of rectified proposal boxes.

operation, Mask-RCNN's proposal locations are not as precise as CenterMask. However, with RPR, the gaps become small.

Considering the improvement brought by our RPR module is mainly around the object's boundary, therefore, we present AP^{bbox} and AP^{mask} along with various fractions of rectified region proposal boxes in Fig. 5. As can be seen, both AP^{bbox} and AP^{mask} curves increase with fractions of rectified proposal boxes in the baseline methods. The improvement is more significant in AP^{bbox} compared to AP^{mask}. Figure 5 further explains the effectiveness of the proposed RPR module. Addressing the robustness of the RPR module in extreme cases with blurred cell boundaries can be a promising direction for future research.

5 Conclusion

In this study, we proposed a region proposal rectification (RPR) module that addresses the challenging incomplete segmentation problem in the top-down instance segmentation of biological images. The proposed approach offers new perspectives to redefine the procedure of biological instance mask generation. The RPR module shows significant improvement in both anchor-based and anchor-free top-down instance segmentation baselines. The effective results on three biological datasets demonstrate that the proposed approach can be served as a solid baseline in instance segmentation of biological images.

References

1. Chang, Q., et al.: Deeprecon: Joint 2d cardiac segmentation and 3d volume reconstruction via a structure-specific generative method. arXiv preprint arXiv:2206.07163 (2022)
2. Chen, H., Qi, X., Yu, L., Dou, Q., Qin, J., Heng, P.A.: DCAN: deep contour-aware networks for object instance segmentation from histology images. Med. Image Anal. **36**, 135–146 (2017)
3. Gao, Y., Zhou, M., Liu, D., Yan, Z., Zhang, S., Metaxas, D.: A data-scalable transformer for medical image segmentation: architecture, model efficiency, and benchmark. arXiv preprint arXiv:2203.00131 (2022)
4. Gao, Y., Zhou, M., Metaxas, D.N.: UTNet: a hybrid transformer architecture for medical image segmentation. In: de Bruijne, M., Cattin, P.C., Cotin, S., Padoy, N., Speidel, S., Zheng, Y., Essert, C. (eds.) MICCAI 2021. LNCS, vol. 12903, pp. 61–71. Springer, Cham (2021). https://doi.org/10.1007/978-3-030-87199-4_6
5. Girshick, R.: Fast R-CNN. In: Proceedings of the IEEE International Conference on Computer Vision, pp. 1440–1448 (2015)
6. He, K., Gkioxari, G., Dollár, P., Girshick, R.: Mask R-CNN. In: Proceedings of the IEEE International Conference on Ccomputer Vision, pp. 2961–2969 (2017)
7. He, K., Zhang, X., Ren, S., Sun, J.: Deep residual learning for image recognition. In: Proceedings of the IEEE Conference on Computer Vision and Pattern Recognition, pp. 770–778 (2016)

8. He, X., Tan, C., Qiao, Y., Tan, V., Metaxas, D., Li, K.: Effective 3d humerus and scapula extraction using low-contrast and high-shape-variability MR data. In: Medical Imaging 2019: Biomedical Applications in Molecular, Structural, and Functional Imaging. vol. 10953, p. 109530O. International Society for Optics and Photonics (2019)
9. Hu, J.B., Guan, A., Zhangli, Q., Sayadi, L.R., Hamdan, U.S., Vyas, R.M.: Harnessing machine-learning to personalize cleft lip markings. Plastic Reconstruct. Surgery-Global Open 8(9S), 150–151 (2020)
10. Irshad, H., et al.: Crowdsourcing image annotation for nucleus detection and segmentation in computational pathology: evaluating experts, automated methods, and the crowd. In: Pacific Symposium on Biocomputing Co-chairs, pp. 294–305. World Scientific (2014)
11. Lee, Y., Park, J.: Centermask: real-time anchor-free instance segmentation. In: Proceedings of the IEEE/CVF Conference on Computer Vision and Pattern Recognition, pp. 13906–13915 (2020)
12. Lin, T.Y., Dollár, P., Girshick, R., He, K., Hariharan, B., Belongie, S.: Feature pyramid networks for object detection. In: Proceedings of the IEEE Conference on Computer Vision and Pattern Recognition, pp. 2117–2125 (2017)
13. Liu, D., Gao, Y., Zhangli, Q., Yan, Z., Zhou, M., Metaxas, D.: Transfusion: multiview divergent fusion for medical image segmentation with transformers. arXiv preprint arXiv:2203.10726 (2022)
14. Liu, D., Ge, C., Xin, Y., Li, Q., Tao, R.: Dispersion correction for optical coherence tomography by the stepped detection algorithm in the fractional Fourier domain. Opt. Express 28(5), 5919–5935 (2020)
15. Liu, D., Liu, J., Liu, Y., Tao, R., Prince, J.L., Carass, A.: Label super resolution for 3d magnetic resonance images using deformable u-net. In: Medical Imaging 2021: Image Processing, vol. 11596, p. 1159628. International Society for Optics and Photonics (2021)
16. Liu, D., Xin, Y., Li, Q., Tao, R.: Dispersion correction for optical coherence tomography by parameter estimation in fractional Fourier domain. In: 2019 IEEE International Conference on Mechatronics and Automation (ICMA), pp. 674–678. IEEE (2019)
17. Liu, D., Yan, Z., Chang, Q., Axel, L., Metaxas, D.N.: Refined deep layer aggregation for multi-disease, multi-view & multi-center cardiac MR segmentation. In: Puyol Antón, E., et al. (eds.) STACOM 2021. LNCS, vol. 13131, pp. 315–322. Springer, Cham (2022). https://doi.org/10.1007/978-3-030-93722-5_34
18. Minervini, M., Fischbach, A., Scharr, H., Tsaftaris, S.A.: Finely-grained annotated datasets for image-based plant phenotyping. Pattern Recogn. Lett. 81, 80–89 (2016)
19. Oda, H., et al.: BESNet: boundary-enhanced segmentation of cells in histopathological images. In: Frangi, A.F., Schnabel, J.A., Davatzikos, C., Alberola-López, C., Fichtinger, G. (eds.) MICCAI 2018. LNCS, vol. 11071, pp. 228–236. Springer, Cham (2018). https://doi.org/10.1007/978-3-030-00934-2_26
20. Pantanowitz, L.: Digital images and the future of digital pathology. J. Pathol. Inform. 1, 15 (2010)
21. Payer, C., Štern, D., Neff, T., Bischof, H., Urschler, M.: Instance segmentation and tracking with cosine embeddings and recurrent hourglass networks. In: Frangi, A.F., Schnabel, J.A., Davatzikos, C., Alberola-López, C., Fichtinger, G. (eds.) MICCAI 2018. LNCS, vol. 11071, pp. 3–11. Springer, Cham (2018). https://doi.org/10.1007/978-3-030-00934-2_1

22. Ren, S., He, K., Girshick, R., Sun, J.: Faster R-CNN: towards real-time object detection with region proposal networks. In: Advances in Neural Information Processing Systems, vol. 28 (2015)
23. Schmidt, U., Weigert, M., Broaddus, C., Myers, G.: Cell detection with star-convex polygons. In: Frangi, A.F., Schnabel, J.A., Davatzikos, C., Alberola-López, C., Fichtinger, G. (eds.) MICCAI 2018. LNCS, vol. 11071, pp. 265–273. Springer, Cham (2018). https://doi.org/10.1007/978-3-030-00934-2_30
24. Tian, Z., Shen, C., Chen, H., He, T.: FCOS: fully convolutional one-stage object detection. In: Proceedings of the IEEE/CVF International Conference on Computer Vision, pp. 9627–9636 (2019)
25. Vaswani, A., et al.: Attention is all you need. In: Advances in Neural Information Processing Systems, vol. 30 (2017)
26. Yi, J., et al.: Object-guided instance segmentation for biological images. In: Proceedings of the AAAI Conference on Artificial Intelligence, vol. 34, pp. 12677–12684 (2020)
27. Yi, J., et al.: Multi-scale cell instance segmentation with keypoint graph based bounding boxes. In: Shen, D., et al. (eds.) MICCAI 2019. LNCS, vol. 11764, pp. 369–377. Springer, Cham (2019). https://doi.org/10.1007/978-3-030-32239-7_41
28. Yi, J., Wu, P., Jiang, M., Huang, Q., Hoeppner, D.J., Metaxas, D.N.: Attentive neural cell instance segmentation. Med. Image Anal. **55**, 228–240 (2019)
29. Zhang, Y., et al.: A multi-branch hybrid transformer network for corneal endothelial cell segmentation. In: de Bruijne, M., et al. (eds.) MICCAI 2021. LNCS, vol. 12901, pp. 99–108. Springer, Cham (2021). https://doi.org/10.1007/978-3-030-87193-2_10
30. Zhou, Y., Onder, O.F., Dou, Q., Tsougenis, E., Chen, H., Heng, P.-A.: CIA-Net: robust nuclei instance segmentation with contour-aware information aggregation. In: Chung, A.C.S., Gee, J.C., Yushkevich, P.A., Bao, S. (eds.) IPMI 2019. LNCS, vol. 11492, pp. 682–693. Springer, Cham (2019). https://doi.org/10.1007/978-3-030-20351-1_53

DeepMIF: Deep Learning Based Cell Profiling for Multispectral Immunofluorescence Images with Graphical User Interface

Yeman Brhane Hagos[1(✉)], Ayse U Akarca[2], Alan Ramsay[3], Riccardo L Rossi[4],
Sabine Pomplun[3], Alessia Moioli[5], Andrea Gianatti[6],
Christopher Mcnamara[10], Alessandro Rambaldi[5,7], Sergio A. Quezada[8,9],
David Linch[9], Giuseppe Gritti[5], Teresa Marafioti[2,3], and Yinyin Yuan[1(✉)]

[1] Division of Molecular Pathology, Centre for Evolution and Cancer,
The Institute of Cancer Research, London, UK
{yeman.hagos,yinyin.yuan}@icr.ac.uk
[2] Cancer Institute, University College London, London, UK
[3] Department of Histopathology, University College Hospitals London, London, UK
[4] Bioinformatics, Istituto Nazionale Genetica Molecolare, Milan, Italy
[5] Hematology Unit, Ospedale Papa Giovanni XXIII, Bergamo, Italy
[6] Pathology Unit, Ospedale Papa Giovanni XXIII, Bergamo, Italy
[7] Department of Oncology and Hematology-Oncology, University of Milan,
Milan, Italy
[8] Cancer Immunology Unit, University College London Cancer Institute, University
College London, London, UK
[9] Research Department of Haematology, University College London Cancer Institute,
University College London, London, UK
[10] Department of Haematology, University College London Hospital, London, UK

Abstract. Multispectral immunofluorescence (M-IF) analysis is used to investigate the cellular landscape of tissue sections and spatial interaction of cells. However, complex makeup of markers in the images hinders the accurate quantification of cell phenotypes. We developed DeepMIF, a new deep learning (DL) based tool with a graphical user interface (GUI) to detect and quantify cell phenotypes on M-IF images, and visualize whole slide image (WSI) and cell phenotypes. To identify cell phenotypes, we detected cells on the deconvoluted images followed by co-expression analysis to classify cells expressing single or multiple markers. We trained, tested and validated our model on $> 50k$ expert single-cell annotations from multiple immune panels on 15 samples of follicular lymphoma patients. Our algorithm obtained a cell classification accuracy and area under the curve (AUC) ≥ 0.98 on an independent validation panel. The cell phenotype identification took on average 27.5 min per WSI, and rendering of the WSI took on average 0.07 minutes. DeepMIF is optimized to run on local computers or high-performance clusters

Supplementary Information The online version contains supplementary material available at https://doi.org/10.1007/978-3-031-16440-8_14.

independent of the host platform. These suggest that the DeepMIF is an accurate and efficient tool for the analysis and visualization of M-IF images, leading to the identification of novel prognostic cell phenotypes in tumours.

Keywords: Deep learning · Multispectral immunofluorescence · Cell detection · Cell classification · Image viewer

1   Introduction

Recent advances in multiplex staining technologies greatly accelerate studies of spatial interaction of cell phenotypes in the tumour microenvironment [1]. These technologies allow detecting multiple proteins at a single cell level on a tissue section at high resolution while preserving their spatial information [1–3].

However, the multiplex images come with complexity for manual analysis by pathologists due to the intermixing of the markers and weak signals [4–6]. Automated artificial intelligence methods such as DL excel at objectively identifying cell phenotypes and generating quantitative features from images [3, 7]. The DL algorithms can be trained end-to-end to extract features which are robust to heterogeneity of signal in M-IF images [8,9]. Previously, commercial software have been used to analyse M-IF images, such as InForm image analysis software [10,11] and Visiopharm [3]. Some studies have used DL to analyse M-IF images [3,12,13]. In [3,12], to detect cell nuclei, DAPI DNA staining images were used. However, DAPI staining is not adequate to capture all cells nuclei, and [12] proposed to use a combination of DNA staining markers, which is costly.

To address these challenges, we developed DeepMIF, a new DL based M-IF image analysis and visualization tool. Our work has the following main contributions:**1)** We developed a highly accurate DL method to identify cell phenotypes on M-IF from its deconvoluted image (DI)s instead of using DAPI that generalizes across multiple panels. **2)** We developed a whole slide M-IF viewer, and DeepMIF could be used from the GUI. Thus our algorithm will be widely accessible to researchers with less/no programming skills. **3)** DeepMIF is easily customizable to allow users to specify cell phenotype of interest in a configuration file or from the GUI. **4)** DeepMIF could easily run on local computers or high-performance clusters independent of the platform and allows parallelization of tasks to speed up execution.

2   Materials

To train and validate our approach, we used diagnostic M-IF images of follicular lymphoma patients. The M-IF images were obtained using Vectra 3 platform at $20x$ magnification and $0.5\,\mu m/pixel$ resolution. The output of Vectra 3 platform contains the M-IF image and DIs (Fig. 1a). To optimize model parameters and test the model, 40327 single cells were annotated by experts from 10 samples

(Table 1). To capture the tissue heterogeneity, the annotations were collected from different regions of the slides. To make sure data from the same patient is not used for training and testing, the training, validation and testing split was done at patient level 60%, 20%, and 20%, respectively. To evaluate the generalizability of the model to other panels, we validated the model on 10038 cells collected from two independent M-IF panels from 5 samples (Table 1). The study was approved by the Ethics Committee (approval number REG. 197/17) and performed following the ethical standards of the 1964 Helsinki declaration and its later amendments. All patients provided written informed consent.

Table 1. The single cell annotation dataset. The model optimization data was extracted from immune T cells panel. Annotations were collected from DI of non-nuclear (CD8, CD4, PD1, CD16 and CD206) and nuclear (FOXP3 and Granulysin) markers. NK/T = Natural killer T cells panel;

—	Model optimizing data			Model optimizing data	
	Training	Validation	Testing	NK/T	Macrophages
Positive	5088	2147	1287	4021	239
Negative	16000	6958	8847	5188	590
DI	CD8, CD4, FOXP3 and PD1			CD16 and Granulysin	CD206

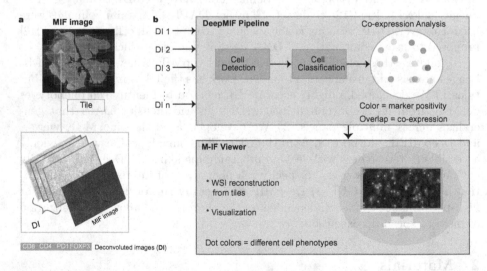

Fig. 1. Schematics of the DeepMIF workflow. **a**) M-IF image and its corresponding DIs. **b**) Components of DeepMIF. DI = deconvoluted image; WSI = whole slide image

3   Methodology

The DeepMIF pipeline has four main sections: cell detection, cell classification, co-expression analysis and WSI viewer (Fig. 1b). The Vectra 3 platform generates M-IF and DIs corresponding to every protein/marker used in the M-IF scanning (Fig. 1a). While the DIs have simple features (negative or positive for a marker), the M-IF image contains complex aggregate features of all markers used. Thus, we applied DL on the DIs followed by co-expression analysis to find cells expressing either single or multiple markers on M-IF images.

3.1   Cell Detection and Classification on Deconvoluted Images

To detect cells on the DIs, we used ConCORDe-Net [9] since the model was designed to give attention to weakly signal markers and touching cells, one of the challenges in M-IF due to co-expression of multiple markers. The model input is a $224 \times 224 \times 3$ pixels image. To discern weakly stained cells and touching cells, the model uses cell count in the training data. Here, the model was trained from scratch using human annotations (Table 1). The model generates a predicted cell nucleus centre probability map image. To converted the probability map to a binary image, we applied 0.8 as a threshold. To fill holes in the binary image, we applied morphological closing as follows:

$$I_{out} = (I_{in} \oplus s) \ominus s, \ where \ s = 5 \ pixels \qquad (1)$$

where I_{in}, I_{out}, s, $\oplus$ and $\ominus$ denote the input image, output image, structuring element, dilation operator and erosion operator, respectively. We excluded objects of area $\leq 10 \ pixel^2$. The center of every object in the binary image is a center of a cell. All the threshold parameters above were optimized on the validation dataset maximizing cell detection F1-score.

To classify cells for a marker positivity on DI, patches of size $20 \times 20 \times 3$ and $28 \times 28 \times 3$ pixels were extracted for nuclear (e.g. FOXP3) and non-nuclear (e.g. CD4) markers, respectively. We used smaller patch sizes for nuclear markers to minimize the effect of background noise. The number of single-cell annotations collected from non-nuclear markers was much higher than that of nuclear markers. To minimize the effect of the imbalance, we trained separate convolutional neural network (CNN) for nuclear markers and non-nuclear markers. InceptionV3 [14] and VGG [15] are among the most commonly used classification CNNs [16]. The models are deep and have a high number of parameters, which can result in overfitting for a small dataset. Thus, we custom designed shallower versions of these CNN with a depth of 5 layers. The first model (**Our model 1**) uses inception model for feature learning section, while the second models (**Our model 2**) uses VGG module. The inception module uses multiple kernels size at a given layer to extract multi-scale features followed by a max-pooling layer, while the VGG module uses a series of two convolutions of the same kernel size followed by a max-pooling layer. The feature learning section starts with a convolution layer of 16 neurons and the number of neurons increases by 16 for every layer added. The classification section consists of two dense layers of $\{200, 2\}$ neurons, with a dropout $(rate = 0.3)$ layer in between. The ReLU activation was used in all layers, but softmax in the last layer to generate a probability. Model parameters were randomly initialized using uniform glorot [17] and optimized using Adam [18], learning rate of 10^{-4} and categorical cross-entropy loss function (Eq. 2). The model was trained for 500 epochs with patience $= 50$ epochs.

$$\text{Loss} = -\frac{1}{n} \sum_{i=1}^{n} (y_i \cdot \log \hat{y}_i + (1 - y_i) \cdot \log (1 - \hat{y}_i)) \tag{2}$$

where $\hat{y}_i$ is the ith value in the model output, y_i is the corresponding target value, and n is the number of cells in the training batch.

3.2   Markers Co-expression Identification

To identify cells co-expressing multiple markers, we first spatially mapped the location of cells positive for the markers onto a single plane. A cell is said to be co-expressing multiple markers if detections on DIs overlap after mapping them onto a single plane. The cell detection algorithm is optimized to find the centre of the nucleus of cells. However, due to the variation of the nature of markers (nuclear or cytoplasmic), the predicted location might slightly vary. We empirically set threshold distance $r = 1.5\,\mu\text{m}$ (about a quarter of lymphocyte diameter). In the rest of the paper, overlapping markers mean within a distance of r. Co-expression analysis was performed as follows.

Suppose we have M-IF panel with n markers $\{m_i : \ i \ \epsilon \ \{1, 2, ...n\}\}$, which will generate n DIs. Suppose, we want to identify cells $(C_{phenotype})$ co-expressing k markers, $M_p = \{m_i : \ i\epsilon\{1, 2, ..., k\}, \ k \leq n\}$ and negative for l markers $M_n = \{m_j : \ j\epsilon\{1, 2, ..., l\}, \ l < n\}$. Distance can only be computed between two points. So, k points are said to be overlapping with each other, if every pair of points are overlapping. The number of combinations (N) is computed as follows:

$$\text{N} = {}^{k}C_2 = \frac{k!}{2!(k-2)!} \quad = \frac{k(k-1)}{2} \tag{3}$$

The combinations are $\{(m_1, m_2), \ (m_1, m_3), \ (m_1, m_4), \ ..., (m_{k-1}, m_k)\}$. The complexity of iterations is $\mathcal{O}(k^2)$. To speed up the computation, we used vectorized forms instead of single cell level looping. The co-expression analysis have N iterations, each with 4 main steps.

Let $CoExp$ is a dictionary of length k with marker name and cells co-expressing the k markers as a key and value, respectively. Initially, the values are set to empty and updated as follows:

Iteration 1:$(m_1, \ m_2)$ combination.

Step 1: Get m_1 and m_2 positive location. Suppose the DI for m_1 has n cells positive for m_1, $U = \{u_i \ \epsilon \ \mathbb{R}^2, i \ \epsilon \ \{1, 2...n\}\}$ and the DI for m_2 has a m cells positive for m_2, $V = \{v_i \epsilon \mathbb{R}^2, i \epsilon \{1, 2...m\}\}$. The u_i and v_i have its own (x, y) location in the image space.

Step 2: Compute distance matrix, $D \epsilon \mathbb{R}^{nxm}$. The distance is defined as follows:

$$D_{ij} = \|u_i - v_j\|_2 = \sqrt{(x_{u_i} - x_{v_j})^2 + (y_{u_i} - y_{v_j})^2} \tag{4}$$

Step 3: Identify cells $Q \subseteq U$ and $P \subseteq V$ which co-express m_1 and m_2. The Q and P are the subset of the original cell collection in which the items in i^{th} location of Q and P are overlapping. Mathematically,

$$\underset{Q\epsilon U, P\epsilon V}{\arg\min A} \, D(U, V) \, : \, \|q_i - p_i\|_2 \leq r, \, for \, q_i\epsilon Q \, and \, p_i\epsilon P \tag{5}$$

Step 4: Update $CoExp$ for m_1 and m_2, i.e., $CoExp[m_1] = Q$ and $CoExp[m_2] = P$.

Steps 1 to 4 will be subsequently applied for the other combinations. If a marker in the current combination was considered in the previous combination, cells positive for that marker which co-express all previous markers will be only considered. For example, for the second combination, (m_1, m_3), Q will be used instead of the original collection U for m_1. Again from (m_1, m_3) combination, a subset of Q will co-express m_3. Then, $CoExp$ will be updated with values for m_1 and m_3. Remove cells form $CoExp$ for m_1, that did not express m_3 and their corresponding m_2 expressing cells. If any of the combinations do not have overlapping markers, the iteration stops and there are no cells that co-express the k markers. Let C be a set of cells co-expressing the k markers, their centre location (X, Y) was computed using Equation (6).

$$X, Y = \frac{\sum_{i=1}^{i=k} X_i}{k}, \frac{\sum_{i=1}^{i=k} Y_i}{k}, \tag{6}$$

where the X_i and Y_i are vectors of x and y location of the markers in $CoExp$, respectively. Finally, $C_{phenotype}$ is a subset of C that doesn't express any of the l markers in M_n. Mathematically,

$$C_{phenotype} = \{c_i\epsilon C, i\epsilon\{1, 2, ..., n\}\} : \|c_i - z_j\|_2 > r|\forall z_j\epsilon Z \tag{7}$$

where Z is a set of locations positive for markers in M_n.

3.3 DeepMIF Graphical User Interface

To make DeepMIF easily useable and interactive for pathologists and the wider research community, we developed a GUI. The GUI has two main components; whole slide M-IF image viewer and DL pipeline (Sup. Fig. 1a). Our tool reconstructs the WSI from its tiles and displays cell phenotypes using the location of tiles in their filename and position of the cells generated using DeepMIF (Fig. 1a, Sup. Fig. 1a-c). The image viewer was developed using an OS independent PyQT Python package. It is interactive and allows batch processing of files. To allow multi-tasking of rendering, visualization and running the DL pipeline in parallel, threading and multiprocessing are employed.

4   Results and Discussion

In this work, we developed DeepMIF, a new DL based M-IF image analysis with GUI. To evaluate the performance of single-cell detection on the DIs, we used recall, precision and F1-score. On a separately held test data, we obtained recall, precision, and F1-score of 0.85, 0.86, and 0.86, respectively. For cell classification, we trained and evaluated our proposed models and fine-tuned ImageNet pretrained VGG16, InceptionV3, ResNet50 and Xception models. All models were trained on the same data from the immune T cells panel (Table 1). On a separately held $> 10k$ test data (Table 1), Our model 2 achieved recall (0.96), the highest among all models (Fig. 2a) and precision of 0.96, same as Our model 1, and VGG16. Using 1000 bootstraps taking 60% of the test data in each bootstrap, the recall estimate of VGG16 and Our model 2 was 0.96, 95% CI (0.95–0.96), and 0.965, 95% CI (0.96–0.97), respectively. These models achieved the same value of AUC (0.96), compared to Xception (0.91), InceptionV3 (0.89) and ResNet50 (0.94) (Sup. Fig. 2a). Our model 2 and Our model 1 achieved 0.98 accuracy (Sup. Fig. 1b), higher than ImageNet pre-trained models. Overall, Our model 2 outperformed all the other models. This could be due to the less number of parameters (Fig. 2a) compared to the other models and thus, less chance of over-fitting. Moreover, due to the reduced number of parameters in Our model 2, it takes less time and memory during training and inference. On an independent natural killer T cells and macrophages panels data, Our model 2 achieved AUC, precision, recall and accuracy values ≥ 0.98 (Fig. 2b, Sup. Fig. 2c-d). This shows Our model 2 is generalizable to other panels and it could be reliably used.

Before applying our co-expression algorithm on M-IF images, we generated and tested it on simulated data (Fig. 2e). A set of points (marker positivity locations) with semi-random (x, y) location were generated for $k = 4$ markers. Our algorithm was able to locate overlapping markers (open circles). We then applied the cell detection, classification and co-expression analysis on M-IF images (Sup. Fig. 3a-b). The whole process took 27.5 (range: 9.4 to 57.7) minutes per WSI depending on the image size, detecting up to 90 millions cell (Fig. 2c, Sup. Fig. 2e).

Although the model was trained on images from immune T cell panel only, DeepMIF accurately identified cell phenotype on NK/T cell panel images which have completely different markers and cell phenotypes (Fig. 2f-g). This shows DeepMIF pipeline is generalizable to multiple panels. In multiplexed staining technologies, color/intensity is the main discriminative feature of cell phenotypes that machine learning algorithms use to differentiate the phenotypes. Though, the M-IF images from different panels could have different colors, the DIs, which our DeepMIF uses as a primary cell detection and marker positivity classification, have only positive (brown) and negative (blue) irrespective of the panel. This makes DeepMIF generalizable across panels. DeepMIF also allows to exploring clinically relevant rare cell types such as CD8+FOXP3+ and CD4+CD8+ cells.

For the image viewer, the average reconstruction and rendering time was 0.07(range: 0.02 to 0.14) minutes for images size ranging from 48.5 million and

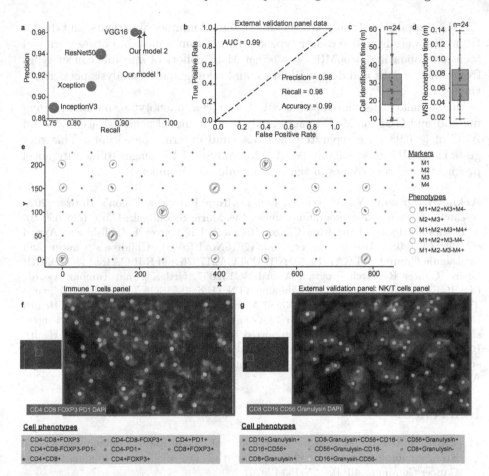

Fig. 2. DeepMIF performance evaluation. **a)** Precision and recall comparison of ImageNet pre-trained model and our models. size = number of parameters. **b)** Performance evaluation of **Our model 2** on external validation panel. **c–d)** Distribution of time taken for cell phenotype identification **(c)** and WSI reconstruction from tiles **(d)** for 24 slides. **e)** Simulated data to test co-expression analysis. **f–g)** Illustrative images for cell phenotype identification on immune T cells **(f)** and validation panel images **(g)**.

388.2 million pixels, respectively (Fig. 2d, Sup. Fig. 1b-c, Sup. Fig. 2f). In addition to the GUI, DeepMIF is packaged using Docker and it can run on high-performance clusters using Docker or Singularity. It is implemented in Python and the code is available at https://github.com/YemanBrhane/DeepMIF. Moreover, DeepMIF can be applied to any multichannel spatial transcriptomics data, such as image mass cytometry (IMC) and CODEX data. These technologies could have up to 40 markers/channels. After detecting cells positive for the markers on their respective channel, our algorithm could be used to identify cells expressing single or multiple markers.

The limitations of this study include the small number of patients, and the M-IF images were from one cancer type generated from same lab. Future work will focus on validating DeepMIF on a larger M-IF cohort of multiple cancer types from different labs and data modalities, and adding spatial analysis packages to the GUI.

In summary, we developed a DL based cell phenotype spatial mapping method and GUI for M-IF images analysis. Our model achieved accuracy and AUC of ≥ 0.98 on a separately held test and external panel data. This suggests DeepMIF could reliably be used to analyse M-IF images to identify novel prognostic cell phenotypes in the tumour microenvironment.

Acknowledgment. Y.H.B received funding from European Union's Horizon 2020 research and innovation programme under the Marie Sklodowska-Curie (No766030). Y.Y acknowledges funding from Cancer Research UK Career Establishment Award (C45982/A21808), Breast Cancer Now (2015NovPR638), Children's Cancer and Leukaemia Group (CCLGA201906), NIH U54 CA217376 and R01 CA185138, CDMRP Breast Cancer Research Program Award BC132057, CRUK Brain Tumour Awards (TARGET-GBM), European Commission ITN (H2020-MSCA-ITN-2019), Wellcome Trust (105104/Z/14/Z), and The Royal Marsden/ICR National Institute of Health Research Biomedical Research Centre. GG and RLR are supported by Gilead Fellowship Program (Ed. 2017). T.M is supported by the UK National Institute of Health Research University College London Hospital Biomedical Research Centre. A.U.A is supported by Cancer Research UK-UCL Centre Cancer Immuno-therapy Accelerator Award.

References

1. Tan, W.C.C., et al.: Overview of multiplex immunohistochemistry/immunofluorescence techniques in the era of cancer immunotherapy. Cancer Commun. **40**(4), 135–153 (2020)
2. Bortolomeazzi, M., et al.: A simpli (single-cell identification from multiplexed images) approach for spatially resolved tissue phenotypingat single-cell resolution. bioRxiv (2021)
3. Yu, W., et al.: A preliminary study of deep-learning algorithm for analyzing multiplex immunofluorescence biomarkers in body fluid cytology specimens. Acta Cytol. **65**(4), 348–353 (2021)
4. Hoyt, C.C.: Multiplex immunofluorescence and multispectral imaging: forming the basis of a clinical test platform for immuno-oncology. Front. Mol. Biosci. **8**, 442 (2021)
5. Lin, J.-R.: Highly multiplexed immunofluorescence imaging of human tissues and tumors using t-CyCIF and conventional optical microscopes. Elife **7**, e31657 (2018)
6. Pulsawatdi, A.V., et al.: A robust multiplex immunofluorescence and digital pathology workflow for the characterisation of the tumour immune microenvironment. Mol. Oncol. **14**(10), 2384–2402 (2020)
7. Hagos, Y.B., et al.: High inter-follicular spatial co-localization of CD8+ FOXP3+ with CD4+ CD8+ cells predicts favorable outcome in follicular lymphoma. Hematol. Oncol. (2022)
8. Dimitriou, N., Arandjelović, O., Caie, P.D.: Deep learning for whole slide image analysis: an overview. Front. Med. **6**, 264 (2019)

9. Hagos, Y.B., Narayanan, P.L., Akarca, A.U., Marafioti, T., Yuan, Y.: ConCORDe-net: cell count regularized convolutional neural network for cell detection in multiplex immunohistochemistry images. In: Shen, D., et al. (eds.) MICCAI 2019. LNCS, vol. 11764, pp. 667–675. Springer, Cham (2019). https://doi.org/10.1007/978-3-030-32239-7_74

10. Sanchez, K., et al.: Multiplex immunofluorescence to measure dynamic changes in tumor-infiltrating lymphocytes and pd-l1 in early-stage breast cancer. Breast Can. Res. **23**(1), 1–15 (2021)

11. Lee, C.-W., Ren, Y.J., Marella, M., Wang, M., Hartke, J., Couto, S.S.: Multiplex immunofluorescence staining and image analysis assay for diffuse large b cell lymphoma. J. Immunol. Methods **478**, 112714 (2020)

12. Maric, D., et al.: Whole-brain tissue mapping toolkit using large-scale highly multiplexed immunofluorescence imaging and deep neural networks. Nat. Commun. **12**(1), 1–12 (2021)

13. Ghahremani, P., et al.: Deep learning-inferred multiplex immunofluorescence for ihc image quantification. bioRxiv, Deepliif (2021)

14. Szegedy, C., Vanhoucke, V., Ioffe, S., Shlens, J., Wojna, Z.: Rethinking the inception architecture for computer vision. In: Proceedings of the IEEE Conference on Computer Vision and Pattern Recognition, pp. 2818–2826 (2016)

15. Simonyan, K., Zisserman, A.: Very deep convolutional networks for large-scale image recognition. arXiv preprint arXiv:1409.1556 (2014)

16. Shu, M.: Deep learning for image classification on very small datasets using transfer learning (2019)

17. Glorot, X., Bengio, Y.: Understanding the difficulty of training deep feedforward neural networks. In: Proceedings of the Thirteenth International Conference on Artificial Intelligence and Statistics, pp. 249–256. JMLR Workshop and Conference Proceedings (2010)

18. Kingma, D.P., Ba, J.: Adam: a method for stochastic optimization. arXiv preprint arXiv:1412.6980 92014)

Capturing Shape Information
with Multi-scale Topological Loss Terms
for 3D Reconstruction

Dominik J. E. Waibel[1,3]📙, Scott Atwell[2]📙, Matthias Meier[2]📙,
Carsten Marr[1]📙, and Bastian Rieck[1,2,3(✉)]📙

[1] Institute of AI for Health, Helmholtz Munich – German Research Centre
for Environmental Health, Neuherberg, Germany
bastian.rieck@helmholtz-muenchen.de
[2] Helmholtz Pioneer Campus, Helmholtz Munich – German Research Centre
for Environmental Health, Neuherberg, Germany
[3] Technical University of Munich, Munich, Germany

Abstract. Reconstructing 3D objects from 2D images is both challenging for our brains and machine learning algorithms. To support this spatial reasoning task, contextual information about the overall shape of an object is critical. However, such information is not captured by established loss terms (e.g. Dice loss). We propose to complement geometrical shape information by including multi-scale topological features, such as connected components, cycles, and voids, in the reconstruction loss. Our method uses cubical complexes to calculate topological features of 3D volume data and employs an optimal transport distance to guide the reconstruction process. This topology-aware loss is fully differentiable, computationally efficient, and can be added to any neural network. We demonstrate the utility of our loss by incorporating it into SHAPR, a model for predicting the 3D cell shape of individual cells based on 2D microscopy images. Using a hybrid loss that leverages both geometrical and topological information of single objects to assess their shape, we find that topological information substantially improves the quality of reconstructions, thus highlighting its ability to extract more relevant features from image datasets.

Keywords: Topological loss · Cubical complex · 3D shape prediction

1 Introduction

Segmentation and reconstruction are common tasks when dealing with imaging data. Especially in the biomedical domain, segmentation accuracy can have a substantial impact on complex downstream tasks, such as a patient's diagnosis and treatment. 3D segmentation is a complex task in itself, requiring the

---

Supplementary Information The online version contains supplementary material available at https://doi.org/10.1007/978-3-031-16440-8_15.

L. Wang et al. (Eds.): MICCAI 2022, LNCS 13434, pp. 150–159, 2022.
https://doi.org/10.1007/978-3-031-16440-8_15

assessment and labelling of each voxel in a volume, which, in turn, necessitates a high-level understanding of the object and its context. However, complexity rapidly increases when attempting to reconstruct a 3D object from a 2D projection since 3D images may often be difficult to obtain. This constitutes an inverse problem with intrinsically ambiguous solutions: each 2D image permits numerous 3D reconstructions, similar to how a shadow alone does not necessarily permit conclusions to be drawn about the corresponding shape. When addressed using machine learning, the solution of such inverse problems can be facilitated by imbuing a model with additional inductive biases about the structural properties of objects. Existing models supply such inductive biases to the reconstruction task mainly via geometry-based objective functions, thus learning a likelihood function $f \colon \mathcal{V} \to \mathbb{R}$, where $f(x)$ for $x \in \mathcal{V}$ denotes the likelihood that a voxel x of the input volume $\mathcal{V}$ is part of the ground truth shape [16]. Loss functions to learn f are evaluated on a per-voxel basis, assessing the differences between the original volume and the predicted volume in terms of overlapping labels. Commonly-used loss functions include binary cross entropy (BCE), Dice loss, and mean squared error (MSE). Despite their expressive power, these loss terms do not capture structural shape properties of the volumes.

Our Contributions. Topological features, i.e. features that characterise data primarily in terms of *connectivity*, have recently started to emerge as a powerful paradigm for complementing existing machine learning methods [11]. They are capable of capturing shape information of objects at multiple scales and along multiple dimensions. In this paper, we leverage such features and integrate them into a novel differentiable 'topology-aware' loss term $\mathcal{L}_T$ that can be used to regularise the shape reconstruction process. Our loss term handles arbitrary shapes, can be computed efficiently, and may be integrated into general deep learning models. We demonstrate the utility of $\mathcal{L}_T$ by combining it with SHAPR [27], a framework for predicting individual cell shapes from 2D microscopy images. The new hybrid variant of SHAPR, making use of both geometry-based and topology-based objective functions, results in improved reconstruction performance along multiple metrics.

2 Related Work

Several deep learning approaches for predicting 3D shapes of single objects from 2D information already exist; we aim to give a brief overview. Previous work includes predicting natural objects such as air planes, cars, and furniture from photographs, creating either meshes [10,28], voxel volumes [3], or point clouds [8]. A challenging biomedical task, due to the occurrence of imaging noise, is tackled by Waibel et al. [27], whose SHAPR model predicts the shape and morphology of individual mammalian cells from 2D microscopy images. Given the multi-scale nature of microscopy images, SHAPR is an ideal use case to analyse the impact of employing additional topology-based loss terms for these reconstruction tasks.

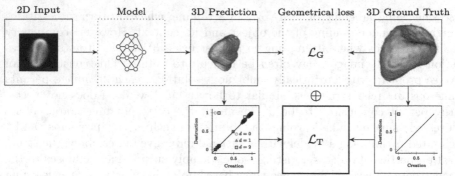

Fig. 1. Given a predicted object and a 3D ground truth object, we calculate topological features using cubical persistent homology, obtaining a set of persistence diagrams. Each point in a persistence diagram denotes the creation and destruction of a d-dimensional topological feature of the given object. We compare these diagrams using $\mathcal{L}_\mathrm{T}$, our novel topology-based loss, combining it with geometrical loss terms such as binary cross entropy (BCE). Dotted components can be swapped out.

Such loss terms constitute a facet of the emerging field of *topological machine learning* and *persistent homology*, its flagship algorithm (see Sect. 3.1 for an introduction). Previous studies have shown great promise in using topological losses for image segmentation tasks or their evaluation [23]. In contrast to our loss, existing work relies on prior knowledge about 'expected' topological features [4], or enforces a pre-defined set of topological features based on comparing segmentations [13,14].

3   Our Method: A Topology-Aware Loss

We propose a topology-aware loss term based on concepts from topological machine learning and optimal transport. The loss term works on the level of individual volumes, leveraging a valid metric between topological descriptors, while remaining efficiently computable. Owing to its generic nature, the loss can be easily integrated into existing architectures; see Fig. 1 for an overview.

3.1   Assessing the Topology of Volumes

Given a volume $\mathcal{V}$, i.e. a d-dimensional tensor of shape $n_1 \times n_2 \times \cdots \times n_d$, we represent it as a *cubical complex* C. A cubical complex contains individual voxels of $\mathcal{V}$ as vertices •, along with connectivity information about their neighbourhoods via edges ⟶, squares ☐, and their higher-dimensional counterparts.[1] Cubical complexes provide a fundamental way to represent volume data

---

[1] Expert readers may recognise that cubical complexes are related to meshes and simplicial complexes but use squares instead of triangles as their building blocks.

and have proven their utility in previous work [22,26]. Topological features of different dimensions are well-studied, comprising connected components (0D), cycles (1D), and voids (2D), for instance. The number of k-dimensional topological features is also referred to as the kth *Betti number* β_k of C. While previous work has shown the efficacy of employing Betti numbers as a topological prior for image segmentation tasks [4,13], the reconstruction tasks we are considering in this paper require a multi-scale perspective that cannot be provided by Betti numbers, which are mere feature counts. We therefore make use of *persistent homology*, a technique for calculating multi-scale topological features [7]. This technique is particularly appropriate in our setting: our model essentially learns a likelihood function $f\colon \mathcal{V} \to \mathbb{R}$. To each voxel $x \in \mathcal{V}$, the function f assigns the likelihood of x being part of an object's shape. For a likelihood threshold $\tau \in \mathbb{R}$, we obtain a cubical complex $C^{(\tau)} := \{x \in \mathcal{V} \mid f(x) \geq \tau\}$ and, consequently, a different set of topological features. Since volumes are finite, their topology only changes at a finite number of thresholds $\tau_1 \geq \ldots \geq \tau_m$, and we obtain a sequence of nested cubical complexes $\emptyset \subseteq C^{(\tau_1)} \subseteq C^{(\tau_2)} \subseteq \cdots \subseteq C^{(\tau_m)} = \mathcal{V}$, known as a *superlevel set filtration*. Persistent homology tracks topological features across all complexes in this filtration, representing each feature as a tuple (τ_i, τ_j), with $\tau_i \geq \tau_j$, indicating the cubical complex in which a feature was being 'created' and 'destroyed,' respectively. The tuples of k-dimensional features, with $0 \leq k \leq d$, are stored in the kth *persistence diagram* $\mathcal{D}_f^{(k)}$ of the data set.[2] Persistence diagrams thus form a multi-scale shape descriptor of all topological features of a dataset. Despite the apparent complexity of filtrations, persistent homology of cubical complexes can be calculated efficiently in practice [26].

Structure of Persistence Diagrams. Persistent homology provides information beyond Betti numbers: instead of enforcing a choice of threshold τ for the likelihood function, which would result in a fixed set of Betti numbers, persistence diagrams encode all thresholds at the same time, thus capturing additional geometrical details about data. Given a tuple (τ_i, τ_j) in a persistence diagram, its *persistence* is defined as $\mathrm{pers}\,(\tau_i, \tau_j) := |\tau_j - \tau_i|$. Persistence indicates the 'scale' over which a topological feature occurs, with large values typically assumed to correspond to more stable features. The sum of all persistence values is known as the *degree-p total persistence*, i.e. $\mathrm{Pers}_p(\mathcal{D}_f) := \sum_{(\tau_i, \tau_j) \in \mathcal{D}_f} |\mathrm{pers}(\tau_i, \tau_j)^p|$. It constitutes a stable summary statistic of topological activity [6].

Comparing Persistence Diagrams. Persistence diagrams can be endowed with a metric by using optimal transport. Given two diagrams $\mathcal{D}$ and $\mathcal{D}'$ containing features of the same dimensionality, their pth *Wasserstein distance* is defined as

$$W_p\,(\mathcal{D}, \mathcal{D}') := \left(\inf_{\eta\colon \mathcal{D} \to \mathcal{D}'} \sum_{x \in \mathcal{D}} \|x - \eta(x)\|_\infty^p \right)^{\frac{1}{p}}, \tag{1}$$

---

[2] We use the subscript f to indicate the corresponding likelihood function; we will drop this for notational convenience when discussing general properties.

where $\eta(\cdot)$ denotes a bijection. Since $\mathcal{D}$ and $\mathcal{D}'$ generally have different cardinalities, we consider them to contain an infinite number of points of the form (τ, τ), i.e. tuples of zero persistence. A suitable $\eta(\cdot)$ can thus always be found. Solving Eq. (1) is practically feasible using modern optimal transport algorithms [9].

Stability. A core property of persistence diagrams is their stability to noise. While different notions of stability exist for persistent homology [6], a recent theorem [25] states that the Wasserstein distance between persistence diagrams of functions $f, f' \colon \mathcal{V} \to \mathbb{R}$ is bounded by their p-norm, i.e.

$$W_p\left(\mathcal{D}_f^{(k)}, \mathcal{D}_{f'}^{(k)}\right) \le C \, \|f - f'\|_p \text{ for } 0 \le k \le d, \tag{2}$$

with $C \in \mathbb{R}_{>0}$ being a constant that depends on the dimensionality of $\mathcal{V}$. Equation (2) implies that gradients obtained from the Wasserstein distance and other topology-based summaries will remain bounded; we will also use it to accelerate topological feature calculations in practice.

Differentiability. Despite the discrete nature of topological features, persistent homology permits the calculation of gradients with respect to parameters of the likelihood function f, thus enabling the use of automatic differentiation schemes [12,17,20]. A seminal work by Carrière et al. [2] proved that optimisation algorithms converge for a wide class of persistence-based functions, thus opening the door towards general topology-based optimisation schemes.

3.2 Loss Term Construction

Given a true likelihood function f and a predicted likelihood function f', our novel generic topology-aware loss term takes the form

$$\mathcal{L}_\mathrm{T}\left(f, f', p\right) := \sum_{i=0}^{d} W_p\left(\mathcal{D}_f^{(i)}, \mathcal{D}_{f'}^{(i)}\right) + \mathrm{Pers}\left(\mathcal{D}_{f'}^{(i)}\right). \tag{3}$$

The first part of Eq. (3) incentivises the model to reduce the distance between f and f' with respect to their topological shape information. The second part incentivises the model to reduce overall topological activity, thus decreasing the noise in the reconstruction. This can be considered as the topological equivalent of reducing the *total variation* of a function [21]. Given a task-specific geometrical loss term $\mathcal{L}_\mathrm{G}$,[3] such as a Dice loss, we obtain a combined loss term as $\mathcal{L} := \mathcal{L}_\mathrm{G} + \lambda \mathcal{L}_\mathrm{T}$, where $\lambda \in \mathbb{R}_{>0}$ controls the impact of the topology-based part. We will use $p = 2$ since Eq. (2) relates $\mathcal{L}_\mathrm{T}$ to the Euclidean distance in this case.

Calculations in Practice. To speed up the calculation of our loss term, we utilise the stability theorem of persistent homology and downsample each volume to $M \times M \times M$ voxels using trilinear interpolation. We provide a theoretical and empirical analysis of the errors introduced by downsampling in the Supplementary Materials. In our experiments, we set $M = 16$, which is sufficiently small to have no negative impact on computational performance while at the same time resulting in empirical errors ≤ 0.1 (measured using Eq. (2) for $p = 2$).

---

[3] We dropped all hyperparameters of the loss term for notational clarity.

4   Experiments

We provide a brief overview of SHAPR before discussing the experimental setup, datasets, and results. SHAPR is a deep learning method to predict 3D shapes of single cells from 2D microscopy images [27]. Given a 2D fluorescent image of a single cell and a corresponding segmentation mask, SHAPR predicts the 3D shape of this cell. The authors suggest to train SHAPR with a combination of Dice and BCE loss, with an additional adversarial training step to improve the predictions of the model. We re-implemented SHAPR using PyTorch [19] to ensure fair comparisons and the seamless integration of our novel loss function $\mathcal{L}_T$, employing 'Weights & Biases' for tracking experiments [1]. Our code and reports are publicly available.[4]

Data. For our experiments, we use the two datasets published with the original SHAPR manuscript [27]. The first dataset comprises 825 red blood cells, imaged in 3D with a confocal microscope [24]. Each cell is assigned to one of nine pre-defined classes: sphero-, stomato-, disco-, echino-, kerato-, knizo-, and acantho-cytes, as well as cell clusters and multilobates. The second dataset contains 887 nuclei of human-induced pluripotent stem cells (iPSCs), counterstained and imaged in 3D with a confocal microscope. Cells were manually segmented to create ground truth objects. Both datasets include 3D volumes of size $64 \times 64 \times 64$, 2D segmentation masks of size 64×64, and fluorescent images of size 64×64.

4.1   Training and Evaluation

We trained our implementation of SHAPR for a maximum of 100 epochs, using early stopping with a patience of 15 epochs, based on the validation loss. For each run, we trained five SHAPR models in a round-robin fashion, partitioning the dataset into five folds with a 60%/20%/20% train/validation/test split, making sure that each 2D input image appears once in the test set. To compare the performance of SHAPR with and without $\mathcal{L}_T$, we used the same hyperparameters for all experiments (initial learning rate of 1×10^{-3}, $\beta_1 = 0.9$, and $\beta_2 = 0.999$ for the ADAM optimiser). We optimised $\lambda \in \{1 \times 10^{-3}, 1 \times 10^{-2}, \ldots, 1 \times 10^2\}$, the regularisation strength parameter for $\mathcal{L}_T$, on an independent dataset, resulting in $\lambda = 0.1$ for all experiments. We also found that evaluating Eq. (3) for each dimension individually leads to superior performance; we thus only calculate Eq. (3) for $i = 2$. Finally, for the training phase, we augmented the data with random horizontal or vertical flipping and 90° rotations with a 33% chance for each augmentation to be applied for a sample. The goal of these augmentations is to increase data variability and prevent overfitting.

Following Waibel et al. [27], we evaluated the performance of SHAPR by calculating (i) the *intersection over union* (IoU) error, (ii) the relative volume error, (iii) the relative surface area error, and (iv) the relative surface roughness error

---

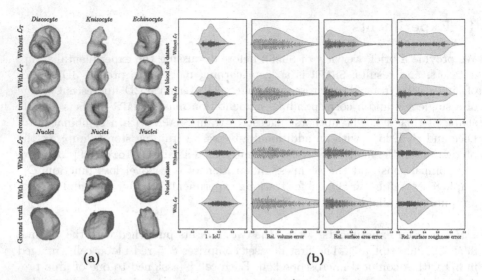

(a)   (b)

Fig. 2. (a) Examples of predictions without (top row) and with (middle row) $\mathcal{L}_T$, our topological loss term. The third row shows ground truth images. (b) $\mathcal{L}_T$ improves predictions in relevant metrics, such as the IoU error, the relative volume error, relative surface area error, and relative surface roughness error.

with respect to the ground truth data, applying Otsu's method [18] for thresholding predicted shapes. We calculate the volume by counting non-zero voxels, the surface area as all voxels on the surface of an object, and the surface roughness as the difference between the surface area of the object and the surface area of the same object after smoothing it with a 3D Gaussian [27].

4.2   Results

To evaluate the benefits of our topology-aware loss, we perform the same experiment twice: first, using a joint BCE and Dice loss [27], followed by adding $\lambda\mathcal{L}_T$. Without $\mathcal{L}_T$, we achieve results comparable to the original publication (IoU, red blood cell data: $0.63 \pm 0.12\%$; IoU, nuclei data: $0.46 \pm 0.16\%$); minor deviations arise from stochasticity and implementation differences between PyTorch and Tensorflow. We observe superior performance in the majority of metrics for both datasets when adding $\mathcal{L}_T$ to the model (see Fig. 2 and Table 1); the performance gains by $\mathcal{L}_T$ are statistically significant in all but one case. Notably, we find that $\mathcal{L}_T$ increases SHAPR's predictive performance unevenly across the classes of the red blood cell dataset (see Fig. 2a). For spherocytes (round cells), only small changes in IoU error, relative volume error, relative surface area error, and relative surface roughness error (7% decrease, 2% decrease, and 3% decrease, respectively) occur, whereas for echinocytes (cells with a spiky surface), we obtain a 27% decrease in IoU error and 7% decrease in relative volume error. Finally, for discocytes (bi-concave cells) and stomatocytes, we obtain a 2% decrease in IoU

Table 1. Median, mean (μ) and standard deviation (σ) of several relative error measures for two datasets (lower values are better; winner shown in **bold**). The $\mathcal{L}_T$ column indicates whether our new loss term was active. We also show the p-value of a paired Wilcoxon signed-rank test between error distributions.

Relative error	$\mathcal{L}_T$	Red blood cell ($n = 825$) Median	$\mu \pm \sigma$	p	Nuclei ($n = 887$) Median	$\mu \pm \sigma$	p
$1 - \mathrm{IoU}$	✗	0.48	0.49 ± 0.09	1.1×10^{-19}	0.62	0.62 ± 0.11	0.5
	✓	**0.47**	**0.47 ± 0.10**		**0.61**	**0.61 ± 0.11**	
Volume	✗	0.31	0.35 ± 0.31	1.2×10^{-47}	0.34	0.48 ± 0.47	4.6×10^{-14}
	✓	**0.26**	**0.29 ± 0.27**		**0.32**	**0.43 ± 0.42**	
Surface area	✗	0.20	0.24 ± 0.20	39.5×10^{-13}	0.21	0.27 ± 0.25	1.7×10^{-8}
	✓	**0.14**	**0.18 ± 0.16**		**0.18**	**0.25 ± 0.24**	
Surface roughness	✗	0.35	0.36 ± 0.24	9.1×10^{-4}	**0.17**	**0.18 ± 0.12**	1.5×10^{-6}
	✓	**0.24**	**0.29 ± 0.22**		0.18	0.19 ± 0.13	

error, a 3% decrease in volume error, an 11% decrease in surface area error, and a 25% decrease in surface roughness error upon adding $\mathcal{L}_T$.

5 Discussion

We propose a novel topology-aware loss term $\mathcal{L}_T$ that can be integrated into existing deep learning models. Our loss term is not restricted to specific types of shapes and may be applied to reconstruction and segmentation tasks. We demonstrate its efficacy in the reconstruction of 3D shapes from 2D microscopy images, where the results of SHAPR are statistically significantly improved in relevant metrics whenever $\mathcal{L}_T$ is jointly optimised together with geometrical loss terms. Notably, $\mathcal{L}_T$ does not optimise classical segmentation/reconstruction metrics, serving instead as an inductive bias for incorporating multi-scale information on topological features. $\mathcal{L}_T$ is computationally efficient and can be adapted to different scenarios by incorporating topological features of a specific dimension. Since our experiments indicate that the calculation of Eq. (3) for a single dimension is sufficient to achieve improved reconstruction results in practice, we will leverage topological duality/symmetry theorems [5] in future work to improve computational efficiency and obtain smaller cubical complexes.

Our analysis of predictive performance across classes of the red blood cell dataset (see Table 1) leads to the assumption that the topological loss term shows the largest reconstruction performance increases on shapes that have complex morphological features, such as echinocytes or bi-concavely shaped cells (discocytes and stomatocytes). This implies that future extensions of the method should incorporate additional geometrical descriptors into the filtration calculation, making use of recent advances in capturing the topology of multivariate shape descriptors [15].

Acknowledgements. We thank Lorenz Lamm, Melanie Schulz, Kalyan Varma Nadimpalli, and Sophia Wagner for their valuable feedback to this manuscript. The authors also are indebted to Teresa Heiss for discussions on the topological changes induced by downsampling volume data.

Author contributions. DW and BR implemented code and conducted experiments. DW, BR, and CM wrote the manuscript. DW created figures and BR the main portrayal of results. SA and MM provided the 3D nuclei dataset. BR supervised the study. All authors have read and approved the manuscript.

Funding Information. Carsten Marr received funding from the European Research Council (ERC) under the European Union's Horizon 2020 Research and Innovation Programme (Grant Agreement 866411).

References

1. Biewald, L.: Experiment tracking with Weights and Biases (2020). https://www.wandb.com/
2. Carrière, M., Chazal, F., Glisse, M., Ike, Y., Kannan, H., Umeda, Y.: Optimizing persistent homology based functions. In: Proceedings of the 38th International Conference on Machine Learning, pp. 1294–1303 (2021)
3. Choy, C.B., Xu, D., Gwak, J.Y., Chen, K., Savarese, S.: 3D-R2N2: a unified approach for single and multi-view 3D object reconstruction. In: Leibe, B., Matas, J., Sebe, N., Welling, M. (eds.) ECCV 2016. LNCS, vol. 9912, pp. 628–644. Springer, Cham (2016). https://doi.org/10.1007/978-3-319-46484-8_38
4. Clough, J., Byrne, N., Oksuz, I., Zimmer, V.A., Schnabel, J.A., King, A.: A topological loss function for deep-learning based image segmentation using persistent homology. IEEE Trans. Pattern Anal. Mach. Intell. (2020)
5. Cohen-Steiner, D., Edelsbrunner, H., Harer, J.: Extending persistence using Poincaré and Lefschetz duality. Found. Comput. Math. **9**(1), 79–103 (2009)
6. Cohen-Steiner, D., Edelsbrunner, H., Harer, J., Mileyko, Y.: Lipschitz functions have L_p-stable persistence. Found. Comput. Math. **10**(2), 127–139 (2010)
7. Edelsbrunner, H., Letscher, D., Zomorodian, A.J.: Topological persistence and simplification. Discrete Comput. Geom. **28**(4), 511–533 (2002)
8. Fan, H., Su, H., Guibas, L.J.: A point set generation network for 3D object reconstruction from a single image. In: Proceedings of the IEEE Conference on Computer Vision and Pattern Recognition (CVPR) (2017)
9. Flamary, R., et al.: POT: python optimal transport. J. Mach. Learn. Res. **22**(78), 1–8 (2021)
10. Gkioxari, G., Malik, J., Johnson, J.: Mesh R-CNN. In: Proceedings of the IEEE/CVF International Conference on Computer Vision (ICCV) (2019)
11. Hensel, F., Moor, M., Rieck, B.: A survey of topological machine learning methods. Front. Artif. Intell. **4**, 681108 (2021)
12. Hofer, C.D., Graf, F., Rieck, B., Niethammer, M., Kwitt, R.: Graph filtration learning. In: Proceedings of the 37th International Conference on Machine Learning (ICML), pp. 4314–4323 (2020)
13. Hu, X., Li, F., Samaras, D., Chen, C.: Topology-preserving deep image segmentation. In: Advances in Neural Information Processing Systems, vol. 32 (2019)

14. Hu, X., Wang, Y., Fuxin, L., Samaras, D., Chen, C.: Topology-aware segmentation using discrete Morse theory. In: International Conference on Learning Representations (2021)

15. Lesnick, M., Wright, M.: Interactive visualization of 2-D persistence modules arXiv:1512.00180 (2015)

16. Minaee, S., Boykov, Y., Porikli, F., Plaza, A., Kehtarnavaz, N., Terzopoulos, D.: Image segmentation using deep learning: A survey. IEEE Trans. Pattern Anal. Mach. Intell. **44**(7), 3523–3542 (2021)

17. Moor, M., Horn, M., Rieck, B., Borgwardt, K.: Topological autoencoders. In: Proceedings of the 37th International Conference on Machine Learning (ICML), pp. 7045–7054 (2020)

18. Otsu, N.: A threshold selection method from gray-level histograms. IEEE Trans. Syst. Man Cybern. **9**(1), 62–66 (1979)

19. Paszke, A., et al.: `PyTorch`: an imperative style, high-performance deep learning library. In: Advances in Neural Information Processing Systems, vol. 32, pp. 8024–8035 (2019)

20. Poulenard, A., Skraba, P., Ovsjanikov, M.: Topological function optimization for continuous shape matching. Comput. Graphics Forum **37**(5), 13–25 (2018)

21. Rieck, B., Leitte, H.: Exploring and comparing clusterings of multivariate data sets using persistent homology. Comput. Graphics Forum **35**(3), 81–90 (2016)

22. Rieck, B., Yates, T., Bock, C., Borgwardt, K., Wolf, G., Turk-Browne, N., Krishnaswamy, S.: Uncovering the topology of time-varying fMRI data using cubical persistence. In: Advances in Neural Information Processing Systems, vol. 33, pp. 6900–6912 (2020)

23. Shit, S., et al.: `clDice` - a novel topology-preserving loss function for tubular structure segmentation. In: Proceedings of the IEEE/CVF Conference on Computer Vision and Pattern Recognition (CVPR), pp. 16560–16569 (2021)

24. Simionato, G., et al.: Red blood cell phenotyping from 3D confocal images using artificial neural networks. PLoS Comput. Biol. **17**(5), 1–17 (2021)

25. Skraba, P., Turner, K.: Wasserstein stability for persistence diagrams. arXiv:2006.16824 (2020)

26. Wagner, H., Chen, C., Vuçini, E.: Efficient computation of persistent homology for cubical data. In: Peikert, R., Hauser, H., Carr, H., Fuchs, R. (eds.) Topological Methods in Data Analysis and Visualization II: Theory, Algorithms, and Applications, pp. 91–106. Springer, Heidelberg (2012). https://doi.org/10.1007/978-3-642-23175-9_7

27. Waibel, D.J.E., Kiermeyer, N., Atwell, S., Sadafi, A., Meier, M., Marr, C.: SHAPR - an AI approach to predict 3D cell shapes from 2D microscopic images bioRxiv:2021.09.29.462353 (2021)

28. Wang, N., Zhang, Y., Li, Z., Fu, Y., Liu, W., Jiang, Y.-G.: Pixel2Mesh: generating 3D mesh models from single RGB images. In: Ferrari, V., Hebert, M., Sminchisescu, C., Weiss, Y. (eds.) ECCV 2018. LNCS, vol. 11215, pp. 55–71. Springer, Cham (2018). https://doi.org/10.1007/978-3-030-01252-6_4

Positron Emission Tomography

MCP-Net: Inter-frame Motion Correction with Patlak Regularization for Whole-body Dynamic PET

Xueqi Guo, Bo Zhou, Xiongchao Chen, Chi Liu, and Nicha C. Dvornek$^{(\boxtimes)}$

Yale University, New Haven, CT 06511, USA
{xueqi.guo,bo.zhou,xiongchao.chen,chi.liu,nicha.dvornek}@yale.edu

Abstract. Inter-frame patient motion introduces spatial misalignment and degrades parametric imaging in whole-body dynamic positron emission tomography (PET). Most current deep learning inter-frame motion correction works consider only the image registration problem, ignoring tracer kinetics. We propose an inter-frame Motion Correction framework with Patlak regularization (MCP-Net) to directly optimize the Patlak fitting error and further improve model performance. The MCP-Net contains three modules: a motion estimation module consisting of a multiple-frame 3-D U-Net with a convolutional long short-term memory layer combined at the bottleneck; an image warping module that performs spatial transformation; and an analytical Patlak module that estimates Patlak fitting with the motion-corrected frames and the individual input function. A Patlak loss penalization term using mean squared percentage fitting error is introduced to the loss function in addition to image similarity measurement and displacement gradient loss. Following motion correction, the parametric images were generated by standard Patlak analysis. Compared with both traditional and deep learning benchmarks, our network further corrected the residual spatial mismatch in the dynamic frames, improved the spatial alignment of Patlak K_i/V_b images, and reduced normalized fitting error. With the utilization of tracer dynamics and enhanced network performance, MCP-Net has the potential for further improving the quantitative accuracy of dynamic PET. Our code is released at https://github.com/gxq1998/MCP-Net.

Keywords: Inter-frame motion correction · Parametric imaging · Tracer kinetics regularization · Whole-body dynamic PET

1 Introduction

Whole-body dynamic positron emission tomography (PET) using 2-deoxy-2-[^{18}F]fluoro-D-glucose (FDG) has emerged as a more accurate glycolytic metabolism measurement in clinical and research protocols [7] than static PET due to

Supplementary Information The online version contains supplementary material available at https://doi.org/10.1007/978-3-031-16440-8_16.

the time dependency of radiotracer uptake [21]. In continuous-bed-motion mode (CBM) [17], an image sequence is typically collected for 90 min starting at the tracer injection and then fitted with voxel-wise kinetic modeling for parametric imaging [22]. For FDG that typically follows irreversible 2-tissue compartmental model, the Patlak plot [18] is a simplified linear model for parametric estimation. The Patlak slope K_i [18], the net uptake rate constant, has been shown to improve oncological lesion identification with higher tumor-to-background and contrast-to-noise ratio [8].

However, patient motion is unpreventable during the long scanning period, which has a harmful impact on parametric imaging [14]. The inter-frame motion caused by body movement and the changes in the long-term cardiac and respiratory motion patterns lead to increased parameter estimation errors. In the whole-body scope, subject motion is non-rigid, complicated, and unpredictable, and the simultaneous presence of high uptake and low uptake organs makes motion correction substantially harder. The significant cross-frame tracer distribution variation also complicates the motion estimation and correction.

Recent breakthroughs in deep learning based image registration have achieved superior performance and computational efficiency over conventional non-rigid registration methods. Spatial-temporal network structures have been applied in motion-related dynamic image sequence registration [10,13,19,24], outperforming single image-pair networks [1,23]. Although multiple-frame analysis has the potential of improving dynamic PET motion correction, most methods still only consider image registration without utilizing tracer kinetics, which could lead to residual misalignment especially for images with low uptake [11]. While the incorporation of kinetic modeling into the registration has been proposed in dynamic contrast-enhanced magnetic resonance imaging [2,15], dynamic PET typically involves more complex tracer dynamics. Pharmacokinetics has been utilized in PET reconstruction [5] and brain registration [11], but such implementation has not been introduced in either deep learning or the whole-body scope.

In this work, we propose an inter-frame Motion Correction framework with Patlak regularization (MCP-Net) for whole-body dynamic PET. An analytical Patlak fitting module is integrated into the framework with Patlak loss penalization introduced to the loss function. We evaluated the proposed model using a simulated dataset and a 9-fold cross-validation on an internal real-patient dataset and compared with traditional and deep learning benchmarks.

2 Methods

2.1 Dataset and Pre-processing

Five healthy and 22 cancer subjects (27 in total) were enrolled at Yale PET Center, with obtained informed consent and Institutional Review Board approval. Each subject underwent a 90-min dynamic multi-frame whole-body PET scan using CBM protocol on a Siemens Biograph mCT with FDG bolus injection [16], obtaining 19 consecutive reconstructed whole-body frames (4×2 min and

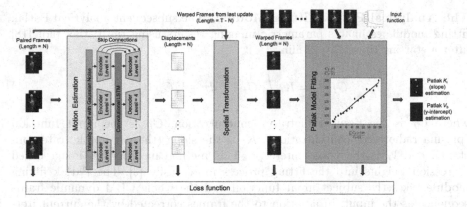

Fig. 1. The overall structure of the proposed motion correction framework MCP-Net.

15 × 5 min) as well as the individual input function. The details of the image acquisition are in Supplementary Fig. S1. In the 22 cancer patients, 57 hypermetabolic regions of interest (ROIs) were selected by a nuclear medicine physician for additional evaluation. Dynamic frames were calibrated to have units of standardized uptake values (SUV). Due to GPU RAM limitation, the input frames were downsampled by a factor of 4 and zero-padded to the same resolution of 128 × 128 × 256 for all the deep learning approaches. The displacements were upsampled back to the original resolution using a spline interpolation (order = 3) before warping the original frames.

2.2   Proposed Network

The MCP-Net consists of a spatial-temporal motion estimation network, a spatial transformation module, and an analytical Patlak fitting module (see Fig. 1).

Spatial-temporal Motion Estimation Network. The dual-channel motion estimation input is a moving frame sequence, each concatenated with the reference frame. To decrease the driving force of high-uptake voxels while also minimize saturation in the local normalized cross-correlation (NCC) loss computation, an intensity cutoff layer is first applied with threshold of SUV = 2.5 and Gaussian noise ($\sigma = 0.01$) added to thresholded voxels [10]. To handle multiple-frame spatial-temporal analysis, the motion estimation module is a concatenated 3-D U-Net [6] with shared weights and a convolutional long short-term memory [20] layer integrated at the bottleneck [10]. This enables information extraction across both adjacent and non-adjacent frames, especially effective for long-duration motion and tracer changes. The number of both encoding and decoding U-Net levels is set to 4, with input sequence length $N = 5$. With the voxel-wise displacement field estimations, the spatial transformation layer warps the input frames and outputs motion compensated frames.

The Analytical Patlak Fitting Module. The subsequent analytical Patlak fitting module estimates parametric imaging results using the Patlak plot [18] after a starting time t* = 20 min,

$$C_T(t) = K_i \int_0^t C_P(\tau)\,d\tau + V_b C_P(t), \tag{1}$$

where C_T is the tissue radiotracer concentration, C_P is the input function (plasma radiotracer concentration), K_i is the slope (the net uptake rate constant), and V_b is the y-axis intercept. This method incorporates image-based regression weights into the fitting process more easily [3]. The Patlak fitting module takes the subject input function and the whole CBM dynamic frame sequence as the input; in addition to the frames corrected by the current iteration, the remaining frames are corrected by the previous update. With the Patlak K_i and V_b estimations, the tracer kinetics information and parametric regularization are introduced to the framework.

The Patlak Penalization in Loss Function. The Patlak penalization by mean squared percentage fitting error (MSPE) is incorporated to the loss function in addition to an image similarity measurement by local NCC and a displacement gradient loss by one-sided forward difference [1],

$$\mathcal{L} = \sum_{i=1}^{N}\left[-NCC\left(F_R, \widehat{F_{Mi}}\right) + \lambda|\triangledown\phi_i|^2\right] + \sum_{j=1}^{T}\alpha MSPE\left(\widehat{F_{Mj}}, \widehat{F_{MjP}}\right), \tag{2}$$

where N is the motion estimation input sequence length, F_R is the reference frame, $\widehat{F_{Mi}}$ is the ith warped frame, λ is the gradient loss regularization factor, ϕ_i is the estimated displacement field for frame i, T is the total number of frames after t*, α is the Patlak penalization factor, $\widehat{F_{Mj}}$ is the jth Patlak input dynamic frame, and $\widehat{F_{MjP}}$ is the jth Patlak fitted dynamic frame.

2.3   Training Details and Baseline Comparison

All 5-min frames were motion corrected with Frame 12 (in the middle of the 5-min scans) as the fixed frame. Five successive frames from the same subject are sent into the motion estimation network as the input sequence, with the remaining 10 frames from the last update and individual input function sent to the Patlak estimation module. Note that the motion estimation inputs are all the original frames without correction, while the remaining frames for Patlak fitting are updated every 50 epochs to provide the latest Patlak error estimation by the currently-trained network. The update cycle is determined from the trade-off between time consumption and network convergence while also avoiding the instability in the early stage of training. A preliminary ablation study of the updating strategy was conducted on a random fold of cross-validation and summarized in Supplementary Table S1.

We included a traditional entropy-based non-rigid registration method implemented by BioImage Suite [9,12] (BIS), a single-pair deep learning registration model Voxelmorph [1] (VXM), and a multiple-frame analysis model [10] (B-convLSTM) as the benchmarks for performance comparison under a 9-fold subject-wise cross-validation. Deep learning approaches were developed using Keras (TensorFlow backend) on an NVIDIA Quadro RTX 8000 GPU and trained using Adam optimizer (learning rate $= 10^{-4}$). The stopping epoch was determined based on the observed minimal validation loss, which was 750 for VXM and 500 for B-convLSTM and MCP-Net. The regularization factor λ of both VXM and B-convLSTM was fixed as 1 [1,10]. The hyperparameters of MCP-Net were set at $\lambda = 0.1$ and $\alpha = 0.1$. A preliminary sensitivity test of λ and α was implemented with results in Supplementary Tables S2 and S3.

2.4   Evaluation Metrics

To directly evaluate motion estimation, we ran a motion simulation test by applying patient-derived motion vector predictions to the selected "motion-free" frames of another subject, since ground-truth motion vectors are not available in real-patient datasets. Specifically, we selected 3 subjects with insignificant motion and treated the frames after motion correction by another well-trained deep learning model VXM-multiframe [10] as motion-free. To achieve realistic simulated motion, we selected another 3 subjects with visually significant motion and used the motion fields also estimated by VXM-multiframe as the ground-truth such that the model for motion generation is independent of the tested models. We calculated the average absolute prediction error in each frame,

$$|\Delta\phi| = \frac{1}{V} \sum_{m=1}^{V} |\phi_{x_m} - \hat{\phi_{x_m}}| + |\phi_{y_m} - \hat{\phi_{y_m}}| + |\phi_{z_m} - \hat{\phi_{z_m}}|, \qquad (3)$$

where V is the total number of voxels per frame, $(\phi_{x_m}, \phi_{y_m}, \phi_{z_m})$ is the ground-truth motion and $(\hat{\phi_{x_m}}, \hat{\phi_{y_m}}, \hat{\phi_{z_m}})$ is the predicted motion. The voxel-wise motion prediction error maps were also visualized.

To assess dynamic frame similarity in real-patient results, we calculated the structural similarity index between the reference frame and the average of all warped moving frames (Avg-to-ref SSIM) in each subject. The K_i and V_b images were generated by the Patlak analysis at the original image resolution. The dynamic frames and K_i/V_b images were overlaid to visualize motion-related mismatch, as both K_i and V_b are motion-sensitive and higher alignment indicates better registration. Whole-body K_i/V_b normalized mutual information (NMI) was computed to measure alignment. To assess Patlak fitting, the normalized weighted mean fitting errors (NFE) were formulated as

$$NFE = \frac{\sum\limits_{k=1}^{T} w_k \left(\widehat{C_T}(t_k) - C_T(t_k)\right)^2}{(T-2) \sum\limits_{k=1}^{T} \left(\frac{w_k C_T(t_k)}{T}\right)^2}, \qquad (4)$$

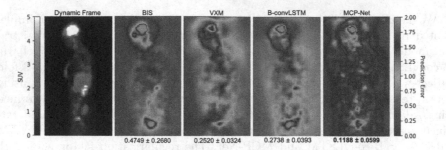

Fig. 2. Sample absolute error maps of predicted motion fields. The subject-wise mean absolute prediction errors (in mm, mean ± standard deviation) are annotated.

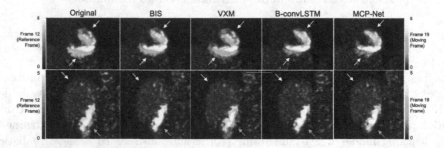

Fig. 3. Overlaid dynamic frames showing inter-frame motion and the correction effects in heart (upper), liver (lower, white arrows), and kidney (lower, cyan arrows). (Color figure online)

where w_k is the fitting weight of time activity curve after decay correction [4], $\widehat{C_T}(t_k)$ is the fitted tissue tracer concentration, $C_T(t_k)$ is the acquired tissue tracer concentration, t_k is the middle acquisition time of the kth frame, and T is the total number of frames after t*. The NFE maps were visualized voxel-wise and the NFE statistics in whole-body, torso, and ROIs were computed. Paired two-tailed t-tests with significance level = 0.05 were used for statistical analysis.

3   Results

3.1   Motion Simulation Test

In Fig. 2, the voxel-wise motion prediction error map of MCP-Net is generally the darkest with reduced hotspots within the body outline and torso organs, indicating decreased inference error. All deep learning models achieved lower motion prediction errors than BIS. MCP-Net significantly decreased motion prediction error compared with other baselines ($p < 0.05$), suggesting improved robustness and prediction accuracy. Sample overlaid dynamic frames demonstrating motion simulation and estimation accuracy are shown in Supplementary Fig. S2.

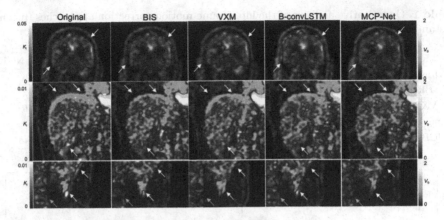

Fig. 4. Overlaid Patlak K_i and V_b images showing motion correction impacts in brain (upper), liver (middle), GI tract (lower, white arrows), and bone (lower, cyan arrows). (Color figure online)

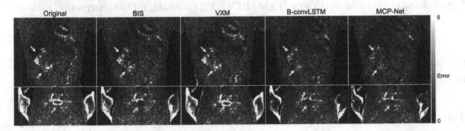

Fig. 5. Sample voxel-wise parametric NFE maps in liver (upper, white arrows), heart (upper, cyan arrows), bladder (lower, white arrows), and hand (lower, cyan arrows). (Color figure online)

3.2 Qualitative Analysis

In Fig. 3, sample overlaid dynamic frame pairs showed inter-frame motion and correction effects for heart, liver, and kidney misalignment. Both single-pair baselines BIS and VXM significantly decreased the misalignment but residual under-correction was still present. While B-convLSTM with multiple-frame analysis further improved motion correction, our proposed MCP-Net achieved the lowest remaining spatial mismatch. Similarly, in Fig. 4, both BIS and VXM reduced the motion-related K_i/V_b misalignment but still had residual mismatch. While B-convLSTM showed improved alignment, the MCP-Net realized the best spatial match at the brain edge, liver dome and the lower edge, gastrointestinal (GI) tract, and bone. Thus, Patlak regularization improved both frame and K_i/V_b spatial alignment. In Fig. 5, using the same color scale, the voxel-wise NFE maps for MCP-Net were generally the darkest with the most reduced bright spots of high fitting error like the heart and liver regions. For the significant motion of

Table 1. Quantitative analysis of the inter-frame motion correction approaches (mean ± standard deviation) with the best results marked **in bold**.

	Avg-to-ref SSIM	Whole-body NFE	Torso NFE	Whole-body K_i/V_b NMI
Original	0.9487 ± 0.0160	0.3634 ± 0.1044	0.7022 ± 0.1079	0.8923 ± 0.0376
BIS	0.9509 ± 0.0149	0.3370 ± 0.0943	0.6908 ± 0.1088	0.9105 ± 0.0362
VXM	0.9446 ± 0.0165	0.3422 ± 0.0977	0.6834 ± 0.1039	0.9067 ± 0.0446
B-convLSTM	0.9513 ± 0.0146	0.2857 ± 0.0836	0.6390 ± 0.1005	0.9281 ± 0.0357
MCP-Net	**0.9523 ± 0.0141**	**0.2840 ± 0.0829**	**0.6197 ± 0.1032**	**0.9295 ± 0.0348**

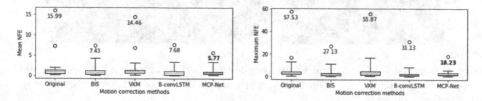

Fig. 6. Mean (left) and maximum (right) ROI NFEs for each motion correction method.

the hand and bladder, which do not strictly follow the 2-tissue compartmental models, the proposed MCP-Net still has the capability to reduce error.

3.3   Quantitative Analysis

Table 1 summarized the quantitative analysis results. Both multiple-frame models achieved substantial improvements in each metric, while the proposed MCP-Net consistently achieved the lowest whole-body and torso NFEs as well as the highest Avg-to-ref SSIM and whole-body K_i/V_b NMI. Compared with BIS and VXM, both B-convLSTM and MCP-Net significantly reduced the NFEs and increased K_i/V_b NMI ($p < 0.05$). The MCP-Net achieved significantly lower torso NFE ($p = 0.027$), higher whole-body K_i/V_b NMI ($p = 0.019$), and improved Avg-to-ref SSIM ($p = 5.01e - 5$) than B-convLSTM. Thus, the MCP-Net with Patlak regularization could further improve parametric imaging with reduced fitting error and enhanced K_i/V_b alignment by directly utilizing tracer kinetics.

   In Fig. 6, box plots show the distributions of the mean and maximum NFE of each ROI. The MCP-Net showed consistent improvement in reducing mean and maximum error as B-convLSTM, but MCP-Net demonstrated stronger reduction for the outliers with extremely high fitting error, suggesting increased robustness.

4   Conclusion

We proposed MCP-Net, a whole-body dynamic PET inter-frame motion correction framework with Patlak penalization. With the integrated analytical Patlak fitting module and Patlak loss regularization, the MCP-Net demonstrated improved motion correction both qualitatively and quantitatively compared with conventional and deep learning benchmarks. This shows the advantage of directly optimizing parameter estimation and utilizing tracer kinetics in multiple-frame motion correction analysis. The proposed MCP-Net has the potential to be applied to other tracers and further developed into a joint end-to-end motion correction and parametric imaging framework. Future directions will include investigating intra-frame motion correction as well as the mismatch problem in attenuation and scatter correction.

Acknowledgements. This work is supported by National Institutes of Health (NIH) through grant R01 CA224140.

References

1. Balakrishnan, G., Zhao, A., Sabuncu, M.R., Guttag, J., Dalca, A.V.: Voxelmorph: a learning framework for deformable medical image registration. IEEE Trans. Med. Imaging **38**(8), 1788–1800 (2019)
2. Bhushan, M., Schnabel, J.A., Risser, L., Heinrich, M.P., Brady, J.M., Jenkinson, M.: Motion correction and parameter estimation in dceMRI sequences: application to colorectal cancer. In: Fichtinger, G., Martel, A., Peters, T. (eds.) MICCAI 2011. LNCS, vol. 6891, pp. 476–483. Springer, Heidelberg (2011). https://doi.org/10.1007/978-3-642-23623-5_60
3. Carson, R.E.: Tracer kinetic modeling in PET. In: Bailey, D.L., Townsend, D.W., Valk, P.E., Maisey, M.N. (eds.) Positron Emission Tomography. Springer, London (2005). https://doi.org/10.1007/1-84628-007-9_6
4. Chen, K., Reiman, E., Lawson, M., Feng, D., Huang, S.C.: Decay correction methods in dynamic pet studies. IEEE Trans. Nucl. Sci. **42**(6), 2173–2179 (1995)
5. Cheng, X.: Improving reconstruction of dynamic PET imaging by utilizing temporal coherence and pharmacokinetics. Ph.D. thesis, Technische Universität München (2015)
6. Çiçek, Ö., Abdulkadir, A., Lienkamp, S.S., Brox, T., Ronneberger, O.: 3D U-Net: learning dense volumetric segmentation from sparse annotation. In: Ourselin, S., Joskowicz, L., Sabuncu, M.R., Unal, G., Wells, W. (eds.) MICCAI 2016. LNCS, vol. 9901, pp. 424–432. Springer, Cham (2016). https://doi.org/10.1007/978-3-319-46723-8_49
7. Dimitrakopoulou-Strauss, A., Pan, L., Sachpekidis, C.: Kinetic modeling and parametric imaging with dynamic pet for oncological applications: general considerations, current clinical applications, and future perspectives. Eur. J. Nucl. Med. Mol. Imaging **48**(1), 21–39 (2021)
8. Fahrni, G., Karakatsanis, N.A., Di Domenicantonio, G., Garibotto, V., Zaidi, H.: Does whole-body patlak 18 f-fdg pet imaging improve lesion detectability in clinical oncology? Eur. Radiol. **29**(9), 4812–4821 (2019)
9. Guo, X., et al.: Inter-pass motion correction for whole-body dynamic parametric pet imaging. In: 2021 Society of Nuclear Medicine and Molecular Imaging Annual Meeting (SNMMI 2021), pp. 1421. SNMMI, Soc Nuclear Med (2021)
10. Guo, X., Zhou, B., Pigg, D., Spottiswoode, B., Casey, M.E., Liu, C., Dvornek, N.C.: Unsupervised inter-frame motion correction for whole-body dynamic PET using convolutional long short-term memory in a convolutional neural network. Med. Image Anal. **80**, 102524 (2022). https://doi.org/10.1016/j.media.2022.102524

11. Jiao, J., Searle, G.E., Tziortzi, A.C., Salinas, C.A., Gunn, R.N., Schnabel, J.A.: Spatio-temporal pharmacokinetic model based registration of 4d pet neuroimaging data. Neuroimage **84**, 225–235 (2014)
12. Joshi, A., et al.: Unified framework for development, deployment and robust testing of neuroimaging algorithms. Neuroinformatics **9**(1), 69–84 (2011)
13. Li, M., Wang, C., Zhang, H., Yang, G.: Mv-ran: multiview recurrent aggregation network for echocardiographic sequences segmentation and full cardiac cycle analysis. Comput. Biol. Med. **120**, 103728 (2020)
14. Lu, Y., et al.: Data-driven voluntary body motion detection and non-rigid event-by-event correction for static and dynamic pet. Phys. Med. Biol. **64**(6), 065002 (2019)
15. Mojica, M., Ebrahimi, M.: Motion correction in dynamic contrast-enhanced magnetic resonance images using pharmacokinetic modeling. In: Medical Imaging 2021: Image Processing, vol. 11596, p. 115962S. International Society for Optics and Photonics (2021)
16. Naganawa, M., et al.: Assessment of population-based input functions for Patlak imaging of whole body dynamic 18 f-fdg pet. EJNMMI Phys. **7**(1), 1–15 (2020)
17. Panin, V., Smith, A., Hu, J., Kehren, F., Casey, M.: Continuous bed motion on clinical scanner: design, data correction, and reconstruction. Phys. Med. Biol. **59**(20), 6153 (2014)
18. Patlak, C.S., Blasberg, R.G., Fenstermacher, J.D.: Graphical evaluation of blood-to-brain transfer constants from multiple-time uptake data. J. Cerebral Blood Flow Metabolism **3**(1), 1–7 (1983)
19. Shi, L., et al.: Automatic inter-frame patient motion correction for dynamic cardiac pet using deep learning. IEEE Trans. Med. Imaging **40**, 3293–3304 (2021)
20. Shi, X., Chen, Z., Wang, H., Yeung, D.Y., Wong, W.K., Woo, W.C.: Convolutional lstm network: A machine learning approach for precipitation nowcasting. arXiv preprint arXiv:1506.04214 (2015)
21. Vaquero, J.J., Kinahan, P.: Positron emission tomography: current challenges and opportunities for technological advances in clinical and preclinical imaging systems. Annu. Rev. Biomed. Eng. **17**, 385–414 (2015)
22. Wang, G., Rahmim, A., Gunn, R.N.: Pet parametric imaging: past, present, and future. IEEE Trans. Radiat. Plasma Med. Sci. **4**(6), 663–675 (2020)
23. Zhao, S., Lau, T., Luo, J., Eric, I., Chang, C., Xu, Y.: Unsupervised 3d end-to-end medical image registration with volume Tweening network. IEEE J. Biomed. Health Inform. **24**(5), 1394–1404 (2019)
24. Zhou, B., Tsai, Y.J., Chen, X., Duncan, J.S., Liu, C.: MDPET: a unified motion correction and denoising adversarial network for low-dose gated pet. IEEE Trans. Med. Imaging **40**, 3154–3164 (2021)

PET Denoising and Uncertainty Estimation Based on NVAE Model Using Quantile Regression Loss

Jianan Cui[1,2], Yutong Xie[3], Anand A. Joshi[4], Kuang Gong[2], Kyungsang Kim[2], Young-Don Son[5], Jong-Hoon Kim[5], Richard Leahy[4], Huafeng Liu[1,6,7(✉)], and Quanzheng Li[2(✉)]

[1] The State Key Laboratory of Modern Optical Instrumentation,
College of Optical Science and Engineering, Zhejiang University,
Hangzhou 310027, Zhejiang, China
liuhf@zju.edu.cn
[2] The Center for Advanced Medical Computing and Analysis,
Massachusetts General Hospital/Harvard Medical School, Boston, MA 02114, USA
li.quanzheng@mgh.harvard.edu
[3] Peking University, Beijing 100871, China
[4] University of Southern California, Los Angeles, CA, USA
[5] The Neuroscience Research Institute, Gachon University of Medicine and Science,
Incheon 21999, South Korea
[6] Jiaxing Key Laboratory of Photonic Sensing and Intelligent Imaging,
Jiaxing 314000, China
[7] Intelligent Optics and Photonics Research Center, Jiaxing Research Institute,
Zhejiang University, Jiaxing 314000, China

Abstract. Deep learning-based methods have shown their superior performance for medical imaging, but their clinical application is still rare. One reason may come from their uncertainty. As data-driven models, deep learning-based methods are sensitive to imperfect data. Thus, it is important to quantify the uncertainty, especially for positron emission tomography (PET) denoising tasks where the noise is very similar to small tumors. In this paper, we proposed a Nouveau variational autoencoder (NVAE) based model using quantile regression loss for simultaneous PET image denoising and uncertainty estimation. Quantile regression loss was performed as the reconstruction loss to avoid the variance shrinkage problem caused by the traditional reconstruction probability loss. The variance and mean can be directly calculated from the estimated quantiles under the Logistic assumption, which is more efficient than Monte Carlo sampling. Experiment based on real ^{11}C-DASB datasets verified that the denoised PET images of the proposed method have a higher mean($\pm$SD) peak signal-to-noise ratio (PSNR)(40.64 ± 5.71) and structural similarity index measure (SSIM) (0.9807 ± 0.0063) than Unet-based denoising (PSNR, 36.18 ± 5.55; SSIM,

---

Supplementary Information The online version contains supplementary material available at https://doi.org/10.1007/978-3-031-16440-8_17.

0.9614 ± 0.0121) and NVAE model using Monte Carlo sampling (PSNR, 37.00 ± 5.35; SSIM, 0.9671 ± 0.0095) methods.

Keywords: PET denoising · Deep learning · Uncertainty · Quantile regression

1   Introduction

Deep learning-based methods have made great progress in the field of medical imaging [4–7]. Although they have achieved superior performance over traditional methods, the reliability of deep learning-based methods has always been questioned as they are data-driven models and work in a black box. Once the testing data is out of the distribution of the training data, the output would be degraded. Therefore, quantifying uncertainty during the inference of deep learning-based methods is of vital importance. Especially in clinical practice, uncertain information can effectively improve the accuracy of diagnosis. Thiagarajan et al. [27] measured uncertainty for the classification of breast histopathological images and verified that high uncertainty data have lower classification accuracy and need human intervention. Hao et al. [11] showed that adding uncertainty information into a graph attention network can improve the classification performance for parapneumonic effusion diagnosis.

In positron emission tomography (PET) image denoising tasks, without prior information from raw data, it is not easy for denoising models to distinguish noise and small tumors as they have very similar structures visually. Small tumors may be eliminated as noise, while some of the noise may be identified as a tumor and retained. If we can quantify the uncertainty for the denoising process, the uncertainty map can provide an additional reference when the radiologists are viewing the denoised PET imaging. Uncertainty has been well studied in the classic PET literature, particularly after Jeffrey Fessler's seminar work [9] in 1997. However, traditional methods [9,21] are not accurate and fast enough. Nowadays, several deep learning-based methods for uncertainty estimation have been proposed, like Bayesian neural networks [18,19,24,26], ensemble methods [17], dropout methods [2,10], and uncertainty aware neural networks [3,20]. For PET image denoising, Sudarshan et al. [26] proposed a robust suDNN to map low-dose PET images to standard-dose PET images and estimate the uncertainty through a Bayesian neural network framework. Cui et al. [8] used a novel neural network, Nouveau variational autoencoder (NVAE) [28], to generate denoising image and uncertainty map based on Monte Carlo sampling.

In this paper, we developed an efficient and effective model for simultaneous PET image denoising and uncertainty estimation. Here, we also utilized NVAE as our network structure due to its superior performance over the traditional VAE model. Compared to the Reference [8], our work has two main contributions:

- Quantile regression loss [1,13,16] was introduced as the reconstruction loss to avoid the variance shrinkage problem of VAE. In VAE, when the conditional

mean network prediction is well-trained (there is no reconstruction error), continued maximizing the log-likelihood will result in the estimated variance approaching zero [1], leading to an artificially narrow output distribution. This will limit the model's generalization ability and reduce sample diversity. Using quantile regression loss to replace log-likelihood can avoid this problem.
– The variance map was directly calculated from the estimated quantiles. Monte Carlo sampling is no longer needed which can save a lot of time and computing resources.

2 Related Work

2.1 Variational Autoencoder (VAE)

VAE [14] is a generative model that is trained to represent the distribution of signal x given the latent variables z which has a known prior distribution $p(z)$. $p(x, z) = p(z)p(x|z)$ represents the true joint distribution of x and z, where $p(x|z)$ is the likelihood function or decoder. Let $q(x)$ be the distribution of x and $q(z|x)$ be the posterior distribution or encoder, then $q(x, z)$ suppose be the estimate of $p(x, z)$. VAE is trained to make $q(x, z)$ close to the true joint distribution $p(x, z)$ by minimizing their KL divergence.

2.2 Nouveau Variational Autoencoder (NVAE)

NVAE [28] is a model recently proposed by NVIDA that can generate high-quality face images as large as 256×256. Through several novel architecture designs, NVAE greatly improved its generative performance for complex signal distribution. A hierarchical multi-scale structure is added between the encoder and the generative model to boost the expressiveness of the approximate posterior $q(z|x)$ and prior $p(z)$. In this hierarchical multi-scale structure, the latent variables of NVAE are separated as L disjoint groups, $z = \{z_1, z_2, \ldots, z_L\}$. Thus, the posterior can be represented as $p(z_1, z_2, \ldots, z_L) = p(z_1) \prod_{l=1}^{L} p(z_i|z_{<l})$ and the prior is $q(z_1, z_2, \ldots, z_L|x) = \prod_{l=1}^{L} q(z_l|x, z_{<l})$. Considering the substantial latent variable groups would make the network hard to optimize and unstable, NVAE proposed the residual normal distributions to parameterize the approximate posterior $q(z_l^i|z_{<l}, x) := \mathcal{N}(\mu_i(z_{<l}) + \Delta\mu_i(z_{<l}, x), \sigma_i(z_{<l}) \cdot \Delta\sigma_i(z_{<l}, x))$ relative to the prior $p(z_l^i|z_{<l}) := \mathcal{N}(\mu_i(z_{<l}), \sigma_i(z_{<l}))$, where z_l^i is the ith variable in z_l. In addition, spectral regularization [30], inverse autoregressive flow [15], depthwise convolutions, squeeze and excitation [12], batch normalization, swish activation [22] were added either to better model the long-range correlations or stable the training.

3 Methods

3.1 Overview

Figure 1 shows the diagram of the proposed simultaneous PET image denoising and uncertainty estimation framework. The NVAE network was trained with supervision by minimizing quantile regression loss and Kullback-Leibler (KL) divergence term. The posterior distribution was assumed to be the Logistic distribution. After training, the location parameter μ and the scale parameter s were acquired from the estimated quantiles. Thus, the mean and variance of the Logistic distribution can be calculated.

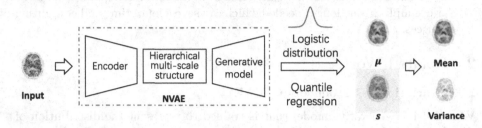

Fig. 1. Diagram of the proposed framework.

3.2   PET Image Denoising

For PET image denoising tasks, given a group of noisy PET images x' and clean PET images x, the conditional log-likelihood function is $\log p(x|x')$. Based on the conditional VAE [25], the variational lower bound of the log-likelihood can be written as:

$$\log p(x'|x) \geq \mathbb{E}_{q(z|x')} \log p(x|x', z) - KL(q(z|x')\|p(z|x')). \tag{1}$$

In this work, we assumed $p(z|x') = p(z)$ that followed Normal distributions. And skip connections were added between the encoder and the generative model to provide information from input x' to the likelihood function $p(x|x', z)$. Thus, the loss can be written as:

$$\mathcal{L}(x) = -\mathbb{E}_{q(z|x')} \log p(x|x', z) + KL(q(z|x')\|p(z)). \tag{2}$$

The first term of the Eq. 2 represents the reconstruction loss $\mathcal{L}_{REC}(x)$ and the second term is the regularization term $\mathcal{L}_{KL}(x)$.

3.3   Quantile Regression Loss

Quantile regression (QR) [16] was proposed by Koenker et al. in 1978, which estimates the nth $(0 < n < 1)$ quantile Q_n by minimizing the problem

$$\min_{\theta} \sum_{t} \rho_n \left(x_t - f_\theta(x'_t) \right), \tag{3}$$

where x'_t and x_t are the tth input and response, respectively. $f_\theta(x'_t)$ represents the NVAE model with parameters θ, which is supposed to be the quantile Q_n after optimizing. ρ_n is the check function:

$$\rho_n(u) = u(nI(u > 0) - (1 - n)I(u < 0)). \tag{4}$$

To avoid the variance shrinkage problem, we replaced the reconstruction loss with the quantile regression loss and calculated the mean and variance of the output distribution by quantiles. We assumed that the output distribution follows the Logistic distribution, which has a cumulative distribution function (CDF) as:

$$F(y; \mu, s) = \frac{1}{1 + e^{-(y-\mu)/s}} \tag{5}$$

where μ is the mean and s is a scale parameter. s has a relation with the variance as $\sigma^2 = \frac{s^2 \pi^2}{3}$. As CDF is equal to n, we can get two quantiles:

$$Q_n = \begin{cases} \mu, n = 0.5 \\ \mu - s, n = \frac{1}{1+e} \approx 0.269 \end{cases} \tag{6}$$

The QR loss aims to estimate the 0.5th quantile and the 0.269th quantile by:

$$\mathcal{L}_{QR}(\boldsymbol{x}) = \sum_t \rho_{0.5}\left(x_t - f_{\theta_{0.5}}(x'_t)\right) + \sum_t \rho_{0.269}\left(x_t - f_{\theta_{0.269}}(x'_t)\right) \tag{7}$$

Thus, the total training loss for the proposed work is

$$\mathcal{L}(\boldsymbol{x}) = \mathcal{L}_{QR}(\boldsymbol{x}) + \mathcal{L}_{KL}(\boldsymbol{x}). \tag{8}$$

4 Experiment

4.1 Dataset

The proposed method was validated on real ^{11}C-DASB datasets, which contain 26 subjects. Each subject was scanned by the HRRT-PET system (Siemens Medical Solutions, Knoxville, TN, USA) with the administered dose of 577.6 ± 41.0 MBq. PET images acquired at 60 min post-injection (matrix size, $256 \times 256 \times 207$; voxel size, 1.21875 mm $\times 1.21875$ mm $\times 1.21875$ mm) were reconstructed by 3D-ordinary ordered subset expectation maximization (OP-OSEM3D) algorithm and attenuation correction was performed. Each subject also has a T1-weighted image scanned by an ultra-high field 7T MRI. We generated the low-quality PET images by down-sampling the list-mode data to a quarter of the original count. In this dataset, 20 subjects were used for training, 3 for validation, and 3 for testing.

4.2 Data Analysis

Supervised denoising using Unet as the network structure was chosen as the baseline to compare the denoising performance with the proposed method (NVAE-QR). We also compared with the work in the Reference [8], which used NVAE for PET image denoising and uncertainty estimation based on Monte Carlo sampling (NVAE-MC). In this work, we evaluated the denoising performance by calculating the peak signal-to-noise ratio (PSNR) and structural similarity index measure (SSIM) [29] using the high-quality PET image as the reference. We used Logistic distribution as the output distribution for NVAE-QR. NVAE-MC used the mixture of discretized Logistic distribution [23] as the output distribution.

The network was trained by 2.5D patch with the size of $3 \times 256 \times 256$. The batch size is 20. The training epochs are 200 and the learning rate is 0.01. All the experiments were performed in Pytorch 1.9.1. The sampling number for NVAE-MC is 500.

Table 1. The PSNR and SSIM of the noisy PET image, the denoising results for Unet, NVAE-MC and NVAE-QR.

Patients	PSNR				SSIM			
	Noisy	Unet	NVAE-MC	NVAE-QR	Noisy PET	Unet	NVAE-MC	NVAE-QR
1	25.76	32.55	33.59	**37.39**	0.8808	0.9518	0.9608	**0.9768**
2	34.10	42.57	43.16	**47.22**	0.8968	0.9750	0.9780	**0.9880**
3	26.10	33.43	34.24	**37.29**	0.8762	0.9572	0.9624	**0.9773**

5   Results

Figure 2 shows one axial slice from the output of our NVAE-QR methods. The network directly estimated the 0.5th quantile and the 0.269th quantile, which are equal to μ and $\mu - s$, respectively. We can get the scale parameter s from the difference image of the 0.5th quantile and the 0.269th quantile, and then calculate the variance image. Figure 3 displays the denoising results for Unet, NVAE-MC, and NVAE-QR. We can see that all the neural network denoised results significantly improved the quality of the low-dose image and even look better than the full-dose image. Among them, our NVAE-QR shows the clearest cortex structure (as the zoom-in subfigures are shown). As ^{11}C has a short half-life and decays fast, ^{11}C-DASB PET images usually have a higher noise level compared to ^{18}F-FDG. Thus, the full-dose PET image shown in Fig. 3 is also noisy and cannot give enough reference for cortex regions. The corresponding

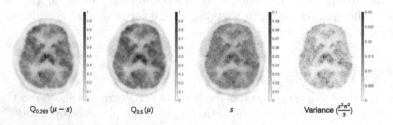

$Q_{0.269} (\mu - s)$ $Q_{0.5} (\mu)$ s Variance $(\frac{s^2\pi^2}{3})$

Fig. 2. The output of our NVAE-QR methods. From left to right: the estimated 0.269th quantile, the estimated 0.5th quantile, the scale parameter s and the variance calculated based on s. The color bar shows the normalized intensity value. (Color figure online)

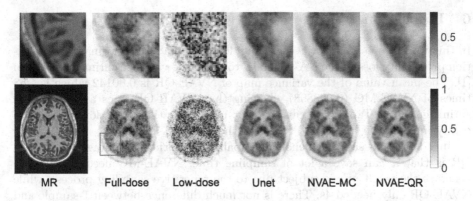

MR   Full-dose   Low-dose   Unet   NVAE-MC   NVAE-QR

Fig. 3. The denoising results of different methods. From left to right: corresponding MR image, full-dose PET image, low-dose PET image, the denoised image using Unet, NVAE-MC and NVAE-QR. The region in the red box was zoomed-in for each image. The color bar shows the normalized intensity value. (Color figure online)

MR is displayed to provide additional references. We also plotted the profile of the denoised results using different methods in Fig. 4. We can see that NVAE-QR matches the high-intensity peak better than the other two methods. The PSNR and SSIM of different denoising methods are listed in Table 1. The proposed NVAE-QR method can achieve the highest mean($\pm$SD) PSNR (40.64 ± 5.71) and SSIM (0.9807 ± 0.0063) compared to Unet (PSNR, 36.18 ± 5.55; SSIM, 0.9614 ± 0.0121) and NVAE-MC (PSNR, 37.00 ± 5.35; SSIM, 0.9671 ± 0.0095). The variance maps of NVAE-MC and NVAE-QR are shown in Fig. 5. The variance of NVAE-MC is lower than NVAE-QR due to the variance shrinkage problem. We also compared the performance of NVAE-MC using Logistic distribution and NVAE-QR using Normal distribution as the ablation study. The PSNR and SSIM in Table 2 show that NVAE-QR using Logistic distribution has the best performance.

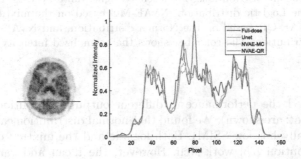

Fig. 4. The profile of the black line for full-dose PET image, the denoised image using Unet, NVAE-MC and NVAE-QR.

6   Discussion

In this work, we used quantile regression loss to replace the original reconstruction probability loss of the NAVE model to avoid the variance shrinkage problem [1]. The mean value of the variance map of NVAE-QR is 0.00142 which is 1.58 times of NVAE-MC (0.000898), showing that NVAR-QR does avoid variance shrinkage. From Table 2 we can see that using quantile regression can significantly improve the PSNR and SSIM for the denoised images.

In addition to superior denoising capability, another advantage for NVAE-QR is that it can save a lot of sampling time. NVAE-MC needed 35min to generate the result of one subject due to the repetitive sampling process, while NVAE-QR only needed 4s. There is not much difference between 1-sample and 500-sample NVAE-QR results. (The comparison is put in the supplementary materials). Thus, NVAE-QR only takes 1/500 percent of the time of NVAE-MC, which is much more efficient.

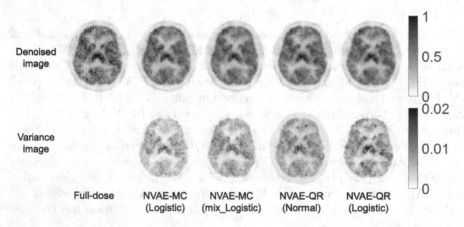

Fig. 5. The denoising PET image and variance map of NVAE-MC and NVAE-QR using different output distributions. From left to right: full-dose PET image, NVAE-MC based on the Logistic distribution, NVAE-MC based on the mixture of Logistic distribution, NVAE-QR based on the Normal distribution, and NVAE-QR based on the Logistic distribution. The color bar shows the normalized intensity value. (Color figure online)

We evaluated the performance of different output distribution models (as Fig. 5 and Table 2 are shown). We found that normal distribution cannot fit PET data well (usually has low SSIM). Both logistic and the mixture of discretized Logistic distribution [23] work well. However, the mean and variance of the mixture of discretized Logistic distribution [23] are hard to calculate as the mixture parameters are learned by the network. Thus, we assumed that the output follows the logistic distribution. We also evaluated the proposed method on whole-body ^{18}F-FDG datasets. The results show that NVAE-QR achieved

Table 2. The PSNR and SSIM of NVAE-MC and NVAE-QR using different output distributions

	Patients	NVAE-MC (Logisitic)	NVAE-MC (mix-Logistic)	NVAE-QR (Normal)	NVAE-QR (Logistic)
PSNR	1	32.92	33.59	**37.59**	37.39
	2	43.26	43.16	46.44	**47.22**
	3	32.49	34.24	37.20	**37.29**
SSIM	1	0.9581	0.9608	0.9497	**0.9768**
	2	0.9801	0.9780	0.9678	**0.9880**
	3	0.9600	0.9624	0.9455	**0.9773**

the highest PSNR, SSIM, and contrast-to-noise ratio (CNR) improvement than Unet and NVAE-MC. The results of the brain datasets and the whole-body datasets show our model works well under this output assumption and has good generalization ability.

7   Conclusion

In this paper, we proposed an NVAE model using quantile regression loss for simultaneous PET denoising and uncertainty estimation. Based on the quantile regression loss, the variance shrinkage problem caused by reconstruction probability loss can be avoided and the sampling time can be saved. The experiment based on real ^{11}C-DASB HRRT-PET dataset verified that the proposed NVAE-QR method outperforms the Unet-based denoising and NVAE-based Monte Carlo sampling. Our future work will focus on more clinical evaluations.

Acknowledgements. This work was supported in part by the National Key Technology Research and Development Program of China (2020AAA0109502), the National Natural Science Foundation of China (U1809204, 62101488), the Key Research and Development Program of Zhejiang Province (2021C03029), the Talent Program of Zhejiang Province (2021R51004) and by China Postdoctoral Science Foundation (2021M692830)

References

1. Akrami, H., Joshi, A.A., Aydore, S., Leahy, R.M.: Addressing variance shrinkage in variational autoencoders using quantile regression. arXiv preprint arXiv:2010.09042 (2020)
2. Ballestar, L.M., Vilaplana, V.: MRI brain tumor segmentation and uncertainty estimation using 3D-UNet architectures. In: Crimi, A., Bakas, S. (eds.) BrainLes 2020. LNCS, vol. 12658, pp. 376–390. Springer, Cham (2021). https://doi.org/10.1007/978-3-030-72084-1_34
3. Bishop, C.M.: Mixture density networks (1994)

4. Cui, J., Gong, K., Guo, N., Kim, K., Liu, H., Li, Q.: Unsupervised pet logan parametric image estimation using conditional deep image prior. Med. Image Anal. **80**, 102519 (2022)
5. Cui, J., et al.: Populational and individual information based pet image denoising using conditional unsupervised learning. Phys. Med. Biol. **66**(15), 155001 (2021)
6. Cui, J., et al.: Pet image denoising using unsupervised deep learning. Eur. J. Nucl. Med. Mol. Imaging **46**(13), 2780–2789 (2019)
7. Cui, J., Gong, K., Han, P., Liu, H., Li, Q.: Unsupervised arterial spin labeling image superresolution via multiscale generative adversarial network. Med. Phys. **49**(4), 2373–2385 (2022)
8. Cui, J., et al.: Pet denoising and uncertainty estimation based on NVAE model. In: 2021 IEEE Nuclear Science Symposium and Medical Imaging Conference Proceedings (NSS/MIC). IEEE (2021)
9. Fessler, J.A.: Approximate variance images for penalized-likelihood image reconstruction. In: 1997 IEEE Nuclear Science Symposium Conference Record, vol. 2, pp. 949–952. IEEE (1997)
10. Gal, Y., Ghahramani, Z.: Dropout as a Bayesian approximation: representing model uncertainty in deep learning. In: International Conference on Machine Learning, pp. 1050–1059. PMLR (2016)
11. Hao, J., et al.: Uncertainty-guided graph attention network for parapneumonic effusion diagnosis. Med. Image Anal. **75**, 102217 (2022)
12. Hu, J., Shen, L., Sun, G.: Squeeze-and-excitation networks. In: Proceedings of the IEEE Conference on Computer Vision and Pattern Recognition, pp. 7132–7141 (2018)
13. Huang, X., Shi, L., Suykens, J.A.: Support vector machine classifier with pinball loss. IEEE Trans. Pattern Anal. Mach. Intell. **36**(5), 984–997 (2013)
14. Kingma, D.P., Welling, M.: Auto-encoding variational Bayes. arXiv preprint arXiv:1312.6114 (2013)
15. Kingma, D.P., Salimans, T., Jozefowicz, R., Chen, X., Sutskever, I., Welling, M.: Improved variational inference with inverse autoregressive flow. In: Advances in Neural Information Processing Systems, vol. 29 (2016)
16. Koenker, R., Bassett Jr, G.: Regression quantiles. Econometrica: J. Econometr. Soc. 33–50 (1978)
17. Lakshminarayanan, B., Pritzel, A., Blundell, C.: Simple and scalable predictive uncertainty estimation using deep ensembles. In: Advances in Neural Information Processing Systems, 30 (2017)
18. Laves, M.H., Ihler, S., Fast, J.F., Kahrs, L.A., Ortmaier, T.: Well-calibrated regression uncertainty in medical imaging with deep learning. In: Medical Imaging with Deep Learning, pp. 393–412. PMLR (2020)
19. MacKay, D.J.: A practical Bayesian framework for backpropagation networks. Neural Comput. **4**(3), 448–472 (1992)
20. Nix, D.A., Weigend, A.S.: Estimating the mean and variance of the target probability distribution. In: Proceedings of 1994 IEEE International Conference on Neural Networks (ICNN 1994), vol. 1, pp. 55–60. IEEE (1994)
21. Qi, J., Leahy, R.M.: A theoretical study of the contrast recovery and variance of map reconstructions from pet data. IEEE Trans. Med. Imaging **18**(4), 293–305 (1999)
22. Ramachandran, P., Zoph, B., Le, Q.V.: Searching for activation functions. arXiv preprint arXiv:1710.05941 (2017)

23. Salimans, T., Karpathy, A., Chen, X., Kingma, D.P.: Pixelcnn++: improving the pixelcnn with discretized logistic mixture likelihood and other modifications. arXiv preprint arXiv:1701.05517 (2017)
24. Sambyal, A.S., Krishnan, N.C., Bathula, D.R.: Towards reducing aleatoric uncertainty for medical imaging tasks. In: 2022 IEEE 19th International Symposium on Biomedical Imaging (ISBI), pp. 1–4. IEEE (2022)
25. Sohn, K., Lee, H., Yan, X.: Learning structured output representation using deep conditional generative models. Advances in Neural Information Processing Systems, vol. 28 (2015)
26. Sudarshan, V.P., Upadhyay, U., Egan, G.F., Chen, Z., Awate, S.P.: Towards lower-dose pet using physics-based uncertainty-aware multimodal learning with robustness to out-of-distribution data. Med. Image Anal. **73**, 102187 (2021)
27. Thiagarajan, P., Khairnar, P., Ghosh, S.: Explanation and use of uncertainty obtained by Bayesian neural network classifiers for breast histopathology images. IEEE Trans. Med. Imaging **41**, 815–825 (2021)
28. Vahdat, A., Kautz, J.: NVAE: a deep hierarchical variational autoencoder. arXiv preprint arXiv:2007.03898 (2020)
29. Wang, Z., Bovik, A.C., Sheikh, H.R., Simoncelli, E.P.: Image quality assessment: from error visibility to structural similarity. IEEE Trans. Image Process. **13**(4), 600–612 (2004)
30. Yoshida, Y., Miyato, T.: Spectral norm regularization for improving the generalizability of deep learning. arXiv preprint arXiv:1705.10941 (2017)

TransEM: Residual Swin-Transformer Based Regularized PET Image Reconstruction

Rui Hu[1] and Huafeng Liu[1,2,3]($\boxtimes$)

[1] State Key Laboratory of Modern Optical Instrumentation,
Department of Optical Engineering, Zhejiang University, Hangzhou 310027, China
liuhf@zju.edu.cn
[2] Jiaxing Key Laboratory of Photonic Sensing & Intelligent Imaging,
Jiaxing 314000, China
[3] Intelligent Optics & Photonics Research Center, Jiaxing Research Institute,
Zhejiang University, Jiaxing 314000, China

Abstract. Positron emission tomography (PET) image reconstruction is an ill-posed inverse problem and suffers from high level of noise due to limited counts received. Recently deep neural networks especially convolutional neural networks (CNN) have been successfully applied to PET image reconstruction. However, the local characteristics of the convolution operator potentially limit the image quality obtained by current CNN-based PET image reconstruction methods. In this paper, we propose a residual swin-transformer based regularizer (RSTR) to incorporate regularization into the iterative reconstruction framework. Specifically, a convolution layer is firstly adopted to extract shallow features, then the deep feature extraction is accomplished by the swin-transformer layer. At last, both deep and shallow features are fused with a residual operation and another convolution layer. Validations on the realistic 3D brain simulated low-count data show that our proposed method outperforms the state-of-the-art methods in both qualitative and quantitative measures.

Keywords: Positron Emission Tomography (PET) · Image reconstruction · Model-based deep learning · Transformer

1 Introduction

Positron Emission Tomography (PET) is one of the irreplaceable tools of functional imaging, which is wildly used in oncology, cardiology, neurology and medical research [1]. However, PET images usually suffer from high level of noise due to many physical degradation factors and the ill-conditioning of PET reconstruction problem.

To reconstruct high-quality PET images, lots of works have been proposed over the last few decades, which can be roughly divided into five categories: 1)traditional analytic methods such as filtered back-projection (FBP [2]) and iterative methods like maximum-likelihood expectation maximization (ML-EM [3]);

L. Wang et al. (Eds.): MICCAI 2022, LNCS 13434, pp. 184–193, 2022.
https://doi.org/10.1007/978-3-031-16440-8_18

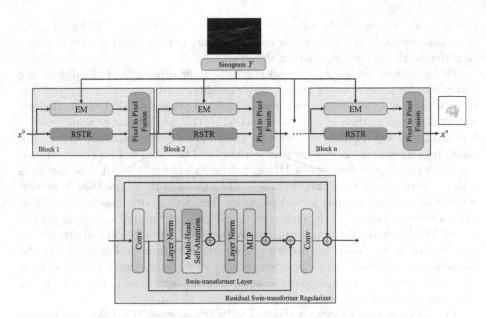

Fig. 1. The overall flow-chart of proposed method. Specifically, TransEM is composed of n blocks. Each block contains EM for image updating, RSTR for regularization and a pixel to pixel fusion operation.

2)prior-incorporative methods; 3)image post-processing (denoising) methods; 4) Penalized Log-Likelihood (PLL) methods and 5)deep learning based methods.

The FBP algorithm is based on the central slice theorem, which can rapidly finish the reconstruction but suffers from heavy noise due to the lack of modeling of physical properties. Iterative algorithms, such as ML-EM modeled the physical properties and improved image quality. However, the excessive noise propagation from the measurements is the biggest disadvantage of ML solution. To further improve the image quality, prior-incorporative reconstruction methods, image post-processing methods and PLL methods have been introduced. The performance of PLL methods [4–6] and prior-incorporative methods like kernel methods [7] are closely related to the hyper-parameters that are often hand-crafted before reconstruction. Post-processing is an effective way to reduce noise such as BM3D [8], non-local mean (NLM) [9] and gaussian filter. However, these methods usually tend to be over-smoothing and time-consuming.

Deep learning (DL) techniques especially supervised learning techniques have recently drawn much attention and shown promising results in PET image reconstruction [10]. Among them, direct learning, DL-based post-denoising and model-based learning are three mainstream approaches. Direct learning [11] methods usually learn the mapping from sinogram to the PET image through deep neural networks (DNN). Because there are no physical constraints, direct learning methods are extremely data-hungry and sometimes unstable. DL-based post-denoising methods [12] are simple to implement, but the final results are very sensitive to the pre-reconstruction algorithms.

By unrolling an iterative reconstruction algorithm, model-based learning shows inspiring results and good interpretability, which has been a promising direction. Gong *et al.* proposed an unrolled network based on 3D U-net and alternating direction method of multipliers (ADMM) [13]. Mehranian *et al.* proposed a forward backward splitting algorithm for Poisson likelihood and unrolled the algorithm into a recurrent neural network with several blocks [14]. Lim *et al.* unrolled the block coordinate descent (BCD) algorithm with U-net [15]. All these methods adopt convolutional neural networks (CNN) to assist in reconstruction. However, a convolution operator has a local receptive field [16], giving rise to that CNNs cannot process long-range dependencies unless passing through a large number of layers. While when layer number increases, the feature resolution and fine details may be lost, which limits the quality of reconstructed images. For this issue, the Transformer [17] is noticed for its strong ability in modeling long-range dependencies of the data and tremendous success in the language domain. Recently, it has also demonstrated promising results in computer vision.

In this paper, we propose a residual swin-transformer [18] based regularizer (RSTR) along with the ML-EM iterative framework, called TransEM, to reconstruct the standard-dose image from low count sinogram. As one of the model-based learning methods (MoDL), TransEM does not need a large training dataset and achieves state-of-the-art results in realistic 3D brain simulation data.

2   Methods and Materials

2.1   Problem Formulation

In PET image reconstruction from sinogram data, The measured data y can be well modeled by a Poisson noise model given by:

$$y \sim Poisson\{\overline{y}\}   s.t. \ \overline{y} = Ax + b \tag{1}$$

where $\overline{y} \in \mathbb{R}^I$ is the mean of the measured data $y \in \mathbb{R}^I$ with y_i representing the i-th detector bin, $x \in \mathbb{R}^J$ is the unknown activity distribution image with x_j representing j-th voxel. $b \in \mathbb{R}^I$ denotes the expectation of scatters and randoms. I is the number of detector pairs and J is the number of pixels. $A \in \mathbb{R}^{I \times J}$ is system response matrix with A_{ij} representing the probabilities of detecting an emission from voxel j at detector i.

Like many other under-determined inverse problem, the unknown image x can be estimated from a Bayesian perspective:

$$\widehat{x} = \arg\max_{x} L(y|x) - \beta R(x) \tag{2}$$

$$L(y|x) = \sum_i y_i \log \overline{y}_i - \overline{y}_i \tag{3}$$

where $L(\boldsymbol{y}|\boldsymbol{x})$ is the Poisson log-likelihood function of measured sinogram data, $R(\boldsymbol{x})$ is the regularization term, β is the parameter that controls the regularization.

The forward-backward splitting(FBS) algorithm [19] and optimization transfer method can be used to solve Eq. (2). FBS algorithm is used to split the objection function into two terms:

$$r^k = x^{k-1} - \alpha\beta\nabla R(x^{k-1}) \tag{4}$$

$$x^k = \arg\max_x L(\boldsymbol{x}|\boldsymbol{y}) - \frac{1}{2\alpha}||x - r^k||^2 \tag{5}$$

where Eq. (4) is a gradient descent update with step size of α and k denotes k-th iteration. In original FBSEM [14], the Eq. (4) was replaced by a Residual CNN [20] unit, while the performance of CNN-based regularizer in long-range dependencies is limited due to their localized receptive fields, which limits the quality of the images obtained. To address this issue, we proposed a residual swin-transformer based regularizer (RSTR) to replace the gradient descent update in Eq. (4):

$$r^k = RSTR(x^{k-1}) \tag{6}$$

Equation (5) can be reformulated with optimize transfer [21] method and EM surrogate [22]:

$$x^k = \arg\max_x \sum_j \hat{x}_{j,EM}^k \ln(x_j) - x_j - \frac{1}{2\alpha \sum_i A_{ij}}(x_j^k - r_j^k)^2 \tag{7}$$

and $\hat{x}_{j,EM}^k$ is given by ML-EM [3] algorithm:

$$\hat{x}_{j,EM}^k = x_j^{k-1}\frac{1}{\sum_i A_{ij}}\sum_i A_{ij}\frac{y_i}{\bar{y}_i} \tag{8}$$

setting the derivative of Eq. (7) to zero, the following closed-form solution can be obtained:

$$x_j^k = \frac{2x_{j,EM}^k}{1 - \frac{r_j^k}{\alpha\sum_i A_{ij}} + \sqrt{(1 - \frac{r_j^k}{\alpha\sum_i A_{ij}})^2 + 4\frac{x_{j,EM}^k}{\alpha\sum_i A_{ij}}}} \tag{9}$$

it can be viewed as a pixel to pixel fusion between regularized reference image r_j^k and ML-EM result $x_{j,EM}^k$. The parameter α was learned from training data.

The whole reconstruction workflow called TransEM is shown in Fig. 1. The TransEM was unrolled to n blocks, where each block consists of two separate steps and a pixel to pixel fusion operation. The two separate steps are a EM step for image update from measured sinogram data and a deep learning step for prior learning using proposed residual swin transformer based regularizer (RSTR) in image domain.

2.2   Residual Swin-Transformer Regularizer

As shown in Fig. 1, the RSTR is a residual block with a Swin Transformer Layer (STL) [18] and two convolutional layers. At first, a 3×3 convolutional layer is used to extract the shallow feature, then a STL is used to extract deep features. At last, another 3×3 convolutional layer is used to aggregate the shallow and deep features with a residual learning operation. STL is based on original Transformer layer and multi-head self-attention (MSA), the input of size $H \times W \times C$ is firstly reshaped to a feature map with size of $\frac{HW}{M^2} \times M^2 \times C$ according to the shifted window mechanism. Then the standard self-attention separately for each window is calculated. After that, a multi-layer perceptron (MLP) with GELU [23] activation are used. Besides, the residual connection is applied for both modules and the LayerNorm (LN) is added before MLP and MSA.

The whole process of RSTR is formulated as:

$$
\begin{aligned}
X_1 &= Conv_{3\times3}(Input) \\
X_2 &= MSA(LN(X_1)) + X_1 \\
X_3 &= MLP(LN(X_2)) + X_2 \\
Output &= Conv_{3\times3}(X3) + X_0
\end{aligned}
\tag{10}
$$

2.3   Implementation Details and Reference Methods

The TransEM was unrolled with ordered subsets (OS) acceleration and implemented using Pytorch 1.7 on a NVIDIA RTX 3090. The number of unrolled Blocks is 60 (10 iterations and 6 subsets). The windowsize of STL (M) is 4. Adam [24] optimizer and Mean square error (MSE) loss between the network outputs and the label images were used during training. The image x^0 was initialized with values of one. The proposed TransEM was compared with conventional ordered subsets expectation maximization (OSEM [25]), maximum a posterior probability expectation maximization algorithm (MAPEM [26]), DeepPET [27] and FBSEM [14]. For both OSEM and MAPEM, 10 iterations and 6 subsets were adopted. The quadratic penalty was used for MAPEM and the β was set to 0.005. Both DeepPET and FBSEM were trained with MSE loss and Adam optimizer. The learning rate was 5e-5, batch size was 4.

3   Experiment and Results

3.1   Experimental Evaluation

Twenty 3D brain phantoms from BrainWeb [28] were used to simulate 2D ^{18}F FDG PET images with the resolution and matrix size of $2.086 \times 2.086 \times 2.031$ mm^3 and $344 \times 344 \times 127$ acquired from a Siemens Biograph mMR. For each phantom, 10 noncontinuous slices were selected from each of the three orthogonal views to generate high count sinograms which were used to reconstruct

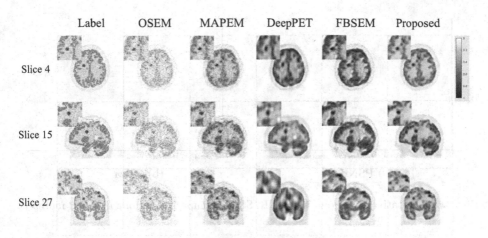

Fig. 2. Reconstruction results of OSEM, MAPEM, DeepPET, FBSEM and proposed TransEM on three orthogonal views of one test brain sample.

the label images and low count sinograms with size of 172×252. The system matrix was simulated with Siddon projection [29]. For high count, $5 * 10^6$ counts and point spread function (PSF) modeling with $2.5mm$ full width at half maximum (FWHM) Gaussian kernels were used, while $5 * 10^5$ counts on average and PSF of $4mm$ were used for low count. The high dose label images were reconstructed from high count sinogram using OSEM algorithm with 10 iterations and 6 subsets. Besides, fifteen hot spheres of radius ranging from 2mm to 8mm were inserted into all phantoms. TransEM has trained with 17 brain samples (510 slices) to map low count sinogram to high dose label PET images, and 2 brain samples (60 slices) for testing and 1 brain sample (30 slices) for validation. To assess reconstruction quality, quantitative comparisons were performed against high dose label images. Both references and reconstructed images were normalized to a maximum of 1. Peak signal to noise ratio (PSNR), structural similarity index (SSIM [30]) and mean contrast recovery coefficients (MCRC) were calculated.

$$MCRC = \frac{1}{N} \sum_{n=1}^{N} \frac{\overline{I_a}}{I_{true}} \qquad (11)$$

where N is the number of pictures which contains the simulated tumors, $\overline{I_a}$ is the average uptake of all the tumor areas in the test phantom.

3.2 Results

Fig. 2 shows three orthogonal views of the reconstructed brain PET images using different methods. It can be observed that the conventional OSEM algorithm suffers from high level noise. MAPEM reduces noise but always shows over-smooth,

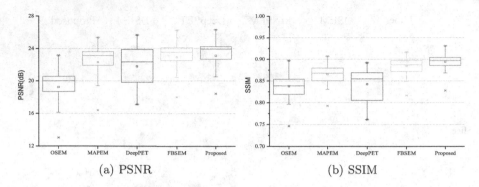

(a) PSNR   (b) SSIM

Fig. 3. Quantitative image quality(PSNR, SSIM) comparison among different methods

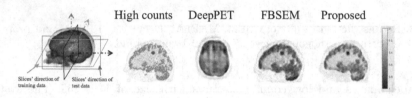

Fig. 4. Robustness analysis on the difference slices' direction between the training set and test set. In this experiment, the training slices are selected from the transverse plane, while the test slices are from the sagittal plane.

resulting in losses of detailed information. As one of the direct learning methods, DeepPET performed not so good. One possible reason is that DeepPET is extremely data-hungry, so poor performance on a small dataset is expected. The FBSEM has a better noise reduction compared to the traditional method OSEM, MAPEM and direct learning method DeepPET, but also has some noises showing up in different regions and some structural information is not well recovered. As seen, the proposed TransEM revealed more cortex structures and preserved edges well compared to other methods. The quantitative results on the test set are demonstrated in Fig. 3 where our proposed method achieves the highest scores among all the methods.

3.3   Robustness Analysis

Besides, to analyze the robustness of the proposed TransEM on different low count levels, we have trained DeepPET, FBSEM, and TransEM on 1/4, 1/100 downsampled data. The training label is reconstructed by OSEM with high count (5e6) data. Each experiment involves retraining and testing. As shown in Table 1, including 1/10 downsampled data results mentioned above, TransEM beats all comparison methods at different counts except DeepPET in 1/100 downsampled situation, while we would like to emphasize that it looks like DeepPET got pretty good PSNR and MCRC, in ultra-low count situation, due to the lack of

Table 1. The PSNR SSIM and MCRC of the test set with different counts level.

Method	Counts=1.25e6 (1/4)			Counts=5e5 (1/10)			Counts=5e4 (1/100)		
	PSNR	SSIM	MCRC	PSNR	SSIM	MCRC	PSNR	SSIM	MCRC
MLEM	19.97±2.69	0.86±0.02	0.6852	19.24±2.34	0.84±0.03	0.5109	15.03±1.93	0.77±0.03	0.1662
MAPEM	22.35±2.26	0.88±0.02	0.8187	22.30±2.25	0.86±0.02	0.7983	17.04±2.23	0.79±0.03	0.3838
DeepPET	20.74±2.05	0.82±0.04	0.7005	21.77±2.13	0.84±0.04	0.6813	**20.69 ± 2.83**	0.82±0.05	**0.6690**
FBSEM	22.52±2.00	0.88±0.01	0.8448	22.94±1.84	0.88±0.02	0.8518	19.16±2.35	0.82±0.03	0.5681
Proposed	**22.61 ± 2.00**	**0.90 ± 0.01**	**0.8578**	**23.10 ± 1.86**	**0.89 ± 0.02**	**0.8718**	20.10±2.47	**0.84 ± 0.03**	0.5765

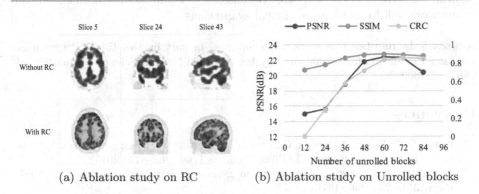

(a) Ablation study on RC   (b) Ablation study on Unrolled blocks

Fig. 5. Ablation study on different settings of TransEM.

physical constraints, the over-fitting of DeepPET is severe and the results are not very reliable which is proved true when we trained the three learning methods with transverse slices and tested with sagittal slices. We selected training slices from the transverse plane and test slices from the sagittal plane to test the generalization ability of three learning-based methods as shown in Fig. 4. It can be observed that the generalization ability of DeepPET is poor.

3.4   Ablation Study and Discussion

Figure 5a shows two residual connection (RC) variants outside STL in RSTR. Without residual connection, the training step is easily falling into sub-optimal solution and is difficult to convergence. The significance of RC also lies in the comparison of reconstruction results.In TransEM proposed in this paper, most of the parameters are learned from training data, however, the number of unrolled blocks is hand-crafted. In this section, the sensitivity of the number of unrolled blocks is analyzed. Due to the limitation of hardware and image size, the number of subsets that we chose is 6, so the number of unrolled blocks is multiples of six. When the number is 60, the TransEM achieves the best performance as shown in Fig 5b, so the number of unrolled blocks is 60 in the experiment in this paper.

4   Conclusions

In this work, we proposed a model-based deep learning method by unrolling the EM algorithm with residual swin-transformer regularizer for low-dose PET image reconstruction. Simulated human brain data were used in the evaluation. Both quantitative and qualitative results show that the proposed TransEM performs better than the FBSEM, DeepPET as well as traditional OSEM and MAPEM regarding PSNR, SSIM and MCRC. Because lack of clinical PET data currently, future work will focus on more clinical evaluations.

Acknowledgements. This work was supported in part by the Talent Program of Zhejiang Province (2021R51004) and by the National Natural Science Foundation of China (U1809204).

References

1. Gunn, R., Slifstein, M., Searle, G., Price, J.: Quantitative imaging of protein targets in the human brain with PET. Phys. Med. Biol. **60**, 363–411 (2015)
2. Brooks, R.A.: Statistical limitations in x-ray reconstructive tomography. Med. Phys. **3**(4), 237–240 (1976)
3. Shepp, L., Vardi, Y.: Maximum likelihood reconstruction for emission tomography. IEEE Trans. Med. Imaging **1**, 113–122 (1982)
4. Xie, N., et al.: Penalized-likelihood PET image reconstruction using 3D structural convolutional sparse coding. IEEE Trans. Biomed. Eng. **69**, 4–14 (2022)
5. Chen, S., Liu, H., Shi, P., Chen, Y.: Sparse representation and dictionary learning penalized image reconstruction for positron emission tomography. Phys. Med. Biol. **60**, 807–823 (2015)
6. Chen, S., Liu, H., Hu, Z., Zhang, H., Shi, P., Chen, Y.: Simultaneous reconstruction and segmentation of dynamic PET via low-rank and sparse matrix decomposition. IEEE Trans. Biomed. Eng. **62**, 1784–1795 (2015)
7. Wang, G., Qi, J.: PET image reconstruction using Kernel method. IEEE Trans. Med. Imaging **34**, 61–71 (2014)
8. Feruglio, P., Vinegoni, C., Gros, J., Sbarbati, A., Weissleder, R.: Block matching 3D random noise filtering for absorption optical projection tomography. Phys. Med. Biol. **55**, 5401 (2010)
9. Dutta, J., Leahy, R., Li, Q.: Non-local means denoising of dynamic PET images. PLoS ONE **8**, e81390 (2013)
10. Reader, A., Corda, G., Mehranian, A., Costa-Luis, C., Ellis, S., Schnabel,: J. Deep learning for PET image reconstruction. IEEE Trans. Radiat. Plasma Med. Sci. **5**, 1–25 (2020)
11. Wang, B., Liu, H.: FBP-Net for direct reconstruction of dynamic PET images. Phys. Med. Biol. **65**, 235008 (2020)
12. Cui, J., et al.: PET image denoising using unsupervised deep learning. Eur. J. Nucl. Med. Mol. Imaging **46**, 2780–2789 (2019)
13. Gong, K., et al.: Iterative PET image reconstruction using convolutional neural network representation. IEEE Trans. Med. Imaging **38**, 675–685 (2018)
14. Mehranian, A., Reader, A.: Model-based deep learning PET image reconstruction using forward-backward splitting expectation-maximization. IEEE Trans. Radiat. Plasma Med. Sci. **5**, 54–64 (2020)

15. Lim, H., Chun, I., Dewaraja, Y., Fessler, J.: Improved low-count quantitative PET reconstruction with an iterative neural network. IEEE Trans. Med. Imaging **39**, 3512–3522 (2020)
16. Dosovitskiy, A., et al..: An image is worth 16x16 words: transformers for image recognition at scale. ArXiv Preprint arXiv:2010.11929 (2020)
17. Vaswani, A., et al.: Attention is all you need. In: Advances in Neural Information Processing Systems 30 (2017)
18. Liu, Z., et al.: Swin transformer: hierarchical vision transformer using shifted windows. In: Proceedings of the IEEE/CVF International Conference on Computer Vision, pp. 10012–10022 (2021)
19. Combettes, P.L., Pesquet, J.C.: Proximal splitting methods in signal processing. In: Bauschke, H., Burachik, R., Combettes, P., Elser, V., Luke, D., Wolkowicz, H. (eds.) Fixed-Point Algorithms for Inverse Problems in Science and Engineering. Springer Optimization and its Applications, vol 49. Springer, New York (2011). https://doi.org/10.1007/978-1-4419-9569-8_10
20. He, K., Zhang, X., Ren, S., Sun, J.: Deep residual learning for image recognition. In: Proceedings of the IEEE Conference on Computer Vision and Pattern Recognition, pp. 770–778 (2016)
21. Wang, G., Qi, J.: Penalized likelihood PET image reconstruction using patch-based edge-preserving regularization. IEEE Trans. Med. Imaging **31**, 2194–2204 (2012)
22. Lange, K., Hunter, D., Yang, I.: Optimization transfer using surrogate objective functions. J. Comput. Graph. Stat. **9**, 1–20 (2000)
23. Hendrycks, D., Gimpel, K.: Gaussian error linear units (GELUs). ArXiv Preprint arXiv:1606.08415 (2016)
24. Kingma, D., Ba, J.: Adam: a method for stochastic optimization. ArXiv Preprint arXiv:1412.6980 (2014)
25. Hudson, H., Larkin, R.: Accelerated image reconstruction using ordered subsets of projection data. IEEE Trans. Med. Imaging **13**, 601–609 (1994)
26. De Pierro, A.: A modified expectation maximization algorithm for penalized likelihood estimation in emission tomography. IEEE Trans. Med. Imaging **14**, 132–137 (1995)
27. Häggström, I., Schmidtlein, C., Campanella, G., Fuchs, T.: DeepPET: a deep encoder-decoder network for directly solving the PET image reconstruction inverse problem. Med. Image Anal. **54**, 253–262 (2019)
28. Cocosco, C., Kollokian, V., Kwan, R., Pike, G., Evans, A.: BrainWeb: online interface to a 3D MRI simulated brain database. Neuroimage **5**, 425 (1997)
29. Siddon, R.: Fast calculation of the exact radiological path for a three-dimensional CT array. Med. Phys. **12**, 252–255 (1985)
30. Wang, Z., Bovik, A., Sheikh, H., Simoncelli, E.: Image quality assessment: from error visibility to structural similarity. IEEE Trans. Image Process. **13**, 600–612 (2004)

Supervised Deep Learning for Head Motion Correction in PET

Tianyi Zeng[1], Jiazhen Zhang[1], Enette Revilla[5], Eléonore V. Lieffrig[1],
Xi Fang[2], Yihuan Lu[6], and John A. Onofrey[1,3,4(✉)]

[1] Department of Radiology and Biomedical Imaging, New Haven, CT, USA
{tianyi.zeng,jiazhen.zhang,eleonore.lieffrig,john.onofrey}@yale.edu
[2] Department of Psychiatry, New Haven, CT, USA
xi.fang@yale.edu
[3] Department of Urology, New Haven, CT, USA
[4] Department of Biomedical Engineering, Yale University, New Haven, CT, USA
[5] University of California, Davis, CA, USA
ecrevilla@ucdavis.edu
[6] United Imaging Healthcare, Shanghai, China
yihuan.lu@united-imaging.com

Abstract. Head movement is a major limitation in brain positron emission tomography (PET) imaging, which results in image artifacts and quantification errors. Head motion correction plays a critical role in quantitative image analysis and diagnosis of nervous system diseases. However, to date, there is no approach that can track head motion continuously without using an external device. Here, we develop a deep learning-based algorithm to predict rigid motion for brain PET by leveraging existing dynamic PET scans with gold-standard motion measurements from external Polaris Vicra tracking. We propose a novel Deep Learning for Head Motion Correction (DL-HMC) methodology that consists of three components: (i) PET input data encoder layers; (ii) regression layers to estimate the six rigid motion transformation parameters; and (iii) feature-wise transformation (FWT) layers to condition the network to tracer time-activity. The input of DL-HMC is sampled pairs of one-second 3D cloud representations of the PET data and the output is the prediction of six rigid transformation motion parameters. We trained this network in a supervised manner using the Vicra motion tracking information as gold-standard. We quantitatively evaluate DL-HMC by comparing to gold-standard Vicra measurements and qualitatively evaluate the reconstructed images as well as perform region of interest standard uptake value (SUV) measurements. An algorithm ablation study was performed to determine the contributions of each of our DL-HMC design choices to network performance. Our results demonstrate accurate motion prediction performance for brain PET using a data-driven registration approach without external motion tracking hardware. All code is publicly available on GitHub: https://github.com/OnofreyLab/dl-hmc_miccai2022.

Supplementary Information The online version contains supplementary material available at https://doi.org/10.1007/978-3-031-16440-8_19.

Keywords: Deep learning · Supervised learning · Data-driven motion correction · Image registration · Brain · PET

1 Introduction

Positron emission tomography (PET) allows clinicians and researchers to study physiological or pathological processes in humans, and in particular the brain [10,15]. However, patient movement during scanning presents a challenge for accurate PET image reconstruction and subsequent quantitative analysis [9]. Head motion during brain PET scans reduces image resolution (sharpness), lowers concentrations in high-uptake regions, and causes mis-estimation in tracer kinetic modeling. Even small magnitude head motion may have a large impact on brain PET quantification. The long duration of PET studies exacerbates this problem, where involuntary movements of the patient are unavoidable and the average head motion can vary from 7 mm [1] in clinical scans to triple this amount for longer research scans. Therefore, the ability to track and correct head motion is critical in PET studies.

For motion correction, a straightforward approach is physical head restraint [5]. However, it does not provide correction once motion occurs and it reduces the level of patient comfort, especially for long research scans. Post-reconstruction registration, the most commonly used approach, cannot correct for motion within one scan period. An alternative method, multi-acquisition-frame [14] divides scan frames at times of motion but cannot correct for frequent motion due to low count statistics in one frame. Neither of these methods can perform motion correction in real-time. To date, the most accurate approach is event-by-event correction using motion information measured by a hardware-based motion tracking (HMT) system such as Polaris Vicra [8]. However, HMT is not generally accepted in clinical use since it usually requires attaching a tracking device to the patient and additional setup time. Frames with inaccurate motion estimates can be excluded, but this increases image noise by discarding data. For HMT, slippage of the attached markers can happen due to non-rigid fixation that can be affected by hair style. Other systems like markerless motion tracking [11] are still under development and have not been validated for PET use. On the other hand, data-driven motion correction methods that are based on PET raw data do not suffer these problems and have been developed and applied in clinical research [13]. Therefore, it is appealing to develop an approach that can perform accurate and robust head motion tracking and estimation based only on PET raw data in real-time during the scan.

Image registration methods [17] that seek to align two or more images offer a data-driven solution for correcting brain motion. While some registration methods use hand-crafted features instead of raw intensities [17], deep learning (DL) techniques, in which neural networks build a hierarchical representation of the data using multiple layers of hidden units [12], allow for the registration methods to learn the features of interest directly from the data. Deep learning methods are of interest because they may be less susceptible to local optima, and they offer highly parallelized implementations conducive to real-time applications.

In this study, we developed a deep learning-based method capable of real-time head motion tracking during brain PET imaging in order to perform rigid motion correction without the aid of external devices. We train our deep learning head motion correction (DL-HMC) network in a supervised manner with one-second 3D point clouds back-projected from clinical patient PET listmode data and use Vicra as gold standard motion estimates. We validate our method in both single subject and multiple subject experiments, and quantitatively compared the synthetic motion information with Vicra gold-standard as well as through qualitative reconstruction image ROI evaluation. We also performed an algorithm ablation study to determine the contributions of each of our strategies.

2   Methods

2.1   Data

We identified 25 ^{18}F-FDG PET scans from a database of brain PET scans acquired on a brain-dedicated Siemens HRRT scanner at the Yale PET Center. The 25 subject group constitutes a diverse patient population that includes 8 cognitive normals, 11 subjects suffering from cocaine dependence, and 6 with cognitive disease. The mean injected activity for these 25 patients is 4.95±0.14 mCi. Eight points forming the vertices of a 10-cm cube centered in the scanner FOV were chosen to describe the motion of the brain, and inter-frame motion was computed by averaging twice the standard deviation of the motion of each of these 8 points [7]. The overall motion of the brain throughout the entire scan (mean±SD) was 12.07±7.12 mm. In addition to the list-mode data, other materials were available such as Polaris Vicra motion tracking information used as motion gold-standard (Sect. 1), T1-weighted MR images and PET-space to MR-space transformation matrices. All PET imaging data is 30 min acquired 60 min post injection.

2.2   Motion Correction Network Structure

Our DL-HMC network architecture (Fig. 1) consists of the following components: (i) two feature extractor blocks to encode the PET input data, which consists of a reference image I_{ref} and moving image I_{mov}; (ii) a regression block to estimate the six rigid transformation motion parameters; and (iii) feature-wise transformation (FWT) layers [3] to condition the network to tracer time-activity. The proposed network architecture uses DenseNet [6] as a feature extractor with shared weights for two input images and concatenates the output features into a single vector. The encoders effectively reduce the 3D image data volumes down to a vector of size 128. The FWT takes the relative difference in time $\Delta t = t_{mov} - t_{ref}$ (in seconds) between the reference and moving images, respectively, as input to a fully connected network and then multiplies the concatenated feature output to this result, which conditions the network to dynamic changes in the PET tracer over time. Finally, the conditioned features are fed into the fully connected regression block to predict the translation and rotation components of the motion $\theta = [t_x, t_y, t_z, r_x, r_y, r_z]$. The network has 11,492,102 trainable parameters.

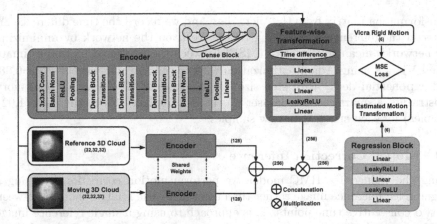

Fig. 1. DL-HMC network architecture. The network takes two one-second 3D point cloud images as input to a feature extraction block (with a DenseNet structure) with shared weights between the reference and moving images. A regression block then estimates the rigid motion transformation parameters. A feature-wise transformation block conditions the network to relative time difference bewteen the reference and moving images.

The input for the network consists of one-second 3D cloud representations of the PET data. The 3D clouds were created by back-projecting the PET listmode data along the line-of-response (LOR) with normalization for scanner sensitivity using MATLAB. We pre-process the 3D cloud data volumes by smoothing and down sampling from $256 \times 256 \times 207$ voxels ($1.22 \times 1.22 \times 1.23\,\mathrm{mm}^3$ voxel spacing) to $32 \times 32 \times 32$ voxels ($9.76 \times 9.76 \times 7.96\,\mathrm{mm}^3$ voxel spacing), which reduces the data memory footprint, increases computational efficiency, and removes image noise. Each one-second 3D cloud has corresponding Vicra motion tracking system (rigid transformation matrix) as gold-standard motion information. We implemented the network in Python (version 3.8) using PyTorch (version 1.7.1) and MONAI (version 0.8). All code is available on GitHub: http:// github.com/OnofreyLab/dl-hmc_miccai2022/

2.3   Network Training Strategy

We perform supervised learning of the DL-HMC network using two input 3D point clouds from two different time points t_{ref} and t_{mov} to predict the relative rigid motion transformation with respect to the Vicra gold-standard. Due to the large number of one-second data input pairs available, we developed an efficient data sub-sampling strategy for model training. From each subject in our training set, we select n_{ref} reference time points from a uniform random distribution over the PET scan duration. For each reference time, we then sample n_{mov} different moving image times using a *uniform sampling strategy*, where moving image times are randomly sampled from a uniform distribution such that $t_{\mathrm{mov}} > t_{\mathrm{ref}}$. For n_{sub} training subjects, this process generates $n_{\mathrm{sub}} \times n_{\mathrm{ref}} \times n_{\mathrm{mov}}$ unique training pairs. In both sampling procedures, we calculate the relative motion transformation matrix from the Vicra data and we record the time difference Δt between the reference and moving times. We train the network by minimizing the network's mean square error (MSE) between the predicted motion estimate $\hat{\theta}$ and Vicra θ using Adam optimization with initial learning rate 5e-4, γ=0.98, and exponential decay with step size 200. Because of GPU and CPU memory constraints, a smart caching dataset was used to replace 25% of the data (1,024 samples) for each epoch with new samples.

2.4   Motion Correction Inference

Using the trained DL-HMC model, we perform motion correction by using a single, fixed reference image rather than computing the relative motion between all two consecutive time points. This approach to using a single reference image avoids accumulation of any errors in the motion correction prediction. In this case, we select the first image time point t_{ref}=3,600 (60 min post injection) as the reference image and predict the motion from this reference to all subsequent one second image frames in the next 30 min (1,800 one-second time points).

3   Results

Due to limitations caused by large amounts of data, hardware memory constraints, and long training times, we performed initial model development using data from a single subject (Sect. 3.1). The results of these pilot experiments informed our model design decisions (Sect. 2.2) as well as training strategy (Sect. 2.3), which we then applied to our multi-subject DL-HMC model (Sect. 3.2).

For all experiments, we quantitatively and qualitatively evaluate motion correction performance. For quantitative assessment, we calculate the MSE between the Vicra gold-standard θ and DL-HMC prediction $\hat{\theta}$ (these are unitless error measurements because they combine translation (mm) and rotation components (degrees)). For qualitative assessment, we reconstruct the PET image using the predicted motion correction information for the whole sequence using Motion-compensation OSEM List-mode Algorithm for Resolution-Recovery Reconstruction (MOLAR) [2] and compare to the Vicra reconstructed image. The same reconstruction parameters were applied using the different DL-HMC and Vicra motion estimates. For a more comprehensive quantitative analysis of the reconstructed PET images, each subject's co-registered MR image was segmented into 109 regions using FreeSurfer [4], which were then merged and into twelve gray matter brain regions of interest (ROIs) and analysed by calculating standard uptake value (SUV). All computations were performed on a server with Intel Xeon Gold 5218 processors, 256 GB RAM, and an NVIDIA Quadro RTX 8000 GPU (48 GB RAM).

3.1   Single Subject Pilot Experiments

To evaluate the feasibility of the proposed method to accurately predict head motion throughout the PET scan duration, we first applied the DL-HMC in

Table 1. DL-HMC ablation study results. Reported values are mean±SD of corresponding dataset.

More Data	FWT	Deep Encoder	Unif. Sampling	Val. MSE	Test MSE
✓	✓	✓	✓	0.070±0.109	**0.035±0.073**
✓	✓	✓	○	**0.029±0.082**	3.530±4.644
✓	✓	○	✓	0.094±0.244	0.058±0.118
✓	✓	○	○	0.139±0.237	0.112±0.179
✓	○	○	✓	0.170±0.227	0.188±0.177
○	✓	○	✓	0.144±0.186	0.143±0.204
○	○	○	○	0.665±0.970	0.786±0.836

single subject ($n_{sub}=1$) experiments and perform a rigorous ablation study to determine the contributions of each of our DL-HMC design choices to network performance. For pilot experiments, we split the subject's entire PET scan time course (1,800 one-second images) into three subsets corresponding to 80/10/10% of the data for training/validation/testing. While using data in this manner from the same subject introduces bias, we utilize a single reference point ($t_{ref} = 3,600$) and register all t_{mov} in the testing set to this image to calculate experimental error independent of the training data, which provides an informative measure of algorithm performance. From the training set, we randomly selected $n_{ref}=1,440$ reference time points. DL-HMC ablation experiments (Table 1) consisted of the following design choices: (i) using a different number moving image time points, $n_{mov}=1$ (1,440 total samples) or $n_{mov}=10$ (14,400 total samples) (see Sect. 2.3); (ii) the inclusion of time information Δt using the FWT layers; (iii) increased depth of the image encoder by changing the DenseNet growth rate from 4 to 32; and (iv) different data sampling strategies, where we compare our *uniform sampling* strategy to a *normal sampling* with moving image times randomly sampled with respect to a normal distribution (right tail) with FWHM equal to 60 s. Our DL-HMC results demonstrated that using a large training dataset ($n_{mov}=10$), FWTs, deep image encoders, and uniform random data sampling provided accurate motion prediction performance with MSE (mean±SD) 0.035±0.073 in the test set. Typical training for one subject with 14,400 training data samples required 10,000 epochs for convergence. Figure 2a shows DL-HMC motion correction predictions nearly identical to Vicra. Reconstructed PET images also appear qualitatively similar between DL-HMC and Vicra (Fig. S1) and both demonstrate similar ROI SUV differences compared to reconstruction with no motion correction (NMC).

3.2 Multi-subject Experiments

Based on the results of the pilot experiments (Sect. 3.1), we verified the generalizability of the proposed network by training on multiple subjects and avoid

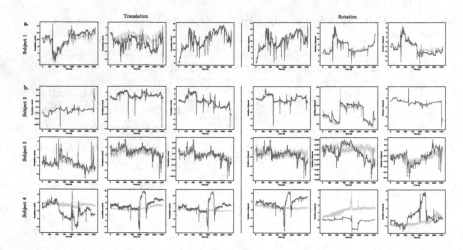

Fig. 2. Motion prediction results. Columns show rigid transformation parameters (from left to right: translation in x, y, z directions and rotation about the x, y, z axes) from DL-HMC (red) and gold-standard Vicra motion tracking (blue). (a) Estimates from single-subject (Subject 1) model experiments and from (b) the multi-subject model in three example test subjects: example case in training set (Subject 2); a good example from the test set (Subject 3, Subject C in Table S1); and a failure case in the test set (Subject 4, Subject D in Table S1). (Color figure online)

bias by evaluating on subjects not included in the training data. Here, we split the patient cohort into training and testing subsets of 20 and 5 subjects, respectively. Training employed the sampling strategy from Sect. 2.3 using n_{sub}=20, n_{ref}=1,800 and n_{mov}=6 (216,000 unique data samples). Using an epoch size 4,096, model training required 20,000 epochs for convergence on the validation set. Figure 2b shows motion prediction results for three example subjects: one subject included in the training set (to test if the model experiences any loss due to increasing the training population) and two subjects from the testing dataset (a good example and the worst performing example). Table S1 shows quantitative results for all test subjects. The results for Subject 2 (mean MSE 0.02) included in the training set show that the network is capable of accurately predicting motion from training subjects even though the motion relative to the reference frame was never used for training. As expected, performance degrades when evaluated on data from the testing set. DL-HMC tracks the Vicra motion estimates for Subject 3 well except for rotation about y (mean MSE is 0.74), but fails to track motion well in Subject 4 (mean MSE is 6.33). Figure 3 shows PET reconstruction results using MOLAR comparing DL-HMC motion results to Vicra and to NMC as well as quantitative ROI SUV evaluation. Subject 3 exhibits DL-HMC reconstruction performance similar to Vicra and shows similar ROI SUV values, although caudate and pallidum ROIs exhibit differences in mean SUV. As for the failure case, the DL-HMC reconstruction result is similar with NMC.

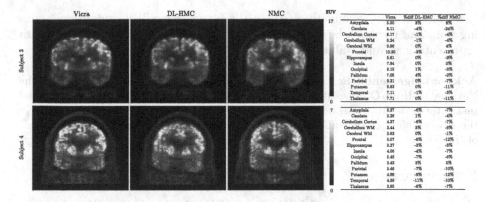

Fig. 3. PET image reconstruction results. MOLAR reconstructed images using Vicra gold-standard motion tracking, the proposed DL-HMC predicted motion correction, and no motion correction (NMC). Subject 3 is an example of successful motion correction using DL-HMC, and Subject 4 represents a failure case. The table on the right shows quantitative SUV difference values evaluated of twelve brain ROIs.

4   Discussion and Conclusion

In this work, we proposed a novel structure of deep neural network to perform head motion estimation using supervised learning. Instead of using one-second reconstructed PET images, which is time-consuming ($\sim$2 min), we use one-second 3D cloud images that take less than ten seconds to generate. DL-HMC is able to extract the motion information from these 3D cloud data with high noise levels (Fig. 1), which otherwise is extremely challenging for both standard, intensity-based registration methods and unsupervised deep learning approached. In contrast to other supervised registration learning approaches that utilize random (synthetic) transformations of the image data to learn the transformation parameters [16], we use an external device, Vicra, to provide supervision. The motion correction task is further complicated by the dynamic nature of PET imaging caused by tracer kinetics. With the help of FWTs, DL-HMC can capture tracer kinetic changes. The success of the uniform sampling strategy (Table 1) indicates that diversity in the training motion (reference and moving time frames are more likely to have larger motion between them with increasing Δt) is import for creating a robust model. Quantitative and qualitative evaluations of pilot and multi-subject experiments demonstrate that the proposed DL-HMC has potential for accurate PET rigid head motion correction.

Limitations of the work include training with a small number of subjects, which prevents the model from generalizing across diverse subject anatomies and motions. Our model may also benefit from a different data representation. While our initial model results indicate capabilities of predicting motion of magnitude $\sim$1mm, our current pre-processing reduces input image resolution to $\sim$10mm^3, which may limit the model's ability to detect motion with smaller magnitudes. Finally, we train and test DL-HMC using a single tracer (FDG), although this is by far the most commonly used. In the future, we will include more training data and test on a larger subject cohort, experiment with alternative data representations, and evaluate DL-HMC on other tracers.

Acknowledgements. Research reported in this publication was supported by the National Institute Of Biomedical Imaging And Bioengineering (NIBIB) of the National Institutes of Health (NIH) under Award Number R21 EB028954. The content is solely the responsibility of the authors and does not necessarily represent the official views of the NIH.

References

1. Beyer, T., Tellmann, L., Nickel, I., Pietrzyk, U.: On the use of positioning aids to reduce misregistration in the head and neck in whole-body PET/CT studies. J. Nucl. Med. **46**(4), 596–602 (2005)
2. Carson, R.E., Barker, W.C., Liow, J.S., Johnson, C.A.: Design of a motion-compensation OSEM list-mode algorithm for resolution-recovery reconstruction for the HRRT. In: 2003 IEEE Nuclear Science Symposium. Conference Record (IEEE Cat. No. 03CH37515), vol. 5, pp. 3281–3285. IEEE (2003)
3. Dumoulin, V., et al.: Feature-wise transformations. Distill **3**(7), e11 (2018)
4. Fischl, B., et al.: Automatically parcellating the human cerebral cortex. Cereb. Cortex **14**(1), 11–22 (2004)
5. Green, M.V., et al.: Head movement in normal subjects during simulated pet brain imaging with and without head restraint. J. Nucl. Med. **35**(9), 1538–1546 (1994)
6. Huang, G., Liu, Z., Van Der Maaten, L., Weinberger, K.Q.: Densely connected convolutional networks. In: Proceedings of the IEEE Conference on Computer Vision and Pattern Recognition, pp. 4700–4708 (2017)
7. Jin, X., Mulnix, T., Gallezot, J.D., Carson, R.E.: Evaluation of motion correction methods in human brain PET imaging-a simulation study based on human motion data. Med. Phys. **40**(10), 102503 (2013)
8. Jin, X., Mulnix, T., Sandiego, C.M., Carson, R.E.: Evaluation of frame-based and event-by-event motion-correction methods for awake monkey brain pet imaging. J. Nucl. Med. **55**(2), 287–293 (2014)
9. Keller, S.H., et al.: Methods for motion correction evaluation using 18f-FDG human brain scans on a high-resolution PET scanner. J. Nucl. Med. **53**(3), 495–504 (2012)
10. Kuang, Z., et al.: Design and performance of SIAT aPET: a uniform high-resolution small animal PET scanner using dual-ended readout detectors. Phys. Med. Biol. **65**(23), 235013 (2020)
11. Kyme, A.Z., Se, S., Meikle, S.R., Fulton, R.R.: Markerless motion estimation for motion-compensated clinical brain imaging. Phys. Med. Biol. **63**(10), 105018 (2018)
12. LeCun, Y., Bengio, Y., Hinton, G.: Deep learning. Nature **521**(7553), 436–444 (2015)
13. Lu, Y., et al.: Data-driven voluntary body motion detection and non-rigid event-by-event correction for static and dynamic PET. Phys. Med. Biol. **64**(6), 065002 (2019)
14. Lu, Y., Naganawa, M., Toyonaga, T., Gallezot, J.D., Fontaine, K., Ren, S., Revilla, E.M., Mulnix, T., Carson, R.E.: Data-driven motion detection and event-by-event correction for brain PET: Comparison with vicra. J. Nucl. Med. **61**(9), 1397–1403 (2020)

15. Rodriguez-Vieitez, E., et al.: Diverging longitudinal changes in astrocytosis and amyloid pet in autosomal dominant Alzheimer's disease. Brain **139**(3), 922–936 (2016). https://doi.org/10.1093/brain/awv404
16. Sloan, J.M., Goatman, K.A., Siebert, J.P.: Learning rigid image registration - utilizing convolutional neural networks for medical image registration. In: Proceedings of the 11th International Joint Conference on Biomedical Engineering Systems and Technologies, pp. 89–99. SCITEPRESS - Science and Technology Publications (2018)
17. Sotiras, A., Davatzikos, C., Paragios, N.: Deformable medical image registration: a survey. IEEE Trans. Med. Imaging **32**(7), 1153–1190 (2013)

Ultrasound Imaging

Adaptive 3D Localization of 2D Freehand Ultrasound Brain Images

Pak-Hei Yeung[1,2]([✉]), Moska Aliasi[3], Monique Haak[3],
the INTERGROWTH-21st Consortium[4], Weidi Xie[5,6],
and Ana I. L. Namburete[2]

[1] Oxford Machine Learning in NeuroImaging Lab, Department of Computer Science,
University of Oxford, Oxford, UK
pak.yeung@pmb.ox.ac.uk
[2] Department of Engineering Science, Institute of Biomedical Engineering,
University of Oxford, Oxford, UK
[3] Division of Fetal Medicine, Department of Obstetrics, Leiden University Medical
Center, 2333, ZA Leiden, The Netherlands
[4] Nuffield Department of Women's and Reproductive Health, University of Oxford,
Oxford, UK
[5] Shanghai Jiao Tong University, Shanghai, China
[6] Visual Geometry Group, Department of Engineering Science, University of Oxford,
Oxford, UK

Abstract. Two-dimensional (2D) freehand ultrasound is the mainstay
in prenatal care and fetal growth monitoring. The task of matching corresponding cross-sectional planes in the 3D anatomy for a given 2D ultrasound brain scan is essential in freehand scanning, but challenging. We
propose AdLocUI, a framework that **Ad**aptively **Loc**alizes 2D **U**ltrasound
Images in the 3D anatomical atlas *without* using any external tracking
sensor. We first train a convolutional neural network with 2D slices sampled from co-aligned 3D ultrasound volumes to predict their locations in
the 3D anatomical atlas. Next, we fine-tune it with 2D freehand ultrasound images using a novel **unsupervised cycle consistency**, which
utilizes the fact that the overall displacement of a sequence of images in
the 3D anatomical atlas is equal to the displacement from the first image
to the last in that sequence. We demonstrate that AdLocUI can adapt to
three different ultrasound datasets, acquired with different machines and
protocols, and achieves significantly better localization accuracy than the
baselines. AdLocUI can be used for sensorless 2D freehand ultrasound
guidance by the bedside. The source code is available at https://github.
com/pakheiyeung/AdLocUI.

Keywords: Freehand ultrasound · Slice to volume registration ·
Domain adaptation

Supplementary Information The online version contains supplementary material
available at https://doi.org/10.1007/978-3-031-16440-8_20.

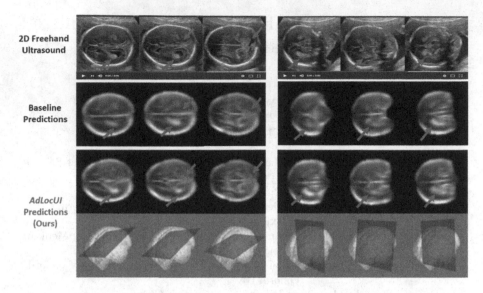

Fig. 1. Localization of 2D freehand ultrasound images in the 3D anatomical atlas (*i.e.* fetal brain). 2D slices sampled from the 3D atlas using image locations predicted by the baseline [23] and `AdLocUI` are presented, where our predictions show better correspondence (*i.e.* emphasized by the red arrows) with the ultrasound images, suggesting more accurate 3D localization prediction by `AdLocUI`. (Color figure online)

1   Introduction

Two-dimensional (2D) freehand ultrasonography is one of the most routinely deployed medical imaging modalities in prenatal care. The nature of ultrasound images is unique when compared to other modalities. While magnetic resonance imaging (MRI) and computerised tomography (CT) capture the complete 3D anatomy, each 2D ultrasound image is just a 2D cross-sectional view of an inherently 3D anatomy. It also differs from other 2D imaging modalities, such as X-ray which captures a projectional view of the 3D body. Such fundamental differences make image localization in the 3D anatomy a unique but important task for 2D freehand ultrasonography, especially for neuroimaging [21] (Fig. 1).

Experienced sonographers are often able to locate the 2D ultrasound images by mentally reconstructing the 3D anatomy [10]. However, training a network to achieve this is very challenging, mainly due to the difficulty of acquiring the training data (*i.e.* 2D freehand ultrasound images and their corresponding locations in the 3D anatomy). In this paper, we overcome this limitation by using only a small number (*i.e.* 50) of 3D ultrasound volumes, co-aligned to a common 3D anatomical atlas, for the training. It can then be fine-tuned by our proposed **unsupervised cycle consistency** to adapt to 2D ultrasound images acquired from different machines and protocols. The *only* manual annotation required in our work is the co-alignment of the 3D training volumes, which could be further automated with volumetric registration algorithms, such as [19].

A related task, namely standard plane detection, has been attempted in numerous prior works, using convolutional neural networks (ConvNet) [1,8,9] and reinforcement learning [5,15]. A recent study [6] extended standard plane detection to a guidance system using an external motion sensor. Despite their excellent performance, the overarching problem of locating a 2D freehand scan in the 3D anatomy remains unexplored. Volumetric reconstruction with motion-tracked probe is another related research topic [17,18]. However, freehand ultrasound scanning of the fetus is challenged by the fact that the subject is not stationary, particularly before the third trimester. A tracking sensor, therefore, can only record the probe position but not the plane position due to the relative motion between the fetus and the probe. This limits the tracking sensors' practical application in our problem setting. Inspired by [13], Yeung et al. [23] proposed to use 2D slices sampled from 3D ultrasound volumes to train a network to predict the 3D locations of 2D ultrasound images. Our work extends this by proposing a framework that adapts the trained network to generalize to 2D ultrasound images acquired from diverse machines and protocols, which are essential for realistic scenarios in which data are acquired from different clinical centres.

In this paper, we propose AdLocUI, a framework that **Ad**aptively **Loc**alizes 2D **U**ltrasound **I**mages in a predefined 3D anatomical atlas (*i.e.* fetal brain). Our work makes the following contributions: *firstly*, we propose a framework for the aforementioned localization task. We demonstrate that a *single* model, trained with minimal manual annotation (*i.e.* co-alignment of a set of 3D volumes), can be fine-tuned in an **unsupervised** manner and adapted to 3 different datasets of ultrasound images, acquired from diverse machines and acquisition protocols differing from those of the training data. *Secondly*, we propose a novel way to fine-tune the trained model to adapt to the target domain 2D ultrasound images, which utilizes the fact that the overall displacement of a sequence of images in the 3D anatomical atlas is equal to the displacement from the first image to the last in that sequence. As our *third* contribution, we show, with ablation studies, that the introduction of our proposed fine-tuning step leads to a significant improvement on localization accuracy when compared to the baseline [23], and that fine-tuned by popular domain adaptation (DA) algorithms [7,16,22]. Our framework can be used for *sensorless* volumetric reconstruction [24] and freehand guidance for training and facilitating more objective analysis and diagnosis.

2   Methods

2.1   Problem Setup

We consider each ultrasound acquisition from different machines as a different domain. In general, given a sequence or set of m 2D ultrasound images, $\mathcal{I} = \{\mathbf{I}_1, \mathbf{I}_2, \ldots, \mathbf{I}_m\}$, acquired from any domain, our goal is to predict their locations, $\mathcal{L}_{Img} = \{\mathbf{L}_1, \mathbf{L}_2, \ldots, \mathbf{L}_m\}$, in a predefined 3D anatomical atlas, $\mathbb{R}^3_{atlas}$.

We formulate this problem in 3 stages (Fig. 2). In *training*, we train a regression ConvNet, $\psi(\cdot; \theta)$, parametrized by θ, with n 2D slices, $\mathcal{S} = \{\mathbf{S}_1, \mathbf{S}_2, \ldots, \mathbf{S}_n\}$,

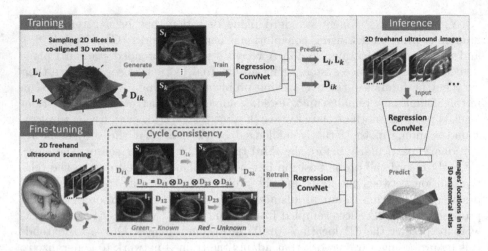

Fig. 2. Pipeline of our proposed framework, `AdLocUI`. During training, 2D slices, $\mathbf{S}_i$, sampled from co-aligned 3D volumes are used to train a regression ConvNet to predict the locations, $\mathbf{L}_i$, and displacement $\mathbf{D}_{ik}$, of the 2D slices in the 3D anatomical atlas. The ConvNet is then fined-tuned **unsupervisedly** with 2D freehand ultrasound images, $\mathbf{I}_i$, based on the proposed cycle consistency. We can then use the fine-tuned ConvNet to localize $\mathbf{I}_i$ of the same domain (*i.e.* acquired with the same machines and protocols) in the predefined 3D anatomical atlas.

sampled from the corresponding plane locations, $\mathcal{L}_S = \{\mathbf{L}_1, \mathbf{L}_2, \ldots, \mathbf{L}_n\}$, of a set of 3D ultrasound volumes co-aligned in $\mathbb{R}^3_{atlas}$. After that, we retrain (*i.e. fine-tune*) $\psi(\cdot; \theta)$ with $\mathcal{S}$ and $\mathcal{I}$, using cycle consistency in an **unsupervised** manner. $\psi(\cdot; \theta)$ can then be used on $\mathcal{I}$ or images of the same domain as $\mathcal{I}$ during *inference*. For clarification, we will refer to 2D slice sampled from the 3D training volumes as $\mathbf{S}$ and the target domain 2D ultrasound image as $\mathbf{I}$.

2.2   Training with Sampled 2D Slices from 3D Volumes

Conventionally, training $\psi(\cdot; \theta)$, requires paired training data (*i.e.* $\{\mathbf{I}_i, \mathbf{L}_i\}$), where $\mathbf{L}_i$ (parameterization of $\mathbf{L}$ is detailed below) needs to be manually annotated, which is very challenging and time-consuming. A prior study [23] proposed to use 2D slices, $\mathcal{S}$, sampled from aligned 3D ultrasound volumes, as the training data. Therefore, the corresponding plane locations, $\mathcal{L}_S$, of the 2D slices are automatically known, voiding the need for further manual annotation. We adopt the same strategy in this study.

Data Preparation Pipeline. We affinely registered a set of 3D ultrasound volumes, to a common predefined anatomical atlas, $\mathbb{R}^3_{atlas}$, either manually, or by alignment algorithms such as [19], followed by minor manual correction. This is the **only** manual annotation required by `AdLocUI`. 2D slices, $\mathcal{S}$, were then randomly sampled from the aligned volumes, using Fibonacci sphere sampling of polar coordinates [13], on the fly during training. The details are described in [23].

Training Objectives. With a set of n paired training data, $\{\mathbf{S}_i, \mathbf{L}_i\}_{i=1}^{n}$, a regression ConvNet, $\psi(\cdot; \theta)$, is trained. $\psi(\cdot; \theta)$ is composed of 3 parts, namely the encoder $\psi_{enc}(\cdot; \theta_{enc})$, location prediction $\psi_{loc}(\cdot; \theta_{loc})$ and displacement prediction $\psi_{disp}(\cdot; \theta_{disp})$. First, $\mathcal{S}$ are randomly augmented by scaling, in-plane translation, contrast adjustment and random noise. A feature vector, $\mathbf{v}_i$, is then generated by the encoder part, $\psi_{enc}(\cdot; \theta_{enc})$, for each $\mathbf{S}_i$:

$$[\mathbf{v}_1, \ \mathbf{v}_2, ..., \ \mathbf{v}_n] = [\psi_{enc}(\mathbf{S}_1; \theta_{enc}), \ \psi_{enc}(\mathbf{S}_2; \theta_{enc}), \ ..., \ \psi_{enc}(\mathbf{S}_n; \theta_{enc})] \qquad (1)$$

Similar to [23], the feature vectors, $\{\mathbf{v}_1, \mathbf{v}_2, \ldots, \mathbf{v}_n\}$, are used to predict the plane locations, $\mathcal{L}_S$, by the location prediction part, $\psi_{loc}(\cdot; \theta_{loc})$:

$$[\hat{\mathbf{L}}_1, \ \hat{\mathbf{L}}_2, ..., \ \hat{\mathbf{L}}_n] = [\psi_{loc}(\mathbf{v}_1; \theta_{loc}), \ \psi_{loc}(\mathbf{v}_2; \theta_{loc}), \ ..., \ \psi_{loc}(\mathbf{v}_n; \theta_{loc})] \qquad (2)$$

where $\hat{\ }$ indicates predicted values. Unlike [23], we simultaneously predict $\mathbf{L}_i$ and the *displacement*, $\mathbf{D}_{ik}$, between each pair of slices, $\mathbf{S}_i$ and $\mathbf{S}_k$, in $\mathbb{R}^3_{atlas}$ by the displacement prediction part, $\psi_{disp}(\cdot; \theta_{disp})$:

$$[..., \ \hat{\mathbf{D}}_{ik}, ..., \ \hat{\mathbf{D}}_{nn}] = [..., \ \psi_{disp}(\mathbf{v}_i, \mathbf{v}_k; \theta_{disp}), \ ..., \ \psi_{disp}(\mathbf{v}_n, \mathbf{v}_n; \theta_{disp})] \qquad (3)$$

Parameterization of L and D. Following the practice of [23], we parameterize the plane location, $\mathbf{L}_i \in \mathcal{D}^{3 \times 3}$, by three anchor points (*i.e.* their x, y and z coordinates), namely the *top right*, *top left* and *bottom right* corners, of $\mathbf{S}_i$. The displacement, $\mathbf{D}_{ik}$, from $\mathbf{S}_i$ to $\mathbf{S}_k$, in $\mathbb{R}^3_{atlas}$ is therefore parameterized as $(\mathbf{L}_i - \mathbf{L}_k)$. There are other parameterization methods, such as Euler angles and quaternions [12,13], which may be investigated in future work.

Training Loss (l_t). We use weighted mean least-squared error (MSE) as the loss function for the multi-task learning:

$$l_t = w_L \cdot \mathrm{MSE}\left(\hat{\mathbf{L}}, \mathbf{L}\right) + w_D \cdot \mathrm{MSE}\left(\hat{\mathbf{D}}, \mathbf{D}\right) \qquad (4)$$

where w_L and w_D are the weights of the respective MSE loss.

2.3 Fine-tuning with 2D Ultrasound Images

The trained ConvNet, $\psi(\cdot; \theta)$, can then be fine-tuned with a new set of m 2D ultrasound images, $\mathcal{I}$, acquired from any domain. The retraining relies on *cycle consistency* and uses both the training data (*i.e.* $\{\mathcal{S}, \mathcal{L}_S\}$) and the new set of images, $\mathcal{I}$, *without* further manual annotation.

Cycle Consistency. Although the plane locations, $\mathcal{L}_{Img}$ of the new $\mathcal{I}$ are unknown, we know, by cycle consistency, that the overall displacement, $\mathbf{D}$, of a sequence of images in $\mathbb{R}^3_{atlas}$ must be equal to $\mathbf{D}$ from the first image to the last of that sequence. For example, as illustrated in Fig. 2, the overall displacement

(i) $\mathbf{S}_i \rightarrow \mathbf{I}_1$ ($\mathbf{D}_{i1}$), and $\mathbf{I}_1 \rightarrow \mathbf{I}_2$ ($\mathbf{D}_{12}$), and $\mathbf{I}_2 \rightarrow \mathbf{I}_3$ ($\mathbf{D}_{23}$), and $\mathbf{I}_3 \rightarrow \mathbf{S}_k$ ($\mathbf{D}_{3k}$) is equal to (ii) $\mathbf{S}_i \rightarrow \mathbf{S}_k$ ($\mathbf{D}_{ik}$). While every $\mathbf{D}$ in (i) is unknown, $\mathbf{D}_{ik}$ in (ii) is known from the original training data. Therefore, we can construct the cycle consistency loss (l_c) with this equality to retrain $\psi(\cdot; \theta)$:

$$l_c = \mathrm{MSE}\left(\hat{\mathbf{D}}_{i1} \otimes \hat{\mathbf{D}}_{12} \otimes \hat{\mathbf{D}}_{23} \otimes \hat{\mathbf{D}}_{3k},\ \mathbf{D}_{ik}\right) \qquad (5)$$

where $\otimes$ depends on the choice of the parameterization of $\mathbf{D}$ and, hence, $\otimes$ is simply *subtraction* here (similar to the derivation of $\mathbf{D}$ from $\mathbf{L}$ described in Sect. 2.2). When predicting two consecutive displacements (*e.g.* $\mathbf{D}_{12}$ and $\mathbf{D}_{23}$), the common image involved (*i.e.* $\mathbf{I}_2$) is augmented differently, which coincides with the recent self-supervised and unsupervised learning studies [2,11,20] that emphasize the importance of data augmentation. Our proposed unsupervised cycle consistency mechanism is also conceptually different from that proposed in other ultrasound imaging studies, such as [4,14].

Fine-Tuning Loss (l_f). Since the goal of AdLocUI is to predict the corresponding plane location, $\mathcal{L}_{Img}$, of $\mathcal{I}$, relying solely on the cycle consistency loss, l_c, (*i.e.* supervise only on $\mathbf{D}$) may diverge the prediction or even fall into trivial solutions [25]. Therefore, we add the original training loss, l_t (Eq. 4), to regulate the retraining and the overall fine-tuning loss, l_f is:

$$l_f = w_c \cdot l_c + l_t \qquad (6)$$

where w_c is the weight of the cycle consistency loss, l_c.

2.4   Inference

The fine-tuned ConvNet, $\psi(\cdot; \theta)$, can be used on the set of 2D ultrasound images, $\mathcal{I}$, or other 2D ultrasound images of the same domain (*i.e.* acquired from the same machine) to predict their corresponding locations, $\mathcal{L}_{Img}$, in the predefined 3D anatomical atlas, $\mathbb{R}^3_{atlas}$:

$$[\hat{\mathbf{L}}_1,\ \hat{\mathbf{L}}_2, ...,\ \hat{\mathbf{L}}_m] = [\psi(\mathbf{I}_1; \theta),\ \psi(\mathbf{I}_2; \theta),\ ...,\ \psi(\mathbf{I}_m; \theta)] \qquad (7)$$

3   Experimental Design

AdLocUI and other baseline approaches were first trained with 2D slices, $\mathcal{S}$, sampled from 50 3D volumes acquired by Philips HD9 (*Training* in Fig. 2). The trained networks was then fine-tuned and evaluated (*Fine-tuning* and *Inference* in Fig. 2) on both volume-sampled 2D images and native 2D freehand images. The training and testing images were acquired from different clinical sites and machines, simulating the cross-domain variance observed in reality. We compared AdLocUI with Yeung et al.[23] and the same fine-tuned by popular unsupervised deep DA methods, namely MK-MMD [16], DANN [7] and CORAL [22]. Their implementation details are in the Supplementary Materials.

Volume-Sampled Testing Images. We tested AdLocUI and other baseline approaches on 2D slices sampled from 17 aligned 3D volumes acquired by GE Voluson E10, which were different from the training volumes (Philips HD9). 3000 slices were sampled from each testing volume. Two evaluation metrics were used, namely the Euclidean distance (ED) between the coordinates of the predicted and ground-truth planes in the $\mathbb{R}^3_{atlas}$ and the dihedral angle (DA) between them.

Native 2D Freehand Images. Images from video sequences of 2D freehand ultrasound brain scans, acquired by GE Voluson E10 and Voluson E8 from two different clinical centers, were tested and qualitatively analyzed. As the ground-truth locations were not available, it was not possible to achieve the same detailed quantitative analysis as the volume-sampled images. We, thus, proposed another quantitative test. As the acquisition of the video sequences was smooth and continuous, the locations of consecutive images should not change abruptly, but show a gradual transition. We quantify such a rate of change (Δc) as:

$$\Delta c = \frac{\text{ED}(\hat{\mathbf{P}}_i, \hat{\mathbf{P}}_{i+1})}{1 - \text{NCC}(\mathbf{I}_i, \mathbf{I}_{i+1})} \tag{8}$$

where $\hat{\mathbf{P}}_i$ are the coordinates of the predicted plane of $\mathbf{I}_i$ and NCC is the normalized cross-correlation. We used normalized (*i.e.* by the mean of Δc) standard deviation (NSTD) to quantify the consistency of Δc throughout the whole video sequence, which should be low ideally. More details of the datasets are in the Supplementary Materials.

4   Results and Discussion

4.1   Volume-Sampled Images

We compared AdLocUI, via ablation studies, to different baseline approaches in two different settings, both corresponding to realistic scenarios.

Firstly, as presented in Table 1a, we considered the scenario where the *same* set of images was used for fine-tuning and then testing. This is relevant when *offline* analysis is performed, where we have sufficient time for fine-tuning with the test images before final analysis. From Table 1a, the original Yeung et al.[23] (*i.e.* without fine-tuning) achieved ED = 71.1 and DA=0.264, which was slightly worse than AdLocUI without fine-tuning (ED = 63.0 and DA = 0.251). The multi-task learning (*i.e.* additional task of predicting $\mathbf{D}_{ij}$) contributed to such improvement. Our proposed fine-tuning step, which does not require any additional manual annotation, contributed to a significant (p<0.05, student's t-test) improvement (ED = 23.7 and DA = 0.198). We also analyzed an *unlikely* situation where we assumed to have the ground-truth locations of the testing images for fine-tuning (*i.e.* retraining) Yeung et al.[23] in a supervised manner. This can be viewed as the *oracle* of the accuracy of the prediction (ED = 11.3 and DA = 0.172).

Table 1. Evaluation results (mean±standard deviation) on volume-sampled 2D images on two settings, 1a and 1b, evaluated by Euclidean distance (ED) and dihedral angle (DA). The voxel size is 0.6*mm*. ↓ indicates lower values being more accurate. * indicates manual annotation being used.

	ED ↓ (voxel)	DA ↓ (rad)	ED ↓ (voxel)	DA ↓ (rad)
Yeung et at.[23]				
without fine-tuning	71.1±29.9	0.264±0.177	70.6±25.3	0.265±0.137
with MK-MMD[16]	71.4±27.0	0.266±0.153	72.6±26.0	0.267±0.140
with CORAL[22]	79.3±29.9	0.276±0.159	80.8±28.1	0.278±0.149
with DANN[7]	72.8±30.5	0.265±0.160	72.4±27.9	0.266±0.143
*supervised fine-tuning	11.3±1.57	0.172±0.055	28.6±14.2	0.202±0.084
AdLocUN (ours)				
without fine-tuning	63.0±29.0	0.251±0.166	62.7±25.0	0.253±0.138
proposed fine-tuning	**23.7±9.01**	**0.198±0.092**	**33.0±15.1**	**0.211±0.097**
	(a) Fine-tune and test on the *same* set of images		(b) *different* set of images	

Secondly, as presented in Table 1, we considered the scenario where *different* sets of images (from the same domain) were used for fine-tuning and testing. This corresponds to *online* prediction, for example scanning guidance, where a set of example images were acquired in advance for fine-tuning . From Table 1, without fine-tuning, Yeung et al.[23] (ED = 70.6 and DA = 0.265) and AdLocUI (ED = 62.7 and DA = 0.253) performed similarly as the first scenario. Compared to the first scenario, a pronounced drop in performance was seen for supervised fine-tuning of Yeung et al.[23] (ED = 28.6 and DA = 0.202) when the fine-tuning and testing images were no longer the same. This had less severe impact to AdLocUI with the proposed fine-tuning (ED = 33.0 and DA = 0.211), which was still significantly ($p<0.05$) better than the baselines. Despite its slightly better performance, supervised fine-tuning requires manually annotated image locations to retrain the network for every new machine or protocol, which is not applicable in practice. On the contrary, AdLocUI just needs the raw 2D images for fine-tuning, which is much more achievable in neuroimaging studies.

Fine-Tuned with Existing DA Methods. We also compared AdLocUI with Yeung et al.[23] fine-tuned by popular unsupervised DA methods (*i.e.* MK-MMD [16], DANN [7] and CORAL [22]). Despite some trials of hyperparameters tuning, as shown in Table 1, their results were still comparable or worse than no fine-tuning. This may be due to the fact that most DA approaches were designed for classification tasks, which may not be directly applicable to our regression task [3]. This further verifies the value of our work.

4.2   Native Freehand Images

In our experiments on native 2D freehand ultrasound images, we used the predicted image locations to sample the corresponding slices from the 3D atlas, to which the 3D training volumes were co-aligned. The sampled slices should match with the corresponding input images for accurate predictions. As shown in Fig. 1, predictions from `AdLocUI` clearly demonstrated a much better match, in terms of similarity and anatomical structures present, with the corresponding input images at different orientations, when compared to Yeung et al.[23]. By our proposed quantitative test (*i.e.* NSTD of Δc) as described in Sect. 3, `AdLocUI` achieved a result of 0.553, which was lower than both Yeung et al.[23] (0.706) and `AdLocUI` without fine-tuning (0.726), suggesting that the predicted localization of `AdLocUI` was more consistent throughout the ultrasound video sequence, which was indicative of the smooth frame-to-frame transitions expected in freehand scanning. Both the qualitative and quantitative results showed `AdLocUI`'s superior performance when being applied on native 2D freehand ultrasound images in practice. More qualitative examples are in the Supplementary Materials.

5 Conclusion

In summary, we propose `AdLocUI`, a framework for localizing 2D ultrasound brain images in the 3D anatomy. By using an intuitive cycle consistency loss, `AdLocUI` can be fine-tuned in an **unsupervised** manner to adapt to images acquired from different machines and protocols. The experiments on three different datasets of ultrasound images demonstrate `AdLocUI`'s generalizability and superior performance to other baseline approaches. As future studies, we would like to extend `AdLocUI` to other anatomies and develop it as an accessible and general *sensorless* freehand ultrasound guidance tool for training novice sonographers to facilitate more contextualized structural analysis and diagnosis.

Acknowledgments. PH. Yeung is grateful for support from the RC Lee Centenary Scholarship. W. Xie is supported by the EPSRC Programme Grant Visual AI (EP/T028572/1). A. Namburete is funded by the UK Royal Academy of Engineering under its Engineering for Development Research Fellowship scheme and the Academy of Medical Sciences. We thank Linde Hesse, Madeleine Wyburd and Nicola Dinsdale for their valuable suggestions and comments about the work.

References

1. Baumgartner, C.F., et al.: SonoNet: real-time detection and localisation of fetal standard scan planes in freehand ultrasound. IEEE Trans. Med. Imaging **36**(11), 2204–2215 (2017)
2. Chen, T., Kornblith, S., Norouzi, M., Hinton, G.: A simple framework for contrastive learning of visual representations. In: International Conference on Machine Learning, pp. 1597–1607. PMLR (2020)
3. Chen, X., Wang, S., Wang, J., Long, M.: Representation subspace distance for domain adaptation regression. In: International Conference on Machine Learning, pp. 1749–1759. PMLR (2021)

4. Delaunay, R., Hu, Y., Vercauteren, T.: An unsupervised approach to ultrasound elastography with end-to-end strain regularisation. In: Martel, A.L., et al. (eds.) MICCAI 2020. LNCS, vol. 12263, pp. 573–582. Springer, Cham (2020). https://doi.org/10.1007/978-3-030-59716-0_55

5. Dou, H., et al.: Agent with warm start and active termination for plane localization in 3D ultrasound. In: Shen, D., et al. (eds.) MICCAI 2019. LNCS, vol. 11768, pp. 290–298. Springer, Cham (2019). https://doi.org/10.1007/978-3-030-32254-0_33

6. Droste, R., Drukker, L., Papageorghiou, A.T., Noble, J.A.: Automatic Probe Movement Guidance for Freehand Obstetric Ultrasound. In: Martel, A.L., et al. (eds.) MICCAI 2020. LNCS, vol. 12263, pp. 583–592. Springer, Cham (2020). https://doi.org/10.1007/978-3-030-59716-0_56

7. Ganin, Y., et al.: Domain-adversarial training of neural networks. J. Mach. Learn. Res. 17(1), 2030–2096 (2016)

8. Gao, Y., Beriwal, S., Craik, R., Papageorghiou, A.T., Noble, J.A.: Label efficient localization of fetal brain biometry planes in ultrasound through metric learning. In: Hu, Y., et al. (eds.) ASMUS/PIPPI -2020. LNCS, vol. 12437, pp. 126–135. Springer, Cham (2020). https://doi.org/10.1007/978-3-030-60334-2_13

9. Gao, Y., Alison Noble, J.: Detection and characterization of the fetal heartbeat in free-hand ultrasound sweeps with weakly-supervised two-streams convolutional networks. In: Descoteaux, M., Maier-Hein, L., Franz, A., Jannin, P., Collins, D.L., Duchesne, S. (eds.) MICCAI 2017. LNCS, vol. 10434, pp. 305–313. Springer, Cham (2017). https://doi.org/10.1007/978-3-319-66185-8_35

10. Gonçalves, L.F., Lee, W., Espinoza, J., Romero, R.: Three- and 4-dimensional ultrasound in obstetric practice: does it help? J. Ultrasound Med. 24(12), 1599–1624 (2005)

11. Grill, J.B., et al.: Bootstrap your own latent-a new approach to self-supervised learning. Adv. Neural. Inf. Process. Syst. 33, 21271–21284 (2020)

12. Hou, B., et al.: Predicting slice-to-volume transformation in presence of arbitrary subject motion. In: Descoteaux, M., Maier-Hein, L., Franz, A., Jannin, P., Collins, D.L., Duchesne, Simon (eds.) MICCAI 2017. LNCS, vol. 10434, pp. 296–304. Springer, Cham (2017). https://doi.org/10.1007/978-3-319-66185-8_34

13. Hou, B., et al.: 3-D reconstruction in canonical co-ordinate space from arbitrarily oriented 2-D images. IEEE Trans. Med. Imaging 37(8), 1737–1750 (2018)

14. K. Z. Tehrani, A., Mirzaei, M., Rivaz, H.: Semi-supervised training of optical flow convolutional neural networks in ultrasound elastography. In: Martel, A.L., et al. (eds.) MICCAI 2020. LNCS, vol. 12263, pp. 504–513. Springer, Cham (2020). https://doi.org/10.1007/978-3-030-59716-0_48

15. Li, K., et al.: Autonomous navigation of an ultrasound probe towards standard scan planes with deep reinforcement learning. In: 2021 IEEE International Conference on Robotics and Automation, pp. 8302–8308. IEEE (2021)

16. Long, M., Cao, Y., Wang, J., Jordan, M.: Learning transferable features with deep adaptation networks. In: International Conference on Machine Learning, pp. 97–105. PMLR (2015)

17. Mohamed, F., Siang, C.V.: A survey on 3D ultrasound reconstruction techniques. In: Artificial Intelligence-Applications in Medicine and Biology, pp. 73–92 (2019)

18. Mozaffari, M.H., Lee, W.S.: Freehand 3-D ultrasound imaging: a systematic review. Ultrasound Med. Biol. 43(10), 2099–2124 (2017)

19. Namburete, A.I., Xie, W., Yaqub, M., Zisserman, A., Noble, J.A.: Fully-automated alignment of 3D fetal brain ultrasound to a canonical reference space using multi-task learning. Med. Image Anal. 46, 1–14 (2018)

20. van den Oord, A., Li, Y., Vinyals, O.: Representation learning with contrastive predictive coding. arXiv preprint arXiv:1807.03748 (2018)
21. Paladini, D., Malinger, G., Monteagudo, A., Pilu, G., Timor-Tritsch, I., Toi, A.: Sonographic examination of the fetal central nervous system: guidelines for performing the 'basic examination' and the 'fetal neurosonogram.' Ultrasound Obstet. Gynecol. **29**(1), 109–116 (2007)
22. Sun, B., Saenko, K.: Deep CORAL: correlation alignment for deep domain adaptation. In: Hua, G., Jégou, H. (eds.) ECCV 2016. LNCS, vol. 9915, pp. 443–450. Springer, Cham (2016). https://doi.org/10.1007/978-3-319-49409-8_35
23. Yeung, P.H., Aliasi, M., Papageorghiou, A.T., Haak, M., Xie, W., Namburete, A.I.: Learning to map 2D ultrasound images into 3D space with minimal human annotation. Med. Image Anal. **70**, 101998 (2021)
24. Yeung, P.H., et al.: ImplicitVol: sensorless 3D ultrasound reconstruction with deep implicit representation. arXiv preprint arXiv:2109.12108 (2021)
25. Zhou, T., Krahenbuhl, P., Aubry, M., Huang, Q., Efros, A.A.: Learning dense correspondence via 3D-guided cycle consistency. In: Proceedings of the IEEE Conference on Computer Vision and Pattern Recognition, pp. 117–126 (2016)

Physically Inspired Constraint for Unsupervised Regularized Ultrasound Elastography

Ali K. Z. Tehrani$^{(\boxtimes)}$ and Hassan Rivaz

Department of Electrical and Computer Engineering, Concordia University,
Montreal, Canada
a_kafaei@encs.concordia.ca, hrivaz@ece.concordia.ca

Abstract. Displacement estimation is a critical step of virtually all Ultrasound Elastography (USE) techniques. Two main features make this task unique compared to the general optical flow problem: the high-frequency nature of ultrasound radio-frequency (RF) data and the governing laws of physics on the displacement field. Recently, the architecture of the optical flow networks has been modified to be able to use RF data. Also, semi-supervised and unsupervised techniques have been employed for USE by considering prior knowledge of displacement continuity in the form of the first- and second-derivative regularizers. Despite these attempts, no work has considered the tissue compression pattern, and displacements in axial and lateral directions have been assumed to be independent. However, tissue motion pattern is governed by laws of physics in USE, rendering the axial and the lateral displacements highly correlated. In this paper, we propose Physically Inspired ConsTraint for Unsupervised Regularized Elastography (PICTURE), where we impose constraints on the Poisson's ratio to improve lateral displacement estimates. Experiments on phantom and *in vivo* data show that PICTURE substantially improves the quality of the lateral displacement estimation. We made the network weights and a demo code available online at code.sonography.ai.

Keywords: Ultrasound elastography · Physically inspired learning · Unsupervised training

1 Introduction

Ultrasound (US) imaging is a popular modality due to its portability and ease-of-use especially in image-guided interventions. Ultrasound Elastography (USE)

Supported by Natural Sciences and Engineering Research Council of Canada (NSERC) Discovery Grant. The Alpinion ultrasound machine was partly funded by Dr. Louis G. Johnson Foundation.

Supplementary Information The online version contains supplementary material available at https://doi.org/10.1007/978-3-031-16440-8_21.

aims to provide stiffness information of the tissue. In USE, an external or internal force deforms the tissue, and US images before and after the tissue deformation are compared to obtain the displacement map. The displacement map is employed to obtain the strain map which reveals the elastic properties of the tissue. Free-hand palpation is a common USE method wherein the external force is applied by the operator using the probe without the need of any external hardware. The quality of the obtained strain map heavily relies on the accuracy of the estimated displacement and many different methods have been developed to obtain high-quality displacement estimation [1,2].

Convolutional Neural Networks (CNN) have shown promising results in optical flow problems. They have been successfully adopted for USE by modifying the architectures to handle high-frequency radio-frequency (RF) data [3,4]. Unsupervised and semi-supervised techniques have also been employed to train the networks using real US data without requiring the ground truth displacements [5–8]. They employed prior knowledge of displacement continuity in the form of the first- and second-derivative regularizers. Despite these attempts, no work has ever considered the tissue compression pattern. The assumptions on the motions in USE can be utilized to provide prior information about the lateral displacement, which is usually poor in free-hand palpation compared to the axial one. In this paper, we propose Physically Inspired ConsTraint for Unsupervised Regularized Elastography (PICTURE), inspired by Hooke's law and constraints on the Poisson's ratio to improve the lateral displacement using the prior knowledge of the compression physics. We show that PICTURE substantially improves the lateral displacement estimation using constraints on the Poisson's ratio.

2   Method

2.1   Hook's Law and Poisson's Ratio

Homogeneous Material: Assuming linear elastic, isotropic, and homogeneous material, Hooke's law can be written for 3 dimensions as [9]:

$$
\begin{bmatrix} \varepsilon_{11} \\ \varepsilon_{22} \\ \varepsilon_{33} \\ 2\varepsilon_{23} \\ 2\varepsilon_{13} \\ 2\varepsilon_{12} \end{bmatrix} = \frac{1}{E} \begin{bmatrix} 1 & -v & -v & 0 & 0 & 0 \\ -v & 1 & -v & 0 & 0 & 0 \\ -v & -v & 1 & 0 & 0 & 0 \\ 0 & 0 & 0 & 2+2v & 0 & 0 \\ 0 & 0 & 0 & 0 & 2+2v & 0 \\ 0 & 0 & 0 & 0 & 0 & 2+2v \end{bmatrix} \begin{bmatrix} \sigma_{11} \\ \sigma_{22} \\ \sigma_{33} \\ \sigma_{23} \\ \sigma_{13} \\ \sigma_{12} \end{bmatrix} \tag{1}
$$

where ε, E and σ represent strain, Young's modulus, and stress, respectively. Also, v is the Poisson's ratio, and depends on the material. ε_{ij} can be obtained by taking the derivative of the displacement in direction i (W_i) with respect to the direction j

$$
\varepsilon_{ij} = \frac{\partial W_i}{\partial j} \tag{2}
$$

where subscripts 1, 2, and 3 denote axial, lateral, and out-of-plane directions, respectively. When a material is compressed in one direction (in USE, it is often the axial direction), it expands in the other directions (in USE, they are lateral and out-of-plane directions). Considering this effect, the lateral and axial strains are not independent anymore. The uniaxial stress can be assumed in free-hand palpation since the operator compresses the tissue downwards and shear stresses on the top are negligible [9]. This assumption leads to the simplification of Eq. 1. All stress components except σ_{11} can be ignored. The strain components are obtained by:

$$\varepsilon_{11} = \frac{\sigma_{11}}{E}, \varepsilon_{22} = -v\frac{\sigma_{11}}{E}, \varepsilon_{33} = -v\frac{\sigma_{11}}{E} \tag{3}$$

This equation indicates that the lateral strain (ε_{22}) can be directly obtained from the axial strain (ε_{11}) and the Poisson's ratio ($\varepsilon_{22} = -v \times \varepsilon_{11}$).

Inhomogeneous Material: When the material is inhomogeneous, the lateral strain (ε_{22}) cannot be directly obtained from Poisson's ratio and the axial strain (ε_{11}) since the assumption of uniaxial compression does not hold everywhere, especially on the borders of the inclusions. Total strain (ε_{ij}) in this case, is obtained by adding the contribution of elastic strain (e_{ij}) and non-elastic eigen-strain (ε_{ij}^*) [10]:

$$\varepsilon_{ij} = e_{ij} + \varepsilon_{ij}^* \tag{4}$$

Eigenstrain is introduced to model the variation of total strain from elastic strain in the presence of inhomogeneity. It is zero inside the inclusions and decays toward zero with increasing distance from the inclusion boundaries [10]. Despite not being able to directly estimate ε_{22} from ε_{11} due to having inhomogeneity (eigenstrain), they are highly correlated and ε_{11} can provide prior information about ε_{22}. Effective Poisson Ratio (EPR) is defined as [11]:

$$v_e = \frac{-\varepsilon_{22}}{\varepsilon_{11}} \tag{5}$$

where EPR (v_e) is obtained by point-by-point division of the lateral and axial strains. Although in inhomogeneous tissues, the EPR differs from the Poisson's ratio of the tissue and temporally, spatially variant, it is still a suitable approx-imator of the Poisson's ratio. It has been used to characterize tissues [11]. The Poisson's ratio range under an arbitrary type of deformation and loading is between 0.2 and 0.5 [12]. Also, EPR has the same range as Poisson's ratio [13]. Therefore, this range can be utilized to improve the lateral displacement quality.

2.2 Physically Inspired ConsTraint for Unsupervised Regularized Elastography (PICTURE)

We propose to utilize EPR as a prior information to improve the estimation of the lateral displacement, which is usually poor in USE. Although the ground-truth value of EPR is not known, the accepted range can be employed as a constraint in unsupervised training. We define a mask (M) to determine the EPR values outside the accepted range as:

$$M(i,j) = \begin{cases} 0 & v_{emin} < \tilde{v}_e(i,j) < v_{emax} \\ 1 & otherwise \end{cases} \tag{6}$$

where v_{emin} and v_{emax} are the minimum and maximum accepted EPR values, and we assume the range to be between 0.1 to 0.6 (to have a small margin of error). In the next step, the following loss is employed to penalize the EPR values outside the accepted range as the following:

$$L_{vd} = |M \otimes (\varepsilon_{22} + <\tilde{v}_e> \times \varepsilon_{11})|_2 \tag{7}$$

where $|.|_2$ denotes the L2 norm, $\otimes$ is the Kronecker product to select the incorrect EPR values, and $<\tilde{v}_e>$ represents the average of EPR values in the accepted range (where $M = 0$) which is obtained by:

$$<\tilde{v}_e> = \frac{\sum_{i,j}(1 - M_{(i,j)}) \otimes v_e}{\sum_{i,j}(1 - M_{(i,j)})} \tag{8}$$

The first-order derivative of v_e are also added to enforce the smoothness of the EPR.

$$L_{vs} = |\frac{\partial v_e}{\partial a}|_1 + \beta \times |\frac{\partial v_e}{\partial l}|_1 \tag{9}$$

where a and l represent the axial and lateral directions, respectively. The parameter β depends on the ratio of the spatial distance between two samples in axial and lateral directions, and is set it to 0.1 similar to [8]. Finally, PICTURE loss is obtained as:

$$L_V = L_{vd} + \lambda_{vs} \times L_{vs} \tag{10}$$

where λ_{vs} is a hyper-parameter that controls the smoothness constraint.

2.3 Unsupervised Training

Let $I_1, I_2 \in \mathbb{R}^{3 \times w \times h}$ be the pre-compression, and post-compression US data each has the width h, height w and the 3 channels of RF data, the imaginary part of the analytic signal and the envelope of RF data, respectively (similar to [8]). The data loss in unsupervised training is the photometric loss obtained by comparing I_1 and warped I_2 ($\tilde{I}_2$) using bi-linear warping by the displacement W which can be defined as [5,8]:

$$L_D = |(I_1 - \tilde{I}_2)|_{1_{N \times N}} \tag{11}$$

where $|.|_1$ denotes the L1 norm, and a window of size $N \times N$ is considered around each sample to reduce the noise caused by warping. We simply set $N = 3$ in this work. The data loss alone results in noisy displacement, and because the derivatives of the displacements are required in USE, smooth displacements are desired. Therefore, regularization of the displacement has been employed. We adopt the regularization method of [8] where the first- and second-order derivatives of displacement (strains and it's first-order derivative) are employed:

$$L_S = L_{s1} + \gamma L_{s2}$$

$$L_{s1} = |\varepsilon_{11} - <\varepsilon_{11}>|_1 + \beta |\varepsilon_{12}|_1 + \frac{1}{2}|\varepsilon_{21}|_1 + \frac{1}{2}\beta |\varepsilon_{22}|_1 \tag{12}$$

$$L_{s2} = \left\{ |(\frac{\partial \varepsilon_{11}}{\partial a})|_1 + \beta |(\frac{\partial \varepsilon_{11}}{\partial l})|_1 + 0.5|(\frac{\partial \varepsilon_{22}}{\partial a})|_1 + 0.5\beta |(\frac{\partial \varepsilon_{22}}{\partial l})|_1 \right\}$$

where L_{s1}, L_{s2} and γ are the first-order smoothness loss, the second-order smoothness loss and the weight associated to the second-order smoothness loss, respectively. The $< . >$ denotes the mean operation, and the hyperparameters are tuned similar to [8].

We propose to add the PICTURE loss as the regularization constraint to improve the lateral displacement quality. Therefore, the final loss used to train the network is:

$$Loss = L_D + \lambda_S L_S + \lambda_V L_V \tag{13}$$

the hyperparameters λ_S and λ_V, control the smoothness and PICTURE loss strength, respectively. It should be mentioned that the PICTURE regularization, similar to other forms of regularization, is only applied during the training and methods such as known operators [14] can be used to apply it during the test.

2.4   Data Collection

Experimental Phantom: A tissue-mimicking breast phantom (Model 059, CIRS: Tissue Simulation & Phantom Technology, Norfolk, VA) was employed for data collection. The elastic modulus of the phantom background was 20 kPa, and the phantom contained several inclusions having at least twice the elastic modulus of the background. An Alpinion E-Cube R12 research US machine (Bothell, WA, USA) with the sampling frequency of 40 MHz and the center frequency of 8 MHz was utilized for data collection of the training and test. To avoid data leakage, different parts of the phantom were imaged for training and test.

***In vivo* Data:** A research Antares Siemens system by a VF 10–5 linear array was employed to collect data with the sampling frequency of 40 MHz and the center frequency of 6.67 MHz. Data was collected at Johns Hopkins Hospital from patients with liver cancer during open-surgical RF thermal ablation. The institutional review board approved the study with the consent of the patients. We selected 600 RF frame pairs of this dataset for the training of networks employed.

2.5   Network Architecture and Training Schedule

We employed MPWC-Net++ (publicly provided in [4]) which showed promising results on both optical flow and USE. This network was a modified variant of PWC-Net [15] to address the high-frequency nature of RF data. The PWC-Net feature extraction part was modified to have less downsampling to reduce loss of information, and the cost volume search range was increased to address the low search range caused by reducing the number of downsampling in the feature extraction layers.

The publicly available pre-trained MPWC-Net++ weights were employed as the initial weights. The network was trained for 20 epochs with the learning rate of 20e-6, which was halved every five epochs, and an Nvidia A100 GPU with 40 GB of memory was utilized for training the network. The tuned hyperparameters

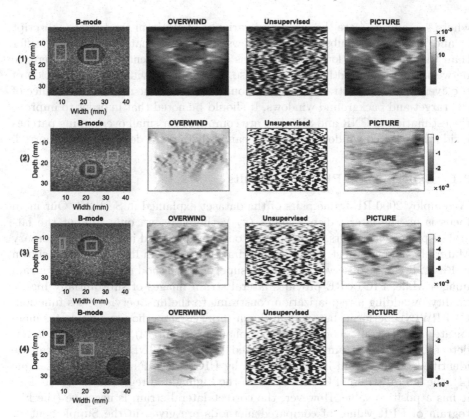

Fig. 1. Lateral strain images in phantom experiments. Rows 1 to 4 correspond to different locations in the phantom.

values can be found in the Supplementary Materials. The network weight and a demo code are publicly available online at code.sonography.ai.

3   Results

PICTURE is compared to OVERWIND, an optimization-based method that uses the initial displacement obtained by Dynamic Programming [2]. OVER-WIND employs total variation for regularization and obtains high-quality sub-pixel displacement [2]. In addition, PICTURE is compared to the regularized unsupervised training of MPWC-Net++ without PICTURE loss ($\lambda_V = 0$ in Eq. 13) which the training loss function becomes similar to [5] but the difference is that a more recent network specifically designed for USE is employed.

Contrast to Noise Ratio (CNR), and Strain Ratio (SR) are employed to quantitatively evaluate the compared methods. CNR and SR are defined as [16]:

$$CNR = \sqrt{\frac{2(\bar{s}_b - \bar{s}_t)^2}{\sigma_b{}^2 + \sigma_t{}^2}}, \qquad SR = \frac{\bar{s}_t}{\bar{s}_b}, \qquad (14)$$

where $\bar{s}_X$, and $\sigma_X{}^2$ are the mean and variance of strain in the target (subscript t) and background (subscript b) windows. Assuming that the target is stiffer than the background, lower SR, which is desired, represents a higher difference between the target and background. Also, CNR can provide a good intuition of the overall quality of strain images by combining both the mean and variance of the target and background windows. It should be noted that in order to improve the estimation of CNR and SR, they are computed for small overlapping patches inside the selected windows, and the mean and standard deviation are reported.

3.1 Experimental Phantom Results

We employ 2000 RF frame pairs of the dataset explained in Sect. 2.4. Our main focus is on the lateral displacement (ε_{22}); therefore, we only present the lateral displacement results, and the axial ones are provided in the Supplementary Materials. The lateral strains of 4 experimental phantom image pairs are shown in Fig. 1. It can be observed that the unsupervised method results in noisy strain images while, PICTURE provides lateral strain images of substantially higher quality by adding a regularization constraint to the unsupervised loss function. OVERWIND performs better than the unsupervised method but estimates inaccurate lateral strain. For instance, in phantom result (2), the inclusion is not detectable by the strain image obtained by OVERWIND whereas, it can be identified by the strain image obtained by PICTURE. Furthermore, in sample (4), the lateral strain of OVERWIND in the highlighted region is incorrect since it has a positive value. However, the correct lateral strain is negative (the histogram of EPR values of compared methods are given in the Supplementary Materials). It should be noted that lateral strain estimation is a more challenging task than the axial one. The evaluated methods provide high-quality axial strain images given in the Supplementary Materials.

3.2 *In Vivo* results

The network was trained with (PICTURE) and without (Unsupervised) the proposed regularizer using *in vivo* dataset. The lateral strain images are illustrated in Fig. 2 (top), and the axial strain images are given as a reference (bottom) for one patient data before liver ablation. It can be observed that PICTURE substantially improves the lateral strain images of the unsupervised method while their axial strain images are virtually similar.

3.3 Quantitative Results

The CNR and SR of the experimental phantom and *in vivo* data results are given in Table 1. In terms of CNR metric, PICTURE substantially outperforms OVER-WIND and the unsupervised method. For *in vivo* data, PICTURE increases the CNR of the unsupervised method from the mean value of 0.73 to 4.27 and has substantially higher CNR than OVERWIND (1.12). In terms of SR, PICTURE

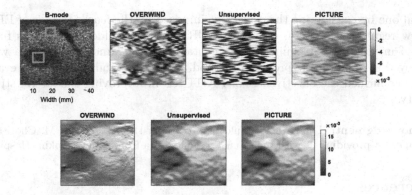

Fig. 2. B-mode and strain images of a patient with liver cancer. Lateral and axial strain images are shown in the top and bottom rows, respectively.

Table 1. Mean and standard deviation of CNR and SR of experimental phantom results. OV, UN, and PIC represent OVERWIND, the unsupervised method, and PICTURE, respectively. Statistical significance is achieved using Friedman's test (p-value < 0.01).

	CNR (higher is better)			SR (lower is better)		
Phantom	OV	UN	PIC	OV	UN	PIC
(1)	3.16±1.45	0.80±0.40	**6.22±1.45**	0.68±0.09	0.57±0.17	**0.35±0.07**
(2)	1.21±0.73	0.38±0.30	**4.72±0.50**	0.86±0.12	10.00±6.80	**0.50±0.07**
(3)	4.19±0.83	0.84±0.38	**5.80±1.46**	0.42±0.07	**0.34±0.18**	0.36±0.05
(4)	9.38±2.53	1.44±0.32	**12.45±0.38**	0.35±0.06	**0.21±0.12**	0.38±0.1
in vivo data	1.12±0.84	0.73±0.54	**4.27±1.12**	1.06±0.30	0.83±0.42	**0.66±0.06**

has the lowest SR in 3 cases, and the unsupervised method has better SR in 2 cases (phantom results 3 and 4). However, the visual results and CNR values indicate that the unsupervised method does not have high-quality lateral strains in those cases. For *in vivo* data, OVERWIND has SR value of 1.06 which means that it incorrectly estimates the target (tumor) has a higher strain value than the background. Whereas unsupervised and PICTURE can detect the lower strain value of the tumor (SR < 1). Also, PICTURE has a lower standard deviation (0.06) compared to unsupervised method (0.42).

4   Conclusions

Advances in several fields such as inverse reconstruction of elasticity modulus and imaging of the effective Poisson's ratio have been hindered because of the low quality of the lateral displacement estimation in USE. This paper takes a step to resolve those issues by incorporating governing laws of physics in USE to improve the lateral strain. We employed the axial displacement to improve the lateral one by considering the constraint imposed by the feasible range of EPR. A new regularization term called PICTURE loss was added to the loss function of unsupervised training. Experimental phantoms and *in vivo* data were employed to validate the proposed method. The visual and quantitative evaluations confirmed the effectiveness of PICTURE in improving the lateral strain quality.

Acknowledgment. The authors would like to thank Drs. E. Boctor, M. Choti and G. Hager for providing us with the *in vivo* patients data from Johns Hopkins Hospital.

References

1. Hall, T.J., et al.: Recent results in nonlinear strain and modulus imaging. Curr. Med. Imaging Rev. **7**(4), 313–327 (2011)
2. Mirzaei, M., Asif, A., Rivaz, H.: Combining total variation regularization with window-based time delay estimation in ultrasound elastography. IEEE Trans. Med. Imaging **38**, 2744–2754 (2019)
3. Tehrani, A.K., Rivaz, H.: Displacement estimation in ultrasound elastography using pyramidal convolutional neural network. IEEE Trans. Ultrason. Ferroelectr. Freq. Control **67**(12), 2629–2639 (2020)
4. Tehrani, A.K.Z., Rivaz, H.: Mpwc-net++: evolution of optical flow pyramidal convolutional neural network for ultrasound elastography. In: Medical Imaging 2021: Ultrasonic Imaging and Tomography, vol. 11602, p. 1160206. International Society for Optics and Photonics (2021)
5. K. Z. Tehrani, A., Mirzaei, M., Rivaz, H.: Semi-supervised training of optical flow convolutional neural networks in ultrasound elastography. In: Martel, A.L., et al. (eds.) MICCAI 2020. LNCS, vol. 12263, pp. 504–513. Springer, Cham (2020). https://doi.org/10.1007/978-3-030-59716-0_48
6. Delaunay, R., Hu, Y., Vercauteren, T.: An unsupervised approach to ultrasound elastography with end-to-end strain regularisation. In: Martel, A.L., et al. (eds.) MICCAI 2020. LNCS, vol. 12263, pp. 573–582. Springer, Cham (2020). https://doi.org/10.1007/978-3-030-59716-0_55
7. Delaunay, R., Hu, Y., Vercauteren, T.: An unsupervised learning approach to ultrasound strain elastography with spatio-temporal consistency. Phys. Med. Biol. **66**, 175031 (2021)
8. Tehrani, A.K., Sharifzadeh, M., Boctor, E., Rivaz, H.: Bi-directional semi-supervised training of convolutional neural networks for ultrasound elastography displacement estimation. IEEE Trans. Ultrason. Ferroelectr. Freq. Control **69**, 1181–1190 (2022)
9. Ugural, A.C., Fenster, S.K.: Advanced Strength and Applied Elasticity. Pearson Education, Englewood Cliffs (2003)
10. Ma, L., Korsunsky, A.M.: The principle of equivalent eigenstrain for inhomogeneous inclusion problems. Int. J. Solids Struct. **51**(25–26), 4477–4484 (2014)
11. Islam, M.T., Chaudhry, A., Tang, S., Tasciotti, E., Righetti, R.: A new method for estimating the effective poisson's ratio in ultrasound poroelastography. IEEE Trans. Med. Imaging **37**(5), 1178–1191 (2018)
12. Mott, P., Roland, C.: Limits to poisson's ratio in isotropic materials-general result for arbitrary deformation. Phys. Scr. **87**(5), 055404 (2013)

13. Righetti, R., Ophir, J., Srinivasan, S., Krouskop, T.A.: The feasibility of using elastography for imaging the poisson's ratio in porous media. Ultrasound Med. Biol. **30**(2), 215–228 (2004)

14. Maier, A.K., et al.: Learning with known operators reduces maximum error bounds. Nat. Mach. Intell. **1**(8), 373–380 (2019)

15. Hur, J., Roth, S.: Iterative residual refinement for joint optical flow and occlusion estimation. In: Proceedings of the IEEE/CVF Conference on Computer Vision and Pattern Recognition, pp. 5754–5763 (2019)

16. Ophir, J., et al.: Elastography: ultrasonic estimation and imaging of the elastic properties of tissues. Proc. Inst. Mech. Eng. [H] **213**(3), 203–233 (1999)

Towards Unsupervised Ultrasound Video Clinical Quality Assessment with Multi-modality Data

He Zhao[1]([✉]), Qingqing Zheng[2], Clare Teng[1], Robail Yasrab[1], Lior Drukker[3,4], Aris T. Papageorghiou[3], and J. Alison Noble[1]

[1] Institute of Biomedical Engineering, University of Oxford, Oxford, UK
he.zhao@eng.ox.ac.uk
[2] Guangdong Provincial Key Laboratory of Computer Vision and Virtual Reality, Shenzhen Institute of Advanced Technology, Chinese Academy of Sciences, Shenzhen, China
[3] Nuffield Department of Women's and Reproductive Health, University of Oxford, Oxford, UK
[4] Department of Obsterics and Gynecology, Tel-Aviv University, Tel Aviv, Israel

Abstract. Video quality assurance is an important topic in obstetric ultrasound imaging to ensure that captured videos are suitable for biometry and fetal health assessment. Previously, one successful objective approach to automated ultrasound image quality assurance has considered it as a supervised learning task of detecting anatomical structures defined by a clinical protocol. In this paper, we propose an alternative and purely data-driven approach that makes effective use of both spatial and temporal information and the model learns from high-quality videos without any anatomy-specific annotations. This makes it attractive for potentially scalable generalisation. In the proposed model, a 3D encoder and decoder pair bi-directionally learns a spatio-temporal representation between the video space and the feature space. A zoom-in module is introduced to encourage the model to focus on the main object in a frame. A further design novelty is the introduction of two additional modalities in model training (sonographer gaze and optical flow derived from the video). Finally, our approach is applied to identify high-quality videos for fetal head circumference measurement in freehand second-trimester ultrasound scans. Extensive experiments are conducted, and the results demonstrate the effectiveness of our approach with an AUC of 0.911.

1 Introduction

Ultrasound imaging is widely used in obstetrics for fetal health assessment due to its portability, low cost, and free radiation. The high dependence on experience, and intra- and inter-observer variability is also well known. For example, it can be difficult for trainee sonographers to localize the appropriate plane for diagnosis because of fetal movement and acoustic shadowing, and even experienced sonographers can struggle to acquire good diagnostic images for subjects with

L. Wang et al. (Eds.): MICCAI 2022, LNCS 13434, pp. 228–237, 2022.
https://doi.org/10.1007/978-3-031-16440-8_22

poor acoustic windows. Assessment and audit of video quality is recommended in clinical guidelines. However, this has to be done by an experienced sonographer which is very time-consuming and labour-intensive and takes clinicians away from treating patients. Despite its importance to clinical practice, hardly any research has been reported on automated video clinical quality assessment.

In this paper, we are interested in video clinical quality assessment which is task-specific for biometric measurement. High clinical quality means the video is suitable for further measurement and analysis. A novel data-driven approach is proposed by learning a model of video quality assessment directly from high-quality data. Our approach learns the spatio-temporal representation between the video and feature space bi-directionally with a reconstruction-based anomaly detection pipeline. The intuition is that a low-quality sample can be detected by its associated large reconstruction error as the sample is not present in the training data. Different from existing supervised image quality assessment methods for ultrasound [1,8,15], our approach makes effective use of both spatial and temporal information and the model learns from high-quality videos without any anatomy-specific annotations. These characteristics make our approach attractive for clinical quality assessment tasks where anatomical annotations are often rare and inaccessible. The contributions of this paper are summarized as follows: (1) To the best of our knowledge, our approach is the first video-based clinical quality assessment method that does not depend on clinical protocol definitions and anatomical annotations. (2) Bi-directional reconstruction between the video and feature spaces prompts our model to learn an informative representation of high-quality data. (3) We propose to use multi-modality data (*i.e.*, optical flow & gaze) in the training stage with the help of an input generator and an auxiliary prediction branch, respectively. This prediction branch further enables our model to highlight informative structures by the predicted gaze.

2   Related Work

Image quality assessment has been studied extensively in image processing with various assessment metrics proposed such as PSNR, SSIM [14], and FID [5]. These image quality metrics focus on image clarity and noise removal. The definition of quality assessment in ultrasound is different in that it needs to factor in clinical context; it is task-specific and aims to ensure that a frame is useful for diagnosis. Prior work has mainly aimed to automate the clinical criteria checklist specified in clinical scanning protocol guideline standards. Early work is reported in [11] and [16]. Wu *et al.* [15] propose two convolutional networks to locate the ROI and detect two anatomies of the fetal abdomen in the 2nd trimester, where a quality score is based on the appearance of the ROI and anatomies. A multi-task Fast R-CNN based quality assessment network for scoring head images is described in [8,9]. In [1], a three-step framework is proposed to give a quality score for the fetal cardiac plane. Firstly, the cardiac four-chamber planes are detected and then a detection network locates the anatomical structures. The authors also propose a classification network that considers two other indices (*i.e.*, view zoom and gain), which is not used in previous studies. A semi-supervised approach using metric learning is proposed in [4] for selecting head planes in low-cost ultrasound probe video. In [12], the authors propose a reinforcement learning method to select images which are amenable to a target task. Although it is not based on clinical criteria, detailed anatomical annotations are still required in training. A recent evaluation of a real-time Artificial Intelligence (AI) based system that automatically keeps track of acquired images and checks images conform to imaging protocol standards is reported in [17] where five experienced sonographers are used as the reference. A specified pre-defined protocol and annotated locations of anatomical structures are required in the aforementioned methods, which limits transferability to new applications.

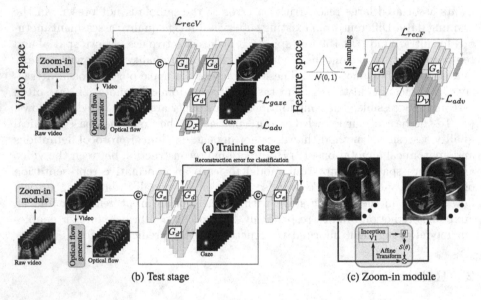

Fig. 1. Flowchart of our approach. (a) Training stage with bi-directional reconstruction loop in video and feature spaces. (b) Test stage with feature reconstruction error for classification. (c) Details of the zoom-in module.

3   Method

Our approach assesses clinical quality of ultrasound videos using only qualified scans without anatomical annotation. We formulate the video quality assessment task as an anomaly detection problem, where low-quality video is regarded as anomalous data. Denote the training dataset as $\mathcal{D}$ with N high-quality training samples only, *i.e.*, $\mathcal{D} = \{x_i, ..., x_N\}$, and a test set $\mathcal{D}_t$, *i.e.*, $\mathcal{D}_t = \{(x_{t_1}, y_1), ..., (x_{t_M}, y_{t_M})\}$ where $y \in \{0, 1\}$ indicates a video label (0 for high quality and 1 for low quality). Our goal is to train a model to learn the distribution of high-quality videos from the training dataset $\mathcal{D}$ and to identify the low-quality video in the test dataset $\mathcal{D}_t$ as anomalous. A three-dimensional encoder G_e and decoder G_d pair is proposed to learn the spatio-temporal representation. The bi-directional information flow between video space and feature space provides feedback for the model during training. This information allows the high-quality data feature representation to be informative and discriminative from that of the low-quality data.

3.1   Model Structure

The pipeline of our approach is shown in Fig. 1. For each given ultrasound video, the main object of interest (e.g., fetal head) is first extracted by the pre-trained zoom-in module. An optical flow generator is followed to estimate an optical flow field describing displacement from the zoomed-in video, which serves as the second modality input in our model. An encoder G_e and decoder G_d pair with 3D convolutional layers is adopted to learn spatio-temporal features from both video-based modalities. Two adversarial reconstruction processes are performed bi-directionally between the video and feature spaces with different alternative combinations of G_e and G_d. Besides video and optical flow, a third modality, gaze, is used by an auxiliary branch to predict where a sonographer looks. Feature reconstruction error is used as the indicator to recognize low-quality data as this will have a large reconstruction error.

Spatial Zoom-In Module and Optical Flow Generator. The goal of the zoom-in module is to extract the spatial region of interest in a video frame. As shown in Fig. 1(c), the original ultrasound video may contain fetal structures (e.g., head) with a low field-of-view occupancy. This may mislead the model as the background has a major influence on overall reconstruction error. Inspired by [6], a zoom-in module is introduced to locate and transform the image to center the region of interest around the fetal structure. Inside the zoom-in module, we use InceptionV1 [13] to learn its affine transformation parameters. This plug-in module is pre-trained with approximate bounding boxes around the fetal structures and is fixed in the following stage. The optical flow generator is developed to capture displacement patterns that characterize the appearance of anatomical structures in videos. We employ the Farneback algorithm [3] with a window size of 3×3 to generate a dense optical flow field. A median filter with a kernel size of 21×21 is applied as pre-processing to reduce the effect of speckle on optical flow field estimation.

Bi-directional Reconstruction Between Two Spaces. As shown in Fig. 1 there are two directional reconstruction processes assisted by adversarial learning. One is video reconstruction following *video → feature → video* by G_e–G_d; the second is feature reconstruction going along with *feature → video → feature* by G_d–G_e. The encoder G_e consists of eight 3D convolutional layers. The first five layers are with kernel size $1 \times 4 \times 4$ and stride $1 \times 2 \times 2$ performing spatial convolution, while the last three layers are with kernel size $4 \times 4 \times 4$ and stride $2 \times 2 \times 2$ performing spatio-temporal convolution leading to a bottleneck feature with size of 1024. The decoder G_d is with symmetrical structure but uses decon-volutional layers instead. The bi-directional information flow helps the model gain better understanding of high-quality videos. Two discriminators (*i.e.*, $D_\mathcal{V}$ and $D_\mathcal{F}$) are also proposed in the video space and feature space, respectively, for generating realistic high-quality data. The discriminator $D_\mathcal{V}$ has the similar structure of encoder and $D_\mathcal{F}$ consists of a stack of fully connected layers with neurons from 64 to 1.

Auxiliary Gaze Branch. Eye-tracking data records sonographer gaze loca-tions during scanning. Trying to predict gaze forces the model to learn the salient regions of interest of high-quality video. To take full advantage of this prior knowledge, we introduce an auxiliary decoder $G_{d'}$ with the same structure as G_d, to learn gaze map. Compared with using the eye-tracking data as addi-tional input, the training scheme as prediction eliminates the requirement for gaze in the test phase. It also enables the model to provide guidance to novice sonographers on where to look and which spatial parts are essential.

3.2   Objective Function

Training is supervised by the bi-directional reconstruction and gaze ground-truth. The encoder $G_e(x, o) : \mathcal{V} \to \mathcal{F}$ takes the video and optical flow as input and transforms them into the feature space. The decoder $G_d(f) : \mathcal{F} \to \mathcal{V}$ converts the feature representation back into the video space. Zero-sum games are played between G_e, G_d and the two discriminators. Our model is trained to solve the following optimization function:

$$\min_{G_e, G_d} \max_{D_\mathcal{F}, D_\mathcal{V}} \mathcal{L} = \omega_{adv}\mathcal{L}_{adv} + \omega_{rec}\mathcal{L}_{rec} + \omega_{gaze}\mathcal{L}_{gaze}, \tag{1}$$

where $\mathcal{L}_{rec}$, $\mathcal{L}_{gaze}$ are the bi-directional reconstruction loss and gaze loss, respec-tively. The adversarial loss function $\mathcal{L}_{adv}$ is defined by the least-squares adver-sarial loss:

$$\mathcal{L}_{adv} = |D_\mathcal{F}(f) - 1|^2 + |D_\mathcal{F}(G_e(x, o))|^2 + |D_\mathcal{V}(x) - 1|^2 + |D_\mathcal{V}(G_d(f))|^2, \tag{2}$$

where x, o are the video and the optical flow, respectively, and f is the feature vector sampled from a standard multivariate Gaussian distribution similarly as in [7]. The adversarial loss aims to learn more realistic reconstructions in both video and feature space by $D_\mathcal{V}$ and $D_\mathcal{F}$, respectively.

Reconstruction Loss. The reconstruction loss allows the encoder-decoder or decoder-encoder models to learn spatio-temporal representations of high-quality videos. Instead of the widely used pixel-wise L1 loss, the structure similarity (SSIM) [14] loss is applied for a perceptual spatial constraint. The bi-directional reconstruction loss $\mathcal{L}_{rec}$ in the video space and feature space is defined as:

$$\mathcal{L}_{rec} = \mathcal{L}_{recV} + \mathcal{L}_{recF}, \tag{3}$$

where $\mathcal{L}_{recV}$ and $\mathcal{L}_{recF}$ are defined as: $\mathcal{L}_{recV} = 1 - SSIM(x, G_d(G_e(x, o)))$ and $\mathcal{L}_{recF} = |G_e(G_d(f), o) - f|$, respectively.

Gaze Loss. We introduce a new loss function for the model to learn the gaze saliency map. The gaze loss aims to minimize the difference between the gaze prediction map and the ground truth and is defined as:

$$\mathcal{L}_{gaze} = |G_{d'}(G_e(x, o)) - g|, \tag{4}$$

where g is the eye gaze ground truth.

4   Experiment and Results

As part of the PULSE study [2], a dataset of 430 subjects with a resolution of 1008×784, including video and gaze data, is used in our experiments. During a scan, an experienced sonographer finds and freezes a biometry plane. The video clip consists of the frozen frame and 2s before freezing and is labeled by the frozen frame type, *e.g.*, transventricular plane (TVP), transcerebellar plane (TCP), abdominal circumference plane (ACP). An approaching the transventricular plane (aTVP) video clip is collected 5–7s before the frozen TVP frame. We collect 430 high-quality TVP video clips (one clip per subject) and 181 low-quality clips. For training, 300 high-quality video clips (TVP) are randomly selected, and the remaining 130 high-quality and 181 low-quality clips are used for test. Each input sample to the model consists of 8 frames sampled from 2s video clips at an 8-frame interval and is further resized to 256×256. Our approach is implemented in PyTorch with a 12 GB TitanX GPU. [1] The model was trained for 200 epochs with an Adam optimizer and the learning rate is set to 0.0002, which is linearly decays to 0 in the last 100 epochs. The loss weights ω_{adv}, ω_{rec} were empirically set to 1 and 10, respectively, to make the value of each loss stay at the same numerical level. The gaze loss weight ω_{gaze} was set to 0.1 based on a parameter study reported in the following section.

Figure 2 presents exemplar frames of high- and low-quality videos together with their dense optical flow field estimated by the optical flow generator. Observe that the different planes have different displacement patterns. For example, for the TVP, the choroid plexus (CP) and brain midline region change the most during scanning; for the TCP, the displacement pattern is high in the cerebellum region. These patterns provide useful additional information for the model to learn the feature representation of high-quality data.

Quantitative Results. We compare our approach with three single-modality methods: a SpatioTemporal Auto-Encoder (STAE) [18], MNAD [10] and an image-based approach which only takes the last frozen frame of the video clip as input. MNAD is a video anomaly detection method which detects anomalous frames in a video. It is obviously unsuitable for our task, thus leading to a rather low performance. Table 1 compares these reference methods with variants of our architecture in terms of the area under the ROC curve (AUC), F1-score, accuracy, sensitivity, and specificity. For all performance metrics, there is a large

---

[1] Code is available at https://github.com/IBMEOX/UltrasoundVQA.

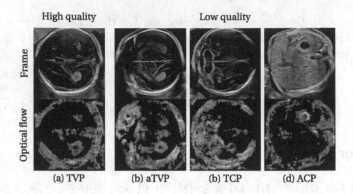

Fig. 2. Exemplar frames and corresponding optical flow fields of high- and low-quality videos from the output of the zoom-in module.

Table 1. Performance of different methods based on the zoomed-in videos with the evaluation metric of AUC, F1 (%), ACC (%), SEN (%) and SPE (%).

Methods			AUC	F1	ACC	SEN	SPE
Single modality		Image-based	0.790 ± 0.006	72.29	71.06	80.11	62.05
		MNAD [10]	0.308 ± 0.009	73.32	57.88	99.45	1.54
		STAE [18]	0.824 ± 0.009	80.46	76.07	84.61	64.18
Multiple modalities	Our approach	Video only	0.863 ± 0.005	82.66	78.78	86.90	67.47
		with Optical flow	0.889 ± 0.006	85.40	82.54	87.69	75.39
		with Gaze	0.886 ± 0.004	84.88	81.67	88.40	72.31
		All modalities	**0.911 ± 0.003**	**86.99**	**84.56**	**88.62**	**78.92**

gap between the image-based and video-based methods, supporting a hypothesis that temporal information is useful to assess clinical quality for clinical tasks. This result is also explainable clinically, the last frozen frame is not always the best diagnostic frame for biometry. The conclusion from this experiment is that including temporal information is helpful to distinguish between task-specific low-quality and high-quality videos. Among the video-based methods, our bi-directional reconstruction approach performs better than single-modality video reconstruction with an improvement of AUC by 4.8%. With the addition of other data modalities, *i.e.*, optical flow, and gaze, the AUC further increases from 0.863 to 0.911, respectively. Moreover, simple perturbations (*e.g.*, flipping, adding Gaussian noise) are applied on test images leading to the AUC of 0.906, which indicates the robustness of our approach. The paired t-test between our approach and STAE [18] is performed with p-value of 8×10^{-5}, which demonstrates the statistically significant benefit of our approach.

Ablation Study. Experiments were performed to study the effect of model components and parameter settings. The top panel of Table 2 demonstrates the effectiveness of the zoom-in module. Observe that a significant improvement is achieved by inclusion of the zoom-in module, with an AUC increase from 0.744 to

0.889. The explanation for this improvement is that the zoom-in module forces the encoder and decoder to concentrate on the essential region of the video instead of reconstructing background pixels which are not of interest. The bottom panel of Table 2 reports model performance for different ω_{gaze}. This additional training guidance further improves the AUC performance of our model from 0.889 to 0.911.

Table 2. Ablation study performance summary of the zoom-in module and different settings of the gaze loss weight. Note models are trained with inputs of video and optical flow.

		AUC	F1	ACC	SEN	SPEC
w/o zoom-in module		0.744	75.39	70.85	86.25	54.39
Zoom-in module		0.889	85.40	82.54	87.69	75.39
Gaze loss	$\omega_{gaze} = 0$	0.889	85.40	82.54	87.69	75.39
	$\omega_{gaze} = 0.1$	**0.911**	**86.99**	**84.56**	88.62	**78.92**
	$\omega_{gaze} = 0.5$	0.899	85.87	82.96	**88.95**	74.62
	$\omega_{gaze} = 1$	0.888	85.25	82.64	86.19	77.69

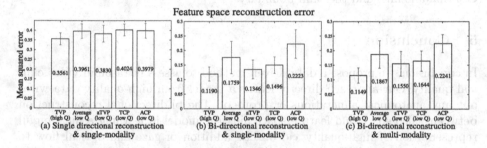

Fig. 3. Reconstruction error in feature space with respect to reconstruction method and modality.

Figure 3 (a)–(c) report the mean and standard deviation of the feature space reconstruction error for the high-quality data (*i.e.*, TVP) and low-quality data (*i.e.*, aTVP, TCP, ACP). The strength of bi-directional reconstruction is demonstrated in Fig. 3(a) and (b). The difference in reconstruction error using a single directional model is very small. Therefore it is not as easy to distinguish between high- and low-quality videos. Conversely, the bi-directional model shows a larger error. The results demonstrate that more information can be learned by the bi-directional reconstruction, thus leading to better performance. The effect of using multi-modality in our model is reported in Fig. 3(b) and (c). The difference in reconstruction error between low quality and high quality is small for the single modality model, especially for aTVP which is the closest video clip to high-quality data. The margin between high- and low-quality data is greater for the multi-modality case. We conclude that the model trained with multi-modal data is able to better distinguish low-quality videos from high-quality videos, compared with just modelling from video alone.

Fig. 4. Three examples of gaze prediction between two consecutive frames.

Gaze Prediction. Our model architecture uses eye gaze in an auxiliary branch instead of an input which allows the model to filter low-quality videos and also performs gaze prediction. Figure 4 shows three example gaze predictions on consecutive test frames. Observe that the gaze predictions mainly focus on the cavum septi pellucidi (CSP) and choroid plexus (CP), which are two anatomical structures that a sonographer pays attention to during scanning. The accuracy of gaze prediction is approximate 89%, where most of the eye gaze falls on CP, CSP, middle line, and the skull boundary.

5   Conclusion

In conclusion, we propose a data-driven method to assess ultrasound video clinical quality. Our approach directly learns a model from high-quality data without any anatomical annotations or protocol. The bi-directional reconstruction between video space and feature space aids the model in learning a meaningful representation of high-quality video. The addition of gaze and optical flow to video improved model performance by providing additional information about clinically important regions. Our approach provides a new idea to evaluate ultrasound video quality in a data-driven fashion without relying on data annotations. It may be readily applied to different task-specific clinical video quality assessment problems.

Acknowledgement. This paper is funded by the ERC (ERC-ADG-2015 694581 project PULSE), the EPSRC (EP/MO13774/1. EP/R013853/1), and the NIHR Biomedical Research Centre funding scheme.

References

1. Dong, J., et al.: A generic quality control framework for fetal ultrasound cardiac four-chamber planes. IEEE J. Biomed. Health Inform. **24**(4), 931–942 (2019)

2. Drukker, L., et al.: Transforming obstetric ultrasound into data science using eye tracking, voice recording, transducer motion and ultrasound video. Sci. Rep. **11**(1), 1–12 (2021)
3. Farnebäck, G.: Two-frame motion estimation based on polynomial expansion. In: Bigun, J., Gustavsson, T. (eds.) SCIA 2003. LNCS, vol. 2749, pp. 363–370. Springer, Heidelberg (2003). https://doi.org/10.1007/3-540-45103-X_50
4. Gao, Y., Beriwal, S., Craik, R., Papageorghiou, A.T., Noble, J.A.: Label efficient localization of fetal brain biometry planes in ultrasound through metric learning. In: Hu, Y., et al. (eds.) ASMUS/PIPPI -2020. LNCS, vol. 12437, pp. 126–135. Springer, Cham (2020). https://doi.org/10.1007/978-3-030-60334-2_13
5. Heusel, M., Ramsauer, H., Unterthiner, T., Nessler, B., Hochreiter, S.: GANs trained by a two time-scale update rule converge to a local Nash equilibrium. In: Advances in Neural Information Processing Systems, vol. 30 (2017)
6. Jaderberg, M., Simonyan, K., Zisserman, A., et al.: Spatial transformer networks. In: Advances in Neural Information Processing Systems, vol. 28, pp. 2017–2025 (2015)
7. Kingma, D.P., Welling, M.: Auto-encoding variational Bayes. In: International Conference on Learning Representations, pp. 1–14 (2014)
8. Lin, Z., et al.: Quality assessment of fetal head ultrasound images based on faster R-CNN. In: Stoyanov, D., et al. (eds.) POCUS/BIVPCS/CuRIOUS/CPM -2018. LNCS, vol. 11042, pp. 38–46. Springer, Cham (2018). https://doi.org/10.1007/978-3-030-01045-4_5
9. Lin, Z., et al.: Multi-task learning for quality assessment of fetal head ultrasound images. Med. Image Anal. **58**, 101548 (2019)
10. Park, H., Noh, J., Ham, B.: Learning memory-guided normality for anomaly detection. In: Proceedings of the IEEE/CVF Conference on Computer Vision and Pattern Recognition, pp. 14372–14381 (2020)
11. Rahmatullah, B., Sarris, I., Papageorghiou, A., Noble, J.A.: Quality control of fetal ultrasound images: Detection of abdomen anatomical landmarks using adaboost. In: 2011 IEEE International Symposium on Biomedical Imaging: From Nano to Macro, pp. 6–9. IEEE (2011)
12. Saeed, S.U., et al.: Learning image quality assessment by reinforcing task amenable data selection. In: Feragen, A., Sommer, S., Schnabel, J., Nielsen, M. (eds.) IPMI 2021. LNCS, vol. 12729, pp. 755–766. Springer, Cham (2021). https://doi.org/10.1007/978-3-030-78191-0_58
13. Szegedy, C., et al.: Going deeper with convolutions. In: Proceedings of the IEEE Conference on Computer Vision and Pattern Recognition, pp. 1–9 (2015)
14. Wang, Z., Bovik, A.C., Sheikh, H.R., Simoncelli, E.P.: Image quality assessment: from error visibility to structural similarity. IEEE Trans. Image Process. **13**(4), 600–612 (2004)
15. Wu, L., Cheng, J.Z., Li, S., Lei, B., Wang, T., Ni, D.: FUIQA: fetal ultrasound image quality assessment with deep convolutional networks. IEEE Trans. Cybern. **47**(5), 1336–1349 (2017)
16. Yaqub, M., Kelly, B., Papageorghiou, A.T., Noble, J.A.: A deep learning solution for automatic fetal neurosonographic diagnostic plane verification using clinical standard constraints. Ultrasound Med. Biol. **43**(12), 2925–2933 (2017)
17. Yaqub, M., et al.: 491 scannav® audit: an AI-powered screening assistant for fetal anatomical ultrasound. Am. J. Obstet. Gynecol. **224**(2), S312 (2021)
18. Zhao, Y., Deng, B., Shen, C., Liu, Y., Lu, H., Hua, X.S.: Spatio-temporal autoencoder for video anomaly detection. In: Proceedings of the 25th ACM International Conference on Multimedia, pp. 1933–1941 (2017)

Key-frame Guided Network for Thyroid Nodule Recognition Using Ultrasound Videos

Yuchen Wang[1], Zhongyu Li[1(✉)], Xiangxiang Cui[1], Liangliang Zhang[1], Xiang Luo[1], Meng Yang[2], and Shi Chang[3(✉)]

[1] School of Software Engineering, Xi'an Jiaotong University, Xi'an, China
zhongyuli@xjtu.edu.cn
[2] Frontline Intelligent Technology (Nanjing) Co., Ltd., Nanjing, China
[3] Department of General Surgery, Xiangya Hospital, Central South University, Changsha, China
changshi@csu.edu.cn

Abstract. Ultrasound examination is widely used in the clinical diagnosis of thyroid nodules (benign/malignant). However, the accuracy relies heavily on radiologist experience. Although deep learning techniques have been investigated for thyroid nodules recognition. Current solutions are mainly based on static ultrasound images, with limited temporal information used and inconsistent with clinical diagnosis. This paper proposes a novel method for the automated recognition of thyroid nodules through an exhaustive exploration of ultrasound videos and key-frames. We first propose a detection-localization framework to automatically identify the clinical key-frame with a typical nodule in each ultrasound video. Based on the localized key-frame, we develop a key-frame guided video classification model for thyroid nodule recognition. Besides, we introduce a motion attention module to help the network focus on significant frames in an ultrasound video, which is consistent with clinical diagnosis. The proposed thyroid nodule recognition framework is validated on clinically collected ultrasound videos, demonstrating superior performance compared with other state-of-the-art methods.

Keywords: Key-frame · Thyroid nodule · Ultrasound video · Video classification · Motion attention

1 Introduction

The incidence of thyroid cancer has continued to increase during the past decades, which is mainly due to the improvement of detection and diagnosis techniques [17]. Generally, thyroid nodules can be divided into two categories: benign and malignant. Ultrasound examinations are usually used in the diagnosis of thyroid nodules. However, the traditional ultrasound examination process relies heavily on radiologist experience. The diagnostic process is time-consuming

© The Author(s), under exclusive license to Springer Nature Switzerland AG 2022
L. Wang et al. (Eds.): MICCAI 2022, LNCS 13434, pp. 238–247, 2022.
https://doi.org/10.1007/978-3-031-16440-8_23

and labor-intensive. Besides, overdiagnosis and overtreatment of thyroid nodules have become a global consensus. Therefore, computer-aided diagnosis (CAD) of thyroid nodules from ultrasound examination is of great significance.

In recent years, many efforts have been made for the CAD of nodules. Handcraft features are firstly used in nodule diagnosis, including Chang et al. [1] extract numerous textural features from nodular lesions and adopt support vector machines (SVM) to select important textural features to classify thyroid nodules. Iakovidis et al. [6] propose a kind of noise-resistant representation for thyroid ultrasound images and use polynomial kernel SVM to classify encoded thyroid ultrasound images. Recently, deep-learning based approaches have been investigated in nodule diagnosis. These works can be summarized into two types by the modality of data. The first type uses static ultrasound images to classify nodule status. For example, Chi et al. [3] use a pre-trained GoogLeNet for feature extraction. The extracted features are then sent to a cost-sensitive random forest classifier to classify nodule status. Li et al. [8] employ an ensembled ResNet-50 [5] and Darknet-19 [9] model to recognize malignant thyroid nodules, the model achieved higher performance in identifying thyroid cancer patients versus skilled radiologists. Song et al. [11] proposed a two-stage network to detect and recognize thyroid nodules. The second type of method uses ultrasound videos to classify nodule status. For example, Wan et al. [14] proposed a hierarchical framework to differentiate pathological types of thyroid nodules from contrast-enhanced ultrasound (CEUS) videos. Chen et al. [2] also adopt CEUS videos to classify breast nodules, in which they adopt 3D convolution and attention mechanism to fuse temporal information of the nodule.

Despite the above methods have been developed, there are mainly three challenges in the CAD of thyroid nodules. Firstly, most methods achieve the classification of thyroid nodules simply based on static 2D ultrasound images. While in clinical diagnosis, radiologists usually achieve diagnostic conclusions based on ultrasound videos, especially through dynamic morphologies and structures of nodules. Secondly, for most methods considering ultrasound videos, they rely on CEUS videos to get clear foreground and background, which are not the most commonly used B-scan ultrasound. Finally, there are no public datasets available for ultrasound video-based thyroid nodule recognition. Especially, it's hard to collect thyroid ultrasound videos with a unified acquisition process by different radiologists.

In this paper, we propose a novel framework for the CAD of thyroid nodules using ultrasound videos. We first develop an automated key-frame localization method to localize the frame with clinically typical thyroid nodules in dynamic ultrasound videos by training a detection-localization model. The model temporally considers texture features of each detected nodule. Subsequently, a key-frame guided network is designed for the classification of ultrasound videos. A motion attention module is introduced into the network to specifically help the network focus on the significant frames in an ultrasound video. Moreover, we collected more than 3000 clinical thyroid ultrasound videos with a unified acquisition process by three radiologists. The proposed framework is validated in the clinical collected dataset, showing promising performance in both key-frame localization and thyroid nodule classification.

2 Method

Overview: As shown in Fig. 1, we propose a novel framework for thyroid nodule diagnosis using ultrasound videos. Our model consists of two stages: key-frame localization stage and ultrasound video classification stage. In the first stage, we identify the position of the key-frame with clinically typical nodules in thyroid ultrasound videos through a detection-localization pipeline. Given an ultrasound video, thyroid nodules in each frame are first detected. Then the key-frame is automatically localized by simultaneously considering detected nodules with texture, spatial and temporal features. After the key-frame localization, we employ a modified C3D network for the classification of re-organized ultrasound videos with the key-frame centered. Especially, a motion attention module is introduced in considering different importance of each frame for the final classification. The whole framework is automated and can investigate information of spatial, temporal, and key-frame of ultrasound video for the classification of thyroid nodules, which is consistent with clinical diagnosis.

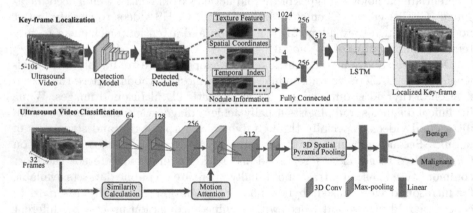

Fig. 1. Overview of our proposed framework for the thyroid nodule classification in ultrasound videos, which consists of two stages: key-frame localization stage and ultrasound video classification stage.

Key-Frame Localization: Previous work [7] has shown that the key-frame is useful in ultrasound video analysis. We notice that radiologists usually need to localize a key-frame with a typical thyroid nodule in supporting the diagnosis and quantitative analysis. Therefore, key-frame localization in ultrasound videos is important in the CAD of thyroid nodules. To utilize this pattern, we firstly propose a new task to localize the key-frame in a thyroid video, where we design a detection-localization framework to localize the key-frame automatically. Specifically, the network structure includes a detection model which detects nodules in each frame and an LSTM network to predict the index of the key-frame in an ultrasound video, i.e., a sequence of images.

For our detection model, we use the Faster-RCNN [10] model for nodule detection and feature extraction in each frame. To obtain features of each detected nodule, we take the output of the FC7 layer in Faster-RCNN as the feature representation for each detected nodule. Then, we use a fully connected (FC) layer to reduce the feature dimension to 256. For each detected nodule, we will also need spatial and temporal information for nodule representation in a video sequence. Inspired by Zhou et al. [18], we use a 5-D vector to represent spatial and temporal information, including four values for the normalized region of interest (ROI) coordinates and one value for the normalized frame index. Then, the 5-D feature is also projected to a 256-D embedding using an FC layer. Finally, we concatenate the two parts to form a 512-D vector which represents both image features and the spatial and temporal embedding for each nodule. The 512-D vector is then fed into the LSTM network to learn temporal relations. Finally, the output of the LSTM network is sent into two FC layers which eventually output a 1-D score for each nodule.

Considering we only have the key-frame index labeled by radiologists, it could be difficult for the network to learn the relationship between ultrasound video and the key-frame index. Therefore, we introduce a regression problem. Specifically, we give each frame a score varying from 0 to 1 to become the key-frame for the network to learn. A label generation procedure is used to make the single key-frame index label into a score sequence label. The score label of the key-frame is set to 1, and the score label of other frames is set from 0 to 1 by calculating the similarity of the current frame and the key-frame. To take full advantage of video data, the similarity includes three parts: image-level similarity, frame index similarity and nodule area IOU (intersection over union) similarity. For image-level similarity, we first calculate the euclidean distance of two frames based on the feature vector extracted in Faster-RCNN. Then we unify them to 0 to 1. For frame index similarity, we calculate the frame index distance between the two frames and unify them to 0 to 1. For IOU similarity, we calculate the IOU of two nodule areas from two frames. Eventually, we average three parts of similarity as our total similarity. Then, the calculated total similarity is used as the score label of each frame for the network to predict. Mean squared error (MSE) loss is adopted for the output score sequence of the network and the score labels.

Ultrasound Video Classification: With the key-frame obtained from the previous stage, we design a key-frame guided ultrasound video classification network for thyroid nodule classification. In this stage, we firstly consider using a C3D backbone for nodule classification. However, due to the limited size of our dataset, the C3D network has encountered severe overfitting on our training data. We finally follow the approach in [2]. Specifically, we remove most of the parameters in the C3D network to construct our lightweight C3D, which could alleviate overfitting. The architecture of the lightweight C3D network backbone includes four 3D convolutional layers, two max-pooling layers, four batch-normalization layers and two fully connected layers. All the 3D convolutional layers are followed by a batch-normalization layer. In addition, the third and the fourth 3D convolutional layer both have a pooling layer behind them. Among them, the first and the second 3D convolutional layer has a stride of $1 \times 1 \times 1$ and $1 \times 2 \times 2$, respectively, while the third and the fourth 3D convolutional layers have a stride of $2 \times 2 \times 2$. All 3D convolutional layers have a kernel size of $3 \times 3 \times 3$ and padding of $1 \times 1 \times 1$. The kernel size of max-pooling layers is $2 \times 2 \times 2$.

By recalling the actual clinical diagnosis of thyroid nodules, radiologists usually determine nodule status by a key-frame to see texture features and its several adjacent frames to see the dynamic morphological change of the thyroid nodule. To incorporate this pattern, we use the key-frame obtained from the previous stage to guide the ultrasound video classification stage. Specifically, to take full advantage of the key-frame, we select T continuous frames with the key-frame in the center of the sequence as our input rather than uniformly sampled frames in other work [2]. T is empirically set to 32 in this work. Besides, we apply the 3D version of the spatial pyramid pooling (SPP) layer [4] to learn multiscale representation. The 3D SPP layer is behind the last pooling layer. Limited by the size of the feature map, we adopt a three-level pyramid (original feature map, $2 \times 2 \times 2, 1 \times 1 \times 1$). Then we concatenate the features to form a multiscale representation of the nodule. Eventually, two FC layers with ReLU activation are appended to give category scores. A dropout layer with the dropout rate of 0.5 is added to alleviate overfitting. We use cross-entropy loss for nodule classification, where the classification loss L_{cls} is formulated by:

$$L_{cls} = -(y_n \cdot \log z_n + (1 - y_n) \cdot \log(1 - z_n)) \tag{1}$$

where n is the batch size, y_n is the label of this batch and z_n is the output of this batch.

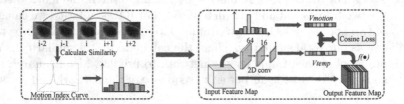

Fig. 2. The structure of the motion attention branch. It uses image similarity to quantify the motion of radiologists. Then it uses convolutional layers to calculate the temporal weights. Cosine loss is appended between temporal weights V_{temp} and the motion vector V_{motion} to optimize parameters.

Motion Attention: We notice that when radiologists find a possible key-frame, they will slow down their motion to observe the nodule, which means the frames in ultrasound video become relatively still. Therefore we design a motion attention module to perform the attention mechanism similar to the radiologists. We use a structure similar to [2] to reassign temporal weights. The motion attention module is added to the end of the first 3D pooling layer. The detailed structure of our motion attention module is shown in Fig. 2. The structure consists of three 2D convolutional layers. The first and the second 2D convolutional layer have a kernel size of 3×3 with a stride of 2×2, while the last 2D convolutional layer has a kernel size of 2×2 with a stride of 1×1. After these convolutional layers, the feature map is reduced to 1 channel. The final output feature map size is $1 \times T \times 1 \times 1$, which could be used as temporal weights. On the other side, we split the whole frame sequence into T (the input temporal dimension) time windows. We use image similarity of these frames to quantify the motion of the radiologist, i.e., high similarity reflects that the radiologist is moving very slowly. We calculate SSIM [15] and histogram similarity within a small interval (frame $i-2, i-1, i+1, i+2$) for frame i. Then we average the results of these two similarity indices to evaluate both pixel-level similarity and structural similarity. We define a motion index to quantify the motion of the radiologist. Motion index M_i for frame i is defined by the average similarity of frame $i-2, i-1, i+1, i+2$. Then we average M_i within each window to represent the motion in this time window. The result vector is defined as V_{motion}. Finally, the learned temporal weights V_{temp} are multiplied with the input feature map in the temporal dimension. Moreover, consistency loss is applied to optimize the temporal weights. Specifically, our loss function L_{motion} is calculated by the cosine similarity between temporal weights V_{temp} and the motion vector V_{motion}. The loss function is expressed as:

$$L_{motion} = 1 - cosine(v_{temp}, v_{motion}) \tag{2}$$

where v_{temp} is the temporal weights, v_{motion} is the calculated motion index vector. Finally, we add L_{motion} to the classification loss L_{cls}, the overall loss L for our nodule classification network could be written as:

$$L = L_{cls} + L_{motion} \tag{3}$$

3 Experiments and Results

Dataset: Our ultrasound video dataset was collected from 2020/04 to 2021/12 at three medical centers, following data cleaning to filter out videos with bad quality. We cropped videos to remove device and patients' information. The devices include three types, i.e., SAMSUNG MEDISON H60, HS50, and X60. All three devices have line array probes with a frequency of 7.5MHz. In the experiment, we only use videos captured in the cross-section direction of the thyroid on thyroid left or right sides. All videos were annotated with key-frame index, nodule ROI position and nodule status (benign/malignant) by two radiologists with over ten years' experience. All the annotations were checked by a third radiologist with over twenty years' experience. Difficult/disagreement samples were decided by three experts together. Finally, 3668 thyroid ultrasound videos were used as our dataset for the key-frame localization stage. For the training of our detection model, we extracted 23219 thyroid images from these videos to train the Faster-RCNN. All images are resized to 500×600 for detection. Then we use these 3668 videos to train the key-frame localization model. We randomly choose 2648 videos for training, 504 videos for validation and 516 videos for testing. The code and data are available at https://github.com/NeuronXJTU/KFGNet.

In the ultrasound video classification stage, due to the extremely unbalanced numbers of benign and malignant nodules, we choose 244 videos from the test set of the previous key-frame localization stage as our dataset, including 125 benign nodule videos and 119 malignant nodule videos. The input of our ultrasound video classification stage is $112 \times 112 \times 32$. We resize each nodule to 112×112 and choose a 32-frame sequence for inputs as mentioned before. In addition, data augmentation including random flip and intensity shift is applied to mitigate overfitting. Considering the limited size of our dataset, 5-fold cross validation is applied to verify our model.

Settings: The model is implemented with PyTorch 1.5.0, using an RTX 2080 Ti GPU. In our experiment, the whole model is randomly initialized with no pretraining. The two stages are trained separately. In the key-frame localization stage, we first train our Faster-RCNN using default settings in the framework [16]. Then we train the LSTM network using Adam optimizer with batch size 64, where the learning rate is set as 0.01 for 20 epochs training. We use the accuracy of different frame distance tolerance to evaluate our model. Specifically, for frame distance D, if the distance between the predicted key-frame and the key-frame label is smaller than D, we define this as a positive sample. Otherwise, it is defined as a negative sample. Then we calculate accuracy to show the prediction results. For the training of ultrasound video classification stage, we use Adam optimizer with the learning rate of $1e-3$ and weight decay of $1e-8$. Batch size is set as 16. After training for 20 epochs, we change the learning rate to $1e-4$ to train another 20 epochs. Then, accuracy, sensitivity, specificity, precision and F1-score are used to evaluate our ultrasound video classification stage.

Experimental Results: To evaluate the proposed method, we conduct a series of comparison and ablation experiments. Since our model contains two stages, we will first evaluate the key-frame localization stage, and then we will evaluate the whole model.

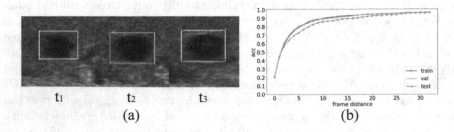

Fig. 3. Results of key-frame localization stage. (a) Detection results of a few frames in a thyroid ultrasound video, where t_2 is the key-frame. (b) Accuracy of key-frame localization with different frame distance tolerance (from 0 to 32).

For our key-frame localization stage, our Faster-RCNN model reaches AP50 of 77.34%, which could verify the effectiveness of our detection model. The key-frame localization results are shown in Fig. 3(b). We calculate the distance between our predicted key-frame and the key-frame label. The results show accuracy with different frame distance tolerance (from 0 to 32). According to the results, our model can reach more than 70% of accuracy within 5 frames error and can reach more than 90% of accuracy within 15 frames error, which is significant for the next ultrasound video classification stage.

We then evaluate the whole model on our dataset. Table 1 shows the results of different methods and our ablation experiments. Since we are using thyroid ultrasound video data, we choose some representative video classification models for comparison, such as C3D [12], R3D [13] and R2plus1D [13]. We choose lightweight C3D as our baseline because our further improvements are based on the lightweight C3D network. The results show that our lightweight C3D backbone achieves the highest accuracy of 68.45% compared with other video classification backbones and gets competitive results in other metrics. Moreover, we design our ablation experiments to verify the effectiveness of the key-frame, 3D SPP and motion attention module, respectively. We first validate the effectiveness of the key-frame. The results show that key-frame guided lightweight C3D outperforms our baseline in all metrics. Specifically, our model has improved 3.2% in accuracy by key-frame, which is mainly because our key-frame has alleviated temporal information redundancy and helped the network focus on significant frames. We then validate 3D SPP and motion attention, respectively. Notably, since the key-frame is our fundamental design and our motion attention module is closely related to the key-frame, we will further validate these two modules based on the key-frame by adding them to our key-frame guided lightweight C3D. Results show that both 3D SPP and motion attention could further improve our network performance. Specifically, the accuracy can get a boost of 2.5% by motion attention and 2.9% by 3D SPP. Finally, we implement our model with key-frame, 3D SPP and motion attention. According to the results, our proposed method outperforms other existing methods by achieving the highest performance in all metrics. Our proposed network outperforms the baseline by 8.2% in accuracy and 7.5% in sensitivity, respectively.

Table 1. Quantitative results of our proposed method with the comparison to other state-of-the-art methods and our ablation experiments.

Methods	Key-frame	3D SPP	Motion attention	Accuracy	Sensitivity	Specificity	Precision	F1-score
C3D [12]				66.78%	70.51%	65.83%	63.27%	65.47%
R3D [13]				67.19%	68.08%	68.45%	70.55%	68.27%
R2plus1D [13]				68.45%	71.37%	66.96%	67.83%	68.75%
lightweight C3D				68.45%	71.06%	66.73%	66.52%	68.13%
lightweight C3D	✓			71.69%	71.94%	71.88%	74.73%	72.76%
lightweight C3D	✓		✓	74.19%	77.88%	72.04%	71.59%	73.90%
lightweight C3D	✓	✓		74.59%	76.67%	75.25%	76.69%	75.52%
Ours	✓	✓	✓	**76.65%**	**78.52%**	**76.36%**	**77.17%**	**77.08%**

4   Conclusions

In this paper, we propose a novel method for computer-aided diagnosis of thyroid nodules using ultrasound videos. To the best of our knowledge, this is the first time to achieve the automated localization of key-frames with typical thyroid nodules in ultrasound videos. The proposed method can locate the key-frame in a thyroid video and use the key-frame to guide the nodule classification. Besides, the motion attention mechanism is introduced to help the network focus on significant frames in a video. As a result, all the designs improve the performance of our network. Our results indicate that the proposed method has significantly outperformed other state-of-the-art methods for thyroid nodule classification on our dataset. The proposed framework can be applied to clinical CAD in reducing doctors' work and improving diagnostic accuracy.

Acknowledgements. This work is partially supported by the National Natural Science Foundation of China under grant No. 61902310 and the Natural Science Basic Research Program of Shaanxi, China under grant 2020JQ030.

References

1. Chang, C.Y., Chen, S.J., Tsai, M.F.: Application of support-vector-machine-based method for feature selection and classification of thyroid nodules in ultrasound images. Pattern Recogn. **43**(10), 3494–3506 (2010)
2. Chen, C., Wang, Y., Niu, J., Liu, X., Li, Q., Gong, X.: Domain knowledge powered deep learning for breast cancer diagnosis based on contrast-enhanced ultrasound videos. IEEE Trans. Med. Imaging **40**(9), 2439–2451 (2021)
3. Chi, J., Walia, E., Babyn, P., Wang, J., Eramian, M.: Thyroid nodule classification in ultrasound images by fine-tuning deep convolutional neural network. J. Digit. Imaging **30**(3), 477–486 (2004)
4. He, K., Zhang, X., Ren, S., Sun, J.: Spatial pyramid pooling in deep convolutional networks for visual recognition. IEEE Trans. Pattern Anal. Mach. Intell. **37**(9), 1904–1916 (2015)
5. He, K., Zhang, X., Ren, S., Sun, J.: Deep residual learning for image recognition. In: Proceedings of the IEEE Conference on Computer Vision and Pattern Recognition, pp. 770–778 (2016)
6. Iakovidis, D.K., Keramidas, E.G., Maroulis, D.: Fusion of fuzzy statistical distributions for classification of thyroid ultrasound patterns. Artif. Intell. Med. **50**(1), 33–41 (2010)
7. Jafari, M.H., et al.: U-land: uncertainty-driven video landmark detection. IEEE Trans. Med. Imaging **41**(4), 793–804 (2021)
8. Li, X., et al.: Diagnosis of thyroid cancer using deep convolutional neural network models applied to sonographic images: a retrospective, multicohort, diagnostic study. Lancet Oncol. **20**(2), 193–201 (2019)
9. Redmon, J., Farhadi, A.: Yolo9000: better, faster, stronger. In: Proceedings of the IEEE Conference on Computer Vision and Pattern Recognition, pp. 7263–7271 (2017)
10. Ren, S., He, K., Girshick, R., Sun, J.: Faster R-CNN: towards real-time object detection with region proposal networks. In: Advances in Neural Information Processing Systems, vol. 28 (2015)

11. Song, W., et al.: Multitask cascade convolution neural networks for automatic thyroid nodule detection and recognition. IEEE J. Biomed. Health Inform. **23**(3), 1215–1224 (2018)
12. Tran, D., Bourdev, L., Fergus, R., Torresani, L., Paluri, M.: Learning spatiotemporal features with 3d convolutional networks. In: Proceedings of the IEEE International Conference on Computer Vision, pp. 4489–4497 (2015)
13. Tran, D., Wang, H., Torresani, L., Ray, J., LeCun, Y., Paluri, M.: A closer look at spatiotemporal convolutions for action recognition. In: Proceedings of the IEEE conference on Computer Vision and Pattern Recognition, pp. 6450–6459 (2018)
14. Wan, P., Chen, F., Liu, C., Kong, W., Zhang, D.: Hierarchical temporal attention network for thyroid nodule recognition using dynamic CEUS imaging. IEEE Trans. Med. Imaging **40**(6), 1646–1660 (2021)
15. Wang, Z., Bovik, A.C., Sheikh, H.R., Simoncelli, E.P.: Image quality assessment: from error visibility to structural similarity. IEEE Trans. Image Process. **13**(4), 600–612 (2004)
16. Yang, J., Lu, J., Batra, D., Parikh, D.: A faster pytorch implementation of faster R-CNN (2017). https://github.com/jwyang/faster-rcnn.pytorch
17. Yu, J., et al.: Lymph node metastasis prediction of papillary thyroid carcinoma based on transfer learning radiomics. Nat. Commun. **11**(1), 1–10 (2020)
18. Zhou, L., Kalantidis, Y., Chen, X., Corso, J.J., Rohrbach, M.: Grounded video description. In: Proceedings of the IEEE/CVF Conference on Computer Vision and Pattern Recognition, pp. 6578–6587 (2019)

Less is More: Adaptive Curriculum Learning for Thyroid Nodule Diagnosis

Haifan Gong[1,3], Hui Cheng[1], Yifan Xie[1], Shuangyi Tan[3,4], Guanqi Chen[1],
Fei Chen[2(✉)], and Guanbin Li[1(✉)]

[1] School of Computer Science and Engineering, Sun Yat-sen University,
Guangdong, China
liguanbin@mail.sysu.edu.cn
[2] Zhujiang Hospital, Southern Medical University, Guangdong, China
gzchenfei@126.com
[3] Shenzhen Research Institute of Big Data, Shenzhen, China
[4] The Chinese University of Hong Kong, Shenzhen, China

Abstract. Thyroid nodule classification aims at determining whether
the nodule is benign or malignant based on a given ultrasound image.
However, the label obtained by the cytological biopsy which is the golden
standard in clinical medicine is not always consistent with the ultrasound
imaging TI-RADS criteria. The information difference between the two
causes the existing deep learning-based classification methods to be inde-
cisive. To solve the *Inconsistent Label* problem, we propose an Adaptive
Curriculum Learning (ACL) framework, which adaptively discovers and
discards the samples with inconsistent labels. Specifically, ACL takes
both hard sample and model certainty into account, and could accurately determine the threshold to distinguish the samples with *Inconsistent Label*. Moreover, we contribute TNCD: a Thyroid Nodule Classification Dataset to facilitate future related research on the thyroid nodules.
Extensive experimental results on TNCD based on three different backbone networks not only demonstrate the superiority of our method but
also prove that the less-is-more principle which strategically discards the
samples with *Inconsistent Label* could yield performance gains. Source
code and data are available at https://github.com/chenghui-666/ACL/.

Keywords: Thyroid nodule · Adaptive curriculum learning ·
Ultrasound imaging · Image classification

1 Introduction

Thyroid nodule is a common clinical disease with an incidence of 19%–68%
in the population, where about 5%–15% of them are malignant [4]. Ultrasonic
image-based diagnosis is the most widely used technique to determine whether
the thyroid nodule is benign or malignant because of its low cost, efficiency, and

---

H. Gong and H. Cheng—Contribute equally to this work.

© The Author(s), under exclusive license to Springer Nature Switzerland AG 2022
L. Wang et al. (Eds.): MICCAI 2022, LNCS 13434, pp. 248–257, 2022.
https://doi.org/10.1007/978-3-031-16440-8_24

sensitivity. However, unlike standardized CT & MRI images, ultrasonic images are taken at variant positions from different angles. Meanwhile, ultrasonic images are susceptible to noise due to their low contrast, which is challenging for inexperienced radiologists to perform diagnoses [5]. Thus, it is valuable to design an accurate computer-aided diagnosis (CAD) system to reduce the performance gap between inexperienced radiologists and experienced ones.

To provide guidance for the diagnosis of thyroid nodule, Tessler et al. [15] have proposed the Thyroid Imaging Reporting And Data System (TI-RADS) which describes five groups of appearance feature-based diagnostic criteria to conduct qualitative analyses for thyroid nodules. Nevertheless, in clinical medicine, the fine needle aspiration (FNA) [12] based cytological biopsy is the golden standard for the diagnosis of the thyroid nodule. In fact, the results of the diagnostic analysis guided by TI-RADS are not necessarily consistent with the judgment based on the golden rule of pathology. TI-RADS, as a diagnostic manual based on the empirical summary, judges the nature of nodules through image features, which means that benign nodules are bound to have some characteristics of malignancy, and malignant nodules must also contain benign morphological features. In terms of probability, the label itself inevitably has uncertainty.

Therefore, the label obtained by the cytological biopsy is not always consistent with that from TI-RADS, and this causes an *Inconsistent Label* problem: the samples with inconsistent labels tend to be harder for the model to fit, which leads to the complexity of the decision plane and harms the generalization of the model. Based on the above concerns, we propose an adaptive curriculum learning framework to resolve these issues. The contribution of this work can be summarized as follow: (1) We propose a curriculum learning-based algorithm to resolve the inconsistent label problem. Specifically, it works by adaptively discovering and discarding the hard samples; (2) We contribute TNCD: a benchmark for the thyroid nodule classification task, to further encourage the research development of thyroid nodule diagnosis. (3) Extensive experiments compared with other state-of-the-art methods have demonstrated the effectiveness of our method, and proving the less-is-more proverbial that end-to-end learning with fewer samples could achieve better performance.

2   Related Work

Thyroid Nodule Diagnosis. Deep neural networks (DNN) have shown their dominance in the field of image representation learning. Based on DNN, Wang et al. [16] proposed an attention-based network that aggregates the extracted features from multiple ultrasound images. Song et al. [14] proposed a hybrid feature cropping network to extract discriminative features for better performance on classification, and this network reduces the negative impacts of local similarities between benign and malignant nodules. Zhao et al. [19] proposed a local and global feature disentangled network to segment and classify the thyroid nodules. To make the automatic diagnosis more accurate and consistent with human cognition, several works [1,9,18] were proposed to integrate domain knowledge for

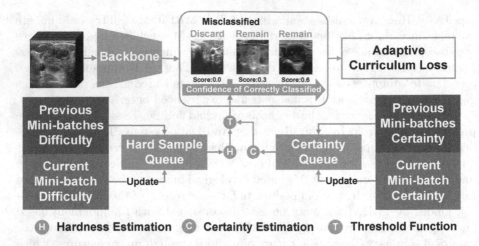

Fig. 1. Overview of the proposed adaptive curriculum learning framework. The orange part shows the training pipeline on a mini-batch. The hard sample estimation queue is shown in blue blocks, while the certainty estimation module is shown in green blocks. (Color figure online)

thyroid nodule diagnosis, such as boundary feature, aspect ratio, echo pattern, orientation, etc. However, all the previous works ignore the *Inconsistent Label* issue. To address this issue, we proposed a curriculum learning-based algorithm to discard the samples adaptively during the neural network training stage.

Curriculum Learning. Curriculum learning [2] is a training strategy that makes models to gradually learn from easy to hard. Many works adopt curriculum learning to improve the generalization or convergence speed of models in the domain of computer vision [17] or natural language processing [13]. Recently, curriculum learning-based approaches [3,11] have been used to overcome the inherent hardness of learning from hard samples, as it automatically decreases the weight of samples based on their difficulty. Lyu et al. [11] proposed to adaptively select samples with a tighter upper bound loss against label corruption. Castells et al. [3] designed SuperLoss that mathematically decreases the contribution of samples with a large loss. Liu et al. [8] proposed a co-correcting framework to relabel the images with dual-network curriculum learning. However, all the above-mentioned methods neither rely on the hard-craft schedule nor ignore the samples with inconsistent labels. Thus, we develop an adaptive curriculum learning paradigm to adaptively discover and discard these samples.

3 Methodology

We propose an adaptive curriculum learning (ACL) framework for thyroid nodule diagnosis, which is shown in Fig. 1. ACL is mainly composed of two parts: a curriculum learning-based sample scheduler and a model certainty estimating function. The idea underlying ACL is to mitigate the *Inconsistent Label* problem by adaptively discovering and discarding the detrimental samples, thus forcing the model to adaptively learn from easy samples to hard samples.

3.1 Hard Sample Discovery with Confidence Queue

The core idea of curriculum learning is to gradually excavate hard samples and adjust their weights adaptively in the process of model training. Therefore, we need to design a function to discriminate the hardness of a sample. Considering that the samples with inconsistent labels tend to be misjudged with high confidence, we first define the set P_c that contains the sample's confidence c_i as:

$$P_c = \{c_0, ..., c_i\} \tag{1}$$

where $c_i = P(x_i|y_i)$. x_i and y_i denote the predicted probability (after Softmax function) and its corresponding label, respectively. i is the index of the sample. c_i ranges from 0 to 1. When $c_i < 0.5$ the model makes incorrect prediction. Thus, the set H of hard samples in current mini-batch c_i' is defined as:

$$H = \{c_i \in P_c | \mathbb{I}(y_i \neq y_i')\} \tag{2}$$

where y_i' is the predicted label. $\mathbb{I}(\cdot)$ is an indicator function that returns true when condition meets, which means the correctly classified i^{th} sample will not enter the hard sample queue. Therefore, the hard sample set H will be fed into the queue to calculate the threshold, which is used to distinguish the samples with the inconsistent label.

To find the hard samples more accurately, we propose the adaptive thresholding function T_{ada}. The tailor-designed T_{ada} can adaptively constrain the model to better learn the easy samples in the early stage, and gradually learn the hard samples in the later stage. As a dynamic threshold, T_{ada} should be able to (1) update in time; (2) estimate with sufficient samples. Thus, we design a hard sample confidence queue Q_h with fixed length L to store the confidence of misclassified samples across batches. This queue is updated every batch by following the first in first out (FIFO) rule, which means we first dequeue the oldest k elements in Q_h, then send the set H into Q_h. Let the queue before updating be $Q_h^{pre}\{c_1, ..., c_l\}$ where the subscripts denote the previous position of the elements, this process is formulated as:

$$Q_h = \begin{cases} \{c_1, ..., c_l, ..., c_{l+k}\}, & l \leq L - k \\ \{c_{l+k-L}, ..., c_l, ..., c_{l+k}\}, & L - k < l < L, \\ \{c_k, ..., c_l, ..., c_{l+k}\}, & l = L \end{cases} \tag{3}$$

where L and l denotes the fixed length and previous length of the queue, respectively. The number of misclassified sample is represented by k. Let μ and σ be the average value and standard deviation of elements in Q_h, the formulation of T_{ada} is defined as:

$$T_{ada} = \mu + \alpha \cdot \sigma \tag{4}$$

where α is a hyper-parameter to trade-off the numbers of the hard samples.

3.2 Model Certainty Estimation with Certainty Queue

Considering that the T_{ada} did not take the model's certainty into concern, which will lead to the inaccurate estimation of T_{ada}, we propose to embedded the model's certainty into the T_{ada} by replacing the hyper-parameter α with a **self-configured & certainty-aware** variable θ. The idea underlying this modification is to use the model's certainty to constrain the standard deviation of difficult sample queues to better estimate difficult samples. As the model certainty can be reflected by the model's prediction, we define the sample certainty $\hat{c}_i$ as:

$$\hat{c}_i = max(x_i) \tag{5}$$

where x_i is the model's prediction after Softmax function. The value of the sample $\hat{c}_i$ ranges from $(0.5, 1)$. The larger value is, the more certain the model is. After that, we follow the idea of a hard sample queue in Sect. 3.1 and propose a certainty queue Q_c to estimate the model's certainty. The difference between Q_c and Q_h is that Q_c uses all the samples in the current mini-batch for updating, while Q_h only updates the queue with the misclassified samples. Since queue length L is set equal to the length of Q_h which is a multiple of batch-size B, letting the queue before updating be $Q_c^{pre}\{\hat{c}_1, ..., \hat{c}_l\}$, this process could be formulated as:

$$Q_c = \begin{cases} \{\hat{c}_1, ..., \hat{c}_l, ..., \hat{c}_{l+B}\}, & l \leq L - B \\ \{\hat{c}_B, ..., \hat{c}_l, ..., \hat{c}_{l+B}\}, & l = L \end{cases} \tag{6}$$

Thus θ is calculated by averaging the elements in queue Q_c with $\theta = \frac{1}{L}\sum_{j=1}^{L} Q_j^c$. Intuitively, the θ should gradually change from 0.5 to 1 as the model's iteration. In the early stage of training, the model is uncertain about the samples, we should discard fewer samples to force the model to learn more imaging features. In the late stage of training, the model is sure about the samples. Thus, we strategically multiply θ and standard deviation σ to embed the model certainty into hard sample selection, forcing the T_{ada} to better distinguish the hard samples. Thus, Eq. 4 is re-written as:

$$T_{ada} = \mu + \theta \cdot \sigma \tag{7}$$

The overall pseudo code to update the T_{ada} is shown in Algorithm 1.

3.3 Loss Function of Adaptive Curriculum Learning

With the T_{ada} and the confidence c_i defined in Equation. 1, the curriculum learning process can be described by adjusting the loss l_i of i-th sample. Let CE be the cross-entropy loss, following the "less is more" proverb, this process is defined as:

$$l_i = \begin{cases} CE(y_i', y_i), & c_i \geq T_{ada} \\ 0, & c_i < T_{ada} \end{cases}, \tag{8}$$

Finally, let B be the batch size, the overall loss L is defined as:

$$L = \sum_{i=1}^{B} l_i. \tag{9}$$

Algorithm 1. Updating T_{ada} in b^{th} batch

Require: $B \in N^+$, the batch size

$\quad$ $X \in \mathbb{R}^{B \times 2}$, the prediction all samples in b^{th} batch

$\quad$ $Y \in \{0,1\}^B$, the labels of all samples in b^{th} batch

$\quad$ $Q_h \in (0, 0.5)^N$, the hard sample queue updated after $(b-1)^{th}$ batch

$\quad$ $Q_c \in (0.5, 1)^N$, the certainty queue updated after $(b-1)^{th}$ batch

Ensure: The updated T_{ada}

$\quad$ $P = softmax(X)$ $\qquad\qquad\qquad$ ▷ The predicted possibility $P \in \mathbb{R}^{B \times 2}$

$\quad$ $Y' = argmax(P[:])$ $\qquad\qquad\qquad$ ▷ The predicted label $Y' \in \{0,1\}^B$

$\quad$ **for** i in range(0,B) **do**

$\qquad$ $C = max(P)$ $\qquad\qquad\qquad\qquad\qquad$ ▷ The set of certainties.

$\qquad$ $dequeue(Q_c, len(C))$ $\qquad\qquad$ ▷ Dequeue the earliest $len(C)$ elements

$\qquad$ $enqueue(Q_c, C)$ $\qquad\qquad$ ▷ Enqueue the probability of the predicted label

$\qquad$ **if** $Y'[i] \neq Y[i]$ **then**

$\qquad\quad$ $H = \{P_i \in P | Y'[i] \neq Y[i]\}$ $\qquad\qquad\qquad$ ▷ The set of difficulty.

$\qquad\quad$ $dequeue(Q_h, len(H))$ $\qquad\qquad$ ▷ Dequeue the earliest element

$\qquad\quad$ $enqueue(Q_h, H)$ $\qquad\quad$ ▷ Enqueue the confidence of misclassified sample

$\qquad$ **end if**

$\quad$ **end for**

$\quad$ $\theta = mean(Q_c)$ $\qquad\qquad\qquad\qquad$ ▷ Estimate the model certainty

$\quad$ $\mu = mean(Q_h)$

$\quad$ $\sigma = std(Q_h)$

$\quad$ $T_{ada} = \mu + \theta \cdot \sigma$ $\qquad\qquad$ ▷ Update T_{ada} with queue C and model certainty

$\quad$ **return** T_{ada}

---

4 TNCD: Benchmark for Thyroid Nodule Classification

To facilitate future research in thyroid nodule diagnosis, we contribute a new Thyroid Nodule Classification Dataset called TNCD, which contains 3493 ultrasound images taken from 2421 patients. According to the results of nodular cytological biopsies, each image is labeled as benign or malignant according to its pathological biopsy result. To verify the performance of the algorithms, the TNCD dataset is divided into the training set and test set by ensuring the images from the same patient only appear in a certain subset. The training set contains 2879 images with 1905 benign and 974 malignant images, while the test set contains 614 images with 378 benign and 236 malignant images.

5 Experiment

5.1 Implementation and Evaluation Metric

The framework is implemented in PyTorch 1.11. All models are trained with NVIDIA 3090 GPU with CUDA 11.3, and initialized by the ImageNet pretrained weights. Stochastic gradient descent is used to optimize our models at an initial learning rate of 0.001, 'Poly' learning rate policy is applied, where $lr = lr_{init} \times (1 - \frac{epoch}{epoch_{total}})^{0.9}$. Batch size and training epoch are set to 16 and

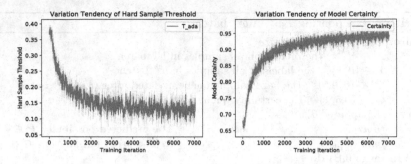

Fig. 2. The visualization result of the T_{ada} and the model certainty θ.

50, respectively. All images are resized to 224×224 with horizontal flip argumentation. We performed oversampling on the malignant samples to avoid the over-fitting of the majority benign samples. It is worth noting that as the training process is not stable initially, we trained the model with the cross entropy loss for the first three epochs, then trained the model with the proposed ACL loss. We use accuracy, precision, recall, F1-score and AUC as metrics.

Table 1. Ablation study of the queue length and the hyper-parameter.

Queue length L	0 (Baseline)	16	32	64
AUC	$77.31_{\pm 1.04}$	$79.24_{\pm 0.98}$	$\mathbf{79.27_{\pm 1.26}}$	$79.18_{\pm 1.17}$
Hyper-parameter α	0	1	2	$\theta(\mathbf{Ours})$
AUC	$79.27_{\pm 1.26}$	$79.66_{\pm 1.13}$	$79.41_{\pm 1.26}$	$\mathbf{79.89_{\pm 0.89}}$

5.2   Ablation Study and Schedule Analysis

All the ablation studies are conducted based on the ResNet18 backbone with 5-fold cross-validation on the AUC score. The ablation study about hard sample queue length is shown in the first two rows of Table 1. To balance the real-time and accuracy of queue updates, we choose 16, 32, and 64 as the length of queue Q_h. We find the length of 32 is appropriate, which achieves the highest AUC value. More importantly, all the AUC scores in this table significantly exceed the baseline by about 2%, showing that discarding the samples with inconsistent labels is useful. The ablation study about the certainty-aware queue is shown in the last two rows of Table 1. By replacing the hyper-parameter α with the certainty-aware variable θ, we achieve better performance while avoiding the laborious hyper-parameter selection.

Moreover, we further visualize the variation tendency of the T_{ada} and the θ in Fig. 2. The T_{ada} is used to discover the hard sample and force the model to learn from easy to hard. The model certainty θ curve gradually increased to 1, which validates our assumption in Sect. 3.2.

Table 2. Comparison with the state of the art methods.

Learning strategy	Backbone	Accuracy	Precision	Recall	F1-score	AUC
Cross entropy	resnet	$70.75_{\pm1.53}$	$61.71_{\pm1.64}$	$68.05_{\pm6.98}$	$64.47_{\pm2.50}$	$77.31_{\pm1.04}$
	densenet	$70.36_{\pm1.21}$	$63.92_{\pm2.33}$	$63.31_{\pm6.28}$	$63.31_{\pm2.49}$	$78.05_{\pm0.42}$
	convnext	$72.29_{\pm1.66}$	$62.94_{\pm2.62}$	$71.19_{\pm8.77}$	$66.36_{\pm2.84}$	$78.38_{\pm1.04}$
CL [11]	resnet	$70.54_{\pm1.32}$	$62.87_{\pm3.62}$	$65.85_{\pm5.27}$	$64.04_{\pm1.70}$	$76.98_{\pm1.16}$
	densenet	$70.03_{\pm0.97}$	$62.44_{\pm3.89}$	$65.25_{\pm7.92}$	$63.31_{\pm2.05}$	$77.27_{\pm0.77}$
	convnext	$72.14_{\pm1.74}$	$60.21_{\pm2.67}$	$\mathbf{75.76_{\pm3.65}}$	$67.00_{\pm1.70}$	$74.37_{\pm2.71}$
SL [3]	resnet	$71.26_{\pm1.82}$	$\mathbf{64.97_{\pm1.73}}$	$64.15_{\pm4.72}$	$64.46_{\pm2.67}$	$78.50_{\pm1.24}$
	densenet	$71.82_{\pm1.66}$	$\mathbf{64.38_{\pm1.81}}$	$66.86_{\pm5.84}$	$65.42_{\pm2.49}$	$78.98_{\pm0.29}$
	convnext	$71.47_{\pm1.53}$	$\mathbf{62.66_{\pm1.33}}$	$68.39_{\pm3.46}$	$65.36_{\pm1.99}$	$77.87_{\pm1.07}$
ACL (Ours)	resnet	$\mathbf{73.28_{\pm0.53}}$	$63.02_{\pm1.86}$	$73.64_{\pm1.90}$	$\mathbf{67.87_{\pm0.40}}$	$\mathbf{79.89_{\pm0.89}}$
	densenet	$\mathbf{72.92_{\pm1.26}}$	$60.74_{\pm3.78}$	$\mathbf{77.80_{\pm4.27}}$	$\mathbf{67.99_{\pm0.88}}$	$\mathbf{79.84_{\pm0.79}}$
	convnext	$\mathbf{72.50_{\pm0.69}}$	$61.19_{\pm1.68}$	$74.75_{\pm3.65}$	$\mathbf{67.21_{\pm0.91}}$	$\mathbf{78.85_{\pm0.99}}$

5.3 Comparison with the State-of-the-arts

The comparison with the state-of-the-art methods are shown in Table 2. These experiments are based on three widely used neural networks (ResNet18 [6], DenseNet121 [7], ConvNeXt-Tiny [10]) power with the advanced curriculum learning based loss functions (Curriculum Loss (CL) [11], SuperLoss (SL) [3])), and the proposed ACL. As shown in this table, the proposed method significantly exceeds the baseline by 3.5% w.r.t averaging AUC score. It also outperforms other curriculum learning-based methods (i.e., SL and CL) that not change the backbone by more than 1% AUC score on average, showing that properly discarding samples is quite effective.

6   Conclusion

We present an adaptive curriculum learning (ACL) framework for thyroid nodule diagnosis to resolve the *Inconsistent Label* problem, which adaptively discovers and discards the hard samples to constrain the neural network to learn from easy to hard. The proposed ACL could be easily embedded into existing neural networks to boost performance. Moreover, we contribute TNCD, a dataset that contains 3464 ultrasonic thyroid images with its cytological benign and malignant labels and pixel-level nodule masks. Extensive experiments have shown that the proposed framework outperforms state-of-the-art methods while unveiling that the "less is more" principle is practical.

Acknowledgement. This work is supported in part by the Chinese Key-Area Research and Development Program of Guangdong Province (2020B0101350001), in part by the Guangdong Basic and Applied Basic Research Foundation (2020B1515020048), in part by the National Natural Science Foundation of China (61976250), in part by the Guangzhou Science and technology project (No. 202102020633), and in part by the Guangdong Provincial Key Laboratory of Big Data Computing, The Chinese University of Hong Kong, Shenzhen.

References

1. Avola, D., Cinque, L., Fagioli, A., Filetti, S., Grani, G., Rodolà, E.: Multimodal feature fusion and knowledge-driven learning via experts consult for thyroid nodule classification. IEEE Trans. Circ. Syst. Video Technol. **32**, 2527–2534 (2021)
2. Bengio, Y., Louradour, J., Collobert, R., Weston, J.: Curriculum learning. In: Danyluk, A.P., Bottou, L., Littman, M.L. (eds.) Proceedings of the 26th Annual International Conference on Machine Learning, ICML 2009, Montreal, Quebec, Canada, 14–18 June 2009. ACM International Conference Proceeding Series, vol. 382, pp. 41–48. ACM (2009)
3. Castells, T., Weinzaepfel, P., Revaud, J.: SuperLoss: a generic loss for robust curriculum learning. In: Advances in Neural Information Processing Systems 33: Annual Conference on Neural Information Processing Systems 2020, NeurIPS 2020, 6–12 December 2020, virtual (2020)
4. Chen, J., You, H., Li, K.: A review of thyroid gland segmentation and thyroid nodule segmentation methods for medical ultrasound images. Comput. Methods Programs Biomed. **185**, 105329 (2020)
5. Gong, H., et al.: Multi-task learning for thyroid nodule segmentation with thyroid region prior. In: 2021 IEEE 18th International Symposium on Biomedical Imaging (ISBI), pp. 257–261. IEEE (2021)
6. He, K., Zhang, X., Ren, S., Sun, J.: Deep residual learning for image recognition. In: 2016 IEEE Conference on Computer Vision and Pattern Recognition, CVPR 2016, Las Vegas, NV, USA, 27–30 June 2016, pp. 770–778 (2016)
7. Huang, G., Liu, Z., van der Maaten, L., Weinberger, K.Q.: Densely connected convolutional networks. In: 2017 IEEE Conference on Computer Vision and Pattern Recognition, CVPR 2017, Honolulu, HI, USA, 21–26 July 2017, pp. 2261–2269 (2017)
8. Liu, J., Li, R., Sun, C.: Co-correcting: noise-tolerant medical image classification via mutual label correction. IEEE Trans. Med. Imaging **40**(12), 3580–3592 (2021)
9. Liu, T., et al.: Automated detection and classification of thyroid nodules in ultrasound images using clinical-knowledge-guided convolutional neural networks. Medical Image Anal. **58**, 101555 (2019)
10. Liu, Z., Mao, H., Wu, C.Y., Feichtenhofer, C., Darrell, T., Xie, S.: A convnet for the 2020s. In: Proceedings of the IEEE/CVF Conference on Computer Vision and Pattern Recognition, pp. 11976–11986 (2022)
11. Lyu, Y., Tsang, I.W.: Curriculum loss: robust learning and generalization against label corruption. In: 8th International Conference on Learning Representations, ICLR 2020, Addis Ababa, Ethiopia, 26–30 April 2020 (2020)
12. Paschke, R., Cantara, S., Crescenzi, A., Jarzab, B., Musholt, T.J., Simoes, M.S.: European thyroid association guidelines regarding thyroid nodule molecular fine-needle aspiration cytology diagnostics. Eur. Thyroid J. **6**(3), 115–129 (2017)
13. Platanios, E.A., Stretcu, O., Neubig, G., Póczos, B., Mitchell, T.M.: Competence-based curriculum learning for neural machine translation. In: Burstein, J., Doran, C., Solorio, T. (eds.) Proceedings of the 2019 Conference of the North American Chapter of the Association for Computational Linguistics: Human Language Technologies, NAACL-HLT 2019, 2–7 June 2019, Minneapolis, MN, USA, vol. 1, pp. 1162–1172. Association for Computational Linguistics (2019)
14. Song, R., Zhang, L., Zhu, C., Liu, J., Yang, J., Zhang, T.: Thyroid nodule ultrasound image classification through hybrid feature cropping network. IEEE Access **8**, 64064–64074 (2020)

15. Tessler, F.N., et al.: ACR thyroid imaging, reporting and data system (TI-RADS): white paper of the ACR TI-RADS committee. J. Am. Coll. Radiol. **14**(5), 587–595 (2017)

16. Wang, L., Zhang, L., Zhu, M., Qi, X., Yi, Z.: Automatic diagnosis for thyroid nodules in ultrasound images by deep neural networks. Medical Image Anal. **61**, 101665 (2020)

17. Wang, Y., Gan, W., Yang, J., Wu, W., Yan, J.: Dynamic curriculum learning for imbalanced data classification. In: 2019 IEEE/CVF International Conference on Computer Vision, ICCV 2019, Seoul, Korea (South), 27 October–2 November 2019, pp. 5016–5025. IEEE (2019)

18. Yang, W., et al.: Integrate domain knowledge in training multi-task cascade deep learning model for benign-malignant thyroid nodule classification on ultrasound images. Eng. Appl. Artif. Intell. **98**, 104064 (2021)

19. Zhao, S.X., Chen, Y., Yang, K.F., Luo, Y., Ma, B.Y., Li, Y.J.: A local and global feature disentangled network: toward classification of benign-malignant thyroid nodules from ultrasound image. IEEE Trans. Med. Imaging (2022)

Localizing the Recurrent Laryngeal Nerve via Ultrasound with a Bayesian Shape Framework

Haoran Dou[3,4], Luyi Han[5,6], Yushuang He[7], Jun Xu[2], Nishant Ravikumar[3,4], Ritse Mann[5,6], Alejandro F. Frangi[3,4,8,9,10], Pew-Thian Yap[11], and Yunzhi Huang[1(✉)]

[1] Institute for AI in Medicine, School of Automation,
Nanjing University of Information Science and Technology, Nanjing, China
yunzhi.huang.scu@gmail.com
[2] Institute for AI in Medicine, School of Artificial Intelligence,
Nanjing University of Information Science and Technology, Nanjing, China
[3] Centre for Computational Imaging and Simulation Technologies in Biomedicine
(CISTIB), School of Computing, University of Leeds, Leeds, UK
[4] Biomedical Imaging Department, Leeds Institute for Cardiovascular and Metabolic
Medicine (LICAMM), School of Medicine, University of Leeds, Leeds, UK
[5] Department of Radiology and Nuclear Medicine, Radboud University Medical
Centre, Nijmegen, The Netherlands
[6] Department of Radiology, Netherlands Cancer Institute (NKI),
Amsterdam, The Netherlands
[7] West China Hospital of Sichuan University, Chengdu, China
[8] Department of Cardiovascular Sciences, KU Leuven, Leuven, Belgium
[9] Department of Electrical Engineering, KU Leuven, Leuven, Belgium
[10] Alan Turing Institute, London, UK
[11] Department of Radiology and Biomedical Research Imaging Center (BRIC),
University of North Carolina, Chapel Hill, USA

Abstract. Tumor infiltration of the recurrent laryngeal nerve (RLN) is a contraindication for robotic thyroidectomy and can be difficult to detect via standard laryngoscopy. Ultrasound (US) is a viable alternative for RLN detection due to its safety and ability to provide real-time feedback. However, the tininess of the RLN, with a diameter typically less than 3 mm, poses significant challenges to the accurate localization of the RLN. In this work, we propose a knowledge-driven framework for RLN localization, mimicking the standard approach surgeons take to identify the RLN according to its surrounding organs. We construct a prior anatomical model based on the inherent relative spatial relationships between organs. Through Bayesian shape alignment (BSA), we obtain the candidate coordinates of the center of a region of interest (ROI) that encloses the RLN. The ROI allows a decreased field of view for determining the refined centroid of the RLN using a dual-path identification network, based on multi-scale semantic information. Experimental

---

H. Dou and L. Han contributed equally to this work.

© The Author(s), under exclusive license to Springer Nature Switzerland AG 2022
L. Wang et al. (Eds.): MICCAI 2022, LNCS 13434, pp. 258–267, 2022.
https://doi.org/10.1007/978-3-031-16440-8_25

results indicate that the proposed method achieves superior hit rates and substantially smaller distance errors compared with state-of-the-art methods.

Keywords: Bayesian shape alignment · Recurrent laryngeal nerve · Localization in ultrasound

1   Introduction

Robotic thyroidectomy safely removes low-risk tumors and is preferred by patients who want a scarless operation with minimal invasiveness [7,17]. A complete pre-operative assessment of the surroundings of the thyroid is critical for accurate surgical planning to prevent unnecessary harm to the internal jugular vein or the recurrent laryngeal nerve (RLN). Currently, laryngoscopy is the only method surgeons can rely on to detect whether the RLN is tumor-infiltrated. However, laryngoscopy determines the RLN indirectly by assessing the activity of the vocal cords [1]. This approach is therefore highly inaccurate and can only distinguish RLN abnormality in about 1–3% patients [3]. Recent clinical trials have turned to ultrasound (US) as an alternative method for pre-operative inspection due to its safety and ability to provide real-time feedback [5].

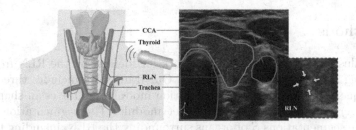

Fig. 1. Ultrasound imaging of bilateral RLNs.

The RLN in the US image is rather tiny relative to organs like the trachea and thyroid (Fig. 1). Therefore, automatic detection of the RLN from an US image is a challenging task. Recent studies [6,15,18] have demonstrated the feasibility of segmenting large nerves from US images, i.e., the sciatic nerve (diameter ranging from 16 to 20 mm [13]) and the median nerve (cross-sectional area ranging from 6.1 to 10.4 mm^2 [10]). These studies propose modifications to basic segmentation models [4,12] to improve segmentation accuracy. For example, van Boxtel et al. [15] investigated the efficacy of a hybrid model on nerve segmentation in US images. Horng et el. [6] integrated a ConvLSTM block [11] at the bottom layer of the U-Net to capture long-term spatial dependencies. Wu et al. [18] employed multi-size kernels and a pyramid architecture to aggregate features for segmentation. Despite these advances, localization of the RLN remains challenging since it is tiny with mean diameter ranging from 1 to 3 mm [16], significantly smaller than the larger nerves mentioned above.

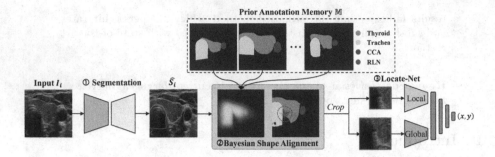

Fig. 2. Overview of the proposed framework.

In this work, we propose a knowledge-driven framework for RLN localization, mimicking the standard approach surgeons take to identify the RLN according to its surrounding organs. Our primary contributions are as follows: (1) We propose the first learning-based framework to identify the RLN from a US image for pre-operative assessment of contraindication for robotic thyroidectomy; (2) We introduce Bayesian shape alignment for geometrical constraints, allowing the utilization of spatial prior knowledge in determining an ROI enclosing the RLN; (3) We introduce Locate-Net, a dual-path network that uses both local and global information to refine the localization of the RLN centroid.

2   Methods

Figure 2 illustrates the proposed framework for identifying the RLN from a US image using anatomical prior knowledge. Our framework includes three coarse-to-fine sequential modules: (1) Segmentation module; (2) Bayesian shape alignment (BSA) module; and (3) Locate-Net module. The segmentation module obtains the segmentations $\hat{S}$ of organs surrounding the RLN, including the common carotid arteries (CCA), thyroid, and trachea. These segmentations form posteriors for the BSA module to infer the candidate coordinates of the RLN. Finally, Locate-Net refines the RLN centroid using local details and global contexts based on the patch centered at the inferred candidate coordinates. Details on the three modules are described in the following sections.

2.1   Bayesian Shape Alignment

To avoid missing the tiny RLN [16] in the midst of significantly larger structures, we introduce a method based on anatomical prior knowledge for RLN detection. Clinically, surgeons recognize the RLN based on its surrounding CCA, thyroid, and trachea [17]. The spatial relationships of these anatomical structures are typically consistent, but not entirely identical, across individuals. Here, we incorporate the spatial relationship into the Bayesian inference with the following mathematical model for a given image I:

$$q(\text{RLN}, \text{SO}|I) \propto p(I|\text{RLN}, \text{SO}) \times p(\text{RLN}|\text{SO}) \times p(\text{SO}) \qquad (1)$$

where SO is a matrix of pixels of a segmentation image, classifying whether each pixel belongs to the surrounding organs (CCA, trachea, thyroid); RLN refers to a set of center points, where each point is specified by a location vector (x, y) for the image matrix. $p(\text{SO})$ is the prior distribution of the segmentation maps of the surrounding organs; and $p(\text{RLN}|\text{SO})$ is the likelihood of the RLN centroid given the segmented matrix of its surrounding organs. $p(\text{SO})$ and $p(\text{RLN}|\text{SO})$ depend on the observed cohort and can be taken as prior knowledge. $p(I|\text{RLN}, \text{SO})$ represents the joint likelihood for the surrounding organs and the RLN's centroid, and is treated as a constant; and $q(\text{RLN}, \text{SO}|I)$ is the likelihood of the RLN centroid and the segmented matrix of its surrounding organs given a particular image I.

In Eq. 1, we aim to predict the RLN's centroid (x, y) given a image I by obtaining the maximum likelihood probability from the priors. The prior distributions for both the RLN centroids and its surrounding segmentation dependent on the given cohort. For each sample I_j from training set, the approximate probability $p_j(\text{RLN}|\text{SO})$ and $p_j(\text{SO})$ attain the maximum value when I_j is most similar to the given sample I. Based on this, we can infer the likelihood RLN's centroids from the samples with similar surrounding segmentation matrix.

Prior Distribution for RLN's Surroundings. Segmenting the organs surrounding the RLN is a prerequisite to determining $p(\text{SO})$. Here, the widely adopted segmentation model, U-Net [12], is employed to segment the CCA, thyroid, and trachea from a US image. The segmentation network takes an US image and outputs the corresponding segmentation maps of the three organs. It comprises an encoder and decoder with a skip-connection to forward the feature representations from each stage of the encoder to the corresponding stage in the decoder. The numbers of feature maps in the encoder are 64, 128, 256, 512, 1024, and similarly in the decoder. Each stage in the segmentation network contains two convolution layers followed by instance normalization [14] and ReLU functions [19]. The training loss function is composed with a cross-entropy loss and a dice similarity coefficient (DSC) loss:

$$\mathcal{L}_{\text{seg}} = \mathcal{L}_{\text{ce}}(\hat{S}, M) + \mathcal{L}_{\text{dsc}}(\hat{S}, M) \tag{2}$$

where $\mathcal{L}_{\text{ce}}$ and $\mathcal{L}_{\text{dsc}}$ refer to cross-entropy loss and DSC loss, respectively.

Alignment-Based Likelihood. Employing the prior sample I_j that is similar in the surrounding masks with the given image I_i to derive the RLN's centroid can derive higher likelihood $p(\text{RLN}|\text{SO})$. However, affected by the probe scanning angles θ, the observations belong to different angle distributions and can not be directly used to construct the priors of RLN's surrounding segmentation, hence, we embed a pre-alignment module to eliminate the influence of θ. The detailed implementation of the proposed alignment-based likelihood infer for the RLN is described in Algorithm 1.

Algorithm 1. Bayesian shape alignment during inference

Input: The predicted segmentation mask $\hat{S}_i$ for a inference sample, a set of mask labels $\mathbb{M} = \{M_j, j \in \mathbb{N}^*\}$ and RLN labels $\mathbb{C} = \{c_j, j \in \mathbb{N}^*\}$ for the training samples

Output: Candidate coordinate C_i of RLN for $\hat{S}_i$

$D[*] = \{d_j, j \in \mathbb{N}^*\}$

$C[*] = \{p_j, j \in \mathbb{N}^*\}$

for corresponding label $\{M_j, c_j\}$ in $\{\mathbb{M}, \mathbb{C}\}$ **do**

$\quad \phi_j \leftarrow \text{Affine}(M_j, \hat{S}_i)$ ▷ shape analysis

$\quad D[j] \leftarrow \text{Dice}(M_j \circ \phi_j, \hat{S}_i)$ ▷ calculate dice metric

$\quad C[j] \leftarrow c_j \circ \phi_j$ ▷ transform centroid of RLN

end for

$index \leftarrow \text{Rank}(D[*])$ ▷ rank dice in the descending order

$C_{sort} \leftarrow \text{Sort}(C[*], index)$ ▷ sort coordinates with dice rank

$C_i \leftarrow \text{AverageTopK}(C_{sort})$ ▷ average the Top-k candidate coordinates

---

Algorithm 1 estimates the likelihood RLN's centroid by searching the similar samples from the priors. We first align the priors to the common angle distribution. Taking each predicted mask $\hat{S}_i$ as the target segmentation and every transversed annotation M_j in the training dataset $\mathbb{M}$ as the moving segmentation, the affine transformation matrix ϕ_j with 6 degrees of freedom (DOF) can be conducted with the mutual information as the similarity metric. After such alignment, the Dice ratio (DSC) between the predicted mask $\hat{S}_i$ and each affined segmentation $M_j \circ \phi_j$ in the training dataset is calculated as the shape similarity score. More similar in the surrounding segmentation correspond to higher likelihood estimation for the entire image and the RLN's centroid. Subsequently, we descend the priors depending on the DSC, and average the RLNs' candidates with the Top-k DSCs to infer the position of RLN for the given image I_i.

2.2   Locate-Net

The BSA module is followed by a dual-path neural network to further refine the centroid of the RLN. Based on the candidate center coordinates of the RLN determined by the BSA module, a global patch with the size of 64×64 and a local patch with the size of 24×24 are cropped from the US image and jointly fed to the refinement network to provide global and local information. The features from the global patch contain global semantics to capture the potential outlier unobserved in the priors. The features from the local patch provide details to help refine the centroid.

In the refinement network, features from the local and global patches are separately extracted with two weight-shared sub-networks. Each sub-network contains three convolutional blocks. After each convolution block, the feature maps are down-sampled with a factor of 2 via the max-pooling layer. The detailed composition of each convolutional block is the same with the encoder in the segmentation network (seen in Sect. 2.1). The outputs of the two sub-networks are then re-scaled to the same size with a adaptive pyramid pooling layer [20], and followed with a concatenation layer and two convolution blocks. The top of the refinement network is three fully connected layers with the hidden units of 512, 64, 2, so that to predict the refined centroid of RLN. The regression loss function for training the refinement network is defined as:

$$\mathcal{L}_{\text{reg}} = \sum_i \mathcal{L}_{s1}(\hat{c}_i - c_i), \tag{3}$$

where $\mathcal{L}_{s1}$ is the smoothed L_1 loss with β of 1.0 indexed for the difference of image pixel $(\Delta x, \Delta y)$, $\hat{c}$ and c denote as the predicted RLN centroid and the ground truth, respectively.

$$\mathcal{L}_{s1}(\Delta x, \Delta y) = \begin{cases} \frac{1}{2\beta}(\Delta x^2 + \Delta y^2) & |\Delta x| + |\Delta y| < 2\beta, \\ |\Delta x| + |\Delta y| - \beta & \text{others}. \end{cases} \tag{4}$$

3 Experiments

3.1 Dataset and Evaluation Metrics

2D ultrasound images were collected with an Aixplorer color Doppler ultrasound device (Hologic Supersonic imagine, AIX en Provence), equipped with a linear array probe with a frequency of 4–15 MHz. A total of 465 patients diagnosed with thyroid cancer by preoperative biopsy and enrolled for thyroidectomy participated in this study. Each patient has both left and right scans of the RLN. Each scan contains a variable number of qualified US frames, ranging from 1 to 4. 325, 46 and 94 subjects were randomly selected for training, validation, and testing, respectively. All images were resampled to a common size of 256 × 256. Manual annotation was contented by three clinical experts and passed through strict quality control from a senior expert.

Performance was quantified using the absolute distance error and the hit rate between the predicted RLN centroid and the ground truth:

$$\text{Dis}(\hat{c}, c) = \|\hat{c} - c\|_1 \tag{5}$$

$$\text{Hit}(\hat{c}, c) = \begin{cases} 1 & \hat{c} \subseteq N_c, \\ 0 & \text{others}, \end{cases} \tag{6}$$

where $\hat{c}$ and c denote as the predicted RLN centroid and the ground truth, respectively. N_c indicates the neighborhood of c with radius r_θ, which is set to be 15 pixels in this work. Lower distance error and higher hit rate correspond to better identification performance.

3.2 Implementation Details

We implemented our method using PyTorch on the Google Colab platform with an NVIDIA Tesla P100 GPU. We trained the segmentation network using the

Table 1. Statistics of competing methods for the testing dataset.

	Methods	Left RLN		Right RLN	
		Distance (*pix*)	Hit Rate (%)	Distance (*pix*)	Hit Rate (%)
Coord-based	ResNet-50 [4]	10.9 ± 9.7	77.5	12.3 ± 8.4	70.0
	SwinT-C [8]	19.7 ± 11.8	42.3	14.4 ± 9.6	59.4
	ConvNeXt-C [9]	16.5 ± 8.2	47.3	14.0 ± 9.5	62.5
Heatmap-based	U-Net [12]	29.3 ± 12.8	11.5	20.9 ± 10.5	31.9
	DeepLab [2]	17.5 ± 8.0	41.2	11.9 ± 7.1	71.3
	SwinT-H [8]	22.7 ± 13.6	30.8	20.2 ± 10.6	35.6
	ConvNeXt-H [9]	12.7 ± 12.1	73.1	13.1 ± 8.7	64.4
	Proposed	**3.49 ± 7.53**	**95.6**	**4.55 ± 7.61**	**92.5**

Adam optimizer with an initial learning rate of 3×10^{-4} and a batch size of 16 for 100 epochs, taking about 3 h. The learning rate was decayed every epoch with a factor of 0.9. The affine matrix in Bayesian shape alignment was initially computed with the center of mass of the masks and iteratively refined with the mutual information metric. For the training of the dual-path refinement network, the learning rate and batch size were set to 1×10^{-3} and 16, respectively. The code for the techniques presented in this study can be found at: https://github.com/wulalago/RLNLocalization

3.3   Comparison Baselines

We compared our method with coordinate and heatmap regression methods. Compared heatmap regression methods include U-Net [12], DeepLab [2], SwinT-H [8], and ConvNeXt-H [9]. Coordinate regression methods include ResNet-50 [4], SwinT-C [8], and ConvNeXt-C [9]. The optimal hyper-parameters of all the baseline methods are obtained based on the grid search strategy. Figure 3 shows example cases of the bilateral RLNs given by the baseline methods. The red and cyan circles mark the annotated ground truth and the predicted centroid of the RLN, respectively. Our method predicts the centroids of the bilateral RLNs with higher accuracy than the baseline methods. Table 1 reports the statistics of the results given by the methods on the testing dataset. The proposed method achieves the lowest distance error with the highest hit rate.

3.4   Ablation Study

We compared three types of centroid refinement methods, including (1) refinement with local information; (2) refinement with global contextual information; and (3) refinement with both local and global features. Table 2 reports the distance errors and hit rates for these settings based on the proposed method. Refinement with local and global information yields the lowest distance error with the highest hit rate.

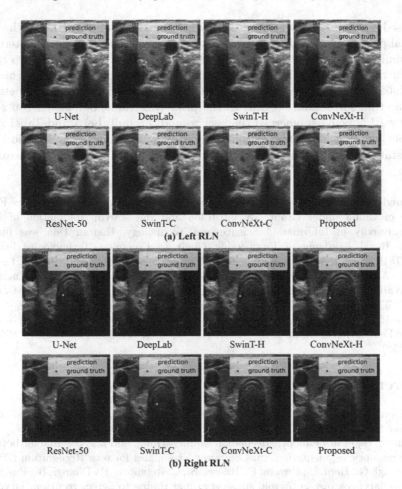

Fig. 3. Example results from competing methods.

Table 2. Statistics for different settings based on the testing dataset.

Methods	Left RLN		Right RLN	
	Distance (pix)	Hit Rate (%)	Distance (pix)	Hit Rate (%)
Initialization	7.52 ± 7.65	89.0	9.70 ± 7.03	84.9
+ Local information	4.45 ± 8.79	91.8	5.47 ± 7.90	88.7
+ Global context	3.58 ± 7.51	94.5	4.42 ± 7.48	91.8
+ Local & global features	**3.49 ± 7.53**	**95.6**	4.55 ± 7.61	**92.5**

4   Conclusion

Inspired by the way surgeons to recognize RLN, we developed a prior knowledge driven framework to automatically identify the tiny RLN from US images. In the proposed pipeline, we first segment the large organs surrounding RLN as the conditional prior, and then using the Bayesian shape alignment model to determine the candidate coordinate close to RLN. Then following the Locate-Net to refine the centriod of RLN with multi-scales patches to extract the local information and global context around the RLN. Leveraging the spatial relationship between RLN and its surrounding organs as the prior constraint, our model can avoid the tiny RLN being submerged the background. From Tabel 1 and Tabel 2, we can conclude that, any combination of our framework achieves the superiority in the distance error and hit rate as compared to the recent coordinate or heatmap regression models.

Acknowledgement. This work was supported by the National Natural Science Foundation of China under Grant No. 62101365 and the startup foundation of Nanjing University of Information Science and Technology. Haoran Dou was funded by the Royal Academy of Engineering Chair in Emerging Technologies Scheme (CiET1819/19). Luyi Han was funded by Chinese Scholarship Council (CSC) scholarship. Alejandro F. Frangi was funded by the Royal Academy of Engineering (INSILEX CiET1819/19), Engineering and Physical Sciences Research Council (EPSRC) programs TUSCA EP/V04799X/1, and the Royal Society Exchange Programme CROSSLINK IES\NSFC\201380. Jun Xu was funded by the National Natural Science Foundation of China (Nos. U1809205, 62171230, 92159301, 61771249, 91959207, 81871352).

References

1. Chandrasekhar, S.S., et al.: Clinical practice guideline: improving voice outcomes after thyroid surgery. Otolaryngol.-Head Neck Surg. **148**, 1–37 (2013)
2. Cheng, B., et al.: Panoptic-deeplab: a simple, strong, and fast baseline for bottom-up panoptic segmentation. In: Computer Vision and Pattern Recognition (2020)
3. Dionigi, G., Boni, L., Rovera, F., Rausei, S., Castelnuovo, P., Dionigi, R.: Postoperative laryngoscopy in thyroid surgery: proper timing to detect recurrent laryngeal nerve injury. Langenbecks Arch. Surg. **395**, 327–331 (2010)
4. He, K., Zhang, X., Ren, S., Sun, J.: Deep residual learning for image recognition. In: Computer Vision and Pattern Recognition (2016)
5. He, Y., Li, Z., Yang, Y., Lei, J., Peng, Y.L.: Preoperative visualized ultrasound assessment of the recurrent laryngeal nerve in thyroid cancer surgery: reliability and risk features by imaging. Can. Manage. Res. **13**, 7057–7066 (2021)
6. Horng, M.H., Yang, C.W., Sun, Y.N., Yang, T.H.: Deepnerve: a new convolutional neural network for the localization and segmentation of the median nerve in ultrasound image sequences. Ultrasound Med. Biol. **46**, 2439–2452 (2020)
7. Lee, J., Chung, W.Y.: Robotic surgery for thyroid disease. Eur. Thyroid J. **2**, 93–101 (2013)
8. Liu, Z., et al.: Swin transformer: hierarchical vision transformer using shifted windows. ArXiv: Computer Vision and Pattern Recognition (2021)
9. Liu, Z., Mao, H., Wu, C.Y., Feichtenhofer, C., Darrell, T., Xie, S.: A convnet for the 2020s. arXiv preprint arXiv:2201.03545 (2022)
10. Meyer, P., Lintingre, P.F., Pesquer, L., Poussange, N., Silvestre, A., Dallaudière, B.: The median nerve at the carpal tunnel ... and elsewhere. J. Belgian Soc. Radiol. **102**, 17–17 (2018)

11. Romera-Paredes, B., Torr, P.H.S.: Recurrent instance segmentation. In: Leibe, B., Matas, J., Sebe, N., Welling, M. (eds.) ECCV 2016. LNCS, vol. 9910, pp. 312–329. Springer, Cham (2016). https://doi.org/10.1007/978-3-319-46466-4_19
12. Ronneberger, O., Fischer, P., Brox, T.: U-Net: convolutional networks for biomedical image segmentation. In: Navab, N., Hornegger, J., Wells, W.M., Frangi, A.F. (eds.) MICCAI 2015. LNCS, vol. 9351, pp. 234–241. Springer, Cham (2015). https://doi.org/10.1007/978-3-319-24574-4_28
13. Tiel, R., Filler, A.G.: Nerve injuries of the lower extremity (2011)
14. Ulyanov, D., Vedaldi, A., Lempitsky, V.: Instance normalization: the missing ingredient for fast stylization. arXiv preprint arXiv:1607.08022 (2016)
15. Van Boxtel, J., Vousten, V., Pluim, J., Rad, N.M.: Hybrid deep neural network for brachial plexus nerve segmentation in ultrasound images. In: 2021 29th European Signal Processing Conference (EUSIPCO), pp. 1246–1250. IEEE (2021)
16. Wojtczak, B., Kaliszewski, K., Sutkowski, K., Bolanowski, M., Barczyński, M.: A functional assessment of anatomical variants of the recurrent laryngeal nerve during thyroidectomies using neuromonitoring. Endocrine **59**(1), 82–89 (2017). https://doi.org/10.1007/s12020-017-1466-3
17. Wong, K.P., Lang, B.H.H.: Endoscopic thyroidectomy: a literature review and update. Current Surgery Reports **1**, 7–15 (2013)
18. Wu, H., Liu, J., Wang, W., Wen, Z., Qin, J.: Region-aware global context modeling for automatic nerve segmentation from ultrasound images. In: National Conference on Artificial Intelligence (2021)
19. Xu, B., Wang, N., Chen, T., Li, M.: Empirical evaluation of rectified activations in convolutional network. arXiv preprint arXiv:1505.00853 (2015)
20. Zhao, H., Shi, J., Qi, X., Wang, X., Jia, J.: Pyramid scene parsing network. In: Proceedings of the IEEE Conference on Computer Vision and Pattern Recognition, pp. 2881–2890 (2017)

Uncertainty-aware Cascade Network for Ultrasound Image Segmentation with Ambiguous Boundary

Yanting Xie[1], Hongen Liao[2], Daoqiang Zhang[1], and Fang Chen[1(✉)]

[1] College of Computer Science and Technology, Nanjing University of Aeronautics and Astronautics, MIIT Key Laboratory of Pattern Analysis and Machine Intelligence, Nanjing 211106, China
chenfang@nuaa.edu.cn

[2] Department of Biomedical Engineering, School of Medicine, Tsinghua University, Beijing 10084, China

Abstract. Ultrasound image segmentation plays an essential role in automatic disease diagnosis. However, to achieve precise ultrasound segmentation is still a challenge caused by the ambiguous lesion boundary and imaging artifacts such as speckles and shadowing noise. Considering that the pixels with high uncertainty generally distributing in the boundary regions of prediction maps, are likely to overlap with the confused regions of ultrasound, we proposed an uncertainty-aware cascade network. Our network uses the confidence map to evaluate the uncertainty of each pixel to enhance the segmentation of ambiguous boundary. On the one hand, the confidence map fuses with the ultrasound features and predicted mask using the adaptive fusion module (AFM) which enriches the context features from different modalities. In addition, the uncertainty attention module (UAM) is proposed based on the confidence map. This module focuses on the influential features with cross attention constrained by the uncertainty of pixels which can extract the localized features of confused ultrasound regions. On the other hand, the recurrent edge correction module (RECM) further improves the segmentation of ambiguous boundary. This module increases the weights of confident features neighboring the uncertainty boundaries in order to refine the predictions of edge pixels with low confidence. We evaluated the proposed method on three public ultrasound datasets and the segmentation results show that our method achieved higher Dice scores and lower Hausdorff distance with more precise boundary details compared with state-of-the-art methods.

Keywords: Uncertainty-aware · Segmentation · Ultrasound · Ambiguous boundary · Confidence map

Supplementary Information The online version contains supplementary material available at https://doi.org/10.1007/978-3-031-16440-8_26.

1   Introduction

Ultrasound (US) imaging is one of the most commonly used diagnosis imaging technologies due to its advantages such as real time, safeness and low cost. The segmentation for US images is of great significance in clinical diagnosis [19]. However, the manual annotation is usually time-consuming, error-prone and subjective, especially under the circumstance with ambiguous boundary [16]. Thus, the automatic segmentation methods which focus on the ambiguous boundary in US images are highly demanded.

Deep learning methods have shown potential abilities in automatic image segmentation, especially the U-Net model with an encoder-decoder architecture. Therefore, most of the existing US segmentation methods are developed based on U-Net [18], such as CR-Unet [8] for transvaginal US, MFP-Unet [11] for left ventricle US, and TUN-Det [14] for thyroid US nodule. However, the shadowing noise and missing/ambiguous boundaries in US images make accurate boundary segmentation a more difficult task than in other modality images [17]. Furthermore, the boundary details will be easily lost due to the encoder-decoder architecture with upsampling operations.

There are plenty of studies which focus on the segmentation of boundary regions. Among them, some methods propose to retain the features in edge regions which constraint the residual features with objective functions [3,9]. For example, RF-Net [17] learns the residual representation of boundaries and transmits it to fine-stage segmentation. While other methods propose to adjust the boundary prediction results through post-processing operations [6,20]. For example, BPR [15] was proposed as a simple post-processing refinement framework based on the results of the existing segmentation models. However, these methods, which mainly emphasize refining the boundary for the task of converting the low-resolution image with clear boundary to a high-quality image, are not applicable for ambiguous or missing boundaries in US segmentation.

Figure 1 demonstrates some cases of US segmentation predictions and the corresponding uncertainty maps from U-Net. The unreliable prediction pixels

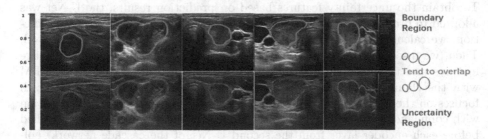

Fig. 1. Schematic diagram of the uncertainty region computed from the prediction results of U-Net. The boundary region of annotation (red) is covered by the corresponding uncertainty map (the value approaches 1 for the pixel with high uncertainty). (Color figure online)

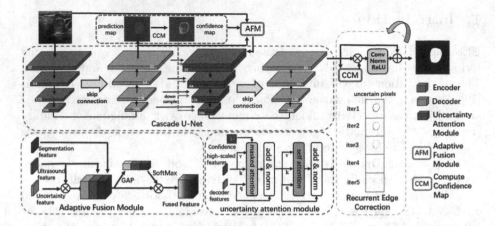

Fig. 2. Architecture of the proposed uncertainty-aware cascade network.

are mostly concentrated in the confusion regions and the boundaries of ultrasound images. Therefore, we tried to improve the segmentation performance of boundary regions based on the uncertainty features. In summary, our main contributions are: (1) we proposed an uncertainty-aware network using the uncertainty of each pixel to enhance the US segmentation; (2) we constructed AFM and UAM based on the confidence map to extract the influential features for confused region segmentation; (3) we established RECM to recurrently adjust the predictions of edge pixels with low confidence; (4) the results on three public US datasets show that our method outperformed various state-of-the-art methods.

2   Methods

2.1   Architecture

The framework of the uncertainty-aware cascade network is shown in Fig. 2. To obtain the uncertainty features based on prediction results, the U-Net was adopted to predict the coarse segmentation. Using the possibility of the prediction, we calculated the confidence map to show the uncertainty of each pixel. Then, we fused the uncertainty features of the confidence map, the US image features and the label features of coarse segmentation adaptively using AFM with the channel attention mechanism. Meanwhile, we adopted UAM which focuses on the features for confused US regions by constraining cross-attention with confidence maps [2]. To utilize the multi-scale features, UAM was applied before each encoder layer from the second U-Net of the cascade network. Following the output of cascade network, we further used the uncertainty features to refine the boundary segmentation. We built RECM to adjust the unreliable boundary pixels by increasing the weights of the confident features neighboring the uncertainty boundaries to correct the uncertainty pixels of the boundaries.

Finally, the segmentation results with the boundary refinement were obtained as the final outputs through the edge correction operation recurrently.

As the pixels around boundaries only occupy a small fraction of the whole image which are difficult to segment, treating all pixels equally may lead to an optimization bias towards the smooth interior areas while underestimating the boundary pixels [15]. To address this problem, the core idea of confidence map is to calculate a weight map for the features, thus to decrease the weights of the features results in the uncertainty predictions [21]. Therefore, we use it in AFM and UAM for features extraction to decrease the weights of the features results in the uncertainty predictions. Simultaneously, we adopt it in RECM to increase the weights of features with high confidence near the boundary pixels with low confidence. In this way, the predictions of the unreliable boundary pixels can be influenced by the confident pixels in the neighboring regions. Therefore, the uncertainty features were fused into the network hierarchically through three new mechanisms including AFM, UAM and RECM.

Computation of the Confidence Map from the Cascade U-Net. The prediction maps are from the output of the cascade U-Net, which here consists of four layers of encoder-decoder blocks. After four times of downsampling and upsampling operations, it predicts the coarse results as the prediction maps. The confidence map is calculated based on the prediction possibility, which denotes the uncertainty of each pixel prediction. Thus, let $S \in \mathbb{R}^{(2 \times w \times h)}$ denote the prediction map which consists of the possibilities belonging to each class, where the sum is 1. When the possibility is close to 0.5, commonly the prediction result is of low confidence. Thus, the confidence map can be calculated as:

$$M_{conf} = 1 - \exp(\frac{-(S_1 - 0.5) \otimes (S_1 - 0.5)}{2 \times std(S_1) \times std(S_1)}), \tag{1}$$

where M_{conf} denotes the confidence map of the prediction map; S_1 represents the possibility map of each pixel belonging to class foreground; std means to calculate the standard deviation of the map; $\otimes$ denotes the element-wise multiplication.

Adaptive Feature Fusion for Uncertainty Features. AFM is adopted to aggregate features adaptively, including the uncertainty confidence map, ultrasound image features and prediction annotation. To adaptively weigh the features of different branches, we introduce the channel attention mechanism inspired by SE-Net [5]. Thus, AFM can rebalance the attention of different features by weighing between the channels with the Squeeze-and-Excite block, which enriches the context features from different modalities as the input.

Uncertainty Attention Module. To concentrate less on the features which cause the uncertain prediction, we use UAM with uncertainty confidence features for the influential features extraction. The module mainly consists of a cross-attention operation and a self-attention operation. During the cross-attention operation, we use the confidence map which focuses on the features with high confidence to correct the predictions of the uncertainty pixels. With the constraints of the confidence map which annotates the uncertainty, these uncertainty pixels are adjusted by computing a global optimum [2].

First, we adopt the 1×1 convolution operation for decoder features of the first U-Net as the query features. Meanwhile, we use the high-scale features from the previous encoder layer as the key and value features of the cross-attention. Based on the cross-attention, we use SoftMax function to calculate the weights of the value features with the matrix multiplication between query and key features. Then, we extract the features based on the weights of the uncertainty confidence map. Thus, the uncertainty cross-attention can be described as:

$$M_{ca} = M_{conf} \otimes SoftMax(\frac{f_q(X)f_k(Y)^T}{\sqrt{d_k}})f_v(Y) + X, \qquad (2)$$

where M_{ca} denotes the output features of the uncertainty cross-attention; X and Y denote the decoder features and high-scale features respectively; f_q, f_k and f_v mean the 1×1 convolution operations; $M_{conf} \in [0,1]^{(1 \times w \times h)}$ denotes the uncertainty confidence map; d_k denotes the dimension of queries and keys; $\otimes$ denotes the element-wise multiplication. Then, after the normalization operation, the self-attention is followed to gather the context features extracted from uncertainty cross-attention following by a normalization operation.

Recurrent Edge Correction with Uncertainty Features. RECM adjusts the pixels with low confidence based on the neighboring pixels with high confidence in order to decrease the weights of the indistinguishable features. The module corrects the unreliable boundary pixels by two recurring steps: (1) calculating the confidence map. (2) adjusting the uncertainty pixels with edge correction operations. We introduce the residual conception, which only calculates the changed information, and adds the original features with skip connection. Moreover, we divide the features through the scaling factors computed by the average pooling for the confidence map to regularize the effect within different sliding windows [21]. Thus, the edge correction operation can be described as:

$$X^l = \sigma(f(M_{conf}^{l-1} \otimes X^{l-1})/(pool(M_{conf}^{l-1}) \times (k \times k)) + X^{l-1}), \qquad (3)$$

where X^l denotes the features after the edge correction operation; l denotes the round of the recurrent iteration; M_{conf} denotes the confidence map; f means the 3×3 convolution operation; σ represents the $ReLU$ activation; $pool$ means the average pooling operation with a $k \times k$ kernel, 1 stride and $\lfloor k/2 \rfloor$ padding; $\otimes$ and $/$ denote the element-wise multiplication and division respectively. And the module will stop when the number of iterations reaches the maximum number, or the change of the confidence map is less than the threshold.

2.2 Objective Function

The loss function consists of three components, including the segmentation losses of two cascade U-Nets and the boundary-aware loss. For segmentation loss, we employ the Dice and Binary Cross-Entropy loss. Moreover, the wrong prediction results of the pixels around the edge region have little influence on the large map. Thus, we employ the Boundary IoU loss function proposed in [1] for our boundary-aware loss. The loss only cares about the pixels in the boundary region, which is more sensitive about the boundary errors for large objects and does not over-penalize errors on smaller objects. Thus, the total loss function can be expressed as the weighted sum of the segmentation loss and the boundary loss, as follows:

$$L_{total} = \alpha(L_{coarse} + L_{fine}) + (1 - \alpha)L_{boundary}, \tag{4}$$

where L_{coarse}, L_{fine} and $L_{boundary}$ denote the loss of two cascade U-Nets and boundary loss respectively. As the weight parameter, we set α to 0.5 in the experiments.

3 Experiments

Dataset. To evaluate the effectiveness of our network, we conducted the experiments on three US image datasets of different organs: (1) the competitive dataset of MICCAI 2020 Challenge named **TN-SCUI** [22], containing 3644 US nodular thyroid images of 3644 patients, with the annotation of nodules labeled by experienced doctors; (2) the fetal ultrasound data **HC18** [4], which is used to measure the fetal head circumferences, composed of a training set of 999 images and a test set of 335 images; (3) the dataset **CAMUS** [7], consisted of the cardiac US images for multi-structure segmentation, from the clinical exams of 500 patients.

Training Details. The proposed network is based on the Pytorch framework and is trained with two GTX 2080 Ti GPUs. We set the batch size to 8 on each GPU. In the training phase, we use the Adaptive moment estimation (Adam) optimizer with 0.9 momentum, weight decay of 10^{-6}. To effectively train the cascade network, we train the first U-Net of the cascade network with the initial learning rate of 10^{-3} for 100 epochs. Then, we freeze the first U-Net and update the other part of the whole network with the learning rate of 10^{-3} for 100 epochs. Finally, we fine-tune the whole network for 100 epochs with the initial learning rate of 10^{-4} multiplied by 0.1 at $70th$ epochs.

Evaluation Metrics. To quantitatively measure the performance, we use six evaluation metrics for US segmentation, including Dice Similarity Coefficient (DSC), Jaccard Index (JI), Recall (REC), Precision (PRC), Hausdorff Distance (HD) and Average Surface Distance (ASD). The first four metrics are used to evaluate the segmentation and the last two metrics are used to measure the boundary distance.

3.1   Comparison with State-of-the-Arts

To evaluate the effectiveness of the proposed method, we compared it with state-of-the-arts for medical image segmentation, namely U-Net [13] and U-Net++ [23]. Besides, three latest boundary-aware methods proposed in MICCAI 2021 are compared, including SAURINet [21] for liver CT, CCBANet [12] for polyp and RF-Net [17] for breast ultrasound.

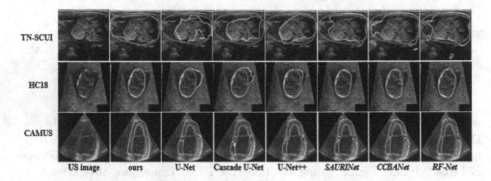

Fig. 3. Segmentation results predicted by different methods (red) and the ground truth (blue) on three datasets. (Color figure online)

Table 1. Comparison results of different methods on **TN-SCUI** and **HC18**.

Method	TN-SCUI				HC18			
	HD↓ (mm)	ASD↓ (mm)	DSC↑ (%)	JI↑ (%)	HD↓ (mm)	ASD↓ (mm)	DSC↑ (%)	JI↑ (%)
U-Net [13]	20.03	5.639	85.87	75.77	7.458	2.206	97.28	94.70
Cascade U-Net [10]	17.14	4.998	86.67	76.99	5.576	1.895	97.44	95.01
U-Net++ [23]	14.81	4.664	88.25	79.37	6.119	1.809	97.64	95.39
SAURINet [21]	14.08	4.549	88.68	80.09	5.123	1.749	97.65	95.41
CCBANet [12]	13.97	4.535	87.49	78.62	4.271	1.707	97.56	95.26
RF-Net [17]	14.05	4.543	88.86	80.32	4.325	1.684	97.67	95.45
proposed	**9.217**	**2.935**	**91.34**	**84.13**	**4.036**	**1.622**	**97.74**	**95.59**

Table 2. Comparison results of different methods on multi-structure ultrasound segmentation in **CAMUS**.

Method	LV_{Endo}				LV_{Epi}			
	HD↓ (mm)	ASD↓ (mm)	DSC↑ (%)	JI↑ (%)	HD↓ (mm)	ASD↓ (mm)	DSC↑ (%)	JI↑ (%)
U-Net	6.522	2.775	90.44	82.76	5.990	1.816	94.38	89.46
Cascade U-Net	6.338	2.786	91.01	83.69	5.938	1.789	94.79	90.18
U-Net++	6.352	2.769	91.25	83.97	5.903	1.781	94.86	90.43
SAURINet	6.347	2.723	91.85	85.16	5.944	1.817	95.24	91.02
CCBANet	6.303	2.642	92.08	85.50	5.855	1.687	95.48	91.42
RF-Net	6.307	2.712	92.05	85.46	5.865	1.777	95.39	91.17
proposed	**5.829**	**2.501**	**92.97**	**87.01**	**5.428**	**1.429**	**96.14**	**92.60**

For quantitative results in Table 1 and Table 2, our proposed approach utilizing uncertainty features achieved the best results in both the segmentation and boundary metrics on all the three datasets. For **TN-SCUI**, compared to the latest three boundary-aware methods, our method achieved a better performance, with a decrease of nearly 4.75 mm and 1.60 mm for HD and ASD, respectively, and an increase of more than 2.48% and 3.81% for DSC and JI, respectively. For **HC18** with the significant foreground features, DSC for all methods was close to 97%. However, our method still achieved the minimum distance error, which validates our method decreases the HD and ASD not only because of the enhancement of segmentation. Moreover, for **CAMUS** with multi-structure segmentation tasks, our method achieved higher DSC and JI as well as lower HD and ASD in each class. Figure 3 illustrates some segmentation results for the qualitative results. The proposed method seems to cover regions of ambiguous boundary more effectively than other boundary-aware methods, which verifies that our method with uncertainty features outperforms others at ultrasound segmentation with ambiguous boundary.

3.2   Ablation Study

To evaluate the effectiveness of the different components of the network, we conducted several ablation experiments on **TN-SCUI**. As shown in Table 3, the modules used in the network greatly improved the performance compared with baseline, where DSC and JI were increased by 5.47% and 8.36%, respectively; HD and ASD were decreased by 10.81 mm and 2.29 mm. Furthermore, when we introduced AFM and UAM gradually, all metrics gained the significantly promotion, which proves that AFM and UAM with uncertainty features can contribute to improving the segmentation performance significantly. For the boundary segmentation, when degrading without either REI or boundary loss, distance-related metrics HD and ASD were increased respectively, which proves that REI and boundary loss can promote the correction of boundary pixels error effectively.

Table 3. Segmentation results on **TN-SCUI** to validate the effectiveness of the different modules adopted in our network.

Cascade	AFM	UAM	RECM	Boundary loss	DSC↑ (%)	JI↑ (%)	REC↑ (%)	PRC↑ (%)	HD↓ (mm)	ASD↓ (mm)
					85.87	75.77	87.94	86.15	20.03	5.639
				✓	86.36	76.40	89.53	85.44	18.45	5.221
			✓		87.62	78.26	90.85	88.93	16.76	4.384
✓					86.67	76.99	88.78	87.10	17.14	4.998
✓	✓				88.32	79.41	90.30	88.86	14.32	4.077
✓	✓	✓			90.02	82.06	92.67	89.11	11.59	3.484
✓	✓	✓		✓	90.64	83.01	**92.87**	89.13	10.54	3.334
✓	✓	✓	✓		90.71	83.24	90.90	91.47	10.37	3.184
✓	✓	✓	✓	✓	**91.34**	**84.13**	91.96	**92.38**	**9.217**	**2.935**

4   Conclusion

In this paper, we have proposed an uncertainty-aware cascade network for ultrasound image segmentation. Our network enchances the segmentation performance in confusion regions and ambiguous boundaries using uncertainty confidence features, which improves the uncertainty region segmentation by decreasing the weights of features causing the uncertain predictions. Therefore, the uncertainty features are fused into the network hierarchically through three new mechanisms including AFM, UAM and RECM. AFM fuses the uncertainty features with other modality features. Then, UAM is introduced to attend the influential features for confused region segmentation. Furthermore, RECM iteratively corrects the pixels with low confidence in the boundaries for boundary refinement. The experiments results have been evaluated in three public ultrasound datasets, which demonstrates that our method significantly outperforms the state-of-the-arts which have achieved better performance in all metrics.

Acknowledgements. The authors acknowledge supports from National Nature Science Foundation of China grants (U20A20389, 61901214, 82027807), China Postdoctoral Science Foundation (2021T140322, 2020M671484), Jiangsu Planned Projects for Postdoctoral Research Funds (2020Z024).

References

1. Cheng, B., Girshick, R., Dollár, P., Berg, A.C., Kirillov, A.: Boundary IoU: improving object-centric image segmentation evaluation. In: Proceedings of the IEEE/CVF Conference on Computer Vision and Pattern Recognition, pp. 15334–15342 (2021)
2. Cheng, B., Misra, I., Schwing, A.G., Kirillov, A., Girdhar, R.: Masked-attention mask transformer for universal image segmentation. arXiv preprint (2021). https://doi.org/10.48550/arXiv.2112.01527
3. Hatamizadeh, A., Terzopoulos, D., Myronenko, A.: End-to-end boundary aware networks for medical image segmentation. In: Suk, H.-I., Liu, M., Yan, P., Lian, C. (eds.) MLMI 2019. LNCS, vol. 11861, pp. 187–194. Springer, Cham (2019). https://doi.org/10.1007/978-3-030-32692-0_22
4. van den Heuvel, T.L., de Bruijn, D., de Korte, C.L., Ginneken, B.V.: Automated measurement of fetal head circumference using 2D ultrasound images. PLoS ONE **13**(8), e0200412 (2018)
5. Hu, J., Shen, L., Sun, G.: Squeeze-and-excitation networks. In: Proceedings of the IEEE Conference on Computer Vision and Pattern Recognition, pp. 7132–7141 (2018)
6. Kirillov, A., Wu, Y., He, K., Girshick, R.: Pointrend: image segmentation as rendering. In: Proceedings of the IEEE/CVF Conference on Computer Vision and Pattern Recognition, pp. 9799–9808 (2020)
7. Leclerc, S., et al.: Deep learning for segmentation using an open large-scale dataset in 2D echocardiography. IEEE Trans. Med. Imaging **38**(9), 2198–2210 (2019)
8. Li, H., et al.: CR-UNET: a composite network for ovary and follicle segmentation in ultrasound images. IEEE J. Biomed. Health Inform. **24**(4), 974–983 (2019)

9. Li, L., Lian, S., Luo, Z., Li, S., Wang, B., Li, S.: Learning consistency- and discrepancy-context for 2D organ segmentation. In: de Bruijne, M., et al. (eds.) MICCAI 2021. LNCS, vol. 12901, pp. 261–270. Springer, Cham (2021). https://doi.org/10.1007/978-3-030-87193-2_25

10. Li, S., Chen, Y., Yang, S., Luo, W.: Cascade dense-unet for prostate segmentation in MR images. In: Huang, D.-S., Bevilacqua, V., Premaratne, P. (eds.) ICIC 2019. LNCS, vol. 11643, pp. 481–490. Springer, Cham (2019). https://doi.org/10.1007/978-3-030-26763-6_46

11. Moradi, S., et al.: MFP-UNET: a novel deep learning based approach for left ventricle segmentation in echocardiography. Physica Medica **67**, 58–69 (2019)

12. Nguyen, T.-C., Nguyen, T.-P., Diep, G.-H., Tran-Dinh, A.-H., Nguyen, T.V., Tran, M.-T.: CCBANet: cascading context and balancing attention for polyp segmentation. In: de Bruijne, M., et al. (eds.) MICCAI 2021. LNCS, vol. 12901, pp. 633–643. Springer, Cham (2021). https://doi.org/10.1007/978-3-030-87193-2_60

13. Ronneberger, O., Fischer, P., Brox, T.: U-Net: convolutional networks for biomedical image segmentation. In: Navab, N., Hornegger, J., Wells, W.M., Frangi, A.F. (eds.) MICCAI 2015. LNCS, vol. 9351, pp. 234–241. Springer, Cham (2015). https://doi.org/10.1007/978-3-319-24574-4_28

14. Shahroudnejad, A., et al.: TUN-Det: a novel network for thyroid ultrasound nodule detection. In: de Bruijne, M., et al. (eds.) MICCAI 2021. LNCS, vol. 12901, pp. 656–667. Springer, Cham (2021). https://doi.org/10.1007/978-3-030-87193-2_62

15. Tang, C., Chen, H., Li, X., Li, J., Zhang, Z., Hu, X.: Look closer to segment better: boundary patch refinement for instance segmentation. In: Proceedings of the IEEE/CVF Conference on Computer Vision and Pattern Recognition, pp. 13926–13935 (2021)

16. Wang, J., Wei, L., Wang, L., Zhou, Q., Zhu, L., Qin, J.: Boundary-aware transformers for skin lesion segmentation. In: de Bruijne, M., et al. (eds.) MICCAI 2021. LNCS, vol. 12901, pp. 206–216. Springer, Cham (2021). https://doi.org/10.1007/978-3-030-87193-2_20

17. Wang, K., Liang, S., Zhang, Yu.: Residual feedback network for breast lesion segmentation in ultrasound image. In: de Bruijne, M., et al. (eds.) MICCAI 2021. LNCS, vol. 12901, pp. 471–481. Springer, Cham (2021). https://doi.org/10.1007/978-3-030-87193-2_45

18. Wang, Z.: Deep learning in medical ultrasound image segmentation: a review. arXiv preprint arXiv:2002.07703 (2020)

19. Xu, Y., Wang, Y., Yuan, J., Cheng, Q., Wang, X., Carson, P.L.: Medical breast ultrasound image segmentation by machine learning. Ultrasonics **91**, 1–9 (2019)

20. Yuan, Y., Xie, J., Chen, X., Wang, J.: SegFix: model-agnostic boundary refinement for segmentation. In: Vedaldi, A., Bischof, H., Brox, T., Frahm, J.-M. (eds.) ECCV 2020. LNCS, vol. 12357, pp. 489–506. Springer, Cham (2020). https://doi.org/10.1007/978-3-030-58610-2_29

21. Zhang, Y., et al.: Multi-phase liver tumor segmentation with spatial aggregation and uncertain region inpainting. In: de Bruijne, M., et al. (eds.) MICCAI 2021. LNCS, vol. 12901, pp. 68–77. Springer, Cham (2021). https://doi.org/10.1007/978-3-030-87193-2_7

22. Zhou, J., Jia, X., Ni, D.: Thyroid nodule segmentation and classification in ultrasound images. In: International Conference on Medical Image Computing and Computer-Assisted Intervention (2020). https://doi.org/10.5281/zenodo.3715942
23. Zhou, Z., Rahman Siddiquee, M.M., Tajbakhsh, N., Liang, J.: UNet++: a nested u-net architecture for medical image segmentation. In: Stoyanov, D., et al. (eds.) DLMIA/ML-CDS -2018. LNCS, vol. 11045, pp. 3–11. Springer, Cham (2018). https://doi.org/10.1007/978-3-030-00889-5_1

BiometryNet: Landmark-based Fetal Biometry Estimation from Standard Ultrasound Planes

Netanell Avisdris[1,2](✉) [iD], Leo Joskowicz[1], Brian Dromey[4,6], Anna L. David[6], Donald M. Peebles[6], Danail Stoyanov[4,5], Dafna Ben Bashat[2,3], and Sophia Bano[4,5]

[1] School of Computer Science and Engineering, The Hebrew University of Jerusalem, Jerusalem, Israel
{netana03,josko}@cs.huji.ac.il
[2] Sagol Brain Institute, Tel Aviv Sourasky Medical Center, Tel Aviv, Israel
[3] Sagol School of Neuroscience and Sackler Faculty of Medicine, Tel Aviv University, Tel Aviv, Israel
[4] Wellcome/EPSRC Centre for Interventional and Surgical Sciences (WEISS), University College London, London, UK
[5] Department of Computer Science, University College London, London, UK
[6] Elizabeth Garrett Anderson Institute for Women's Health, University College London, London, UK

Abstract. Fetal growth assessment from ultrasound is based on a few biometric measurements that are performed manually and assessed relative to the expected gestational age. Reliable biometry estimation depends on the precise detection of landmarks in standard ultrasound planes. Manual annotation can be time-consuming and operator dependent task, and may results in high measurements variability. Existing methods for automatic fetal biometry rely on initial automatic fetal structure segmentation followed by geometric landmark detection. However, segmentation annotations are time-consuming and may be inaccurate, and landmark detection requires developing measurement-specific geometric methods. This paper describes BiometryNet, an end-to-end landmark regression framework for fetal biometry estimation that overcomes these limitations. It includes a novel Dynamic Orientation Determination (DOD) method for enforcing measurement-specific orientation consistency during network training. DOD reduces variabilities in network training, increases landmark localization accuracy, thus yields accurate and robust biometric measurements. To validate our method, we assembled a dataset of 3,398 ultrasound images from 1,829 subjects acquired in three clinical sites with seven different ultrasound devices. Comparison and cross-validation of three different biometric measurements on two independent datasets shows that BiometryNet is robust and yields accurate measurements whose errors

---

Supplementary Information The online version contains supplementary material available at https://doi.org/10.1007/978-3-031-16440-8_27.

are lower than the clinically permissible errors, outperforming other existing automated biometry estimation methods. Code is available at https://github.com/netanellavisdris/fetalbiometry.

Keywords: Fetal biometry estimation · Fetal ultrasound · Anatomical landmarks' localisation · Computer-assisted diagnosis

1 Introduction

Ultrasound (US) based estimation of fetal biometry is widely used to monitor fetal growth assessed relative to the expected gestational age and to diagnose prenatal abnormalities. Reliable estimation of fetal biometry depends on the localization of fetal landmarks on standard planes (SPs) by the sonographer. Common SPs include the trans-ventricular plane to measure the fetal head circumference, the trans-abdominal plane to measure the fetal abdominal circumference, and femoral plane to measure the femur length. Obtaining manual measurements can be time-consuming and operator-dependent, especially for trainees [9], and results in high inter-and intra-operator variability [13]. In fetal biometry, inter-operator measurements variability range between $\pm 4.9\%$ and $\pm 11.1\%$ and an intra-operator variability between $\pm 3\%$ and $\pm 6.6\%$ [19]. This variability contributes to biometry uncertainty and hampers fetal growth evaluation in the clinic. Automating fetal biometry can reduce measurement variability and improve fetal monitoring and clinical decision making.

Numerous methods have been developed for automatic computation of different measurements in US-based fetal biometry [21], e.g., biparietal diameter [1,24], head circumference [12], and femur length [14]. Recently, methods for comprehensive biometry required for fetal weight estimation have been proposed [6,16]. Similar methods have been developed for other imaging modalities, e.g., fetal MRI [5] and 3D US [17]. These methods rely on obtaining segmentation masks to train fetal anatomy segmentation models, which is time-consuming, and on developing geometric methods for each measurement.

An alternative approach is the detection of landmarks directly on the image without relying on segmentation masks. The advantages of this approach are that it follows the clinical workflow – the sonographer locates on the two landmarks required for biometric measurement directly on the image, and that obtaining ground-truth data is fast and straightforward. Landmark-based approaches have been proposed for various medical imaging modalities [23], e.g. CT and MRI, to quantify lesions progression [20], for fetal MRI biometry estimation [4], and for fetal landmark detection in US using reinforcement learning agents [2]. However, this approach has not been used for automating fetal biometry in US SPs.

Automating fetal US biometry presents numerous challenges. First, imaging quality varies across different US devices, heterogeneous in overall appearance, particularly regarding gain and zoom. Second, some fetal anatomical structures may become difficult to image with increasing gestational age. Third, anatomical structure position, size, orientation, and appearance present significant variability (Fig. 1). Since the fetus can lie in any of a wide variety of positions, anatomical landmarks can be in orientations that are off the horizontal. Finally, biometric parameters have different geometric characteristics and performed on different SPs, thus each requires its own individual method.

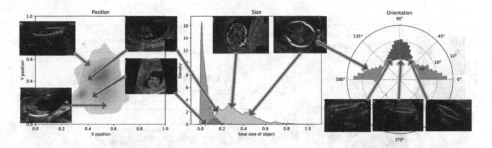

Fig. 1. Fetal biometry variability for the head (red) and femur (blue) SPs. The graphs show (left to right) the distributions of the position (structure center point), size (structure area with respect to image area) and orientation (structure angle with respect to horizontal plane). Sample US image inserts illustrate the distribution. (Color figure online)

We propose BiometryNet, an end-to-end framework that automates US fetal biometry for multiple fetal structures using direct landmark detection that overcomes these challenges. Unlike other methods [1,6,17,21,24], BiometryNet only requires measurement landmark annotations for training. The main contributions of our work are:

- We show for the first time that US fetal biometry can be automated with high accuracy using only landmark annotations that can be acquired easily. We demonstrate our approach on a large fetal biometry dataset of 3,398 US images from 1,820 subjects acquired by various operators and US devices at multiple clinical centers.
- We propose a novel Dynamic Orientation Determination (DOD) method to determine measurement-wise orientation and provide consistent landmark class for various measurements. We show that DOD is robust for variabilities in the SPs orientations, leading to improved biometry estimates and generalization on unseen datasets.

2 Method

We propose BiometryNet, a framework for the estimation of fetal US biometry using a landmark regression convolution neural network (Fig. 2). BiometryNet locates two landmark points on an US image for three biometric parameters:

biparietal diameter (BPD) and occipito-frontal diameter (OFD) in the trans-ventricular (head) plane, and femur length (FL) in the femur plane. It includes Dynamic Orientation Determination (DOD) used during training for consistent landmark class. At inference time, the trained BiometryNet predicts two biometry landmarks, followed by scale recovery in order to estimate image resolution needed to compute the actual biometric measure.

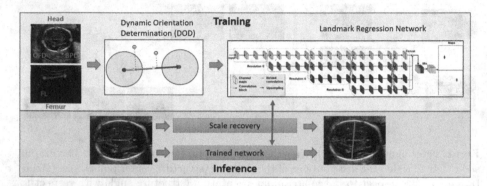

Fig. 2. BiometryNet framework. Top: during training, annotated head and femur planes are fed into the DOD module and to the landmark regression network to predict two landmarks per biometric measurement. Bottom: during inference, the trained model predicts the landmarks followed by scale recovery for biometric measurements estimation.

2.1   Landmark Regression Network

The landmark regression network is a modified HRNet [22], trained to predict a heat map for each landmark defined by a Gaussian function centered at the landmark coordinates whose co-variance describes the landmark location uncertainty. We used HRNet since it has achieved state-of-the-art performance for computer vision tasks, e.g. object detection, semantic segmentation, face landmark detection and human pose estimation. HRNet is a Convolutional Neural Network that combines the representations of multi-scale high-to-low resolution parallel streams into a single stream. The representations are then input to a two-layer convolution classifier. The first layer combines the feature maps of all four resolutions; the second layer computes a Gaussian heat map for each of the two landmarks. One network is trained for each biometric measurement (two landmarks points) with the Mean Squared Error loss between the Gaussian maps created from the ground-truth landmarks and the predicted heat maps. At inference time, the two landmarks' locations are defined by the coordinates of the pixel with the maximal value on each heat map.

To compensate for the high variability in acquisition orientation and object scales in fetal US images (Fig. 1), two training time augmentations are used:

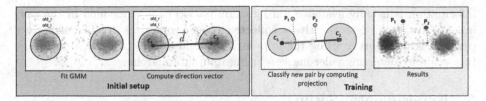

Fig. 3. Illustration of Dynamic Orientation Determination (DOD). Left: *Initial setup stage, measurement direction vector computation between GMM centroids fitted to normalized landmark points*; Right: *Training stage, re-assignment of each landmark pair class by projecting the landmarks on the direction vector and ordering them.*

1) rotations around the image center at randomly sampled angles in the range $[-180, 180]°$ followed by cropping to preserve a fixed image size; 2) image scaling at randomly sampled scales in the range $[-5, +5]\%$.

2.2 Dynamic Orientation Determination (DOD)

Since fetal structure may appear in various orientations (Fig. 1) and CNN are not rotation-invariant, orientation variability must be handled properly. A common approach to handle such variability is augmentation. However, rotation augmentation may cause landmark class labeling (e.g. left/right landmarks) to be inconsistent with image coordinates, i.e. the left and right points may be erroneously switched, which will hamper network training (Fig. 1 Supp.). This inconsistency can be corrected by landmark class reassignment (LCR) [4] to preserve horizontal (left/right) landmark class consistency after augmentation. However, different biometric measurements may have different spatial orientation, e.g., OFD is mostly vertical and BPD is mostly horizontal.

To overcome this issue, we introduced Dynamic Orientation Determination (DOD), a method that determine measurement-wise orientations and perform class reassignment accordingly, instead of computing only the horizontal measurement landmark pairs as in [4]. DOD consists of two stages (Fig. 3). In *initial setup* stage, biometry orientation is determined. First, Gaussian Mixture Model of two Gaussians was fitted onto the ground-truth landmarks of training dataset of each biometric measurements with Expectation-Maximization algorithm [8]. Next, biometry orientation is computed as directional vector between the two Gaussian centroids, $\vec{d} = \overrightarrow{C_1 C_2}$. In the network *training* stage, the learned orientation is used to enforce consistency. After all augmentations are performed, each resulting biometric measurement landmark pair $(P = p_1, p_2)$ is projected on the directional vector $r_i = (p_i \cdot \vec{d})/|\vec{d}|$ and then ordered according to its projection $sort(|r_i|)$ to obtain their reassigned class.

2.3 Scale Recovery

To obtain actual measurements that can be compared to those obtained in the clinic, scale conversion from pixel to millimeter units is required. While this information is usually available during examination or is embedded in the raw image data, some retrospectively collected images may lack it. Therefore, we perform scale recovery using the approach presented in [6]. Briefly, it recovers true scale by detecting ruler markers using template matching.

3   Experimental Setup

Datasets and Annotations: we use two public datasets, Fetal Planes (FP) [7] and HC18 [12]. FP [7] was originally designed for US SPs classification challenge. The US images were acquired on six US devices: three GE Voluson E6, one Voluson S8, one Voluson S10 and one Aloka at two clinical sites in Barcelona, Spain. Since not all images in FP qualified as SPs for fetal biometry [18], we selected 1,638 (909 subjects) fetal head and 761 (630 subjects) fetal femur SPs. Not all subjects are included in both planes datasets, resulting in a total of 2,399 images from 1,014 unique subjects. An obstetrician then manually annotated the landmarks on each image with the VIA annotation tool [10]. On average, each plane annotation for landmarks took 20 s, which is far less than 70 s required for manual structure delineation.HC18 [12] was designed for fetal head circumference (HC) challenge. The US images were acquired with two US devices: GE Voulson E8 and 730, in one clinical site in the Netherlands. All HC18 training set, 999 (806 subjects) fetal head SPs, were annotated with a HC measurement. We computed the BPD and OFD biometric measurements from the major and minor axes of an ellipse by least-square fitting [11] onto the ground-truth mask.

Evaluation Metrics: we use the mean and median of L_1 difference, bias and agreement. For two sets of n biometric measurements, $M_1 = \{m_i^1\}$, $M_2 = \{m_i^2\}$, let m_i^1 and m_i^2 ($1 \leq i \leq n$) be two measurement values, the ground-truth and the computed one, respectively.The difference between each pair of measurements is defined as $d_i = m_i^1 - m_i^2$. The mean and median differences for M_1, M_2 are defined as $\overline{L_1}(M_1, M_2) = 1/n \sum_{i=1}^{n} |d_i|$ and $\widetilde{L_1}(M_1, M_2) = median_i(|d_i|)$, respectively. We use the Bland-Altman method [3] to estimate the bias and agreement between two biometry measurement sets. Agreement is defined by the 95% confidence interval $CI_{95}(M_1, M_2) = 1.96 \times \sqrt{1/n \sum_{i=1}^{n} (\overline{L_1}(M_1, M_2) - d_i)^2}$. The measurements bias is defined as $Bias(M_1, M_2) = 1/n \sum_{i=1}^{n} d_i$.

Study Setup: the two datasets FP and HC18 were split into training and test sets. For the FP head and femur SPs, we selected 757 (449 subjects) and 437 (368 subjects) images for training and 881 (460 subjects) and 324 (262 subjects) images for testing, respectively. For a fair comparison of head planes in FP and HC18, we selected from HC18, similar number of 737 images (600 subjects) for training. The remaining 262 images (206 subjects) were used for the test set.BiometryNet was implemented in PyTorch and trained for 200 epochs in about 2 h on a single NVIDIA 1080Ti GPU with a batch size of 16 using the ADAM optimizer [15], an initial learning rate of 10^{-4} and a drop factor of 0.2 in epochs 10, 40, 90, and 150. For validation, a comparison to four networks

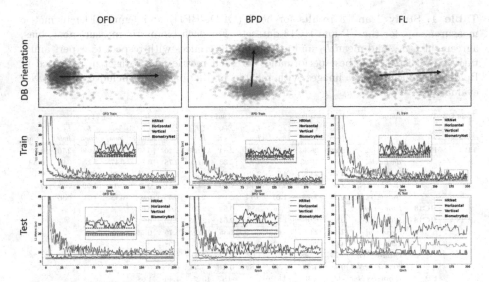

Fig. 4. Effect of learned dynamic orientation (first row) on training (2nd row) and inference (3rd row) for three measurements (columns) on convergence (yellow boxes): OFD, BPD and FL, in the FP dataset. Four models were trained: *HRNet* (black), with *horizontal* (blue) fixed orientation, *vertical* (green) fixed orientation and *BiometryNet* with DOD (red). Dotted lines denote the best performing epoch metric for each model. (Color figure online)

was performed: (a) Vanilla HRNet [22]; (b) HRNet with fixed horizontal orientation determination; (c) HRNet with fixed vertical orientation determination for biometric measurements with horizontal orientation (OFD, FL) and vertical orientation (BPD); and, (d) FMLNet [4], which is an HRNet with fixed horizontal orientation determination, test-time augmentation and a method for prediction reliability estimation.

4   Results

We conducted three experimental studies on the FP and HC18 datasets to quantify the performance of BiometryNet and compare it to other existing methods.

Study 1: Effect of DOD on training: we evaluated the effect of DOD on training and inference dynamics on three biometric measurements: OFD, BPD, and FL in the FP dataset. OFD and FL have mostly horizontal orientations and BPD has mostly vertical orientation. Figure 4 shows the results. Note that for all biometric measurements, the learned orientation is similar to the preferred orientation. BiometryNet converged faster and performed better than networks trained on fixed orientations of both the training and test sets, similar to those with the preferred fixed orientation, and better than the Vanilla HRNet, which

Table 1. Study 2 and 3 results for head (OFD, BPD) and femur (FL) biometric measurements for the FP and HC18 datasets. For each biometric measurement, bias, agreement CI_{95}, and mean $\overline{L_1}$ and median $\widetilde{L_1}$ differences with respect to expert annotations are listed. The best performance for each metric and dataset in indicated in Bold. (*) indicates only images with reliable predictions were included in FMLNet evaluation.

Train DB	Test DB	Method	Head - OFD				Head - BPD				Femur - FL			
			Bias [mm]	CI_{95} [mm]	$\overline{L_1}$ [mm]	$\widetilde{L_1}$ [mm]	Bias [mm]	CI_{95} [mm]	$\overline{L_1}$ [mm]	$\widetilde{L_1}$ [mm]	Bias [mm]	CI_{95} [mm]	$\overline{L_1}$ [mm]	$\widetilde{L_1}$ [mm]
FP	FP	HRNet [22]	6.23	26.40	6.30	3.30	2.84	22.57	3.20	0.80	1.80	18.40	2.70	0.62
		Horizontal	2.65	10.23	2.87	1.90	2.36	21.60	2.78	0.76	0.17	3.27	0.99	**0.59**
		Vertical	4.73	23.51	4.86	2.46	0.77	8.28	1.28	0.65	0.33	10.27	1.47	0.65
		FMLNet* [4]	1.96	7.80	2.16	1.43	1.30	14.56	1.71	0.65	**0.14**	**3.00**	1.02	0.68
		BiometryNet	**0.21**	**2.75**	**1.01**	**0.71**	**0.04**	**2.50**	**0.77**	**0.58**	0.18	3.03	**0.97**	0.62
	HC18	BiometryNet	2.31	5.21	2.46	1.85	0.84	2.70	1.06	0.91				
HC18	HC18	HRNet [22]	0.64	6.01	1.51	0.92	2.64	21.48	3.10	0.71				
		Horizontal	2.82	23.9	3.69	0.93	1.35	12.86	1.75	**0.59**				
		Vertical	4.02	29.15	4.92	0.97	0.50	5.13	0.98	0.65				
		FMLNet* [4]	2.23	17.48	2.61	1.02	0.73	4.00	0.93	0.64				
		BiometryNet	**0.56**	**4.43**	**1.39**	**0.84**	**0.16**	**3.54**	**0.88**	0.61				
	FP	BiometryNet	-3.24	6.01	3.54	2.72	-1.11	3.35	1.40	1.08				

performed poorly. This advantage becomes more evident when the landmarks' locations are more disperse, e.g. for FL. This shows that DOD provides robustness with respect to orientation variability and yields an improved performance.

Study 2: Performance comparison: we evaluate the performance of BiometryNet on the FP and HC18 datasets. Table 1 lists the results. HRNet performed poorly on all biometric measurements, with a high CI_{95} and error. Fixed orientation determination yielded better results in preferred orientation of measurement, i.e. horizontal in OFD and FL, and vertical in BPD. FMLNet [4] performed better than fixed horizontal in all cases, but at the expense of discarding 8% of test inputs in average. BiometryNet outperformed other methods in OFD and BPD biometric measurements in all metrics. While FL has a slightly better bias and CI_{95} in FMLNet, considering only included cases by all methods, the paired t-test ($p = 0.02$) shows that BiometryNet outperforms all other methods, including FMLNet.

BiometryNet yields a median error (<0.84 mm (OFD), <0.61 mm (BPD) and <0.62 mm (FL)) that is better than the error reported in [6] (1.30 mm (OFD), 0.80 mm (BPD) and 2.1 mm (FL)). In addition, the results are better than [1], which was the best BPD performer in a 2022 review on fetal US biometry [21], that achieved a mean error of 2.33 mm, bias of 1.49 mm and CI_{95} of 5.55 mm. Furthermore, the variance of all methods except BiometryNet is higher than the reported inter-observer variability [24] of 5.0 mm (OFD), 3.0 mm (BPD) and 4.3 mm (FL) [19]. These results suggest that overall BiometryNet performs better and is more stable (lower variance) than the existing methods.

Study 3: Impact of training dataset: to demonstrate the generalization capabilities of BiometryNet, we analyzed its performance by cross-validation on unseen datasets. For this purpose, we train the OFD and BPD models on FP dataset and test each on HC18 dataset, and vice versa. Table 1 lists the results. Note that training on one dataset and testing on the other (rows 6 and 12) results in high mean and median errors, with significant and complementary (2.31 mm vs -3.24 mm in OFD, 0.81 mm vs -1.11 mm in BPD) bias and acceptable variance. In contrast, testing on the same dataset (rows 5 and 11) results in low bias, but similar variance (CI_{95}) as before. This bias can be explained by the differences in annotation protocol between the two datasets. In HC18, the landmark annotations lie between the outer contours of the skull, while in FP, they are marked in the middle of the fetal skull contour, thus resulting in a consistent bias (Fig. 2 supp.). Clinically, both protocols are acceptable, and their selection depends on the specific clinical site. We also observe that using FP annotations for network training produced better and more consistent results than using those of HC18. This may occur because HC18 annotations are extracted from HC ellipse rather than annotated directly at the BPD/OFD landmarks. We conclude from these results that BiometryNet is capable of generalization, as it can learn to annotate like the annotation protocol, and can be tuned for use across many sites and protocols.

5   Conclusions

We proposed BiometryNet, an end-to-end network for automatic fetal biometry estimation from standard US planes. BiometryNet only required anatomical landmarks annotations for biometric measurements prediction without the need of any geometric methods as post-processing. To overcome the variability that is inherently present in the acquired US planes, we introduced a novel dynamic orientation determination mechanism which enforced measurement-wise orientation consistency in network training. This resulted in reduced variability and improved landmarks' localization, thus leading to more accurate biometric measurements compared to the state-of-the-art methods. Through the analysis of two large and independent datasets, we demonstrated the generalization ability of our proposed method. Moreover, BiometryNet resulted in minimal error which is lower than the clinically permissible error [19], thus showing the potential for clinical translation to improve fetal growth assessment.

In future work, we plan to analyze the abdominal plane and its measurement using BiometryNet. Furthermore, BiometryNet assumes SP is already available for the measurement, which is not always the case in clinical settings. Therefore, we will design a holistic network to jointly learn SP selection and fetal biometry.

Acknowledgements. This research was partly supported by the Wellcome/EPSRC Centre for Interventional and Surgical Sciences (WEISS) [203145/Z/16/Z]; the Engineering and Physical Sciences Research Council (EPSRC) [EP/P027938/1, EP/R004080/1, EP/P012841/1]; the Royal Academy of Engineering Chair in Emerging Technologies Scheme, and Horizon 2020 FET Open [863146]; Kamin Grants [63418, 72126] from the Israel Innovation Authority.

References

1. Al-Bander, B., Alzahrani, T., Alzahrani, S., Williams, B.M., Zheng, Y.: Improving fetal head contour detection by object localisation with deep learning. In: Zheng, Y., Williams, B.M., Chen, K. (eds.) MIUA 2019. CCIS, vol. 1065, pp. 142–150. Springer, Cham (2020). https://doi.org/10.1007/978-3-030-39343-4_12
2. Alansary, A., et al.: Evaluating reinforcement learning agents for anatomical landmark detection. Med. Image Anal. **53**, 156–164 (2019)
3. Altman, D.G., Bland, J.M.: Measurement in medicine: the analysis of method comparison studies. J. Roy. Stat. Soc. Ser. D (The Statistician) **32**(3), 307–317 (1983)
4. Avisdris, N., Ben Bashat, D., Ben-Sira, L., Joskowicz, L.: Fetal brain MRI measurements using a deep learning landmark network with reliability estimation. In: Sudre, C.H., et al. (eds.) UNSURE/PIPPI -2021. LNCS, vol. 12959, pp. 210–220. Springer, Cham (2021). https://doi.org/10.1007/978-3-030-87735-4_20
5. Avisdris, N., et al.: Automatic linear measurements of the fetal brain with deep neural networks. Int. J. Comput. Assist. Radiol. Surg. **16**, 1481–1492 (2021)
6. Bano, S., et al.: AutoFB: automating fetal biometry estimation from standard ultrasound planes. In: de Bruijne, M., et al. (eds.) MICCAI 2021. LNCS, vol. 12907, pp. 228–238. Springer, Cham (2021). https://doi.org/10.1007/978-3-030-87234-2_22
7. Burgos-Artizzu, X.P., et al.: Evaluation of deep convolutional neural networks for automatic classification of common maternal fetal ultrasound planes. Sci. Rep. **10**(1), 1–12 (2020)
8. Dempster, A.P., Laird, N.M., Rubin, D.B.: Maximum likelihood from incomplete data via the em algorithm. J. Roy. Stat. Soc. Ser. B **39**(1), 1–22 (1977)
9. Dromey, B.P., et al.: Dimensionless squared jerk: an objective differential to assess experienced and novice probe movement in obstetric ultrasound. Prenat. Diagn. **41**, 271–277 (2020)
10. Dutta, A., Zisserman, A.: The via annotation software for images, audio and video. In: Proceedings of the 27th ACM International Conference on Multimedia, pp. 2276–2279 (2019)
11. Fitzgibbon, A.W., Pilu, M., Fisher, R.B.: Direct least squares fitting of ellipses. In: Proceedings of the International Conference on Pattern Recognition, vol. 1, pp. 253–257. IEEE (1996)
12. van den Heuvel, T.L., de Bruijn, D., de Korte, C.L., Ginneken, B.V.: Automated measurement of fetal head circumference using 2D ultrasound images. PLoS ONE **13**(8), e0200412 (2018)
13. Joskowicz, L., Cohen, D., Caplan, N., Sosna, J.: Inter-observer variability of manual contour delineation of structures in CT. Eur. Radiol. **29**(3), 1391–1399 (2019)
14. Khan, N.H., Tegnander, E., Dreier, J.M., Eik-Nes, S., Torp, H., Kiss, G.: Automatic detection and measurement of fetal biparietal diameter and femur length-feasibility on a portable ultrasound device. Open J. Obstetr. Gynecol. **7**(3), 334–350 (2017)
15. Kingma, D.P., Ba, J.: Adam: a method for stochastic optimization. In: Proceedings of the International Conference on Learning Representations (2015)
16. Prieto, J.C., et al.: An automated framework for image classification and segmentation of fetal ultrasound images for gestational age estimation. In: Medical Imaging 2021: Image Processing, vol. 11596, p. 115961N. International Society for Optics and Photonics (2021)

17. Ryou, H., Yaqub, M., Cavallaro, A., Papageorghiou, A.T., Noble, J.A.: Automated 3D ultrasound image analysis for first trimester assessment of fetal health. Phys. Med. Biol. **64**(18), 185010 (2019)
18. Salomon, L., Winer, N., Bernard, J., Ville, Y.: A score-based method for quality control of fetal images at routine second-trimester ultrasound examination. Prenat. Diagn. **28**(9), 822–827 (2008)
19. Sarris, I., et al.: Intra-and interobserver variability in fetal ultrasound measurements. Ultrasound Obstetr. Gynecol. **39**(3), 266–273 (2012)
20. Tang, Y., et al.: Lesion segmentation and RECIST diameter prediction via click-driven attention and dual-path connection. In: de Bruijne, M., et al. (eds.) MICCAI 2021. LNCS, vol. 12902, pp. 341–351. Springer, Cham (2021). https://doi.org/10.1007/978-3-030-87196-3_32
21. Torres, H.R., et al.: A review of image processing methods for fetal head and brain analysis in ultrasound images. Comput. Methods Programs Biomed. **215**, 106629 (2022)
22. Wang, J., et al.: Deep high-resolution representation learning for visual recognition. IEEE Trans. Pattern Anal. Mach. Intell. **43**, 3349–3364 (2019)
23. Zhang, J., Liu, M., Shen, D.: Detecting anatomical landmarks from limited medical imaging data using two-stage task-oriented deep neural networks. IEEE Trans. Pattern Anal. Mach. Intell. **26**(10), 4753–4764 (2017)
24. Zhang, L., Dudley, N.J., Lambrou, T., Allinson, N., Ye, X.: Automatic image quality assessment and measurement of fetal head in two-dimensional ultrasound image. J. Med. Imaging (Bellingham) **4**(2), 024001 (2017)

Deep Motion Network for Freehand 3D Ultrasound Reconstruction

Mingyuan Luo[1,2,3], Xin Yang[1,2,3], Hongzhang Wang[1,2,3], Liwei Du[1,2,3], and Dong Ni[1,2,3(✉)]

[1] National-Regional Key Technology Engineering Laboratory for Medical Ultrasound, School of Biomedical Engineering, Health Science Center, Shenzhen University, Shenzhen, China
nidong@szu.edu.cn
[2] Medical Ultrasound Image Computing (MUSIC) Laboratory, Shenzhen University, Shenzhen, China
[3] Marshall Laboratory of Biomedical Engineering, Shenzhen University, Shenzhen, China

Abstract. Freehand 3D ultrasound (US) has important clinical value due to its low cost and unrestricted field of view. Recently deep learning algorithms have removed its dependence on bulky and expensive external positioning devices. However, improving reconstruction accuracy is still hampered by difficult elevational displacement estimation and large cumulative drift. In this context, we propose a novel deep motion network (MoNet) that integrates images and a lightweight sensor known as the inertial measurement unit (IMU) from a velocity perspective to alleviate the obstacles mentioned above. Our contribution is two-fold. First, we introduce IMU acceleration for the first time to estimate elevational displacements outside the plane. We propose a temporal and multi-branch structure to mine the valuable information of low signal-to-noise ratio (SNR) acceleration. Second, we propose a multi-modal online self-supervised strategy that leverages IMU information as weak labels for adaptive optimization to reduce drift errors and further ameliorate the impacts of acceleration noise. Experiments show that our proposed method achieves the superior reconstruction performance, exceeding state-of-the-art methods across the board.

Keywords: Inertial measurement unit · Online learning · Freehand 3D ultrasound

1 Introduction

Three-dimensional (3D) ultrasound (US) is widely used because of its intuitive visuals, easy interaction and rich clinical information. Freehand 3D US offers flexibility and simplicity over mechanical probes or electronic phased arrays [5].

M. Luo and X. Yang—Contribute equally to this work.

© The Author(s), under exclusive license to Springer Nature Switzerland AG 2022
L. Wang et al. (Eds.): MICCAI 2022, LNCS 13434, pp. 290–299, 2022.
https://doi.org/10.1007/978-3-031-16440-8_28

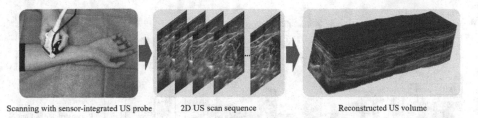

Scanning with sensor-integrated US probe   2D US scan sequence   Reconstructed US volume

Fig. 1. Pipeline of freehand 3D US reconstruction with a lightweight inertial measurement unit (IMU) sensor.

It typically reconstructs the volume by calculating the relative positions of a series of US images. Recently, freehand reconstruction techniques have moved away from complex and costly external positioning systems previously used to obtain high-precision positions [2,7,11,12]. However, improving reconstruction accuracy remains difficult as these techniques only rely on images to infer relative positions. Specifically, the difficulty in estimating elevational displacement between images and the accumulation of drift errors make the reconstruction very challenging. In this regard, lightweight sensors are expected to avoid the disadvantages of traditional position sensors while improving the deep learning based reconstruction performance, as illustrated in Fig. 1.

Freehand 3D US reconstruction has been studied for over half a century [10]. Early solutions mainly relied on complex and expensive external positioning systems to accurately calculate image locations [8–10]. The non-sensor scheme is mainly speckle decorrelation [13], which uses speckle correlation between adjacent images to estimate relative motion and decomposes it into in-plane and out-of-plane parts. However, the reconstruction quality is susceptible to scan rate and angle [9]. With the development of deep learning technology [6], Prevost et al. [12] first used a convolutional neural network (CNN) to estimate the relative motion of US images. Guo et al. [2] proposed a deep contextual learning network (DCL-Net) to mine the correlation information of US video clips for 3D reconstruction. Luo et al. [7] designed an online learning framework (OLF) that improves reconstruction performance by utilizing consistency constraints and shape priors. Although effective, the reconstruction performance based on deep learning still faces challenges such as difficult elevational displacement estimation and large cumulative drift.

Compared to complicated positioning systems, the lightweight sensor called inertial measurement unit (IMU) is inexpensive and takes up less space (Fig. 1). IMU integrates triaxial accelerometer, gyroscope and magnetometer sensors to measure an object's triaxial orientation and acceleration [1]. Integrating an IMU does not increase US scanning complexity. Prevost et al. [11] first demonstrated the promise of boosting reconstruction performance by simply concatenating the IMU orientation with the fully connected layer of neural networks, due to the low signal-to-noise ratio (SNR) of the IMU acceleration.

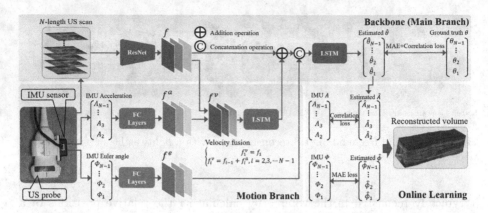

Fig. 2. Overview of our lightweight sensor-based deep motion network (MoNet).

In this study, we propose a novel lightweight sensor-based deep motion network (MoNet) for freehand 3D US reconstruction. Our contribution is two-fold. First, we equip a lightweight IMU sensor and exploit the IMU acceleration and orientation for the first time to improve image-based reconstruction performance. We propose a temporal and multi-branch structure from a velocity perspective to mine the valuable information of low-SNR acceleration. Second, we propose a multi-modal online self-supervised strategy that leverages IMU information as weak label for adaptive optimization to reduce drift errors and further ameliorate the impacts of acceleration noise. We thoroughly validate the efficacy and generalizability of MoNet on the collected arm and carotid scans. Experimental results show that MoNet achieves state-of-the-art reconstruction performance by fully utilizing the IMU information and deeply fusing it with image content.

2   Methodology

We define the N-length scan as $I = \{I_i | i = 1, 2, \cdots, N\}$, and for image I_i, the corresponding orientation and acceleration vector provided by the IMU as $O_i = (O_x, O_y, O_z)_i$ and $A_i = (A_x, A_y, A_z)_i$, respectively. The O_i is based on the east-north-up coordinate system, and the Euler angle $\Phi_i = (\Phi_x, \Phi_y, \Phi_z)_i$ between the images I_i and I_{i+1} can be calculated as

$$\Phi_i = M^{-1}(M(O_i)^{-1} * M(O_{i+1})), \quad i = 1, 2, \cdots, N-1, \tag{1}$$

where $M(\cdot)$ converts the orientation vector into a 3×3 rotation matrix and $M^{-1}(\cdot)$ denotes the inverse operation of $M(\cdot)$. For the A_i, we first subtract the component of the gravity direction g_i computed from O_i. We also adjust the mean value of acceleration to zero to reduce the influence of noise. The calculation can be expressed as

$$A_i \leftarrow (A_i - g_i) - \frac{1}{N}\sum_i (A_i - g_i), \quad i = 1, 2, \cdots, N. \tag{2}$$

Figure 2 illustrates the proposed lightweight sensor-based deep motion network (MoNet). MoNet takes all adjacent images $\{(I_i, I_{i+1})|i = 1, 2, \cdots, N - 1\}$, the acceleration $\{A_i|i = 2, 3, \cdots, N - 1\}$ and the Euler angle $\{\Phi_i|i = 1, 2, \cdots, N - 1\}$ as inputs to estimate the relative transformation parameters $\theta = \{\theta_i|i = 1, 2, \cdots, N - 1\}$, where θ_i indicates 3 translations $t_i = (t_x, t_y, t_z)_i$ and 3 rotation degrees $\phi_i = (\phi_x, \phi_y, \phi_z)_i$, respectively. It contains a temporal and multi-branch structure for mining valuable IMU information. Furthermore, the multi-modal online self-supervised strategy is used to improve estimation accuracy further.

2.1 Temporal and Multi-branch Structure for IMU Fusion

As shown in Fig. 2, we construct the MoNet using ResNet [3] and LSTM [4]. ResNet is a powerful feature extraction network that is commonly used to design networks for various tasks. LSTM is used to process temporal information, memorizing the knowledge of all historical images as contextual information to help estimate future parameters.

Estimating out-of-plane elevational displacements from images alone is a huge challenge. In this study, we introduce IMU acceleration for the first time to address this challenge. We first argue that the output features of the ResNet with adjacent images as input implicitly contain relative distance information between images. Second, scanning speed can be represented by relative distance, assuming a constant sampling time between adjacent images. Hence, the IMU acceleration should be associated with the features containing velocity information, allowing complementary learning through a multi-branch structure implementation.

Within the multi-branch structure as shown in Fig. 2, we map the processed acceleration to a high-dimensional space using multiple fully connected layers and reshape it into 2D features for easy combination with image features. The acceleration feature f^a is then added to the implied velocity feature f to construct the IMU velocity feature f^v, which can be expressed as

$$\begin{cases} f_1^v = f_1, \\ f_i^v = f_{i-1} + f_i^a, i = 2, 3, \cdots, N - 1. \end{cases} \quad (3)$$

Subsequently, to minimize the impact of acceleration noise on network performance in short sequence intervals, we feed f^v into a LSTM to enhance the velocity features using the temporal context information. The LSTM output is merged into the main branch and added to the ResNet output. By fusing the IMU acceleration, the multi-branch structure provides a better estimation of elevational displacements. Furthermore, the Euler angle calculated from IMU orientation is fed into multiple fully connected layers and concatenated to the LSTM input in the main branch to enhance the Euler angle estimation in the relative transformation parameters.

In the training phase, the loss function of MoNet contains two items. The first item minimizes the mean absolute error (MAE) between the estimated transformation parameters $\hat{\theta}$ and ground truth θ. The second item is the Pearson correlation loss from [2], which aids in learning the general trend of the scan.

$$L = \|\hat{\theta} - \theta\|_1 + (1 - \frac{\mathbf{Cov}(\hat{\theta}, \theta)}{\sigma(\hat{\theta})\sigma(\theta)}), \tag{4}$$

where $\|\cdot\|_1$ calculates L1 normalization, $\mathbf{Cov}$ denotes the covariance, and σ indicates the standard deviation.

2.2   Multi-modal Online Self-supervised Strategy

Most previous 3D reconstruction methods [2,11,12] relied solely on offline network training and direct online inference. This strategy often fails to handle scans with a different distribution than the training data. Online self-supervised learning can address this challenge by leveraging adaptive optimization and valuable prior knowledge. In this study, we propose a multi-modal online self-supervised strategy that leverages IMU information as weak labels for adaptive optimization to reduce drift errors and further ameliorate the impacts of acceleration noise. Specifically, as shown in Fig. 2, the IMU acceleration and Euler angle are used as weak labels for iterative optimization after estimating the transformation parameters using the trained MoNet. The estimated acceleration $\hat{A}$ at the centroid of each image is calculated from the estimated translations $\hat{t}$ and scaled to match the mean-zeroed IMU acceleration.

$$\hat{A}_i = (\hat{t}_{i-1}^{-1} + \hat{t}_i) - \frac{1}{N-2} \sum_i (\hat{t}_{i-1}^{-1} + \hat{t}_i), \quad i = 2, 3, \cdots, N-1, \tag{5}$$

where $\hat{t}_{i-1}^{-1}$ denotes the translations in the inversion of $\hat{\theta}_{i-1}$. The optimization loss L_{online} is split into two components: acceleration and Euler angle. We measure the difference between the estimated acceleration $\hat{A}$ and IMU acceleration A with the Pearson correlation loss. This exploits the correct trend of IMU acceleration over a wide range of each scan to improve the MoNet estimation and ameliorate the impacts of noise. Meanwhile, the MAE loss constrains the difference between the estimated Euler angle $\hat{\phi}$ and IMU Euler angle Φ.

$$L_{online} = (1 - \frac{\mathbf{Cov}(\hat{A}, A)}{\sigma(\hat{A})\sigma(A)}) + \|\hat{\phi} - \Phi\|_1 \tag{6}$$

3   Experiments

Materials and Implementation. We built a data acquisition system to acquire all US scans and corresponding IMU data. The system consists of a portable US machine, an IMU sensor (WT901C-232, WitMotion ShenZhen Co., Ltd., China) and an electromagnetic (EM) positioning transmitter/receiver. We acquired US images with a linear probe at 10 MHz and bound the IMU sensor to the probe to obtain the acceleration and orientation information. We also connected the EM receiver to the probe and utilized the EM positioning system

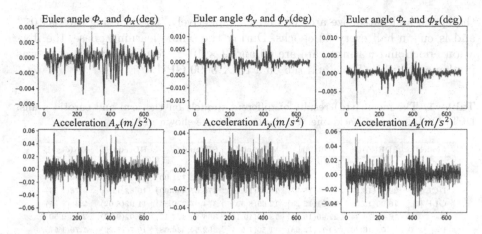

Fig. 3. Comparison of IMU data (Φ and A, blue line) and EM positioning data (ϕ and A, red line). The abscissa of each subfigure indicates the image index. (Color figure online)

to trace the scan route accurately. The US image depth is set as 3.5 cm, the IMU measurement resolution is 5×10^{-4} g/LSB (acceleration) and $0.5°$ (orientation), and the EM positioning resolution is 1.4 mm (position) and $0.5°$ (orientation). We calibrated the entire system to acquire precise transformation parameters while minimizing EM positioning interference with the IMU. As shown in Fig. 3, we analyzed the acceleration and Euler angle calculated by IMU data and compared them to the EM positioning. It can be observed that the acceleration is much more noisy at a single point compared to the Euler angle, but has a correct trend over a wide range.

We constructed two datasets including arm and carotid using the acquisition system for evaluation. The arm dataset contains 250 scans from 41 volunteers with an average length of 94.83 mm. Scanning tactics included linear, curved, fast-and-slow and loop scans to mimic complex real-world situations. The carotid dataset contains 160 scans from 40 volunteers, with an average length of 53.71 mm. Only linear scans were performed due to the narrow pathway and the tissue's deformable tendency. The size of all scanned images is 478×522 pixel, and the image spacing is 0.075×0.075 mm^2. The local IRB approves the collection and use of data.

We randomly divided the arm and carotid datasets into 196/54 and 136/24 scans based on volunteer level to construct the training/test set. All images were scaled down to 0.6 times their original size. To increase the network's robustness and prevent overfitting, we conducted random augmentation of each scan, including subsequence intercepting, interval sampling, and sequence inversion. Each training scan was randomly augmented to 40 sequences and regenerated at each epoch to further improve the model generalizability. Each test scan was randomly augmented to 10 fixed sequences to mimic complex real-world situations. The Adam optimizer is used to optimize the MoNet. In the training phase, the epoch and batch size are 200 and 1, respectively. The learning rate is 10^{-4} and is cut in half every 30 epochs. During the online learning phase, the iteration epoch and learning rate are 60 and 2×10^{-6}, respectively. All code was implemented in PyTorch and ran on a RTX 3090 GPU.

Table 1. The mean (std) results of different models on the arm and carotid scans. DCL: DCL-Net, Bk: Backbone. The best results are shown in blue.

Models	FDR(%)↓	ADR(%)↓	MD(mm)↓	SD(mm)↓	HD(mm)↓	EA(deg)↓
	Arm scans					
CNN [11]	31.84(18.35)	37.58(18.02)	27.31(19.34)	765.02(721.00)	26.45(19.42)	1.96(1.70)
DCL [2]	20.17(13.37)	26.05(15.57)	16.75(11.70)	476.67(440.90)	15.82(11.50)	2.78(2.93)
OLF [7]	15.00(13.09)	20.91(12.23)	12.69(8.30)	374.07(350.84)	11.92(8.02)	2.38(2.25)
Bk	16.42(14.24)	22.40(16.13)	13.10(10.15)	394.90(427.16)	11.92(9.22)	2.29(2.50)
Bk+IMU	14.05(10.36)	20.12(12.63)	11.56(7.54)	352.54(334.08)	10.76(7.20)	1.75(1.57)
MoNet	12.75(9.05)	19.05(11.46)	10.24(7.36)	332.29(316.36)	9.40(7.13)	1.55(1.46)
	Carotid scans					
CNN [11]	31.88(15.76)	39.71(14.88)	17.63(9.88)	493.71(449.95)	16.66(9.92)	2.31(1.79)
DCL [2]	24.66(12.11)	30.06(12.26)	13.43(7.30)	362.28(296.41)	12.79(7.44)	2.54(1.60)
OLF [7]	20.08(14.72)	29.21(14.99)	11.01(6.76)	326.91(317.36)	10.38(6.53)	2.59(1.58)
Bk	20.55(18.73)	30.74(19.09)	11.06(7.84)	318.38(306.10)	10.03(6.73)	2.61(1.72)
Bk+IMU	17.78(11.50)	27.47(13.05)	9.73(4.83)	285.99(239.24)	9.14(4.83)	2.18(1.43)
MoNet	15.67(8.37)	25.08(9.34)	8.89(4.31)	258.83(208.12)	8.28(4.29)	1.50(0.98)

Quantitative and Qualitative Analysis. To demonstrate the efficacy of our method, we performed the comparison with three SOTA approaches including CNN [11], DCL-Net [2], and OLF [7]. CNN used images, calculated optical flow and IMU Euler angles as input, whereas DCL-Net and OLF only used scanned images. Note that DCL-Net was modified to estimate the transformation parameters of adjacent images rather than the average parameters of several images to achieve better performance. Meanwhile, OLF's shape prior module was removed because muscles and vessels do not have prominent shape features. In this study, six criteria, including final drift rate (FDR), average drift rate (ADR), maximum drift (MD), sum of drift (SD), symmetric Hausdorff distance (HD), and mean error of angle (EA) are used to evaluate the performance (all criteria refer to [7] except EA). Furthermore, our ablation experiments compare Backbone (ResNet+LSTM), Backbone+IMU, and full MoNet (Backbone+IMU+Online) to validate the efficacy of IMU fusion and online learning strategy.

Table 1 shows that our MoNet outperforms previous approaches on all metrics significantly (*t*-test, $p < 0.05$) for both arm and carotid scans. We note that the CNN incorporating IMU Euler angles [11] outperforms other sensorless approaches [2,7] in terms of EA metric, verifying the effectiveness of IMU integration. However, the simple combination of CNN and IMU results in the lowest performance on other metrics. In addition, the OLF [7] and proposed MoNet outperform other methods [2,11] on most metrics, illustrating the importance of online learning. The ablation experiments further demonstrate that both IMU fusion and online learning strategy greatly improve the reconstruction accuracy.

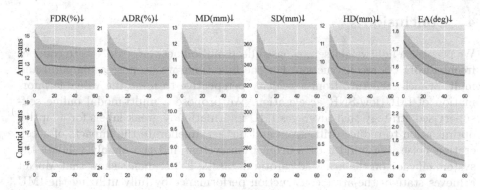

Fig. 4. Metric decline curves (with 95% confidence interval) for online learning strategy. The abscissa and ordinate represent the number of iterations and the value of metrics.

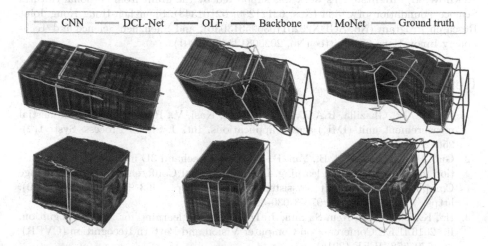

Fig. 5. Typical reconstruction cases on arm (Row I) and carotid (Row II) scans.

We further illustrate the metric decline curves when using online learning strategy in Fig. 4. For both arm and carotid, the online learning substantially reduces all metrics and the most significant reductions are 12.64% of HD (arm) and 31.19% of EA (carotid). This further demonstrates the efficacy of our proposed online learning strategy. Figure 5 visualizes six typical results to show the difference between our MoNet and other methods. It can be observed that our proposed MoNet achieves the closest reconstruction outcomes to ground truth compared to the Backbone or other methods.

4   Conclusion

We propose a lightweight sensor-based deep motion network (MoNet) to conduct freehand 3D US reconstruction. For the first time, we propose a temporal and multi-branch structure from a velocity perspective to mine the valuable information of IMU low-SNR acceleration. We propose a multi-modal online self-supervised strategy that leverages IMU information as weak labels for adaptive optimization to reduce drift errors and further ameliorate the impacts of acceleration noise. We build a data acquisition system and thoroughly validate the system efficacy on the arm and carotid datasets. Experiments show that MoNet achieves state-of-the-art reconstruction performance by fully utilizing the IMU information and deeply fusing it with image content. Future research will focus on extending this network to more anatomical structures.

Acknowledgements. This work was supported by the grant from National Natural Science Foundation of China (Nos. 62171290, 62101343), Shenzhen-Hong Kong Joint Research Program (No. SGDX20201103095613036), and Shenzhen Science and Technology Innovations Committee (No. 20200812143441001).

References

1. Ahmad, N., Ghazilla, R.A.R., Khairi, N.M., Kasi, V.: Reviews on various inertial measurement unit (IMU) sensor applications. Int. J. Signal Process. Syst. **1**(2), 256–262 (2013)
2. Guo, H., Xu, S., Wood, B., Yan, P.: Sensorless freehand 3D ultrasound reconstruction via deep contextual learning. In: International Conference on Medical Image Computing and Computer-Assisted Intervention, pp. 463–472. Springer (2020). https://doi.org/10.1007/978-3-030-59716-0_44
3. He, K., Zhang, X., Ren, S., Sun, J.: Deep residual learning for image recognition. In: 2016 IEEE Conference on Computer Vision and Pattern Recognition (CVPR), pp. 770–778. IEEE (2016)
4. Hochreiter, S., Schmidhuber, J.: Long short-term memory. Neural Comput. **9**(8), 1735–1780 (1997)
5. Huang, Q., Zeng, Z.: A review on real-time 3D ultrasound imaging technology. In: BioMed Research International 2017 (2017)
6. LeCun, Y., Bengio, Y., Hinton, G.: Deep learning. Nature **521**(7553), 436–444 (2015)
7. Luo, M., et al.: Self context and shape prior for sensorless freehand 3D ultrasound reconstruction. In: International Conference on Medical Image Computing and Computer-Assisted Intervention, pp. 201–210. Springer (2021). https://doi.org/10.1007/978-3-030-87231-1_20
8. Mercier, L., LangØ, T., Lindseth, F., Collins, D.L.: A review of calibration techniques for freehand 3-D ultrasound systems. Ultrasound Med. Biol. **31**, 449–471 (2005)
9. Mohamed, F., Siang, C.V.: A survey on 3D ultrasound reconstruction techniques. Artif. Intell.-Appl. Med. Biol. (2019)
10. Mozaffari, M.H., Lee, W.S.: Freehand 3-D ultrasound imaging: a systematic review. Ultrasound Med. Biol. **43**(10), 2099–2124 (2017)

11. Prevost, R., et al.: 3D freehand ultrasound without external tracking using deep learning. Med. Image Anal. **48**, 187–202 (2018)
12. Prevost, R., Salehi, M., Sprung, J., Ladikos, A., Bauer, R., Wein, W.: Deep learning for sensorless 3D freehand ultrasound imaging. In: International Conference on Medical Image Computing and Computer-Assisted Intervention, pp. 628–636. Springer (2017). https://doi.org/10.1007/978-3-319-66185-8_71
13. Tuthill, T.A., Krücker, J., Fowlkes, J.B., Carson, P.L.: Automated three-dimensional us frame positioning computed from elevational speckle decorrelation. Radiology **209**(2), 575–582 (1998)

Agent with Tangent-Based Formulation and Anatomical Perception for Standard Plane Localization in 3D Ultrasound

Yuxin Zou[1,2,3], Haoran Dou[4,5], Yuhao Huang[1,2,3], Xin Yang[1,2,3], Jikuan Qian[6], Chaojiong Zhen[7], Xiaodan Ji[7], Nishant Ravikumar[4,5], Guoqiang Chen[7], Weijun Huang[7], Alejandro F. Frangi[4,5,8,9], and Dong Ni[1,2,3(✉)]

[1] National-Regional Key Technology Engineering Laboratory
for Medical Ultrasound, School of Biomedical Engineering, Health Science Center,
Shenzhen University, Shenzhen, China
nidong@szu.edu.cn
[2] Medical Ultrasound Image Computing (MUSIC) Laboratory, Shenzhen University,
Shenzhen, China
[3] Marshall Laboratory of Biomedical Engineering,
Shenzhen University, Shenzhen, China
[4] Centre for Computational Imaging and Simulation Technologies in Biomedicine
(CISTIB), School of Computing, University of Leeds, Leeds, UK
[5] Biomedical Imaging Department, Leeds Institute for Cardiovascular and Metabolic
Medicine (LICAMM), School of Medicine, University of Leeds, Leeds, UK
[6] Shenzhen RayShape Medical Technology Co., Ltd., Shenzhen, China
[7] Department of Ultrasound, The First People's Hospital of Foshan, Foshan, China
[8] Departments of Cardiovascular Sciences and Electrical Engineering, KU Leuven,
Leuven, Belgium
[9] Alan Turing Institute, London, UK

Abstract. Standard plane (SP) localization is essential in routine clinical ultrasound (US) diagnosis. Compared to 2D US, 3D US can acquire multiple view planes in one scan and provide complete anatomy with the addition of coronal plane. However, manually navigating SPs in 3D US is laborious and biased due to the orientation variability and huge search space. In this study, we introduce a novel reinforcement learning (RL) framework for automatic SP localization in 3D US. Our contribution is three-fold. First, we formulate SP localization in 3D US as a tangent-point-based problem in RL to restructure the action space and significantly reduce the search space. Second, we design an auxiliary task learning strategy to enhance the model's ability to recognize subtle differences crossing Non-SPs and SPs in plane search. Finally, we propose a spatial-anatomical reward to effectively guide learning trajectories by exploiting spatial and anatomical information simultaneously. We explore the efficacy of our approach on localizing four SPs on uterus and fetal brain datasets. The experiments indicate that our approach achieves a high localization accuracy as well as robust performance.

Y. Zou and H. Dou—Contribute equally to this work.

Keywords: Reinforcement learning · Standard plane localization · Ultrasound

1 Introduction

Ultrasound (US) is the primary scanning method in routine diagnosis due to its lack of radiation, real-time imaging, low cost and high mobility [2]. As the preliminary step in US diagnosis, acquiring standard plane (SP) provides anatomical content for subsequent bio-marker measurement and abnormal diagnosis. Compared with the 2D US, 3D US shows natural superiority in acquiring multiple view planes via a single scan and providing complete and fruitful 3D information [4]. Furthermore, 3D US enables the sonographer to obtain additional SP that is unavailable using the 2D US owing to bony pelvis [15], e.g., the coronal plane of the uterus, which is important for assessing uterine abnormalities. However, manually localizing SP is laborious and biased due to the huge search space and orientation variability of 3D US. The internal invisibility of US volume makes it further difficult for sonographers to search the vast 3D space. Hence, developing an automatic approach for localizing SP in 3D US is highly desirable to relieve the burden of sonographers and reduce operator dependency.

Regression of plane parameters or transformation matrix is a common strategy for 3D SP localization [3,10,12,19]. Chykeyuk et al. [3] proposed a random forest method to regress plane parameters in 3D echocardiography. Li et al. [10] introduced a deep neural network to localize fetal brain planes by computing transformation matrix iteratively. Lorenz et al. [12] proposed to extract the abdomen plane through anatomical landmark detection and align them to a fetal organ model. Most recently, Yeung et al. [19] designed an annotation-efficient approach to learn the mapping between the 2D images and 3D space in US. However, all aforementioned methods are limited by the difficulty in optimizing a highly abstract mapping function [18].

Recently, reinforcement learning (RL) shows great potential in addressing the SP localization problem by its specific reward mechanism and interactive planning [1]. Dou et al. [4,17] first proposed the RL-based framework for localizing SP in 3D US. They designed a registration-based warm-up strategy to address the large orientation variability of US volume and provide effective initialization for the agent in RL. In their follow-up work [18], they embedded neural network searching in the RL optimization and designed a multi-agent collaborative system for multi-SP navigation. Motivated by [4,17], several works [8,9] employed the RL to achieve autonomous navigation of US probe towards SP. Although these approaches achieved high performance in SP localization, several issues are still required to be addressed. First, current studies [4,17,18] rely on initial registration to ensure data orientation consistency. They are easily trapped when pre-registration fails. Second, most studies [1,4,17,18] designed an eight-dimensional action space in terms of angle and distance, where the coupling among the directional cosines in the formula and the huge search space make the optimization difficult. Third, existing RL systems [1,4,17,18] are only driven by the plane-movement-based reward function, lacking the perception and guidance of anatomical structures.

To address the outstanding issues mentioned above, we introduce a novel RL-based framework for automatic SP localization in 3D US. In particular, we define a new tangent-point-based plane formulation in RL to restructure the action space and significantly reduce the search space; we design an auxiliary task learning strategy to enhance the model's ability to recognize subtle differences crossing Non-SPs and SPs in plane search; we propose a spatial-anatomical reward to effectively guide learning trajectories by exploiting spatial and anatomical information simultaneously.

2   Method

As shown in Fig. 1, our proposed SP localization framework is based on RL, where the *agent* (neural network) interacts with the *environment* (3D US Volume) to learn an optimal SP searching policy with the maximum accumulated *reward*. Additionally, we equip the RL framework with an auxiliary task to predict the similarity of the current state and target state, thus boosting the model's recognition ability. An imitation learning module is leveraged to initialize the agent in RL framework for speeding up the optimization.

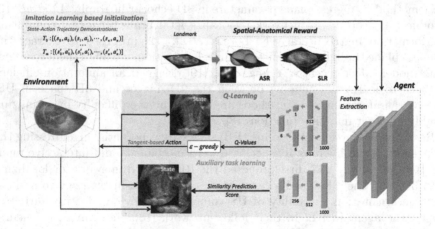

Fig. 1. Overview of the proposed SP localization framework. SLR: spatial location reward; ASR: anatomical structure reward.

2.1   Reinforcement Learning for Plane Localization

Formulation of the SP localization is essential for optimizing the RL framework. Previous works [1,4,17,18] modeled the plane movement by adjusting the plane function in terms of normal and distance (see Fig. 2). However, the coupling among the directional cosines $(cos^2(\alpha) + cos^2(\beta) + cos^2(\gamma) = 1)$ makes actions

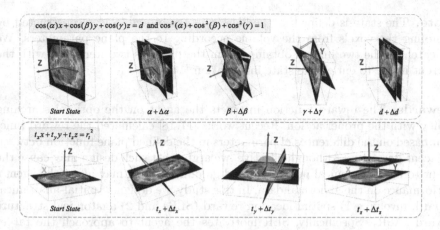

Fig. 2. Comparison of our formulation (bottom) and previous one (top). Previous formulation controls the plane movement by adjusting directional cosines (α, β, γ) and the distance to the origin (d). Instead, our design modifies the plane movement by translating the coordinate (t_x, t_y, t_z) of the tangent point.

dependent and unable to reflect the model's objective accurately, resulting in obstacles to agent learning. Furthermore, the RL training can easily fail without the pre-registration processing [4] to limit orientation variability and search space [17]. This study proposes a novel tangent-point-based formulation for SP localization in RL. Our formulation builds a simplified and mutual-independent action space to improve the optimization of the RL framework, enabling accurate SP localization even within the unaligned US environment. Figure 2 illustrates the comparison of our formulation and that of previous works. We discovered that any view plane in the 3D space can be defined uniquely as its tangent point (t_x, t_y, t_z) on the sphere centering in the origin with the radius of r_t, where $r_t^2 = t_x^2 + t_y^2 + t_z^2$. The plane function can be written as $t_x x + t_y y + t_z z = r_t^2$. Therefore, SP localization can be re-formulated into the tangent point searching task, where the action space only contains the translation of the coordinate of the tangent point. The proposed formulation is unrestricted by directional cosines coupling with less action space than the previous ones $(6 < 8)$, facilitating agent learning. We explain the details of the elements in the RL here.

Action. The action space is defined as $\{\pm a_{t_x}, \pm a_{t_y}, \pm a_{t_z}\}$ based on our formulation. Given an action in step i, the tangent point coordinate can be modified accordingly, e.g. $t_x^{i+1} = t_x^i + a_{t_x}$. We noticed experimentally that the image content is sensitive to the step size when the corresponding sphere radius is small. To address this issue, we model the agent-environment interaction as a multi-stage motion process by progressively scaling down the step size from 1.0 to 0.01 when the agent appears to oscillate for three steps. We terminate the agent searching at 60 steps.

State. The state is defined as the 2D US image of size 224^2 reconstructed by sampling the voxels from the volume according to the plane parameters. We concatenate the two images obtained from the previous two iterations with the current image to enrich the state information [14].

Rewards. The reward function instructs the agent on the optimal searching policy with the proper action. Recent works [17,18] calculated the reward function based on the differences of parameters in the defined plane function between adjacent iterations. Although effective, we argue that such design may cause the agent to lack anatomical perception and guidance, which may affect the agent's performance on the abnormal data. In this study, we design a spatial-anatomical reward, involving 1) spatial location reward (SLR) and 2) anatomical structure reward (ASR). Specifically, SLR motivates the agent to approach the target location by minimizing the Euclidean distance of the plane parameters between the current plane and target plane, while ASR encourages the agent to perceive anatomical information. We construct the heatmap with a Gaussian kernel at anatomical landmarks (see Fig. 1) to calculate the ASR. The reward can be defined as:

$$r = sgn(\| P_{t-1} - P_g \|_2 - \| P_t - P_g \|_2) + sgn(\mid I_t - I_g \mid - \mid I_{t-1} - I_g \mid) \quad (1)$$

where $sgn(\cdot)$ is the sign function, P_t and P_g indicate the tangent point parameters of the prediction plane and the target plane, respectively. Likewise, I_t and I_g represent the sum of the heatmap value corresponding to the prediction plane and the target plane, respectively.

Loss Function. Similar to [17,18], we perform the dueling Q-learning [16] to train the agent. Given the prioritized replay buffer $\mathcal{M}$, which stores the transitions of each step, including state s, action a, reward r, and next state s', the loss function for the Q-learning part of our framework can be defined as:

$$\mathcal{L}_Q(\omega) = \mathbb{E}_{s,r,a,s' \sim U(\mathcal{M})}(r + \gamma Q_{target}(s', \underset{a'}{argmax}\, Q(s', a'; \omega); \omega') - Q(s, a; \omega))^2 \quad (2)$$

where γ is the discount factor that balances the importance of current and future rewards. s, s' a and a' are the state and action in the current/next step. In this study, the current and target Q-network share the same network architecture (i.e. ResNet [5]), and w and w' are their parameters. During training, the target Q-network copied the parameters of the current Q-network every 1800 steps.

2.2 Auxiliary Task of State-Content Similarity Prediction

Localizing SPs in 3D US is challenging due to the low inter-class variability between SPs and non-SPs in the searching procedure and high intra-class variability of SPs. Most approaches [10,17,18] lack the proper strategy to use the image-level content information (e.g., anatomical priors), resulting in inefficient data utilization and agent learning. Auxiliary tasks for RL [7,13] could improve learning efficiency and boost the performance by learning the fine-grained representations. To facilitate the agent to learn the content representations, we design an auxiliary task of state-content similarity prediction (SCSP). As shown in Fig. 1, we utilize an additional regression branch in the agent network to predict the similarity of the current state to the target state. The content similarity is measured by normalized cross-correlation (NCC) [20]. The loss function for the auxiliary task part of our framework is defined as:

$$\mathcal{L}_A(\omega) = \mathbb{E}_{s \sim U(\mathcal{M})} \parallel Score_{gt}(s, s_{gt}) - Score_{pre}(s; \omega) \parallel_2 \qquad (3)$$

where $Score_{gt}(s, s_{gt})$ is the NCC between the current state s and the target state s_{gt}; $Score_{pre}(s; \omega)$ is the NCC score predicted by SCSP. Overall, the total loss function of our proposed RL framework is $\mathcal{L} = \mathcal{L}_Q + \delta \mathcal{L}_A$, where $\delta = 0.5$ is the weight to balance the importance of Q-learning loss and auxiliary task loss.

2.3   Imitation Learning Based Initialization

It is difficult for the agent to obtain effective samples during interacting with the unaligned US environment because the replay buffer will store a number of futile data during the agent exploring the 3D space. It might reduce the agent learning efficiency even harm the performance. [6] pointed out that imitation learning could effectively address this issue by pre-training the agent to ensure it could gain enough knowledge before exploring the environment, thus boosting the learning efficiency. Therefore, we adopt imitation learning as an initialization of the agent. Specifically, we first randomly select 20 initial tangent points in each training data and then approach the target plane by taking the optimal action in terms of the distance to the target tangent point. This can imitate the expert's operation and obtain a number of effective demonstrated state-action trajectories (e.g., $(s_0, a_0), (s_1, a_1), \ldots, (s_n, a_n)$). After that, we perform the supervised learning with the cross-entropy loss on the agent based on the randomly sampled state-action pair. With a well-trained agent based on imitation learning initialization, the learning of the RL framework can be eased and accelerated.

3   Experimental Result

3.1   Materials and Implementation Details

We validated our proposed method on four SPs in two datasets, including the coronal (C) plane in the uterus and the trans-ventricular (TV), trans-thalamic (TT), and trans-cerebellar (TC) plane in the fetal brain. The uterus dataset has 363 normal patients and 45 abnormal patients (Congenital Uterine Anomalies, CUAs) with an average volume size of $432 \times 377 \times 217$ and spacing of $0.3 \times 0.3 \times 0.3$ mm^3; the fetal brain dataset has 432 patients with an average volume size of $270 \times 207 \times 235$ and spacing of $0.5 \times 0.5 \times 0.5$ mm^3. Six experienced sonographers manually annotated SPs and landmarks using the Pair annotation software package [11] under strict quality control. We randomly split each dataset

Table 1. Quantitative comparison of different methods on SP localization. C_N and C_P mean the coronal plane of normal and abnormal uteruses, respectively. (mean $\pm$ std)

Metrics		Methods					
		RG_{single}	RG_{ITN}	$Regist$	RL_{AVP}	RL_{WSADT}	RL_{Ours}
C_N	Ang($°$)	16.24 $\pm$ 9.72	29.61 $\pm$ 24.49	15.77 $\pm$ 14.34	49.15 $\pm$ 13.26	15.71 $\pm$ 14.99	**10.36 $\pm$ 11.92**
	Dis(mm)	2.48 $\pm$ 2.07	**0.83 $\pm$ 0.75**	1.94 $\pm$ 1.90	2.86 $\pm$ 2.10	1.83 $\pm$ 1.91	0.88 $\pm$ 0.84
	SSIM	0.10 $\pm$ 0.07	0.55 $\pm$ 0.11	0.46 $\pm$ 0.10	0.28 $\pm$ 0.06	0.48 $\pm$ 0.12	**0.61 $\pm$ 0.19**
	NCC	0.51 $\pm$ 0.17	0.64 $\pm$ 0.16	0.69 $\pm$ 0.14	0.36 $\pm$ 0.16	0.70 $\pm$ 0.16	**0.74 $\pm$ 0.18**
C_P	Ang($°$)	16.25 $\pm$ 8.16	29.98 $\pm$ 25.67	21.79 $\pm$ 19.30	52.58 $\pm$ 13.07	21.22 $\pm$ 19.20	**11.90 $\pm$ 5.78**
	Dis(mm)	2.88 $\pm$ 2.37	1.50 $\pm$ 1.26	2.64 $\pm$ 2.57	4.30 $\pm$ 2.67	2.76 $\pm$ 2.53	**1.48 $\pm$ 1.35**
	SSIM	0.09 $\pm$ 0.08	0.51 $\pm$ 0.12	0.41 $\pm$ 0.10	0.27 $\pm$ 0.06	0.41 $\pm$ 0.11	**0.52 $\pm$ 0.14**
	NCC	0.49 $\pm$ 0.18	0.58 $\pm$ 0.17	0.61 $\pm$ 0.17	0.30 $\pm$ 0.19	0.61 $\pm$ 0.17	**0.62 $\pm$ 0.20**
TT	Ang($°$)	30.46 $\pm$ 21.05	21.15 $\pm$ 20.46	14.37 $\pm$ 13.42	54.05 $\pm$ 15.35	**10.48 $\pm$ 5.80**	10.89 $\pm$ 7.70
	Dis(mm)	3.53 $\pm$ 2.19	0.94 $\pm$ 0.75	2.12 $\pm$ 1.42	4.34 $\pm$ 2.97	2.02 $\pm$ 1.33	**0.80 $\pm$ 0.93**
	SSIM	0.58 $\pm$ 0.14	0.85 $\pm$ 0.05	0.83 $\pm$ 0.09	0.64 $\pm$ 0.06	0.78 $\pm$ 0.06	**0.92 $\pm$ 0.06**
	NCC	0.51 $\pm$ 0.27	0.57 $\pm$ 0.17	**0.83 $\pm$ 0.13**	0.44 $\pm$ 0.10	0.78 $\pm$ 0.14	0.78 $\pm$ 0.22
TV	Ang($°$)	38.78 $\pm$ 25.40	26.80 $\pm$ 25.55	13.40 $\pm$ 4.68	53.77 $\pm$ 14.58	10.39 $\pm$ 4.03	**8.65 $\pm$ 7.10**
	Dis(mm)	7.44 $\pm$ 5.99	1.43 $\pm$ 0.98	2.68 $\pm$ 1.58	4.27 $\pm$ 2.73	2.48 $\pm$ 1.27	**1.16 $\pm$ 2.45**
	SSIM	0.58 $\pm$ 0.11	0.85 $\pm$ 0.05	0.71 $\pm$ 0.11	0.64 $\pm$ 0.06	0.66 $\pm$ 0.14	**0.92 $\pm$ 0.06**
	NCC	0.53 $\pm$ 0.18	0.56 $\pm$ 0.16	0.56 $\pm$ 0.27	0.43 $\pm$ 0.11	0.57 $\pm$ 0.28	**0.78 $\pm$ 0.25**
TC	Ang($°$)	33.08 $\pm$ 21.18	27.21 $\pm$ 23.83	16.24 $\pm$ 13.57	52.70 $\pm$ 16.03	10.26 $\pm$ 7.25	**9.75 $\pm$ 8.45**
	Dis(mm)	3.82 $\pm$ 3.30	1.26 $\pm$ 1.06	3.47 $\pm$ 2.39	4.20 $\pm$ 2.65	2.52 $\pm$ 2.13	**0.88 $\pm$ 1.15**
	SSIM	0.59 $\pm$ 0.13	0.84 $\pm$ 0.05	0.68 $\pm$ 0.18	0.64 $\pm$ 0.07	0.64 $\pm$ 0.14	**0.88 $\pm$ 0.09**
	NCC	0.56 $\pm$ 0.22	0.55 $\pm$ 0.16	0.55 $\pm$ 0.29	0.45 $\pm$ 0.12	0.55 $\pm$ 0.30	**0.69 $\pm$ 0.25**

Table 2. Ablation study for analyzing SCSP and ASR.

Strategy		C_N				C_P			
SCSP	ASR	Ang(o)↓	Dis(mm)↓	SSIM↑	NCC↑	Ang(o)↓	Dis(mm)↓	SSIM↑	NCC↑
✗	✗	14.11 $\pm$ 11.08	0.91 $\pm$ 0.87	0.57 $\pm$ 0.17	0.69 $\pm$ 0.17	15.57 $\pm$ 10.95	1.45 $\pm$ 1.25	0.51 $\pm$ 0.14	0.59 $\pm$ 0.17
✓	✗	11.83 $\pm$ 13.54	0.84 $\pm$ 0.74	0.58 $\pm$ 0.18	0.70 $\pm$ 0.19	13.80 $\pm$ 9.13	1.63 $\pm$ 1.61	0.52 $\pm$ 0.14	0.59 $\pm$ 0.22
✗	✓	12.72 $\pm$ 10.78	**0.80 $\pm$ 0.72**	0.59 $\pm$ 0.16	0.70 $\pm$ 0.17	14.09 $\pm$ 7.89	**1.27 $\pm$ 1.07**	0.51 $\pm$ 0.14	0.59 $\pm$ 0.20
✓	✓	**10.36 $\pm$ 11.92**	0.88 $\pm$ 0.84	**0.61 $\pm$ 0.19**	**0.74 $\pm$ 0.18**	**11.90 $\pm$ 5.78**	1.48 $\pm$ 1.35	**0.52 $\pm$ 0.13**	**0.62 $\pm$ 0.20**

for training, validating, testing of 290, 20, 53 in the uterus, and 330, 30, 72 in the fetal brain, respectively. To verify the generalizability of our method, we only involve the healthy subjects in our training dataset and test the 45 CUAs patients independently.

In this study, we implemented our method by PyTorch using a standard PC with an NVIDIA RTX 2080Ti GPU. We trained the model through Adam optimizer with a learning rate of 5e−5 and a batch size of 32 for 100 epochs. The discount factor γ in Eq. 2 was set as 0.85. The size of the prioritized Replay Buffer was set as 15000. The $\epsilon - greedy$ exploration strategy was set according to [17]. We calculated the mean (μ) and standard deviation (σ) of target tangent point locations in the training dataset and randomly initialized start points for training within $\mu \pm 2\sigma$ to capture 95% variability approximately. For testing, the origin was set as the initial tangent point.

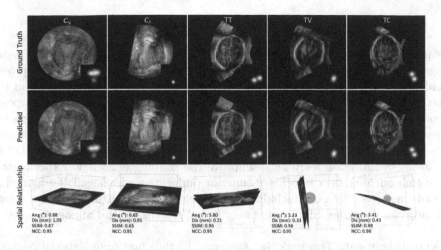

Fig. 3. Visual example results of our methods. The first row shows the ground truth of five SPs; the second row shows the predicted plane with its landmark heatmap in the Lower right corner; the third row shows the 3D spatial relationship between ground truth (red) and prediction (green). (Color figure online)

3.2   Quantitative and Qualitative Analysis

To demonstrate the efficacy of our proposed method, we performed the comparison with five SOTA approaches including regression-based, (i.e., RG_{Single}, RG_{ITN} [10]), registration-based (i.e., $Regist$ [4]), and RL-based methods (i.e., RL_{AVP} [1], RL_{WSADT} [17]). Four criteria, including the spatial metrics (angle and distance between two planes, Ang & Dis) and content metrics (Structural Similarity Index and Normalized Cross-correlation, SSIM & NCC), were used to evaluate the performance.

As shown in Table 1, our proposed method outperforms all of the others on most of the metrics, indicating the superior ability of our method in SP localization tasks. Specifically, we can observe that RL gains large boosting in performance through pre-registration to ensure orientation consistency (RL_{AVP} vs. RL_{WSADT}). In comparison, our new formulation could enable the RL algorithm to achieve superiority even without pre-registration. Additionally, prior RL-based methods fail easily in the abnormal dataset (RL_{WSADT} in C_P). On the contrary, our method obtains consistent performance on both normal and abnormal datasets. Table 2 shows the results of the ablation study to investigate the impact of each designed module. It can be observed that SCSP improves the generalizability of the model by enhancing the recognition of the SPs and non-SPs. It is beneficial to compose ASR with the basic reward SLR to boost agents' perception of anatomical structures, which enables our model to generalize external abnormal uterus dataset having significant content differences with the normal one. Visual illustration of the results of our method in Fig. 3 also shows the extent of the SP localization performance associated with the quantitative measures reported in Table 1.

4   Conclusion

We proposed a novel RL framework for SP localization in 3D US. We define a tangent-point-based plane formulation to restructure action space and improve agent optimization within unaligned US environment. This formulation can be extended to similar tasks in other modalities, e.g., CT or MRI. We propose a content-aware regression auxiliary task to improve the agent's robustness to noisy US environment. In addition, we design a spatial-anatomical reward to provide both spatial and anatomical knowledge for the agent. Moreover, we initialize the agent by imitation learning to improve the training efficiency. Experiments show that our method can achieve superior performance for localizing four SPs in two unaligned datasets including abnormal cases, which indicates its great potential for localizing SPs in randomly initialized spaces and abnormal cases.

Acknowledgement. This work was supported by the grant from National Natural Science Foundation of China (Nos. 62171290, 62101343), Shenzhen-Hong Kong Joint Research Program (No. SGDX20201103095613036), Shenzhen Science and Technology Innovations Committee (No. 20200812143441001), the Royal Academy of Engineering (INSILEX CiET1819/19), the Royal Society Exchange Programme CROSSLINK IES\NSFC\201380, and Engineering and Physical Sciences Research Council (EPSRC) programs TUSCA EP/V04799X/1.

References

1. Alansary, A., et al.: Automatic view planning with multi-scale deep reinforcement learning agents. In: Frangi, A.F., Schnabel, J.A., Davatzikos, C., Alberola-López, C., Fichtinger, G. (eds.) MICCAI 2018. LNCS, vol. 11070, pp. 277–285. Springer, Cham (2018). https://doi.org/10.1007/978-3-030-00928-1_32
2. Beyer, T., et al.: What scans we will read: imaging instrumentation trends in clinical oncology. Cancer Imaging **20**(1), 1–38 (2020)
3. Chykeyuk, K., Yaqub, M., Noble, J.A.: Class-specific regression random forest for accurate extraction of standard planes from 3D echocardiography. In: International MICCAI Workshop on Medical Computer Vision, pp. 53–62. Springer (2013). https://doi.org/10.1007/978-3-319-05530-5_6
4. Dou, H., et al.: Agent with warm start and active termination for plane localization in 3D ultrasound. In: International Conference on Medical Image Computing and Computer-Assisted Intervention, pp. 290–298. Springer (2019). https://doi.org/10.1007/978-3-030-32254-0_33
5. He, K., Zhang, X., Ren, S., Sun, J.: Deep residual learning for image recognition. In: Proceedings of the IEEE Conference on Computer Vision and Pattern Recognition, pp. 770–778 (2016)
6. Hester, T., et al.: Deep q-learning from demonstrations. In: Proceedings of the AAAI Conference on Artificial Intelligence, vol. 32 (2018)
7. Jaderberg, M., et al.: Reinforcement learning with unsupervised auxiliary tasks. arXiv preprint arXiv:1611.05397 (2016)
8. Li, K., et al.: Autonomous navigation of an ultrasound probe towards standard scan planes with deep reinforcement learning. In: 2021 IEEE International Conference on Robotics and Automation (ICRA), pp. 8302–8308. IEEE (2021)

9. Li, K., Xu, Y., Wang, J., Ni, D., Liu, L., Meng, M.Q.H.: Image-guided navigation of a robotic ultrasound probe for autonomous spinal sonography using a shadow-aware dual-agent framework. IEEE Trans. Med. Robot. Bionics **4**, 130–144 (2021)
10. Li, Y., Khanal, B., Hou, B., Alansary, A., et al.: Standard plane detection in 3D fetal ultrasound using an iterative transformation network. In: International MICCAI Workshop on Medical Computer Vision, pp. 392–400. Springer (2018). https://doi.org/10.1007/978-3-030-00928-1_45
11. Liang, J., et al.: Sketch guided and progressive growing GAN for realistic and editable ultrasound image synthesis. Med. Image Anal. **79**, 102461 (2022)
12. Lorenz, C., et al.: Automated abdominal plane and circumference estimation in 3D us for fetal screening. In: Medical Imaging 2018: Image Processing, vol. 10574, p. 105740I. International Society for Optics and Photonics (2018)
13. Mirowski, P., et al.: Learning to navigate in complex environments. arXiv preprint arXiv:1611.03673 (2016)
14. Mnih, V., et al.: Human-level control through deep reinforcement learning. Nature **518**(7540), 529–533 (2015)
15. Turkgeldi, E., Urman, B., Ata, B.: Role of three-dimensional ultrasound in gynecology. J. Obstetr. Gynecol. India **65**(3), 146–154 (2015)
16. Wang, Z., Schaul, T., Hessel, M., Hasselt, H., Lanctot, M., Freitas, N.: Dueling network architectures for deep reinforcement learning. In: International Conference on Machine Learning, pp. 1995–2003. PMLR (2016)
17. Yang, X., et al.: Agent with warm start and adaptive dynamic termination for plane localization in 3D ultrasound. IEEE Trans. Med. Imaging **40**, 1950–1961 (2021)
18. Yang, X., et al.: Searching collaborative agents for multi-plane localization in 3D ultrasound. Med. Image Anal. **72**, 102119 (2021)
19. Yeung, P.H., Aliasi, M., Papageorghiou, A.T., Haak, M., Xie, W., Namburete, A.I.: Learning to map 2D ultrasound images into 3D space with minimal human annotation. Med. Image Anal. **70**, 101998 (2021)
20. Yoo, J.C., Han, T.H.: Fast normalized cross-correlation. Circ. Syst. Sig. Process. **28**(6), 819–843 (2009)

Weakly-Supervised High-Fidelity Ultrasound Video Synthesis with Feature Decoupling

Jiamin Liang[1,2,3], Xin Yang[1,2,3], Yuhao Huang[1,2,3], Kai Liu[1,2,3],
Xinrui Zhou[1,2,3], Xindi Hu[4], Zehui Lin[4], Huanjia Luo[5], Yuanji Zhang[6],
Yi Xiong[6], and Dong Ni[1,2,3(✉)]

[1] National-Regional Key Technology Engineering Laboratory for Medical
Ultrasound, School of Biomedical Engineering, Health Science Center,
Shenzhen University, Shenzhen, China
nidong@szu.edu.cn
[2] Medical Ultrasound Image Computing (MUSIC) Laboratory,
Shenzhen University, Shenzhen, China
[3] Marshall Laboratory of Biomedical Engineering, Shenzhen University,
Shenzhen, China
[4] Shenzhen RayShape Medical Technology Co., Ltd, Shenzhen, China
[5] Huizhou Central People's Hospital, Huizhou, Guangdong, China
[6] Department of Ultrasound, Luohu People's Hospital, Shenzhen, China

Abstract. Ultrasound (US) is widely used for its advantages of real-time imaging, radiation-free and portability. In clinical practice, analysis and diagnosis often rely on US sequences rather than a single image to obtain dynamic anatomical information. This is challenging for novices to learn because practicing with adequate videos from patients is clinically unpractical. In this paper, we propose a novel framework to synthesize high-fidelity US videos. Specifically, the synthesis videos are generated by animating source content images based on the motion of given driving videos. Our highlights are three-fold. First, leveraging the advantages of self- and fully-supervised learning, our proposed system is trained in weakly-supervised manner for keypoint detection. These keypoints then provide vital information for handling complex high dynamic motions in US videos. Second, we decouple content and texture learning using the dual decoders to effectively reduce the model learning difficulty. Last, we adopt the adversarial training strategy with GAN losses for further improving the sharpness of the generated videos, narrowing the gap between real and synthesis videos. We validate our method on a large in-house pelvic dataset with high dynamic motion. Extensive evaluation metrics and user study prove the effectiveness of our proposed method.

1 Introduction

Ultrasound (US) videos can provide more diagnostic information flow compared to static images, thus being popular in various clinical scenarios. Sonographers

---

J. Liang and X. Yang—Contribute equally to this work.

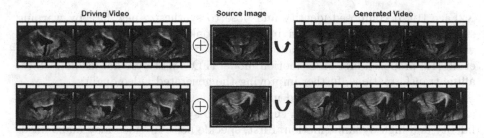

Fig. 1. Our task is to transfer the motion from the driving video to the static source image, thus obtaining the generated US video.

require to learn through abundant US video scans for gaining experiences and improving diagnostic ability. However, acquisition of plenty of US sequences with teaching and diagnostic significance is unpractical in clinic. Specifically, scanning high-quality US videos including numerous frames is time-consuming, also, operator- and device-dependent. Besides, some positive cases and rare diseases have a limited amount in clinical practice, which results in their collecting difficulties. Hence, synthesizing US videos with high fidelity and dynamic motion is highly desirable to assist in clinical training.

In the related studies, lots of generative adversarial network (GAN) [1] based approaches have been explored to synthesize medical images [3,7,13]. Though synthesizing realistic images, these methods focus on image-level static information, without considering information flow between frames, and thus cannot be directly used in video synthesis task. To date, several video-based synthesis methods have been proposed, and they can be roughly classified into two types.

Unconditional Video Synthesis (UVS). Most UVS methods took random noise as input and learned both content and motion information with high complexity. The most common UVS approaches set different vectors for learning image content and motion, respectively [10,14,16]. However, due to the lack of informative driving signals, a large degree of distortion may occur as generated frames increase or motions get complex. Thus, these methods cannot handle the long-time or large-movement-range video generations.

Conditional Video Synthesis (CVS). Compared to UVS, CVS took additional content or motion as input, thus improving the synthesis quality. Realistic face video simulation based on 3D face model is one focus of CVS research [21]. Then, inspired by the image-to-image translation framework, a video-to-video system using large-scale data and paired segmentation maps was proposed to synthesize high-resolution and temporally consistent videos [17]. These methods depend on strong priors or annotations, which limits their applicability in medical, especially US, video synthesis tasks. Most recently, some annotation-free methods were proposed to transfer motions among images by taking static source images and driving videos as the *condition*. Specifically, source image and driving video were used as appearance and action information, respectively.

X2Face [19] decomposed identity and pose to synthesize new face by warping static images according to the driving video. Monkey-Net [11] employed unsupervised learning to detect sparse motion-specific keypoints. Following [11], Siarohin et al. [12] proposed first order motion model (FOMM) to predict keypoint local affine transformations, further improving the generated video quality.

Though the above-mentioned methods have been validated on human pose and face datasets, they are still challenging to synthesize US videos with high fidelity and high dynamic motion. First, speckle noise in video may make unsupervised models fail in perceiving anatomical areas, thus causing severe image distortion. Moreover, US videos usually contain structures of varying size or intensity representation, and patient movements cannot be strictly controlled during US scanning. This will result in very complex and uncertain motion trajectories, making model learning difficult.

In this paper, we propose a novel framework for high-fidelity US video synthesis. The proposed framework animates static source images for video generation by extracting motion information from given driving videos (see Fig. 1). We believe the proposed framework is the first US video synthesis system. Our contributions are three-fold. First, we leverage weakly-supervised learning to predict the keypoints, thus capturing the complex high dynamic motions in US videos. Note that we only need few keypoint annotations during training, and the rest can be learned by the model automatically. Second, we carefully design a two-branch architecture to learn content and texture separately, thus simplifying model optimization. Last, we adopt adversarial learning and GAN losses to further enhance the sharpness of generated frames. Validation experiments and user study demonstrate the efficacy of the proposed framework.

2   Methodology

Figure 2 shows our proposed framework for high-fidelity US video synthesis. Our task is to animate the static source image (**S**) via the motion information provided by the driving video (**D**). In our proposed system, we first train a keypoint detector to predict the points and their affine transformations in weakly-supervised manner. Second, a motion prediction network is equipped for estimating the deformation and occlusion maps. Last, a generator with dual-branch decoder and a discriminator are introduced for high-frequency information learning, thus ensuring high-quality video generation.

2.1   Weakly-Supervised Training for Motion Estimation

The locations of keypoints reflect the relative motion relationship between frames, and thus detecting them can help the model learn the motion transformation. In this study, based on the pure self-supervised keypoint detection [12], we further add several supervised keypoints for providing vital anatomical information to benefit the model learning. Hence, the training of keypoint detection is

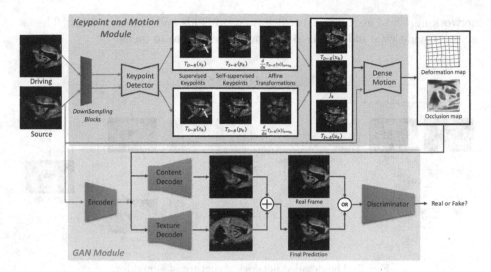

Fig. 2. Our proposed framework. In the *supervised keypoints*, red (left) and yellow (right) arrows indicate the lower edge of the symphysis and the bladder neck. (Color figure online)

considered as weakly-supervised learning. Specifically, as shown in Fig. 2, the keypoint detector uses source and driving frames as input, and locates the keypoints in two ways. The one way is to learn the keypoints in an self-supervised way through the Thin Plate Splines (TPS) deformations (refer to [12]). Another way is to detect the anatomical points with manual annotation in a fully-supervised manner. Besides, the affine transformations are also predicted by the detector to provide first-order motion information ($\frac{d}{du}$ in Fig. 2) of each detected keypoint. Similar to FOMM [12], giving the transformations ($\frac{d}{du}$ in Fig. 2) considering the assumed reference frame $\mathbf{R}$, the Jacobian matrix (J_k) can be obtained to help predict motions between $\mathbf{S}$ and $\mathbf{D}$. u_k is the coordinates of k_{th} keypoint.

For self-supervised keypoints learning, the equivariance losses $\mathcal{L}_{\mathrm{eq}}$ in terms of displacements and affine transformations are calculated as Eq. 1 and Eq. 2.

$$\mathcal{L}_{\mathrm{eq1}} = \|T_{\mathbf{X}\leftarrow\mathbf{R}}\,(p_k) - T_{\mathbf{X}\leftarrow\mathbf{Y}} \circ T_{\mathbf{Y}\leftarrow\mathbf{R}}\,(p_k)\|_1 , \tag{1}$$

$$\mathcal{L}_{\mathrm{eq2}} = \left\| 1 - \left(T'_{\mathbf{X}\leftarrow\mathbf{R}}(p)\big|_{p=p_k} \right)^{-1} \left(T'_{\mathbf{X}\leftarrow\mathbf{Y}}(p)\big|_{p=T_{\mathbf{Y}\leftarrow\mathbf{R}}(p_k)} \right) \left(T'_{\mathbf{Y}\leftarrow\mathbf{R}}(p)\big|_{p=p_k} \right) \right\|_1 , \tag{2}$$

$$\mathcal{L}_{\mathrm{eq}} = \mathcal{L}_{\mathrm{eq1}} + \mathcal{L}_{\mathrm{eq2}}, \tag{3}$$

where X and Y denote the driving/source frames, and the frames after TPS transformation of X. p_k denotes the k_{th} coordinates of the self-supervised points.

For supervised part, we use the L2 loss to constrain the differences between true and predicted heatmaps, which can be calculated by:

$$\mathcal{L}_{\mathrm{key}} = \|T_{\mathbf{X}\leftarrow\mathbf{R}}\,(s_k) - Heatmap\,(s_k)\|_2, \tag{4}$$

where s_k denotes the k_{th} coordinates of the supervised keypoint. Then, taking the source image and output of keypoint detector as input, we use the dense motion network in [12] to learn the dense deformation fields and occlusion maps. Theses maps provide vital indication to tell the model where to focus.

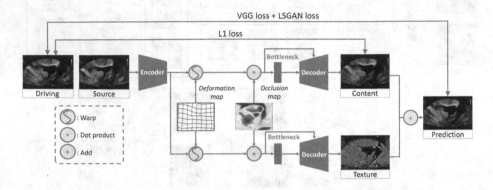

Fig. 3. The detailed network structure of generator.

2.2   Dual-Decoder Generator for Content and Texture Decoupling

Content and texture are the two vital elements that may influence the visual quality of frame/video. Most previous studies, taking deformation and occlusion maps as input, adopted a unified path for simultaneously learning content and high-frequency texture. This architecture design requires the model to decode the highly-coupled features, which may easily cause high-frequency information (i.e., texture) loss, and thus resulting blurry videos. Besides, the lower-size maps may further aggravate this problem in the upsampling stage. In this study, we propose a dual-decoder architecture to decouple the content and texture learning, thus reducing the learning difficulty of the network effectively.

Figure 3 presents the structure of generator. The inputs are the source image, and deformation&occlusion maps predicted by the dense motion network. The intermediate features are then fed to each upsampling layer of the decoder to strengthen the learning of the deformation information, i.e., the two maps. The final prediction image is obtained by adding the pixel values of the content and texture images. The learning mode is driven by the carefully-designed loss functions. For content learning, we use *L1 reconstruction loss* to restrict pixel-level consistency between the driving image and predicted content. For texture part, due to unavailability of its ground truth, we adopt feature reconstruction VGG loss [5] to constrain the similarity of driving frame and the final prediction with texture information. The two losses are calculated on multiple resolutions obtained by *downsample* operations, including 256×256, 128×128, 64×64 and 32×32, which can be written as follows:

$$L_{rec_{L1}} = \sum_{i=0}^{I} \|Down_i(\mathbf{D}) - Down_i(G_c(\mathbf{S}))\|_1,\tag{5}$$

$$L_{recv_{GG}} = \sum_{i=0}^{I} \sum_{j=1}^{J} \|VGG_j(Down_i(\mathbf{D})) - VGG_j(Down_i(G_f(\mathbf{S})))\|_1, \quad (6)$$

where $Down_i$ denotes i_{th} downsample, VGG_j is the j_{th} activation layer of VGG network. G_c and G_f are the content image and final prediction, respectively.

2.3 Adversarial Learning and GAN Loss for Sharpness Improvement

Though the above designs have provided the informative estimation of motion, content and texture, the synthesis videos still cannot meet the clinical training requirements due to finer details loss when compared to ground truth. Thus, the adversarial training strategy is further introduced to improve the sharpness of the generated videos. Specifically, we add a discriminator to judge the differences between reconstructed and real frames, that is, forcing the generator to learn and synthesize more realistic frames to 'cheat' the discriminator. The input of the discriminator is generated or real frame and the output is a probability map, predicting the trueness of the frame. We train the generator and discriminator (Dis) using LSGAN loss [8] for learning stability (see Eq. 7 and 8).

$$L_G^{LSGAN} = E\left[(Dis(G_f(\mathbf{S})) - 1)^2\right] \quad (7)$$

$$L_{Dis}^{LSGAN} = E\left[(Dis(\mathbf{D}) - 1)^2\right] + E\left[Dis(G_f(\mathbf{S}))^2\right] \quad (8)$$

Further, the feature matching loss [18] is adopted to encourage the similar intermediate representation of the discriminator, which can be written as Eq. 9:

$$L_{feat} = \sum_{i=0}^{I} \|Dis_i(\mathbf{D}) - Dis_i(G_{final}(\mathbf{S}))\|_1, \quad (9)$$

where Dis_i denotes for the i_{th} intermediate outputs of the discriminator.

3 Experiments and Results

Materials and Implementation Details. We evaluate on pelvic video dataset using endosonography. Two keypoints (the lower edge of the symphysis and bladder neck) were manually annotated on each frame by experts using the Pair annotation software package [6] (see Fig. 2). Totally 169 videos were collected, with 134 for training and 35 for testing. Each video contains 37 to 88 frames, which are resized and padded to 256×256. We implemented our method in *Pytorch* and trained the system by Adam optimizer for 50 epochs, using a standard PC with four NVIDIA TITAN 2080 GPU. The batch size is 20 and the learning rate is set as 0.0002. The number of self-supervised keypoints is set to 10. The keypoint detection network and dense motion network employ U-Net [9] structure with five downsampling and upsampling blocks. The bottleneck contains the structure of 6 residual blocks with two convolution layers, while the

Table 1. Quantitative result of compared methods

Methods	Reconstruction					Prediction	
	L1 Loss↓	FID↓	LPIPS↓	PSNR↑	FVD↓	FID↓	FVD↓
M-Net [11]	0.0416	17.78	0.0120	33.05	619.50	20.32	737.44
FOMM [12]	0.0249	15.96	0.0065	33.51	405.63	18.90	658.12
Ours-P	**0.0222**	15.66	0.0059	33.66	415.77	18.66	575.90
Ours-PT	0.0224	15.39	0.0056	33.66	372.52	18.41	571.26
Ours-PTG	0.0225	**14.53**	**0.0044**	**33.68**	**324.95**	**17.82**	**552.80**

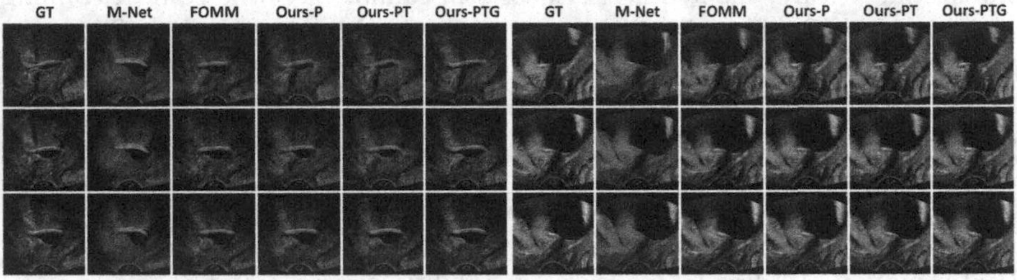

Fig. 4. Visualization results of two typical cases for reconstruction task.

discriminator adopts the structure of PatchGAN [4] with four convolution layers. The weights of losses $\mathcal{L}_{eq}$, $\mathcal{L}_{key}$, $L_{rec_{L1}}$, $L_{rec_{VGG}}$, L_G^{LSGAN}, L_{Dis}^{LSGAN}, L_{feat} are 10, 100, 10, 10, 1, 1, 10, respectively.

Quantitative and Qualitative Analysis. We evaluated the performance on two tasks, including reconstruction and prediction. For the reconstruction task, we considered the test videos as driving videos and their intermediate frames as source images. For the prediction task, we randomly choose a video from test set as driving video and an intermediate frame from another test video as source image. It is noted that the ground truth (GT) in the reconstruction task is the test video itself, while in the prediction task, GT is unavailable. In this study, five metrics were adopted to evaluate the reconstruction task, including 1) $\mathcal{L}_1$ Loss for pixel-level absolute distance calculation, 2) Frechet Inception Distance (FID) [2] for image quality assessment in feature level, 3) Learned Perceptual Image Patch Similarity (LPIPS) [20] for statistics of feature similarity, 4) Peak Signal to Noise Ratio (PSNR) for image quality assessment in image level, 5) Frechet Video Distance (FVD) [15] for temporal coherence evaluation in video level. For the prediction task, only FID and FVD were leveraged, since other metrics required pair GT and synthesis videos. Figure 4 and Fig. 5 shows our qualitative results on reconstruction and prediction task, respectively. Ours-P, ours-PT and ours-PTG denote our ablation studies, including gradually adding keypoint supervision ('-P'), texture decoder ('-T') and GAN loss ('-G') to the plain FOMM. To use the same source image and driving video, ours-PTG achieve the comparable results with GT frames on reconstruction task. Compared to other FOMM on prediction

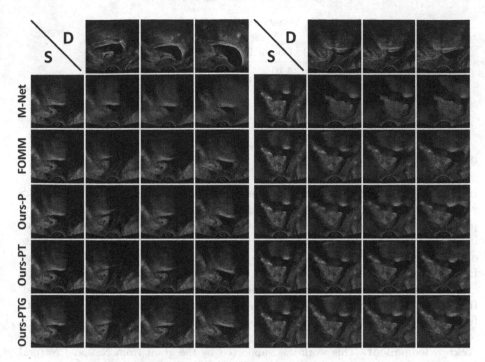

Fig. 5. Result visualization for prediction task. D: driving frames; S: source frame.

task, ours-P performs better on the area near the annotated keypoints. Further, with texture enhanced and GAN loss enforced, ours-PTG realizes sharper synthesized frames with high fidelity and consistency between frames. The quantitative results in Table 1 are in accordance with the visualization results. Our proposed method with keypoint supervision, dual decoder and GAN loss achieves the best performance.

User Study. To further investigate the quality of synthesis videos, we conducted a user study. Four experienced doctors were asked to rate each giving video in 5 levels. Level 5 means the video looks the most realstic. Three types of videos (GT, FOMM, ours-PTG) were giving, with each selecting 10 videos. Finally, the average level of the each type was calculated, which was 4.60, 4.15 and 4.65 for videos of GT, FOMM, ours-PTG. The details are presented in Table 2. With the similar average level of the GT and ours-PTG, we can conclude that the videos synthesized by our method are realistic enough.

318   J. Liang et al.

Table 2. The quantitative results of user study

Settings	Doctor 1	Doctor 2	Doctor 3	Doctor 4	Average
GT	4.70	4.10	4.60	5.00	4.60
FOMM	4.60	2.40	4.60	5.00	4.15
Ours-PTG	5.00	3.90	4.80	4.90	4.65

4   Conclusions

In this paper, we propose a novel framework for synthesizing high-fidelity US videos to address the challenge of lacking adequate US sequences for training junior doctors. The videos are synthesized by animating the content in any source images according to the motion of given driving videos. Extensive experiments on one large pelvic dataset validate the effectiveness of each of our key designs. Besides, user study indicates that videos generated by our framework scored close to the real ones, showing the clinical availability of our proposed method. In the future, we will explore the framework in more challenging datasets to further validate its generality.

Acknowledgement. This work was supported by the grant from National Natural Science Foundation of China (Nos. 62171290, 62101343), Shenzhen-Hong Kong Joint Research Program (No. SGDX20201103095613036), and Shenzhen Science and Technology Innovations Committee (No. 20200812143441001).

References

1. Goodfellow, I., Pouget-Abadie, J., et al.: Generative adversarial nets. In: NeurIPS, pp. 2672–2680 (2014)
2. Heusel, M., Ramsauer, H., et al.: GANs trained by a two time-scale update rule converge to a local Nash equilibrium. In: NeurIPS, pp. 6626–6637 (2017)
3. Hu, Y., et al.: Freehand ultrasound image simulation with spatially-conditioned generative adversarial networks. In: Cardoso, M.J., et al. (eds.) CMMI/SWITCH/RAMBO -2017. LNCS, vol. 10555, pp. 105–115. Springer, Cham (2017). https://doi.org/10.1007/978-3-319-67564-0_11
4. Isola, P., Zhu, J.Y., Zhou, T., Efros, A.A.: Image-to-image translation with conditional adversarial networks. In: Proceedings of the IEEE Conference on Computer Vision and Pattern Recognition, pp. 1125–1134 (2017)
5. Johnson, J., Alahi, A., Fei-Fei, L.: Perceptual losses for real-time style transfer and super-resolution. In: Leibe, B., Matas, J., Sebe, N., Welling, M. (eds.) ECCV 2016. LNCS, vol. 9906, pp. 694–711. Springer, Cham (2016). https://doi.org/10.1007/978-3-319-46475-6_43
6. Liang, J., et al.: Sketch guided and progressive growing GAN for realistic and editable ultrasound image synthesis. Med. Image Anal. **79**, 102461 (2022)
7. Liang, J., et al.: Synthesis and edition of ultrasound images via sketch guided progressive growing GANs. In: 2020 IEEE 17th International Symposium on Biomedical Imaging (ISBI), pp. 1793–1797. IEEE (2020)

8. Mao, X., Li, Q., Xie, H., Lau, R.Y., Wang, Z., Smolley, S.P.: Least squares generative adversarial networks. In: Proceedings of the IEEE International Conference on Computer Vision, pp. 2794–2802 (2017)

9. Ronneberger, O., Fischer, P., Brox, T.: U-Net: convolutional networks for biomedical image segmentation. In: Navab, N., Hornegger, J., Wells, W.M., Frangi, A.F. (eds.) MICCAI 2015. LNCS, vol. 9351, pp. 234–241. Springer, Cham (2015). https://doi.org/10.1007/978-3-319-24574-4_28

10. Saito, M., Matsumoto, E., Saito, S.: Temporal generative adversarial nets with singular value clipping. In: Proceedings of the IEEE International Conference on Computer Vision, pp. 2830–2839 (2017)

11. Siarohin, A., Lathuilière, S., Tulyakov, S., Ricci, E., Sebe, N.: Animating arbitrary objects via deep motion transfer. In: Proceedings of the IEEE/CVF Conference on Computer Vision and Pattern Recognition, pp. 2377–2386 (2019)

12. Siarohin, A., Lathuilière, S., Tulyakov, S., Ricci, E., Sebe, N.: First order motion model for image animation. Adv. Neural Inf. Process. Syst. 32 (2019)

13. Tom, F., et al.: Simulating patho-realistic ultrasound images using deep generative networks with adversarial learning. In: ISBI, pp. 1174–1177. IEEE (2018)

14. Tulyakov, S., Liu, M.Y., Yang, X., Kautz, J.: MoCoGAN: decomposing motion and content for video generation. In: Proceedings of the IEEE Conference on Computer Vision and Pattern Recognition, pp. 1526–1535 (2018)

15. Unterthiner, T., van Steenkiste, S., Kurach, K., Marinier, R., Michalski, M., Gelly, S.: Towards accurate generative models of video: a new metric & challenges. arXiv preprint arXiv:1812.01717 (2018)

16. Vondrick, C., Pirsiavash, H., Torralba, A.: Generating videos with scene dynamics. Adv. Neural Inf. Process. Syst. 29 (2016)

17. Wang, T.C., et al.: Video-to-video synthesis. arXiv preprint arXiv:1808.06601 (2018)

18. Wang, T.C., Liu, M.Y., Zhu, J.Y., Tao, A., Kautz, J., Catanzaro, B.: High-resolution image synthesis and semantic manipulation with conditional GANs. In: Proceedings of the IEEE Conference on Computer Vision and Pattern Recognition, pp. 8798–8807 (2018)

19. Wiles, O., Koepke, A., Zisserman, A.: X2Face: a network for controlling face generation using images, audio, and pose codes. In: Proceedings of the European Conference on Computer Vision (ECCV), pp. 670–686 (2018)

20. Zhang, R., Isola, P., Efros, A.A., Shechtman, E., Wang, O.: The unreasonable effectiveness of deep features as a perceptual metric. In: Proceedings of the IEEE Conference on Computer Vision and Pattern Recognition, pp. 586–595 (2018)

21. Zollhöfer, M., et al.: State of the art on monocular 3D face reconstruction, tracking, and applications. In: Computer Graphics Forum, vol. 37, pp. 523–550. Wiley Online Library (2018)

Class Impression for Data-Free Incremental Learning

Sana Ayromlou[1], Purang Abolmaesumi[1], Teresa Tsang[2], and Xiaoxiao Li[1(✉)]

[1] The University of British Columbia, Vancouver, BC, Canada
{s.ayromlou,xiaoxiao}@ece.ubc.ca
[2] Vancouver General Hospital, Vancouver, BC, Canada

Abstract. Standard deep learning-based classification approaches require collecting all samples from all classes in advance and are trained offline. This paradigm may not be practical in real-world clinical applications, where new classes are incrementally introduced through the addition of new data. Class incremental learning is a strategy allowing learning from such data. However, a major challenge is catastrophic forgetting, i.e., performance degradation on previous classes when adapting a trained model to new data. To alleviate this challenge, prior methodologies save a portion of training data that require perpetual storage, which may introduce privacy issues. Here, we propose a novel data-free class incremental learning framework that first synthesizes data from the model trained on previous classes to generate a `Class Impression`. Subsequently, it updates the model by combining the synthesized data with new class data. Furthermore, we incorporate a cosine normalized Cross-entropy loss to mitigate the adverse effects of the imbalance, a margin loss to increase separation among previous classes and new ones, and an intra-domain contrastive loss to generalize the model trained on the synthesized data to real data. We compare our proposed framework with state-of-the-art methods in class incremental learning, where we demonstrate improvement in accuracy for the classification of 11,062 echocardiography cine series of patients. Code is available at https://github.com/sanaAyrml/Class-Impresion-for-Data-free-Incremental-Learning

1 Introduction

Deep learning classification models for medical imaging tasks have shown promising performance. Most of these models usually require collecting all training data and defining the tasks at the beginning. However, while highly desirable, it is impractical to train a deep learning model only once during deployment and then expect it to perform well on all future data, which may not be well represented in the training data. One promising solution is to allow the system to perform class incremental learning (a subset of continual learning or lifelong learning),

Supplementary Information The online version contains supplementary material available at https://doi.org/10.1007/978-3-031-16440-8_31.

i.e., adapting the deployed model to the newly collected data from new classes. Unfortunately, catastrophic forgetting [4] occurs when a deep learning model overwrites past knowledge when training on new data.

Recent efforts to address catastrophic forgetting mainly include the following three categories: 1) Replay methods, which alleviate forgetting by replaying some stored samples from previous tasks [3,7,9,17,18]; 2) Regularization-based methods, which use defined regularization terms such as additional losses to preserve prior learned knowledge while updating on new tasks [10,13,16,26]; 3) Parameter isolation methods, which allocate a fixed part of a static architecture for each task and only update that part during training [1,19]. These techniques have been mainly deployed in the natural image domain, and the solution for medical image analysis is under-explored [23]. Among these approaches, rehearsal-based strategy has been reported to achieve the best results [7]. Still, it requires accessing either the entire data or a portion of data representations used for training the previous model by saving them with more complex memory systems. It then performs re-training on the saved data with new data. This approach is less practical in medical imaging applications due to privacy regulations of data storage.

To complement storing past data, data-free rehearsal (pseudo-rehearsal) strategies are recently proposed, in which the external memory is replaced with a model that is capable of generating samples from the past [11,20,22]. However, the existing data-free rehearsal methods in class-incremental learning perform poorly for medical images (seen from our experiment results in Sect. 3) without considering their unique properties. We reveal the **challenges** are: 1) generating synthetic images with high fidelity and preserving class-specific information from medical images is challenging; 2) mitigating the domain shift between generated and real images may not be straightforward in medical image classification; and 3) creating a robust decision boundary under imbalanced class distributions may be subject to significant uncertainty.

It is practical yet challenging to deploy class-incremental learning for medical image analysis. To the best of our knowledge, no existing data-free rehearsal-based class incremental learning work on *deep neural networks* is specifically designed for medical image analysis. Motivated by the observation that medical imaging samples within a categorical classification task normally share similar anatomical landmarks, we propose a novel class-incremental learning pipeline that 1) restores `Class Impression`, *i.e.*, generating prototypical synthetic images with high quality for each class using the frozen weights of the existing model, 2) mitigates the domain shift between class-wise synthesized images and original images by defining the *intra-domain contrastive loss*, which empowers `Class Impression` in addressing the catastrophic forgetting problem, and 3) leverages a novel *cosine normalized cross-entropy loss* for imbalance issue and a *margin loss* to encourage robust decision boundary to regularize `Class Impression` for handling catastrophic forgetting and encouraging better generalization. We conduct extensive comparison experiments and ablation analysis on the echocardiogram view classification task to demonstrate the efficacy.

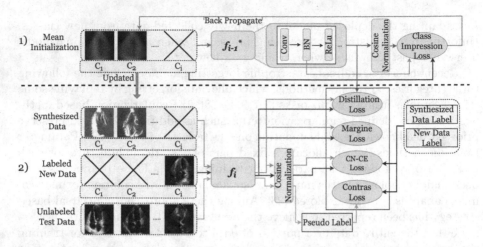

Fig. 1. Class Impression consists of two main iterative steps to perform class incremental classification: 1) Synthesize samples images for each past class from the frozen model trained on the previous task f_{i-1}^* by back-propagating using Eq. (1) with class mean as initialization. 2) Update the model on new tasks. We utilize the distillation training method to leverage information from the previous model [7,13]. We add Cosine Normalization cross-entropy loss (Eq. (4)) and Margin loss over latent representation of synthesized images and labeled new data (Eq. (5)), to overcome data unbalance issue and catastrophic forgetting of past tasks, respectively. Furthermore, we introduce a novel Intra-domain Conservative loss (Eq. (6)) as a semi-supervised domain adaption technique between synthesized data and original data to mitigate the domain shift.

2 Method

Problem Setting. The general class incremental learning considers a sequence of classification tasks, where in each task, new classes are added over time to a prior set of classes. The objective is to maintain high classification accuracy across all classification tasks. Let us denote $x^t \in \mathcal{X}^t$ as the input image, $y^t \in \mathcal{Y}^t$ as the class label w.r.t. the task t, and we have $\{\mathcal{Y}^t\} \subset \{\mathcal{Y}^{t+1}\}$. In rehearsal-based class incremental learning, the generalization error of all seen tasks is

$$\sum_{t=1}^{T} \mathbb{E}_{(x^t,y^t)\sim(\mathcal{X}^t,\mathcal{Y}^t)} \left[\ell(f_t(x^t;\theta), y^t)\right],$$

with loss function ℓ, classifier parameter θ, the current task T, and the model f_t trained in task t. While under data-free setting, there is no access to data $(\mathcal{X}^t, \mathcal{Y}^t)$ for $t < T$.

Overview of Our Pipeline. Figure 1 shows the whole pipeline of our proposed method. We have two stages for each task. In the first stage, we synthesize images from values saved in the frozen model trained on the previous task to employ them as replay data by seizing a genuine class-wise impression instead of saving them. In the second stage, we perform distilled class incremental training on the data using the new classes and synthesized data with proposed novel losses to 1) learn features of new classes, 2) preserve features comprehended from prior classes during previous tasks, and 3) maximize distances between the distribution of the new and previous classes in the latent space. Next, we will introduce each innovative component in our pipeline.

2.1 Class Impression

Different from [22] that trains a model to synthesize images without considering preserving class-specific information, we are motivated by recent work, DeepInversion [25], which was originally formulated to distill knowledge from a trained model for transfer learning. Given a randomly initialized input $\hat{x} \in \mathbb{R}^{B \times H \times W \times C}$ where B, H, W, C are the batch size, height, width, and number of channels, respectively, a target label y, the image is synthesized by optimizing

$$\min_{\hat{x}} \mathcal{L}_{\mathrm{CE}}(\hat{x}, y) + \mathcal{R}(\hat{x}), \tag{1}$$

where $\mathcal{L}_{\mathrm{CE}}(\cdot)$ is cross-entropy loss, and $\mathcal{R}(\cdot)$ is the regularization to improve the fidelity of the synthetic images. Specifically, following DeepInversion [25] and DeepDream [14], we have

$$\mathcal{R}(\hat{x}) = \alpha_{\mathrm{tv}} \mathcal{R}_{\mathrm{TV}}(\hat{x}) + \alpha_{\ell_2} \mathcal{R}_{\ell_2}(\hat{x}) + \alpha_{\mathrm{bn}} \mathcal{R}_{\mathrm{BN}}(\hat{x}, \mathcal{X}), \tag{2}$$

where αs are scaling factors, $\mathcal{R}_{\mathrm{TV}}(\cdot)$ and $\mathcal{R}_{\ell_2}(\cdot)$ penalize the total variance and the ℓ_2 norm of the generated image batch $\hat{x}$, respectively. $\mathcal{R}_{\mathrm{BN}}(\cdot, \cdot)$ is for matching the batch normalization (BN) statistic in trained model with the original images and defined as

$$\mathcal{R}_{\mathrm{BN}} = \sum_l \|\mu_l(\hat{x} - \mathbb{E}(\mu_l(x)|\mathcal{X})\|_2 + \sum_l \|\sigma_l^2(\hat{x} - \mathbb{E}(\sigma_l^2(x)|\mathcal{X})\|_2, \tag{3}$$

where μ_l and σ_l^2 are the batch-wise mean and variance estimates of feature maps corresponding to the l-th BN layer. To inject class-specific impression to the synthetic images without violating privacy regulations (such as re-identification), we assume the averaged image of each class $\bar{x}_k^t$ ($k \in \mathcal{Y}^t$) is available to initialize the optimization of $\hat{x}$ in Eq. (1). It is worth noting that, Class Impression aims to *generate* images following the distributions of the past class, rather than reconstructing the training data points as model inversion attacks does [6,8,24], thus Class Impression aims to meet certain privacy requirements imposed on storing medical data.

2.2 Novel Losses

Although we can leverage Class Impression, a.k.a the synthetic data of the past classes to conduct rehearsal distillation-based training, which mitigates catastrophic forgetting, class weights of old classes still may be ill-updated and mismatched with the updated representation space [27]. Therefore, we propose to use a modified classification loss, *i.e.*, *cosine normalized cross-entropy loss*, and two additional regularization terms, *i.e.*, *margin loss*, and *intra-domain contrastive loss* to improve the utility of `Class Impression`.

Cosine Normalized Cross-Entropy Loss. Classifier bias commonly exists in class incremental learning, because data in the new classes are more abundantly available or mostly have better quality [27]. In classification task, the Softmax operation yields the prediction probably of class k as $p_i(x) = \exp(\theta_i^\top f(x) + b_k)/\sum_j \exp(\theta_j^\top f(x) + b_i)$, which $f(\cdot)$ is feature extractor, and θ_k and b_k are class embedding and bias weights. Due to class imbalance, the magnitudes of embedding and bias of the new class can be significantly higher than the past classes. Cosine normalization has been widely used in vision tasks [5,7,15] to eliminate the bias caused by the significant difference in magnitudes. Thus, following the above-mentioned work [7], we add the following *Cosine Normalized Cross-entropy* (CNCE) loss for classification with the past and new classes at the current task t:

$$\mathcal{L}_{\text{CNCE}} = -\sum_{k=1}^{|\mathcal{Y}^t|} y_k \log \left(\frac{\exp(\eta \langle \bar{\theta}_k, \bar{f}(x) \rangle)}{\sum_j \exp(\eta \langle \bar{\theta}_j, \bar{f}(x) \rangle)} \right), \tag{4}$$

where $\bar{v} = v/\|v\|_2$ indicates the unit normalized vector, $\langle \cdot, \cdot \rangle$ measures the cosine similarity of two vectors, and η is the temperature hyperparameter. Further, `Class Impression` can generate an equal number of data for each past class as that of the new class to alleviate the imbalanced issue.

Margin Loss. Representation overlapping is another inherent problem in class incremental learning [27]. Margin loss uses a margin to compare samples representations distances, and is used in few-shot learning [12] and non-data-free class incremental learning [7]. To avoid the ambiguities between the past and new classes, we are the first to explore margin loss in data-free class incremental learning that encourage separating the decision boundary of the new class from the old ones. At the current task t, margin loss is written as

$$\mathcal{L}_{\text{margin}} = \sum_{k=1}^{|\mathcal{Y}^{t-1}|} \max \left(m - \langle \bar{\theta}, \bar{f}(x) \rangle + \langle \bar{\theta}^k, \bar{f}(x) \rangle, 0 \right), \tag{5}$$

where x are the synthesized images that are used as anchors of the classes seen in the previous tasks' distribution, m is the margin for tolerance, $\bar{\theta}$ is the embedding vector of x's true class, and $\bar{\theta}^k$ is the embedding vector of the new class, which is viewed as negatives for x. A larger m encourages a larger separation.

Intra-domain Contrastive Loss. We notice that directly applying the synthetic medical images for rehearsal may not generalize well to classify the original data. Motivated by semi-supervised domain adaption [21], we aim to align the domain shift between the source $\mathcal{S}$ (*i.e.*, synthetic images) and target $\mathcal{T}$ (*i.e.*, unlabeled testing data in the new task). The centroid of the images from the source domain belonging to class k is defined as $c_k^\mathcal{S} = \sum_i \mathbb{1}_{\{y_i^S = k\}} f(x_i^s) / \sum_i \mathbb{1}_{\{y_i^s = k\}}$. Then, we assign the pseudo label for the unlabeled target samples using the currently updated classifier. An intra-domain contrastive loss can pull the source and target samples in the same class together and push apart the centroids of different classes, which is written as (at task t):

$$\mathcal{L}_{\text{contras}}(c_k^\mathcal{S}, c_k^\mathcal{T}) = -\log \frac{\exp(\tau \langle \bar{c}_k^\mathcal{S}, \bar{c}_k^\mathcal{T} \rangle)}{\exp(\tau \langle \bar{c}_k^\mathcal{S}, \bar{c}_k^\mathcal{T} \rangle) + \sum_{\substack{j=1 \\ \mathcal{Q} \in \{\mathcal{S}, \mathcal{T}\}}}^{|\mathcal{Y}^{t-1}|} \mathbb{1}_{\{j \neq k\}} \exp(\tau \langle \bar{c}_k^\mathcal{Q}, \bar{c}_k^\mathcal{T} \rangle)}, \quad (6)$$

where τ is the temperature hyperparameter in $\exp(\cdot)$.

Altogether, the total loss used to train the new model for recognizing the new class while maintaining the old knowledge is given by:

$$\mathcal{L}_{total} = \mathcal{L}_{\text{CNCE}} + \alpha_{\text{dist}} \mathcal{L}_{\text{dist}} + \alpha_{\text{margin}} \mathcal{L}_{\text{margin}} + \alpha_{\text{contras}} \mathcal{L}_{\text{contras}}, \quad (7)$$

where α are tunable scaling factors, and $\mathcal{L}_{\text{dist}} = 1 - \langle \bar{f}^*(x), \bar{f}(x) \rangle$ with $\bar{f}^*$ as the old model, is the distillation loss widely used in class incremental learning [7,13].

3 Experiments

3.1 Datasets and Experimental Settings

Dataset: Heart echo data utilized in this paper come from several investigations at our local institution, randomly chosen from the hospital picture archiving system, with authorization from the Information Privacy Office and Clinical Medical Research Ethics Board. These cines are captured by six devices: GE Vivid 7, Vivid i, Vivid E9, Philips iE33, Sonosite, and Sequoia. Our dataset contains 11,062 cines (videos) of 2151 unique patients diagnosed with various heart diseases, with an average of 48 frames in each. An experienced cardiologist labeled gathered cines as five different views. The view distribution is shown in Supplementary Table 1. We chose our task as a test-bed to evaluate our innovations. In contrast to many other medical imaging classification problems, the labels associated with standard echo views are less ambiguous, less noisy, and anatomically interpretable, making the analysis of classification results easier and its failure modes tractable. Finally, we split the data into training, validation, and test sets based on the subject with the ratio of 70%, 20%, and 10%, respectively.

Experimental Settings: We perform a four-task class incremental learning, with a two-way classification at the beginning and adding in one new class at each task. As the number of data points is relatively low compared to natural image's benchmark datasets, the classification model of Class Impression is a ResNet-based convolutional neural network with three residual blocks, each

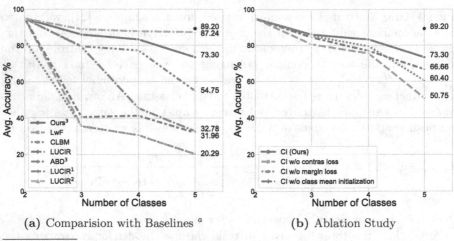

(a) Comparision with Baselines [a]   (b) Ablation Study

---

[a] 1. With corset data; 2. With weighted
corset data; 3. With synthesized data

Fig. 2. Testing accuracies of four tasks. It shows the classification accuracies on the
heart echo test dataset comparing with (a) baselines of class-incremental learning and
(b) ablation study on different configurations of proposed framework. $\star$ indicates the
accuracy of Oracle model, $i.e.$, training all the classes offline w/o class-incremental setting. Class Impression shows consistently higher accuracy with an average of 31.34%
increase after the final task compared to the SOTA data-free incremental learning
(ABD).

containing two layers. All models are implemented with PyTorch and trained on
one NVIDIA Tesla V100 GPU with 16GB of memory.

As mentioned in Sect. 2, our implementation contains two main stages for
each task. We **freeze** model weights for the image synthesis stage. We use
Adam optimizer and optimize the batch of 40 images with a learning rate of
0.01 for 2000 epochs. In the stage of incremental learning with a new class, we
update model weights again with the SGD optimizer and continue to learn on
each new task for 30 epochs with a batch size of 40. We search the optimal
hyper-parameters using Weights & Biases Sweeps, an automated hyperparameter searching software [2]. The best chosen hyperparameters are detailed in
Supplementary.

3.2 Comparison with Baselines

We compare Class Impression with the best-performed data-free baselines and
a non-data-free baseline that saves coreset data in the incremental learning setting by implementing them on our heart echo dataset.

The baseline methods included in this study are listed as follows: **LwF** [13]
uses distillation-based training to overcome catastrophic forgetting among different tasks. **ABD** [22] generates synthesized images of classes in the prior task.

CLBM [23] fits Gaussian mixture models to save information extracted from data points in each class. **LUCIR** [7] is a state-of-the-art rehearsal-based method that saves a coreset of data points from each seen class and replays them as anchors of their respective class distribution to maximize the distance between the distribution of classes in the latent space.

The results are given in Fig. 2a. **LWF**, reaching 20.29% accuracy, completely fails to consider the imbalance issue among classes in different tasks and distinguish between inter-task classes. **ABD** is a recent work that shares a similar data synthesis idea with us for class incremental learning. However, its final task accuracy is only 32.78%, much worse than `Class Impression`. Note that our innovations over **ABD** are multifold, lying in utilizing the unique class-specific information in medical images: 1) we initialize batches for the image synthesis step with the mean of each class; and 2) we mitigate the domain shift between class-wise synthesized images and original images by defining the *intra-domain contrastive loss*. **CLBM** overfits to new data feature distribution and fails to distinguish it from the old ones, yielding poor classification accuracy. **LUCIR** saves auxiliary information (*i.e.*, coreset data of old classes) and performs the closest to `Class Impression`. If we implement it without storing any data or saving a determined number of data as coreset from each class, it reaches the accuracy of 54.75% and `Class Impression` fairly outperforms it. However, if we use a weighted sampler in **LUCIR** to increase the saved samples' effect, it exceeds `Class Impression`. This result is expected due to intrinsic information loss in the data-free setting. In comparison, `Class Impression` results substantially outperform prior class incremental data-free settings by boosting 31.34% accuracy on the all seen classes in the final task and standing on 73.3% accuracy over five classes. The synthetic images generated by `Class Impression` are presented in Supplementary.

3.3 Ablation Studies

We perform extensive ablation studies to expose the impact of different losses in the final performance. The results are given in Fig. 2b. 1) *Impact of domain adaption:* We omit intra-domain contrastive loss (Eq. (4)) to observe the effect of the gap between the domain of synthesized images and original images. As seen in Fig. 2b, it results in the worst performance compared to other settings. 2) *Impact of inter-class separation:* When we omit margin loss (Eq. (5)), the model does not increase the distance of data points from previous tasks and new tasks, which also leads to a significant accuracy drop. 3) *Impact of mean initialization:* We initialize input images with random Gaussian noise instead of the mean of each class in the synthesis stage. Therefore, the model fails to capture the true impression of each class, and performance reduces.

4   Conclusion

In this work, we propose `Class Impression`, a novel data-free class incremental learning framework. In `Class Impression`, instead of saving data from classes in the earlier tasks that are not available for training in the new task, we synthesize class-specific images from the frozen model trained on the last task. Following, we continue training on new classes and synthesized images using the proposed novel losses to alleviate catastrophic forgetting, imbalanced data issues among new and past classes, and domain shift between new synthesized and original images of old classes. Experimental results for echocardiography cines classification on the large-scale dataset validate `Class Impression` out-performs the SOTA methods in data-free class incremental learning with an improbable gap of 31.34% accuracy in the final task and get comparable results with the SOTA data-saving rehearsal-based methods.

Our proposed method shows the potential to apply incremental learning in many healthcare applications that cannot save data due to memory constraints or privacy issues. It is common in clinical deployment that a client inherits a trained model without having access to its training data. Our design enables the client to refine the model with new tasks. For our future work, we plan to combine our work with other practical settings in the real world in the medical domain (*e.g.*, testing on different medical datasets) and further improve the pipeline to meet clinical-preferred performance.

Acknowledgement. This work is supported in part by the Natural Sciences and Engineering Research Council of Canada (NSERC), the Canadian Institutes of Health Research (CIHR), and NVIDIA Hardware Award. We thank Dr. Hongxu Yin at NVIDIA research for his insightful suggestions.

References

1. Aljundi, R., Chakravarty, P., Tuytelaars, T.: Expert gate: lifelong learning with a network of experts. In: Proceedings of the IEEE Conference on Computer Vision and Pattern Recognition, pp. 3366–3375 (2017)
2. Biewald, L.: Experiment tracking with weights and biases (2020). https://www.wandb.com/, software available from wandb.com
3. Chaudhry, A., et al.: Continual learning with tiny episodic memories (2019)
4. Delange, M., et al.: A continual learning survey: defying forgetting in classification tasks. IEEE Trans. Patt. Anal. Mach. Intell. **44**, 3366–3385 (2021)
5. Gidaris, S., Komodakis, N.: Dynamic few-shot visual learning without forgetting. In: Proceedings of the IEEE Conference on Computer Vision and Pattern Recognition, pp. 4367–4375 (2018)
6. Hatamizadeh, A., et al.: Do gradient inversion attacks make federated learning unsafe? arXiv preprint arXiv:2202.06924 (2022)
7. Hou, S., Pan, X., Loy, C.C., Wang, Z., Lin, D.: Learning a unified classifier incrementally via rebalancing. In: Proceedings of the IEEE/CVF Conference on Computer Vision and Pattern Recognition, pp. 831–839 (2019)
8. Huang, Y., Gupta, S., Song, Z., Li, K., Arora, S.: Evaluating gradient inversion attacks and defenses in federated learning. Adv. Neural Inf. Process. Syst. **34**, 7232–7241 (2021)
9. Isele, D., Cosgun, A.: Selective experience replay for lifelong learning. In: Proceedings of the AAAI Conference on Artificial Intelligence, vol. 32 (2018)

10. Jung, H., Ju, J., Jung, M., Kim, J.: Less-forgetting learning in deep neural networks. arXiv preprint arXiv:1607.00122 (2016)
11. Lavda, F., Ramapuram, J., Gregorova, M., Kalousis, A.: Continual classification learning using generative models. arXiv preprint arXiv:1810.10612 (2018)
12. Li, A., Huang, W., Lan, X., Feng, J., Li, Z., Wang, L.: Boosting few-shot learning with adaptive margin loss. In: Proceedings of the IEEE/CVF Conference on Computer Vision and Pattern Recognition, pp. 12576–12584 (2020)
13. Li, Z., Hoiem, D.: Learning without forgetting. IEEE Trans. Pattern Anal. Mach. Intell. **40**(12), 2935–2947 (2017)
14. Mordvintsev, A., Olah, C., Tyka, M.: Inceptionism: Going deeper into neural networks (2015)
15. Qi, H., Brown, M., Lowe, D.G.: Low-shot learning with imprinted weights. In: Proceedings of the IEEE Conference on Computer Vision and Pattern Recognition, pp. 5822–5830 (2018)
16. Rannen, A., Aljundi, R., Blaschko, M.B., Tuytelaars, T.: Encoder based lifelong learning. In: Proceedings of the IEEE International Conference on Computer Vision, pp. 1320–1328 (2017)
17. Rebuffi, S.A., Kolesnikov, A., Sperl, G., Lampert, C.H.: iCaRL: incremental classifier and representation learning. In: Proceedings of the IEEE Conference on Computer Vision and Pattern Recognition, pp. 2001–2010 (2017)
18. Rolnick, D., Ahuja, A., Schwarz, J., Lillicrap, T., Wayne, G.: Experience replay for continual learning. Adv. Neural Inf. Process. Syst. **32** (2019)
19. Serra, J., Suris, D., Miron, M., Karatzoglou, A.: Overcoming catastrophic forgetting with hard attention to the task. In: International Conference on Machine Learning, pp. 4548–4557. PMLR (2018)
20. Shin, H., Lee, J.K., Kim, J., Kim, J.: Continual learning with deep generative replay. Adv. Neural Inf. Process. Syst. **30** (2017)
21. Singh, A.: CLDA: contrastive learning for semi-supervised domain adaptation. Adv. Neural Inf. Process. Syst. **34**, 5089–5101 (2021)
22. Smith, J., Hsu, Y.C., Balloch, J., Shen, Y., Jin, H., Kira, Z.: Always be dreaming: a new approach for data-free class-incremental learning. In: Proceedings of the IEEE/CVF International Conference on Computer Vision, pp. 9374–9384 (2021)
23. Yang, Y., Cui, Z., Xu, J., Zhong, C., Wang, R., Zheng, W.-S.: Continual learning with Bayesian model based on a fixed pre-trained feature extractor. In: de Bruijne, M., et al. (eds.) MICCAI 2021. LNCS, vol. 12905, pp. 397–406. Springer, Cham (2021). https://doi.org/10.1007/978-3-030-87240-3_38
24. Yin, H., Mallya, A., Vahdat, A., Alvarez, J.M., Kautz, J., Molchanov, P.: See through gradients: Image batch recovery via grad inversion. In: Proceedings of the IEEE/CVF Conference on Computer Vision and Pattern Recognition, pp. 16337–16346 (2021)
25. Yin, H., et al.: Dreaming to distill: data-free knowledge transfer via deep inversion. In: Proceedings of the IEEE/CVF Conference on Computer Vision and Pattern Recognition, pp. 8715–8724 (2020)
26. Zhang, J., et al.: Class-incremental learning via deep model consolidation. In: Proceedings of the IEEE/CVF Winter Conference on Applications of Computer Vision, pp. 1131–1140 (2020)
27. Zhu, F., Cheng, Z., Zhang, X.Y., Liu, C.l.: Class-incremental learning via dual augmentation. Adv. Neural Inf. Process. Syst. **34**, 14306–14318 (2021)

Simultaneous Bone and Shadow Segmentation Network Using Task Correspondence Consistency

Aimon Rahman[1]([⊠]), Jeya Maria Jose Valanarasu[1], Ilker Hacihaliloglu[2], and Vishal M. Patel[1]

[1] Johns Hopkins University, Baltimore, USA
arahma30@jhu.edu
[2] University of British Columbia, Vancouver, Canada

Abstract. Segmenting both bone surface and the corresponding acoustic shadow are fundamental tasks in ultrasound (US) guided orthopedic procedures. However, these tasks are challenging due to minimal and blurred bone surface response in US images, cross-machine discrepancy, imaging artifacts, and low signal-to-noise ratio. Notably, bone shadows are caused by a significant acoustic impedance mismatch between the soft tissue and bone surfaces. To leverage these complementary features between these highly related tasks, we propose a single end-to-end network with a shared transformer-based encoder and task independent decoders for simultaneous bone and shadow segmentation. To share complementary features, we propose a cross task feature transfer block which learns to transfer meaningful features from decoder of shadow segmentation to that of bone segmentation and vice-versa. We also introduce a correspondence consistency loss which makes sure that network utilizes the inter-dependency between the bone surface and its corresponding shadow to refine the segmentation. Validation against expert annotations shows that the method outperforms the previous state-of-the-art for both bone surface and shadow segmentation.

Keywords: Multi-task · Ultrasound · Bone segmentation · Shadow segmentation

1 Introduction

There has been a significant interest in incorporating ultrasound (US) imaging for computer assisted orthopedic surgery (CAOS) procedures owing to its non-invasive, radiation-free, and cost-effective nature. However, due to bone surfaces appearing only several millimeters (mm) in thickness along with noisy artifacts, researchers have been focusing on developing automated bone segmentation and enhancement methods [7]. These bone surfaces generally have the highest intensity in US images which is then followed by a low-intensity region, namely bone shadows. Bone shadow is the result of a high acoustic impedance mismatch

© The Author(s), under exclusive license to Springer Nature Switzerland AG 2022
L. Wang et al. (Eds.): MICCAI 2022, LNCS 13434, pp. 330–339, 2022.
https://doi.org/10.1007/978-3-031-16440-8_32

between the bone surface and the adjacent soft tissue, which reflects the US signal to the transducer. The bone shadow information is essential to guide the orthopedic surgeon to a standardized viewing plane with minimal noise and artifacts. Hence, both bone surface and shadow segmentation are crucial to CAOS procedures.

Recent literature on bone and shadow segmentation focus on learning individual networks for each problem separately [1–3,13]. However, in [11], Wang et al. [11] proposed a pre-enhancement network that leverages bone shadow information for bone surface segmentation. The bone shadow was obtained using a bone shadow enhancement method where a signal transmission map is constructed from the local phase bone image features [6]. The enhanced bone shadow information has also been used in [12] where a multi-task learning-based method to segment bone shadow region is proposed.

It should be noted that bone shadow is a signal void that indicates the loss of energy as US waves propagate through bone tissues. Thus, the quality of bone surface segmentation can have major impact on shadow segmentation accuracy and vice-versa. However, existing works do not fully exploit the structure of these highly related tasks. Despite being closely-related, existing top networks for bone and shadow segmentation have significantly different and specialized architectures. Our proposed method explores the idea of exploiting shared features for a more compact network and taking advantage of interactions between the two tasks to generate a better feature representation. We hypothesize that the interrelation between bone and shadow response in US images can be leveraged to significantly improve the quality of both learned networks. In summary, we present the following contributions in this paper:

- We are the first to integrate two highly-related homogeneous tasks into a single framework for unified bone surface and shadow segmentation. The common encoder brings powerful synergy across both tasks when extracting shared deep features for the two tightly-coupled problems.
- We propose a cross task feature transfer block to extract complementary features at decoders to improve the quality of performance in the multi-task learning framework.
- We propose a task correspondence consistency loss to further regularize the network by ensuring the transitivity between the two related predictions.
- We conduct extensive experiments using the in vivo US scans of knee, femur, distal radius, spine, and tibia bones collected using two US machines and demonstrate that the proposed method is competitive with other individual specialized state-of-the-art methods.

2   Method

2.1   Preliminaries

Instead of using only B-mode US scan as input, the proposed network takes the concatenation of three filtered images along with the original B-mode US scan

$(US(x, y))$. The filtered images are shown in Fig. 1(a)–(d). This has been done to reduce the domain discrepancy between the images obtained using different US machine settings or different orientations of the transducer. During the extraction of filtered images we have used the original parameters and constant values described in [6,8]. The Local Phase Tensor Image $(LPT(x, y))$ is computed by defining odd and even filter responses using [8]. Local Phase Bone Image $LP(x, y)$ is computed using: $LP(x, y) = LPT(x, y) \times LPE(x, y) \times \text{LwP} A(x, y)$, where $LPE(x, y)$ and $LwPA(x, y)$ represent the local phase energy and local weighted mean phase angle image features, respectively. These two features are computed using monogenic signal theory as [6]. Bone Shadow Enhanced image $BSE(x, y)$ is obtained by modeling the interaction of Ultrasound signal at position (x,y) within the tissues as scattering and attenuation information using the method proposed in [6],

$$BSE(x, y) = [(CM_{LP}(x, y) - \rho)/[max(US_A(x, y), \epsilon)]^\delta] + \rho$$

Here the confidence map is denoted by $CM_{LP}(x, y)$ which is obtained by modeling the US signal propagation inside the tissue considering bone feature in local phase bone image LP(x, y). $US_A(x, y)$ maximizes the visibility of bone features with high intensity inside a local region. δ represents the tissue attenuation coefficient. ρ is related to echogenicity confining the bone surface and ϵ is a small constant to avoid division by zero.

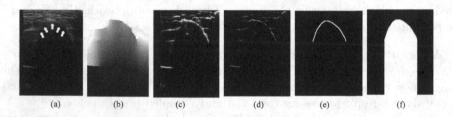

(a)   (b)   (c)   (d)   (e)   (f)

Fig. 1. (a) B-mode US scan. Thick white arrows point to the bone response in US image. (b) LPT (c) LP (d) BSE (e) Bone Surface Segmentation and (f) Bone Shadow Segmentation.

2.2   Network Architecture

We propose Shadow and Surface Segmentation Network (SSNet) for simultaneous bone surface and shadow segmentation from US images which is illustrated in Fig. 2. SSNet is composed of a shared LeViT-based encoder to extract global and long-range spatial features and two CNN-based decoders with a cross task feature transfer block to leverage complementary features between the two tasks.

(i) LeViT-based Shared Encoder: The shared encoder for bone and shadow surface segmentation is built based on the LeViT architecture [5]. The encoder part consists of four 3×3 convolution layers with stride 2 initially followed by three transformer blocks. Features from the convolution layers are forwarded to the LeViT transformer blocks which require fewer floating-point operations (FLOPs) than ViTs [4]. The local and global features at different scales are exploited by concatenating the features from both transformer and convolution layers.

(ii) CNN-based Decoders: The decoder part of the network consists of two separate branches for bone surface and shadow segmentation. Inspired by UNet [10], the features from decoders are concatenated with skip connection to effectively reuse spatial information of feature maps. The resolution from the previous layers is recovered using the cascaded upsampling technique similar to UNet. The decoder blocks consist of a 3×3 convolution, batch normalization layer followed by a ReLU layer.

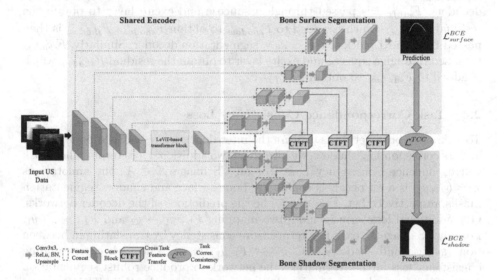

Fig. 2. An overview of the proposed SSNet for simultaneous bone surface and shadow segmentation from US images.

2.3   Cross Task Feature Transfer Block

To leverage the joint-learning capabilities of these two highly-related tasks, we propose a cross task feature transfer (CTFT) block used in between the two decoders. CTFT extracts complementary features from the two decoder branches using a squeeze and excitation block [9] and forwards them to the next decoder blocks of respective branches. We use squeeze and excitation block to learn which features of the surface segmentation decoder would help in segmenting bone shadow and vice-versa. Squeeze and excite enables dynamic channel-wise feature re-calibration thus help extract features that contributes to the complementary task. The details of CTFT are illustrated in Fig. 3. It takes in two inputs: $F_{surface}$

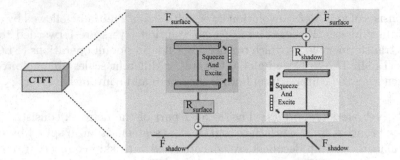

Fig. 3. An overview of the Cross Task Feature Transfer Block.

and F_{shadow} corresponding to the feature maps of bone surface and shadow decoders. $F_{surface}$ is passed through a squeeze and excite layer to obtain the residual $R_{surface}$ which is added to F_{shadow} to obtain $\hat{F}_{shadow}$. $\hat{F}_{shadow}$ is then passed to the next block of the shadow segmentation decoder. Similarly, F_{shadow} is passed through a squeeze and excite layer to obtain the residual R_{shadow} which is added to $F_{surface}$ to obtain $\hat{F}_{surface}$.

2.4   Task Correspondence Consistency Loss

To guarantee both networks capture the inter-dependency between bone surface and its corresponding shadow, we introduce two additional loss terms called Task Correspondence Consistency Loss. For an US image $X \in \mathcal{X}$, the annotations $Y = (y_1, y_2)$ is a set of labels containing bone surface and shadow segmentation masks, respectively. Let, $\hat{Y} = (\hat{y_1}, \hat{y_2})$ be the predictions of the decoder networks. Our additional loss term includes two mapping $F_1 : y_1 \rightarrow y_2$ and $F_2 : y_2 \rightarrow y_1$. For any US image X, each loss term ensure consistency by translating in between bone surface and shadows, i.e., $y_1 \rightarrow F_1(y_1) \approx y_2$. The task corresponding consistency loss further regularizes the network to produce robust segmentation masks for both task and prevent them to contradict each other. The proposed Task Correspondence Consistency Loss $\mathcal{L}^{TCC}(X, Y)$ is defined as:

$$\mathcal{L}^{TCC}(X, Y) = \mathcal{L}^{BCE}(y_1, F_2(\hat{y_2})) + \mathcal{L}^{BCE}(y_2, F_1(\hat{y_1})).$$

3   Experiments and Results

Dataset: The study includes 25 healthy volunteers with the approval of the institutional review board (IRB). Total 1042 different US images have been collected using SonixTouch US machine (Analogic Corporation, Peabody, MA, USA) with 2D C5-2/60 curvilinear and L14-5 linear transducer. For independent testing, 3 new subjects have been included in the study. Using handheld wireless US scans (Clarius C3, ClariusMobile Health Corporation, BC, Canada), a total of 185 scans have been collected. Depending on the depth setting, scan resolution varies between 0.1 mm to 0.15 mm. As both transducer and reconstruction pipelines are different, Clarius have low image quality. The scans include knee, femur, radius, and spine data and all of them are manually segmented by an expert ultrasonographer. For the Sonix dataset, a random 80:20 split has been applied based on the subject, making the final training set with 834 samples and the test set with 208 samples.

Implementation Details: SSNet is trained using a batch size of 32. For training both branches, a two-step training phase is adapted. Each of these steps are trained until convergence. The weights and bias of the network are optimized using Adam optimizer with a learning rate of 10^{-4}. All US scans and their corresponding masks are resized to 224×224 pixels and rescaled between 0 to 1. All transformer blocks in the LeViT architecture were pre-trained on ImageNet-1k. The overall loss function we use to train the multi-task network is,

$$\mathcal{L}^{total}(X,Y) = \mathcal{L}^{BCE}(y_1,\hat{y_1}) + \mathcal{L}^{BCE}(y_2,\hat{y_2}) + \mathcal{L}^{TCC}(X,Y).$$

Binary-cross entropy loss has been used between the prediction and the ground truth, which is expressed as,

$$\mathcal{L}_{CE(p,\hat{p})} = - \left(\frac{1}{wh} \sum_{x=0}^{w-1} \sum_{y=0}^{h-1} (p(x,y)\log(\hat{p}(x,y))) + (1-p(x,y))\log(1-\hat{p}(x,y)) \right).$$

Here, w and h represents the dimension of ultrasound scan, $p(x,y)$ denotes the pixel in scan and $\hat{p}(x,y)$ denotes the output prediction at a specific location (x,y). Test images can be forwarded through the network for both tasks in one shot. The experiments are carried out on a Linux workstation with Intel 3.50 GHz CPU and a 12GB NVidia Titan Xp GPU using the PyTorch framework. Dice coefficients are used to measure the segmentation performance of different methods.

Quantitative Comparison: For bone shadow segmentation, we compare the performance of our proposed method with that of UNet [10], MFG-CNN [11], and PSPGAN MTL [12]. PSPGAN MTL is the current state-of-the-art for bone shadow segmentation. For bone surface segmentation, we compare with UNet [10], MFG-CNN [11] without the classification labels, and LPT+GCT [13]. All the methods are trained using the same training dataset as used to train the proposed method. PSPGAN-MTL uses a conditional shape discriminator to enforce bone interval boundaries which provides more accurate and robust bone segmentation. Instead of using bone interval boundaries during the training, we enforce the boundary from the bone surface segmentation mask during inference instead. Average test results are shown in Table 1. It can be observed that the shared network SSNet outperforms the current state-of-the-art [12] and individual networks for both bone and shadow segmentation (paired t-test < 0.05).

Qualitative Comparison: We present sample qualitative results in Fig. 4 for both bone surface and shadow segmentation. It can be observed that the current state-of-the-art methods result in either missed shadow regions or disjoint bone segmentation maps. As our proposed method uses the inter-dependency between

Table 1. Results averaged over 5 folds. Numbers correspond to dice score with standard deviation. Boldface numbers indicate the best segmentation performance.

Method	SonixTouch		Clarius	
	Surface (%)	Shadow (%)	Surface (%)	Shadow (%)
UNet [10]	76.01 ± 0.20	88.33 ± 0.06	75.11 ± 0.31	84.03 ± 0.14
MFG-CNN [11]	81.05 ± 0.06	–	82.23 ± 0.14	–
LPT + GCT [13]	81.65 ± 0.10	–	83.05 ± 0.21	–
PSPGAN-MTL [12]	–	93.49 ± 0.06	–	91.01 ± 0.18
SSNet + CTFT + TCC loss (ours)	**87.03 ± 0.21**	**96.18 ± 0.43**	**83.33 ± 0.31**	**93.01 ± 0.23**

these tasks, we see a significant improvement with less discrepancies compared to the ground truth annotations.

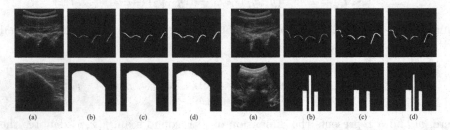

Fig. 4. Top Row - Bone surface segmentation. Bottom Row - Bone shadow segmentation. (a) Input US scan (b) Ground Truth (c) Output from current state-of-the-art [13] (surface), [12] (shadow) (d) Ours.

4   Discussion

Ablation Study: To understand the contribution of each individual module in the proposed SSNet, we conduct an ablation study and report it in Table 2. It can be observed that addition of CTFT helps improve the performance of both surface and shadow segmentation by injecting complementary features to the respective decoders. Also, using the propose task consistency ($\mathcal{L}^{TCC}$) further regularizes the network and boosts the segmentation performance.

Importance of Joint Learning: Qualitative results in Fig. 5 shows the importance of the joint learning framework. The result from cascaded network demonstrates that the faulty output from either of the network can produce wrong corresponding prediction. Cascaded network corresponds to using a deep network to predict the bone shadow map from bone surface segmentation map and vice-versa. For example, missing or joint boundaries in bone surface segmentation may result in wrong bone intervals in shadow network as demonstrated in the top row of Fig. 5. Similarly, over or under-segmented bone shadow predictions may produce faulty surface estimations. However, as each of the decoders

Table 2. Ablation study. Numbers correspond to dice score.

Method	SonixTouch		Clarius	
	Surface (%)	Shadow (%)	Surface (%)	Shadow (%)
SSNet (Base)	82.95 ± 0.13	93.34 ± 0.06	81.71 ± 0.20	90.94 ± 0.22
SSNet + CTFT	84.03 ± 0.11	94.88 ± 0.16	81.13 ± 0.19	92.43 ± 0.18
SSNet + CTFT + $\mathcal{L}^{TCC}$ (ours)	$\mathbf{87.03 \pm 0.21}$	$\mathbf{96.18 \pm 0.43}$	$\mathbf{83.33 \pm 0.31}$	$\mathbf{93.01 \pm 0.23}$

in our network is specialized for their respective task and further regularized by ensuring cross-task consistency, our network produces more consistent results.

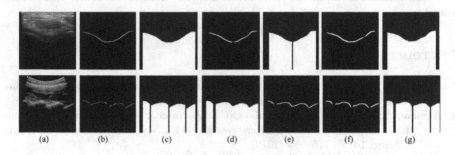

(a)   (b)   (c)   (d)   (e)   (f)   (g)

Fig. 5. (a) Input US scan (b) Surface ground truth (c) Shadow ground truth (d) Top row corresponds to output from an individual bone surface segmentation network and bottom row corresponds to output from an individual bone shadow segmentation network (e) Top row corresponds to cascaded shadow segmentation output generated using the segmentation from individual network and bottom row corresponds to cascaded surface segmentation output generated using the segmentation from individual network (f) Surface output from ours (g) Shadow output from ours.

Effectiveness of CTFT: In Table 3, we show that adding CTFT to the base network improves the segmentation performance. To further validate the claim, we conduct more experiments as seen in Table 3. It can be observed that adding CTFT to a joint-UNet architecture results in a boost in performance.

Table 3. Ablation study. All results are reported in Dice score.

Method	SonixTouch		Clarius	
	Surface (%)	Shadow (%)	Surface (%)	Shadow (%)
Joint-UNet	76.45 ± 0.03	86.06 ± 0.15	75.11 ± 0.33	84.01 ± 0.17
Joint-UNet + CTFT	77.19 ± 0.17	89.01 ± 0.15	75.81 ± 0.21	84.71 ± 0.11

5   Conclusion

Accurate, complete, and robust bone and shadow segmentation are important to make ultrasound an essential imaging modality in clinically acceptable orthopedics procedures. In this paper, we propose an end-to-end network to simultaneously perform robust and accurate bone and shadow segmentation by leveraging complementary features between the two tasks. The main novelty of our work lies in (1) the first systematic design of exploiting interrelation between two tasks to improve both bone and shadow segmentation, and (2) the design of fusion method of CNN and vision transformer to leverage multi-task learning while optimizing accuracy-efficiency trade-off. We believe the multi-task learning framework is an important contribution to the field of US-based orthopedic procedures.

References

1. Alsinan, A., Vives, M., Patel, V., Hacihaliloglu, I.: Spine surface segmentation from ultrasound using multi-feature guided CNN. CAOS **3**, 6–10 (2019)
2. Alsinan, A.Z., Patel, V.M., Hacihaliloglu, I.: Automatic segmentation of bone surfaces from ultrasound using a filter-layer-guided CNN. Int. J. Comput. Assist. Radiol. Surg. **14**(5), 775–783 (2019)
3. Alsinan, A.Z., Patel, V.M., Hacihaliloglu, I.: Bone shadow segmentation from ultrasound data for orthopedic surgery using GAN. Int. J. Comput. Assist. Radiol. Surg. **15**(9), 1477–1485 (2020)
4. Dosovitskiy, A., et al.: An image is worth 16 × 16 words: transformers for image recognition at scale. arXiv preprint arXiv:2010.11929 (2020)
5. Graham, B., et al.: LeViT: a vision transformer in convnet's clothing for faster inference. arXiv preprint arXiv:2104.01136 (2021)
6. Hacihaliloglu, I.: Enhancement of bone shadow region using local phase-based ultrasound transmission maps. Int. J. Comput. Assisted Radiol. Surg. **12**(6), 951–960 (2017)
7. Hacihaliloglu, I.: Ultrasound imaging and segmentation of bone surfaces: a review. Technology **5**(02), 74–80 (2017)
8. Hacihaliloglu, I., Rasoulian, A., Rohling, R.N., Abolmaesumi, P.: Local phase tensor features for 3-D ultrasound to statistical shape+ pose spine model registration. IEEE Trans. Med. Imaging **33**(11), 2167–2179 (2014)
9. Hu, J., Shen, L., Sun, G.: Squeeze-and-excitation networks. In: Proceedings of the IEEE Conference on Computer Vision and Pattern Recognition, pp. 7132–7141 (2018)
10. Ronneberger, O., Fischer, P., Brox, T.: U-net: Convolutional networks for biomedical image segmentation. In: International Conference on Medical Image Computing and Computer-Assisted Intervention, pp. 234–241. Springer (2015). https://doi.org/10.1007/978-3-319-24574-4_28
11. Wang, P., Patel, V.M., Hacihaliloglu, I.: Simultaneous segmentation and classification of bone surfaces from ultrasound using a multi-feature guided CNN. In: Frangi, A.F., Schnabel, J.A., Davatzikos, C., Alberola-López, C., Fichtinger, G. (eds.) MICCAI 2018. LNCS, vol. 11073, pp. 134–142. Springer, Cham (2018). https://doi.org/10.1007/978-3-030-00937-3_16

12. Wang, P., Vives, M., Patel, V.M., Hacihaliloglu, I.: Robust bone shadow segmentation from 2D ultrasound through task decomposition. In: Martel, A.L., et al. (eds.) MICCAI 2020. LNCS, vol. 12266, pp. 805–814. Springer, Cham (2020). https://doi.org/10.1007/978-3-030-59725-2_78
13. Wang, P., Vives, M., Patel, V.M., Hacihaliloglu, I.: Robust real-time bone surfaces segmentation from ultrasound using a local phase tensor-guided CNN. Int. J. Comput. Assist. Radiol. Surg. 15, 1127–1135 (2020)

Contrastive Learning for Echocardiographic View Integration

Li-Hsin Cheng, Xiaowu Sun, and Rob J. van der Geest$^{(\boxtimes)}$

Division of Image Processing, Department of Radiology, Leiden University Medical Center, Leiden, The Netherlands
R.J.van_der_Geest@lumc.nl

Abstract. In this work, we aimed to tackle the challenge of fusing information from multiple echocardiographic views, mimicking cardiologists making diagnoses with an integrative approach. For this purpose, we used the available information provided in the CAMUS dataset to experiment combining 2D complementary views to derive 3D information of left ventricular (LV) volume. We proposed intra-subject and inter-subject volume contrastive losses with varying margin to encode heterogeneous input views to a shared view-invariant volume-relevant feature space, where feature fusion can be facilitated. The results demonstrated that the proposed contrastive losses successfully improved the integration of complementary information from the input views, achieving significantly better volume predictive performance (MAE: 10.96 ml, RMSE: 14.75 ml, R^2: 0.88) than that of the late-fusion baseline without contrastive losses (MAE: 13.17 ml, RMSE: 17.91 ml, R^2: 0.83). Code available at: https://github.com/LishinC/VCN.

Keywords: Contrastive learning · Multi-view integration · Echocardiogram · Left ventricular volume regression

1 Introduction

2D echocardiography is a major imaging modality for first-line cardiac function assessment and diagnosis of cardiovascular disease [1]. An echocardiographic examination usually contains multiple 2D images or cine loops from different viewpoints. To make the diagnosis, cardiologists often need to integrate information from multiple views. Mimicking such multi-view integration process is an critical challenge in automating echocardiography interpretation.

Limited by the available data (Sect. 3.1), we experimented specifically the objective of predicting LV volume using apical 2-chamber (A2C) and apical 4-chamber (A4C) views. Indeed volume regression is different from automated diagnosis, and only two input views are available instead of all possible views. However, it is an excellent scheme to investigate view integration, since the LV volume is a 3D information which can only

---

Supplementary Information The online version contains supplementary material available at https://doi.org/10.1007/978-3-031-16440-8_33.

L. Wang et al. (Eds.): MICCAI 2022, LNCS 13434, pp. 340–349, 2022.
https://doi.org/10.1007/978-3-031-16440-8_33

be accurately predicted by combining complementary information from the two 2D views. Concerning automated LV volume prediction, there are many prior studies in deriving LV volume with a segmentation approach [2–4]. However, the purpose of this study is to pave the way for the general problem of view integration in echocardiographic classification or regression tasks, and the volume prediction accuracy is used as a measure to assess view integration performance.

There are no existing studies in view integration for echocardiography volume regression. Therefore, we refer to classic view integration methods developed in other domains. The early-fusion architecture [5, 6] concatenates multiple input images along the channel dimension and processes the image stack with a single encoder. This simple architecture works for integrating anatomically similar images, but would not generalize well to combining multiple visually distinct echocardiographic views. Therefore, in this work, we adopted a late-fusion architecture [5–8], processing images from each view with a dedicated encoder branch, fusing the extracted features at a late stage, then predicting the final output with the fused feature.

However, a late-fusion architecture alone does not guarantee good performance. We therefore propose to leverage contrastive learning to fuse features from multiple views effectively. Contrastive learning has been widely applied to pre-train feature extractors for deriving a better feature representation [9, 10]. Importantly, recent studies [11] and [12] further applied contrastive learning to align video clips of a common object from different viewpoints, concerning human action videos and echocardiography, respectively. The core idea was to match frames at the same time point that contain relevant information to each other, and delineate frames within the same video clip of a viewpoint that contain distinct temporal information. This can be achieved, surprisingly, without any label information. By contrasting frame pairs, the encoder learns a temporal-disentangled and viewpoint-invariant feature representation. We further expanded the idea and applied it to improve the integration of echocardiographic views. Specifically, we aim to investigate if late fusion can be facilitated by contrastive learning mapping heterogeneous input views into a common feature space.

The contribution of the work is two-fold. Firstly, to the best of our knowledge, we are the first to apply contrastive learning for the purpose of multi-view integration. Secondly, we developed intra- and inter- subject volume contrastive losses with varying margin to encourage extraction of view-invariant volume-relevant features, which, in turn, benefits multi-view integration.

2 Methods

2.1 Volume Contrastive Network

As shown in Fig. 1 (a), the Volume Contrastive Network (VCN) consists of two Encoder branches, two Head blocks, and a Merging block. The encoders are each a ResNet50 [13]. For the Head block, we experimented with different settings. In the final VCN, it is simply a L2 normalization layer, mapping the extracted features from the encoders to a unit hypersphere for calculation of volume contrastive loss. Finally, the Merging block concatenates the extracted A2C and A4C features along the channel dimension, and outputs the LV volume prediction with a single linear layer. With no contrastive losses and only the regression loss as Eq. (1), a 2-branch late-fusion baseline model can be built:

$$L_{\text{reg}} = \frac{1}{N} \sum_i^N (y_i - \hat{y}_i)^2 \tag{1}$$

where N is the number of training subjects, y_i is the ground truth volume and $\hat{y}_i$ is the prediction for subject i.

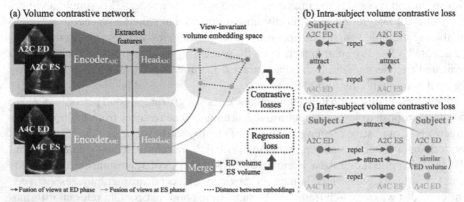

Fig. 1. Volume contrastive network (VCN) and contrastive losses. (a) The A2C and A4C frames at the same cardiac phase are combined to predict the LV volume at that phase. (b,c) The intra- and inter-subject volume contrastive losses encode heterogeneous input views to a common space where feature fusion can be facilitated.

2.2 Volume Contrastive Losses

By further adding volume contrastive losses, we constructed the VCN for better feature extraction and thus feature fusion. The final loss function of the VCN is described in Eq. (2), which consists of regression loss, intra-subject volume contrastive loss, and inter-subject volume contrastive loss, with λ_1 and λ_2 chosen empirically to be 1000.

$$L = L_{\text{reg}} + \lambda_1 L_{\text{intra}} + \lambda_2 L_{\text{inter}} \tag{2}$$

Intra-subject Volume Contrastive Loss. The main concept of the loss is illustrated in Fig. 1 (b). Considering the A2C and A4C cine loops from the same subject, despite the neighboring frames within the same cine loop from the same view resemble each other, the images at the end-diastolic (ED) and end-systolic (ES) phases actually encode very different temporal and volume information. One correspond to the largest and the other the smallest LV volume within the cardiac cycle. In an ideal embedding space that is highly relevant to the prediction objective of LV volume, the two embeddings should be far away from each other. Therefore, the ED-ES frame pairs from the same view are defined as negative pairs. The squared Euclidean distance between the embeddings of two images x_a and x_b is first described as Eq. (3):

$$\text{distance}(x_a, \ x_b) = \|\phi_a(x_a) - \phi_b(x_b)\|_2^2 \tag{3}$$

where $\phi_a(\cdot)$ and $\phi_b(\cdot)$ are the Encoders corresponding to the views of images x_a and x_b. Then, the summarized distances of the two negative pairs for subject i can be described as Eq. (4), which should be maximized.

$$D_{\text{neg}}(i) = \text{distance}\left(x_i^{A2C,ED}, \ x_i^{A2C,ES}\right) + \text{distance}\left(x_i^{A4C,ED}, \ x_i^{A4C,ES}\right) \tag{4}$$

On the other hand, although visually distinct, the A2C and A4C images at the same cardiac phase actually encode related information, which both describe the LV volume of the same subject at the same phase. Therefore, the A2C-A4C image pair at the same cardiac phase is defined as a positive pair, and their embeddings should be pulled closer. The summarized distances of the two positive pairs for subject i is described as Eq. (5).

$$D_{\text{pos}}(i) = \text{distance}\left(x_i^{A2C,ED}, \ x_i^{A4C,ED}\right) + \text{distance}\left(x_i^{A2C,ES}, \ x_i^{A4C,ES}\right) \tag{5}$$

Finally, the intra-subject volume contrastive loss is completed as Eq. (6), which encourages that the distances of the positive pairs would be at least smaller than that of the negative pairs by a certain margin.

$$L_{\text{intra}} = \sum_i^N \left[D_{\text{pos}}(i) - D_{\text{neg}}(i) + \alpha(i)\right]_+ \tag{6}$$

where the margin $\alpha(i) = \left(Vd_{\text{neg}}(i) - Vd_{\text{pos}}(i)\right) \times 0.005$. $Vd_{\text{neg}}(i)$ is the LV volume difference between the images in the negative pairs, which is the ED-ES volume difference, and $Vd_{\text{pos}}(i)$ the volume difference in positive pairs, which is 0. In previous works [9, 11], the margin was fixed at 0.2. Here we propose a varying margin $\alpha(i)$ based on the volume difference scaled by 0.005, such that the margin would center around 0.25. With the varying margin, negative pairs that have larger volume differences would be pushed further apart, while negative pairs that actually have smaller volume differences are allowed to stay just sufficiently apart. Such varying margin encourages a more delicate feature disentanglement. Note that the loss is clamped at zero, since pushing the embeddings of the negative pairs infinitely apart is unnecessary.

Inter-subject Volume Contrastive Loss. Under a similar spirit, we developed the inter-subject volume contrastive loss to provide even more diverse contrasting pairs and encourage even better feature disentanglement. The concept is illustrated in Fig. 1 (c), using the ED phase as an example: Although the ED frames from different subjects look different, their embeddings should be similar as long as the two images encode similar LV volume. Specifically, considering the frame at phase p of subject i, we find a random subject i' from the batch in each training iteration which has a similar volume at phase p to form a positive pair; While the negative pair is formed within subject i with the corresponding frame at the counter phase p'. (When p is ED phase, p' implies ES phase, and vice versa.) The distances of the positive and negative pairs can thus be described as Eq. (7) and (8), forming the inter-subject volume contrastive as Eq. (9):

$$D_{\text{pos}}(i, p) = \text{distance}\left(x_i^{A2C,p}, \ x_{i'}^{A2C,p}\right) + \text{distance}\left(x_i^{A4C,p}, \ x_{i'}^{A4C,p}\right) \tag{7}$$

$$D_{\text{neg}}(i, p) = \text{distance}\left(x_i^{A2C,p}, \ x_i^{A2C,p'}\right) + \text{distance}\left(x_i^{A4C,p}, \ x_i^{A4C,p'}\right) \tag{8}$$

$$L_{\text{inter}} = \sum_i^N \frac{1}{2} \sum_{p \in [ED,ES]} \left[D_{\text{pos}}(i, p) - D_{\text{neg}}(i, p) + \alpha(i, p)\right]_+ \tag{9}$$

where the margin $\alpha(i, p) = \left(Vd_{\text{neg}}(i, p) - Vd_{\text{pos}}(i, p)\right) \times 0.005$. $Vd_{\text{neg}}(i, p)$ here is still the volume difference between ED and ES, but $Vd_{\text{pos}}(i, p)$ becomes the volume difference between subjects i and i' at phase p. Note that since the calculation of inter-subject loss was repeated over the ED and ES phases, we divided it by 2 to maintain an identical scale as the intra-subject loss.

3 Experiments and Results

3.1 Experiment Settings

Data. The publically available CAMUS dataset [2] was used in this study. The released data contains 450 subjects. For each subject, the A2C and A4C views are available, each being a video clip either starting from ED to ES or from ES to ED. The LV volume of the ED and ES phases were provided, estimated by the Simpson's biplane method of discs.

The raw images in the dataset have varying sizes with a fixed grid resolution of 0.308 mm × 0.154 mm. We center-cropped and resized the images, such that each image becomes 256×256 pixel^2 with fixed grid resolution of 1.482 mm × 0.741 mm. The intensity of the images was divided by 255, so the processed images have intensity ranging from 0 to 1. During training, we applied on-the-fly augmentation to the images, including random shift, rotation, and multiplicative noise. We did not include random scaling or elastic transformation since the resized LV would no longer correspond to the LV volume ground truth.

Metrics and Statistical Test. We used the metrics Mean Absolute Error (MAE), Root Mean Square Error (RMSE), and coefficient of determination (R^2) to evaluate the performance of LV volume regression. The presented results are averaged over all test subjects' ED and ES phases. When comparing if one method significantly outperforms another, we sample with replacement 90% of the test subjects 1000 times. Each time, the difference between the two methods in terms of MAE, RMSE, and R^2 can be calculated. For each of the three metrics, if the 95% confidence interval does not contain 0, we reject the null hypothesis that the two methods are equal in terms of the metric.

Implementation Details. Five-fold cross test-validation was adopted. Specifically, the 450 subjects in the dataset were split into 5 folds. For the kth iteration, fold k was used as the testing set, and fold (k + 1) was used as the validation set, while the rest folds are used as the training set. The presented results are the averaged test performance. For fair comparison and maximizing the reproducibility, in all the experiments, all the Encoder blocks have the same weight initialization, and the Head and Merging blocks in two-view models also have identical weight initialization. The initial model weights, as well as the final built models, were provided in our GitHub repository. The Adam [14] optimizer was used for training, with learning rate set to 10^{-4} and weight decay set to 10^{-8}. The batch size was 16 and the models were trained for 2000 epochs with early stop.

3.2 Results

Comparison of VCN with Baselines. Rows 1–6 of Table 1 reports the performance of several baselines and the proposed VCN. There are no state-of-the-art methods of view integration in echocardiography. Therefore, we mainly compared VCN with classic view integration methods proposed in other domains – the early-fusion (#3) and late-fusion (#4) approaches. Additionally, the performance of a recent Transformer-based approach [8] (#5) is presented as a reference. All the comparisons are supported by statistical test with the detailed confidence interval provided in the supplementary. Firstly, if adopting the simple early-fusion setting (#3), the performance was even worse than that of using only the A4C view (#2). It is possible that if the complementary information from each view was not properly extracted and combined, the model would not even benefit from the extra input information that was provided. Secondly, the late-fusion baseline (#4) was better than using only A2C (#1), but not significantly different from the A4C model (#2). Although assigning a dedicated encoder for each view and fusing extracted features at a later stage made the model perform at least as good as the better view among the inputs, such architecture alone did not guarantee maximal utilization of all the complementary information from both input views. Finally, the proposed VCN (#6) significantly outperformed all the baseline models (#1–5), achieving MAE, RMSE, and R^2 of 10.96 ml, 14.75 ml, and 0.88. The VCN has the same architecture as the late-fusion baseline, but the additional volume contrastive losses further improved view integration.

Ablation Study on Contrastive Loss Variations. Under the same network architecture of two input views and two-branch late fusion, we experimented with different variations of the contrastive losses as shown in rows 7–9 of Table 1. Firstly, we found that each of the contrastive loss components (#7–8) resulted in better performance than the baselines (#1–5). Secondly, although the differences are not statistically significant, using only the intra-subject (#7) or inter-subject (#8) loss both resulted in a lower averaged performance than including both losses (#6). Finally, we experimented with intra-subject "phase" contrast (#9). This is a similar setting as intra-subject volume contrast (#7), but with a fixed margin of 0.2 as in the original time-contrastive network [11]. It did not outperform intra-subject volume contrast (#7), demonstrating that our varying margin based on volume difference did encourage better feature disentanglement.

Table 1. LV volume predictive performance.

#	Network	Input	MAE (ml)	RMSE (ml)	R^2
1	ResNet50	Single view (A2C)	14.27	19.93	0.788
2	ResNet50	Single view (A4C)	13.14	18.15	0.824
3	ResNet50 (Early-fusion baseline)	Two views concat.	14.50	19.78	0.791
4	Late-fusion baseline	Two views separated	13.17	17.91	0.829
5	Transformer based approach	Two views separated	12.57	18.67	0.807
6	Proposed VCN	Two views separated	**10.96**	**14.75**	**0.884**
7	Intra-subject loss only	Two views separated	11.33	15.78	0.867
8	Inter-subject loss only	Two views separated	11.59	15.41	0.873
9	Intra-subject "phase" contrast	Two views separated	11.80	16.39	0.856
10	ResNet50 + inter-subject loss	Single view (A2C)	13.50	18.83	0.811
11	ResNet50 + inter-subject loss	Single view (A4C)	12.86	17.63	0.834

However, intra-subject phase contrast (#9) could still improve multi-view integration as compared to the baselines (#1–5) without requiring the volume information at all. This setting would become useful in integrating more echocardiography views, where the phase could be known by electrocardiography (ECG), but the views are not volume relevant or when the volume is unknown. Note that we did not try inter-subject phase contrast since finding the positive pair would already require the volume information.

Performance Improvement Brought by View Integration. In rows 10–11 of Table 1, the performance is reported when using each of the single views with the inter-subject contrastive loss. Although the differences are not significant, it can be seen that, compared to the plain single-view models (# 1,2), the inter-subject loss improved the averaged performance (# 10,11) by extracting volume-relevant features. However, inter-subject loss using two views (# 8) still significantly outperformed using only single views (# 10,11). This indicated that the improved performance in the two-view settings was brought not only by the contrastive loss extracting volume-relevant features, but also by proper integration of the features from both views within a common feature space.

Further Analyses of VCN. The prediction-versus-ground truth scatter plot of the VCN is shown in Fig. S1(a), with the Pearson correlation coefficient being 0.94. The Bland–Altman plot is shown in Fig. S1(b), with the bias being -0.94 (ml) and the standard deviation being 9.87 (ml). Both plots indicate that the prediction agrees well with the ground truth without systematic under- or over- estimation of the LV volume.

With tSNE [15], we further visualized the extracted features of the late-fusion base-line and the VCN to investigate the impact of contrastive losses on feature extraction. By comparing Fig. 2 (a) to (b), it can be seen that, with volume contrastive losses, the embeddings of the A2C and A4C frames from the same phase became combined in one cluster. Furthermore, the comparison of Fig. 2 (c) to (d) indicates that the volume contrastive losses encourage better feature disentanglement, as the embeddings are bet-ter sorted according to the volume. Even if the late-fusion baseline was trained on the objective of LV volume regression, thus having full access to the volume information, the embedding was far less well sorted as that of the VCN. Finally, in the unit-hypersphere space where the extracted features were projected to by the Head block, we calculated the Euclidean distance between the embeddings of A2C ES, A2C ED, A4C ES, and A4C ED. The distances were averaged over all test subjects and presented in Fig. 2 (e, f). It can be seen that the contrastive losses successfully pushed apart the embeddings of the ED and ES frames, and pulled the complementary views at the same phase together. This again confirmed the extraction of view-invariant and volume-relevant features.

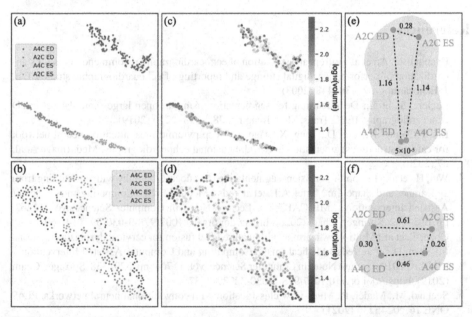

Fig. 2. Feature analysis. The upper row presents the result for the late-fusion baseline, and the lower row for the VCN. (a, b) are tSNE visualization of extracted feature colored by view-phase; (c, d) colored by volume. (e, f) are the averaged Euclidean distances between the embeddings. (Color figure online)

In summary, with the contrastive losses, the heterogeneous input views are mapped to the same view-invariant and volume-relevant feature space. It is likely that the features from different views are more easily fused within this common space, thus resulting in an improved performance in predicting the 3D information of LV volume.

4   Conclusion

In this work, we tackled the challenge of fusing information from multiple 2D echocardiographic views to derive 3D information of left ventricular (LV) volume. To the best of our knowledge, we are the first to apply contrastive learning for the purpose of multiview integration. We developed intra- and inter- subject volume contrastive losses with varying margin, encoding heterogeneous input views to the same view-invariant volume-relevant feature space, where feature fusion can be facilitated. The results demonstrated that the proposed contrastive losses successfully improved the fusion of complementary information from visually distinct views to achieve better volume predictive performance. Further data and experiments are required to verify if the method generalizes well to integrating more than two views and predicting other objectives.

Acknowledgement. The work of LC was supported by the RISE-WELL project under H2020 Marie Skłodowska-Curie Actions.

References

1. Evangelista, A., et al.: European association of echocardiography recommendations for standardization of performance, digital storage and reporting of echocardiographic studies. Eur. J. Echocardiogr. **9**, 438–448 (2008)
2. Leclerc, S., et al.: Deep learning for segmentation using an open large-scale dataset in 2D echocardiography. IEEE Trans. Med. Imaging. **38**, 2198–2210 (2019)
3. Liu, F., Wang, K., Liu, D., Yang, X., Tian, J.: Deep pyramid local attention neural network for cardiac structure segmentation in two-dimensional echocardiography. Med. Image Anal. **67**,(2020)
4. Wei, H., et al.: Temporal-consistent segmentation of echocardiography with co-learning from appearance and shape. In: Martel, A.L., et al. (eds.) Medical Image Computing and Computer Assisted Intervention – MICCAI 2020. Lecture Notes in Computer Science, vol. 12262, pp. 623–632. Springer, Cham (2020). https://doi.org/10.1007/978-3-030-59713-9_60
5. Chen, T., et al.: Multi-view learning with feature level fusion for cervical dysplasia diagnosis. In: Shen, D., et al. (eds.) Medical Image Computing and Computer Assisted Intervention – MICCAI 2019. Lecture Notes in Computer Science, vol. 11764, pp. 329–338. Springer, Cham (2019). https://doi.org/10.1007/978-3-030-32239-7_37
6. Seeland, M., Mäder, P.: Multi-view classification with convolutional neural networks. PLoS ONE **16**, e0245230 (2021)
7. Wu, N., et al.: Deep neural networks improve radiologists' performance in breast cancer screening. IEEE Trans. Med. Imaging. **39**, 1184–1194 (2020). https://doi.org/10.1109/TMI. 2019.2945514
8. van Tulder, G., Tong, Y., Marchiori, E.: Multi-view analysis of unregistered medical images using cross-view transformers. In: de Bruijne, M., et al. (eds.) Medical Image Computing and Computer Assisted Intervention – MICCAI 2021. Lecture Notes in Computer Science, vol. 12903, pp. 104–113. Springer, Cham (2021). https://doi.org/10.1007/978-3-030-87199-4_10
9. Schroff, F., Kalenichenko, D., Philbin, J.: FaceNet: a unified embedding for face recognition and clustering. In: 2015 IEEE Conference on Computer Vision and Pattern Recognition (CVPR), pp. 815–823 (2015)

10. Chen, T., Kornblith, S., Norouzi, M., Hinton, G.: A simple framework for contrastive learning of visual representations. In: 37th International Conference on Machine Learning. pp. 1597–1607, PMLR (2020)

11. Sermanet, P., et al.: Time-contrastive networks: self-supervised learning from video. In: 2018 IEEE International Conference on Robotics and Automation (ICRA), pp. 1134–1141 (2018)

12. Dezaki, F.T., et al.: Echo-SyncNet: self-supervised cardiac view synchronization in echocardiography. IEEE Trans. Med. Imaging. **40**, 2092–2104 (2021)

13. He, K., Zhang, X., Ren, S., Sun, J.: Deep residual learning for image recognition. In: 2016 IEEE Conference on Computer Vision and Pattern Recognition (CVPR), pp. 770–778 (2016)

14. Kingma, D.P., Ba, J.L.: Adam: a method for stochastic optimization. In: 3rd International Conference on Learning Representations, ICLR 2015 - Conference Track Proceedings. International Conference on Learning Representations, ICLR (2015)

15. Van Der Maaten, L., Hinton, G.: Visualizing data using t-SNE. J. Mach. Learn. Res. **9**, 2579–2625 (2008)

BabyNet: Residual Transformer Module for Birth Weight Prediction on Fetal Ultrasound Video

Szymon Płotka[1,2(✉)], Michal K. Grzeszczyk[1],
Robert Brawura-Biskupski-Samaha[3], Paweł Gutaj[4], Michał Lipa[5],
Tomasz Trzciński[6], and Arkadiusz Sitek[1]

[1] Sano Centre for Computational Medicine, Cracow, Poland
s.plotka@sanoscience.org
[2] Informatics Institute, University of Amsterdam, Amsterdam, The Netherlands
[3] The Medical Centre of Postgraduate Education, Warsaw, Poland
[4] Poznan University of Medical Sciences, Poznan, Poland
[5] Medical University of Warsaw, Warsaw, Poland
[6] Warsaw University of Technology, Warsaw, Poland

Abstract. Predicting fetal weight at birth is an important aspect of perinatal care, particularly in the context of antenatal management, which includes the planned timing and the mode of delivery. Accurate prediction of weight using prenatal ultrasound is challenging as it requires images of specific fetal body parts during advanced pregnancy which is difficult to capture due to poor quality of images caused by the lack of amniotic fluid. As a consequence, predictions which rely on standard methods often suffer from significant errors. In this paper we propose the Residual Transformer Module which extends a 3D ResNet-based network for analysis of $2D + t$ spatio-temporal ultrasound video scans. Our end-to-end method, called BabyNet, automatically predicts fetal birth weight based on fetal ultrasound video scans. We evaluate BabyNet using a dedicated clinical set comprising 225 2D fetal ultrasound videos of pregnancies from 75 patients performed one day prior to delivery. Experimental results show that BabyNet outperforms several state-of-the-art methods and estimates the weight at birth with accuracy comparable to human experts. Furthermore, combining estimates provided by human experts with those computed by BabyNet yields the best results, outperforming either of other methods by a significant margin. The source code of BabyNet is available at https://github.com/SanoScience/BabyNet.

Keywords: Deep learning · Fetal birth weight · Transformer

1 Introduction

Fetal birth weight (FBW) is a significant indicator of perinatal health prognosis. Accurate prediction of FBW, as well as gestational age, complications in pregnancy, and maternal physical parameters are critical in determining the best

---

S. Płotka and M. K. Grzeszczyk — Authors contributed equally.

L. Wang et al. (Eds.): MICCAI 2022, LNCS 13434, pp. 350–359, 2022.
https://doi.org/10.1007/978-3-031-16440-8_34

method of delivery (natural or Cesarean). These factors are widely used as a part of the hospital admission procedure in the world [14]. However, FBW prediction is a challenging task, requiring highly visible fetal body standard planes, which can only be identified by experienced sonographers. Unfortunately, weight predictions provided by experienced sonographers are often imprecise, with up to 10% mean absolute percentage errors. Currently, FBW is estimated on the basis of fetal biometric measurements of body organs – head circumference (HC), biparietal diameter (BPD), abdominal circumference (AC), femur length (FL), which are used as the input to heuristic formulae [6,11].

In recent years, machine learning-based methods have been proposed as a possible means of automating FBW prediction. Lu et al. [9,10] presents a solution based on an ensemble model consisting of Random Forest, XGBoost and LightGBM algorithms. Tao et al. [20] use a hybrid-LSTM network model [24] for temporal data analysis. Convolutional neural network (CNN)-based models are also proposed to estimate fetal weight based on ultrasound images [2,5] or videos [12,13]. However, such methods do not rely on the true FBW as the ground truth, but instead predict it through heuristic formulae using estimated fetal body-part biometrics, which is prone to errors.

Recently, Transformers [22] have been proposed as an alternative architecture to CNNs, and have achieved competitive performance for many computer vision tasks e.g. Vision Transformer (ViT) for image classification [3] or Video Vision Transformer (ViViT) for video recognition [1]. Transformers utilize the Multi-Head Self-Attention (MHSA) mechanism to learn the global context between input sequence elements. Unfortunately, due to their high computational complexity, Transformers require a large amount of training data and long training times. Many methods have been developed to bridge the gap between sample-efficient learning with a high inductive bias of CNNs and performance but data-inefficient Transformers. Hybrid models utilizing CNN layers and Transformer blocks have also been introduced [4,8,15].

In this paper we utilize Transformers for direct estimations of fetal weights from US videos. We implement this solution as an extension of a 3D ResNet-based network [21] with a Residual Transformer Module (RTM) called BabyNet. The RTM allows local and global feature representation through residual connections and utilization of convolutional layers. This representation is refined through the global self-attention mechanism included inside RTM. BabyNet is a hybrid neural network that efficiently bridges CNNs and Transformers for $2D + t$ spatio-temporal ultrasound video scans analysis to directly predict fetal birth weight. The main contribution of our work is as follows: (1) We provide an end-to-end method for birth weight estimation based directly on fetal ultrasound video scans, (2) We introduce a novel Residual Transformer Module by adding temporal position encoding to 3D MHSA in 3D ResNet-based neural network, (3) To the best of our knowledge, BabyNet is the first framework to automate fetal birth weight prediction on fetal ultrasound video scans trained and validated with data acquired one day prior to delivery.

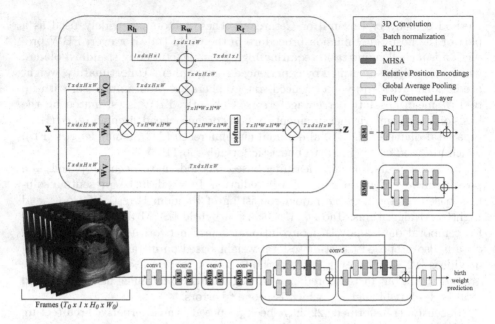

Fig. 1. The overview of proposed BabyNet for FBW estimation from fetal US video scans. In BabyNet, we replace two Residual Modules of 3D ResNet-18 with two Residual Transformer Modules (RTM) containing 3D Multi-Head Self-Attention (MHSA) with Relative Positional Encoding (RPE). RPE is calculated as the sum of height (R_h), width (R_w) and temporal (R_t) position encodings. For clarity, only one attention head is presented. The model takes 16 frames as the input to make a single-segment prediction. All frames for a given patient are divided into non-overlapping 16-frame segments and a patient-level prediction is obtained by averaging all segment predictions.

2   Method

The overview of our method for end-to-end FBW prediction is presented in Fig. 1. We use 3D ResNet-18 for high-level US feature extraction. The RTM is designed to learn local and global feature representation with 3D Multi-Head Self-Attention mechanism and convolutional layers. We replace the last two residual modules of ResNet with RTMs.

2.1   Feature Extraction

We employ 3D ResNet-18 [21] as the base network to extract high-level $2D + t$ spatio-temporal US feature representations. The initial input to the network is US video sequence $S_{US} \in \mathbb{R}^{T_0 \times 1 \times H_0 \times W_0}$ of height H_0, width W_0 and frame number T_0. It is transformed via convolutional residual modules to a low-resolution feature map sequence $S'_{US} \in \mathbb{R}^{T_1 \times D_1 \times H_1 \times W_1}$, where $T_1 = T_0/4$, $D_1 = 512$, $H_1 = H_0/8$, and $W_1 = W_0/8$. Multi-channel, low-resolution feature map sequences are fed to the RTM.

2.2 Residual Transformer Module

Residual modules are constructed from a layer followed by a rectified linear unit (ReLU) and Batch Normalization. This structure is repeated two or three times with a skip connection of the input added to the output of the previous layers [7]. To include global low-resolution feature map context processing via a self-attention mechanism we design RTM in a similar manner to BoT [19]. Our RTM extends BoT to 3D space by adding temporal position encoding [17] to 3D Multi-Head Self-Attention. BoT utilizes MHSA instead of 3×3 convolution in the residual bottleneck module, created to decrease the computational complexity in deeper ResNet architectures. 3D ResNets are often shallower and do not contain Bottleneck blocks. Thus, to utilize the self-attention mechanism in shallower ResNets we replace the last convolutional layer in the residual module with MHSA, and define RTM as:

$$y = BN\left(MHSA(\sigma(BN(Conv(x)) + x\right) \qquad (1)$$

where x and y are input and output of the RTM respectively, $Conv$ denotes the convolutional layer, BN is Batch Normalization and σ stands for ReLU.

2.3 3D Multi-Head Self-Attention

To learn multiple attention representations at different positions, instead of performing a single attention, many self-attention heads (Multi-Head Self-Attention) are jointly trained with their outputs concatenated [22]. Since such operation is permutation-invariant, positional encoding r needs to be added to include positional information. Depending on the application, absolute (e.g. sinusoidal) or relative positional encodings (RPE) [17], recently identified as a better fit for vision tasks [23], can be used. To process $2D+t$ US videos with MHSA we add temporal positional encoding to the 2D RPE and compute positional encoding r as the sum of $R_h \in \mathbb{R}^{1\times D\times H\times 1}$, $R_w \in \mathbb{R}^{1\times D\times 1\times W}$ and $R_t \in \mathbb{R}^{T\times D\times 1\times 1}$, the height, width and temporal positional encodings respectively. Finally, we compute the 3D MHSA output of $S_{US}^{''} \in \mathbb{R}^{T\times D\times H\times W}$ input as:

$$MHSA\left(S_{US}^{''}\right) = concat\left[softmax\left(\frac{Q_i(K_i + r)^T}{\sqrt{d}}\right)V_i\right] \qquad (2)$$

where $T = \frac{T_1}{2}$, $D = D_1$, $H = \frac{H_1}{2}$, $W = \frac{W_1}{2}$, Q_i, K_i, V_i are queries, keys and values for the ith attention head calculated from $W_Q(S_{US}^{''})$, $W_K(S_{US}^{''})$ and $W_V(S_{US}^{''})$ $1\times1\times1$ 3D convolutions performed over input $S_{US}^{''}$ and d is D divided by the number of heads.

3 Experiments

In this section, we describe our dataset and present architectural details of BabyNet. We compare BabyNet's performance with other $2D+t$ spatio-temporal

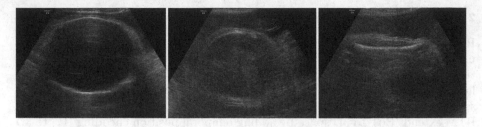

Fig. 2. Sample US frames extracted from fetal US videos. The frames show the fetal body part standard planes of the head, abdomen and femur respectively, going from left to right. Images obtained several hours before delivery are of lower quality than at earlier stages of pregnancy due to the lack of amniotic fluid.

video analysis methods and with results obtained from clinicians. We show, through an ablation study, the importance of BabyNet components that have been added or replaced in 3D ResNet-18.

Dataset and Pre-processing. Ethical Committee approval was obtained for all subjects enrolled in the study. The dataset consists of 225 2D fetal ultrasound video scans in standard plane view of fetal head, abdomen, and femur. The multi-centre dataset was obtained from 75 pregnant women aged 21 to 42 and acquired through routine US examinations less than 24 h prior to delivery. The data was acquired by three experienced sonographers using GE Voluson E6 and S10 devices. Each US video scan is stored in DICOM file format, captured in two resolutions: 960×720 and 852×1136 pixels. The number of frames is between 463 and 1448, with a mean of 852. The US videos were obtained in sector scan sweep mode with frame per second (FPS) between 24 and 37. For each video, we resample pixel spacing to 0.2×0.2 mm. As the ground truth, we use the true fetal weight measured at birth. The ground truth values were between 2085 and 4995, with a mean of 3454 grams [g].

Implementation Details. We adopt 3D ResNet-18 [21] as our base neural network. Table 1 presents the architectural details of BabyNet, as compared to 3D ResNet-18. BabyNet comprises a 3D convolutional stem followed by *conv* stages: three with two residual modules each, and one final stage implemented with two RTMs. The output of the final RTM is global average pooled (GAP) and fed to the fully-connected (FC) layer with one neuron (512 input weights) for fetal birth weight prediction. We implement our model with PyTorch and train it using an NVIDIA RTX 2080 Ti 24GB GPU with a mini-batch size of 2 and an initial learning rate of 1×10^{-4} with a step decay by a factor of $g = 0.1$ every 160th epochs until convergence over 200 epochs. To minimize the Mean Squared Error (MSE) loss function, we employ an ADAM optimizer with 1×10^{-4} weight decay. During training, we apply data augmentation including rotate ($\pm 25°$), random brightness and contrast, horizontal flip, image compression and blur for each mini-batch. We retain height and width ratio and resize video frames to

Table 1. Comparison of ResNet3D-18 and BabyNet architectures. We replace the last two residual modules of 3D ResNet-18 with two Residual Transformer Modules containing a 3D MHSA instead of the second 3×3 3D convolution.

Stage name	Output size	3D ResNet-18	BabyNet
conv1	$T_0 \times \frac{H_0}{2} \times \frac{W_0}{2}$	$3 \times 7 \times 7, 64$, stride $1 \times 2 \times 2$	
conv2	$T_0 \times \frac{H_0}{2} \times \frac{W_0}{2}$	$\begin{bmatrix} 3 \times 3 \times 3, 64 \\ 3 \times 3 \times 3, 64 \end{bmatrix} \times 2$	$\begin{bmatrix} 3 \times 3 \times 3, 64 \\ 3 \times 3 \times 3, 64 \end{bmatrix} \times 2$
conv3	$\frac{T_0}{2} \times \frac{H_0}{4} \times \frac{W_0}{4}$	$\begin{bmatrix} 3 \times 3 \times 3, 128 \\ 3 \times 3 \times 3, 128 \end{bmatrix} \times 2$	$\begin{bmatrix} 3 \times 3 \times 3, 128 \\ 3 \times 3 \times 3, 128 \end{bmatrix} \times 2$
conv4	$\frac{T_0}{4} \times \frac{H_0}{8} \times \frac{W_0}{8}$	$\begin{bmatrix} 3 \times 3 \times 3, 256 \\ 3 \times 3 \times 3, 256 \end{bmatrix} \times 2$	$\begin{bmatrix} 3 \times 3 \times 3, 256 \\ 3 \times 3 \times 3, 256 \end{bmatrix} \times 2$
conv5	$\frac{T_0}{8} \times \frac{H_0}{16} \times \frac{W_0}{16}$	$\begin{bmatrix} 3 \times 3 \times 3, 512 \\ 3 \times 3 \times 3, 512 \end{bmatrix} \times 2$	$\overbrace{\begin{bmatrix} 3 \times 3 \times 3, 512 \\ \textbf{MHSA} \end{bmatrix}}^{RTM} \times 2$
	$1 \times 1 \times 1$	Global Avg Pooling, FC layer	

64×64 ($H_0 \times W_0$) with padding. The number of attention heads is empirically set to 4, while the temporal sequence length T_0 is 16. Thus, BabyNet transforms US input sequence $S_{US} \in \mathbb{R}^{16 \times 1 \times 64 \times 64}$ to the output $O_{S_{US}} \in \mathbb{R}^1$ of predicted fetal birth weights. We perform 5-fold cross-validation (CV) to compare and verify the robustness of the regression algorithm. We ensure that data from a single patient appears only in a single fold. As measurement metrics, we use Root Mean Square Error (RMSE), Mean Absolute Error (MAE), and Mean Absolute Percentage Error (MAPE) to evaluate the regression performance.

Comparison with Clinicians and State-of-the-Art Algorithms. We compare BabyNet with several $2D + t$ spatio-temporal video analysis methods. In particular, we compare it with results obtained by clinicians in [18] as well as results obtained by clinicians for the dataset used in this work. We also present results for Video Vision Transformer (ViViT) [1] and test the hybrid approach of 2D ResNet-50 as a convolutional feature extractor (without GAP and FC layers) to ViViT network. Finally, we utilize a vanilla 3D ResNet-18 [21]. We train all models in the same fashion as BabyNet.

Table 2 presents a comparison of 5-fold CV results for all tested methods. Results for machine learning methods are out-of-fold predictions. Combination of estimations performed by clinicians with estimations provided by BabyNet is the most accurate, with MAE of 180 ± 156 (max p-value < 0.001), RMSE of 237 ± 145 (max p-value < 0.001), and MAPE of 5.2 ± 4.6 (max p-value < 0.001). Max p-value is the maximum paired dual sided p-value computed for results of the "Clinicians (this work) & BabyNet" method and other methods listed in Table 2.

Table 2. Five-fold cross-validation results and comparison of state-of-the-art methods. The mean of Mean Absolute Error (MAE), Root Mean Square Error (RMSE) and Mean Absolute Percentage Error (MAPE) across all folds are reported.

Method	mMAE [g]	mRMSE [g]	mMAPE [%]
Clinicians (from [18])	-	-	7.9 ± 6.8
Clinicians (this work)	213 ± 155	264 ± 158	6.3 ± 4.8
ViViT [1]	361 ± 244	444 ± 230	10.6 ± 7.3
2D ResNet + ViViT	344 ± 241	426 ± 226	10.3 ± 7.2
3D ResNet-18 [21]	328 ± 234	421 ± 225	10.1 ± 7.1
BabyNet	254 ± 230	341 ± 215	7.5 ± 6.6
Clinicians (this work) & BabyNet	$\mathbf{180 \pm 156}$	$\mathbf{237 \pm 145}$	$\mathbf{5.2 \pm 4.6}$

We did not detect a statistically significant difference between the performance of clinicians measured in [18] and our algorithm (p-value = 0.6). Estimations provided by clinicians in our study seem to be better than those provided by clinicians in [18] (p-value = 0.04) and BabyNet (p-value = 0.07). Out of all neural networks investigated in this work, the hybrid approach of utilizing 3D convolutions and 3D MHSA within RTM as a part of 3D ResNet-18 outperforms other methods based on plain CNNs, plain Transformer or CNN+Transformer networks.

We noted that the best results were obtained by averaging estimations provided by clinicians and by BabyNet. The performance of the ensemble of clinicians & BabyNet was better by 18% compared to clinicians alone in terms of mMAPE, which is a clear indication of added value and potential clinical benefits of BabyNet.

Ablation Study. We conducted an ablation study to show the effectiveness of novel components within BabyNet. In this experiment, we employ 3D ResNet-18 as the base neural network for $2D + t$ spatio-temporal US video scan analysis. To learn multiple relationships and enable capture of richer interpretations of the US video sequence, we integrate CNN and Transformer by swapping the last convolutional layer in the residual module for MHSA. To further enhance $2D + t$ spatio-temporal feature representation in space and time, we add temporal position encoding (TPE). Table 3 demonstrates that the combination of CNN with a Transformer-based module, MHSA and temporal position encoding improves performance of the weight-estimation task directly from US video scan.

Table 3. Ablation study.

Method	mMAE [g] ↓	mRMSE [g] ↓	mMAPE [%] ↓
3D ResNet-18 (base)	328 ± 234	421 ± 225	10.1 ± 7.1
+ RTM	277 ± 228	374 ± 221	8.1 ± 7.0
+ RTM + TPE (ours)	$\mathbf{254 \pm 230}$	$\mathbf{341 \pm 215}$	$\mathbf{7.5 \pm 6.6}$

4 Discussion

In this work we were not able to match the performance of the clinicians in estimating fetal weight (mMAPE 7.5% vs. 6.3%); however, clinicians who worked with us and provided measurements are top experts in performing biometric measurements. On the other hand, we were able to match the performance of clinicians reported in [18] (7.5% vs. 7.9% p-value = 0.6). The training data set was relatively small and we expect to significantly improve the performance of BabyNet by using more data in future work.

The method presented here can be characterized as end-to-end. Due to $2D+t$ spatio-temporal feature processing it does not require standard plane detection which substantially reduces the workload involved in performing the estimation of FBW. In clinical practice, BabyNet can be used as an aid for clinicians in their decision-making process regarding the type of delivery. According to literature [16,18] the heavier the child, the greater the likelihood of Cesarean delivery. Serious complications may arise when a heavy child's FBW is misjudged. Under these circumstances, if natural delivery is decided upon severe complications for both mother and child may arise.

This work has certain limitations. A relatively small number of patients was used in the study, which can affect the accuracy and generalization of results. A related issue is that the patient population is limited and we do not know if BabyNet would work on a different population (e.g. different race). The algorithm is trained and evaluated on short clips of US videos recorded by clinicians. To operate in a clinical setting, further effort would be needed to create a system that extracts appropriate clips for BabyNet analysis.

5 Conclusions

In this paper we presented an extension of the 3D ResNet-based network with a Residual Transformer Module (RTM), named BabyNet, for $2D + t$ spatio-temporal fetal ultrasound video scan analysis. The proposed framework is an end-to-end method that automatically performs fetal birth weight prediction. This is done without the need for finding standard planes in ultrasound video scans, which are required in the classical method of estimating fetal weight. Combining classical and BabyNet estimations provides the best results, significantly outperforming top expert clinicians who use available commercial tools. Our method has the potential to help clinicians select – on the basis of US examination – the type of delivery which is safest for the mother and the child. Future work includes testing BabyNet on external datasets which are preferably acquired using different devices and by operators with different levels of experience. Moreover, we plan to use multimodal data – combine the fetal US video and clinical data to improve the performance and robustness of the model.

Acknowledgements. This work is supported by the European Union's Horizon 2020 research and innovation programme under grant agreement Sano No 857533 and the International Research Agendas programme of the Foundation for Polish Science, co-financed by the European Union under the European Regional Development Fund. We would like to thank Piotr Nowakowski for his assistance with proofreading the manuscript.

References

1. Arnab, A., Dehghani, M., Heigold, G., Sun, C., Lučić, M., Schmid, C.: ViVit: a video vision transformer. In: Proceedings of the IEEE/CVF International Conference on Computer Vision (ICCV), pp. 6836–6846 (2021)
2. Bano, S., et al.: AutoFB: automating fetal biometry estimation from standard ultrasound planes. In: de Bruijne, M., et al. (eds.) MICCAI 2021. LNCS, vol. 12907, pp. 228–238. Springer, Cham (2021). https://doi.org/10.1007/978-3-030-87234-2_22
3. Dosovitskiy, A., et al.: An image is worth 16x16 words: transformers for image recognition at scale. In: International Conference on Learning Representations (2021)
4. d'Ascoli, S., Touvron, H., Leavitt, M.L., Morcos, A.S., Biroli, G., Sagun, L.: ConViT: improving vision transformers with soft convolutional inductive biases. In: International Conference on Machine Learning, pp. 2286–2296. PMLR (2021)
5. Feng, M., Wan, L., Li, Z., Qing, L., Qi, X.: Fetal weight estimation via ultrasound using machine learning. IEEE Access **7**, 87783–87791 (2019)
6. Hadlock, F.P., Harrist, R., Sharman, R.S., Deter, R.L., Park, S.K.: Estimation of fetal weight with the use of head, body, and femur measurements-a prospective study. Am. J. Obstet. Gynecol. **151**(3), 333–337 (1985)
7. He, K., Zhang, X., Ren, S., Sun, J.: Deep residual learning for image recognition. In: Proceedings of the IEEE conference on computer vision and pattern recognition, pp. 770–778 (2016)
8. Liu, Y., Sun, G., Qiu, Y., Zhang, L., Chhatkuli, A., Van Gool, L.: Transformer in convolutional neural networks. arXiv preprint arXiv:2106.03180 (2021)
9. Lu, Y., Fu, X., Chen, F., Wong, K.K.: Prediction of fetal weight at varying gestational age in the absence of ultrasound examination using ensemble learning. Artif. Intell. Med. **102**, 101748 (2020)
10. Lu, Y., Zhang, X., Fu, X., Chen, F., Wong, K.K.: Ensemble machine learning for estimating fetal weight at varying gestational age. In: Proceedings of the AAAI conference on artificial intelligence, vol. 33, pp. 9522–9527 (2019)
11. Milner, J., Arezina, J.: The accuracy of ultrasound estimation of fetal weight in comparison to birth weight: a systematic review. Ultrasound **26**(1), 32–41 (2018)
12. Płotka, S., Klasa, et al.: Deep learning fetal ultrasound video model match human observers in biometric measurements. Phys. Med. Biol. **67**(4), 045013 (2022)
13. Płotka, S., et al.: FetalNet: multi-task deep learning framework for fetal ultrasound biometric measurements. In: Mantoro, T., Lee, M., Ayu, M.A., Wong, K.W., Hidayanto, A.N. (eds.) ICONIP 2021. CCIS, vol. 1517, pp. 257–265. Springer, Cham (2021). https://doi.org/10.1007/978-3-030-92310-5_30
14. Pressman, E.K., Bienstock, J.L., Blakemore, K.J., Martin, S.A., Callan, N.A.: Prediction of birth weight by ultrasound in the third trimester. Obstet. Gynecol. **95**(4), 502–506 (2000)

15. Reynaud, H., Vlontzos, A., Hou, B., Beqiri, A., Leeson, P., Kainz, B.: Ultrasound video transformers for cardiac ejection fraction estimation. In: de Bruijne, M., et al. (eds.) MICCAI 2021. LNCS, vol. 12906, pp. 495–505. Springer, Cham (2021). https://doi.org/10.1007/978-3-030-87231-1_48

16. Scioscia, M., Vimercati, A., Ceci, O., Vicino, M., Selvaggi, L.E.: Estimation of birth weight by two-dimensional ultrasonography: a critical appraisal of its accuracy. Obstet. Gynecol. **111**(1), 57–65 (2008)

17. Shaw, P., Uszkoreit, J., Vaswani, A.: Self-attention with relative position representations. arXiv preprint arXiv:1803.02155 (2018)

18. Sherman, D.J., Arieli, S., Tovbin, J., Siegel, G., Caspi, E., Bukovsky, I.: A comparison of clinical and ultrasonic estimation of fetal weight. Obstet. Gynecol. **91**(2), 212–217 (1998)

19. Srinivas, A., Lin, T.Y., Parmar, N., Shlens, J., Abbeel, P., Vaswani, A.: Bottleneck transformers for visual recognition. In: Proceedings of the IEEE/CVF conference on computer vision and pattern recognition, pp. 16519–16529 (2021)

20. Tao, J., Yuan, Z., Sun, L., Yu, K., Zhang, Z.: Fetal birthweight prediction with measured data by a temporal machine learning method. BMC Med. Inform. Decis. Mak. **21**(1), 1–10 (2021)

21. Tran, D., Wang, H., Torresani, L., Ray, J., LeCun, Y., Paluri, M.: A closer look at spatiotemporal convolutions for action recognition. In: Proceedings of the IEEE conference on Computer Vision and Pattern Recognition, pp. 6450–6459 (2018)

22. Vaswani, A., et al.: Attention is all you need. In: Advances in Neural Information Processing Systems, pp. 5998–6008 (2017)

23. Wu, K., Peng, H., Chen, M., Fu, J., Chao, H.: Rethinking and improving relative position encoding for vision transformer. In: Proceedings of the IEEE/CVF International Conference on Computer Vision, pp. 10033–10041 (2021)

24. Xingjian, S., Chen, Z., Wang, H., Yeung, D.Y., Wong, W.K., Woo, W.: Convolutional LSTM network: a machine learning approach for precipitation nowcasting. In: Advances in Neural Information Processing Systems, pp. 802–810 (2015)

EchoGNN: Explainable Ejection Fraction Estimation with Graph Neural Networks

Masoud Mokhtari[1] ⓘ, Teresa Tsang[2], Purang Abolmaesumi[1(✉)],
and Renjie Liao[1(✉)]

[1] Electrical and Computer Engineering, University of British Columbia,
Vancouver, BC, Canada
{masoud,purang,rjliao}@ece.ubc.ca
[2] Vancouver General Hospital, Vancouver, BC, Canada
t.tsang@ubc.ca

Abstract. Ejection fraction (EF) is a key indicator of cardiac function, allowing identification of patients prone to heart dysfunctions such as heart failure. EF is estimated from cardiac ultrasound videos known as echocardiograms (echo) by manually tracing the left ventricle and estimating its volume on certain frames. These estimations exhibit high inter-observer variability due to the manual process and varying video quality. Such sources of inaccuracy and the need for rapid assessment necessitate reliable and explainable machine learning techniques. In this work, we introduce EchoGNN, a model based on graph neural networks (GNNs) to estimate EF from echo videos. Our model first infers a latent echo-graph from the frames of one or multiple echo cine series. It then estimates weights over nodes and edges of this graph, indicating the importance of individual frames that aid EF estimation. A GNN regressor uses this weighted graph to predict EF. We show, qualitatively and quantitatively, that the learned graph weights provide explainability through identification of critical frames for EF estimation, which can be used to determine when human intervention is required. On EchoNet-Dynamic public EF dataset, EchoGNN achieves EF prediction performance that is on par with state of the art and provides explainability, which is crucial given the high inter-observer variability inherent in this task. Our source code is publicly available at: https://github.com/MasoudMo/echognn.

Keywords: Ultrasound · Ejection fraction · Cardiac imaging · Explainable models · Graph Neural Networks · Deep learning

1 Introduction

Ejection fraction (EF) is a ratio indicating the volume of blood pumped by the heart. This measurement is crucial in monitoring cardiovascular health and is a

Supplementary Information The online version contains supplementary material available at https://doi.org/10.1007/978-3-031-16440-8_35.

potential indicator of heart failure [9,17]. EF is computed using the stroke volume, which is the blood volume difference in the Left Ventricle (LV) during the End-Systolic (ES) and End-Diastolic (ED) phases of the cardiac cycle denoted by ESV and EDV, respectively [2]. These volumes are estimated from ultrasound videos of the heart, *i.e.* echocardiograms (echo), which involves detecting the frames corresponding to ES and ED and tracing the LV region. The manual process of detecting the correct frames and making proper traces is prone to human error. Therefore, the American Society of Echocardiography recommends performing EF estimation for up to 5 cardiac cycles and averaging the results [16]. However, this guideline is seldom followed in practice, and a single representative beat is selected for evaluation instead. This results in inter-observer variations from 7.6% to 13.9% in the EF ratio [18].

Automatic EF estimation techniques aid professionals by adding another layer of verification. Additionally, with the emergence of Point-of-Care Ultrasound (POCUS) imaging devices, which are routinely used by less experienced echo users, automation of clinical measurements such as EF is further needed [1]. However, to be adopted broadly, such automation techniques must be explainable to detect when human intervention is required. Different machine learning (ML) architectures have been proposed to perform automatic EF estimation [10,12,18,21,23], most of which lack reliable explainability mechanisms. Some of these models fail to provide the model's confidence on their predictions [18,21,23] or have low accuracy due to unrealistic data augmentation during training and over-reliance on ground truth labels [21].

In this work, we introduce EchoGNN, a novel deep learning model for explainable EF estimation. Our approach first infers a latent graph between frames of one or multiple echo cine series. It then estimates EF based on this latent graph via Graph Neural Networks (GNNs) [22], which are a class of deep learning models that efficiently capture graph data. To the best of our knowledge, our work is the first one that investigates GNNs in the context of ultrasound videos and EF estimation. Moreover, our work brings explainability through latent graph learning, inspiring further work in this domain. Our contributions are threefold:

- We introduce EchoGNN, a novel deep learning model for explainable EF estimation through GNN-based latent graph learning.
- We present a weakly-supervised training pipeline for EF estimation without direct reliance on ground truth ES/ED frame labels.
- Our model has a much lower number of parameters compared to prior work, significantly reducing computational and memory requirements.

2   Related Work

Most prior works use Convolutional Neural Networks (CNNs) in their EF estimation pipeline [10,12,18,21]. Ouyang et al. [18] uses ResNet-based (2+1)D convolutions [24] to estimate and average EF for all possible 32-frame clips in an echo, while Kazemi Esfeh et al. [12] uses a similar approach under the Bayesian Neural Networks (BNNs) setting. Recent work uses the encoder of ResNetAE [8] to reduce data dimensionality before using transformers [25] to jointly perform ES/ED frame detection and EF estimation [21]. While these methods show different levels of accuracy and success in predicting EF, they either lack explainability or significantly rely on accurate clinical labels, which are inherently noisy and subject to significant inter-observer variability. As an example, the transformer-based approach requires ES/ED frame index labels in addition to EF labels in its training pipeline [21]. Lastly, while Kazemi Esfeh et al. and Jafari et al. [10,12] report uncertainty on their predictions, they still lack explainable indicators as to why models fail or succeed for different cases. Our proposed framework based on GNNs aims to alleviate these shortcomings. It provides explainability by only relying on EF labels and not requiring ES/ED frame labels in a supervised manner. Lastly, as an added advantage, the number of parameters for our model is significantly less than prior work, which is highly desirable for deploying such models on mobile clinical devices.

3   Methodology

We consider the following supervised problem for EF estimation: assume for each patient $i \in [N]$ in dataset D, there is a ground truth EF ratio $y^i \in \mathbb{R}$, and there are K number of echo videos $x_k^i \in \mathbb{R}^{T \times W \times H}$, where $k \in [K]$, T is the number of frames, and H and W are the height and width of each frame. The goal of our model is to learn a function $f : \mathbb{R}^{K \times T \times H \times W} \to \mathbb{R}$ to estimate EF from echo videos. For notational simplicity and since our evaluation dataset only contains one video per patient, we assume that $K = 1$. However, it must be noted that our model is flexible in this regard and can handle multiple videos per patient.

3.1   EchoGNN Architecture

As shown in Fig. 1, EchoGNN is composed of three main components: Video Encoder, Attention Encoder, and Graph Regressor. In the following subsections, we discuss the details pertaining to each component.

Video Encoder. The original echo videos are high-dimensional and must be mapped into lower-dimensional embeddings to reduce memory footprint and remove redundant information.

The Video Encoder is used to learn a mapping $f_{ve} : R^{T \times H \times W} \to R^{T \times d}$ from input echo videos $x^i \in \mathbb{R}^{T \times W \times H}$ to d-dimensional embeddings $h_j^i \in \mathbb{R}^d$, where $j \in [T]$ is the frame number. The temporal dimension is preserved because the Attention Encoder requires embeddings for all frames to produce interpretable weights over them. We use a custom network consisting of 3D convolutions and residual connections to use both the spatial and temporal information in the video in generating the embeddings. This network's architecture is provided in the supp. material. Lastly, following [25], periodic positional encodings are added to the generated frame embeddings to encode the sequential nature of video data.

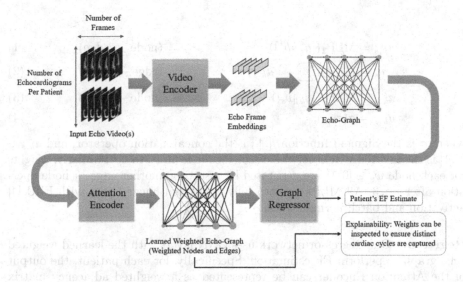

Fig. 1. EchoGNN has three main components. (1) Video Encoder: encodes video frames into vector embeddings while preserving the temporal dimension; (2) Attention Encoder: infers weights over the nodes (video frames) and edges (relationships among frames) of the echo-graph; (3) Graph Regressor: estimates EF using the inferred weighted graph; this figure shows an example where each patient has an apical two-chamber (AP2) and an apical four-chamber (AP4) echo video.

Attention Encoder. For each patient, we construct an *echo-graph*, which is a complete graph where each node corresponds to a frame in the echo video, and the edges show the non-Euclidean relationship between these frames. Formally, we denote the echo-graph with $G_{echo}(V, E)$ where V is the set of nodes corresponding to echo frames such that $|V| = T$, and E is the set of edges between the nodes to show the relationship between video frames such that if $v_1, v_2 \in V$ are connected, then $e_{v_1,v_2} \in E$. We use the frame embeddings from our Video Encoder as node features of G_{echo}. That is, $\{h_1^i, h_2^i, ..., h_T^i\}$ are the set of features for $\{v_1, v_2, ..., v_T\}$. These embeddings can be represented as a matrix $H^i \in \mathbb{R}^{T \times d}$ such that each row is the embedding for a frame in the echo video for patient i.

Inspired by [14], we propose using GNNs to learn and assign weights to both edges and nodes of the echo-graph. The edge and node weights are learned to encode the importance of each frame (node weights) and the relationships among frames (edge weights) for the final EF estimation.

The Attention Encoder infers weights over edges and nodes of the echo-graph using message passing based GNNs [7]. A single message passing step is enough for each node to capture information from all other nodes due to echo-graph being a complete graph. More specifically, the following operations are used to obtain weights over each edge e_{v_k,v_s}:

$$u_{k,s} = \text{MLP}_1([h_k^i \| h_s^i]) \qquad\qquad \text{(node} \rightarrow \text{edge)} \qquad (1)$$

$$v_s = \text{MLP}_2(\sum_{k \neq s} u_{k,s}) \qquad\qquad \text{(edge} \rightarrow \text{node)} \qquad (2)$$

$$z_{k,s} = \text{MLP}_3([v_k \| v_s]) \qquad\qquad \text{(node} \rightarrow \text{edge)} \qquad (3)$$

$$a_{k,s} = \sigma(z_{k,s}), \qquad\qquad\qquad\qquad\qquad\qquad\quad (4)$$

where σ is the Sigmoid function, $[.\|.]$ is the concatenation operator, and $a_{k,s} \in [0,1]$ is the inferred weight for the directed edge from v_k to v_s. Similarly, weights for each node $w_s \in [0,1]$ are generated by inserting another edge $\rightarrow$ node operation after Eq. 3. All MLPs use two fully connected linear layers with ELU [4] activation and batch normalization.

Regressor. Our Regressor network uses GNN layers with the learned weighted echo-graph to perform EF estimation. Specifically, for each patient, the output of the Attention Encoder can be represented as a weighted adjacency matrix $A \in [0,1]^{T \times T}$ and a node weight vector $w \in [0,1]^T$. The Regressor uses A to generate embeddings over frames of the echo video:

$$H^l = g^l(A, H^{l-1}), \quad l = 1, ..., L \qquad (5)$$

where $H^l \in \mathbb{R}^{T * d_g}$ is the matrix of learned node embeddings at layer l, H^0 is the matrix of frame embeddings from the Video Encoder, and g^l is composed of a Graph Convolutional Network (GCN) layer followed by batch normalization and ELU activation [15]. To represent the whole graph with a single vector embedding, the node embeddings are averaged using the frame weights w generated by the Attention Encoder:

$$h_{\text{graph}}^i = \frac{\sum_{j=1}^T w_j * H_j^l}{\sum_{j=1}^T w_j}, \qquad (6)$$

where $H_j^l \in \mathbb{R}^d$ is the jth row of H^l, and w_j is the jth scalar weight in the frame weight vector. h_{graph}^i is mapped into an EF estimate using an MLP with two fully connected linear layers, ELU activation and batch normalization.

Learning Algorithm. The model is differentiable in an end-to-end manner. Therefore, we use gradient descent with Mean-Absolute-Error (MAE) between predicted EF estimates $\tilde{y}^i$ and ground truth EF values $y^i \in Y$ as the optimization objective, which is computed as $L = \frac{1}{N} \sum_{i=1}^N |\tilde{y}^i - y^i|$.

4 Experiments

4.1 Dataset

We use EchoNet-Dynamic public EF dataset consisting of 10,030 AP4 echo videos obtained between 2016 and 2018 at Stanford University Hospital. Each echo frame has a dimension of 112×112, and the dataset provides ESV, EDV, contour tracings of LV, and EF ratios for each patient [18]. We use the provided splits in the dataset from mutually exclusive patients, including 7465 samples for training, 1288 samples for validation, and 1277 samples for testing. The data distribution in the training set is unbalanced with only 12.7% of samples having EF ratio below 40%. Clinically, however, such patients are most critical to be detected for timely intervention [3,11].

Frame Sampling: To stay within reasonable memory requirements, we use a fixed number of frames per echo denoted by T_{fixed}. During training, we uniformly sample an initial frame index j in $[1, T_{\text{total}}^i - T_{\text{fixed}}]$, where T_{total}^i is the total number of frames in echo video i. We then use T_{fixed} samples starting from j. Following [18], we set T_{fixed} to 64 and use zero padding in the temporal dimension when $T_{\text{total}}^i < T_{\text{fixed}}$. During test time, we extract multiple back to back clips with each clip containing T_{fixed} frames and the first clip starting from index 0. We use zero padding in the temporal dimension if $T_{\text{total}}^i < T_{\text{fixed}}$ and overlap the last clip with the previous one if the last clip overshoots T_{total}^i. We set T_{fixed} to 64 and independently estimate EF for each clip and report the average prediction.

Data Augmentation: Occasionally, AP4 echo is zoomed in on the LV region for certain clinical studies [5,20]. To allow learning of this under-represented distribution, we augment our training set by using a fixed cropping window of 90×72 centered at the top of each frame and interpolating the result to achieve the original 112×112 dimension, which creates the desired zoom-in effect.

4.2 Implementation

The Video Encoder uses custom convolution blocks with 16, 32, 64, 128, and 256 channels. The Attention Encoder uses a hidden dimension of 128 for MLP layers, and the Regressor uses 3-layer GNN with 128, 64 and 32 hidden dimensions followed by an MLP with a hidden dimension of 16. We use the Adam optimizer [13] with a learning rate of 1e-4, a batch size of 80, and 2500 training epochs. Our framework is implemented using PyTorch [19] and PyG [6], and the training was performed on two Nvidia Titan V GPUs. **Pretraining:** We use ES/ED index labels in a pretraining step to train the Video Encoder and the Attention Encoder to give higher weights to ES and ED frames. **Classification Loss:** We bin the EF values into 4 ranges $[0 - 30], (30, 40], (40, 55], (55, 100]$ and use a cross-entropy loss encouraging the model to learn EF's clinical categories [3].

4.3 Results and Discussion

Explainability. The key advantage of EchoGNN over prior work is the explainability it provides through the learned weights on the echo-graph. As shown in Fig. 2, the learned weights can indicate when human intervention is required. We observe two different scenarios: (1) the model learns the periodic nature of echo videos and assigns larger weights to frames and edges that are in between ES and ED phases before performing EF estimation. This means that the location of ES and ED can be approximated using these weights as illustrated in Fig. 2. (2) The model cannot detect the location of ES and ED frames and distributes weights more evenly. We see that in these cases, we have either an atypical zoomed-in AP4 echo or an echo where the LV is not entirely visible and is cropped. In such cases, an expert can evaluate the video and determine if new videos must be obtained. More explainability examples are provided in the supp. material.

To quantitatively measure the explainability of EchoGNN, for the cases where the model learns the periodic nature of the data (1173 samples out of 1277), we use the average frame distance (aFD) as in [21], which is computed as $aFD = \frac{1}{N} \sum_{i=1}^{N} |j_i - \tilde{j}_i|$ with j_i and $\tilde{j}_i$ being the true and approximated indices, respectively, for sample i. As shown in Table 1, our model achieves better ED aFD and comparable ES aFD without using ground-truth ES/ED locations for training, whereas Reynaud et al. [21] uses such supervision. This shows the explainability power of EchoGNN. aFD computation details are provided in the supp. material.

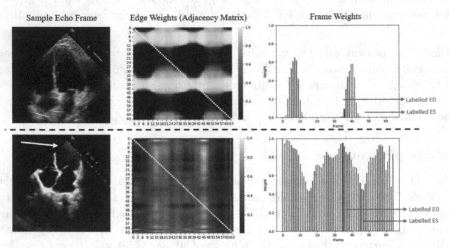

Fig. 2. (Top) An example where the model has learned the periodic nature of the data, and the learned weights allow identification of ES/ED locations. (Bottom) Another example where the LV region is cropped (as shown by the arrow), and learned weights are distributed more evenly indicating the need for expert intervention.

EF Estimation. To evaluate the error in predicted EF values, we use Mean-Absolute-Error (MAE). Additionally, as a measure of the amount of explained variance in the data, we report the model's R^2 score. Moreover, we report the F_1 score for the task of indicating whether EF values are lower than 40%, which is a strong indicator of heart failure [11].

As shown in Table 1, our model significantly outperforms [21] without direct supervision of ES and ED frame locations during training. Our model has similar predictive performances as [12] with a much lower number of parameters and the added benefit of explainability through the learned latent graph structures. EchoNet (AF) [18] requires large amounts of RAM due to sampling all 32-frame clips in a video, making us unable to train and evaluate the model. Because of this we only report results from the paper and cannot produce additional metrics such as F_1 score which is not originally reported, and hence we show this with N/A in Table 1. This model's weak performance compared to our model shows the sensitivity of EchoNet (AF) to frame locations in a clip. Lastly, our model has a significantly lower number of parameters, making it desirable for deployment on mobile clinical devices. Our model's EF scatter plot and confusion matrix are provided in the supp. material.

Table 1. Summary of quantitative results. Lower values are better for all metrics besides R^2 and F_1. EchoNet (AF) averages predictions on all possible 32-frame clips in a sampled video. Transformer (R) and (M) are transformer-based models with different sampling techniques. The Bayesian model uses BNNs. We mark the models that cannot predict ES/ED locations as "-" in the aFD metric. EchoGNN is the only model that provides explainability and ES/ED location estimations without direct supervision.

Model	R^2	MAE	F_1 <40%	ES aFD	ED aFD	#params ($\times 10^6$)
EchoNet (AF) [18]	0.4	7.35	N/A	-	-	31.5
Transformer (R) [21]	0.48	6.76	0.70	**2.86**	7.88	346.8
Transformer (M) [21]	0.52	5.95	0.55	3.35	7.17	346.8
Bayesian [12]	0.75	4.46	0.77	-	-	31.5
EchoGNN (ours)	**0.76**	**4.45**	**0.78**	4.15	**3.68**	**1.7**

4.4 Ablation Study

In Table 2, we see that the classification loss improves model's performance for under-represented samples, while pretraining and data augmentation reduce EF error and increase the model's ability to represent the variance in data.

Table 2. Ablation study results. Aug., Class., and Pretrain columns indicate if the model uses data augmentation, classification loss and pretraining, respectively. We see that the classification loss improves performance for under-represented groups, while pretraining and data augmentation reduce overall EF error.

Aug	Class	Pretrain	R^2	MAE	F_1 <40%
✓	✗	✗	0.75	4.48	0.76
✓	✓	✗	0.74	4.59	0.77
✓	✗	✓	0.75	4.47	0.73
✗	✓	✓	0.75	4.47	0.77
✓	✓	✓	**0.76**	**4.45**	**0.78**

5   Limitations

While our model outperforms prior works for EF estimation and also provides explainability, there are certain limitations that can be addressed in future work. Firstly, while the explainability provided over frames and edges of the echo-graph allows identification of cases that need closer inspection, they do not allow finding regions of each frame that the model is uncertain about. We argue that an attention map over the pixels in each frame can further help with explainability. Secondly, creating a complete graph for long videos leads to large memory cost. While this is not an issue for echo, where videos are relatively short, alternative graph construction methods should be considered for longer videos.

6   Conclusion

In this work, we introduce a deep learning model that provides the benefit of explainability via GNN-based latent graph learning. While we showcased the success of our framework for EF estimation, we argue that the same pipeline could be used for other datasets and problems, introducing a new paradigm for video processing and prediction tasks from clinical data and beyond.

Acknowledgements. This research was supported in part by the Natural Sciences and Engineering Research Council of Canada (NSERC), the Canadian Institutes of Health Research (CIHR) and computational resources provided by Advanced Research Computing at the University of British Columbia.

References

1. Amaral, C., Ralston, D., Becker, T.: Prehospital point-of-care ultrasound: a transformative technology. SAGE Open Med. **8**, 2050312120932706 (2020)
2. Bamira, D., Picard, M.: Imaging: echocardiology-assessment of cardiac structure and function. In: Vasan, R.S., Sawyer, D.B. (eds.) Encyclopedia of Cardiovascular Research and Medicine, pp. 35–54. Elsevier, Oxford (2018)
3. Carroll, M.: Ejection fraction: Normal range, low range, and treatment (2021). https://www.healthline.com/health/ejection-fraction
4. Clevert, D.A., Unterthiner, T., Hochreiter, S.: Fast and accurate deep network learning by exponential linear units (ELUs). arXiv: Learning (2016)
5. Ferraioli, D., Santoro, G., Bellino, M., Citro, R.: Ventricular septal defect complicating inferior acute myocardial infarction: a case of percutaneous closure. J. Cardiovas. Echogr. **29**(1), 17–19 (2019)
6. Fey, M., Lenssen, J.E.: Fast graph representation learning with PyTorch geometric. In: ICLR Workshop on Representation Learning on Graphs and Manifolds (2019)
7. Gilmer, J., Schoenholz, S.S., Riley, P.F., Vinyals, O., Dahl, G.E.: Neural message passing for quantum chemistry. CoRR abs/1704.01212 (2017)
8. Hou, B.: ResNetAE (2019). https://github.com/farrell236/ResNetAE
9. Huang, H., et al.: Accuracy of left ventricular ejection fraction by contemporary multiple gated acquisition scanning in patients with cancer: comparison with cardiovascular magnetic resonance. J. Cardiovas. Magn. Reson. **19**(1), 34 (2017)

10. Jafari, M.H., Woudenberg, N.V., Luong, C., Abolmaesumi, P., Tsang, T.: Deep Bayesian image segmentation for a more robust ejection fraction estimation. In: 2021 IEEE 18th International Symposium on Biomedical Imaging (ISBI), pp. 1264–1268 (2021)
11. Kalogeropoulos, A.P., et al.: Characteristics and outcomes of adult outpatients with heart failure and improved or recovered ejection fraction. JAMA Cardiol. **1**(5), 510–518 (2016)
12. Kazemi Esfeh, M.M., Luong, C., Behnami, D., Tsang, T., Abolmaesumi, P.: A deep Bayesian video analysis framework: towards a more robust estimation of ejection fraction. In: Martel, A.L., et al. (eds.) MICCAI 2020. LNCS, vol. 12262, pp. 582–590. Springer, Cham (2020). https://doi.org/10.1007/978-3-030-59713-9_56
13. Kingma, D., Ba, J.: Adam: a method for stochastic optimization. In: International Conference on Learning Representations (2014)
14. Kipf, T., Fetaya, E., Wang, K.C., Welling, M., Zemel, R.: Neural relational inference for interacting systems. In: Proceedings of the 35th International Conference on Machine Learning (2018)
15. Kipf, T.N., Welling, M.: Semi-supervised classification with graph convolutional networks. arXiv preprint arXiv:1609.02907 (2016)
16. Lang, R.M., et al.: Recommendations for cardiac chamber quantification by echocardiography in adults: an update from the American society of echocardiography and the European association of cardiovascular imaging. J. Am. Soc. Echocardiogr. **28**(1), 1-39.e14 (2015)
17. Loehr, L., Rosamond, W., Chang, P., Folsom, A., Chambless, L.: Heart failure incidence and survival (from the atherosclerosis risk in communities study). Am. J. Cardiol. **101**(7), 1016–1022 (2008)
18. Ouyang, D., et al.: Video-based AI for beat-to-beat assessment of cardiac function. Nature **580**(7802), 252–256 (2020)
19. Paszke, A., et al.: PyTorch: an imperative style, high-performance deep learning library. In: Wallach, H., Larochelle, H., Beygelzimer, A., d'Alché-Buc, F., Fox, E., Garnett, R. (eds.) Advances in Neural Information Processing Systems 32, pp. 8024–8035. Curran Associates, Inc. (2019)
20. Patil, V., Patil, H.: Isolated non-compaction cardiomyopathy presented with ventricular tachycardia. Heart views **12**(2), 74–78 (2011)
21. Reynaud, H., Vlontzos, A., Hou, B., Beqiri, A., Leeson, P., Kainz, Bernhard: Ultrasound video transformers for cardiac ejection fraction estimation. In: de Bruijne, M., et al. (eds.) MICCAI 2021. LNCS, vol. 12906, pp. 495–505. Springer, Cham (2021). https://doi.org/10.1007/978-3-030-87231-1_48
22. Scarselli, F., Gori, M., Tsoi, A.C., Hagenbuchner, M., Monfardini, G.: The graph neural network model. IEEE Trans. Neural Networks **20**(1), 61–80 (2008)
23. Smistad, E., et al.: Real-time automatic ejection fraction and foreshortening detection using deep learning. IEEE Trans. Ultrason. Ferroelectr. Freq. Control **67**(12), 2595–2604 (2020)
24. Tran, D., Wang, H., Torresani, L., Ray, J., LeCun, Y., Paluri, M.: A closer look at spatiotemporal convolutions for action recognition. CoRR abs/1711.11248 (2017)
25. Vaswani, A., et al.: Attention is all you need. CoRR abs/1706.03762 (2017)

EchoCoTr: Estimation of the Left Ventricular Ejection Fraction from Spatiotemporal Echocardiography

Rand Muhtaseb[(✉)] [ID] and Mohammad Yaqub [ID]

Mohamed Bin Zayed University of Artificial Intelligence,
Abu Dhabi, United Arab Emirates
{rand.muhtaseb,mohammad.yaqub}@mbzuai.ac.ae

Abstract. Learning spatiotemporal features is an important task for efficient video understanding especially in medical images such as echocardiograms. Convolutional neural networks (CNNs) and more recent vision transformers (ViTs) are the most commonly used methods with limitations per each. CNNs are good at capturing local context but fail to learn global information across video frames. On the other hand, vision transformers can incorporate global details and long sequences but are computationally expensive and typically require more data to train. In this paper, we propose a method that addresses the limitations we typically face when training on medical video data such as echocardiographic scans. The algorithm we propose (EchoCoTr) utilizes the strength of vision transformers and CNNs to tackle the problem of estimating the left ventricular ejection fraction (LVEF) on ultrasound videos. We demonstrate how the proposed method outperforms state-of-the-art work to-date on the EchoNet-Dynamic dataset with MAE of 3.95 and R^2 of 0.82. These results show noticeable improvement compared to all published research. In addition, we show extensive ablations and comparisons with several algorithms, including ViT and BERT. The code is available at https://github.com/BioMedIA-MBZUAI/EchoCoTr.

Keywords: Transformers · Deep learning · Echocardiography · Ejection fraction · Heart failure

1 Introduction

In medical imaging, there are different imaging modalities that are crucial to real-time clinical assessment and visualization. An example of this is echocardiography, which produces spatiotemporal data made of a sequence of two-dimensional (2D) images. When dealing with spatiotemporal data, it is essential to learn the spatial information as well as take into account the temporal factor in these sequences for an accurate diagnosis. In order to detect abnormalities and certain diseases, cardiologists also tend to take into consideration the temporal information when measuring the left ventricular ejection fraction (LVEF) or while

© The Author(s), under exclusive license to Springer Nature Switzerland AG 2022
L. Wang et al. (Eds.): MICCAI 2022, LNCS 13434, pp. 370–379, 2022.
https://doi.org/10.1007/978-3-031-16440-8_36

assessing heart wall motion [5]. LVEF can be measured as the difference in the left ventricle volume at end-diastole and end-systole divided by the end-diastolic volume estimated from the apical four-chamber (a4c) or apical-two chamber (a2c) views of the heart. LVEF is an important biomarker that can predict heart failure (HF), which is a serious condition that can be caused when the heart cannot pump enough blood and consequently, oxygen to other parts of the body. In 2018, heart failure contributed to 13.4% of the recorded deaths in the United States [16]. Early diagnosis of HF will help cardiologists prescribe medications and encourage patients to have effective lifestyles [18]. Heart failure is typically diagnosed if LVEF is less than the normal range (50–80%). Echocardiography is the most common imaging modality used to assess cardiac function by measuring the left ventricle volume, wall thickness and LVEF since it is real-time, low-cost, ionizing radiation free, portable and a highly sensitive tool compared to other modalities. However, ultrasound technology has many drawbacks, such as operator-dependence, noise, artifacts and decreased contrast that may affect its quality which could lead to a high inter- and intra- observer variability in the diagnosis [17].

In this paper, we study the impact of different CNNs and transformer models to estimate left ventricle ejection fraction (LVEF) from ultrasound videos. Convolutional neural networks (CNNs) have shown great success when training the models to tackle problems in medical or natural images. However, vision transformers have shown that they may be good contenders to CNNs when solving certain image analysis problems. There are major differences between the two approaches. CNNs have limited receptive fields in the initial layers, but can progressively enlarge the field of view through convolution operations. In contrast, vision transformers (ViTs), can have the entire field of view starting from the initial layers through the self-attention process. However, unlike CNNs, ViTs do not have inductive bias and hence typically require a large amount of data to train on which is not always available especially in medical imaging. A research study shows that the initial layers of a ViT cannot acquire local information if the dataset is small, which highly impacts the model accuracy [9]. Hence, having a method that combines the strengths of both CNNs and ViTs, to work efficiently with spatiotemporal data in medical imaging assessment, is of great value.

Our contribution in this work is three fold:

- We propose EchoCoTr (**Echo Co**nvolutional **Tr**ansformer) which is a method that is able to analyze echocardiography video sequences by combining the strength of CNNs and vision transformers to accurately estimate the heart's ejection fraction. Even though EchoCoTr is adapted from UniFormer [6] which worked on natural video datasets, some changes were made to address the challenging problems we face such as proper frame sampling.
- We show how our proposed method outperforms all published work to-date on a large scale public dataset [8,10], which does not require: 1) information regarding the position of end-systolic (ES) and end-diastolic (ED) frames, 2) segmentation masks as EchoNet-Dynamic's beat-to-beat pipeline [8], and 3) a pre-defined length of the cardiac scan.

- We compare our proposed method with several existing deep learning algorithms and perform thorough ablation studies to provide a deep discussion of the results.

2   Related Works

Many research papers [11,13,14,19] were introduced to improve the segmentation of the left ventricle to accurately estimate ejection fraction. Silva et al. [12] used a 3D CNN with residual learning blocks to estimate ejection fraction from transthoracic echocardiography (TTE) exams. Ouyang et al. [8] proposed a deep learning approach to estimate the beat-to-beat ejection fraction and predict heart failure with reduced ejection fraction (HFrEF) by combining the semantic segmentation results and the clip-level ejection fraction prediction using spatiotemporal CNN [15]. Recently, Reynaud et al. [10] proposed a transformer model based on residual auto-encoder to reduce the dimensions followed by Bidirectional Encoder Representations from Transformers (BERT) for end-systolic (ES) and end-diastolic (ED) frame detection and ejection fraction estimation. Understanding spatiotemporal data using transformers can also be found in other medical imaging domains. Latest research areas have been focusing on using transformers to diagnose COVID-19 [4,20,21] and perform 3D image segmentation of multi-organ and on brain tumor datasets [2].

A recent work was proposed by Li et al. [6] in a modified transformer version that combines the strengths of 3D CNNs and spatiotemporal transformers. The UniFormer has three main components. The first component is Dynamic Position Embeddings (DPE) which maintains the spatiotemporal positions of the video tokens by applying 3D depthwise convolution without padding. The second component is Multi-Head Relation Aggregator (MHRA) which learns the local token relations to ignore the redundancy due to the small differences found in adjacent frames in the initial layers. However, in the last two stages, MHRA learns the global token affinity, which is similar to the self-attention scheme. The last component is Feed Forward Network (FFN) which has two linear layers.

3   Methods

In this section, we describe the frames sampling approach, model architecture and the proposed method when estimating ejection fraction from echocardiographic videos.

3.1   Frames Sampling

Deep learning networks require a fixed number of video frames from each scan. However, EchoNet-Dynamic videos contain one or more cardiac cycles, which also vary in the number of frames per cycle (approximately 20-30 frames). Moreover, the differences between the adjacent video frames are small. Because of

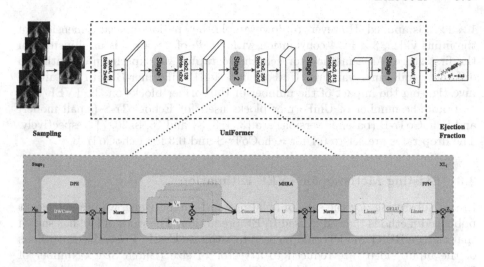

Fig. 1. The overall architecture of EchoCoTr is based on UniFormer [6]. Echocardiographic videos will be first sampled, to introduce dissimilarity between the frames, then fed to the UniFormer model to predict the LVEF for the entire video sequence.

that, we had to perform a video frame sampling by experimenting with different number of frames {32, 36, 40} and uniform frequencies {2, 4, 6} adapted by [8]. The sampling operation starts with a random clip within the range of [0 - (Number of original video frames - (Number of sampling video frames - 1) * Sampling frequency)]. Prior to that, in the case of short videos, frames filled with zeros will be added to the end of the video. The strength of using video sampling techniques replaces the traditional methods that clinicians do, which requires knowing the location of ES and ED frames before calculating the LVEF. In addition to that, as the location of ES and ED frames are already known beforehand, we also experimented with only selecting ES and ED frames from the video to check if these are sufficient to give an adequate LVEF prediction. A summary of some experiments related to video sampling is found in Table 2.

3.2 Architecture Overview

EchoCoTr builds on UniFormer [6] to address both the challenges of the local redundant features and the complex dependency among the video frames in the cardiac echo scans. Subtle differences between adjacent frames make it important that the network selects the most representative frames when estimating LVEF. Therefore, we had to adapt an architecture that effectively learns the local features without redundancy in the adjacent frames while capturing the global information along the video. An illustration of the overall architecture is found in Fig. 1. Before feeding the ultrasound videos to the UniFormer model to generate LVEF prediction, we sample the video frames to introduce dissimilarity and make sure that there is no redundancy between the neighboring frames. Before each stage in the UniFormer model, $1 \times 2 \times 2$ convolution with stride of

$1 \times 2 \times 2$ is applied. However, to downsample the spatiotemporal dimensions of the input video, $3 \times 4 \times 4$ convolution with stride of $2 \times 4 \times 4$ is used instead in the first stage. As a method for echocardiography, we experimented with two different UniFormer variants: UniFormer-S and UniFormer-B with the aim of investigating the impact of the number of UniFormer blocks on the LVEF estimation. The number of UniFormer blocks used for EchoCoTr-S (small model) and EchoCoTr-B (baseline version) are {3, 4, 8, 3} and {5, 8, 20, 7}, respectively. The drop rates are set to 0.1 for EchoCoTr-S and 0.3 for EchoCoTr-B.

3.3   Existing Methods for LVEF Estimation

In this subsection, for the sake of ablations and comparisons, we present recent published methods that addressed LVEF prediction. The work of [10] has shown that using a BERT model could be used to estimate LVEF. First, the dimensions of the input videos are reduced to a vector of size (Batch Size × Number of Frames) × 1024 using a ResNetAE [3] encoder. Two sampling strategies were introduced by [10]. The first is mirroring (M), which places the repeated sequence between the ES and ED frames after the last annotated frame. The second strategy is random sampling (R), which adds up 10-70% of the distance between the two annotated frames before and after the sampled frames from a heart cycle. However, the result that was reported did not outperform [8] that used a spatiotemporal convolution based ResNet (ResNet (2+1)D) [15]. Therefore, we compare our proposed method with the BERT method [10] and with other transformer models, such as DistilBERT and ViT.

4   Experiments

In this section, we aim to give a brief summary of the dataset used and experimental setup that we had for our experiments.

4.1   Datasets

EchoNet-Dynamic. [7] is the largest publicly available dataset of echocardiographic scans for the apical four-chamber (a4c) view of the heart acquired from the Stanford University Hospital. It consists of 10,030 videos in total. Each video consists of a sequence of 112×112 grayscale images and traces for the left ventricle end-systole (ES) and end-systole (ED) frames. In addition, every video is labelled with the corresponding end-systolic volume (ESV), end-diastolic volume (EDV) and ejection fraction (EF).

4.2   Experimental Setup

The data split sizes for training, validation and testing are 7460, 1288 and 1277, respectively. This is the same split chosen by [7]. All selected hyperparameters are optimized experimentally. The evaluation metrics used are mean absolute error (MAE), root mean squared error (RMSE) and R-squared (R^2). In addition to that, we also compare the floating point operations (FLOPs) values for the different models using fvcore package [1].

EchoCoTr Experiments: EchoCoTr models are trained on an NVIDIA A100 GPU for 45 epochs. The batch sizes used for EchoCoTr-S and EchoCoTr-B are 25 and 16, respectively. AdamW is used as an optimizer with a value of 1e-4 for both the learning rate and weight decay. Both models were pretrained on the Kinetics-400 dataset with different pretraining strategies. EchoCoTr-S is pretrained on $16 \times 1 \times 4$ frames with sampling stride of 8. However, the weights used for EchoCoTr-B is $32 \times 1 \times 4$ frames with sampling stride of 4. Frame resolutions are kept as same as in the original public dataset (112×112).

Other Experiments. BERT, DistilBERT and ViT models are trained for 5 epochs with batch size of 2, which is small because of the large model size. AdamW is used as an optimizer with a learning rate of 1e-5 and weight decay of 1e-2. Images are padded to be 128×128 in size to facilitate fair comparison and easy integration for the three models. The Hugging Face Python library is used for the transformer experiments.

Table 1. Comparison with the state-of-the-art results on EchoNet-Dynamic dataset. "R." and "M" are the sampling methods proposed by [10], which refer to random and mirroring sampling. EchoNet-Dynamic (1) predicts the clip-level LVEF using 32 frames. EchoNet-Dynamic (2) uses the segmentation and clip-level LVEF outputs to evaluate the beat-to-beat LVEF estimation for the entire video sequence. One sample from the testing dataset is used to calculate the FLOPs.

Model	No. of frames	FLOPs	MAE ↓	RMSE ↓	R^2 ↑
UVT R. [10]	128	130.00G	6.77	8.70	0.48
UVT M. [10]	128	130.00G	5.95	8.38	0.52
R3D [8]	32	92.273G	4.22	5.62	0.79
MC3 [8]	32	97.656G	4.54	5.97	0.77
EchoNet-Dynamic [8] (1)	32	91.974G	4.22	5.56	0.79
EchoNet-Dynamic [8] (2)	beat-to-beat	-	4.05	5.32	0.81
EchoCoTr-B	36	44.907G	**3.98**	**5.34**	**0.81**
EchoCoTr-S	36	19.611G	**3.95**	**5.17**	**0.82**

5   Results

As Table 1 shows, our EchoCoTr-S model, which was trained on only 36 frames with sampling frequency of 4 (3.95 MAE), outperforms the state-of-the-art results reported by [8,10]. It is also noticeable from the results that the

EchoCoTr-S experiment (3.95 MAE) performed slightly better than EchoCoTr-B (3.98 MAE). We test the effect of various sampling frequencies and sizes on the LVEF prediction. Results in Table 2 show that a sampling frequency of 4 frames achieves the best result for both small and baseline models. In addition, the optimal number of frames is found to be 36 for both models. Surprisingly, training both EchoCoTr-S and EchoCoTr-B models on only two frames (ES and ED) from each video achieves lower yet satisfactory results (4.432 and 4.494 MAE).

Table 2 also displays the results of our experiments that we performed using BERT, DistilBERT and ViT. We only report the experiments for the mirroring sampling strategy, as it achieved better results than the random one in [10]. Results suggest that the BERT model with the mirroring sampling on 36 and 128 frames (5.788 and 5.950 MAE, respectively) [10] performs better than DistilBERT and ViT when estimating LVEF. Moreover, reducing the number of frames to 36 was negatively impacting DistilBERT's MAE score the most (6.689).

Table 2. Ablation study: Summary of experiments performed on the EchoNet-Dynamic Dataset using EchoCoTr and transformer models. The sampling strategy used for BERT, DistilBERT and ViT experiments is mirroring [10]. 2* refers to the two video frames used, which are ES and ED.

Model	Frequency	No. of frames	Batch size	MAE ↓	RMSE ↓	R^2 ↑
BERT	-	36	2	5.788	8.137	0.545
BERT [10]	-	128	2	5.950	8.380	0.520
DistilBERT	-	36	2	6.689	9.234	0.414
DistilBERT	-	128	2	6.430	8.940	0.451
ViT	-	36	2	6.454	8.955	0.448
ViT	-	128	2	6.527	9.053	0.436
EchoCoTr-S	-	2*	25	4.432	5.998	0.759
EchoCoTr-S	2	36	25	4.168	5.541	0.795
EchoCoTr-S	4	32	25	3.966	5.290	0.813
EchoCoTr-S	4	36	25	**3.947**	**5.174**	**0.821**
EchoCoTr-S	4	40	25	4.010	5.326	0.810
EchoCoTr-S	6	36	25	4.135	5.434	0.803
EchoCoTr-B	-	2*	16	4.494	6.205	0.743
EchoCoTr-B	2	36	16	4.184	5.590	0.791
EchoCoTr-B	4	36	16	**3.980**	**5.342**	**0.809**
EchoCoTr-B	6	36	16	4.068	5.410	0.804

6   Discussion

In this paper, we propose EchoCoTr which is a method that combines the strengths of 3D CNNs and vision transformers for spatiotemporal echocardiography assessment in order to estimate LVEF on ultrasound videos.

The results in Table 1 show that the model trained using EchoCoTr-S on only 36 frames with a uniform sampling frequency of 4 (3.95 MAE), outperforms the state-of-the-art results reported by EchoNet-Dynamic on the beat-to-beat pipeline for LVEF prediction (4.05 MAE). In addition, unlike EchoNet-Dynamic, our method does not require the segmentation masks. Furthermore, our score is also better than the result that EchoNet-Dynamic stated for 32 frames and a sampling frequency of 2 frames (4.22 MAE). As illustrated in Table 2, a proper video sampling strategy plays a role in improving the results when using EchoCoTr models. This might be due to the different details that the model attends to spatially and temporally. For instance, not all adjacent frames might be needed during training and frames from multiple heart cycles are likely needed to provide a better temporal representation. Furthermore, we think that 36 frames with sampling frequency of 4 is found to be an ideal configuration to the problem at hand, because it covered multiple cardiac cycles (4-5 cycles) while skipping redundant and similar frames in most of the videos found in the EchoNet-Dynamic dataset. Hence, this has led to a more accurate estimation of LVEF prediction for the entire video. In fact, the frame sampling strategy we propose is aligned with the clinical guidelines that suggest estimating LVEF from up to 5 cardiac cycles.

Another remarkable result found is that EchoCoTr achieves satisfactory LVEF estimations when trained on only two frames (ES and ED). Due to its design, it ignores the local redundant features but learns the long-range dependencies. This follows the same methodology that clinicians do when calculating the EDV and ESV values to estimate LVEF.

It is also clearly seen from Table 2 that training on 36 frames achieves comparable results to 128 frames for BERT, DistilBERT and ViT models. However, all these experiments did not perform as well as our proposed method. We hypothesize that these models could not capture the temporal information as effectively as our proposed method while learning the local features within different frames. We believe that EchoCoTr-B performed marginally less than EchoCoTr-S due to its large architectural size that might be an overkill for the LVEF estimation problem.

7   Conclusion

We propose EchoCoTr which utilizes CNNs' discriminative spatial ability with transformers' temporal perception to estimate LVEF from a set of sampled frames from multiple heart cycles. The method outperforms other recent work when estimating ejection fraction on the EchoNet-Dynamic dataset. The goal of this paper is not to comprehensively study the performance of different transformer models, but to compare their performances with our CNN-Transformer method on spatiotemporal image analysis. For future work, it is valuable to study the effect of self-supervision on EchoCoTr's performance by using the unlabelled frames from each video. EchoNet-Dynamic dataset size proved to be enough to produce good results using EchoCoTr and spatiotemporal convolutional neural networks. Furthermore, it is also worth experimenting with the impact of performance on smaller datasets and datasets with abnormal motion of the heart.

Acknowledgments. We thank Mohamed Bin Zayed University of Artificial Intelligence (MBZUAI) for providing funding for this study, and Mohamed Saeed for providing his support.

References

1. Facebookresearch: fvcore: flop counter for pyTorch models. https://github.com/facebookresearch/fvcore/blob/main/docs/flop_count.md
2. Hatamizadeh, A., et al.: UNETR: transformers for 3D medical image segmentation (2021)
3. Hou, B.: ResNetAE-https://github.com/farrell236/resnetae (2019). https://github.com/farrell236/ResNetAE
4. Hsu, C.C., Chen, G.L., Wu, M.H.: Visual transformer with statistical test for COVID-19 classification (2021)
5. Lara Hernandez, K.A., Rienmüller, T., Baumgartner, D., Baumgartner, C.: Deep learning in spatiotemporal cardiac imaging: a review of methodologies and clinical usability. Comput. Biol. Med. **130**, 104200 (2021). https://doi.org/10.1016/j.compbiomed.2020.104200. https://www.sciencedirect.com/science/article/pii/S001048252030531X
6. Li, K., et al.: UNIFORMER: unified transformer for efficient spatiotemporal representation learning (2022)
7. Ouyang, D., et al.: EchoNet-Dynamic: a large new cardiac motion video data resource for medical machine learning. In: NeurIPS ML4H Workshop, Vancouver, BC, Canada (2019)
8. Ouyang, D., et al.: Video-based AI for beat-to-beat assessment of cardiac function. Nature **580**(7802), 252–256 (2020). https://doi.org/10.1038/s41586-020-2145-8
9. Raghu, M., Unterthiner, T., Kornblith, S., Zhang, C., Dosovitskiy, A.: Do vision transformers see like convolutional neural networks? (2021)
10. Reynaud, H., Vlontzos, A., Hou, B., Beqiri, A., Leeson, P., Kainz, B.: Ultrasound video transformers for cardiac ejection fraction estimation (2021)
11. Saeed, M., Muhtaseb, R., Yaqub, M.: Contrastive pretraining for echocardiography segmentation with limited data (2022). https://doi.org/10.48550/ARXIV.2201.07219. https://arxiv.org/abs/2201.07219
12. Silva, J.F., Silva, J.M., Guerra, A., Matos, S., Costa, C.: Ejection fraction classification in transthoracic echocardiography using a deep learning approach. In: 2018 IEEE 31st International Symposium on Computer-Based Medical Systems (CBMS), pp. 123–128 (2018). https://doi.org/10.1109/CBMS.2018.00029

13. Smistad, E., et al.: Real-time automatic ejection fraction and foreshortening detection using deep learning. IEEE Trans. Ultrason. Ferroelectr. Freq. Control **67**(12), 2595–2604 (2020). https://doi.org/10.1109/TUFFC.2020.2981037

14. Smistad, E., Østvik, A., Salte, I.M., Leclerc, S., Bernard, O., Lovstakken, L.: Fully automatic real-time ejection fraction and mapse measurements in 2D echocardiography using deep neural networks. In: 2018 IEEE International Ultrasonics Symposium (IUS), pp. 1–4 (2018). https://doi.org/10.1109/ULTSYM.2018.8579886

15. Tran, D., Wang, H., Torresani, L., Ray, J., LeCun, Y., Paluri, M.: A closer look at spatiotemporal convolutions for action recognition. In: 2018 IEEE/CVF Conference on Computer Vision and Pattern Recognition, pp. 6450–6459 (2018)

16. Virani, S.S., et al.: Heart disease and stroke statistics—2020 update: a report from the american heart association. Circulation **141**(9), 139–596 (2020). https://doi.org/10.1161/cir.0000000000000757. https://doi.org/10.1161/cir.0000000000000757

17. Voorhees, A., Han, H.C.: Biomechanics of cardiac function. Compr. Physiol. **5**(4), 1623–1644 (2015). https://doi.org/10.1002/cphy.c140070

18. Wang, Y., et al.: Early detection of heart failure with varying prediction windows by structured and unstructured data in electronic health records. In: 37th Annual International Conference of the IEEE Engineering in Medicine and Biology Society, EMBC 2015, Milan, Italy, 25–29 August 2015, pp. 2530–2533. IEEE (2015). https://doi.org/10.1109/EMBC.2015.7318907. https://doi.org/10.1109/EMBC.2015.7318907

19. Zhang, J., et al.: Fully automated echocardiogram interpretation in clinical practice: feasibility and diagnostic accuracy. Circulation **138**, 1623–1635 (10 2018). https://doi.org/10.1161/CIRCULATIONAHA.118.034338

20. Zhang, L., Wen, Y.: MIA-COV19D: a transformer-based framework for COVID19 classification in chest CTs (2021). https://doi.org/10.13140/RG.2.2.12992.05125

21. Zhang, L., Wen, Y.: A transformer-based framework for automatic COVID19 diagnosis in chest CTs. In: 2021 IEEE/CVF International Conference on Computer Vision Workshops (ICCVW), pp. 513–518 (2021). https://doi.org/10.1109/ICCVW54120.2021.00063

Light-weight Spatio-Temporal Graphs for Segmentation and Ejection Fraction Prediction in Cardiac Ultrasound

Sarina Thomas[1], Andrew Gilbert[2], and Guy Ben-Yosef[3(✉)]

[1] University of Oslo, Oslo, Norway
[2] GE Vingmed Ultrasound, Oslo, Norway
[3] GE Research, Niskayuna, NY, USA
guy.ben-yosef@ge.com

Abstract. Accurate and consistent predictions of echocardiography parameters are important for cardiovascular diagnosis and treatment. In particular, segmentations of the left ventricle can be used to derive ventricular volume, ejection fraction (EF) and other relevant measurements. In this paper we propose a new automated method called EchoGraphs for predicting ejection fraction and segmenting the left ventricle by detecting anatomical keypoints. Models for direct coordinate regression based on Graph Convolutional Networks (GCNs) are used to detect the keypoints. GCNs can learn to represent the cardiac shape based on local appearance of each keypoint, as well as global spatial and temporal structures of all keypoints combined. We evaluate our EchoGraphs model on the EchoNet benchmark dataset. Compared to semantic segmentation, GCNs show accurate segmentation and improvements in robustness and inference run-time. EF is computed simultaneously to segmentations and our method also obtains state-of-the-art ejection fraction estimation. Source code is available online: https://github.com/guybenyosef/EchoGraphs.

Keywords: Graph convolutional networks · Segmentation · Ejection fraction · Ultrasound · Echocardiography

1 Introduction

Heart failure continues to be the leading cause of hospitalization and death worldwide, lending an urgency to personalized and prospective care solutions [19]. Cardiovascular ultrasound (or echocardiography) is the most frequently

---

S. Thomas and A. Gilbert contributed equally

Supplementary Information The online version contains supplementary material available at https://doi.org/10.1007/978-3-031-16440-8_37.

used method for diagnosing heart disease due to its wide availability, low cost, real-time feedback, and lack of ionizing radiation.

Reduced left ventricle outflow – an important marker of heart failure – is measured by the ejection fraction (EF). EF describes the volumetric blood fraction pumped by the heart in each heart cycle and can be estimated by the ratio between the maximal volume (occurring at the end diastole phase of the cardiac cycle) and the minimal volume (occurring at the end systole phase). These volume estimates are typically derived from a segmentation of the myocardial border of the left ventricle. Segmentations of the myocardial border are also useful for many other downstream tasks such as foreshortening detection during acquisition [20] or as an initialization for strain measurement [14]. Due to their frequent use and high prognostic value, accurate and robust automation of left ventricle segmentation and EF measurement are high priority tasks for modern echocardiography systems.

1.1 Prior Work

Several previous works have shown highly accurate automation results using deep learning for both left ventricle segmentation [4,9,11,13,15,20] and direct EF estimation [10,15,17]. For segmentation, previous works have mostly relied on semantic segmentation, which outputs a pixel-wise classification of an input image. In some cases, extra modules were included to implicitly include shape constraints [13,16], but in general these methods do not explicitly optimize the shape of interest. This is sub-optimal for a problem such as left ventricle segmentation because the shape is consistent between patients, and shape variations that do occur are critical for many diagnoses [2,12]. Additionally, annotations are typically provided as keypoints, making keypoint regression a more natural form of learning.

The state-of-the-art for semantic segmentation in medical imaging is the nnU-Net [8], a learning pipeline with a U-Net backbone. The success of the nnU-Net stems from its augmentations and automatic optimization of many network hyper-parameters based on dataset characteristics.

Graph convolutional networks (GCNs) have been gaining popularity as a learning method to integrate multi-modal data that may not be grid-structured [1]. However, GCNs are also ideally suited for predicting spatio-temporal keypoint locations across time based on image or video features. For these problems the graph nodes represent the keypoints and the graph edges represent the learned relationship between points. GCNs have achieved state-of-the-art results in problems such as pose prediction in video [23] and also segmentation in several medical imaging problems [6,21]. In this work, we adapt graph convolutional approaches for echocardiography segmentation.

1.2 Contributions:

Given an echocardiography video loop of the left ventricle we use GCNs to demonstrate accurate automation of two relevant tasks for heart failure diagnosis: **(1) left ventricle segmentation** at end diastole (ED) and end systole (ES) phases of the cardiac cycle and **(2) ejection fraction estimation**. To our knowledge, this is the first work to apply graph convolutional approaches to these tasks and we show several advantages compared to prior works:

- **Accuracy:** We demonstrate highly accurate segmentation and state-of-the-art ejection fraction prediction.
- **Robustness**: We demonstrate that the explicit shape encoding of GCNs leads to fewer segmentation outliers.
- **Speed**: Model run-time is an important consideration for echocardiography measurement tools since algorithms may be implemented on point of care systems with variable computational resources. We achieve decreased run-time relative to semantic segmentation using the GCN segmentation approach.
- **Landmark prediction:** The predicted graph nodes can be directly tied to important left ventricle landmarks such as the apex and basal points which are required for volume estimation and other downstream tasks. Semantic segmentation requires an extra module or rules-based analysis to identify these landmarks.
- **Related tasks are predicted by a single model:** Segmentation and EF measurement predictions are processed together based on a single multi-frame encoder. Such an approach leads to improved performance, accuracy (since these tasks contribute to each other), and interpretability of clinical predictions.

2   Method

Ejection fraction estimation requires the prediction of the left ventricle endocardial border at two points in the cardiac cycle: end-diastole (ED) and end-systole (ES). Sec. 2.1 describes the building blocks of the proposed approach while Sec. 2.2 describes how those blocks can be combined for segmentation and EF prediction.

2.1   Building Blocks

Our method consists of four components: a CNN encoder that outputs a feature vector, a decoding graph that regresses the keypoints based on the feature representations, and two regression layers that directly outputs a value for the ejection fraction or a classification of the frame. The proposed method is completely modular and different networks can be substituted for each component.

Graph Convolutional Point Decoder. The left ventricle is an anatomical shape that can be described by a closed contour and approximated by a finite number of points sampled from the contour. Given a single ultrasound frame, we can interpret the contour of the left ventricle as an undirected graph $G = (V, E)$. Nodes $V = \{v_i | i = 1, ..., N\}$ represent the contour points and E represent

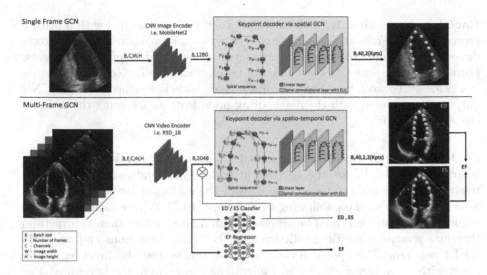

Fig. 1. Overview of the proposed method Single frame GCN (top): The output of the CNN encoder is forwarded to the GCN with four spiral convolution layers that regresses a coordinate vector for each keypoint. Multi-frame GCN (bottom): The image sequence consisting of F frames is fed into a CNN video encoder that outputs a feature representation. This feature representation is passed to a regressor module to predict the EF value and the spatio-temporal GCN that outputs keypoint coordinates for the two key frames. An ED/ES classifier is optionally added when the location of those frames is unknown (Sec. 2.2)

the connections between the points. Spatial changes of one contour point most likely affect the neighboring points but may also affect other points that are not in direct proximity. Graph convolutional neural networks (GCNs) can be seen as a generalization of CNNs that do not require a fixed grid but can operate on any non-Euclidean structured data by aggregating the information of the neighbors using the edges and applying a weighting term [5]. While several graph network models can be used, the proposed method relies on spiral convolutions [3]. This operator enforces a fixed ordering of neighboring nodes during message passing to compute node updates with $x_i^k = \gamma^k \left(\|_{j \in S(i,l)} x_j^{k-1} \right)$ where $S(i, l)$ is the fixed spiral concatenation of the neighboring nodes x_j and γ is a multi-layer perceptron. Spiral connections were chosen because they can explicitly model an inductive bias of neighboring nodes and are computationally efficient. Although the approach was inspired by closed mesh structures and the spiral was defined on the mesh vertices, it can be also applied to circular structures like the left ventricle by defining the starting index and then generating the sequence in a clock-wise manner. The proposed graph decoder architecture consists of one initial dense layer that further compresses the input feature vector followed by four spiral convolution layers that are complemented by an exponential linear activation unit. In the last layer, two values are predicted for each node that represent the coordinate pixel position in the image.

Encoder. In the input layer of the graph, each node is assigned with a feature representation. From the original image or video information, a distinct lower dimensional feature vector must be extracted to meet these input requirements. For that purpose, any CNN network can be used and the choice of architecture is a trade-off between speed and accuracy. Each node is assigned with the CNN output concatenated with the neighboring node features following the order of the spiral sequence.

EF Regressor. The ejection fraction is defined as $EF = (EDV - ESV)/EDV$ where EDV and ESV are the volumes at end-diastole and end-systole respectively. While the EF can be estimated from the extracted keypoints using the Simpson biplane method, following earlier work [10,15,17], we found that more accurate EF prediction could be obtained from a direct estimation. Our method therefore generates one EF prediction from keypoint predictions and one from the EF regressor. This approach yields accurate results from the direct regression along with a confidence check and explainable results from the keypoints. The proposed method uses a 4-layer multi-perceptron network (each linear layer is followed by an exponential linear activation unit), which takes the feature vector from the encoder and outputs a single predicted EF value.

ES/ED Classifier. EF estimation from an unlabeled video requires estimation of the ES and ED frames to know where segmentation should be applied. For predicting the ES and ED frame indices we use another multi-perceptron network based on 4 linear layers, in which each layer is followed by normalization and ReLU activation. Similar to [17], the network outputs two arrays that represent the likelihood of each frame to be the ES or ED. A weighted cross-entropy loss is then applied to match each array against the ground truth index location.

2.2   EchoGraphs - Left Ventricle Segmentation and EF Prediction

Single Frame Segmentation. An image encoder and graph point decoder can be used to predict the pixel location $(x, y) \in R^2$ of each keypoint $v_i \in V$ given a single image frame as shown in the top part of Fig. 1. Based on the shape constraint enforced by the GCN configuration, the output is a closed contour along the myocardial border that represents a segmentation of the left ventricle.

Multi-Frame Segmentation and EF Prediction with Known ED/ES. To measure EF, multiple input frames must be analyzed. We extend the proposed single frame approach discussed above to optimize keypoint contours on both ED and ES frames. One key property of the sequence is the shape consistency of the left ventricle between consecutive frames. Taking a similar approach to previous work on body pose estimation [24], each graph node at ED is connected to the corresponding node in ES to model the temporal connections. Adding these temporal edges between two consecutive frames can help to enforce consistency between the predicted segmentations.

For this approach, the R(2+1)D video encoder [22] is used for generating the feature vector. This network takes as input a sequence of 16 frames where the first frame is ED and the last is ES. Including the intermediary frames gives better results than using a two frame approach with only ED and ES, indicating the extra context helps with learning. This approach requires manual identification of ED and ES frames. The output of the encoder serves as the input of the EF regression network and the graph decoder. EF prediction in this approach comes from both the keypoints and an EF regressor attached to the feature vector.

Multi-Frame Segmentation and EF Prediction from Unknown ED/ES.
If ED and ES are unknown, we demonstrate two possible approaches. First, the above approaches can be combined in a two-stage solution where the single-frame model first predicts keypoints for each frame. Those keypoints allow the computation of ventricle volumes and following the approach of [15], negative and positive peaks of the volumes can be identified. Subsequently, the multi-frame model can be applied to each peak pair to estimate the EF.

In the second approach, an ED/ES classifier is added that takes the encoder output and predicts the occurrence of the ED/ES frames in the sequence. The classifier output is concatenated with the feature vector from the encoder as input for the graph decoder. If a ED or ES frame is detected, the output of the decoder resembles the respective ventricle contours. During inference, a sliding window approach is applied to process the entire video and EF results are averaged across the sequence. The multi-frame approaches with/without the ED/ES classifier are shown at the bottom of Fig. 1.

3   Experiments and Results

Following research questions were asked in this project:

Q1 How accurate, efficient, and robust is segmentation of a single frame using GCNs? (sec. 3.2)
Q2 Given a single heart cycle video with labeled ED and ES frames, can we predict EF along with keypoints on the ED and ES frames? (sec. 3.3)
Q3 Given an unlabeled video with one or more cycles, can we predict the EF and ED/ES keypoints? (sec. 3.3)

Experiments to answer these questions are detailed below. Implementation details are in the supplementary material and source code to reproduce the given results is on Github: https://github.com/guybenyosef/EchoGraphs .

3.1   Dataset

All Echographs models were trained and evaluated on the EchoNet open-access dataset [15]. The dataset consists of 10,030 echocardiography videos of healthy and pathological patients. All videos have two frames labeled - the ED and ES

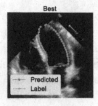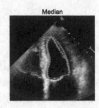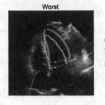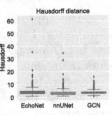

Fig. 2. Left: Best, median, and worst results from the EchoGraphs single-frame segmentation network. The model prediction in the worst case appears to be more accurate than the label. **Right:** Hausdorff distance (in pixels) box plot of segmentation results. Compared to semantic segmentation, the EchoGraphs (with MobileNet2 backbone) is more robust.

frame for one selected cycle. The 40 annotated keypoints provide an approximation of the left ventricle contour plus 2 additional keypoints for the basal and apex point. Furthermore, the dataset provided EF values for each sequence. The dataset authors provide splits of the data into 80% training, 10% validation and 10% test sets to allow direct comparison. Evaluations of all methods were performed on the same independent test set not seen during training.

3.2 Segmentation

To answer Q1 the single-frame model approach (Sec. 2.2) was trained on all annotated frames from the EchoNet dataset. Three different encoder backbones were tested for the EchoGraphs model to evaluate the trade-off between runtime and accuracy: MobilenetV2 [18], ResNet18, and ResNet50 [7]. We compare to two semantic segmentation algorithms: the DeepLabv3 approach from EchoNet [15] and the nnU-Net [8]. Results are shown in Table 1 where all approaches were compared on Dice score, mean keypoint error, performance, and memory size. The EchoNet dataset does not have real image sizes so to calculate keypoint error, coordinates were normalized by image dimensions. Example contours are shown in Fig. 2. Dice results were all found to be significantly different using a Wilcoxon signed-rank test ($p_{wilcoxon} \ll 0.01$).

Table 1. Segmentation accuracy and performance for different methods evaluated on the EchoNet [15] test set with 1264 patients and two annotated frames (ED and ES) each. MKE = mean keypoint error (mean L1 error in %). Runtime is measured in msec per frame for a single forward pass of the model without preprocessing or augmentation.

Model	Backbone	Dice (%)	MKE (%)	Runtime [cpu/gpu]	Parameters
EchoNet [15]	DeepLabV3	91.7 ± 4.2	2.5 ± 1.2	33.65/4.94	39.6 M
nnU-Net [8]	U-Net	$\mathbf{92.8 \pm 3.6}$	2.3 ± 1.2	14.86/1.05	7.3 M
EchoGraphs (ours)	MobileNetv2	91.6 ± 4.0	2.3 ± 1.0	$\mathbf{2.45}$/0.68	$\mathbf{4.92\ M}$
EchoGraphs (ours)	ResNet18	91.8 ± 4.0	2.3 ± 1.0	2.68/$\mathbf{0.46}$	12.1 M
EchoGraphs (ours)	ResNet50	92.1 ± 3.8	$\mathbf{2.2 \pm 0.9}$	6.73/1.05	27.1 M

3.3   EF Prediction

The approaches described in Sec. 2.2 were applied to the problem of EF prediction to answer Q2/Q3. Our methods were compared to the best results given by [15] and [17]. Results are shown in Table 2 and all approaches are compared on mean absolute error (MAE), root mean squared error (RMSE), and correlation (R^2) averaged over all patients.

Table 2. EF prediction results of the EchoGraphs models evaluated on 1264 patients. The top section of the table shows results from prediction on a single heartbeat while the bottom shows performance given a video with one or more cycles. The multi-frame EchoGraphs allows EF prediction based on the keypoints and the direct regression. Both results are listed for the single heartbeat while only regression results are listed for the whole video. The EchoGraphs approach with peak computation required one initial run of the single-frame approach. In four cases no peaks could be found and the method failed. Only the best approaches from [15] and [17] are listed.

Method	Input	Frames	MAE	RMSE	R^2
EchoNet (MC3) [15]	single heartbeat	32	4.22	5.56	0.79
Transformer (M.) [17]	single heartbeat	128	5.32	7.23	0.64
Regression only (ours)	single heartbeat	16	4.28	5.75	0.72
EchoGraphs (ours) using keypoints	single heartbeat	16	4.66	6.30	0.73
EchoGraphs (ours) with regression head	single heartbeat	16	**4.01**	**5.36**	**0.81**
EchoNet [15]	whole video	-	**4.05**	**5.32**	**0.81**
Transformer [17]	whole video	-	5.95	8.38	0.52
EchoGraphs (ours) - Peak computation	whole video	-	4.30	5.86	0.65
EchoGraphs (ours) - ED/ES classifier	whole video	-	4.23	5.67	0.79

4   Discussion and Conclusion

In this work, we have proposed a graph convolutional neural network for segmenting the myocardial border of the left ventricle and predicting ejection fraction for echocardiography videos. For the task of segmentation, our EchoGraphs method reaches comparable accuracy results in Dice score and mean keypoint error to state-of-the-art methods while achieving considerably better run-time performance. These results show graph convolutional networks are a more suitable method for segmentation when performance is critical. In addition to being faster, EchoGraphs are more robust, as demonstrated by the Hausdorff distance box plots in Fig. 2. Most failure cases could be attributed to low image quality or false annotations (Fig. 2 - worst). The robustness of the EchoGraphs can be attributed to the explicit shape encoding in the graph structure while the runtime is reduced because the decoding path is simpler.

Although segmentation accuracy is slightly below nnU-Net, the nnU-Net pipeline contains test-time augmentations and an abundance of hyperparameter optimizations based on dataset characteristics. These same optimizations could be applied to EchoGraphs and likely further improve performance.

We achieve state-of-the-art results for EF prediction from echocardiography clips. We demonstrate an interpretable approach based on the volume estimation from the predicted keypoint segmentations, and a slightly more accurate black-box approach based on direct EF estimation from the encoder feature vector. Our results show that a GCN-based multi-task approach for simultaneously learning both keypoints and clinical measurements can achieve high accuracy for all tasks and outperforms direct regression ($p_{wilcoxon} \ll 0.01$). We present two approaches for EF prediction from videos and both approaches achieve results comparable to previous methods while simultaneously predicting left ventricle segmentations. The EF errors for each of our EchoGraphs models were significantly below the 7-13% inter-observer error range reported in [15].

The proposed approach may provide more efficient and accurate measurement systems for commercial scanner systems. In the future, we aim to extend the approach to other clinical measures. The predicted keypoints provide important information that can directly be utilized for other applications such as foreshortening detection and strain analysis.

References

1. Ahmedt-Aristizabal, D., Armin, M.A., Denman, S., Fookes, C., Petersson, L.: Graph-based deep learning for medical diagnosis and analysis: past, present and future. Sensors **21**(14), 4758 (2021). https://doi.org/10.3390/s21144758
2. Baltabaeva, A., et al.: Regional left ventricular deformation and geometry analysis provides insights in myocardial remodelling in mild to moderate hypertension. Eur. J. Echocardiogr. **9**(4), 501–508 (2008). https://doi.org/10.1016/j.euje.2007.08.004
3. Bouritsas, G., Bokhnyak, S., Ploumpis, S., Bronstein, M., Zafeiriou, S.: Neural 3D morphable models: spiral convolutional networks for 3D shape representation learning and generation. In: The IEEE International Conference on Computer Vision (ICCV) (2019)
4. Gilbert, A., Marciniak, M., Rodero, C., Lamata, P., Samset, E., Mcleod, K.: Generating synthetic labeled data from existing anatomical models: an example with echocardiography segmentation. IEEE Trans. Med. Imaging **40**(10), 2783–2794 (2021). https://doi.org/10.1109/TMI.2021.3051806
5. Gong, S., Chen, L., Bronstein, M., Zafeiriou, S.: SpiralNet++: a fast and highly efficient mesh convolution operator. In: Proceedings of the IEEE International Conference on Computer Vision Workshops (CVPR) (2019)
6. Gopinath, K., Desrosiers, C., Lombaert, H.: Graph domain adaptation for alignment-invariant brain surface segmentation. In: Sudre, C.H., et al. (eds.) UNSURE/GRAIL -2020. LNCS, vol. 12443, pp. 152–163. Springer, Cham (2020). https://doi.org/10.1007/978-3-030-60365-6_15
7. He, K., Zhang, X., Ren, S., Sun, J.: Deep residual learning for image recognition. In: Proceedings of the IEEE conference on computer vision and pattern recognition, pp. 770–778 (2016). https://doi.org/10.1109/CVPR.2016.90

8. Isensee, F., Jaeger, P.F., Kohl, S.A., Petersen, J., Maier-Hein, K.H.: nnU-Net: a self-configuring method for deep learning-based biomedical image segmentation. Nat. Methods **18**(2), 203–211 (2021). https://doi.org/10.1038/s41592-020-01008-z

9. Jafari, M.H., et al.: A unified framework integrating recurrent fully-convolutional networks and optical flow for segmentation of the left ventricle in echocardiography data. In: Stoyanov, D., et al. (eds.) DLMIA/ML-CDS -2018. LNCS, vol. 11045, pp. 29–37. Springer, Cham (2018). https://doi.org/10.1007/978-3-030-00889-5_4

10. Kazemi Esfeh, M.M., Luong, C., Behnami, D., Tsang, T., Abolmaesumi, P.: A deep Bayesian video analysis framework: towards a more robust estimation of ejection fraction. In: Martel, A.L., et al. (eds.) MICCAI 2020. LNCS, vol. 12262, pp. 582–590. Springer, Cham (2020). https://doi.org/10.1007/978-3-030-59713-9_56

11. Leclerc, S., et al.: Deep Learning Segmentation in 2D echocardiography using the CAMUS dataset : automatic assessment of the anatomical shape validity. In: International Conference Medical Imaging with Deep Learning - Extended Abstract Track (2019)

12. Marciniak, M., et al.: Septal curvature as a robust and reproducible marker for basal septal hypertrophy. J. Hypertens. **39**(7), 1421 (2021). https://doi.org/10.1097/HJH.0000000000002813

13. Oktay, O., et al.: Anatomically constrained neural networks (ACNNs): application to cardiac image enhancement and segmentation. IEEE Trans. Med. Imaging **37**(2), 384–395 (2017)

14. Østvik, A., Smistad, E., Espeland, T., Berg, E.A.R., Lovstakken, L.: Automatic myocardial strain imaging in echocardiography using deep learning. In: Stoyanov, D., et al. (eds.) DLMIA/ML-CDS -2018. LNCS, vol. 11045, pp. 309–316. Springer, Cham (2018). https://doi.org/10.1007/978-3-030-00889-5_35

15. Ouyang, D., et al.: Interpretable AI for beat-to-beat cardiac function assessment. Nature **580**(7802), 252–256 (2020). https://doi.org/10.1038/s41586-020-2145-8

16. Payer, C., Štern, D., Bischof, H., Urschler, M.: Integrating spatial configuration into heatmap regression based CNNs for landmark localization. Med. Image Anal. **54**, 207–219 (2019). https://doi.org/10.1016/j.media.2019.03.007

17. Reynaud, H., Vlontzos, A., Hou, B., Beqiri, A., Leeson, P., Kainz, Bernhard: Ultrasound video transformers for cardiac ejection fraction estimation. In: de Bruijne, M., et al. (eds.) MICCAI 2021. LNCS, vol. 12906, pp. 495–505. Springer, Cham (2021). https://doi.org/10.1007/978-3-030-87231-1_48

18. Sandler, M., Howard, A., Zhu, M., Zhmoginov, A., Chen, L.C.: MobileNetV2: inverted residuals and linear bottlenecks. In: Proceedings of the IEEE Conference on Computer Vision and Pattern Recognition, pp. 4510–4520 (2018). https://doi.org/10.1109/CVPR.2018.00474

19. Savarese, G., Stolfo, D., Sinagra, G., Lund, L.H.: Heart failure with mid-range or mildly reduced ejection fraction. Nature Rev. Cardiol. **19**, 100–116 (2022). https://doi.org/10.1038/s41569-021-00605-5

20. Smistad, E., et al.: Real-time automatic ejection fraction and foreshortening detection using deep learning. IEEE Trans. Ultrason. Ferroelectr. Freq. Control **67**(12), 2595–2604 (2020). https://doi.org/10.1109/TUFFC.2020.2981037

21. Tian, Z., et al.: Graph-convolutional-network-based interactive prostate segmentation in MR images. Med. Phys. **47**(9), 4164–4176 (2020)

22. Tran, D., Wang, H., Torresani, L., Ray, J., LeCun, Y., Paluri, M.: A closer look at spatiotemporal convolutions for action recognition. In: Proceedings of the IEEE Conference on Computer Vision and Pattern Recognition, pp. 6450–6459 (2018)

23. Wang, J., Yan, S., Xiong, Y., Lin, D.: Motion guided 3D pose estimation from videos. In: Vedaldi, A., Bischof, H., Brox, T., Frahm, J.-M. (eds.) ECCV 2020. LNCS, vol. 12358, pp. 764–780. Springer, Cham (2020). https://doi.org/10.1007/978-3-030-58601-0_45
24. Yan, S., Xiong, Y., D, L.: Spatial temporal graph convolutional networks for skeleton-based action recognition. In: Proceedings of the AAAI Conference Artificial Intelligence (2018)

Rethinking Breast Lesion Segmentation in Ultrasound: A New Video Dataset and A Baseline Network

Jialu Li[1,2], Qingqing Zheng[2], Mingshuang Li[2], Ping Liu[2], Qiong Wang[2(✉)], Litao Sun[3(✉)], and Lei Zhu[4,5]

[1] University of Chinese Academy of Sciences, Beijing, China
[2] Guangdong Provincial Key Laboratory of Computer Vision and Virtual Reality, Shenzhen Institute of Advanced Technology, Chinese Academy of Sciences, Shenzhen, China
wangqiong@siat.ac.cn
[3] Zhejiang Provincial People's Hospital, Hangzhou, China
litaosun1971@sina.com
[4] The Hong Kong University of Science and Technology (Guangzhou), Guangzhou, China
[5] The Hong Kong University of Science and Technology, Hong Kong, China

Abstract. Automatic breast lesion segmentation in ultrasound (US) videos is an essential prerequisite for early diagnosis and treatment. This challenging task remains under-explored due to the lack of availability of annotated US video dataset. Though recent works have achieved better performance in natural video object segmentation by introducing promising Transformer architectures, they still suffer from spatial inconsistency as well as huge computational costs. Therefore, in this paper, we first present a new benchmark dataset designed for US video segmentation. Then, we propose a dynamic parallel spatial-temporal Transformer (DPSTT) to improve the performance of lesion segmentation in US videos with higher computational efficiency. Specifically, the proposed DPSTT disentangles the non-local Transformer along the temporal and spatial dimensions, respectively. The temporal Transformer attends temporal lesion movement on different frames at the same regions, and the spatial Transformer focuses on similar context information between the previous and the current frames. Furthermore, we propose a dynamic selection scheme to effectively sample the most relevant frames from all the past frames, and thus prevent out of memory during inference. Finally, we conduct extensive experiments to evaluate the efficacy of the proposed DPSTT on the new US video benchmark dataset.

1 Introduction

Automatic segmentation of breast lesions in ultrasound (US) video is essential for computer-aided clinical examination and treatment [5]. Compared with the

J. Li and Q. Zheng—Contributed equally to this work.

© The Author(s), under exclusive license to Springer Nature Switzerland AG 2022
L. Wang et al. (Eds.): MICCAI 2022, LNCS 13434, pp. 391–400, 2022.
https://doi.org/10.1007/978-3-031-16440-8_38

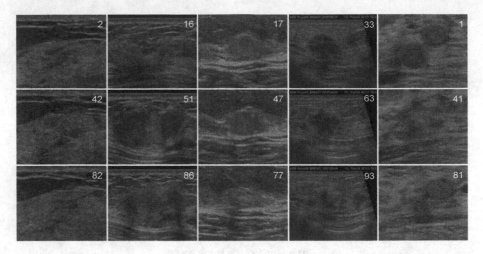

Fig. 1. Each column contains sample frames from a video in the breast lesion segmentation dataset, with high-quality pixel-level annotations marked in red. (Color figure online)

image segmentation, the segmentation in US video is more in line with the practice as it provides additional temporal information for the target object. It can be formulated as a binary labeling problem aiming to automatically segment target lesions in pixel level from a breast US video. This challenging task is rarely explored due to the lack of availability of published annotated US video datasets.

Although many convolutional neural networks (CNN), such as U-Net [9] and its variants [10,13], have achieved outstanding performance on various benchmarks by learning robust representative features for US image segmentation. Directly applying these image segmentation methods to independently process each US video frame may fail to capture temporal context information and result in temporal inconsistency. Recently, Transformers become increasingly popular in video object segmentation tasks [3]. To model long-range relationships, Transformers employ a self-attention mechanism to calculate pairwise similarities between all input units. As a representative, space-time memory (STM) [7] leverages a memory network to read relevant information from a temporal buffer of all preceding frames. The STM performs dense matching in the feature space to capture context information with an unlimited receptive field. However, the non-local property of STM may result in mismatching since that lesions in US videos usually appear in local neighborhoods across memory frames. In addition, the memory would increase linearly with the length of videos during inference, which inevitably brings huge computational costs and may encounter memory overflow.

To tackle the above challenges, we first introduce a new US video dataset with accurate frame-wise annotation in pixel level for breast lesion segmentation; see Fig. 1 for examples. Then, we propose a Dynamic Parallel Spatial-Temporal

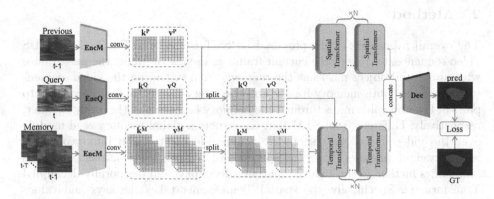

Fig. 2. Overview of the proposed DPSTT framework. Our network consists of two encoders (a memory encoder for the past frames, and a query encoder for the current frame), a parallel pair of spatially- and temporally-decoupled Transformer and a decoder. The memory encoder takes an RGB image and its corresponding lesion mask as input, whilst the query encoder only takes an RGB image. Here we repeat the memory encoder for the previous frame for better visualization.

Transformer (DPSTT) framework for US video segmentation. Specifically, following STM, we first extract pairs of key and value embedding from the current frame and all frames in the memory with a convolution-based encoder. Subsequently, we split the memory module into two parallel temporally- and spatially-decoupled Transformer blocks. In the temporally-decoupled block, the obtained key maps are spatially divided into multiple non-overlapped patches, and the attention is only calculated in the same regions between embedding of the current frame and those of memory frames. Such a temporal operation makes the modeling of pixel movements of breast lesions easier. By contrast, the spatially-decoupled block calculates the attention between the embedding of the current frame and that of the previous one in a non-local manner, which models the global similarity of stationary background texture between two adjacent frames. Moreover, to prevent unlimited growth of memory during inference, we also develop a non-uniform adaptive memory selection scheme to dynamically update the frames in the memory based on the similarity metric. In summary, the contributions of our method are threefold: (1) We are the first to present an annotated benchmark dataset specifically designed for the task of breast lesion segmentation in US videos, which would promote the progress of the medical video process. (2) We propose a Dynamic Parallel Spatial Temporal Transformer (DPSTT) framework for US video segmentation to improve lesion segmentation performance with higher computational efficiency. (3) We have conducted extensive experiments to evaluate the proposed DPSTT. Experimental results demonstrate that our method outperforms state of the arts by a large margin.

2   Method

The overall framework of the proposed DPSTT is shown in Fig. 2. Given a US video sequence, we regard the current frame as the *query* frame, the past frames with annotated object masks as the *memory* frames. During the video segmentation process, both memory frames and the query frame are first encoded into pairs of key and value maps through the memory encoder and the query encoder, respectively. Different from STM that constructs a global memory read module over the video space, we disentangle the non-local attention into two parallel lightweight modules along the spatial and temporal dimensions. The keys and values further go through the spatially-decoupled and temporally-decoupled Transformers. Specifically, the spatial Transformer takes the keys and values from the query and the previous frames to extract the global background context information, while the temporal Transformer takes the keys and values at the same local regions from the query and memory frames to aggregate the temporal movement of target objects at the same time. The outputs of the spatial and temporal Transformers are finally sent to the decoder, which estimates the target mask for the query frame.

2.1   Query and Memory Encoder

Both the query and memory encoders share the same structure except for the input. Similar to STM, we utilize the ResNet50 [4] as the backbone network and modify the first convolutional layer to take a 4-channel input for the memory encoder. Then two parallel convolutional layers are utilized to further embed the backbone network output into a pair of key and value maps by reducing its channel size to 1/8 and 1/2, respectively. We denote by $\mathbf{k}^Q \in \mathbb{R}^{H \times W \times C/8}$ and $\mathbf{v}^Q \in \mathbb{R}^{H \times W \times C/2}$ the key and the value maps for the query frame, where H is the height, W is the width and C represents the channel size of the feature map. Similarly, each individual of T memory frames ($T \geq 1$) is independently embedded into key and value maps. The resulting key and value maps are represented as $\mathbf{k}^M \in \mathbb{R}^{T \times H \times W \times C/8}$ and $\mathbf{v}^M \in \mathbb{R}^{T \times H \times W \times C/2}$. For ease of description, we also denote the corresponding key and value maps of the previous frame by $\mathbf{k}^P$ and $\mathbf{v}^P$, which have the same resolution as $\mathbf{k}^Q$ and $\mathbf{v}^Q$.

2.2   Parallel Spatial Temporal Transformer

Different from the memory read module in STM that simultaneously processes similarity matching between all pixels of the query frame and memory frames, we disentangle this expensive module into two much easier components: a temporally-decoupled Transformer for extracting local features along the temporal dimension, and a spatially-decoupled Transformer block for capturing global features between the query frame and its previous frame in a non-local manner.

For the temporal Transformer, given the memory key $\mathbf{k}^M$ and the query key $\mathbf{k}^Q$, we split them into s^2 non-overlapped patches along both height and width dimensions. Each region is represented by $\mathbf{k}_{ij}^{M_k} \in \mathbb{R}^{H/s \times W/s \times C/8}, k \in [1, T]$ for the memory and $\mathbf{k}_{ij}^Q \in \mathbb{R}^{H/s \times W/s \times C/8}$ for the query respectively, where $i, j \in [1, s]$ denote the index of the local region. We then group the local memory regions by temporal dimension, i.e., $P_{ij}^M = \{\mathbf{k}_{ij}^{M_1}, \cdots, \mathbf{k}_{ij}^{M_T}\}$. Then the temporal Transformer measures the local similarity with:

$$f(P_{ij}^{M_k}, \mathbf{k}_{ij}^Q) = \text{Softmax}(\exp(P_{ij}^{M_k} \otimes \mathbf{k}_{ij}^Q)), \tag{1}$$

where $\otimes$ denotes the dot product. With the soft weights, the memory values are subsequently retrieved by a weighted summation as follows:

$$\mathbf{v}_{ij}^T = \sum_{k=1}^T f(P_{ij}^{M_k}, \mathbf{k}_{ij}^Q)\mathbf{v}_{ij}^{M_k}. \tag{2}$$

The resulting $\mathbf{v}_{ij}^T$ concatenated with the query value at the same location, is further organized into a new tensor according to its location index to produce the temporal Transformer output $\mathbf{y}^T$. By doing so, continuous movements of the target object in a smaller spatial region can be detected without the disturbance of redundant temporal features.

For the spatial Transformer, we assume the previous frame has less movement or appearance difference compared with the query frame. The previous frame with its estimated mask would help provide coarse guidance for the query frame. Therefore, the similarity matching between the previous and the query frame is performed in a non-local manner with

$$f(\mathbf{k}^Q, \mathbf{k}^P) = \text{Softmax}(\exp(\mathbf{k}^Q \otimes \mathbf{k}^P)). \tag{3}$$

Then the output of the spatial Transformer is generated by

$$\mathbf{y}^S = [\mathbf{v}^Q, f(\mathbf{k}^Q, \mathbf{k}^P)\mathbf{v}^P]. \tag{4}$$

In this way, the spatial Transformer pays more attention to the global static background context information. Finally, these two decoupled spatial and temporal Transformers are calculated in parallel and their outputs $\mathbf{y}^S$ and $\mathbf{y}^T$ are concatenated and further refined by a convolutional operation.

2.3 Decoder

The decoder takes the refined output of the decoupled spatial and temporal Transformers to estimate the lesion mask for the query frame. We follow the refinement module in [7] to build the decoder, which upscales the feature map gradually by a set of residual convolutional blocks. Finally, We minimize the binary cross-entropy(BCE) loss and the dice loss between the object masks $\hat{Y}$ and the ground truth labels Y.

2.4 Dynamic Memory Selection

Though spatial and temporal Transformers benefit from storing enough information in the memory frames, storing all the past frames is impossible and may

Table 1. Quantitative comparison with different methods on the proposed dataset.

Methods	Jaccard	Dice	Precision	Recall	FPS
UNet [9]	62.47 ± 0.53	73.03 ± 0.36	79.46 ± 0.20	72.72 ± 0.45	**88.18**
UNet++ [13]	61.24 ± 0.73	71.79 ± 0.53	82.80 ± 0.04	68.84 ± 1.09	40.9
TransUNet [2]	53.58 ± 0.37	65.47 ± 0.21	71.67 ± 0.13	66.82 ± 0.20	65.1
SETR [12]	54.80 ± 0.68	66.49 ± 0.59	75.33 ± 0.15	66.43 ± 1.04	21.61
OSVOS [8]	56.74 ± 0.59	70.98 ± 0.33	77.78 ± 0.92	64.04 ± 0.98	27.25
ViViT [1]	54.46 ± 0.32	67.39 ± 0.29	75.54 ± 0.03	66.83 ± 0.59	24.33
STM [7]	68.58 ± 0.56	78.62 ± 0.43	82.01 ± 0.35	79.10 ± 0.44	23.17
AFB-URR [6]	70.34 ± 0.25	80.18 ± 0.15	80.08 ± 0.32	**85.91 ± 0.15**	11.84
Ours	**73.64 ± 0.18**	**82.55 ± 0.20**	**83.89 ± 0.13**	84.55 ± 0.29	30.5

lead to memory overflow. To eliminate unnecessary features, we propose a simple yet effective selection mechanism to dynamically update the memory frames. We maintain a fixed K memory frames for segmenting the tth query frame if $t > K$, or all of the past frames as memory frames if $t \leq K$. Then we update the memory buffer by selecting the most K relevant frames. For example, assume that we have memory frames M for segmenting the tth frame $(t > K)$, when moving forward to the $(t+1)^{th}$ frame, we adopt the cosine metric and sort the resulting similarity values with

$$\text{Sort}\{Cos(\mathbf{k}^{Q_{t+1}}, \mathbf{k}^{M_k}), Cos(\mathbf{k}^{Q_{t+1}}, \mathbf{k}^{M_t})\}, k \in [1, K]. \tag{5}$$

Then the memory frames can be updated by adding the tth frame at the tail and removing the one with the least similarity value. It is noteworthy that our dynamic memory selection speeds up the temporal attention calculation, and performs online adaptation without additional training.

Time Complexity. With such a pipeline, we significantly reduce the computational complexity of memory read module in STM from $\mathcal{O}(TH^2W^2C)$ into $\mathcal{O}(KH^2W^2C/(s^4))$ for the temporally-decoupled block and $\mathcal{O}(H^2W^2C)$ for the spatially-decoupled block. Although $T = 3$ is chosen in the training process, T would increase linearly with the video length during inference, which would be much larger than a predetermined K. In addition, the computation of the temporal Transformer would be more efficient when s becomes larger.

3 Experiments

3.1 Dataset and Implementation

Here we describe the newly collected dataset, specifically designed for the task of breast lesion segmentation in US videos. Sample frames of the breast US videos are shown in Fig. 1. The breast US dataset comprises 63 video sequences, one video sequence per person, 4619 frames annotated with pixel-level ground truth by experts. These videos are collected from different US devices and their spatial resolution varies from 580×600 to 600×800. To ease training, we further crop the video sequences to a spatial resolution of 300×200. For quantitative comparison, we employ several widely used segmentation evaluation metrics, namely, Jaccard similarity coefficient (Jaccard), Dice similarity coefficient (Dice), Precision and Recall; see [11] for their definitions. Moreover, we adopt five-fold cross-validation on our dataset to statistically test different video segmentation methods.

We implement our network using the PyTorch framework with an NVIDIA RTX 3090 graphics card. In our experiments, all the input US frames are empirically resized to 240×240 and the training epoch is set to 100. During training, we sample $T(T = 3)$ temporally ordered frames with random skip N frames ($N \leq 5$) from a US video. We set the batch size to 4 and learning rate to $1e - 4$. We use the binary cross-entropy(BCE) loss and the dice loss with the weight of 0.5 and 0.5 during the training process. For the temporal Transformer, we set s to be 2. During inference, when the size of memory frames exceeds K ($K = 10$), the dynamic selection mechanism is activated to eliminate the redundant frame for the memory.

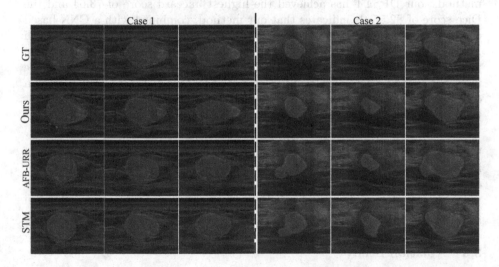

Fig. 3. Visual comparison with competitive video-based methods on two breast lesion cases.

3.2 Comparison with State-of-the-Art Methods

Quantitative Comparisons. As shown in Table 1, we qualitatively compare our method with state-of-the-art methods, including image-based segmentation methods (UNet [9], UNet++ [13], TransUNet [2] and SERT [12]) and video-based

Table 2. Ablation study on different transformer combination strategies. T denotes the temporal block and S is the spatial block. $\times N$ denotes repeating N times.

Stacking strategies	Jaccard	Dice	Precision	Recall
S(x1)	70.92 ± 0.15	80.07 ± 0.19	81.63 ± 0.25	82.77 ± 0.66
T(x1)	71.09 ± 0.15	80.24 ± 0.21	83.61 ± 0.26	80.88 ± 0.43
S-T(x1)	72.64 ± 0.18	81.58 ± 0.23	83.63 ± 0.11	82.99 ± 0.47
T-S(x1)	72.86 ± 0.18	81.86 ± 0.21	82.75 ± 0.08	84.02 ± 0.44
T‖S(x1)	$\mathbf{73.64 \pm 0.18}$	$\mathbf{82.55 \pm 0.20}$	$\mathbf{83.89 \pm 0.13}$	$\mathbf{84.55 \pm 0.29}$
S-T(x3)	72.03 ± 0.18	81.22 ± 0.19	82.69 ± 0.20	83.07 ± 0.25
T-S(x3)	72.72 ± 0.22	81.68 ± 0.29	83.18 ± 0.09	83.67 ± 0.61
T‖S(x3)	72.15 ± 0.29	81.64 ± 0.24	83.11 ± 0.47	83.10 ± 0.15

segmentation methods (OSVOS [8], ViViT [1], STM [7], AFB-URR [6]). From the results, we can observe that the video-based methods are prone to outperform image-based methods with higher evaluation scores, which demonstrates that leveraging temporal information provides promising benefits for breast lesion segmentation in US videos. More importantly, among all video-based segmentation methods, our DPSTT has achieved the highest Jaccard score of 73.64 and the Dice score of 82.55. It indicates that our method, combined with a CNN-based encoder and spatial-temporal Transformers, is able to simultaneously learn both high- and low-level cues and thus achieves significant improvements over those pure Transformer methods, such as SERT and ViViT. Table 1 also reports the inference speed performance of different methods. Due to the parallel operation of the decoupled Transformers, our method reduces much redundant computation and thus runs the fastest compared with other video-based approaches.

Qualitative Comparisons. Figure 3 visualizes the qualitative comparison of lesion masks among different video segmentation methods. We can observe that our method can provide more precise masks than STM and AFB-URR with more consistent boundaries. This is because our dynamic selection mechanism provides the most relevant memory and preserves the spatial consistency.

3.3   Ablation Study

The Effect of Transformers. We evaluate the effect of different Transformers by removing the spatial and temporal blocks separately in Table 2. It shows that the combination of both modules consistently results in better performance. This is because any decoupled Transformer can't simultaneously capture both stationary texture and moving information. We further compare different stacking strategies in the row 3–5. It shows that stacking such two different Transformers in parallel performs better than in an interweaving way, no matter starting from spatial or temporal blocks. Moreover, it is also observed that only one parallel temporal and spatial blocks are good enough to capture representative features.

Table 3. Ablation study on different memory selection strategies.

Sample strategies	Jaccard	Dice	Precision	Recall
Skip memory	73.06 ± 0.19	82.10 ± 0.21	83.61 ± 0.16	84.13 ± 0.30
Random memory	72.76 ± 0.16	81.94 ± 0.19	83.04 ± 0.09	83.95 ± 0.30
Dynamic memory	$\mathbf{73.64 \pm 0.18}$	$\mathbf{82.55 \pm 0.20}$	$\mathbf{83.89 \pm 0.13}$	$\mathbf{84.55 \pm 0.29}$

The Effect of Dynamic Memory. We investigate different memory selection strategies by comparing the segmentation performance with skip memory (every five frames) in STM, random memory of fixed size as well as our dynamic memory in Table 3. The results show that the random memory performs worst than the other two strategies. This phenomenon verifies our assumption that good enough memory can provide benefits for segmentation performance.

4 Conclusion

In this paper, we present the first pixel-wise annotated benchmark dataset for breast lesion segmentation in US videos. Then a Dynamic Parallel Spatial-Temporal Transformer framework is proposed for US video segmentation. Moreover, an efficient dynamic memory selection is further developed based on the similarity metric to prevent memory overflow. Finally, we conduct extensive experiments to evaluate the efficacy of our method.

Acknowledgments. This work was supported by the National Natural Science Foundation of China (No. 12026604, No. 62072452 and No. 61902275), the Regional Joint Fund of Guangdong under Grant (No. 2021B1515120011), the Key Fundamental Research Program of Shenzhen under Grant (No. JCYJ20200109115627045 and No. JCYJ20200109114233670) and in part by Pazhou Lab, Guangzhou 510320, China.

References

1. Arnab, A., Dehghani, M., Heigold, G., Sun, C., Lučić, M., Schmid, C.: Vivit: a video vision transformer. In: Proceedings of the IEEE/CVF International Conference on Computer Vision, pp. 6836–6846 (2021)
2. Chen, J., et al.: TransUNet: transformers make strong encoders for medical image segmentation. CoRR, abs/2102.04306 (2021)
3. Duke, B., Ahmed, A., Wolf, C., Aarabi, P., Taylor, G.W.: SSTVOS: sparse spatiotemporal transformers for video object segmentation. In: Proceedings of the IEEE/CVF Conference on Computer Vision and Pattern Recognition (CVPR), pp. 5912–5921 (2021)
4. He, K., Zhang, X., Ren, S., Sun, J.: Deep residual learning for image recognition. In: Proceedings of the IEEE Conference on Computer Vision and Pattern Recognition (CVPR), pp. 770–778, June 2016
5. Huang, Q., Huang, Y., Luo, Y., Yuan, F., Li, X.: Segmentation of breast ultrasound image with semantic classification of superpixels. Med. Image Anal. **61**, 101657 (2020)

6. Liang, Y., Li, X., Jafari, N., Chen, Q.: Video object segmentation with adaptive feature bank and uncertain-region refinement. In: Annual Conference on Neural Information Processing Systems (NeurIPS) (2020)

7. Oh, S.W., Lee, J.-Y., Xu, N., Kim, S.J.: Video object segmentation using space-time memory networks. In: Proceedings of the IEEE/CVF International Conference on Computer Vision (ICCV), pp. 9226–9235 (2019)

8. Perazzi, F., Khoreva, A., Benenson, R., Schiele, B., Sorkine-Hornung, A.: Learning video object segmentation from static images. In: Proceedings of the IEEE Conference on Computer Vision and Pattern Recognition (CVPR), pp. 2663–2672 (2017)

9. Ronneberger, O., Fischer, P., Brox, T.: U-net: convolutional networks for biomedical image segmentation. In: Navab, N., Hornegger, J., Wells, W.M., Frangi, A.F. (eds.) MICCAI 2015. LNCS, vol. 9351, pp. 234–241. Springer, Cham (2015). https://doi.org/10.1007/978-3-319-24574-4_28

10. Schlemper, J.: Attention gated networks: learning to leverage salient regions in medical images. Med. Image Anal. **53**, 197–207 (2019)

11. Wang, Y., et al.: Deep attentional features for prostate segmentation in ultrasound. In: Frangi, A.F., Schnabel, J.A., Davatzikos, C., Alberola-López, C., Fichtinger, G. (eds.) MICCAI 2018. LNCS, vol. 11073, pp. 523–530. Springer, Cham (2018). https://doi.org/10.1007/978-3-030-00937-3_60

12. Zheng, S., et al.: Rethinking semantic segmentation from a sequence-to-sequence perspective with transformers. In: Proceedings of the IEEE/CVF Conference on Computer Vision and Pattern Recognition (CVPR), pp. 6881–6890 (2021)

13. Zhou, Z., Rahman Siddiquee, M.M., Tajbakhsh, N., Liang, J.: UNet++: a nested U-net architecture for medical image segmentation. In: Stoyanov, D., et al. (eds.) DLMIA/ML-CDS -2018. LNCS, vol. 11045, pp. 3–11. Springer, Cham (2018). https://doi.org/10.1007/978-3-030-00889-5_1

MIRST-DM: Multi-instance RST
with Drop-Max Layer for Robust Classification
of Breast Cancer

Shoukun Sun(iD), Min Xian(✉)(iD), Aleksandar Vakanski(iD), and Hossny Ghanem(iD)

Department of Computer Science, University of Idaho, Idaho Falls, USA
{ssun,mxian,vakanski}@uidaho.edu, ghan9472@vandals.uidaho.edu

Abstract. Robust self-training (RST) can augment the adversarial robustness of image classification models without significantly sacrificing models' generalizability. However, RST and other state-of-the-art defense approaches failed to preserve the generalizability and reproduce their good adversarial robustness on small medical image sets. In this work, we propose the Multi-instance RST with drop-max layer, namely MIRST-DM, which involves a sequence of iteratively generated adversarial instances during training to learn smoother decision boundaries on small datasets. The proposed drop-max layer eliminates unstable features and helps learn representations that are robust to image perturbations. The proposed approach was validated using a small breast ultrasound dataset with 1,190 images. The results demonstrate that the proposed approach achieves state-of-the-art adversarial robustness against three prevalent attacks.

Keywords: Adversarial robustness · Robust self-training · Breast ultrasound

1 Introduction

Deep neural networks (DNNs) have achieved unprecedented performance in medical image analysis; however, existing approaches lack robustness to both natural and adversarial image perturbations [1], which makes it difficult to deploy them in an open-world environment. In this work, we focus on improving the adversarial robustness of deep learning-based models for medical image classification. Varies defense approaches were developed to overcome DNNs' vulnerability to adversarial samples by incorporating adversarial samples into training to improve the smoothness of a model's decision boundary [1–6]. Existing approaches were proposed on natural image sets, and no study has been conducted to improve the adversarial robustness of medical systems. Most natural image sets are large, e.g., the CIFAR-10 dataset has 6k images, and the ImageNet has more than 14 million images, while typical medical image datasets [7, 8] are usually much smaller than natural image datasets. The small medical datasets make it difficult for adversarial training to converge to a smooth decision boundary; hence established approaches cannot reproduce their good adversarial robustness on medical image sets. Furthermore, previous research showed that a tradeoff exists between the adversarial

© The Author(s), under exclusive license to Springer Nature Switzerland AG 2022
L. Wang et al. (Eds.): MICCAI 2022, LNCS 13434, pp. 401–410, 2022.
https://doi.org/10.1007/978-3-031-16440-8_39

robustness and generalization of a DNN [4]; and some defense approaches [1] have a dramatic decrease in their generalizability.

To overcome the challenges in the existing defense approach, we propose the multi-instance robust self-training with the drop-max layer to augment DNNs' adversarial robustness on small medical image sets. We are inspired by the finding that training with a series of adversarial samples could lead to smoother decision boundaries and achieve higher adversarial robustness. The proposed approach utilizes multiple adversarial instances from a sequence of images generated iteratively from a multi-step attack; and it increases the number of training samples and encodes the smooth transitions among adversarial samples. Furthermore, we propose the drop-max layer to replace the first pooling layer to remove unstable features at an early stage. We validate different approaches using a small breast ultrasound dataset [7, 8]. The primary contributions of this study are summarized below.

- The proposed approach uses a sequence of adversarial samples during training and significantly improves the adversarial robustness of the conventional RST approach using a small image set.
- The proposed drop-max layer removes non-robust features and greatly improves the adversarial robustness of RST approaches against the Carlini and Wagner attack and Projected Gradient Descent attacks.
- The pretrained backbone network using contrast learning improves both the generalization and adversarial robustness of a DNN model.

2 Related Works

2.1 Adversarial Attacks and Defenses

Adversarial attacks can be categorized into white-box and black-box attacks. A white-box attack generates adversarial examples directly using parameters from the target neural network; on the contrary, a black-box attack is applied on a surrogate model instead of accessing the actual target model. Attacks can be targeted and untargeted. Targeted attacks fool models to produce intended classification output, while untargeted attacks generate adversarial examples that can be misclassified to any class which differs from the true label. In this study, we focus on defending targeted white-box attacks.

Fast Gradient Sign Method (FGSM) [1] computes the gradients of a loss function with respect to the target image, then uses the gradients as perturbations and adds them to each pixel. FGSM is also called the one-step first-order attack because it only calculates the first-order gradient once to generate adversarial examples. Projected Gradient Descent (PGD) [9] iteratively updates perturbations based on the gradients with respect to the adversarial image by n steps. In each loop, PGD works like FGSM but with a smaller step size while updating perturbations. After each loop, it cuts perturbation values that are larger than the allowed maximum perturbation ϵ. Carlini and Wagner (CW) [10] has three implementations: L_0, L_1, and L_∞, and we use the L_∞ version in this study. Instead of using cross-entropy loss function, CW applies a new loss function to find stronger adversarial examples and produces smaller perturbations. The framework of CW with L_∞ setting is similar to the PGD attack excepting the loss function (Fig. 1).

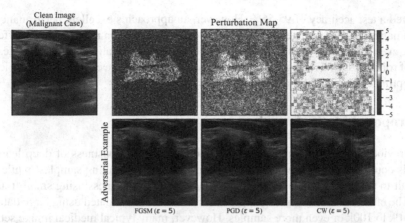

Fig. 1. Adversarial samples. The first row presents perturbations generated by three attacks. The second row shows the corresponding adversarial samples. The adversarial examples are misclassified to benign cases.

The two most popular defense approaches are regularization and training with adversarial samples. Adversarial Training (AT) [9] trains DNNs with adversarial examples generated with the model parameters on the current epoch. Classifiers trained with AT could increase robustness, but it costs a significant decrease of a model's generalization ability. Gradient Regularization (GR) [2] introduces the L_p norm of gradients with respect to the input into the loss function. The model trained with the additional gradient term could produce smoother classification boundaries. GR conducts double backpropagation and needs more computations and memory. Locally-Linear Regularization (LLR) [3] regularizes the classifier to be locally linear using the first-order Taylor expansion of a loss function. Tradeoff-inspired Adversarial Defense via Surrogate-loss minimization (TRADES) [4] is motivated to reduce the tradeoff between standard and adversarial accuracies using a classification-calibrated surrogate loss as the regularization term. The TRADES solves the problem of AT by adding a soft regularization term to minimize the difference of outputs between the clean image and the crafted image given. Robust Self-Training (RST) [5, 6] was first proposed to utilize unlabeled images with the semi-supervised learning framework to improve the adversarial robustness. For making fair comparison with other defense approaches, we only consider the supervised RST which uses only labeled images and a loss function with the standard cross-entropy loss and the adversarial loss.

2.2 Breast Ultrasound Image Classification

Breast ultrasound (BUS) was recommended as a primary imaging tool or supplemental screening with mammography to improve the sensitivity of cancer detection in women with dense breasts [11–13]. Recent research [14–17] demonstrated that BUS images with advanced DNNs could achieve high sensitivity and specificity for breast cancer detection. Zhang et al. [17] proposed a multitask DNN to segment and classify breast tumor in BUS images simultaneously. The approach was validated using 647 images and achieved a test accuracy of 95.56%. However, an approach's excellent performance on BUS images from one image set often degrades significantly on images from a different set, or even on images from the same set with minor perturbations. This indicates the lack of robustness of existing approaches which undermines the confidence of clinicians in adopting these computer-aided diagnosis systems.

3 Proposed Method

The previous work [6] demonstrated that the adversarial robustness of deep learning models could be improved with the increasing number of training samples, while it is difficult to achieve high generalization and adversarial robustness using small training sets. The effectiveness of existing approaches was usually validated using large datasets with 10k to 100k or even more samples. However, many typical medical image sets [7, 8] only have a few hundred to thousand images, and applying previous approaches, e.g., TRADES and RST, achieves poor robustness. Inspired by RST, we propose a novel self-training approach that applies the newly proposed drop-max layer and involves multiple adversarial samples during training to smooth the decision boundaries.

3.1 Multi-instance RST

Let $\{(x_i, y_i)\}_{i=1}^n$ be a labeled dataset, and f_θ be a parametric model to be learned during the training to map x_i to y_i. . The general RST approach for supervised learning aims to minimize a combination of a standard loss (L_{std}) and an adversarial loss (L_{adv}),

$$L_\theta = \underbrace{\frac{1}{n}\sum_{i=1}^n l(f_\theta(x_i), y_i)}_{L_{std}} + \underbrace{\frac{1}{n}\sum_{i=1}^n max_{\bar{x}\in D(x_i)} l(f_\theta(\bar{x}), y_i)}_{L_{adv}} \quad (1)$$

where $l(\cdot)$ denotes a standard loss function used in model training, e.g., the cross-entropy function; and $D(x_i)$ is a set of adversarial samples of x_i.

In Eq. (1), L_{adv} only counts the most aggressive adversarial instances from $D(x_i)$ for each clean image. When there is a large difference between x and $\bar{x}$, it is difficult for a model to converge to a smooth classification boundary that encloses both x and the most aggressive $\bar{x}$ using a small number of training images. Our motivation is to enable the visibility of the smooth transition from a clean image to the most aggressive adversarial instance during the training. We propose the Multi-instance RST (MIRST) to overcome existing challenges by involving a sequence of adversarial instances to speed the model convergence and enhance the adversarial robustness. The loss function of the proposed MIRST is defined by

$$L_\theta^{MI} = \frac{1}{n}\sum_{i=1}^n l(f_\theta(x_i), y_i) + \alpha \cdot \frac{1}{n}\sum_{i=1}^n \sum_{j=1}^m \beta_j \cdot l(f_\theta(\bar{x}_j), y_i) \quad (2)$$

where α balances the standard loss and the adversarial loss, β_j denotes the weight for the loss of the j th adversarial instance $\bar{x}_j$, and m is the number of adversarial instances.

In this work, we applied a T-step PGD attack to generate adversarial instances,

$$x_{t+1}^{adv} = \Pi_{x\pm\epsilon}\left(x_t^{adv} + \gamma \cdot sign\left(\nabla_x l\left(f_\theta\left(x_t^{adv}\right), y\right)\right)\right), t = 1, 2, \cdots, T \quad (3)$$

where x_t^{adv} is the t th adversarial instance and x_1^{adv} is the original clean image; the $sign(\cdot)$ function returns the sign of a value; $\Pi_{x\pm\epsilon}(\cdot)$ operator projects values to the range $[x-\epsilon, x+\epsilon]$; and γ is the step size. In experiments, T is set to 10, and $\overline{x}_j$ is x_{2j+1}^{adv} (Fig. 2).

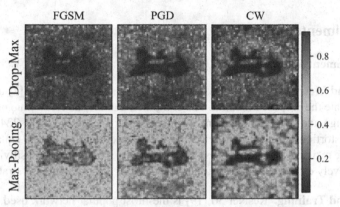

Fig. 2. Different residual maps calculated using the max-pooling layer and drop-max layer. Each residual map shows the difference between a clean image's feature map and its adversarial image's feature map. Note that all channels are added to generate residual maps.

3.2 Drop-Max Layer

The max-pooling is a popular operation in convolutional neural networks (CNNs) to downsample feature maps and extract the most salient features. However, those maximum values are sensitive to image perturbations. To overcome this challenge, we propose the drop-max layer to remove unstable features at the early stage of CNNs.

The drop-max layer removes the maximum value and selects the second largest value into the next layer. Most white-box attacks utilize the gradient $\nabla_x \mathcal{L}(f_\theta(x), y)$ to find perturbations that fool the model to produce the wrong output. Because of the max-pooling layers, perturbations were transmitted to the final decision layer through the unstable maximum values. We replace the first max-pooling layer with the proposed drop-max layer to depress the chance of letting perturbed values get into the next layers.

3.3 SimCLR Pretraining

The SimCLR [18] is a semi-supervised learning framework that was proposed to learn high-quality image representations using a small labeled image set. SimCLR samples a minibatch with the size of N and pair each image with an augmented image. By treating each pair as a positive pair, the rest $2(N-1)$ images are treated as negative. The normalized temperature-scaled cross-entropy (NT-Xent) is used to calculate loss across all positive pairs,

$$l_{simclr}(z_i, z_j) = -\log \frac{\exp(sim(z_i, z_j)/\tau)}{\sum_{k=1}^{2N} \mathbb{1}_{[k\neq i]} \exp(sim(z_i, z_k)/\tau)}, \tag{4}$$

where z_i and z_j are the outputs two image samples in a positive pair, $\text{sim}(\cdot)$ is the cosine similarity function, $\mathbb{1}_{[k \neq i]}$ is an indicator function that returns 1 iff $k \neq i$, and τ is a constant. Minimizing l_{simclr} leads to similar outputs of images in positive pairs and increased differences in outputs between positive and negative images.

4   Experimental Results

4.1   Experiment Setup

Datasets and Metrics. We apply two B-mode BUS image sets, BUSI [7] and BUSIS [8], to evaluate the proposed method. The combined dataset has 1,190 images, of which 726 are benign and 464 are malignant. All images are resized to 224×224 pixels. To avoid the distortion of tumor shape, we apply zero-padding to generate square images before image resizing. The 5-fold cross-validation with F1-score and sensitivity are used to quantitatively evaluate the adversarial robustness of different defense strategies.

Network and Training. ResNet-50 [19] is the most popular network used to validate the effectiveness of different defense strategies [9, 20, 21], and we use it as the baseline image classifier in all experiments. All approaches are trained for 100 epochs using the Adam optimizer with a learning rate of 0.0001 and a batch size of 8.

Adversarial Attack Settings. We employ three adversarial attack approaches, FGSM [1], PGD [9], and CW [10]. All these attacks are bounded by $\epsilon = 0.0196(5/255)$ with respect to the L_∞ norm. The number of the maximum iterations of PGD and CW is set to 20 and 10, respectively, and the step sizes are both 0.001.

Defense Methods and Parameters. We implement the AT [9], GR [2], LLR [3], TRADES [4], and RST [5, 6]. The weight of adversarial loss in GR, TRADES, and RST is set to 1 by experiments. In LLR, the weight of the locally linearity measure and gradient magnitude term is set to 3 and 4, respectively. MIRST-DM uses weight 1 for the adversarial loss for a fair comparison with RST. The weights for the four adversarial examples in MIRST-DM follow a descending series, i.e., $\beta = [0.34, 0.28, 0.22, 0.16]$, which sums to be 1.

4.2   The Effectiveness of Multiple-Instance RST

The primary difference between RST and the proposed MIRST is the number of adversarial samples involved in the training. In this section, we compare their performance against three attack methods. ResNet50 is used as the image classifier for the baseline, RST, and MIRST and pre-trained using ImageNet. The baseline model uses the CE loss. The adversarial robustness is evaluated using the F1 score and sensitivity on adversarial images from three attacking approaches. Note that all metrics listed in Tables 1, 2, 3 are the average values of the results from 5-fold cross-validation.

Table 1. Test performance of the baseline model, RST, and MIRST.

	Attack	Baseline	RST	MIRST
F1 score	No attack	**0.798**	0.757	0.748
	FGSM	0.014	0.519	**0.542**
	PGD	0.000	0.496	**0.516**
	CW	0.000	0.482	**0.498**
Sensitivity	No attack	**0.786**	0.711	0.713
	FGSM	0.017	0.495	**0.528**
	PGD	0.000	0.478	**0.513**
	CW	0.000	0.463	**0.492**

In Table 1, the values in the 'No attack' row are calculated using clean test images, while values in other rows are from adversarial images. The F1 score and sensitivity of the baseline model drop significantly under the three –attack approaches, which demonstrates the poor adversarial robustness of the baseline model. For example, the PGD and CW attacks reduce the baseline model's F1 score to 0. Both RST and MIRST achieve comparable generalization and greatly improve the adversarial robustness of the baseline model against the FGSM, PGD, and CW attacks. MIRST achieves higher F1 scores than those of RST against all three attacks. MIRST improves RST's sensitivity values against the FGSM, PGD, and CW attacks by 6.74%, 7.17%, and 6.22%.

Table 2. Test performance of the models using SimCLR pretrained model.

	Attack	Baseline	GR	AT	LLR	TRADES	RST	MI-RST
F1 score	No attack	0.831	0.817	0.489	–	0.822	0.802	**0.830**
	FGSM	0.231	0.198	0.253	–	0.576	0.620	**0.640**
	PGD	0.000	0.000	0.096	–	0.366	0.425	**0.544**
	CW	0.000	0.000	0.479	–	0.458	0.467	**0.512**
Sensitivity	No attack	0.827	0.815	0.344	–	0.780	0.762	**0.805**
	FGSM	0.284	0.245	0.267	–	0.522	0.604	**0.622**
	PGD	0.000	0.000	0.083	–	0.379	0.420	**0.543**
	CW	0.000	0.000	0.336	–	0.467	0.463	**0.504**

'-' in the LLR column denotes unavailable values because the training did not converge.

4.3 The Effectiveness of the SimCLR Pretrained Model

We compare the generalization ability and adversarial robustness of the baseline, GR, AT, LLR, TREADS, RST, and MIRST pretrained using the SimCLR loss on ImageNet. All results in Table 1 are from models pretrained using the CE loss on ImageNet. As shown in Table 2, SimCLR improves the generalizability (F1 scores) of the baseline, RST, and MI-RST by 4.14%, 5.87%, and 10.93%. In addition, SimCLR can significantly improve the adversarial robustness of the proposed MIRST, e.g., MIRST's F1 scores against FGSM, PGD, and CW attacks increased by 18.06%, 5.46%, and 2.84%.

Table 3. Results of RST and MI-RST with (w/) and without (w/o) the drop-max layer.

		RST		MIRST	
	Attack	w/o DM	w/ DM	w/o DM	w/ DM
F1 score	No attack	0.802	**0.825**	**0.830**	0.823
	FGSM	0.620	**0.641**	0.640	**0.655**
	PGD	0.425	**0.580**	0.544	**0.586**
	CW	0.467	**0.740**	0.512	**0.734**
Sensitivity	No attack	0.762	**0.806**	**0.805**	0.799
	FGSM	0.604	**0.628**	0.622	**0.650**
	PGD	0.420	**0.571**	0.543	**0.587**
	CW	0.463	**0.743**	0.504	**0.720**

4.4   The Effectiveness of the Drop-Max Layer

We compare the results of the RST and MIRST with and without the proposed drop-max (DM) layer. The DM layer is applied to replace the first max-pooling layer of ResNet50. As shown in Table 3, the F1 scores of RST with the DM layer against the FGSM, PGD, and CW are improved by 3.38%, 36.66%, and 58.51%, respectively. The DM layer also increases the F1 score of RST on clean images by 2.89%. The DM layer does not improve MIRST's generalization on clean images. But it improves the adversarial robustness of MIRST against all three attacks. E.g., the F1 score of MIRST-DM against the CW attack is 43.42% higher than that of MIRST without the DM layer; and the F1 score of MIRST-DM against the PGD attack increased by 7.65%.

5   Conclusion

In this study, we propose the MI-RST approach to improve the adversarial robustness of DNNs and validate it using a breast ultrasound (BUS) image set. The proposed MI-RST achieves higher adversarial robustness than RST using a small BUS image set, and its generalizability is comparable to RST. The proposed drop-max layer removes unstable features at the early stage of model training and significantly improves the adversarial robustness of both RST and MI-RST against FGSM, PGD, and CW attacks. The pre-trained model using SimCLR leads to improved generalizability and adversarial robustness of MI-RST. This work provides a comprehensive view of the performance of state-of-the-art defense approaches on a small medical image set. It can help develop more robust and trustworthy computer-aided diagnosis systems in an open-world environment.

References

1. Goodfellow, I.J., Shlens, J., Szegedy, C.: Explaining and harnessing adversarial examples. arXiv preprint arXiv:1412.6572 (2014)
2. Drucker, H., Cun, Y.L.: Double backpropagation increasing generalization performance. In: IJCNN-91-Seattle International Joint Conference on Neural Networks, vol. 2, pp. 145–150 (1991). https://doi.org/10.1109/IJCNN.1991.155328
3. Qin, C., et al.: Adversarial robustness through local linearization. Adv. Neural. Inf. Process. Syst. **32**, 13847–13856 (2019)
4. Zhang, H., Yu, Y., Jiao, J., Xing, E., El Ghaoui, L., Jordan, M.: Theoretically principled trade-off between robustness and accuracy. In: International Conference on Machine Learning, pp. 7472–7482. PMLR (2019)
5. Carmon, Y., Raghunathan, A., Schmidt, L., Duchi, J.C., Liang, P.S.: Unlabeled data improves adversarial robustness. In: Advances in Neural Information Processing Systems, vol. 32 (2019)
6. Raghunathan, A., Xie, S.M., Yang, F., Duchi, J., Liang, P.: Understanding and mitigating the tradeoff between robustness and accuracy. In: Proceedings of the 37th International Conference on Machine Learning, pp. 7909–7919. PMLR (2020)
7. Al-Dhabyani, W., Gomaa, M., Khaled, H., Fahmy, A.: Dataset of breast ultrasound images. Data Brief **28**, 104863 (2020). https://doi.org/10.1016/j.dib.2019.104863
8. Xian, M., et al.: BUSIS: a benchmark for breast ultrasound image segmentation. arXiv preprint arXiv:1801.03182 [cs] (2021)
9. Madry, A., Makelov, A., Schmidt, L., Tsipras, D., Vladu, A.: Towards deep learning models resistant to adversarial attacks. In: Presented at the International Conference on Learning Representations, 15 Feb 2018 (2018)
10. Carlini, N., Wagner, D.: Towards evaluating the robustness of neural networks. In: 2017 IEEE Symposium on Security and Privacy (SP), pp. 39–57 (2017). https://doi.org/10.1109/SP.2017.49
11. Lehman, C.D., Lee, C.I., Loving, V.A., Portillo, M.S., Peacock, S., DeMartini, W.B.: Accuracy and value of breast ultrasound for primary imaging evaluation of symptomatic women 30–39 years of age. Am. J. Roentgenol. **199**, 1169–1177 (2012). https://doi.org/10.2214/AJR.12.8842
12. Okello, J., Kisembo, H., Bugeza, S., Galukande, M.: Breast cancer detection using sonography in women with mammographically dense breasts. BMC Med. Imaging **14**, 41 (2014). https://doi.org/10.1186/s12880-014-0041-0
13. Burkett, B.J., Hanemann, C.W.: A review of supplemental screening ultrasound for breast cancer: certain populations of women with dense breast tissue may benefit. Acad. Radiol. **23**, 1604–1609 (2016). https://doi.org/10.1016/j.acra.2016.05.017
14. Shia, W.-C., Chen, D.-R.: Classification of malignant tumors in breast ultrasound using a pretrained deep residual network model and support vector machine. Comput. Med. Imaging Graph. **87**, 101829 (2021). https://doi.org/10.1016/j.compmedimag.2020.101829
15. Xie, J., et al.: A novel approach with dual-sampling convolutional neural network for ultrasound image classification of breast tumors. Phys. Med. Biol. **65** (2020)

16. Zhuang, Z., Yang, Z., Zhuang, S., Joseph Raj, A.N., Yuan, Y., Nersisson, R.: Multi-features-based automated breast tumor diagnosis using ultrasound image and support vector machine. Comput. Intell. Neurosci. **2021**, e9980326 (2021). https://doi.org/10.1155/2021/9980326

17. Zhang, G., Zhao, K., Hong, Y., Qiu, X., Zhang, K., Wei, B.: SHA-MTL: soft and hard attention multi-task learning for automated breast cancer ultrasound image segmentation and classification. Int. J. Comput. Assist. Radiol. Surg. **16**(10), 1719–1725 (2021). https://doi.org/10.1007/s11548-021-02445-7

18. Chen, T., Kornblith, S., Norouzi, M., Hinton, G.: A simple framework for contrastive learning of visual representations. In: International Conference on Machine Learning, pp. 1597–1607. PMLR (2020)

19. He, K., Zhang, X., Ren, S., Sun, J.: Deep residual learning for image recognition. In: Presented at the Proceedings of the IEEE Conference on Computer Vision and Pattern Recognition (2016)

20. Yang, Y.-Y., Rashtchian, C., Zhang, H., Salakhutdinov, R., Chaudhuri, K.: A closer look at accuracy vs. robustness. arXiv preprint arXiv:2003.02460 [cs, stat]. (2020)

21. Ma, X., et al.: Understanding adversarial attacks on deep learning based medical image analysis systems. Pattern Recogn. **110**, 107332 (2021). https://doi.org/10.1016/j.patcog.2020.107332

Towards Confident Detection of Prostate Cancer Using High Resolution Micro-ultrasound

Mahdi Gilany[1]([✉]), Paul Wilson[1], Amoon Jamzad[1], Fahimeh Fooladgar[2],
Minh Nguyen Nhat To[2], Brian Wodlinger[3], Purang Abolmaesumi[2],
and Parvin Mousavi[1]

[1] School of Computing, Queen's University, Kingston, Canada
`mahdi.gilany@queensu.ca`
[2] Department of Electrical and Computer Engineering,
University of British Columbia, Vancouver, Canada
[3] Exact Imaging, Markham, Canada

Abstract. MOTIVATION: Detection of prostate cancer during transrectal ultrasound-guided biopsy is challenging. The highly heterogeneous appearance of cancer, presence of ultrasound artefacts, and noise all contribute to these difficulties. Recent advancements in high-frequency ultrasound imaging - micro-ultrasound - have drastically increased the capability of tissue imaging at high resolution. Our aim is to investigate the development of a robust deep learning model specifically for micro-ultrasound-guided prostate cancer biopsy. For the model to be clinically adopted, a key challenge is to design a solution that can confidently identify the cancer, while learning from coarse histopathology measurements of biopsy samples that introduce weak labels. METHODS: We use a dataset of micro-ultrasound images acquired from 194 patients, who underwent prostate biopsy. We train a deep model using a co-teaching paradigm to handle noise in labels, together with an evidential deep learning method for uncertainty estimation. We evaluate the performance of our model using the clinically relevant metric of accuracy vs. confidence. RESULTS: Our model achieves a well-calibrated estimation of predictive uncertainty with area under the curve of 88%. The use of co-teaching and evidential deep learning in combination yields significantly better uncertainty estimation than either alone. We also provide a detailed comparison against state-of-the-art in uncertainty estimation.

Keywords: Prostate cancer · Micro-ultrasound · Uncertainty · Weak labels

1 Introduction

Prostate cancer (PCa) is the second most common cancer in men worldwide [18]. The standard of care for diagnosing PCa is histopathological analysis of tissue samples obtained via systematic prostate biopsy under trans-rectal ultrasound

L. Wang et al. (Eds.): MICCAI 2022, LNCS 13434, pp. 411–420, 2022.
https://doi.org/10.1007/978-3-031-16440-8_40

(TRUS) guidance. TRUS is used for anatomical navigation rather than cancer targeting. The appearance of cancer on ultrasound is highly heterogeneous and is further affected by imaging artifacts and noise, resulting in low sensitivity and specificity in PCa detection based on ultrasound alone.

Substantial previous literature and large multi-center trials report low sensitivity of systematic TRUS biopsy. In [3], authors compare diagnostic accuracy of TRUS biopsy and multi-parametric MRI (mp-MRI). They report sensitivity of systematic TRUS biopsy as low as 42–55% compared to 88–96% for mp-MRI. However, they report low specificity of 36–46% for mp-MRI compared to 94–98% for TRUS.

Fusion of mp-MRI imaging with ultrasound can enable targeted biopsy by identifying cancerous lesions in the prostate [13,17]. Fusion biopsy involves either manual or semi-automated registration of lesions identified in mp-MRI with real-time TRUS. This process can be time-consuming and inaccurate due to registration errors and patient motion. It is therefore highly desirable to improve the capability of biopsy targeting using ultrasound imaging alone at the point of care.

The recent development of high frequency "micro-ultrasound" technology allows for the visualization of tissue at higher resolution than conventional ultrasound. A qualitative scoring system based on visual analysis of micro-ultrasound images called the PRI-MUS (prostate risk identification using micro-ultrasound) protocol [6] has been proposed to estimate PCa likelihood. Several studies have shown that micro-ultrasound can detect PCa with sensitivity comparable to that of mp-MRI using this grading system [2,4]. A recent systematic review and meta analysis analyzing 13 published studies with 1,125 total participants found that micro-ultrasound guided prostate biopsy and mp-MRI imaging targeted prostate biopsy resulted in comparable detection rates for PCa [19]. Research on this technology is in early stages and relatively few quantitative methods are reported. Rohrbach et al. [14] use a combination of manual feature selection with machine learning as the first quantitative approach to this problem. Shao et al. [16] use a deep learning strategy with a three-player minimax game to tackle data source heterogeneity. While these studies show significant potential of micro-ultrasound as a diagnostic tool for PCa, methods to-date primarily focus on improving accuracy for cancer prediction. We argue that in addition, confidence in detection of cancer can play a significant role for adoption of this technology to ensure that predictions can be clinically trusted. Towards this end, we propose to address several key challenges.

Machine learning models built from ultrasound data rely on ground truth labels from histopathology that are coarse and only approximately describe the spatial distribution of cancer in a biopsy core [11,14,16]. The lack of finer labels cause two challenges: first, labels assigned to patches of ultrasound images in a biopsy core may not match the ground truth tissue, resulting in weak labels; second, biopsies include other types of tissue such as fibromuscular cells, benign prostatic hyperplasia and precancerous changes. Many of these tissues are unlabeled in a histopathology report, which will result in out-of-distribution (OOD) data. Therefore, effective learning models for micro-ultrasound data should be robust to label noise and OOD samples.

Several solutions have been presented to address the above issues, mainly by quantifying the uncertainty of predictions [1,5,12]. Predictive uncertainty can be used as a tool to discard unreliable and OOD samples. Evidential deep learning (EDL) [15] and ensemble methods [12] are amongst such approaches. In particular, evidential learning is computationally light, run-time efficient and theoretically grounded, hence it fits our clinical purpose here. Learning from noise in labels (i.e. weak labels) has also been addressed before using methods that 1) estimate noise; 2) modify the learning objective function, or 3) use alternative optimization [8]. Among these, co-teaching [9] has been shown to be a successful baseline that can be easily integrated with any uncertainty quantification method.

In this paper, for the first time, we propose a learning model for PCa detection using micro-ultrasound that can provide an estimate of its predictive confidence and is robust to weak labels and OOD data. We address label noise using co-teaching and utilize evidential learning to estimate uncertainty for OOD rejection, resulting in confident detection of PCa. We assess our approach by examining the classification accuracy and uncertainty calibration (i.e. the tendency of the model to have high levels of certainty on correct predictions). We compare our methodology to a variety of uncertainty methods with and without co-teaching and demonstrate significant improvements over baseline. We show that applying an adjustable threshold to discard uncertain predictions yields great improvements in accuracy. By allowing correct and confident predictions, our approach could provide clinicians with a powerful tool for computer-assisted cancer detection from ultrasound.

2 Materials and Methods

2.1 Data

Data is obtained from 2,335 biopsy cores of 198 patients who underwent transrectal ultrasound-guided prostate biopsy through a clinical trial and after institutional ethics approval is provided. A 29 MHz micro-ultrasound system and transducer (ExactVu, Markham) was used for data acquisition. A single sagittal ultrasound image composed of 512 lateral radio frequency (RF) lines was obtained prior to the firing of the biopsy gun for each core. Primary and secondary Gleason grades, together with an estimate of the fraction of cancer relative to the total core area (the so-called "involvement of cancer") are also provided for each patient. We under-sampled benign cores in order to obtain an equal proportion of cancerous and benign cores during training and evaluation, resulting in 300 benign and 300 cancerous cores, respectively. As in [14], we exclude cores with involvement less than 40% to learn from data that better represents PCa. We hold out the data from 27 patients as a test set, with the remaining 161 used for training and cross-validation.

Pre-processing: For each RF ultrasound image, a rectangular region of interest (ROI) corresponding to the approximate needle trace area is determined by using

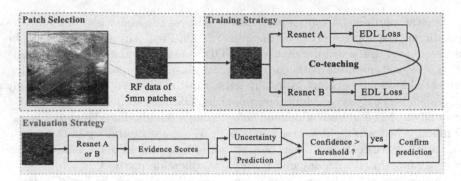

Fig. 1. Top left: Patches are extracted from the needle region. Top Right: during training, "clean" examples are selected by the peer model for training updates. Bottom: The model predicts evidence scores which are used to calculate predictions and uncertainty. Predictions with high uncertainty are rejected. (Color figure online)

the angle and location of the probe-mounted needle relative to the imaging plane (Fig. 1, yellow region). This ROI is intersected with a manually drawn prostate segmentation mask to exclude non-prostatic tissue. Overlapping patches are extracted corresponding to 5 mm × 5 mm tissue regions with an overlap of 90% covering the ROI. These patches are up-sampled in the lateral direction and down-sampled in the axial direction by factors of 5 to obtain a uniform physical spacing of pixels in both directions. This results in a patch of 256 by 256 pixels. Ultrasound data in each patch are normalized to a mean of 0 and standard deviation of 1. Patches are assigned a binary label of 0 (benign) or 1 (cancerous) depending on the pathology of the core. The patches and their associated labels are inputs to our learning algorithms.

2.2 Methodology

We propose a micro-ultrasound PCa detection learning model that is robust to challenges associated with weak labels and OOD samples. In this section, we first define the problem followed by descriptions of co-teaching as a strategy for dealing with weak labels. Next, we incorporate evidential deep for quantifying prediction uncertainty and excluding suspected OOD data. Finally, we present evaluation metrics to assess our methods.

Weak Labels and OOD: Let $X_i = \{x_1, x_2, ..., x_{n_i}\}$ refer to a biopsy core where n_i number of patches extracted from needle region (Fig. 1). For each biopsy core X_i, pathology reports a label Y_i and the length of cancer L_i in core, which is a rough estimate between zero and the biopsy sample length. Following previous work in PCa detection [11,14], we assign coarse pathology labels Y_i to all extracted patches $\{x_1, x_2, ..., x_{n_i}\}$ due to the lack of finer patch-level labels. Therefore, many assigned labels to patches may not necessarily match with the ground truth and they are inherently weak. Additionally, other tissue than cancer, present in the core, does not have any gold standard labels. Therefore, there is also OOD data.

Co-teaching: We propose to use a state-of-the-art method, co-teaching, to address label noise for micro-ultrasound data [9]. For weak label methods, we rely on the findings of [11] showing the success of co-teaching method, and [20], which found that co-teaching significantly out-performed other methods such as robust loss functions. This approach simultaneously trains two similar neural networks with different weight initializations. According to the theory of co-teaching, neural networks initially learn simpler and cleaner samples then overfit to noisy input. Therefore, during each iteration, each network picks a subset of samples with lower loss values as potentially clean data and trains the other network with those samples. In a batch of data with size N, only $R(e) * N$ number of samples are selected by each network as clean samples, where $R(e)$ is the ratio of selection starting from 1 and gradually decreasing to a fixed value $1 - \gamma$. Formally we have $R(e) = 1 - \min(\frac{e}{e_{\max}}, \gamma)$, where $\gamma \in [0, 1]$ is a hyperparameter, and e and $e_{\max}$ are the current and maximum number of epochs, respectively. Using two networks prevents confirmation bias from arising.

Evidential Deep Learning: Evidential deep learning (EDL) [15] uses the concepts of *belief* and *evidence* to formalize the notion of uncertainty in deep learning. A neural network is used to learn the parameters of a prior distribution for the class likelihoods instead of point estimates of these likelihoods. Given a binary classification problem where $P(y = 1|x_i) = p_i$, instead of estimating p_i, the network estimates parameters e_0, e_1 such that $p_i \sim \text{Beta}(e_0+1, e_1+1)$. These parameters are then referred to as evidence scores for the classes, and used to generate a belief mass and uncertainty assignment, via $b_0 = \frac{e_0}{S}, b_1 = \frac{e_1}{S}, U = \frac{2}{S}$, where $S = \sum_{i=0}^{1} e_i + 1$. Note that $b_0 + b_1 + U = 1$. U ranges between 0 and 1 and is inversely proportional to our overall level of belief or evidence for each class. It is worth mentioning that term confidence is also used often instead of uncertainty with confidence being $1 - U$.

The network is trained to minimize an objective function based on its Bayes Risk as an estimator of the likelihoods p_i. If the network produces evidences e_0, e_1 for sample i, the loss and predicted uncertainty for this sample are

$$\mathcal{L}_i = \sum_{i=1}^{n} E_{p_i \sim \text{Beta}(e_0+e_1)}\big(|p_i - y_i|^2\big), U_i = \frac{2}{e_0 + e_1 + 2}, \tag{1}$$

where e_0 and e_1 are the network outputs. The loss also incorporates a KL divergence term, which encourages higher uncertainty on predictions that do not contribute to data fit. The method offers a combination of speed (requiring only a single forward pass for inference) and well-calibrated uncertainty estimation with a solid theoretical foundation.

Table 1. Effect of co-teaching on accuracy and calibration error.

Method	AUC	Sensitivity	Specificity	Patch B-accuracy	ECE
EDL	**88.27**	71.32	84.80	67.47	0.1989
	± 2.66	± 1.23	± 7.01	± 2.47	± 0.0142
EDL + Co-teaching	87.76	67.38	88.20	**71.25**	**0.1379**
(ours)	± 1.82	± 4.91	± 6.85	± 1.16	± 0.0258

Clinical Evaluation Metrics: The goal of our model is to provide the operator with clinically relevant information, such as real-time identification of potential biopsy targets. It should also state the degree of confidence in its predictions such that the operator can decide when to accept the model's suggestions or defer to their own experience. To measure these success criteria, we propose several evaluation metrics.

Accuracy reported at the level of patches (the basic input to the model) can be misleading due to weak labeling (some correct predictions are recorded as incorrect because of incorrect labels). Therefore, we propose accuracy reported at the level of biopsy cores as a more relevant alternative. We determine core-based accuracy using core-wise predictions aggregated from patch-wise predictions for the core. Specifically, the average of patch predicted labels is used as a probability score that cancer exists in the core [20,21]. To model uncertainty at the core level, patch-wise predictions that do not meet a specified confidence threshold are ignored when calculating this score, and if more than 40% of the patch predictions for a core fall below this threshold, the entire core prediction is considered "uncertain".

We also use "uncertainty calibration", a metric that assesses how accurate and representative the predicted uncertainty or confidence is (in terms of true likelihood). To compute calibration, we compute Expected Calibration Error (ECE) [7], which measures the correspondence between predictive confidence and empirical accuracy. ECE is calculated by grouping the predictions so that each prediction falls into one of the S equal bins produced between zero and one based on its confidence score:

$$\text{ECE} = \sum_{s=1}^{S} \frac{n_s}{N} |\text{acc}(s) - \text{conf}(s)|, \tag{2}$$

where S denotes the number of bins (10 used in this paper), n_s the number of predictions in bin s, N the total number of predictions, and $\text{acc}(s)$ and $\text{conf}(s)$ the relative accuracy and average confidence of bin s, respectively.

3   Experiments and Results

From all data, 161 patients (392 cores, 12664 patches) are used for training and a further 40 patients are used as a validation set for model selection and tuning.

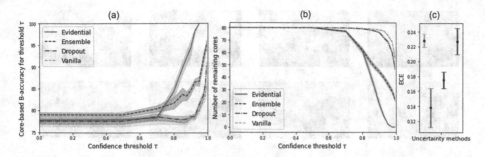

Fig. 2. Left: accuracy vs. confidence plot. As we increase the confidence threshold τ and retain only confident predictions, the balanced accuracy increases accordingly. Middle: The number of remaining cores following exclusion based on the confidence threshold. Right: the Expected Calibration Error (ECE) error bar plot for all presented uncertainty quantification methods (lower is better).

We hold out a set of randomly selected, mutually exclusive, patients as test set (27 patients, 80 cores, 2808 patches). All experiments, except for the ensemble method, are repeated nine times with three different validation sets, each with three different initializations; the average of all runs is reported. For the ensemble method, as suggested in [12], five different models with different initialization are used for estimating true prediction probabilities, $p(y_i|x_i)$. This process is done with five different validation sets, resulting in a total of 25 runs. As a backbone network, we modify ResNet18 [10] by using only half of the layers in each residual block. We found this reduction in layers to improve model performance, likely by reducing overfitting. Two copies of modified ResNet with different initializations are used for the co-teaching framework. For our choice of γ, we emprically found 0.4 to be the best. We employ the NovoGrad optimizer with learning rate of 1e-4.

3.1 Effect of Co-teaching

To determine the effects of weak labels and the added value of co-teaching, we design an experiment comparing EDL with co-teaching to EDL alone. Table 1 shows a promising improvement in both ECE score and patch-based balanced accuracy (Patch B-accuracy) when the co-teaching is employed. We report sensitivity, specificity and area under the curve (AUC) metrics for cores. Counterintuitively, we observe that gains in patch-wise accuracy with co-teaching are not reflected in these metrics. We hypothesize that the averaging from patch-wise to core-wise predictions may sufficiently smooth the effects of noisy labels at this level. We emphasize that the AUC for *both* methods is at least 10% higher than AUC achieved using conventional ultrasound machines [11], underlining the strong capabilities of high-frequency ultrasound.

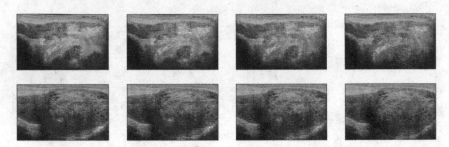

Fig. 3. Heatmaps representing predictions of cancer (red) or benign (blue). The confidence threshold is increased from left to right as $[0.7, 0.8, 0.85, 0.9]$, progressively excluding more uncertain predictions. The top row is from cancerous core with Gleason score 4 + 3; the bottom row is from a benign core. (Color figure online)

3.2 Comparison of Uncertainty Methods

Quantification of predictive uncertainty could help clinical decision making during the biopsy procedure by only relying on highly confident predictions and discarding OOD and suspect samples. We examine EDL predictive uncertainty using *accuracy vs. confidence plots* in this section, and illustrate how it may be utilised to eliminate uncertain predictions while achieving high accuracy on the confident ones. Then, we compare EDL predictive uncertainty with MC Dropout [5] and deep ensemble [12] methods.

In our *accuracy vs. confidence plot*, Fig. 2 (a), we plot core-based balanced accuracy as a function of the confidence threshold $\tau \in [0, 1]$ used to filter out underconfident patch-level predictions. Patches with predicted confidence less than τ, i.e. predictive uncertainty more than $1 - \tau$, are discarded. If at least 60% of extracted patches for a biopsy core remain, the average of the remaining patch predictions is used as core-based prediction. We observe the increase in core-based accuracy as the threshold increases, showing that confident predictions tend to be correct. As shown in Fig. 2 (b), there is a natural trade-off, with increased threshold values also resulting in increased numbers of rejected cores, yet with well-calibrated uncertainty methods it is not necessary to discard a high fraction of cores in order for uncertainty thresholding to result in meaningful accuracy gains. In Fig. 2 (c), we compare the quality of predictive uncertainty of all methods via ECE score. Our experiments show that EDL achieves the best calibration error while providing the best balance between high accuracy and core retention at different threshold levels.

3.3 Model Demonstration

As a proof-of-concept for the clinical utility of our method, we applied our model as a sliding window over entire RF images and generated a heatmap, where red corresponds to a prediction of cancer and blue to a prediction of benign. Uncertainty thresholds at various levels were applied to discard uncertain predictions

- discarded predictions had their opacity decreased to 0. These maps were over-laid over the corresponding B-mode images to visualize the spread of cancer. An example of heatmaps for a cancerous and benign core are shown in Fig. 3. The cancerous image shows a large amount of red which focuses on two main regions as the confidence threshold increases. By the results of Fig. 1, we can say that these loci are very likely to be cancerous lesions and good biopsy targets. The benign image, on the other hand, shows a dominance of blue, with two small red areas that disappear as the threshold increases. These are most likely areas of OOD features on which the model correctly reported high levels of uncertainty. These images show the subjective quality of our model's performance and the utility of an adjustable uncertainty threshold.

4   Conclusion

We proposed a model for confident PCa detection using micro-ultrasound. We employed co-teaching to improve robustness to label noise, and used eviden-tial deep learning to model the predictive uncertainty of the model. We find these strategies to yield a significant improvement over baseline in the clini-cally relevant metrics of accuracy vs. confidence. Our model provides crucial confidence information to interventionists weighing the recommendations of the model against their own expertise, which can be critical for the adoption of precision biopsy targeting using TRUS.

Acknowledgement. This work was supported by the Natural Sciences and Engi-neering Research Council of Canada (NSERC) and the Canadian Institutes of Health Research (CIHR).

References

1. Abdar, M., et al.: A review of uncertainty quantification in deep learning: tech-niques, applications and challenges. Inf. Fusion **76**, 243–297 (2021)
2. Abouassaly, R., Klein, E.A., El-Shefai, A., Stephenson, A.: Impact of using 29 mhz high-resolution micro-ultrasound in real-time targeting of transrectal prostate biopsies: initial experience. World J. Urol. **38**(5), 1201–1206 (2020)
3. Ahmed, H.U., et al.: Diagnostic accuracy of multi-parametric MRI and TRUS biopsy in prostate cancer (PROMIS): a paired validating confirmatory study. Lancet **389**(10071), 815–822 (2017)
4. Eure, G., Fanney, D., Lin, J., Wodlinger, B., Ghai, S.: Comparison of conven-tional transrectal ultrasound, magnetic resonance imaging, and micro-ultrasound for visualizing prostate cancer in an active surveillance population: a feasibility study. Can. Urol. Assoc. J. **13**(3), E70 (2019)
5. Gal, Y., Ghahramani, Z.: Dropout as a bayesian approximation: representing model uncertainty in deep learning. In: International Conference on Machine Learning, pp. 1050–1059. PMLR (2016)
6. Ghai, S., et al.: Assessing cancer risk on novel 29 mhz micro-ultrasound images of the prostate: creation of the micro-ultrasound protocol for prostate risk identifica-tion. J. Urol. **196**(2), 562–569 (2016)

7. Guo, C., Pleiss, G., Sun, Y., Weinberger, K.Q.: On calibration of modern neural networks. In: International Conference on Machine Learning, pp. 1321–1330. PMLR (2017)
8. Han, B., et al.: A survey of label-noise representation learning: Past, present and future. arXiv preprint arXiv:2011.04406 (2020)
9. Han, B., et al.: Co-teaching: robust training of deep neural networks with extremely noisy labels. Adv. Neural Inf. Process. Syst. **31** (2018)
10. He, K., Zhang, X., Ren, S., Sun, J.: Deep residual learning for image recognition. In: Proceedings of the IEEE conference on computer vision and pattern recognition, pp. 770–778 (2016)
11. Javadi, G., et al.: Training deep networks for prostate cancer diagnosis using coarse histopathological labels. In: de Bruijne, M., et al. (eds.) MICCAI 2021. LNCS, vol. 12908, pp. 680–689. Springer, Cham (2021). https://doi.org/10.1007/978-3-030-87237-3_65
12. Lakshminarayanan, B., Pritzel, A., Blundell, C.: Simple and scalable predictive uncertainty estimation using deep ensembles. Adv. Neural Inf. Process. Syst. **30** (2017)
13. Rai, B.P., Mayerhofer, C., Somani, B.K., Kallidonis, P., Nagele, U., Tokas, T.: Magnetic resonance imaging/ultrasound fusion-guided transperineal versus magnetic resonance imaging/ultrasound fusion-guided transrectal prostate biopsy-a systematic review. Eur. Urol. Oncol. **4**(6), 904–913 (2021)
14. Rohrbach, D., Wodlinger, B., Wen, J., Mamou, J., Feleppa, E.: High-frequency quantitative ultrasound for imaging prostate cancer using a novel micro-ultrasound scanner. Ultrasound in Med. Biol. **44**(7), 1341–1354 (2018)
15. Sensoy, M., Kaplan, L., Kandemir, M.: Evidential deep learning to quantify classification uncertainty. Adv. Neural Inf. Process. Syst. **31** (2018)
16. Shao, Y., Wang, J., Wodlinger, B., Salcudean, S.E.: Improving prostate cancer (PCA) classification performance by using three-player minimax game to reduce data source heterogeneity. IEEE Trans. Med. Imaging **39**(10), 3148–3158 (2020)
17. Siddiqui, M.M., et al.: Magnetic resonance imaging/ultrasound-fusion biopsy significantly upgrades prostate cancer versus systematic 12-core transrectal ultrasound biopsy. Eur. Urol. **64**(5), 713–719 (2013)
18. Smith, L., Bryan, S., De, P., et al.: Canadian cancer statistics advisory committee. Can. Can. Stat. **2018** (2018)
19. Sountoulides, P.: Micro-ultrasound-guided vs multiparametric magnetic resonance imaging-targeted biopsy in the detection of prostate cancer: a systematic review and meta-analysis. J. Urol. **205**(5), 1254–1262 (2021)
20. To, M.N.N., et al.: Increasing diagnostic yield of prostate cancer during ultrasound guided biopsy in the presence of label noise (2022)
21. To, M.N.N., et al.: Coarse label refinement for improving prostate cancer detection in ultrasound imaging. Int. J. Comput. Assis. Radiol. Surg. **17**(5), 841–847 (2022)

Video Data Analysis

Unsupervised Contrastive Learning of Image Representations from Ultrasound Videos with Hard Negative Mining

Soumen Basu[1]([✉])(iD), Somanshu Singla[1], Mayank Gupta[1], Pratyaksha Rana[2], Pankaj Gupta[2], and Chetan Arora[1]

[1] Indian Institute of Technology, Delhi, India
soumen.basu@cse.iitd.ac.in
[2] Postgraduate Institute of Medical Education and Research, Chandigarh, India

Abstract. Rich temporal information and variations in viewpoints make video data an attractive choice for learning image representations using unsupervised contrastive learning (UCL) techniques. State-of-the-art (SOTA) contrastive learning techniques consider frames within a video as positives in the embedding space, whereas the frames from other videos are considered negatives. We observe that unlike multiple views of an object in natural scene videos, an Ultrasound (US) video captures different 2D slices of an organ. Hence, there is almost no similarity between the temporally distant frames of even the same US video. In this paper we propose to instead utilize such frames as hard negatives. We advocate mining both intra-video and cross-video negatives in a hardness-sensitive negative mining curriculum in a UCL framework to learn rich image representations. We deploy our framework to learn the representations of Gallbladder (GB) malignancy from US videos. We also construct the first large-scale US video dataset containing 64 videos and 15,800 frames for learning GB representations. We show that the standard ResNet50 backbone trained with our framework improves the accuracy of models pretrained with SOTA UCL techniques as well as supervised pretrained models on ImageNet for the GB malignancy detection task by 2–6%. We further validate the generalizability of our method on a publicly available lung US image dataset of COVID-19 pathologies and show an improvement of 1.5% compared to SOTA. Source code, dataset, and models are available at https://gbc-iitd.github.io/usucl.

Keywords: Contrastive learning · Ultrasound · Negative mining

Supplementary Information The online version contains supplementary material available at https://doi.org/10.1007/978-3-031-16440-8_41.

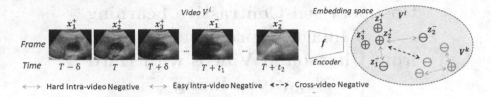

Fig. 1. We motivate the use of intra-video negatives in contrastive learning. Based on the visibility of a pathology in the intra-video samples, negatives can be sampled. The frames in range $[T - \delta, T + \delta]$ in video V^i has stones and malignant wall thickening visible for a small δ. A slightly distant frame $T + t_1$ shows a GB, but the malignant wall thickening is not visible. This sample acts as a hard negative. The viewing plane further changes in frame $T + t_2$ and GB becomes invisible.

1   Introduction

Due to their remarkable performance, Deep Neural Networks (DNNs) have become defacto standard for a wide range of medical image analysis tasks in recent years [4,6]. However, lack of annotated medical data due to the specialized nature of annotations, and the data privacy issues restrict the applicability of supervised learning of DNNs in medical imaging. Although pretraining on large natural image datasets yields a performance boost for downstream tasks on medical data [3,13], the large domain gap between the natural and medical images remains a bottleneck. Recent works are increasingly going beyond the supervised setup and exploiting unsupervised techniques to compensate for the lack of annotated data [10,19]. Broadly, there are two prominent categories of representation learning techniques for leveraging unlabeled data. In the pretext task-based method, the DNNs are pretrained with some spatial tasks such as image rotation prediction [22] or temporal tasks such as video clip order prediction [26] to learn efficient image representation. On the other hand, contrastive methods [10] try to distinguish between different views of image samples to learn robust representation without labels. Visual representations learned by contrastive learning have been shown to outperform the supervised pretraining on large annotated data in terms of accuracy on the downstream prediction tasks [10,19].

Video data contains rich variations in viewpoints and natural temporal information for objects making it suitable for going beyond image-level contrastive learning. Additionally, the abundance of unlabeled video data makes it an attractive choice for learning representations. Recent works are attempting to exploit the video data to learn robust image-level representations [12,25]. We observe that current SOTA techniques for image representation learning from videos, such as USCL [12] suggest that images coming from the same video are too close to be considered negatives (*similarity conflict*). USCL advocates considering only cross-video samples as negatives to avoid the similarity conflict. While similarity conflict is prevalent for intra-video samples of natural video datasets like action recognition, where each video contains a distinct action, the US videos are inherently different. The frames of a US video contain both types of images where pathology is visible or absent. We argue that frames from the same video where the pathology is absent can be used as hard negatives for the positive samples with the visible pathology. Figure 1 shows the positive and negative frames from the same US video. The temporal distance between the frames acts as a proxy to the hardness. Negative samples that are temporally closer to the positives contain higher similarities with the positives and are harder to differentiate in the embedding space. We propose an unsupervised contrastive learning framework to exploit both the intra-video and cross-video negatives for learning robust visual representations from US videos. We design a hardness-sensitive negative mining curriculum to lower the distance between the anchor and negatives gradually. Due to its unsupervised nature, our technique can be used for pretraining a backbone on any US video dataset for superior downstream performance.

We deploy our video contrastive learning framework to pretrain a neural network before supervised fine-tuning to identify GB malignancy in US images. Due to its non-ionizing radiation, low cost, and accessibility, US is a popular non-invasive diagnostic modality for patients with suspected GB pathology. Although there are prior works involving DNNs to detect GB afflictions such as polyp or stones [9,21,23], there is limited prior work on using DNNs to detect GB malignancy in US images [5]. Unlike detecting stones or polyps, identifying GB malignancy from the routine US is challenging for radiologists [17,18]. We observed that ImageNet pretrained classifiers perform even worse than radiologists. We used an in-house abdominal US video dataset to pretrain our model. Our contrastive learning-based pretrained model surpasses human radiologists and SOTA contrastive learning methods on GB malignancy classification.

We also validate our framework on a public lung US dataset, POCUS [8], containing COVID-19 and Pneumonia samples. Pretraining our model on public lung US videos, and finetuning for the downstream classification shows improvement over ImageNet pretraining and the current SOTA contrastive techniques.

Contributions: The key contributions of this work are:

- We design an unsupervised contrastive learning technique for US videos to exploit both cross-video and intra-video negatives for rich representation learning. We further use a hardness-sensitive negative mining curriculum to boost the performance of our contrastive learning framework.
- We deploy our framework to solve a novel GB malignancy classification problem from US images. We also validate the efficacy of our technique on a publicly available lung US dataset for COVID detection.
- We are contributing the first US video dataset of 64 videos and 15800 frames containing both malignant and non-malignant GB towards the development of representation learning from medical US videos.

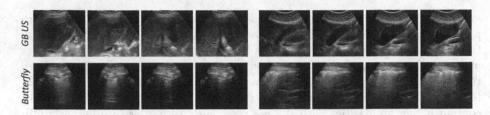

Fig. 2. Sample video sequences from the GB US video and the Butterfly [1] datasets. Two sequences of size 4 is shown on the left and right for each dataset.

2   Datasets

2.1   In-house US Dataset for Gallbladder Cancer

The transabdominal US video dataset is acquired at the Postgraduate Institute of Medical Education and Research (PGIMER), Chandigarh, India. The PGIMER ethics committee approved the study.

Video Data: Radiologists with 2–8 years of experience in abdominal sonography acquired the data. The US videos were obtained after at least 6 h of fasting using a 1–5 MHz curved array transducer (C-1-5D, Logiq S8, GE Healthcare). The scanning intended to include the entire GB and the lesion or pathology. The frame rate was 29 fps. The length of the videos varied from 43 to 888 frames depending on the GB distension and size of the lesion. The dataset consists of 32 malignant and 32 non-malignant videos containing a total of 12,251 and 3,549 frames, respectively. Note that we do not use the video level labels in our setup. We cropped the video frames from the center to anonymize the patient information and annotations. The processed video frames were of size 360×480 pixels. Figure 2 shows some samples from the video data. We are releasing this large scale video dataset for the community.

Image Data: We use the publicly contributed GBCU dataset [5] consisting of 1255 US images from 218 patients. The dataset consists of 990 non-malignant (171 patients with normal and benign GB) and 265 malignant (47 patients) GB images. The images were labeled as normal, benign, or malignant, and such labels were biopsy-proven. We use this dataset for finetuning and report 10-fold cross-validation. Note that the patients recorded in the video dataset are not included in this image dataset to ensure generalization.

2.2   Public Lung US Dataset for COVID-19

Video Data: We use the public lung US video dataset, Butterfly [1]. Butterfly consists of 22 US videos containing 1533 images of size 658×758 pixels of the lung. The dataset was collected using a Resona 7T machine.

Image Data: We use the publicly available POCUS [8] dataset consisting of a total of 2116 lung US images, of which 655, 349, and 1112 images are of COVID-19, bacterial pneumonia, and healthy control, respectively.

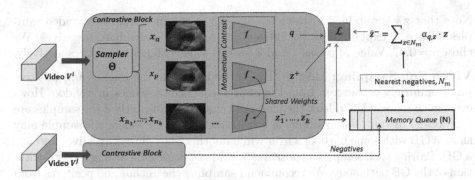

Fig. 3. Overview of the proposed contrastive loss, $\mathcal{L}$. An anchor **q** and another temporally close sample $\mathbf{z}^+$ from the same video are used as positive pairs. Given the set of cross-video negatives N, and the intra-video negatives $\mathbf{z}_j^-$, we compute $\hat{\mathbf{z}}^-$ from the m most similar cross-video negatives to the anchor. The intra-video samples $\mathbf{z}_j^-$ and $\hat{\mathbf{z}}^-$ are considered as negatives to the anchor.

3   Our Method

Contrastive Learning Setup: Suppose, $\mathbf{V}^i = \{\mathbf{x}_j\}_{j=1}^{M^i}$ is the i-th video in the video dataset consisting of M^i frames where $\mathbf{x}_j$ is the j-th individual frame. We sample an anchor image, $\mathbf{x}_a$, a positive image $\mathbf{x}_p$, and k negative frames $\mathbf{x}_{n_1}, \ldots, \mathbf{x}_{n_k}$ from a video using a sampler Θ. We encode the samples using a backbone f followed by a two layer MLP, g that creates a 128 dimensional embedding vector. We denote the embedding vectors as:

$$\mathbf{q} = g(f(\mathbf{x}_a)), \qquad \mathbf{z}^+ = g(f(\mathbf{x}_p)), \quad \text{and} \qquad \mathbf{z}_j^- = g(f(\mathbf{x}_{n_j})). \qquad (1)$$

We maximize the agreement between (positive, anchor) and minimize between (anchor, negatives) pairs in the embedding space. Let N be the set of cross video negatives generated from other videos in the dataset. To exploit the cross-video negatives, we calculate the normalized similarity measure between **q** and **z** for all $\mathbf{z} \in N$:

$$\alpha_{\mathbf{q},\mathbf{z}} = \frac{\exp\left(s(\mathbf{q}, \mathbf{z})/\tau\right)}{\sum_{\mathbf{z}_c \in N} \exp\left(s(\mathbf{q}, \mathbf{z}_c)/\tau\right)}, \qquad (2)$$

where $s(\mathbf{a}, \mathbf{b}) = \mathbf{a} \cdot \mathbf{b}/(\|\mathbf{a}\|_2 \|\mathbf{b}\|_2)$ is the cosine similarity and τ is a temperature scaling parameter. We then use the $\alpha_{\mathbf{q},\mathbf{z}}$ to rank the cross-video negatives according to their similarity with the anchor. Note that, with increasing similarity, the hardness of the negatives increase. We pick the top-n hardest cross-video negatives, N_m, and compute $\hat{\mathbf{z}}^- = \sum_{\mathbf{z} \in N_m} \alpha_{\mathbf{q},\mathbf{z}}\mathbf{z}$. Finally, we minimize the loss,

$$\mathcal{L} = -\log \frac{\exp\left(s(\mathbf{q}, \mathbf{z}^+)/\tau\right)}{\exp\left(s(\mathbf{q}, \mathbf{z}^+)/\tau\right) + \sum_{j=1}^{k} \exp\left(s(\mathbf{q}, \mathbf{z}_j^-)/\tau\right) + \exp\left(s(\mathbf{q}, \hat{\mathbf{z}}^-)/\tau\right)}. \qquad (3)$$

Note that $\mathbf{z}_j^-$ is obtained intra-video, and $\hat{\mathbf{z}}^-$ is obtained from inter-video samples. Hence, $\mathcal{L}$ exploits both the intra-video and cross-video hard negatives. We chose $\tau = 0.07$. Value of n was 4 and 2 for GB videos and Butterfly, respectively.

Video Sub-Sampling: Most SOTA methods sample the anchor and positive pairs uniformly at random from the entire sequence of frames in a video. However, in the case of US videos, the view may change significantly if the samples are temporally distant. For example, in a transabdominal US video, one sample may show a GB with some parts of a liver while another may show only a liver and not a GB. Pairing such samples as positives would not work for learning a representation of the GB pathology. We recommend sampling the anchor and positives from a temporally close interval. We use a sampler, $\Theta : \mathbf{V} \rightarrow (\mathbf{x}_a, \mathbf{x}_p, \{\mathbf{x}_{n_1}, \ldots, \mathbf{x}_{n_k}\})$ to get the anchor $(\mathbf{x}_a)$, positive $(\mathbf{x}_p)$, and k negative frames $(\mathbf{x}_{n_1}, \ldots, \mathbf{x}_{n_k})$ from a video $\mathbf{V} = \{\mathbf{x}_j\}_{j=1}^{M}$. The indices of the anchor, positive, and negative frames are sampled as following:

$$a \sim U([1, M]), \qquad p \sim U([a - \delta, a + \delta] \setminus \{a\}),$$
$$n_1, \ldots, n_k \overset{\text{i.i.d.}}{\sim} U([1, M] \setminus [a - \Delta, a + \Delta])$$

where $U(I)$ denotes sampling uniformly at random from interval I. We vary Δ between the Δ_h and Δ_l during the curriculum to adjust the hardness of the mined negatives. Also, $1 \le \delta \ll M$ and $\Delta_l \le \Delta \le \Delta_h < M$.

Curriculum-based Negative Mining: We use the negative samples in a hardness-sensitive order for effective learning. The model would initially learn to distinguish anchors from distant negatives and then gradually closer and thus harder negatives will be introduced. We start the training with only cross-video negatives and minimize the loss term,

$$\mathcal{L}_{\text{cross}} = -\log \frac{\exp\left(s(\mathbf{q}, \mathbf{z}^+)/\tau\right)}{\exp\left(s(\mathbf{q}, \mathbf{z}^+)/\tau\right) + \exp\left(s(\mathbf{q}, \hat{\mathbf{z}}^-)/\tau\right)}. \tag{4}$$

We then gradually start using the loss in Eq. (3) to introduce intra-video negatives, which are more challenging to distinguish from the anchor than the cross-video negatives. We initially keep the $\Delta = \Delta_h = \lceil M/5 \rceil$ used in Eq. (4) for sampling the negatives and ensure the anchor and negatives are at least Δ frames apart temporally, and the hardness is comparatively lower. We gradually lower the Δ using a cosine annealing during the later phase of training to introduce harder negatives. We chose $\delta = 3$, $k = 3$, and $\Delta_l = 7$ in our experiments.

4   Experiments and Results

Experimental Setup: We use a machine with Intel Xeon Gold 5218@2.30 GHz processor and 4 Nvidia Tesla V100 GPUs for our experiments. We pretrain a ResNet50 encoder using SGD with LR 0.003, weight decay 10^{-4}, and momentum

Table 1. The fine-tuning performance of ResNet50 model in classifying malignant vs. non-malignant GBs from US images. We report accuracy, specificity, and sensitivity.

Method	Acc.	Spec.	Sens.
Pretrained on [14]	0.867 ± 0.070	0.926 ± 0.069	0.672 ± 0.147
SimCLR [10]	0.897 ± 0.040	0.912 ± 0.055	0.874 ± 0.067
SimSiam [11]	0.900 ± 0.052	0.913 ± 0.059	0.861 ± 0.061
BYOL [15]	0.844 ± 0.129	0.871 ± 0.144	0.739 ± 0.178
MoCo v2 [19]	0.886 ± 0.061	0.893 ± 0.078	0.871 ± 0.094
Cycle-Contrast [25]	0.861 ± 0.087	0.867 ± 0.098	0.844 ± 0.097
USCL [12]	0.901 ± 0.047	0.923 ± 0.041	0.831 ± 0.072
Ours	**0.921 ± 0.034**	**0.926 ± 0.043**	**0.900 ± 0.046**

Table 2. Comparison of finetuning performance of ResNet using the SOTA USCL, ImageNet pretraining, and our method on POCUS. We used the official finetuning script used by USCL. The pretraining was done on Butterfly dataset. The USCL official script reports the average accuracy over 5 runs. **C**, **P**, and **R** denote COVID-19, Pneumonia, and Regular respectively.

Method	Accuracy			
	Overall	C	P	R
Pretrained [14]	0.842	0.795	0.786	0.886
SimCLR	0.864	0.832	0.894	0.871
MoCo v2	0.848	0.797	0.814	0.889
USCL	0.907	0.861	0.903	0.935
Ours	**0.922**	**0.892**	**0.951**	0.931

Table 3. We asked expert radiologists to classify GB malignancy for the test set of GBCU containing 80 non-malignant, and 42 malignant GB US images. Radiologists were not allowed access to any other patient data. The performance of the expert radiologists is comparable to that reported in the literature [7, 16].

Method	Acc.	Spec.	Sens.
Radiologist A	0.816	0.873	0.707
Radiologist B	0.784	0.811	0.732
USCL	0.812	0.838	0.762
Pretrained [14]	0.787	0.875	0.619
Ours	**0.877**	**0.900**	**0.833**

0.9 for 60 epochs with batch size 32. We used a grid-search strategy to select the sampling hyper-parameters. We use a cosine annealing of the LR. The parameters of the anchor and positive encoders are updated using momentum contrast with momentum coefficient, $m = 0.999$. Size of the queue for cross-video negative set is $|N| = 96$ for GB videos and $|N| = 66$ for Butterfly. We fine-tune for 30 epochs with batch size of 64 and an SGD optimizer with weight decay $5 \cdot 10^{-4}$. The remaining hyper-parameters are set similar to that of the pretraining phase.

Comparison with SOTA: We compare the ResNet50 [20] backbone pretrained on our contrastive learning framework with ImageNet pretraining, SOTA UCL techniques SimCLR [10], SimSiam [11], MoCo [19], BYOL [15], and SOTA image representation learning from video methods: Cycle-Contrast [25] and USCL [12]. USCL is specialized for pretraining on the US datasets. We note the performance of our pretraining framework for the GB malignancy classification task in Table 1. Our method gives 92.1% overall accuracy which is 2% higher than SOTA

Table 4. Significance of joint mining of intra, and cross video negatives. While the individual mining techniques match SOTA performance in GB malignancy, pretraining with proposed joint mining surpasses the current SOTA.

Type of negative used		Acc.	Spec.	Sens.
Cross-video	Intra-video			
✓		0.890 ± 0.062	0.897 ± 0.061	0.869 ± 0.108
	✓	0.893 ± 0.057	0.904 ± 0.059	0.835 ± 0.109
✓	✓	0.921 ± 0.034	0.926 ± 0.043	0.900 ± 0.046

Table 5. Effectiveness of our curriculum-based negative mining. The other alternative, curricula based trained models, lag significantly in GB malignancy classification.

Method	Acc.	Spec.	Sens.
Proposed curriculum	0.921 ± 0.034	0.926 ± 0.043	0.900 ± 0.046
Anti-curriculum	0.887 ± 0.064	0.902 ± 0.056	0.836 ± 0.097
Control-curriculum	0.897 ± 0.067	0.918 ± 0.062	0.810 ± 0.114

and 90% accuracy on malignant samples (sensitivity) which is 7% higher than USCL. Our method also outperforms human experts significantly for detecting GB malignancy from US images (Table 3). We show the performance comparison on the POCUS dataset in Table 2 and observe that our method surpasses the SOTA USCL pretraining by 1.5%. Figure S1 in the supplementary material shows the Grad-CAM [24] visuals of the last conv layer to demonstrate that the attention regions of contrastive backbones are more precise and clinically relevant.

Generality of our Method: We have shown our method's efficacy on two different tasks - (1) GB malignancy detection from abdominal US and (2) COVID-19 detection from lung US, which establishes the generality of our method on US modality. We also performed preliminary analysis on the performance of a ResNet50 classifier in detecting COVID-19 from a public CT dataset [27]. We pretrained the model on another CT dataset [2]. The (accuracy, specificity, sensitivity) for our method was (0.80, 0.81, 0.80) as compared to (0.73, 0.72, 0.74) of ImageNet pretraining, and (0.78, 0.81, 0.76) of USCL. The results are indicative of the generality of our method across modalities.

Ablation Study: (1) **Significance of Mining Intra-Video Hard Negatives:** In Table 4 we observe that when the intra-video negatives are not used, the performance of malignancy detection of our method becomes comparable to that of Cycle-Contrast and USCL; both methods use only cross-video negatives. On the other hand, if only intra-video negatives are used, the model performance becomes similar to that of the SOTA image contrastive techniques. This shows the importance of mining both intra-video and cross-video negatives in achieving the performance boost. (2) **Effectiveness of Curriculum-based Negative**

Mining: We propose to use increasing order of hardness for negative mining during the training. To assert the effectiveness of such a curriculum, we compare the curriculum with two possible alternatives - (i) *anti-curriculum* initially trains with harder negatives and progressively lowers the hardness of the negatives, and (ii) *control-curriculum* does not order the negatives according to their hardness. We initially train the model with temporally close intra-video negatives during the anti-curriculum and gradually start sampling temporally distant negatives. During the last few epochs, only the cross-video negatives are used. Table 5 shows the performance comparison of the proposed hardness-sensitive curriculum over the two alternative curricula. (3) **Sensitivity of Hyper-parameters:** Fig. 4 shows the sensitivity of three important pretraining hyper-parameters on the accuracy of the downstream task for our method.

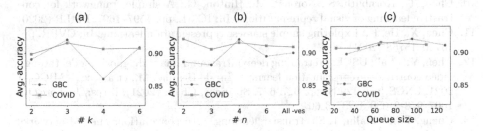

Fig. 4. Sensitivity of pretraining hyper-parameters - (a) number of intra-video negatives (k) (b) number of top cross-video negatives (n), and (c) queue size ($|N|$) - on downstream accuracy. Mean cross-val accuracy is shown for GB Cancer and COVID.

5   Conclusion

We introduce the first large-scale US video dataset for learning GB malignancy representation and propose an efficient UCL framework that exploits both intra-video and cross-video negatives through a hardness-aware curriculum. Our framework surpasses the human experts, imageNet-pretrained DNNs, and DNNs pretrained with SOTA contrastive learning methods specialized for US modality.

References

1. Butterfly videos. https://www.butterflynetwork.com/index.html, Accessed: 2 Mar 2022
2. Afshar, P., et al.: Covid-CT-MD, Covid-19 computed tomography scan dataset applicable in machine learning and deep learning. Sci. Data **8**(1), 1–8 (2021)
3. Alzubaidi, L., et al.: Towards a better understanding of transfer learning for medical imaging: a case study. Appl. Sci. **10**(13), 4523 (2020)
4. Ardila, D., et al.: End-to-end lung cancer screening with three-dimensional deep learning on low-dose chest computed tomography. Nat. Med. **25**(6), 954–961 (2019)

5. Basu, S., Gupta, M., Rana, P., Gupta, P., Arora, C.: Surpassing the human accuracy: detecting gallbladder cancer from USG images with curriculum learning. In: Proceedings of the IEEE/CVF Conference on Computer Vision and Pattern Recognition (CVPR), pp. 20886–20896 (2022)
6. Bejnordi, B.E., et al.: Diagnostic assessment of deep learning algorithms for detection of lymph node metastases in women with breast cancer. Jama **318**(22), 2199–2210 (2017)
7. Bo, X., et al.: Diagnostic accuracy of imaging modalities in differentiating xanthogranulomatous cholecystitis from gallbladder cancer. Ann. Transl. Med. **7**(22), 627 (2019)
8. Born, J., et al.: POCOVID-Net: automatic detection of COVID-19 from a new lung ultrasound imaging dataset (pocus). arXiv preprint arXiv:2004.12084 (2020)
9. Chen, T., et al.: Computer-aided diagnosis of gallbladder polyps based on high resolution ultrasonography. Comput. Methods Programs Biomed. **185**, 105118 (2020)
10. Chen, T., Kornblith, S., Norouzi, M., Hinton, G.: A simple framework for contrastive learning of visual representations. In: ICML, pp. 1597–1607. PMLR (2020)
11. Chen, X., He, K.: Exploring simple siamese representation learning. In: CVPR, pp. 15750–15758 (2021)
12. Chen, Y., et al.: USCL: pretraining deep ultrasound image diagnosis model through video contrastive representation learning. In: de Bruijne, M., et al. (eds.) MICCAI 2021. LNCS, vol. 12908, pp. 627–637. Springer, Cham (2021). https://doi.org/10.1007/978-3-030-87237-3_60
13. Cheng, P.M., Malhi, H.S.: Transfer learning with convolutional neural networks for classification of abdominal ultrasound images. J. Digit. Imaging **30**(2), 234–243 (2017)
14. Deng, J., Dong, W., Socher, R., Li, L.J., Li, K., Fei-Fei, L.: Imagenet: a large-scale hierarchical image database. In: CVPR, pp. 248–255 (2009)
15. Grill, J.B., et al.: Bootstrap your own latent-a new approach to self-supervised learning. NIPS **33**, 21271–21284 (2020)
16. Gupta, P., Kumar, M., Sharma, V., Dutta, U., Sandhu, M.S.: Evaluation of gallbladder wall thickening: a multimodality imaging approach. Expert Rev. Gastroenterol. Hepatol. **14**(6), 463–473 (2020)
17. Gupta, P., et al.: Gallbladder reporting and data system (gb-rads) for risk stratification of gallbladder wall thickening on ultrasonography: an international expert consensus. Abdom. Radiol., 1–12 (2021)
18. Gupta, P., et al.: Imaging-based algorithmic approach to gallbladder wall thickening. World J. Gastroenterol. **26**(40), 6163 (2020)
19. He, K., Fan, H., Wu, Y., Xie, S., Girshick, R.: Momentum contrast for unsupervised visual representation learning. In: CVPR, pp. 9729–9738 (2020)
20. He, K., Zhang, X., Ren, S., Sun, J.: Deep residual learning for image recognition. In: CVPR, pp. 770–778 (2016)
21. Jeong, Y., et al.: Deep learning-based decision support system for the diagnosis of neoplastic gallbladder polyps on ultrasonography: preliminary results. Sci. Rep. **10**(1), 1–10 (2020)
22. Komodakis, N., Gidaris, S.: Unsupervised representation learning by predicting image rotations. In: International Conference on Learning Representations (ICLR) (2018)
23. Lian, J., et al.: Automatic gallbladder and gallstone regions segmentation in ultrasound image. Int. J. Comput. Assist. Radiol. Surg. **12**(4), 553–568 (2017). https://doi.org/10.1007/s11548-016-1515-z

24. Selvaraju, R.R., Cogswell, M., Das, A., Vedantam, R., Parikh, D., Batra, D.: Grad-cam: visual explanations from deep networks via gradient-based localization. In: Proceedings of the IEEE international conference on computer vision, pp. 618–626 (2017)

25. Wu, H., Wang, X.: Contrastive learning of image representations with cross-video cycle-consistency. In: ICCV, pp. 10149–10159 (2021)

26. Xu, D., Xiao, J., Zhao, Z., Shao, J., Xie, D., Zhuang, Y.: Self-supervised spatiotemporal learning via video clip order prediction. In: Proceedings of the IEEE/CVF Conference on Computer Vision and Pattern Recognition, pp. 10334–10343 (2019)

27. Yang, X., He, X., Zhao, J., Zhang, Y., Zhang, S., Xie, P.: Covid-CT-dataset: a CT scan dataset about covid-19. arXiv preprint arXiv:2003.13865 (2020)

An Advanced Deep Learning Framework for Video-Based Diagnosis of ASD

Miaomiao Cai[1], Mingxing Li[1], Zhiwei Xiong[1,2]($\boxtimes$), Pengju Zhao[3], Enyao Li[3], and Jiulai Tang[4]

[1] University of Science and Technology of China, Hefei, China
zwxiong@ustc.edu.cn
[2] Institute of Artificial Intelligence, Hefei Comprehensive National Science Center, Hefei, China
[3] The Fifth Affiliated Hospital of Zhengzhou University, Zhengzhou, China
[4] The First Affiliated Hospital of Anhui Medical University, Hefei, China

Abstract. Autism spectrum disorder (ASD) is one of the most common neurodevelopmental disorders, which impairs the communication and interaction ability of patients. Intensive intervention in early ASD can effectively improve symptoms, so the diagnosis of ASD children receives significant attention. However, clinical assessment relies on experienced diagnosticians, which makes the diagnosis of ASD children difficult to popularize, especially in remote areas. In this paper, we propose a simple yet effective pipeline to diagnose ASD children, which comprises a convenient and fast strategy of video acquisition and an advanced deep learning framework. In our framework, firstly, we extract sufficient head-related features from the collected videos by a generic toolbox. Secondly, we propose a head-related characteristic (HRC) attention mechanism to select the most discriminative disease-related features adaptively. Finally, a convolutional neural network is used to diagnose ASD children by exploring the temporal information from the selected features. We also build a video dataset based on our strategy of video acquisition that contains 82 children to verify the effectiveness of the proposed pipeline. Experiments on this dataset show that our deep learning framework achieves a superior performance of ASD children diagnosis. The code and dataset will be available at https://github.com/xiaotaiyangcmm/DASD.

Keywords: Autism spectrum disorder · Deep learning · Attention mechanism · Video analysis

1 Introduction

According to statistics from the World Health Organization, 1 in 160 children in the world has Autism Spectrum Disorder (ASD) [4]. ASD is a complex neu-

Supplementary Information The online version contains supplementary material available at https://doi.org/10.1007/978-3-031-16440-8_42.

rodevelopmental disease that affects the development of the patient's brain and can cause significant deficits in social interaction, communication, interests, and behavior [1]. With children growing up, these deficits will make their lives challenging. Fortunately, researches show that early intensive intervention can improve ASD symptoms effectively [9,16]. Therefore, the diagnosis of children with ASD is critical to ensuring a healthy life for each child.

Clinical assessment is a common diagnostic tool to help psychologists and psychiatrists make empirical diagnoses. For example, Autism Diagnosis Observation Schedule-2 (ADOS-2) [10] is a representative clinical assessment method, which lasts roughly an hour. However, clinical assessment has difficulty in popularizing due to a shortage of qualified diagnosticians, especially in remote areas.

In recent years, researchers look for more convenient and efficient methods to diagnose ASD children by machine learning techniques. Many researchers focus on the atypical behavior patterns and facial emotional responsiveness in social interaction, including abnormalities in eye contact [8], head motion [18], facial expression [7], etc. Besides, researchers often utilize machine learning with images or videos of children in interaction to diagnose children with ASD. For images, spatiotemporal motion information is ignored [15]. In contrast, video analysis is more popular because it contains spatiotemporal information. However, most existing works extract insufficient features from videos, which limits the accuracy of diagnosis. For example, Li et al. [7] only extracted 22 facial features. On the other hand, many works handle temporal information in a simple way, such as calculating the average and standard deviation of the features of all frames [7] or counting the number of frames that meet the ideal conditions [19], which do not make full use of temporal information.

To better diagnose ASD children, we propose a simple yet effective pipeline. First of all, we design a fast and convenient video acquisition scheme by mobile phone. Then we develop an advanced deep learning framework to realize the binary classification of ASD children and typically developing (TD) children. In our framework, a generic toolbox is used to extract sufficient head-related features (709 dimensions) from the video, which contain most of the appearance and behavior features related to the head of the child. Then, we design a head-related characteristic (HRC) attention mechanism to select the most discriminative disease-related features. Finally, a convolutional neural network (CNN) is used to explore the temporal information from our selected features. In a real-world environment, one can fast diagnose whether a child has ASD by shooting a few seconds of video following our specifications (see Fig. 1).

The main contributions of our method are summarized in three aspects: (1) We propose a simple yet effective pipeline to diagnose ASD children, which comprises a convenient and fast video acquisition strategy and an advanced deep learning framework. The proposed pipeline is not limited to professional clinical environments and can be used for remote diagnosis in general environments, like home. (2) An HRC attention mechanism is proposed to capture the most discriminative disease-related features adaptively, which significantly promotes the diagnosis accuracy using different CNNs for binary classification. (3) We will release a video dataset that records the responsiveness of 82 children in social interaction, where participating children have been professionally tested by clinical assessment.

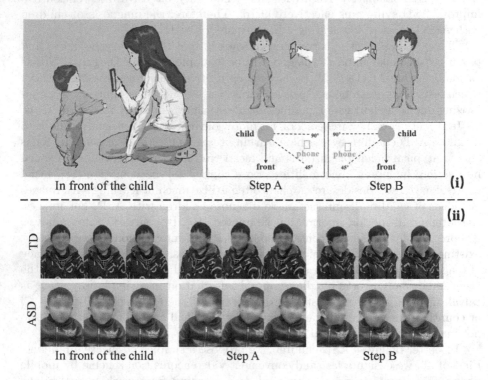

Fig. 1. Video acquisition. (i) Firstly, the parent points the phone directly in front of the child and attracts the child's attention. Then the parent moves the phone to child's left front (Step A) and right front (Step B) respectively and re-attract attention. The parent can repeat Step A and Step B twice or more. (ii) Examples of frames from ASD and TD children's videos.

2   Methodology

In this section, we firstly introduce our strategy of video acquisition and our dataset (see Fig. 1). Then we elaborate on our advanced deep learning framework, which is illustrated in Fig. 2.

2.1   Video Acquisition of Children

In order to make the diagnosis of ASD children convenient and fast, we propose a strategy of video acquisition, which is shown in Fig. 1(i). In our strategy, firstly,

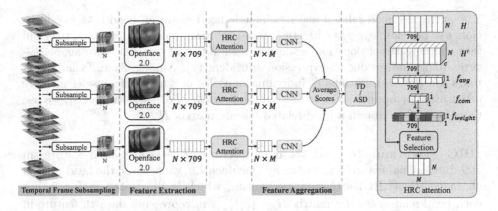

Fig. 2. An overview of our advanced deep learning framework.

the parent points the phone directly in front of the child and attracts the child's attention by calling the child's name or using a toy. Then the parent repeats Step A and Step B twice or more. Step A: move the phone to the child's left front and re-attract attention; Step B: move the phone to the child's right front and re-attract attention. During the video acquisition, it is necessary to ensure the child's entire head is within the phone's shooting range. In addition, if the child shows no behavior response in the process of attracting attention, the parent can skip to the next step.

A total of 82 children (ASD: 57; TD: 25) finish the experiments with their parents at home, and they all consent to use their data for our research. In our dataset, the average length of acquired videos is 18.74s, which shows that our strategy takes less time than clinical assessment. The frame rate of our acquired videos is 25 FPS. All diagnostic labels (ASD or TD) are provided by the ADOS-2, which have been done independently of our experiments. Examples of frames from ASD and TD children's videos are shown in Fig. 1(ii).

2.2 Advanced Deep Learning Framework

Temporal Frame Subsampling. Since there is no constraint on the length of children's videos, we design a temporal frame subsampling method to adapt videos with different lengths. Firstly, the video is equally divided into T segments. In the i-th segment, we sample a snippet s_i that consists of consecutive N frames. The first frame of each snippet is sampled by a symmetric beta distribution $Beta(\gamma, \gamma)$, where γ is the dispersion of the probability distribution [12]. Finally we can get a group of snippets $S = \{s_i\}_{i=1}^{T}$.

Head-Related Feature Extraction. We use Openface 2.0 toolbox [2], which can extract sufficient head-related features (709 dimensions in our experiments).

The extracted head-related features include head position, head rotation direction, eye position, eye-gaze direction, facial position, facial action units, the rigid face shape features (location, scale and rotation) and non-rigid face shape features (deformation due to expression and identity). Among them, facial action units are the basic actions of individual muscles or groups of muscles and are often used for human facial expression analysis [3]. For each snippet s_i, we use Openface 2.0 to obtain a head-related feature matrix $H \in \mathbb{R}^{1 \times N \times 709}$.

HRC Attention. To select the most discriminative head-related features in 709-dimensional features extracted by Openface 2.0, we propose the head-related characteristic (HRC) attention mechanism, which is illustrated in Fig. 2. For each head-related feature matrix $H = \{v_i\}_{i=1}^{709}$, v_i represents the i-th feature in H. First of all, we use a convolution module $F_{cov}(\cdot) : H \rightarrow H' \in \mathbb{R}^{c \times N \times 709}$ to increase the channel dimension, where H' is the deep feature and c is the number of channels. Then we compress H' into the average vector $f_{avg} \in \mathbb{R}^{1 \times 1 \times 709}$ through a global average pooling operation. After that, with the help of the fully connected layer, we compress f_{avg} into the compressed vector $f_{com} \in \mathbb{R}^{1 \times 1 \times \lambda}$, where λ is the compression dimension, and then stretch f_{com} into $f_{weight} \in \mathbb{R}^{1 \times 1 \times 709}$, where f_{weight} is the weight of head-related features. Then we define a selection function $F_{sel}(\cdot)$ to select M features with the largest weights in H according to f_{weight}. Ultimately, we can obtain a descending dimension head-related feature matrix $V \in \mathbb{R}^{1 \times N \times M}$. $F_{sel}(\cdot)$ is defined as follows:

$$V = F_{sel}(H, f_{weight}) = \{v_j\}, \; if \; j \; ranks \; top \; M \; in \; f_{weight} \tag{1}$$

Feature Aggregation and Classification. Obtaining the descending dimension head-related feature matrix $V \in \mathbb{R}^{1 \times M \times 709}$, we utilize a CNN to determine whether the child has ASD. Note that the CNN can be replaced by existing classification networks in our framework. Through the CNN, we can get the confidence scores of a group of snippets $S = \{s_i\}_{i=1}^{T}$ that the child has ASD. Then we aggregate the confidence scores by the average operation to output the final confidence score from 0 to 1. During the inference phase, we set a threshold (0.5) to binarize the final confidence score. Our framework outputs 'ASD' when the final confidence score is greater than this threshold, and 'TD' otherwise.

3   Experiments and Results

3.1   Implementation Details

With the help of Openface 2.0, we delete the frames whose landmark detection confidence are less than 0.75. In our setting, the number of segments T, the number of frames in each snippet N, the number of channels in the deep feature c, the number of head-related features with the largest weight selected by the HRC attention M and the compression dimension in the compressed vector λ are set to 4, 32, 64, 100 and 45 respectively. Following [12], the dispersion of the probability distribution γ is set to 2. We utilize the ResNet-50 [5] as the CNN and we adopt Bottleneck [5] in F_{cov}.

Our experiments are implemented on Pytorch. We utilize Adam optimizer [6] with the learning rate of 10^{-3}, and the batch size of 4 on one NVIDIA TitanXP GPU for 10000 epochs. To balance the inequality of numbers between classes, we utilize a higher class weight (2.28) to the TD class. During the inference phase, we extract the middle snippet of each segment. We adopt the 3-fold cross-validation to demonstrate the superiority and generalization of our method on Accuracy (Acc.), F1-score, Specificity (Spe.), and Sensitivity (Sen.) metrics.

Table 1. Quantitative comparison with baseline methods in the 3-fold cross-validation.

Method	Acc. (%)	F1(%)	Spe. (%)	Sen. (%)	AUC (%)
ResNet-50 w/ LDA	65.74	74.28	51.85	71.93	61.89
ResNet-50 w/ RF	70.63	81.16	23.61	91.23	57.42
ResNet-50 w/ KNN	70.68	44.52	84.21	39.35	61.78
ResNet-50 w/ LR	70.77	81.29	24.54	91.23	57.88
ResNet-50 w/ SVM	75.62	84.63	28.24	96.49	62.37
Li *et al.* [7]	80.51	87.40	44.44	**96.49**	70.47
Ours	**95.06**	**91.90**	**96.48**	92.59	**94.54**

Table 2. Components analysis on the head-related feature extraction and the HRC attention in the 3-fold cross-validation.

Head-related feature extraction	HRC	Acc. (%)	F1 (%)	Spe. (%)	Sen. (%)	AUC (%)
✗	✗	78.09	47.41	77.65	88.89	83.27
✓	✗	81.70	62.63	81.99	84.92	83.46
✓	✓	**95.06**	**91.90**	**96.48**	**92.59**	**94.54**

3.2 Experimental Results

We construct several baseline methods. 1) We use five basic classifiers to diagnose ASD children, including Linear Discriminant Analysis (LDA), Random Forest (RF), K-Nearest Neighbor (KNN), Logistics Regression (LR), and Support Vector Machines (SVM). We take the output of our pre-trained ResNet-50 without the HRC attention as the input of basic classifiers. 2) We reproduce Li *et al.* [7], which designs an end-to-end system for ASD classification using 22-dimensional facial attributes. As shown in Table 1, our advanced deep learning framework achieves the best performance in diagnosing ASD children, compared with other methods. The accuracy on diagnosis is improved by 14.55% compared with the most competitive method.

3.3   Analysis and Discussion

Components Analysis. We adopt ResNet-50 as the CNN to demonstrate the effectiveness of our proposed method. We perform comparative experiments to analyze the impacts of each component as follows: 1) Without the head-related feature extraction and the HRC attention, we directly extract the features of each frame by the CNN and average the confidence score. 2) Without the HRC attention, we extract the head-related feature matrix H from each snippet by Openface 2.0. 3) With the head-related feature extraction and the HRC attention, we select the most discriminative head-related features for the CNN. As listed in Table 2, we can observe that both head-related feature extraction and the HRC attention have positive effects on the performance of diagnosis of ASD children.

Table 3. Hyperparameter analysis on different number of head-related features with the largest weight selected by the HRC attention in the 3-fold cross-validation.

Number of features	Acc. (%)	F1 (%)	Spe. (%)	Sen. (%)	AUC (%)
50	91.40	83.22	92.54	**93.33**	92.93
100	**95.06**	**91.90**	**96.48**	92.59	**94.54**
150	91.36	85.93	94.71	85.24	89.9
200	90.17	83.25	93.16	83.57	88.36

Table 4. Hyperparameter analysis on different number of frames in each snippet in the 3-fold cross-validation.

Number of frames	Acc. (%)	F1 (%)	Spe. (%)	Sen. (%)	AUC (%)
1	89.07	82.50	92.95	81.98	87.47
2	91.40	86.48	96.30	81.85	89.07
3	92.59	88.07	**96.67**	86.15	91.41
4	**95.06**	**91.90**	96.48	**92.59**	**94.54**
5	92.59	88.24	96.30	85.19	90.74

Hyperparameter Analysis. The number of head-related features with the largest weights M is the important parameter in the HRC attention. Therefore, we conduct the experiments on different M to determine the optimal number of head-related features, and the results are shown in Table 3. It can be found that when $M = 100$, the performance is the best. In addition, we also conduct the experiments on different number of segments N. Considering the minimum number of frames in the dataset is 167 and the number of frames in each snippet is set to 32, the maximum number of segments is 5. As listed in Table 4, we can observe that our framework achieves the best performance when the number of segments is set to 4.

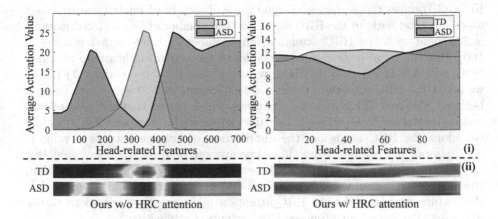

Fig. 3. Visual analysis for the HRC attention. (i) The average activation value, which is calculated on one of the validation sets of the 3-fold cross-validation. The larger the average activation value, the greater contribution of the head-related features to the diagnosis result. (ii) Some examples of the activation heatmap obtained by Grad-CAM [14]. Combining (i) and (ii), with the HRC attention, the most discriminative disease-related features are selected and have uniform and high responses.

Table 5. Robustness analysis on different CNNs in the 3-fold cross-validation.

Method	Acc. (%)	F1 (%)	Spe. (%)	Sen. (%)	AUC (%)
Mobilenetv2 [13]	82.85	64.56	85.37	87.88	86.63
Mobilenetv2 w/ HRC attention	93.83	89.95	96.39	88.43	92.41
ResNeXt [17]	81.70	60.56	82.43	86.11	84.27
ResNeXt w/ HRC attention	93.83	89.95	96.39	88.43	92.41
Espnetv2 [11]	79.28	58.73	83.57	78.35	80.96
Espnetv2 w/ HRC attention	95.06	91.37	96.67	91.53	94.10

Visual Analysis. For further analysis of the HRC attention, we define the average activation value of each head-related feature based on Grad-CAM [14], which represents the contribution to the diagnosis for each head-related feature. The average activation value is calculated on one of the validation sets of the 3-fold cross-validation. Specifically, for each snippet, we can obtain the head-related feature matrix H and the descending dimension head-related feature matrix V. Then we utilize Grad-CAM to generate the activation heatmap for both of them, and then sum the value of activation heatmap in each head-related feature to obtain the activation value. Finally, we average the activation value in all snippets to obtain the average activation value of each head-related feature. Figure 3(i) shows the average activation value of each head-related feature based on our method without the HRC attention (the number of head-related features is 709) and with the HRC attention (the number of head-related features is 100). Besides, we also show some examples of the activation heatmap obtained by Grad-CAM in Fig. 3(ii). In Fig. 3, we can obtain two observations. 1) Before we adopt the HRC attention, the average activation value has a significant gap between ASD and TD in some feature areas, which proves that the head-related features extracted by Openface 2.0 are discriminative for ASD and TD. 2) Before we adopt the HRC attention, the distribution of average activation value is not uniform, and some features have low average activation values, providing less contribution to the diagnosis. However, after we add the HRC attention, the average activation value has uniform and high response, which proves that the features extracted by the HRC attention make great contributions to the diagnosis. Therefore, our proposed HRC attention is effective.

Robustness Analysis. In order to analyze the robustness of the HRC attention, Mobilenetv2 [13], ResNext [17] and Espnetv2 [11] are used to replace ResNet-50 respectively, and the results are shown in Table 5. After adding the HRC attention, the performances of all methods are improved, so it can be concluded that the HRC attention has strong robustness. Among them, Espnetv2 obtain the highest performance, with the accuracy rate of 95.06%.

4   Conclusion

We propose a simple yet effective pipeline to diagnose ASD children, which consists of a convenient and fast strategy for video acquisition and an advanced deep learning framework. Firstly, we collect a video dataset that contains 82 children with professional clinical assessment, which will be released to facilitate the research in this field. Secondly, our framework uses a generic toolbox to extract sufficient head-related features and then utilizes an HRC attention mechanism to select the most discriminative disease-related features. Then a CNN is used to diagnose ASD children by exploring the temporal information from selected features. Experiments show that our pipeline achieves superior diagnostic results on the above dataset. In a real-world environment, parents can get a valid diagnosis result of their child by our pipeline. Also, our pipeline can be efficiently deployed on mobile phones to assist remote diagnosis.

Acknowledgement. This work was supported in part by the National Key R&D Program of China under Grant 2017YFA0700800, the National Natural Science Foundation of China under Grant 62021001, and the University Synergy Innovation Program of Anhui Province No. GXXT-2019-025.

References

1. Association, A.P., et al.: Diagnostic and statistical manual of mental disorders (DSM-5®). American Psychiatric Publishing (2013)
2. Baltrusaitis, T., Zadeh, A., Lim, Y.C., Morency, L.P.: Openface 2.0: facial behavior analysis toolkit. In: 2018 13th IEEE International Conference on Automatic Face & Gesture Recognition (FG 2018), pp. 59–66. IEEE (2018)
3. Ekman, P., Friesen, W.V.: Facial action coding system. Environ. Psychol. Nonverbal Behav. (1978)
4. Elsabbagh, M., et al.: Global prevalence of autism and other pervasive developmental disorders. Autism Res. **5**(3), 160–179 (2012)
5. He, K., Zhang, X., Ren, S., Sun, J.: Deep residual learning for image recognition. In: Proceedings of the IEEE Conference on Computer Vision and Pattern Recognition, pp. 770–778 (2016)
6. Kingma, D.P., Ba, J.: Adam: a method for stochastic optimization. arXiv preprint arXiv:1412.6980 (2014)
7. Li, B., et al.: A facial affect analysis system for autism spectrum disorder. In: 2019 IEEE International Conference on Image Processing (ICIP), pp. 4549–4553. IEEE (2019)
8. Li, J., Zhong, Y., Han, J., Ouyang, G., Li, X., Liu, H.: Classifying ASD children with LSTM based on raw videos. Neurocomputing **390**, 226–238 (2020)
9. Liu, X., Wu, Q., Zhao, W., Luo, X.: Technology-facilitated diagnosis and treatment of individuals with autism spectrum disorder: an engineering perspective. Appl. Sci. **7**(10), 1051 (2017)
10. Lord, C., et al.: The autism diagnostic observation schedule-generic: a standard measure of social and communication deficits associated with the spectrum of autism. J. Autism Dev. Disord. **30**(3), 205–223 (2000)
11. Mehta, S., Rastegari, M., Shapiro, L., Hajishirzi, H.: Espnetv2: a light-weight, power efficient, and general purpose convolutional neural network. In: Proceedings of the IEEE/CVF Conference on Computer Vision and Pattern Recognition, pp. 9190–9200 (2019)
12. Pérez-García, F., Scott, C., Sparks, R., Diehl, B., Ourselin, S.: Transfer learning of deep spatiotemporal networks to model arbitrarily long videos of seizures. In: de Bruijne, M., et al. (eds.) MICCAI 2021. LNCS, vol. 12905, pp. 334–344. Springer, Cham (2021). https://doi.org/10.1007/978-3-030-87240-3_32
13. Sandler, M., Howard, A., Zhu, M., Zhmoginov, A., Chen, L.C.: Mobilenetv 2: inverted residuals and linear bottlenecks. In: Proceedings of the IEEE Conference on Computer Vision and Pattern Recognition, pp. 4510–4520 (2018)
14. Selvaraju, R.R., Cogswell, M., Das, A., Vedantam, R., Parikh, D., Batra, D.: Gradcam: visual explanations from deep networks via gradient-based localization. In: Proceedings of the IEEE International Conference on Computer Vision, pp. 618–626 (2017)
15. Tamilarasi, F.C., Shanmugam, J.: Convolutional neural network based autism classification. In: 2020 5th International Conference on Communication and Electronics Systems (ICCES), pp. 1208–1212. IEEE (2020)
16. Warren, Z., McPheeters, M.L., Sathe, N., Foss-Feig, J.H., Glasser, A., Veenstra-VanderWeele, J.: A systematic review of early intensive intervention for autism spectrum disorders. Pediatrics **127**(5), e1303–e1311 (2011)
17. Xie, S., Girshick, R., Dollár, P., Tu, Z., He, K.: Aggregated residual transformations for deep neural networks. In: Proceedings of the IEEE Conference on Computer Vision and Pattern Recognition, pp. 1492–1500 (2017)

18. Zhao, Z., et al.: Atypical head movement during face-to-face interaction in children with autism spectrum disorder. Autism Res. **14**(6), 1197–1208 (2021)
19. Zhao, Z., et al.: Identifying autism with head movement features by implementing machine learning algorithms. J. Autism Dev. Disord. **52**, 1–12 (2021). https://doi.org/10.1007/s10803-021-05179-2

Automating Blastocyst Formation and Quality Prediction in Time-Lapse Imaging with Adaptive Key Frame Selection

Tingting Chen[1,2], Yi Cheng[1,2], Jinhong Wang[1,2], Zhaoxia Yang[3],
Wenhao Zheng[1,2], Danny Z. Chen[4], and Jian Wu[5(✉)]

[1] College of Computer Science and Technology, Zhejiang University,
Hangzhou 310027, China
[2] Real Doctor AI Research Centre, Zhejiang University, Hangzhou, China
[3] Alibaba Group, Hangzhou, China
[4] Department of Computer Science and Engineering, University of Notre Dame,
Notre Dame, IN 46556, USA
[5] Second Affiliated Hospital School of Medicine, School of Public Health,
and Institute of Wenzhou, Zhejiang University, Hangzhou 310058, China
wujian2000@zju.edu.cn

Abstract. Effective approaches for accurately predicting the developmental potential of embryos and selecting suitable embryos for blastocyst culture are critically needed. Many deep learning (DL) based methods for time-lapse monitoring (TLM) videos have been proposed to tackle this problem. Although fruitful, these methods are either ineffective when processing long TLM videos, or need extra annotations to determine the morphokinetics parameters of embryos. In this paper, we propose Adaptive Key Frame Selection (AdaKFS), a new framework that adaptively selects informative frames on per-input basis to predict blastocyst formation using TLM videos at the cleavage stage on day 3. For each time step, a policy network decides whether to use or skip the current frame. Further, a prediction network generates prediction using the morphokinetics features of the selected frames. We efficiently train and enhance the frame selection process by using a Gumbel-Softmax sampling approach and a reward function, respectively. Comprehensive experiments on a large TLM video dataset verify the performance superiority of our new method over state-of-the-art methods.

Keywords: Adaptive Key Frame Selection · Morphokinetics parameters · Blastocyst formation prediction · TLM videos

1 Introduction

In vitro fertilization (IVF) is one of the most common methods for infertility [6]. For improving the efficacy of IVF, embryo selection and transfer are key

---

T. Chen and Y. Cheng–Equal contribution.

© The Author(s), under exclusive license to Springer Nature Switzerland AG 2022
L. Wang et al. (Eds.): MICCAI 2022, LNCS 13434, pp. 445–455, 2022.
https://doi.org/10.1007/978-3-031-16440-8_43

procedures. Clinically, embryos are evaluated by embryologists and transferred at the cleavage stage on day 3 (D3) or blastocyst stage on day 5 or 6 (D5/6) post-fertilization. Studies have shown that blastocyst transfer can improve the implantation rate and pregnancy rate of embryos [20]. However, long-term in vitro culture may reduce the developmental potential of embryos, and there also exists a risk of embryo development to blastocyst stage failure. Therefore, it is particularly important to evaluate embryos early, and select embryos with high possibility to form blastocysts [3] and suitable for extended culture, thus helping improve the success rate of IVF.

Time-lapse monitoring (TLM) is an emerging and powerful tool for embryo assessment and selection, in which embryos are cultured in incubators with built-in microscopes to automatically acquire images every 5–20 min at a certain focus and magnification [13]. This process provides stable video data to continuously observe the dynamic embryo development without removing embryos from controlled environmental conditions. However, embryologists often analyze TLM videos manually, which is cumbersome and subjective, and suffers from large inter- and intra-observer variances. To assist embryologists effectively analyze TLM videos and accurately recognize high-quality embryos, automatic embryo selection methods are highly desired for Computer-Aided Diagnosis (CAD).

Recently, many deep learning (DL) methods were proposed for embryo selection by automatically analyzing TLM videos [1,8,9,14–16,21,23]. Generally, these methods are either for embryo quality grading [1,8,9,23] or embryo development stage classification [14–16]. Embryo quality grading can be conducted using D3 or D5 TLM videos, and embryos are often classified into good-quality or poor-quality (transfer or discard). Development stage classification is typically a sequential prediction task, which recognizes each stage of the embryo development process by dynamic programming [14], two-stream model [16], or temporal learning [15]. Although these methods improved performances greatly, they still suffer a drawback that they did not fully consider morphological and kinetic parameters of early embryo development, and thus may incur low practicability and applicability. In IVF clinics, morphokinetics parameters [5,12], such as morphological images and time durations of various embryo development stages (see Fig. 1), are key indicators helping embryologists perform embryo selection, and they are highly related with the transplantation outcome. Studies with different time-lapse equipment also reported improved prediction accuracy of embryo implantation by analyzing the morphokinetics of human embryos at early cleavage stages [4,18,19]. In [11], five key morphokinetic features of embryos were automatically measured with a unified pipeline of five convolutional neural networks (CNNs). In [13], a temporal stream model and a spatial stream model were designed to capture kinetic parameters and morphological features respectively, which were then integrated together to predict blastocyst formation. But, to include both morphological and kinetic parameters in prediction models, these methods require the input frames to be manually annotated, such as annotating cell stages, fragmentation scores, or cell boundaries [11,13]. Thus, they are not fully automated and need several pre-processing steps. Further, those extra

Fig. 1. A conceptual overview of our AdaKFS approach, which focuses on selecting multiple informative key frames that may contain different embryo development stages, aiming for performance gain and correct prediction. The top texts are for the pronuclei appearance (PNA), pronuclei fading (PNF), 2–5 cell, and 8-cell cleavage stages.

annotations are time-consuming, error-prone, and subjective. Moreover, these methods often directly process the whole long TLM videos (>700 frames per video), which sometimes provide irrelevant/redundant information for recognizing embryo quality and may degrade performances as informative frames can be overwhelmed by uninformative ones in such long videos.

To address the above issues, we take a new approach for blastocyst formation prediction, by performing targeted TLM video analysis and automatically determining morphokinetic parameters. We explore how to adaptively select a small number of informative frames on the per-video basis to produce correct predictions (Fig. 1). For model training, the selected frames are expected to contain different embryo development stages in order to allow us to properly utilize their morphokinetic features. However, this is particularly challenging since there is no supervision indicating which frames are important (in specific stages) and TLM videos are generally weakly-labeled (with only one label for a whole video).

In this paper, we propose AdaKFS, a novel approach to learn how to adaptively select key frames conditioned on the input for predicting blastocyst formation and blastocyst quality on day 3 (D3). Specifically, at each time step of a TLM video, a policy network examines the current frame and decides to use or drop it. Then a prediction network generates prediction using the selected frames by combining their morphological and kinetic features. As the use-or-drop decision function is discrete and non-differentiable, we apply an efficient Gumbel-Softmax sampling strategy [7] to help model training. To further enhance the frame selection, we seek to maximize a reward function that encourages predictions to be more confident when including the current frame. Our proposed method is fully automated and introduces morphokinetic parameters without requiring any extra annotations. Our method is also targeted, and adaptively selects a small number of key frames towards performance gain and accurate prediction. To validate AdaKFS, we build a large time-lapse embryo video dataset on D3. Extensive experiments show that our method outperforms the known methods and achieves state-of-the-art performance on blastocyst formation prediction.

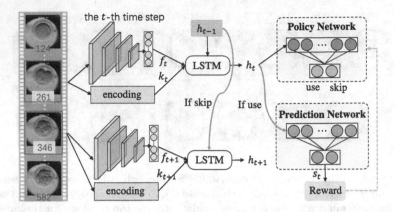

Fig. 2. An overview of our proposed AdaKFS model. The numbers under the frames are their indices in the original TLM video. We encode these numbers as kinetic features.

The main contributions of our work are as follows. (1) We propose a novel method, AdaKFS, to accurately predict blastocyst formation and blastocyst quality using TLM videos on D3. Our model adatively selects a small number of key frames to perform effective TLM video analysis and introduces morphokinetic parameters of embryos automatically. (2) We efficiently train our model with the Gumbel-Softmax sampling, and facilitate frame selection by maximizing a reward function. (3) We conduct extensive experiments on a large TLM video dataset to verify the superiority of our AdaKFS over state-of-the-art methods.

2   Method

We seek to develop an effective key frame selection strategy to produce correct blastocyst formation prediction using a small number of frames and their morphokinetic parameters, without any extra annotations. To this end, we propose AdaKFS to adaptively select informative frames toward performance gain and correct prediction. Figure 2 shows an overview of our new framework.

Given a video which is a sequence of T frames, we have their feature representations $(f_1, f_2, \ldots, f_T)$. To explore the temporal causality across different time steps of the video, we employ a Long Short-Term Memory (LSTM) module in our AdaKFS. Specifically, at the t-th time step, the LSTM module takes the features f_t of the current frame, the previous hidden states h_{t-1}, previous cell states c_{t-1}, and the kinetic parameter embeddings k_t of the current frame as input, and computes the current hidden states h_t and cell states c_t:

$$h_t, c_t = LSTM([f_t, k_t], h_{t-1}, c_{t-1}), \tag{1}$$

where f_t and k_t are concatenated. Conditioned on the hidden states h_t, a policy network produces a binary policy vector to determine to keep or drop the current frame. If keeping it, a prediction network further uses this h_t for classification. If dropping it, we skip the current hidden states h_t (i.e., skip this frame), and compute the hidden states of next frame. Note that f_t is the morphological image features of embryos and k_t is the corresponding embedded kinetic parameters. These two are complementary markers for embryo selection and blastocyst prediction, and thus we integrate them together in our AdaKFS model to effectively select key frames and accurately predict blastocyst formation.

Below we elaborate the components of AdaKFS in detail.

2.1 Policy Network

The policy network aims to make decisions on using or skipping each frame of an input video. Here, a key problem is that the policy decisions are discrete, thus making it difficult to train the network as the backpropagation algorithm cannot be applied to non-differentiable layers. In this work, we adopt Gumbel-Softmax sampling [7] to deal with this non-differentiability, which is a simple yet effective method that replaces an original non-differentiable sample from a discrete distribution by a differentiable sample from a corresponding Gumbel-Softmax distribution. Drawing samples from the Gumbel-Softmax distribution enables us to directly optimize the discrete policy with standard backpropagation. Specifically, given the hidden states h_t, we first generate the logits $z_t \in \mathbb{R}^2$ using one fully-connected layer, and then apply Gumbel-Softmax sampling to perform a continuous and differentiable approximation to the discrete decisions:

$$p_{i,t} = \frac{\exp((\log z_{i,t} + g_{i,t})/\tau)}{\sum_{j \in \{0,1\}} \exp((\log z_{j,t} + g_{j,t})/\tau)}, \tag{2}$$

where $i \in \{0,1\}$ indicates a skipping or using decision, $g_{i,t}$ is an i.i.d. sample drawn from the standard Gumbel-Softmax distribution $Gumbel(0,1)$, and τ is the temperature parameter that controls the discreteness of p_t. As $\tau \to 0$, samples from the Gumbel-Softmax distribution are identical to samples from the discrete distribution (i.e., p_t becomes a one-hot vector). As $\tau \to \infty$, p_t converges to a uniform distribution. During the backward process, we calculate the gradient of the continuous Gumbel-Softmax (Eq. (2)) to approximate the gradient of the discrete samples in our policy network.

2.2 Prediction Network

With the selected frames, the prediction network produces the classification output for blastocyst and non-blastocyst formation prediction. It maps the hidden states h_t (if selected) to output $s_t \in \mathbb{R}^C$ using one fully-connected layer, where $C = 2$ is the number of classes. A *softmax* function is further applied to normalize s_t and generate probability scores for each class. Note that we produce the blastocyst formation predictions following the perspective of clinics, and we combine the morphological and kinetic features of the selected frames and utilize an LSTM layer to capture the temporal causality of embryo development. The prediction network is optimized with a cross-entropy loss using predictions after the policy network interacts with all the input frames. Specifically,

$$L_{cls} = -\sum_{c=1}^{C} y^c \log(s_{T_s}^c), \qquad (3)$$

where T_s denotes the final number of selected frames for an input video, and y is the corresponding one-hot encoded ground truth label.

2.3 Loss Function

Since no supervision is given to indicate whether any single frame is informative, we introduce a reward function to further facilitate the frame selection process. Motivated by [17], the reward function evaluates the potential information gain brought by the current selected frame, and the goal is that including such a frame is expected to help improve the performance and produce more accurate predictions. Formally, the reward function can be described as follows:

$$r_t = \max\{0, d_t - \max_{t' \in [0,t-1]} d_{t'}\}. \qquad (4)$$

Here, $d_t = s_t^{gt} - \max\{s_t^{c'} \mid c' \neq gt\}$ is the difference between the probability score of the ground truth class (denoted as gt) and the largest one of the other classes, and this is to enforce the score of the ground truth class to be larger than the other classes by a margin. Further, the reward function in Eq. (4) encourages that including the current selected frame can receive an increased reward, and is higher than including the previous selected frame. Such an operation can be viewed as a proxy that constrains and measures whether the selected frame brings additional information for identifying the correct classes.

With the above reward function, our AdaKFS can be trained using the following overall loss function:

$$L = L_{cls} + \lambda L_{rwd}, \qquad (5)$$

where L_{rwd} is the reward loss for facilitating the frame selection process with a form of $\sum_{t=0}^{T_s} r_t$, and λ is a hyper-parameter that controls the relative importance of L_{cls} and L_{rwd}.

3 Experimental Results

Dataset. Our experiments are conducted on a dataset of 3300 human embryo time-lapse image sequences (videos), each recording the first three days' development of a fertilized ovum before the embryo is cultured to the blastocyst stage. Image frames were acquired every 5 min with a fixed focal plane, and totally one video may have 700–900 frames. The label for a video is only the blastocyst or nonblastocyst outcome based on the Gardner scoring system [2], and we do not

Table 1. Quantitative comparison with state-of-the-art methods on the test set.

Method	ACC (%)	SEN (%)	SPE (%)	PPV (%)	NPV (%)	F1 (%)	AUC (%)
STEM [13]	70.61	85.71	46.46	71.72	67.44	69.23	71.00
8-layer CNN [23]	69.39	84.24	45.67	71.07	64.77	68.06	70.00
AdaKFS (ours)	**72.42**	**87.68**	**51.18**	**72.76**	**71.43**	**71.03**	**73.01**

Table 2. Quantitative analysis of different components on the test set. "Policy" denotes the policy network for key frame selection, "Reward" is the reward loss guiding the frame selection process, and "Kinetics" means the kinetic parameter embeddings for blastocyst formation prediction. "#SF" is the average number of selected frames.

Method	Policy	Reward	Kinetics	ACC(%)	SEN(%)	SPE(%)	PPV(%)	NPV(%)	F1(%)	AUC(%)	#SF
LSTM	–	–	–	65.15	79.80	41.73	68.49	56.52	63.75	66.93	32
AdaKFS	✓			67.88	83.25	47.24	70.82	60.82	66.93	68.67	14.4
AdaKFS	✓	✓		70.61	84.73	48.03	72.08	66.67	69.42	71.25	9.08
AdaKFS	✓	✓	✓	**72.42**	**87.68**	**51.18**	**72.76**	**71.43**	**71.03**	**73.01**	6.25

have any other annotations. We split the dataset into training, validation, and test sets with a ratio of 8:1:1, and all the results are evaluated on the test set.

Evaluation Metrics. We evaluate the prediction performance using the metrics of accuracy (ACC), sensitivity (SEN), specificity (SPE), positive prediction value (PPV), negative prediction value (NPV), F1 score, and area under the receiver operator characteristic curve (AUC).

Implementation Details. We adopt PyTorch for implementation and use SGD for optimization with a momentum of 0.9, a weight decay of $1e-4$, and $\lambda = 1$. We train the network for 75 epochs with a batch size of 3. We follow a step-wise learning rate scheduler with an initial learning rate of $1e-3$ and decay by 0.1 every 25 epochs. We uniformly sample $T = 32$ frames from each video as input, and the input dimension is 224×224. Random cropping, flipping, and rotating are used for data augmentation during training. Center cropping is used during inference. We use ResNet-50 (until the penultimate layer) as the image morphological feature extractor, and the kinetic parameters are approximated by frame indices and are encoded by the positional encoding [22] method. Both the f_t and k_t are vectors of 2048 dimensions. We use a one-layer LSTM with 2048 hidden units, and the temperature τ is set to 1.

Comparison with Known Methods. We implement and adapt several state-of-the-art methods for comparison. (1) STEM [13]: It needs to obtain the cell stages first and use almost all the frames of a video. Kinetic and morphological features are modeled by a temporal stream model (600 frames) and a spatial stream model (35 frames) respectively, and are integrated by an ensemble model STEM to attain the final results. (2) 8-layer CNN [23]: It manually opts 3 focal point images by correlation calculation to form a single 'RGB' image, and utilizes an 8-layer CNN (AlexNet [10]) to predict the discard or transfer destiny

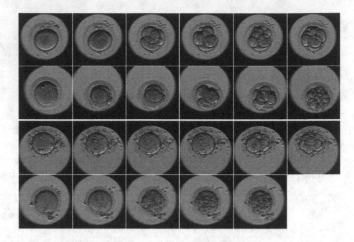

Fig. 3. Visualization of our AdaKFS frame selection results. The top two rows are for the blastocyst class, and the bottom two rows are for the nonblastocyst class.

of embryos on D3. Results are reported in Table 1, and one can see that our AdaKFS outperforms all of them, especially in sensitivity and specificity, which demonstrates the effectiveness of our method. This also shows that focusing on informative contents by selecting key frames from a long TLM video can facilitate the performance greatly. Moreover, without any annotations indicating the embryo development stages, our method can adaptively and automatically introduce morphokinetic parameters for accurate blastocyst formation prediction.

Ablation Study of Our Method. We conduct an ablation study to examine the effects of our proposed components. (1) LSTM: not performing frame selection and directly utilizing LSTM to predict results. (2) Different configurations of AdaKFS: with policy network, with policy network and reward function, and with both of them and the kinetic parameter embeddings. Table 2 reports the detailed ablation study results, and several observations can be made. (a) Compared with the baseline method, LSTM, our frame selection scheme (policy network) achieves a considerably better performance, with improvement of 2.73%, 3.45%, and 5.51% in accuracy, sensitivity, and specificity, respectively. This shows that our main idea for adaptively selecting key frames to predict blastocyst formation is effective, and utilizing information from all the input can be counterproductive as informative frames are often overwhelmed by uninformative ones in long TLM videos. (b) The recognition performance and #SF are further improved with the reward function, which shows that L_{rwd} is in fact a good proxy for constraining the frame selection towards information and performance gain. (c) Integrating morphological features and kinetic parameters is also important for blastocyst formation prediction, and the sensitivity, specificity, and NPV are improved by 2.95%, 3.15%, and 4.76%, respectively. (d) Our final AdaKFS surpasses the baseline model by a large margin, and it selects a small number (∼6) of key frames and reduces the impact of uninformative ones.

Qualitative Evaluation. We visualize some frame selection results by our AdaKFS. As Fig. 3 shows, even though without extra annotations, AdaKFS can still select a small number of key frames to make accurate predictions. For example, for the blastocyst class, AdaKFS can select informative frames of different embryo development stages, such as 2–5 cell and 8-cell stages, which allows us to properly analyze these frames with their morphological and kinetic parameters in a clinical perspective, thus predicting accurate blastocyst formation. For the nonblastocyst class, AdaKFS can also find key frames with abnormal cleavage. Moreover, for different videos, we can select different numbers of frames, which are ranging from 5 to 8.

4 Conclusions

In this paper, we explored blastocyst formation prediction effectively and clinically, by performing targeted TLM video analysis and introducing morphokinetic parameters without extra annotations. We proposed AdaKFS, a novel approach to learn how to adaptively select a small number of key frames for accurately predicting blastocyst formation and blastocyst quality on D3. The Gumbel-Softmax sampling strategy allows us to directly optimize our discrete policy with standard backpropagation, and our reward function facilitates the frame selection process towards information gain and performance improvement. Our method is fully automated and targeted. Experiments on a large TLM video dataset validated the superiority of our new method over state-of-the-art methods.

Acknowledgment. This research was partially supported by National Key R&D Program of China under grant No. 2019YFC0118802, National Natural Science Foundation of China under grants No. 62176231 and No. 62106218, Zhejiang Public Welfare Technology Research Project under grant No. LGF20F020013, Wenzhou Bureau of Science and Technology of China (No. Y2020082). D. Z. Chen's research was supported in part by NSF Grant CCF-1617735.

References

1. Abbasi, M., Saeedi, P., Au, J., Havelock, J.: A deep learning approach for prediction of IVF implantation outcome from day 3 and day 5 time-lapse human embryo image sequences. In: 2021 IEEE International Conference on Image Processing (ICIP), pp. 289–293. IEEE (2021)
2. Gardner, D.K., Lane, M., Stevens, J., Schlenker, T., Schoolcraft, W.B.: Blastocyst score affects implantation and pregnancy outcome: towards a single blastocyst transfer. Fertil. Steril. **73**(6), 1155–1158 (2000)
3. Glujovsky, D., Farquhar, C., Retamar, A.M.Q., Sedo, C.R.A., Blake, D.: Cleavage stage versus blastocyst stage embryo transfer in assisted reproductive technology. Cochrane Database Syst. Rev. (6) (2016)
4. Herrero, J., Tejera, A., Albert, C., Vidal, C., de los Santos, M.J., Meseguer, M.: A time to look back: analysis of morphokinetic characteristics of human embryo development. Fertil. Steril. **100**(6), 1602–1609 (2013)

5. Holte, J., et al.: Construction of an evidence-based integrated morphology cleavage embryo score for implantation potential of embryos scored and transferred on day 2 after oocyte retrieval. Hum. Reprod. **22**(2), 548–557 (2007)

6. Huang, B., et al.: Elevated progesterone levels on the day of oocyte maturation may affect top quality embryo IVF cycles. PLOS ONE **11**(1), e0145895 (2016)

7. Jang, E., Gu, S., Poole, B.: Categorical reparametrization with Gumbel-Softmax. In: Proceedings International Conference on Learning Representations (ICLR), April 2017. https://openreview.net/pdf?id=rkE3y85ee

8. Khosravi, P., et al.: Deep learning enables robust assessment and selection of human blastocysts after in vitro fertilization. NPJ Digital Med. **2**(1), 1–9 (2019)

9. Kragh, M.F., Rimestad, J., Berntsen, J., Karstoft, H.: Automatic grading of human blastocysts from time-lapse imaging. Comput. Biol. Med. **115**, 103494 (2019)

10. Krizhevsky, A., Sutskever, I., Hinton, G.E.: ImageNet classification with deep convolutional neural networks. Adv. Neural Inf. Process. Syst. **25** (2012)

11. Leahy, B.D., et al.: Automated measurements of key morphological features of human embryos for IVF. In: Martel, A.L., et al. (eds.) MICCAI 2020. LNCS, vol. 12265, pp. 25–35. Springer, Cham (2020). https://doi.org/10.1007/978-3-030-59722-1_3

12. Lemmen, J., Agerholm, I., Ziebe, S.: Kinetic markers of human embryo quality using time-lapse recordings of IVF/ICSI-fertilized oocytes. Reprod. Biomed. Online **17**(3), 385–391 (2008)

13. Liao, Q., et al.: Development of deep learning algorithms for predicting blastocyst formation and quality by time-lapse monitoring. Commun. Biol. **4**(1), 1–9 (2021)

14. Liu, Z., et al.: Multi-task deep learning with dynamic programming for embryo early development stage classification from time-lapse videos. IEEE Access **7**, 122153–122163 (2019)

15. Lockhart, L., Saeedi, P., Au, J., Havelock, J.: Automating embryo development stage detection in time-lapse imaging with synergic loss and temporal learning. In: de Bruijne, M., et al. (eds.) MICCAI 2021. LNCS, vol. 12905, pp. 540–549. Springer, Cham (2021). https://doi.org/10.1007/978-3-030-87240-3_52

16. Lukyanenko, S., et al.: Developmental stage classification of embryos using two-stream neural network with linear-chain conditional random field. In: de Bruijne, M., et al. (eds.) MICCAI 2021. LNCS, vol. 12908, pp. 363–372. Springer, Cham (2021). https://doi.org/10.1007/978-3-030-87237-3_35

17. Ma, S., Sigal, L., Sclaroff, S.: Learning activity progression in LSTMs for activity detection and early detection. In: Proceedings of the IEEE Conference on Computer Vision and Pattern Recognition, pp. 1942–1950 (2016)

18. Meseguer, M., Herrero, J., Tejera, A., Hilligsøe, K.M., Ramsing, N.B., Remohí, J.: The use of morphokinetics as a predictor of embryo implantation†. Hum. Reprod. **26**(10), 2658–2671 (2011). https://doi.org/10.1093/humrep/der256

19. Motato, Y., de los Santos, M.J., Escriba, M.J., Ruiz, B.A., Remohí, J., Meseguer, M.: Morphokinetic analysis and embryonic prediction for blastocyst formation through an integrated time-lapse system. Fertil. Steril. **105**(2), 376–384 (2016)

20. Papanikolaou, E.G., et al.: Live birth rate is significantly higher after blastocyst transfer than after cleavage-stage embryo transfer when at least four embryos are available on day 3 of embryo culture. a randomized prospective study. Hum. Reprod. **20**(11), 3198–3203 (2005)

21. Tran, D., Cooke, S., Illingworth, P.J., Gardner, D.K.: Deep learning as a predictive tool for fetal heart pregnancy following time-lapse incubation and blastocyst transfer. Hum. Reprod. **34**(6), 1011–1018 (2019)

22. Vaswani, A., et al.: Attention is all you need. Adv. Neural Inf. Process. Syst. **30** (2017)
23. Zeman, A., Maerten, A.-S., Mengels, A., Sharon, L.F., Spiessens, C., de Beeck, Hans Op: Deep learning for human embryo classification at the cleavage stage (Day 3). In: Del Bimbo, A., et al. (eds.) ICPR 2021. LNCS, vol. 12661, pp. 278–292. Springer, Cham (2021). https://doi.org/10.1007/978-3-030-68763-2_21

Semi-supervised Spatial Temporal Attention Network for Video Polyp Segmentation

Xinkai Zhao[1], Zhenhua Wu[1], Shuangyi Tan[2,3], De-Jun Fan[4], Zhen Li[3], Xiang Wan[3,5], and Guanbin Li[1(✉)]

[1] School of Computer Science and Engineering, Sun Yat-sen University, Guangzhou, China
liguanbin@mail.sysu.edu.cn
[2] Shenzhen Research Institute of Big Data, Shenzhen, China
[3] The Chinese University of Hong Kong, Shenzhen, China
[4] The Sixth Affiliated Hospital, Sun Yat-sen University, Guangzhou, China
[5] Pazhou Lab, Guangzhou, China

Abstract. Deep learning-based polyp segmentation approaches have achieved great success in image datasets. However, the frame-by-frame annotation of polyp videos requires a large amount of workload, which limits the application of polyp segmentation algorithms in clinical videos. In this paper, we address the semi-supervised video polyp segmentation task, which requires only sparsely annotated frames to train a video polyp segmentation network. We propose a novel spatial-temporal attention network which is composed of Temporal Local Context Attention (TLCA) module and Proximity Frame Time-Space Attention (PFTSA) module. Specifically, TLCA module is to refine the prediction of the current frame using the prediction results of the nearby frames in the video clip. PFTSA module utilizes a simple yet powerful hybrid transformer architecture to capture long-range dependencies in time and space efficiently. Combined with consistency constraints, the network fuses representations of proximity frames at different scales to generate pseudo-masks for unlabeled images. We further propose a pseudo-mask-based training method. Additionally, we re-masked a subset of LDPolypVideo and applied it as a semi-supervised polyp segmentation dataset for our experiments. Experimental results show that our proposed semi-supervised approach can outperform existing image-level semi-supervised and fully supervised methods with sparse annotation at a speed of 135 fps. The code is available at github.com/ShinkaiZ/SSTAN.

Keywords: Polyp segmentation · Semi-supervised learning · Medical image segmentation

Supplementary Information The online version contains supplementary material available at https://doi.org/10.1007/978-3-031-16440-8_44.

1   Introduction

Colorectal Cancer (CRC) has become a worldwide human health threat especially for people over fifty years old. In 2021, 147,000 people in United State were diagnosed with this disease, while 53,200 among them died from it [18]. Most CRCs develop from intestinal polyps (adenomas and serrated type), which means the detection and treatment of polyps with colonoscopy is exceedingly significant for the prevention and screening [6]. Clinically, the diagnosis of polyps was completed by an experienced endoscopist, which suffers from a high labor cost and may lead to the omission of diagnosis. With the development of artificial intelligence, many automatic polyp segmentation methods were proposed for ancillary diagnosis and made remarkable progress. Inspired by the great progress achieved by fully convolutional network (FCN) [1], UNet [20], ResUnet [2], UNet++ [31] and ResUNet++ [10] were firstly applied to the polyp segmentation task. Later with the development of attention and transformer [23], ACSNet [29], PraNet [9] and SANet [26] were presented. Inspired by vision transformer [8], which is a novel structure adopting the transformer to computer vision task, Polyp-PVT [7] was soon suggested. All these deep learning based medical segmentation methods mainly focus on the polyp segmentation at the image level, which means they ignore the temporal consistency in endoscopic videos. To better integrate temporal information, video polyp segmentation methods such as Hybrid CNN [19] and PNS-Net [12] were presented recently.

However, the outstanding performances achieved by above supervised models all depend on a large amount of image annotations. In reality, annotation of polyp images and videos would be labor-intensive and resource-intensive. Different from nature images, the labels of medical images require experts in related fields to be annotated and refined. Moreover, for each endoscopic video, many video frames describing a similar content are included, which causes repetitive work and the consistency of manual labels is hard to be guaranteed. Therefore, many semi-supervised polyp segmentation models are suggested, which reduce their requirements for the amount of labeled data and try to fully utilize the unlabelled data. For example, interpolation consistency training method [25] and its improvements [14,17,27,28,30] employ and predict the unlabelled data with the assumption that there is consistency between adjacent labeled data and unlabelled data. Nevertheless, all semi-supervised methods simply consider the consistency and complete the segmentation at the image-level, which ignores the consistency between consecutive frames in video clips.

Considering the labeling difficulty and the utilization of the consistency between consecutive video frames, in this paper, we address the semi-supervised video polyp segmentation task with sparsely annotated frames as well as unlabelled frames and proposed Semi-Supervised Spatial Temporal Attention Network (SSTAN). In our work, we consider both the temporal consistency between video frames and the spatial information contained in each frame with semi-supervised transformer block and vision transformer block, respectively. For evaluation, we applied our model and other cutting-edge models on the subset of LDPolypVideo dataset [15] with masks re-annotated by us. In our experiments,

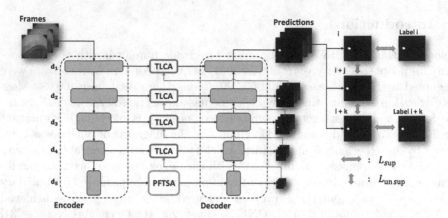

Fig. 1. The overview of our approach for semi-supervised video polyps segmentation, which consist of four Temporal Local Context Attention (TLCA) module in the skip connections with a Proximity Frame Temporal-Spatial Attention (PFTSA) module in the bottom layer.

SSTAN requires only 10% of sparse annotations even to outperform existing fully supervised methods on public benchmarks.

Generally, our contributions are four-folds: (1) We creatively address a semi-supervised video polyp segmentation task, which requires the model to be trained under the supervision of a few sparsely annotated video frames and a large number of unlabeled video frames. (2) To both exploit the temporal and spatial features, we propose a novel Semi-Supervised Spatial Temporal Attention Network (SSTAN) with Temporal Local Context Attention (TLCA) and Proximity Frame Time-Space Attention (PFTSA). Additionally, we suggest a corresponding guided training flow consisted with two stages, which allows the model to generate pseudo labels for unlabeled frames under the supervision of labeled data firstly and be finetuned with both true label and pseudo labels. (3) We relabelled and provided corresponding masks to partial video frames from the LDPolypVideo dataset, which was originally labeled with bounding boxes. With dense video frames, the partial re-annotated dataset could be served as one of the few semi-supervised video polyp segmentation datasets. (4) We evaluated and compared our model with both image and video polyp segmentation models and our SSTAN significantly outperformed existing state-of-the-art fully supervised methods with limited labels (e.g., 10% ground truth labels) (Fig. 1).

2   Method

This paper is targeted at tackling the semi-supervised video polyps segmentation task. Suppose we have a colonoscopy video clip which is constituted by n frames $X = \{x_i\}_{i=1}^{n}$ for training, including M frames with pixel-wise annotations, donated as L, and other $N - M$ frames without annotations, donated as

U. The goal of this task is to train the video segmentation model using L and U, thus reducing the dependency on annotations in the training process. The framework of our approach is shown in Fig. 3, which is based on ResUnet [10] as the framework like ACSNet [29]. In order to fuse the proximity frame information at different layers, the TLCA module is placed in each skip link. Moreover, we utilize the PFTSA module to capture contextual information in both time and space at the bottom layer. Finally, we use consistency loss to constrain the unlabeled frames in the sparsely annotated video frames.

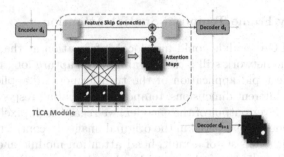

Fig. 2. Temporal local context attention module

2.1   Temporal Local Context Attention

The goal of Temporal Local Context Attention(TLCA) module is to exploit the prediction differences of adjacent frames to focus the network attention on regions that are harder to predict accurately, thus refining the decoding results. As shown in Fig. 2, for the outputs of encoder layer d, donated as $\{\mathcal{E}_d(x_t)\}_{t=1}^{n}$, we leverage the predictions $\{\mathcal{P}_{d+1}(x_t)\}_{t=1}^{n}$ of the decoder layer $d+1$ to calculate the attention map for each frame. Specifically, the attention map of frame x_i is donated as follow:

$$\mathcal{M}_i^d = \frac{1}{n-1}\sum_{t\neq i}(|\mathcal{P}_{d+1}(x_t) - \mathcal{P}_{d+1}(x_i)|) \tag{1}$$

where d represents the depth, t stands for the frames except the current frame i. We calculate the absolute difference between the prediction of the current frame and the prediction of nearby frames. For each pixel in the image, when the prediction of different frames is similar, the attention map is close to 0. Conversely, when the prediction differs significantly between frames, the attention map is close to 1, representing that this position needs to be better refined in the next decoder layer. Finally, the attention enhanced feature is used as input to the previous layer, to optimize the output of the higher resolution mask.

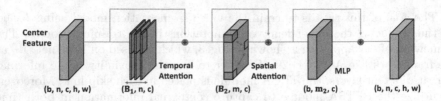

Fig. 3. Proximity Frame Temporal-Spatial Attention Module. The b, n, c, h, w stands for batch size, frames number, channel number, height and width, respectively.

2.2 Proximity Frame Temporal-Spatial Attention

Although the TLCA module could fuse local information at the same position across frames, the network still lacks the ability to capture long-term contexts. Motivated by the rapid application of the transformer, we applied multi-head attention in two different dimensions, temporal and spatial, respectively. Specifically, for the last layer output of the encoder, we regard each pixel in the feature map as the embedding of a patch in the original image. In contrast to the vanilla transformer, which consists of a multi-head attention module and an MLP, we borrow the idea from [5] to use two multi-head attention modules to capture spatial and temporal contextual dependencies. For feature $\mathcal{E}_5(x) \in \mathbb{R}^{b*n*c*h*w}$, we firstly reshape it to $\mathbb{R}^{B_1*n*c}$, where $B_1 = b*h*w$, then calculate the multi-head attention across n frames. Consequently, the feature is re-arranged to $\mathbb{R}^{B_2*m*c}$, where $B_2 = b*n, m = h*w$. And another multi-head attention is calculated within each image. Finally, after the MLP module, the output is used as the input of decoder.

2.3 Loss Function

Our loss function is divided into supervised and unsupervised parts. The supervised loss function is formulated as follow:

$$\mathcal{L}_{sup} = \frac{1}{2 * |L| * |D|} \sum_{x_n \in L} \sum_{d \in D} (Dice\left(\mathcal{P}_d(x_n), y_d\right) + CE\left(\mathcal{P}_d(x_n), y_d\right)), \quad (2)$$

where y_d is the ground truth of the labeled image which is down-scaled to the feature size of the corresponding layer d. $Dice(\cdot)$ is dice loss and $CE(\cdot)$ is binary cross entropy loss. L_{sup} is used to calculate between prediction $\mathcal{P}_d(x_n)$ and ground truth y_d of frames which have been labeled.

The unsupervised loss function can be formulated as follow:

$$\mathcal{L}_{unsup} = \frac{1}{|X| * |D|} \sum_{x_n \in X} \sum_{d \in D} SmoothL1\left(\mathcal{P}_d(x_n), \mathcal{P}_d(x_{n+1})\right) \quad (3)$$

To compute consistency, L_{unsup} is calculated between the current frame x_n and the next frame x_{n+1} except the last frame in a video clip.

2.4   Training Flow

The whole network is trained following the end-to-end scheme in two stages: *i) Pretraining phase* We used the training data for semi-supervised training of our model with $L_{pretrain} = \frac{1}{2}(\mathcal{L}_{sup} + \mathcal{L}_{unsup})$. *ii) Finetuning phase* The model pretrained in the first stage was applied to generate pseudo labels for the unlabeled frames in the training set. With training data as well as both true labels and pseudo labels of all frames, the model was supervised finetuned with loss function L_{sup} subsequently.

3   Experiments

3.1   Datasets and Implementation

Datasets. Commonly used polyp segmentation datasets including five benchmarks (Kvasir [11], CVC-ClinicDB [3], EndoScene [24], ETIS-Larib Polyp DB [21] and CVC-ColonDB [4]) are image-based, which contain selected frames from video clips. For video polyp segmentation task, due to the expensive cost of video annotation, the only currently knowable video polyp segmentation dataset, i.e., ASU-Mayo, contains video with dense frames and is annotated with masks [22]. However, ASU-Mayo is not publicly accessible, which means other datasets are desired for training models. Meanwhile, LDPolypVideo [15] and SUN Colonoscopy Video Database [16] are two recent video polyp dectection datasets fully annotated with bounding boxes. LDPolypVideo contains 160 video clips with 15397 dense video frames describing polyps in more variety under different bowel environments. To adapt LDPolypVideo to our task, we re-masked 60 videos out of 160 videos in LDPolypVideo for training and testing. The details of our re-masked dataset are described in supplementary material.

Training and Testing. In our experiment, the partial masked 36 videos and the following fully annotated 12 videos in re-masked LDPolypVideo were applied as training data and validation data, respectively. The initial learning rate, batch size and optimizer applied in our model training is $1e^{-4}$, 4, and AdamW [13], respectively. Every 11 frames with the first frame and the last frames masked in each video were resized to 256×256 as a single input. The model was pretrained for 100 epochs and finetuned for 50 epochs. Same parameters and the last 12 fully annotated videos were used for evaluation. When testing, our approach achieves a speed of about 135fps on a single Nvidia Tesla V100 GPU.

State-of-the-Art Models. We compared our model with other state-of-the-art models mainly in three types: (1) Image-based Supervised Model (ACSNet [29], SANet [26], PVT [7]); (2) Video-based Supervised Model (PNS [12]) and (3) Image-based Semi-Supervised Model (URPC [14], CLCC [30]). We trained the Image-based Semi-Supervised Model in an end-to-end way under their default settings. Models in other types were retrained in two stages similarly to training

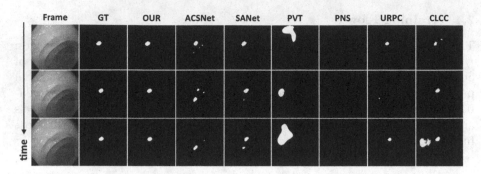

Fig. 4. Qualitative results of different models on LDPolypVideo testing set.

Table 1. The results and comparison with other state-of-the-art methods. The highest score is highlighted in black bold.

Model	Labeled	Unlabeled	Accuracy	MAE	F1-Score	F2-Score	mIoU
ACSNet	10%		0.984	0.016	0.396	0.411	0.658
	10%	90%	0.983	0.017	0.332	0.338	0.631
SANet	10%		0.986	0.014	0.405	0.399	0.665
	10%	90%	0.982	0.018	0.396	0.391	0.665
PVT	10%		0.966	0.034	0.149	0.177	0.538
	10%	90%	0.953	0.047	0.165	0.214	0.531
PNSNet	10%	90%	0.989	0.011	0.314	0.296	0.628
URPC	10%	90%	0.984	0.016	0.370	0.389	0.648
CLCC	10%	90%	0.987	0.013	0.366	0.367	0.657
Ours	10%	90%	**0.990**	**0.010**	**0.482**	**0.486**	**0.700**

setting: *i) Pretraining phase* We used the annotated 10% data for supervised training of the model under their default settings. *ii) Finetuning phase* We used the model obtained in the previous step to predict the remaining 90% of our datasets and got the corresponding masks. These masks were used as pseudo-labels for 90% of the data, and then we trained the model using both data with pseudo-labels and data with ground truth. For fair comparison, we trained the first stage over 100 epochs and the second stage over 50 epochs and the result of all models in two stages have been tested except PNS, which is a video-based model while the first stage of its default training process utilizing images.

3.2 Qualitative Evaluation

In Fig. 4, we provide the visualization results of our model and other compared models on the testing set of re-annotated LDPolypVideo. We selected three adjacent frames for visualization. Our model has two main advantages: (1) our model has the ability to locate and segment the polyps in many conditions,

Table 2. The results of ablation study. The highest score is highlighted in black bold.

Model	Accuracy	MAE	F1-Score	F2-Score	mIoU
Baseline	0.979	0.021	0.306	0.300	0.619
Baseline+PFTSA	0.975	0.015	0.410	0.432	0.665
Baseline+PFTSA+TLCA	0.988	0.012	0.432	0.431	0.686
Baseline+PFTSA+TLCA+Finetuning	**0.990**	**0.010**	**0.482**	**0.486**	**0.700**

such as motion blur, different lighting, complex environment with reflections and bubbles, *etc.*. (2) Our model can consistently predict polyps among consecutive frames because the information of adjacent frames is taken into account. More visualization results is shown in supplementary material.

3.3 Quantitative Evaluation

For quantitative evaluation, we selected six metrics: Accuracy, MAE, F1-Score (Dice), F2-Score and mean IoU (mIoU). The results of our model and other state-of-the-art models are shown in Table 1. Our model outperformed all three types of models under the same data setting over all metrics. Specially, our model improves the Dice, F2-Score and mIoU achieved by other models by 8.6%, 7.5% and 4.2%, respectively. This result indicates that our model utilizes the 90% unlabeled data better than other image-based models as well as the video-based supervised model by considering the consistency between consecutive frames. Additionally, two notable results are worth mentioning. One is that the performance of PVT is remarkably worse than other convolution-based models, which demonstrates the perspective shown in [8] that the performance of vision transformer highly depends on the size of training data. The other is that F1-score, F2-score and mIoU are unsatisfactory as the original LDPolypVideo is a challenging dataset that contains various polyps under complex colonial environment [15]. For more experimental results, see supplementary materials.

3.4 Ablation Study

In order to verify the effectiveness of our proposed modules, we conducted ablation experiments on the same testing dataset. The baseline model is the ResUNet framework, and we evaluated module effectiveness by adding components. Specifically, we gradually added PFTSA at the bottom layer, TLCA modules at the skip links, and finetuning at the training phase.

Effectiveness of PFTSA. We trained the baseline both with PFTSA and without PFTSA. The results are shown in the first and second line of Table 2. We found that results with PFTSA performed better. The improvements suggest that PFTSA improves performance by using spatial and temporal information.

Effectiveness of TLCA. Similarly, we investigated the contribution of TLCA by introducing the module additionally. The results are shown in the third line of

Table 2. Compared to the model with PFTSA, F1-score and mIoU of the model were increased by 2.2% and 2.1% respectively, which indicates the attention mechanism can enable the model to focus on the hard regions.

Effectiveness of Finetuning. Notably, the above experiments were only trained in pretraining phase. To analyze the effectiveness of our training process, we additionally performed finetuning on the model with both PFTSA and TLCA. The improvement suggests that introducing pseudo labels and performing supervised training are necessary for increasing performance.

4   Conclusion

In this paper, we defined the semi-supervised polyp video segmentation task and proposed an accurate and novel network SSTAN, which exploits the spatial and temporal information from the proximity frames in endoscope videos with PFTSA and explores the hard regions with TLCA. Additionally, we produced and applied a re-masked sub-dataset of LDPolypVideo, which could be served as the first challenging dataset for semi-supervised polyp video segmentation task. Experiment results demonstrate that our SSTAN outperformed other state-of-the-art methods including image-based supervised model, image-based semi-supervised model and video-based supervised model under the same data setting with real time speed (135 fps). In future work, we will further explore a better performance of SSTAN on semi-supervised tasks for video polyp segmentation.

Acknowledgment. This work was supported in part by the Guangdong Basic and Applied Basic Research Foundation (No. 2020B1515020048), in part by the National Natural Science Foundation of China (No. 61976250), in part by the Guangzhou Science and technology project (No. 202102020633), in part by the Chinese Key-Area Research and Development Program of Guangdong Province (2020B0101350001), and in part by the Guangdong Provincial Key Laboratory of Big Data Computing, The Chinese University of Hong Kong, Shenzhen.

References

1. Akbari, M., et al.: Polyp segmentation in colonoscopy images using fully convolutional network. In: 2018 40th Annual International Conference of the IEEE Engineering in Medicine and Biology Society (EMBC), pp. 69–72. IEEE (2018)
2. Alam, S., Tomar, N.K., Thakur, A., Jha, D., Rauniyar, A.: Automatic polyp segmentation using u-net-resnet50. arXiv preprint arXiv:2012.15247 (2020)
3. Bernal, J., Sánchez, F.J., Fernández-Esparrach, G., Gil, D., Rodríguez, C., Vilariño, F.: Wm-dova maps for accurate polyp highlighting in colonoscopy: Validation vs. saliency maps from physicians. Computerized Med. Imaging Graph. **43**, 99–111 (2015)
4. Bernal, J., Sánchez, J., Vilarino, F.: Towards automatic polyp detection with a polyp appearance model. Pattern Recogn. **45**(9), 3166–3182 (2012)
5. Bertasius, G., Wang, H., Torresani, L.: Is space-time attention all you need for video understanding. arXiv preprint arXiv:2102.05095 2(3), 4 (2021)

6. Buskermolen, M., et al.: Impact of surgical versus endoscopic management of complex nonmalignant polyps in a colorectal cancer screening program. Endoscopy (2022)
7. Dong, B., Wang, W., Fan, D.P., Li, J., Fu, H., Shao, L.: Polyp-pvt: polyp segmentation with pyramid vision transformers. arXiv preprint arXiv:2108.06932 (2021)
8. Dosovitskiy, A., et al.: An image is worth 16x16 words: transformers for image recognition at scale. arXiv preprint arXiv:2010.11929 (2020)
9. Fan, D.-P., Ji, G.-P., Zhou, T., Chen, G., Fu, H., Shen, J., Shao, L.: PraNet: parallel reverse attention network for polyp segmentation. In: Martel, A.L., Abolmaesumi, P., Stoyanov, D., Mateus, D., Zuluaga, M.A., Zhou, S.K., Racoceanu, D., Joskowicz, L. (eds.) MICCAI 2020. LNCS, vol. 12266, pp. 263–273. Springer, Cham (2020). https://doi.org/10.1007/978-3-030-59725-2_26
10. Jha, D., Smedsrud, P.H., Johansen, D., de Lange, T., Johansen, H.D., Halvorsen, P., Riegler, M.A.: A comprehensive study on colorectal polyp segmentation with resunet++, conditional random field and test-time augmentation. IEEE J. Biomed. Health Inform. **25**(6), 2029–2040 (2021)
11. Jha, D., et al.: Kvasir-SEG: a segmented polyp dataset. In: Ro, Y.M., et al. (eds.) MMM 2020. LNCS, vol. 11962, pp. 451–462. Springer, Cham (2020). https://doi.org/10.1007/978-3-030-37734-2_37
12. Ji, G.-P., et al.: Progressively normalized self-attention network for video polyp segmentation. In: de Bruijne, M., et al. (eds.) MICCAI 2021. LNCS, vol. 12901, pp. 142–152. Springer, Cham (2021). https://doi.org/10.1007/978-3-030-87193-2_14
13. Loshchilov, I., Hutter, F.: Decoupled weight decay regularization. arXiv preprint arXiv:1711.05101 (2017)
14. Luo, X., et al.: Efficient semi-supervised gross target volume of nasopharyngeal carcinoma segmentation via uncertainty rectified pyramid consistency. In: de Bruijne, M., et al. (eds.) MICCAI 2021. LNCS, vol. 12902, pp. 318–329. Springer, Cham (2021). https://doi.org/10.1007/978-3-030-87196-3_30
15. Ma, Y., Chen, X., Cheng, K., Li, Y., Sun, B.: LDPolypVideo benchmark: a large-scale colonoscopy video dataset of diverse polyps. In: de Bruijne, M., et al. (eds.) MICCAI 2021. LNCS, vol. 12905, pp. 387–396. Springer, Cham (2021). https://doi.org/10.1007/978-3-030-87240-3_37
16. Misawa, M., et al.: Development of a computer-aided detection system for colonoscopy and a publicly accessible large colonoscopy video database (with video). Gastrointestinal Endoscopy **93**(4), 960–967 (2021)
17. Pandey, P., Pai, A., Bhatt, N., Das, P., Makharia, G., AP, P., et al.: Contrastive semi-supervised learning for 2d medical image segmentation. arXiv preprint arXiv:2106.06801 (2021)
18. Patel, S.G., et al.: Updates on age to start and stop colorectal cancer screening: recommendations from the us multi-society task force on colorectal cancer. Gastroenterology **162**(1), 285–299 (2022)
19. Puyal, J.G.-B., et al.: Endoscopic polyp segmentation using a hybrid 2D/3D CNN. In: Martel, A.L., et al. (eds.) MICCAI 2020. LNCS, vol. 12266, pp. 295–305. Springer, Cham (2020). https://doi.org/10.1007/978-3-030-59725-2_29
20. Ronneberger, O., Fischer, P., Brox, T.: U-Net: convolutional networks for biomedical image segmentation. In: Navab, N., Hornegger, J., Wells, W.M., Frangi, A.F. (eds.) MICCAI 2015. LNCS, vol. 9351, pp. 234–241. Springer, Cham (2015). https://doi.org/10.1007/978-3-319-24574-4_28
21. Silva, J., Histace, A., Romain, O., Dray, X., Granado, B.: Toward embedded detection of polyps in WCE images for early diagnosis of colorectal cancer. Int. J. Comput. Assist. Radiol. Surg. **9**(2), 283–293 (2014)

22. Tajbakhsh, N., Gurudu, S.R., Liang, J.: Automated polyp detection in colonoscopy videos using shape and context information. IEEE Trans. Med. Imaging **35**(2), 630–644 (2015)

23. Vaswani, A., et al.: Attention is all you need. Advances in neural information processing systems 30 (2017)

24. Vázquez, D., et al.: A benchmark for endoluminal scene segmentation of colonoscopy images. J. Healthcare Eng. 2017 (2017)

25. Verma, V., Kawaguchi, K., Lamb, A., Kannala, J., Bengio, Y., Lopez-Paz, D.: Interpolation consistency training for semi-supervised learning. arXiv preprint arXiv:1903.03825 (2019)

26. Wei, J., Hu, Y., Zhang, R., Li, Z., Zhou, S.K., Cui, S.: Shallow attention network for polyp segmentation. In: de Bruijne, M., et al. (eds.) MICCAI 2021. LNCS, vol. 12901, pp. 699–708. Springer, Cham (2021). https://doi.org/10.1007/978-3-030-87193-2_66

27. Xiang, J., Li, Z., Wang, W., Xia, Q., Zhang, S.: Self-ensembling contrastive learning for semi-supervised medical image segmentation. arXiv preprint arXiv:2105.12924 (2021)

28. You, C., Zhou, Y., Zhao, R., Staib, L., Duncan, J.S.: Simcvd: Simple contrastive voxel-wise representation distillation for semi-supervised medical image segmentation. arXiv preprint arXiv:2108.06227 (2021)

29. Zhang, R., Li, G., Li, Z., Cui, S., Qian, D., Yu, Y.: Adaptive context selection for polyp segmentation. In: Martel, A.L., et al. (eds.) MICCAI 2020. LNCS, vol. 12266, pp. 253–262. Springer, Cham (2020). https://doi.org/10.1007/978-3-030-59725-2_25

30. Zhao, X., Fang, C., Fan, D.J., Lin, X., Gao, F., Li, G.: Cross-level contrastive learning and consistency constraint for semi-supervised medical image segmentation. arXiv preprint arXiv:2202.04074 (2022)

31. Zhou, Z., Rahman Siddiquee, M.M., Tajbakhsh, N., Liang, J.: UNet++: a nested U-Net architecture for medical image segmentation. In: Stoyanov, D., et al. (eds.) DLMIA/ML-CDS -2018. LNCS, vol. 11045, pp. 3–11. Springer, Cham (2018). https://doi.org/10.1007/978-3-030-00889-5_1

Geometric Constraints for Self-supervised Monocular Depth Estimation on Laparoscopic Images with Dual-task Consistency

Wenda Li[1], Yuichiro Hayashi[1], Masahiro Oda[1,2], Takayuki Kitasaka[3], Kazunari Misawa[4], and Kensaku Mori[1,5,6(✉)]

[1] Graduate School of Informatics, Nagoya University, Furou-cho, Chikusa-ku, Nagoya, Aichi 464-8601, Japan
Kensaku@is.nagoya-u.ac.jp
[2] Information and Communications, Nagoya University, Furou-cho, Chikusa-ku, Nagoya, Aichi 464-8601, Japan
[3] Faculty of Information Science, Aichi Institute of Technology, Yakusacho, Toyota, Aichi 470-0392, Japan
[4] Aichi Cancer Center Hospital, Chikusa-ku, Nagoya, Aichi 464-8681, Japan
[5] Information Technology Center, Nagoya University, Furou-cho, Chikusa-ku, Nagoya, Aichi 464-8601, Japan
[6] Research Center of Medical Bigdata, National Institute of Informatics, Hitotsubashi, Chiyoda-ku, Tokyo 101-8430, Japan

Abstract. Depth values are essential information to automate surgical robots and achieve Augmented Reality technology for minimally invasive surgery. Although depth-pose self-supervised monocular depth estimation performs impressively for autonomous driving scenarios, it is more challenging to predict accurate depth values for laparoscopic images due to the following two aspects: (i) the laparoscope's motions contain many rotations, leading to pose estimation difficulties for the depth-pose learning strategy; (ii) the smooth surface reduces photometric error even if the matching pixels are inaccurate between adjacent frames. This paper proposes a novel self-supervised monocular depth estimation for laparoscopic images with geometric constraints. We predict the scene coordinates as an auxiliary task and construct dual-task consistency between the predicted depth maps and scene coordinates under a unified camera coordinate system to achieve pixel-level geometric constraints. We extend the pose estimation into a Siamese process to provide stronger and more balanced geometric constraints in a depth-pose learning strategy by leveraging the order of the adjacent frames in a video sequence. We also design a weight mask for depth estimation based on our consistency to alleviate the interference from predictions with low confidence. The experimental results showed that the proposed method outperformed the

Supplementary Information The online version contains supplementary material available at https://doi.org/10.1007/978-3-031-16440-8_45.

baseline on depth and pose estimation. Our code is available at https://github.com/MoriLabNU/GCDepthL.

Keywords: Monocular depth estimation · Self-supervised learning · Laparoscopic images

1   Introduction

Augmented-reality-assisted minimally invasive surgery (ARAMIS) and robotic-assisted minimally invasive surgery (RAMIS) are two options for solving challenges in laparoscopic surgery, such as the fulcrum effect and the narrow field of view [6,22,25]. RAMIS has become the preferred approach for laparoscopic surgery. Depth values are necessary information to achieve the 3D reconstruction of organs in the abdominal cavity for AR technology [22] and the automation of surgical robots [12].

Monocular self-supervised depth estimation has also recently become a critical tool due to its low computational complexity and impressive performance without ground-truth during training [20,24,27]. As one of the earliest works, Garg et al. [5] estimated the disparity map from the left view of stereo images and reconstructed the left image by a corresponding right image to achieve a self-supervised learning strategy. Unfortunately, this self-supervised learning strategy still required stereo image datasets during training. Zhou et al. [28] first leveraged the structure-from-motion theory [4] to achieve a depth-pose self-supervised learning strategy for monocular depth estimation. Godard et al. [7] optimized this method through minimum photometric loss and introduced auto-masking in the loss function and achieved a state-of-the-art performance. More recent works adopted this method as a baseline and improved results by introducing more auxiliary information from other tasks [3,8,13]. A few methods considered self-supervised monocular depth estimation for laparoscopic images. Huang et al. [10] introduced the generative adversarial network into the self-supervised learning strategy that required stereo images as input of a depth estimation network. Li et al. [16] described the differences between autonomous driving scenes and laparoscopic scenes and chose the depth-pose self-supervised learning strategy with a nested structural network and a non-local block, having high computational complexity to improve the depth estimation results.

This work proposes a novel monocular self-supervised depth estimation for laparoscopic images by analyzing the following two aspects of the differences between autonomous driving and laparoscopic scenes. First, the motions of laparoscopes have many complex rotations of six degrees of freedom (6-DOF); there are no significant changes in pitch and the z-axis of 6-DOF for cars in autonomous driving scenes, which simplifies the motion pattern of motion and pose estimation. Second, unlike the autonomous driving frame with rich features, the smooth surface of organs occupies most of the regions in a laparoscopic frame. The photometric error becomes small even if the pixels are matched

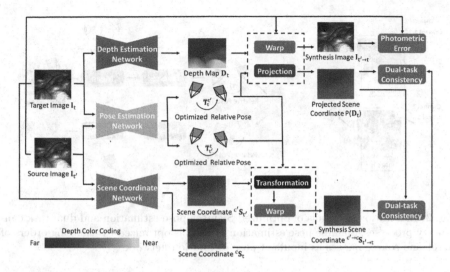

Fig. 1. Overview of our depth-pose self-supervised monocular depth estimation framework: Our three-branch method consists of depth estimation, pose estimation, and scene coordinate prediction. Loss function includes photometric error for depth estimation and dual-task consistency loss based on depth estimation and scene coordinate prediction. Scene coordinate contains 3D coordinates (X, Y, Z) of input image under camera coordinate system in three channels.

inaccurately between adjacent frames. Therefore, we introduce geometric constraints into the self-supervised depth estimation on laparoscopic images based on the scene coordinate predictions as an auxiliary task with consistency. The different tasks obtain various levels of information and complement each other during training. In addition, we propose several innovations for entire scheme's performance.

This paper's contributions can be summarized as follows: (i) We propose a novel self-supervised monocular depth estimation with three task branches, including depth estimation, pose estimation, and scene coordinate prediction with novel consistency loss functions under a camera coordinate system; (ii) We adopt an optimized Siamese pose estimation process to provide stronger and more balanced geometric constraints; (iii) We propose a consistency-based weight mask that reduces interference from low-confidence predictions.

2   Method

2.1   Self-supervised Learning

Following the previous methods [7,19,28], we adopt the depth-pose self-supervised learning strategy for depth estimation. Our enire proposed self-supervised learning strategy is illustrated in Fig. 1. In this strategy, the depth estimation network predicts depth map $\mathbf{D}_t$ from target image $\mathbf{I}_t$, where t denotes

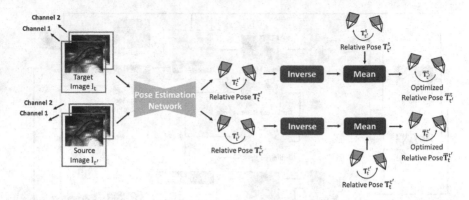

Fig. 2. Illustration of details of optimized Siamese pose estimation and dual-task consistency processes. Siamese pose estimation process is optimized by changing orders of target and source images as inputs of pose estimation network.

the moment when the frame appears in the video sequence. Source image $\mathbf{I}_{t'}$ is the adjacent image of $\mathbf{I}_t$ in the video sequence. $\mathbf{I}_t$ and $\mathbf{I}_{t'}$ are the inputs of the pose estimation to predict transformation matrix $\mathbf{T}_t^{t'}$, which represents the rigid relative pose of the laparoscope from views $\mathbf{I}_t$ to $\mathbf{I}_{t'}$.

To overcome the challenge of pose estimation for laparoscopic images, we optimize the pose estimation process by emphasizing the order of the adjacent frames in the video sequence. We exchange the order of $\mathbf{I}_t$ and $\mathbf{I}_{t'}$ as the input of the pose estimation network as shown in Fig. 2. The pose estimation outputs are transformation matrix $\mathbf{T}_t^{t'}$ and $\mathbf{T}_{t'}^t$. We average $\mathbf{T}_t^{t'}$ and the inverse of $\mathbf{T}_{t'}^t$ to obtain optimized relative pose $\overline{\mathbf{T}}_t^{t'}$ by $\overline{\mathbf{T}}_t^{t'} = \frac{1}{2}\left(\mathbf{T}_t^{t'} + \left(\mathbf{T}_{t'}^t\right)^{-1}\right)$. As shown in Fig. 2, we design a Siamese pose estimate process to estimate optimized relative pose $\overline{\mathbf{T}}_{t'}^t$ to provide stronger and more balanced geometric constraints for pose estimation instead of estimating single optimized relative poses in the previous work [15]. $\overline{\mathbf{T}}_{t'}^t$ is used in the dual-task consistency described in Sect. 2.2. Then $\overline{\mathbf{T}}_t^{t'}$ matches the pixels in $\mathbf{I}_t$ and $\mathbf{I}_{t'}$ by

$$p_{t'} = \mathbf{K}\overline{\mathbf{T}}_t^{t'}\mathbf{D}(p_t)\mathbf{K}^{-1}p_t, \tag{1}$$

where p_t and $p_{t'}$ are the pixel coordinates in $\mathbf{I}_t$ and $\mathbf{I}_{t'}$. $\mathbf{D}(p_t)$ is the predicted depth value on the location with the pixel coordinates p_t. $\mathbf{K}$ is the intrinsic parameter matrix of the larparoscope. The synthesis image $\mathbf{I}_{t' \to t}$ is generated by $\mathbf{I}_{t' \to t}(p_t) = \mathbf{I}_{t'}(p_{t'})$. Then the minimized photometric error can be formulated:

$$E\left(\mathbf{I}_t, \mathbf{I}_{t' \to t}\right) = \frac{\alpha}{2}\left(1 - \text{SSIM}\left(\mathbf{I}_t, \mathbf{I}_{t' \to t}\right)\right) + (1 - \alpha)\left\|\mathbf{I}_t - \mathbf{I}_{t' \to t}\right\|_1, \tag{2}$$

$$\mathcal{L}_p = \min_{t'} E\left(\mathbf{I}_t, \mathbf{I}_{t' \to t}\right), \tag{3}$$

where α is set to 0.85 as baseline [7] for structured similarity (SSIM) [26] and an L1-norm operator. $\mathbf{I}_{t'}$ is the adjacent images of $\mathbf{I}_t$ as $\mathbf{I}_{t'} \in \{\mathbf{I}_{t-1}, \mathbf{I}_{t+1}\}$.

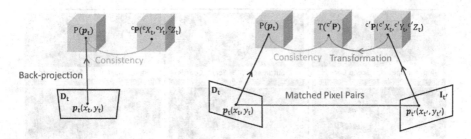

Fig. 3. Dual-task consistency construction process: (a) consistency between depth estimation and scene coordinate prediction through back-projection with estimated depth maps and (b) consistency between predicted scene coordinates by matched pixel pairs and transformation of camera coordinate systems.

2.2 Dual-task Consistency Loss and Weight Mask

Scene coordinate network is designed to estimate the 3D coordinates in the world coordinate system under the supervised learning strategy described in previous researches [17,18]. To introduce scene coordinate prediction in the self-supervised learning strategy and construct consistency with depth estimation, we adopt the scene coordinate network to predict the 3D coordinates under the dynamic camera coordinate system. We fix the camera coordinate system in the center of the end of laparoscope. The camera coordinate system moves along with the laparoscope at different moments. As shown in Fig. 1, $\mathbf{I}_t$ and $\mathbf{I}_{t'}$ are fed to the scene coordinate network, and corresponding scene coordinates $^c\mathbf{S}_t$ and $^{c'}\mathbf{S}_{t'}$ are output. $^c\mathbf{S}_t$ represents the 3D coordinates under camera coordinate system c predicted from the frame at moment t, and $^{c'}\mathbf{S}_{t'}$ represents the 3D coordinates under the camera coordinate system c′ predicted from the frame at moment t′.

Instead of sharing the feature maps to build cooperation between different tasks [8], we propose two types of consistency based on scene coordinate prediction and depth estimation and construct dual-task consistency loss. First, we utilize back-projection to predict the 3D coordinates under the current camera coordinate system based on estimated depth map $\mathbf{D}_t$ by

$$\mathbf{P}\left(\boldsymbol{p}_t\right) = \mathbf{K}^{-1}\mathbf{D}(\boldsymbol{p}_t)\boldsymbol{p}_t, \tag{4}$$

where $\mathbf{P}\left(\boldsymbol{p}_t\right)$ is the projected 3D coordinates corresponding to pixel coordinates $\boldsymbol{p}_t$ in $\mathbf{D}_t$. The back-projection process is shown in Fig. 3(a), where $^c\mathbf{P}$ denotes 3D coordinates under camera coordinate system c in predicted scene coordinates $^c\mathbf{S}_t$ from the scene coordinate network. All projected 3D coordinates $\mathbf{P}\left(\boldsymbol{p}_t\right)$ of pixel coordinates $\boldsymbol{p}_t$ in $\mathbf{D}_t$ form projected scene coordinate $\mathbf{P}\left(\mathbf{D}_t\right)$. Moreover, as shown in Fig. 3(b), we utilized predicted rigid relative pose $\overline{\mathbf{T}}_{t'}^t$ to transform predicted scene coordinates $^{c'}\mathbf{S}_{t'}$ from camera coordinate system c to camera

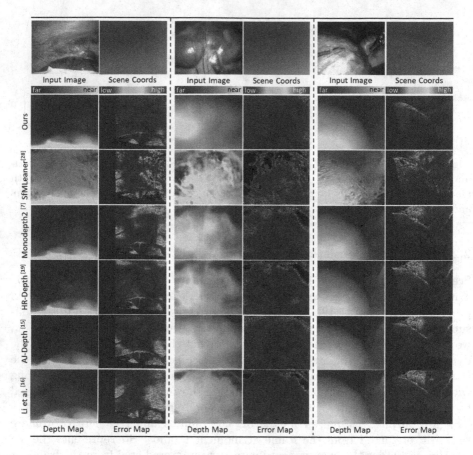

Fig. 4. Comparison of qualitative results for depth estimation: First row shows proposed method's input images and predicted scene coordinates. Images are estimated depth maps and error maps based on absolute relative error metrics from second row to last row.

coordinate system c' by $\mathrm{T}\left({}^{c'}\mathbf{S}_{t'}\right) = \overline{\mathbf{T}}_{t'}^{t}\,{}^{c'}\mathbf{S}_{t'}$. Then we generate synthesis scene coordinate ${}^{c' \to c}\mathbf{S}_{t' \to t}$ by

$$
{}^{c' \to c}\mathbf{S}_{t' \to t}\,(\boldsymbol{p}_t) = \left(\overline{\mathbf{T}}_{t'}^{t}\,{}^{c'}\mathbf{S}_{t'}\right)(\boldsymbol{p}_{t'}), \tag{5}
$$

where $\overline{\mathbf{T}}_{t'}^{t}$ is the predicted relative pose from the pose estimation. $\boldsymbol{p}_t$ and $\boldsymbol{p}_{t'}$ are matched pixel pairs according to Eq. 1. As shown in Fig. 3, the dual-task consistency loss can be calculated based on two consistencies:

$$
\mathcal{L}_{consistency} = \left\|{}^{c}\mathbf{S}_t - \mathbf{P}\left(\mathbf{D}_t\right)\right\|_1 + \left\|{}^{c' \to c}\mathbf{S}_{t' \to t} - \mathbf{P}\left(\mathbf{D}_t\right)\right\|_1. \tag{6}
$$

Table 1. Comparison of proposed model with existing models for depth estimation.

	Abs Rel	Sq Rel	RMSE	RMSE log	$\delta < 1.25$	$\delta < 1.25^2$	$\delta < 1.25^3$
SfMLearner [28]	0.100	2.539	11.916	0.138	0.910	0.977	0.993
Monodepth2 [7]	0.075	0.827	7.538	0.100	0.943	0.995	0.999
HR-Depth [19]	0.076	0.864	7.718	0.103	0.941	0.995	**1.000**
AJ-Depth [15]	0.069	0.745	7.072	0.093	0.953	0.995	**1.000**
Li et al. [16]	0.066	0.715	6.684	0.089	0.952	0.995	0.999
Ours	**0.062**	**0.654**	**6.649**	**0.086**	**0.956**	**0.997**	**1.000**

Inspired by the self-discovered mask [2], we propose weight mask M to alleviate the interference from predictions with low confidence by

$$M = {}^c\mathbf{S}_t - {}^{c' \to c}\mathbf{S}_{t' \to t}. \tag{7}$$

Our final loss is $\mathcal{L}_{final} = (1 - M)\,\mathcal{L}_p + \mu\mathcal{L}_{consistency} + \lambda\mathcal{L}_{smooth}$, where weight mask M is normalized in $[0, 1]$ and $\mathcal{L}_{smooth}$ is the smoothness term in the baseline [7].

3 Experiments and Results

3.1 Datasets and Evaluation Metrics

We adopted the SCARED [1] datasets with depth values as ground-truth for all the experiments. The datasets included nine various scenes in 35 laparoscopic stereo videos. Based on the video sequence, we divided SCARED at a 10:1:1 ratio for each scene. The datasets split was 47,373, 4,810, and 4,810 frames for training, validation, and test, respectively. Due to the limitations of the computation resources, we downsampled images as 320 × 256 pixels at a quarter of the images' original size in SCARED [1].

For evaluation, we followed the baseline [7] and used seven classical metrics for depth evaluation. In addition, we adopted the 5-frame-snippets metric, as in SfMLearner [28] to evaluate the estimated rigid relative poses.

3.2 Implementation Details

We implemented our model using PyTorch library [21]. We trained the networks with Adam [14] for 25 epochs with a learning rate of 1.0×10^{-4}, dropped by a scale factor of 10 after 15 epochs. The batch size was 12, and μ and λ in the final loss function were set to 0.1 and 1.0×10^{-3}. Furthermore, we set the cap of predicted depth to 200mm. Following the baseline [7], all the methods in our experiments shared identical basic parameter settings.

We adopted ResNet-18 [9] with pretrained weights on ImageNet [23] as the encoder module for the three models in this work. The depth estimation network's decoder also followed the baseline [7]. Our proposed method took about 12 h for training on a single NVIDIA Quadro RTX 8000 GPU.

Table 2. Comparison of proposed model with existing models for rotation evaluation: Average in last row represents results based on test datasets over all scenes. Results consist of Mean(°) ± Standard Deviation of error.

	SfMLearner [28]	Monodepth2 [7]	HR-Depth [19]	AJ-Depth [15]	Li et al. [16]	Ours
Scene1	0.652±0.375	0.751±0.362	0.758±0.376	0.742±0.361	0.686±0.321	**0.390±0.262**
Scene2	1.286±1.524	1.412±1.491	1.410±1.487	1.385±1.482	1.389±1.411	**0.888±1.313**
Scene3	0.732±0.342	0.757±0.344	0.773±0.345	0.771±0.346	0.796±0.329	**0.481±0.338**
Scene4	0.522±0.284	0.658±0.274	0.651±0.273	0.638±0.272	0.635±0.257	**0.194±0.282**
Scene5	0.863±0.383	0.986±0.345	0.994±0.354	1.011±0.356	1.020±0.390	**0.570±0.440**
Scene6	0.570±0.512	0.768±0.494	0.766±0.492	0.738±0.498	0.757±0.496	**0.509±0.552**
Scene7	0.691±0.565	0.838±0.556	0.845±0.562	0.846±0.566	0.829±0.527	**0.526±0.467**
Scene8	0.884±0.370	0.984±0.345	0.993±0.346	0.965±0.345	1.008±0.345	**0.580±0.306**
Scene9	0.675±0.417	0.786±0.415	0.778±0.423	0.777±0.430	0.772±0.420	**0.255±0.282**
Total	0.794±0.752	0.919±0.733	0.922±0.733	0.911±0.734	0.918±0.707	**0.531±0.662**

Table 3. Ablation results for contribution of each component in proposed method based on depth estimation.

	Abs Rel	Sq Rel	RMSE	RMSE log	$\delta < 1.25$	$\delta < 1.25^2$	$\delta < 1.25^3$
Ours w/o novel pose	0.063	0.673	6.710	0.087	0.955	0.996	**1.000**
Ours w/o scene coords	0.081	0.966	8.063	0.106	0.933	0.933	0.999
Ours w/o consis term1	0.063	0.663	6.680	0.088	0.953	0.996	**1.000**
Ours w/o consis term2	0.064	0.666	**6.640**	0.088	0.953	0.996	**1.000**
Ours w/o mask	0.063	0.671	6.739	0.087	0.955	0.996	**1.000**
Ours (full)	**0.062**	**0.654**	6.649	**0.086**	**0.956**	**0.997**	1.000

3.3 Comparison Results

We compared the proposed method with the existing methods [7,15,16,19,28] that were retrained on the SCARED datasets [1]. Table 1 showed the quantitative results for the depth estimation in seven metrics used in the baseline [7]. We compared the quantitative results for the estimated depth maps with error maps in Fig. 4. The error maps were calculated by the absolute relative error metric, identical as the first metric in Table 1. For visualization, we equivalently applied color maps to all the error maps. For pose estimation, we test the predicted rotation results on each scene following the rotation matrices [11], as shown in Table 2. We also visualized the point clouds of the estimated depth maps (see supplementary materials).

3.4 Ablation Study

To confirm and analyze the contribution of our various components in the proposed method, we performed an ablation study based on the same seven metrics for depth estimation. For the dual-task consistency loss, we considered the first term in Eq. 6 as consistency term 1 called as consis term1, while the second term in Eq. 6 is consistency term 2 named as consis term2 in Table 3. Also, we replaced the optimized Siamese pose estimation process with the baseline process in the baseline [7], and the result was shown as ours w/o novel pose in Table 3. Since the consistency and mask were based on the scene coordinate prediction, ours w/o scene coords represented that our proposed method was evaluated only with the optimized Siamese pose process.

4   Discussion and Conclusions

Organ surfaces create large smooth regions in the laparoscopic images. In Fig. 4, the proposed method and four others [7,15,16,19] predict smooth depth maps from the laparoscopic images. Although these estimated depth maps look qualitatively similar, the error maps reveal mistakes hidden in the smooth regions. In particular, in the organ surface's marginal zone, where the corresponding depth values start to change, the proposed method has better depth predictions based on the error maps in Fig. 4. Moreover, Table 1 shows that the proposed method outperforms the other methods on seven metrics for depth evaluation. In addition, for pose estimation, many rotations of the laparoscope's motions complicate the predictions of rigid relative poses. Table 2 shows that our proposed method outperforms the other methods on rotation predictions. Moreover, according to the ablation study, the results show that the full proposed method has noticeable improvement when it combines each component. In particular, scene coordinate prediction greatly enhances the proposed method. Its limitations include a relatively sluggish performance for pose estimation on rotations based on the standard deviation of error in Table 2.

In conclusion, we introduce the scene coordinate prediction to the depth-pose monocular self-supervised learning strategy under an optimized Siamese pose estimation process. We also propose dual-task consistency between depth estimation and scene coordinate prediction with a novel weight mask. These contributions provide geometric constraints for depth estimation on laparoscopic images. Our experimental results showed that the proposed method performs better depth estimation and pose estimation on rotation predictions.

Acknowledgments. The authors are grateful for the support from JST CREST Grant Number JPMJCR20D5; MEXT/JSPS KAKENHI Grant Numbers 17H00867, 26108006, and 21K19898; JSPS Bilateral International Collaboration Grants; and CIBoG program of Nagoya University from the MEXT WISE program.

References

1. Allan, M., et al.: Stereo correspondence and reconstruction of endoscopic data challenge. arXiv preprint arXiv:2101.01133 (2021)
2. Bian, J., Li, Z., Wang, N., Zhan, H., Shen, C., Cheng, M.M., Reid, I.: Unsupervised scale-consistent depth and ego-motion learning from monocular video. In: Advances in Neural Information Processing Systems, vol. 32 (2019)

3. Dai, Q., Patil, V., Hecker, S., Dai, D., Van Gool, L., Schindler, K.: Self-supervised object motion and depth estimation from video. In: Proceedings of the IEEE/CVF Conference on Computer Vision and Pattern Recognition (CVPR) Workshops (2020)
4. Furukawa, Y., Curless, B., Seitz, S.M., Szeliski, R.: Towards internet-scale multi-view stereo. In: 2010 IEEE Computer Society Conference on Computer Vision and Pattern Recognition, pp. 1434–1441 (2010)
5. Garg, R., B.G., V.K., Carneiro, G., Reid, I.: Unsupervised CNN for single view depth estimation: geometry to the rescue. In: Leibe, B., Matas, J., Sebe, N., Welling, M. (eds.) ECCV 2016. LNCS, vol. 9912, pp. 740–756. Springer, Cham (2016). https://doi.org/10.1007/978-3-319-46484-8_45
6. Geis, W.P.: Head-mounted video monitor for global visual access in mini-invasive surgery. Surg. Endosc. **10**(7), 768–770 (1996)
7. Godard, C., Mac Aodha, O., Firman, M., Brostow, G.J.: Digging into self-supervised monocular depth estimation. In: 2019 IEEE/CVF International Conference on Computer Vision (ICCV), pp. 3827–3837. IEEE (2019)
8. Guizilini, V., Hou, R., Li, J., Ambrus, R., Gaidon, A.: Semantically-guided representation learning for self-supervised monocular depth. In: International Conference on Learning Representations (2020)
9. He, K., Zhang, X., Ren, S., Sun, J.: Deep residual learning for image recognition. In: Proceedings of the IEEE Conference on Computer Vision and Pattern Recognition, pp. 770–778 (2016)
10. Huang, B., et al.: Self-supervised generative adversarial network for depth estimation in laparoscopic images. In: de Bruijne, M., et al. (eds.) MICCAI 2021. LNCS, vol. 12904, pp. 227–237. Springer, Cham (2021). https://doi.org/10.1007/978-3-030-87202-1_22
11. Huynh, D.Q.: Metrics for 3D rotations: Comparison and analysis. Journal of Mathematical Imaging and Vision **35**(2), 155–164 (2009)
12. Hwang, M., et al.: Applying depth-sensing to automated surgical manipulation with a da Vinci robot. In: 2020 International Symposium on Medical Robotics (ISMR), pp. 22–29. IEEE (2020)
13. Johnston, A., Carneiro, G.: Self-supervised monocular trained depth estimation using self-attention and discrete disparity volume. In: 2020 IEEE/CVF Conference on Computer Vision and Pattern Recognition (CVPR), pp. 4755–4764. IEEE (2020)
14. Kingma, D.P., Ba, J.: Adam: a method for stochastic optimization. arXiv preprint arXiv:1412.6980 (2014)
15. Li, W., Hayashi, Y., Oda, M., Kitasaka, T., Misawa, K., Kensaku, M.: Attention Guided Self-supervised Monocular Depth Estimation Based on Joint Depth-pose Loss for Laparoscopic Images. Computer Assisted Radiology and Surgery (2022)
16. Li, W., Hayashi, Y., Oda, M., Kitasaka, T., Misawa, K., Mori, K.: Spatially variant biases considered self-supervised depth estimation based on laparoscopic videos. Computer Methods in Biomechanics and Biomedical Engineering: Imaging & Visualization, pp. 1–9 (2021)
17. Li, X., Wang, S., Zhao, Y., Verbeek, J., Kannala, J.: Hierarchical scene coordinate classification and regression for visual localization. In: 2020 IEEE/CVF Conference on Computer Vision and Pattern Recognition (CVPR), pp. 11980–11989. IEEE (2020)
18. Li, X., Ylioinas, J., Verbeek, J., Kannala, J.: Scene coordinate regression with angle-based reprojection loss for camera relocalization. In: Proceedings of the European Conference on Computer Vision (ECCV) Workshops, pp. 1–16 (2018)

19. Lyu, X., et al.: Hr-depth: High resolution self-supervised monocular depth estimation. arXiv preprint arXiv:2012.07356 6 (2020)
20. Ming, Y., Meng, X., Fan, C., Yu, H.: Deep learning for monocular depth estimation: a review. Neurocomputing **438**, 14–33 (2021)
21. Paszke, A., et al.: Automatic differentiation in pytorch. In: NIPS 2017 Workshop on Autodiff (2017)
22. Qian, L., Zhang, X., Deguet, A., Kazanzides, P.: ARAMIS: augmented reality assistance for minimally invasive surgery using a head-mounted display. In: Shen, D., Liu, T., Peters, T.M., Staib, L.H., Essert, C., Zhou, S., Yap, P.-T., Khan, A. (eds.) MICCAI 2019. LNCS, vol. 11768, pp. 74–82. Springer, Cham (2019). https://doi.org/10.1007/978-3-030-32254-0_9
23. Russakovsky, O., Deng, J., Su, H., Krause, J., Satheesh, S., Ma, S., Huang, Z., Karpathy, A., Khosla, A., Bernstein, M., et al.: Imagenet large scale visual recognition challenge. Int. J. Comput. Vision **115**(3), 211–252 (2015)
24. Tian, Y., Hu, X.: Monocular depth estimation based on a single image: a literature review. In: Twelfth International Conference on Graphics and Image Processing (ICGIP), vol. 11720, pp. 584–593. International Society for Optics and Photonics, SPIE (2021)
25. Vecchio, R., MacFayden, B., Palazzo, F.: History of laparoscopic surgery. Panminerva Med. **42**(1), 87–90 (2000)
26. Wang, Z., Bovik, A., Sheikh, H., Simoncelli, E.: Image quality assessment: from error visibility to structural similarity. IEEE Trans. Image Process. **13**(4), 600–612 (2004)
27. Zhao, C.Q., Sun, Q.Y., Zhang, C.Z., Tang, Y., Qian, F.: Monocular depth estimation based on deep learning: an overview. Sci. China Technol. Sci. **63**(9), 1612–1627 (2020). https://doi.org/10.1007/s11431-020-1582-8
28. Zhou, T., Brown, M., Snavely, N., Lowe, D.G.: Unsupervised learning of depth and ego-motion from video. In: Proceedings of the IEEE Conference on Computer Vision and Pattern Recognition (CVPR), pp. 1851–1858 (2017)

Recurrent Implicit Neural Graph for Deformable Tracking in Endoscopic Videos

Adam Schmidt[1]([⊠]) [iD], Omid Mohareri[2], Simon DiMaio[2],
and Septimiu E. Salcudean[1]

[1] Department of Electrical and Computer Engineering, The University of British Columbia, Vancouver, BC V6T 1Z4, Canada
adamschmidt@ece.ubc.ca
[2] Advanced Research, Intuitive Surgical, Sunnyvale, CA 94086, USA

Abstract. Tracking points in robotic assisted surgery will help to enable models in augmented reality and image guidance applications. For these applications, both speed and accuracy are critical. Current dense convolutional neural networks can be costly, especially so when we only desire to track user defined regions. Faster methods use keypoints and their movement as a way to estimate flow in an image. In this paper we introduce a recurrent implicit neural graph (RING) which estimates flow efficiently. RING interpolates the flow at any selected query points with a implicit neural representation (also known as coordinate-based representation) that takes the surrounding points and history of the tracked (query) points as input. RING is able to track an arbitrary number of image points. We demonstrate that RING estimates point motion better than methods that do not use a state. We evaluate RING both photometrically and using ground truth depth data. Finally we demonstrate RING's real-time effectiveness in timing experiments.

Keywords: Tissue tracking · Coordinate-based MLP · Graph neural networks

1 Introduction

Real-time tracking of points in endoscopy will enable mapping the environment as it deforms and has many applications in navigation, image guidance, and surgical perception [8,15]. These applications include mapping for colonoscopy [37], augmented reality for surgery [12], heart motion estimation [19], and surgical

This work was supported by Intuitive Surgical.

Supplementary Information The online version contains supplementary material available at https://doi.org/10.1007/978-3-031-16440-8_46.

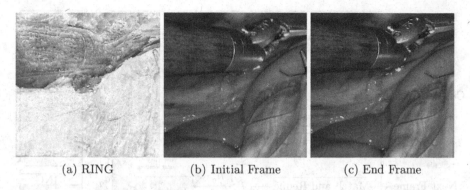

(a) RING   (b) Initial Frame   (c) End Frame

Fig. 1. Optical flow tracked using RING, see supplementary material for more examples. Note how RING separates the instrument motion from background tissue motion.

perception [15]. We are interested in a model that accounts for the transformations in the environment which include instrument and tissue motion. One approach to this involves masking the instruments [9] and using two separate models for the instruments and tissue. Our approach uses a single model that is more general and has the potential to better handle all situations (e.g. instruments behind tissue, and new instruments or devices such as a tissue collection bag). We leave instruments in our training set and we design RING with this in mind.

Current tissue models either deform state over time frame by frame [15,27], use Kalman filtering [7], or CNNs [24]. In order to create a robust map of the environment, we believe each tracked point should hold a state as well. We introduce a model that can track an arbitrary number of points over time. We then test our model both visually on multiple datasets and with ground truth pixel motions from the SCARED dataset [1]. With our Recurrent Implicit Neural Graph (RING), we present a new way to track points using a novel temporal memory for each tracked point without significantly increasing computation cost. In RING, each point's transformation is an implicit neural representation [26] conditioned on its state and neighbors.

2 Related Work

RING involves concepts from works on surgical tracking and mapping, point clouds, deformation estimation, and implicit neural representation.

Surgical Tracking and Mapping: Surgical tracking and mapping looks to reconstruct or map the surgical environment. Works use CNNs to estimate depth [34], and reconstruct rigid scenes [37]. Relevant to optical flow, Shao et al. [24] introduce appearance flow using a CNN for estimating egomotion in rigid endoscopy. For works that track surfaces, many use surgical features [7].

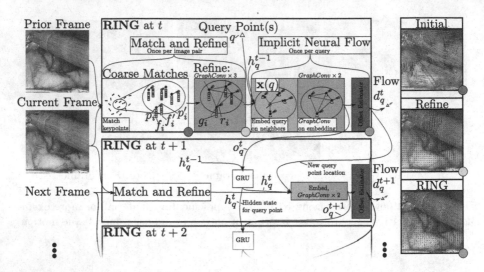

Fig. 2. For each frame, RING takes in an image pair. Sparse keypoints are detected and matched between frames. These matches are fed to a graph neural network $GraphConv$ that refines and outputs new displacements $r_i \in \mathbb{R}^2$, and descriptors $g_i \in \mathbb{R}^c$. For each tracked query point q we create an implicit neural representation dependent on the surrounding keypoints and the history of the query h_q^{t-1}. This state is carried over time using an RNN. Images on the right are the flow estimates evaluated using a grid of query points for each stage (coarse matching, refinement, and RING).

Region tracking then uses these features with underlying models that use rigid transforms [36], embedded deformation [38], or splines [8]. Some look to do both tracking and mapping, and use triangular meshing [20] or mosaicking [38]. RING focuses on making tracking fast and robust without forcing surface constraints.

Point Clouds: These networks operate on point clouds using pooling, introduced in PointNet [17,18]. Other methods transform positions of the cloud and edges dynamically [33], and then pool. We want an estimate that depends on the neighbors. We use attention [30] which has been adapted to graphs [31] (Fig. 2).

Depth, Flow and Deformation: Like our work, depth, flow, and deformation models can use sparse matches for estimation. In order of increasing problem complexity, first we have the problem of depth estimation. Keypoint matches can be passed into a CNN for depth infilling [25]. For dense rigid correspondence, DenseGAP [13] use anchor point matches, and for optical flow RAFT [29] uses all-pairs correspondence on images. To make optical flow correspondence more efficient, Jiang et al. [11] use sparse convolutions on top-k pixel correspondences over whole images, while He et al. [10] create a correspondence vector field from sparse matches. Finally, for 3D motion estimation, embedded deformation graphs are used for non-rigid tracking [3].

Implicit Neural Representations: The concept behind implicit neural representations was introduced concurrently in two separate works [26,28]. Instead of a using a discrete grid, these represent a signal as a function that maps coordinates to values. These are used for modeling point clouds locally [6], signed distance functions [5], and radiance fields [4].

Novelty and Significance: RING extends a recent approach [22] where deformation of a query is determined by correspondence neighbors using an implicit neural representation. RING extends this by adding in temporal history from a RNN as a novel means to condition an implicit neural representation. RING uses sparse correspondences and history in tandem to represent flow over time. Using RING, we can run inference without requiring training to fit an implicit neural representation per scene.

3   Methods

RING consists of three steps, with the first two being based off of prior work [22]. First, we detect and describe the keypoints for each image $(I^t, I^{t+1}, \ldots)$ in a sequence of images. We use ReTRo [23], but our model could use any classical descriptor [14], learned ones with pose supervision [32], or those for surgical images [7]. Then we match keypoints, and refine these matches with a neural network. This refinement step results in a graph of keypoints with new displacements, and features dependent on those nearby (can be thought of as a meta-feature with wider influence). Finally, for each query point we use the nearby matches, position, and a hidden state to act as input to an implicit neural representation that estimates the query's motion. This hidden state acts as a temporal memory that is carried through time with a gated recurrent unit (GRU).

Detection and Description. After detecting, describing, and initial matching between frames I^t, I^{t+1}, we have a set of N correspondence pairs with positions p_i, p_i' and feature descriptors $f_i, f_i', \{i \in 1, 2, \ldots, N\} = \mathcal{V}, f_i \in \mathbb{R}^c$. These points are used to create a graph with edges that are connected based on distance in the image.

Matching and Refinement. This initial match graph is then refined. That means we calculate new features and refined displacement estimates for each match. We could use a RANSAC scheme if we had a rigid environment, but our data is non-rigid. SuperGlue [21] or GMSMatch [2] could possibly be adapted but we do not want to discard possible information, and instead refine points and outliers while also enabling features to become a function of those around them. RING takes the initial match graph as input, using graph attention to calculate new features and move outliers to fit the underlying deformation. This layer outputs a set of features and new displacements $\{g_i \in \mathbb{R}^c, r_i \in \mathbb{R}^2\}_{i \in \mathcal{V}}$.

To get these new features, we first embed the position and feature pair of each correspondence into a graph. For each node:

$$b_i = \phi_2(p_i) + \phi_2(p'_i) + \gamma_a(f_i) + \gamma_b(f'_i) + \phi_1(\|p_i - p'_i\|_2) \tag{1}$$

We use a positional encoding layer, $\phi_{dim} : \mathbb{R}^{dim} \to \mathbb{R}^c$, to encode the positions and distances of each node [28]. γ_* is a linear layer followed by a ReLU, where different subscripts for different instances. Now we have features b_i for each correspondence and can use these in a graph attention network.

Edges $\mathcal{E}$ are chosen that connect each point with its k-neighbors in the initial image. For each frame these are updated as the detected points change.

Our graph attention has a query, $q_{att} \in \mathbb{R}^c$, for each node and a set of values for itself and its neighbors, $\mathbf{v} \in \mathbb{R}^{c \times k}$. These are each multiplied by matrices $\mathbf{W}_q, \mathbf{W}_v \in \mathbb{R}^{c \times c}$. The attention operation returns a vector in $\mathbb{R}^c$ that mixes the values of neighbors together adaptively.

$$\alpha_j = \text{softmax}_j(\mathbf{W}_q q_{att} \cdot \mathbf{W}_v v_j) \in \mathbb{R} \tag{2}$$

$$Attn(q_{att}, \{v_1, v_2, ...v_k\}) = \sum_j \alpha_j v_j \in \mathbb{R}^c \tag{3}$$

For graph refinement, we encode each neighbor's relative position in our graph attention similarly to the work of some others [31], with the difference being that we add in a relative positional embedding to let the network select based on position. This embedding that includes relative position is denoted by $\mathbf{m_i}$, which is a set of k points for each node i:

$$\mathbf{m}_i = \{b_j + \phi_2(p_i - p_j) \,|\, j : (i, j) \in \mathcal{E}\} \tag{4}$$

$$GraphConv(b_i) = \gamma_g(Attn(b_i, \mathbf{m}_i)) + \gamma_f(b_i) \in \mathbb{R}^c \tag{5}$$

We use three *GraphConv* layers to create the output features, g_i, that will be used for neural flow interpolation and refined displacement estimates. We estimate a refined flow for each vertex as $r_i = linear(\gamma_h(g_i))$. We select three layers to provide a reasonable balance between increasing receptive field and computation cost. At this stage for each detected keypoint we have an updated flow estimate along with a feature that will be used for flow interpolation.

Recurrent Neural Interpolation. After we have a graph of refined keypoints, we then want to estimate deformation for each query point, q. We use a implicit neural representation [26,28] to estimate tissue movement at any query position using a graph attention network [31] of the neighbors. This implicit neural representation for each query point only depends on the k refined neighbor points (distant information is gathered by the earlier refinement step), the hidden temporal state $h^{t-1}(q)$ of the query point q, and a small image feature at q. The information at the query point is broadcast to each of these neighbors, run through two graph convolutions and then pooled. We include image information at q by querying a lightweight feature map $\mathbf{L}_q = ConvRELU(ConvRELU(I^t))_q$,

Table 1. Models used. Control estimates 0 movement. Bary: barycentric interpolation. Refinement denotes use of our graph refinement step.

	RING	RINGNornn	BaryRefine	Refine	Bary	Nearest	Control
RNN	✓	✗	✗	✗	✗	✗	✗
Interpolation	Neural	Neural	Bary	Nearest	Bary	Nearest	✗
Refinement	✓	✓	✓	✓	✗	✗	✗

where $ConvReLU$ is a 3×3 convolutional layer followed by a ReLU. This only needs to be calculated at each query point and requires sampling a 5×5 window.

We estimate the flow as the sum of a base offset and the residual estimate from the implicit neural representation function. The base offset is a simple interpolation of the neighbor offsets. By having this base offset, we can aid learning similarly to how a skip connection helps learn the residual in CNNs. The interpolated base offset is the barycentric interpolation on the Delaunay triangulation of the refined neighbor node displacements. Now for the flow function; indexing by $s(q)_j$ means gathering the feature from the jth nearest keypoint neighbor of query q, $\mathcal{N}_{(q)_j}$. We embed the relative position of the query point and its distance onto the graph of its nearest keypoints:

$$s(q)_j = \mathcal{N}_{(q)_j} \in \mathcal{V} \quad (6)$$

$$\mathbf{w}(q) = \left\{\phi_2(p_{s(q)_j}) + \phi_2(r_{s(q)_j}) + g_{s(q)_j} \,|\, j \in [1,k]\right\} \in \mathbb{R}^{k \times c} \quad (7)$$

$$\mathbf{e}(q) = \left\{\phi_1(\|p_{s(q)_j} - q\|_2) + \phi_2(p_{s(q)_j} - q) + \phi_2(q) + \mathbf{L}_q \,|\, j \in [1,k]\right\} \in \mathbb{R}^{k \times c} \quad (8)$$

$$\mathbf{x}(q) = \mathbf{w}(q) + \mathbf{e}(q) \in \mathbb{R}^{k \times c} \quad (9)$$

This is a means to broadcast information from the query onto a graph. Then this graph $\mathbf{x}(q) \in \mathbb{R}^{k \times c}$ is treated as a k-clique for graph convolution:

$$o_q^t = \frac{1}{k}\Sigma_i GraphConv\left(GraphConv\left(\mathbf{x}(q) + h_q^{t-1}\right)\right) \quad (10)$$

$$h_q^t = GRU(o_q^t + h_q^{t-1}) \quad (11)$$

$$d_q^t = linear\left(\gamma_d\left(o_q^t\right)\right) + barycentric^t(q) \in \mathbb{R}^2 \quad (12)$$

We compress the k-clique together with a sum pooling into a single vector $o_q^t \in \mathbb{R}^c$. A GRU maintains state alongside each query point. For a new query, we set the prior hidden state to $h_q^{t-1} = \mathbf{0}$. The output state, $o_q^t \in \mathbb{R}^c$, is passed along with history h_q^{t-1} into the GRU. Flow, d_q^t, is estimated by passing o_q^t through a convolution and a linear layer and adding it to the base offset.

Embedding relative position allows weighting based on direction/relative location, while embedding distance gives the network a direct value to ease calculation. This formulation with attention enables the network to decide how much a correspondence should affect flow of a query. For example, instrument features should not affect tissue feature movement as is demonstrated in Fig. 1.

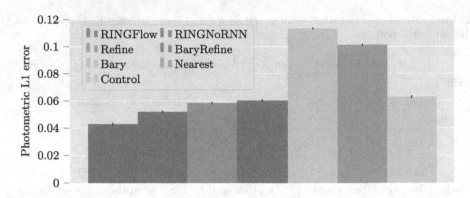

Fig. 3. Photometric error on porcine dataset.

Since our model only needs temporal recurrence for each query point, the overhead for tracking temporally stays low, unlike that of a convolutional LSTM. For training, we mix L_1 and Structural Similarity Index Measure (SSIM) with $\alpha = 0.85$. I_{flow} is the resampled initial image according to the flow:

$$\mathcal{L}_{im} = \alpha\frac{1 - SSIM(I_{flow}^{t-1}, I^t)}{2} + (1 - \alpha)\|I_{flow}^{t-1} - I^t\|_1. \tag{13}$$

4   Experiments

We train RING on a porcine dataset from clinical labs with an Xi surgical system (Porcine). This dataset has 8 rectified stereo videos with a resolution of 1280×1080 for each frame. We use two videos for testing and the other 6 for training resulting in $90,402$ frames available for testing and $275,534$ for training. Videos average 12.5 min in length, with a frame rate 30 Hz. We first train the ReTRo [23] descriptor on the dataset using relative pose supervision. Afterwards, we train RING, using temporal sequences 5 frames long and randomly skipping between $(1, 30)$ frames, with a total lag between start and end frames between $(\frac{1}{6}, 5)$ seconds. Training samples are cropped to 256×256 images, and we densely sample query points to have as much information as possible for each training sample. We set $k = 4$ for both the graph and flow network, and use a channel size of $c = 64$. We use a batch size of 2 and a learning rate of 10^{-4} to train our model. Training takes approximately two days on a 1080 Ti. We test photometrically on the test split of the Porcine dataset and demonstrate its generalization to the SCARED [1], EndoSLAM [16], and Hamlyn [35] datasets. We then test pixel tracking error on the SCARED dataset using ground truth. For evaluation we densely sample query points. We compare different interpolation models shown in Table 1.

SCARED Synchronization. The SCARED dataset has sequences with keyframes and estimated depth estimated using structured light. We use it for

Table 2. Photometric L_1 errors demonstrating generalization to other datasets. Standard error of the mean is in parentheses (compact form).

Dataset	RING	RINGnornn	Refine	BaryRefine	Bary	Nearest	Control
EndoSLAM	**0.056(1)**	0.060(1)	0.0661(9)	0.0675(9)	0.0873(9)	0.0784(8)	0.086(1)
Hamlyn	**0.0487(7)**	0.0648(7)	0.0753(8)	0.0787(8)	0.1636(7)	0.1489(6)	0.082(1)
SCARED	**0.0427(7)**	0.0489(7)	0.0564(7)	0.0575(8)	0.0898(8)	0.0816(6)	0.097(1)

Table 3. Pixel tracking error on 5-length sequences from the SCARED dataset. $\pm$ denotes standard error of mean.

RING	RINGNornn	BaryRefine	Refine
$3.897 \pm 0.002\,\mathrm{px}$	$3.914 \pm 0.002\,\mathrm{px}$	$7.256 \pm 0.006\,\mathrm{px}$	$7.131 \pm 0.006\,\mathrm{px}$

estimating rigid flow. Due to synchronization issues between instrument kinematics and camera [1], we synchronize pose using image features. We detect SIFT keypoints and use the OpenCV Perspective-n-Point algorithm to estimate correspondence between the keyframe and each frame used in our test sequence. Occluded points are discarded with a depth test.

5 Results

We first present our photometric results on the internal porcine dataset. L_1 error is calculated by estimating optical flow for every pixel in the image through a sequence of five frames with random skip factors uniformly sampled from $(1, 30)$. The final pixel location is used to warp the initial frame to the final frame, and the mean absolute difference between these frames is the L_1 error. Due to occlusions, and surfaces being non-diffuse this error will not be zero. Figure 3 shows RING's performance photometrically on the porcine dataset in terms of L_1 error. Relative performance remains the same when testing on other datasets, shown in Table 2. Interestingly, as the porcine dataset has less movement, the control method of zero movement outperforms the noisy and unrefined brute-force methods (barycentric, nearest).

Our pixel errors on the SCARED dataset are shown in Table 3. RING has a mean distance error of 3.987 pixels on the sample set. These results demonstrate RING performs better than other tested interpolation methods on this rigid transformation dataset. See the supplementary material for images of this data.

Timing. We time RING on a 1080 Ti to evaluate its feasibility for real-time applications. Results are in Table 4. Refinement time includes every operation after coarse matching and before a query point is given. Flow querying time includes everything after the refinement step: calculation of $\mathbf{L}$, Delaunay triangulation, the GRU, and the implicit neural flow calculation. We can track 1024 arbitrary points using 256 correspondence keypoints in $0.97 + 5.00 = 5.97$ ms, so our method can be used for real-time tracking.

Table 4. Timings in ms for our model evaluated on images with varying numbers of keypoints and tracked query points.

	Refinement Time			Flow Querying Time		
	Query Points			Query Points		
Keypoints	1024	4096	16384	1024	4096	16384
128	0.82 ± 0.005	0.85 ± 0.009	0.94 ± 0.014	3.26 ± 0.02	7.37 ± 0.06	26.16 ± 0.14
256	0.97 ± 0.017	0.84 ± 0.007	0.90 ± 0.013	5.00 ± 0.09	8.48 ± 0.05	27.41 ± 0.14
512	0.86 ± 0.010	0.84 ± 0.008	0.87 ± 0.012	6.71 ± 0.08	10.93 ± 0.09	31.02 ± 0.17
1024	1.74 ± 0.007	1.68 ± 0.006	1.72 ± 0.005	11.50 ± 0.16	15.88 ± 0.15	36.27 ± 0.12

6   Conclusion

We introduce RING, a recurrent implicit neural graph for tracking arbitrary query points and their state through endoscopic videos. We demonstrate our tracking on image sequences on four different datasets and show its performance generalization capability. Then we report results on pixel tracking errors. Finally we justify RING's viability for real-time applications. Further work will focus on dealing with specularities, extending to 3D and dealing with occlusion.

References

1. Allan, M., et al.: Stereo correspondence and reconstruction of endoscopic data challenge. arXiv:2101.01133 [cs] (2021)
2. Bian, J.-W., et al.: GMS: grid-based motion statistics for fast, ultra-robust feature correspondence. Int. J. Comput. Vis. **128**(6), 1580–1593 (2019). https://doi.org/10.1007/s11263-019-01280-3
3. Božič, A., Palafox, P., Zollhöfer, M., Thies, J., Dai, A., Nießner, M.: Neural deformation graphs for globally-consistent non-rigid reconstruction. In: CVPR (2021)
4. Du, Y., Zhang, Y., Yu, H.X., Tenenbaum, J.B., Wu, J.: Neural radiance flow for 4D view synthesis and video processing. In: ICCV, pp. 14324–14334 (2021)
5. Erler, P., Guerrero, P., Ohrhallinger, S., Mitra, N.J., Wimmer, M.: Points2Surf learning implicit surfaces from point clouds. In: ECCV (2020)
6. Feng, W., Li, J., Cai, H., Luo, X., Zhang, J.: Neural points: point cloud representation with neural fields. arXiv:2112.04148 [cs] (2021)
7. Giannarou, S., Visentini-Scarzanella, M., Yang, G.: Probabilistic tracking of affine-invariant anisotropic regions. IEEE Trans. Patt. Anal. Mach. Intell. **35**(1), 130–143 (2013). https://doi.org/10.1109/TPAMI.2012.81
8. Giannarou, S., Ye, M., Gras, G., Leibrandt, K., Marcus, H.J., Yang, G.-Z.: Vision-based deformation recovery for intraoperative force estimation of tool–tissue interaction for neurosurgery. Int. J. Comput. Assist. Radiol. Surg. **11**(6), 929–936 (2016). https://doi.org/10.1007/s11548-016-1361-z
9. González, C., Bravo-Sánchez, L., Arbelaez, P.: ISINet: An instance-based approach for sdurgical instrument segmentation. In: MICCAI (2020)
10. He, K., Zhao, Y., Liu, Z., Li, D., Ma, X.: Whole-pixel registration of non-rigid images using correspondences interpolation on sparse feature seeds. Vis. Comput. **38**(5), 1815–1832 (2021). https://doi.org/10.1007/s00371-021-02107-4

11. Jiang, S., Lu, Y., Li, H., Hartley, R.: Learning optical flow from a few matches. In: CVPR, pp. 16587–16595. IEEE, Nashville, TN, USA (2021)
12. Kalia, M., Mathur, P., Tsang, K., Black, P., Navab, N., Salcudean, S.: Evaluation of a marker-less, intra-operative, augmented reality guidance system for robot-assisted laparoscopic radical prostatectomy. Int. J. Comput. Assist. Radiol. Surg. **15**(7), 1225–1233 (2020). https://doi.org/10.1007/s11548-020-02181-4
13. Kuang, Z., Li, J., He, M., Wang, T., Zhao, Y.: DenseGAP: graph-structured dense correspondence learning with anchor points. arXiv:2112.06910 [cs] (2021)
14. Lowe, D.G.: Distinctive image features from scale-invariant keypoints. Int. J. Comput. Vis. **60**(2), 91–110 (2004)
15. Lu, J., Jayakumari, A., Richter, F., Li, Y., Yip, M.C.: Super deep: a surgical perception framework for robotic tissue manipulation using deep learning for feature extraction. In: ICRA. IEEE (2021)
16. Ozyoruk, K.B., et al.: EndoSLAM dataset and an unsupervised monocular visual odometry and depth estimation approach for endoscopic videos. Med. Image Anal. **71**, 102058 (2021)
17. Qi, C.R., Su, H., Kaichun, M., Guibas, L.J.: PointNet: deep learning on point sets for 3D classification and segmentation. In: 2017 IEEE Conference on Computer Vision and Pattern Recognition (CVPR), pp. 77–85. IEEE, Honolulu, HI (2017). https://doi.org/10.1109/CVPR.2017.16
18. Qi, C.R., Yi, L., Su, H., Guibas, L.J.: Pointnet++: deep hierarchical feature learning on point sets in a metric space. In: NeurIPS (2017)
19. Richa, R., Bó, A.P., Poignet, P.: Towards robust 3D visual tracking for motion compensation in beating heart surgery. Med. Image Anal. **15**(3), 302–315 (2011)
20. Rodríguez, J.J.G., Lamarca, J., Morlana, J., Tardós, J.D., Montiel, J.M.M.: SD-DefSLAM: semi-direct monocular SLAM for deformable and intracorporeal scenes. arXiv:2010.09409 [cs] (2020)
21. Sarlin, P.E., DeTone, D., Malisiewicz, T., Rabinovich, A.: SuperGlue: learning feature matching with graph neural networks. In: CVPR (2020)
22. Schmidt, A., Mohareri, O., DiMaio, S.P., Salcudean, S.E.: Fast graph refinement and implicit neural representation for tissue tracking. In: ICRA (2022)
23. Schmidt, A., Salcudean, S.E.: Real-time rotated convolutional descriptor for surgical environments. In: MICCAI (2021)
24. Shao, S., et al.: Self-supervised monocular depth and ego-motion estimation in endoscopy: appearance flow to the rescue. arXiv:2112.08122 [cs] (2021)
25. Sinha, A., Murez, Z., Bartolozzi, J., Badrinarayanan, V., Rabinovich, A.: Deltas: depth estimation by learning triangulation and densification of sparse points. In: ECCV (2020)
26. Sitzmann, V., Martel, J.N.P., Bergman, A.W., Lindell, D.B., Wetzstein, G.: Implicit neural representations with periodic activation functions. In: NeurIPS (2020)
27. Song, J., Wang, J., Zhao, L., Huang, S., Dissanayake, G.: MIS-SLAM: real-time large-scale dense deformable SLAM system in minimal invasive surgery based on heterogeneous computing. IEEE Robot. Autom. Lett. **3**(4), 4068–4075 (2018)
28. Tancik, M., et al.: Fourier features let networks learn high frequency functions in low dimensional domains. In: NeurIPS (2020)
29. Teed, Z., Deng, J.: RAFT: recurrent all-pairs field transforms for optical flow. In: Vedaldi, A., Bischof, H., Brox, T., Frahm, J.-M. (eds.) ECCV 2020. LNCS, vol. 12347, pp. 402–419. Springer, Cham (2020). https://doi.org/10.1007/978-3-030-58536-5_24

30. Vaswani, A., et al.: Attention is all you need. In: NeurIPS (2017)
31. Velickovic, P., Cucurull, G., Casanova, A., Romero, A., Lio', P., Bengio, Y.: Graph attention networks. In: ICLR (2018). https://doi.org/10.17863/CAM.48429
32. Wang, Q., Zhou, X., Hariharan, B., Snavely, N.: Learning feature descriptors using camera pose supervision. In: Computer Vision – ECCV 2020 (2020)
33. Wang, Y., Sun, Y., Liu, Z., Sarma, S.E., Bronstein, M.M., Solomon, J.M.: Dynamic graph CNN for learning on point clouds. ACM Trans. Graph. **38**(5), 1–12 (2019)
34. Yang, Z., Simon, R., Li, Y., Linte, C.A.: Dense depth estimation from stereo endoscopy videos using unsupervised optical flow methods. In: Papież, B.W., et al. (eds.) MIUA 2021. LNCS, vol. 12722, pp. 337–349. Springer, Cham (2021). https://doi.org/10.1007/978-3-030-80432-9_26
35. Ye, M., Johns, E., Handa, A., Zhang, L., Pratt, P., Yang, G.Z.: Self-supervised siamese learning on stereo image pairs for depth estimation in robotic surgery. arXiv:1705.08260 [cs] (2017)
36. Yip, M.C., Lowe, D.G., Salcudean, S.E., Rohling, R.N., Nguan, C.Y.: Tissue tracking and registration for image-guided surgery. IEEE Trans. Med. Imaging **31**(11), 2169–2182 (2012)
37. Zhang, Y., et al.: ColDE: a depth estimation framework for colonoscopy reconstruction. arXiv:2111.10371 [cs, eess] (2021)
38. Zhou, H., Jayender, J.: EMDQ-SLAM: real-time high-resolution reconstruction of soft tissue surface from stereo laparoscopy videos. In: de Bruijne, M., et al. (eds.) MICCAI 2021. LNCS, vol. 12904, pp. 331–340. Springer, Cham (2021). https://doi.org/10.1007/978-3-030-87202-1_32

Pose-Based Tremor Classification
for Parkinson's Disease Diagnosis
from Video

Haozheng Zhang[1], Edmond S. L. Ho[2], Francis Xiatian Zhang[1],
and Hubert P. H. Shum[1(✉)]

[1] Durham University, Durham, UK
{haozheng.zhang,xiatian.zhang,hubert.shum}@durham.ac.uk
[2] University of Glasgow, Glasgow, UK
Shu-Lim.Ho@glasgow.ac.uk

Abstract. Parkinson's disease (PD) is a progressive neurodegenerative
disorder that results in a variety of motor dysfunction symptoms, including tremors, bradykinesia, rigidity and postural instability. The diagnosis
of PD mainly relies on clinical experience rather than a definite medical test, and the diagnostic accuracy is only about 73–84% since it is
challenged by the subjective opinions or experiences of different medical
experts. Therefore, an efficient and interpretable automatic PD diagnosis
system is valuable for supporting clinicians with more robust diagnostic
decision-making. To this end, we propose to classify Parkinson's tremor
since it is one of the most predominant symptoms of PD with strong
generalizability. Different from other computer-aided time and resource-
consuming Parkinson's Tremor (PT) classification systems that rely on
wearable sensors, we propose SPAPNet, which only requires consumer-
grade non-intrusive video recording of camera-facing human movements
as input to provide undiagnosed patients with low-cost PT classification
results as a PD warning sign. For the first time, we propose to use a
novel attention module with a lightweight pyramidal channel-squeezing-
fusion architecture to extract relevant PT information and filter the noise
efficiently. This design aids in improving both classification performance
and system interpretability. Experimental results show that our system
outperforms state-of-the-arts by achieving a balanced accuracy of 90.9%
and an F1-score of 90.6% in classifying PT with the non-PT class.

Keywords: Parkinson's diagnosis · Tremor analysis · Graph neural
network · Attention mechanism · Deep learning

1 Introduction

Parkinson's disease (PD) is a progressive neurodegenerative disorder characterized by a variety of life-changing motor dysfunction symptoms, including

The original version of this chapter has been revised. The name of the third author
has been corrected. A correction to this chapter can be found at
https://doi.org/10.1007/978-3-031-16440-8_71

Supplementary Information The online version contains supplementary material
available at https://doi.org/10.1007/978-3-031-16440-8_47.

tremor, bradykinesia (slow of movement), rigidity (limb stiffness), impaired balance and gait [14]. According to pathological studies, the motor deficits of PD are mainly caused by the loss of dopamine due to the degeneration of dopamine neurons in patients [20]. As the second most common neurological disorder, the diagnosis of PD mainly relies on clinical criteria based on the parkinsonian symptoms (e.g., tremor, bradykinesia), medical history, and l-dopa or dopamine response [10,21,30]. However, the clinical diagnostic accuracy of PD is only about 73–84% [25] since the diagnostic performance is challenged by the subjective opinions or experiences of different medical experts [19]. Therefore, an efficient and interpretable automatic PD diagnosis system is valuable for supporting clinicians with more robust diagnostic decision-making.

Recent machine learning and deep learning-based methods achieved impressive performance in PD diagnosis by analyzing the neuroimaging, cerebrospinal fluid, speech signals, gait pattern [1], and hand tremors. Although neuroimagings [33] or cerebrospinal fluid [29] based models perform well, they face a problem of high cost and intrusive. As for the non-intrusive methods, current speech-based models [7] are limited by their generalizability, as the language and pronunciation habits of people in different regions and countries vary significantly. Several studies [11,24] indicate that gait disturbance is less likely to be the main symptom in patients with early-onset PD, but more than 70% of those patients present at least one type of tremors [3,22,24]. Hence we believe that detecting PD by diagnosing Parkinson's Tremor (PT) is a more generalizable approach compared with other methods. Conventional hand tremors-based studies [12] achieve promising performance by using a deep learning network on wearable sensors data to detect PD. However, using wearable sensors is still time and resource-consuming [12], and requires careful synchronization of data captured from different sensors.

For the first time, we propose a graph neural network for diagnosing PD by PT classification as it effectively learns the spatial relationship between body joints from graph-structured data. Inspired by the information gain analysis [8] and the clinician observation [9] that PT usually occurs only on one side of the early stage PD patient's upper body, we propose a novel attention module with a lightweight pyramidal channel-squeezing-fusion architecture to capture the self, short and long-range joint information specific to PT and filter noise. This design aids in improving both classification performance and system interpretability. Our system only requires consumer-grade non-intrusive video recordings and outperforms state-of-the-arts by achieving a balanced accuracy of 90.9% and an F1-score of 90.6% in classifying PT with non-PT class. Our work demonstrates the effectiveness and efficiency of computer-assisted technologies in supporting the diagnosis of PD non-intrusively, and provides a PT classification warning sign for supporting the diagnosis of PD in the resource-limited regions where the clinical resources are not abundant. Our source code is available at: https://github.com/mattz10966/SPAPNet.

2   Method

As shown in Fig. 1, the input consists of video recordings of each participant sitting in a chair in a normal upright position with various poses (e.g., tapping with the contralateral hand in the rhythm). We extract the human joint position features from the RGB video by OpenPose algorithm [4]. These human joint position features are passed to the Spatial Pyramidal Attention Parkinson's tremor classification Network (SPAPNet) for diagnosis.

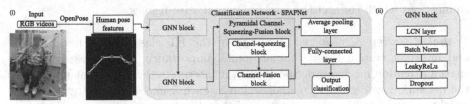

Fig. 1. (i) The overview of our proposed framework. (ii) The design of each GNN block.

2.1   Pose Extraction

We first extract 2D skeleton features from the video sequences. Each frame is fed to OpenPose [4] due to its robust and efficient performance in detecting the 2D joint landmarks for people in normal upright positions. We do not estimate the 3D human pose as in [16], since the state-of-the-art 3D pose estimation methods still introduce noise while processing the 2D information to 3D [5, 18,27], which is not suitable for sensitive features like the tremor. We extract 18 OpenPose-skeleton format [4] landmarks with 2D coordinate (x, y) and a confidence score c indicating the estimation reliability by the OpenPose, but only use the seven upper body landmarks (seen in Fig. 3) for PT classification, because PT usually tends to occur on the upper body, especially the hands and arms [26]. This approach eliminates less relevant features to help reduce model bias and improve efficiency. In addition, we do not include the head joint considering the participant's privacy, since the face is generally occluded in the medical video. We implement normalization to reduce the bias from the underlying differences between the videos to tackle overfitting risk. To remove the participants' global translation, we center the participant's pose per frame by aligning the center of the triangle of the neck and two hip joints as the global origin. Then, we represent all joints as a relative value to the global origin.

2.2   Classification Network

We propose a *Spatial Pyramidal Attention Parkinson's tremor classification Network (SPAPNet)* for PT diagnosis. The proposed SPAPNet consists of a graph neural network with the spatial attention mechanism and a novel pyramidal channel-squeezing-fusion block to enhance the attention mechanism.

Graph Neural Network with Spatial Attention Mechanism:

Graph Neural Network (GNN): We propose to use the graph neural network to diagnose PD by classifying PT, since it effectively learns the spatial relationship between human joints from graph-structured data (e.g., human poses). To this end, we follow [31] to apply a pose graph $G = (V, E)$ aligned with the human skeletal graph to structure human pose data in the graph domain. In this graph, $\{V = v_{pq}\}$ denotes the joints positions, where v_{pq} represents the p-th joint at q-th frame. The edge set E includes: (1) the intra-skeleton connection each frame designed by the natural connections of human joints. (2) the inter-frame connections which connect the joints in consecutive frames.

Spatial Attention Mechanism: To improve the PT classification performance and interpret system the by human joints' importance, we propose using the spatial attention mechanism. Specifically, it interprets the important joints that the network considers in PT classification at each frame and video by attention weights and the temporal aggregation of the attention weights, respectively.

We adopt the locally connected network (LCN) [6] to learn joint i's attention weight from its relationship between other joints. This method overcomes the representation power limitation that different joints share the same weight set in the vanilla graph convolutional network (GCN) [13]. In addition, it enables the system to learn joint i's attention from its relationship between other joints. The basic formulation is as follows:

$$\mathbf{h_i} = \sigma \left(\sum_{j \in \mathcal{N}^i} \mathbf{W}_j^i \mathbf{x}_j \hat{a}_{ij} \right) \tag{1}$$

where $\mathbf{W}_j^i$ is the learnable attention weight between the target joint i and the related joint j, $\hat{a}_{ij}$ is the corresponding element in the adjacency matrix, $\mathbf{x}_j$ is the input features of node j, $\mathcal{N}^i$ is the set of connected nodes for node i, σ is an activation function, and $\mathbf{h}_i$ is the updated features of node i.

Pyramidal Channel-Squeezing-Fusion Block (PCSF): As an extension of the spatial attention module, we propose a novel lightweight inverted pyramid architecture consisting of a *channel-squeezing block* and a *channel-fusion block* to extract relevant PT information and filter noise. This is motivated by two findings: (i) Information Gain analysis [8] shows that the information gain decreases exponentially with increasing distance between graph nodes; (ii) clinical observation [9] shows that PT usually occurs only on one side of the PD patient's upper body, such that the information relevancy between two arms should be reduced. Our proposed design does not require learnable parameters, such that it prevents overfitting problems. As illustrated in Fig. 2, we introduce the proposed PCSF by comparing it with the vanilla weight-sharing strategy in GCN [13]. In PCSF, the final attention weight for joint-1 is learned from the information between the target joint 1 and the relevant joints 2,3,...,7 after a series of channel squeezing and fusion operations. Conversely, the vanilla weight-sharing mechanism can not learn from the joint-wise relevancy since all joints share the same set of weights.

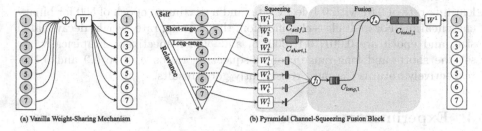

(a) Vanilla Weight-Sharing Mechanism   (b) Pyramidal Channel-Squeezing Fusion Block

Fig. 2. The architectures of (a) Vanilla weight-sharing mechanism in GCN [13], (b) proposed Pyramidal Channel-Squeezing-Fusion (PCSF) mechanism. Both architectures are taking the joint node 1, the right wrist as an example. Other nodes refer to Fig. 3.

The Channel-Squeezing Block: To capture the relevant information specific to PT and filter noise, we hypothesize that (i) the short-range joints (i.e., on the same side of the body) contain slightly less relevant information compared with the target joint itself based on the information gain analysis; (ii) the long-range nodes (i.e., not on the same side of the body) contains much less information relevant to PT classification based on the clinician observation [2,9]. Hence, we propose the following channel-squeezing operation to reach the above hypothesis:

Suppose node m to be the target node, node k to be the relevant node of m, such that the shortest path between two nodes in the graph domain is $k - a$. We propose Eq. 2 to determine the output channel size of the relevant node k:

$$C_{out,k} = b \times C_{in}, \quad |k - m| \leq 2 \quad and \quad C_{out,k} = d^{|k-m|}C_{in}, \quad |k - m| > 2 \quad (2)$$

where b, d are the channel-squeezing ratios for short-range and long-range node, respectively. $b, d \in [0, 1]$ and $b \gg d$. $C_{out,k}$ is the output channel size of node k. $|\cdot|$ is the distance between node m and k in the graph domain.

The Channel-Fusion Block: To fuse the relevancy information of the target joint m from different ranges, we propose a two-stage fusion process to first fuse long-range features from less-related joints by f_l, then fuse all features by f_a:

$$\mathbf{h_m} = f_a[\mathbf{h_{slef}}, \mathbf{h_{short}}, f_l(\mathbf{h_{long,p}})]\mathbf{W^m} \quad (3)$$

where $\mathbf{h_{long,p}}$ is features of long-range related node p, $\mathbf{h_{short}}$ and $\mathbf{h_{slef}}$ are features of short-range related nodes and self-range node, respectively. $\mathbf{W^a}$ is the final weight of node m.

Implementation Details: As shown in Fig. 1, we use two GNN blocks (64, 128 output channel size respectively) with each consisting of an LCN layer, a batch normalization layer, an LeakyReLU layer (0.2 alpha), and a dropout layer (0.2 rates). After two GNN blocks, we apply a PCSF block, a global average pooling layer and a fully connected layer. We use the focal-loss [15] as the loss function for overcoming class imbalance in multiclass classification task. The optimizer is chosen as Adam, and we train the model with a batch size of 16, a learning rate of 0.01 with 0.1 decay rate, and a maximum epoch of 500 for binary classification; For multiclass classification, the learning rate, weight decay, batch size, and epoch are 0.001, 0.1, 500, 8, and 500, respectively. Empirically, we set the short- and long-range channel-squeezing ratios b, d to 0.9 and 0.125, respectively, returns the most consistently good results.

3 Experiments

Our experiments were run on a PC with Ubuntu 18.04 and an NVIDIA GeForce RTX 3080. Our system is low-cost as it only requires an average GPU memory usage of 1.48 gigabytes for training. The total model training time on the TIM-TREMOR dataset is about ten hours, including human pose features extractions from RGB videos. It only takes about 48s for the PT classification of 1000 frames 30FPS video recording($\sim$33s), which can be employed in interactive-time diagnosis.

The Dataset: We verify our model on a publicly available TIM-TREMOR (Technology in Motion Tremor Dataset) dataset [23]. The dataset consists of 917 video recordings from 55 participants sitting in a chair and performing a set of 21 tasks, and videos range from 18 s to 112 s. There are 579 videos that present different types of tremors, including 105 PT, 182 Essential Tremor (ET), 88 Functional Tremor (FT), and 204 Dystonic Tremor (DT) videos. Another 60 videos have no tremor during the assessment. The remaining 278 videos with ambiguous diagnosis results are labeled as "Other".

Setup: We first eliminated inconsistent videos to avoid label noise, that is, (i) videos with motion tasks recorded only on a minor subset of participants; (ii) videos with ambiguous diagnosis label -"other". Then, we clip each video into samples of 100 frames each, with the number of clips depending on the length of the successive video frames where the participant is not occluded by the interaction with the clinician. Each clip inherits the label of the source video and is considered an individual sample. A voting system [16,17] is employed to obtain the video-level classification results. This clipping-and-voting mechanism increases the robustness of the system and augments the sample size for training. We employ a 5-fold cross-validation to evaluate our proposed system.

To evaluate the generalizability of the proposed method, we validate our system not only on the binary classification (i.e., classify PT label with non-PT labels), but also on a more challenging multiclass classification task that classifies samples with five tremor labels (PT, ET, FT, DT, and No tremor). We report the mean and standard deviation among all cross-validation for the following metrics: the metrics for the binary classification includes the accuracy (AC), sensitivity (SE), specificity (SP), and F1-Score; the metrics for the multiclass classification are AC and per-class and macro average F1-score, SE and SP.

Table 1. The comparisons on the binary classification (PT v.s. non-PT) task and the summarized multiclass classification (PT v.s. ET v.s DT v.s FT v.s non-tremor) results.

Method		Binary classification			
		AC	SE	SP	F1
CNN-LSTM [28]		81.0	n/a	79.0	80.0
LSTM [28]		80.0	n/a	79.0	79.0
SVM-1 [28]		53.0	n/a	63.0	55.0
ST-GCN [31]		87.7 ± 3.8	88.3 ± 5.3	87.4 ± 3.1	87.0 ± 4.4
CNN-Conv1D		81.6 ± 5.7	83.4 ± 9.1	80.7 ± 4.4	80.3 ± 6.0
Decision Tree		74.5 ± 4.7	73.4 ± 5.7	75.8 ± 4.0	73.6 ± 4.6
SVM		64.3 ± 5.4	62.2 ± 7.5	66.7 ± 4.6	63.1 ± 7.1
Ours	SPAPNet - full	**90.9 ± 3.4**	**90.7 ± 5.0**	**91.3 ± 2.3**	**90.6 ± 3.7**
	w/o PCSF	88.4 ± 4.5	90.4 ± 6.9	87.0 ± 3.7	87.5 ± 5.2
	w/o Attention	82.6 ± 5.3	82.7 ± 6.0	82.8 ± 5.1	81.3 ± 6.8
		Multiclass classification			
ST-GCN [31]		70.3 ± 6.9	69.5 ± 6.4	90.7 ± 5.4	67.9 ± 6.7
CNN-Conv1D		63.1 ± 6.5	59.5 ± 5.6	90.8 ± 7.4	61.9 ± 8.3
Decision tree		54.3 ± 5.7	49.0 ± 7.3	92.3 ± 5.4	55.5 ± 6.5
SVM		47.6 ± 6.4	45.7 ± 6.9	91.6 ± 6.1	52.1 ± 7.2
Ours	SPAPNet - full	**73.3 ± 6.8**	**72.8 ± 5.1**	**92.3 ± 4.1**	**70.7 ± 6.5**
	w/o PCSF	69.1 ± 6.9	69.9 ± 4.0	88.2 ± 4.6	65.7 ± 7.1
	w/o Attention	65.9 ± 6.8	64.2 ± 5.5	90.4 ± 7.9	65.0 ± 7.9

Comparison with Other Methods: To evaluate the effectiveness of our system, we compare our results with the following state-of-the-art video-based PT classification methods: (i) CNN-LSTM [28]: This method uses a CNN-LSTM model to classify the PT and non-PT classes from hand landmarks extracted by MediaPipe [32], their data is videos from the TIM-TREMOR dataset; (ii) SVM-1 [28]: This is a support vector machine model proposed to classify the PT and non-PT classes by the same features in [28]; (iii) LSTM [28]: This is an LSTM deep neural network proposed to classify the PT and non-PT classes by the same features in [28]; (iv) ST-GCN [31]: This is a spatial and temporal graph convolutional neural network for classification tasks on human pose data. For works in [28], we only report the performance in their work since the source code is not publicly available. To compare the effectiveness of our system with conventional methods, we implement a CNN with 1D convolutional layers (CNN-Conv1D) [28] and two machine learning-based methods, namely Decision Tree (DT) and SVM.

From the binary classification result in Table 1, our full system outperforms state-out-of-the-arts [28,31] and other implemented methods. Our AC, SE, SP, and F1 achieves over 90% with standard deviations less than 5%, which indicates the effectiveness and robustness in classifying PT class with non-PT class. Our system achieves better performance by only applying spatial convolution instead of a more deep architecture like spatial-temporal convolution modeling method, ST-GCN [31]. The result validates that our proposed PCSF block effectively improves classification performance and mitigates the overfitting risk in small datasets. Moreover, although our system is designed for binary classification purposes, the full system also shows effectiveness and generalizability by outperforming others in the multiclass classification task. The high macro-average SP showed relatively reliable performance in identifying people without corresponding tremor labels. Improving the multiclass classification AC and SE is scheduled in our future work.

Ablation Studies: We perform an ablation to evaluate whether there is any adverse effect caused by the proposed PCSF block or the whole attention module. From the rows of "Ours" in Table 1, we observe the effectiveness of the PCSF block and attention module from the performance reduction across all metrics when eliminating the PCSF or the whole attention module for both classification tasks. In addition, we observe the stability of using the full system as it has smaller standard deviations than its variants. Besides, we can observe that the vanilla GNN (i.e., SPAPNet w/o Attention) presents better performance than CNN-Con2D in both classification tasks. It demonstrates the effectiveness of learning human pose features in the graph domain. Moreover, the results show the advantage of deep learning networks by comparing them with two machine learning-based methods, which are decision tree and SVM.

Qualitative Analysis: Figure 3a visualizes the interpretability of our system by presenting the mean attention weights of each skeleton joint among all cross-validation. We notice that the mean attention weights of 'Right Wrist' and 'Left Wrist' are significantly higher than others on both classification tasks. It indicates our system pays more attention to the movements of participants' wrists. In addition, the attention weight of 'Neck' is lower than others significantly. One possible reason is that the participants are sitting on the chair, and their neck joint has the smallest global variance during the whole video.

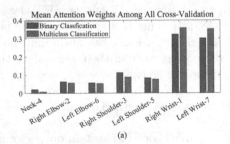 

Fig. 3. (a) The mean attention weights of different joints among all cross-validation for both classification tasks; (b) the visualization of the attention weights at a single example frame. The joint index numbers in (b) corresponds to (a); (b$_1$) One frame in a successful diagnosis; (b$_2$) One frame in a false diagnosis.

We also analyze the situation in which our method fails or succeeds. Figure 3 b$_1$ is a frame in a successful diagnosed example of a PT patient. Consistent with the clinician PT diagnosis based on right hand resting tremor, the right wrist node contributes the most attention. Figure 3 b_2 is a frame in misdiagnosis, and the attention is incorrectly dominated by the mis-detected joint position of the right elbow from the pose extraction algorithm. Therefore, it highlights the importance of improving pose extraction performance for future work.

4   Conclusion

In this work, we propose a novel interpretable method SPAPNet to diagnose Parkinson's from the consumer-grade RGB video recordings. Our system outperforms state-of-the-arts by achieving an accuracy of 90.9% and an F1-score of 90.6%. The proposed attention module aids in improving both classification performance and system interpretability. Our proposed novel lightweight pyramidal channel-squeezing-fusion block effectively learns the self, short and long-range relevant information specific to Parkinson's tremor and filters irrelevant noise. Our system shows the potential to support non-intrusive PD diagnosis from human pose videos. Since our system only requires the consumer-grade human pose videos as input, it provides a way for diagnosis of PD in the resource-limited regions where the clinical experts are not abundant. In addition, our system shows potential for remote diagnosis of PD in special situations (e.g., COVID-19 epidemic) and automatic monitoring of PT symptoms during daily life for PD diagnosis.

References

1. Alle, S., Priyakumar, U.D.: Linear prediction residual for efficient diagnosis of Parkinson's disease from gait. In: de Bruijne, M., et al. (eds.) MICCAI 2021. LNCS, vol. 12905, pp. 614–623. Springer, Cham (2021). https://doi.org/10.1007/978-3-030-87240-3_59
2. Bhat, S., Acharya, U.R., Hagiwara, Y., Dadmehr, N., Adeli, H.: Parkinson's disease: cause factors, measurable indicators, and early diagnosis. In: Computers in Biology and Medicine, vol. 102, pp. 234–241. (2018)
3. Beitz, J. M.: Parkinson's disease: a review. Front. Biosci. (Schol. Ed.). **6**, 65–74. (2014)
4. Cao, Z., Hidalgo, G., Simon, T., Wei, S.-E., Sheikh, Y.: OpenPose: realtime multi-person 2D pose estimation using part affinity fields. arXiv e-prints, arXiv:1812.08008 (2018)
5. Chen, C., Ramanan, D.: 3D human pose estimation = 2D pose estimation + matching. In: the IEEE Conference on Computer Vision and Pattern Recognition (CVPR), pp. 7035–7043 (2017)
6. Ci, H., Ma, X., Wang C., Wang, Y.: Locally connected network for monocular 3D human pose estimation. In: IEEE Trans. Pattern Anal. Mach. Intell. **44**(3), 1429–1442 (2022)
7. Vásquez-Correa, J.C., Arias-Vergara, T., Orozco-Arroyave, J.R., Eskofier, B., Klucken, J., Nöth, E.: Multimodal assessment of Parkinson's disease: a deep learning approach. IEEE J. Biomed. Health Inform. **23**(4), 1618–1630 (2019)

8. Li, S., Gao, Z., Lin, H.: LookHOPs: light multi-order convolution and pooling for graph classification. arXiv preprint arXiv:2012.15741 (2020)
9. Fahn, S.: Description of Parkinson's disease as a clinical syndrome. Ann. N. Y. Acad. Sci. **991**, 1–14 (2003)
10. Gibb, W.R., Lees, A.J.: The relevance of the Lewy body to the pathogenesis of idiopathic Parkinson's disease. In: J. Neurol. Neurosurg. Psychiatry **51**, 745–52 (1988)
11. Hausdorff J.M.: Gait dynamics in Parkinson's disease: common and distinct behavior among stride length, gait variability, and fractal-like scaling. Chaos (Woodbury, N.Y.) **19**(2), 026113 (2009)
12. Hssayeni, M.D., Jimenez-Shahed, J., Burack, M.A., Ghoraani, B.: Wearable sensors for estimation of Parkinsonian tremor severity during free body movements. Sensors (Basel, Switzerland) **19**(19), 4215 (2019)
13. Kipf, N., Welling, M.: Semi-supervised classification with graph convolutional networks. In: ICLR (2017)
14. Patel, S., Lorincz, K., Hughes, R., et al.: Monitoring motor fluctuations in patients with Parkinson's disease using wearable sensors. IEEE Trans. Inf. Technol. Biomed. **13**(6), 864–873 (2009)
15. Lin, T.Y., Goyal, P., Girshick, R., He, K., Dollár, P.: Focal loss for dense object detection. In: CVPR, pp. 2980–2988 (2017)
16. Lu, M., et al.: Vision-based estimation of MDS-UPDRS gait scores for assessing Parkinson's disease motor severity. In: Martel, A.L., et al. (eds.) MICCAI 2020. LNCS, vol. 12263, pp. 637–647. Springer, Cham (2020). https://doi.org/10.1007/978-3-030-59716-0_61
17. Lu, M., Zhao, Q., Poston, K., Sullivan, L.,et al.: Quantifying Parkinson's disease motor severity under uncertainty using MDS-UPDRS videos. Med. Image Anal. **73** (2021)
18. Luvizon, D.C., Picard, D., Tabia, H.: 2D/3D pose estimation and action recognition using multitask deep learning. In: the IEEE Conference on Computer Vision and Pattern Recognition (CVPR), pp. 5137–5146 (2018)
19. Massano, J., Bhatia, K.P.: Clinical approach to Parkinson's disease: features, diagnosis, and principles of management. Cold Spring Harbor Perspect. Med. **2**(6), a008870 (2012)
20. Mhyre, T.R., Boyd, J.T., Hamill, R.W., Maguire-Zeiss, K.A.: Parkinson's disease. Subcell. Biochem. **65**, 389–455 (2012)
21. Mostafa, S.A., et al.: Examining multiple feature evaluation and classification methods for improving the diagnosis of Parkinson's disease, In: Cognitive Systems Research, vol. 54, pp. 90–99 (2019)
22. Pasquini, J., et al.: Progression of tremor in early stages of Parkinson's disease: a clinical and neuroimaging study. Brain **141**(3), 811–821 (2018)
23. Pintea, S.L., Zheng, J., Li, X., Bank, P., van Hilten, J.J., van Gemert, J.C.: Hand-tremor frequency estimation in videos. In: ECCV Workshops, vol. 11134, no. 6, pp. 213–228 (2018)
24. Rizek, P., Kumar, N., Jog, M.S.: An update on the diagnosis and treatment of Parkinson disease. CMAJ: Can. Med. Assoc. J. **188**(16), 1157–1165 (2016)
25. Rizzo, G., Copetti, M., Arcuti, S., Martino, D., Fontana, A., Logroscino, G.: Accuracy of clinical diagnosis of Parkinson disease: a systematic review and meta-analysis. Neurology **9**; **86**(6), 566–576 (2016)
26. Sveinbjornsdottir, S.: The clinical symptoms of Parkinson's disease. In: J. Neurochem. **139**, 318–324 (2016)

27. Wang, J., Yan, S., Xiong, Y., Lin, D.: Motion guided 3D pose estimation from videos. In: Vedaldi, A., Bischof, H., Brox, T., Frahm, J.-M. (eds.) ECCV 2020. LNCS, vol. 12358, pp. 764–780. Springer, Cham (2020). https://doi.org/10.1007/978-3-030-58601-0_45

28. Wang, X., Garg, S., Tran, S.N., Bai, Q., Alty, J.: Hand tremor detection in videos with cluttered background using neural network based approaches. Health Inf. Sci. Syst. **9**(1), 1–14 (2021). https://doi.org/10.1007/s13755-021-00159-3

29. Wang, W., Lee, J., Harrou, F., Sun, Y.: Early detection of Parkinson's disease using deep learning and machine learning. IEEE Access **8**, 147635–147646 (2020)

30. Wirdefeldt, K., Adami, H.O., Cole, P., Trichopoulos, D., Mandel, J.: Epidemiology and etiology of Parkinson's disease: a review of the evidence. Eur. J. Epidemiol. **26**(Suppl 1), S1–58 (2011)

31. Yan, S., Xiong, Y., Lin, D.: Spatial temporal graph convolutional networks for skeleton-based action recognition. In: AAAI Conference on Artificial Intelligence (2018)

32. Zhang, F., et al.: MediaPipe hands: on-device real-time hand tracking. arXiv preprint arXiv:2006.10214 (2020)

33. Zhang, L., Wang, M., Liu, M., Zhang, D.: A survey on deep learning for neuroimaging-based brain disorder analysis. Front. Neurosci. **14** (2020)

Image Segmentation I

Neural Annotation Refinement: Development of a New 3D Dataset for Adrenal Gland Analysis

Jiancheng Yang[1,2], Rui Shi[1], Udaranga Wickramasinghe[2], Qikui Zhu[3,4],
Bingbing Ni[1(✉)], and Pascal Fua[2]

[1] Shanghai Jiao Tong University, Shanghai, China
nibingbing@sjtu.edu.cn
[2] EPFL, Lausanne, Switzerland
[3] Department of Computer and Data Science, Case Western Reserve University,
Cleveland, OH, USA
[4] Department of Biomedical Engineering, Case Western Reserve University,
Cleveland, OH, USA

Abstract. The human annotations are imperfect, especially when produced by junior practitioners. Multi-expert consensus is usually regarded as golden standard, while this annotation protocol is too expensive to implement in many real-world projects. In this study, we propose a method to refine human annotation, named *Neural Annotation Refinement (NeAR)*. It is based on a learnable implicit function, which decodes a latent vector into represented shape. By integrating the appearance as an input of implicit functions, the appearance-aware NeAR fixes the annotation artefacts. Our method is demonstrated on the application of adrenal gland analysis. We first show that the NeAR can repair distorted golden standards on a public adrenal gland segmentation dataset. Besides, we develop a new Adrenal gLand ANalysis (ALAN) dataset with the proposed NeAR, where each case consists of a 3D shape of adrenal gland and its diagnosis label (normal vs. abnormal) assigned by experts. We show that models trained on the shapes repaired by the NeAR can diagnose adrenal glands better than the original ones. The ALAN dataset will be open-source, with 1,594 shapes for adrenal gland diagnosis, which serves as a new benchmark for medical shape analysis. Code and dataset are available at https://github.com/M3DV/NeAR.

Keywords: Neural annotation refinement · Adrenal gland · ALAN dataset · Geometric deep learning · Shape analysis

---

J. Yang and R. Shi—These authors have contributed equally.

Supplementary Information The online version contains supplementary material available at https://doi.org/10.1007/978-3-031-16440-8_48.

1 Introduction

Deep learning has enjoyed a great success in medical image analysis, but large annotated datasets are required to achieve this [1,5–7,12]. Unfortunately, such datasets are difficult to obtain in part because human annotations are known to be imperfect [11,24]. In medical image segmentation, multi-expert consensus is employed as golden standard, where the agreement of multiple annotators is regarded as ground truth. Nevertheless, this protocol involving multiple medical experts is often too time-consuming and expensive to achieve in practice. In those cases, there are often high-frequency artefacts and false positive/negative in human segmentation. Please refer to Fig. 1 (a) for illustration.

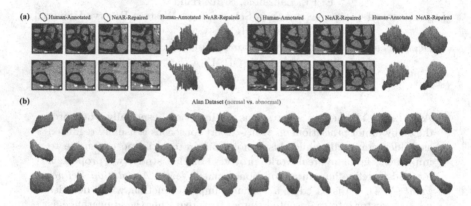

Fig. 1. The ALAN dataset. It features 1,594 adrenal glands, each one of which has been tagged by human experts as normal or abnormal. The normal ones are shown in green and the abnormal in red. Best viewed on screen. **(a)** Images with human and NeAR-repaired annotations, in red and blue contours respectively, and the corresponding 3D visualization. **(b)** The repaired ALAN Dataset. (Color figure online)

In this paper, we introduce *Neural Annotation Refinement (NeAR)*, an approach to automatically correcting human-annotated segmentation databases, so that networks trained using the corrected database perform better than those trained using the original one. Our method is developed based on the fact that a neural network with appropriate inductive bias could serve as a deep prior [8,25]. By leveraging the recent advance in implicit surface modeling [2,16,20] that uses a neural network (*e.g.*, MLP and CNN [22]) as a mapping from spatial coordinates to a shape representation, the NeAR learns data-efficient implicit functions as a shape prior of the target annotations, which can be used to repair human annotations. To make the repaired segmentation appearance-aware, we integrate the appearance as an input of the implicit function. As illustrated in Fig. 1 (a), the repaired segmentation by the proposed NeAR is visually appealing. We will further show that the repairing can be used to improve downstream applications.

Our method is demonstrated on the application of adrenal gland analysis. We first show that the NeAR can repair distorted golden standards on a public

adrenal gland segmentation dataset, consisting of 100 cases. The NeAR outperforms standard segmentation methods quantitatively in terms of the repaired
annotation quality. Furthermore, we apply the NeAR to repair a new Adrenal
gLand ANalysis (ALAN) dataset of 1,584 cases, where each adrenal gland is segmented by 1 clinician and diagnosed—as normal or abnormal—by 2 clinicians
and 1 senior endocrinologist. In other words, the diagnosis label is quite reliable
whereas the segmentation exhibits problems as shown in Fig. 1 (a). As shown
in Fig. 1 (b), NeAR can effectively repair these segmentations, as evidenced by
the fact that models trained on the shapes repaired by the NeAR can better
diagnose adrenal glands (normal vs. abnormal) than the original ones.

As an independent contribution, the ALAN dataset will be open-source, with
NeAR-repaired shapes of adrenal glands and the corresponding diagnosis labels
(normal vs. abnormal), as illustrated in Fig. 1 (b). This shape classification
benchmark with 1,594 high-quality 3D models will be of interest for medical
image analysis and geometric deep learning research community.[1]

2   Method

In this section, we first briefly review deep implicit surface, an emerging technique in 3D vision. We then introduce how this technique can be applied to
repair human annotated segmentation labels, and propose the Neural Annotation Refinement (NeAR) based on appearance-aware implicit surface model.

2.1   Deep Implicit Surfaces

Implicit surface modeling [2,16,20] maps spatial coordinates to shape representations with a neural network. Typically, the shape representation could be either
binary occupancy or signed/unsigned distance. For simplicity, we use occupancy
fields [16] in this study, while the whole framework can be easily applied on
distance functions [20]. In implicit surface modeling, a 3D shape is first encoded
with a c-dimensional latent vector $\mathbf{z} \in \mathbb{R}^c$, and a continuous representation of
the shape is then obtained by learning a mapping:

$$\mathcal{F}(\mathbf{z}, \mathbf{p}) = o : \mathbb{R}^c \times \mathbb{R}^3 \rightarrow [0, 1]. \tag{1}$$

Here, a c-dimensional latent vector $\mathbf{z} \in \mathbb{R}^c$ and coordinates of a query point
$\mathbf{p} \in \mathbb{R}^3$ are inputted into a neural network $\mathcal{F}$–typically multi-layer perceptron
(MLP)–to classify whether the query point is inside or outside the represented
shape, with the occupancy probability o close to 1 for $\mathbf{p}$ inside the shape and 0
otherwise. With a thresholding parameter t, the underlying surface is implicitly
represented by the decision boundary $\mathcal{F}(\mathbf{z}, \mathbf{p}) = t$. For model training, we apply
auto-decoding [20], an encoder-free approach where a learnable latent vector $\mathbf{z}$
of each shape is directly taken as input, jointly optimized with the parameters

---

[1] Code and dataset are available at https://github.com/M3DV/NeAR.

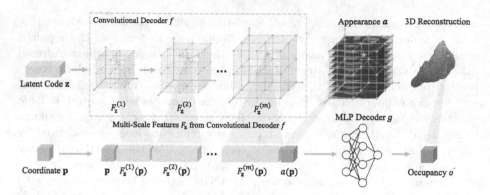

Fig. 2. Neural Annotation Refinement (NeAR). Given a learnable latent vector, it builds multi-scale feature maps F_z by a convolutional decoder f. A query coordinate $\mathbf{p}$ aggregates global and local features $F_z^{(1)}, F_z^{(2)}, ..., F_z^{(m)}$, with its appearance a from image. Finally, these point-wise features are fed into a light MLP g for occupancy prediction o to reconstruct appearance-aware surface.

of $\mathcal{F}$ through back-propagation. The number of latent vectors is equal to the number of training shape samples.

The deep implicit models have achieved a great success in a wide range of applications, *e.g.*, shape modeling [2,10,16,20], 3D reconstruction [3,26] and differentiable rendering [17,18]. The deep implicit surface serves as a deep prior [8,25] for shape modeling, thus can be used as a tool to refine annotations, as the implicit reconstructions tend to remove high-frequency artefacts introduced by human annotators. However, standard implicit surface methods are not aware of the appearance, thus the reconstructed surfaces could be misaligned with the actual boundaries. It motivates us to propose the appearance-aware implicit surface model for annotation refinement. Moreover, as the MLP-based implicit functions tend to be data-hungry, which is hard to be satisfied in medical imaging scenario, we introduce the convolutional architecture with multi-scale features to reconstruct the shapes.

2.2   Neural Annotation Refinement

Appearance-Aware Annotation Refinement. The standard deep implicit surface takes spatial coordinates as input; Although the learned shape prior is able to reconstruct a high-quality surface, the reconstructed surface is possible to be misaligned with the actual boundaries. To make the implicit model appearance-aware, we employ a simple strategy by changing the input of the implicit function from spatial coordinates $\mathbf{p}$ to $\mathbf{p}$ with its appearance a, *i.e.*,

$$\mathcal{F}(\mathbf{z}, \mathbf{p}, a) = o : \mathbb{R}^c \times \mathbb{R}^3 \times \mathbb{R} \to [0, 1], \tag{2}$$

where a short for $a(\mathbf{p})$ denotes the image appearance at the position $\mathbf{p}$, *e.g.*, Hounsfield Units in computed tomography. As will be shown, this simple modification leads to significant improvement over shape-only implicit models in both annotation refinement and downstream applications.

Network Architecture. As the data size is generally small in medical imaging applications, standard MLP-based implicit functions can be hard to train. To improve the data efficiency of MLP-based implicit functions, we introduce a convolutional decoder with multi-scale feature aggregation into the deep pipeline, inspired by [3,22,29]. As illustrated in Fig. 2, a latent vector $\mathbf{z}$ is first transformed by a convolutional decoder f into multi-scale feature maps,

$$F_{\mathbf{z}} = [F_{\mathbf{z}}^{(1)}, F_{\mathbf{z}}^{(2)}, \cdots, F_{\mathbf{z}}^{(m)}] = f(\mathbf{z}). \tag{3}$$

In our experiments, the resolution of largest feature map $F_{\mathbf{z}}^{(m)}$ is $32 \times 32 \times 32$.

For a query point $\mathbf{p}$, it obtains its features $F_{\mathbf{z}}^{(1)}(\mathbf{p}), F_{\mathbf{z}}^{(2)}(\mathbf{p}), \cdots, F_{\mathbf{z}}^{(m)}(\mathbf{p})$ by trilinear interpolation from the multi-scale maps. To make the model appearance-aware, we further integrate the appearance $a = a(\mathbf{p})$ as an input of the implicit function. To be concrete, the coordinates and the point-wise features, are concatenated and transformed into the occupancy o through a light MLP g,

$$o = \mathcal{F}(\mathbf{z}, \mathbf{p}, a) = g(\mathbf{p}, F_{\mathbf{z}}^{(1)}(\mathbf{p}), F_{\mathbf{z}}^{(2)}(\mathbf{p}), \cdots, F_{\mathbf{z}}^{(m)}(\mathbf{p}), a(\mathbf{p})). \tag{4}$$

Model Training and Inference. We treat the shape implicitly as occupancy field and train the model via auto-decoding [20]. The shape loss is measured by binary cross entropy (BCE) between predicted occupancy o and ground-truth occupancy $\hat{o}$. Different from standard auto-encoding technique, the auto-decoding is encoder-free. We thus add regularization loss, the l_2-norm of the latent code. In total, the training loss is weighted by λ ($\lambda = 0.01$ in our experiments),

$$\mathcal{L} = BCE(o, \hat{o}) + \lambda \cdot ||\mathbf{z}||_2. \tag{5}$$

The flexibility of implicit functions enables different training resolution from actual resolution. At training stage, we sample $64 \times 64 \times 64$ meshgrid coordinates from full-resolution $128 \times 128 \times 128$ input volumes to reduce training cost. The training meshgrid is added by a random Gaussian noise $\mathcal{N}(0, 0.01^2)$, whose occupancy labels are sampled from the full-resolution ground truth. We utilize an Adam optimizer [13] with an initial learning rate of 0.001 and train the model for 1,500 epochs. At inference stage, we sample full-resolution uniform meshgrid to reconstruct surfaces, *i.e.*, repaired annotations in this study.

Counterpart. Segmentation models [23] with image as input to refine the source masks, *e.g.*, 3D ResNet-based FCN [9,14] (Seg-FCN) and 3D UNet [4] (Seg-UNet), are used as counterparts. They are trained with human-annotated segmentation masks, and try to output refined annotations. Note that the label refinement counterparts are trained with the same datasets.

3   Datasets

3.1   Distorting a Golden Standard Segmentation Dataset

In order to quantitatively analyze the performance of annotation refinement, we synthesize distorted segmentation masks from golden standard. Here, we use the public AbdomenCT-1K [15], an abdominal CT organ segmentation dataset, which is annotated under multi-expert consensus protocol and thus can be regarded as golden standard. We use the adrenal gland subset[2], containing 100 adrenal glands from 50 patients. For each case, we calculate the center of left and right adrenal gland respectively, and center-crop the left and right adrenal gland into $128 \times 128 \times 128$ volumes with a normalized spacing of $1mm^3$. The resulting dataset has 100 cases with golden standard segmentation of adrenal glands. For image pre-processing, we clip the Hounsfield Units using soft-organ window [-60, 140] and then normalize to [0,1].

To synthesize distorted segmentation masks, we randomly add or cut out cubes on the boundary. We then apply random dilation or erosion operation to the shape followed by adding small salt-and-pepper noises. The resulting distorted masks are demonstrated in Fig. 3, which imitate imperfect human annotations, including high-frequency artefacts (unsmooth boundaries) and false positive/negative. The average Dice between distorted masks and ground truth is 0.71, with a lower bound of 0.65 and an upper bound of 0.75.

3.2   ALAN Dataset: A New 3D Dataset for Adrenal Gland Analysis

In this study, we introduce a new 3D Adrenal gLand ANalysis dataset, named ALAN. It consists of computed tomography (CT) scans from 792 patients (*i.e.*, 1,584 left and right adrenal glands). Each case is annotated with a segmentation mask and a binary diagnosis label (normal vs. abnormal). The segmentation mask is annotated by a single clinician using 3D Slicer software. As the boundary of adrenal gland–soft organ–is difficult to identify, and the segmentation is made slice-by-slice, the resulting 3D segmentation is imperfect with potential errors, *e.g.*, inconsistent cross-slice segmentation, high-frequency artefacts and human mistakes. Different from the segmentation masks, the diagnosis labels are independently made by 2 clinicians, and confirmed by 1 senior endocrinologist when diagnoses of the 2 clinicians disagree. We pre-process the dataset from raw 792 CT scans into 1,584 3D image cubes of $128 \times 128 \times 128$ following Sect. 3.1.

As the segmentation mask of adrenal glands is imperfect, we repair the annotation with the proposed NeAR. To demonstrate the usefulness of repairing, we run 3D convolutional networks with the shapes of adrenal glands as inputs, to output the diagnosis labels. The networks are trained with the ALAN dataset, with training/validation/test split of 1,188/98/298 on a patient level. As will be shown in Sect. 4.2, the adrenal gland shapes repaired by NeAR could be better classified than the human annotated ones.

---

[2] https://github.com/JunMa11/AbdomenCT-1K

Table 1. Segmentation repairing on the distorted golden standard dataset.
We compare the counterparts (Seg-FCN and Seg-UNet), NeAR w/ shape only (S),
and NeAR w/ shape and appearance (S+A) in Dice Similarity Coefficient (DSC) and
Normalized Surface Dice (NSD) over 5 trials.

Metrics	Seg-FCN	Seg-UNet	NeAR (S)	NeAR (S+A)
DSC (%, ↑)	79.56 ± 0.45	78.70 ± 0.45	78.79 ± 0.45	$\mathbf{81.07 \pm 0.22}$
NSD (%, ↑)	89.54 ± 0.33	87.71 ± 0.90	87.96 ± 0.51	$\mathbf{91.22 \pm 0.12}$

The ALAN dataset will be open-source, with 1,594 cases of NeAR-repaired, high-quality 3D models of adrenal glands together with the corresponding diagnosis labels. As there are only a few publicly available medical shape datasets [27,30] (see supplementary materials for a comparison), our dataset will be a valuable addition to the medical image analysis and geometric deep learning community.

4 Experiments

4.1 Quantitative Experiments on Distorted Golden Standards

Experiment Setting. All our experiments are implemented with PyTorch 1.8 [21]. To quantitatively analyze the performance of the proposed NeAR method on repairing segmentation annotations, we implement several methods on the distorted golden standard segmentation dataset, including

- **NeAR (S+A)**: The full proposed method;
- **NeAR (S)**: The shape-only NeAR model without appearance a as input;
- **Seg-FCN/Seg-UNet**: Segmentation counterparts, see Sect. 2.2.

All these methods are trained with all 100 cases, consisting of image and distorted segmentation mask, and evaluated by comparing the similarity between the model-predicted and golden standard segmentation masks. Best models are selected with the lowest training loss. The evaluation is based on volume-based Dice Similarity Coefficient (DSC), and surface-based Normalized Surface Dice (NSD) [19] with a distance tolerance of 1.0.

The segmentation models need to maintain 3D feature maps in the encoder, and thus take much larger memory and computation under the same training resolution as the NeAR. We use a slightly different training schedule. We observed that the number of training iterations of these segmentation models is smaller than the NeAR. Therefore, we utilize an Adam optimizer [13] with an initial learning rate of 0.001 for 100 epochs, delaying the learning rate by 0.1 after 50 and 75 epochs. Longer training schedule does not lead to higher performance.

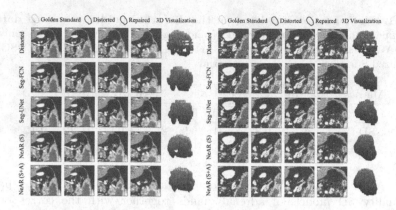

Fig. 3. Visualization of repaired annotations. Contours of adrenal glands are shown on image slices. Red are distorted, yellow are golden standard, and blue are repaired. The 3D visualization is shown on the right side. (Color figure online)

Results. As depicted in Table 1, the NeAR (S+A) surpasses all the other methods on both DSC and NSD, especially in surface-based method (NSD). NeAR (S) underperforms NeAR (S+A) as well as the standard segmentation method Seg-FCN and Seg-UNet, indicating that appearance-awareness boosts the repair performance significantly. Figure 3 shows contours of adrenal gland on image slices and 3D visualization of repaired annotations for each method. As shown by the contours on image slices, NeAR (S+A) can repair the distorted annotations more accurately and fix distortions that other methods fail to repair.

Moreover, we add manual smoothing as a baseline, including morphological closing and connected components filtering. We tried several settings, and the highest Dice is 76.90%, much lower than neural methods.

4.2   Adrenal Diagnosis on the Repaired ALAN Dataset

Experiment Setting. As described in Sect. 3.2, the segmentation masks in the ALAN dataset are imperfect. We utilize 4 different methods to repair the 3D adrenal gland analysis dataset, standard segmentation methods Seg-FCN and Seg-UNet as the baseline methods, NeAR (S) and NeAR (S+A). These methods are conducted in the same settings as that in Sect. 4.1 respectively. As there are no golden standard segmentation masks in the ALAN dataset, we only provide the qualitative results by visualizing the repaired segmentation masks in the supplementary materials.

To quantitatively analyze the annotation repairing quality, we conduct shape classification experiments on the human-annotated and model-repaired ALAN dataset. ResNet [9] variants with 2D/3D/ACS [28] convolutions are implemented to classify the shapes into binary diagnosis labels (normal vs. abnormal). The shapes of $128 \times 128 \times 128$ are resized to the size of $48 \times 48 \times 48$ as model inputs. For model training, we utilize an Adam optimizer [13] with an initial learning rate of 0.001 for 50 epochs, delaying the learning rate by 0.1 after 25 and 40 epochs. We use cross-entropy loss, and report area under ROC curve (AUC) as the evaluation metric. Best models are selected with lowest validation loss. We repeat experiments for 5 trials for each setting.

Results. As depicted in Table 2, models trained with shapes repaired by the NeAR (S+A) can diagnose the adrenal glands better than other methods, as well as the human annotated imperfect ones. Notably, standard segmentation methods (Seg-FCN and Seg-UNet) deliver worse shape classification results than NeAR (S) and raw human annotation, though the segmentation methods produce better shape repairing results than NeAR (S) in Sect. 4.1. This implies that the learned prior of deep implicit surfaces can be particularly useful for downstream applications.

Table 2. Shape classification on the ALAN dataset. We repair the 3D shapes of adrenal glands using standard segmentation (Seg-FCN and Seg-UNet), NeAR w/ shape only (S), and NeAR w/ shape and appearance (S+A). ResNet-18 and ResNet-50 variants are trained to classify the 3D shapes of adrenal glands (normal vs. abnormal) on the human-annotated and the repaired datasets. We report mean and standard deviation of AUC (%, ↑) on the test set over 5 trials.

Networks	Human-annotated	Seg-FCN	Seg-UNet	NeAR (S)	NeAR (S+A)
ResNet-18 [9] (2D)	68.35 ± 2.53	65.17 ± 2.21	64.68 ± 2.45	65.95 ± 0.83	**69.69 ± 1.44**
ResNet-18 [9] (3D)	89.77 ± 1.20	86.27 ± 1.91	86.55 ± 0.89	88.64 ± 1.24	**90.38 ± 0.57**
ResNet-18 [9] (ACS [28])	90.10 ± 0.90	87.02 ± 2.20	86.83 ± 2.00	89.22 ± 1.08	**91.11 ± 0.35**
ResNet-50 [9] (2D)	66.36 ± 2.56	64.88 ± 3.47	66.06 ± 2.79	69.04 ± 3.11	**69.94 ± 1.18**
ResNet-50 [9] (3D)	89.72 ± 1.33	85.64 ± 1.59	84.92 ± 1.08	88.76 ± 0.91	**89.78 ± 0.79**
ResNet-50 [9] (ACS [28])	90.13 ± 0.40	85.91 ± 2.11	82.28 ± 2.34	89.42 ± 1.35	**90.72 ± 0.72**

5   Conclusion

This study addresses a practical problem in medical image analysis: how to repair the imperfect segmentation. We propose Neural Annotation Refinement, an appearance-aware implicit method, whose values are validated in repairing segmentation and downstream applications. Moreover, the ALAN dataset for 3D shape classification will be an addition for the research community. There are limitations in the current study, *e.g.*, validated on adrenal glands only. We will test the NeAR on sparse annotations and small objects in the future research.

Acknowledgment. This work was supported by National Science Foundation of China (U20B2072, 61976137), supported in part by a Swiss National Science Foundation grant, and also supported in part by Grant YG2021ZD18 from Shanghai Jiao Tong University Medical Engineering Cross Research.

References

1. Ardila, D., et al.: End-to-end lung cancer screening with three-dimensional deep learning on low-dose chest computed tomography. Nat. Med. **25**(6), 954–961 (2019)
2. Chen, Z., Zhang, H.: Learning implicit fields for generative shape modeling. In: Conference on Computer Vision and Pattern Recognition, pp. 5939–5948 (2019)
3. Chibane, J., Alldieck, T., Pons-Moll, G.: Implicit functions in feature space for 3D shape reconstruction and completion. In: Conference on Computer Vision and Pattern Recognition, pp. 6970–6981 (2020)
4. Çiçek, Ö., Abdulkadir, A., Lienkamp, S.S., Brox, T., Ronneberger, O.: 3D u-net: learning dense volumetric segmentation from sparse annotation. In: Ourselin, S., Joskowicz, L., Sabuncu, M.R., Unal, G., Wells, W. (eds.) MICCAI 2016. LNCS, vol. 9901, pp. 424–432. Springer, Cham (2016). https://doi.org/10.1007/978-3-319-46723-8_49
5. Esteva, A., et al.: Deep learning-enabled medical computer vision. NPJ Digit. Med. **4**(1), 1–9 (2021)
6. Esteva, A., et al.: Dermatologist-level classification of skin cancer with deep neural networks. Nature **542**(7639), 115–118 (2017)
7. Gulshan, V., et al.: Development and validation of a deep learning algorithm for detection of diabetic retinopathy in retinal fundus photographs. JAMA **316**(22), 2402–2410 (2016)
8. Hanocka, R., Metzer, G., Giryes, R., Cohen-Or, D.: Point2Mesh: a self-prior for deformable meshes. In: ACM SIGGRAPH (2020)
9. He, K., Zhang, X., Ren, S., Sun, J.: Deep residual learning for image recognition. In: Conference on Computer Vision and Pattern Recognition, pp. 770–778 (2016)
10. Huang, X., et al.: Representation-agnostic shape fields. In: International Conference on Learning Representations (2022)
11. Karimi, D., Dou, H., Warfield, S.K., Gholipour, A.: Deep learning with noisy labels: exploring techniques and remedies in medical image analysis. Med. Image Anal. **65**, 101759 (2020)
12. Kermany, D.S., et al.: Identifying medical diagnoses and treatable diseases by image-based deep learning. Cell **172**(5), 1122–1131 (2018)
13. Kingma, D.P., Ba, J.: Adam: a method for stochastic optimization. arXiv Preprint (2014)
14. Long, J., Shelhamer, E., Darrell, T.: Fully convolutional networks for semantic segmentation. In: Conference on Computer Vision and Pattern Recognition, pp. 3431–3440 (2015)
15. Ma, J., et al.: Abdomenct-1k: is abdominal organ segmentation a solved problem? IEEE Trans. Pattern Anal. Mach. Intell. (2021)
16. Mescheder, L., Oechsle, M., Niemeyer, M., Nowozin, S., Geiger, A.: Occupancy networks: learning 3d reconstruction in function space. In: Conference on Computer Vision and Pattern Recognition, pp. 4460–4470 (2019)
17. Mildenhall, B., Srinivasan, P.P., Tancik, M., Barron, J.T., Ramamoorthi, R., Ng, R.: NeRF: representing scenes as neural radiance fields for view synthesis. In: Vedaldi, A., Bischof, H., Brox, T., Frahm, J.-M. (eds.) ECCV 2020. LNCS, vol. 12346, pp. 405–421. Springer, Cham (2020). https://doi.org/10.1007/978-3-030-58452-8_24
18. Niemeyer, M., Geiger, A.: Giraffe: representing scenes as compositional generative neural feature fields. In: International Conference on Computer Vision, pp. 11453–11464 (2021)

19. Nikolov, S., et al.: Deep learning to achieve clinically applicable segmentation of head and neck anatomy for radiotherapy. arXiv Preprint (2018)
20. Park, J.J., Florence, P., Straub, J., Newcombe, R., Lovegrove, S.: DeepSDF: learning continuous signed distance functions for shape representation. In: Conference on Computer Vision and Pattern Recognition, pp. 165–174 (2019)
21. Paszke, A., et al.: Pytorch: an imperative style, high-performance deep learning library. In: Advances in Neural Information Processing Systems, vol. 32 (2019)
22. Peng, S., Niemeyer, M., Mescheder, L., Pollefeys, M., Geiger, A.: Convolutional occupancy networks. In: Vedaldi, A., Bischof, H., Brox, T., Frahm, J.-M. (eds.) ECCV 2020. LNCS, vol. 12348, pp. 523–540. Springer, Cham (2020). https://doi.org/10.1007/978-3-030-58580-8_31
23. Rajchl, M., et al.: DeepCut: object segmentation from bounding box annotations using convolutional neural networks. IEEE Trans. Med. Imaging **36**(2), 674–683 (2016)
24. Tajbakhsh, N., Jeyaseelan, L., Li, Q., Chiang, J.N., Wu, Z., Ding, X.: Embracing imperfect datasets: a review of deep learning solutions for medical image segmentation. Med. Image Anal. **63**, 101693 (2020)
25. Ulyanov, D., Vedaldi, A., Lempitsky, V.: Deep image prior. In: Conference on Computer Vision and Pattern Recognition (2018)
26. Xu, Q., Wang, W., Ceylan, D., Mech, R., Neumann, U.: DISN: deep implicit surface network for high-quality single-view 3D reconstruction. In: Advances in Neural Information Processing Systems, vol. 32 (2019)
27. Yang, J., Gu, S., Wei, D., Pfister, H., Ni, B.: RibSeg dataset and strong point cloud baselines for rib segmentation from CT scans. In: de Bruijne, M., et al. (eds.) MICCAI 2021. LNCS, vol. 12901, pp. 611–621. Springer, Cham (2021). https://doi.org/10.1007/978-3-030-87193-2_58
28. Yang, J., et al.: Reinventing 2D convolutions for 3D images. IEEE J. Biomed. Health Inform. **25**(8), 3009–3018 (2021)
29. Yang, J., Wickramasinghe, U., Ni, B., Fua, P.: ImplicitAtlas: learning deformable shape templates in medical imaging. In: Conference on Computer Vision and Pattern Recognition, pp. 15861–15871 (2022)
30. Yang, X., Xia, D., Kin, T., Igarashi, T.: Intra: 3D intracranial aneurysm dataset for deep learning. In: Conference on Computer Vision and Pattern Recognition, pp. 2656–2666 (2020)

Few-shot Medical Image Segmentation Regularized with Self-reference and Contrastive Learning

Runze Wang, Qin Zhou, and Guoyan Zheng[✉]

Institute of Medical Robotics, School of Biomedical Engineering, Shanghai Jiao Tong University, No. 800, Dongchuan Road, Shanghai 200240, China
guoyan.zheng@sjtu.edu.cn

Abstract. Despite the great progress made by deep convolutional neural networks (CNN) in medical image segmentation, they typically require a large amount of expert-level accurate, densely-annotated images for training and are difficult to generalize to unseen object categories. Few-shot learning has thus been proposed to address the challenges by learning to transfer knowledge from a few annotated support examples. In this paper, we propose a new prototype-based few-shot segmentation method. Unlike previous works, where query features are compared with the learned support prototypes to generate segmentation over the query images, we propose a self-reference regularization where we further compare support features with the learned support prototypes to generate segmentation over the support images. By this, we argue for that the learned support prototypes should be representative for each semantic class and meanwhile discriminative for different classes, not only for query images but also for support images. We additionally introduce contrastive learning to impose intra-class cohesion and inter-class separation between support and query features. Results from experiments conducted on two publicly available datasets demonstrated the superior performance of the proposed method over the state-of-the-art (SOTA).

Keywords: Few-shot · Medical image segmentation · Self-reference · Contrastive learning

1 Introduction

Medical image segmentation is a prerequisite for many clinical applications including disease diagnosis, surgical planning and computer assisted interventions. Recently, deep-learning based methods, in particular convolutional neural networks (CNN), have revolutionized the landscape in automatic medical image segmentation [3,8]. However, the success of deep CNNs relies heavily on the

This study was partially supported by Shanghai Municipal S&T Commission via Project 20511105205 and by the Natural Science Foundation of China via project U20A20199.

availability of a large amount of expert-level accurate, densely-annotated images for training, which are time-consuming, labor-intensive and expensive to obtain. Besides their hunger for training data, these models also suffer from poor generalizability to unseen classes. To deal with the challenges, few-shot segmentation (FSS) methods [5,10–13,15,16] have been proposed to learn how to distill discriminative representation of an unseen class from a few labeled samples, typically denoted as support images, to guide semantic segmentation for unlabeled images with novel classes, known as query images.

Few-shot medical image segmentation is receiving increasing interest recently [9,14]. For example, Roy et al. [9] proposed the 'Squeeze & Excitation' modules to facilitate the interaction between support and query images in order to perform few-shot organ segmentation. There exist other attempts that are based on non-parametric learning framework such as prototype networks [7,17,18]. Wang et al. [17] proposed PANet which uses a prototype alignment regularization between support and query to learn a better class-specific global prototype representation. Ouyang et al. [7] designed an adaptive local prototype pooling module for prototypical networks to boost the performance of few-shot medical image segmentation. They additionally introduced a superpixel-based pseudo label generation method to remove the requirement of manual annotations for training. Inspired by their work, Yu et al. [18] proposed a location-sensitive local prototype network to leverage spatial prior for few-shot image segmentation.

The aforementioned non-parametric learning framework-based methods conduct segmentation over the query images by matching query features to the learned support prototypes. We argue for that the learned support prototypes should be representative for each semantic class and meanwhile discriminative for different classes for both support and query images. To this end, we propose a self-reference regularization where we further compare support features with the learned support prototypes to generate segmentation over the support images. We additionally introduce contrastive learning to impose intra-class cohesion and inter-class separation between support and query features. Our contributions can be summarized as follows:

- We propose a self-reference regularization to learn better support prototypes that are representative for both support and query images, leading to better segmentation performance.
- We incorporate contrastive learning into our framework to improve feature discrimination by imposing intra-class cohesion and inter-class separation between support and query features.
- We conduct experiments on two public datasets to evaluate the performance of the present method.

2 Methodology

2.1 Problem Setting

In FSS, we need to train a segmentation model on a dataset $\mathcal{D}_{train}$ and evaluate on a dataset $\mathcal{D}_{test}$. Suppose the semantic category set in $\mathcal{D}_{train}$ is $\mathcal{C}_{seen}$ and the

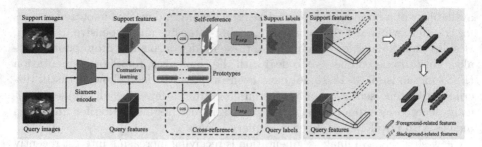

Fig. 1. Left: the proposed FSS framework with contrastive learning and self-reference regularization. Right: illustration of the contrastive learning used in our framework.

category set in $\mathcal{D}_{test}$ is $\mathcal{C}_{unseen}$, there is no overlap between training set and test set, i.e., $\mathcal{C}_{seen} \cap \mathcal{C}_{unseen} = \emptyset$. Please note that the background class is denoted as c_0 and it does not count toward $\mathcal{C}_{seen}$ or $\mathcal{C}_{unseen}$.

Following previous definitions in FSS [7,17,18], we adopt an episodic paradigm to set a K-shot segmentation task. Each episode consists of a support set $\mathcal{S}$ and a query set $\mathcal{Q}$ for a specific class c. At training stage, for one episode, the support set $\mathcal{S}_{train}$ contains K image-mask pairs, i.e., $\mathcal{S}_{train} = \{(I_k^s, M_k^s)\}_{k=1}^K$, where I_k^s indicates the kth image and M_k^s represents the corresponding labeled binary mask for class c. The query set contains N^q pairs of query image and labeled binary mask for the same class, i.e., $\mathcal{Q}_{train} = \{(I_j^q, M_j^q)\}_{j=1}^{N^q}$. After training our model, we evaluate its performance on $\mathcal{D}_{test}$. For each testing episode, our model is evaluated on the query set $\mathcal{Q}_{test}$ given the support set $\mathcal{S}_{test}$.

2.2 Local Prototype-Based Segmentation

Figure 1 (left) presents an overview of the proposed FSS framework. For each training episode, the support image I_k^s and query image I_j^q are first embedded into feature space $\mathcal{F}(I_k^s)$ and $\mathcal{F}(I_j^q) \in \mathbb{R}^{D \times H \times W}$ respectively by the shared Siamese encoder $\mathcal{F}(\cdot)$. D, H, W represents channel depth, height and width of the feature maps, respectively. Local prototypes are then extracted for both the foreground class c and the background class c_0. In our method, we generate the adaptive local prototypes according to [7]. Specifically, taking the foreground class as an example, we average-pool the support features with a pooling window size (L_H, L_W). Accordingly, the labeled binary support mask is scaled to a size of $(\frac{H}{L_H}, \frac{W}{L_W})$. Then each pixel on the average-pooled foreground feature maps is denoted as a local prototype $P_{k,n}^c \in \mathbb{R}^{D \times 1 \times 1}$. Similarly, we can obtain the prototypes $P_{k,m}^{c_0} \in \mathbb{R}^{D \times 1 \times 1}$ for the background class. Then we collect them into a prototype ensemble $\mathcal{P} = \{\{P_{k,m}^{c_0}\}_{m=1}^{N_{c_0}}, \{P_{k,n}^c\}_{n=1}^{N_c}\}$, where N_{c_0} and N_c denote the total number of prototypes for the background and the foreground classes, respectively. Each prototype in $\mathcal{P}$ explicitly represents a local region on the masked support features. Therefore, it enables to preserve rich intra-class local information. The segmentation for the query image is essentially achieved by matching the local features in the query image to the generated local prototype ensemble. Mathematically, the similarity between the query feature at spatial location (h, w) and each local prototype of the background and foreground class is calculated as:

$$S_{j,m}^{co}(h, w) = \mu P_{k,m}^{co} \odot \mathcal{F}(I_j^q)(h, w), \quad S_{j,n}^{c}(h, w) = \mu P_{k,n}^{c} \odot \mathcal{F}(I_j^q)(h, w) \quad (1)$$

where $a \odot b = \frac{\langle a, b \rangle}{\|a\|_2 \|b\|_2}$ and μ is a multiplier helping gradients to back-propagate and is empirically set to 20 according to [17].

We then compute $\mathbf{V}_j^{co}(h, w) = \underset{m}{softmax}(\{S_{j,m}^{co}(h, w)\}_{m=1}^{N_{co}})$ and $\mathbf{V}_j^{c}(h, w) = \underset{n}{softmax}(\{S_{j,n}^{c}(h, w)\}_{n=1}^{N_c})$, where $\underset{m}{softmax}(\{S_{j,m}^{co}(h, w)\}_{m=1}^{N_{co}})$ refers to the operation of first stacking all $S_{j,m}^{co}(h, w)$'s and then computing softmax function to get a probability vector at location (h, w). We further compute class-wise similarities S_j^{co} and S_j^{c} by weighted averaging:

$$S_j^{co}(h, w) = \sum_{m=1}^{N_{co}}(S_{j,m}^{co}(h, w) \cdot \mathbf{V}_j^{co}(h, w)[m]) \quad (2)$$

$$S_j^{c}(h, w) = \sum_{n=1}^{N_c}(S_{j,n}^{c}(h, w) \cdot \mathbf{V}_j^{c}(h, w)[n]) \quad (3)$$

Finally, the predicted segmentation probabilities are given by $Y_j^q(h, w, \hat{c}) = \underset{\hat{c}}{softmax}[S_j^{co}(h, w), S_j^{c}(h, w)]$, where $\hat{c} = \{c_0, c\}$. We employ the cross-entropy loss $\mathcal{L}_j^q$ to supervise the training process, which is calculated as:

$$\mathcal{L}_j^q = -\frac{1}{HW} \sum_h^H \sum_w^W \sum_{\hat{c}} M_j^q(h, w, \hat{c}) log(Y_j^q(h, w, \hat{c})) \quad (4)$$

2.3 Self-reference Regularization

The inspiration for the self-reference is based on the assumption that the prototypes that better represent support features help to achieve better segmentation results on the query image. Existing methods only calculate similarities between learned prototypes and query features, which neglects the supervision from the support image. Besides the cross-reference matching between the learned support prototypes and query features, we propose a self-reference regularization, i.e., training the model to segment the support image by matching the learned support prototypes with support features. By this, we argue for that the learned support prototypes should be representative for each semantic class and meanwhile discriminative for different classes, not only for query image but also for support image. This is done by computing the local similarity maps of the support features as:

$$S_{k,m}^{co}(h, w) = \mu P_{k,m}^{co} \odot \mathcal{F}(I_k^s)(h, w), \quad S_{k,n}^{c}(h, w) = \mu P_{k,n}^{c} \odot \mathcal{F}(I_k^s)(h, w) \quad (5)$$

Similarly, we can calculate the self-reference class-wise similarities $S_k^{co}(h, w)$ and $S_k^c(h, w)$ following Eq. (2) and (3).

The predicted segmentation probabilities of the support image is then calculated as $Y_k^s(h, w, \hat{c}) = \underset{\hat{c}}{softmax}[S_k^{co}(h, w), S_k^c(h, w)]$. Our self-reference regularization loss is then defined as the cross-entropy loss calculated on the support image:

$$\mathcal{L}_k^s = -\frac{1}{HW} \sum_h^H \sum_w^W \sum_{\hat{c}} M_k^s(h, w, \hat{c}) log(Y_k^s(h, w, \hat{c})) \tag{6}$$

2.4   Contrastive Learning

Accurate few-shot segmentation relies on intra-class similarity and inter-class distinction between support features and query features. To this end, we propose to leverage contrastive learning to regularize the foreground-related and background-related features from both support and query images. This is done by respectively clustering these features to a compact space regardless of their distributions while reducing the clusters overlap, as shown in Fig. 1 (right). Concretely, we used the masked average pooling to extract foreground- and background-related features. Taking foreground as an example, the foreground-related features on the support and query feature space are respectively expressed as:

$$h_k^{s,c} = \frac{\sum_{h,w} \mathcal{F}(I_k^s)(h, w) M_k^{s,c}(h, w)}{\sum_{h,w} M_k^{s,c}(h, w)}, h_j^{q,c} = \frac{\sum_{h,w} \mathcal{F}(I_j^q)(h, w) M_j^{q,c}(h, w)}{\sum_{h,w} M_j^{q,c}(h, w)} \tag{7}$$

Similarly, we can obtain the background-related features on the support and query feature space. Denote (t_u, t_v) as a pair of features, which is a positive pair when t_u and t_v belong to the same category and otherwise negative pair. We employ the InfoNCE [1] to perform the contrastive learning. The InfoNCE loss function for each positive pair of (t_u, t_v) is defined as:

$$l(t_u, t_v) = -log \frac{exp(t_u \odot t_v / \tau)}{\sum_{w=1, w \neq u}^{2R} \mathbb{1}(t_u, t_w) exp(t_u \odot t_w / \tau)} \tag{8}$$

where R represents the number of both foreground-related and background-related features; $\mathbb{1}(t_u, t_w)$ is respectively 0 and 1 for positive and negative pairs; τ denotes the temperature parameter and is empirically set as 0.05. The final contrastive loss $\mathcal{L}_c$ is the average of $l(t_u, t_v)$ over all positive pairs:

$$\mathcal{L}_c = \sum_{u=1}^{2R} \sum_{v=u+1}^{2R} \frac{(1 - \mathbb{1}(t_u, t_v)) l(t_u, t_v)}{B(R, 2) \times 2} \tag{9}$$

where $B(R, 2)$ is the number of combinations. The overall objective function of our method is as follows:

$$\mathcal{L} = \mathcal{L}_j^q + \lambda_1 \mathcal{L}_k^s + \lambda_2 \mathcal{L}_c \tag{10}$$

where $\{\lambda_1, \lambda_2\}$ are parameters controlling the relative weights of different losses, which are empirically set as $\{1, 0.1\}$.

Table 1. Quantitative comparison between our method and other SOTA methods.

Comparison results on Abd-CT dataset					
Method	Upper		Lower		Average
	Liver	Spleen	Kidney(L)	Kidney(R)	
SE-Net [9]	0.27	0.23	32.83	14.34	11.91
PANet [17]	38.42	29.59	32.34	17.37	29.43
GCN-DE [12]	46.77	56.53	**68.13**	**75.50**	61.73
SSL-ALPNet [7]	**73.65**	60.25	63.34	54.82	63.02
Ours	73.63	**67.36**	67.39	63.37	**67.94**
Comparison results on Abd-MRI dataset					
Method	Upper		Lower		Average
	Liver	Spleen	Kidney(L)	Kidney(R)	
SE-Net [9]	27.43	51.80	62.11	61.32	50.66
PANet [17]	42.26	50.90	53.45	38.64	46.33
GCN-DE [12]	49.47	60.63	76.07	83.03	67.30
SSL-ALPNet [7]	73.05	67.02	73.63	78.39	73.02
Ours	**75.55**	**73.73**	**77.07**	**84.24**	**77.65**

2.5 Superpixel-Based Self-supervised Learning

In this work, we employ the superpixel-based self-supervised learning proposed in [7] to train our network without the requirement of any manual annotations for training. Specifically, we can obtain a superpixel-based pseudo-label for each support image. We then perform geometric and intensity transformation on support image and mask to get the corresponding query image and mask (for mask, we only apply geometric transformation). After that, the obtained support and query images and their associated masks are fed into our network for end-to-end training. After training, for each testing episode, a support image is fed to our trained model together with its manual annotations in order to predict the segmentation for a query image.

3 Experiments

3.1 Experimental Setup

Datasets: We evaluate the proposed method on abdominal organs segmentation task with two publicly available datasets: abdominal CT (Abd-CT) dataset from MICCAI 2015 Multi-Atlas Abdomen Labeling challenge [6] and abdominal MRI (Abd-MRI) dataset from ISBI 2019 Combined Healthy Abdominal Organ Segmentation Challenge [4]. The Abd-CT dataset consists of 30 3D abdominal CT scans while the Abd-MRI dataset contains 20 3D T2 MRI scans. We are aiming to segment four organs from both datasets, i.e., *live, spleen, left* and *right kidney.*

Table 2. Ablation studies on Abd-MRI dataset.

Method	$\mathcal{L}_k^s$	$\mathcal{L}_c$	Upper		Lower		Average
			Liver	Spleen	Kidney(L)	Kidney(R)	
No regularization	–	–	73.05	67.02	73.63	78.39	73.02
+ Self-reference	✓	–	74.59	70.13	76.92	82.41	76.01
+ Contrastive learning	-	✓	74.17	69.84	75.77	80.08	74.97
Ours	✓	✓	**75.55**	**73.73**	**77.07**	**84.24**	**77.65**

All 3D images are reformatted as 2D slices and scaled to a size of 256×256 pixels for training and testing. It is worth to note that to evaluate generalization ability to unseen testing classes, we force the testing classes to be completely invisible by removing any images containing the test classes from the training dataset. Specifically, since {*liver, spleen*} appear in the upper abdomen region while {*left/right kideney*} usually appear in the lower abdomen region, we separate the extracted 2D slices of each data into *upper* and *lower* abdomen groups such that slices from one group will only be used as either training or testing dataset. When we train the model with *upper* abdomen group, the *lower* abdomen group is used for evaluation and vice versa. To simulate the scarcity of labeled data in clinical practice, all our experiments are performed under 1-way 1-shot setting. To evaluate 2D segmentation on 3D images, we follow the well-established evaluation protocol in [9]. All experiments are performed with five-fold cross-validation and quantified with the commonly used Dice Similarity Coefficient (DSC).

Implementation Details: The proposed approach is implemented in PyTorch. The Siamese encoder is a pre-trained ResNet101 [2]. The average pooling window (L_H, L_W) is empirically set to 4×4 for training and 2×2 for testing. At training stage, we use the stochastic gradient descent (SGD) optimizer with a batch size of 1 and set the learning rate to $1e - 3$ with a stepping decay rate of 0.98 per 1000 iterations. The total number of iterations is set to 100,000. The end-to-end training takes on average 6 h to finish on an Nvidia RTX 3090 graphics card.

3.2   Comparison with the State-of-the-Art (SOTA) Methods

We compared our method with the SOTA approaches including PANet [17], SE-Net [9], GCN-DE [12], and SSL-ALPNet [7]. The PANet is a popular prototype network on nature images while the SE-Net, GCN-DE, and SSL-ALPNet are recent SOTA methods for few-shot medical image segmentation. For a fair comparison, we used the same configuration as used in [7]. As shown in Table 1, the proposed method achieved the best DSC of 67.94% when evaluated on the Abd-CT dataset. In comparison with the second-best method (SSL-ALPNet), the average DSC achieved by our method increased 4.92%. When evaluated on the Abd-MRI dataset, a similar performance improvement was observed. Specifically, our method achieved the best segmentation performance on each

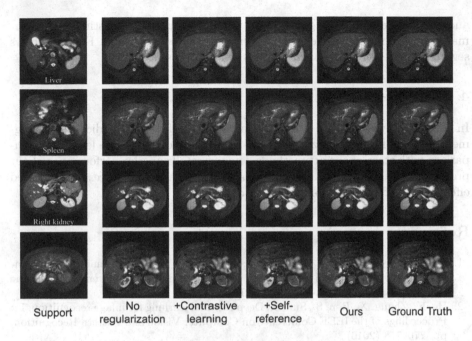

| Support | No regularization | +Contrastive learning | +Self-reference | Ours | Ground Truth |

Fig. 2. Qualitative comparison of segmentation results obtained from ablation study.

abdominal organ which were significantly better than the second-best method (SSL-ALPNet) (77.65% vs. 73.02% in terms of average DSC). We further conducted a paired t-test with a two-sided 0.01 level of significance to compare our method with the second-best method. On Abd-CT dataset, we obtained a p-value of $2.0e-9$ while on Abd-MRI dataset, we obtained a p-value of $1.6e-5$, demonstrating a statistically significant performance improvement. Quantitative results on both datasets demonstrated the effectiveness of our proposed approach on few-shot medical image segmentation.

3.3 Ablation Studies

To investigate the effectiveness of self-reference and contrastive learning regularization in our method, we conducted an ablation study on the Abd-MRI dataset. The quantitative results of this study are presented in Table 2. From this table, we can see that without any regularization, the worst results were obtained with an average DSC of 73.02%. By only incorporating contrastive learning regularization, we observed an 1.95% increase of average DSC. In contrast, by only incorporating the self-reference regularization, a 2.99% increase of average DSC was observed, indicating the effectiveness of self-reference regularization. By adding the contrastive learning regularization together with the self-reference regularization, a 3.63% increase of average DSC across all abdominal organs was achieved, which demonstrated that self-reference regularization and contrastive learning regularization were synergistically boosting the performance of our method for few-shot medical image segmentation. Figure 2 shows segmentation examples obtained from the ablation study.

4   Conclusion

In this paper, we proposed a new prototype-based few-shot medical image segmentation method regularized with self-reference and contrastive learning. Comparison with state-of-the-art methods demonstrated superior performance of our proposed method. Quantitative and qualitative ablation study results validated effectiveness of each key component in our method.

References

1. Chen, T., Kornblith, S., Norouzi, M., Hinton, G.: A simple framework for contrastive learning of visual representations. In: International Conference on Machine Learning, pp. 1597–1607. PMLR (2020)
2. He, K., Zhang, X., Ren, S., Sun, J.: Deep residual learning for image recognition. In: Proceedings of the IEEE Conference on Computer Vision and Pattern Recognition, pp. 770–778 (2016)
3. Isensee, F., Jaeger, P.F., Kohl, S.A., Petersen, J., Maier-Hein, K.H.: nnU-net: a self-configuring method for deep learning-based biomedical image segmentation. Nat. methods 18(2), 203–211 (2021)
4. Kavur, A.E., et al.: Chaos challenge-combined (CT-MR) healthy abdominal organ segmentation. Med Image Anal. 69, 101950 (2021)
5. Kim, S., An, S., Chikontwe, P., Park, S.H.: Bidirectional RNN-based few shot learning for 3d medical image segmentation. In: Proceedings of the AAAI Conference on Artificial Intelligence, vol. 35, pp. 1808–1816 (2021)
6. Landman, B., Xu, Z., Igelsias, J., Styner, M., Langerak, T., Klein, A.: Miccai multi-atlas labeling beyond the cranial vault-workshop and challenge. In: Proceedings of MICCAI Multi-Atlas Labeling Beyond Cranial Vault-Workshop Challenge, vol. 5, p. 12 (2015)
7. Ouyang, C., Biffi, C., Chen, C., Kart, T., Qiu, H., Rueckert, D.: Self-supervision with superpixels: training few-shot medical image segmentation without annotation. In: Vedaldi, A., Bischof, H., Brox, T., Frahm, J.-M. (eds.) ECCV 2020. LNCS, vol. 12374, pp. 762–780. Springer, Cham (2020). https://doi.org/10.1007/978-3-030-58526-6_45
8. Ronneberger, O., Fischer, P., Brox, T.: U-net: convolutional networks for biomedical image segmentation. In: Navab, N., Hornegger, J., Wells, W.M., Frangi, A.F. (eds.) MICCAI 2015. LNCS, vol. 9351, pp. 234–241. Springer, Cham (2015). https://doi.org/10.1007/978-3-319-24574-4_28
9. Roy, A.G., Siddiqui, S., Pölsterl, S., Navab, N., Wachinger, C.: 'Squeeze & excite' guided few-shot segmentation of volumetric images. Med. Image Anal. 59, 101587 (2020)
10. Shaban, A., Bansal, S., Liu, Z., Essa, I., Boots, B.: One-shot learning for semantic segmentation. arXiv preprint arXiv:1709.03410 (2017)
11. Snell, J., Swersky, K., Zemel, R.: Prototypical networks for few-shot learning. Adv. Neural Inf. Process. Syst. 30, 4080–4090 (2017)

12. Sun, L., et al.: Few-shot medical image segmentation using a global correlation network with discriminative embedding. Comput. Biol. Med. **140**, 105067 (2022)
13. Sung, F., Yang, Y., Zhang, L., Xiang, T., Torr, P.H., Hospedales, T.M.: Learning to compare: relation network for few-shot learning. In: Proceedings of the IEEE Conference on Computer Vision and Pattern Recognition, pp. 1199–1208 (2018)
14. Tajbakhsh, N., Jeyaseelan, L., Li, Q., Chiang, J.N., Wu, Z., Ding, X.: Embracing imperfect datasets: a review of deep learning solutions for medical image segmentation. Med. Image Anal. **63**, 101693 (2020)
15. Tang, H., Liu, X., Sun, S., Yan, X., Xie, X.: Recurrent mask refinement for few-shot medical image segmentation. In: Proceedings of the IEEE/CVF International Conference on Computer Vision, pp. 3918–3928 (2021)
16. Vinyals, O., Blundell, C., Lillicrap, T., Wierstra, D., et al.: Matching networks for one shot learning. Adv. Neural Inf. Process. Syst. **29**, 3637–3645 (2016)
17. Wang, K., Liew, J.H., Zou, Y., Zhou, D., Feng, J.: Panet: few-shot image semantic segmentation with prototype alignment. In: Proceedings of the IEEE/CVF International Conference on Computer Vision, pp. 9197–9206 (2019)
18. Yu, Q., Dang, K., Tajbakhsh, N., Terzopoulos, D., Ding, X.: A location-sensitive local prototype network for few-shot medical image segmentation. In: 2021 IEEE 18th International Symposium on Biomedical Imaging (ISBI), pp. 262–266. IEEE (2021)

Shape-Aware Weakly/Semi-Supervised Optic Disc and Cup Segmentation with Regional/Marginal Consistency

Yanda Meng[1], Xu Chen[2], Hongrun Zhang[1], Yitian Zhao[3], Dongxu Gao[4], Barbra Hamill[5], Godhuli Patri[6], Tunde Peto[5], Savita Madhusudhan[6], and Yalin Zheng[1,7(✉)]

[1] Department of Eye and Vision Science, University of Liverpool, Liverpool, UK
yalin.zheng@liverpool.ac.uk
[2] Department of Medicine, University of Cambridge, Cambridge, UK
[3] Cixi Institute of Biomedical Engineering, Ningbo Institute of Industrial Technology, Chinese Academy of Sciences, Ningbo, China
[4] School of Computing, University of Portsmouth, Portsmouth, UK
[5] St Paul's Eye Unit, Liverpool University Hospitals NHS Foundation Trust, Liverpool, UK
[6] School of Medicine, Dentistry and Biomedical Sciences, Queen's University Belfast, Belfast, UK
[7] Liverpool Centre for Cardiovascular Science, University of Liverpool and Liverpool Heart and Chest Hospital, Liverpool, UK

Abstract. Glaucoma is a chronic eye disease that permanently impairs vision. Vertical cup to disc ratio ($vCDR$) is essential for glaucoma screening. Thus, accurately segmenting the optic disc (OD) and optic cup (OC) from colour fundus images is essential. Previous fully-supervised methods achieved accurate segmentation results; then, they calculated the $vCDR$ with offline post-processing step. However, a large set of labeled segmentation images are required for the training, which is costly and time-consuming. To solve this, we propose a weakly/semi-supervised framework with the benefits of geometric associations and specific domain knowledge between pixel-wise segmentation probability map (PM), geometry-aware modified signed distance function representations ($mSDF$), and local boundary region of interest characteristics (B-ROI). Firstly, we propose a dual consistency regularisation based semi-supervised paradigm, where the regional and marginal consistency benefits the proposed model from the objects' inherent region and boundary coherence of a large amount of unlabeled data. Secondly, for the first time, we exploit the domain-specific knowledge between the boundary and region in terms of the perimeter and area of an oval shape of OD & OC, where a differentiable $vCDR$ estimating module is proposed for the end-to-end training. Thus, our model does not need any offline post-process to generate $vCDR$. Furthermore, without requiring any additional laborious annotations, the supervision on $vCDR$ can serve as a weakly-supervision for OD & OC region and boundary segmentation. Experiments on six large-scale datasets demonstrate that our

L. Wang et al. (Eds.): MICCAI 2022, LNCS 13434, pp. 524–534, 2022.
https://doi.org/10.1007/978-3-031-16440-8_50

method outperforms state-of-the-art semi-supervised approaches for segmentation of the optic disc and optic cup, and estimation of $vCDR$ for glaucoma assessment in colour fundus images, respectively. The implementation code is made available. (https://github.com/smallmax00/Share_aware_Weakly-Semi_ODOC_seg)

Keywords: Optic disc and cup segmentation ·
Weakly/semi-supervised learning

1 Introduction

The relative size of the OD and the OC in fundus images can be used to assess glaucomatous damage to the optic nerve head [3]. As a general rule, a greater $vCDR$ indicates a higher risk of developing glaucoma and vice versa [23]. Thus, accurate OD & OC segmentation is critical for glaucoma assessment via $vCDR$ measurement. Recently, numerous deep learning-based segmentation models [3,17–19,21,23,26] have been proposed, significantly improving the OD & OC segmentation accuracy. However, they still use a fully supervised paradigm, which requires large annotations which is time-consuming, laborious and costly. Semi-supervised learning frameworks [10,15,16] can obtain high-quality segmentation results by directly learning from a small set of labeled data and a large set of unlabeled data. Numerous of them have been developed to investigate unsupervised consistency regularisation. For instance, they introduced noises at the data-level [25,28] into unlabeled samples and required consistency between model predictions on the original and perturbed data. Furthermore, the feature-level of perturbations are incorporated into multiple output branches [10,16], to ensure the consistency of model predictions across output branches. On the contrary, the consistency regularisation at task-level in semi-supervised learning has received little attention until recently in a variety of computer vision tasks, including crowd counting [20], 3D object detection [13], and 3D medical image segmentation [15]. For example, if we can map the predictions of different tasks into the same predefined space and then evaluate them using the same criterion, the results will undoubtedly be less than optimal, as there are prediction perturbations between tasks. To this end, we learned a dual-task level of geometric consistency via PM segmentation and $mSDF$ regress. Additionally, we investigated the boundary quality of consistency regularisation at the task-level as the second consistency learning. Specifically, we derived the B-ROI masks from the PM segmentation and $mSDF$ regress branches, respectively. Then the supervised and unsupervised losses are applied to learn more accurate boundary segmentation results with the help of labeled and unlabeled data. Note that a high-quality object boundary is more critical than that of the regional pixel-wise coverage in medical image segmentation tasks [21]. On the other hand, previous weakly supervised learning methods [8,9,11] segmented images using bounding boxes [9], scribbles [11], or image-level tags [8] rather than pixel-by-pixel annotation, which alleviates the burden of annotations. Differently, in this work, we

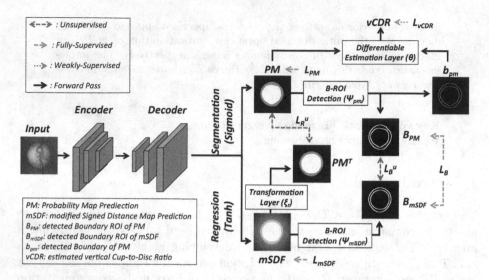

Fig. 1. Overview of the proposed weakly/semi-supervised learning pipeline. PM and $mSDF$ both have two channels to represent the output of OC and OD. We overlapped them for better visualisation.

investigated the task-specific domain knowledge of oval shape for the OD & OC segmentation task. Along with the estimated region and boundary predictions of OD & OC, we proposed a novel differentiable $vCDR$ estimation layer. As a result, our model is capable of estimating the $vCDR$ end-to-end on the basis of OD & OC segmentation. Simultaneously, the information gain from $vCDR$ ground truth can weakly-supervise the segmentation process for both region and boundary of OD & OC.

Despite human graders' instinctive use of both domains, previous methods approach to segment biomedical images frequently overlooked the underlying relationships between the region and boundary characteristics. This article demonstrates how to rationally leverage geometric associations between OD & OC in terms of region and boundary on semi-supervised consistency learning and differentiable weakly-supervised $vCDR$ estimation.

2   Methods

Figure 1 depicts an overview of the proposed learning pipeline, which consists of two tasks of PM segmentation and $mSDF$ regression. The geometric associations of two tasks in terms of the region and boundary are exploited in the proposed weakly/semi-supervised learning manner, respectively. The details are elaborated as follows.

2.1 Modified Signed Distance Function ($mSDF$)

Previous works [15,27] adopted SDF to represent the target mask in segmentation tasks because it enables the network to learn a distance-aware representation $w.r.t$ the object boundary, emphasising the spatial perception of the input images. Inspired by [6], we propose a modified Signed Distance Function ($mSDF$), which is defined as:

$$mSDF(x) = \begin{cases} 1, & x \in B_{in} \\ 0, & x \in \Delta B \\ -\inf_{y \in \Delta B} \|x - y\|_2, & x \in B_{out} \end{cases} \tag{1}$$

where $\|x - y\|_2$ is the Euclidean distance between pixel x and y. Besides, B_{out}, B_{in} and ΔB, denote the outside, inside and boundary of the object, respectively. Different from the classic SDF, outside each object, $mSDF$ takes negative values, proportional to the distance from the boundary, while it is simply 1 inside of the object and 0 on the boundary. In this way, dual tasks can acquire the coherent semantic features, meanwhile the $mSDF$ regression task benefits from the distance-aware spatial information supervision.

2.2 Dual Consistency Regularisation of Semi-Supervision

Under semi-supervised conditions, the dual consistency regularisation imposes regional and marginal consistency at the task level. As for region-wise consistency, similar to [15,20,27], we propose a transformation layer to convert the $mSDF$ to PM in a differentiable way. To be precise, the region-wise transformation layer ξ_r is defined as:

$$\xi_r(z) = 2 * Sigmoid(K \cdot ReLu(z)) - 1, \tag{2}$$

where z denotes the $mSDF$ value at pixel x; K is a very large value; $Sigmoid$ and $ReLu$ are the non-linear activation functions. Note that, sigmoid activation function is used because we treat OC & OD segmentation as two binary segmentation in two output channels. The larger K value indicates a closer approximation, and it is adopted as 5000 in this work. With Eq. 2, we can obtain the transformed segmentation maps PM^t, for example, $PM^t = \xi_r(mSDF)$. For all of the unlabeled input, we apply a $Dice$ loss (L_{R^u}) between PM and PM^t to enforce the unsupervised regional consistency regularisation.

Concerning the boundary-wise consistency, we derive the spatial gradient of PM and $mSDF$, as the respectively estimated contours. Previous studies [2,21] have proven that such narrow contours with a width of one pixel are challenging to optimise due to the extremely unbalanced foreground and background, resulting in weakened consistency regularisations. Rather than focusing exclusively on the thin contour locations, we consider the ROI within a certain distance (boundary width) of the corresponding estimated contours. A simple yet efficient B-ROI detection layer (ψ) is proposed for PM and $mSDF$. For example, ψ_{PM} and ψ_{mSDF} are defined as:

$$\psi_{PM} = PM + Maxpooling2D(-PM), \tag{3}$$

$$\psi_{mSDF} = \xi_r(mSDF) + Maxpooling2D\big(-\xi_r(mSDF)\big), \tag{4}$$

It is worth noting that the output width of ψ can be determined by varying the kernel size, stride, and padding value of the Maxpooling2D operation. We empirically set the output boundary width of ψ_{PM} and ψ_{mSDF} to 4 pixels in this work. After ψ_{PM} and ψ_{mSDF}, we refer to such B-ROI of PM and $mSDF$ as B_{pm} and B_{mSDF}, respectively. Ideally, B_{PM} and B_{mSDF} should be close enough to one another. Thus, a $Dice$ loss (L_{B^u}) between B_{PM} and B_{mSDD} is applied to enforce the unsupervised marginal consistency regularisation of unlabeled data. Meanwhile, we apply a $Dice$ loss (L_B) on both B_{PM} and B_{mSDF} to supervise the dual boundary predictions of labeled data.

2.3   Differentiable $vCDR$ estimation of Weakly Supervision

Because the shape of OD & OC are oval-like [23], previous methods adopt to offline post-process the segmentation predictions with ellipse fitting to improve the segmentation accuracy [3], or to calculate the $vCDR$ using the approximated diameters of the OD & OC in long axis [17, 18, 21]. However, they overlooked the underlying supervision value of it in OD & OC segmentation task. To address this issue, we take advantage of the specific domain knowledge between the boundary and region in terms of the perimeter and area of an oval-like shape to approximate the $vCDR$ in a differentiable way. To be precise, the $vCDR$ is defined as the ratio of dividing the measured diameters of the cup by disc in the long axis. While, such ratio can also be estimated given the size of perimeter and the area of OD and OC. According to the $Euler's\ Method$ [12], the area (A_o) and perimeter (P_o) of the oval shape are defined as:

$$A_o = \pi \cdot a \cdot b, \tag{5}$$

$$P_o = \pi \cdot \sqrt{2(a^2 + b^2)}. \tag{6}$$

where a and b denote the semi-axis of the long and short axis of oval shape, respectively. We approximate A_o with the summed pixel value of PM, which can be regarded as the area of oval shape in pixel level. Furthermore, we derive the spatial gradient of PM via the B-ROI detection layer (ψ_{PM}), to detect the boundary (b_{pm}) with width $= 1$. Then the summed pixel values of b_{pm} is approximately regarded as P_o. With Eq. 5 and Eq. 6, we can approximate a with A_o and P_o, such as:

$$a = \sqrt{\frac{(P_o)^2 + \sqrt{(4\pi A_o + (P_o)^2) \cdot |(4\pi A_o - (P_o)^2))|}}{4\pi^2}}), \tag{7}$$

where $|\cdot|$ is used to prevent sqrt from returning a negative value during the initial learning period. Given Eq. 7, we can calculate the OD long semi-axis (a^{OD}) and the OC long semi-axis (a^{OC}) with the respective P_o and A_o. Then, the $vCDR$ estimation layer θ can be defined as:

$$\theta(vCDR) = \frac{a^{OC} + e^{-6}}{a^{OD} + e^{-6}}, \tag{8}$$

where, e^{-6} is added to avoid dividing by zero errors. Given the prediction of $vCDR$, we apply a MSE loss (L_{vCDR}) between the prediction and ground truth to fully-supervise the $vCDR$ estimation and weakly-supervise the OD & OC segmentation.

3   Experiments

3.1   Datasets and Implementation Details

SEG dataset: following the previous methods [19,21], we pooled 2,068 images from five public available datasets (Refuge [23], Drishti-GS [24], ORIGA [29], RIGA [1], RIM-ONE [4]). These five datasets provide the fundus images and the ground truth masks, then we generate the corresponding ground truth of $mSDF$, B_{PM}, B_{mSDF} and $vCDR$ with Eq. 1, 3, 4 and 8. Following the previous methods [19,21], 613 fundus images were randomly selected as the test dataset, leaving the other 1,315 images for training and 140 images for validation.

UKBB Dataset: The UK Biobank[1] is a large-scale biomedical database and research resource, that contains detailed health information on half a million participants from the United Kingdom. Participants were scanned using the TOPCON 3D OCT 1000 Mk2 camera (Topcon Inc, Japan). There are 117,832 fundus images with $vCDR$ scalars are available, of which 38,421 are randomly selected as the weakly/semi-supervised training dataset, and the rest 79,411 are used as test datasets.

Implementation: We cropped the image of 256 × 256 pixels with the same way of [17,19,21], then randomly rotated and flipped the training dataset with a probability of 0.5. The rotation ranges from −20 to 20 degree. The stochastic gradient descent with a momentum of 0.9 is used to optimise the overall parameters. We trained the model around 10,000 iterations for all the experiments, with a learning rate of 1e-2 and a step decay rate of 0.999 every 100 iterations. The batch size was set as 56, consisting of 28 labeled and 28 unlabeled images. A backbone network [5] is used for ours and all the compared methods. All the training processes were performed on a server with four *GEFORCE RTX 3090 24GiB GPUs*, and all the test experiments were conducted on a workstation with *Intel(R) Xeon(R) W-2104 CPU* and *Geforce RTX 2080Ti GPU* with 11GB memory. We use the output of the *PM* as the segmentation result, and

---

[1] https://www.ukbiobank.ac.uk/.

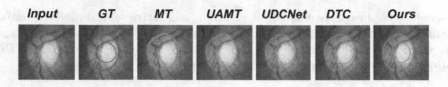

Fig. 2. Qualitative results of *OD* & *OC* segmentation in *SEG* test dataset. We compare our model with *MT* [25], *UAMT* [28], *UDCNet* [10] and *DTC* [15].

Table 1. Quantitative segmentation results of *OD* & *OC* and glaucoma assessment on *SEG* and *UKBB* test datasets. The performance is reported as *Dice* (%), *BIoU* (%), *Corr* and *MAE*. 95% confidence intervals are presented in the brackets, respectively. The implementation of the compared semi-supervised state-of-the-art works is mainly based on an open-source codebase [14].

Methods	SEG (OC)		SEG (OD)		SEG (vCDR)		UKBB (vCDR)	
	Dice(%) ↑	BIoU(%) ↑	Dice(%) ↑	BIoU(%) ↑	MAE ↓	Corr ↑	MAE ↓	Corr ↑
MT [25]	84.1	78.2	94.3	86.5	0.091	0.683	0.145	0.307
	(81.8, 85.7)	(77.0, 79.6)	(94.0, 94.7)	(85.0, 87.3)	(0.080, 0.099)	(0.641, 0.701)	(0.139, 0.150)	(0.276, 0.340)
UAMT [28]	85.3	80.2	95.2	86.4	0.075	0.692	0.134	0.339
	(82.8, 86.9)	(79.0, 81.7)	(94.7, 95.6)	(85.1, 87.7)	(0.063, 0.081)	(0.642, 0.723)	(0.127, 0.139)	(0.301, 0.361)
URPC [16]	86.1	81.2	96.0	87.3	0.067	0.701	0.126	0.361
	(83.1, 87.2)	(79.6, 82.0)	(95.4, 96.3)	(85.0, 87.9)	(0.059, 0.073)	(0.659, 0.742)	(0.121, 0.135)	(0.337, 0.382)
DTC [15]	86.1	81.1	96.1	87.0	0.065	0.703	0.126	0.364
	(83.0, 87.4)	(79.5, 82.8)	(95.3, 96.4)	(85.2, 87.8)	(0.060, 0.072)	(0.661, 0.739)	(0.120, 0.137)	(0.339, 0.389)
UDCNet [10]	86.2	81.4	96.2	87.1	0.067	0.714	0.127	0.389
	(83.3, 87.1)	(79.6, 83.0)	(95.7, 96.5)	(85.6, 87.9)	(0.059, 0.071)	(0.663, 0.742)	(0.119, 0.135)	(0.365, 0.412)
Ours (Semi)	**87.1**	**83.4**	**97.2**	**89.3**	**0.052**	**0.817**	**0.102**	**0.453**
	(86.4, 87.8)	(81.0, 85.5)	(97.1, 97.3)	(88.2, 89.9)	(0.049, 0.056)	(0.777, 0.852)	(0.099, 0.104)	(0.439, 0.477)

a fixed threshold 0.5 is employed to get a binary mask. For a fair comparison, we do not use any post-processing or ensemble methods. Given the previously discussed loss function terms, we defined the overall loss function as:

$$L_{overall} = L_{PM} + L_{mSDF} + L_B + \lambda * (L_{R^u} + L_{B^u} + L_{vCDR}) \qquad (9)$$

where L_{PM} is *Dice* loss for supervised segmentation, L_{mSDF} is *MSE* loss for supervised regression. λ is adopted from [7] as the time-dependent Gaussian ramp-up weighting coefficient to account for the trade-off between the supervised, unsupervised, and weakly-supervised losses. This avoids the network getting stuck in a degenerate solution during the initial training period. Because no meaningful prediction of the unlabeled data, as well as *vCDR*, are obtained.

4   Results

In this section, we show qualitative (Fig. 2) and quantitative results (Tab. 1) of the *OD* & *OC* segmentation and glaucoma assessment tasks. Dice similarity score (*Dice*) and boundary intersection-over-union (*BIoU*) [2] are used as the segmentation accuracy metrics; Mean Absolute Error (*MAE*) and Pearson's correlation coefficients [22] (*Corr*) are used as the *vCDR* estimation metrics. The

Table 2. Ablation study on weakly/semi-supervision components. The performance is reported as *Dice* (%), *BIoU* (%), *MAE*, and *Corr*.

Methods	SEG (OC)		SEG (OD)		UKBB (vCDR)	
	Dice (%) ↑	BIoU(%) ↑	Dice(%) ↑	BIoU(%) ↑	MAE↓	Corr↑
w/o L_{Ru}	85.7	80.6	95.9	86.6	0.151	0.319
w/o L_{Bu}	86.1	81.1	96.1	87.0	0.133	0.338
w/ Both	86.5	82.1	96.5	88.0	0.127	0.341
w/ L_{vCDR}	86.7	82.6	96.7	88.5	0.112	0.410
w/ $L_{Bu}+L_{vCDR}$	86.9	82.9	96.7	88.6	0.109	0.427
w/ $L_{Ru}+L_{vCDR}$	86.9	82.8	96.6	88.7	0.105	0.439
Ours (Label-only)	80.3	70.5	91.2	75.5	0.631	0.112
Ours (Semi)	**87.1**	**83.4**	**97.2**	**89.3**	**0.102**	**0.453**

best result in each category is highlighted in bold. 95% confidence intervals were generated by using 2000 sample bootstrapping.

Optic Disc and Cup Segmentation. In Table 1, we present the results that are trained with 5% of *SEG* training dataset and all of *UKBB* training dataset. *Ours (Semi)* obtains an average 87.1% and 97.2% *Dice* on *OC* and *OD* segmentation, respectively, outperforms data-level consistency regularisation based methods *MT* [25], *UAMT* [28] by 3.3% and 2.1%, outperforms feature-level regularisation based methods *URPC* [16], *UDCNet* [10] by 1.2% and 1.0%.

Clinical Evaluation. Along with assessing computer vision evaluation metrics, we evaluated our method's performance via *vCDR* in glaucoma assessment. Table 1 illustrates the *vCDR* evaluation results on *SEG* and *UKBB* test dataset respectively. The *UKBB (vCDR)* has 79,411 test images, which is significantly larger than the *SEG (vCDR)* (619 images). Therefore, the performance on *UKBB (vCDR)* may more accurately reflect the situation in real-world. Specifically, *Ours (semi)* achieved the best performance of 0.102 *MAE*, which outperforms *UDCNet* [10] by 19.7%. Please note that, the segmentation-unlabeled 38,421 images of *UKBB* training dataset also serve as the fully supervision for *vCDR* estimation.

Ablation Study. We conducted extensive ablation studies, and all the results demonstrate our model's effectiveness. To illustrate, the ablation results for weakly/semi-supervision components are shown in Tab. 2. Specifically, we conduct experiments to evaluate the effectiveness of the proposed dual consistency regularisation in a semi-supervised manner and the propose differentiable *vCDR* estimation module in a weakly-supervised manner. We represent our model that is trained with only 5 % *SEG* training data as *Ours (Label-only)*. Firstly, we retain the same model structure and eliminate the *vCDR* estimation loss to focus on the dual consistency regularisation losses (*w/ Both*). Following that, we remove the region-wise unsupervised loss (*w/o L_{Ru}*), boundary-wise unsupervised loss (*w/o L_{Bu}*) respectively. Secondly, we remove both of the consistency losses and only apply the weakly-supervised *vCDR* estimation loss (*w/ L_{vCDR}*). Then we add the other two unsupervised consistency losses individually ($w/$ $L_{B^u}+L_{vCDR}$ and $w/$ $L_{R^u}+L_{vCDR}$) to see if the performance are boosted. Table 2 demonstrates that the proposed unsupervised dual consistency losses and weakly supervised loss can improve the model by 6.7 % and 6.9 % *Dice* respectively for *OD* & *OC* segmentation. Particularly, the boundary-wide unsupervised loss can increase the model by 15.1 % *BIoU*, which leads to a better boundary segmentation quality. The weakly supervised loss can bring a large improvement of 82.2 % *MAE* of *vCDR* estimation, which is the ultimate goal for *OD* & *OC* segmentation task *w.r.t* clinic application.

5   Conclusion

We propose a novel weakly/semi-supervised segmentation framework. The geometric associations and specific domain knowledge between the modified signed distance function representations, object boundary characteristics, and pixelwise probability map features are exploited in the proposed semi-supervised consistency regularisations, and weakly-supervised guidance. Our experiments have demonstrated that the proposed model can effectively leverage semantic region features and spatial boundary features for segmentation of optic disc & optic cup and *vCDR* estimation of glaucoma assessment from retinal images.

References

1. Almazroa, A., et al.: Retinal fundus images for glaucoma analysis: the RIGA dataset. In: Medical Imaging 2018: Imaging Informatics for Healthcare, Research, and Applications, vol. 10579, p. 105790B. International Society for Optics and Photonics (2018)
2. Cheng, B., Girshick, R., Dollár, P., Berg, A.C., Kirillov, A.: Boundary IoU: improving object-centric image segmentation evaluation. In: Proceedings of the IEEE Conference on Computer Vision and Pattern Recognition (2021)
3. Fu, H., Cheng, J., Xu, Y., Wong, D.W.K., Liu, J., Cao, X.: Joint optic disc and cup segmentation based on multi-label deep network and polar transformation. IEEE Trans. Med. Imaging **37**(7), 1597–1605 (2018)
4. Fumero, F., Alayón, S., Sanchez, J.L., Sigut, J., Gonzalez-Hernandez, M.: RIM-ONE: an open retinal image database for optic nerve evaluation. In: 24th International Symposium on Computer-Based Medical Systems (CBMS), pp. 1–6. IEEE (2011)
5. Gao, S., Cheng, M.M., Zhao, K., Zhang, X.Y., Yang, M.H., Torr, P.H.: Res2net: a new multi-scale backbone architecture. IEEE Trans. Pattern Anal. Mach. Intell. **43**, 652–662 (2019)
6. Jiang, W., Kolotouros, N., Pavlakos, G., Zhou, X., Daniilidis, K.: Coherent reconstruction of multiple humans from a single image. In: Proceedings of the IEEE/CVF Conference on Computer Vision and Pattern Recognition, pp. 5579–5588 (2020)
7. Laine, S., Aila, T.: Temporal ensembling for semi-supervised learning. In: International Conference on Learning Representations (ICLR) (2017)

8. Lee, J., Kim, E., Lee, S., Lee, J., Yoon, S.: Ficklenet: weakly and semi-supervised semantic image segmentation using stochastic inference. In: Proceedings of the IEEE/CVF Conference on Computer Vision and Pattern Recognition, pp. 5267–5276 (2019)

9. Lee, J., Yi, J., Shin, C., Yoon, S.: Bbam: bounding box attribution map for weakly supervised semantic and instance segmentation. In: Proceedings of the IEEE/CVF conference on Computer Vision and Pattern Recognition, pp. 2643–2652 (2021)

10. Li, Y., Luo, L., Lin, H., Chen, H., Heng, P.-A.: Dual-consistency semi-supervised learning with uncertainty quantification for COVID-19 lesion segmentation from CT images. In: de Bruijne, M., et al. (eds.) MICCAI 2021. LNCS, vol. 12902, pp. 199–209. Springer, Cham (2021). https://doi.org/10.1007/978-3-030-87196-3_19

11. Liu, X., et al.: Weakly supervised segmentation of COVID19 infection with scribble annotation on CT images. Pattern Recogn. **122**, 108341 (2022)

12. Lockwood, E.: Length of ellipse. Math. Gaz. **16**(220), 269–270 (1932)

13. Lu, Y., et al.: Taskology: utilizing task relations at scale. In: Proceedings of the IEEE/CVF Conference on Computer Vision and Pattern Recognition, pp. 8700–8709 (2021)

14. Luo, X.: Ssl4mis (2020). https://github.com/hilab-git/ssl4mis

15. Luo, X., Chen, J., Song, T., Wang, G.: Semi-supervised medical image segmentation through dual-task consistency. In: Proceedings of the AAAI Conference on Artificial Intelligence, vol. 35, pp. 8801–8809 (2021)

16. Luo, X., et al.: Efficient semi-supervised gross target volume of nasopharyngeal carcinoma segmentation via uncertainty rectified pyramid consistency. In: de Bruijne, M., et al. (eds.) MICCAI 2021. LNCS, vol. 12902, pp. 318–329. Springer, Cham (2021). https://doi.org/10.1007/978-3-030-87196-3_30

17. Meng, Y., et al.: Regression of instance boundary by aggregated CNN and GCN. In: Vedaldi, A., Bischof, H., Brox, T., Frahm, J.-M. (eds.) ECCV 2020. LNCS, vol. 12353, pp. 190–207. Springer, Cham (2020). https://doi.org/10.1007/978-3-030-58598-3_12

18. Meng, Y., et al.: CNN-GCN aggregation enabled boundary regression for biomedical image segmentation. In: Martel, A.L., et al. (eds.) MICCAI 2020. LNCS, vol. 12264, pp. 352–362. Springer, Cham (2020). https://doi.org/10.1007/978-3-030-59719-1_35

19. Meng, Y., et al.: Bi-GCN: boundary-aware input-dependent graph convolution network for biomedical image segmentation. In: 32nd British Machine Vision Conference: BMVC 2021. British Machine Vision Association (2021)

20. Meng, Y., et al.: Spatial uncertainty-aware semi-supervised crowd counting. In: Proceedings of the IEEE/CVF International Conference on Computer Vision, pp. 15549–15559 (2021)

21. Meng, Y., et al.: Graph-based region and boundary aggregation for biomedical image segmentation. IEEE Trans. Med. Imaging **41**, 690–701 (2021)

22. Mukaka, M.M.: A guide to appropriate use of correlation coefficient in medical research. Malawi Med. J. **24**(3), 69–71 (2012)

23. Orlando, J.I., et al.: REFUGE challenge: a unified framework for evaluating automated methods for glaucoma assessment from fundus photographs. Med. Image Anal. **59**, 101570 (2020)

24. Sivaswamy, J., Krishnadas, S., Joshi, G.D., Jain, M., Tabish, A.U.S.: Drishti-GS: retinal image dataset for optic nerve head (ONH) segmentation. In: 2014 IEEE 11th International Symposium on Biomedical Imaging (ISBI), pp. 53–56. IEEE (2014)

25. Tarvainen, A., Valpola, H.: Mean teachers are better role models: weight-averaged consistency targets improve semi-supervised deep learning results. In: Advances in Neural Information Processing Systems, pp. 1195–1204 (2017)
26. Wu, J., Wang, K., Shang, Z., Xu, J., Ding, D., Li, X., Yang, G.: Oval shape constraint based optic disc and cup segmentation in fundus photographs. In: BMVC, p. 265 (2019)
27. Xue, Y., et al.: Shape-aware organ segmentation by predicting signed distance maps. In: Proceedings of the AAAI Conference on Artificial Intelligence, vol. 34, pp. 12565–12572 (2020)
28. Yu, L., Wang, S., Li, X., Fu, C.-W., Heng, P.-A.: Uncertainty-aware self-ensembling model for semi-supervised 3D left atrium segmentation. In: Shen, D., et al. (eds.) MICCAI 2019. LNCS, vol. 11765, pp. 605–613. Springer, Cham (2019). https://doi.org/10.1007/978-3-030-32245-8_67
29. Zhang, Z., et al.: ORIGA-light: An online retinal fundus image database for glaucoma analysis and research. In: 2010 Annual International Conference of the IEEE Engineering in Medicine and Biology, pp. 3065–3068. IEEE (2010)

Accurate and Robust Lesion RECIST Diameter Prediction and Segmentation with Transformers

Youbao Tang[1]([✉]), Ning Zhang[1], Yirui Wang[1], Shenghua He[1], Mei Han[1], Jing Xiao[2], and Ruei-Sung Lin[1]

[1] PAII Inc., Palo Alto, CA, USA
tybxiaobao@gmail.com
[2] Ping An Technology, Shenzhen, China

Abstract. Automatically measuring lesion/tumor size with RECIST (Response Evaluation Criteria In Solid Tumors) diameters and segmentation is important for computer-aided diagnosis. Although it has been studied in recent years, there is still space to improve its accuracy and robustness, such as (1) enhancing features by incorporating rich contextual information while keeping a high spatial resolution and (2) involving new tasks and losses for joint optimization. To reach this goal, this paper proposes a transformer-based network (MeaFormer, **Mea**surement trans**Former**) for lesion RECIST diameter prediction and segmentation (LRDPS). It is formulated as three correlative and complementary tasks: lesion segmentation, heatmap prediction, and keypoint regression. To the best of our knowledge, it is the first time to use keypoint regression for RECIST diameter prediction. MeaFormer can enhance high-resolution features by employing transformers to capture their long-range dependencies. Two consistency losses are introduced to explicitly build relationships among these tasks for better optimization. Experiments show that MeaFormer achieves the state-of-the-art performance of LRDPS on the large-scale DeepLesion dataset and produces promising results of two downstream clinic-relevant tasks, *i.e.*, 3D lesion segmentation and RECIST assessment in longitudinal studies.

Keywords: RECIST diameter prediction · Lesion segmentation · Transformers · Keypoint regression

1 Introduction

When reading computed tomography (CT) scans, an important step for radiologists is to measure the size of found lesions. Accurately measuring the lesions is crucial in precisely assessing the lesion growth rates across different time points. As such, it plays an important role in monitoring disease progression and making therapeutic plan. Currently, the most widely-used clinical guideline of lesion measurement is bidimensional RECIST (Response Evaluation Criteria In Solid

L. Wang et al. (Eds.): MICCAI 2022, LNCS 13434, pp. 535–544, 2022.
https://doi.org/10.1007/978-3-031-16440-8_51

Tumors) [8] diameters. Manually labeling the RECIST diameters is tedious, time-consuming, and prone to be inconsistent among different observers [22]. To overcome these issues, Tang *et al.* [16] first presented a semi-automatic RECIST diameter labeling approach. It has been demonstrated that segmentation can be considered as a more precise measurement than RECIST diameters to assess treatment response [1,14]. Therefore, some great progresses [17,18] have been made recently to further improve the performance of RECIST diameter prediction and incorporate lesion segmentation simultaneously.

The previous works [17,18] tried to build powerful convolutional neural networks (CNN) through sophisticated designs to learn discriminative features. Although they achieved promising performances on lesion RECIST diameter prediction and segmentation (LRDPS), there are two obvious limitations. First, they failed to fully exploit the features' long-range dependencies due to the inherent locality of convolutional operations, which is crucial for pixel-wise prediction tasks, *e.g.*, lesion segmentation and heatmap prediction. Second, they only produced a single RECIST diameter output based on heatmap prediction. This would lead to unsatisfactory results when the lesions are difficult to identify.

On the other hand, transformer is designed to model sequence-to-sequence predictions in natural language processing tasks [19], which is able to capture the long-range dependencies of the input sequences. Recently, it has been successfully applied to tasks of computer vision [5,7] and medical image segmentation [4,11,23], which attracts tremendous attentions increasingly. Hence, to address the above limitations, we propose a transformer-based network (MeaFormer, **Mea**surement trans**Former**) for LRDPS in this paper, where three correlative and comprementary tasks are involved in including lesion segmentation, heatmap prediction, and keypoint regression. Three main contributions are made in MeaFormer to push it into achieving accurate and robust results of LRDPS: (1) transformers are employed to model the long-range dependencies of the high-resolution features extracted by a small CNN backbone. By incorporating rich contextual information, the enhanced high-resolution features facilitate accurate lesion segmentation and heatmap prediction results. (2) To the best of knowledge, it is the first time to use keypoint regression for RECIST diameter prediction and obtain RECIST diameters directly from segmentations. Thus, three types of RECIST diameter predictions are produced by MeaFormer in total instead of a single one. Fusing them helps to achieve a more robust outcome. (3) Two consistency losses are introduced to explicitly build relationships among these tasks. A joint optimization using them facilitates MeaFormer with an more optimal solution. Furthermore, extensive experiments on the large-scale DeepLesion dataset show that the proposed MeaFormer achieves the state-of-the-art performance of LRDPS.

2   Method

As done in [17,18], we also develop a click-based automatic LRDPS system with two steps, whose pipeline is presented in Fig. 1(a). Given a CT image and a click

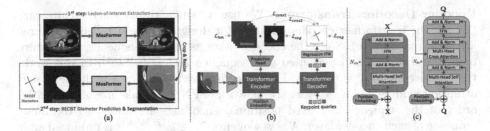

Fig. 1. System overview. (a) The pipeline of our click-based automatic LRDPS system with separately trained MeaFormer models for step 1 and step 2, respectively. (b) The architecture of the proposed network MeaFormer used at step 2. (c) The detailed structures of MeaFormer's encoder and decoder. The MeaFormer used at step 1 has the same architecture except the following differences: (i) two queries for box prediction at step 1 rather than four at step 2 and (ii) no consistency losses (*i.e.*, $\mathcal{L}_{cons1}$ and $\mathcal{L}_{cons2}$) used for training at step 1. All figures are best viewed in color. (Color figure online)

guidance (the red spot) within the lesion, the top-left and bottom-right corners (the green circles) of a bounding box (the green dotted box) are predicted to indicate the lesion region at the 1st step. A lesion-of-interest (LOI, the region in the magenta box) is extracted, whose center is the predicted box and whose width is two times the extent of the predicted box's long side. As such, sufficient context information is preserved in a LOI. The LOI is then cropped and resized to 256×256. At the 2nd step, the results of LRDPS are obtained based on the resized LOI. The proposed network MeaFormer is used at both steps.

2.1 The Architecture of MeaFormer

Figure 1(b) shows the architecture of MeaFormer. We borrowed idea from DETR [5] where transformers are applied on a CNN-based feature map instead of the image input. MeaFormer contains four main components, including a CNN backbone for feature extraction, an encoder-decoder transformer, a CNN-based prediction head for lesion segmentation and heatmap prediction, and a regression feed-forward network (FFN) for box/keypoint prediction at the $1^{st}/2^{nd}$ step.

Backbone. Given an image $\mathbf{I}_{ct} \in \mathbb{R}^{H_0 \times W_0}$ of an original CT image at the 1st step or a resized LOI CT image at the 2nd step, we first generate a click image $\mathbf{I}_c$ and a distance transform image $\mathbf{I}_d$ based on the human click guidance following [17,18]. A 3-channel image $\mathbf{I} \in \mathbb{R}^{3 \times H_0 \times W_0}$ is constructed by concatenating $\mathbf{I}_{ct}$, $\mathbf{I}_c$, and $\mathbf{I}_d$, which serves as an input of the backbone. To reduce the computation cost at the 1st step, the original CT image is resized to 256×256. Thus, $H_0 = W_0 = 256$ in this work. Here, we choose HRNet-W48 [20] as the backbone for feature extraction. As we know that the features' spatial and low-level information are crucial to getting accurate pixel-wise predictions, thus only the first three stages of HRNet-W48 is adopted to generate a low-level and high-resolution feature map $\mathbf{F} \in \mathbb{R}^{C \times H \times W}$, where $C = 48, H = \frac{H_0}{4}, W = \frac{W_0}{4}$.

Encoder-Decoder Transformer. We use a vanilla transformer architecture [19] for our transformer encoder and decoder design, whose detailed structures are shown in Fig. 1(c). Since the encoder takes as input a sequence, the feature map $\mathbf{F}$ is flattened and permuted to a sequence $\mathbf{X} \in \mathbb{R}^{(H \cdot W) \times C}$. In this work, the encoder has $N_{en} = 6$ layers. Each encoder layer contains a multi-head self-attention module and a feed-forward network (FFN). To make use of the spatial order of the sequence, the fixed positional encodings are added to the input sequence of each encoder layer. A new sequence $\mathbf{X}' \in \mathbb{R}^{(H \cdot W) \times C}$ is produced after forwarding N_{en} encoder layers. The decoder aims to transform a learnable query matrix $\mathbf{Q} \in \mathbb{R}^{N_q \times C}$ that contains N_q query embeddings of size C using multi-head self- and encoder-decoder attention mechanisms. It consists of $N_{de} = 6$ layers. Each layer takes as input $\mathbf{X}'$ and $\mathbf{Q}$, and outputs an updated $\mathbf{Q}$. Similarly to the encoder, the positional encodings are added to the input of each decoder layer. After forwarding N_{de} decoder layers, the final updated query matrix $\mathbf{Q}$ is token as input of the regression FFN. We set $N_q = 2$ and $N_q = 4$ at the 1st and 2nd step, respectively. That is because two corners/four keypoints are required for box/keypoint prediction.

Prediction Head. A CNN-based prediction head is attached to the transformer encoder for lesion segmentation and heatmap prediction. Before feeding the sequence $\mathbf{X}' \in \mathbb{R}^{(H \cdot W) \times C}$ into the prediction head, we first permute and reshape $\mathbf{X}'$ to a feature map $\mathbf{F}' \in \mathbb{R}^{C \times H \times W}$. The prediction head consists of sequential layers: $conv(kn = 32, ks = 3, st = 1)$, $deconv(32, 4, 2)$, $conv(32, 3, 1)$, $deconv(32, 4, 2)$, and $conv(5, 1, 1)$, where $conv(*)$, $deconv(*)$, kn, ks, and st represent convolutional layer, deconvolutional layer, kernel number, kernel size, and stride, respectively. Each layer is followed by a batch normalization and a ReLU except the last one. Therefore, the output of the prediction head $\mathbf{O} \in \mathbb{R}^{5 \times H_0 \times W_0}$ has the same resolution to the input image. One channel of $\mathbf{O}$ is the lesion segmentation result $\mathbf{S}$ and the other four channels are the predicted heatmaps $\mathbf{M}$.

Regression FFN. To get the box/keypoint prediction results, a regression FFN is attached to the transformer decoder. It consists of a 2-layer perceptron with ReLU activation function and hidden dimension $d = 96$, and a linear projection layer with two output nodes for predicting the corner/keypoint coordinate (x, y) using a softmax function. As done in [5], we also add the regression FFN after each transformer decoder layer to introduce auxiliary losses for model optimization. All regression FFNs share their parameters.

2.2 Model Optimization

The porposed MeaFormer has three task-related losses to optimize. The lesion segmentation loss $\mathcal{L}_{seg}$ is the summation of a binary cross entropy loss $\mathcal{L}_{bce}$ and an IoU loss $\mathcal{L}_{iou}$ [13], $i.e.$, $\mathcal{L}_{seg} = \mathcal{L}_{bce} + \mathcal{L}_{iou}$. The same procedure as [15] is conducted to construct initial and updated lesion pseudo masks as supervision for $\mathcal{L}_{seg}$ optimization. For heatmap prediction, the objective function $\mathcal{L}_{hm}$ is a mean squared error loss $\mathcal{L}_{mse}$ that measures the errors between the predicted heatmaps and the ground truth heatmaps, which are four 2D Gaussian maps (with a standard deviation of 5 pixels) centered on the endpoints of RECIST annotations. For keypoint regression, the objective function $\mathcal{L}_{reg}$ is a L1 loss $\mathcal{L}_1$ that is adopted to calculate the errors between the predicted keypoint coordinates produced by N_{de} regression FFNs and the ground truth coordinates of the RECIST diameters' endpoints.

Besides these individual losses, this work also introduces two consistency losses to explicitly build two relationships among different tasks. One relationship is built between the tasks of keypoint regression and heatmap prediction. Both of them are conducted for RECIST diameter prediction, thus their outputs should be as consistent as possible. Let (x_i, y_i) denote the ith keypoint's predicted coordinate produced by the keypoint regression task, so $\mathbf{M}_{i,y_i,x_i}$ means the value of the ith predicted heatmap at location (x_i, y_i). To make the outputs of keypoint regression and heatmap prediction as consistent as possible, (x_i, y_i) should be as close as possible to the maximum location of the ith predicted heatmap, meaning that the error between $\mathbf{M}_{i,y_i,x_i}$ and 1 should be as small as possible. The other relationship is built between the tasks of keypoint regression and lesion segmentation. In an ideal situation, the predicted keypoints should be located at the boundaries of the lesion segmentation. We first binarize the segmentation result by $\mathbf{S} \geq 0.5$, and then perform a distance transformation on the binary mask to get a distance map $\mathbf{D}$. Therefore, to make the results of keypoint regression and lesion segmentation as consistent as possible, the error between $\mathbf{D}_{y_i,x_i}$ and 0 should be as small as possible. L1 losses are used to compute the aforementioned two errors, which are denoted as $\mathcal{L}_{cons1}$ and $\mathcal{L}_{cons2}$, respectively. The final objective function for model optimization is defined as

$$\mathcal{L} = \lambda_1 \mathcal{L}_{seg} + \lambda_2 \mathcal{L}_{hm} + \lambda_3 \mathcal{L}_{reg} + \lambda_4 \mathcal{L}_{cons1} + \lambda_5 \mathcal{L}_{cons2}, \tag{1}$$

where we set $\lambda_1 = 1$, $\lambda_2 = 10$, $\lambda_3 = 1$, $\lambda_4 = 0.01$, and $\lambda_5 = 0.01$ to balance the magnitude of different losses in this work.

Implementation Details. MeaFormer is implemented in PyTorch 1.6 [12] and the CNN backbone is initialized with ImaeNet [6] pre-trained weights. Adam optimizer [10] with an initial learning rate of 0.001 and default settings (*e.g.*, betas=(0.9, 0.999)) is used to train the model for 200 epochs reduced by 0.1 at epoch 100 and 150. The training batch size is 16. The following operations are randomly conducted for data augmentation: scaling, cropping, rotating, brightness and contrast adjusting, and Gaussian blurring. The MeaFormer models used at two steps are trained separately. Following [15], the one at the 2nd step is trained three rounds with the iteratively updated lesion pseudo masks as supervisions for weakly-supervised lesion segmentation learning.

3   Experiments

Dataset and Evaluation Metrics. A large-scale DeepLesion dataset [21][1] is used to train and test the proposed MeaFormer. It collects 32,735 lesions

---

[1] https://nihcc.app.box.com/v/DeepLesion.

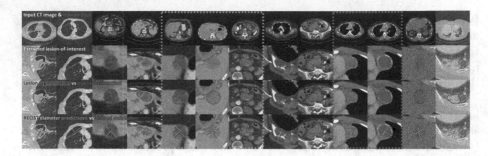

Fig. 2. Qualitative results of our system. Each column gives an example, where the content of each row has been described with texts. The predicted RECIST diameters shown in the fourth row with different colors are obtained from three different tasks, including segmentation, heatmap prediction, and keypoint regression. The orange dotted box shows three examples with imperfect manual diameter annotations. The magenta dotted box shows a lesion pair collected from the same patient at different time points, where the manual annotations of the left lesion are incorrect. (Color figure online)

Table 1. Results of different methods for LRDPS on the DeepLesion test set in terms of model size (*i.e.*, the parameter number, the unit is million), Dice (%), and long/short diameter length error (mm). The mean and standard deviation are reported. Red and blue texts indicate rank 1 and 2, respectively.

Method	Size	Dice	Heatmaps		Segmentation		Regression		Fusion	
			Long	Short	Long	Short	Long	Short	Long	Short
Cai *et al.* [2]	-	90.6±8.9	-	-	-	-	-	-	-	-
AHRNet [15]	-	92.6±4.3	-	-	-	-	-	-	-	-
Tang *et al.* [16]	-	-	1.9±2.2	1.6±1.9	-	-	-	-	-	-
SEENet [18]	-	91.2±3.9	1.7±2.0	1.6±1.8	-	-	-	-	-	-
nnUNet [9]	-	90.7±5.0	2.1±2.0	1.8±1.7	-	-	-	-	-	-
PDNet [17]	-	92.4±4.5	1.7±1.5	1.5±1.4	-	-	-	-	-	-
Swin-Unet [4]	84.0	91.0±5.1	1.9±1.9	2.0±3.7	2.0±1.8	1.8±2.2	-	-	1.9±1.8	1.7±2.5
SegTran [11]	134.8	91.9±5.2	1.8±1.5	1.9±3.1	1.8±1.7	1.7±2.1	-	-	1.7±1.6	1.7±2.2
TransFuse [23]	26.1	92.0±4.9	1.8±1.4	1.8±2.0	1.7±1.6	1.5±2.1	-	-	1.7±1.5	1.6±1.8
Ours	18.3	92.7±4.3	1.6±1.4	1.4±1.6	1.6±1.3	1.5±1.5	1.9±1.5	1.7±1.9	1.6±1.3	1.4±1.5

from 10, 594 studies of 4, 427 patients. There are a variety of lesion types in this dataset, such as lung nodules, liver tumors, enlarged lymph nodes, and so on. All lesion are annotated by bidimensional RECIST diameters telling their sizes and locations. As done in [17, 18], 1, 000 lesion images from 500 patients are manually segmented as a test set. The rest patient data are used for training (80%) and validation (20%). The same evaluation metrics to [17, 18] are adopted to calculate the quantitative results, including the pixel-wise dice coefficient (Dice) for lesion segmentation and the differences between the diameter lengths (mm) of the predictions and manual annotations for RECIST diameter prediction.

Experimental Results. Figure 2 displays several qualitative results produced by our system. We observe that (1) the lesions are well located at the center of the extracted LOIs, meaning that the proposed network can accurately predict the

Table 2. Results of different settings of our network on the DeepLesion test set.

Method	Size	Dice	Heatmaps		Regression	
			Long	Short	Long	Short
HRNet$_{regression}$	39.2	-	-	-	3.0±2.3	2.1±2.2
HRNet$_{heatmap}$	70.4	91.4±5.7	1.9±1.7	1.9±2.4	-	-
HRNet*+TranE	17.6	92.1±4.9	1.7±1.6	1.7±2.1	-	-
HRNet*+TranE+TranD($\mathcal{L}_1$)	18.3	92.5±4.4	1.7±1.7	1.6±1.7	2.3±1.9	2.0±2.2
HRNet*+TranE+TranD($\mathcal{L}_1+\mathcal{L}_{cons1}$)	18.3	92.5±4.5	1.7±1.5	1.5±1.7	1.9±1.6	1.8±2.0
HRNet*+TranE+TranD($\mathcal{L}_1+\mathcal{L}_{cons1}+\mathcal{L}_{cons2}$)	18.3	92.7±4.3	1.6±1.4	1.4±1.6	1.9±1.5	1.7±1.9

corners of the lesion bounding boxes. A prediction is considered as correct when the IoU of the predicted box and the ground truth box is larger than 0.5. On the 1000 test lesions, we achieve an accuracy of 99.1% surpassing the previous work [18] by about 2%. (2) Our automatic results are close to the manual annotations and the diameter predictions produced by different tasks are nearly consistent, which visually demonstrate the effectiveness of our system and the contributions of the proposed consistency losses. (3) For some cases (*e.g.*, the examples in the orange dotted box), even the manual diameter annotations are not very precise, our automatic predictions can mitigate this issue. (4) For some cases (the left example in the magenta dotted box), the lesions' boundaries are unclear for some areas, resulting in incorrect manual annotations, but the automatic results can correct them. (5) Although our system works well on most of cases, it still faces some difficulties when the lesions' boundaries/shapes are heavily vague/irregular (the examples in the last two columns).

The quantitative comparisons of our system with previous approaches on these tasks [2,9,15–18] and three transformer-based medical image segmentation approaches [4,11,23] are presented in Table 1. The listed results of [2,15–18] are copied from their related papers. The results of nnUnet [9] are copied from [17]. For [4,11,23], we train them for heatmap prediction and lesion segmentation at the 2nd step using the same data as ours for fair comparisons. We observe that (1) Our MeaFormer has the smallest model size but achieves the best performance on all tasks, demonstrating its effectiveness for these tasks. (2) Better segmentation results produce better RECIST diameter predictions from segmentation. Sometimes, it even outperforms the heatmap-based prediction. This demonstrates that segmentation is a reliable way to predict RECIST diameters. Specifically, the RECIST diameters are obtained by first finding the longest diameter (long axis) from a lesion segmentation, and then calculating its longest perpendicular diameter (short axis). (3) More reliable RECIST diameter lengths can be obtained after fusing the predictions from different tasks, which mimics the behavior of radiologists making a consistent decision together when they have different observations. In this work, we find that the following fusion strategy achieves the best performance: (i) use prediction from segmentation as the reference, (ii) select a prediction from another task that has the

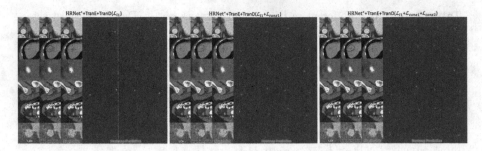

Fig. 3. Visual comparisons of the results produced by the proposed network that is trained with or without the consistency losses. The red curves and spots are the manually annotated lesion masks and RECIST diameters' endpoints. The blue curves are the automatic lesion segmentation results. The green spots are the predicted RECIST diameters' endpoints by keypoint regression. (Color figure online)

smallest length difference compared to the reference, (iii) average their lengths to estimate the lesion size.

Ablation Studies. The proposed network is built based on HRNet by gradually integrating a transformer encdoer (TranE) and a transformer decoder (TranD). Besides, two new consistency losses ($\mathcal{L}_{cons1}$ and $\mathcal{L}_{cons2}$) are introduced for model optimization. Although only the first three stages of HRNet (HRNet*) are used in this work, we also adopt the full HRNet for keypoint regression (HRNet$_{regression}$) by adding a global average pooling layer and a fully connected layer, and lesion segmentation and heatmap prediction (HRNet$_{heatmap}$) by adding a UNet-like decoder and skip connections. Table 2 lists the results of different settings. We observe that (1) the performance of all tasks are consistently improved after gradually introducing different components, demonstrating the effectiveness and contributions of each component for these tasks. (2) After simply adding a transformer encoder (HRNet*+TranE), the performance gets a big improvement compared to HRNet$_{heatmap}$, meaning that the encoder can well capture the long-range dependencies of low-level features to enhance their representation ability. (3) After introducing the consistency losses, all tasks' results are improved, especially for keypoint regression when adding $\mathcal{L}_{cons1}$ and lesion segmentation when adding $\mathcal{L}_{cons2}$. Figure 3 provides visual evidences to show the effectiveness of the proposed consistency losses, where the results of lesion segmentation and keypoint regression become closer to manual annotations and the predicted heatmaps become more concentrated and reliable after adding them.

Downstream Tasks. Two straightforward downstream clinic-relevant tasks can be conducted based on our results, which are 3D lesion segmentation and RECIST assessment in longitudinal studies. For 3D lesion segmentation, 200 lesions selected from above manually segmented 1,000 lesions are fully annotated with 3D masks following [2]. We run our system on these lesions slice-by-slice and stack their 2D segmentation results to form their 3D segmentations. This work achieves a mean Dice score of 85.6% remarkably surpassing the previous work [2] by 9.2%. For RECIST assessment in longitudinal studies, 480 lesion pairs from the test set of the DLS dataset [3][2] are used for evaluation, which are excluded from our training data. The CT scans of each pair are collected at different time points from the same patient. For each lesion pair, we first get the lesions' RECIST diameters using our system. Then we compute its tumor response class, as complete response, partial response, progressive disease, or stable disease, of the manual RECIST and our automated RECIST assessments, based on RECIST version 1.1 [8]. On the 480 test lesion pairs, we achieve an accuracy of 91.7% for the tumor response classification, suggesting that our system can help clinicians to annotate sequential RECIST measurements with minimal human effort.

4 Conclusions

In this work, we propose a transformer-based network for lesion RECIST diameter prediction and segmentation. It leverages the long-range dependencies learning ability of transformers to enhance features. Besides, three tasks are performed and jointly trained, and their relationships are explicitly built by introducing two new consistency losses. All of these facilitate our system to produce accurate and robust results. Hence, it can serve as a useful tool for clinicians to precisely measure tumor sizes with minimal effort and may provide high positive clinical values on oncologic imaging analysis workflows.

References

1. Bretschi, M., et al.: Assessing treatment response of osteolytic lesions by manual volumetry, automatic segmentation, and RECIST in experimental bone metastases. Acad. Radiol. **21**(9), 1177–1184 (2014)
2. Cai, J., et al.: Accurate weakly-supervised deep lesion segmentation using large-scale clinical annotations: slice-propagated 3D mask generation from 2D RECIST. In: Frangi, A.F., Schnabel, J.A., Davatzikos, C., Alberola-López, C., Fichtinger, G. (eds.) MICCAI 2018. LNCS, vol. 11073, pp. 396–404. Springer, Cham (2018). https://doi.org/10.1007/978-3-030-00937-3_46
3. Cai, J., et al.: Deep lesion tracker: Monitoring lesions in 4d longitudinal imaging studies. In: CVPR, pp. 15159–15169 (2021)
4. Cao, H., et al.: Swin-unet: unet-like pure transformer for medical image segmentation. arXiv preprint arXiv:2105.05537 (2021)
5. Carion, N., Massa, F., Synnaeve, G., Usunier, N., Kirillov, A., Zagoruyko, S.: End-to-end object detection with transformers. In: Vedaldi, A., Bischof, H., Brox, T., Frahm, J.-M. (eds.) ECCV 2020. LNCS, vol. 12346, pp. 213–229. Springer, Cham (2020). https://doi.org/10.1007/978-3-030-58452-8_13
6. Deng, J., Dong, W., Socher, R., Li, L., Li, K., Li, F.: Imagenet: a large-scale hierarchical image database. In: CVPR, pp. 248–255 (2009)
7. Dosovitskiy, A., et al.: An image is worth 16 × 16 words: transformers for image recognition at scale. arXiv preprint arXiv:2010.11929 (2020)

---

[2] https://github.com/JimmyCai91/DLT.

8. Eisenhauer, E.A., et al.: New response evaluation criteria in solid tumours: revised RECIST guideline (version 1.1). Eur. J. Cancer **45**(2), 228–247 (2009)

9. Isensee, F., et al.: nnU-net: self-adapting framework for u-net-based medical image segmentation. arXiv preprint arXiv:1809.10486 (2018)

10. Kingma, D.P., Ba, J.: Adam: a method for stochastic optimization. arXiv preprint arXiv:1412.6980 (2014)

11. Li, S., Sui, X., Luo, X., Xu, X., Liu, Y., Goh, R.S.M.: Medical image segmentation using squeeze-and-expansion transformers. In: IJCAI, pp. 807–815 (2021)

12. Paszke, A., et al.: Pytorch: An imperative style, high-performance deep learning library. In: NeurIPS, pp. 8024–8035 (2019)

13. Rahman, M.A., Wang, Y.: Optimizing intersection-over-union in deep neural networks for image segmentation. In: Bebis, G., et al. (eds.) ISVC 2016. LNCS, vol. 10072, pp. 234–244. Springer, Cham (2016). https://doi.org/10.1007/978-3-319-50835-1_22

14. Rothe, J.H., et al.: Size determination and response assessment of liver metastases with computed tomography-comparison of RECIST and volumetric algorithms. Eur. J. Radiol. **82**(11), 1831–1839 (2013)

15. Tang, Y., et al.: Weakly-supervised universal lesion segmentation with regional level set loss. In: de Bruijne, M., et al. (eds.) MICCAI 2021. LNCS, vol. 12902, pp. 515–525. Springer, Cham (2021). https://doi.org/10.1007/978-3-030-87196-3_48

16. Tang, Y., Harrison, A.P., Bagheri, M., Xiao, J., Summers, R.M.: Semi-automatic RECIST labeling on CT scans with cascaded convolutional neural networks. In: Frangi, A.F., Schnabel, J.A., Davatzikos, C., Alberola-López, C., Fichtinger, G. (eds.) MICCAI 2018. LNCS, vol. 11073, pp. 405–413. Springer, Cham (2018). https://doi.org/10.1007/978-3-030-00937-3_47

17. Tang, Y., et al.: Lesion segmentation and RECIST diameter prediction via click-driven attention and dual-path connection. In: de Bruijne, M., et al. (eds.) MICCAI 2021. LNCS, vol. 12902, pp. 341–351. Springer, Cham (2021). https://doi.org/10.1007/978-3-030-87196-3_32

18. Tang, Y., Yan, K., Xiao, J., Summers, R.M.: One click lesion RECIST measurement and segmentation on CT scans. In: Martel, A.L., et al. (eds.) MICCAI 2020. LNCS, vol. 12264, pp. 573–583. Springer, Cham (2020). https://doi.org/10.1007/978-3-030-59719-1_56

19. Vaswani, A., et al.: Attention is all you need. NeurIPS **30** (2017)

20. Wang, J., et al.: Deep high-resolution representation learning for visual recognition. IEEE Trans. Pattern Anal. Mach. Intell. **10**(2020), 3349–3364 (2020)

21. Yan, K., Wang, X., Lu, L., Summers, R.M.: DeepLesion: automated mining of large-scale lesion annotations and universal lesion detection with deep learning. J. Med. Imaging **5**(3), 036501 (2018)

22. Yoon, S.H., Kim, K.W., Goo, J.M., Kim, D.W., Hahn, S.: Observer variability in recist-based tumour burden measurements: a meta-analysis. Eur. J. Cancer **53**, 5–15 (2016)

23. Zhang, Y., Liu, H., Hu, Q.: TransFuse: fusing transformers and CNNs for medical image segmentation. In: de Bruijne, M., et al. (eds.) MICCAI 2021. LNCS, vol. 12901, pp. 14–24. Springer, Cham (2021). https://doi.org/10.1007/978-3-030-87193-2_2

DeSD: Self-Supervised Learning with Deep Self-Distillation for 3D Medical Image Segmentation

Yiwen Ye[1], Jianpeng Zhang[1], Ziyang Chen[1], and Yong Xia[1,2,3(✉)]

[1] National Engineering Laboratory for Integrated Aero-Space-Ground-Ocean Big Data Application Technology, School of Computer Science and Engineering, Northwestern Polytechnical University, Xi'an 710072, China
{ywye,james.zhang}@mail.nwpu.edu.cn, yxia@nwpu.edu.cn
[2] Ningbo Institute of Northwestern Polytechnical University, Ningbo 315048, China
[3] Research & Development Institute of Northwestern Polytechnical University in Shenzhen, Shenzhen 518057, China

Abstract. Self-supervised learning (SSL), enabling advanced performance with few annotations, has demonstrated a proven successful in medical image segmentation. Usually, SSL relies on measuring the similarity of features obtained at the deepest layer to attract the features of positive pairs or repulse the features of negative pairs, and then may suffer from the weak supervision at shallow layers. To address this issue, we reformulate SSL in a Deep Self-Distillation (DeSD) manner to improve the representation quality of both shallow and deep layers. Specifically, the DeSD model is composed of an online student network and a momentum teacher network, both being stacked by multiple sub-encoders. The features produced by each sub-encoder in the student network are trained to match the features produced by the teacher network. Such a deep self-distillation supervision is able to improve the representation quality of all sub-encoders, including both shallow ones and deep ones. We pre-train the DeSD model on a large-scale unlabeled dataset and evaluate it on seven downstream segmentation tasks. Our results indicate that the proposed DeSD model achieves superior pre-training performance over existing SSL methods, setting the new state of the art. The code is available at https://github.com/yeerwen/DeSD.

Keywords: Self-supervised learning · Deep self-distillation · Medical image segmentation

1 Introduction

Y. Ye and J. Zhang—Contributed equally.

Supplementary Information The online version contains supplementary material available at https://doi.org/10.1007/978-3-031-16440-8_52.

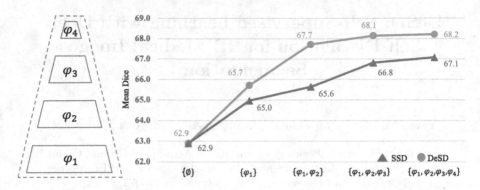

Fig. 1. Single Self-Distillation (SSD) vs. Deep Self-Distillation (DeSD). The encoder is divided into four sub-encoders, φ_1, φ_2, φ_3, and φ_4. $\{\phi\}$: training from scratch; $\{\varphi_i\}$: initializing φ_i with pre-training weights from deep self-distillation (orange) or single self-distillation (blue). Here we use the hepatic vessel and tumor segmentation as the downstream task. (Color figure online)

Medical image segmentation plays an essential role in computer-aided diagnosis [2,15,23]. Although deep learning achieves great success on many computer vision tasks, medical image segmentation remains challenging due to the hunger of deep models for expensive voxel-wise dense annotations [11,16,17].

Recently, self-supervised learning (SSL), which does not rely on large-scale annotations [20,21,25], has delivered proven performance that is competitive or even superior to supervised learning [4,7,9,10,12,13,22]. SimCLR [7] makes the output vectors of the same image's two views similar while the output vectors of different images repulsive. MoCo [9,13] sets up a dictionary as a queue to store and update representations of negative samples and alleviates the heavy dependence on the large batch size via a momentum encoder. BYOL [12] and SimSiam [10] ignore the negative samples and employ an asymmetric structure, *i.e.*, adding a prediction head, for self-distillation. Meanwhile, the momentum encoder and stop-gradient operation are useful to avoid trivial solutions. Similarly, DINO [5] integrates the multi-crop strategy [4] and self-distillation, and devises the centering and sharpening operations to further avoid collapse. For medical image domain, Models Genesis (MG) [25] adopts image reconstruction, where the input image is randomly augmented by four transformations, as the pretext task to learn powerful representations. Preservational Contrastive Representation Learning (PCRL) [24] jointly uses contrastive learning and image reconstruction to preserve both global and local representations. In these solutions, the similarity measurement is exerted on the features obtained at the deepest layer to attract the positive pairs, or repulse the negative pairs, or reconstruct the corrupted images, resulting in the weak constraint at shallow layers.

To address this issue, we propose a **D**eep **S**elf-**D**istillation (DeSD) based SSL method for 3D medical image segmentation, aiming to boost the representation quality of all shallow and high layers. Specifically, we adopt a pair of Siamese networks consisting of an online student encoder and a momentum teacher encoder,

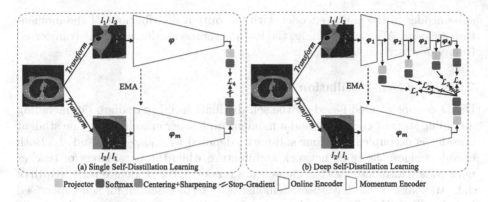

Fig. 2. Two types of SSL methods. (a) Single self-distillation learning: The output distribution obtained from the student encoder is trained to match that obtained from the teacher encoder. (b) Proposed deep self-distillation learning (DeSD): The student encoder is decoupled into four sub-encoders, each performing a single self-distillation learning.

which are fed with the two transformations of the same image, respectively. The student encoder is divided into multiple sub-encoders, each being optimized to match the output distribution obtained with the teacher encoder. Such a fine-grained optimization contributes for the strong representations across all layers, including the shallow ones. To verify the effectiveness of deep self-distillation, we decouple the encoder into four sub-encoders, and evaluate the pre-training performance of part of sub-encoders in Fig. 1. The proposed deep self-distillation outperforms the single self-distillation, especially in shallow layers. We further evaluate the proposed DeSD on seven downstream 3D segmentation datasets, and it achieves the state-of-the-art segmentation performance.

Our contributions are three-fold: (1) we propose a simple but effective SSL method called DeSD to ease the annotation cost by using free unlabeled data for 3D medical image segmentation; (2) we focus on the weak representation issue in shallow layers and address it using the deep self-distillation strategy; and (3) the proposed DeSD method produces a strong pre-training model that achieves the state-of-the-art performance on seven 3D medical image segmentation tasks.

2 Method

2.1 Overview

Our DeSD method follows the two-step SSL paradigm, *i.e.*, self-supervised representation learning and fully-supervised downstream fine-tuning. DeSD contains an online encoder and a momentum encoder (see Fig. 2). The online encoder is further divided into four sub-encoders that produce multiple intermediate representations. The objective of DeSD is to match the output distribution of each sub-encoder in the online encoder with the output distributions of the momentum encoder. After pre-training, the learned representation ability is transferred to any downstream tasks.

2.2   Deep Self-Distillation

DeSD is implemented based on the self-distillation SSL paradigm [5], including an online student encoder φ and a momentum teacher encoder φ_m. The student encoder is decoupled into four sub-parts, denoted by φ_1, φ_2, φ_3, and φ_4. Both encoders share the same network architecture while the parameters of teacher network are formulated as the momentum version of the student one. A wealth of data transformations have been demonstrated to be essential for self-supervised learning [7,8]. Hence, strong data transformations are employed for this study, including flipping, scaling, Gaussian noise, Gaussian blur, image brightness, and image contrasting, to generate two views I_1 and I_2 as the input of Siamese networks. During each iteration, I_1 and I_2 pass through four sub-encoders in turn, and then each output feature from these sub-encoders is transformed into a feature vector by the global average pooling. Subsequently, each sub-encoder is followed by a multi-layer perceptron (MLP) projector (with four layers) and a softmax function to project the feature vectors to a high-dimensional latent space. Each of the first two MLP layers has 2048 neurons followed by the batch normalization (BN) and Gaussian error linear units (GELU) activation. The bottleneck layer has 256 neurons without BN and GELU. The last MLP layer increases the number of neurons to K and employs the weight normalization [19] to accelerate the training. In the meantime, I_2 and I_1 pass through the momentum teacher encoder, and the obtained feature vectors are fed to the MLP projector, which is followed by the centering and sharpening operations [5], and a softmax function. The output is treated as the supervision signal for those target vectors produced by four sub-encoders in the online encoder. The loss function is based on the symmetrized cross-entropy loss, shown as follows

$$\arg\min \mathbb{E}_{I_1,I_2 \in D_u} \Big\{ \sum_{i=1}^{4} [-f(I_2; \varphi_m) \log(f(I_1; \langle \varphi_1, ..., \varphi_i \rangle))$$
$$-f(I_1; \varphi_m) \log(f(I_2; \langle \varphi_1, ..., \varphi_i \rangle))] \Big\}, \tag{1}$$

where D_u is a large-scale unlabeled dataset, $f(\cdot; \cdot)$ presents the feedforward process that generates output vectors, and $\langle \cdot \rangle$ is a set of parameters used in this process. Note that the MLP parameters are ignored in this equation for simplicity.

The above loss function is only used to update the online encoder. The following exponential moving average (EMA) strategy [13] is adopted to update the momentum encoder φ_m in each iteration

$$\varphi_m \leftarrow m\varphi_m + (1 - m)\varphi, \tag{2}$$

where m is the momentum coefficient that is initialized to 0.996 and gradually increased to 1 according to the cosine schedule [12].

2.3 Downstream Transfer Learning

To adapt the DeSD pre-trained momentum encoder to a downstream segmentation task, we stack a CNN-based decoder at the end of it. The decoder parameters are initialized randomly. This segmentation network is trained in an supervised manner to minimize the sum of Dice loss and binary cross entropy loss.

Table 1. Overview of eight datasets used for this study.

	Upstream	Downstream						
Dataset	DeepLesion	Liver	Kidney	HepaV	Pancreas	Colon	Lung	Spleen
Organ	✕	✓	✓	✓	✓	✕	✕	✓
Tumor	✕	✓	✓	✓	✓	✓	✓	✕
Train	10,594	104	168	242	224	100	50	32
Test	0	27	42	61	57	26	13	9

Table 2. Quantitative results on seven 3D segmentation datasets. We compare the Dice (%) on each dataset and average Dice (%) of all datasets. Δ refers to the performance improvement compared to the training from scratch (TFS). The best results are highlighted in bold.

Method	Liver		Kidney		HepaV		Pancreas		Colon		Lung		Spleen		Average
	Dice	Δ	Dice	Δ	Dice	Δ	Dice	Δ	Dice	Δ	Dice	Δ	Dice	Δ	
TFS	77.2	0.0	83.7	0.0	62.9	0.0	66.6	0.0	31.0	0.0	54.8	0.0	95.2	0.0	67.3
MG [25]	77.8	+0.6	86.8	+3.1	63.4	+0.5	69.6	+3.0	36.6	+5.6	60.0	+5.2	95.3	+0.1	69.9
SimSiam [10]	79.9	+2.7	87.4	+3.7	66.5	+3.6	66.3	−0.3	35.5	+4.5	64.2	+9.4	**96.1**	**+0.9**	70.8
BYOL [12]	81.1	+3.9	87.1	+3.4	65.6	+2.7	69.3	+2.7	37.9	+6.9	63.4	+8.6	95.9	+0.7	71.5
PCRL [24]	80.4	+3.2	87.0	+3.3	66.9	+4.0	70.5	+3.9	40.6	+9.6	63.8	+9.0	95.8	+0.6	72.1
DINO [5]	81.0	+3.8	86.9	+3.2	67.6	+4.7	**70.6**	**+4.0**	44.3	+13.3	67.6	+12.8	96.0	+0.8	73.4
DeSD	**81.9**	**+4.7**	**89.2**	**+5.5**	**68.2**	**+5.3**	**70.6**	**+4.0**	**51.9**	**+20.9**	**72.7**	**+17.9**	96.0	+0.8	**75.8**

2.4 Architecture Details

For this study, we used the 3D ResNet-50 as the online and momentum encoders and adopted four decoder blocks to gradually restore the spatial resolution. In each decoder block, the input feature is first up-sampled by a 3D transpose convolution layer, then added to the feature maps obtained by passing the output of the corresponded encoder block through a 3D convolution block, and finally processed by a 3D residual convolution block. The ASPP module [6] is inserted between the encoder and decoder, and a $1 \times 1 \times 1$ convolution layer is placed behind the decoder as the segmentation head for label prediction. In the segmentation network, the LeakyReLU activation is adopted to substitute for ReLU and the instance normalization is used to replace the BN.

3   Experiments and Results

3.1   Datasets and Evaluation Metrics

Datasets. The datasets used for this study consist of two parts: A large-scale unlabeled dataset and seven labeled downstream datasets. The DeepLesion dataset, used for SSL, is a large-scale dataset with 10,594 CT scans collected from 4,427 unique patients. Seven 3D medical image segmentation datasets are used to evaluate the per-trained model. The Liver dataset and Kidney dataset are from LiTS [3] and KiTS [14], respectively. The other five datasets, inlcuding the Hepatic Vessel (HepaV) dataset, Pancreas dataset, Colon dataset, Lung dataset, and Spleen dataset, are from Medical Segmentation Decathlon (MSD) [1]. More details were given in Table 1.

Table 3. Ablation study of four self-distillation losses. We adopt the Dice (%) and average Dice (%) as performance metrics. The best performance on each dataset is highlighted in bold.

Method	Liver	Kidney	HepaV	Pancreas	Colon	Lung	Spleen	Average
TFS	77.2	83.7	62.9	66.6	31.0	54.8	95.2	67.3
DeSD w/ $\mathcal{L}_4$	80.8	86.9	67.0	70.6	40.7	62.2	95.7	72.0
DeSD w/ $\mathcal{L}_4, \mathcal{L}_3$	81.5	86.9	67.6	69.9	39.4	67.2	95.9	72.6
DeSD w/ $\mathcal{L}_4, \mathcal{L}_3, \mathcal{L}_2$	81.2	87.3	**67.7**	68.9	44.6	66.2	95.8	73.1
DeSD w/ $\mathcal{L}_4, \mathcal{L}_3, \mathcal{L}_2, \mathcal{L}_1$	**81.7**	**88.1**	66.8	**70.9**	**49.9**	**69.7**	**96.0**	**74.7**

Evaluation Metrics. The Dice similarity coefficient (Dice), which measures the overlap ratio of the segmentation prediction and ground truth, is employed to evaluate the segmentation models.

3.2   Implementation Details

We adopted the SGD optimizer and set the batch size to 192, the dimensions of target vectors *i.e.*, K, to 60,000, and the maximum training iterations to 195,300. Following [22], we randomly cropped $16 \times 96 \times 96$ patches. Note that two positive patches have content overlaps during the cropping. A warm-up strategy is performed at the first 10 epochs to gradually increase the learning rate from 0 to 0.3, which is then decreased to 0.048 in the subsequent training according to the cosine schedule [18]. During the fine-tuning, we set the learning rate to a smaller value of 0.01, the patch size to $64 \times 192 \times 192$, the batch size to 2, and the maximum number of training iterations to approximately 25,000 for all downstream tasks.

3.3   Results

Comparing to other SSL Methods. The proposed DeSD was compared to five advanced SSL methods, including BYOL [12], SimSiam [10], DINO [5],

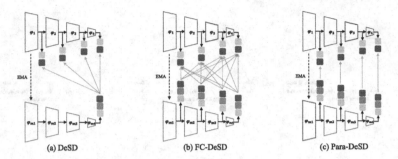

(a) DeSD   (b) FC-DeSD   (c) Para-DeSD

Fig. 3. Diagram of DeSD, FC-DeSD, and Para-DeSD. We use arrows to point from the supervised signal to the target vector.

Table 4. Performance of three deep supervision schemes, SSD, and TFS. SSD presents single self-distillation learning. Both Dice (%) and average Dice (%) are used for evaluation, and the best performance is highlighted in bold.

Method	Liver	Kidney	HepaV	Pancreas	Colon	Lung	Spleen	Average
TFS	77.2	83.7	62.9	66.6	31.0	54.8	95.2	67.3
SSD	80.8	88.4	67.1	70.1	41.6	64.7	95.8	72.6
FC-DeSD	81.5	89.1	**68.7**	69.1	40.8	72.3	**96.1**	73.9
Para-DeSD	81.0	87.5	65.3	68.4	34.6	66.9	95.1	71.3
DeSD	**81.9**	**89.2**	68.2	**70.6**	**51.9**	**72.7**	96.0	**75.8**

MG [25], and PCRL [24]. For a fair comparison, all these SSL methods were pre-trained on the same unlabeled dataset. Table 2 lists the performance of DeSD and other competitors on seven datasets. It shows that the pre-trained parameters generated by the SSL methods can effectively facilitate the model to produce better segmentation performance than random initialization (*i.e.*, TFS), demonstrating the effectiveness of SSL. More importantly, DeSD obtains the highest Dice on six datasets, especially on the Colon dataset and Lung dataset, where our DeSD beats DINO [5], the second-best method, by 7.6% and 5.1%, respectively. For the other one dataset, DeSD achieves the second-best performance, slightly lower than that of SimSiam [10]. Overall, our DeSD achieves the highest average Dice of 75.8%, which is 2.4% higher than the second-best method DINO.

Ablation on Deep Self-Distillation. The proposed deep self-distillation contains four loss items, varying from the shallow to deep layers. To verify the effectiveness of each self-distillation loss, we sequentially added self-distillation losses from the deepest layer ($\mathcal{L}_4$) to the shallowest one ($\mathcal{L}_1$), and evaluated their performance on seven downstream datasets. We set the maximum pre-training iterations to 65,100 for the sake of computational simplicity. The ablation results in Table 3 show that the proposed DeSD achieves better segmentation performance when more self-distillation losses are used. The DeSD with full deep self-distillation outperforms the single distillation based DeSD up to 2.7% average Dice over seven downstream tasks.

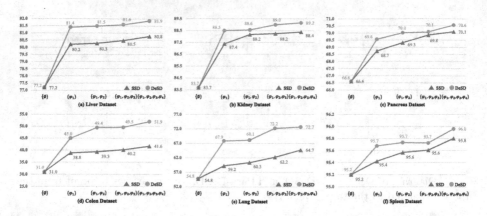

Fig. 4. Resutls of SSD and DeSD on the other six datasets. The settings are consistent with Fig. 1.

Table 5. Performance of TFS, SSD, and DeSD on seven downstream datasets with 10% or 100% annotations. The Dice (%) and average Dice (%) are used for evaluation, and the best performance is highlighted in bold.

Method	10% annotations								100% annotations							
	Liver	Kidney	HepaV	Pancreas	Colon	Lung	Spleen	Average	Liver	Kidney	HepaV	Pancreas	Colon	Lung	Spleen	Average
TFS	66.5	63.7	58.7	47.4	2.4	28.9	74.4	48.9	77.2	83.7	62.9	66.6	31.0	54.8	95.2	67.3
SSD	72.1	68.7	60.8	51.6	**8.4**	30.5	72.2	52.0	80.8	88.4	67.1	70.1	41.6	64.7	95.8	72.6
DeSD	**73.3**	**71.4**	**62.1**	**52.1**	8.2	**30.8**	**91.4**	**55.6**	**81.9**	**89.2**	**68.2**	**70.6**	**51.9**	**72.7**	**96.0**	**75.8**

Comparison of Different Deep Self-Distillation Variants. Our DeSD adopts only one supervision signal produced by the deepest block of the momentum encoder (see Fig. 3(a)). We also compare this deep-distillation method to other two variants, including a fully connected deep self-distillation (FC-DeSD) and a parallel deep self-distillation (Para-DeSD). FC-DeSD decouples both online encoder and momentum encoder into four sub-encoders, and the output of each momentum sub-encoder is regarded as the supervision signal of all target vectors obtained by four online sub-encoders (see Fig. 3(b)). FC-DeSD aims to achieve a dense consistency of all online and momentum sub-encoders, leading to totally 16 loss items. By contrast, Para-DeSD imposes the consistency restrictions between the matched sub-encoders that have the same depth in the online and momentum encoders (see Fig. 3(c)). The results in Table 4 show that the performance of Para-DeSD is generally lower than that of single self-distillation learning (SSD) on seven datasets, suggesting that the parallel constraints even hinder the representation learning. Both FC-DeSD and DeSD are effective to improve the segmentation performance. Considering the trade-off between complexity and performance, we advocate to use DeSD for self-supervised representation learning.

Downstream with Fewer Annotations. We reported the performance of TFS, SSD, and our DeSD on seven datasets with 10% or 100% annotations, as shown in Table 5. As expected, when decreasing the downstream annotations from 100% to 10%, each method suffers from a significant performance drop. However, our DeSD not only achieves the best performance on seven datasets with 100% annotations, but also maintains the advanced performance when there are only 10% annotations.

Sufficient Representation Learning with DeSD. To evaluate the representation quality of all layers, we decoupled the pre-training weights of SSD/DeSD into four parts, φ_1, φ_2, φ_3, and φ_4, and gradually initialized the downstream model from the shallow layers to deep layers using pre-trained parameters. As shown in Fig. 4, the proposed DeSD outperforms the SSD pre-training across all pre-trained layers. The results reveal that the proposed deep self-distillation strategy is able to boost the feature representation quality, not only for deep layers but also shallow layers.

4 Conclusion

The single self-distillation based SSL suffers from the weak supervision in shallow layers, resulting in the insufficient representation learning. To address this issue, we propose a deep self-distillation based SSL method called DeSD that aims to improve the representation quality of all layers, especially for shallow layers. We pre-trained DeSD on a large-scale upstream dataset and evaluated it on the seven downstream datasets. Extensive experiments were conducted to demonstrate the effectiveness of the proposed DeSD. Meanwhile, our DeSD achieves the superior performance over other advanced SSL methods, setting a new record.

Acknowledgements. This work was supported in part by the National Natural Science Foundation of China under Grants 62171377, in part by the Key Research and Development Program of Shaanxi Province under Grant 2022GY-084, and in part by the Natural Science Foundation of Ningbo City, China, under Grant 2021J052.

References

1. Antonelli, M., et al.: The medical segmentation decathlon. arXiv preprint arXiv: 2106.05735 (2021)
2. Asgari Taghanaki, S., Abhishek, K., Cohen, J.P., Cohen-Adad, J., Hamarneh, G.: Deep semantic segmentation of natural and medical images: a review. Artif. Intell. Rev. **54**(1), 137–178 (2020). https://doi.org/10.1007/s10462-020-09854-1
3. Bilic, P., et al.: The liver tumor segmentation benchmark (lits). arXiv preprint arXiv:1901.04056 (2019)
4. Caron, M., Misra, I., Mairal, J., Goyal, P., Bojanowski, P., Joulin, A.: Unsupervised learning of visual features by contrasting cluster assignments. Adv. Neural. Inf. Process. Syst. **33**, 9912–9924 (2020)
5. Caron, M., et al.: Emerging properties in self-supervised vision transformers. In: Proceedings of the IEEE/CVF International Conference on Computer Vision, pp. 9650–9660 (2021)

6. Chen, L.C., Papandreou, G., Kokkinos, I., Murphy, K., Yuille, A.L.: Deeplab: semantic image segmentation with deep convolutional nets, atrous convolution, and fully connected CRFs. IEEE Trans. Pattern Anal. Mach. Intell. **40**(4), 834–848 (2017)

7. Chen, T., Kornblith, S., Norouzi, M., Hinton, G.: A simple framework for contrastive learning of visual representations. In: International Conference on Machine Learning, pp. 1597–1607. PMLR (2020)

8. Chen, T., Kornblith, S., Swersky, K., Norouzi, M., Hinton, G.E.: Big self-supervised models are strong semi-supervised learners. Adv. Neural. Inf. Process. Syst. **33**, 22243–22255 (2020)

9. Chen, X., Fan, H., Girshick, R., He, K.: Improved baselines with momentum contrastive learning. arXiv preprint arXiv:2003.04297 (2020)

10. Chen, X., He, K.: Exploring simple SIAMESE representation learning. In: Proceedings of the IEEE/CVF Conference on Computer Vision and Pattern Recognition, pp. 15750–15758 (2021)

11. Ghesu, F.C., et al.: Self-supervised learning from 100 million médical images. arXiv preprint arXiv:2201.01283 (2022)

12. Grill, J.B., et al.: Bootstrap your own latent-a new approach to self-supervised learning. Adv. Neural. Inf. Process. Syst. **33**, 21271–21284 (2020)

13. He, K., Fan, H., Wu, Y., Xie, S., Girshick, R.: Momentum contrast for unsupervised visual representation learning. In: Proceedings of the IEEE/CVF Conference on Computer Vision and Pattern Recognition, pp. 9729–9738 (2020)

14. Heller, N., et al.: The state of the art in kidney and kidney tumor segmentation in contrast-enhanced CT imaging: results of the kits19 challenge. Med. Image Anal. **67**, 101821 (2021)

15. Isensee, F., Jaeger, P.F., Kohl, S.A., Petersen, J., Maier-Hein, K.H.: NNU-net: a self-configuring method for deep learning-based biomedical image segmentation. Nat. Methods **18**(2), 203–211 (2021)

16. Işın, A., Direkoğlu, C., Şah, M.: Review of MRI-based brain tumor image segmentation using deep learning methods. Procedia Comput. Sci. **102**, 317–324 (2016)

17. Liu, X., Song, L., Liu, S., Zhang, Y.: A review of deep-learning-based medical image segmentation methods. Sustainability **13**(3), 1224 (2021)

18. Loshchilov, I., Hutter, F.: SGDR: stochastic gradient descent with warm restarts. arXiv preprint arXiv:1608.03983 (2016)

19. Salimans, T., Kingma, D.P.: Weight normalization: a simple reparameterization to accelerate training of deep neural networks. In: Advances in Neural Information Processing Systems, vol. 29 (2016)

20. Tang, Y., et al.: Self-supervised pre-training of SWIN transformers for 3D medical image analysis. arXiv preprint arXiv:2111.14791 (2021)

21. Wang, Y., Zhang, Q., Wang, Y., Yang, J., Lin, Z.: Chaos is a ladder: a new understanding of contrastive learning. In: International Conference on Learning Representations (2022)

22. Xie, Y., Zhang, J., Liao, Z., Xia, Y., Shen, C.: PGL: prior-guided local self-supervised learning for 3d medical image segmentation. arXiv preprint arXiv:2011.12640 (2020)

23. Zhang, J., Xie, Y., Zhang, P., Chen, H., Xia, Y., Shen, C.: Light-weight hybrid convolutional network for liver tumor segmentation. In: IJCAI, vol. 19, pp. 4271–4277 (2019)

24. Zhou, H.Y., Lu, C., Yang, S., Han, X., Yu, Y.: Preservational learning improves self-supervised medical image models by reconstructing diverse contexts. In: Proceedings of the IEEE/CVF International Conference on Computer Vision, pp. 3499–3509 (2021)
25. Zhou, Z., Sodha, V., Pang, J., Gotway, M.B., Liang, J.: Models genesis. Med. Image Anal. **67**, 101840 (2021)

Self-supervised 3D Anatomy Segmentation Using Self-distilled Masked Image Transformer (SMIT)

Jue Jiang[1], Neelam Tyagi[1], Kathryn Tringale[2], Christopher Crane[2], and Harini Veeraraghavan[1(✉)]

[1] Department of Medical Physics, Memorial Sloan Kettering Cancer Center, New York, USA
veerarah@mskcc.org
[2] Department of Radiation Oncology, Memorial Sloan Kettering Cancer Center, New York, USA

Abstract. Vision transformers efficiently model long-range context and thus have demonstrated impressive accuracy gains in several image analysis tasks including segmentation. However, such methods need large labeled datasets for training, which is hard to obtain for medical image analysis. Self-supervised learning (SSL) has demonstrated success in medical image segmentation using convolutional networks. In this work, we developed a self-distillation learning with masked image modeling method to perform SSL for vision transformers (SMIT) applied to 3D multi-organ segmentation from CT and MRI. Our contribution combines a dense pixel-wise regression pretext task performed within masked patches called masked image prediction with masked patch token distillation to pre-train vision transformers. Our approach is more accurate and requires fewer fine tuning datasets than other pretext tasks. Unlike prior methods, which typically used image sets arising from disease sites and imaging modalities corresponding to the target tasks, we used 3,643 CT scans (602,708 images) arising from head and neck, lung, and kidney cancers as well as COVID-19 for pre-training and applied it to abdominal organs segmentation from MRI pancreatic cancer patients as well as publicly available 13 different abdominal organs segmentation from CT. Our method showed clear accuracy improvement (average DSC of 0.875 from MRI and 0.878 from CT) with reduced requirement for fine-tuning datasets over commonly used pretext tasks. Extensive comparisons against multiple current SSL methods were done. Our code is available at: https://github.com/harveerar/SMIT.git.

Keywords: Self-supervised learning · Segmentation · Self-distillation · Masked image modeling · Masked embedding transformer

Supplementary Information The online version contains supplementary material available at https://doi.org/10.1007/978-3-031-16440-8_53.

1   Introduction

Vision transformers (ViT) [1] efficiently model long range contextual information using multi-head self attention mechanism, making them robust to occlusions, image noise, as well as domain and image contrast differences. Hence, ViTs have shown to produce more accurate medical image segmentation than convolutional neural networks (CNN) [2,3]. However, ViT requires a large number of labeled training datasets that are not commonly available in medical applications. Self-supervised learning (SSL) overcomes the afore-mentioned requirement by extracting visual information inherent in images from large unlabeled datasets by using pre-defined, annotation free pretext tasks as surrogate supervision signals for pre-training [4–6]. Once pre-trained, the model can be re-purposed for a variety of tasks by fine-tuning with relatively few labeled sets.

The choice of pretext tasks is crucial for SSL to successfully mine useful image information. Image denoising to recover images from their corrupted versions using CNN-based autoencoders [7,8], pseudo labels [8–10], and contrastive learning [11–14] using CNNs have been used as pretext tasks in medical image applications. Data augmentation strategies including jigsaw puzzles [11,15], restoration of image contrast and local texture [7], predicting image rotations [5], and prediction of masked image slices [16] have also been successfully used as pretext tasks for medical image segmentation with convolutional networks. However, CNNs are less effective than transformers in their capacity to model long-range context. Hence, we combined ViT with SSL using masked image modeling (MIM) and self-distillation of concurrently trained teacher and student networks.

MIM has been combined with transformers in natural image analysis [17–19,19–21]. Knowledge distillation with concurrently trained teacher has also been used for medical image segmentation by leveraging different imaging modalities (CT and MRI) [22,23]. Self-distillation differs from knowledge distillation in it's use of different augmented views of the same image [24]. It has been used for medical image classification [10] by combining contrastive learning with CNN encoders.

Prior works have shown the ability to achieve highly accurate natural image classification and segmentation [19,24] by combining self-distillation of a pair of teacher and student transformer encoders using MIM. It was also shown that combining global and local patch token embeddings [19] improved accuracy compared to pretext tasks that only extracted class tokens [CLS] to model global image embedding [24]. However, these methods ignored the dense pixel dependencies, which is essential for dense prediction tasks like segmentation. Hence, we introduced masked image prediction (MIP) pretext task to predict pixel intensities within masked patches combined with the local and global embedding tasks for medical image segmentation.

Our Contributions Include: (i) SSL using MIM and self-distillation approach combining masked image prediction, masked patch token distillation, and global image token distillation for CT and MRI organs segmentation using transformers. (ii) a simple linear projection layer for medical image reconstruction to speed

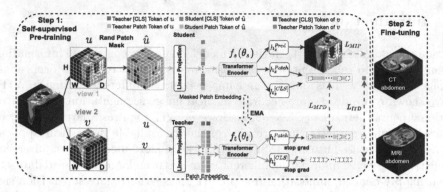

Fig. 1. SMIT: Self-distillation with masked image modeling for transformers using SSL. Two augmented views of 3D image patches are passed to a student (with masking) and teacher (without masking) networks. Teacher regularizes the student to extract the masked patch tokens through masked patch token distillation (MPD). Masked image prediction (MIP) and global image token [CLS] prediction (ITD) are additional pretext tasks. The teacher uses exponential moving average (EMA) for parameter updates.

up pre-training, which we show is more accurate than multi-layer decoder. (iii) SSL pre-training using large 3,643 3D CTs arising from a variety of disease sites including head and neck, chest, and abdomen with different cancers (lung, naso/oropharynx, kidney) and COVID-19 applied to CT and MRI segmentation. (iv) Evaluation of various pretext tasks using transformer encoders related to fine tuning data size requirements and segmentation accuracy.

2   Method

Goal: Extract a universal representation of images for dense prediction tasks, given an unlabeled dataset of Q images.

Approach: A visual tokenizer $f_s(\theta_s)$ implemented as a transformer encoder is learned via self-distillation using MIM pretext tasks in order to convert an image x into image tokens $\{x_i\}_{i=1}^N$, N being the sequence length. MIM pretext tasks include masked image prediction (MIP) and masked patch token distillation (MPD). Self distillation is performed by concurrently training an online teacher tokenizer model $f_t(\theta_t)$ with the same network structure as $f_s(\theta_s)$ serving as the student model. In addition, global image token distillation (ITD) pretext task is done to match the global tokens extracted by f_t and f_s [24].

Suppose $\{u, v\}$ are two augmented views of a 3D image x. N image patches are extracted from the images to create a sequence of image tokens [1], say $u = \{u_i\}_{i=1}^N$. The image tokens are then corrupted by randomly masking image tokens based on a binary vector $m = \{m_i\}_{i=1}^N \in \{0, 1\}$ with a probability p and then replacing with mask token [20] $e_{[MASK]}$ such that as $\tilde{u} = m \odot u$ with $\tilde{u}_i = e_{[MASK]}$ at $m_i = 1$ and $\tilde{u}_i = u_i$ at $m_i = 0$. The second augmented view v is also corrupted but using a different mask vector instance m' as $\tilde{v} = m' \odot v$.

Dense Pixel Dependency Modeling Using MIP: MIP involves recovering the original image view u from corrupted $\tilde{u}$, as $\hat{u} = h_s^{Pred}(f_s(\tilde{u}, \theta_s))$, where h_s^{Pred} decodes the visual tokens produced by a visual tokenizer $f_s(\theta_s)$ into images (see Fig. 1). MIP involves dense pixel regression of image intensities within masked patches using the context of unmasked patches. The MIP loss is computed as (dotted green arrow in Fig. 1):

$$L_{MIP} = \sum_i^N E \|m_i \cdot (h_s^{Pred}(f_s(\tilde{u}_i, \theta_s))) - u_i\|_1 \tag{1}$$

h_s^{Pred} is a linear projection with one layer for dense pixel regression. A symmetrized loss using v and $\tilde{v}$ is combined to compute the total loss for L_{MIP}.

Masked Patch Token Self-distillation (MPD): MPD is accomplished by optimizing a teacher $f_t(\theta_t)$ and a student visual tokenizer $f_s(\theta_s)$ such that the student network predicts the tokens of the teacher network. The student network f_s tokenizes the corrupted version of an image $\tilde{u}$ to generate visual tokens $\phi' = \{\phi_i'\}_{i=1}^N$. The teacher network f_t tokenizes the uncorrupted version of the same image u to generate visual tokens $\phi = \{\phi_i\}_{i=1}^N$. Similar to MIP, MPD focuses on accurate prediction of the masked patch tokens. Therefore, the loss is computed from masked portions (i.e. $m_i = 1$) using cross-entropy of the predicted patch tokens (dotted red arrow in Fig. 1):

$$L_{MPD} = -\sum_{i=1}^N m_i \cdot P_t^{Patch}(u_i, \theta_t) log(P_s^{Patch}(\tilde{u}_i, \theta_s)), \tag{2}$$

where P_s^{Patch} and P_t^{Patch} are the patch token distributions for student and teacher networks. They are computed by applying *softmax* to the outputs of h_s^{Patch} and h_t^{Patch}. The sharpness of the token distribution is controlled using a temperature term $\tau_s > 0$ and $\tau_t > 0$ for the student and teacher networks, respectively. Mathematically, such a sharpening can expressed as (using notation for the student network parameters) as:

$$P_s^{Patch}(u, \theta_s) = \frac{exp(h_s^{Patch}(f_s(u_j, \theta_s))/\tau_s}{\sum_{j=1}^K exp(h_s^{Patch}(f_s(u_j, \theta_s))/\tau_s}. \tag{3}$$

A symmetrized cross entropy loss corresponding to the other view v and $\tilde{v}$ is also computed and averaged to compute the total loss for MPD.

Global Image Token Self-distillation (ITD): ITD is done by matching the global image embedding or class tokens [CLS] distribution $P_s^{[CLS]}$ extracted from the corrupted view $\tilde{u}$ by student transformer network using $h_s^{[CLS]}(f_s(\theta_s, \tilde{u}))$ with the token distribution $P_t^{[CLS]}$ extracted from the uncorrupted and different view v by the teacher network using $h_t^{[CLS]}(f_t(\theta_t, v))$ (shown by dotted blue arrow in Fig. 1) as:

$$L_{ITD} = -\sum_{i=1}^N m_i \cdot P_t^{[CLS]}(v_i, \theta_t) log(P_s^{[CLS]}(\tilde{u}_i, \theta_s)) \tag{4}$$

Table 1. Accuracy on BTCV standard challenge test set. SP: spleen, RK/LK: right & left kidney, GB: gall bladder, ESO: esophagus, LV: liver, STO: stomach, AOR: aorta, IVC: inferior vena cava, SPV: portal & splenic vein, Pan: Pancreas, AG: Adrenals.

Method	SP	RK	LK	GB	ESO	LV	STO	AOR	IVC	SPV	Pan	AG	AVG
ASPP [29]	0.935	0.892	0.914	0.689	0.760	0.953	0.812	0.918	0.807	0.695	0.720	0.629	0.811
nnUnet [30]	0.942	0.894	0.910	0.704	0.723	0.948	0.824	0.877	0.782	0.720	0.680	0.616	0.802
TrsUnet [31]	0.952	0.927	0.929	0.662	0.757	0.969	0.889	0.920	0.833	0.791	0.775	0.637	0.838
CoTr [2]	0.958	0.921	0.936	0.700	0.764	0.963	0.854	0.920	0.838	0.787	0.775	0.694	0.844
UNETR [3]	**0.968**	0.924	0.941	0.750	0.766	0.971	0.913	0.890	0.847	0.788	0.767	0.741	0.856
SMIT(rand)	0.959	0.921	0.947	0.746	0.802	0.972	0.916	0.917	0.848	0.797	0.817	0.711	0.850
SMIT(SSL)	0.967	**0.945**	**0.948**	**0.826**	**0.822**	**0.976**	**0.934**	**0.921**	**0.864**	**0.827**	**0.851**	**0.754**	**0.878**

Sharpening transforms are applied to $P_t^{[CLS]}$ and $P_s^{[CLS]}$ similar to Eq. 4. A symmetrized cross entropy loss corresponding to the corrupted view $\tilde{v}$ and another u is also computed and averaged to compute the total loss for L_{ITD}.

Online Teacher Network Update: Teacher network parameters were updated using exponential moving average (EMA) with momentum update, and shown to be feasible for SSL [19,24] as: $\theta_t = \lambda_m \theta_t + (1 - \lambda_m)\theta_s$, where λ_m is momentum, which was updated using a cosine schedule from 0.996 to 1 during training. The total loss was, $L_{total} = L_{MIP} + \lambda_{MPD} L_{MPD} + \lambda_{ITD} L_{ITD}$.

Implementation Details: All the networks were implemented using the Pytorch library and trained on 4 Nvidia GTX V100. SSL optimization was done using ADAMw with a cosine learning rate scheduler trained for 400 epochs with an initial learning rate of 0.0002 and warmup for 30 epochs. $\lambda_{MPD} = 0.1$, $\lambda_{ITD} = 0.1$ were set experimentally. A default mask ratio of 0.7 was used. Centering and sharpening operations reduced chances of degenerate solutions [24]. τ_s was set to 0.1 and τ_t was linearly warmed up from 0.04 to 0.07 in the first 30 epochs. SWIN-small backbone [25] with 768 embedding, window size of $4 \times 4 \times 4$, patch size of 2 was used. The 1-layer decoder was implemented with a linear projection layer with the same number of output channels as input image size. The network had 28.19M parameters. Following pre-training, only the student network was retained for fine-tuning and testing.

3   Experiments and Results

Training Dataset: SSL pre-training was performed using 3,643 CT patient scans containing 602,708 images. Images were sourced from patients with head and neck (N = 837) and lung cancers (N = 1455) from internal and external [26], as well as those with kidney cancers [27] (N = 710), and COVID-19 [28] (N = 650). GPU limitation was addressed for training, fine-tuning, and testing by image resampling ($1.5 \times 1.5 \times 2$ mm voxel size) and cropping ($128 \times 128 \times 128$) to enclose the body region. Augmented views for SSL training was produced through randomly cropped $96 \times 96 \times 96$ volumes, which resulted in $6 \times 6 \times 6$ image patch

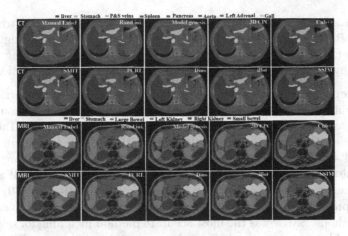

Fig. 2. Segmentation performance of different methods on MRI abdomen organs.

tokens. A sliding window strategy with half window overlap was used for testing [2,3]. Dataset I and pre-training CT datasets were pre-processed with intensity rescaling [−175 HU to 250 HU]. Dataset II (MRI) was subjected to histogram standardization, intensity clipping [0, 2000], and intensity normalization [0, 1].

CT Abdomen Organ Segmentation (Dataset I): The pre-trained networks were fine-tuned to generate volumetric segmentation of 13 different abdominal organs from contrast-enhanced CT (CECT) scans using publicly available beyond the cranial vault (BTCV) [32] dataset. Randomly selected 21 images are used for training and the remaining used for validation. Furthermore, blinded testing of 20 CECTs evaluated on the grand challenge website is also reported.

MRI Upper Abdominal Organs Segmentation (Dataset II): The SSL network was evaluated for segmenting abdominal organs at risk for pancreatic cancer radiation treatment, which included stomach, small and large bowel, liver, and kidneys. No MRI or pancreatic cancer scans were used for SSL pre-training. Ninety two 3D T2-weighted MRIs (TR/TE = 1300/87 ms, voxel size of $1 \times 1 \times 2 \, \text{mm}^3$, FOV of $400 \times 450 \times 250 \, \text{mm}^3$) and acquired with pnuematic compression belt to suppress breathing motion were analyzed. Fine tuning used five-fold cross-validation and results from the validation folds not used in training are reported.

Experimental Comparisons: SMIT was compared against representative SSL medical image analysis methods. Results from representative published methods on the BTCV testing set [2,3,30] are also reported. The SSL comparison methods were chosen to evaluate the impact of the pretext task on segmentation accuracy and included (a) local texture and semantics modeling using model genesis [7], (b) jigsaw puzzles [15], (c) contrastive learning [14] with (a),(b), (c) implemented on CNN backbone, (d) self-distillation using whole image reconstruction [24], (e) masked patch reconstruction [18] without self-distillation, (f) MIM using self-distillation [19] with (d),(e), and (f) implemented in a SWIN transformer backbone. Random initialization results are shown for benchmarking purposes using both CNN and SWIN backbones. Identical training and testing sets were used with hyper-parameters adopted from their default implementation.

CT Segmentation Accuracy: As shown in Table 1, SMIT outperformed representative published methods including transformer based segmentation [2,3,31]. SMIT was also more accurate than all evaluated SSL methods (Table 2) for most organs. Prior-guided contrast learning (PRCL) [14] was more accurate than SMIT only for gall bladder (0.797 vs. 0.787). SMIT was more accurate than self-distillation with MIM [19] (average DSC of 0.848 vs. 0.833) as well as masked image reconstruction without distillation [18] (0.848 vs. 0.830). Figure 2 shows a representative case with multiple organs segmentations produced by the various methods. SMIT was the most accurate method including for organs with highly variable appearance and size such as the stomach and esophagus.

MRI Segmentation Accuracy: SMIT was more accurate than all other SSL-based methods for all evaluated organs (Table 2). SMIT produced more accurate segmentations than other methods even for small bowel, a difficult organ to segment due to the presence of closely packed bowel loops. Figure 2 shows a representative MRI case with segmentations produced by the various methods.

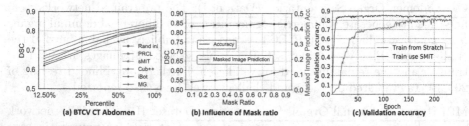

Fig. 3. (a) Impact of SSL task on fine-tuning sizes, (b) impact of mask ratio on masked image prediction and segmentation accuracy, (c) training convergence.

Ablation Experiments: All ablation and design experiments (1 layer decoder vs. multi-layer or ML decoder) were performed using the BTCV dataset and used the SWIN-backbone as used for SMIT. ML decoder was implemented with five transpose convolution layers for up-sampling back to the input image resolution. Figure 4 shows the accuracy comparisons of networks pre-trained with different tasks including full image reconstruction, contrastive losses, pseudo labels [33], and various combination of the losses ($L_{MIP}, L_{MPD}, L_{ITD}$). As shown, the accuracies for all the methods was similar for large organs depicting good contrast that include liver, spleen, left and right kidney (Fig. 4(I)). On the other hand, organs with low soft tissue contrast and high variability (Fig. 4(II)) and small organs (Fig. 4(III)) show larger differences in accuracies between methods with SMIT achieving more accurate segmentations. Major blood vessels Fig. 4(IV) also depict segmentation accuracy differences across methods, albeit less so than for small organs and those with low soft-tissue contrast. Importantly, both full image reconstruction and multi-layer decoder based MIP (ML-MIP) were less accurate than SMIT, which uses masked image prediction with 1-layer linear projection decoder (Fig. 4 (II,III,IV)). MPD was the least accurate for organs with low soft-tissue contrast and high variability (Fig. 4(II)), which was improved slightly by adding global image distillation (ITD). MIP alone (using 1-layer decoder) was similarly accurate as SMIT and more accurate than other pretext task based segmentation including ITD [24], MPD+ITD [19]. Lower MSE loss indicates better reconstruction as shown in Fig. 4 using 1-layer vs. multi-layer decoder.

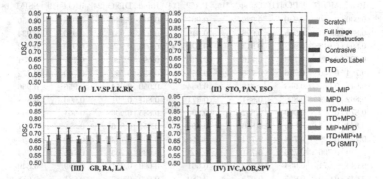

Fig. 4. Accuracy variations by organ types using different pretext tasks. MIM pretext tasks are MIP using 1-layer decoder, ML-MIP using multi-layer decoder, MPD, and ITD combined with MIP or MPD.

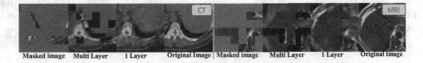

Fig. 5. Reconstructed images using 1-layer vs. multi-layer decoder trained with SMIT from masked images (0.7 masking ratio).

Impact of Pretext Tasks on Sample Size for Fine Tuning: SMIT was more accurate than all other SSL methods irrespective of sample size used for fine-tuning (Fig. 3(a)) and achieved faster convergence (Fig. 3(c)). It outperformed iBot [19], which uses MPD and ITD, indicating effectiveness of MIP for SSL.

Impact of Mask Ratio on Accuracy: Figure 3(b) shows the impact of mask ratio (percentage of masked patches) in the corrupted image for both the accuracy of masked image reconstruction (computed as mean square error [MSE]) as well as segmentation (computed using DSC metric). Accuracy increased initially with the mask ratio and then stabilized. Image reconstruction error also increased slightly with mask ratio. Figure 5 shows a representative CT and MRI reconstruction produced using default and multi-layer decoder, wherein our method was more accurate even in highly textured portions of the images containing multiple organs (additional examples are shown in Supplementary Fig 1). SMIT using 1-layer decoder was more accurate than multi-layer decoder (MSE of 0.061 vs. 0.32) for CT (N=10 cases) and 92 MRI (MSE of 0.062 vs. 0.34).

Table 2. CT and MRI segmentation accuracy comparisons to SSL methods. Rand-random; LB-Large bowel, SB - Small bowel.

Mod	Organ	CNN					SWIN				
		Rand	MG [7]	CPC [11]	Cub++ [15]	PRCL [14]	Rand	DINO [24]	iBOT [19]	SSIM [18]	SMIT
CT	Sp	0.930	0.950	0.940	0.926	0.937	0.944	0.946	0.948	0.950	**0.963**
	RK	0.892	0.934	0.916	0.928	0.919	0.926	0.931	0.936	0.934	**0.950**
	LK	0.894	0.918	0.903	0.914	0.921	0.905	0.913	0.919	0.913	**0.943**
	GB	0.605	0.639	0.718	0.715	**0.797**	0.694	0.730	0.777	0.761	0.787
	ESO	0.744	0.739	0.756	0.768	0.759	0.732	0.752	0.760	0.772	**0.772**
	LV	0.947	0.967	0.953	0.946	0.954	0.950	0.954	0.956	0.956	**0.970**
	STO	0.862	0.879	0.896	0.881	0.877	0.861	0.891	0.900	0.898	**0.903**
	AOR	0.875	0.909	0.900	0.892	0.894	0.885	0.906	0.901	0.905	**0.913**
	IVC	0.844	0.882	0.855	0.866	0.851	0.851	0.866	0.879	0.867	**0.871**
	SPV	0.727	0.739	0.731	0.734	0.760	0.725	0.752	0.759	0.754	**0.784**
	Pan	0.719	0.706	0.726	0.731	0.693	0.688	0.763	0.755	0.764	**0.810**
	RA	0.644	0.671	0.655	0.665	0.661	0.660	0.651	0.659	0.640	**0.669**
	LA	0.648	0.640	0.655	0.675	0.680	0.590	0.680	0.681	0.678	**0.687**
	AVG.	0.795	0.813	0.816	0.819	0.823	0.801	0.826	0.833	0.830	**0.848**
MR	LV	0.921	0.936	0.925	0.920	0.930	0.922	0.920	0.939	0.937	**0.942**
	LB	0.786	0.824	0.824	0.813	0.823	0.818	0.804	0.833	0.835	**0.855**
	SB	0.688	0.741	0.745	0.735	0.745	0.708	0.729	0.744	0.759	**0.775**
	STO	0.702	0.745	0.769	0.783	0.793	0.732	0.750	0.783	0.775	**0.812**
	LK	0.827	0.832	0.876	0.866	0.876	0.837	0.911	0.883	0.874	**0.936**
	RK	0.866	0.886	0.863	0.861	0.871	0.845	0.896	0.906	0.871	**0.930**
	AVG.	0.798	0.827	0.834	0.830	0.840	0.810	0.835	0.848	0.842	**0.875**

4 Discussion and Conclusion

In this work, we demonstrated the potential for SSL with 3D transformers for medical image segmentation. Our approach, which leverages CT volumes arising from highly disparate body locations and diseases produced more accurate segmentations from CT and MRI scans than current SSL-based methods, especially for hard to segment organs with high appearance variability and small sizes. Importantly, masked image dense prediction improved segmentation accuracy with reduced requirement of fine tuning dataset size. Although pre-training used CT, the network showed ability to segment on T2-weighted MRI because T2-weighted MRI also captures anatomic information like CT. Higher soft-tissue contrast on MRI, histogram standarization to harmonize MRIs, combined with the use of transformers, known to be robust to domain differences [34], aided generalization with fine tuning.

References

1. Dosovitskiy, A., et al.: An image is worth 16x16 words: transformers for image recognition at scale. In: International Conference on Learning Representations (2021)
2. Xie, Y., Zhang, J., Shen, C., Xia, Y.: COTR: efficiently bridging CNN and transformer for 3D medical image segmentation. In: Medical Image Computing and Computer Assisted Intervention, pp. 171–180 (2021)
3. Hatamizadeh, A., Tang, Y., Nath, V., Yang, D., Myronenko, A., Landman, B., Roth, H.R., Xu, D.: UNETR: transformers for 3D medical image segmentation. In: IEEE/CVF Winter Conference on Applications of Computer Vision, pp. 1748–1758 (2022)
4. Noroozi, M., Favaro, P.: Unsupervised learning of visual representations by solving jigsaw puzzles. In: Leibe, B., Matas, J., Sebe, N., Welling, M. (eds.) ECCV 2016. LNCS, vol. 9910, pp. 69–84. Springer, Cham (2016). https://doi.org/10.1007/978-3-319-46466-4_5
5. Komodakis, N., Gidaris, S.: Unsupervised representation learning by predicting image rotations. In: International Conference on Learning Representations (2018)
6. He, K., Fan, H., Wu, Y., Xie, S., Girshick, R.: Momentum contrast for unsupervised visual representation learning. In: Proceedings of the IEEE/CVF Conference Computer Vision and Pattern Recognition, pp. 9729–9738 (2020)
7. Zhou, Z., Sodha, V., Pang, J., Gotway, M.B., Liang, J.: Models genesis. Med. Image Anal. **67**, 101840 (2021)
8. Haghighi, F., Hosseinzadeh Taher, M.R., Zhou, Z., Gotway, M.B., Liang, J.: Learning semantics-enriched representation via self-discovery, self-classification, and self-restoration. In: Martel, A.L., et al. (eds.) MICCAI 2020. LNCS, vol. 12261, pp. 137–147. Springer, Cham (2020). https://doi.org/10.1007/978-3-030-59710-8_14
9. Chen, L., Bentley, P., Mori, K., Misawa, K., Fujiwara, M., Rueckert, D.: Self-supervised learning for medical image analysis using image context restoration. Med. Image Anal. **58**, 101539 (2019)
10. Sun, J., Wei, D., Ma, K., Wang, L., Zheng, Y.: Unsupervised representation learning meets pseudo-label supervised self-distillation: a new approach to rare disease classification. In: de Bruijne, M., et al. (eds.) MICCAI 2021. LNCS, vol. 12905, pp. 519–529. Springer, Cham (2021). https://doi.org/10.1007/978-3-030-87240-3_50
11. Taleb, A., et al.: 3 D self-supervised methods for medical imaging. In: Advances in Neural Information Processing Systems, vol. 33, pp. 18158–18172 (2020)
12. Chaitanya, K., Erdil, E., Karani, N., Konukoglu, E.: Contrastive learning of global and local features for medical image segmentation with limited annotations. In: Advances in Neural Information Processing Systems, vol. 33, pp. 12546–12558 (2020)
13. Feng, R., Zhou, Z., Gotway, M.B., Liang, J.: Parts2Whole: self-supervised contrastive learning via reconstruction. In: Albarqouni, S., et al. (eds.) DART/DCL -2020. LNCS, vol. 12444, pp. 85–95. Springer, Cham (2020). https://doi.org/10.1007/978-3-030-60548-3_9
14. Zhou, H.Y., Lu, C., Yang, S., Han, X., Yu, Y.: Preservational learning improves self-supervised medical image models by reconstructing diverse contexts. In: IEEE/CVF International Conference on Computer Vision, pp. 3499–3509 (2021)
15. Zhu, J., Li, Y., Hu, Y., Ma, K., Zhou, S.K., Zheng, Y.: Rubik's cube+: a self-supervised feature learning framework for 3 D medical image analysis. Med. Image Anal. **64**, 101746 (2020)

16. Jun, E., Jeong, S., Heo, D.W., Suk, H.I.: Medical transformer: universal brain encoder for 3 D MRI analysis. arXiv preprint arXiv:2104.13633 (2021)

17. Li, Z., et al.: MST: masked self-supervised transformer for visual representation. In: Advances in Neural Information Processing Systems, vol. 34, pp. 13165–13176 (2021)

18. Xie, Z., et al.: SIMMIM: a simple framework for masked image modeling. In: Proceedings of the IEEE/CVF Conference on Computer Vision and Pattern Recognition, pp. 9653–9663 (2022)

19. Zhou, J., et al.: Image BERT pre-training with online tokenizer. In: International Conference on Learning Representations (2022)

20. Bao, H., Dong, L., Wei, F.: BEi T: BERT pre-training of image transformers. arXiv preprint arXiv:2106.08254 (2021)

21. He, K., Chen, X., Xie, S., Li, Y., Dollár, P., Girshick, R.: Masked autoencoders are scalable vision learners. In: Proceedings of the IEEE/CVF Conference on Computer Vision and Pattern Recognition, pp. 16000–16009 (2022)

22. Li, K., Yu, L., Wang, S., Heng, P.A.: Towards cross-modality medical image segmentation with online mutual knowledge distillation. In: Proceedings of the AAAI, vol. 34, no. 01, pp. 775–783 (2020)

23. Jiang, J., Rimner, A., Deasy, J.O., Veeraraghavan, H.: Unpaired cross-modality educed distillation (CMEDL) for medical image segmentation. IEEE Trans. Med. Imaging **41**, 1057–1068 (2021)

24. Caron, M., et al.: Emerging properties in self-supervised vision transformers. In: IEEE/CVF International Conference on Computer Vision, pp. 9650–9660 (2021)

25. Liu, Z., et al.: SWIN transformer: hierarchical vision transformer using shifted windows. In: IEEE International Conference on Computer Vision, pp. 10012–10022 (2021)

26. Aerts, H., et al.: Data from NSCLC-radiomics. The Cancer Imaging Archive (2015)

27. Akin, O., et al.: Radiology data from the cancer genome atlas kidney renal clear cell carcinoma [tcga-kirc] collection. The Cancer Imaging Archive (2016)

28. Harmon, S.A., et al.: Artificial intelligence for the detection of COVID-19 pneumonia on chest CT using multinational datasets. Nature Commun. **11**(1), 1–7 (2020)

29. Chen, L.C., Zhu, Y., Papandreou, G., Schroff, F., Adam, H.: Encoder-decoder with atrous separable convolution for semantic image segmentation. In: Proceedings of the European Conference on Computer Vision, pp. 801–818 (2018)

30. Isensee, F., Jaeger, P.F., Kohl, S.A., Petersen, J., Maier-Hein, K.H.: nn U-Net: a self-configuring method for deep learning-based biomedical image segmentation. Nat. Meth. **18**(2), 203–211 (2021)

31. Chen, J., et al.: Transunet: transformers make strong encoders for medical image segmentation. arXiv preprint arXiv:2102.04306 (2021)

32. de Bruijne, M., et al. (eds.): MICCAI 2021. LNCS, vol. 12901. Springer, Cham (2021). https://doi.org/10.1007/978-3-030-87193-2

33. Chen, X., Xie, S., He, K.: An empirical study of training self-supervised vision transformers. In: IEEE/CVF International Conference on Computer Vision, pp. 9640–9649 (2021)

34. Naseer, M.M., et al.: Intriguing properties of vision transformers. In: Advances in Neural Information Processing Systems, vol. 34 (2021)

DeepRecon: Joint 2D Cardiac Segmentation and 3D Volume Reconstruction via a Structure-Specific Generative Method

Qi Chang[1(✉)], Zhennan Yan[2], Mu Zhou[2], Di Liu[1], Khalid Sawalha[3],
Meng Ye[1], Qilong Zhangli[1], Mikael Kanski[4,5], Subhi Al'Aref[3], Leon Axel[5],
and Dimitris Metaxas[1]

[1] Rutgers University, Piscataway, NJ 08854, USA
qc58@rutgers.edu
[2] SenseBrain Research, Princeton, USA
[3] Department of Medicine, Division of Cardiology. University of Arkansas
for Medical Sciences, Little Rock, AR, USA
[4] Clinical Physiology, Department of Clinical Sciences Lund, Lund University,
Skåne University Hospital, Lund, Sweden
[5] Department of Radiology, New York University, New York, NY 10016, USA

Abstract. Joint 2D cardiac segmentation and 3D volume reconstruction are fundamental in building statistical cardiac anatomy models and understanding functional mechanisms from motion patterns. However, due to the low through-plane resolution of cine MR and high inter-subject variance, accurately segmenting cardiac images and reconstructing the 3D volume are challenging. In this study, we propose an end-to-end latent-space-based framework, DeepRecon, that generates multiple clinically essential outcomes, including accurate image segmentation, synthetic high-resolution 3D image, and 3D reconstructed volume. Our method identifies the optimal latent representation of the cine image that contains accurate semantic information for cardiac structures. In particular, our model jointly generates synthetic images with accurate semantic information and segmentation of the cardiac structures using the optimal latent representation. We further explore downstream applications of 3D shape reconstruction and 4D motion pattern adaptation by the different latent-space manipulation strategies. The simultaneously generated high-resolution images present a high interpretable value to assess the cardiac shape and motion. Experimental results demonstrate the effectiveness of our approach on multiple fronts including 2D segmentation, 3D reconstruction, downstream 4D motion pattern adaption performance.

Keywords: 3D reconstruction · Cardiac MRI · GAN · Latent space

Supplementary Information The online version contains supplementary material available at https://doi.org/10.1007/978-3-031-16440-8_54.

1   Introduction

Comprehensive image-based assessment of cardiac structure and motion through 3D heart modeling is essential for early detection, cardiac function understanding, and treatment planning of cardiovascular diseases (CVD) [2,12]. As a standard clinical diagnostic tool, cine magnetic resonance imaging (cMRI) has been used to characterize the complex shape and motion of the heart. cMRI presents multiple advances, including the high temporal and in-plane resolution, minimal radiation exposure, and improved soft tissue definition [19]. Yet conventional practice acquires a stack of 2D short-axis (SAX) slices with large between-slice spacing, so the accurate heart tissue segmentation and 3D image-based heart modeling is challenging due to the missing structure information.

Heart modeling from cMRI typically consists of carefully-designed steps, including image segmentation [5,16,28] and 3D reconstruction [3]. Deep learning has shown its progress in the segmentation of cardiac structures [4,15], which addresses the challenges of analyzing the complex and variable shape of the heart and ill-defined borders in MR images. After obtaining 2D segmentation, 3D reconstruction can be implemented by subsequent interpretations between neighboring slices. Conventional approaches [7,13] often struggle when significant anatomical changes appear in the consecutive slices. For instance, deformable models have been proposed for 3D surface construction of left ventricular (LV) wall and motion tracking [25,26]. Yet the parameter initialization is sensitive, making it difficult to generalize across clinical settings. Despite that 3D high-resolution image acquisition and generation are gaining momentum to assess disease status [3,12,23], the integrative analysis of MR data enables high-quality MR image segmentation, reconstruction, and subsequent interpretation has not been explicitly addressed.

In this study, we propose an end-to-end, latent-space-based framework, DeepRecon, that generates multiple clinically essential outcomes, including accurate image segmentation, synthetic high-resolution 3D image, and 3D reconstructed volume (see Fig. 1). Our method could jointly generate 2D segmentation and 3D volume (by interpolating latent codes) simultaneously in the evaluation stage. Thus, we do not require another step to reconstruct the 3D volume from the sparse 2D segmentations. Meanwhile, the simultaneously generated synthetic images present a high interpretable value to assess the shape and motion of cardiology. Our study draws inspiration from StyleGANs [10,11], where a synthetic image can be generated from a random latent code. Our findings are built upon the rationale that the latent code can be used to reconstruct the realistic synthetic image and simultaneously generate accurate segmentation [14,20]. Experimental results demonstrate the effectiveness of our approach on 2D segmentation, 3D reconstruction, and 4D motion pattern adaptation performance.

2   Method

Figure 1 illustrates the end-to-end framework of DeepRecon that learns a latent space from MR imaging to yield a broad range of outcomes, including generation of high-quality 2D cine image and corresponding segmentation, high-resolution 3D

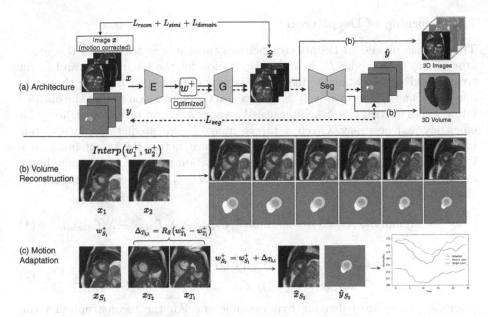

Fig. 1. (a) illustrates the architecture of DeepRecon. The black arrow workflow demonstrates the hybrid inversion method to acquire the optimized latent code. The black dash workflow shows the segmentation training stage, and the red workflow shows the 3D image and volume reconstruction process. (b) shows a 3D volume reconstruction (both images and masks) by interpolating the latent code of adjacent slices x_1 and x_2. (c) shows a source case x_{S_1} can adapt the motion pattern extracted from temporal frames x_{T_2} and x_{T_1} of a target case, so the source's synthetic motion has similar volume changes as the target. Best viewed in color. (Color figure online)

reconstructed volume, and 4D motion adaptation of the heart. We first describe the architecture design and the learning process and then elaborate on latent-space-based 3D reconstruction and motion adaptation.

2.1 DeepRecon Architecture

Our architecture consists of a latent-code encoder E, a MR image generator G followed by a segmentation network Seg, as shown in Fig. 1 (a). The E takes an real MR image x as input and outputs its latent code representation w^+. The optional motion correction is described in [6,24]. Then, G can generate synthetic image $\hat{x}$ from the w^+, and Seg produces the segmentation $\hat{y}$. As an intuitive downstream application, we can interpolate the latent codes of two neighboring MR slices to produce 3D images and masks by stacking continuous synthetic outputs (spatial domain synthesize), as shown in Fig. 1 (b). Furthermore, we show that the manipulation of latent codes enables a 4D motion adaptation that can transfer a motion pattern of one subject to another subject (temporal domain synthesize), as shown in Fig. 1 (c) and described in Sect. 2.3.

2.2   Learning of DeepRecon

The training process of DeepRecon includes three stages: training of the generator G and the encoder E, hybrid optimization for the latent code, and latent space based segmentation module. The training of the G and E follow the methods in [11] and [20], respectively. Then, we use GAN inversion to find the optimal latent codes for real cine SAX images. We adopt a hybrid inversion strategy for efficiency and accuracy. Given a target image x, we predict the latent code $w^+ = E(x)$. The w^+ is then optimized by reconstructing the target image. We formulate the objective function of the optimization by three losses, including a reconstruction term L_{smooth}, a similarity term L_{simi}, and a domain regularization term L_{domain}.

$$w^{+*} = \underset{w^+}{\arg\min} \mathcal{L}(x, G(w^+)) = \underset{w^+}{\arg\min}(\lambda_1 \mathcal{L}_{recon} + \lambda_2 \mathcal{L}_{simi} + \lambda_3 \mathcal{L}_{domain}) \quad (1)$$

$$\begin{aligned} \mathcal{L}_{recon} &= \mathcal{L}_{LPIPS}(x, G(w^+)) + \|ROI(x - G(w^+))\|_2^2, \\ \mathcal{L}_{simi} &= - L_{NCC}(x, G(w^+)), \mathcal{L}_{domain} = \|w^+ - E(G(w^+))\|_2^2 \end{aligned} \quad (2)$$

where $\lambda_1, \lambda_2, \lambda_3$ are balancing hyperparameters. For the reconstruction term, we use the Learned Perceptual Image Patch Similarity (LPIPS) distance [27] to encourage smooth generator mapping from latent codes. We also include a ROI-based regularization by a weighted L2 term to encourage the similarity in the ROI. For the similarity term, we adopt a normalized local cross-correlation (NCC) metric [1] to ensure robustness for intensity-variant cine images. The last term regularizes the optimization trajectory to stay in the training domain and keep the interpolation of latent-space vectors smoothness [29].

We store the optimized latent codes of training samples for training the Seg (e.g., U-Net [21]). The Seg takes synthetic images $\hat{x} = G(w^{+*})$ as input and train the network with the Cross-Entropy(CE) and DICE loss [21,22]. The loss of the segmentation task is defined as $\mathcal{L}_{seg} = \mathcal{L}_{ce} + \mathcal{L}_{dice}$.

2.3   3D Reconstruction and 4D Motion Adaptation

After learning of the DeepRecon, we use the learned model towards 3D shape reconstruction and 4D motion adaptation that take fully advantage of the learned latent space for the MR images. Our key motivation is that, by identifying the optimal latent-space representation, the spatial interpolation of two neighboring SAX slices can be achieved by generating images from the interpolation of their corresponding latent codes (see Fig. 1 (b)). In this way, DeepRecon is able to output a smooth super-resolution cine image volume and the corresponding 3D heart shape from the generated segmentations.

Beyond the spatial interpolation, we can adapt a motion pattern of a target subject x_T to a source subject x_S. In this way, we can synthesize and visualize a healthy-heart motion of a diseased subject and compare with its real motion pattern in an intuitive manner. The motion adaptation is demonstrated in Fig. 1 (c). Formally, we define the motion adaptation module as:

$$\hat{x}_{S_{i+1}} = G(w_{S_0}^+ + \sum_{n=0}^{i} \mathcal{R}_S \Delta_{T_{n+1,n}}) \qquad (3)$$

where $\hat{x}_{S_{i+1}}$ is the generated source images in time $i+1$; $w_{S_0}^+$ is the latent code for x_{S_0}; $\Delta_{T_{n+1,n}} = (w_{T_{n+1}}^+ - w_{T_n}^+)$ and $w_{T_n}^+$ is the latent code for target subject in time n. Because the size of heart varies, $\mathcal{R}_S$ represents the resampling function that align the number of target slices to the number of source slices.

3 Experiments

We evaluate multiple outputs of DeepRecon including latent-space-based 2D segmentation (Sect. 3.1), 3D volume reconstruction (Sect. 3.2), and motion adaptation (Sect. 3.3).

Dataset: The UK Biobank dataset [18] consists of SAX and LAX cine CMR images of normal subjects. Cardiac structures, LV cavity (LVC), LV myocardium (LVM), and right-ventricle cavity (RVC) were manually annotated on SAX images at the end-diastolic (ED) and end-systolic (ES) cardiac phases [18]. We use 6,846 cases containing 3,569,990 2D SAX MR images as a pre-training subset. We adopt the first 1,010 annotated subjects and split them into two sets of 810/200 for training and validation of DeepRecon. We select another 100 cases from the UK Biobank as the testing set that has no overlap with the pre-training, training and validation subsets. Besides, two cardiologists annotated and verified the LAX images of 50 testing cases to evaluate the 3D volume reconstruction task. Finally, we validate the motion adaptation on a private dataset with diseased cases to assess the motion patterns among various cardiac functional diseases.

3.1 Latent-space-based 2D Segmentation

Settings: We first evaluate the generative segmentation method based on the latent representation of MR images. The purpose of this task is to ensure the generated 2D segmentation is accurate enough to reconstruct 3D cardiac shape precisely. We pre-train the MR image generator G on the pre-training subset based on StyleGAN2 method [11]. The training took 14 days with 4 RTX 8000 GPUs and achieved Fid50k score of 18.09. We perform the following experiments for comparison. 1) *DirectSeg*. We train a segmentation network with the same architecture as the *Seg* in our method directly on the real images. This result shows the approximate upper bound of the segmentation task. 2) *3D-Unet*. In this method, we evaluate the 3D-Unet segmentation on the original low-resolution Cine data. Since there is no high-resolution 3D data for training the 3D-UNet, it can not be directly applied to the generated high-resolution 3D images to obtain the 3D segmentation volume. 3) *SemanticGAN* [14]. In this method, the architecture of the generator is extended to output the image and segmentation at the same time (no additional segmentation network is required). 4) $W^+SegNet$. A variant of our method keeps the same architecture except the

Table 1. Segmentation results by various latent-code-based methods compared with a direct segmentation from real images: mean (standard deviation).

Method	LVC		LVM		RVC	
	DICE↑	HD95↓	DICE↑	HD95↓	DICE↑	HD95↓
DirectSeg	0.928(0.04)	2.31(9.8)	0.861(0.03)	1.38(3.5)	0.892(0.04)	4.69(15.8)
3D-UNet	0.938(0.046)	3.78(11.4)	0.861(0.03)	2.31(1.8)	0.90(0.03)	5.79(3.9)
SemanticGAN	0.891(0.05)	5.23(7.1)	0.787(0.04)	3.11(1.9)	0.843(0.05)	4.77(4.2)
$W^+SegNet$	0.895(0.05)	5.97(9.5)	0.789(0.06)	3.11(2.7)	0.822(0.06)	6.33(6.2)
$DeepRecon_{no}$	0.895(0.04)	2.37(8.1)	0.792(0.04)	1.87(5.8)	0.847(0.05)	2.33(5.6)
$DeepRecon_{1k}$	**0.926(0.04)**	**1.25(0.8)**	0.835(0.05)	**1.27(1.7)**	0.883(0.04)	**1.51(4.4)**
$DeepRecon_{10k}$	0.925(0.04)	3.15(14.8)	**0.858(0.03)**	2.14(9.1)	**0.890(0.04)**	2.70(10.2)

Seg network takes latent code as input to directly predict the segmentation. 5) $DeepRecon_{no}$. The proposed method without the hybrid latent code optimization. 6) $DeepRecon_{1k}$, $DeepRecon_{10k}$. These two settings of the proposed method use the latent code generated by the encoder E, followed by 1k and 10k optimization steps, respectively. We train all the models in 2D and use 3D DICE and 95% quantile of Hausdorff distance (HD95) for evaluation.

Result: We report the quantitative segmentation results in Table 1, and illustrates a representative example in Fig. 2. Table 1 shows that DeepRecon consistently outperforms the other latent-space-based methods and achieves similar performance as the upper bound. The proposed $DeepRecon_{1k}$ performs the best overall, especially in HD95, because more accurate image reconstruction with fine details helps to optimize the segmentation network. The $DeepRecon_{10k}$ further improves the DICE score of LVM while it drops in terms of HD95 (may due to overfitting) and takes 10x time to retrieve the optimized latent code. Thus, the $DeepRecon_{1k}$ presents a good trade-off between the accuracy and efficiency and is used for evaluation in following experiments. We also observe that other latent-space-based methods tend to have significantly worse results for the LVM compared with the LVC and RVC. A possible reason is that the sub-optimal latent code predicted from the encoder is challenging to accurately reconstruct such a thin annular shape. Our $DeepRecon_{1k}$, $DeepRecon_{10k}$ are statistically better than SematicGAN in all metrics ($p < 0.05$) and comparable with Direct-Seg ($p > 0.05$) in most metrics. Additionally, we measure the image quality of the ground-truth and synthetic images using the averaged peak signal-to-noise ratio (PSNR) and structural similarity index (SSIM) in Fig. 2. The results show the improvement of the synthesized image quality.

3.2   3D Volume Reconstruction

Settings: We evaluate the reconstructed 3D cardiac shape continuity from the interpolated latent codes. Since 3D MR image and segmentation volume are unavailable, we utilize the LAX annotations and calculate the overlapping accuracy (2D DICE) of the intersection areas, i.e., the intersection of the reconstructed

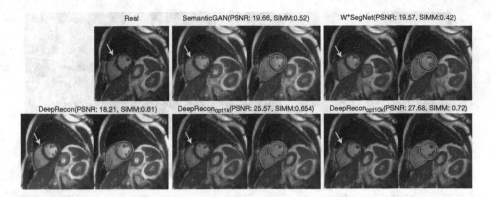

Fig. 2. Segmentation results of different latent-space-based models. Each group shows the synthetic image and corresponding segmentation. The red lines are the ground truth boundaries, and the green lines are the predictions. We notice that the sub-optimal latent codes may differ in the cardiac region, especially thin structures. (Color figure online)

Table 2. Evaluation of reconstructed 3D volumes in terms of the DICE score of their intersections on each LAX plane.

Method	Average DICE	2ch view DICE	3ch view DICE	4ch view DICE
Original	0.780 ± 0.111	0.787 ± 0.091	0.793 ± 0.105	0.766 ± 0.128
Linear Interp	0.781 ± 0.080	0.797 ± 0.051	0.773 ± 0.070	0.768 ± 0.102
CPD [17]	0.790 ± 0.099	0.803 ± 0.084	$\mathbf{0.815 \pm 0.094}$	0.767 ± 0.109
$DeepRecon_{no}$	0.806 ± 0.111	0.830 ± 0.069	0.799 ± 0.111	0.787 ± 0.091
$DeepRecon_{1k}$	$\mathbf{0.817 \pm 0.097}$	$\mathbf{0.848 \pm 0.056}$	0.802 ± 0.141	$\mathbf{0.797 \pm 0.091}$
$DeepRecon_{10k}$	0.809 ± 0.094	0.839 ± 0.053	0.800 ± 0.136	0.787 ± 0.090

3D volume and the LAX slice. We correct the misalignment for each SAX slice based on the method described in [24]. The LAX slices usually include 2-chamber (2ch), 3-chamber (3ch), and 4-chamber (4ch) views. The following experiments are performed: 1) Original. The intersections of tiles of the original SAX annotations and each LAX view. 2) Linear Interpolation. 3) Coherent Point Drifting (CPD). The CPD algorithm [17] can construct 3D surface based on a 3D point cloud and the deformable registration. 4) $DeepRecon_{no}, DeepRecon_{1k}, DeepRecon_{10k}$ experiments follow the same configuration described in 3.1. The DICE scores on different views and their average score are computed.

Result: In Table 2, the DICE scores measure the accuracy for the LVC region between the LAX annotation and the intersection of 3D reconstructed volume and the corresponding LAX plane. We also show three examples in Fig. 3 for each LAX view. Overall, our method achieves improved performance in each view compared with other approaches. We observe that the SAX slices are not complete compared to the LAX slices in the basal and apex region, but our methods still achieve a better performance in 2ch and 4ch views on average.

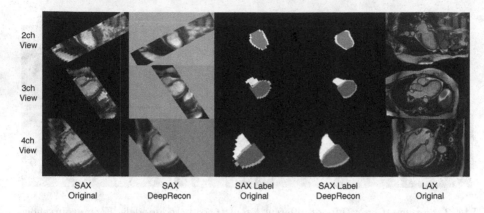

Fig. 3. Visualization of the cross-sections of reconstructed 3D images and label volumes by DeepRecon in different LAX views (last column). The first and third columns show the original low-resolution SAX images and labels. The second and fourth columns show the high-resolution reconstructions from the proposed method.

3.3   Motion Pattern Adaptation

Settings: We further perform an exploratory analysis to assess the cardiac 4D motion adaptation qualitatively. We extract a target case's motion pattern and assign such motion pattern to the initial shape of a source heart. First, we select two random healthy cases from the UK Biobank dataset. Second, we use one normal case as the target and one diseased case from our private dataset as the source. The diseased heart has shown severe mitral regurgitation with significant LV dilation and decreased function.

Results: The volume changes of the LVC over time within a full cardiac cycle are presented in Fig. 4. The healthy example (Fig. 4 left) shows the consistency of cavity volume change. By transferring the cardiac motion pattern from the target case to the source shape, the motion of the source heart (the blue Adapted curve) becomes similar to the target case (the green curve) while the heart scale remains the same. In the second experiment, shown in Fig. 4 right, we can synthesize a normal-like motion for the source diseased heart (the blue curve),

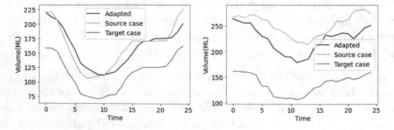

Fig. 4. Two examples of motion adaptation: normal-to-normal (left) and diseased-to-normal (right). The motions are plotted by volume changes of LVC in a cardiac cycle. (Color figure online)

which shows a more efficient contraction than its real motion (the orange curve). The ejection fraction of the source case is significantly smaller than the adapted motion. Such motion adaptation method provides a unique tool to potentially help cardiologists analyze functional differences between various cases (see video clips in the supplementary).

4   Conclusion

Integrative analysis of cMRI is of great clinical significance in cardiac function understanding and assessment. This paper proposes an end-to-end latent-space-based generative method, DeepRecon, that generates multiple outcomes, including 2D image segmentation, 3D reconstructed volume, and extended motion pattern adaptation. Our findings show that the learned latent representation can lead to high-level performance on cMRI feature analysis. In particular, our approach opens up new perspectives on building scalable 3D/4D synthetic cardiac models for cardiac functional research. In the future, we will consider Transformer-based approaches [8,9,15] and investigate a large-scale study to validate our approach. We also plan to examine pathological identification based on the learned latent space.

References

1. Avants, B.B., Tustison, N.J., Song, G., Cook, P.A., Klein, A., Gee, J.C.: A reproducible evaluation of ants similarity metric performance in brain image registration. Neuroimage **54**(3), 2033–2044 (2011)
2. Awori, J., et al.: 3D models improve understanding of congenital heart disease. 3D Print. Med. **7**(1), 1–9 (2021)
3. Biffi, C., et al.: 3D high-resolution cardiac segmentation reconstruction from 2D views using conditional variational autoencoders. In: 2019 IEEE 16th International Symposium on Biomedical Imaging (ISBI 2019), pp. 1643–1646. IEEE (2019)
4. Campello, V.M., et al.: Multi-centre, multi-vendor and multi-disease cardiac segmentation: the M&MS challenge. IEEE Trans. Med. Imaging **40**(12), 3543–3554 (2021)
5. Chang, Q., Yan, Z., Lou, Y., Axel, L., Metaxas, D.N.: Soft-label guided semi-supervised learning for bi-ventricle segmentation in cardiac cine MRI. In: 2020 IEEE 17th International Symposium on Biomedical Imaging (ISBI), pp. 1752–1755. IEEE (2020)
6. Chang, Q., et al.: An unsupervised 3D recurrent neural network for slice misalignment correction in cardiac MR imaging. In: Puyol Antón, E., et al. (eds.) STACOM 2021. LNCS, vol. 13131, pp. 141–150. Springer, Cham (2022). https://doi.org/10.1007/978-3-030-93722-5_16
7. Frakes, D.H., et al.: A new method for registration-based medical image interpolation. IEEE Trans. Med. Imaging **27**(3), 370–377 (2008)
8. Gao, Y., Zhou, M., Liu, D., Yan, Z., Zhang, S., Metaxas, D.: A data-scalable transformer for medical image segmentation: architecture, model efficiency, and benchmark. arXiv preprint arXiv:2203.00131 (2022)

9. Gao, Y., Zhou, M., Metaxas, D.N.: UTNet: a hybrid transformer architecture for medical image segmentation. In: de Bruijne, M., et al. (eds.) MICCAI 2021. LNCS, vol. 12903, pp. 61–71. Springer, Cham (2021). https://doi.org/10.1007/978-3-030-87199-4_6

10. Karras, T., Laine, S., Aila, T.: A style-based generator architecture for generative adversarial networks. In: Proceedings of the IEEE/CVF Conference on Computer Vision and Pattern Recognition, pp. 4401–4410 (2019)

11. Karras, T., Laine, S., Aittala, M., Hellsten, J., Lehtinen, J., Aila, T.: Analyzing and improving the image quality of stylegan. In: Proceedings of the IEEE/CVF Conference on Computer Vision and Pattern Recognition, pp. 8110–8119 (2020)

12. Küstner, T., et al.: CINENET: deep learning-based 3d cardiac cine MRI reconstruction with multi-coil complex-valued 4d spatiotemporal convolutions. Sci. Rep. **10**(1), 1–13 (2020)

13. Leng, J., Xu, G., Zhang, Y.: Medical image interpolation based on multi-resolution registration. Comput. Math. Appl. **66**(1), 1–18 (2013)

14. Li, D., Yang, J., Kreis, K., Torralba, A., Fidler, S.: Semantic segmentation with generative models: semi-supervised learning and strong out-of-domain generalization. In: Proceedings of the IEEE/CVF Conference on Computer Vision and Pattern Recognition, pp. 8300–8311 (2021)

15. Liu, D., et al.: Transfusion: multi-view divergent fusion for medical image segmentation with transformers. arXiv preprint arXiv:2203.10726 (2022)

16. Liu, D., Yan, Z., Chang, Q., Axel, L., Metaxas, D.N.: Refined deep layer aggregation for multi-disease, multi-view & multi-center cardiac MR segmentation. In: Puyol Antón, E., et al. (eds.) STACOM 2021. LNCS, vol. 13131, pp. 315–322. Springer, Cham (2022). https://doi.org/10.1007/978-3-030-93722-5_34

17. Myronenko, A., Song, X.: Point set registration: coherent point drift. IEEE Trans. Pattern Anal. Mach. Intell. **32**(12), 2262–2275 (2010)

18. Petersen, S.E., et al.: UK biobank's cardiovascular magnetic resonance protocol. J. Cardiovascular Magnet. Reson. **18**(1), 1–7 (2015)

19. Prakash, A., Powell, A.J., Geva, T.: Multimodality noninvasive imaging for assessment of congenital heart disease. Circul. Cardiovascular Imaging **3**(1), 112–125 (2010)

20. Richardson, E., et al.: Encoding in style: a stylegan encoder for image-to-image translation. In: Proceedings of the IEEE/CVF Conference on Computer Vision and Pattern Recognition, pp. 2287–2296 (2021)

21. Ronneberger, O., Fischer, P., Brox, T.: U-Net: convolutional networks for biomedical image segmentation. In: Navab, N., Hornegger, J., Wells, W.M., Frangi, A.F. (eds.) MICCAI 2015. LNCS, vol. 9351, pp. 234–241. Springer, Cham (2015). https://doi.org/10.1007/978-3-319-24574-4_28

22. Sudre, C.H., Li, W., Vercauteren, T., Ourselin, S., Jorge Cardoso, M.: Generalised dice overlap as a deep learning loss function for highly unbalanced segmentations. In: Cardoso, M.J., et al. (eds.) DLMIA/ML-CDS -2017. LNCS, vol. 10553, pp. 240–248. Springer, Cham (2017). https://doi.org/10.1007/978-3-319-67558-9_28

23. Xia, Y., Ravikumar, N., Greenwood, J.P., Neubauer, S., Petersen, S.E., Frangi, A.F.: Super-resolution of cardiac MR cine imaging using conditional GANs and unsupervised transfer learning. Med. Image Anal. **71**, 102037 (2021)

24. Yang, D., Wu, P., Tan, C., Pohl, K.M., Axel, L., Metaxas, D.: 3D motion modeling and reconstruction of left ventricle wall in cardiac MRI. In: Pop, M., Wright, G.A. (eds.) FIMH 2017. LNCS, vol. 10263, pp. 481–492. Springer, Cham (2017). https://doi.org/10.1007/978-3-319-59448-4_46

25. Ye, M., et al.: Deeptag: an unsupervised deep learning method for motion tracking on cardiac tagging magnetic resonance images. In: Proceedings of the IEEE/CVF Conference on Computer Vision and Pattern Recognition, pp. 7261–7271 (2021)
26. Yu, Y., Zhang, S., Li, K., Metaxas, D., Axel, L.: Deformable models with sparsity constraints for cardiac motion analysis. Med. Image Anal. **18**(6), 927–937 (2014)
27. Zhang, R., Isola, P., Efros, A.A., Shechtman, E., Wang, O.: The unreasonable effectiveness of deep features as a perceptual metric. In: Proceedings of the IEEE Conference on Computer Vision and Pattern Recognition, pp. 586–595 (2018)
28. Zhangli, Q., et al.: Region proposal rectification towards robust instance segmentation of biological images. arXiv preprint arXiv:2203.02846 (2022)
29. Zhu, J., Shen, Y., Zhao, D., Zhou, B.: In-domain GAN inversion for real image editing. In: Vedaldi, A., Bischof, H., Brox, T., Frahm, J.-M. (eds.) ECCV 2020. LNCS, vol. 12362, pp. 592–608. Springer, Cham (2020). https://doi.org/10.1007/978-3-030-58520-4_35

Online Easy Example Mining
for Weakly-Supervised Gland
Segmentation from Histology Images

Yi Li[1,2], Yiduo Yu[1], Yiwen Zou[1], Tianqi Xiang[1],
and Xiaomeng Li[1,2(✉)]

[1] Department of Electronic and Computer Engineering, The Hong Kong University
of Science and Technology, Hong Kong, China
eexmli@ust.hk
[2] HKUST Shenzhen Research Institute, Shenzhen, China

Abstract. Developing an AI-assisted gland segmentation method from
histology images is critical for automatic cancer diagnosis and prognosis;
however, the high cost of pixel-level annotations hinders its applications
to broader diseases. Existing weakly-supervised semantic segmentation
methods in computer vision achieve degenerative results for gland segmentation, since the characteristics and problems of glandular datasets
are different from general object datasets. We observe that, unlike natural
images, the key problem with histology images is the confusion of classes
owning to morphological homogeneity and low color contrast among different tissues. To this end, we propose a novel method *Online Easy Example Mining* (OEEM) that encourages the network to focus on credible
supervision signals rather than noisy signals, therefore mitigating the
influence of inevitable false predictions in pseudo-masks. According to
the characteristics of glandular datasets, we design a strong framework
for gland segmentation. Our results exceed many fully-supervised methods and weakly-supervised methods for gland segmentation over 4.6%
and 6.04% at mIoU, respectively. Code is available at https://github.
com/xmed-lab/OEEM.

Keywords: Online Easy Example Mining · Histology image · Gland
segmentation · Wealy-supervised semantic segmentation

1 Introduction

Accurate gland segmentation is one crucial prerequisite step to obtain reliable
morphological statistics that indicate the aggressiveness of tumors. With the
advent of deep learning and whole slide imaging, considerable efforts have been
devoted to developing automatic semantic segmentation algorithms from histology images [13]. These methods require massive training data with pixel-wise

---

Y. Li and Y. Yu—Co-first authors.

© The Author(s), under exclusive license to Springer Nature Switzerland AG 2022
L. Wang et al. (Eds.): MICCAI 2022, LNCS 13434, pp. 578–587, 2022.
https://doi.org/10.1007/978-3-031-16440-8_55

annotations from expert pathologists [3,10,24]. However, obtaining pixel-wise annotation for histology images is expensive and labor-intensive. To reduce the annotation cost, designing a weakly-supervised segmentation method that only requires a patch-level label is highly desirable.

Fig. 1. (a): Examples of VOC (general dataset) and GlaS (glandular dataset). The blue region refers to glandular tissues, and the green region refers to non-glandular tissues. The characteristics of GlaS are morphological homogeneity, obvious overlaps, and low color contrast among different tissues. (b): Confusion regions (highlighted in cyan) in weakly-supervised gland segmentation. (Color figure online)

To our best knowledge, there are no prior studies for weakly-supervised gland segmentation from histology images. For other medical datasets, weakly-supervised segmentation methods are mainly based on multiple instance learning (MIL) [4,21,22], which requires at least two types of image-level labels to train the classifier.

However, this method is not applicable to our task since all our training images contain glandular tissues, *i.e.*, we only have one type of image-level label. Another limitation of MIL is the low quality of the pseudo-mask, which is block-like and coarse-grained because MIL regards all pixels within one patch as the same class. For general weakly-supervised semantic segmentation (WSSS) approaches in computer vision, the pseudo-mask is more fine-grained with pixel-level prediction via CAM [25]. Nevertheless, algorithms in general WSSS [1,2,5,17,23] do not suit glandular datasets because its core problem is *local activation* resulting from different representations in one object. While for glandular datasets, the key problem is *confusion among classes*, owning to the morphological homogeneity, obvious overlap, and low color contrast of targets.

As shown in Fig. 1 (a), compared to the natural images with apparent color differences, our gland images have a similar color distribution and morphological affinity between different tissues. For these confusing regions in Fig. 1 (b), techniques in general object datasets like saliency detection [23] and affinity learning [1] are invalid because these methods require *salient differences* between targets and background.

To solve the confusion problem and avoid the above issues, our key idea is that the network should highlight the training with credible supervision and down-weight the learning with noisy signals. To this end, we propose the Online

Easy Example Mining (OEEM) to distinguish easy and confusing examples in the optimization. Specifically, we develop a metric based on the normalized loss to achieve this goal, where pixels with lower losses are dynamically assigned higher weights in a batch.

Notably, our method is different from the existing online hard example mining methods [9,11]. For instance, online hard example mining [11] and focal loss [9] in object detection are hard to transfer to weakly supervised scenarios, since they amplify the noise in pseudo-mask.

Moreover, we design a powerful framework for weakly-supervised gland segmentation and report its fully-supervised result of the segmentation stage. With this strong baseline, our method excels many previous fully supervised methods [14–16] on the GlaS [12] dataset, notably outperforming the prior best method [16] by 4.6% on mIoU. Importantly, even with such a high backbone, our proposed OEEM further increases the performance by around 2.0% mIoU in weakly settings. And our weakly-supervised result surpasses the influential and general WSSS methods [2,6,18] by over 6.04% at mIoU.

The main contributions of our work are summarized as follows:

- We point out that the key problem of gland segmentation is the confusion caused by the homogeneity of histology images, rather than the local activation problem that most WSSS methods in computer vision try to solve.
- We propose the Online Easy Example Mining (OEEM) to mine the credible supervision signals in pseudo-mask with proposed normalized loss, thus mitigating the damage of confused supervisions for gland segmentation.
- We design a strong framework for gland segmentation. Our fully-supervised and proposed weakly-supervised OEEM surpasses the existing fully- and weakly-supervised methods for gland segmentation, respectively.

2   Method

2.1   Overall Framework

This part introduces the overall pipeline of weakly-supervised gland segmentation, consisting of two stages. As shown in Fig. 2, our framework starts from the classification stage, which is trained using patch-level supervision only. Then we synthesize the pseudo pixel-level mask based on CAM [25] for the training set. The pseudo-masks with original images are then passed to the segmentation stage in the manner of fully-supervised segmentation. To reduce the adverse impacts resulting from the noise in pseudo-masks, we adopt the proposed OEEM during the optimization of the segmentation model. Note that only the segmentation network is used to generate final predictions. The details of these two stages are shown below:

Classification: We denote the input image as $X \in \mathbb{R}^{C \times H \times W}$, and its patch-level label as Y, where Y is a one-hot vector of $[y_1, y_2, ..., y_n]$ and n is the number of classes in the dataset. $feat = f_{cls}(X, \phi_{feat})$ is the predicted feature map via

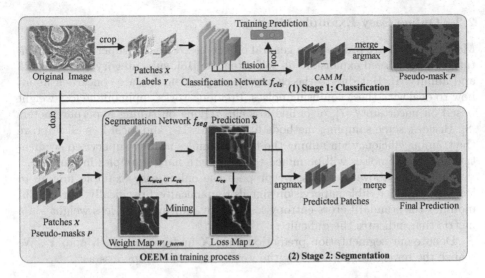

Fig. 2. Overview of our proposed weakly-supervised gland segmentation method with OEEM. (a) Classification pipeline for pseudo-mask generation from CAM. (b) Segmentation pipeline. We use weighted cross-entropy loss $\mathcal{L}_{wce}$ with weight map W_{l_norm} for multi-label patches. Here, the glandular tissues are shown in blue and non-glandular tissues are shown in green. (Color figure online)

network f_{cls} and its parameters ϕ_{feat} except that of classifier. Note that feature maps of last three stages are fused with interpolations before the classifier for better representation. Then we get the CAM $M \in \mathbb{R}^{n \times H \times W}$ by multiply the weights of classifier ϕ_{cls} to $feat$ without average pooling as:

$$M = f_{cls}(X, \phi_{feat}) \cdot \phi_{cls} \qquad (1)$$

The idea of CAM is that the feature maps of CNN architecture contain spatial information of the activated regions in the image, where the classification model is paying attention to. We apply argmax operation on M along the category dimension and get a 2-dim pseudo-mask $P \in \mathbb{R}^{H \times W}$ as Eq. 2. P is subsequently sent to segmentation stage.

$$P = \text{argmax}(M_{:,h,w}), \forall h, w \qquad (2)$$

Segmentation: We now train the segmentation model in a fully-supervised manner using pseudo-mask P. Denoting the segmentation network as f_{seg} with parameters ϕ_{seg}, the eventual prediction result $\tilde{X}$ is derived as $\tilde{X} = f_{seg}(X, \phi_{seg})$. Due to the inevitable noisy responses in pseudo-mask, the supervision P introduces many confusing signals to the optimization of segmentation. To cope with this issue, we need to direct supervised learning by weakening the guidance in the confusing region. Based on this motivation, we propose the OEEM to reweight the loss map for better usage of credible and clean supervision.

2.2　Online Easy Example Mining

Many solutions are proposed in general object-based weakly-supervised segmentation, such as seed expansion [5], self-attention [18], sub-category clustering [2] and affinity [1]. But due to the changed core problem, we are concerned about how to deal with these confusing noises. Previous works apply offline loss weight based on uncertainty [7], or online loss clip relying on tuning hyperparameters [8]. Besides, some sampling methods like OHEM [11], and focal loss [9] improve the training efficiency via mining the hard examples in fully-supervised segmentation. But the noises will be mined together with hard examples in our case.

Unlike the above methods, we propose the online easy example mining to learn from the credible supervision signals dynamically. Specifically, our OEEM modifies the standard cross-entropy loss $\mathcal{L}_{ce}$ by multiplying a loss weight via a metric that indicates the difficulty.

Denote our segmentation prediction map $\tilde{X}$ and ground truth map Y. We realize the reweighting scheme by the weighted cross-entropy loss as:

$$\mathcal{L}_{wce} = -\sum_{j=0}^{w}\sum_{i=0}^{h} W_{i,j} \cdot \log \frac{\exp(\tilde{X}_{Y_{i,j},i,j})}{\sum_{k=1}^{C}(\exp \tilde{X}_{k,i,j})} \cdot 1 \tag{3}$$

where $W \in \mathbb{R}^{H \times W}$ is the loss weight. To get this loss weight, we pick the loss scattered on loss map $L \in \mathbb{R}^{H \times W}$ and confidence on predicted score map as metrics to indicate the learning difficulty. And base on these metrics, we propose four types of loss weight maps to mine the easy examples.

The first two weight types are based on the metric of confidence. The motivation of Eq. 4 is that easy examples are usually of high confidence. We firstly apply softmax operation sm on the category dimension to normalize the score to $[0, 1]$, and select the maximum value as metric to form the weight map W_{c_max}. The second type Eq. 5 uses the difference of confidence as the metric, since comparable confidences indicate harder examples.

$$W_{c\_max} = \max((sm(\tilde{X}_{:,h,w}))), \forall h, w \tag{4}$$

$$W_{c\_diff} = \max((sm(\tilde{X}_{:,h,w}))) - \min((sm(\tilde{X}_{:,h,w}))), \forall h, w \tag{5}$$

The other two types are based on the loss value. Different from the confidence, the loss is obtained from both confidence and pseudo-ground-truth with more information. The noises with high confidences on the false category have high loss values, and those pixels supervised by clean labels have lower loss values. To get higher loss weight for easy examples, we apply a minus sign to the loss map L and deploy the softmax function sm on the hw dimension with a division of its mean value. We name this process to normalized loss as Eq. 6. At last, we combine max confidence and normalized loss as Eq. 7.

$$W_{l\_norm} = \frac{sm(-L)}{\text{mean}(sm(-L))} \tag{6}$$

$$W_{lc\_mix} = \frac{\text{sm}(-L)}{\text{mean}(\text{sm}(-L))} \cdot \max((\text{sm}(\tilde{X}_{:,h,w}))), \forall h, w \qquad (7)$$

Empirical experience suggests that W_{l_norm} in Eq. 6 performs best. So we select it as the metric of reweighting. And note that some images only contain one type of artifact that should not yield any noise. Hence, we use original cross-entropy loss $\mathcal{L}_{ce}$ without OEEM for images with number of classes $n = 1$. The final loss of segmentation is then expressed as:

$$\mathcal{L} = \begin{cases} \mathcal{L}_{wce} & n > 1, s.t. W = W_{l\_norm} \\ \mathcal{L}_{ce} & n = 1. \end{cases} \qquad (8)$$

2.3 Network Training

Our model is implemented with PyTorch and is trained with one NVIDIA GeForce RTX 3090 card. For the classification part, we adopt ResNet38 [19] as the backbone. We use an SGD optimizer with a polynomial decay policy at a learning rate of 0.01. The batch size is 20, and the model is trained for 20 epochs. Data augmentation includes random flip, random resized crop, and all patches are normalized by the calculated mean and variance of the GlaS dataset. We also utilize the multi-scale test with scales of [1, 1.25, 1.5, 1.75, 2] for CAM generation. For the segmentation part, we use PSPNet [24] with backbone ResNet38. The optimizer is SGD in poly scheduler at learning rate $5e - 3$, the batch size is 32, and the model is trained for 10000 iterations. Data augmentation includes random flip, random crop, and distortion. In the inference process, we apply a multi-scale test with scales of [0.75, 1, 1.25, 1.5, 1.75, 2, 2.5, 3] at crop size 320 and stride 256 for robust results. Note that all the weakly-supervised methods in Table 1 deploy the same settings for fair comparisons.

3 Experiments

3.1 Dataset

We carry out experiments on the Gland Segmentation in Histology Images Challenge (GlaS) Dataset [12]. It contains 165 images derived from 16 Hematoxylin, and Eosin (H&E) stained histological Whole Slide Images (WSIs) of stage T3 or T42 colorectal adenocarcinoma.

Following previous works [14–16], we split the data into 85 training images and 80 test images, which are separated by patients as original dataset without patch shuffle. There is no classifiable image-level label, since glands exist in each image. So we crop patches at side 112 and stride 56 to get balanced patch-level labels from masks, with a one-hot label indicating whether it contains glandular and non-glandular tissues for each patch. Note that all the patches are merged to the original sizes for evaluation in the metric of mIoU.

Table 1. Results of gland segmentation on the GlaS dataset. "-" refers to not reported.

Method	Backbone	Supervision	mIoU (%)	Dice (%)	F1 (%)
Unet [10]	Unet	Fully	65.34	79.04	77.78
Res-UNet [20]	Res-UNet	Fully	65.95	79.48	78.83
MedT [14]	Vision transformer	Fully	69.61	82.08	81.02
KiU-Net [15]	KiU-Net	Fully	71.31	83.25	–
UCTransNet [16]	UCTransNet	Fully	82.24	90.25	–
Ours w/o OEEM	PSPNet & ResNet38	Fully	**86.84**	**92.96**	**93.24**
SEAM [17]	PSPNet & ResNet38	Weakly	66.11	79.59	79.50
Adv-CAM [6]	PSPNet & ResNet38	Weakly	68.54	81.33	81.36
SC-CAM [2]	PSPNet & ResNet38	Weakly	71.52	83.40	83.32
Ours w/o OEEM	PSPNet & ResNet38	Weakly	75.64	86.13	82.36
OEEM	PSPNet & ResNet38	Weakly	**77.56**	**87.36**	**87.35**

3.2   Compare with State-of-the-Arts

Compare with Fully-Supervised Methods. We compare the final results after the segmentation step in Table 1. The result of our method without OEEM shows that we have already constructed a robust baseline model that excels in many fully-supervised settings like Unet [10] and MedT [14]. This suggests that our classification model based on ResNet38 with a multi-test mechanism performs quite well for the pseudo-mask generation.

Compare with Weakly-Supervised Methods. In Table 1, we firstly propose a powerful baseline, whose fully-supervised result is 86.84%, significantly beyond previous state-of-the-arts. Based on this framework, our weakly-supervised result is higher than most fully-supervised methods. Even under such a high baseline, our OEEM still works fine and increases our baseline from 75.64% to 77.56%. We also experimented with other influential weakly-supervised methods in the general object segmentation domain, such as SEAM, SC-CAM, and Adv-CAM. There is a large margin of at least 6.04% comparing to the proposed OEEM method. This is because the confusion owing to morphological homogeneity, low color contrast and serious overlap of tissue cells obstructs the network learning, leading to low quality pseudo-masks of classification stage.

Visualization. Here we show some qualitative visualization results compared to SC-CAM [2] in Fig. 3. The SC-CAM prediction fails to clearly capture the underlying patterns, causing the predicted glandular tissues to be tied up with each other(first and third row) or eroded in between(second row). This suggests that SC-CAM is unsuitable for the GlaS dataset and has trouble distinguishing the confusing boundary regions. In contrast, our OEEM prediction is more accurate and smooth, which seems quite similar to the fully-supervised result.

3.3   Ablation Study

Performance Gains in Overall Framework. We show the performances gains in the framework by listing the results of different predictions. The SEAM

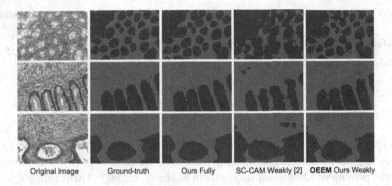

Original Image   Ground-truth   Ours Fully   SC-CAM Weakly [2]   **OEEM** Ours Weakly

Fig. 3. Qualitative results compared with ground-truth, fully and other weakly results. The glandular tissues are shown in blue and non-glandular tissues are shown in green. (Color figure online)

is different from our framework in the classification stage, with a drop at mIoU 15.89% owning to the shifted core problem in the histology dataset. The performance gain of our framework from CAM to pseudo-mask and segmentation prediction are 2.12%, 9.64% respectively. Note that OEEM shares the same pseudo-mask with our baseline and improves the performance by about 2% (Table 2).

Table 2. Performance of the framework at metric mIoU (%). CAM denotes the output of the classification stage on training set. Pseudo-mask is the refined CAM after using the patch-level labels to eliminate the non-existing tissues. Prediction is the result of the segmentation state on testing set.

Method	CAM	Pseudo-mask	Prediction
SEAM [17]	52.03	60.48	66.11
ours w/o OEEM	67.92	70.04	75.64
OEEM			**77.56**

Effectiveness of OEEM with Normalized Loss. For the segmentation part, we compare four OEEM weight metrics and OHEM [11] with our baseline result in Table 3. Unlike hard example mining in fully supervised learning [11], pseudo-masks from weakly supervision exist massive noise. It means hard samples and false samples are intertwined and indistinguishable. So we see that OHEM even introduces a performance drop due to the noise included. Thus, we mine the easy samples to make the supervision credible and mitigate the influence of noise from hard samples. Among which, *normalized loss* performs the best. This could be attributed to the help of pseudo ground-truth in computing the weight metrics. Additionally, normalization via softmax amplifies the loss gaps and emphasizes the clean samples more. Compared to the baseline model, our OEEM strategy improves 1.92% in mIoU, which is essential to our pipeline.

Table 3. Segmentation results of reweighting metrics in OEEM with baselines.

Metric	Baseline	OHEM [11]	W_{c_max}	W_{c_diff}	W_{l_norm}	W_{lc_mix}
mIoU (%)	75.64	75.49	75.93	75.43	**77.56**	77.19

4 Conclusion

This paper proposes a novel online easy example mining method for weakly-supervised gland segmentation from histology images, where only patch-level labels are provided. Our main motivation is that, unlike natural images, the key problem of histology images is the confusion among classes due to its low color contrast among different tissues, making it challenging for gland segmentation. Such a property degenerates many existing weakly-supervised methods in computer vision. Our proposed OEEM focuses on training with credible supervision and down-weight the training with noisy signals. Experimental results demonstrated that our method can outperform other weakly-supervised methods by a large margin.

Acknowledgement. This work was supported by Shenzhen Municipal Central Government Guides Local Science and Technology Development Special Funded Projects under 2021Szvup139 and Foshan HKUST Projects under FSUST21-HKUST11E.

References

1. Ahn, J., Kwak, S.: Learning pixel-level semantic affinity with image-level supervision for weakly supervised semantic segmentation. In: CVPR, pp. 4981–4990 (2018)
2. Chang, Y.T., Wang, Q., Hung, W.C., Piramuthu, R., Tsai, Y.H., Yang, M.H.: Weakly-supervised semantic segmentation via sub-category exploration. In: CVPR, pp. 8991–9000 (2020)
3. Chen, L.C., Papandreou, G., Kokkinos, I., Murphy, K., Yuille, A.L.: Deeplab: semantic image segmentation with deep convolutional nets, atrous convolution, and fully connected crfs. IEEE Trans. Pattern Anal. Mach. Intell. **40**(4), 834–848 (2017)
4. Jia, Z., Huang, X., Eric, I., Chang, C., Xu, Y.: Constrained deep weak supervision for histopathology image segmentation. IEEE Trans. Med. Imaging **36**(11), 2376–2388 (2017)
5. Kolesnikov, A., Lampert, C.H.: Seed, expand and constrain: three principles for weakly-supervised image segmentation. In: Leibe, B., Matas, J., Sebe, N., Welling, M. (eds.) ECCV 2016. LNCS, vol. 9908, pp. 695–711. Springer, Cham (2016). https://doi.org/10.1007/978-3-319-46493-0_42
6. Lee, J., Kim, E., Yoon, S.: Anti-adversarially manipulated attributions for weakly and semi-supervised semantic segmentation. In: Proceedings of the IEEE/CVF Conference on Computer Vision and Pattern Recognition, pp. 4071–4080 (2021)
7. Li, Y., Duan, Y., Kuang, Z., Chen, Y., Zhang, W., Li, X.: Uncertainty estimation via response scaling for pseudo-mask noise mitigation in weakly-supervised semantic segmentation. In: AAAI (2022)

8. Li, Y., Kuang, Z., Liu, L., Chen, Y., Zhang, W.: Pseudo-mask matters in weakly-supervised semantic segmentation. In: ICCV, pp. 6964–6973 (2021)
9. Lin, T.Y., Goyal, P., Girshick, R., He, K., Dollár, P.: Focal loss for dense object detection. In: ICCV, pp. 2980–2988 (2017)
10. Ronneberger, O., Fischer, P., Brox, T.: U-net: convolutional networks for biomedical image segmentation. In: Navab, N., Hornegger, J., Wells, W.M., Frangi, A.F. (eds.) MICCAI 2015. LNCS, vol. 9351, pp. 234–241. Springer, Cham (2015). https://doi.org/10.1007/978-3-319-24574-4_28
11. Shrivastava, A., Gupta, A., Girshick, R.: Training region-based object detectors with online hard example mining. In: CVPR, pp. 761–769 (2016)
12. Sirinukunwattana, K., et al.: Gland segmentation in colon histology images: The glas challenge contest. Med. Image Anal. 35, 489–502 (2017)
13. Srinidhi, C.L., Ciga, O., Martel, A.L.: Deep neural network models for computational histopathology: a survey. Med. Image Anal. 67, 101813 (2021)
14. Valanarasu, J.M.J., Oza, P., Hacihaliloglu, I., Patel, V.M.: Medical transformer: gated axial-attention for medical image segmentation. In: de Bruijne, M., et al. (eds.) MICCAI 2021. LNCS, vol. 12901, pp. 36–46. Springer, Cham (2021). https://doi.org/10.1007/978-3-030-87193-2_4
15. Valanarasu, J.M.J., Sindagi, V.A., Hacihaliloglu, I., Patel, V.M.: Kiu-net: Overcomplete convolutional architectures for biomedical image and volumetric segmentation. IEEE Trans. Med. Imaging 41(4), 965–976 (2021)
16. Wang, H., Cao, P., Wang, J., Zaiane, O.R.: Uctransnet: rethinking the skip connections in u-net from a channel-wise perspective with transformer. In: AAAI (2022)
17. Wang, Y., Zhang, J., Kan, M., Shan, S., Chen, X.: Self-supervised equivariant attention mechanism for weakly supervised semantic segmentation. In: CVPR, pp. 12275–12284 (2020)
18. Wang, Y., Zhang, J., Kan, M., Shan, S., Chen, X.: Self-supervised equivariant attention mechanism for weakly supervised semantic segmentation. In: CVPR, June 2020
19. Wu, Z., Shen, C., Van Den Hengel, A.: Wider or deeper: Revisiting the resnet model for visual recognition. Pattern Recogn. 90, 119–133 (2019)
20. Xiao, X., Lian, S., Luo, Z., Li, S.: Weighted res-unet for high-quality retina vessel segmentation. In: 2018 9th International Conference on Information Technology in Medicine and Education (ITME), pp. 327–331. IEEE (2018)
21. Xu, G., et al.: Camel: a weakly supervised learning framework for histopathology image segmentation. In: Proceedings of the IEEE/CVF International Conference on Computer Vision, pp. 10682–10691 (2019)
22. Xu, Y., et al.: Deep learning of feature representation with multiple instance learning for medical image analysis. In: 2014 IEEE international conference on acoustics, speech and signal processing (ICASSP), pp. 1626–1630. IEEE (2014)
23. Zeng, Y., Zhuge, Y., Lu, H., Zhang, L.: Joint learning of saliency detection and weakly supervised semantic segmentation. In: ICCV, pp. 7223–7233 (2019)
24. Zhao, H., Shi, J., Qi, X., Wang, X., Jia, J.: Pyramid scene parsing network. In: Proceedings of the IEEE Conference on Computer Vision and Pattern Recognition, pp. 2881–2890 (2017)
25. Zhou, B., Khosla, A., Lapedriza, A., Oliva, A., Torralba, A.: Learning deep features for discriminative localization. In: CVPR, pp. 2921–2929 (2016)

Joint Class-Affinity Loss Correction
for Robust Medical Image Segmentation
with Noisy Labels

Xiaoqing Guo⬮ and Yixuan Yuan(✉)⬮

Department of Electrical Engineering, City Univeristy of Hong Kong,
Kowloon Tong, Hong Kong
xiaoqiguo2-c@my.cityu.edu.hk, yxyuan.ee@cityu.edu.hk

Abstract. Noisy labels collected with limited annotation cost prevent
medical image segmentation algorithms from learning precise semantic
correlations. Previous segmentation arts of learning with noisy labels
merely perform a pixel-wise manner to preserve semantics, such as pixel-
wise label correction, but neglect the pair-wise manner. In fact, we
observe that the pair-wise manner capturing affinity relations between
pixels can greatly reduce the label noise rate. Motivated by this observation, we present a novel perspective for noisy mitigation by incorporating
both pixel-wise and pair-wise manners, where supervisions are derived
from noisy class and affinity labels, respectively. Unifying the pixel-wise
and pair-wise manners, we propose a robust Joint Class-Affinity Segmentation (JCAS) framework to combat label noise issues in medical image
segmentation. Considering the affinity in pair-wise manner incorporates
contextual dependencies, a differentiated affinity reasoning (DAR) module is devised to rectify the pixel-wise segmentation prediction by reasoning about intra-class and inter-class affinity relations. To further enhance
the noise resistance, a class-affinity loss correction (CALC) strategy is
designed to correct supervision signals via the modeled noise label distributions in class and affinity labels. Meanwhile, CALC strategy interacts
the pixel-wise and pair-wise manners through the theoretically derived
consistency regularization. Extensive experiments under both synthetic
and real-world noisy labels corroborate the efficacy of the proposed JCAS
framework with a minimum gap towards the upper bound performance.
The source code is available at https://github.com/CityU-AIM-Group/
JCAS.

Keywords: Class and affinity · Loss correction · Noisy label

1 Introduction

Image segmentation, as one of the most essential tasks in medical image analysis, has received lots of attention over the last decades. This task aims to assign

Supplementary Information The online version contains supplementary material
available at https://doi.org/10.1007/978-3-031-16440-8_56.

L. Wang et al. (Eds.): MICCAI 2022, LNCS 13434, pp. 588–598, 2022.
https://doi.org/10.1007/978-3-031-16440-8_56

a semantic label for each pixel, further benefiting various clinical applications such as treatment planning and surgical navigation [9]. Deep learning algorithms based on convolutional neural networks (CNNs) have achieved remarkable progress in medical image segmentation, but they require a large amount of training data with precise pixel-level annotations that are extremely expensive and labor-intensive to obtain [10]. With limited budgets and efforts, the resulting dataset would be noisy, and the presence of label noises may mislead the segmentation model to memorize wrong semantic correlations, resulting in severely degraded generalizability [8,23]. Hence, developing medical image segmentation techniques that are robust to noisy labels in training data is of great importance.

Solutions towards noisy label issues in image classification tasks have been extensively explored [11, 15,17,22,23], while pixel-wise label noises in segmentation tasks have not been well-studied, especially for medical image analysis. Previous solutions for medical image segmentation with noisy labels can be summarized into three aspects. Firstly, some researchers model the noisy label distribution through either the confusion matrix [20] or noise transition matrix (NTM) [6,7], and then leverage the modeled distribution for pixel-wise loss corrections. Secondly, pixel-wise label refurbishments are implemented by the spatial label smoothing regularization [19] or the convex combination with superpixel predictions [10]. Thirdly, pixel-wise resampling and reweighting strategies are designed to concentrate the segmentation model on learning reliable pixels. For instance, Tri-network et al. [21] contains three collaborative networks and adaptively selects informative samples according to the consensus between predictions from different networks. Wang et al. [16] leverage meta-learning to automatically estimate an importance map, thereby mining reliable information from important pixels.

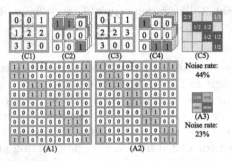

Fig. 1. A toy example to illustrate the comparison between pixel-wise class label (C) and pair-wise affinity label (A). (C1, C2) True class label and the one-hot encoding. (C3, C4) Noisy class label and the one-hot encoding. (C5) Class-level noise transition matrix with noise rate of 44%. (A1) True affinity label. (A2) Noisy affinity label. (A3) Affinity-level noise transition matrix with noise rate of 23%. (Color figure online)

Despite the impressive performance in promoting generalizability, almost all existing image segmentation methods tackle label noise issues merely in a pixel-wise manner. *Complementing the widely utilized pixel-wise manner, we make the first effort in exploiting the affinity relation between pixels within an image for noisy mitigation in a pair-wise manner.* Unlike pixel-wise manner that regularizes pixels with class label (Fig. 1 C1-4), pair-wise manner constrains relations between pixels with affinity label (Fig. 1 A1-2), indicating whether two pixels belong to the same category. The motivation behind this conception is to reduce the ratio of label noises. Intuitively, if one pixel in a pair is mislabeled (e.g. the

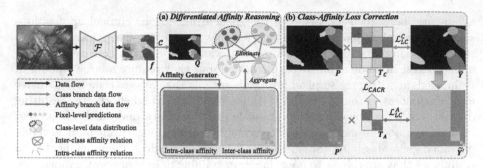

Fig. 2. Illustration of Joint Class-Affinity Segmentation (JCAS) framework, including (a) differentiated affinity reasoning and (b) class-affinity loss correction.

red rectangle in Fig. 1) or even both pixels are mislabeled (e.g. the orange rectangle in Fig. 1), the affinity label of this pair might be correct, thereby reducing the noise rate (e.g. from 44% to 23% in Fig. 1). Moreover, affinity relations in pair-wise manner comprehensively incorporate intra-class and inter-class contextual dependencies, and thus it may be beneficial to explicitly differentiate them for correlated information propagation and irrelevant information elimination.

Unifying the pixel-wise and pair-wise manners, we propose a robust Joint Class-Affinity Segmentation (JCAS) framework to combat label noise issues in medical image segmentation. JCAS framework has two supervision signals, derived from noisy class labels and noisy affinity labels, for regularizing pixel-wise predictions and pair-wise affinity relations, respectively. These two supervision signals in JCAS are complementary to each other since the pixel-wise one preserves semantics and the pair-wise one reduces noise rate. Pair-wise affinity relations derived at the feature level model the contextual dependencies, indicating the correlation between any two pixels in a pair. Considering differentiated contextual dependencies can prevent undesirable aggregations, *we devise a differentiated affinity reasoning (DAR) module to guide the refinement of pixel-wise predictions with differentiated affinity relations.* DAR module differentiates affinity relations to explicitly aggregate intra-class correlated information and eliminate inter-class irrelevant information. *To further correct both pixel-wise and pair-wise supervision signals, we design a class-affinity loss correction (CALC) strategy.* This strategy models noise label distributions in class labels and affinity labels as two NTMs for loss correction, meanwhile, it unifies the pixel-wise and pair-wise supervisions through the theoretically derived consistency regularization, thereby facilitating the noise resistance. Extensive experiments under both synthetic and real-world noisy labels demonstrate the effectiveness of the proposed JCAS framework with a minimum gap towards the upper bound performance.

2   Joint Class-Affinity Segmentation Framework

The proposed Joint Class-Affinity Segmentation (JCAS) framework is illustrated in Fig. 2. Formally, we have access to training images $\mathcal{X} = \{ \boldsymbol{X} \in \mathbb{R}^{H \times W \times 3} \}$ with spatial dimension of $H \times W$. The corresponding one-hot encoding of pixel-wise noisy labels is denoted as $\mathcal{Y} = \{\widetilde{Y} \in \mathbb{R}^{H \times W \times C}\}$, where C indicates the number of classes. We aim to learn a segmentation network that is robust to label noises in $\mathcal{Y}$ during the training process and could derive clean labels for test data. Given an input training image X, a feature map $f \in \mathbb{R}^{h \times w \times d}$ is first computed from the feature extractor $\mathcal{F}$. Note that h, w, and d denote the height, width, and channel number of the feature map. Then, the feature map is passed through two branches for estimating pixel-wise predictions (upper branch in Fig. 2) and pair-wise affinity relations (lower branch in Fig. 2), respectively.

In the upper branch, a classifier $\mathcal{C}$ with softmax is used to produce the coarse segmentation result Q. In the lower branch, an affinity generator is introduced to generate the affinity map $P' \in [0,1]^{n \times n}$ where $n = h \times w$, and the generator is formulated as $P'(k_1, k_2) = norm(\frac{f(i_1, j_1)^\top f(i_2, j_2)}{\|f(i_1,j_1)\|_2 \|f(i_1,j_1)\|_2})$. $(i., j.)$ is the coordinate of a pixel in feature map, and (k_1, k_2) is the coordinate in affinity map. Note that k_1 and (i_1, j_1) denote the position of the same pixel. The operator $norm(\cdot)$ performs normalization along each row to ensure affinity relations towards pixel k_1 are summed to 1, i.e., $\sum_{k_2}^{n} P'(k_1, k_2) = 1$. The obtained affinity map P' measures feature similarity between two pixels. Since intra-class pixels share the similar semantic features, intra-class pixel pairs usually show large similarity scores in P', which highlights these pixel pairs belonging to the same class. Hence, P' reveals the intra-class affinity relations. Then, we devise a differentiated affinity reasoning (DAR) module (Fig. 2(a), Sect. 2.1) to obtain refined segmentation result P, where the affinity map P' derived in the lower branch is leveraged to guide the refinement of previously generated coarse segmentation result Q in the upper branch. Both pixel-wise segmentation prediction P and pair-wise affinity map P' are regularized through the proposed class-affinity loss correction (CALC) strategy (Fig. 2(b), Sect. 2.2). The optimized JCAS framework produces the refined segmentation result P as the final prediction in test phase.

2.1 Differentiated Affinity Reasoning (DAR)

In the image segmentation task, each image is equipped with a ground truth map, indicating pixel-wise semantic class label. Pixel-wise supervision signal cannot regularize the segmentation network to model the contextual dependencies from isolated pixels. Hence, we incorporate the contextual dependency embedded in the pair-wise affinity map P' to guide the refinement of the pixel-wise segmentation result Q. Moreover, different from existing affinity methods [18,24] that aggregates contextual information as a mixture and may introduce undesirable contextual aggregations, we propose a differentiated affinity reasoning (DAR) module to explicitly distinguish intra-class and inter-class contextual dependencies and leverage the differentiated contexts to rectify segmentation predictions.

In addition to previously calculated pair-wise affinity map P' that represents intra-class affinity relation, we infer the reverse affinity map $P'_{re} = norm(1 - P')$. The reverse affinity map measures the dissimilarity between two pixels and reveals the inter-class affinity relations. The proposed DAR module performs intra-class and inter-class affinity reasonings, respectively. To be specific, the intra-class affinity reasoning aims to aggregate correlated information according to the intra-class affinity relations P', and the inter-class affinity reasoning aims to eliminate irrelevant information according to the inter-class affinity relations P'_{re}, which can be formulated as:

$$P_{intra}(k_1) = P(k_1) + \sum_{k_2}^{n} P'(k_1, k_2)Q(k_2); P_{inter}(k_1) = P(k_1) - \sum_{k_2}^{n} P'_{re}(k_1, k_2)Q(k_2).$$

$$(1)$$

The refined pixel-wise prediction P is obtained through combining both intra-class and inter-class affinity reasoning results, i.e., $P = \frac{1}{2}(P_{intra} + P_{inter})$. With the proposed DAR module, the correct predictions are strengthened, and the incorrect segmentation results are debiased and rectified.

2.2 Class-Affinity Loss Correction (CALC)

In multi-class image segmentation task, the widely used cross entropy loss is computed in a pixel-wise manner and formulated as $\mathcal{L}_{CE}^{C} = -\sum_{k}^{H \times W} \widetilde{Y}(k) \log P(k)$. However, directly minimizing the empirical risk of training data with respect to noisy labels $\widetilde{Y}$ will lead to severely degraded generalizability. To reduce the noise rate, we introduce the pair-wise manner, and the corresponding affinity label is derived by $Y'(k1, k2) = Y(k1)^{\top} Y(k2)$. Only if two pixels share the same category, the value in the affinity label Y' will be 1, otherwise Y' will be 0. Although the pair-wise manner can greatly reduce the noise rate compared to the pixel-wise manner as demonstrated in Fig. 1, there still exist noises, and thus the binary entropy loss $\mathcal{L}_{Bi}^{A} = -\sum_{k}^{H \times W} \widetilde{Y}(k) \log P'(k) + (1 - \widetilde{Y}(k)) \log(1 - P'(k))$ for affinity map supervision cannot guarantee the robustness of segmentation model towards label noises, resulting in biased semantic correlations. To facilitate the noise tolerance of L_{CE}^{C} and L_{Bi}^{A}, we devise the class-affinity loss correction (CALC) strategy, including the class-level loss correction $\mathcal{L}_{LC}^{C}$ and affinity-level loss correction $\mathcal{L}_{LC}^{A}$. Meanwhile, a theoretically derived class-affinity consistency regularization $\mathcal{L}_{CACR}$ is advanced to unify pixel-wise and pair-wise supervisions.

Class-Level Loss Correction. We model the label noise distributions in noisy class labels through a noise transition matrix (NTM) $T_C \in [0, 1]^{C \times C}$, which specifies the probability of clean label m translating to noisy label n via $T_C(m, n) = p(\widetilde{Y} = n | Y = m)$. Hence, the probability of one pixel being predicted as $\widetilde{Y} = n$ is computed by $p(\widetilde{Y} = n) = \sum_{m=1}^{C} p(Y = m) \cdot T_C(m, n)$, where $p(Y)$ is the clean class probability. Then the modeled noise label distribution is exploited to correct the supervision signal (i.e. L_{CE}^{C}) derived from noisy labels via $\mathcal{L}_{LC}^{C} = -\sum_{k}^{H \times W} \widetilde{Y}(k) \log[P(k)T_C]$. This corrected loss encourages the consistency between noisy translated predictions and noisy class labels. Therefore, once the true NTM is obtained, the desired estimation of clean class predictions can be recovered by the output of segmentation model P. For the estimation of the true NTM, we exploit the volume minimization regularization in [11].

Affinity-Level Loss Correction. Similar to the class-level NTM, affinity-level NTM is defined as $T_A \in [0, 1]^{2 \times 2}$, modeling the probability of clean affinity

Fig. 3. Illustration of dataset with different kinds of label noises. (Color figure online)

labels flipping to noisy affinity labels. Then, we exploit the modeled label noise distribution NTM to rectify the supervision signal (i.e. L_{Bi}^A) for affinity relation learning. Therefore, the affinity-level loss correction is formulated as $\mathcal{L}_{LC}^A = -\sum_k^{H \times W} \widetilde{Y}(k) \log[P'(k)T_A] + (1 - \widetilde{Y}(k)) \log(1 - P'(k)T_A)$.

Class-Affinity Consistency Regularization. To unify the pixel-wise and pair-wise supervisions, we bridge the class-level and affinity-level NTMs in Theorem 1. A theoretical proof for the Theorem is provided in *supplementary*. Hence, the class-affinity consistency regularization is defined as $\mathcal{L}_{CACR} = \|T_{C \to A} - T_A\|_2$.

Combining the above defined losses, we obtain the joint loss of the proposed JCAS framwork as: $\mathcal{L} = \mathcal{L}_{LC}^C + \mathcal{L}_{LC}^A + \lambda \mathcal{L}_{CACR}$, which interacts the pixel-wise and pair-wise manners. Note that λ is the weighting factor of $\mathcal{L}_{CACR}$.

Theorem 1. *Assume that the class distribution of dataset denoting proportions of pixel number is $\mathcal{N} = [N_1, N_2, ..., N_C]$, and the noise is class-dependent[1]. Given a class-level NTM T_C, the translated affinity-level NTM $T_{C \to A}$ is calculated by*

$$T_{C \to A}(0,0) = 1 - T_{C \to A}(0,1), \ T_{C \to A}(0,1) = \frac{\sum_m \left[N_m \sum_n T_C(m,n)\right]^2 - \sum_m (N_m)^2 \|T_C\|_2^2}{\sum_m \left[N_m (\sum_m N_m - N_m)\right]},$$
$$T_{C \to A}(1,0) = 1 - T_{C \to A}(1,1), \ T_{C \to A}(1,1) = \frac{\sum_m (N_m)^2 \|T_C\|_2^2}{\sum_m (N_m)^2}.$$

$$(2)$$

3   Experiments

Dataset. We validate the proposed JCAS method on the surgical instrument dataset Endovis18 [1]. It consists of 2384 images annotated with the instrument part labels, and the label space includes shaft, wrist and clasper classes, as shown in Fig. 3. The dataset is split into 1639 training images and 596 test images following [5]. Each image is resized into a resolution of 256×320 in preprocessing.

Noise Patterns. To comprehensively verify the robustness of JCAS, we conduct experiments with both ***synthetic label noise*** (i.e., *elipse, symmetric* and *asymmetric* noises) and ***real-world label noise*** (i.e., *noisy pseudo labels in source-free domain adaptation (SFDA)*), as compared in Fig. 3. Specifically, the ellipse noisy label is a kind of weak annotation generated by drawing the minimal ellipse given the true segmentation label, greatly reducing the manual annotation cost. To simulate errors in the annotation process, ellipse labels are randomly

---

[1] Real-world label noises can be well approximated via class-dependent noises [4,6,11].

Table 1. Comparison under four label noises. Best and second best results are **highlighted** and underlined. 'w/ Affinity' introduces pair-wise supervision $\mathcal{L}_{Bi}^{A}$ to backbone.

Noises	Method	Shaft		Wrist		Clasper		Average	
		Dice (%)	Jac (%)	Dice (%)	Jac (%)	Dice (%)	Jac (%)	Dice (%)	Jac (%)
	Upper bound	88.740	81.699	65.045	52.627	70.531	56.618	74.772	63.648
Ellipse	RAUNet (19') [13]	83.137	74.139	56.941	43.215	61.081	45.883	67.053	54.412
	LWANet (20') [12]	81.945	72.735	53.626	40.886	**64.364**	**49.781**	66.645	54.468
	CSS (21') [14]	84.577	**75.736**	57.597	43.687	63.686	48.347	68.620	55.923
	MTCL (21') [19]	72.719	60.540	39.386	27.474	49.662	35.085	53.922	41.033
	SR (21') [23]	79.966	69.621	53.540	39.747	60.179	44.775	64.561	51.381
	VolMin (21') [11]	81.320	70.758	60.470	46.408	58.203	42.524	66.664	53.230
	Baseline [3]	79.021	68.097	42.069	29.582	55.489	40.175	58.860	45.951
	w/ Affinity	82.158	72.339	49.128	35.455	58.933	43.594	63.406	50.463
	w/ DAR	82.698	72.992	52.207	38.442	61.544	46.027	65.483	52.487
	w/ CALC	82.973	73.126	61.885	47.527	60.416	44.821	68.425	55.158
	Ours (JCAS)	**84.683**	75.378	**65.599**	**51.623**	63.871	48.356	**71.384**	**58.452**
Symmetric	RAUNet (19') [13]	68.044	54.397	31.581	20.676	41.302	27.819	46.976	34.297
	LWANet (20') [12]	0.294	0.150	10.089	5.908	10.228	5.489	6.870	3.849
	CSS (21') [14]	86.555	78.451	32.363	20.767	53.364	37.901	57.427	45.706
	MTCL (21') [19]	78.480	67.855	50.011	38.013	55.515	40.411	61.336	48.760
	SR (21') [23]	86.648	78.823	58.217	46.870	64.643	50.120	69.836	58.604
	VolMin (21') [11]	86.811	78.834	63.712	51.259	66.604	52.096	72.376	60.730
	Baseline [3]	85.021	76.419	57.026	44.563	63.255	48.395	68.434	56.459
	Ours (JCAS)	**88.285**	**80.692**	**65.759**	**53.487**	68.129	53.821	**74.058**	**62.667**
Asymmetric	RAUNet (19') [13]	87.255	79.983	59.462	46.639	67.347	52.801	71.355	59.808
	LWANet (20') [12]	0.015	0.007	40.548	30.683	9.060	4.825	16.541	11.838
	CSS (21') [14]	**89.825**	**83.543**	43.743	30.569	**69.285**	**54.758**	67.618	56.290
	MTCL (21') [19]	74.544	62.525	41.433	30.533	48.077	33.676	54.685	42.244
	SR (21') [23]	86.360	78.055	62.854	49.651	65.483	50.962	71.566	59.556
	VolMin (21') [11]	86.840	78.796	63.345	51.137	65.220	50.996	71.802	60.310
	Baseline [3]	84.497	75.607	58.717	46.060	61.662	46.770	68.292	56.146
	Ours (JCAS)	88.247	80.730	**67.298**	**54.922**	67.686	53.436	**74.410**	**63.029**
SFDA	RAUNet (19') [13]	73.370	61.568	56.063	42.570	45.979	31.720	58.471	45.286
	LWANet (20') [12]	75.377	64.457	53.203	39.799	48.558	34.191	59.046	46.149
	CSS (21') [14]	74.419	64.261	**61.765**	**47.880**	45.749	31.709	60.644	47.950
	MTCL (21') [19]	72.289	60.346	51.095	37.972	38.762	25.567	54.048	41.295
	SR (21') [23]	75.992	64.835	57.370	43.863	40.471	27.388	57.944	45.362
	VolMin (21') [11]	**76.641**	65.063	58.285	44.389	41.780	28.324	58.902	45.925
	Baseline [3]	76.107	64.858	56.259	42.740	41.364	28.091	57.910	45.230
	Ours (JCAS)	76.540	**65.300**	59.904	46.104	**48.725**	**34.283**	**61.723**	**48.562**

dilated and eroded. Moreover, two commonly used label noises in the machine learning field, including symmetric and asymmetric noises with the rate of 0.5 [11,23], are used to evaluate JCAS. Furthermore, we introduce Endovis17 [2] containing 1800 annotated images with domain shift to Endovis18, and generate realistic noisy labels from source only model trained on Endovis17.

Implementation. The proposed JCAS framework is implemented with PyTorch on Nvidia 2080Ti. DeepLabV2 [3] with the pre-trained encoder ResNet101 is our segmentation backbone. The initial learning rate is set as 1e−4 for the pre-trained encoder and 1e-3 for the rest of trainable parameters. We adopt a batch size of

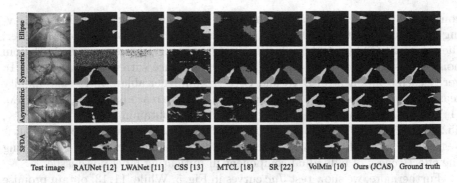

Fig. 4. Comparison of segmentation results.

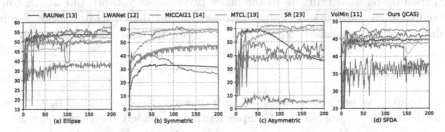

Fig. 5. Curve of test Jac vs. epoch with four different types of noise labels.

3 and the maximum epoch number of 200. The weighting factor λ is 0.01. The segmentation performance is assessed by $Dice$ and Jac scores.

Experiment Results. Experimental comparison results under four types of label noises are presented in Table 1, in which we list the performance of upper bound (i.e., model trained with clean labels), three state-of-the-arts [12–14] in instrument segmentation, three label noise methods [11,19,23], our backbone [3], and the proposed JCAS. For a fair comparison, we reimplement [11,19,23] using the same backbone [3]. Compared with the aforementioned baselines, JCAS shows the minimum performance gap with the upper bound under all kinds of label noises, demonstrating the robustness of JCAS. Despite the satisfactory performance under ellipse and SFDA noises, LWANet [12] cannot deal with the other two types of noises, resulting in 6.870% and 16.541% $Dice$ scores. In contrast, JCAS shows comparable result to the upper bound with only 0.981% and 0.388% Jac gaps under symmetric and asymmetric label noises. We further illustrate typical surgical instrument segmentation results in Fig. 4, validating the superiority of JCAS over baseline methods in the qualitative aspect.

To analyze the influence of JCAS, we then conduct ablation study under ellipse noises. With the pair-wise manner ('w/ Affinity'), the noise rate of supervision signals is greatly reduced, yielding an increment of 4.512% in Jac, while the increased memory overhead is negligible (from 780.71MB to 784.67MB). The devised DAR module ('w/ DAR') is also verified to be effective in differentiating contexture dependencies for the refinement of segmentation predictions, achieving an improvement of 9.207% Jac score compared to the backbone. Moreover, the proposed CALC strategy further rectifies supervision signals derived from noisy labels and boosts the segmentation performance with 5.965% Jac gain. To verify each component in DAR and CALC, we further ablate intra-class affinity reasoning (1st item in Eq. (1)), inter-class affinity reasoning (2nd item in Eq. (1)), $\mathcal{L}_{LC}^C$, $\mathcal{L}_{LC}^A$, and $\mathcal{L}_{CACR}$ under ellipse noises, obtaining 55.795%, 56.180%, 55.203%, 55.179%, 56.612% Jac. The performance of ablating each component is degraded compared to 58.452% Jac achieved by our method (Table 1), verifying the effectiveness of individual component in mitigating label noise issue.

Furthermore, we show test Jac curves in Fig. 5. While [11,13] obtain promise results under ellipse and SFDA noises, they reach a high Jac in the early stage and then decrease, overfitting to the other two noises. Notably, our JCAS converges to high performance under four noises and demonstrates more stable training process compared to [12,14,19], verifying its noise-resistant property.

4   Conclusion

In this paper, we propose a robust JCAS framework to combat label noise issues in medical image segmentation. Complementing the widely used pixel-wise manner, we introduce the pair-wise manner by capturing affinity relations among pixels to reduce noise rate. Then a DAR module is devised to rectify pixel-wise segmentation predictions by reasoning about intra-class and inter-class affinity relations. We further design a CALC strategy to unify pixel-wise and pair-wise supervisions, and facilitate noise tolerances of both supervisions. Extensive experiments under four noisy labels corroborate the noise immunity of JCAS.

Acknowledgments. This work was supported by Hong Kong Research Grants Council (RGC) Early Career Scheme grant 21207420 (CityU 9048179) and Hong Kong Research Grants Council (RGC) General Research Fund 11211221 (CityU 9043152).

References

1. Allan, M., et al.: 2018 robotic scene segmentation challenge. arXiv preprint arXiv:2001.11190 (2020)
2. Allan, M., et al.: 2017 robotic instrument segmentation challenge. arXiv preprint arXiv:1902.06426 (2019)
3. Chen, L.C., Papandreou, G., Kokkinos, I., Murphy, K., Yuille, A.L.: Deeplab: semantic image segmentation with deep convolutional nets, atrous convolution, and fully connected CRFs. IEEE Trans. Pattern Anal. Mach. Intell. **40**(4), 834–848 (2017)
4. Cheng, J., Liu, T., Ramamohanarao, K., Tao, D.: Learning with bounded instance and label-dependent label noise. In: ICML, pp. 1789–1799. PMLR (2020)
5. González, C., Bravo-Sánchez, L., Arbelaez, P.: ISINet: an instance-based approach for surgical instrument segmentation. In: Martel, A.L., et al. (eds.) MICCAI 2020. LNCS, vol. 12263, pp. 595–605. Springer, Cham (2020). https://doi.org/10.1007/978-3-030-59716-0_57

6. Guo, X., Liu, J., Liu, T., Yuan, Y.: Simt: handling open-set noise for domain adaptive semantic segmentation. In: CVPR (2022)
7. Guo, X., Yang, C., Li, B., Yuan, Y.: Metacorrection: domain-aware meta loss correction for unsupervised domain adaptation in semantic segmentation. In: CVPR, pp. 3927–3936 (2021)
8. Karimi, D., Dou, H., Warfield, S.K., Gholipour, A.: Deep learning with noisy labels: Exploring techniques and remedies in medical image analysis. Med. Image Anal. **65**, 101759 (2020)
9. Karimi, D., Vasylechko, S.D., Gholipour, A.: Convolution-free medical image segmentation using transformers. In: de Bruijne, M., et al. (eds.) MICCAI 2021. LNCS, vol. 12901, pp. 78–88. Springer, Cham (2021). https://doi.org/10.1007/978-3-030-87193-2_8
10. Li, S., Gao, Z., He, X.: Superpixel-guided iterative learning from noisy labels for medical image segmentation. In: de Bruijne, M., Cattin, P.C., Cotin, S., Padoy, N., Speidel, S., Zheng, Y., Essert, C. (eds.) MICCAI 2021. LNCS, vol. 12901, pp. 525–535. Springer, Cham (2021). https://doi.org/10.1007/978-3-030-87193-2_50
11. Li, X., Liu, T., Han, B., Niu, G., Sugiyama, M.: Provably end-to-end label-noise learning without anchor points. In: ICML, pp. 6403–6413 (2021)
12. Ni, Z.L., Bian, G.B., Hou, Z.G., Zhou, X.H., Xie, X.L., Li, Z.: Attention-guided lightweight network for real-time segmentation of robotic surgical instruments. In: ICRA, pp. 9939–9945. IEEE (2020)
13. Ni, Z.-L., et al.: RAUNet: residual attention U-Net for semantic segmentation of cataract surgical instruments. In: Gedeon, T., Wong, K.W., Lee, M. (eds.) ICONIP 2019. LNCS, vol. 11954, pp. 139–149. Springer, Cham (2019). https://doi.org/10.1007/978-3-030-36711-4_13
14. Pissas, T., Ravasio, C.S., Cruz, L.D., Bergeles, C.: Effective semantic segmentation in cataract surgery: What matters most? In: MICCAI. pp. 509–518. Springer (2021)
15. Shu, J., et al.: Meta-weight-net: learning an explicit mapping for sample weighting. In: NeurIPS, pp. 1919–1930 (2019)
16. Wang, J., Zhou, S., Fang, C., Wang, L., Wang, J.: Meta corrupted pixels mining for medical image segmentation. In: Martel, A.L., et al. (eds.) MICCAI 2020. LNCS, vol. 12261, pp. 335–345. Springer, Cham (2020). https://doi.org/10.1007/978-3-030-59710-8_33
17. Wu, S et al.: Class2simi: a noise reduction perspective on learning with noisy labels. In: ICML, pp. 11285–11295 (2021)
18. Xu, L., Ouyang, W., Bennamoun, M., Boussaid, F., Sohel, F., Xu, D.: Leveraging auxiliary tasks with affinity learning for weakly supervised semantic segmentation. In: ICCV, pp. 6984–6993 (2021)
19. Xu, Z., et al.: Noisy labels are treasure: mean-teacher-assisted confident learning for hepatic vessel segmentation. In: de Bruijne, M., et al. (eds.) MICCAI 2021. LNCS, vol. 12901, pp. 3–13. Springer, Cham (2021). https://doi.org/10.1007/978-3-030-87193-2_1
20. Zhang, L., et al.: Disentangling human error from ground truth in segmentation of medical images. NeurIPS **33**, 15750–15762 (2020)
21. Zhang, T., Yu, L., Hu, N., Lv, S., Gu, S.: Robust medical image segmentation from non-expert annotations with tri-network. In: Martel, A.L., et al. (eds.) MICCAI 2020. LNCS, vol. 12264, pp. 249–258. Springer, Cham (2020). https://doi.org/10.1007/978-3-030-59719-1_25
22. Zhang, Z., Zhang, H., Arik, S.O., Lee, H., Pfister, T.: Distilling effective supervision from severe label noise. In: CVPR, pp. 9294–9303 (2020)

23. Zhou, X., Liu, X., Wang, C., Zhai, D., Jiang, J., Ji, X.: Learning with noisy labels via sparse regularization. In: ICCV, pp. 72–81 (2021)
24. Zhu, X., et al.: Weakly supervised 3d semantic segmentation using cross-image consensus and inter-voxel affinity relations. In: ICCV, pp. 2834–2844 (2021)

Task-Relevant Feature Replenishment for Cross-Centre Polyp Segmentation

Yutian Shen[1], Ye Lu[1], Xiao Jia[2], Fan Bai[1], and Max Q.-H. Meng[1,3(✉)]

[1] Department of Electronic Engineering, The Chinese University of Hong Kong, Sha Tin, Hong Kong
[2] Department of Radiation Oncology, Stanford University, Stanford, CA, USA
[3] Department of Electronic and Electrical Engineering, The Southern University of Science and Technology, Shenzhen, China
max.meng@sustech.edu.cn

Abstract. Colonoscopy images from different centres usually exhibit appearance variations, making the models trained on one domain unable to generalize well to another. To tackle this issue, we propose a novel Task-relevant Feature Replenishment based Network (TRFR-Net) for cross-centre polyp segmentation via retrieving task-relevant knowledge for sufficient discrimination capability with style variations alleviated. Specifically, we first design a domain-invariant feature decomposition (DIFD) module placed after each encoding block to extract domain-shared information for segmentation. Then we develop a task-relevant feature replenishment (TRFR) module to distill informative context from the residual features of each DIFD module and dynamically aggregate these task-relevant parts, providing extra information for generalized segmentation learning. To further bridge the domain gap leveraging structural similarity, we devise a Polyp-aware Adversarial Learning (PPAL) module to align prediction feature distribution, where more emphasis is imposed on the polyp-related alignment. Experimental results on three public datasets demonstrate the effectiveness of our proposed algorithm. The code is available at: https://github.com/CathyS1996/TRFRNet.

Keywords: Colonoscopy · Polyp segmentation · Domain adaptation

1 Introduction

Colorectal cancer (CRC) has become the second leading cause of cancer-related death around the world in 2021 [13], the risk of which can be reduced by early diagnosis and treatment of precancerous polyps via colonoscopy screening [9]. Despite the success of deep-learning based methods for automated polyp segmentation, their performance usually degrades when applied to new data acquired from different centres, due to the notable domain shift caused by various scanners or imaging protocols [1,3], as illustrated in Fig. 1(a).

To alleviate the domain discrepancy as shown in Fig. 1(b)(i), a feasible solution is unsupervised domain adaptation (UDA). Ganin *et al.* [4] developed

L. Wang et al. (Eds.): MICCAI 2022, LNCS 13434, pp. 599–608, 2022.
https://doi.org/10.1007/978-3-031-16440-8_57

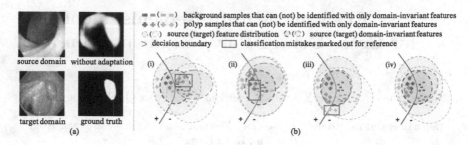

Fig. 1. (a) Illustration of domain shift. (b) Illustration of: (i) original data distribution; (ii) extreme classical feature adaptation; (iii) extreme domain-invariant feature adaptation; (iv) feature adaptation in our method. (Color figure online)

domain-adversarial neural networks to align feature distribution between source and target images. Tsai *et al.* [16] proposed to perform adaptation at different feature levels via employing adversarial learning in the output space. These approaches paid equal attention to all semantic features, which may potentially lead to negative alignment for segmentation task. As in Fig. 1(b)(ii), equivalent distribution are guaranteed on the overall feature space but the domain-invariant part remains inconsistent. Zhou *et al.* [20] integrated style regularization in the network to reduce variations thereby reducing the domain discrepancy. Wang *et al.* [19] aligned the domain-invariant features via the domain-specific decomposition and suppression. Despite their effectiveness in UDA, these normalization-based methods are task-ignorant and will unavoidably overlook the task-relevant knowledge enclosed in the domain-specific part, which however is useful for polyp segmentation [3]. As in Fig. 1(b)(iii), the domain-invariant features are well aligned leaving out the domain-specific part, but error occurs due to the loss of task-relevant knowledge. On the contrary, our proposed method aligns domain-invariant distribution while retaining attention for task-related domain-specific features, thus ensuring better classifications as in Fig. 1(b)(iv).

In this paper, as mentioned above, we propose a Task-relevant Feature Replenishment based Network (TRFR-Net) to tackle existing problems in UDA, eliminating domain shifts in multi-centre colonoscopy images while retaining sufficient discrimination capability. Specifically, we first develop a Domain-invariant Feature Decomposition (DIFD) module to reduce style variations. Then we design a task-relevant feature replenishment (TRFR) module that disentangles informative context for polyp segmentation from the residual domain-specific features of DIFD, providing extra information for generalized segmentation. Meanwhile, considering structural similarities in polyp segmentation maps, polyp-aware adversarial learning (PAAL) is employed to bridge the domain gap by aligning features in output space, where more attention are paid on the feature alignment of potential polyp region. Extensive experiments with ablation studies over three public datasets have demonstrated the superiority of our TRFR-Net, obtaining improvements of 8.86% to 22.87% in *Dice* compared with the model trained on only source data in four adaptation settings.

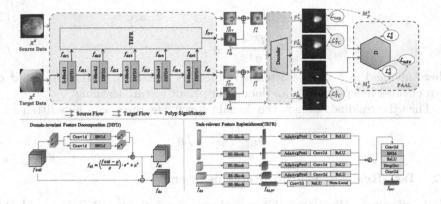

Fig. 2. Overview of our proposed TRFR-Net. The bottom part illustrates domain-invariant feature decomposition (DIFD) module and task-relevant feature replenishment (TRFR) module.

2 Methodology

The architecture of the proposed TRFR-Net is illustrated in Fig. 2, which contains a generator and a discriminator for adversarial learning. The generator employs an encoder-decoder framework, where the ResNet-34 [5] comprising five encoding blocks is adopted as the feature extractor and the decoder branch also has five blocks consisting of two Conv-BN-ReLu combinations and an upsample operation each. The discriminator is composed of two Conv-LeakyReLu combinations followed by an upsample operation and a convolutional classifier.

The DIFD modules are placed after each encoding block, which decompose the input features to domain-invariant portion (f_{di}) and side-out domain-specific portion (f_{ds}). The TRFR module takes in the domain-specific features and output combined task-relevant features (f_{trr}) for context replenishment. Then the replenished domain-invariant features (f_+) are delivered to the decoder sub-network for segmentation predictions (p_+). In PAAL, the discriminator adapts features in the output space to enhance inter-domain spatial similarities.

2.1 Domain-Invariant Feature Decomposition (DIFD)

Instance Normalization (IN) [17] can be viewed as a kind of style transfer that holds the potential to enhance generalization ability on unseen domains by reducing feature dissimilarity [7]. We adapt IN in our DIFD to obtain domain-invariant features to narrow the inter-domain discrepancy.

Different from IN which directly learns the new mean and standard deviation parameters for each instance, we propose to recalibrate them with guidance of channel attention. Given the input features $feat \in \mathbb{R}^{C \times H \times W}$ with original means and standard deviations $\{\mu, \sigma\} \in \mathbb{R}^{C \times 2}$, we have the recalibrated value $\mu^\star$ and $\sigma^\star$ and domain-invariant features f_{di} as:

$$\mu^{j\star} = h(\mu^j, \sigma^j) \cdot \mu^j, \quad j = 1, 2, ..., C \tag{1}$$

$$\sigma^{j\star} = g(\mu^j, \sigma^j) \cdot \sigma^j, \quad j = 1, 2, ..., C \tag{2}$$

$$f_{di}^j = \sigma^{j\star} \cdot \frac{feat^j - \mu^j}{\sigma^j} + \mu^{j\star}, \quad j = 1, 2, ..., C \tag{3}$$

where $h(\cdot)$ and $g(\cdot)$ are the attention functions that learn to scale μ and σ of each channel independently for domain-invariant feature learning.

Then the residual, namely the domain-specific features, can be written as:

$$f_{ds} = feat - f_{di} \tag{4}$$

2.2   Task-Relevant Feature Replenishment

While effectively alleviating the cross-domain variations, DIFD inevitably filters out some task-relevant information encoded in domain-specific features thus leading to degradation of discrimination capability [12]. Therefore, we propose the TRFR module to adaptively distill informative features useful for polyp segmentation from domain-specific features for feature replenishment.

Firstly, we incorporate the squeeze and excitation (SE) [6] block to disentangle the task-relevant features from features filtered by the DIFD module. The domain-specific features are squeezed to a single vector that is successively learnt by fully connected layers. Leveraging inter-dependencies between channels and attention of individual channels, these learnt channel-wise weights enable us to enhance the essential context and suppress the uninstructive ones on the channel level. Given the input domain-specific features from i^{th} DIFD module $f_{ds_i} \in \mathbb{R}^{C \times H \times W}$, the disentangled features $f_{ds\_tr_i}$ can be formulated as:

$$f_{ds\_tr_i}^j = \Psi^j(f_{ds_i}) \cdot f_{ds_i}^j, \quad j = 1, 2, ..., C \tag{5}$$

where $\Psi(\cdot)$ is the squeeze and excitation function that learns weights for each channel to extract task-relevant features.

Then as illustrated in Fig. 2, we utilize an AdaAvgPool-Conv-ReLU combination block to extract local context information from shallower semantic layers. We also use a Conv-ReLU combination followed by a non-local block [18] to extract global context information from the bottom encoding block to intensify the features with long-range dependency. Finally, after concatenation, a convolution block of Conv-BN-ReLU-Conv combination is developed to dynamically aggregate these distilled task-relevant features of different semantic levels to obtain the final effective task-relevant content for polyp segmentation.

Inspired by [11], we argue that the feature augmented by task-relevant information f_+ is more discriminative than the pure domain-invariant feature f_{di}, resulting in a more certain prediction with a smaller entropy. Therefore, we propose the TRFR Constraint Loss (TCLoss) to advance the feature disentanglement in TRFR. To achieve this, we separately forward the replenished features f_+ and domain-invariant features f_{di} to decoder sub-network and obtain the corresponding segmentation prediction p_+ and p_{di} as in Fig. 2. Then the TCLoss for source (target) domain can be formulated as:

$$\mathcal{L}_{TC}^{s(t)} = ln(1 + exp(\frac{1}{H \times W} \sum_{i=1}^{H} \sum_{j=1}^{W} (\mathcal{I}(p_+^{s(t)}) - \mathcal{I}(p_{di}^{s(t)}))[i,j])) \tag{6}$$

where the $\mathcal{I}(\cdot)$ denotes entropy map calculated via: $\mathcal{I}(p) = -p \cdot log(p)$, given a prediction map $p \in \mathbb{R}^{H \times W}$.

2.3   Polyp-Aware Adversarial Learning (PAAL)

Since polyp segmentation has structured outputs with spatial similarities, we develop PAAL in the output space to further bridge the inter-domain gap. Considering the polyp region carries more significance but is usually under-represented due to the class-imbalance issue in our task, we argue that the alignment should be more emphasized on potential polyp regions..

To achieve this, we first derive a polyp significance index mask $M_p \in \mathbb{R}^{H \times W}$ from the output prediction $p_+ \in \mathbb{R}^{H \times W}$ of segmentation network, which can be formulated as:

$$M_p[i,j] = \begin{cases} 1, & if \ p_+[i,j] \geqslant 0.5 \\ w_{bg}, & o/w \end{cases} \tag{7}$$

where w_{bg} is a weight between 0 to 1 controlling the significance of predicted background region alignment.

Then with output from discriminator $D(p_+^t)$, the PAALoss for generator is modified as:

$$\mathcal{L}_{adv} = M_p^t \odot \mathcal{L}_{BCE}(D(p_+^t), l_{src}) \tag{8}$$

where $\mathcal{L}_{BCE}(\cdot)$ denotes a binary cross entropy (BCE) loss to encourage correct class predictions at each pixel, $\odot$ denotes pixel-wise production. l_{src} represents ground-truth mask full of source label (0).

Similarly, the PAALoss for discriminator can be formulated as:

$$\mathcal{L}_d = \mathcal{L}_d^s + \mathcal{L}_d^t = M_p^s \odot \mathcal{L}_{BCE}(D(p_+^s), l_{src}) + M_p^t \odot \mathcal{L}_{BCE}(D(p_+^t), l_{trg}) \tag{9}$$

where l_{trg} represents ground-truth mask full of target label (1).

2.4   Overall Network Training

For supervised segmentation learning in source domain, we employ a segmentation loss consisting of a BCE loss for pixel-wise correct class labels and a dice loss to predict and correct higher-order inconsistencies for images. Denoting the segmentation ground truth of source data as y^s, the supervised segmentation is defined as:

$$\mathcal{L}_{seg} = \mathcal{L}_{BCE}(p_+^s, y^s) + \mathcal{L}_{Dice}(p_+^s, y^s) \tag{10}$$

Hence, the overall training loss for the segmentation generator is composed of the segmentation loss with the afore-mentioned PAALoss, and the TCLoss is only used to train the TRFR module, which are formulated as:

$$\mathcal{L}_G = \mathcal{L}_{seg} + \lambda_{adv}\mathcal{L}_{adv} \tag{11}$$

$$\mathcal{L}_{TC} = \lambda_{TC}(\mathcal{L}_{TC}^s + \mathcal{L}_{TC}^t) \tag{12}$$

where λ_{adv} and λ_{TC} are the weights used to control the significance of PPAL module and TRFR module. $\mathcal{L}_{TC}^s$ and $\mathcal{L}_{TC}^t$ represent TCLoss for source domain and target domain respectively, as defined in Eq. 6. $\mathcal{L}_{adv}$ represents PAALoss as defined in Eq. 8.

In the meantime, the discriminator is trained with PPALoss defined in Eq. 9. The segmentation generator and the discriminator are trained in the adversarial learning manner and are updated in turn until convergence.

3 Experiments

3.1 Experimental Settings

Datasets. Experiments are conducted on three benchmark polyp segmentation datasets: Kvasir-SEG [8], ETIS-Larib [14] and CVC-Colon DB [15]. The first dateset consists of 1000 images and includes more noise with time information on images. The latter two datasets separately contains 196 annotated images and 300 annotated frames with various polyps and different illuminations.

These three datasets are extracted from the colonoscopy sequences captured by different centres. For each dataset, 70% of the dataset is splited as training set, 10% as validation set, and the remaining 20% as test set. In each adaptation setting, the ground truth masks of target images are used for validation and performance evaluation only, which are not accessible to the network during training. Each image is resized to 256×256 with random horizontal and vertical flips and randomly cropped to 224×224 for training, while being resized to 256×256 for inference stage.

Implementation Details and Evaluation Metrics. The Pytorch framework is adopted to implement our algorithm. We utilize stochastic gradient descent (SGD) to optimize the model with a momentum of 0.9 and weight decay of 10^{-5}. The learning rate for generator and discriminator are respectively initialized as 10^{-3} and 10^{-5}, which are both decreased by a factor $(epoch/num_{epoch})^{0.9}$. The significance of predicted background region alignment w_{bg} is assigned as 0.5 for simplicity. λ_{adv} and λ_{TC} are set as 0.001 and 0.01, respectively. All experiments are run on an NVIDIA GeForce RTX 2080 Ti GPU with batch size of 4 and the maximum training epoch is set as 150.

For evaluation, we adopt seven commonly used metrics for medical image segmentation tasks, including *Recall (Rec), Specificity (Spec), Dice Coefficient (Dice), F2 Score (F2), Intersection-over-Union for Polyp (IoUp), Intersection-over-Union for Background (IoUb) and Mean IoU (mIoU)*.

Table 1. Quantitative results on the Kvasir-SEG dataset and ETIS-Larib dataset. Best and second best results are highlighted and underlined.

Method	Kvasir-SEG → ETIS-Larib							ETIS-Larib → Kvasir-SEG						
	Rec	Spec	Dice	F2	IoUp	IoUb	mIoU	Rec	Spec	Dice	F2	IoUp	IoUb	mIoU
Source Only	50.55	94.78	41.80	43.45	35.67	93.84	64.76	67.04	94.18	58.78	62.04	45.57	87.90	66.73
DANN(JMLR'15) [4]	68.25	94.01	40.63	50.79	30.63	93.36	61.99	63.17	98.86	68.12	64.55	57.41	91.23	74.32
AdaptSeg(CVPR'18) [16]	72.15	96.16	58.42	63.86	49.62	95.79	72.71	69.77	97.47	70.86	68.70	60.00	90.95	75.47
CLAN(CVPR'19) [10]	61.81	94.40	48.87	53.25	41.45	93.87	67.66	63.44	98.29	67.28	64.09	55.18	90.90	73.04
IntraDA(CVPR'20) [11]	68.35	96.88	56.91	62.45	48.62	96.51	72.57	53.73	99.56	62.19	56.56	51.71	90.68	71.20
Li et al.(ICIP'21) [2]	59.72	97.63	51.08	54.77	43.13	96.94	70.04	57.14	98.56	61.93	58.40	49.96	90.50	70.23
MixStyle(ICLR'21) [20]	70.66	95.89	56.79	62.24	48.31	95.49	71.90	66.89	98.10	69.18	67.06	58.57	91.04	74.80
TRFR-Net(Ours)	74.55	98.05	64.67	69.44	56.11	97.63	76.87	70.49	97.77	72.22	70.01	61.36	91.31	76.33

3.2 Comparison with State-of-the-Arts

Experiments are conducted to compare the proposed TRFR-Net with DANN [4], AdaptSeg [16], IntraDA [11], CLAN [10], Li et al. [2] and MixStyle [20]. For a fair comparison, all models are trained and tested on the same split train/valid/test sets with data preparation mentioned in Sec. 3.1. And the comparisons are implemented based on the released code and settings in original literature.

Experiments on the Kvasir-SEG Dataset and ETIS-Larib Dataset. In this section, comprehensive evaluation for cross-centre adaptation is conducted in both directions, i.e., from Kvasir-SEG to ETIS-Larib and from ETIS-Larib to Kvasir-SEG. As shown in Table 1, UDA based methods [2,10,11,16,20] demonstrate higher segmentation performance compared to the the model trained with only source data (denoted as "Source Only"), which proves the effectiveness of domain adaption in cross-centre polyp segmentation. Among these, our method achieves the best performance with a *Dice* of 64.67% obtaining an improvement of 6.25% to 24.04% over other methods when adapting CVC-Colon DB to ETIS-Larib and a *Dice* of 72.22% with an improvement of 1.36% to 10.29% in reserve direction. Besides, our model achieves the highest *IoUp* of 45.11% and 68.24%, showing the superiority of polyp region segmentation. Some results are shown in Fig. 3 for visual comparison, and our proposed model consistently generate more accurate segmentation predictions for the polyps of various sizes and shapes.

Experiments on the CVC-Colon DB Dataset and ETIS-Larib Dataset. In this section, two-direction adaptations are also conducted on a different combination of datasets, i.e., CVC-Colon DB and ETIS-Larib, to prove the robustness of our method. As shown in Table 2, our proposed model again outperforms all state-of-the-art methods with a *Dice* of 55.36% adapting CVC-Colon DB to ETIS-Larib and a *Dice* of 78.23% adapting in opposite direction.

3.3 Ablation Study

The ablation experiments are conducted on the CVC-Colon DB and ETIS-Larib dataset to verify the effectiveness and necessity of each module. The results are

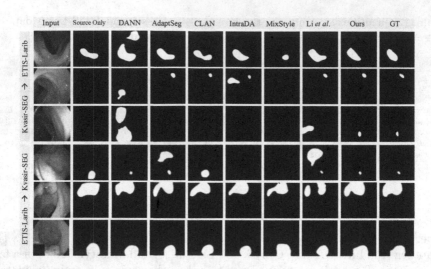

Fig. 3. Examples of polyp segmentation results on the Kvasir-SEG dataset and ETIS-Larib dataset.

Table 2. Quantitative results and ablation study on the CVC-Colon DB Dataset and ETIS-Larib Dataset. Best and second best results are highlighted and underlined.

Method	CVC-Colon DB → ETIS-Larib							ETIS-Larib → CVC-Colon DB						
	Rec	Spec	Dice	F2	IoUp	IoUb	mIoU	Rec	Spec	Dice	F2	IoUp	IoUb	mIoU
Source Only	42.88	**99.38**	44.11	43.15	37.22	97.41	67.31	67.18	<u>99.64</u>	69.37	67.61	58.60	98.23	78.41
DANN(JMLR'15) [4]	51.72	98.57	46.58	48.19	37.02	96.92	66.97	71.31	99.14	71.43	70.88	59.92	98.10	79.01
AdaptSeg(CVPR'18) [16]	56.05	99.00	51.28	52.91	42.00	97.18	69.69	78.58	99.05	75.86	76.86	64.03	98.26	81.15
CLAN(CVPR'19) [10]	48.53	97.69	43.44	45.48	35.29	96.27	65.78	53.49	99.59	62.68	56.27	49.11	98.13	73.62
IntraDA(CVPR'20) [11]	53.02	<u>99.34</u>	49.49	50.66	39.75	**97.68**	68.72	69.70	**99.83**	74.71	71.35	64.97	98.53	81.75
Li et al.(ICIP'21) [2]	38.15	99.01	38.22	37.95	31.63	97.05	64.34	60.83	99.56	63.44	61.38	51.76	98.01	74.89
MixStyle(ICLR'21) [20]	57.69	98.79	53.75	54.73	45.11	<u>97.57</u>	**71.34**	78.29	99.12	<u>76.05</u>	76.16	64.63	98.23	81.43
TRFR-Net(Ours)	**65.90**	98.18	**55.36**	**58.59**	**45.11**	97.07	<u>71.09</u>	**84.29**	99.00	**78.23**	<u>81.07</u>	**68.24**	<u>98.56</u>	**83.40**
Baseline (B)	55.35	98.83	49.70	51.24	40.46	97.12	68.79	77.54	98.21	71.22	73.88	60.49	97.59	79.04
B+DIFD (B1)	56.09	98.90	49.73	52.06	40.58	97.18	68.88	75.14	99.25	74.82	74.55	62.48	98.36	80.42
B1+TRFR (B2)	56.57	98.91	50.43	52.62	41.03	97.23	69.13	**88.56**	98.66	75.80	**82.04**	64.38	98.29	81.34
B2 + TCLoss (B3)	<u>61.73</u>	98.31	<u>54.55</u>	<u>56.56</u>	<u>44.25</u>	97.05	70.65	75.43	99.45	<u>76.05</u>	75.38	<u>66.13</u>	**98.59**	<u>82.36</u>

presented in Table 2. In specific, "B" denotes a vanilla encoder-decoder framework as generator and a discriminator with basic loss functions; "B1" plugs five DIFD modules into "B"; "B2" further integrates the TRFR module in "B 1; and "B3" introduces TCLoss based on "B2". Results show that our algorithm has witnessed performance improvements by sequentially integrating DIFD module, TRFR module, TCLoss and PAALoss, increasing the *Dice* by 0.03%, 0.70%, 4.12% and 0.81% when adapting CVC-Colon DB to ETIS-Larib and by 3.60%, 0.98%, 0.25% and 2.18% reversely.

4   Conclusion

In this work, we propose a novel style normalization and task-relevant feature replenishment network named TRFR-Net that employs adversarial training for cross-centre polyp segmentation. Our model takes advantage of domain-invariant features and task-relevant features with the devised DIFD and TRFR module, improving generalization ability while retaining discrimination capability. We further align the feature distribution in segmentation prediction in a polyp-aware manner with the proposed PPAL. Extensive experiments and ablation studies have demonstrated the superiority of our proposed algorithm and effectiveness of each module.

Acknowledgements. This work was supported by National Key R&D Program of China with Grant No.2019YFB1312400, Hong Kong RGC CRF Grant C4063-18G and Hong Kong RGC GRF Grant # 14211420.

References

1. Chen, J., Li, Y., Ma, K., Zheng, Y.: Generative adversarial networks for video-to-video domain adaptation. In: Proceedings of the AAAI Conference on Artificial Intelligence, vol. 34, pp. 3462–3469 (2020)
2. Diao, L., Guo, H., Zhou, Y., He, Y.: Bridging the gap between outputs: domain adaptation for lung cancer IHC segmentation. In: 2021 IEEE International Conference on Image Processing (ICIP), pp. 6–10. IEEE (2021)
3. Dong, J., Cong, Y., Sun, G., Zhong, B., Xu, X.: What can be transferred: unsupervised domain adaptation for endoscopic lesions segmentation. In: Proceedings of the IEEE/CVF Conference on Computer Vision and Pattern Recognition, pp. 4023–4032 (2020)
4. Ganin, Y., et al.: Domain-adversarial training of neural networks. J. Mach. Learn. Res. **17**(1), 2030–2096 (2016)
5. He, K., Zhang, X., Ren, S., Sun, J.: Deep residual learning for image recognition. In: Proceedings of the IEEE Conference on Computer Vision and Pattern Recognition, pp. 770–778 (2016)
6. Hu, J., Shen, L., Sun, G.: Squeeze-and-excitation networks. In: Proceedings of the IEEE Conference on Computer Vision and Pattern Recognition, pp. 7132–7141 (2018)
7. Huang, X., Belongie, S.: Arbitrary style transfer in real-time with adaptive instance normalization. In: Proceedings of the IEEE International Conference on Computer Vision, pp. 1501–1510 (2017)
8. Jha, D., et al.: Kvasir-SEG: a segmented polyp dataset. In: Ro, Y.M., et al. (eds.) MMM 2020. LNCS, vol. 11962, pp. 451–462. Springer, Cham (2020). https://doi.org/10.1007/978-3-030-37734-2_37
9. Kim, S.Y., et al.: Colonoscopy versus fecal immunochemical test for reducing colorectal cancer risk: a population-based case-control study. Clin. Transl. Gastroenterol. **12**(5), e00350 (2021)
10. Luo, Y., Zheng, L., Guan, T., Yu, J., Yang, Y.: Taking a closer look at domain shift: category-level adversaries for semantics consistent domain adaptation. In: Proceedings of the IEEE/CVF Conference on Computer Vision and Pattern Recognition, pp. 2507–2516 (2019)

11. Pan, F., Shin, I., Rameau, F., Lee, S., Kweon, I.S.: Unsupervised intra-domain adaptation for semantic segmentation through self-supervision. In: Proceedings of the IEEE/CVF Conference on Computer Vision and Pattern Recognition, pp. 3764–3773 (2020)

12. Pan, X., Luo, P., Shi, J., Tang, X.: Two at once: enhancing learning and generalization capacities via ibn-net. In: Proceedings of the European Conference on Computer Vision (ECCV), pp. 464–479 (2018)

13. Siegel, R.L., Miller, K.D., Fuchs, H.E., Jemal, A.: Cancer statistics. CA: Can. J. Clin. (2022)

14. Silva, J., Histace, A., Romain, O., Dray, X., Granado, B.: Toward embedded detection of polyps in WCE images for early diagnosis of colorectal cancer. Int. J. Comput. Assist. Radiol. Surg. 9(2), 283–293 (2014)

15. Tajbakhsh, N., Gurudu, S.R., Liang, J.: Automated polyp detection in colonoscopy videos using shape and context information. IEEE Trans. Med. Imaging 35(2), 630–644 (2015)

16. Tsai, Y.H., Hung, W.C., Schulter, S., Sohn, K., Yang, M.H., Chandraker, M.: Learning to adapt structured output space for semantic segmentation. In: Proceedings of the IEEE Conference on Computer Vision and Pattern Recognition, pp. 7472–7481 (2018)

17. Ulyanov, D., Vedaldi, A., Lempitsky, V.: Instance normalization: the missing ingredient for fast stylization (2016)

18. Wang, X., Girshick, R., Gupta, A., He, K.: Non-local neural networks. In: Proceedings of the IEEE Conference on Computer Vision and Pattern Recognition, pp. 7794–7803 (2018)

19. Wang, Y., et al.: Domain-specific suppression for adaptive object detection. In: Proceedings of the IEEE/CVF Conference on Computer Vision and Pattern Recognition, pp. 9603–9612 (2021)

20. Zhou, K., Yang, Y., Qiao, Y., Xiang, T.: Mixstyle neural networks for domain generalization and adaptation. arXiv:2107.02053 (2021)

Vol2Flow: Segment 3D Volumes Using a Sequence of Registration Flows

Adeleh Bitarafan[1], Mohammad Farid Azampour[1,2], Kian Bakhtari[1],
Mahdieh Soleymani Baghshah[1(✉)], Matthias Keicher[2], and Nassir Navab[2,3]

[1] Sharif University of Technology, Tehran, Iran
soleymani@sharif.edu
[2] Computer Aided Medical Procedures, Technical University of Munich,
Munich, Germany
[3] Computer Aided Medical Procedures, Johns Hopkins University,
Baltimore, USA

Abstract. This work proposes a self-supervised algorithm to segment
each arbitrary anatomical structure in a 3D medical image produced
under various acquisition conditions, dealing with domain shift problems
and generalizability. Furthermore, we advocate an interactive setting in
the inference time, where the self-supervised model trained on unlabeled
volumes should be directly applicable to segment each test volume given
the user-provided single slice annotation. To this end, we learn a novel 3D
registration network, namely **Vol2Flow**, from the perspective of image
sequence registration to find 2D displacement fields between all adjacent
slices within a 3D medical volume together. Specifically, we present a
novel 3D CNN-based architecture that finds a series of registration flows
between consecutive slices within a whole volume, resulting in a dense
displacement field. A new self-supervised algorithm is proposed to learn
the transformations or registration fields between the series of 2D images
of a 3D volume. Consequently, we enable gradually propagating the user-
provided single slice annotation to other slices of a volume in the inference
time. We demonstrate that our model substantially outperforms related
methods on various medical image segmentation tasks through several
experiments on different medical image segmentation datasets. Code is
available at https://github.com/AdelehBitarafan/Vol2Flow.

Keywords: Self-supervised learning · Semi-automatic segmentation ·
Image sequence registration · Self-supervised algorithm

1 Introduction

In medical image analysis, multi-organ segmentation in three-dimensional (3D)
images is a critical task in radiation therapy planning and tumor resection surg-
eries [13]. In the current literature, numerous methods based on convolution

Supplementary Information The online version contains supplementary material
available at https://doi.org/10.1007/978-3-031-16440-8_58.

neural networks convolution neural network (CNN) have become dominant in the medical image segmentation task [8,9,17,19]. However, most segmentation models fall into the supervised learning paradigm, which requires many manually labeled data for training. Labeling data brings a substantial additional burden on users to annotate 3D volumes. Another limitation of supervised approaches is generalizability to classes (organs) unseen during training. Additionally, when employed on different test sets, the robustness to inter-scanner variability or discrepancies in acquisition systems is another challenge for supervised methods. Although many successful attempts in the semi-supervised learning paradigm have been presented to alleviate the dependency on manual annotations [5,7,26], they still lack generalizability to both new organs and different test images.

In this work, we propose a new self-supervised algorithm to deal with domain shift problems and generalizability. Specifically, we aim to learn a 3D registration network from the perspective of image sequence registration [2] to find two-dimensional (2D) displacement fields between all adjacent slices within a 3D volume together. We denominate this network as **Vol2Flow**. To the best of our knowledge, this is the first study to register 2D image sequences of a volume together, which can be effective in solving various medical image analysis tasks in different learning paradigms. Contrary to traditional algorithms for the registration of 2D image sequences [2,16], we develop **Vol2Flow** based on 3D CNN models to output a dense displacement field (DDF), including a sequence of 2D displacement fields. To this end, we learn effective visual representation from unlabeled volumes by solving the image sequence registration problem as a proxy task. Ultimately, **Vol2Flow** can be employed to segment each arbitrary anatomical structure in a volume using an interactive setting similar to Sli2Vol [27]. However, Sli2Vol can not model the long-range dependencies between slices and ignore global 3D context information within the whole volume since it finds 2D displacement fields by only using two adjacent slices without employing the whole context. **Vol2Flow** overcome this weakness by proposing a 3D network to model 3D spatial contextual information within the whole volume. Besides, we present an effective base classifier in the test time to clean pseudo labels generated in each round, alleviating error accumulation in mask propagation. Finally, comprehensive experiments demonstrate the superiority of **Vol2Flow** against Sli2Vol and other related methods.

1.1 Related Works

To enhance generalizability and alleviate the burden of manual annotation in 3D training data while preserving the performance, recently self-supervised learning (SSL) paradigms in an interactive setting have attracted more attention [24, 27,28]. In General, the goal is to learn effective visual representation from a large number of unlabeled volumes by solving a pretext task. Then, the learned representation is employed to tackle the segmentation task using fine-tuning on data annotated by a user in the inference time [24,28] or without fine-tuning [27].

Different ways of user interaction are proposed in the literature. For example, Zang et al. [28] exploits full-annotation of some slices (2D images) in a volume, but they employ user interactions as guidance for dealing with the training set rather than test images. Wang et al. [24] propose to use user-provided bounding boxes or scribbles for dealing with test images. However, this approach probably fails on new organs and different test images. More recently, Yeung et al. [27] propose a self-supervised method, termed as Sli2Vol, to segment any arbitrary organ in a 3D volume, given that the user annotates only a single slice within the test volume. To produce a dense 3D segmentation, they propagate 2D segmentation masks between adjacent slices within a volume. Label propagation is done by learning transformation patterns between neighboring slices via solving a pairwise slice reconstruction task. However, Sli2Vol exhibits limitations for modeling the long-range dependencies and global 3D contexts within volumes (or sequences of slices) since they do not utilize whole information in a 3D image. Although related works developed with level-set [29], random forest [25], or medical image registration using optical flow [10,12,15] or unsupervised approaches [3,18], can be applied for the propagation of a 2D mask between slices within a volume, they still suffer from the same shortcomings as Sli2Vol.

2   Method

We aim to learn a self-supervised algorithm directly applicable in segmenting each volume given the user-provided single slice annotation. Assume a huge number of unlabeled volumes as the training set are available, $\{X^{(1)}, X^{(2)}, ..., X^{(N)}\}$, where N indicates the number of training data. In general, we can consider each $X^{(n)}$ as a sequence of slices (i.e. 2D images) $X^{(n)} = (x_1, x_2, ..., x_D)$, comprising of D consecutive slices in which $x_d \in \mathbb{R}^{W \times H}$ (H and W show the height and width of slices, respectively). Thus, a volume can seen as a streaming data drawn from a continuously evolving visual domain [4]. Subsequently, in the inference time, we advocate an interactive setting where the self-supervised model learned on unlabeled training volumes is employed to produce a dense segmentation mask $Y = (y_1, y_2, ..., y_D)$ for each test volume $X \in \mathbb{R}^{D \times W \times H}$ ($y_d \in \{0, 1\}^{W \times H}$ denotes the segmentation mask of slice d for a specified organ), provided that y_s is available. To this end, we propagate y_s to other slices by prepared transformations between all adjacent slices. However, the most common ways are finding a transformation pattern only using two slices and training a 2D CNN model [3,10,27]. Unlike existing approaches, we learn a 3D registration network from the viewpoint of the image sequence registration task [2] that finds a sequence of transformations or flow patterns together from a volume. Figure 1 outlines a graphical presentation of the proposed model, **Vol2Flow**. In the following, the architecture and learning algorithm will be introduced in Sect. 2.1. Then, mask propagation using **Vol2Flow** will be elaborated in Sect. 2.2.

2.1   Vol2Flow Network and Self-Supervised Learning

Architecture. We develop **Vol2Flow** that gets the volume $X = (x_1, x_2, ..., x_D)$ as input and outputs two DDFs, $\Phi^f = \left(\phi^f_{1,2}, \phi^f_{2,3}, ..., \phi^f_{D-1,D}\right)$ and $\Phi^b = (\phi^b_{2,1}, \phi^b_{3,2}, ..., \phi^b_{D,D-1})$, containing a sequence of 2D displacement fields in the direction of forward and backward, respectively to propagate information in two directions between all pairs of adjacent slices within a volume.

Architecture is based on 3D-UNet structures [8] similar to VoxelMorph [3]. However, VoxelMorph-2D (or 3D) takes two slices (or volumes) as input and outputs one 2D displacement field (or one 3D DDF) between moving and target images to map all pixels (or voxels) of the moving image into the target one. In contrast, **Vol2Flow** outputs two DDFs of shape $D \times W \times H \times 2$ from one 3D input to map all pixels in a sequence of slices. Thus, we designed the architecture by adding two separate heads responsible for generating Φ^f and Φ^b. Further details of **Vol2Flow** network are given in the Supplementary Materials.

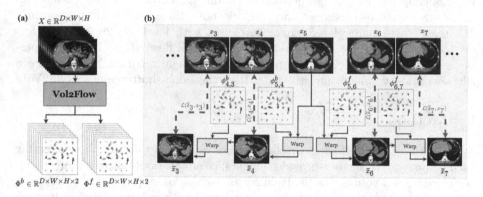

Fig. 1. (a) an overview of the **Vol2Flow** network, (b) the learning process of the proposed self-supervised method where $s = 5$, and $M = 2$.

Learning. We utilize Φ^f and Φ^b to construct neighboring slices around each slice by applying corresponding DDF on a source slice. In particular, for each source slice x_s, the goal is to generate M prior and M subsequent neighboring slices, $\{x_{s-M}, ..., x_{s-2}, x_{s-1}\}$ and $\{x_{s+1}, x_{s+2}, ..., x_{s+M}\}$, respectively. To this end, for each subsequent slice x_{s+m} $(m = 1, ..., M)$, we calculate the deformed moving image $\tilde{x}_{s+m}$ by sequentially applying Φ^f on x_s to the m-th moving image ($\tilde{x}_{s+m} = x_s \circ \phi^f_{s,s+1} \circ \phi^f_{s+1,s+2} \circ ... \circ \phi^f_{s+m-1,s+m}$). Similarly, for each prior slice x_{s-m}, we calculate the deformed moving image $\tilde{x}_{s-m}$ as $x_s \circ \phi^b_{s,s-1} \circ \phi^b_{s-1,s-2} \circ ... \circ \phi^b_{s-m+1,s-m}$, where $\mathcal{I} \circ \phi$ represents transforming an 2D image $\mathcal{I}$ by transformation ϕ. Finally, we minimize the loss function $\mathcal{L}(\tilde{x}_d, x_d)$ for each $x_d \in X^{(n)}$. Figure 1 (b) outlines the learning process, where $M = 2$ and $s = 5$.

In this work, we profit from structural similarity index (SSIM) to measure the similarity accounting for the difference both in low and high-frequency features between the two images. Besides, an edge-preserving loss is applied to emphasize the boundary of anatomical structures, which play a critical role in the segmentation task. We first detect the edge map of each original slice using the Canny edge detector [6]. Then, the edge-preserving loss is given as the mean of the pixel-wise product of the binary edge map and the reconstruction error. Thus, the overall loss function can be mathematically presented as:

$$\mathcal{L}(\tilde{x}_d, x_d) = \lambda \left(1 - \text{SSIM}(\tilde{x}_d, x_d)\right) + (1 - \lambda) \frac{\sum_{i=1}^{H} \sum_{j=1}^{W} C(x_d)_{i,j} |\tilde{x}_{d,i,j} - x_{d,i,j}|}{HW} \tag{1}$$

where C denotes the Canny operator and λ is a hyperparameter defining the importance of the edge-preserving loss with regard to SSIM. Further details of the algorithm of the learning process are given in the Supplementary Materials.

2.2 Mask Propagation

In this section, we aim to employ **Vol2Flow** learned on unlabeled training volumes for segmenting any arbitrary organ in a test volume, $X \in \mathbb{R}^{D \times W \times H}$, and producing a dense segmentation mask $Y = (y_1, y_2, ..., y_D)$ for a specified organ, given that y_s is provided by an annotator. To achieve this goal, we sequentially apply Φ^b and Φ^f on y_s to generate pseudo label $\tilde{y}_d$ for other slices. The schematic illustration of mask propagation strategy is depicted in the Supplementary Materials. However, mask propagation leads to accumulating errors due to generating synthetic labels. To tackle this error popagation problem, we introduce an effective refinement function, $f(.)$, to correct each $\tilde{y}_d$ (i.e., $y_d = f(\tilde{y}_d)$) after each step of mask propagation, resulting in boosting the performance. Thus, the final mask propagation strategy from s-th slice to m-th slice can be given as $y_m = f(f \cdots f(f(y_s \circ \phi^f_{s,s+1}) \circ \phi^f_{s+1,s+2}) \circ ...) \circ \phi^f_{m-1,m})$ for $m > s$, and $y_m = f(f \cdots f(f(y_s \circ \phi^b_{s,s-1}) \circ \phi^b_{s-1,s-2}) \circ ...) \circ \phi^b_{m+1,m})$ for $m < s$.

In [27], authors present $f(.)$ based on a heuristic algorithm. Specifically, for cleaning $\tilde{y}_d$, they create two binary regions, $P = y_{d-1}$ and $N = \Omega(y_{d-1}) - y_{d-1}$ (Ω refers to dilation morphological operator), as positive and negative class samples, respectively. Then, each of the predicted foreground pixels of $\tilde{y}_d$ can be re-classified according to its distance to the mean of these two classes. However, their algorithm might fail to classify linearly separable data as it is based on the mean of classes only. Furthermore, we found positive class samples come from the same distribution since all depend on a specific organ, while negative ones might be sampled from various organs, coming from different distributions. Thus, the supposed classification problem is not necessarily linearly separable. To overcome this problem, we learn an efficient non-linear classifier based on support vector machine (SVM) with the RBF kernel. Particularly, we train the SVM-based classifier on foreground pixels of P as positive class samples and N as negative ones. Besides, in contrast to [27], we create P according to just the real label of the source slice, not the pseudo label of other slices. Thus, we set $P = y_s$ fixed in each round of propagation, considerably reducing false-positive errors in mask propagation. Furthermore, since N is made according to pseudo labels, we weight negative samples regarding their predicted probability.

3 Experimental Setup

In this work, we evaluate **Vol2Flow** in the mask propagation task, where it should be directly applicable to segment each arbitrary anatomical structure in a test volume given the user-provided single slice annotation. To demonstrate the network generalization ability to domain shift problem, similar to [27], we train the network on three publicly CT datasets in an unsupervised-manner and segment chest-abdominal organs in test volumes of the other three ones given user-provided single slice annotation.

Datasets. Following [27], we train **Vol2Flow** on three large-scale CT datasets, containing 300 volumes from C4KC-KiTS [11], 86 from CT-LN [21], and 82 from CT-Pancreas [20] and test on Sliver07 [23], CHAOS [14], 3Dircadb-01, and 3Dircadb-02 [22] datasets. However, any annotations of training datasets are not used during the training, but the user-provided single slice annotation of each test volume is employed as guidance for segmenting the same volume. Moreover, Synapse multi-organ segmentation dataset[1] including 50 volumes are taken as validation dataset to set hyper-parameters. Furthermore, since inputs of **Vol2Flow** must be the same size, all test and training volumes are resized in $128 \times 128 \times 400$ pixels per patient, including a set of thorax slices.

Compared Methods. To evaluate, we compare **Vol2Flow** against related existing approaches, including: 1) 3D-UNet [8] in a fully supervised setup which is trained on volumes of validation dataset, 2) optical flow [10], 3) Voxel-Morph [3], and 4) Sli2Vol [27] which are trained on unlabeled training datasets as **Vol2Flow**. Adam optimizer with the learning rate of 0.0001 for 500 epochs is used to train all methods. Moreover, known results from fully supervised state-of-the-art (SOTA) methods [1,14] are reported, demonstrating upper bounds given a large set of fully-annotated data. However, they work only in the same domain setting, where the training and testing data come from the same domain.

4   Results and Discussion

Following [27], the slice with the largest annotation (i.e., s_L) is chosen as the user-provided annotated slice. Through our experiments, we find selecting one of the ± 4 slices around s_L can also preserve segmentation performance. For example, selecting the central slice of the target organ, located in $[s_L - 4, s_L + 4]$, results in 92.3 DSC on Sliver07, while selecting slices out of this range does not provide comparable results. The effects of other Hyper-parameters, like M and λ (set 5 and 0.5, respectively), are also investigated in the Supplementary Materials.

The comparison between the mentioned methods on different test datasets is presented in Table 1. To investigate the effect of the test-time classification strategy in mask propagation, we assess **Vol2Flow** against the absence and presence of this strategy, termed as Vol2Flow^{-tc} and Vol2Flow^{+tc}, respectively. Similarly, results of Sli2Vol in two cases of Sli2Vol^{-tc} and Sli2Vol^{+tc} are also reported. The comparison between Vol2Flow^{+tc}, SOTA, and 3D-UNet trained on the same domain of test data (values in braces) shows **Vol2Flow** has close

---

[1] https://www.synapse.org/#!Synapse:syn3193805/wiki/217789.

Table 1. Comparison results (the average DSC ± standard deviation) of different methods on various test datasets. The best results are highlighted in bold, and the average of all results is reported in the last column. Note: OF: optical flow, VXM: VoxelMorph, S2V: Sli2Vol, V2F: Vol2Flow, GB: gallbladder, SG: surrenal-gland.

Test dataset	Organ (# vol)	SOTA	3D UNet	OF	VXM	$S2V^{-tc}$	$S2V^{+tc}$	$V2F^{-tc}$	$V2F^{+tc}$
Sliver07	Liver (20)	94.8 [1]	62.05 {93.5}	65.2 ± 8.8	57.2 ± 9.8	74.8 ± 7.4	91.3 ± 3.2	70.97 ± 3.62	**92.63** ± 5.7
CHAOS	Liver (20)	97.8 [14]	66.69 {92.8}	72.0 ± 9.9	66.5 ± 10.5	77.8 ± 8.4	**91.0** ± 2.9	78.55 ± 7.00	85.58 ± 3.5
3D-IRCADb-01 and 3D-IRCADb-02	Liver (22)	96.5 [1]	65.85 {90.5}	68.4 ± 9.4	60.5 ± 9.7	73.9 ± 8.5	88.2 ± 3.0	73.82 ± 5.15	**88.4** ± 4.05
	Kidney (17)	-	-	73.6 ± 14.6	70.1 ± 18.6	86.8 ± 15.7	**91.4** ± 4.8	89.85 ± 5.49	89.2 ± 5.268
	Lung (12)	-	-	33.6 ± 18.0	38.7 ± 21.2	48.8 ± 25.6	81.4 ± 28.5	66.63 ± 16.61	**88.07** ± 6.4
	Spleen (41)	-	-	72.9 ± 14.5	61.5 ± 19.5	85.8 ± 13	**90.2** ± 9.5	84.00 ± 9.58	88.35 ± 5.68
	Pancreas (4)	-	-	21.9 ± 12.6	28.3 ± 11.0	53.9 ± 7.1	58.2 ± 4.6	58.82 ± 8.49	**63.49** ± 9.24
	Heart (3)	-	-	32.2 ± 11.6	20.3 ± 6.5	49.4 ± 12.3	75.9 ± 10.9	80.51 ± 2.74	**89.17** ± 3.58
	GB (8)	-	-	24.6 ± 12.4	20.2 ± 12.2	68.5 ± 13.8	68.9 ± 9.9	67.13 ± 6.32	**69.08** ± 9.59
	SG (11)	-	-	22.1 ± 12.6	41.1 ± 15.3	58.3 ± 16.6	48.4 ± 13.5	59.69 ± 11.74	**68.06** ± 9.37
Average		-	-	48.65 ± 23.37	46.44 ± 19.12	67.8 ± 12.84	78.5 ± 9.08	73.00 ± 7.67	**82.20** ± 6.23

results to those of the fully supervised methods trained on the same domain of the testing dataset. However, SOTA and 3D-UNet require many manually annotated samples for training, bringing a significant additional burden on users to annotate volumes. Even, they are not generalizable to unseen objects and different test data, leading to not-applicability in the clinical area. This can be verified by comparing the results of 3D-UNet in two scenarios, where it is trained and tested in different domains, and the same domain (values in braces). As observed, **Vol2Flow** outperforms 3D-UNet tested on data coming from different domains on the liver segmentation task although trained in a supervised setting. Thus, it confirms **Vol2Flow** is dealing with domain shift and generalizability. Besides, the high performance of $Vol2Flow^{-tc}$, in terms of both DSC and standard deviation, compared to optical flow, VoxelMorph, and $Sli2Vol^{-tc}$ (by more than 5% on average) reveals 2D displacement fields inferred using global 3D context are more effective for mask propagation. In fact, applying 3D spatial information in **Vol2Flow** leads to modeling global 3D context information within the whole volume, yielding strong performance in tracking target structures. Also, it helps in registering slices with a larger thickness (see results on Sliver07, which has a slice thickness up to 5 mm). Furthermore, $Vol2Flow^{+tc}$ outperforms $Sli2Vol^{+tc}$ significantly and achieves 3.7 higher DSC and 2.8 smaller standard deviation on average, revealing superior performance in refining pseudo labels. To analyze the efficiency of the proposed test-time classification, we illustrate Fig. 2. It demonstrates segmentation results gained by **Vol2FLow** when pseudo labels in each round of propagation are amended by our test-time classification (column (d)) and introduced by Sli2Vol [27] (column (c)). According to blue arrows, ours can successfully handle boundaries and amend pseudo labels. Besides, our test-time classification can also deal with incorrect manual annotations. For example, it can detect the hepatic veins in the liver, which are incorrectly annotated as liver by a user (see yellow arrows in Fig. 2). Further experiments and qualitative examples are brought in the Supplementary Materials.

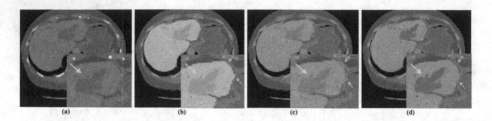

Fig. 2. Visual comparison of the segmentation mask refined by our method (d) and introduced by Sli2Vol [27] (c) on the liver organ of 3Dircadb-01 dataset. (a) and (b) show the raw image, and annotated by a user, respectively. The yellow arrows indicate the hepatic veins in the liver. The blue arrows show pixels that are incorrectly predicted. (Color figure online)

To investigate the performance of non-registration-based methods against **Vol2Flow**, we considered two cases. In the first one, only a single annotated slice in each test volume is used to fine-tune a pre-trained 2D-UNet in the inference time to segment unlabeled slices of test volumes. The second case considers a 3D-UNet in the semi-automated setup, where test volumes with a single slice annotation are utilized to train the 3D-UNet. However, both cases yield weak performances, especially for small organs (e.g., 59.7 and 62.1 DSC on kidneys for the first and second cases, respectively), and their inference time is high due to their test-time training requirement (almost 200 s per slice (s/sl), while the inference time of **Vol2Flow** is about 0.58 s/sl).

5 Conclusion

We proposed a self-supervised algorithm for 3D image registration to find 2D displacement fields between all adjacent slices within a whole volume together, resulting in a sequence of transformations or registration fields. To the best of our knowledge, the proposed model, **Vol2Flow**, is the first model that takes a 3D volume as input and outputs a 3D displacement field. In this work, the output of **Vol2Flow** is employed to segment each arbitrary anatomical structure in a 3D medical image by gradually propagating the 2D segmentation mask provided by a user between other slices. Experimental results on test volumes, coming from the domain different from training set, revealed the superior performance of **Vol2Flow** in generalizability and accuracy against other related methods. Consequently, this work approved, **Vol2Flow** has a strong potential to alleviate the cost of annotating 3D images while preserving the performance and possible applications in the clinical cases when no set of fully-annotated samples exists.

Acknowledgements. The authors were partially supported by the grant NPRP-11S-1219- 170106 from the Qatar National Research Fund (a member of the Qatar Foundation). The findings herein are however solely the responsibility of the authors.

References

1. Ahmad, M., et al.: Deep belief network modeling for automatic liver segmentation. IEEE Access **7**, 20585–20595 (2019)
2. Arganda-Carreras, I., et al.: Non-rigid consistent registration of 2D image sequences. Phys. Med. Biol. **55**(20), 6215 (2010)
3. Balakrishnan, G., Zhao, A., Sabuncu, M.R., Guttag, J., Dalca, A.V.: Voxelmorph: a learning framework for deformable medical image registration. IEEE Trans. Med. Imaging **38**(8), 1788–1800 (2019)
4. Bitarafan, A., Baghshah, M.S., Gheisari, M.: Incremental evolving domain adaptation. IEEE Trans. Knowl. Data Eng. **28**(8), 2128–2141 (2016)
5. Bitarafan, A., Nikdan, M., Baghshah, M.S.: 3D image segmentation with sparse annotation by self-training and internal registration. IEEE J. Biomed. Health Inform. **25**(7), 2665–2672 (2020)
6. Canny, J.: A computational approach to edge detection. IEEE Trans. Pattern Anal. Mach. Intell. **6**, 679–698 (1986)
7. Chen, S., Bortsova, G., García-Uceda Juárez, A., van Tulder, G., de Bruijne, M.: Multi-task attention-based semi-supervised learning for medical image segmentation. In: Shen, D., et al. (eds.) MICCAI 2019. LNCS, vol. 11766, pp. 457–465. Springer, Cham (2019). https://doi.org/10.1007/978-3-030-32248-9_51
8. Çiçek, Ö., Abdulkadir, A., Lienkamp, S.S., Brox, T., Ronneberger, O.: 3D U-net: learning dense volumetric segmentation from sparse annotation. In: Ourselin, S., Joskowicz, L., Sabuncu, M.R., Unal, G., Wells, W. (eds.) MICCAI 2016. LNCS, vol. 9901, pp. 424–432. Springer, Cham (2016). https://doi.org/10.1007/978-3-319-46723-8_49
9. Conze, P.H., et al.: Abdominal multi-organ segmentation with cascaded convolutional and adversarial deep networks. Artif. Intell. Med. **117**, 102109 (2021)
10. Farnebäck, G.: Two-frame motion estimation based on polynomial expansion. In: Bigun, J., Gustavsson, T. (eds.) SCIA 2003. LNCS, vol. 2749, pp. 363–370. Springer, Heidelberg (2003). https://doi.org/10.1007/3-540-45103-X_50
11. Heller, N., et al.: Data from c4kc-kits [data set]. Cancer Imaging Arch. **10** (2019)
12. Hermann, S., Werner, R.: High accuracy optical flow for 3D medical image registration using the census cost function. In: Klette, R., Rivera, M., Satoh, S. (eds.) PSIVT 2013. LNCS, vol. 8333, pp. 23–35. Springer, Heidelberg (2014). https://doi.org/10.1007/978-3-642-53842-1_3
13. Hesamian, M.H., Jia, W., He, X., Kennedy, P.: Deep learning techniques for medical image segmentation: achievements and challenges. J. Digit. Imaging **32**(4), 582–596 (2019)
14. Kavur, A.E., et al.: Chaos challenge-combined (CT-MR) healthy abdominal organ segmentation. Med. Image Anal. **69**, 101950 (2021)
15. Keeling, S.L., Ring, W.: Medical image registration and interpolation by optical flow with maximal rigidity. J. Math. Imaging Vis. **23**(1), 47–65 (2005)
16. Li, Z., Dong, Z., Yu, A., He, Z., Zhu, X.: A robust image sequence registration algorithm for videosar combining surf with inter-frame processing. In: IGARSS 2019–2019 IEEE International Geoscience and Remote Sensing Symposium, pp. 2794–2797. IEEE (2019)

17. Liu, X., Song, L., Liu, S., Zhang, Y.: A review of deep-learning-based medical image segmentation methods. Sustainability **13**(3), 1224 (2021)
18. Mocanu, S., Moody, A.R., Khademi, A.: FlowREG: fast deformable unsupervised medical image registration using optical flow. arXiv preprint arXiv:2101.09639 (2021)
19. Radiuk, P.: Applying 3D U-net architecture to the task of multi-organ segmentation in computed tomography. Appl. Comput. Syst. **25**(1), 43–50 (2020)
20. Roth, H., Farag, A., Turkbey, E., Lu, L., Liu, J., Summers, R.: Data from pancreas-CT (2016)
21. Roth, H., et al.: A new 2.5 d representation for lymph node detection in CT. Cancer Imaging Arch. (2018)
22. Soler, L., et al.: 3D image reconstruction for comparison of algorithm database: a patient specific anatomical and medical image database. Technical report, IRCAD, Strasbourg, France (2010)
23. Van Ginneken, B., Heimann, T., Styner, M.: 3D segmentation in the clinic: a grand challenge. In: MICCAI workshop on 3D segmentation in the clinic: a grand challenge, vol. 1, pp. 7–15 (2007)
24. Wang, G., et al.: Interactive medical image segmentation using deep learning with image-specific fine tuning. IEEE Trans. Med. Imaging **37**(7), 1562–1573 (2018)
25. Wang, G., et al.: Slic-Seg: slice-by-slice segmentation propagation of the placenta in fetal MRI using one-plane scribbles and online learning. In: Navab, N., Hornegger, J., Wells, W.M., Frangi, A.F. (eds.) MICCAI 2015. LNCS, vol. 9351, pp. 29–37. Springer, Cham (2015). https://doi.org/10.1007/978-3-319-24574-4_4
26. Xia, Y., et al.: 3D semi-supervised learning with uncertainty-aware multi-view co-training. In: Proceedings of the IEEE/CVF Winter Conference on Applications of Computer Vision, pp. 3646–3655 (2020)
27. Yeung, P.-H., Namburete, A.I.L., Xie, W.: Sli2Vol: annotate a 3D volume from a single slice with self-supervised learning. In: de Bruijne, M., et al. (eds.) MICCAI 2021. LNCS, vol. 12902, pp. 69–79. Springer, Cham (2021). https://doi.org/10.1007/978-3-030-87196-3_7
28. Zhang, X., Xie, W., Huang, C., Zhang, Y., Wang, Y.: Self-supervised tumor segmentation through layer decomposition. arXiv preprint arXiv:2109.03230 (2021)
29. Zheng, Z., Zhang, X., Xu, H., Liang, W., Zheng, S., Shi, Y.: A unified level set framework combining hybrid algorithms for liver and liver tumor segmentation in CT images. In: BioMed research International 2018 (2018)

Parameter-Free Latent Space Transformer for Zero-Shot Bidirectional Cross-modality Liver Segmentation

Yang Li[1,2], Beiji Zou[1], Yulan Dai[1], Chengzhang Zhu[1(✉)], Fan Yang[3], Xin Li[3],
Harrison X. Bai[4], and Zhicheng Jiao[2]

[1] School of Computer Science and Engineering, Central South University,
Changsha, Hunan, China
chzhzhu@csu.edu.cn
[2] Department of Diagnostic Imaging, The Warren Alpert Medical School, Brown University,
Providence, RI, USA
[3] AIQ, Abu Dhabi, UAE
[4] Department of Radiology and Radiological Sciences,
Johns Hopkins University School of Medicine, Baltimore, MD, USA

Abstract. In this paper, we address the domain shift in cross CT-MR liver segmentation task with a latent space investigation. Domain adaptation between modalities is of significant importance in clinical practice, as different diagnostic procedures require different imaging modalities, such as CT and MR. Thus, training a convolutional neural network (CNN) with one modality may not be sufficient for application in another one. Most domain adaptation methods need to use data and ground truths of both source and target domain in the training process. Different from these techniques, we propose a zero-shot bidirectional cross-modality liver segmentation method by investigating a parameter-free latent space through the prior knowledge from CT and MR images. Experiments on the CHAOS, the subset of LiTS and the local TACE datasets demonstrate that our method can well deal with the problem of CNN failure caused by domain shift and yields promising segmentation results.

Keywords: Cross-modality liver segmentation · Latent space transformer · Parameter-free · Zero-shot

1 Introduction

Automatic liver segmentation from multi-modal images is essential for liver disease assessment, diagnosis and personalized treatment planning in clinic settings [1, 2]. Convolutional neural networks (CNNs) have achieved great success in abdominal liver image segmentation [3, 4]. However, these models usually tend to fail when applied on cross

Supplementary Information The online version contains supplementary material available at
https://doi.org/10.1007/978-3-031-16440-8_59.

modalities due to the different intensity distributions and contrasts of liver images, as shown in Fig. 1.

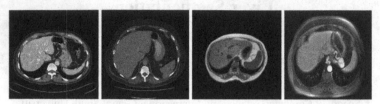

Fig. 1. Examples of liver image over different modalities, from left to right are CT in the CHAOS, CT in the subset of LiTS, MR T1 inphase in the CHAOS and MR T1 enhance in TACE datasets, respectively.

A naive way to address this problem is to collect images and their annotations of new modality to fine-tune the model trained on existing modality [5] or jointly train another model from scratch with the known modality [6]. However, this solution is expensive and infeasible, making it less practical in source-limited settings. Unsupervised domain adaptation (UDA) tackles this challenge by transferring knowledge from source modality to target modality without extra manual annotation [7]. Recent researches on UDA based cross-modality segmentation rely on generative adversarial networks (GANs) [8] and its variants [9], whose objective is to align features of different modalities in pixel-level and semantic-level to force the segmentation network to learn domain-invariant representation and achieve more robust cross-modality performance [10]. However, it's usually challenging to balance the loss terms for domain alignment and segmentation during the joint optimization. In addition, there is a method that synthesized intermediate representation from multi-modal images to improve the generalization capacity of cross modalities segmentation modal [11]. UDA image segmentation has also been proposed to address domain shift by searching domain-invariant features, such as shape feature [12]. As a fact that the organs usually show consistent shape between modalities, Pham et.al [13] proposed to use liver contour prior knowledge for cross MR-CT liver segmentation and got a satisfying result of CT liver segmentation Dice 75.3% on the MR trained CNN.

Inspired by the ideas of generating intermediate modality and learning domain-invariant features, we investigate a common latent space that maximizes the similarity and minimizes the domain shift between CT and MR liver images by a parameter-free latent space transformer (LST) so that get satisfying zero-shot bidirectional cross-modality liver segmentation performance. **Our main contributions are:** 1) Our work provides a new insight into the cross modalities liver segmentation task: parameterized modality transfer and domain-invariant feature learning are not necessary, the domain shift could also be addressed by parameter-free latent space feature mining. 2) We propose a parameter-free yet effective cross modalities latent space transformer (LST), which projects CT and MR images into a common space based on the prior knowledge of intensity distribution in liver. 3) We construct a new MR dataset called TACE that consists of 24 abdominal MR T1 enhance volumes with liver annotation. 4) Comprehensive experiments on the CHAOS, the subset of LiTS and the local TACE datasets demonstrate that our method can get promising zero-shot bidirectional cross CT-MR liver segmentation results.

2 Method

To simplify the cross-modality liver segmentation process and avoid consuming more manually labeled liver ground truths and learnable parameters, we aim to formulate a parameter-free latent space transformer that projects the CT and MR liver image to a common space to minimize the domain gap between them so that get the satisfying zero-shot cross-modality liver segmentation results. The overview of our proposed method is shown in Fig. 2.

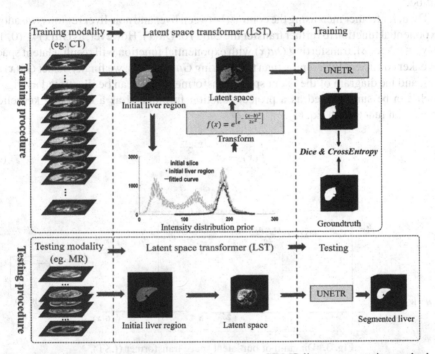

Fig. 2. Overview of our zero-shot bidirectional cross CT-MR liver segmentation method.

Owing to the property of CT and MR scannings, the certain organ such as liver intensity distribution lies in a certain/rough range and always in line with normal distribution [14, 15], we propose a hypothesis that the latent space of CT and MR liver images satisfy the following two conditions: 1) The latent space can effectively exclude complex non-liver areas and highlight liver region; 2) The pixels whose intensity locates at the intensity range of live and close to the mean liver grayscale have higher transferred pixel values, otherwise have lower values.

To meet the conditions, we first seek a continuous function $G(x)$ that meets: ① $G(x)$ is in the semi-closed interval $(0, 1]$, i.e., $G(x) \in (0, 1]$; ② $G(x)$ reaches maxima 1 when pixel value x equals to the mean value of liver intensity μ; ③ $G(x)$ is monotonically increase and decrease when x is smaller and larger than the mean liver grayscale denoted as μ, respectively. Among the well-known functions, Gaussian function shown in Eq. (1) and Quadratic function shown in Eq. (2) can fit these properties well.

$$Gu(x) = e^{-\frac{(x-\mu)^2}{2\delta^2}}$$ (1)

$$Qu(x) = \frac{-[x - (\mu - 2\delta)][x - (\mu + 2\delta)]}{4\delta}$$ (2)

where μ and δ are the mean and variance for the fitted normal distribution curve of the partial liver intensity distribution, respectively, which can be observed by least square method.

Then, for further increasing the contrast between liver and non-liver regions, we adopt a exponential function to further transfer the $Gu(x)$ or $Qu(x)$. However, as $Gu(x) \in (0, 1]$, $Qu(x) \in (-\infty, \delta]$, transferring $Qu(x)$ with exponential function will result a latent space of weaker consistent liver region than transferring $Gu(x)$. Thus, we finally select $Gu(x)$ as $G(x)$, and the diagram of the latent space transformer (LST) can be illustrated as Fig. 3, which can be summarized as a project function formulated as a Gaussian kernelled exponential function in Eq. (3).

$$f(x) = e^{e^{-\frac{(x-\mu)^2}{2\delta^2}}}$$ (3)

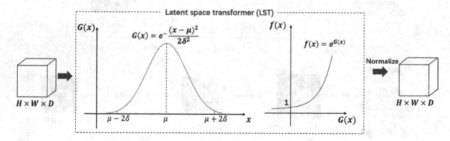

Fig. 3. Diagram of our latent space transformer (LST).

Figure 4 shows examples of the latent space transfer results, in which (a) gives a partial CT and MR liver regions; (b) the intensity distribution prior corresponds to (a); (c) reminding liver slices; (d) the latent space corresponds to (c); (e) the intensity distribution of (d). The results in Fig. 4 indicate that our proposed method can greatly minimize the domain shift between CT and MR images and further help to get satisfying zero-shot cross-modality liver segmentations.

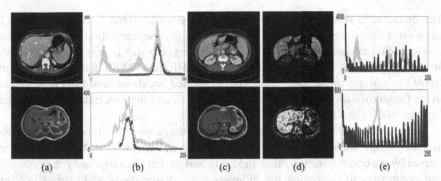

| (a) | (b) | (c) | (d) | (e) |

Fig. 4. Examples of the latent space transfer results. (The upper and bottom rows represent CT and MR images, respectively. In (b), the green and blue curves are the actual histogram distribution of slice and liver region, respectively, the red curve is the histogram normal distribution fitting of the liver region. In (e), the green and blue curves are the histogram distribution of the original slice and its latent space, respectively.) (Color figure online)

3 Experiments and Results

- **Dataset**

  We use three datasets including the public CHAOS dataset [16] consisting of 20 MR T1 In-phase and 20 CT images, the subset of LiTS dataset [17] containing 20 CT images and the locally constructed TACE dataset consisting of 24 MR T1 enhance images for cross-modality liver segmentation experiments.

- **Implementations**

  The latest and superior architecture UNETR [18] with cross-entropy and Dice loss is used as segmentation backbone. For data processing, we use the 3D volumes, cropped to $96 \times 96 \times 96$ and normalized to $[0, 1]$. For testing, we adopt the sliding window strategy with an overlap of 0.8. The segmentation performance is reported in terms of the Dice similarity coefficient (Dice).

- **Experimental Settings**

  We consider three experimental settings. **Setting 1):** To access the superior liver segmentation performance of the backbone, we train and test the backbone over a single modality image, i.e., CT or MR image. **Setting 2):** To highlight the severe domain shift between modalities, we consider the situation when no domain adaptation is conducted. Thus, we train our backbone over one modality and test it over other unlabeled modalities, i.e., zero-shot segmentation. **Setting 3):** To evaluate the effectiveness of latent space in cross-modality liver segmentation, we conduct the LST before liver segmentation with the same train and test strategy as setting 2). First, we use Quadratic function Eq. (2) as the kernel of the project function, whose μ and δ are captured by the intensity distribution in a circle area of the initial liver. We refer this setting as CQ kernel. Secondly, we use the same projection as CQ kernel, but the μ and δ are captured by the intensity prior of initial liver region. We refer this setting as IQ kernel. Thirdly, we evaluate our proposed parameter-free latent space capture method, i.e., the project function (Eq. (3)) used Gaussian as kernel, which is referred as IG kernel.

- **Results and Discussions**

The quantitative results of our experiments are given in Table 1, 2, and 3. Table 1 shows that the backbone is able to get satisfying liver segmentation results over the single labeled modality while failing when applying zero-shot liver segmentation over cross-modality with Dice of 3.77% from CT to MR and 12.98% from MR to CT in CHAOS dataset. Furthermore, the CHAOS trained backbone also fails to segment livers from cross-site images, such as the sub LiTS and the TACE datasets although they are in the same modality.

Table 2 gives the liver segmentation results of the proposed method over the cross-modality image. It can be observed that the LST can well deal with the backbone failure caused by the domain shift in cross-modality and the data heterogeneity in cross-site and contributes to improving the bidirectional cross-modality and cross-site liver segmentation accuracy as the LST pushes the images in different modalities and sites to a common latent space. Additionally, Table 2 shows that the setting with IG kernel gets the superior result that achieves Dice of 71.99% when conducting zero-shot CT to MR liver segmentation and 86.25% MR to CT liver segmentation in CHAOS. Besides, the MR to CT liver segmentation Dice in setting with IG kernel is much higher than the reported Dice of 75.3% in [13] over the same dataset. In Table 2, the setting with IQ kernel and CQ kernel get the second and third best results, respectively. It may of the reasons from two aspects. One is that the intensity distribution in liver region is more capable to represents the liver prior knowledge than that in a circled liver area. The other is that the intensity distribution of liver conforms to a Gaussian distribution so that the Gaussian kernel outperforms the Quadratic kernel although they are monotonic consistent. The visual comparison among the latent space generated by CQ, IQ and IG kernels-based project function is shown in Fig. 5, which also indicate that the IG kernel gets the best common latent space of CT and MR image, while CQ and IQ kernels cause the loss of liver structure information.

Table 3 shows the liver segmentation results of our proposed method over the single modality. It indicates that our method can get satisfying performance in a single modality, especially in cross-site CT liver segmentation accuracy, which further demonstrates the robust generalization capability of our latent space.

Table 1. Performances of backbone over the single-modality, cross-modality and cross-site images.

Methods	Modality	Train CHAOS	Val CHAOS	Test CHAOS	Dice (%)	Test sub LiTS	Dice (%)	Test TACE	Dice (%)
Backbone Setting1	CT → CT	13 CT	2 CT	5 CT	97.08	20 CT	85.07	–	–
	MR → MR	13 MR	2 MR	5 MR	87.03	–	–	24 MR	41.09
Backbone Setting2	CT → MR	18 CT	2 CT	20 MR	4.52	–	–	24 MR	37.56
	MR → CT	18 MR	2 MR	20 CT	13.24	20 CT	43.24	–	–

Table 2. Performances of different project function kernels over the cross-modality and cross-site images.

Methods	Modality	Train CHAOS	Val CHAOS	Test CHAOS	Dice (%)	Test sub LiTS	Dice (%)	Test TACE	Dice (%)
CQ kernel	CT → MR	18 CT	2 CT	20 MR	55.58	–	–	24 MR	47.66
Setting3	MR → CT	18 MR	2 MR	20 CT	82.55	20 CT	76.63	–	–
IQ kernel	CT → MR	18 CT	2 CT	20 MR	71.50	–	–	24 MR	71.55
Setting3	MR → CT	18 MR	2 MR	20 CT	85.00	20 CT	71.06	–	–
IG kernel	CT → MR	18 CT	2 CT	20 MR	**71.99**	–	–	24 MR	**73.24**
Setting3	MR → CT	18 MR	2 MR	20 CT	**86.25**	20 CT	**83.17**	–	–

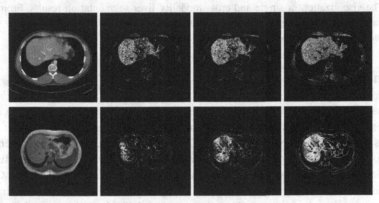

Fig. 5. The visual comparisons among the latent space, from the left to right are original image, the latent space captured by CQ, IQ and IG kernel-based LST, respectively. (The upper and bottom rows are CT and MR images, respectively.)

Table 3. Performances of different project function kernels over the single modality image.

Methods	Modality	Train CHAOS	Val CHAOS	Test CHAOS	Dice (%)	Test sub LiTS	Dice (%)	Test TACE	Dice (%)
CQ kernel	CT → CT	13 CT	2 CT	5 CT	96.80	20 CT	83.67	–	–
Setting3	MR → MR	13 MR	2 MR	5 MR	79.82	–	–	24 MR	45.63
IQ kernel	CT → CT	13 CT	2 CT	5 CT	**96.99**	20 CT	86.70	–	–
Setting3	MR → MR	13 MR	2 MR	5 MR	74.52	–	–	24 MR	64.77
IG kernel	CT → CT	13 CT	2 CT	5 CT	96.84	20 CT	**93.03**	–	–
Setting3	MR → MR	13 MR	2 MR	5 MR	**76.71**	–	–	24 MR	**66.70**

Figure 6 gives the liver segmentation results of our LST-based zero-shot bidirectional cross-modality method, which show that the proposed LST can get satisfying performance on both single and cross-modality liver segmentation.

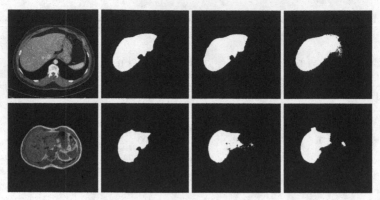

Fig. 6. The visualization of single and cross-modality liver segmentation results. From left to right denote the CT/MR images, the liver Ground truth, the results of CNN trained by CT/MR images and CNN trained by MR/CT images, respectively.

4   Conclusion

In this paper, we present a LST that transfers the CT and MR liver images to a common latent space to minimize the domain shift between CT and MR modalities so that improves the generalization capability of CNN in cross-modality liver segmentation. The proposed LST is simple and parameter-free. It is designed by a project function with a Gaussian kernel based on the fact that the liver intensity distribution in CT and MR lies in a certain/rough range and is always in line with normal distribution. This work provides a new insight for researching the cross-modality liver segmentation method. Experimental results of over CT and MR images in the CHAOS, the subset of LiTS and locally constructed TACE datasets indicate that the latent space generated by our LST is capable to address the domain shift and get promising liver segmentation results over single modality, zero-shot bidirectional cross-modality and cross-site. Future work will expand the idea of our work to different image spaces for investigating more abundant modality-invariant features and further improve the cross-modality liver segmentation performance.

Acknowledgements. This work is supported by the National Key R&D Program of China (2018AAA0102100), International Science and Technology Innovation Joint Base of Machine Vision and Medical Image Processing in Hunan Province (2021CB1013), the Scientific and Technological Innovation Leading Plan of High-tech Industry of Hunan Province (2020GK2021) , the 111 project under grant no. B18059, the Fundamental Research Funds for the Central Universities of Central South University.

References

1. Ackaouy, A., Courty, N., Vallée, E., Commowick, O., Barillot, C., Galassi, F.: Unsupervised domain adaptation with optimal transport in multi-site segmentation of multiple sclerosis lesions from MRI data. Front. Comput. Neurosci. **14**, 19 (2020)
2. Seo, H., Huang, C., Bassenne, M., Xiao, R., Xing, L.: Modified U-Net (mU-Net) with incorporation of object-dependent high level features for improved liver and liver-tumor segmentation in CT images. IEEE Trans. Med. Imaging **39**(5), 1316–1325 (2020)
3. Dou, Q., Chen, H., Jin, Y., Yu, L., Qin, J., Heng, P.A.: 3D deeply supervised network for automatic liver segmentation from CT volumes. In: Ourselin, S., et al. (eds) Medical Image Computing and Computer-Assisted Intervention – MICCAI 2016. MICCAI 2016. Lecture Notes in Computer Science, vol. 9901. Springer, Cham (2016). https://doi.org/10.1007/978-3-319-46723-8_18
4. Li, X.-M., Chen, H., Qi, X., Dou, Q., Fu, C.-W., Heng, P.-A.: H-DenseUNet: hybrid densely connected UNet for liver and tumor segmentation from CT volumes. IEEE Trans. Med. Imaging **37**(12), 2663–2674 (2018)
5. Zakazov, I., Shirokikh, B., Chernyavskiy, A., Belyaev, M.: Anatomy of domain shift impact on U-Net layers in MRI segmentation. In: de Bruijne, M., et al. (eds.) Medical Image Computing and Computer Assisted Intervention – MICCAI 2021: 24th International Conference, Strasbourg, France, September 27–October 1, 2021, Proceedings, Part III, pp. 211–220. Springer International Publishing, Cham (2021). https://doi.org/10.1007/978-3-030-87199-4_20
6. Chen, C., Dou, Q., Chen, H., Heng, P.-A.: Semantic-aware generative adversarial nets for unsupervised domain adaptation in chest X-ray segmentation. In: Shi, Y., Suk, H.-I., Liu, M. (eds.) MLMI 2018. LNCS, vol. 11046, pp. 143–151. Springer, Cham (2018). https://doi.org/10.1007/978-3-030-00919-9_17
7. Zeng, G., et al.: Semantic consistent unsupervised domain adaptation for cross-modality medical image segmentation. In: de Bruijne, M., et al. (eds.) Medical Image Computing and Computer Assisted Intervention – MICCAI 2021. Lecture Notes in Computer Science, vol. 12903, pp. 201–210. Springer, Cham (2021). https://doi.org/10.1007/978-3-030-87199-4_19
8. Goodfellow, I., et al.: Generative adversarial nets. Adv. Neural. Inf. Process. Syst. (2014). https://doi.org/10.1145/3422622
9. Zhu, J.-Y., Park, T., Isola, P., Efros, A.-A.: Unpaired image-to-image translation using cycle-consistent adversarial networks. In: Proceedings of the IEEE International Conference on Computer Vision, pp. 2223–2232. IEEE (2017)
10. Chen, C., Dou, Q., Chen, H., Qin, J., Heng, P.-A.: Unsupervised bidirectional cross-modality adaptation via deeply synergistic image and feature alignment for medical image segmentation. IEEE Trans. Med. Imaging **39**(7), 2494–2505 (2020)
11. Gu, R., Zhang, J., Huang, R., Lei, W., Wang, G., Zhang, S.: Domain composition and attention for unseen-domain generalizable medical image segmentation. In: de Bruijne, M., et al. (eds.) Medical Image Computing and Computer Assisted Intervention – MICCAI 2021. Lecture Notes in Computer Science, vol. 12903, pp. 241–250. Springer, Cham (2021). https://doi.org/10.1007/978-3-030-87199-4_23
12. Geirhos, R., Rubisch, P., Michaelis, C., Bethge, M., Wichmann, F.A., Brendel, W.: Imagenet-trained CNNs are biased towards texture; increasing shape bias improves accuracy and robustness. In: International Conference on Learning Representations, pp. 1–22 (2019)
13. Pham, D.-D., Dovletov, G., Pauli, J.: Liver segmentation in CT with MRI data: zero-shot domain adaptation by contour extraction and shape priors. In: 2020 IEEE 17th International Symposium on Biomedical Imaging (ISBI), pp. 1538–1542. IEEE (2020)
14. Lu, X., Wu, J., Ren, X., et al.: The study and application of the improved re gion growing algorithm for liver segmentation. Optik **125**(9), 2142–2147 (2014)

15. Liao, M., et al.: Automatic liver segmentation from abdominal CT volumes using graph cuts and border marching. Comput. Methods Programs Biomed. **143**, 1–12 (2017)
16. CHAOS - Combined (CT-MR) Healthy Abdominal Organ Segmentation. https://chaos.grand-challenge.org/Data/. Accessed 4 Apr 2021
17. LiTS-Liver tumor segmentation challenge. https://competitions.codalab.org/competitions/17094. Accessed 27 Apr 2018
18. Hatamizadeh, A., et al.: UNETR: transformers for 3D medical image segmentation. In: Proceedings of the IEEE/CVF Winter Conference on Applications of Computer Vision, pp. 574–584. IEEE (2022)

Using Guided Self-Attention with Local Information for Polyp Segmentation

Linghan Cai[1], Meijing Wu[2], Lijiang Chen[1(✉)], Wenpei Bai[2], Min Yang[2], Shuchang Lyu[1], and Qi Zhao[1]

[1] Institute of Electronic Information Engineering, Beihang University, Beijing, China
chenlijiang@buaa.edu.cn
[2] Department of Gynecology and Obstetrics, Beijing Shijitan Hospital, Capital Medical University, Beijing, China

Abstract. Automatic and precise polyp segmentation is crucial for the early diagnosis of colorectal cancer. Existing polyp segmentation methods are mostly based on convolutional neural networks (CNNs), which usually utilize the global features to enhance local features through well-designed modules, thereby dealing with the diversity of polyps. Although CNN-based methods achieve impressive results, they are powerless to model explicit long-range relations, which limits their performance. Different from CNN, Transformer has a strong capability of modeling long-range relations owing to self-attention. However, self-attention always spreads attention to unexpected regions and the Transformer's ability of local feature extraction is insufficient, resulting in inaccurate localization and fuzzy boundary. To address these issues, we propose PPFormer for accurate polyp segmentation. Specifically, we first adopt a shallow CNN encoder and a deep Transformer encoder to extract rich features. In the decoder, we present the PP-guided self-attention that uses prediction maps to guide self-attention to focus on the hard regions so as to enhance the model's perception of polyp boundary. Meanwhile, the Local-to-Global mechanism is designed to encourage the Transformer to capture more information in the local-window for better polyp localization. Extensive experiments on five challenging datasets show that PPFormer outperforms other advanced methods and achieves state-of-the-art results with six metrics, i.e. mean Dice and mean IoU.

Keywords: Colorectal cancer · Polyp segmentation · Transformer · Local-to-Global mechanism · PP-guided self-attention

1 Introduction

Colorectal cancer (CRC) is the third most common malignancy in the world and induces nearly 1 million deaths in 2020 [16]. Colorectal polyps are believed the precursors for CRCs [9], so the early detection of polyps is crucial to improving

---

L. Cai and M. Wu—Contributed equally to this work.

L. Wang et al. (Eds.): MICCAI 2022, LNCS 13434, pp. 629–638, 2022.
https://doi.org/10.1007/978-3-031-16440-8_60

the five-year survival rate of patients. Although colonoscopy can provide information on the appearance and localization of polyps, it requires expensive labor resources and remains a high miss-detection rate. Hence, it is of great practical significance to realize automatic and precise polyp segmentation.

Polyp segmentation has been significantly prospered by recent advances in convolutional neural networks (CNNs). FCN [1] replaces the fully connected layers with convolutional layers in the neural network, achieving end-to-end polyp segmentation. To improve detail retention, UNet [13] adopts a symmetric encoder-decoder structure with skip-connections to restore feature maps, and has become a basic framework for biomedical image segmentation [9,24,25]. Although these networks achieve impressive results, CNN-based approaches are powerless to model explicit long-range relations due to the local receptive fields of convolution operation, which limits their performance. To tackle the problem, some methods [12,22] adopt well-designed modules to enhance long-range relations. PraNet [7] aggregates high-level features to generate global maps and utilizes them to establish the relationship between areas and boundaries through the reverse attention modules. Nevertheless, these methods do not pay attention to the process of obtaining global features, which leads to misclassification.

On the other hand, Transformer, an architecture that consists of self-attention has obtained excellent performance in many computer vision tasks [4, 8]. Compared with CNN-based methods, TransUNet [3], TransFuse [23] have made great progress in biomedical image segmentation by utilizing Transformer's long-range modeling ability. But these methods still have weaknesses in polyp segmentation: (1) In the self-attention mechanism, each pixel directly acts on the other pixels. This procedure may cause the misguided spread of attention from the discriminative regions to unexpected areas, resulting in inaccurate localization. Figure 1 shows an example. (2) Some Transformer-based methods [19,21] frequently adopt down-sampling operations to reduce memory and computation complexity. The loss of local information in the process leads to the fuzzy boundary.

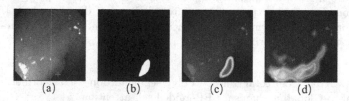

(a)   (b)   (c)   (d)

Fig. 1. Illustration of attention maps. (a) is the input image, the interesting pixel is marked by '+'. (b) is the ground truth. (c) shows the attention map learned by PP-guided self-attention. (d) presents the attention map learned by vanilla self-attention.

To this end, we propose PPFormer to exploit Transformer in polyp segmentation task. PPFormer is an encoder-decoder framework, in which the encoder consists of a deep Transformer branch and a shallow CNN branch so as to extract rich features. For the problem of self-attention, we present the PP-guided

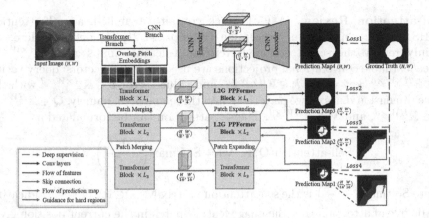

Fig. 2. Overview of the proposed PPFormer. $(\frac{H}{n}, \frac{W}{n})$ represents the size of image or feature map. L_i denotes the number of Transformer blocks. Patch Merging uses a convolutional layer to merge image patches and increase feature dimension. Patch Expanding up-samples patches and decreases their feature dimension.

self-attention that uses prediction maps to guide self-attention to focus on the hard regions. To localize polyp accurately, we introduce the Local-to-Global (L2G) mechanism to make the Transformer obtain more local features. Moreover, the L2G mechanism can facilitate the boundary localization of PP-guided self-attention. In summary, our contributions mainly include: (1) We propose PPFormer for accurate polyp segmentation, which takes advantage of the Transformer's long-range modeling ability and CNN's local feature extraction. (2) We present the PP-guided self-attention to enhance the model's perception of polyp boundary. (3) L2G mechanism is designed to capture more information in the local-window for better polyp localization. (4) Extensive experiments demonstrate that PPFormer outperforms other advanced polyp segmentation methods, and achieves state-of-the-art (SOTA) results on five challenging datasets.

2   Method

Overall, PPFormer is an encoder-decoder architecture and generates prediction maps at different levels. As shown in Fig. 2, PPFormer's encoder consists of two parallel branches: (1) Transformer encoder for global feature extraction. We adopt Convolution Vision Transformer (CvT) [21] to build Transformer encoder. Thanks to CvT's removal of position encoding, our model supports input images of various sizes. (2) CNN encoder is used to obtain more low-level features for better pixel-level segmentation. We adopt the first two blocks of VGG-16 [15] to build it. PPFormer's decoder includes two stages: (1) In the first stage, the model predicts coarse results with high-level features and uses the prediction maps to guide self-attention in the L2G PPFormer blocks. (2) In the second stage, the low-level features from the CNN encoder are applied to refine the segmentation results. The details of each module will be introduced as follows.

Self-attention Review. A CvT block contains a multi-head self-attention (MHSA) and a multi-layer perception (refer to [4,21] for details). Here, we mainly review the self-attention. Given input feature maps $x \in \mathbb{R}^{H \times W \times C}$, three learnable convolutional projections are used to derive vectors: query vector $q \in \mathbb{R}^{H \times W \times d}$, key vector $k \in \mathbb{R}^{H \times W \times d}$, and value vector $v \in \mathbb{R}^{H \times W \times d}$ with the same dimension d. Next, we pack them into three matrices, namely, $\mathbf{Q} \in \mathbb{R}^{HW \times d}$, $\mathbf{K} \in \mathbb{R}^{HW \times d}$, and $\mathbf{V} \in \mathbb{R}^{HW \times d}$. The self-attention can be formulated as:

$$\text{Self-attention}(\mathbf{Q}, \mathbf{K}, \mathbf{V}) = \text{Softmax}\left(\frac{\mathbf{Q}\mathbf{K}^T}{\sqrt{d}}\right)\mathbf{V} \tag{1}$$

where $\text{Softmax}\left(\frac{\mathbf{Q}\mathbf{K}^T}{\sqrt{d}}\right)$ is the self-attention matrix $\mathbf{M}_{\text{SA}} \in \mathbb{R}^{HW \times HW}$, indicating the degree of attention that the image feature patch in the current position gives other patches. As the extension of self-attention, MHSA divides x into h groups and merges the results of self-attention in each group to obtain the output.

PP-Guided Self-Attention. We use high-level features to generate prediction maps in low resolutions (the sigmoid function is not used now). The patch-level segmentation result scores each image patch, a high score in absolute value represents the patch is likely to belong to the foreground (polyp) or background. On the contrary, a low score indicates that the attribution of the patch is difficult to determine, which frequently occurs on the boundary of a polyp. Therefore, guidance-attention matrix $\mathbf{M}_{\text{GA}}$ is proposed to guide these patches:

$$\mathbf{M}_{\text{GA}} = \alpha \left(\mathbf{P}_f \mathbf{P}_f^T \odot \mathbf{P}_f \mathbf{P}_f^T\right) + 1 \tag{2}$$

where $\mathbf{P}_f \in \mathbb{R}^{HW \times 1}$ is the resized and flattened prediction map, $\| \odot \|$ represents the element-wise product. α indicates the importance of the guidance-attention to self-attention and is set as 1e-2 in our experiments. $\mathbf{M}_{\text{GA}} \in \mathbb{R}^{HW \times HW}$ focuses on the uncertain regions and requires them to establish relations with the high-score patches rather than other uncertain regions so as to determine their attribution. Then, we fuse $\mathbf{M}_{\text{GA}}$ and $\mathbf{M}_{\text{SA}}$ to calculate PP-guided self-attention:

$$\text{PP-Self-attention}(\mathbf{Q}, \mathbf{K}, \mathbf{V}, \mathbf{P}) = (\mathbf{M}_{\text{SA}} \odot \mathbf{M}_{\text{GA}})\mathbf{V} \tag{3}$$

Compared with vanilla self-attention, PP-guided self-attention utilizes the prediction map as guidance information, making the model focus on the hard regions. As shown in the PP-guided self-attention of Fig. 3, our method determines clear boundaries. Because of the $\mathbf{P}_f \mathbf{P}_f^T$ operation in Eq. 2, we name the module PP-guided self-attention and the block PPFormer block.

Local-to-Global Mechanism. To reduce memory and computation complexity, CvT adopts squeezed convolutional projections to obtain k and v. However, they are not suitable for use in the decoder due to the loss of local information. Hence, we design the L2G mechanism to capture more information in the local-window with low memory usage.

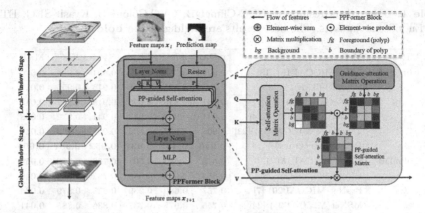

Fig. 3. The structure of the L2G PPFormer block. The red boxes in the PP-guided self-attention represent the relationship between boundaries and target regions. (Color figure online)

Figure 3 illustrates the L2G mechanism in a L2G PPFormer block, which consists of a local-window stage and a global-window stage. In the former stage, we split the input feature maps $x \in \mathbb{R}^{H \times W \times C}$ into $s \times s$ non-overlapping windows: $x \rightarrow \{x_1, x_2, \dots, x_{s \times s}\}$, where each window is of size $\frac{H}{s} \times \frac{W}{s} \times C$, s is the stride of the global-window stage's squeezed convolutional projections. Next, we perform the PPFormer block within each local-window independently. Importantly, we use convolutional projections with stride=1 in the local-window stage to retain more local features for better polyp localization. In the global-window stage, another PPFormer block is used to model long-range relations.

Loss Function. PPFormer is trained end-to-end with weighted IoU loss and binary cross-entropy (BCE) loss, $\mathcal{L} = \mathcal{L}_{\text{IoU}}^{w} + \mathcal{L}_{\text{BCE}}^{w}$. As defined in [20], we increase the weight of boundary pixels, and the effectiveness has been validated in their work. Deep supervision is applied for each prediction map {e.g. $\mathbf{P}_1$, $\mathbf{P}_2$, $\mathbf{P}_3$ and $\mathbf{P}_4$} in training. We use the sigmoid function to activate prediction maps {e.g. $\mathbf{P}_{s1}$, $\mathbf{P}_{s2}$, $\mathbf{P}_{s3}$, and $\mathbf{P}_{s4}$} and up-sample them to the same size as the ground truth $\mathbf{GT}$. Thus, the total loss can be formulated as: $\mathcal{L}_{total} = \sum_{i=1}^{i=4} \mathcal{L}(\mathbf{GT}, \mathbf{P}_{si})$.

3 Experiments

3.1 Experiments on Polyp Segmentation

Datasets and Evaluation Metrics. We evaluate PPFormer on five public polyp segmentation datasets: CVC-ClinicDB [2], CVC-ColonDB [17], Kvasir-SEG [10], ETIS [14] and EndoScene [18]. We follow the same training strategy as in [7,24]: the training set has 1450 images, including 550 samples from CVC-ClinicDB and 900 samples from Kvasir-SEG. A total of 798 images from the above two seen datasets and the other three unseen datasets are used for testing.

Table 1. Comparison results on CVC-ClinicDB, CVC-ColonDB, Kvasir-SEG, ETIS and EndoScene datasets. The best results are highlighted in **bold**.

Datasets	Methods	mDice	mIoU	F_β^w	S_α	E_ϕ^{max}	MAE
ClinicDB	UNet(MICCAI'15) [13]	0.823	0.755	0.812	0.891	0.954	0.020
	UNet++(TMI'19) [25]	0.885	0.825	0.878	0.915	0.955	0.017
	PraNet(MICCAI'20) [7]	0.901	0.845	0.896	0.919	0.961	0.015
	MSNet(MICCAI'21) [24]	0.921	0.879	0.914	0.941	0.972	0.008
	TransFuse(MICCAI'21) [23]	0.908	0.857	0.902	0.935	0.963	0.011
	PPFormer(Ours)	**0.946**	**0.902**	**0.937**	**0.952**	**0.987**	**0.006**
ColonDB	UNet(MICCAI'15) [13]	0.515	0.453	0.501	0.709	0.780	0.059
	UNet++(TMI'19) [25]	0.653	0.578	0.633	0.782	0.792	0.046
	PraNet(MICCAI'20) [7]	0.757	0.680	0.739	0.835	0.879	0.034
	MSNet(MICCAI'21) [24]	0.755	0.678	0.737	0.836	0.883	0.041
	TransFuse(MICCAI'21) [23]	0.790	0.710	0.756	0.858	0.893	**0.033**
	PPFormer(Ours)	**0.832**	**0.756**	**0.771**	**0.877**	**0.924**	**0.033**
Kvasir	UNet(MICCAI'15) [13]	0.817	0.753	0.789	0.857	0.899	0.051
	UNet++(TMI'19) [25]	0.838	0.765	0.802	0.864	0.902	0.048
	PraNet(MICCAI'20) [7]	0.896	0.840	0.886	0.909	0.939	0.029
	MSNet(MICCAI'21) [24]	0.907	0.862	0.893	0.922	0.944	0.028
	TransFuse(MICCAI'21) [23]	0.915	0.860	0.906	0.919	0.958	**0.023**
	PPFormer(Ours)	**0.930**	**0.879**	**0.921**	**0.929**	**0.963**	**0.023**
ETIS	UNet(MICCAI'15) [13]	0.407	0.344	0.371	0.680	0.644	0.036
	UNet++(TMI'19) [25]	0.506	0.438	0.722	0.696	0.722	0.030
	PraNet(MICCAI'20) [7]	0.733	0.665	0.696	0.827	0.868	0.016
	MSNet(MICCAI'21) [24]	0.719	0.664	0.678	0.840	0.830	0.020
	TransFuse(MICCAI'21) [23]	0.748	0.657	0.695	0.850	0.882	0.018
	PPFormer(Ours)	**0.791**	**0.706**	**0.749**	**0.876**	**0.907**	**0.013**
EndoScene	UNet(MICCAI'15) [13]	0.712	0.631	0.675	0.838	0.867	0.022
	UNet++(TMI'19) [25]	0.794	0.718	0.776	0.870	0.894	0.013
	PraNet(MICCAI'20) [7]	0.868	0.795	0.839	0.911	0.947	0.009
	MSNet(MICCAI'21) [24]	0.869	0.807	0.849	0.925	0.943	0.010
	TransFuse(MICCAI'21) [23]	0.893	0.825	0.872	0.934	0.965	0.007
	PPFormer(Ours)	**0.919**	**0.857**	**0.903**	**0.942**	**0.979**	**0.005**

We adopt six metrics for quantitative evaluation: mean Dice score (mDice), mean IoU score (mIoU), mean absolute error (MAE), weighted F_β-measure (F_β^w) [11], enhanced-alignment measure (E_ϕ^{max}) [6], and structure measure (S_α) [5]. Among these evaluation metrics, the lower score is better for MAE and the higher score is better for the others.

Implementation Details. Our model is implemented based on PyTorch framework and trained for 60 epochs with a batch size of 8 on an NVIDIA GeForce RTX 3090 GPU. The resolution of each image is resized to 352×352, we employ random scaling, horizontal flip, and random rotation to augment data. Adam optimization algorithm is used to optimize the trainable parameters with a

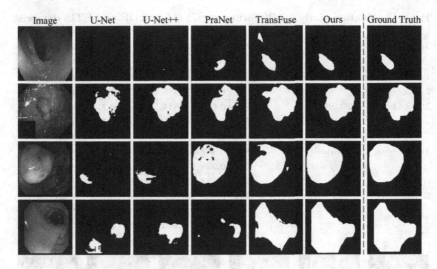

Fig. 4. Qualitative results of different methods.

momentum beta1 of 0.5, a momentum beta2 of 0.999, and a learning rate of 5e-5. The threshold of 0.5 is set for $\mathbf{P}_{s4}$ to obtain the final segmentation results.

Quantitative and Qualitative Evaluation. We compare our PPFormer with five advanced methods, including UNet [13], UNet++ [25], PraNet [7], MSNet [24] and TransFuse [23]. To ensure fairness, we obtain the experimental results in their papers or rerun their released code under the same training strategy.

Table 1 illustrates the quantitative results, in which PPFormer outperforms other approaches and achieves SOTA results on five datasets. In particular, PPFormer achieves significant improvements on CVC-ColonDB and ETIS with a gain of 4.6% and 4.1% in mIoU, respectively. Figure 4 provides the visible results of different methods. It can be seen that our proposed method has better performance in localizing and segmenting polyps of different sizes and various shapes.

3.2 Ablation Study

To evaluate the effectiveness of each module in PPFormer, we design the ablation experiments on the seen and unseen datasets, the quantitative and qualitative results are shown in Table 2 and Fig. 5, respectively. Backbone represents the basic combination of the Transformer branch and CNN branch. Firstly, we remove the CNN encoder branch and use $\mathbf{P}_{s3}$ as result. The mDice decreases from 0.916 to 0.901 and S_{α} decreases from 0.923 to 0.904 on CVC-ClincDB. From Table 2, we find that the results of $\mathbf{P}_{s4}$ are consistently better than $\mathbf{P}_{s3}$ in the settings 3, 4, and 5, which note the low-level features from CNN are effective

Table 2. Ablation study for PPFormer on CVC-ClinicDB and ETIS datasets.

Settings	P_{si}	ClinicDB (seen)			ETIS (unseen)		
		mDice	mIoU	S_α	mDice	mIoU	S_α
1. Only Transformer encoder branch	P_{s3}	0.901	0.827	0.904	0.693	0.611	0.785
2. Backbone	P_{s4}	0.916	0.831	0.923	0.715	0.626	0.827
3. Backbone + L2G Block	P_{s1}	0.915	0.834	0.924	0.712	0.624	0.825
	P_{s3}	0.931	0.865	0.936	0.719	0.630	0.838
	P_{s4}	0.933	0.879	0.938	0.723	0.633	0.841
4. Backbone + PPFormer Block	P_{s1}	0.907	0.829	0.914	0.717	0.635	0.836
	P_{s3}	0.928	0.875	0.932	0.755	0.677	0.857
	P_{s4}	0.934	0.893	0.941	0.761	0.684	0.862
5. Backbone + L2G PPFormer Block	P_{s1}	0.915	0.854	0.918	0.713	0.627	0.835
	P_{s3}	0.940	0.898	0.945	0.784	0.704	0.871
	P_{s4}	**0.946**	**0.902**	**0.952**	**0.791**	**0.706**	**0.876**

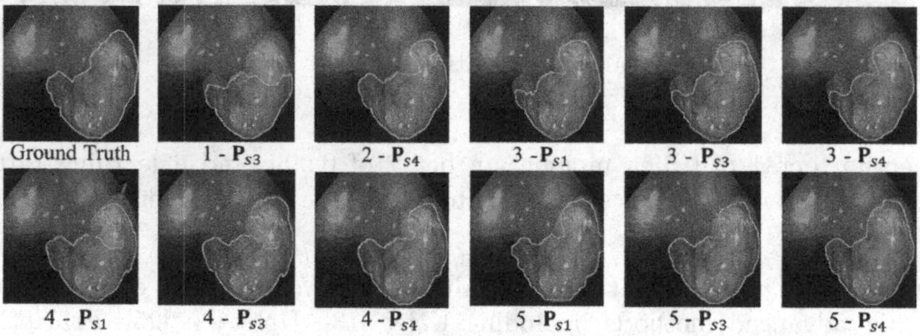

Fig. 5. Visual comparison of ablation study. The numbers correspond to the settings in Table 2. The pink area represents differences between the results and ground truth. (Color figure online)

to improve segmentation performance. We further investigate the effectiveness of the L2G mechanism and the PP-Guided self-attention. Table 2 shows that they are beneficial for polyp segmentation and the latter module has better performance on the unseen dataset. When we adopt the L2G PPFormer block in the backbone, the mDice significantly improves with a gain of 3.0% and 7.6% on CVC-ClinicDB and ETIS, respectively. Besides, Fig. 5 intuitively displays the effectiveness of each module, it can be seen that the L2G mechanism can capture more local information, and PP-guided self-attention can enhance the model's perception of hard regions so as to adjust the segmentation results. Finally, the combination of these modules can achieve accurate polyp segmentation.

4   Conclusion

In this paper, we propose a novel architecture PPFormer for automatic polyp segmentation. Specifically, we design the PP-guided self-attention to enhance the model's perception of polyp boundary. The L2G mechanism is proposed to improve Transformer's attention to local information. Extensive experiments demonstrate that PPFormer outperforms other advanced methods and achieves SOTA results on five challenging datasets, especially on unseen datasets. Moreover, PP-guided self-attention and L2G mechanism are flexible modules, we hope our work can contribute to the vision community to explore more impressive methods in other tasks such as instance segmentation or cross-domain learning.

Acknowledgements. This project was partly supported by the National Natural Science Foundation of China (Grant No. 62072021), the Fundamental Research Funds for the Central Universities (Grant No. YWF-22-L-532), and the Beijing Hospitals Authority'Ascent Plan (Grant No. DFL20190701).

References

1. Akbari, M., et al.: Polyp segmentation in colonoscopy images using fully convolutional network. In: 2018 40th Annual International Conference of the IEEE Engineering in Medicine and Biology Society (EMBC), pp. 69–72. IEEE (2018)
2. Bernal, J., Sánchez, F.J., Fernández-Esparrach, G., Gil, D., Rodríguez, C., Vilariño, F.: WM-DOVA maps for accurate polyp highlighting in colonoscopy: validation vs. saliency maps from physicians. Comput. Med. Imaging Graph. **43**, 99–111 (2015)
3. Chen, J., et al.: Transunet: Transformers make strong encoders for medical image segmentation. arXiv preprint arXiv:2102.04306 (2021)
4. Dosovitskiy, A., et al.: An image is worth 16 × 16 words: transformers for image recognition at scale. In: ICLR (2021)
5. Fan, D.P., Cheng, M.M., Liu, Y., Li, T., Borji, A.: Structure-measure: a new way to evaluate foreground maps. In: Proceedings of the IEEE International Conference on Computer Vision, pp. 4548–4557 (2017)
6. Fan, D.P., Gong, C., Cao, Y., Ren, B., Cheng, M.M., Borji, A.: Enhanced-alignment measure for binary foreground map evaluation. In: Proceedings of the Twenty-Seventh International Joint Conference on Artificial Intelligence, IJCAI-18, pp. 698–704. International Joint Conferences on Artificial Intelligence Organization (2018)
7. Fan, D.-P., et al.: PraNet: parallel reverse attention network for polyp segmentation. In: Martel, A.L., et al. (eds.) MICCAI 2020. LNCS, vol. 12266, pp. 263–273. Springer, Cham (2020). https://doi.org/10.1007/978-3-030-59725-2_26
8. Han, K., et al.: A survey on vision transformer. IEEE Trans. Pattern Anal. Mach. Intell. (2022)
9. Jha, D., et al.: A comprehensive study on colorectal polyp segmentation with resunet++, conditional random field and test-time augmentation. IEEE J. Biomed. Health Inf. **25**(6), 2029–2040 (2021)
10. Jha, D., et al.: Kvasir-SEG: a segmented polyp dataset. In: Ro, Y.M., et al. (eds.) MMM 2020. LNCS, vol. 11962, pp. 451–462. Springer, Cham (2020). https://doi.org/10.1007/978-3-030-37734-2_37
11. Margolin, R., Zelnik-Manor, L., Tal, A.: How to evaluate foreground maps? In: Proceedings of the IEEE Conference on Computer Vision and Pattern Recognition, pp. 248–255 (2014)

12. Nguyen, T.-C., Nguyen, T.-P., Diep, G.-H., Tran-Dinh, A.-H., Nguyen, T.V., Tran, M.-T.: CCBANet: cascading context and balancing attention for polyp segmentation. In: de Bruijne, M., et al. (eds.) MICCAI 2021. LNCS, vol. 12901, pp. 633–643. Springer, Cham (2021). https://doi.org/10.1007/978-3-030-87193-2_60

13. Ronneberger, O., Fischer, P., Brox, T.: U-net: convolutional networks for biomedical image segmentation. In: Navab, N., Hornegger, J., Wells, W.M., Frangi, A.F. (eds.) MICCAI 2015. LNCS, vol. 9351, pp. 234–241. Springer, Cham (2015). https://doi.org/10.1007/978-3-319-24574-4_28

14. Silva, J., Histace, A., Romain, O., Dray, X., Granado, B.: Toward embedded detection of polyps in WCE images for early diagnosis of colorectal cancer. Int. J. Comput. Assist. Radiol. Surg. 9(2), 283–293 (2014)

15. Simonyan, K., Zisserman, A.: Very deep convolutional networks for large-scale image recognition. In: ICLR (2015)

16. Sung, H., Ferlay, J., Siegel, R.L., Laversanne, M., Soerjomataram, I., Jemal, A., Bray, F.: Global cancer statistics 2020: GLOBOCAN estimates of incidence and mortality worldwide for 36 cancers in 185 countries. CA: A Cancer J. Clin. 71(3), 209–249 (2021)

17. Tajbakhsh, N., Gurudu, S.R., Liang, J.: Automated polyp detection in colonoscopy videos using shape and context information. IEEE Trans. Med. Imaging 35(2), 630–644 (2015). https://doi.org/10.1109/TMI.2015.2487997

18. Vázquez, D., et al.: A benchmark for endoluminal scene segmentation of colonoscopy images. J. Healthc. Eng. 2017 (2017)

19. Wang, W., et al.: Pvtv 2: improved baselines with pyramid vision transformer. Comput. Vis. Media 8(3), 1–10 (2022)

20. Wei, J., Wang, S., Huang, Q.: F^{3}net: fusion, feedback and focus for salient object detection. In: Proceedings of the AAAI Conference on Artificial Intelligence, vol. 34, pp. 12321–12328 (2020)

21. Wu, H., et al.: CVT: introducing convolutions to vision transformers. In: Proceedings of the IEEE/CVF International Conference on Computer Vision, pp. 22–31 (2021)

22. Zhang, R., Li, G., Li, Z., Cui, S., Qian, D., Yu, Y.: Adaptive context selection for polyp segmentation. In: Martel, A.L., et al. (eds.) MICCAI 2020. LNCS, vol. 12266, pp. 253–262. Springer, Cham (2020). https://doi.org/10.1007/978-3-030-59725-2_25

23. Zhang, Y., Liu, H., Hu, Q.: TransFuse: fusing transformers and CNNs for medical image segmentation. In: de Bruijne, M., et al. (eds.) MICCAI 2021. LNCS, vol. 12901, pp. 14–24. Springer, Cham (2021). https://doi.org/10.1007/978-3-030-87193-2_2

24. Zhao, X., Zhang, L., Lu, H.: Automatic polyp segmentation via multi-scale subtraction network. In: de Bruijne, M., et al. (eds.) MICCAI 2021. LNCS, vol. 12901, pp. 120–130. Springer, Cham (2021). https://doi.org/10.1007/978-3-030-87193-2_12

25. Zhou, Z., Siddiquee, M.M.R., Tajbakhsh, N., Liang, J.: Unet++: redesigning skip connections to exploit multiscale features in image segmentation. IEEE Trans. Med. Imaging 39(6), 1856–1867 (2019). https://doi.org/10.1109/TMI.2019.2959609

Momentum Contrastive Voxel-Wise Representation Learning for Semi-supervised Volumetric Medical Image Segmentation

Chenyu You[1(✉)], Ruihan Zhao[2], Lawrence H. Staib[1,3,4], and James S. Duncan[1,3,4]

[1] Electrical Engineering, Yale University, New Haven, CT, USA
chenyu.you@yale.edu
[2] Electrical and Computer Engineering, The University of Texas at Austin, Austin, TX, USA
[3] Radiology and Biomedical Imaging, Yale School of Medicine, New Haven, CT, USA
[4] Biomedical Engineering, Yale University, New Haven, CT, USA

Abstract. Contrastive learning (CL) aims to learn useful representation without relying on expert annotations in the context of medical image segmentation. Existing approaches mainly contrast a single positive vector (*i.e.*, an augmentation of the same image) against a set of negatives within the entire remainder of the batch by simply mapping all input features into the same constant vector. Despite the impressive empirical performance, those methods have the following shortcomings: (1) it remains a formidable challenge to prevent the collapsing problems to trivial solutions; and (2) we argue that not all voxels within the same image are equally positive since there exist the dissimilar anatomical structures with the same image. In this work, we present a novel **C**ontrastive **V**oxel-wise **R**epresentation **L**earning (CVRL) method to effectively learn low-level and high-level features by capturing 3D spatial context and rich anatomical information along both the feature and the batch dimensions. Specifically, we first introduce a novel CL strategy to ensure feature diversity promotion among the 3D representation dimensions. We train the framework through bi-level contrastive optimization (*i.e.*, low-level and high-level) on 3D images. Experiments on two benchmark datasets and different labeled settings demonstrate the superiority of our proposed framework. More importantly, we also prove that our method inherits the benefit of hardness-aware property from the standard CL approaches.

Keywords: Contrastive learning · Semi-supervised learning · Medical image segmentation

Supplementary Information The online version contains supplementary material available at https://doi.org/10.1007/978-3-031-16440-8_61.

1   Introduction

Learning from just a few labeled examples while leveraging a large amount of unlabeled data is a long-standing pursuit in the machine learning community, which is especially crucial for the medical imaging domain. Generating reliable manual annotations of 3D imaging data at scale is expensive, time-consuming, and may require domain-specific expertise. Due to privacy concerns, another challenge in medical imaging is relatively small training datasets.

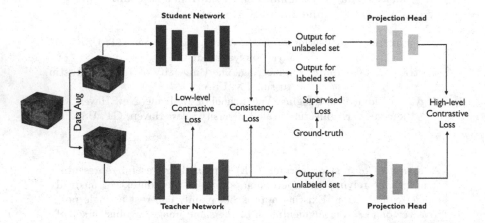

Fig. 1. Overview of CVRL architecture. We learn rich dense voxel-wise representations by exploiting high-level context between voxels and volumetric regions and low-level correlations in both batch and feature dimensions in a semi-supervised manner.

In the medical imaging domain, substantial efforts [1,2,4,13,16,19,22,30–33,35,36] have been devoted to incorporating unlabeled data to improve network performance due to the limited 3D data and annotations. The most common training techniques are adversarial learning and consistency loss as regularization terms to encourage unsupervised mapping. Recently, contrastive learning (CL) has drawn considerable attention to learning useful representations without expert supervision and shown remarkable performance in the medical image analysis domain [3,8,34]. The central idea [3,5,6,14,15,18,25,28,29] is to learn powerful representations invariant to data augmentations that maximize the agreement between instance embeddings from different augmentations of the same images. The major stream of subsequent work focuses on the choice of dissimilar pairs, which determine the quality of learned representations. The loss function used to contrast is chosen from several options, such as InfoNCE [20], Triplet [27], and so on. However, while remarkable, those methods assume that the repulsive effect of negatives can avoid collapsing along all dimensions to trivial solutions by explicitly using positive and negative pairs in the loss function. However, it has been empirically observed that such design may still collapse along certain dimensions (*i.e.*, *dimensional collapse*), as noted in [9,26]. Such scenarios can happen in predefined augmentations, which usually lead to

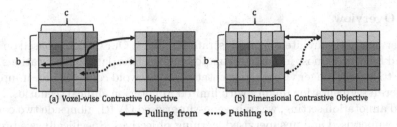

Fig. 2. Comparison of (a) Voxel-wise Contrastive Objective (*i.e.*, batch dimension), and (b) Dimensional Contrastive Objective (*i.e.*, feature dimension). b denotes batch size and c is the feature dimension.

better performance due to the inter-instance constraints while usually ignoring anatomically feasibility in the transformation.

In this paper, we present CVRL, a novel end-to-end semi-supervised framework to learn high-level contexts and local-level features in both the batch and the feature directions for 3D medical image segmentation. One **blessing** comes from the recent finding [10] in the context of image classification. The authors note that applying strong augmentation along the feature dimension may result in the dimensional collapse in CL. In other words, the augmented images are not "standardized" well and may easily admits collapsed solutions (*e.g.*, generating the same vector for all 3D scans), making it challenging or even infeasible in real-world clinical practice. Three **key aspects** distinguish from the recent success [3]. First, the standard CL encourages instance-level representation diversity within the batch. By contrast, we propose an anatomy-informed regularization among the feature dimension, as an intra-instance constraint to encourage feature diversity for its improved robustness, as illustrated in Fig. 2. This design is appealing: (1) our idea is rather plug-and-play and can be easily compatible with existing inter-instance constraints; and (2) it inherits the strength of CL in learning useful representations to improve the feature spaces' discriminative capability (See Appendix). Second, we propose to perform low-level contrast in a lower-dimensional 3D subspace, which could capture rich anatomic information; and (3) existing methods mainly perform local contrast in the image-level space, which may usually lead to sub-optimal segmentation quality due to the lack of spatial information. In contrast, if the proposed method can learn more generic representation from 3D context, it will unlock the appealing prospect of 3D nature in medical images (*i.e.*, 3D volumetric scans). We propose an additional high-level contrast to exploit distinctive features in the embedding feature space by designing a new 3D projection head to encode 3D features. We also theoretically show our dimensional contrastive learning inherits the hardness-aware property in Appendix. The results demonstrate that our segmentation network outperforms the state-of-the-art methods on two benchmark datasets, and generates object segmentation with high-quality global shapes.

1.1   Overview

An overview of the architecture is illustrated in Fig. 1. Our CVRL is based on GCL [3], and follows its most important components such as data augmentations. Our goal is to learn stronger visual representations that avoid collapsing for improving the overall segmentation quality with limited annotation clinical scenarios. In the limited annotation setting, we train semi-supervised CVRL alongside two components - supervised and unsupervised learning objectives. Specifically, we propose a novel voxel-wise representation learning algorithm to learn low-level and high-level representations from 3D unlabeled data by regularizing the embedding space and exploring the geometric and spatial context of training voxels.

In our problem setting, we consider a set of training data (3D images) including N labeled data and M unlabeled data, where $N \ll M$. For simplicity of exposition, we denote limited label data as $\mathcal{D}_l = \{(\mathbf{x}_i, y_i)\}_{i=1}^N$, and abundant unlabeled data as $\mathcal{D}_u = \{(\mathbf{x}_i)\}_{i=N+1}^{N+M}$, where $\mathbf{x}_i \in \mathbb{R}^{H \times W \times D}$ are volume inputs, and $y_i \in \{0,1\}^{H \times W \times D}$ are ground-truth labels. Specifically, we adopt V-Net [35] as the network backbone $F(\cdot)$, which consists of an encoder network and a decoder network. To maximize mutual information between latent representations, we design a projection head, that comprises one encoder network which share the similar architecture to the prior encoder network.

1.2   Unsupervised Contrastive Learning

A key component of CVRL is the ability to capture rich voxel-wise representations of high dimensional data by contrastive distillation. CVRL trains on the contrastive objective as an auxiliary loss during the volume batch updates. We utilize two contrastive learning objectives: (i) voxel-wise contrastive objective (ii) dimensional contrastive objective, each applied on a low-level feature and a high-level feature. The resulting combined training objective greatly improves the quality of learned representations.

First we establish some notations which will assist in explaining our approach. We denote a batch of input image $x_1 \cdots x_b$, the teacher encoder network f, the student encoder network g and a set of data augmentation transformations T (e.g. random flipping, random rotation, random brightness, random contrast, random zooming, cube rearrangement and cube rotation). Here f and g use the same encoder architecture $e(\cdot)$ as introduced in Sect. 1.1, but with different parameters. $z^f \in \mathbb{R}^{h \times w \times d \times c} = f(t(x)))$ is a feature volume produced by the student encoder, whereas $z^g = g(t'(x))$ is the corresponding feature volume produced by the teacher encoder, under a different random transformation $t' \neq t$.

Voxel-Wise Contrastive Objective. Using standard contrastive learning, we encourage the feature extractor to produce representations that are invariant under data augmentations. On the other hand, features should still preserve locality: different voxels in a feature volume should contain their unique information. Specifically, as the learned feature volumes are divided into slices, we pull the pairs of voxels that come from two augmentations of the same image closer; voxels at different locations or from different images are pushed away. To learn a feature extractor that unlocks the desired properties, we use InfoNCE loss [20]:

$$\mathcal{L}_q = -\log \frac{\exp(q \cdot k_+/\tau)}{\exp(q \cdot k_+/\tau) + \sum_{k\in\mathcal{K}_-} \exp(q \cdot k/\tau)} \qquad (1)$$

The query $q \in \mathbb{R}^c$ is a voxel in a student feature volume z^f, and key $k \in \mathbb{R}^c$ comes from the teacher feature volume z^g. In particular, k_+, the positive key, is the teacher feature voxel corresponding to the same location in the same image as the query q. The set $\mathcal{K}_-$ contains all other keys in the mini-batch, from different locations and different inputs. τ is a temperature hyper-parameter.

To obtain the voxel-wise contrastive loss, we take the average over the set of query voxels $\mathcal{Q}_v$ consisting of all feature voxels in the mini-batch of student feature volumes:

$$\mathcal{L}_v = \frac{1}{|\mathcal{Q}_v|} \sum_{q\in\mathcal{Q}_v} \mathcal{L}_q \qquad (2)$$

Dimensional Contrastive Objective. Motivated by recent findings on dimensional collapse in contrastive learning [9,10], we propose a dimensional contrastive objective to encourage different dimensions/channels in the feature voxels to contain diverse information. Given a batch of student feature volumes of shape $b{\times}h{\times}w{\times}d{\times}c$, we group the first 4 dimensions to obtain a set of dimensional queries: $q \in \mathcal{Q}_d \subset \mathbb{R}^{(b\times h\times w\times d)}$ where $|\mathcal{Q}_d| = c$, the number of channels in the feature volume. We define the $\mathcal{K} = \{k_+\} \cup \mathcal{K}_-$ in the same way, but using the corresponding batch feature volumes from the teacher encoder. In the dimensional contrastive setting, k_+ is defined as the key vector that corresponds to the same feature dimension as the query q. The dimensional contrastive loss is the average over all query dimensions:

$$\mathcal{L}_d = \frac{1}{c} \sum_{q\in\mathcal{Q}_d} \mathcal{L}_q \qquad (3)$$

We theoretically show our dimensional contrastive learning inherits the hardness-aware property in Appendix.

Consistency Loss $\mathcal{L}_c$. Recent work [11,24] show that using an exponential moving average (EMA) over network parameters is empirically shown to improve training stability and models' final performance. With this insight, we introduce an EMA teacher model with parameters θ as the moving-average of the parameters θ' from the original student network. Specifically, the architecture of EMA model follows the original model. At training step t, the update rule follows $\theta_t = m\theta_{t-1} + (1 - m)\theta'_t$, where $m \in [0, 1)$ is momentum parameter. On the unlabeled set, we perform different perturbation operations on the unlabeled input volume sample x^u, e.g. adding noise ϵ. To encourage training stability and performance improvements, we define consistency loss as:

$$\mathcal{L}^{\text{con}} = \mathcal{L}_{\text{mse}}\left(g\left(x^u; \theta, \epsilon\right), f\left(x^u; \theta', \epsilon'\right)\right), \qquad (4)$$

where $\mathcal{L}_{\mathrm{mse}}$ is the mean squared error loss.

Overall Training Objective. Our overall learning objective is to minimize a combination of supervised and unsupervised losses. On the labeled data, the supervised training objective is the linear combination of cross-entropy loss and dice loss. On the unlabeled dataset, unsupervised training objective consist of the consistency loss $\mathcal{L}_c$, high-level contrastive loss $\mathcal{L}^{\mathrm{high}}$ (*i.e.*, the linear combination of $\mathcal{L}_v^{\mathrm{high}}$ and $\mathcal{L}_d^{\mathrm{high}}$), and low-level contrastive loss $\mathcal{L}^{\mathrm{low}}$ (*i.e.*, the linear combination of $\mathcal{L}_v^{\mathrm{low}}$ and $\mathcal{L}_d^{\mathrm{low}}$). The overall loss function is:

$$\mathcal{L} = \mathcal{L}^{\mathrm{sup}} + \alpha\mathcal{L}^{\mathrm{high}} + \beta\mathcal{L}^{\mathrm{low}} + \gamma\mathcal{L}^{\mathrm{con}} \tag{5}$$

where α, β, γ are hyperparameters that balance each term.

Table 1. Quantitative segmentation results on the LA dataset. The backbone network of all evaluated methods are V-Net.

Method	# scans used		Metrics			
	Labeled	Unlabeled	Dice [%]	Jaccard [%]	ASD [voxel]	95HD [voxel]
V-Net [17]	80	0	91.14	83.82	1.52	5.75
V-Net	16	0	86.03	76.06	3.51	14.26
DAN [36]	16	64	87.52	78.29	2.42	9.01
DAP [37]	16	64	87.89	78.72	2.74	9.29
UA-MT [35]	16	64	88.88	80.21	2.26	7.32
LG-ER-MT [7]	16	64	89.56	81.22	2.06	7.29
SASSNet [12]	16	64	89.27	80.82	3.13	8.83
Chaitanya et al. [3]	16	64	89.94	81.82	2.66	7.23
CVRL(ours)	16	64	**90.45**	**83.02**	**1.81**	**6.56**
V-Net [17]	8	0	79.99	68.12	5.48	21.11
DAN [36]	8	72	80.87	70.65	3.72	15.96
DAP [37]	8	72	81.89	71.23	3.80	15.81
UA-MT [35]	8	72	84.25	73.48	3.36	13.84
LG-ER-MT [7]	8	72	85.43	74.95	3.75	15.01
SASSNet [12]	8	72	86.81	76.92	3.94	12.54
Chaitanya et al. [3]	8	72	84.95	74.77	3.70	10.68
CVRL(ours)	8	72	**88.56**	**78.89**	**2.81**	**8.22**

2 Experiments

Dataset and Pre-processing. We conduct our experiments on two benchmark datasets: the Left Atrium (LA) dataset from Atrial Segmentation Challenge[1] and the NIH pancreas CT dataset [21]. The LA dataset includes 100 3D gadolinium-enhanced MR imaging scans with annotations. The isotropic resolution of the

---

[1] http://atriaseg2018.cardiacatlas.org/.

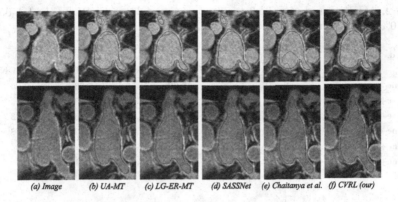

(a) Image   (b) UA-MT   (c) LG-ER-MT   (d) SASSNet   (e) Chaitanya et al.   (f) CVRL (our)

Fig. 3. Visual comparisons with other methods. As observed, our CVRL achieves superior performance with more accurate borders and shapes. Red and blue lines denote output predictions and ground-truth, respectively.

scan is of $0.625 \times 0.625 \times 0.625\text{mm}^3$. We use 80 scans for training, and 20 scans for evaluation. For pre-processing, we crop all the scans at the heart region and normalized them into zero and unit variance with the size of sub-volumes $112 \times 112 \times 80\text{mm}^3$. The pancreas dataset consists of 82 contrast-enhanced abdominal CT scans. We use the same experimental setting [16] to randomly select 62 scans for training, and 20 scans for evaluation. For pre-processing, we first rescale the intensities of the CT images into the window $[-125, 275]$ HU [38], and then re-sample all the data to a isotropic resolution of $1.0 \times 1.0 \times 1.0\text{mm}^3$. We crop all the scans at the pancreas region and normalized into zero and unit variance with the size of sub-volumes $96 \times 96 \times 96\text{mm}^3$. In this study, we conduct all experiments on LA and pancreas dataset under 10% and 20% labeled ratios.

Implementation Details. In our framework, we use V-Net as the network backbone for two networks. For data augmentation, we use standard data augmentation techniques [23,35]. We empirically set the hyper-parameters $\alpha, \beta, \gamma, \tau$ as $0.1, 0.1, 0.1, 1.0$, respectively. We use SGD optimizer with a momentum 0.9 and weight decay 0.0005 to optimize the network parameters. The initial learning rate is set as 0.01 and divided by 10 every 3000 iterations. For EMA updates, we follow the experimental setting in [35], where the EMA decay rate α is set to 0.999. We use the time-dependent Gaussian warming-up function $\Psi_{con}(t) = \exp\left(-5\left(1 - t/t_{\max}\right)^2\right)$ to ramp up parameters, where t and t_{max} denote the current and the maximum training step, respectively. For fairness, all evaluated methods are implemented in PyTorch, and trained for 10000 iterations on an NVIDIA 3090Ti GPU with batch size 6. In the testing stage, we adopt four metrics to evaluate the segmentation performance, including Dice coefficient (Dice), Jaccard Index (Jaccard), 95% Hausdorff Distance (95HD), and Average Symmetric Surface Distance (ASD).

Comparison with Other Semi-supervised Methods. We evaluate our CVRL with several state-of-the-art semi-supervised segmentation methods on

Table 2. Ablation study for the key component modules of CVRL on the LA dataset with 10% annotation ratio (8 labeled and 72 unlabeled).

Method	# scans used		Metrics			
	Labeled	Unlabeled	Dice[%]	Jaccard[%]	ASD[voxel]	95HD[voxel]
Baseline	8	72	83.09	71.75	5.53	19.65
Baseline+$\mathcal{L}^{high}$	8	72	87.46	78.12	3.03	9.99
Baseline+$\mathcal{L}^{low}$	8	72	87.24	77.49	3.36	10.13
Baseline+$\mathcal{L}^{con}$	8	72	85.72	75.31	4.72	13.18
Baseline+$\mathcal{L}^{high}$+$\mathcal{L}^{low}$	8	72	88.14	78.38	3.02	9.58
Baseline+$\mathcal{L}^{high}$+$\mathcal{L}^{low}$+$\mathcal{L}^{con}$	8	72	88.56	78.89	2.81	8.22

different amounts of labeled data, including V-Net [17], DAN [36], DAP [37], UA-MT [35], LG-ER-MT [7], SASSNet [12], and Chaitanya *et al.* [3]. Table 1 compares our segmentation results with other methods.

We first conduct experiments under 20% annotation ratios (16 labeled and 64 unlabeled). Under this setting, most above approaches achieve superior segmentation performance. CVRL gives better performance thanks to its low-level and high-level voxel-wise feature extraction. In particular, our proposed method outperforms other end-to-end semi-supervised methods in Dice (90.45%), Jaccard (83.02%), ASD (1.81), and 95HD (6.56).

To further evaluate the effectiveness of CVRL, we compare it with other methods in 10% annotation ratio (8 labeled and 72 unlabeled), as reported in Table 1. We observe consistent performance improvements over state-of-the-arts, in terms of Dice (88.56%), and Jaccard (78.89%). This evidence that i). taking voxel samples with contrastive learning yields better voxel embeddings; ii) both high-level and low-level relations are informative cues in both batch and feature dimension; iii) utilizing dimensional contrast is capable of consistently helping improve the segmentation performance. Leveraging all these aspects, it can observe consistent performance gains. As shown in Fig. 3, our method is capable of generating more accurate segmentation, considering the fact the improvement in such setting is difficult. This demonstrates i) the necessity of comprehensively considering both high-level and low-level contrast in both batch and feature dimension; and ii) efficacy of both inter-instance and intra-instance constraints. We also assess the performance of CVRL on Pancreas. We provide detailed evaluation results on Pancreas in Appendix Table 3. We find that CVRL significantly outperforms all the state-of-the-art methods by a significant margin. We noticed that our proposed CVRL could improve results by an especially significant margin, with up to 3.25–5.21% relative improvement in Dice.

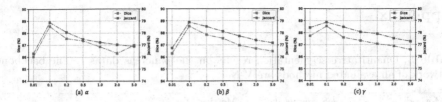

Fig. 4. Ablation results on hyper-parameters. For hyper-parameter selection, we perform grid search of α, β, γ from $\{0.001, 0.1, 0.2, 0.5, 1.0, 2.0, 5.0\}$. We observe $\alpha = \beta = \gamma$ is the best selection.

Ablation Study. We perform ablation experiments to validate the effectiveness of major components in our proposed method, including high-level and low-level contrastive strategy, and consistency loss. The quantitative results is reported in Table 2. We compare CVRL with its five variants under 10% annotation ratio (8 labeled and 72 unlabeled). Specially, the Baseline model refers to MT [24]. We gradually incorporate $\mathcal{L}^{high}$, $\mathcal{L}^{low}$, $\mathcal{L}^{con}$, denoted as Baseline+$\mathcal{L}^{low}$, Baseline+$\mathcal{L}^{high}$, Baseline+$\mathcal{L}^{con}$, Baseline+$\mathcal{L}^{low}$+$\mathcal{L}^{high}$, Baseline+$\mathcal{L}^{low}$+$\mathcal{L}^{high}$+ $\mathcal{L}^{con}$ (CVRL), respectively. As shown in the table, the Baseline network achieve 83.09%, 71.75%, 5.53, 19.65 in terms of Dice, Jaccard, ASD, and 95HD. With the progressive introduction of $\mathcal{L}^{high}$, $\mathcal{L}^{low}$, $\mathcal{L}^{con}$, our proposed algorithm enjoys consistently improvement gains over the Baseline network, boosting Dice and Jaccard by 5.47%, 7.14%, respectively. Also, the metrics ASD and 95HD are reduced by 2.72 and 11.43, respectively. This further validates the effectiveness of each key component. We summarize the effects of hyperparameters in Fig. 4.

3 Conclusion

In this work, we propose CVRL, a semi-supervised contrastive representation distillation framework by leveraging low-level and high-level cues to learn voxel-wise representations for volumetric medical image segmentation. Specifically, we propose to use voxel-wise contrastive and dimensional contrastive learning to ensure diversity promotion and exploit complex relations among training voxels. We also show the hardness-aware property is a key property for the success of our proposed dimensional contrastive learning. Experimental results demonstrate that our model yields state-of-the-art performance with generating more accurate boundaries with very limited annotations.

Appendix

Table 3. Quantitative segmentation results on the pancreas dataset. The backbone network of all evaluated methods are V-Net.

Method	# Scans used		Metrics			
	Labeled	Unlabeled	Dice[%]	Jaccard[%]	ASD[voxel]	95HD[voxel]
V-Net [17]	62	0	77.84	64.78	3.73	8.92
V-Net	12	0	62.42	48.06	4.77	22.34
DAN [36]	12	50	68.67	53.97	3.07	15.78
DAP [37]	12	50	71.29	56.69	2.82	16.31
MT [24]	12	50	71.29	56.69	2.82	16.31
LG-ER-MT [7]	12	50	71.27	54.34	4.29	16.14
UA-MT [35]	12	50	72.43	57.91	4.25	11.01
SASSNet [12]	12	50	70.47	55.74	4.26	10.95
Chaitanya et al. [3]	12	50	70.79	55.76	6.08	15.35
CVRL (ours)	12	50	**76.68**	**61.16**	**3.19**	**8.24**

Table 4. More Ablation study on the LA dataset for voxel-wise contrastive objective $\mathcal{L}_v$ and dimensional contrastive objective $\mathcal{L}_d$ (8 labeled and 72 unlabeled). We can observe our dimensional contrastive objective can be considered as the complementary to voxel-wise contrastive objective. This demonstrates the importance of dimensional contrastive objective, which provides good performance gains.

Method	High Level		Low Level		Metrics			
	$\mathcal{L}_v$	$\mathcal{L}_d$	$\mathcal{L}_v$	$\mathcal{L}_d$	Dice[%]	Jaccard[%]	ASD[voxel]	95HD[voxel]
CVRL	✓	-	✓	-	87.93	78.01	2.97	9.63
CVRL	-	✓	-	✓	87.87	77.89	3.21	10.02
CVRL	✓	✓	✓	✓	88.56	78.89	2.81	8.22

A   Hardness-aware Property of the Contrastive Losses

Recent work [26] has studies the property of standard contrastive objective (*i.e.*, InfoNCE). For better illustration, we reproduce the contrastive objective defined in Sect. 1.2 as follows:

$$\mathcal{L}_q = -\log \frac{\exp(q \cdot k_+/\tau)}{\exp(q \cdot k_+/\tau) + \sum_{k \in \mathcal{K}_-} \exp(q \cdot k/\tau)}$$

Given query vector q, and a set of key vectors $\mathcal{K}$, the InfoNCE loss can be understood as maximizing/minimizing the positive score $\exp(q \cdot k_+/\tau)$/negative score $\exp(q \cdot k/\tau)$. Concretely, $\mathcal{L}_q = -\log P_+$ where P_i is the probability of q matched to k_i:

$$P_i = \frac{\exp(q \cdot k_i/\tau)}{\sum_{k \in \mathcal{K}} \exp(q \cdot k/\tau)}$$

Next, we show that InfoNCE has the *hardness-aware* property compared to a more naïve contrastive loss $\mathcal{L}'_q$ whose object is also to maximize the similarity between the query q and the positive key k_+:

$$\mathcal{L}'_q = -q \cdot k_+ + \lambda \sum_{k \in \mathcal{K}_-} q \cdot k$$

We analyze the derivative with respect to the positive key k_+ and any negative key k_-:

$$\frac{\partial \mathcal{L}_q}{\partial k_+} = -\frac{[\sum_{k \in \mathcal{K}} \exp(q \cdot k/\tau)] \exp(q \cdot k_+/\tau) - [\exp(q \cdot k_+/\tau)]^2}{P_+ [\sum_{k \in \mathcal{K}} \exp(q \cdot k/\tau)]^2} \cdot \frac{q}{\tau},$$

$$= -\frac{\sum_{k \in \mathcal{K}_-} \exp(q \cdot k/\tau)}{\sum_{k \in \mathcal{K}} \exp(q \cdot k/\tau)} \cdot \frac{q}{\tau} = -\frac{q}{\tau} \sum_{k \neq +} P_k,$$

$$\frac{\partial \mathcal{L}_q}{\partial k_-} = -\frac{-\exp(q \cdot k_+/\tau) \exp(q \cdot k_-/\tau)}{P_+ [\sum_{k \in \mathcal{K}} \exp(q \cdot k/\tau)]^2} \cdot \frac{q}{\tau} = \frac{q}{\tau} P_-,$$

$$\frac{\partial \mathcal{L}'_q}{\partial k_+} = -q, \quad \frac{\partial \mathcal{L}'_q}{\partial k_-} = \lambda q.$$

We can observe that the derivative of $\mathcal{L}_q$ with respect to any negative sample k_- is proportional to the exponential term $\exp(q \cdot k_-/\tau)$, indicating *hardness-aware* property. On the other hand, $\mathcal{L}'_q$ is not *hardness-aware* because each negative key is weighted the same (Table 4).

In Sect. 1.2, both voxel-wise and dimensional contrastive objectives use the InfoNCE loss, and thus benefit from the hardness-aware property. (1) **Voxel-wise Contrastive Objective**, we define queries and keys as:

$$q = f(t(x))_i, \quad k_i = g(t'(x))_i, \quad k_j = g(t'(x))_j,$$

where i and j denote voxel indices. k_j is a feature voxel at a different location, which is considered as a negative key. $\mathcal{L}_v$ essentially pushes the k_j away from q more strongly when they are close. This encourages the representations to contain unique local information. (2) **Dimensional Contrastive Objective**: for brevity, here we denote i and j as dimension index. $\mathcal{L}_d$ encourages each dimension of the features to encode dissimilar information and prevents dimensional collapse [25].

References

1. Bai, W., Chen, C., Tarroni, G., Duan, J., Guitton, F., Petersen, S.E., Guo, Y., Matthews, P.M., Rueckert, D.: Self-supervised learning for cardiac MR image segmentation by anatomical position prediction. In: Shen, D., Liu, T., Peters, T.M., Staib, L.H., Essert, C., Zhou, S., Yap, P.-T., Khan, A. (eds.) MICCAI 2019. LNCS, vol. 11765, pp. 541–549. Springer, Cham (2019). https://doi.org/10.1007/978-3-030-32245-8_60
2. Bortsova, G., Dubost, F., Hogeweg, L., Katramados, I., de Bruijne, M.: Semi-supervised medical image segmentation via learning consistency under transformations. In: Shen, D., Liu, T., Peters, T.M., Staib, L.H., Essert, C., Zhou, S., Yap, P.-T., Khan, A. (eds.) MICCAI 2019. LNCS, vol. 11769, pp. 810–818. Springer, Cham (2019). https://doi.org/10.1007/978-3-030-32226-7_90
3. Chaitanya, K., Erdil, E., Karani, N., Konukoglu, E.: Contrastive learning of global and local features for medical image segmentation with limited annotations. In: NeurIPS (2020)
4. Chen, S., Bortsova, G., García-Uceda Juárez, A., van Tulder, G., de Bruijne, M.: Multi-task attention-based semi-supervised learning for medical image segmentation. In: Shen, D., et al. (eds.) MICCAI 2019. LNCS, vol. 11766, pp. 457–465. Springer, Cham (2019). https://doi.org/10.1007/978-3-030-32248-9_51
5. Chen, T., Kornblith, S., Norouzi, M., Hinton, G.: A simple framework for contrastive learning of visual representations. In: ICML, pp. 1597–1607. PMLR (2020)
6. Hadsell, R., Chopra, S., LeCun, Y.: Dimensionality reduction by learning an invariant mapping. In: CVPR, vol. 2, pp. 1735–1742. IEEE (2006)
7. Hang, W., et al.: Local and global structure-aware entropy regularized mean teacher model for 3D left atrium segmentation. In: Martel, A.L., et al. (eds.) Local and global structure-aware entropy regularized mean teacher model for 3d left atrium segmentation. LNCS, vol. 12261, pp. 562–571. Springer, Cham (2020). https://doi.org/10.1007/978-3-030-59710-8_55
8. Hu, X., Zeng, D., Xu, X., Shi, Y.: Semi-supervised contrastive learning for label-efficient medical image segmentation. In: de Bruijne, M., Cattin, P.C., Cotin, S., Padoy, N., Speidel, S., Zheng, Y., Essert, C. (eds.) Semi-supervised contrastive learning for label-efficient medical image segmentation. LNCS, vol. 12902, pp. 481–490. Springer, Cham (2021). https://doi.org/10.1007/978-3-030-87196-3_45
9. Hua, T., Wang, W., Xue, Z., Ren, S., Wang, Y., Zhao, H.: On feature decorrelation in self-supervised learning. In: ICCV, pp. 9598–9608 (2021)
10. Jing, L., Vincent, P., LeCun, Y., Tian, Y.: Understanding dimensional collapse in contrastive self-supervised learning. arXiv preprint arXiv:2110.09348 (2021)
11. Laine, S., Aila, T.: Temporal ensembling for semi-supervised learning. arXiv preprint arXiv:1610.02242 (2016)
12. Li, S., Zhang, C., He, X.: Shape-aware semi-supervised 3D semantic segmentation for medical images. In: Martel, A.L., Abolmaesumi, P., Stoyanov, D., Mateus, D., Zuluaga, M.A., Zhou, S.K., Racoceanu, D., Joskowicz, L. (eds.) MICCAI 2020. LNCS, vol. 12261, pp. 552–561. Springer, Cham (2020). https://doi.org/10.1007/978-3-030-59710-8_54
13. Li, X., Yu, L., Chen, H., Fu, C.W., Heng, P.A.: Semi-supervised skin lesion segmentation via transformation consistent self-ensembling model. arXiv preprint arXiv:1808.03887 (2018)
14. Liu, F., et al.: Graph-in-graph network for automatic gene ontology description generation. arXiv preprint arXiv:2206.05311 (2022)

15. Liu, F., You, C., Wu, X., Ge, S., Sun, X., et al.: Auto-encoding knowledge graph for unsupervised medical report generation. In: Advances in Neural Information Processing Systems (NeurIPS) (2021)
16. Luo, X., Chen, J., Song, T., Wang, G.: Semi-supervised medical image segmentation through dual-task consistency. In: AAAI (2020)
17. Milletari, F., Navab, N., Ahmadi, S.A.: V-net: fully convolutional neural networks for volumetric medical image segmentation. In: 3DV, pp. 565–571. IEEE (2016)
18. Misra, I., Maaten, L.v.d.: Self-supervised learning of pretext-invariant representations. In: CVPR, pp. 6707–6717 (2020)
19. Nie, D., Gao, Y., Wang, L., Shen, D.: Asdnet: Attention based semi-supervised deep networks for medical image segmentation. In: MICCAI. pp. 370–378. Springer (2018)
20. Oord, A.v.d., Li, Y., Vinyals, O.: Representation learning with contrastive predictive coding. arXiv preprint arXiv:1807.03748 (2018)
21. Roth, H.R., Farag, A., Turkbey, E., Lu, L., Liu, J., Summers, R.M.: Data from pancreas-ct. the cancer imaging archive (2016)
22. Sun, S., Han, K., Kong, D., You, C., Xie, X.: Mirnf: medical image registration via neural fields. arXiv preprint arXiv:2206.03111 (2022)
23. Taleb, A., et al.: 3d self-supervised methods for medical imaging. In: NeurIPS, pp. 18158–18172 (2020)
24. Tarvainen, A., Valpola, H.: Mean teachers are better role models: weight-averaged consistency targets improve semi-supervised deep learning results. In: NeurIPS, pp. 1195–1204 (2017)
25. Tian, Y., Krishnan, D., Isola, P.: Contrastive multiview coding. arXiv preprint arXiv:1906.05849 (2019)
26. Wang, F., Liu, H.: Understanding the behaviour of contrastive loss. In: CVPR, pp. 2495–2504 (2021)
27. Wang, X., Gupta, A.: Unsupervised learning of visual representations using videos. In: ICCV, pp. 2794–2802 (2015)
28. Wu, Z., Xiong, Y., Stella, X.Y., Lin, D.: Unsupervised feature learning via non-parametric instance discrimination. In: CVPR (2018)
29. You, C., Chen, N., Zou, Y.: Self-supervised contrastive cross-modality representation learning for spoken question answering. arXiv preprint arXiv:2109.03381 (2021)
30. You, C., Dai, W., Staib, L., Duncan, J.S.: Bootstrapping semi-supervised medical image segmentation with anatomical-aware contrastive distillation. arXiv preprint arXiv:2206.02307 (2022)
31. You, C., et al.: Incremental learning meets transfer learning: application to multi-site prostate MRI segmentation. arXiv preprint arXiv:2206.01369 (2022)
32. You, C., Yang, J., Chapiro, J., Duncan, J.S.: Unsupervised wasserstein distance guided domain adaptation for 3D multi-domain liver segmentation. In: Cardoso, J., et al. (eds.) IMIMIC/MIL3ID/LABELS -2020. LNCS, vol. 12446, pp. 155–163. Springer, Cham (2020). https://doi.org/10.1007/978-3-030-61166-8_17
33. You, C., Zhao, R., Liu, F., Chinchali, S., Topcu, U., Staib, L., Duncan, J.S.: Class-aware generative adversarial transformers for medical image segmentation. arXiv preprint arXiv:2201.10737 (2022)
34. You, C., Zhou, Y., Zhao, R., Staib, L., Duncan, J.S.: SimCVD: simple contrastive voxel-wise representation distillation for semi-supervised medical image segmentation. IEEE Trans. Med. Imaging, 2022 (2022)

35. Yu, L., Wang, S., Li, X., Fu, C.-W., Heng, P.-A.: Uncertainty-aware self-ensembling model for semi-supervised 3D left atrium segmentation. In: Shen, D., Liu, T., Peters, T.M., Staib, L.H., Essert, C., Zhou, S., Yap, P.-T., Khan, A. (eds.) MICCAI 2019. LNCS, vol. 11765, pp. 605–613. Springer, Cham (2019). https://doi.org/10.1007/978-3-030-32245-8_67

36. Zhang, Y., Yang, L., Chen, J., Fredericksen, M., Hughes, D.P., Chen, D.Z.: Deep adversarial networks for biomedical image segmentation utilizing unannotated images. In: Descoteaux, M., Maier-Hein, L., Franz, A., Jannin, P., Collins, D.L., Duchesne, S. (eds.) MICCAI 2017. LNCS, vol. 10435, pp. 408–416. Springer, Cham (2017). https://doi.org/10.1007/978-3-319-66179-7_47

37. Zheng, H., Lin, L., Hu, H., Zhang, Q., Chen, Q., Iwamoto, Y., Han, X., Chen, Y.-W., Tong, R., Wu, J.: Semi-supervised segmentation of liver using adversarial learning with deep atlas prior. In: Shen, D., Liu, T., Peters, T.M., Staib, L.H., Essert, C., Zhou, S., Yap, P.-T., Khan, A. (eds.) MICCAI 2019. LNCS, vol. 11769, pp. 148–156. Springer, Cham (2019). https://doi.org/10.1007/978-3-030-32226-7_17

38. Zhou, Y., et al.: Prior-aware neural network for partially-supervised multi-organ segmentation. In: ICCV, pp. 10672–10681 (2019)

Context-Aware Voxel-Wise Contrastive Learning for Label Efficient Multi-organ Segmentation

Peng Liu and Guoyan Zheng[✉]

Institute of Medical Robotics, School of Biomedical Engineering,
Shanghai Jiao Tong University, No. 800, Dongchuan Road, Shanghai 200240, China
guoyan.zheng@sjtu.edu.cn

Abstract. Medical image segmentation is a prerequisite for many clinical applications including disease diagnosis, surgical planning and computer assisted interventions. Due to the challenges in obtaining expert-level accurate, densely annotated multi-organ dataset, existing datasets for multi-organ segmentation either have small number of samples, or only have annotations of a few organs instead of all organs, which are termed as partially labeled data. There exist previous attempts to develop label efficient segmentation method to make use of these partially labeled dataset for improving the performance of multi-organ segmentation. However, most of these methods suffer from the limitation that they only use the labeled information in the dataset without taking advantage of the large amount of unlabeled data. To this end, we propose a context-aware voxel-wise contrastive learning method to take full advantage of both labeled and unlabeled data in partially labeled dataset for an improvement of multi-organ segmentation performance. Experimental Results demonstrated that our proposed method achieved superior performance than other state-of-the-art methods.

Keywords: Multi-organ segmentation · Label efficient · Contrastive learning · Context-aware

1 Introduction

Multi-organ segmentation is a prerequisite for many clinical applications including disease diagnosis, surgical planning and computer assisted interventions [5]. Recently, deep learning-based methods such as convolutional neural networks (CNN) have made remarkable progress in solving multi-organ segmentation tasks

This study was partially supported by Shanghai Municipal S&T Commission via Project 20511105205, by the Natural Science Foundation of China via project U20A20199, and by the key program of the medical engineering interdisciplinary research fund of Shanghai Jiao Tong University via project YG2019ZDA22 and YG2019ZDB09.

L. Wang et al. (Eds.): MICCAI 2022, LNCS 13434, pp. 653–662, 2022.
https://doi.org/10.1007/978-3-031-16440-8_62

[1,2,11,12,15,16]. However, they typically require a large amount of expert-level accurate, densely-annotated data for training. Annotating large amount of medical image data, especially when pixel-level annotations of multiple organs in the dataset are required, is challenging. Some may choose to annotate one or a few out of the many organs in order to save time and efforts. We term such dataset as partially labeled dataset. Actually, there exist many openly available partially labeled dataset [7,18] but very few fully annotated dataset [10]. Therefore, how to make use of partially labeled dataset to train a multi-organ segmentation model has become a practical problem.

Training a multi-organ segmentation model from partially labeled dataset is receiving increasing interest recently [3,17,20]. A naive way to solve this problem is to train multiple networks by separating the partially labeled dataset into several fully labeled subsets and training a network on each subset for a specific segmentation task [9,14,19]. However, although such methods are simple, they usually lead to much larger computational complexity and hardware consumption. Alternatively, one can design a multi-head network, composing of a shared encoder and multiple task-specific decoders where each decoder can be used to segment one specific organ [20]. During training, when any partially labeled data is fed to the network, weights for the shared encoder will be updated together with one of the decoder heads. Such methods reduce the computational complexity to a certain extent, but they require multiple inferences in order to generate segmentation of all organs in a dataset. Additionally, they also suffer from the design flexibility issue as any time when a new organ is needed to be segmented, we have to add one more decoder head. This has motivated the recent development of end-to-end networks to solve the problem. For example, Zhang et al. [20] proposed a Dynamic on-Demand Network (DoDNet), consisting of a shared encoder-decoder architecture, a task encoding module, a controller for generating dynamic convolution filters, and a single but dynamic segmentation head. Inspired by conditional generative adversarial networks (cGAN) [13], Dmitriev et al. [3] proposed conditional U-Net [16] for multi-organ segmentation. Shi et al. [17] proposed to take advantage of marginal loss and exclusion loss for partially supervised multi-organ segmentation.

Despite significant progress, however, it is still challenging for existing methods to solve the problem and there are great potential to improve the performance for the following reasons. First, most of previously introduced methods only use labeled information in the partially labeled dataset without taking advantage of a large amount of unlabeled information in the dataset. Second, due to GPU memory restrictions caused by moving to fully 3D, most of previously introduced methods adopted patch/subvolume-based strategy to train a model to segment multiple organs from 3D dataset. Then, depending on which patch an organ lies in, the prediction of the same organ may be different, due to the change of context, leading to inconsistent predictions.

To this end, we propose context-aware voxel-wise contrastive learning method for label efficient multi-organ segmentation from partially labeled dataset. Contrastive learning [6] have proven to be an effective method to learn feature representations that are invariant to different views of the same instance. This is done

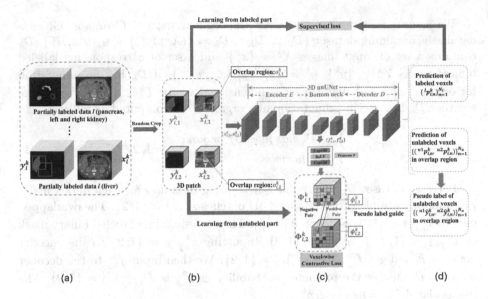

Fig. 1. The overview of the proposed context-aware voxel-wise contrastive learning segmentation framework.(a) Partially labeled data and ground truth. (b) 3D patches and ground truth label sampled from partially labeled data. (c) Voxel-wise Contrastive Learning (d) Predictions for both labeled and unlabeled parts.

by pulling closer the positive pairs and pushing away negative pairs. Different from previous works, here we propose to use contrastive learning to take full advantage of unlabeled data in the partially labeled data. Our contributions can be summarized as follows:

- We propose a label efficient method for multi-organ segmentation from partially labeled data. Our method can take full advantage of both labeled and unlabeled information in partially labeled dataset for an improvement of multi-organ segmentation performance.
- We propose a context-aware voxel-wise contrastive learning method that can learn better feature representation of unlabeled data in the partially labeled dataset. Our method is network-agnostic.
- We conduct comprehensive experiments to validate the performance of the proposed method.

2   Method

Figure 1 shows the overall architecture of our method. From this figure, one can see that there are two branches, i.e., one for labeled voxels and the other for unlabeled voxels. For labeled voxels, we compute Cross Entropy(CE) loss and Dice loss. For unlabeled part, we compute a context-aware voxel-wise contrastive learning loss.

We assume that our task is to get the segmentation of C organs. Given a database containing dataset $\{\mathcal{D}_0, ..., \mathcal{D}_K\}$, $\mathcal{D}_k = \{(X^k; Y^k)\}, k \in \{0, ..., K\}$. $\mathcal{D}_k$ contains a set of input images $X^k = \{x_i^k\}$ and a set of corresponding labeled binary masks $Y^k = \{y_i^k\}$, $y_i^k = \{y_i^{k,0}, y_i^{k,1}, ..., y_i^{k,C}\}$, if $\mathcal{D}_k$ has no annotation for organ c, $y_i^{k,c} = \emptyset$. We use a $C-$dimensional vector $T^k \in \{0,1\}^C$ to denote whether $\mathcal{D}_k$ has specific annotation of a organ, T^k is computed as follows:

$$T^{k,c} = \begin{cases} 1, & \mathcal{D}_k \ has \ label \ of \ organ \ c \\ 0, & otherwise. \end{cases} \quad c = 1, 2, ...C \quad (1)$$

For each dataset $\mathcal{D}_k$, we shuffle our training data and for each data i in $\mathcal{D}_k$ we randomly sample two overlapped 3D patches $x_{i,j}^k, j = \{1,2\}$. The overlapped part in $x_{i,j}^k, j = \{1,2\}$ is denoted as $o_{i,j}^k$. The corresponding labeled binary mask of $x_{i,j}^k, j = \{1,2\}$ is $y_{i,j}^k, j = \{1,2\}$. Inputting $x_{i,j}^k, j = \{1,2\}$ to the encoder network E and get $f_{i,j}^k = E(x_{i,j}^k), j = \{1,2\}$. We then input $f_{i,j}^k$ to the decoder network D and get the predicted probability as $p_{i,j}^k = D(f_{i,j}^k), j = \{1,2\}$. The pseudo label $\hat{y}_{i,j}^k = argmax(p_{i,j}^k)$.

2.1   Supervised Losses for Labeled Voxels

We group prediction of labeled voxels from $p_{i,1}^k$ and $p_{i,2}^k$ into a set $\{^l p_{i,n}^k\}_{n=1}^{N_l}$, N_l is the number of labeled voxels. The corresponding ground truth label of $\{^l p_{i,n}^k\}_{n=1}^{N_l}$ is $\{^l y_{i,n}^k\}_{n=1}^{N_l}$. Specifically, for those labeled voxels in the overlapped region, prediction and ground truth label will be counted twice since those voxels have two different predictions in different patches. Formally, we can compute supervised loss $\mathcal{L}_{Sup}$ as follows:

$$\mathcal{L}_{Sup} = \frac{1}{N_l} \sum_{n=1}^{N_l} (- \sum_{c=1}^{C} T^{k,c} \cdot {}^l y_{i,n}^{k,c} log({}^l p_{i,n}^{k,c}) + \sum_{c=1}^{C} T^{k,c} (1 - 2 \cdot \frac{{}^l y_{i,n}^{k,c} \cdot {}^l p_{i,n}^{k,c}}{{}^l y_{i,n}^{k,c} + {}^l p_{i,n}^{k,c}})) \quad (2)$$

2.2   Context-Aware Contrastive Learning Loss for Unlabeled Voxels

When patch/subvolume-based strategy is used to train a network, predictions of a voxel may be different when the voxel lies in different patches due to the differences of context information. We propose to use a context-aware contrastive learning to minimize such an inconsistency, which then allows us to take advantage of the large amount of unlabeled data in the partially labeled dataset.

Concretely, at each training iteration, after we feed the two overlapped 3D patches to our network to get predictions, we group prediction of unlabeled voxels in the overlapped region from $p_{i,1}^k$ and $p_{i,2}^k$ as a set $\{(^{u1} p_{i,n}^k, ^{u2} p_{i,n}^k)\}_{n=1}^{N_u}$, where N_u is the number of unlabeled voxels in the overlapped region. The corresponding pseudo labels of $\{(^{u1} p_{i,n}^k, ^{u2} p_{i,n}^k)\}_{n=1}^{N_u}$ are $\{(^{u1} \hat{y}_{i,n}^k, ^{u2} \hat{y}_{i,n}^k)\}_{n=1}^{N_u}$. Moreover, we need to downsample $\{(^{u1}p^k_{i,n}, {}^{u2}p^k_{i,n})\}^{N_u}_{n=1}$ and $\{(^{u1}\hat{y}^k_{i,n}, {}^{u2}\hat{y}^k_{i,n})\}^{N_u}_{n=1}$ as the feature maps of the overlapped region is obtained after downsampling to $1/16$ of the original resolution. After downsampling $\{(^{u1}p^k_{i,n}, {}^{u2}p^k_{i,n})\}^{N_u}_{n=1}$ and $\{(^{u1}\hat{y}^k_{i,n}, {}^{u2}\hat{y}^k_{i,n})\}^{N_u}_{n=1}$, we get $\{(^{u1}\tilde{p}^k_{i,n}, {}^{u2}\tilde{p}^k_{i,n})\}^{N_{uo}}_{n=1}$ and $\{(^{u1}\tilde{\hat{y}}^k_{i,n}, {}^{u2}\tilde{\hat{y}}^k_{i,n})\}^{N_{uo}}_{n=1}$, where $N_{uo} = N_u/16^3$. In order to get the voxel-wise feature for contrastive learning, we use a projector P as shown in Fig. 1 to project $f^k_{i,j}$ to a 128-dimensional feature $\Phi^k_{i,j} = P(f^k_{i,j})$. We denote the feature of the overlapped region as $\phi^k_{i,j}$. We then select feature of unlabeled voxels from $\phi^k_{i,1}$ and $\phi^k_{i,2}$ as a feature set $\{(^{u1}\phi^k_{i,n}, {}^{u2}\phi^k_{i,n})\}^{N_{uo}}_{n=1}$. Since $^{u1}\phi^k_{i,n}$ and $^{u2}\phi^k_{i,n}$ belong to the same voxel, we want the corresponding features to be close. Here, we use contrastive learning to achieve this goal. As shown in Fig. 1(c), we take $^{u1}\phi^k_{i,n}$ and $^{u2}\phi^k_{i,n}$ as the positive pair. Features at different locations and having different pseudo labels are regarded as negative pairs. After that, for $\{(^{u1}\phi^k_{i,n}, {}^{u2}\phi^k_{i,n})\}^{N_{uo}}_{n=1}$, we can obtain the maximum classification probabilities corresponding to the features i.e., $\{(max(^{u1}\tilde{p}^k_{i,n}), max(^{u2}\tilde{p}^k_{i,n}))\}^{N_{uo}}_{n=1}$ which are used as their confidences. Obviously, for a voxel n in the overlapped region, we get respectively two features $(^{u1}\phi^k_{i,n}, {}^{u2}\phi^k_{i,n})$ and two confidences $(max(^{u1}\tilde{p}^k_{i,n}), max(^{u2}\tilde{p}^k_{i,n}))$ from predictions from two patches. Because the features with higher confidence are generally more accurate, the features with lower confidence should be aligned to the features with higher confidence. To this end, we design a Directional Contrastive Loss (DC Loss) to train our network in order to align features for the same voxel obtained from different patch predictions. We additionally require that the confidence of the aligned features should be greater than a certain threshold to ensure the quality of the aligned features. Formally, the DC Loss $\mathcal{L}_{dc}$ is computed as follow:

$$\mathcal{L}_{dc}(^{u1}\phi^k_{i,n}, {}^{u2}\phi^k_{i,n}) = \mathcal{M}_d(n) \cdot \log \frac{r(^{u1}\phi^k_{i,n}, {}^{u2}\phi^k_{i,n})}{r(^{u1}\phi^k_{i,n}, {}^{u2}\phi^k_{i,n}) + \sum_{\phi_{ne} \in \mathcal{F}_u} r(^{u1}\phi^k_{i,n}, \phi_{ne})} \tag{3}$$

$$\mathcal{M}_d(n) = \mathbf{1}\{max(^{u1}\tilde{p}^k_{i,n}) < max(^{u2}\tilde{p}^k_{i,n})\} \cdot \mathbf{1}\{\gamma < max(^{u2}\tilde{p}^k_{i,n})\} \tag{4}$$

$$\mathcal{L}_{CL} = -\frac{1}{N_{uo}} \sum_{n=1}^{N_{uo}} (\mathcal{L}_{dc}(^{u1}\phi^k_{i,n}, {}^{u2}\phi^k_{i,n}) + \mathcal{L}_{dc}(^{u2}\phi^k_{i,n}, {}^{u1}\phi^k_{i,n})) \tag{5}$$

where $r(\cdot, \cdot)$ is an exponential function of the cosine similarity $s(\cdot, \cdot)$ between two features with a temperature τ, i.e., $r(^{u1}\phi^k_{i,n}, {}^{u2}\phi^k_{i,n}) = exp(s(^{u1}\phi^k_{i,n}, {}^{u2}\phi^k_{i,n}))/\tau$; $\mathcal{F}_u$ represents the set of negative samples; ϕ_{ne} represents a negative sample; $\mathcal{M}_d(n)$ is a binary mask to select the region where the predicted probability in $^{u2}\phi^k_{i,n}$ is not only greater than the predicted probability of $^{u1}\phi^k_{i,n}$ but also greater than the threshold γ; $\mathcal{L}_{CL}$ represents the overall context-aware contrastive learning (CL) loss.

Table 1. A summary description of our used datasets.

Name	Source dataset	Number	Annotated organs
$\mathcal{D}_0$	MALBCVWC [10]	30	All organs
$\mathcal{D}_1$	Decathlon-Liver [18]	131	Liver
$\mathcal{D}_2$	Decathlon-Spleen [18]	41	Spleen
$\mathcal{D}_3$	Decathlon-Pancreas [18]	281	Pancreas
$\mathcal{D}_4$	KiTS [7]	210	Left kidney, right kidney

2.3 Overall Loss Function

Our overall loss function contains the supervised loss for the labeled data and the CL loss for unlabeled part as follows:

$$\mathcal{L} = \mathcal{L}_{Sup} + \lambda \mathcal{L}_{CL} \tag{6}$$

2.4 Implementation Details

We choose 3D nnUNet [8] as our backbone network. We chose a patch size of [160, 160, 96]. We empirically set γ to 0.6 and λ to 0.1. In total we train our network 600 epochs. For each epoch, we use 250 batches and per batch, we sample two pairs of patches with overlapped regions. We use Adam optimizer and set the initial learning rate to 0.01. Whenever the loss reduction is less than 0.001 in a consecutive 10 epochs, the learning rate decays by 20%. We use Dice similarity coefficient (DSC) and Hausdorff distance (HD95;mm) as metrics to evaluate the performance of different methods. All methods were implemented in python using PyTorch framework and evaluated on a NVIDIA Tesla V100 GPU.

3   Experiments

3.1   Dataset

We use five CT datasets (details as shown in Table 1) in our experiments and choose liver, spleen, pancreas, left kidney and right kidney as the segmentation targets. The spatial resolution of all these datasets are resampled to $(1 \times 1 \times 3) mm^3$. We randomly split each dataset into training(60%), validation(20%) and testing(20%).

3.2   Comparing to State-of-the-Art Methods

We compared the performance of the proposed method with three SOTA methods [4,17,21]. As $\mathcal{D}_0$ contains segmentation of all organs, we trained a model on this dataset and treated as the baseline. All other methods were trained with

Table 2. DSC (%) obtained by different Methods. L:Liver, S:Spleen, P:Pancreas, RK: Right Kidney, LK: Left Kidney.

Method	L$\in\mathcal{D}_0$	L$\in\mathcal{D}_1$	S$\in\mathcal{D}_0$	S$\in\mathcal{D}_2$	P$\in\mathcal{D}_0$	P$\in\mathcal{D}_3$	RK$\in\mathcal{D}_0$	LK$\in\mathcal{D}_0$	RK$\in\mathcal{D}_4$	LK$\in\mathcal{D}_4$	All
Baseline	96.7	93.1	**95.8**	94.0	70.5	65.8	90.9	**94.4**	92.8	86.2	88.0
PaNN [21]	96.5	94.8	95.2	**95.1**	67.9	80.1	94.2	80.3	**96.5**	92.6	89.3
PIPO [4]	96.4	92.2	93.8	93.5	77.5	76.4	94.2	94.6	93.4	89.3	90.1
DoDNet [20]	96.7	95.1	95.5	94.8	79.1	69.0	94.5	94.7	94.0	91.6	90.5
Shi et al. [17]	96.5	95.2	95.4	94.5	74.4	78.3	94.4	94.4	94.1	91.1	90.8
Ours	**96.7**	**95.7**	95.4	94.6	**80.6**	**83.6**	**94.6**	**94.6**	94.8	**93.9**	**92.5**

Table 3. The Hausdorff distances (mm) obtained by different Methods. L:Liver, S:Spleen, P:Pancreas, RK: Right Kidney, LK: Left Kidney.

Method	L$\in\mathcal{D}_0$	L$\in\mathcal{D}_1$	S$\in\mathcal{D}_0$	S$\in\mathcal{D}_2$	P$\in\mathcal{D}_0$	P$\in\mathcal{D}_3$	RK$\in\mathcal{D}_0$	LK$\in\mathcal{D}_0$	RK$\in\mathcal{D}_4$	LK$\in\mathcal{D}_4$	All
Baseline	1.78	7.70	1.08	3.08	9.63	14.06	3.44	1.31	7.86	13.42	6.34
PaNN [21]	2.14	5.64	1.25	**1.43**	14.33	5.75	1.50	5.24	**1.39**	7.57	4.62
PIPO [4]	1.98	6.57	2.49	2.20	5.35	7.40	1.57	1.33	6.57	7.54	4.30
DoDNet [20]	1.71	2.95	1.17	1.47	4.22	0.00	1.37	1.25	2.80	4.45	2.81
Shi et al. [17]	1.98	2.37	1.25	1.63	6.47	5.39	1.41	1.45	2.88	6.07	3.09
Ours	**1.71**	**2.55**	**1.17**	1.44	**3.56**	**4.30**	**1.37**	**1.31**	2.33	**2.63**	**2.24**

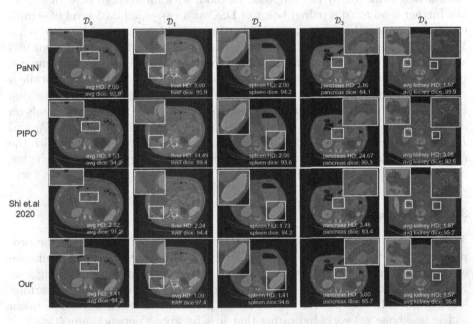

Fig. 2. The comparison of segmentation results from different methods. The red area represents the liver, the yellow area represents the spleen, the cyan area represents the pancreas, the green and blue areas represent the right and left kidneys, respectively. The edge with deeper color means the ground truth. (Color figure online)

Table 4. Performance obtained by UNet as the backbone network. UNet-CL:UNet with contrastive learning, L:Liver, S:Spleen, P:Pancreas, RK:Right Kidney, LK:Left Kidney.

	$L \in \mathcal{D}_0$	$L \in \mathcal{D}_1$	$S \in \mathcal{D}_0$	$S \in \mathcal{D}_2$	$P \in \mathcal{D}_0$	$P \in \mathcal{D}_3$	$RK \in \mathcal{D}_0$	$LK \in \mathcal{D}_0$	$RK \in \mathcal{D}_4$	$LK \in \mathcal{D}_4$	All
UNet [16](DSC)	96.1	94.0	93.7	85.6	76.5	77.4	**94.2**	**94.6**	93.9	89.1	89.5
UNet [16](HD)	2.46	**4.42**	2.23	7.80	5.50	7.07	**1.41**	**1.39**	6.28	**7.56**	4.61
UNet-CL(DSC)	**96.4**	**94.9**	**95.0**	**94.1**	**76.8**	**81.4**	93.8	94.4	**94.7**	**91.1**	**91.3**
UNet-CL(HD)	**2.09**	7.04	**1.25**	**1.63**	**4.51**	**5.34**	1.77	1.51	**2.36**	7.86	**3.54**

$\mathcal{D}_0 + \mathcal{D}_1 + \mathcal{D}_2 + \mathcal{D}_3 + \mathcal{D}_4$. Table 2 and Table 3 shows the comparison results. Specifically, the Prior-aware Neural Network (PaNN) [21] achieved slightly better results than the baseline as it only added a prior-aware loss to learn from partially labeled data. The pyramid input and pyramid output (PIPO) [4] further improved the segmentation results over the PaNN method by developing a multi-scale structure as well as target adaptive loss to enable learning from partially labeled data. Shi et al. [17] proposed marginal and exclusion loss in combination with the nnUNet [8] architecture to leverage the partially labeled data, and achieved a better performance than both PaNN and PIPO methods. DoDNet [20] achieved better results than both PaNN and PIPO methods but its performance was slightly worse than the method introduced in [17]. The best results were achieved by the proposed method, with an average DSC of 92.5%. We further conducted a paired t-test of DSC at a two-sided 0.05 level of significance to compare the results achieved by the second-best method [17] and ours. We obtained a p-value of 0.028, which demonstrated that the improvement was statistically significant. It is worth to note that our method achieved a comparable performance when segmenting large organs such as liver and spleen while a significantly better performance when segmenting small organs such as pancreas. Figure 2 shows several segmentation examples achieved by different methods on different datasets. From this figure, one can see that in both dataset $\mathcal{D}_0$ and $\mathcal{D}_3$ the pancreas segmentation of our method have a better consistency with the ground truth. In dataset $\mathcal{D}_1$, the spleen segmentation of our method has a higher overlap ratio with the ground truth.

3.3   Ablation Study

To evaluate the influence of backbone network on the performance of the proposed method, we replaced nnUNet by UNet [16]. Table 4 shows the performance of UNet with or without using the proposed voxel-wise contrastive learning loss. From this table, one can see that the proposed voxel-wise contrastive learning loss significantly improve the segmentation performance when UNet was taken as the backbone network, indicating that it is backbone network-agnostic.

4   Conclusion

This paper addressed the problem of multi-organ segmentation from partially labeled dataset. A context-aware voxel-wise contrastive learning method was proposed to make full use of partially labeled dataset for multi-organ segmentation. Our method can take full advantage of both labeled and unlabeled data in partially labeled dataset for an improvement of multi-organ segmentation performance. It is backbone network-agnostic and holds the potential to be used with other segmentation networks for performance improvement.

References

1. Cao, H., et al.: Swin-unet: unet-like pure transformer for medical image segmentation. arXiv preprint arXiv:2105.05537 (2021)
2. Chen, J., et al.: Transunet: Transformers make strong encoders for medical image segmentation. arXiv preprint arXiv:2102.04306 (2021)
3. Dmitriev, K., Kaufman, A.E.: Learning multi-class segmentations from single-class datasets. In: Proceedings of the IEEE/CVF Conference on Computer Vision and Pattern Recognition, pp. 9501–9511 (2019)
4. Fang, X., Yan, P.: Multi-organ segmentation over partially labeled datasets with multi-scale feature abstraction. IEEE Trans. Med. Imaging **39**(11), 3619–3629 (2020)
5. Gibson, E., et al.: Automatic multi-organ segmentation on abdominal CT with dense v-networks. IEEE Trans. Med. Imaging **37**(8), 1822–1834 (2018)
6. Hadsell, R., Chopra, S., LeCun, Y.: Dimensionality reduction by learning an invariant mapping. In: 2006 IEEE Computer Society Conference on Computer Vision and Pattern Recognition (CVPR 2006), vol. 2, pp. 1735–1742. IEEE (2006)
7. Heller, N., et al.: The kits19 challenge data: 300 kidney tumor cases with clinical context, CT semantic segmentations, and surgical outcomes. arXiv preprint arXiv:1904.00445 (2019)
8. Isensee, F., Jaeger, P.F., Kohl, S.A., Petersen, J., Maier-Hein, K.H.: NNU-net: a self-configuring method for deep learning-based biomedical image segmentation. Nat. Methods **18**(2), 203–211 (2021)
9. Isensee, F., Jäger, P.F., Kohl, S.A., Petersen, J., Maier-Hein, K.H.: Automated design of deep learning methods for biomedical image segmentation. arXiv preprint arXiv:1904.08128 (2019)
10. Landman, B., Xu, Z., Igelsias, J.E., Styner, M., Langerak, T., Klein, A.: Miccai multi-atlas labeling beyond the cranial vault-workshop and challenge. In: Proceedings of MICCAI: multi-atlas labeling beyond cranial vault-workshop challenge (2015)
11. Long, J., Shelhamer, E., Darrell, T.: Fully convolutional networks for semantic segmentation. In: Proceedings of the IEEE Conference on Computer Vision and Pattern Recognition, pp. 3431–3440 (2015)
12. Milletari, F., Navab, N., Ahmadi, S.A.: V-net: fully convolutional neural networks for volumetric medical image segmentation. In: 2016 Fourth International Conference on 3D Vision (3DV), pp. 565–571. IEEE (2016)
13. Mirza, M., Osindero, S.: Conditional generative adversarial nets. arXiv preprint arXiv:1411.1784 (2014)

14. Myronenko, A., Hatamizadeh, A.: 3d kidneys and kidney tumor semantic segmentation using boundary-aware networks. arXiv preprint arXiv:1909.06684 (2019)
15. Oktay, O., et al.: Attention u-net: learning where to look for the pancreas. arXiv preprint arXiv:1804.03999 (2018)
16. Ronneberger, O., Fischer, P., Brox, T.: U-net: convolutional networks for biomedical image segmentation. In: Navab, N., Hornegger, J., Wells, W.M., Frangi, A.F. (eds.) MICCAI 2015. LNCS, vol. 9351, pp. 234–241. Springer, Cham (2015). https://doi.org/10.1007/978-3-319-24574-4_28
17. Shi, G., Xiao, L., Chen, Y., Zhou, S.K.: Marginal loss and exclusion loss for partially supervised multi-organ segmentation. Med. Image Anal. **70**, 101979 (2021)
18. Simpson, A.L., et al.: A large annotated medical image dataset for the development and evaluation of segmentation algorithms. arXiv preprint arXiv:1902.09063 (2019)
19. Yu, Q., Shi, Y., Sun, J., Gao, Y., Zhu, J., Dai, Y.: Crossbar-net: a novel convolutional neural network for kidney tumor segmentation in CT images. IEEE Trans. Image Process. 1 (2019)
20. Zhang, J., Xie, Y., Xia, Y., Shen, C.: Dodnet: learning to segment multi-organ and tumors from multiple partially labeled datasets. In: Proceedings of the IEEE/CVF Conference on Computer Vision and Pattern Recognition, pp. 1195–1204 (2021)
21. Zhou, Y., et al.: Prior-aware neural network for partially-supervised multi-organ segmentation. In: Proceedings of the IEEE/CVF International Conference on Computer Vision, pp. 10672–10681 (2019)

Vector Quantisation for Robust Segmentation

Ainkaran Santhirasekaram[1(✉)], Avinash Kori[1], Mathias Winkler[2],
Andrea Rockall[2], and Ben Glocker[1]

[1] Department of Computing, Imperial College London, London, UK
a.santhirasekaram19@imperial.ac.uk
[2] Department of Surgery and Cancer, Imperial College London, London, UK

Abstract. The reliability of segmentation models in the medical domain depends on the model's robustness to perturbations in the input space. Robustness is a particular challenge in medical imaging exhibiting various sources of image noise, corruptions, and domain shifts. Obtaining robustness is often attempted via simulating heterogeneous environments, either heuristically in the form of data augmentation or by learning to generate specific perturbations in an adversarial manner. We propose and justify that learning a discrete representation in a low dimensional embedding space improves robustness of a segmentation model. This is achieved with a dictionary learning method called vector quantisation. We use a set of experiments designed to analyse robustness in both the latent and output space under domain shift and noise perturbations in the input space. We adapt the popular UNet architecture, inserting a quantisation block in the bottleneck. We demonstrate improved segmentation accuracy and better robustness on three segmentation tasks. Code is available at https://github.com/AinkaranSanthi/Vector-Quantisation-for-Robust-Segmentation.

Keywords: Robustness · Vector quantisation · Semantic segmentation

1 Introduction

Segmentation of medical images is important in both aiding diagnosis and treatment planning [10]. Deep learning, based on convolutional neural networks (CNNs), has significantly improved segmentation performance and is now the most widely used approach for automated segmentation [10]. However, it is well established in the literature that these models are not significantly robust to perturbations in the input whether that be noise or a domain shift [2,11]. This is particularly relevant in the medical domain whereby images are acquired from many sources with varying protocols and hence different image characteristics

---

A. Santhirasekaram and A. Kori—Joint first authors.

Supplementary Information The online version contains supplementary material available at https://doi.org/10.1007/978-3-031-16440-8_63.

[3]. There have been various methods developed in the literature to increase robustness of the model most of which are based on simulating perturbations in the input space during training [21]. For example, one can achieve this heuristically through various data augmentation strategies of the training data. One can also train a model to learn to generate data to have an adversarial effect on the performance of a model [12,18].

The vector quantised variational auto-encoder (VQ-VAE) was proposed as a generative model which learns a discrete representation in the latent space via a method called vector quantisation [19]. This is claimed to circumvent the issue of posterior collapse in the VAE [19]. This model has been especially exploited in the field of image generation including text-to-image [4–6,14].

We note that current methods have not explored how to improve the design of a segmentation model so that it is inherently more robust to input perturbations [3]. We take inspiration from the VQ-VAE and hypothesise that deep segmentation models are more robust and accurate when mapping the input data to a discrete latent space.

1.1 Contribution

We propose quantisation of the latent space of any segmentation network architecture, mapping the input images to a lower dimensional embedding space increasing robustness to perturbation in the input space. We provide a thorough justification for this claim under a set of laid out assumptions. We then derive an empirically driven upper bound for maximum allowed shift in the latent space due to perturbation for robustness to hold. We finally support our claim by demonstrating through a set experiments how robustness and performance of the popular UNet architecture [15] is improved with a quantised latent space. Our experiments look at two forms of perturbations to highlight our claim in the form of domain shift and noise. We focus on anatomical segmentation which benefits most from a quantised latent space, because the spatial variability of human anatomy is structured and quantisation in the bottleneck aims to help to capture this by constraining the space where the features can reside.

2 Methods

2.1 Robustness and Network Assumptions

Given an input x, we first define a function $f(x)$ to represent the transformed input due to perturbation. This is a generic function in order to account for various types of perturbations ranging from a re-normalisation function to a non-linear mapping. We therefore now denote the perturbation to be $\delta(x) = f(x) - x$ which can represent noise or domain shift. The aim in this work is to find a way to learn a model (Φ) with weights w to be robust against $\delta(x)$ and construct an uncorrupted segmentation y from the perturbed input $f(x)$.

Assumption 1. *Assuming a small value for $\delta(x)$, we can then approximate $\Phi(x + \delta(x))$ with a first order Taylor expansion as follows: $\Phi(x + \delta(x)) = \Phi(x) + \delta(x)^T \nabla_x \Phi$. Therefore, the training framework should optimize for $argmin_w [\Phi(x + \delta(x)) - \Phi(x)]$ to be robust.*

Assumption 2. *In this work we assume that the segmentation network can be decomposed into an encoder (Φ_e) and decoder (Φ_d) such that $\Phi = \Phi_d \circ \Phi_e$, where $\Phi_e : \mathcal{X} \to \mathcal{E}$ maps from image space to a lower dimensional embedding space and $\Phi_d : \mathcal{E} \to \mathcal{Y}$ maps the embedding space back to segmentation space.*

2.2 Quantisation for Robustness

Formally, with the quantisation block our segmentation network Φ now decomposes as $\Phi_d \circ \Phi_q \circ \Phi_e$, where Φ_e, Φ_d, Φ_q corresponds to the encoder, decoder, and quantisation blocks. Φ_q maps the embedding vectors (e) from the continuous embedding space output of $\Phi_e(x)$ to quantised vectors (z_q). The goal of the quantisation block is to remove unnecessary information in the latent space by collapsing a continuous latent space to a set of discrete vectors.

The quantisation process initially requires us to define a codebook ($c \in \mathcal{R}^{K \times D}$. K is the size of the codebook and D is the dimensionality of each codebook vector $l_i \in \mathcal{R}^D$. We then define a discrete uniform prior and learn a categorical distribution $\mathbb{P}(z \mid x)$ with one-hot probabilities determined by the mapping of each embedding vector in e to the nearest codebook vector l_k which form z_q as follows [19]:

$$\mathbb{P}(z = k \mid x) = \begin{cases} 1 & \text{for} \quad k =_i \|\Phi_e(x) - l_i\|_2 \\ 0 & \text{otherwise} \end{cases} \tag{1}$$

Backpropagation through the non-differentiable quantisation block requires straight-through gradient approximation whereby one copies the gradients from z_q to the encoder output (e) which is used to update the codebook. This allows the entire model to be trained end-to-end with the following loss function [19]:

$$\mathcal{L}_{total} = \mathcal{L}_{Dice}(\hat{y}, y) + \mathcal{L}_{CE}(\hat{y}, y) + \|sg(\Phi_e(x)) - l\|_2 + \beta\|\Phi_e(x) - sg(l)\|_2 \tag{2}$$

The first two terms in Eq. 2 correspond to the Dice and cross entropy loss between the predicted segmentation ($\hat{y}$) and label (y). The third term updates the codebook by moving the codebook vectors (l_i) towards the output of the encoder. The fourth term in Eq. 2 is defined as a commitment loss weighted by β [19] . A stop gradient (sg) is applied to constrain the update to the appropriate operand.

Based on Assumption 1, we get, $\Phi_q(\Phi_e(x + \delta(x))) = \Phi_q(\Phi_e(x) + \delta(x)^T \nabla_x \Phi_e(x))$.

We claim, quantisation pushes $\delta(x)^T \nabla_w \Phi_e(x)$ to 0 and thereby enforces $\Phi_q(\Phi_e(x + \delta(x))) = \Phi_q(\Phi_e(x))$. This claim holds true, if we make the following assumption:

Assumption 3. *We assume if $\|\Phi_e(x) - l_i\|_2 > 0$; then x is absolutely perturbed by $\delta(x)$. This means a codebook c with dimensionality D contains the minimal number of codebook vectors K to fully capture all possible semantics in the latent space i.e., complete. We also assume c is uniformly distributed on the surface of a D-dimensional hypersphere. Therefore, the space on the hypersphere which lie between c represents only perturbations of c. We denote the entire surface of the hypersphere as Z and $\Phi_e(x)$ only generates e which only lies on Z.*

Finally, if the decoder (Φ_d) is only a function of the quantised representation (z_q) then given our Assumption 3, $\Phi(x + \delta(x)) = \Phi(x)$. However, if Φ_d is a function of z and output of each scale from the encoder (s) like in the UNet, then the effect on the output of the model by $\delta(x)$ is only reduced. Yet, this maybe beneficial in practise where the codebook is not complete.

2.3   Perturbation Bounds

A codebook has the advantage to allow us to derive a limit for the shift in latent space which represents the boundary between perturbation and a true semantic shift for the data distribution which we sample, given Assumption 3. This can be defined as the maximum perturbation allowed around a single codebook vector denoted r and calculated empirically as half the average distance between a codebook vector (l_i) and its nearest neighbour (l_{i+1}) across the whole of c as follows:

$$r = \frac{\sum_{i=0}^{i=K-1} \frac{1}{2}(\|l_i - l_{i+1}\|_2)}{K-1} \tag{3}$$

Uniformity also allows to state no matter what the shift along the surface of Z, one will always be at least a distance r from the closest codebook vector l_k.

Next, for simplicity observe a single vector from the output of $\Phi_e(x)$ and $\Phi_e(x + \delta(x))$ denoted e_j and $e_j + \Delta$. We can combine Eq. 3 and the first order Taylor expansion of $\Phi_e(x + \delta(x))$ to theoretically express r in terms of $\delta(x)$ as follows:

$$r > \|\delta(x)^T \nabla_x e_j\|_2 \tag{4}$$

Therefore to affect an output of the quantisation block Φ_q, a perturbation $\delta(x)$ should lead to a change in the embedding space (e) greater than r whose upper bound expressed in terms of $\delta(x)$ is derived in Eq. 4.

2.4   Implementation Details and Data

Architecture: We consider the UNet as our benchmark segmentation architecture and for the proposed architecture, *VQ-UNet*, we add a vector quantisation block at the bottleneck layer of the baseline UNet. Our codebook size (K) is 1024 each of dimension (D) 256. We consider both 2D and 3D UNets. In the encoder we double the number of feature channels from 32 and 16 at the first level to 512 and 256 at the bottleneck, respectively for 2D and 3D. Each scale of the encoder and decoder consist of a single pre-activation residual block [7], with group normalisation [22] and Swish activation [13].

Training: We fine-tuned the hyper-parameter β in the loss function Eq. 3 to be 0.25. The loss function for training the UNet is the sum of the first two terms of Eq. 2 (Dice/cross entropy). We train with batch-size of 10 and 2 for the 2D and 3D tasks, respectively. We apply the same spatial augmentation strategy for all models, and use Adam optimisation with a base learning rate of 0.0001 and weight decay of 0.05 [8]. We train all models for a maximum of 500 epochs on three NVIDIA RTX 2080 GPUs.

Datasets: We use the following three datasets for our experimental study:

Abdomen: We use the Beyond the Cranial Vault (BTCV) consisting of 30 CT scans with 13 labels acquired from a single domain (Vanderbilt University Medical Center) [9]. All images were normalised to 0–1 and resampled to 1.5 ×1.5× 2 mm. We randomly crop 96 × 96 × 96 patches for training.

Prostate: The prostate dataset originates from the NCI-ISBI13 Challenge [1]. It consists of 60 T2 weighted MRI scans of which half come from Boston Medical Centre (BMC) acquired on a 1.5T scanner with an endorectal coil and the other half is acquired from Radboud University Nijmegen Medical Centre (RUNMC) on a 3T scanner with a surface coil [1]. All images were re-sampled to 0.5 × 0.5 × 1.5 mm and z-score normalized. We centre crop to 192 × 192 × 64.

Chest-X-ray: We use the NIH Chest X-ray dataset [20] with annotations provided by [17] and the Japanese Society of Radiological Technology (JSRT) dataset [16] for domain shift analysis; there are 100 and 154 annotated images, respectively. Images were resized to 512 × 512 pixels and normalised to 0–1.

3 Experiments

3.1 Codebook Study

We first analyse whether Assumption 3 holds by calculating r based on Eq. 3 and its standard deviation. We note there is a very large standard deviation around r ranging from 0.0011 to 0.0021 for all 5 datasets (Table 2). This suggests the 5 codebooks are not uniformly distributed i.e., incomplete. Hence, we cannot reliably assume that a shift in latent space greater than r represents the boundary between a meaningful semantic shift and perturbation. Therefore, r is obsolete, and we can only denote r_i; the distance for each codebook vector (l_i) to its nearest neighbour. r_i allows us to at least represent the maximally allowed perturbation in the latent space for each learnt codebook vector (Table 1).

Table 1. Mean $r \pm 1$ standard deviation for all 5 datasets

NIH	JRST	Abdomen	BMC	RUNMC
0.001 ± 0.011	0.002 ± 0.014	0.011 ± 0.018	0.015 ± 0.021	0.012 ± 0.019

3.2 Domain Shift Study

We tackle domain shift from the angle of model design through incorporation of a vector quantisation block in the UNet bottleneck. We evaluate how segmentation performance of the VQ-UNet differs from the UNet on a single domain and across domain for the chest X-ray and prostate datasets on two evaluation metrics: : Dice score and 95% Hausdorff distance in mm (HD95). We randomly split a

Table 2. Mean Dice and HD95 on the validation sets for a single domain and test set across domain. The arrow represents the domain shift

Chest X-ray

	JRST		NIH		JRST→NIH		NIH→JRST	
	Dice	HD95	Dice	HD95	Dice	HD95	Dice	HD95
UNet	0.93	7.31	0.96	6.80	0.95	7.12	0.82	8.27
VQ-UNet	**0.94**	**7.21**	**0.970**	**6.01**	**0.96**	**6.51**	**0.85**	**7.79**

Prostate

	BMC		RUNMC		BMC→RUNMC		RUNMC→BMC	
	Dice	HD95	Dice	HD95	Dice	HD95	Dice	HD95
UNet	0.80	8.42	**0.824**	7.84	0.55	33.3	0.62	25.7
VQ-UNet	**0.82**	**7.82**	0.822	**7.11**	**0.59**	**31.5**	**0.71**	**21.4**

single domain in the prostate dataset into 24 for training and 6 for validation and use the best trained model based on the Dice score for testing on the second domain (30). For the NIH and JRST chest X-ray datasets, we randomly select 20 and 30 samples respectively for validation to find the best model to test on the second domain.

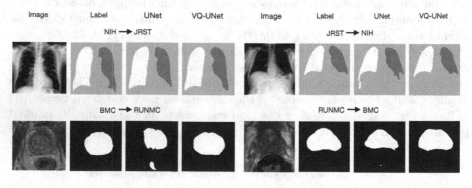

Fig. 1. Sampled image input and segmentation output for 2 domain shifts in chest X-ray (top row) and prostate (bottom row)

Overall, the VQ-UNet improved the segmentation performance both on the validation set and test set from a different domain for both prostate and chest X-ray (Table 2). We note the UNet Dice score reduces to 0.82 and 0.93 compared to 0.85 from 0.94 for the VQ-UNet when shifting domain from JRST to NIH (Table 2). For prostate, there is a significant domain shift and we note a significant drop in Dice score and HD95 distances when testing on a different domain for both the UNet and VQ-UNet (Table 2). However, VQ-UNet appears to be more robust to this domain shift. This is particularly noted when testing on the BMC dataset after training the VQ-UNet on RUNMC (Table 2). The drop in performance albeit improved compared the UNet, is due to an incomplete codebook. It is highly likely the data from the test set maps to e which is a distance greater than r_i of the nearest codebook vector (l_k). This suggest e is a perturbed version of a discrete point on the hypersphere which is not in our incomplete codebook. Nonetheless, in Fig. 1 we note the smoother, anatomically more plausible segmentation map of the VQ-UNet compared to the UNet.

3.3 Perturbation Study

We compare how much the latent space changes in both models with different perturbations in the input space for three datasets (abdomen, NIH, BMC). There are myriad of perturbations one can apply in the input space, so we choose three different types of noise perturbations (Gaussian, salt and pepper, and Poisson noise) under 5 noise levels ranging from 0% to 30% to justify our claim of robustness.

To evaluate the effect of noise on the latent space of the trained models, we sample 100 different noise vectors for each image at each noise level, and observe the variance in the latent space on the validation set. Table 3 describes the average variance of latent space features in both models across all noise levels for each type of noise. It can seen that latent space features in VQ-UNet are not significantly changed (close to 0 variance) under various types of noise. The results are visualised in Fig. 2 whereby the latent space of the VQ-UNet does not significantly change compared to the UNet under the addition of up to 30% Gaussian noise in the NIH dataset. Therefore, given Eq. 4, noise levels of up to 30% is leading to a shift in the latent space of the VQ-UNet less than r_i.

Fig. 2. Variance heatmap of UNet(left) and VQ-UNet(right) latent space under 4 Gaussian noise levels for the NIH dataset. X-axis indicates a unique subset of features from a latent space, Y-axis corresponds to 100 randomly sampled test set images, and value at each location indicates the variance of a specific feature for a given image across 100 test time augmentations with Gaussian noise.

Table 3. Average latent space variance in both the models for all three datasets.

	Abdominal CT			Chest X-ray			Prostate		
	Gauss. Noise	S &P Noise	Poisson noise	Gauss. Noise	S &P Noise	Poisson noise	Gauss. Noise	S &P Noise	Poisson noise
UNet	0.46	0.44	0.46	0.51	0.43	0.47	0.56	0.51	0.51
VQ-UNet	3e–4	5e–5	2e–4	2e–4	1e–4	3e–4	1e–4	6e–5	8e–5

In our analysis of the output space, Table 4 indicates the effect of Gaussian perturbation on Dice scores on the in-domain validation set. It demonstrates the Dice scores are more stable in the VQ-UNet compared to the UNet for all three datasets up to 30% noise. We highlight this result further in Fig. 3 which demonstrates that the segmentation maps produced by the VQ-UNet under the addition of 30% Gaussian noise do not change visually compared to the UNet. We make similar findings for salt & pepper noise and Poisson noise (see supplementary material).

| Image | UNet | VQ-UNet | Image(30%) | UNet(30%) | VQ-UNet(30%) |

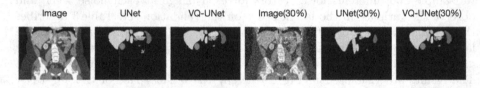

Fig. 3. Sampled Abdomen input image and segmentation output for UNet and VQ-UNet under 0% (1st 3 columns) and 30% (2nd 3 columns) for s&p noise

Overall, the perturbation experiments show that quantisation helps in mitigating the effect of noise perturbation on the latent space, thereby generating non-corrupted segmentation maps. This is in contrast to the prostate domain

Table 4. Gaussian noise perturbation on all 3 datasets

	Dice @0%	Dice @1%	Dice @10%	Dice @20%	Dice @30%
Chest X-ray NIH dataset					
UNet	0.95 ± 0.02	0.96 ± 0.02	0.95 ± 0.03	0.95 ± 0.03	0.95 ± 0.03
VQ-UNet	**0.97 ± 0.01**	**0.97 ± 0.01**	**0.97 ± 0.01**	**0.96 ± 0.02**	**0.96 ± 0.02**
Abdominal CT					
UNet	0.77 ± 0.01	0.76 ± 0.02	0.77 ± 0.04	0.76 ± 0.04	0.75 ± 0.08
VQ-UNet	**0.80 ± 0.01**	**0.79 ± 0.01**	**0.80 ± 0.01**	**0.80 ± 0.02**	**0.79 ± 0.02**
Prostate BMC dataset					
UNet	0.80 ± 0.02	0.81 ± 0.02	0.80 ± 0.03	0.78 ± 0.03	0.77 ± 0.06
VQ-UNet	**0.82 ± 0.02**	**0.82 ± 0.02**	**0.82 ± 0.02**	**0.82 ± 0.03**	**0.80 ± 0.04**

shift experiments whereby the domain shift generates a shift in the latent space larger than r_i for each codebook vector or maps to perturbations from discrete points not present in the codebook.

4   Conclusion

We propose and justify that given a segmentation architecture which maps the input space to a low dimensional embedding space, learning a discrete latent space via quantisation improves robustness of the segmentation model. We highlight quantisation to be especially useful in the task of anatomical segmentation where the output space is structured and hence the codebook metaphorically behaves like an atlas in latent space. This however also possibly limits quantisation in highly variable segmentation tasks such as tumour segmentation.

For future work, other architectures under various other perturbations such as adversarial perturbations will be explored. We also note the limitation of having a uniform prior during training in this work and aim to further increase robustness by jointly training a VQ model with an auto-regressive prior.

Acknowledgements. This work was supported and funded by Cancer Research UK (CRUK) (C309/A28804) and UKRI centre for Doctoral Training in Safe and Trusted AI (EP/S023356/1).

References

1. Bloch, N., et al.: NCI-ISBI 2013 challenge: automated segmentation of prostate structures. Can. Imaging Arch. **370**, 6 (2015)
2. Carlini, N., Wagner, D.: Towards evaluating the robustness of neural networks. In: 2017 IEEE symposium on security and privacy (SP), pp. 39–57. IEEE (2017)
3. Chen, Y.: Towards to robust and generalized medical image segmentation framework. arXiv preprint arXiv:2108.03823 (2021)
4. Ding, M., et al.: Cogview: mastering text-to-image generation via transformers. Adv. Neural Inf. Process. Syst. **34**, 19822–19835 (2021)
5. Esser, P., Rombach, R., Ommer, B.: Taming transformers for high-resolution image synthesis. In: Proceedings of the IEEE/CVF Conference on Computer Vision and Pattern Recognition, pp. 12873–12883 (2021)
6. Gu, S., et al.: Vector quantized diffusion model for text-to-image synthesis. arXiv preprint arXiv:2111.14822 (2021)
7. He, K., Zhang, X., Ren, S., Sun, J.: Identity mappings in deep residual networks. In: Leibe, B., Matas, J., Sebe, N., Welling, M. (eds.) ECCV 2016. LNCS, vol. 9908, pp. 630–645. Springer, Cham (2016). https://doi.org/10.1007/978-3-319-46493-0_38
8. Kingma, D.P., Ba, J.: Adam: a method for stochastic optimization. arXiv preprint arXiv:1412.6980 (2014)
9. Landman, B., Xu, Z., Igelsias, J., Styner, M., Langerak, T., Klein, A.: Miccai multi-atlas labeling beyond the cranial vault-workshop and challenge. In: Proceedings of MICCAI Multi-Atlas Labeling Beyond Cranial Vault-Workshop Challenge, vol. 5, p. 12 (2015)

10. Lei, T., Wang, R., Wan, Y., Zhang, B., Meng, H., Nandi, A.K.: Medical image segmentation using deep learning: a survey. arXiv preprint arXiv:2009.13120 (2020)
11. Moosavi-Dezfooli, S.M., Fawzi, A., Fawzi, O., Frossard, P.: Universal adversarial perturbations. In: Proceedings of the IEEE Conference on Computer Vision and Pattern Recognition, pp. 1765–1773 (2017)
12. Mummadi, C.K., Brox, T., Metzen, J.H.: Defending against universal perturbations with shared adversarial training. In: Proceedings of the IEEE/CVF International Conference on Computer Vision, pp. 4928–4937 (2019)
13. Ramachandran, P., Zoph, B., Le, Q.V.: Searching for activation functions. arXiv preprint arXiv:1710.05941 (2017)
14. Ramesh, A., et al.: Zero-shot text-to-image generation. In: International Conference on Machine Learning, pp. 8821–8831. PMLR (2021)
15. Ronneberger, O., Fischer, P., Brox, T.: U-net: convolutional networks for biomedical image segmentation. In: Navab, N., Hornegger, J., Wells, W.M., Frangi, A.F. (eds.) MICCAI 2015. LNCS, vol. 9351, pp. 234–241. Springer, Cham (2015). https://doi.org/10.1007/978-3-319-24574-4_28
16. Shiraishi, J., et al.: Development of a digital image database for chest radiographs with and without a lung nodule: receiver operating characteristic analysis of radiologists' detection of pulmonary nodules. Am. J. Roentgenol. 174(1), 71–74 (2000)
17. Tang, Y.B., Tang, Y.X., Xiao, J., Summers, R.M.: Xlsor: a robust and accurate lung segmentor on chest x-rays using criss-cross attention and customized radiorealistic abnormalities generation. In: International Conference on Medical Imaging with Deep Learning, pp. 457–467. PMLR (2019)
18. Tramer, F., Boneh, D.: Adversarial training and robustness for multiple perturbations. Adv. Neural Inf. Process. Syst. 32 (2019)
19. Van Den Oord, A., Vinyals, O., et al.: Neural discrete representation learning. Adv. Neural Inf. Process. Syst. 30 (2017)
20. Wang, X., Peng, Y., Lu, L., Lu, Z., Bagheri, M., Summers, R.M.: Chestx-ray8: hospital-scale chest x-ray database and benchmarks on weakly-supervised classification and localization of common thorax diseases. In: Proceedings of the IEEE Conference on Computer Vision and Pattern Recognition, pp. 2097–2106 (2017)
21. Wiles, O., Gowal, S., Stimberg, F., Alvise-Rebuffi, S., Ktena, I., Cemgil, T., et al.: A fine-grained analysis on distribution shift. arXiv preprint arXiv:2110.11328 (2021)
22. Wu, Y., He, K.: Group normalization. In: Proceedings of the European conference on computer vision (ECCV), pp. 3–19 (2018)

A Hybrid Propagation Network for Interactive Volumetric Image Segmentation

Luyue Shi[1], Xuanye Zhang[1], Yunbi Liu[1,2]([✉]), and Xiaoguang Han[1,2]([✉])

[1] Shenzhen Research Institute of Big Data, Shenzhen, China
ybliu1994@gmail.com, hanxiaoguang@cuhk.edu.cn
[2] School of Science and Engineering, The Chinese University of Hong Kong,
Shenzhen, China

Abstract. Interactive segmentation is of great importance in clinical practice for correcting and refining the automated segmentation by involving additional user hints, e.g., scribbles and clicks. Currently, interactive segmentation methods for 2D medical images are well studied, while seldom works are conducted on 3D medical volumetric data. Given a 3D volumetric image, the user interaction can only be performed on a few slices, thus the key issue is how to propagate the information over the entire volume for spatial-consistent segmentation. In this paper, we propose a novel hybrid propagation network for interactive segmentation of 3D medical images. Our proposed method consists of two key designs, including a *slice propagation network* (denoted as SPN) for transferring user hints to adjacent slices to guide the segmentation slice-by-slice and a *volume propagation network* (denoted as VPN) for propagating user hints over the entire volume in a global manner. Specifically, as for SPN, we adopt a memory-augmented network, which utilizes the information of segmented slices (memory slices) to propagate interaction information. To use interaction information propagated by VPN, a *feature-enhanced memory module* is designed, in which the volume segmentation information from the latent space of VPN is introduced into the memory module of SPN. In such a way, the interactive segmentation can leverage both advantages of volume and slice propagation, thus improving the volume segmentation results. We perform experiments on two commonly-used 3D medical datasets, with the experimental results indicating that our method outperforms the state-of-the-art methods. Our code is available at https://github.com/luyueshi/Hybrid-Propagation.

Keywords: Interactive segmentation · Hybrid propagation · 3D medical images

---

Supplementary Information The online version contains supplementary material available at https://doi.org/10.1007/978-3-031-16440-8_64.

1   Introduction

Medical image segmentation is a fundamental procedure for many medical applications, such as measurement of lesions, diagnosis and treatment. However, segmenting medical images, especially 3D volumetric data, is particularly difficult due to the anatomy, pathology, and imaging variation. Although many fully-automated segmentation methods [4,8,13] have been proposed for 3D medical images, they often deliver sub-optimal results without human corrections. Interactive segmentation allows additional user hints, *e.g.,* scribbles, clicks and bounding boxes, to make necessary corrections for the automated segmentation results, which is indispensable in many real-world medical applications.

For interactive volumetric segmentation, once a user hint is provided on a particular slice according to initial/current segmentation, the segmentation of entire volume needs to be refined. This process generally repeats several times until the segmentation result is satisfactory. In this process, how to propagate the user interaction information from the interacted slice to the entire volume is essential. As for 3D medical volumetric data, the propagation of interactive information can start from the interacted slice, pass to the next adjacent one, and so on slice by slice in both forward and backward directions. Also it can be done directly on the entire volume. For convenience, we regard the former as slice propagation and the latter as volume propagation. And we simply divide existing interactive volumetric segmentation methods into *slice propagation-based* [2,7,17,18] and *volume propagation-based* [10–12]. Slice propagation-based methods can process high-resolution volume data at the 2D level by employing 2D CNNs. However, the 3D information is ignored and the interactive information tends to get weaker and weaker during propagation for these slice propagation-based methods. Volume propagation-based methods generally design 3D networks to holistically segment voxels and refine entire volume at a time using the user interaction information as extra input. This kind of methods consider the 3D structures by learning volume features. However, they obviously require significantly more parameters and high memory capacity, and thus often have degraded performance on small datasets and need extra user input to label the bounding box of ROIs for cropping volumes before segmentation.

In this paper, to take full advantage of two segmentation propagation methods, we propose a novel hybrid propagation network for interactive segmentation of 3D medical images. Our proposed method consists of a slice propagation network(denoted as SPN) for slice-by-slice segmentation by propagating the interaction information from one slice to the entire volume, and a volume propagation network(denoted as VPN) for propagating user hints over the entire volume in a global manner. Specifically, we adopt a memory-augmented network which consists of an interaction module and a memory module as our SPN to learn the slice features and predict the segmentation result of every slice. Besides, it also generates the target bounding box for cropping volume patch as the input of VPN to reduce the memory burden. The VPN helps propagate the user guidance at the volume level and produces the spatial-consistent features to guide the slice propagation of SPN. In such a hybrid propagation mode, the segmentation model is

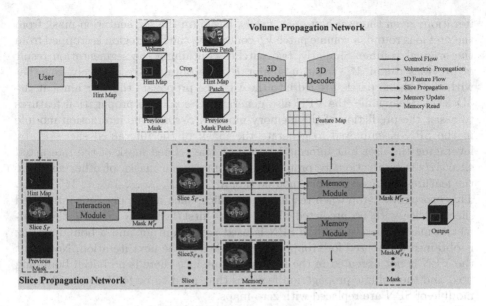

Fig. 1. Pipeline of hybrid propagation network. The hybrid propagation network consists of a 2D SPN and a 3D VPN. The VPN will produce spatial-consistent features to assist the slice propagation of SPN.

expected to be more robust with improved performance. Experiments are performed on multiple medical datasets, with results suggesting the effectiveness of the proposed method.

2 Methodology

For a given volume data, the user first selects an arbitrary slice and gives the hints (e.g., clicks or scribbles), then our framework predicts the initial mask of the entire volume. In the following, the user examines the segmentation results and decides to give a new hint to start next iteration (round) or stop the interaction process. Let $V \in \mathbb{R}^{H \times W \times Z}$ be the input volumetric image, which has Z slices with spatial size $H \times W$. We denote r as the current interaction round, the index of user interacted frame in r-th round is i^r, the i-th slice of the volume is S_i. The segmentation mask of i-th slice and the entire mask after the r-th round is denoted as M_i^r and M^r, respectively.

2.1 Overview

In our work, we propose a hybrid propagation network for interactive segmentation, which leverages both advantages of slice propagation and volume propagation strategies. As shown in Fig. 1, our network consists of a volume propagation network (VPN) and a slice propagation network (SPN), where the SPN contains an interaction module and a feature enhanced memory module. For each iteration, given the user hint map, *firstly*, based on the segmentation mask from the previous round, a volume patch V_p^r containing the ROI region is cropped from the original volume. Similarly, two patches containing the segmentation result of previous round M_p^{r-1} and user hint H_p^r are obtained respectively, together with the volume patch, are fed into the VPN to propagate the user hints at the 3D level. Meanwhile, the VPN also generates the volume propagation features to assist the prediction of the memory module. *Second*, the interaction module in the SPN is employed to generate the mask of the interacted slice $M_{i^r}^r$ by leveraging the user hint information. *Third*, the refined mask of the interacted slice $M_{i^r}^r$ is bidirectionally propagated to obtain the masks of other slices by the feature-enhanced memory module (i.e. $M_{i^r+1}^r, M_{i^r+2}^r, ..., M_{i^r-1}^r, M_{i^r-2}^r, ...$). This process will stop when reaches a stop slice, such as the previous interacted slice, a slice with no predicted object or the first/last slice. *Finally*, the volumetric mask generated by the SPN is used as the output and a bounding box is obtained to be used for cropping the patches in the next iteration. Note that the VPN is not executed in the first iteration since there is no initial bounding box, and the volume propagation features that need to be fed into the memory module of SPN are replaced with zero-maps.

2.2   Volume Propagation Network

The VPN uses a 3D-ResUNet [9] as the backbone, and its input consists of three volume patches: the cropped medical volume patch V_p^r, the mask patch M_p^{r-1} and the user hint map H_p^r. The user hint input is a double-channel 3D binary mask for foreground and background tips. The outputs of VPN are the volumetric segmentation result and features containing volume propagation information. The features F^V at the decoder of VPN are extracted as the additional input of the memory module of SPN, and the output mask of VPN is only used for training the network.

2.3   Slice Propagation Network

The SPN consists of an interaction module and a feature enhanced memory module, where the interacation module is used to refine the user interacted slice and the memory module is used to propagate the mask $M_{i^r}^r$ bidirectionally to segment other slices. Here we propose a novel feature enhanced memory module to leverage the volume propagation features to help the SPN segmentation.

Interaction Module. We use DeepLabV3+ [1] as the backbone of the interaction module of SPN. The inputs of the interaction module consist of the grayscale interacted slice of current round S_{i^r}, the slice mask predicted in the previous round $M_{i^r}^{r-1}$, and the positive/negative hint masks. Note that in the first round, $M_{i^r}^{r-1}$ is initialized as a zero-map with same size as S_{i^r}.

Feature Enhanced Memory Module. After the interacted slice S_{i^r} is segmented by the interaction module, our feature-enhanced memory module learns from the features of segmented slices and volume propagation features to produce corresponding masks in subsequent slices. We design the memory module based on STCN [3], which is extended by the space-time memory [14]. During propagation, we consider the segmented slices as memory slices, which are used to predict the mask of to-be-segmented (query) slice. The prediction of memory module for segmentation contains the following two steps.

Key-Value Embedding and Memory Reading. The key-value embedding module consists of a key encoder f_{Enc}^k and a value encoder f_{Enc}^v. A feature extraction step is performed to generate the key feature of query slice $k^Q \in \mathbb{R}^{C^k \times HW}$ and the key $k^M \in \mathbb{R}^{C^k \times DHW}$ and value features $v^M \in \mathbb{R}^{C^v \times DHW}$ of memory slices. Therein, C^k, C^v and D are the channel number of key feature, the channel number of value feature, and the number of memory slices, respectively. Through similarity measuring, we can compute the pairwise affinity matrix A and the softmax-normalized affinity matrix W for query key and memory keys, where $A, W \in \mathbb{R}^{DHW \times HW}$ with:

$$A = (k^M)^T k^Q, W_{ij} = \frac{exp(A_{ij})}{\Sigma_p(exp(A_{pj}))}, \tag{1}$$

The value of W_{ij} measures the matching probability between i-th position in memory and j-th position in query. With the normalized affinity matrix W, the query value is calculated as:

$$v^Q = v^M W. \tag{2}$$

Feature-Enhanced Decoding. In our work, we propose to introduce the volume propagation features from the decoder of the VPN into the memory module to guide segmentation. Through position embedding for locating the query slice index in the F^V, we extract the corresponding features for query slice F_q^V from the volumetric features F^V, followed by a convolution operation for feature converting. The query slice feature F_s^Q obtained by f_{Enc}^k, together with query value v^Q and the extracted volume propagation feature F_v^Q for query slice, are fed into a decoder f_{Dec} to generate the segmentation mask of the query slice:

$$M_q = f_{Dec}(F_s^Q, v^Q, F_v^Q). \tag{3}$$

Note that since the input of our VPN is a volume patch obtained by cropping and resizing, the extracted volumetric feature F_v^Q for query slice is firstly restored to the original size and position before being fed into f_{Dec}.

2.4 Implementation

We implement our method on the PyTorch. On each datasets, the training process can be separated into 4 steps: 1) Train interaction module of SPN: During training, the previous round masks are simulated by schemes such as morphology transforms on ground truth masks. We use the weights trained on video object segmentation tasks [2,3] for initialization and train it for 1,000 epochs using Adam with learning rate 1e–5. 2) Pre-train VPN and memory module of SPN: Semantic segmentation loss is used to pre-train the encoder and decoder in VPN. We directly use Xavier [5] methods to initialize the network and train it for 500 epochs with Adam and learning rate 1e–3. For the memory module, we first train the memory module without VPN features. Specifically, we randomly sample 3 slices from a volume as a training sample, where the first slice is used as memory slice and slice-by-slice segment another two slices. Besides, the pre-trained weights on video object segmentation is used for initialization and optimizer Adam with learning rate 1e–5 is used to train the model for 500 epochs. 3) Train the decoder of memory module: in this step, the decoder with VPN feature is trained based on the pre-trained weights of VPN and weights of key/value encoders. 4) Joint train the whole model: we load the weights of VPN and memory module trained in previous steps, and fine-tune the VPN and memory module for 300 epoches. Adam is adopted with learning rate 1e–5.

3   Experiments

3.1   Datasets and Experimental Setup

Datasets. We conduct our experiments for 4 segmentation tasks using two public 3D CT datasets, including MSD [15] and KiTS19 [6] to evaluate the effectiveness of our proposed method. The MSD dataset includes ten subsets with different anatomy of interests. We select two challenge subsets about colon and lung cancer from the MSD dataset in our experiments. The colon cancer dataset consists of 126 volumes separated into 100/26 for training/test. The lung subset contains 96 volumes separated into 43/21 for training/test. As for the KiTS19 dataset, 210 CT scans with annotations of kidney and kidney tumor are used and separated into 168/42 for training/test.

Scribble Simulation. Scribbles give a set of pixels to label 'foreground' or 'background' by mouse clicking, which is user-friendly interaction way. Our scribbles are simulated according to the ground-truth masks by simple binary operations. In the first segmentation round, we first randomly generate simulated scribbles on an arbitrary slice and feed it into the segmentation model to segment ROI regions for all the slices. In the following rounds, we select one of the worst slices to generate new simulated scribbles. In this work, our method mainly simulates the scribbles. Actually, other interaction ways, such as clicks, are also applied to our method.

Experimental Setup. Two groups of experiments are conducted. *In the first group*, we compare our hybrid propagation network with other competing methods, including the baseline of our method, nnIU-Net [8], DeepIGeoS [16], and Mem3d [18]. The baseline is the SPN-only counterpart of our method. nnIU-Net is a modified nnU-Net for interactive segmentation as implemented by [18]. Here we denote it as nnIU-Net for convenience. Among these methods, both Baseline and Mem3d adopt the memory-augmented network segmentation for slice propagation, while nnIU-Net and DeepIGeos employ 3D segmentation CNNs for

Table 1. Quantitative performance (DSC%) on KiTS19 and MSD datasets.

Methods	Propagation	KiTS19-Kidney	KiTS19-Tumor	MSD-Lung	MSD-Colon
nnIU-Net [8]	Volume	94.5	86.3	73.9	68.1
DeepIGeoS [16]	Volume	95.7	87.6	76.6	72.3
Mem3d [18]	Slice	96.9	88.2	80.9	79.7
Baseline/SPN	Slice	96.8	88.0	82.4	82.2
Ours	Hybrid	**97.2**	**92.1**	**86.9**	**87.3**

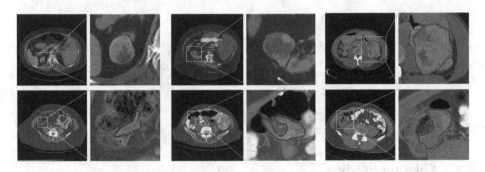

Fig. 2. Visual segmentation results. The red, green, blue boundaries indicate ground truth, the results of baseline and our method, respectively. (Color figure online)

volume propagation. Only our method involves both slice and volume propagation networks for hybrid propagation. *In the second group*, we conduct the ablation study to verify the help of VPN features at different layers for slice segmentation propagation of our SPN, and thus verify the effectiveness of hybrid propagation on interactive volumetric segmentation. Besides, we also investigate the impact of the number of interactions on segmentation performance.

3.2 Comparison with Previous Methods

Table 1 reports the quantitative results of our method and recent competing methods, *i.e.*, Baseline, Interactive nnU-Net [8], DeepIGeoS [16], and Mem3d [18]. Following the previous work [18], we report the results at 6th round. As reported in Table 1, our method achieves the best performance on both two datasets and four segmentation tasks, including segmenting kidney and kidney tumor from KiTS19 dataset and segmenting lung and colon cancer regions from MSD dataset. Especially for the kidney tumor and colon cancer region segmentation, our method improves 3.9 percent point and 5.1 percent point by a large margin than the second-best results obtained by Mem3d and our Baseline method, respectively. These results indicate the superiority of our method to other interaction volumetric segmentation methods involving only one propagation way. We also show the visual results of our method, Baseline method and the ground truth segmentations in Fig. 2. The visual result shown in Fig. 2 also suggests the effectiveness of the hybrid propagation network of our method.

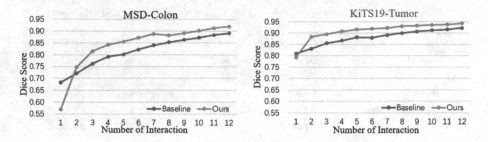

Fig. 3. The segmentation performance with respect to number of interactions.

Table 2. Evaluation on the impact of different VPN features on the segmentation.

Method	MSD-Colon
Baseline/SPN	82.2
Baseline + VPN (last)	85.5
Baseline + VPN (middle)	**87.3**

3.3   Ablation Study

Number of Interactions. Every time a user gives a hint on a single slice, the interaction segmentation network will refine the volume segmentation result at a time. Figure 3 shows the segmentation performance of our method and baseline on the MSD-Colon and KiTS19-Tumor datasets with different numbers of inter-action. It can be seen that our proposed method achieves better performance than the SPN-only baseline method in each iteration except the first iteration due to the lack of volume propagation features, indicating the superiority of the proposed hybrid propagation.

VPN Features at Different Layers. During training and inference phases, our method extracts the VPN features to the SPN for guiding segmentation. We simply investigate the impact of the VPN features extracted from different lay-ers of VPN decoder using the MSD-Colon dateset. Table 2 reports the segmenta-tion performance of the baseline method without adding VPN features and our method with adding the VPN features from the last and middle layers, respec-tively. From the results in Table 2, we can infer that the introduction of VPN features is helpful. Besides, the middle down-scaled VPN features with compact semantic information is more effective than the last VPN features at the orig-inal scale with the VPN input. Note that before being fed into the SPN, the corresponding query slice feature need be extracted from the VPN features and restored to the same size with the query slice according to position embedding.

3.4   User Study

We conducted a user study to evaluate our algorithm in real applications. We invited 5 radiologists who were given 20 min to get familiar with the tools and then annotated 5 CT scans for multiple rounds until achieved user-satisfied results. We evaluated four methods: a. completely manual annotation, b. traditional methods-assisted annotation, c. our baseline-assisted annotation, d. our hybrid network-assisted annotation. The average annotation time and number of user-interacted slices are (minutes/slices) 25.1/27.4, 16.7/21.8, 7.3/7.3, 4.5/4.7, respectively, which show the outperformance of our method in real applications.

4 Conclusion

In this work, we proposed a hybrid propagation network for interactive 3D medical images segmentation. Different from other methods which involves only one propagation when a user hint is provided, both of slice and volume propagation networks are included in our method. These two networks collaborate with each other for segmentation. The SPN employs a memory-augmented network to encode the slice images and segmentation masks, and segment the ROI slice by slice. Besides, it also predicts the target bounding box used to generate the input patch of our VPN. Our VPN can encode the volume information and generate the spatial-consistent features to assist the slice propagation of SPN. Experiments on multiple 3D medical datasets show that our method is superior than other methods and the proposed strategy is effective. However, requiring model training for specific data is still a limitation, which is also a common limitation for learning-based methods. In the trial, the model can be trained and updated as user interacts. And we will focus on solving this issue in the future work.

Acknowledgements. This work was supported by Chinese Key-Area Research and Development Program of Guangdong Province (2020B0101350001) and the Guangdong Provincial Key Laboratory of Big Data Computing, The Chinese University of Hong Kong, Shenzhen. It was also supported by NSFC-61931024 and Shenzhen Sustainable Development Project(KCXFZ20201221173008022). We thank the ITSO in CUHKSZ for their High-Performance Computing Services.

References

1. Chen, L.C., Zhu, Y., Papandreou, G., Schroff, F., Adam, H.: Encoder-decoder with atrous separable convolution for semantic image segmentation. In: Proceedings of the European Conference on Computer Vision (ECCV), pp. 801–818 (2018)
2. Cheng, H.K., Tai, Y.W., Tang, C.K.: Modular interactive video object segmentation: interaction-to-mask, propagation and difference-aware fusion. In: Proceedings of the IEEE/CVF Conference on Computer Vision and Pattern Recognition, pp. 5559–5568 (2021)
3. Cheng, H.K., Tai, Y.W., Tang, C.K.: Rethinking space-time networks with improved memory coverage for efficient video object segmentation. Adv. Neural Inf. Process. Syst. **34**, 11781–11794 (2021)
4. Dou, Q., et al.: 3d deeply supervised network for automated segmentation of volumetric medical images. Med. Image Anal. **41**, 40–54 (2017)

5. Glorot, X., Bengio, Y.: Understanding the difficulty of training deep feedforward neural networks. In: Proceedings of the Thirteenth international Conference on Artificial Intelligence and Statistics, pp. 249–256. JMLR Workshop and Conference Proceedings (2010)
6. Heller, N., et al.: The kits19 challenge data: 300 kidney tumor cases with clinical context, CT semantic segmentations, and surgical outcomes. arXiv preprint arXiv:1904.00445 (2019)
7. Heo, Y., Koh, Y.J., Kim, C.S.: Guided interactive video object segmentation using reliability-based attention maps. In: Proceedings of the IEEE/CVF Conference on Computer Vision and Pattern Recognition, pp. 7322–7330 (2021)
8. Isensee, F., et al.: nnU-net: Self-adapting framework for u-net-based medical image segmentation. arXiv preprint arXiv:1809.10486 (2018)
9. Lee, K., Zung, J., Li, P., Jain, V., Seung, H.S.: Superhuman accuracy on the snemi3d connectomics challenge. arXiv preprint arXiv:1706.00120 (2017)
10. Li, W., et al.: Interactive medical image segmentation with self-adaptive confidence calibration. arXiv preprint arXiv:2111.07716 (2021)
11. Liao, X., et al.: Iteratively-refined interactive 3d medical image segmentation with multi-agent reinforcement learning. In: Proceedings of the IEEE/CVF Conference on Computer Vision and Pattern Recognition, pp. 9394–9402 (2020)
12. Ma, C., et al.: Boundary-aware supervoxel-level iteratively refined interactive 3d image segmentation with multi-agent reinforcement learning. IEEE Trans. Med. Imaging 40(10), 2563–2574 (2020)
13. Milletari, F., Navab, N., Ahmadi, S.A.: V-net: fully convolutional neural networks for volumetric medical image segmentation. In: 2016 Fourth International Conference on 3D vision (3DV), pp. 565–571. IEEE (2016)
14. Oh, S.W., Lee, J.Y., Xu, N., Kim, S.J.: Video object segmentation using space-time memory networks. In: Proceedings of the IEEE/CVF International Conference on Computer Vision, pp. 9226–9235 (2019)
15. Simpson, A.L., et al.: A large annotated medical image dataset for the development and evaluation of segmentation algorithms. arXiv preprint arXiv:1902.09063 (2019)
16. Wang, G., et al.: Deepigeos: a deep interactive geodesic framework for medical image segmentation. IEEE Trans. Pattern Anal. Mach. intell. 41(7), 1559–1572 (2018)
17. Yin, Z., Zheng, J., Luo, W., Qian, S., Zhang, H., Gao, S.: Learning to recommend frame for interactive video object segmentation in the wild. In: Proceedings of the IEEE/CVF Conference on Computer Vision and Pattern Recognition, pp. 15445–15454 (2021)
18. Zhou, T., Li, L., Bredell, G., Li, J., Konukoglu, E.: Quality-aware memory network for interactive volumetric image segmentation. In: de Bruijne, M., et al. (eds.) MICCAI 2021. LNCS, vol. 12902, pp. 560–570. Springer, Cham (2021). https://doi.org/10.1007/978-3-030-87196-3_52

SelfMix: A Self-adaptive Data Augmentation Method for Lesion Segmentation

Qikui Zhu[1], Yanqing Wang[2], Lei Yin[5], Jiancheng Yang[3], Fei Liao[4], and Shuo Li[1(✉)]

[1] Department of Biomedical Engineering and Computer and Data Science, Case Western Reserve University, Cleveland, OH, USA
QikuiZhu@163.com, slishuo@gmail.com
[2] Department of Gynecology, Renmin Hospital of Wuhan University, Wuhan, China
yanqingwang543@gmail.com
[3] Shanghai Jiao Tong University, Shanghai, China
jekyll4168@sjtu.edu.cn
[4] Department of Gastroenterology, Renmin Hospital of Wuhan University, Wuhan, China
feiliao@whu.edu.cn
[5] China Nanhu Academy of Electronics and Information Technology, Jiaxing, China
yinlei915@163.com

Abstract. Deep learning-based methods have obtained promising results in various organ segmentation tasks, due to their effectiveness in learning feature representation. However, accurate segmentation of lesions can still be challenging due to 1) the lesions provide less information than normal organs; 2) the available number of labeled lesions is more limited than normal organs; 3) the morphology, shape, and size of lesions are more diverse than normal organs. To increase the number of lesion samples and further boost the performance of various lesion segmentation, in this paper, we propose a simple but effective lesion-aware data augmentation method called Self-adaptive Data Augmentation (SelfMix). Compared with existing data augmentation methods, such as Mixup, CutMix, and CarveMix, our proposed SelfMix have three-fold advances: 1) Solving the challenges that the generated tumor images are facing the problem of distortion by absorbing both tumor and non-tumor information; 2) SelfMix is tumor-aware, which can adaptively adjust the fusing weights of each lesion voxels based on the geometry and size information from the tumor itself; 3) SelfMix is the first one that notices non-tumor information. To evaluate the proposed data augmentation method, experiments were performed on two public lesion segmentation datasets. The results show that our method improves the lesion segmentation accuracy compared with other data augmentation approaches.

Keywords: Lesions segmentation · Data augmentation · Tumor-aware

1 Introduction

Deep convolutional neural networks (DCNNs) have obtained promising performance on various medical image segmentation tasks [8,9], which promotes the

L. Wang et al. (Eds.): MICCAI 2022, LNCS 13434, pp. 683–692, 2022.
https://doi.org/10.1007/978-3-031-16440-8_65

development of automated computer-aided medical image analysis. However, CNNs based methods are data-hungry, which makes the performance of methods vulnerable to the amount of training data. This phenomenon is particularly obvious when dealing with various lesions, due to 1) lesions typically contain less feature information than normal organs. 2) Lesion annotations are pricey and labor-intensive, which require extensive domain knowledge from biomedical experts. This leads to proving enough labeled lesions data is very hard. 3) The morphology, shape, and size of lesions are more diverse than normal organs, which further increases the difficulty of lesion segmentation. An effective lesions generation method is urgently needed to boost the performance of lesion segmentation. In this paper, we focus on addressing the urgent needs and propose a novel data augmentation framework through better utilizing the lesions and normal image information to improve the performance of lesion segmentation.

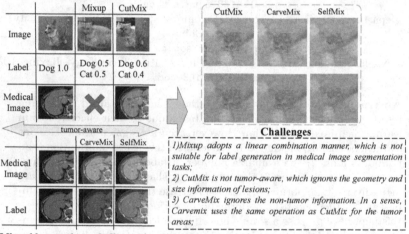

Fig. 1. Challenges in various image generation methods. Our proposed SelfMix addresses those challenges by absorbing both tumor and non-tumor information adaptively. The natural image samples are cited from paper [5]. The images generated by CutMix and CarveMix are the same, due to CarveMix having the same operation (directly replaces) as CutMix when CarveMix does not scale the size of the tumor.

Data augmentation is a widely used strategy that enlarges the amounts of training samples for overcoming the challenge of lacking sufficient training data. Typically, augmented data is generated by transformation operation, including rotation, flipping, adding noise, random crop, from existing training data [2]. However, the diversity of data generated via those basic image transformations is always limited. To overcome the above challenges, many researchers try to generate synthesizing images by utilizing Generative Adversarial Networks (GANs) [10]. There is no denying that the invention of GANs marks a major milestone in generating image synthesis, and the generated natural images are more and more realistic. However, different from natural images, medical images contain more complex structural and content information, and the generated medical images are facing the problem of distortion. Meanwhile, there is room for improvement in the generated medical images and clinical applications. To overcome those challenges, other types of data augmentation methods have been developed by utilizing annotated data, such as Mixup [6], CutMix [5], CarveMix [7], which could generate more realistic samples. Specifically, Mixup adopts a linear combination manner, which linearly combines two annotated images for creating augmented training images. Differently, CutMix adopts a nonlinear combination manner, which first extracts one region from one image and then the extracted region nonlinearly combines with other images. The annotations are still linearly combined according to the proportion of each image. To make the model aware of the lesion, CarveMix is proposed which stochastically combines two existing labeled images based on the shape and location of lesions to generate new labeled samples.

Although the above data augmentation methods could generate sufficient training data and improve the performance of CNN-based models, there still exists a huge gap between true lesions and generated lesions. As shown in Fig. 1, 1) Mixup is designed for classification tasks and is not suitable for segmentation tasks, particularly for medical image segmentation. 2) CutMix directly pastes one region with other images, which ignores the structure and information of the lesion itself and leads to the generated image is unnatural and heterogeneous. 3)Although the CarveMix is tumor-aware, which ignores the non-tumor information and adopts the same operation as CutMix for the tumor areas generation in a sense. To simultaneously obtain diverse training data and overcome the above challenges, in this paper, a simpler and more effective data augmentation method is developed. Specifically, given a training image with corresponding tumor label, we first extract the region of lesion according to the lesion location and geometry provided by label, and then the extracted tumor region adaptive fuses with a non-tumor region in other images and generate a new training data with tumor information. Remarkably, except for considering the tumor information, our proposed method also absorbs the non-tumor information and adaptively adjusts the fusing weights of each tumor voxels. And the annotation of the generated image in the new region is replaced by the corresponding labels of the original tumor as well. In the above-mentioned way, we could generate new labeled images for network training. Since the combination is achieved based on the information from both tumor and non-tumor, we call our method Self-adaptive Data Augmentation (Self-Mix). We evaluate the proposed data augmentation method on two public lesion segmentation datasets. The results show that our method improves the lesion segmentation accuracy compared with other data augmentation approaches.

Summary, our detailed contributions are as follow:

- Compared with Mixup, CutMix, CarveMix, our proposed method is the first one that notices non-tumor information.
- Our proposed method is tumor-aware, which avoids the challenge of distortion problems in the generated tumor images.

– Experimental results demonstrate that our method improves the lesion segmentation accuracy compared with other data augmentation approaches.

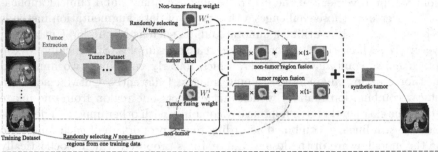

Step.1: Extracting tumor, selecting non-tumor regions from training dataset.   Step.2: Fusing tumor with non-tumor region by utilizing fusing weights   Step3: generating synthetic tumor.

Fig. 2. A graphical illustration of the image generation procedure in SelfMix.

2   Method

2.1   Self-adaptive Data Augmentation

Figure 2 is the graphical illustration of the synthetic images and annotations generating procedure, which consists of multi-steps. Specifically, given the training image dataset $\{(X_1, Y_1), ..., (X_N, Y_N)\}$, where (X_i, Y_i) is the i-th image with corresponding label, and N is the total number of images. We first extract the region of tumors with corresponding annotations from training image based on the annotation for constructing tumor dataset $\{(t_1, l_1), ..., (t_K, l_K)\}$, where K is the total number of tumors.

By utilizing those extracted tumors and corresponding labels, SelfMix can generate various tumors for training images. Mathematically, the normalized distance maps D_t^i and D_n^i for the ith tumor and non-tumor region are first computed by the distance Dis_t^i, Dis_n^i between each voxel and the tumor boundary.

$$D_t^i = \frac{Dis_t^i - \min(Dis_t^i)}{\max(Dis_t^i) - \min(Dis_t^i)}, D_n^i = \frac{Dis_n^i - \min(Dis_n^i)}{\max(Dis_n^i) - \min(Dis_n^i)}, \quad (1)$$

Afterward, the fusing weights of the tumor region and non-tumor region are computed based on the information proved by the distance maps. In addition, to guarantee the consistency between tumor and label, SelfMix ensures the tumor information occupies a higher weight than the non-tumor region in fusing weights (larger than 0.50), which makes tumor features occupy the main component inside the synthetic tumor.

$$W_t^i = (1 - \delta) \times D_t^i + \delta, W_n^i = (1 - \delta) \times D_n^i + \delta, \quad (2)$$

where, $\delta \sim U(0.5, 1)$ controls the fusing weight.

Once the fusion weight W_t^i, W_n^i are obtained, we can generate diverse and distortion free new image with corresponding tumor label by fusing the extracted tumor region t_i with randomly selected non-tumor region X_t^p from images X_t. Mathematically, the synthetic lesion X'^p_t and annotation Y'^p_t are generated as follows:

$$X'^p_t = W_n^i \odot X_t^p + (1 - W_n^i) \odot t_i + W_t^i \odot t_i + (1 - W_t^i) \odot X_t^p \qquad (3)$$

$$Y'^p_t = l_i \qquad (4)$$

where, $\odot$ denotes voxel wise multiplication, X_t^p with same size as the lesion t_i is a randomly selected non-tumor region from images X_t. The non-tumor region is selected from the normal tissue where tumors can grow. Specifically, in our paper, the non-tumor regions were randomly selected from the normal liver or kidney tissues. This setting makes the tumor generated by our method clinically appropriate and reasonable. The complete SelfMix algorithm for generating the sets of synthetic lesion and annotations is summarized in Algorithm 1.

Algorithm 1. SelfMix

Input: Training images with corresponding annotations $\{(X_1, Y_1), (X_2, Y_2), ..., (X_N, Y_N)\}$, the desired number of synthetic lesion region $\mathcal{T}$ for each training data (X_i, Y_i).

Output: Synthetic training data $\{(X'_1, Y'_1), (X'_2, Y'_2), ..., (X'_N, Y'_N)\}$, each synthetic training date contains additional $\mathcal{T}$ synthetic lesions.

for (X_i, Y_i) in $\{(X_1, Y_1), (X_2, Y_2), ..., (X_N, Y_N)\}$ **do**

  1) Randomly selecting $\mathcal{T}$ lesion regions from the tumor dataset;

  2) Randomly selecting $\mathcal{T}$ non-tumor regions from (X_i, Y_i);

  3) Computing the fusing weights W_t^i, W_n^i for each tumor and non-tumor region by Eq. 1 and Eq. 2;

  4) Fusing the $\mathcal{T}$ lesion regions with $\mathcal{T}$ non-tumor regions for generating synthetic lesion regions by Eq. 3 and Eq. 4;

end for

Return (X'_i, Y'_i)

Table 1. The statistics of datasets adopted in our study.

Dataset	Volume number			Tumor number	
	Training	Testing	Total	Befor augmentation	After augmentation
LiTS	104	26	130	684	2057
KiTS19	168	42	210	129	1827

3   Experiments

3.1   Datasets and Implementation Details

Datasets: To evaluate the proposed method, we performed experiments on the public Liver Tumor Segmentation (LiTS) dataset [1] and KiTS19 challenge data [3]. The LiTS data contains 130 CT scans for training and 70 CT scans for evaluation. Each CT scan has the same resolution of 512×512 pixels but with varied slice thicknesses. The ground truth is only provided for the training set. In our experiment, we randomly selected 26 (20%) images from 130 CT scans as the testing set and the rest of the scans as the training set. KiTS19 is a publicly available dataset for kidney tumor segmentation, which consists of 210 3D abdominal CT images with kidney tumor subtypes and segmentations of kidney and kidney tumors. These CT images are from more than 50 institutions and scanned with different CT scanners and acquisition protocols. In our experiment, we randomly split the published 210 images into a training set with 168 images and a testing set with 42 images.

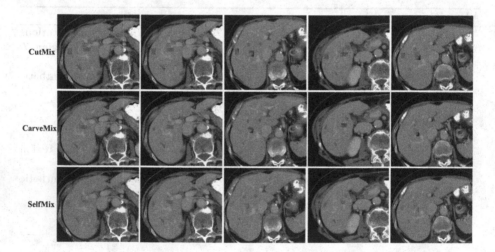

Fig. 3. Qualitative comparison with augmented samples produced by various data augmentation methods. Both samples and samples with labels are listed. Readers better zoom in to see the difference in detail.

Implementation Details: Following the setting in previous work [7], in this work, we also choose to perform offline data augmentation. The desired number of synthetic lesions generated by the three methods as listed in Table 1. Parts of tumors generated are shown in Fig. 3. Notable, for a fair comparison with other methods, the selected location of the non-tumor region was same in compared methods, and the standard 3D segmentation network, named Vnet, as the baseline segmentation model. Before training, the image intensity is windowed by $[-100, 400]$ for liver tumors, $[-160, 240]$ for kidney tumors. Each slice is resized to 512×512 and then randomly cropped to 256×256 for training. The Adam [4] is used for optimization with an initial learning rate of 5e−4. To evaluate the effectiveness of the data augmentation, we also compare with the default traditional data augmentation (TDA) including rotation, scaling, mirroring, elastic deformation, intensity perturbation. The maximum number of training epochs was set to 500 for the two datasets.

3.2   Experimental Results

Results on the LiTS/KiTS19 Dataset: To quantitatively evaluate the effectiveness of methods, we compute the means and standard deviations of the Dice coefficients of the segmentation results on the same test set. The results of the proposed method and comparison methods are shown in Table 2. As it can be seen from the Table 2, the proposed model achieves the highest improvements on the two tumor segmentation tasks compared to other data augmentation methods, which convincingly demonstrates the effectiveness of SelfMix in exploring and integrating tumor information. It is worth noting that the CutMix even degrades the segmentation performance, which indicates that CutMix may not be suitable for tumor segmentation.

We also evaluate the performance of the model from the aspect of quality. The segmentation results on a representative test scan are shown in Fig. 4. We can see that SelfMix produced better segmentation results than the competing methods, which further proves the effectiveness of SelfMix.

Table 2. Means and standard deviations of the Dice coefficients (%) of the segmentation results on the test set for the LiTS/KiTS19.

Dataset	Mean dice ± std/improvement over baseline (%)			
	TDA	CutMix	CarveMix	SelfMix
LiTS	55.41 ± 26.84	55.09 ± 27.49/−0.32	58.79 ± 24.80/+3.38	62.08 ± 22.36/ +6.67
KiTS19	44.92 ± 31.83	47.89 ± 31.22/+2.97	55.56 ± 25.86/+10.64	56.60 ± 23.02/+10.68

3.3   Effectiveness Analysis Using SelfMix:

We also demonstrate the potentials of SelfMix in an extremely low-data regime via additional ablations on KiTS19. Particularly, we randomly select 25%, 50%, 75% of data from the training set same as before as training data, and evaluate the performance of the model on the same testing data. The results of the proposed method and comparison methods are shown in Table 3. As it can be seen from the Table 3, SelfMix assists the baseline model to achieve higher Dice

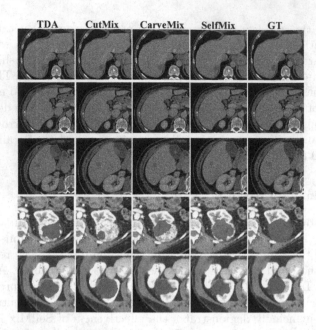

Fig. 4. Qualitative comparisons with the same model under various data augmentation methods.

coefficients and outperform the competing methods. Specifically, SelfMix can improve 13.16%, 8.42%, 5.41%, and 11.68% under 25%, 50%, 75%, and 100% training data, which convincingly demonstrates the effectiveness of SelfMix in learning tumor feature representation.

Table 3. Means and standard deviations of the Dice coefficients (%) of the segmentation results on the test set for the KiTS19.

KiTS19	Mean dice ± std/improvement over baseline (%)			
	TAD	CutMix	CarveMix	SelfMix
25%	28.28 ± 25.32	31.47 ± 23.28/+3.19	41.46 ± 26.42/+12.88	41.74 ± 25.01/ +13.46
50%	42.54 ± 27.63	45.46 ± 28.63/+2.92	48.65 ± 28.09/+6.11	50.96 ± 29.14/+8.42
75%	48.12 ± 30.52	47.70 ± 27.49/−0.42	52.59 ± 26.53/+4.47	53.53 ± 25.20/+5.41
100%	44.92 ± 31.83	47.89 ± 31.22/+2.97	55.56 ± 25.86/+10.64	56.60 ± 23.02/+11.68

3.4 Relationship with Mixup, CutMix and CarveMix

To analyze the difference and relationship between the four types of data augmentation methods, in this section, we summarize and compare the synthetic samples generation procedures of them. Note that, in this paper, we just consider the application scenarios that generate the synthetic lesion voxelwise samples for enlarging the number of lesion samples. Mixup and CutMix are unaware of lesions, where the data generation does not pay more attention to the region of the lesion and is not be specifically designed for synthetic lesion generation. Specifically, Mixup linearly combines the two images at the voxel, which ignores the shape and location of the lesion and the generation of annotations is not suitable for the lesion segmentation task. CutMix adopts a nonlinear combination manner, which extracts one region from one image and directly combines with other images, the generated image is mixed and unnatural. Compared with Mixup and CutMix, CarveMix adopts a lesion-aware manner, and the synthetic lesion is determined by the lesion location and geometry given by the annotation. However, CarveMix only considers the lesion information and ignores the information from the non-tumor region, which makes the synthetic lesion cannot fusing into the new image naturally. In addition, CarveMix adopts the same operation as CutMix for the tumor areas generation. Our proposed SelfMix addresses these limitations from three aspects: 1) Different from synthesizing images, the tumor generated by our proposed model is directly constructed by the true tumor information, which avoids the content of generated tumor suffering from distortion. 2) Both tumor information and non-tumor information (from combining images) are considered during two image voxels fusing, which further avoids the distortion that exists in the fusing region. 3) The fusing weights are adaptively computed by the structure and geometry of the lesion itself, which can be adapted to the tumor with various sizes and distributions and further avoids the distortion bring by the tumor itself. In summary, the generation of images and annotation are more in line with the actual lesion situation and avoid distortion problems.

4   Conclusion

In this paper, we propose a simple but effective tumor-aware data augmentation named SelfMix. Compared with existing data augmentation methods, such as Mixup, CutMix, and CarveMix, our proposed SelfMix have three-fold advances: 1) Solving the challenges that the generated medical images are facing the problem of distortion; 2) SelfMix is tumor-aware, which can adaptively adjust the fusing weights of each lesion voxels based on the geometry and size information from the tumor itself; 3) Expect for the tumor information, the non-tumor information is also be considered, which makes the generating lesions are more reasonable. Experiments were performed on two public lesion segmentation datasets. The results show that our method improves the lesion segmentation accuracy compared with other data augmentation approaches.

References

1. Bilic, P., et al.: The liver tumor segmentation benchmark (LiTS). arXiv preprint arXiv:1901.04056 (2019)
2. Chaitanya, K., et al.: Semi-supervised task-driven data augmentation for medical image segmentation. Med. Image Anal. **68**, 101934 (2021)

3. Heller, N., et al.: The kits19 challenge data: 300 kidney tumor cases with clinical context, CT semantic segmentations, and surgical outcomes. arXiv preprint arXiv:1904.00445 (2019)
4. Kingma, D.P., Ba, J.: Adam: a method for stochastic optimization. arXiv preprint arXiv:1412.6980 (2014)
5. Yun, S., Han, D., Oh, S.J., Chun, S., Choe, J., Yoo, Y.: CutMix: regularization strategy to train strong classifiers with localizable features. In: Proceedings of the IEEE/CVF International Conference on Computer Vision, pp. 6023–6032 (2019)
6. Zhang, H., Cisse, M., Dauphin, Y.N., Lopez-Paz, D.: mixup: Beyond empirical risk minimization. arXiv preprint arXiv:1710.09412 (2017)
7. Zhang, X., et al.: CarveMix: a simple data augmentation method for brain lesion segmentation. In: de Bruijne, M., et al. (eds.) MICCAI 2021. LNCS, vol. 12901, pp. 196–205. Springer, Cham (2021). https://doi.org/10.1007/978-3-030-87193-2_19
8. Zhu, Q., Du, B., Yan, P.: Boundary-weighted domain adaptive neural network for prostate MR image segmentation. IEEE Trans. Med. Imaging **39**(3), 753–763 (2019)
9. Zhu, Q., Wang, Y., Du, B., Yan, P.: OASIS: one-pass aligned atlas set for medical image segmentation. Neurocomputing **470**, 130–138 (2022)
10. Zou, D., Zhu, Q., Yan, P.: Unsupervised domain adaptation with dual-scheme fusion network for medical image segmentation. In: IJCAI, pp. 3291–3298 (2020)

Bi-directional Encoding for Explicit Centerline Segmentation by Fully-Convolutional Networks

Ilyas Sirazitdinov[1,2], Axel Saalbach[1], Heinrich Schulz[1], and Dmitry V. Dylov[2(✉)]

[1] Philips Research, Hamburg, Germany
{ilyas.sirazitdinov,axel.saalbach,heinrich.schulz}@philips.com
[2] Skolkovo Institute of Science and Technology, Moscow, Russia
d.dylov@skoltech.ru

Abstract. Localization of tube-shaped objects is an important topic in medical imaging. Previously it was mainly addressed via dense segmentation that may produce inconsistent results for long and narrow objects. In our work, we propose a point-based approach for explicit centerline segmentation that can be learned by fully-convolutional networks. We propose a new bi-directional encoding scheme that does not require any autoregressive blocks and is robust to various shapes and orientations of lines, being adaptive to the number of points in their centerlines. We present extensive evaluation of our approach on synthetic and real data (chest x-ray and coronary angiography) and show its advantage over the state-of-the-art segmentation models.

Keywords: Tube-shaped segmentation · Centerline segmentation · Bi-directional encoding · Computer-assisted intervention · Catheter tracking

1 Introduction

Tube-shaped objects are widespread in healthcare. They can be informally divided into two groups: anatomical tube-shaped objects and medical devices. The anatomical group includes blood vessels, veins, arteries. Medical devices entail tubes, catheters, and wires, mainly used either for diagnostic or for interventional purposes. Precise detection and localization of such objects is an important clinical topic, *e.g.*, segmentation of coronary arteries helps to diagnose vessel narrowing [4]; automatic catheter and guidewire localization is the important part of robot-assisted interventions that are guided by fluoroscopy [17,18]; localization and tip detection of the central venous catheter helps to recognize malposition cases [7], capable of causing severe complications. Endotracheal tubes,

---

Supplementary Information The online version contains supplementary material available at https://doi.org/10.1007/978-3-031-16440-8_66.

tracheostomy tubes, chest tubes, nasogastric tubes, *etc.* [3,16] are all frequently engaged in clinical practice, with chest x-ray being used for inserting and guiding the object in a precise and a controllable manner.

The conventional way of localizing tube-shaped objects is a semantic segmentation that produces a binary mask [8,9,17,18]. Zhou et al. proposed an encoder-decoder network with recurrent residual blocks [18] and with the attention mechanisms [17] to address a guidewire segmentation and tracking in endovascular aneurysm repair problem. A U-Net model with the spatial location priors was used in [9]. The endotracheal tube was segmented by U-Net with the help of synthetic data in [3]. Various catheters and tubes were segmented in pediatric x-ray images using a scale-recurrent network [15]. Such models may be followed by some post-processing algorithms that try to eliminate or merge individual connected components to reconstruct the true shape of a device [1]. In contrast to all these methods that operate with a binary mask, we propose a different data structure for the efficient segmentation of tube-shaped objects, *i.e.*, a centerline built with n connected points. *The main contribution of our work* is a n-landmarks-based centerline model that can be directly predicted by fully-convolutional networks. We propose a coordinate order encoding scheme that can be learned by the neural network without any ambiguity. Moreover, all predictions of the network can be easily interpreted without any post-processing.

2   Method

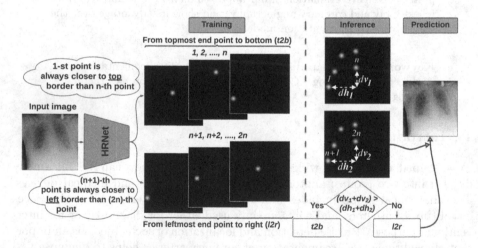

Fig. 1. Bi-directional encoding scheme. During the training, we predict n points from the topmost endpoint to the bottom, and n points from the leftmost endpoint to the right edge. During the inference, we pick one of the encodings based on the horizontal and the vertical distances to the predicted endpoints.

Localization via segmentation is a common approach in medical imaging which is usually performed by predicting $h \times w$-grid mask for each object with each cell belonging to a specific class. It is an efficient way of localizing convex-shape objects, *e.g.*, organs, bones, *etc.* Small errors for convex-shape objects, holes in masks, can be easily recovered by morphological operations. The tube-shaped objects, in contrast to convex-shape ones, are narrow and long. Hence, a misclassification of a few pixels may lead to inconsistent line prediction, requiring multiple connected components either to be discarded or to be connected together. In our work, we overcome this problem by predicting the explicit centerline of the tube-shaped objects.

Naturally, a narrow tube-shaped object can be approximated as its centerline. The centerline can be presented as a vector of points $(p_1, p_2, \ldots, p_n)$ with the pre-defined connectivity: p_i and p_{i+1} connect with an edge, $1 \le i \le n-1$. In our model, we fix n to be identical for all tubes regardless of their shape and length, which allows predicting the coordinates directly by a fully-convolutional network without any autoregressive modules. The choice of n-points is the following: p_1 and p_n are defined as endpoints, and the points from p_2 to p_{n-1} are uniformly sampled from on centerline, so $d(p_i, p_{i+1}) = d(p_{i+1}, p_{i+2})$, where d is Euclidian distance, $1 \le i \le n-2$.

Centerline Encoding. Direct $(p_1, p_2, \ldots, p_n)$ and reverse $(p_n, p_{n-1}, \ldots, p_1)$ orders are both valid for the centerline representation. Thus, there is a need to establish an encoding scheme that will tackle the ambiguity. One can notice, that some encoding schemes can be based on the ordering of points from the starting point to the tipping point. It can be a working solution for tubes, where we can identify if p_1 or p_n is the tip, *e.g.*, endotracheal tube. However, such annotations may be missing or tube-shaped objects can be bi-directional. Therefore, there is a need to address a more general case, where we do not know which point is the tip. The proposed encoding scheme mimics the human annotation behavior, when the points are labeled from one of the endpoints to the others, *i.e.*, from the leftmost endpoint towards the second endpoint (p_1 is closer to the left border than p_n, denoted as $l2r$) and from the topmost endpoint to the remaining endpoint (p_1 is closer to the top border than p_n, denoted as $t2b$). The bi-directional encoding is crucial because it tackles ambiguous cases, *e.g.*, when the points have identical horizontal or vertical coordinates (see Supplementary material). The only uncertain case of the bi-directional encoding is $p_1 = p_n$, *i.e.*, a rare case of closed contour.

Training and Inference. Figure 1 shows the training and inference schemes of our model. During the training, we predict $2n$ heatmaps $(\hat{y})$, where $\hat{y}_0, \hat{y}_1, \ldots, \hat{y}_n$ are encoded from the topmost endpoint, and $\hat{y}_{n+1}, \hat{y}_{n+2}, \ldots, \hat{y}_{2n}$ are encoded from the leftmost endpoint. We use the standard heatmap regression loss to supervise our model:

$$L = \frac{1}{2nhw} \sum_{k=1}^{2n} \sum_{i=1}^{h} \sum_{j=1}^{w} W_{kij} (y_{kij} - \hat{y}_{kij})^2 \tag{1}$$

where h, w are the height and the width of the predicted heatmap, y is the ground-true heatmap, $\hat{y}$ is the predicted heatmap, $W = \frac{y}{max(y)} \times s$ is the spatial-wise scaling tensor of size $2n \times h \times w$ with a scaling coefficient s. We calculate $\hat{y}$ in the following way: $\hat{y} = g(\frac{\tilde{y}}{\sqrt{hw}})$, where $\tilde{y}$ is the output of the final convolutional layer without any activation, g is a softmax calculated along the flattened feature map, and the $\sqrt{hw}$ normalization is used to avoid pushing softmax to the regions with the small gradients. We skip the loss function calculation, when the horizontal coordinates of the endpoints are closer than some threshold t for the $t2b$ encoding and do the same for the vertical coordinates and the $l2r$ encoding.

During the inference, we sharpen the distribution of $\hat{y}$ by reducing the normalization constant: $\hat{y} = g(\frac{\tilde{y}}{\sqrt{hw/4}})$. The barycenter coordinates of $\hat{y}$ are the predicted coordinates of points $(\hat{p}_1, \hat{p}_2, \ldots, \hat{p}_{2n})$.

3   Experiments

3.1   Data

Synthetic Data. We used synthetic data to develop the bi-directional encoding scheme and compare it to unidirectional encodings. We generated 2000 lines of various shapes and its $90°C$ rotated versions: semicircles ($\cap$ and $\subset$ icons), waves ($\int$ and $\sim$ icons), and lines ($|$ and $-$ icons, see Supplementary material).

Real Data: Chest X-ray Catheters and Tubes. We used 6364 images from CliP data [11] with the unique central venous catheter (CVC), 2994 with the endotracheal tube (ETT), 3177 with the nasogastric tube (NGT). The original centerline points were uniformly resampled, approximated as a static 8px width line on 512×512 resolution.

Semi-synthetic Data: Coronary Angiography. Semi-synthetic coronary angiography was used to evaluate blood vessels segmentation. We generated 175 synthetic coronary trees with a realistic cardiac background. For each image, we generated left anterior descending artery (LAD), left circumflex artery (LCX), diagonal 1 (D1), and left marginal arteries (M1).

3.2   Encoding Configuration

HRNet [10] was used as the encoder network, taking images of size 512×512 and producing $n = 31$ heatmaps of size 128×128. Each ground-truth heatmap was a rasterized 2-dimensional Gaussian with a diagonal covariance matrix with $\sigma = 2$ for 128×128. We set $s = 100$ in Eq. (1) and ignored loss calculation for $t \leq 5$. All the results were obtained on a 5-fold cross-validation (patient-wise for chest x-ray), the metrics were averaged for the last 3 epochs.

3.3 Results

We evaluated models using conventional landmark detection and segmentation metrics: successful detection rate (SDR) shows the fraction of points predicted within the ground truth radius (5px), Hausdorff distance (HD) calculated for the vectors of centerline points, and Dice score that was calculated for the masks restored from n predicted and the ground truth points. Table 1 shows the comparison of models trained using the unidirectional ($l2r$ or $t2b$) and the

Table 1. The comparison of coordinate encoding schemes for synthetic data.

sort	SDR ↑	HD ↓	Dice ↑	SDR↑	HD ↓	Dice ↑
	semicircle(∩)			*semicircle* (⊂)		
l2r	**1.000±0.000**	**0.478±0.019**	**0.987±0.001**	0.335±0.129	13.756±2.477	0.224±0.104
t2b	0.300±0.170	14.413±2.984	0.186±0.141	**1.000±0.000**	**0.515±0.016**	**0.987±0.002**
l2r&t2b	**1.000±0.000**	0.513±0.042	0.986±0.001	**1.000±0.000**	0.589±0.034	**0.984±0.002**
	wave (∫)			*wave*(∼)		
l2r	**1.000±0.000**	**0.532±0.017**	**0.977±0.002**	0.156±0.013	21.207±0.544	0.150±0.009
t2b	0.166+0.010	19.325±0.997	0.161±0.016	**1.000±0.000**	**0.570⊥0.010**	**0.978±0.001**
l2r&t2b	**1.000±0.000**	0.642±0.046	**0.975±0.004**	**1.000±0.000**	0.833±0.332	0.969±0.014
	line (−)			*line* (∣)		
l2r	**1.000±0.000**	**0.193±0.009**	**0.989±0.001**	0.810±0.038	4.923±0.443	0.858±0.018
t2b	0.807±0.018	5.214±0.442	0.855±0.019	**1.000±0.000**	**0.186±0.004**	**0.989±0.002**
l2r&t2b	**1.000±0.000**	0.213±0.010	**0.989±0.001**	**1.000±0.000**	0.199±0.009	**0.988±0.002**

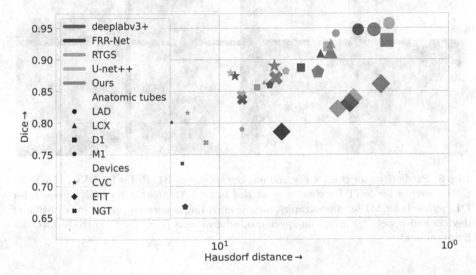

Fig. 2. Performance of models on medical data. x axis is inversed log-scaled Hausdorff distance (lower is better), y axis is Dice score (higher is better). The size of markers is proportional to $(1/\#ccs^2)$ (larger is better). Compare the same marker shapes (*e.g.*, rhombi for ETT). See the data in Supplemental material as a table.

bi-directional encodings (*l2r&t2b*). All models were evaluated only on cases that may be challenging for some encoding schemes. We can notice that *t2b* models were poorly trained with ∩, ∫, | shapes and *l2r* with the remaining shapes. In contrast, *l2r&t2b* encoding behaved almost as *t2b* on ∩, ∫, | and *l2r* on the remaining shapes. *Thus, l2r&t2b, agnostic to the ambiguous placement of the endpoints, was selected as a default encoding scheme for further experiments.*

We also trained and evaluated our model with *l2r&t2b* encoding on medical imaging datasets with chest x-ray and coronary angiography, comparing the result with the state-of-the-art models: FRR-Net [18] and RTGS [17] (which tackled a similar problem of segmentation of real-time catheters and tracking them in endovascular aneurysm repair), deeplabv3+ [2] (high performance in natural image segmentation), and U-net++ [19] (efficient model for numerous medical imaging tasks). Because all of the models perform semantic segmentation, we compared their performance in terms of segmentation metrics: Dice score, Hausdorff distance, number of predicted connected components ($\#ccs$), the fraction of prediction where $\#ccs \neq 1$. For our model, we restored a binary mask from n predicted points by putting a line with constant width (8px for 512×512) between the adjacent points.

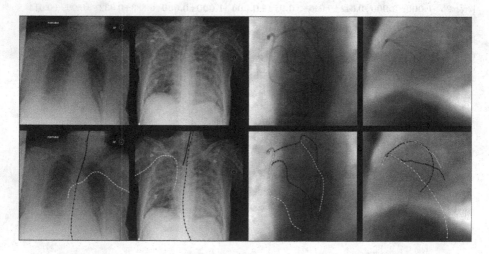

Fig. 3. Predictions for chest x-ray and angiography, $n = 31$. *Red* is for CVC, *blue* is for ETT, *green* is for NGT for chest x-rays. *Red* is for LAD, *blue* is for LCX, *green* is for D1, *yellow* is for M1 for angiography. Simple encoding generated precise localization of devices and vessels, ignoring non-specific tubular objects (*e.g.*, chest electrodes). (Color figure online)

Figure 2 compares the models. As can be noticed, our model outperformed deeplabv3+, FRR-Net, RTGS, and was competitive to U-net++ in Dice and Hausdorff distance. As expected, and confirmed in Fig. 3, our model always predicted a single completely connected component, unlike the other methods.

3.4 Ablation Study

Table 2 shows the results as a function of different number of centerline points. We can notice that our model was agnostic to the number of centerline points and showed almost identical results, regardless of whether it was trained to predict 15 or 47 points. We can also visually inspect the predictions and confirm adequate localization for both 15 and 47 centerline points in Fig. 4. Some rare exceptions can be found in Fig. 5. We also performed a pairwise comparison for our coordinate extraction method and the standard *maximum likelihood* point extraction (*i.e.*, a point with the highest value in the heatmap). We did not find the statistical difference for SDR; yet, our method was better in 12 pairs for HD, and 21 pairs for Dice score.

Table 2. Dependence of metrics on # of points used to approximate the centerline.

# points	SDR ↑	HD ↓	Dice ↑	SDR ↑	HD ↓	Dice ↑
	CVC			*ETT*		
15	0.847±0.005	5.897±0.142	0.888±0.002	0.976±0.007	1.921±0.108	0.862±0.004
31	0.848±0.008	5.796±0.398	0.890±0.004	0.975±0.008	1.978±0.133	0.861±0.004
47	0.844±0.009	5.677±0.355	0.882±0.004	0.977±0.008	1.958±0.175	0.861±0.005
	NGT			*LAD*		
15	0.843±0.006	6.218±0.432	0.866±0.003	0.977±0.015	3.555±0.533	0.920±0.013
31	0.852±0.014	5.717±0.671	0.871±0.005	0.991±0.017	2.120±0.972	0.947±0.026
47	0.844±0.013	5.651±0.716	0.870±0.005	0.988±0.021	1.863±1.159	0.947±0.029
	LCX			*D1*		
15	0.866±0.059	5.018±0.654	0.872±0.012	0.980±0.016	2.213±0.268	0.934±0.014
31	0.914±0.028	3.277±0.603	0.912±0.015	0.985±0.018	1.857±0.467	0.930±0.021
47	0.923±0.023	3.088±0.825	0.905±0.018	0.981±0.017	1.770±0.306	0.929±0.020

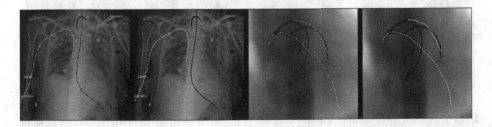

Fig. 4. Predictions for chest x-ray and angiography, $n = 15$ for the 1st and 3rd image, $n = 47$ for the 2nd and 4th image. *Red* is for CVC, *blue* is for ETT, *green* is for NGT for chest x-rays. *Red* is for LAD, *blue* is for LCX, *green* is for D1, *yellow* is for M1 for angiography. (Color figure online)

4   Discussion

In our work, we addressed the problem of localization of tube-shaped objects by explicit heatmap regression of centerline coordinates. Our model followed the idea of landmark detection and pose estimation models [10] that detect static landmarks in images, *e.g.*, wrist digits or elbow key-point. In contrast, however, our model needs only 2 static endpoints to operate, treating the remaining $n-2$ points as dynamic. We may assume it requires some implicit estimation of the length of the tubular objects and a consequent uniform sampling of points. We may also assume that the length estimation requires large receptive field of the model. The evaluation of different receptive fields and encoders will be addressed elsewhere. In some sense, our work is closer to the segmentation models that operate with contours or some prior shapes [5,12,14]. Similarly, our method is based on a prior n-points-based centerline model with the known connectivity.

The number of points in the centerline, n, is an important parameter of our model. Obviously, if n is small and the shape of the line is complex, then the linear interpolation of points may be a very coarse approximation of the line. We can notice such behavior for LCX in Table 2, where the performance increases with the number of points. Nevertheless, we found that $n = 15, 31, 47$ were good enough to tackle the segmentation of tubes, catheters, and arteries. A more flexible point detection approach, evaluating optimal n implicitly, will be the subject of future work.

One limitation of our model is the static width of predicted objects. While such a limitation may not be critical for thin objects, the thick ones may be predicted poorly. This issue can be improved via a straightforward estimation of the width from the variance of the heatmaps.

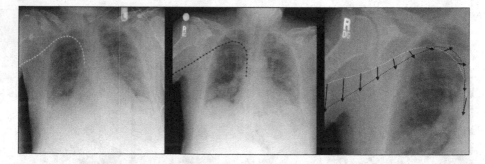

Fig. 5. A use-case example for tracking CVC position in time. *Left* image shows patient at a time step t, *middle* at a time step $t+1$, *right* shows the projected CVC from t (*red*) to $t+1$ (*green*). *Blue* arrows show the displacement of the uniformly sampled points of catheter, obtained via image registration from t to $t+1$. Given our model consistently predicts single connected component ($\#ccs = 1$), we expect no false positives for the frame-to-frame tracking and an excellent real-time performance in the IR applications. (Color figure online)

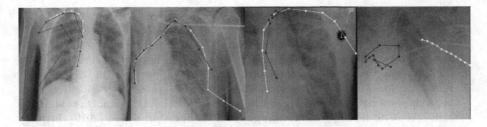

Fig. 6. Failure cases for CVC prediciton (*green*) shown against the ground truth (*red*). Note how a wrong starting point or a different catheter managed to mislead the model. (Color figure online)

Our encoding scheme might appear redundant because it requires $2n$ points to predict n points. For instance, a different origin point may tackle the ambiguity in x and y axes, *e.g.*, $(0,0)$-point. However, such observations can be easily addressed with a counterexample, *e.g.*, a diagonal line crossing $(0,0)$. Another way of the n-based encoding is to encode *w.r.t.* some static point, *i.e.*, $n/2$-th point for the odd number of points. Our preliminary experiments did not succeed with that; yet, we consider this direction to be worthwhile for future efforts.

We believe our approach can be valuable for computer-assisted diagnostic and surgical needs, *e.g.*, it could track the position of a central venous catheter in time, helping prevent the malposition [13]. The model can be incorporated into interventional monitoring systems, *e.g.*, to track the position of the device during the catheterization of coronary arteries [6] or during the catheter-based ablation [20] (see the use case in Fig. 5).

5 Conclusions

In our work, we presented a new approach for deep learning-based centerline localization. We proposed a bi-directional encoding scheme to address ambiguous cases in coordinate encoding and showed its efficiency for different object shapes and lengths. Our approach was evaluated both on foreign devices (tubes, catheters, etc.) and on anatomic objects (arteries), proving successful in localizing them on x-ray images.

The segmentation metrics were competitive to those of the state-of-the-art segmentation models which are known to be prone to break the long tubular objects into pieces. On the opposite, our model invariably predicted a single connected line and was always superior in terms of consistency. We also showed that our model was agnostic to the number of points set during the training, promising better localization of more complex lines and tracking trajectories.

References

1. Ambrosini, P., Ruijters, D., Niessen, W.J., Moelker, A., van Walsum, T.: Fully automatic and real-time catheter segmentation in x-ray fluoroscopy. In:

Descoteaux, M., et al. (eds.) MICCAI 2017. LNCS, vol. 10434, pp. 577–585. Springer, Cham (2017). https://doi.org/10.1007/978-3-319-66185-8_65

2. Chen, L.C., Zhu, Y., Papandreou, G., Schroff, F., Adam, H.: Encoder-decoder with atrous separable convolution for semantic image segmentation. In: Proceedings of the European conference on computer vision (ECCV), pp. 801–818 (2018)

3. Frid-Adar, M., Amer, R., Greenspan, H.: Endotracheal tube detection and segmentation in chest radiographs using synthetic data. In: Shen, D., Shen, D., et al. (eds.) MICCAI 2019. LNCS, vol. 11769, pp. 784–792. Springer, Cham (2019). https://doi.org/10.1007/978-3-030-32226-7_87

4. Pan, L.S., Li, C.W., Su, S.F., Tay, S.Y., Tran, Q.V., Chan, W.P.: Coronary artery segmentation under class imbalance using a u-net based architecture on computed tomography angiography images. Sci. Rep. **11**(1), 1–7 (2021)

5. Peng, S., Jiang, W., Pi, H., Li, X., Bao, H., Zhou, X.: Deep snake for real-time instance segmentation. In: Proceedings of the IEEE Computer Society Conference on Computer Vision and Pattern Recognition, pp. 8530–8539 (2020). https://doi.org/10.1109/CVPR42600.2020.00856

6. Pothineni, N.V., et al.: Coronary artery injury related to catheter ablation of cardiac arrhythmias: a systematic review. J. Cardiovasc. Electrophysiol. **30**(1), 92–101 (2019)

7. Sirazitdinov, I., Lenga, M., Baltruschat, I.M., Dylov, D.V., Saalbach, A.: Landmark constellation models for central venous catheter malposition detection. In: 2021 IEEE 18th International Symposium on Biomedical Imaging (ISBI), pp. 1132–1136. IEEE (2021)

8. Sirazitdinov, I., Schulz, H., Saalbach, A., Renisch, S., Dylov, D.V.: Tubular shape aware data generation for segmentation in medical imaging. Int. J. Comput. Assist. Radiol. Surg., 1–9 (2022)

9. Subramanian, V., Wang, H., Wu, J.T., Wong, K.C.L., Sharma, A., Syeda-Mahmood, T.: Automated detection and type classification of central venous catheters in chest x-rays. In: Shen, D., et al. (eds.) MICCAI 2019. LNCS, vol. 11769, pp. 522–530. Springer, Cham (2019). https://doi.org/10.1007/978-3-030-32226-7_58

10. Sun, K., et al.: High-resolution representations for labeling pixels and regions. arXiv preprint arXiv:1904.04514 (2019)

11. Tang, J.S., et al.: Clip, catheter and line position dataset. Sci. Data **8**(1), 1–7 (2021)

12. Wei, F., Sun, X., Li, H., Wang, J., Lin, S.: Point-set anchors for object detection, instance segmentation and pose estimation. In: Vedaldi, A., Bischof, H., Brox, T., Frahm, J.-M. (eds.) ECCV 2020. LNCS, vol. 12355, pp. 527–544. Springer, Cham (2020). https://doi.org/10.1007/978-3-030-58607-2_31

13. Wood, B.J., et al.: Navigation with electromagnetic tracking for interventional radiology procedures: a feasibility study. J. Vasc. Intervent. Radiol. **16**(4), 493–505 (2005)

14. Xie, E., et al.: PolarMask: Single shot instance segmentation with polar representation. In: Proceedings of the IEEE Computer Society Conference on Computer Vision and Pattern Recognition, vol. 1, pp. 12190–12199 (2020). https://doi.org/10.1109/CVPR42600.2020.01221

15. Yi, X., Adams, S., Babyn, P., Elnajmi, A.: Automatic catheter and tube detection in pediatric x-ray images using a scale-recurrent network and synthetic data. J. Digital Imaging **33**(1), 181–190 (2020)

16. Yi, X., Adams, S.J., Henderson, R.D., Babyn, P.: Computer-aided assessment of catheters and tubes on radiographs: how good is artificial intelligence for assessment? Radiol. Artif. Intell. **2**(1), e190082 (2020)

17. Zhou, Y.-J., et al.: Real-time guidewire segmentation and tracking in endovascular aneurysm repair. In: Gedeon, T., Wong, K.W., Lee, M. (eds.) ICONIP 2019. LNCS, vol. 11953, pp. 491–500. Springer, Cham (2019). https://doi.org/10.1007/978-3-030-36708-4_40

18. Zhou, Y.J., Xie, X.L., Hou, Z.G., Bian, G.B., Liu, S.Q., Zhou, X.H.: Frr-net: fast recurrent residual networks for real-time catheter segmentation and tracking in endovascular aneurysm repair. In: 2020 IEEE 17th International Symposium on Biomedical Imaging (ISBI), pp. 961–964. IEEE (2020)

19. Zhou, Z., Siddiquee, M.M.R., Tajbakhsh, N., Liang, J.: Unet++: redesigning skip connections to exploit multiscale features in image segmentation. IEEE Trans. Med. Imaging **39**(6), 1856–1867 (2019)

20. Zolotarev, A.M., et al.: Optical mapping-validated machine learning improves atrial fibrillation driver detection by multi-electrode mapping. Circul. Arrhythmia Electrophysiol. **13**(10), e008249 (2020)

Transforming the Interactive Segmentation for Medical Imaging

Wentao Liu[1], Chaofan Ma[1], Yuhuan Yang[1], Weidi Xie[1,2], and Ya Zhang[1,2(✉)]

[1] Cooperative Medianet Innovation Center, Shanghai Jiao Tong University,
Shanghai, China
ya_zhang@sjtu.edu.cn
[2] Shanghai AI Laboratory, Shanghai, China

Abstract. The goal of this paper is to interactively refine the automatic segmentation on challenging structures that fall behind human performance, either due to the scarcity of available annotations or the difficulty nature of the problem itself, for example, on segmenting cancer or small organs. Specifically, we propose a novel **T**ransformer-based architecture for **I**nteractive **S**egmentation (**TIS**), that treats the refinement task as a procedure for grouping pixels with similar features to those clicks given by the end users. Our proposed architecture is composed of Transformer Decoder variants, which naturally fulfills feature comparison with the attention mechanisms. In contrast to existing approaches, our proposed TIS is not limited to binary segmentations, and allows the user to edit masks for arbitrary number of categories. To validate the proposed approach, we conduct extensive experiments on three challenging datasets and demonstrate superior performance over the existing state-of-the-art methods. The project page is: https://wtliu7.github.io/tis/.

Keywords: Interactive segmentation · Transformer

1 Introduction

In medical image analysis, segmentation is undoubtedly one of the most widely researched problems in the literature. The goal is to identify the structure of interest (SOI) with pixel level accuracy, acquiring rich information, such as the position, size, and texture statistics, to assist clinicians for making assessments on diseases and better treatment plans.

In the recent years, tremendous progress has been made for *fully-automatic* segmentations by training deep neural networks on large-scale datasets in a *supervised manner*, for example, FCN [6], UNet [11], nnU-Net [4]. Occasionally, such heavily-supervised approaches have already approached similar performance level as human expert. However, apart from the well-solved problems, one critical issue remains, **what else can we do to improve models' usability on the challenging scenarios**, where automatic predictions significantly under-perform humans, either due to the lack of large-scale training set, or the difficulty nature of problem, for example, on cancer segmentation.

L. Wang et al. (Eds.): MICCAI 2022, LNCS 13434, pp. 704–713, 2022.
https://doi.org/10.1007/978-3-031-16440-8_67

One potential solution is interactive segmentation, with the goal of refining the automatic predictions by only a few user inputs, *e.g.* clicks, scribbles, boundary delineation, etc. In the literature, such line of research involves a long list of seminal works, including the early attempts that took inspiration from mathematics and topology, adopting variational methods [3,10] to group pixels that share certain common features as the users' initialisation, *e.g.* intensity, texture, contrast, etc. However, such variational approaches usually involve heavy parameter-tuning and long inference time (*i.e.* tens of minutes for large volumes), thus limiting its practical usefulness. Till recently, approaches based on deep learning become popular, by transforming users' annotations into certain distance maps, such as euclidean [5], gaussian [9] or geodesic distance maps [7,13], the ConvNets are trained to exploit such information together with images; concurrently, a set of works have also considered to ease the interaction process, for example, [7,9] only requires to click on extreme points and [14] use both positive and negative points.

Here, we continue this vein of research, and propose a novel **Transformer**-based architecture for **Interactive Segmentation**, termed as **TIS**. In particular, for images that end up with unsatisfactory predictions, our proposed TIS only requires a few clicks from the end users, each pixel on the image only needs to compare with these "examplar" clicks, and copy the label information from its closest click. Such "compare-and-copy" procedure can be elegantly achieved by adopting a variant of Transformer Decoder. Notably, in contrast to the existing approaches that can only segment single structure at a time, our TIS allows the end users to edit arbitrary number of categories simultaneously, given each is provided with at least one examplar click. We conduct evaluations on three challenging datasets and demonstrate superior performance over the state-of-the-art approaches.

2 Methods

In this paper, we consider a practical scenario for segmenting challenging structures in medical images, that is, to enable end users to correct the model's prediction with only *a few clicks* during inference time.

2.1 Problem Scenario

Given a **training set** of n image-mask pairs, $\mathcal{D}_{\text{train}} = \{(\mathcal{I}_1, y_1), \ldots, (\mathcal{I}_n, y_n)\}$, where $\mathcal{I} \in \mathbb{R}^{H \times W \times D}$ and $y \in \mathbb{R}^{H \times W \times D \times C}$, with H, W, D, C denoting height, width, depth, and number of categories, respectively. Our goal is to train a segmentation model that can not only give automatic predictions, but also allow the end users to refine the predictions during **inference time**:

$$\hat{y} = \Phi_{\text{REF}}(\Phi_{\text{ENC}}(\mathcal{I}; \Theta_e), \mathcal{A}; \Theta_r) \in \mathbb{R}^{H \times W \times D \times C}, \tag{1}$$

where $\hat{y}$ denotes the final prediction, $\mathcal{A} = \{(p_1, c_k), \ldots, (p_n, c_k)\}$ refers the user's interaction in the form of pixel clicks, with $p_i \in \mathbb{R}^3$ denoting the spatial position for each given click, and $c_i \in \mathbb{R}^C$ referring the semantic category for the

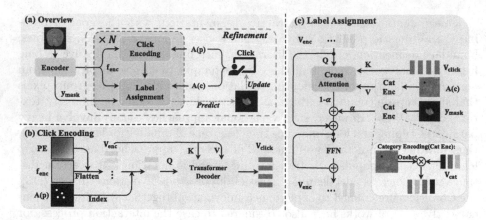

Fig. 1. Structure of our method. (a) Overview of the whole framework. (b) Structure of click encoding module. (d) Structure of label assignment module.

annotated pixel. In the following sections, we will detail the building blocks of our proposed architecture (as shown in Fig. 1(a)), namely, an encoder network (Φ_{ENC}, parameterized with Θ_e) that extracts image features, and provides automatic structure segmentations; and a refinement module (Φ_{REF}, parameterized with Θ_r) that refines its prediction with the provided clicks from end users through *click encoding* and *label assignment*. Generally, the outputs from the encoder are architecture-agnostic, and experts can continuously interact with the refinement module until being satisfied.

2.2   Encoder (Φ_{ENC})

As for image encoder, we adopt the popular nnU-Net [4], that maps the input images to segmentation masks:

$$\{y_{mask},\ f_{enc}\} = \Phi_{ENC}(\mathcal{I};\ \Theta_e),\tag{2}$$

where $y_{mask} \in \mathbb{R}^{H \times W \times D \times C}$ refers to the output mask with C categories, and $f_{enc} \in \mathbb{R}^{\frac{H}{2} \times \frac{W}{2} \times \frac{D}{2} \times m}$ denotes the dense feature embeddings from the penultimate layer of nnU-Net. During training, the encoder is simply trained with standard pixelwise cross-entropy loss.

2.3   Refinement (Φ_{REF})

At a high-level, our method is based on the intuition that users' click can be treated as a set of "examplars", and each pixel to be segmented can simply compare with these "examplars", and copy the category information from its closest clicks. Technically, we adopt an architecture that interleaves Transformer Decoder variants, alternating between *click encoding* and *label assignment*, as detailed below.

Tokenization: To start with, we vectorize the encoder's output encodings:

$$\mathcal{V}_{\text{enc}} = \phi_{\text{flatten}}(f_{\text{enc}}) + \phi_{\text{PE}}(\Omega), \tag{3}$$

where ϕ_{flatten} refers to a reshape operation, and ϕ_{PE} refers to the learnable positional encodings for a dense 3D grid (Ω), $\mathcal{V}_{\text{enc}} \in \mathbb{R}^{HWD \times m}$ ends up to be the tokenized vector sequences of the encoder embeddings.

Click Encoding: To incorporate the users' feedback in refinement, we encode these clicks into vectors:

$$\mathcal{V}_{\text{click}} = \phi_{\text{index}}(f_{\text{enc}}, \mathcal{A}(p)), \tag{4}$$

$$\mathcal{V}_{\text{click}} = \psi_{\text{T-Dec}}(\underbrace{W_1^q \cdot \mathcal{V}_{\text{click}}}_{\text{Query}}, \underbrace{W_1^k \cdot \mathcal{V}_{\text{enc}}}_{\text{Key}}, \underbrace{W_1^v \cdot \mathcal{V}_{\text{enc}}}_{\text{Value}}), \tag{5}$$

where ϕ_{index} refers to an indexing function that simply pick out the vectors from the dense feature map, based on corresponding spatial locations of the clicks. To avoid notation abuse, we use $\mathcal{V}_{\text{click}} \in \mathbb{R}^{k \times m}$ to represent the results from indexing initial click embeddings, and the one after enrichment from a standard Transformer Decoder ($\psi_{\text{T-Dec}}$), with input *Query* derived from a linear projection of the click embeddings, while *Key* and *Value* are generated by applying two different linear transformations on the encoder's outputs.

In specific, the Transformer Decoder consists of multi-head cross-attention (MHCA), multi-head self-attention (MHSA), a feed-forward network (FFN), and residual connections, which effectively enriches the click embeddings by aggregating information from the encoder outputs. For more details, we would refer the readers to the original Transformer paper [12].

Label Assignment: Here, we construct a "compare-and-copy" mechanism, that assigns labels to each pixel based on two factors: (1) the similarity between pixels and users' clicks, (2) the weighting of the automatic segmentation.

Specifically, we adopt a Transformer Decoder variant, as shown below:

$$\mathcal{V}_{\text{enc}} = \alpha \cdot \psi_{\text{T-Dec}}(\underbrace{W_2^q \cdot \mathcal{V}_{\text{enc}}}_{\text{Query}}, \underbrace{W_2^k \cdot \mathcal{V}_{\text{click}}}_{\text{Key}}, \underbrace{\phi_{\text{CE}}(\mathcal{A}(c))}_{\text{Value}}) + (1 - \alpha) \cdot \phi_{\text{CE}}(y_{\text{mask}}),$$

where $\phi_{\text{CE}}(\cdot)$ refers to a projection (accomplished by a learnable MLP) on the category labels to high-dimensional embeddings, operating on both user's click and automatic segmentations, these embeddings are then used for constructing the *Value* in Transformer Decoder. As for *Query* and *Key*, they are computed by applying linear transformations on the dense features and click embeddings respectively. **Note that**, with such architecture design, the cross attention effectively computes a similarity matching between each pixel ($\mathcal{V}_{\text{enc}}$) and users' click ($\mathcal{V}_{\text{click}}$), and copying back the "category" information, balanced with a *learnable* weighting scalar (α) between predictions and user's clicks.

Training: As mentioned above, features after label assignment now have incorporated the category information obtained from both automatic segmentation and clicks. To properly train the model, we simulate the user interactions at training stage, where clicks are sampled based on the discrepancy between automatic prediction and the groundtruth annotations, *i.e.* erroneous predictions. After stacking 6 layers of *click encoding* and *label assignment* modules, we adopt a **linear MLP layer** to read out the segmentation labels, and train it with pixelwise cross-entropy loss.

Discussion: Inspired by the observation that pixels of the same category should ideally be clustered together in some high-dimensional space, we thus adopt a variant of Transformer Decoder, which naturally facilitates the "compare-and-copy" mechanism, *i.e.* compute similarity between pixels and user's click, then copy the category information correspondingly. Note that, such procedure works in the same manner for segmentation of arbitrary class, this is in contrast to the existing approaches that are only limited to work for binary segmentation.

3   Experiments

3.1   Datasets

In this paper, we conduct experiments on the Medical Segmentation Decathlon (MSD) datasets [1]. Specifically, we focus on three challenging subsets:

Lung (Training set).   consists of preoperative thin-section CT scans from 63 patients with non-small cell lung cancer. The goal is to segment the tumors within the lung (L1). We randomly split into 50 cases for training and the rest 13 cases for evaluation.

Colon (Training set).   consists of 126 portal venous phase CT scans of patients undergoing resection of primary colon cancer. The goal is to segment the colon cancer primaries (L1). 100 cases are split for training randomly and the remaining 26 for evaluation.

Pancreas (Training set).   consists of 281 portal venous phase CT scans of patients undergoing resection of pancreatic masses. The goal is to segment *both* pancreatic parenchyma (L1) and pancreatic tumor (L2). 224 cases are randomly picked for training and the remaining 57 for evaluation.

3.2   Evaluation Metrics

For quantitative evaluation, we employ Dice Similarity Coefficient (DSC):

$$\text{DSC}\left(\mathcal{R}_p, \mathcal{R}_g\right) = \frac{2\left|\mathcal{R}_p \cap \mathcal{R}_g\right|}{\left|\mathcal{R}_p\right| + \left|\mathcal{R}_g\right|}, \tag{6}$$

where $\mathcal{R}_p, \mathcal{R}_g$ represent the region of prediction and the ground-truth, respectively. $|\cdot|$ is the number of pixels/voxels in the corresponding region. And the goal is thus to get a higher accuracy with less user clicks.

Table 1. Performances of different methods on three datasets with 10 clicks.

Metric	Method	Year	Lung	Colon	Pancreas	
			L1	L1	L1	L2
Dice	Automatic [4]	2018	64.99	44.84	82.16	49.34
	InterCNN [2]	2018	$80.07_{\pm 2.65}$	$69.58_{\pm 2.97}$	$82.31_{\pm 3.28}$	$74.17_{\pm 2.91}$
	DeepIGeoS [13]	2019	$81.74_{\pm 1.72}$	$70.61_{\pm 2.46}$	$82.77_{\pm 1.51}$	$75.36_{\pm 2.60}$
	BS-IRIS [8]	2020	$81.67_{\pm 2.14}$	$71.27_{\pm 1.82}$	$85.16_{\pm 1.34}$	$76.49_{\pm 2.48}$
	MIDeepSeg [7]	2021	$82.31_{\pm 3.58}$	$71.89_{\pm 3.09}$	$84.69_{\pm 4.03}$	$70.34_{\pm 4.36}$
	Ours	2022	$\mathbf{85.07}_{\pm 1.55}$	$\mathbf{73.03}_{\pm 1.68}$	$\mathbf{87.72}_{\pm 1.28}$	$\mathbf{77.91}_{\pm 2.07}$

3.3 Implementation Details

We use nnU-Net [4] as our encoder, and retrain it on corresponding datasets under the default settings. According to the official code of nnU-Net[1], the setting we used to train it is that the "network" is "3d-fullres", the "network-trainer" is "nnUNetTrainerV2" and leave other options as default. Due to the complexity of Transformer and the cost of memory, we used feature of the penultimate layer of nnU-Net. In practice, the feature will be cropped based on the automatic segmentation and clicks before processed by our model.

In practice, the feature will be cropped based on the automatic segmentation and clicks before processed by our model. In the experiment, we train our model for 200 epochs. It is optimized using AdamW optimizer, starting with a learning rate of 10^{-2}, and decreasing with a rate factor 0.9 every 10 epochs. For more details, please see supplementary materials.

4 Results

4.1 User Interactions Simulation

Following previous works [7,8,13], we also adopt a robust agent to simulate the user clicks. The clicking positions are chosen as the center region of the largest mis-segmented regions according to the ground-truth. For each clicking step, a small disturbance ϵ (10 pixels) is added on each click's positions to imitate the behavior of a real user and force the model to be more robust. Additionally, in cases when the centroid is not within the mis-segmented region, then we pick an arbitrary point in the non-boundary region as the click.

4.2 Comparisons with State-of-the-Art

Performance on Different Datasets: As shown in Tabel 1, given 10 clicks, our approach achieves the best performance in all three challenging datasets. It is worth noting that the "Automatic" row shows the results from state-of-the-art automatic segmentation model (nnU-Net [4]), while our proposed TIS can improve the prediction by a large margin with only a few clicks.

---

[1] https://github.com/MIC-DKFZ/nnUNet..

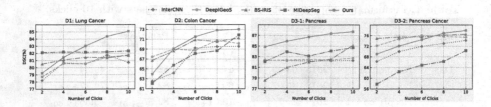

Fig. 2. Improvements in one interactive sequence of different methods on three datasets (four structures). Note that figures with gray background are two different structures in the same dataset. This figure is best viewed on pdf.

Improvements in One Interaction Sequence: In Fig. 2, we plot the results with multi-round refinement for different approaches. As can be seen, despite all interactive segmentation approaches have shown improvements with interaction, our proposed TIS maintains the growing trend with more clicks available, and substantially outperforms the others in the end. Specifically, for datasets that have small regions and heterogeneous appearance (for example, cancers), our method has smoother and more robust refinements through interaction.

4.3   Ablation Study

In this section, we perform a detailed ablation study by removing the component from TIS. All the ablation experiments are performed on the Pancreas dataset.

Table 2. Quantitive ablation study on critical modules.

Modules		5 clicks		10 clicks	
Click encoding	Label assignment	Pancreas	Cancer	Pancreas	Cancer
✗	✓	82.74	66.74	83.32	71.52
✓	✗	81.23	70.54	80.78	69.82
✓	✓	**86.15**	**72.82**	**87.72**	**77.91**

Effect of Click Encoding: The main purpose of click encoding is to add context information to the click embeddings. To validate its effect, we only index embeddings, but do not encode them through Transformer Decoder ($\psi_{\text{T-Dec}}$). As shown in Table 2, the performance has a severe recession, due to the lack of context information, especially after feature update of label assignment, the network degrades, refining only a small area around the click.

Effect of Label Assignment: In this part, we **do not** encode the category label as *Value*, rather, use a MLP projection, as normally did in standard transformer. Through a stack of Transformer layers, the cross-attention still computes the similarity between pixels and clicks, but unable to directly copy the label

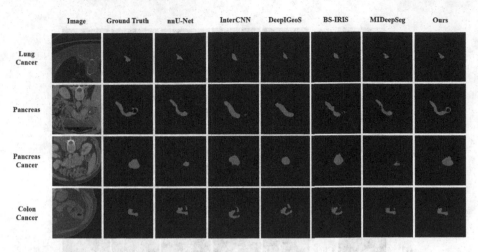

Fig. 3. Visualization of qualitative comparison on three datasets (four structures). All interactive methods are provided with 10 clicks.

information. And at the end, the click embeddings obtained from click encoding are used as classifiers to segment based on similarity. In order to make a fair comparison, we still use the weighting scalar (α) to combine the automatic segmentation and the Transformer segmentation. As shown in Table 2, the performance has dropped drastically. With the number of clicks increasing, it even gets worse. In practice, despite we click at the mis-segmented region, the network is still unable to correct it.

4.4 Visualization of Results

Figure 3 shows a comparison of the final segmentation results for the automatic nnU-net and four interactive methods. It can be seen that the state-of-the-art automatic segmentation method nnU-net often fails in these challenging scenarios, showing the potential of interactive segmentation methods. And our method, with the same 10 clicks provided, have a more detailed segmentation and largest performance improvements compared with all interactive methods, especially for some small regions like lung cancer and colon cancer.

4.5 Visualization of the Interaction Process

Figure 4 shows the interaction process, where two examples from Pancreas dataset are detailed. For each step, we provide the mis-segmented region ("Error"), the click position ("Click") and the prediction of our method ("Pred"). The performance improves as the number of clicks increasing, with the mis-segmented region decreases alongside.

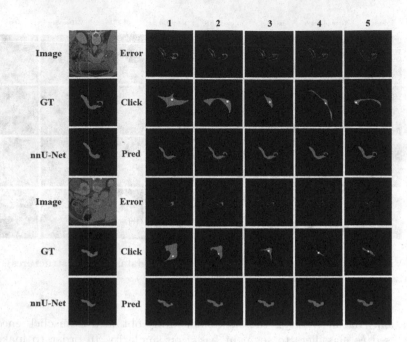

Fig. 4. Visualization of the interaction process with 5 clicks. Two examples are shown.

5   Conclusion

We propose a novel Transformer-based framework (**TIS**) for interactive segmentation. It is designed for a realistic and challenging scenario, where automatic segmentations largely under-perform human performance. The core idea is to treat the users' clicks as "examplars", and our proposed method is able to segment SOI by comparing each pixel on the image with the provided clicks, and copy the label information from them. Specifically, our method interleaves two variants of Transformer Decoders, alternating between *click encoding* and *label assignment*. We validate our method on three challenging datasets and demonstrate superior performance over the existing state-of-the-art methods. Additionally, our methods breaks through the limitation that previous methods can only complete single classification.

References

1. Antonelli, M., et al.: The medical segmentation decathlon. arXiv preprint arXiv:2106.05735 (2021)
2. Bredell, G., Tanner, C., Konukoglu, E.: Iterative interaction training for segmentation editing networks. In: Shi, Y., Suk, H.-I., Liu, M. (eds.) MLMI 2018. LNCS, vol. 11046, pp. 363–370. Springer, Cham (2018). https://doi.org/10.1007/978-3-030-00919-9_42

3. Chan, T.F., Vese, L.A.: Active contours without edges. IEEE Trans. Image Process. **10**(2), 266–277 (2001)
4. Isensee, F., Jaeger, P.F., Kohl, S.A.A., Petersen, J., Maier-Hein, K.H.: nnU-net: a self-configuring method for deep learning-based biomedical image segmentation. Nat Methods **18**(2), 203–211 (2020)
5. Li, Z., Chen, Q., Koltun, V.: Interactive image segmentation with latent diversity. In: Proceedings of the IEEE Conference on Computer Vision and Pattern Recognition, pp. 577–585 (2018)
6. Long, J., Shelhamer, E., Darrell, T.: Fully convolutional models for semantic segmentation. In: Proceedings of the IEEE Conference on Computer Vision and Pattern Recognition (2015)
7. Luo, X., et al.: Mideepseg: minimally interactive segmentation of unseen objects from medical images using deep learning. Med. Image Anal. **72**, 102102 (2021)
8. Ma, C., et al.: Boundary-aware supervoxel-level iteratively refined interactive 3d image segmentation with multi-agent reinforcement learning. IEEE Trans. Med. Imaging **40**(10), 2563–2574 (2020)
9. Maninis, K.K., Caelles, S., Pont-Tuset, J., Van Gool, L.: Deep extreme cut: from extreme points to object segmentation. In: Proceedings of the IEEE Conference on Computer Vision and Pattern Recognition, pp. 616–625 (2018)
10. Mumford, D., Shah, J.: Optimal approximations by piecewise smooth functions and associated variational problems. Commun. Pure Appl. Math. **42**(5), 577–685 (1989)
11. Ronneberger, O., Fischer, P., Brox, T.: U-net: convolutional networks for biomedical image segmentation. In: Proceedings of the International Conference on Medical Image Computing and Computer Assisted Intervention (2015)
12. Vaswani, A., et al.: Attention is all you need. In: Advances in Neural Information Processing Systems (2017)
13. Wang, G., et al.: Deepigeos: a deep interactive geodesic framework for medical image segmentation. IEEE Trans. Pattern Anal. Mach. Intell. **41**(7), 1559–1572 (2018)
14. Zhang, S., Liew, J.H., Wei, Y., Wei, S., Zhao, Y.: Interactive object segmentation with inside-outside guidance. In: Proceedings of the IEEE Conference on Computer Vision and Pattern Recognition, pp. 12234–12244 (2020)

Learning Incrementally to Segment Multiple Organs in a CT Image

Pengbo Liu[1,2], Xia Wang[3], Mengsi Fan[3], Hongli Pan[3], Minmin Yin[3], Xiaohong Zhu[3], Dandan Du[3], Xiaoying Zhao[3], Li Xiao[2], Lian Ding[4], Xingwang Wu[3], and S. Kevin Zhou[1,2(✉)]

[1] Center for Medical Imaging, Robotics, Analytic Computing and Learning (MIRACLE), School of Biomedical Engineering and Suzhou Institute for Advanced Research, University of Science and Technology of China, Suzhou, China
skevinzhou@ustc.edu.cn
[2] Key Lab of Intelligent Information Processing of Chinese Academy of Sciences (CAS), Institute of Computing Technology, CAS, Beijing, China
[3] The First Affiliated Hospital of Anhui Medical University, Anhui, China
[4] Huawei Cloud Computing Technology Co. Ltd., Dongguan, China

Abstract. There exists a large number of datasets for organ segmentation, which are partially annotated and sequentially constructed. A typical dataset is constructed at a certain time by curating medical images and annotating the organs of interest. In other words, new datasets with annotations of new organ categories are built over time. To unleash the potential behind these partially labeled, sequentially-constructed datasets, we propose to incrementally learn a multi-organ segmentation model. In each incremental learning (IL) stage, we lose the access to previous data and annotations, whose knowledge is assumingly captured by the current model, and gain the access to a new dataset with annotations of new organ categories, from which we learn to update the organ segmentation model to include the new organs. While IL is notorious for its 'catastrophic forgetting' weakness in the context of natural image analysis, we experimentally discover that such a weakness mostly disappears for CT multi-organ segmentation. To further stabilize the model performance across the IL stages, we introduce a *light memory module* and some loss functions to restrain the representation of different categories in feature space, aggregating feature representation of the same class and separating feature representation of different classes. Extensive experiments on five open-sourced datasets are conducted to illustrate the effectiveness of our method.

Keywords: Incremental learning · Partially labeled datasets · Multi-organ segmentation

1 Introduction

While most natural image datasets [3,10] are completely labeled for common categories, fully annotated medical image datasets are scarce, especially for

L. Wang et al. (Eds.): MICCAI 2022, LNCS 13434, pp. 714–724, 2022.
https://doi.org/10.1007/978-3-031-16440-8_68

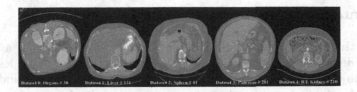

Fig. 1. Number of cases in different partially labeled datasets for different tasks.

a multi-organ segmentation (MOS) task [29] that requires pixel-wise annotations, as constructing such a dataset requires professional knowledge of different anatomical structures [28,29]. Fortunately, there exist many partially labeled datasets [1,5,24] for organ segmentation. Another dimension associated with these datasets is that they are constructed sequentially at different sites. Our goal is to train **a single multi-organ segmentation model from partially labelled, sequentially constructed datasets**. To achieve such a goal, we have to address two issues. (i) The first issue arising from *partial labeling* is knowledge conflict, that is, labels in different datasets have conflicts, *e.g.*, the liver is marked as foreground in Dataset 1 but as background in Datasets 2–4, as shown in Fig. 1. (ii) The second issue arising from *sequential construction* is data availability, that is, the datasets are not simultaneously available for learning. What could be even worse is that, due to security concern, these datasets are not allowed to be transferred across the border of the curating institutes; only the model parameters are sharable.

There has been some emerging research [4,21,27,30] that successfully handles knowledge conflict and trains a single model from pooled datasets for improved performance in multi-organ segmentation, proving that the unlabeled data in partially labeled datasets is also helpful for learning. However, these approaches conduct model learning in a batch model based and hence unable to be applied to deal with sequential construction. To deal with both issues, we hereby propose a novel multi-organ segmentation approach based on *the principle of incremental learning (IL)*, which is a staged learning method that has an access to the data available at current learning stage, while losing the access to the data available in previous stages.

Our main contributions are summarized as below:

- We make the first attempt in the literature to merge partially labeled datasets in medical image scenario using IL method, addressing the issues of knowledge conflict and data availability, and possibly security concern.
- To combat the 'catastrophic forgetting' problem that commonly plagues IL, we introduce a light memory module [7] to store the prototypical representation of different organ categories and corresponding loss functions to make different organs more distinguishable in feature space.
- Our extensive experiments on five open-source organ datasets achieve comparable performance to state-of-the-art (SOTA) batch methods which can access all datasets in training phase, unleashing the great potential of IL in multiple organ segmentation.

2   Related Work

MOS with Partially Labelled Datasets. Zhou *et al.* [30] learn a segmentation model in the case of partial labeling by adding a prior-aware loss in the learning objective to match the distribution between the unlabeled and labeled datasets. In [4], first multi-scale features at various depths are hierarchically incorporated for image segmentation and then a unified segmentation strategy is developed to train three separate datasets together, and finally multi-organ segmentation is achieved by learning from the union of partially labeled and fully labeled datasets. Zhang *et al.* [27] propose a dynamic on-demand network (DoDNet) that learns to segment multiple organs and tumors on partially labeled datasets, which embedded dynamically generated filter by a task encoding module into an encoder-decoder architecture. Shi *et al.* [21] encode knowledge from different organs into a single multi-class segmentation model by introducing two simple but effective loss functions, *Marginal* loss and *Exclusion* loss.

Incremental Learning. IL has been studied for object recognition [8,9,11,19] and detection [15,22,23], also segmentation [2,17,18,25]. The main challenge in IL is the so-called 'catastrophic forgetting' [16]: how to keep the performance on old classes while learning new ones? Methods based on parameter isolation [20,26] and data replay [13,19] are all with limited scalability or privacy issues. Regularization based method is the most ideal direction in IL community. In natural image segmentation, Cermelli et al. [2] solved knowledge conflicts existing in other IL methods [9,17] by remodeling old and new categories into background in loss functions, achieving a performance improvement. In 2D medical image segmentation, Ozdemir and Goksel [18] made some attempts using the IL methods used in natural images directly, with only two categories, and it mainly focuses on verifying the possibility of transferring the knowledge learned in the first category with more images to a second category with less images. In this paper, we apply IL to multiple organ segmentation for the first time.

3   Method

3.1   IL for MOS

Framework of IL. The overview of the tth stage of IL in our method is shown in Fig. 2. Given a pair of 3D input image and ground truth, $\{x^t, y^t\} \in \{\mathcal{X}^t, \mathcal{C}^t\}$, we firstly process x^t by the model in current stage, $f_{\theta_t}(\cdot)$ with trainable parameters θ_t, getting the output $q^t = f_{\theta_t}(x^t)$. And we assume that each image x^t is composed by a set of voxels x_i^t with constant cardinality $|\mathcal{I}| = N$. The whole label space $\mathcal{Y}^t$ cross all t stages is expanded from $\mathcal{Y}^{t-1}$ with new classes added in current stage $(\mathcal{C}^t)$, $\mathcal{Y}^t = \mathcal{Y}^{t-1} \cup \mathcal{C}^t = \mathcal{C}^1 \cup ... \cup \mathcal{C}^t$. Note that the annotations of the old categories $\mathcal{Y}^{t-1}$ will be inaccessible in the new stage under ideal IL settings. For preserving the knowledge of old categories in regularization based method, we process x^t by the saved old model $f_{\theta_{t-1}}(\cdot)$ with frozen parameters θ_{t-1} and get $q^{t-1} = f_{\theta_{t-1}}(x^t)$ as the pseudo label. Knowledge distillation loss,

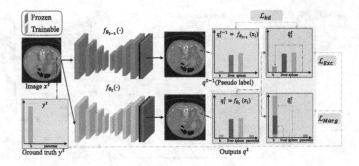

Fig. 2. Overview of the tth stage of IL in multi-organ segmentation.

$\mathcal{L}_{kd}$, is introduced in IL setting to keep old knowledge learned from previous stages. Trainable θ_t in the tth stage is expanded from θ_{t-1} with Θ_t to segment new categories, $\theta_t = \theta_{t-1} \cup \Theta_t$.

Avoiding Knowledge Conflict in IL. The structures of old classes in $\mathcal{X}^t$, are marked as background in $\mathcal{C}^t$. And the new structures also do not exist in $\mathcal{Y}^{t-1}$, that is new structures are marked as background in pseudo label. If we directly use q^t to compute segmentation loss for new classes, and knowledge distillation loss for old classes, these conflicts between prediction and ground truth break the whole training process. So referring to marginal loss in MargExc [21], we modify the prediction q^t to $\hat{q}^t$ and $\tilde{q}^t$, as shown in Fig. 2 and Eqs. (1) and (2):

$$\hat{q}^t_{i,j} = \begin{cases} \exp(q^t_{i,b} + \sum_{c\in\mathcal{C}^t} q^t_{i,c})/\sum_{c\in\mathcal{Y}^t\cup b}\exp(q^t_{i,c}) & \text{if } j = b \\ \exp(q^t_{i,j})/\sum_{c\in\mathcal{Y}^t\cup b}\exp(q^t_{i,c}) & \text{if } j \in \mathcal{Y}^{t-1} \end{cases} \quad (1)$$

$$\tilde{q}^t_{i,j} = \begin{cases} \exp(q^t_{i,b} + \sum_{c\in\mathcal{Y}^{t-1}} q^t_{i,c})/\sum_{c\in\mathcal{Y}^t\cup b}\exp(q^t_{i,c}) & \text{if } j = b \\ 0 & \text{if } j \in \mathcal{Y}^{t-1} \\ \exp(q^t_{i,j})/\sum_{c\in\mathcal{Y}^t\cup b}\exp(q^t_{i,c}) & \text{if } j \in \mathcal{C}^t \end{cases} \quad (2)$$

where b means background. Then the probability of classes not marked in ground truth or pseudo label will not be broken during training.

3.2 Memory Module

As shown in Fig. 3, representation $\mathcal{R}$ is feature maps out of decoder, with shape of $C \times D \times H \times W$, where C means the number of channels in $\mathcal{R}$. To further mitigate 'knowledge forgetting' in IL setting, we introduce a light memory module $\mathcal{M}$ of size $|\mathcal{Y}^t| \times C$ in feature space between decoder and segmentation head, $\mathfrak{H}$, to remember the representation of each class. The size of $\mathcal{M}$ is updated by more $|\mathcal{C}^t| \times C$ on $|\mathcal{Y}^{t-1}| \times C$ after the tth stage. Then based on $\mathcal{M}$ we can add some constraints in feature space to improve the IL learning progress.

During training of each stage, with the position supplied by ground truth, we can acquire the voxel representation of corresponding new organs in feature

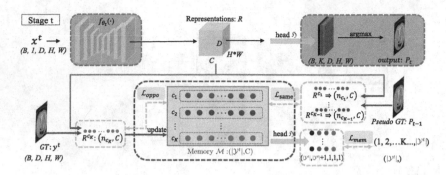

Fig. 3. Diagram of the memory module $\mathcal{M}$ in feature space between decoder and segmentation head. Based on label, we can take n_{c_K} voxels' representation from $\mathcal{R}$, $\mathcal{R}^{c_K}$:(n_{c_K}, C), to update $\mathcal{M}$ or calculate loss function.

map $\mathcal{R}$. Then new class c in $\mathcal{M}$ can be updated via moving average after each iteration:

$$\mathcal{M}_k^c = (1 - m_k) \cdot \mathcal{M}_{k-1}^c + m_k \cdot \mathcal{R}_k^c, \quad m_k = \frac{9m_0}{10} \cdot (1 - \frac{k}{K})^p + \frac{m_0}{10}, \quad (3)$$

where m is the momentum, k denotes the current number of iterations, and K is the total number of iterations of training. p and m_0 are set as 0.9 empirically. After each stage of training ends, the mean representation of new organ of category c in that stage is saved into the memory $\mathcal{M}$ as $\mathcal{M}^c$.

When we have $\mathcal{M}$ to save the mean representation of each class, we can introduce more regularization to constrain the learning of feature space. In this paper, we introduce l_{mem}, l_{same} and l_{oppo}:

$$\mathcal{L}_{mem} = \mathcal{L}_{ce}(\mathfrak{H}(reshape(\mathcal{M})), range(1, |\mathcal{Y}^t| + 1)) \quad (4)$$

$$\mathcal{L}_{same} = \sum_{c_0 \in \mathcal{Y}^{t-1}} \mathcal{L}_{cos}(\mathcal{M}^{c_o}, \mathcal{R}^{c_o}, 1) \quad (5)$$

$$\mathcal{L}_{oppo} = \sum_{c_n \in \mathcal{C}^t} (\mathcal{L}_{cos}(\mathcal{R}^b, \mathcal{R}^{c_n}, -1) + \sum_{c_0 \in \mathcal{Y}^{t-1}} \mathcal{L}_{cos}(\mathcal{M}^{c_o}, \mathcal{R}^{c_n}, -1)) \quad (6)$$

In Eq. (4), *reshape* is used to change $\mathcal{M}$ to the size of $|\mathcal{Y}^t| \times C \times 1 \times 1 \times 1$, which can be regarded as $|\mathcal{Y}^t|$ voxels belong to $|\mathcal{Y}^t|$ classes. $range(1, |\mathcal{Y}^t| + 1)$ can be seen as corresponding ground truth. Through the shared segmentation head $\mathfrak{H}$, features of classes in current stage are going to center around the mean representation in $\mathcal{M}$. Through l_{mem}, we constrain the learned feature of different classes in different stages more stable. The mean representation of old classes are treated as a kind of replay without privacy concerns. In Eqs. (5) and (6), c_o and c_n refer to old and new classes, respectively. Using Cosine Embedding Loss, $\mathcal{L}_{cos}$, we can explicitly restrain the feature of old class close to $\mathcal{M}^{c_o}$, and the feature of new class away from all $\mathcal{M}^{c_o}$.

Table 1. A summary of five benchmark datasets used in our experiments. [T] means there are tumor labels in original dataset and we merge them into corresponding organs.

Phase	Datasets	Modality	# of labeled volumes	Annotated organs	Mean spacing (z, y, x)	Source
Training & Val	Dataset0 (F)	CT	30	Five organs	(3.0, 0.76, 0.76)	Abdomen in [1]
	Dataset1 (P_1)	CT	131	Liver [T]	(1.0, 0.77, 0.77)	Task03 in [24]
	Dataset2 (P_2)	CT	41	Spleen	(1.6, 0.79, 0.79)	Task09 in [24]
	Dataset3 (P_3)	CT	281	Pancreas [T]	(2.5, 0.80, 0.80)	Task07 in [24]
	Dataset4 (P_4)	CT	210	L&R Kidneys [T]	(0.8, 0.78, 0.78)	KiTS [5]
	All	CT	693	Five organs	(1.7, 0.79, 0.79)	-
Testing	CLINIC	CT	107	Five organs	(1.2, 0.74, 0.74)	Private
	Amos	CT	200	Five organs	(5.0, 0.74, 0.74)	Temporarily private
	Pan	CT	56	Five organs	(2.6, 0.82, 0.82)	FLARE 21 [14]

4 Experiments

4.1 Setup

Datasets and preprocessing. To compare with our base method, MargExc [21], we choose the same five organs and datasets in our experiments, including liver, spleen, pancreas, right kidney and left kidney. In addition, we find three more independent datasets for testing to give a comprehensive evaluation. The details of these datasets are shown in Table 1.

We preprocess all datasets to a unified spacing (2.41, 1.63, 1.63) and normalize them with mean and std of 90.9 and 65.5 respectively. We respectively split five training datasets into 5 folds and randomly select one fold as validation set. For our main IL setting, five organs are learned in four stages: liver $(F+P_1) \rightarrow$ spleen $(F+P_2) \rightarrow$ pancreas $(F+P_3) \rightarrow$ R/L kidney $(F+P_4)$. The annotations of different organs in dataset F are used separately in our IL setting.

Implementation Details. We implement our experiments based on 3D lowres version of nnU-Net[1] [6] and also refer to MONAI[2] during our algorithm development. The patch-size and batch-size are set as (80, 160, 128) and 2, respectively, in our experiments. We train the network with the same optimizer and learning rate policy as nnU-Net for 350 epochs. The initial learning rate of the first stage and followed stages are set to 3e-4 and 15e-5.

Baseline Methods. Intuitively, we train a 5-class segmentation model ϕ_F on dataset F directly. And to use more partially labeled datasets, we train 4 models separately for different organs, too, i.e., ϕ_{F+P_*}. To simulate different organs are collected sequentially, simple fine-tuning (FT) and some SOTA IL methods (LwF [9], ILT [17] and MiB [2]) are also implemented. In the end, to evaluate our performance in actual usage scenarios, we compare our method to the upper bound results from MargExc [21]. Since we also use the marginal loss in IL, we call our method MargExcIL.

---

[1] github.com/mic-dkfz/nnunet.
[2] https://monai.io/.

Table 2. In the last stage(4th), the DC and HD95 of the segmentation results of different methods. MargExc [21] is the upper bound method training all datasets in the meantime. '-' means no result.

Training form	Methods	Organs DC/HD95 ($F + P_i$)											
		Liver		Spleen		Pancreas		R Kidney		L Kidney		Mean	
		DC	HD	DC	HD	DC	HD	DC	HD	DC	HD	DC	HD
Trained separated	ϕ_F (Five organs)	.953	10.28	.953	1.93	.721	8.25	.895	5.82	.839	13.41	.872	7.94
	ϕ_{F+P_1} (Liver)	.967	5.89	-	-	-	-	-	-	-	-	.936	8.25
	ϕ_{F+P_2} (Spleen)	-	-	.954	20.20	-	-	-	-	-	-		
	ϕ_{F+P_3} (Pancreas)	-	-	-	-	.842	5.13	-	-	-	-		
	ϕ_{F+P_4} (Kidneys)	-	-	-	-	-	-	.968	5.18	.950	4.86		
One model	FT	.000	-	.000	-	.000	-	.970	6.502	.963	2.018	.387	-
	LwF [9]	.001	190.33	.906	2.22	.792	5.91	.966	7.70	.948	7.22	.723	42.68
	ILT [17]	.000	170.77	.914	2.05	.772	8.40	.969	1.41	.948	4.06	.721	37.34
	MiB [2]	.966	6.76	.961	1.26	.817	6.56	.966	3.77	.946	7.22	.931	5.11
Ours	MargExcIL	.965	7.98	.962	1.30	.835	5.51	.968	1.40	.959	2.37	.938	3.71
Upper bound	MargExc [21]	.962	7.01	.965	1.15	.848	4.83	.969	1.39	.965	3.96	**.942**	**3.67**

Performance Metrics. We use Dice coefficient (DC) and 95th percentile Hausdorff distance (HD95) to evaluate results.

4.2 Results and Discussions

Comparison with Baseline Methods. In IL setting, performance of batch learning of all categories is seen as the upper bound for comparison. Because joint learning can access all knowledge at the meantime, it is possible to fit the distribution of the whole dataset. We regard MargExc [21] as the counterpart batch method in MOS, which obtains the DC of 0.942 and HD95 of 3.67 when training all five training datasets together, as in Table 2.

When we do not aggregate these partially labeled data together, there are some limitations in performance. The 5-class segmentation model ϕ_F only trained on small scale 'fully' annotated dataset F, can not generalize well to all validation datasets due to the scale of the dataset F. The metrics of DC and HD95 are all much worse than upper bound. When we train four models, ϕ_{F+P_*}, one model per organ segmentation task trained on corresponding datasets ($F+P_*$), then all datasets can be used. We can get much better performance than ϕ_F on DC metric, but also bad HD95 metric. Higher HD95 means more false positive predictions out of our trained models. Furthermore, training separately is also poor in scalability and efficiency when the categories grow in the future.

When we aggregate these partially labeled datasets together sequentially, the most intuitive method FT is the worst. It has no preservation of the old knowledge because there is no restraint for it. LwF [9] and ILT [17] perform better than FT, but 'knowledge conflict' limits the performance of LwF and ILT when the stage of IL is more than 3, *i.e.*, the liver knowledge in the 1st stage can not be kept in the 4th stage. We check the output of the models trained via LwF

Table 3. The DC and HD95 of the segmentation results. The best and second result is shown in **bold** and red. S* means *$*^{th}$ stage in IL setting. '-' means **No Access** to the classes in that stage.

| Setting | Organs | DC/HD95 Model$_{S*}$ on Validation Sets | | | | | | | | Model$_{S3}$ on Testing Datasets | | | | | |
| | | S0 | | S1 | | S2 | | S3 | | CLINIC | | AMOS | | Pan | |
		DC	HD	DC	HD	DC	HD	DC	HD	DC	HD	DC	HD	DC	HD
MargExc− IL$_{swin}$ (woMem)	Liver	.965	5.51	.959	20.10	.958	20.86	.957	7.24	.971	3.33	.937	10.68	.977	2.00
	Spleen	-	-	.958	2.11	.960	2.12	.962	1.19	.953	5.88	.865	6.93	.965	1.66
	Pancreas	-	-	-	-	.827	6.02	.809	6.85	.853	5.80	.610	21.91	.809	6.85
	R Kidney	-	-	-	-	-	-	.966	1.46	.945	6.80	.837	7.10	.942	3.88
	L Kidney	-	-	-	-	-	-	.959	2.29	.941	6.83	.872	7.64	.948	4.41
	mean	.965	5.51	.959	11.11	.915	9.67	.931	3.81	.933	5.73	.824	10.85	.928	3.76
MargExc− IL$_{swin}$	Liver	.965	3.60	.962	7.33	.959	8.08	.958	9.04	.970	3.46	.950	4.08	.974	2.42
	Spleen	-	-	.961	1.24	.964	1.18	.963	1.15	.953	3.50	.882	6.00	.966	1.58
	Pancreas	-	-	-	-	.826	5.21	.816	5.65	.847	6.24	.640	31.31	.817	5.71
	R Kidney	-	-	-	-	-	-	.964	3.49	.942	7.31	.883	6.43	.941	4.63
	L Kidney	-	-	-	-	-	-	.953	2.59	.933	8.94	.867	8.96	.951	3.60
	mean	.965	3.60	.962	4.28	.916	4.821	.931	4.38	.929	5.89	.844	11.36	.930	3.59
MargExcIL (woMem)	Liver	.967	5.89	.965	14.99	.962	17.45	.965	6.32	.972	4.72	.948	4.66	.979	1.83
	Spleen	-	-	.963	1.21	.956	2.42	.963	1.17	.957	12.39	.885	23.77	.971	1.19
	Pancreas	-	-	-	-	.840	5.72	.836	5.67	.865	5.21	.687	17.62	.838	5.48
	R Kidney	-	-	-	-	-	-	.968	1.63	.945	5.44	.870	6.94	.937	3.71
	L Kidney	-	-	-	-	-	-	.957	2.51	.941	5.98	.875	4.22	.944	3.74
	mean	**.967**	5.89	**.964**	8.10	.919	8.53	.938	**3.46**	**.936**	6.75	.853	11.44	.934	3.19
MargExcIL (Ours)	Liver	.967	2.83	.966	3.41	.966	7.05	.965	7.98	.971	3.27	.947	4.85	.978	1.86
	Spleen	-	-	.962	1.18	.962	1.21	.962	1.30	.956	4.60	.888	6.27	.969	1.26
	Pancreas	-	-	-	-	.837	5.32	.835	5.51	.865	5.13	.711	16.78	.839	5.14
	R Kidney	-	-	-	-	-	-	.968	1.40	.946	6.14	.846	7.44	.943	3.48
	L Kidney	-	-	-	-	-	-	.959	2.37	.942	5.86	.872	12.20	.935	3.05
	mean	**.967**	**2.83**	**.964**	**2.30**	.922	4.53	.938	3.71	**.936**	5.00	.853	**9.51**	**.935**	**3.05**
MargExc [21] (Upper Bound)	Liver	.967	5.89	.966	6.90	.968	2.79	.962	7.01	.965	3.04	.952	4.05	.981	1.63
	Spleen	-	-	.950	5.86	.959	2.15	.965	1.15	.948	3.01	.896	9.24	.970	1.26
	Pancreas	-	-	-	-	.841	5.92	.848	4.83	.862	5.67	.677	20.41	.849	4.94
	R Kidney	-	-	-	-	-	-	.969	1.39	.950	2.17	.854	6.65	.918	7.84
	L Kidney	-	-	-	-	-	-	.965	3.96	.943	2.28	.898	10.64	.935	6.39
	mean	**.967**	5.89	.958	6.38	**.923**	**3.62**	**.942**	3.67	.934	**3.23**	**.855**	10.20	.931	4.41

and ILT, finding that old organs' logit is overwhelmed by the logit of background as the training stages progress. MiB [2] can get a good result compared with LwF and ILT because of remodeling background and foreground in training phase, thus avoiding the 'knowledge conflict' problem.

MargExc [21] also solves the 'knowledge conflict' problem, which is the most harmful factor in aggregating partially labeled dataset. Based on MargExc, our MargExcIL also performs well on DC and HD95, better than all other methods, *e.g.* MiB or the models trained separated for all organs, approaching upper bound result (DC: 0.938 vs 0.942 & HD95: 3.71 vs 3.67). In '*Model$_{S3}$ on Testing Datasets*' part in Table 3, MargExcIL even performs better than MargExc [21]. These results prove IL might have a practical potential in clinical scenario.

Effectiveness of Memory Module. In Table 3, we also show the results of the 4 intermediate stages of our method, in '$Model_{S*}$ on Validation Sets' part. '$(woMem)$' means our method without memory module and corresponding loss functions. '$_{swin}$' means that we modify encoder of our network designed by nnUNet to Swin Transformer [12], which can also assist in proving the effectiveness of our memory module. Without memory module, we can also obtain the same level performance in last stage, but it's *not stable in the middle stages*, e.g., liver's HD95 get worse dramatically in stage 2 and stage 3. This uncertainty factor in our IL system is not acceptable. We believe that this phenomenon is caused by the variation in the image distribution or field-of-view (FOV) in different datasets. Our memory module stores a prior knowledge of old class to stabilize the whole IL system. Compared with MargExc [21], we also achieve a comparable performance.

5   Conclusion

To unleash the potential from a collection of partially labeled datasets and to settle the efficiency, storage, and ethical issues in current methods, we introduce an incremental learning (IL) mechanism with a practical *four*-stage setting and verify the implementation potential of IL in MOS. IL methods have a natural adaptability to medical image scenarios due to the relatively fixed anatomical structure of human body. The introduced light memory module and loss functions can also stabilize the IL system in practice via constraining the representation of different categories in feature space. We believe that IL holds a great promise in addressing the challenges in real clinics.

References

1. Bennett, L., et al.: 2015 miccai multi-atlas labeling beyond the cranial vault - workshop and challenge (2015). https://doi.org/10.7303/syn3193805
2. Cermelli, F., Mancini, M., Bulo, S.R., Ricci, E., Caputo, B.: Modeling the background for incremental learning in semantic segmentation. In: Proceedings of the IEEE/CVF Conference on Computer Vision and Pattern Recognition, pp. 9233–9242 (2020)
3. Deng, J., Dong, W., Socher, R., Li, L.J., Li, K., Fei-Fei, L.: Imagenet: a large-scale hierarchical image database. In: 2009 IEEE Conference on Computer Vision and Pattern Recognition, pp. 248–255. IEEE (2009)
4. Fang, X., Yan, P.: Multi-organ segmentation over partially labeled datasets with multi-scale feature abstraction. IEEE Trans. Med. Imaging **39**(11), 3619–3629 (2020)
5. Heller, N., et al.: The kits19 challenge data: 300 kidney tumor cases with clinical context, CT semantic segmentations, and surgical outcomes. arXiv:1904.00445 (2019)
6. Isensee, F., Jaeger, P.F., Kohl, S.A., Petersen, J., Maier-Hein, K.H.: nnu-net: a self-configuring method for deep learning-based biomedical image segmentation. Nat. Methods **18**(2), 203–211 (2021)

7. Jin, Z., et al.: Mining contextual information beyond image for semantic segmentation. In: Proceedings of the IEEE/CVF International Conference on Computer Vision, pp. 7231–7241 (2021)

8. Kirkpatrick, J., et al.: Overcoming catastrophic forgetting in neural networks. Proc. Natl. Acad. Sci. **114**(13), 3521–3526 (2017)

9. Li, Z., Hoiem, D.: Learning without forgetting. IEEE Trans. Pattern Anal. Mach. Intell. **40**(12), 2935–2947 (2017)

10. Lin, T.-Y., et al.: Microsoft COCO: common objects in context. In: Fleet, D., Pajdla, T., Schiele, B., Tuytelaars, T. (eds.) ECCV 2014. LNCS, vol. 8693, pp. 740–755. Springer, Cham (2014). https://doi.org/10.1007/978-3-319-10602-1_48

11. Liu, Y., Schiele, B., Sun, Q.: Meta-aggregating networks for class-incremental learning. arXiv preprint arXiv:2010.05063 (2020)

12. Liu, Z., et al.: Swin transformer: hierarchical vision transformer using shifted windows. In: Proceedings of the IEEE/CVF International Conference on Computer Vision, pp. 10012–10022 (2021)

13. Lopez-Paz, D., Ranzato, M.: Gradient episodic memory for continual learning. Advances in neural information processing systems 30 (2017)

14. Ma, J., et al.: Abdomenct-1k: Is abdominal organ segmentation a solved problem. IEEE Trans. Pattern Anal. Mach. Intell., 1 (2021). https://doi.org/10.1109/TPAMI.2021.3100536

15. Marra, F., Saltori, C., Boato, G., Verdoliva, L.: Incremental learning for the detection and classification of gan-generated images. In: 2019 IEEE International Workshop on Information Forensics and Security (WIFS), pp. 1–6 (2019). https://doi.org/10.1109/WIFS47025.2019.9035099

16. McCloskey, M., Cohen, N.J.: Catastrophic interference in connectionist networks: the sequential learning problem. In: Psychology of learning and motivation, vol. 24, pp. 109–165. Elsevier (1989)

17. Michieli, U., Zanuttigh, P.: Incremental learning techniques for semantic segmentation. In: Proceedings of the IEEE/CVF International Conference on Computer Vision Workshops (2019)

18. Ozdemir, F., Goksel, O.: Extending pretrained segmentation networks with additional anatomical structures. Int. J. Comput. Assist. Radiol. Surg. **14**(7), 1187–1195 (2019). https://doi.org/10.1007/s11548-019-01984-4

19. Rebuffi, S.A., Kolesnikov, A., Sperl, G., Lampert, C.H.: icarl: incremental classifier and representation learning. In: Proceedings of the IEEE conference on Computer Vision and Pattern Recognition, pp. 2001–2010 (2017)

20. Rusu, A.A., et al.: Progressive neural networks. arXiv preprint arXiv:1606.04671 (2016)

21. Shi, G., Xiao, L., Chen, Y., Zhou, S.K.: Marginal loss and exclusion loss for partially supervised multi-organ segmentation. Medical Image Analysis, p. 101979 (2021)

22. Shi, K., Bao, H., Ma, N.: Forward vehicle detection based on incremental learning and fast R-CNN. In: 2017 13th International Conference on Computational Intelligence and Security (CIS), pp. 73–76 (2017). https://doi.org/10.1109/CIS.2017.00024

23. Shmelkov, K., Schmid, C., Alahari, K.: Incremental learning of object detectors without catastrophic forgetting. In: Proceedings of the IEEE International Conference on Computer Vision, pp. 3400–3409 (2017)

24. Simpson, A.L., et al.: A large annotated medical image dataset for the development and evaluation of segmentation algorithms. arXiv:1902.09063 (2019)

25. Tasar, O., Tarabalka, Y., Alliez, P.: Incremental learning for semantic segmentation of large-scale remote sensing data. IEEE J. Sel. Topics Appl. Earth Observ. Remote Sens. **12**(9), 3524–3537 (2019)
26. Xu, J., Zhu, Z.: Reinforced continual learning. Advances in Neural Information Processing Systems 31 (2018)
27. Zhang, J., Xie, Y., Xia, Y., Shen, C.: Dodnet: learning to segment multi-organ and tumors from multiple partially labeled datasets. In: Proceedings of the IEEE/CVF Conference on Computer Vision and Pattern Recognition, pp. 1195–1204 (2021)
28. Zhou, S.K., et al.: A review of deep learning in medical imaging: Imaging traits, technology trends, case studies with progress highlights, and future promises. Proceedings of the IEEE (2021)
29. Zhou, S.K., Rueckert, D., Fichtinger, G.: Handbook of Medical Image Computing and Computer Assisted Intervention. Academic Press (2019)
30. Zhou, Y., et al.: Prior-aware neural network for partially-supervised multi-organ segmentation. In: Proceedings of the IEEE/CVF International Conference on Computer Vision, pp. 10672–10681 (2019)

Harnessing Deep Bladder Tumor Segmentation with Logical Clinical Knowledge

Xiao Huang[1], Xiaodong Yue[1,2(✉)], Zhikang Xu[1], and Yufei Chen[3]

[1] School of Computer Engineering and Science, Shanghai University, Shanghai, China
[2] Artificial Intelligence Institute of Shanghai University, Shanghai University, Shanghai, China
yswantfly@shu.edu.cn
[3] College of Electronics and Information Engineering, Tongji University, Shanghai, China

Abstract. Segmentation of bladder tumors from Magnetic Resonance (MR) images is important for early detection and auxiliary diagnosis of bladder cancer. Deep Convolutional Neural Networks (DCNNs) have been widely used for bladder tumor segmentation but the DCNN-based tumor segmentation over-depends on data training and neglects the clinical knowledge. From a clinical point of view, a bladder tumor must rely on the bladder wall to survive and grow, and the domain prior is very helpful for bladder tumor localization. Aiming at the problem, we propose a novel bladder tumor segmentation method in which the clinical logic rules of bladder tumor and wall are incorporated into DCNNs and make the segmentation of DCNN harnessed by the clinical rules. The logic rules provide a semantic and friendly knowledge representation for human clinicians, which are easy to set and understand. Moreover, fusing the logic rules of clinical knowledge facilitates to reduce the data dependency of the segmentation network and achieve precise segmentation results even with limited labeled training images. Experiments on the bladder MR images from the cooperative hospital validate the effectiveness of the proposed tumor segmentation method.

Keywords: Bladder tumor segmentation · Deep convolutional neural network · Logic rules of clinical knowledge

1 Introduction

Bladder cancer is one of common urological tumors. Early detection and removal of bladder tumors is crucial for bladder cancer treatments. Tumor segmentation of Magnetic Resonance (MR) images is the key technology to implement the intelligent detection and measurement of bladder tumors. Due to the superiority of image feature learning, Deep Convolutional Neural Networks (DCNNs) have

L. Wang et al. (Eds.): MICCAI 2022, LNCS 13434, pp. 725–735, 2022.
https://doi.org/10.1007/978-3-031-16440-8_69

been widely used to analyze bladder MR images for bladder tumor segmentation [13,15], detection [1,20] and auxiliary diagnosis [7,9].

To improve the model interpretation and reduce the data dependency, researchers tried to involve the domain knowledge including the size, shape and spatial priors into DCNNs for medical image segmentation [11,16,17,22,23]. From the view of domain knowledge utilization, the DCNN-based bladder tumor segmentation methods can be divided into two categories of data-driven and data-knowledge fusion methods. The pure data-driven segmentation methods directly construct tumor segmentation models based on only labeled training images. Ge et al. [8] and Dolz et al. [5] combined dilated convolution to improve the bladder tumor segmentation model. The data-driven segmentation methods over depend on the data training and cannot be applied in the scenarios with insufficient labeled medical images. In contrast, data-knowledge fusion methods incorporate domain knowledge into the tumor segmentation models and are less dependent on labeled image data. Huang et al. formulated the domain priors of bladder tumor size and location distribution with the attention mechanism and integrated the priors into DCNN to constrain the tumor segmentation [10]. Li et al. utilized an autoencoder network to learn the semantic features of bladder as priors and then incorporated the priors into the segmentation network [13] .

Although involving domain priors into DCNNs can improve the segmentation performances, the related data-knowledge fusion methods still suffered two drawbacks. First, the knowledges are represented in the forms of parameter setting, optimization constraints, attention mechanism and probability distribution, which are difficult for the knowledge acquisition from clinicians. For example, it is difficult for human doctors to accurately describe and understand the constraints of priors for model optimization. Second, the extraction of some knowledges still requires abundant labeled data, such as the priors of attentions and probability distributions learnt from abundant labeled images.

To tackle the drawbacks of knowledge representation, in this paper, we propose a novel bladder tumor segmentation method in which the logic rules of clinical knowledge are incorporated into DCNNs. As a natural way of human thinking, logic rules provide a semantic and human-friendly knowledge representation. It has been verified that the symbolic logic rules can be effectively fused into a deep neural networks to improve its classification performances [4,21]. Zhang et al. [24] used logic rules to classify the stage of bladder tumor cancer with good results, but their method cannot be directly used for segmentation task. In the proposed method, we first extract the clinical knowledge of bladder tumors and walls in the form of logic rules from the segmentation masks of ground-truth. Then we train a graph convolutional network to embed the logic rules into a latent feature space. After that, we reconstruct the loss function of segmentation network to minimize the difference between logic rule embeddings of the ground-truth segmentation and the predicted segmentation, and thereby use the logic rules to guide the tumor segmentation of the network.

To the best of our knowledge, the related works of involving logic rules into DCNNs for medical image segmentation are very limited. Comparing with the other knowledge representations, the logic rules of clinical knowledge are more semantic and friendly to human clinicians. Moreover, fusing the logic rules of clinical knowledge facilitates to reduce the data dependency of the segmentation network and achieve precise segmentation results even with limited labeled training images. Experiments on the bladder MR images from the cooperative hospital validate the effectiveness of the proposed tumor segmentation method.

2 Method

In this section, we introduce how to integrate the clinical logic rules into DCNNs to guide the bladder tumor segmentation. As shown in Fig. 1, the framework of the proposed segmentation method consists of two parts. The left part is a backbone segmentation network, such as a U-Net, and the right part is the clinical logic knowledge extraction model. First, we extract the logic rules related to bladder tumor and bladder wall from both ground-truth and predicted segmentation masks. Then we transform the logic rules into graphs and use a graph convolution network to embed them into a latent feature space. Through reducing the gap between the latent features of the logic rules induced by the ground-truth and the predicted segmentation, we make the segmentation results consistent with the logic rules. The overall loss function of segmentation is listed below, in which the first term is used to measure the segmentation error and the second one is to measure the logic rule consistency, β is the balance factor.

$$L_{total} = L_{segment} + \beta L_{rule}. \tag{1}$$

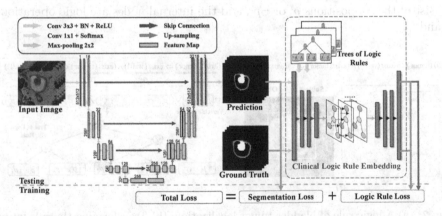

Fig. 1. Framework of the proposed bladder tumor segmentation method, in which the segmentation network is harnessed by logic rules.

2.1 Constructing Logic Rules for Bladder Tumor Localization

From a clinical point of view, a bladder tumor must rely on the bladder wall to survive and grow. The clinical knowledge that tumors are attached to the bladder wall can help us to localize the bladder tumors. The logic rule of bladder tumor localization is defined as a propositional formula. A propositional formula F is a combination of propositional variables connected by logical connectives $\{\neg, \wedge, \vee, \Rightarrow, \Leftrightarrow\}$. Let $p^1, p^2, ..., p^n$ be n propositional variables appearing in the propositional formula F, p^i is a statement that is either true or false. Setting values of the propositional variables which map the formula to true or false is called an assignment. We define two types of propositions for bladder tumor localization as follows.

- **Existence Proposition** indicates whether an object exists in a segmentation mask, e.g. *exist*(tumor) and *exist*(bladder wall).
- **Spatial Proposition** indicates the relative spatial relationships of two objects, which include $\{in,\ out,\ nearby\}$, e.g. *in*(tumor, wall), *out*(tumor, wall) and *nearby*(tumor, wall).

Combining the existence and spatial propositions, we can construct the logic rules of bladder tumor localization, such as $(exist(\text{tumor}) \Rightarrow exist(\text{wall})) \wedge$ $((exist(\text{tumor}) \Leftrightarrow in(\text{tumor, wall}))$ to indicate that there exists a tumor inside the bladder wall. '$\Rightarrow$' and '$\Leftrightarrow$' are the logic implications and the rule can be equally transformed into the formula of propositions $(\neg exist(\text{tumor}) \vee (exist(\text{wall}) \wedge in(\text{tumor,wall}))) \wedge (\neg in(\text{tumor,wall}) \vee exist(\text{tumor}))$. Adopting p^1, p^2 and p^3 to briefly denote the propositions $exist(\text{tumor})$, $exist(\text{wall})$ and $in(\text{tumor, box})$, we can obtain the rule as $(\neg p^1 \vee (p^2 \wedge p^3)) \wedge (\neg p^3 \wedge p^1)$. Furthermore, we can structurally represent the propositional formula by a tree, in which the leaf nodes consist of the propositions p^i or $\neg p^i$, and the internal nodes are logic operations $\wedge$ and $\vee$.

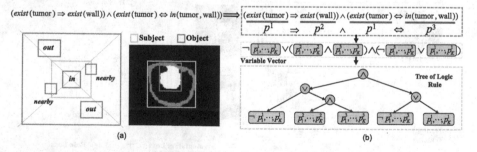

Fig. 2. (a) A logic rule of bladder tumor localization. (b) Transforming the rule into a formula of K-dimensional propositional variables and constructing the tree of rule.

In addition, the binary propositional variables of a logic rule reflect the information of the entire image, which are too coarse to represent the detailed information of bladder tumors. For example, the binary proposition $exist(\text{tumor})$

can only indicate whether the tumor exists, but cannot indicate where the tumor exists. Therefore, we further extend a binary propositional variable p^i to a K-dimensional vector $p_1^i, ..., p_k^i, ..., p_K^i$, in which each element p_k^i indicates whether the tumor exists in the kth local region in the image. In the DCNN-based image segmentation, we generate the vector of propositional variables through inputting a medical image into the multiple max-pooling module. Summarizing all the binary propositional variables of local regions in the vector, we can compute the propositional variable p^i of the entire image.

$$p^i = \begin{cases} false, & \text{if } \sum_{k=1}^{K} p_k^i = 0 \\ true, & \text{otherwise} \end{cases} \tag{2}$$

The workflow to form the representation of the logic rules of bladder tumor is shown in Fig. 2(b).

2.2   Embedding Logic Rules into Latent Features

As mentioned above, for a clinical logic rule of propositional formula, we can represent the rule by a tree and utilize the Graph Convolutional Network (GCN) [12] to embed the tree of rule into a latent feature space. In the feature space, we can measure the difference between the rule embeddings of ground-truth segmentation and the predicted segmentation produced by DCNNs. The GCN for embedding the logic rules is constructed as

$$Z^{(l+1)} = \sigma\left(\tilde{D}^{-\frac{1}{2}}\tilde{A}\tilde{D}^{-\frac{1}{2}}Z^{(l)}W^{(l)}\right), \tag{3}$$

where $Z^{(l)}$ is the embedding matrix output by layer l-1, and $Z^{(0)}$ is constructed as a combination of a global embedding vector and the embedding vectors of all the tree nodes. A is the adjacency matrix of the tree of the rule, $\tilde{A} = A + I$, I is a identity matrix. This transformation enables the adjacency matrix A to consider the influences caused by the nodes themselves. $\tilde{D}$ is the in-out degree matrix, $\tilde{D}_{ii} = \sum_j \tilde{A}_{ij}$. $\tilde{D}^{-\frac{1}{2}}\tilde{A}\tilde{D}^{-\frac{1}{2}}$ denotes the adjacency matrix normalized by the in-out degree. The trainable weight parameter matrix of the current layer is denoted by W, and σ indicates the activation function.

Moreover, in order to learn the GCN weights W, we implement a binary classification task to pre-train GCN. As shown in the blue area of Fig. 3, given a logic rule, we construct its truth table and accordingly generate multiple logic rules of K-dimensional propositional variables. We label each input segmentation mask as positive or negative. If the segmentation mask corresponds to a true value, it is labeled as positive, otherwise it is labeled as negative. Besides the ground-truth segmentation masks in the training dataset which are labeled as positive, we augment a number of negative segmentation masks through making the masks violate the rules.

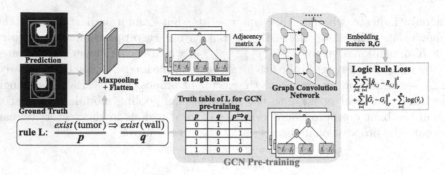

Fig. 3. Embedding logic rules into latent features with GCN to construct the rule loss.

2.3   Optimization of Segmentation Network with Logic Rules

To guide the tumor segmentation network with the clinical logic rules, we define a loss function of rules L_{rule} to measure the distance between the predicted segmentation and ground-truth segmentation based on the feature embedding of logic rules.

$$L_{rule} = \sum_{j=1}^{n}\sum_{i=1}^{m}\left\|\hat{R}_{i,j} - R_{i,j}\right\|_{F}^{2} + \sum_{i=1}^{m}\left\|\hat{G}_i - G_i\right\|_{F}^{2} - \sum_{i=1}^{m}\log(\hat{v}_i), \qquad (4)$$

where $\|\cdot\|_F$ is the Frobenius norm of matrix.

Given m labeled training images, the rule loss function consists of three terms. The first and second terms are used to keep the logic rule extracted from the predicted segmentation of DCNN consistent with the rule extracted from the ground truth segmentation. For the logic rule extracted from the ground truth segmentation of the ith image, suppose Z_i is the feature embedding matrix of the rule output by the last layer of GCN, $R_i \subset Z_i$ is the submatrix of the embedded feature vectors of the propositional variables in the rule, $R_{i,j}$ is the embedded feature vector of the propositional variable j in the rules. Correspondingly, $\hat{Z}_i$ is the feature embedding matrix of the rules extracted from the predicted segmentation of DCNN and $\hat{R}_{i,j}$ denotes the embedded feature vector of the propositional variable j in the rules of predicted segmentation. Obviously, the first term is used to measure the difference between the propositional variables of the logic rules from ground truth and predicted segmentations. In the second part, G_i is global logic rule embedding of the i-th ground truth segmentation obtained from the corresponding row of Z_i, and $\hat{G}_i$ represents the global logic rule embedding of the predicted segmentation. The third part is used to guarantee that the logic rule extracted from the predicted segmentation is correct, in which $\hat{v}_i$ is the binary classification result (true or false) of the feature vector of rule output by GCN.

Besides the rule loss, we adopt both *cross-entropy* and *dice* measurements to implement the segmentation loss. The loss function for optimizing the backbone segmentation network is $L_{segment} = L_{ce} + 0.01L_{dice}$, in which L_{ce} and L_{dice} denote cross-entropy loss and dice loss respectively.

3 Experiments

We conduct experiments on a bladder tumor data set that contains 387 MR bladder images (slices) of 14 patients with the segmentation labels of background, bladder wall and tumor. We use 290 images of 10 patients for training and 97 images of 4 patients for testing. We use *Dice similarity coefficient (Dice)* and *Average symmetric surface distance (Assd)* to evaluate the segmentation results. To verify the universal effectiveness of the proposed method, we plug the clinical logic rules into three state-of-the-art medical image segmentation networks, U-Net, ResUnet and DenseUnet. All these networks are trained from scratch by employing the Adam optimizer with $\beta \in [0.9, 1]$. We randomly initialize the weights of the networks and set the learning rates to 1e-3.

3.1 Test of Segmentation Enhancement by Logic Rules

First, we verify that fusing clinical logic rules into DCNNs can generally enhance the DCNN-based segmentation. Abbreviating the propositions *exist*(tumor), *exist*(wall), *in*(tumor, box), *out*(tumor, box) and *nearby*(tumor, box) to a, b, c, d, e respectively. According to experiences, clinicians can simply set up the following three logic rules for bladder tumor localization. r1: $a \Rightarrow b$; r2: $(a \Rightarrow b) \wedge (a \Leftrightarrow c) \wedge (a \Leftrightarrow \neg d)$; r3: $(a \Rightarrow b) \wedge (a \Leftrightarrow c) \wedge (a \Leftrightarrow \neg d) \wedge (a \Leftrightarrow e)$. Integrating these logic rules into U-Net, ResUnet and DenseUnet for bladder tumor and wall segmentation, Table 1 presents the evaluations of the segmentation results produced by backbone networks and networks with logic rules. We can find that for different kinds of DCNNs, fusing logic rules into the networks can generally improve the segmentations of both bladder wall and tumor.

Table 1. Evaluations of segmentations produced by DCNNs and DCNNs with rules.

Method	Dice ↑		Assd ↓	
	Wall	Tumor	Wall	Tumor
U-Net				
Base	0.881±0.005	0.758±0.010	0.495±0.074	4.793±1.364
Base+rule	**0.889±0.004**	**0.765±0.005**	**0.407±0.026**	**3.579±0.658**
ResUnet				
Base	0.875±0.012	0.748±0.015	0.500±0.082	3.635±0.921
Base+rule	**0.879±0.001**	**0.764±0.003**	**0.459±0.001**	**3.532±0.757**
DenseUnet				
Base	0.878±0.007	0.775±0.008	0.437±0.015	**2.541±0.084**
Base+rule	**0.884±0.003**	**0.783±0.010**	**0.351±0.008**	2.898±0.052

Besides the accuracy improvement, we also validate that fusing the logical clinical knowledge is helpful to reduce the data dependency of DCNNs for image segmentation. Based on the varying ratios of training labeled images (12.5%, 25%, 50%, 100%), we perform U-Net, ResUnet, DenseUnet and all the networks with the rules of r1-3 for tumor segmentation. As shown in Fig. 4, it is obvious that the segmentations produced by DCNNs with logic rules outperform the base models on the partial labeled training images. Especially when the training data are very limited (12.5% and 25%), the clinical logic rules can guide DCNNs to greatly improve their segmentation performances.

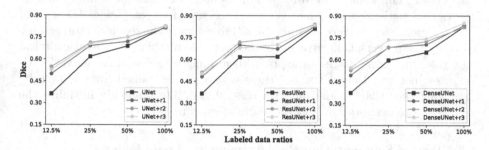

Fig. 4. Comparison of DCNN-based segmentations with and without rules based on varying ratios of training images.

We also visualize the segmentation results produced by U-Net and U-Net with the rule of r3 under varying ratios of training images in Fig. 5. We can find that the misclassified tissues by U-Net are far from the bladder. The possible reasons are the tissues have similar intensities and shape to tumor and wall. In contrast, harnessed by the clinical logic rules, the U-Net with rules can mitigate the misclassification and give cleaner segmentation results. In addition, guided by the rules of spatial relation, U-Net can accurately detect the relative position between the tumor and bladder wall. As shown in Fig. 5, for the tumors closely

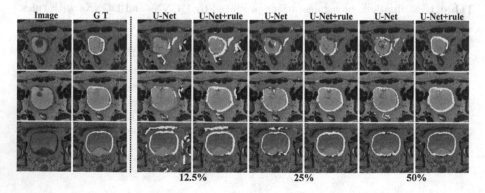

Fig. 5. Visualization of the bladder tumor and wall segmentations produced by U-Net and U-Net with rules under different ratios of training images.

attached to the bladder wall, the U-Net with rules can accurately segment the tumors but the base U-Net often confuses the tumor and bladder wall.

3.2 Comparison with Other Segmentation Methods

To further verify the superiority of fusing logic rules into DCNN-based segmentation, we compare the proposed method with 9 state-of-the-art image segmentation methods including 10 data-driven deep neural networks and one data-knowledge fusion segmentation method that involves attention priors (U-net + Attention [10]). For fair comparison, we use 50% training images for build up all the segmentation models. Table.2 shows the detailed experimental results.

Table 2. Comparison with other image segmentation methods.

Method	Dice ↑		Assd ↓	
	Wall	Tumor	Wall	Tumor
UNet++ [26]	0.775	0.601	4.867	4.787
AttGateUNet [18]	0.727	0.540	2.381	9.335
MAnet [6]	**0.803**	0.628	<u>1.846</u>	7.064
DeepLabV3 [2]	0.635	0.541	2.214	4.201
DeepLabV3+ [3]	0.763	0.569	1.884	4.904
U-Net+Attention [10]	0.770	0.674	3.408	3.850
BW-Net [13]	0.786	0.631	2.965	4.012
MD-Net [8]	0.767	0.644	2.103	4.158
U-Net [19]	0.762	0.618	3.646	5.056
ResUnet [25]	0.714	0.583	2.390	7.601
DenseUnet [14]	0.724	0.575	3.041	8.589
UNet+rule	<u>0.797</u>	<u>0.693</u>	2.307	**2.976**
ResUnet+rule	0.757	0.646	**1.404**	5.962
DenseUnet+rule	0.774	**0.708**	3.864	<u>3.714</u>

It can be observed that our method achieves competitive performance against other segmentation methods. Comparing with all the data-driven segmentation methods, our method achieves best performance in term of *Assd*, and in term of *Dice* on Tumor, which validate the superiority of fusing logic rules. In addition, across all evaluation metric, our method outperforms data-knowledge fusion method U-net+Attention. The major drawbacks of U-net+Attention is that its prior representation is based on attention mechanism that needs sufficient training images to formulate. Moreover, comparing with the attention mechanism learnt from the labeled data, the logic rules are semantic knowledge and can be conveniently acquired from human clinicians.

4   Conclusion

The DCNN-based bladder tumor segmentation methods rely on labeled training data and ignore the clinical knowledge. To tackle this problem, this paper proposes a novel bladder tumor segmentation method by fusing clinical logic rules of bladder tumor and wall. We first extract the logic rules from segmentation masks and then embed the logic rules into latent features using GCN. Through reducing the gap between the logic rule embeddings of the ground-truth segmentation and the predicted segmentation, the rules can guide the DCNN to produce precise segmentation results. Our future work will focus on the semi-supervised medical image segmentation with logic rules of domain knowledge.

Acknowledgments. This work was supported by National Natural Science Foundation of China (Serial Nos. 61976134, 62173252, 61991410) and Natural Science Foundation of Shanghai (NO 21ZR1423900).

References

1. Cha, K.H., et al.: Computer-aided detection of bladder masses in CT urography (CTU). In: Medical Imaging 2017: Computer-Aided Diagnosis, vol. 10134, p. 1013403. International Society for Optics and Photonics (2017)
2. Chen, L.C., Papandreou, G., Schroff, F., Adam, H.: Rethinking atrous convolution for semantic image segmentation. arXiv preprint arXiv:1706.05587 (2017)
3. Chen, L.-C., Zhu, Y., Papandreou, G., Schroff, F., Adam, H.: Encoder-decoder with atrous separable convolution for semantic image segmentation. In: Ferrari, V., Hebert, M., Sminchisescu, C., Weiss, Y. (eds.) ECCV 2018. Encoder-decoder with atrous separable convolution for semantic image segmentation, vol. 11211, pp. 833–851. Springer, Cham (2018). https://doi.org/10.1007/978-3-030-01234-2_49
4. Dash, T., Srinivasan, A., Vig, L.: Incorporating symbolic domain knowledge into graph neural networks. Mach. Learn. **110**(7), 1609–1636 (2021). https://doi.org/10.1007/s10994-021-05966-z
5. Dolz, J., et al.: Multiregion segmentation of bladder cancer structures in MRI with progressive dilated convolutional networks. Med. Phys. **45**(12), 5482–5493 (2018)
6. Fan, T., Wang, G., Li, Y., Wang, H.: Ma-net: a multi-scale attention network for liver and tumor segmentation. IEEE Access **8**, 179656–179665 (2020)
7. Garapati, S.S., et al.: Urinary bladder cancer staging in CT urography using machine learning. Med. Phys. **44**(11), 5814–5823 (2017)
8. Ge, R., et al.: Md-unet: Multi-input dilated u-shape neural network for segmentation of bladder cancer. Comput. Biol. Chem. **93**, 107510 (2021)
9. Gosnell, M.E., Polikarpov, D.M., Goldys, E.M., Zvyagin, A.V., Gillatt, D.A.: Computer-assisted cystoscopy diagnosis of bladder cancer. In: Urologic Oncology: Seminars and Original Investigations, vol. 36, pp. 8–e9. Elsevier (2018)
10. Huang, X., Yue, X., Xu, Z., Chen, Y.: Integrating general and specific priors into deep convolutional neural networks for bladder tumor segmentation. In: 2021 International Joint Conference on Neural Networks (IJCNN), pp. 1–8. IEEE (2021)
11. Kervadec, H., Dolz, J., Tang, M., Granger, E., Boykov, Y., Ayed, I.B.: Constrained-CNN losses for weakly supervised segmentation. Med. Image Anal. **54**, 88–99 (2019)

12. Kipf, T.N., Welling, M.: Semi-supervised classification with graph convolutional networks. arXiv preprint arXiv:1609.02907 (2016)
13. Li, R., Chen, H., Gong, G., Wang, L.: Bladder wall segmentation in MRI images via deep learning and anatomical constraints. In: 2020 42nd Annual International Conference of the IEEE Engineering in Medicine & Biology Society (EMBC), pp. 1629–1632. IEEE (2020)
14. Li, X., Chen, H., Qi, X., Dou, Q., Fu, C.W., Heng, P.A.: H-denseunet: hybrid densely connected unet for liver and tumor segmentation from CT volumes. IEEE Trans. Med. Imaging **37**(12), 2663–2674 (2018)
15. Ma, X., et al.: U-net based deep learning bladder segmentation in CT urography. Med. Phys. **46**(4), 1752–1765 (2019)
16. Mirikharaji, Z., Hamarneh, G.: Star shape prior in fully convolutional networks for skin lesion segmentation. In: Frangi, A.F., Schnabel, J.A., Davatzikos, C., Alberola-López, C., Fichtinger, G. (eds.) MICCAI 2018. LNCS, vol. 11073, pp. 737–745. Springer, Cham (2018). https://doi.org/10.1007/978-3-030-00937-3_84
17. Oda, H., et al.: BESNet: boundary-enhanced segmentation of cells in histopathological images. In: Frangi, A.F., Schnabel, J.A., Davatzikos, C., Alberola-López, C., Fichtinger, G. (eds.) MICCAI 2018. LNCS, vol. 11071, pp. 228–236. Springer, Cham (2018). https://doi.org/10.1007/978-3-030-00934-2_26
18. Oktay, O., et al.: Attention u-net: Learning where to look for the pancreas. arXiv preprint arXiv:1804.03999 (2018)
19. Ronneberger, O., Fischer, P., Brox, T.: U-Net: convolutional networks for biomedical image segmentation. In: Navab, N., Hornegger, J., Wells, W.M., Frangi, A.F. (eds.) MICCAI 2015. LNCS, vol. 9351, pp. 234–241. Springer, Cham (2015). https://doi.org/10.1007/978-3-319-24574-4_28
20. Shkolyar, E., Jia, X., Chang, T.C., Trivedi, D., Mach, K.E., Meng, M.Q.H., Xing, L., Liao, J.C.: Augmented bladder tumor detection using deep learning. Eur. Urol. **76**(6), 714–718 (2019)
21. Xie, Y., Xu, Z., Kankanhalli, M.S., Meel, K.S., Soh, H.: Embedding symbolic knowledge into deep networks. Advances in neural information processing systems 32 (2019)
22. Yan, S., Tai, X.C., Liu, J., Huang, H.Y.: Convexity shape prior for level set-based image segmentation method. IEEE Trans. Image Process. **29**, 7141–7152 (2020)
23. Yue, Q., Luo, X., Ye, Q., Xu, L., Zhuang, X.: Cardiac segmentation from LGE MRI using deep neural network incorporating shape and spatial priors. In: Shen, D., Liu, T., Peters, T.M., Staib, L.H., Essert, C., Zhou, S., Yap, P.-T., Khan, A. (eds.) MICCAI 2019. LNCS, vol. 11765, pp. 559–567. Springer, Cham (2019). https://doi.org/10.1007/978-3-030-32245-8_62
24. Zhang, C., Yue, X., Chen, Y., Lv, Y.: Integrating diagnosis rules into deep neural networks for bladder cancer staging. In: Proceedings of the 29th ACM International Conference on Information & Knowledge Management, pp. 2301–2304 (2020)
25. Zhang, Z., Liu, Q., Wang, Y.: Road extraction by deep residual u-net. IEEE Geosci. Remote Sens. Lett. **15**(5), 749–753 (2018)
26. Zhou, Z., Rahman Siddiquee, M.M., Tajbakhsh, N., Liang, J.: UNet++: a nested U-Net architecture for medical image segmentation. In: Stoyanov, D., Taylor, Z., Carneiro, G., Syeda-Mahmood, T., Martel, A., Maier-Hein, L., Tavares, J.M.R.S., Bradley, A., Papa, J.P., Belagiannis, V., Nascimento, J.C., Lu, Z., Conjeti, S., Moradi, M., Greenspan, H., Madabhushi, A. (eds.) DLMIA/ML-CDS-2018. LNCS, vol. 11045, pp. 3–11. Springer, Cham (2018). https://doi.org/10.1007/978-3-030-00889-5_1

Test-Time Adaptation with Shape Moments for Image Segmentation

Mathilde Bateson[✉], Herve Lombaert, and Ismail Ben Ayed

ETS Montréal, Montreal, Canada
`mathilde.bateson.1@ens.etsmtl.ca`

Abstract. Supervised learning is well-known to fail at generalization under distribution shifts. In typical clinical settings, the source data is inaccessible and the target distribution is represented with a handful of samples: adaptation can only happen at test time on a few (or even a single) subject(s). We investigate test-time *single-subject adaptation* for segmentation, and propose a *shape-guided entropy minimization* objective for tackling this task. During inference for a single testing subject, our loss is minimized with respect to the batch normalization's scale and bias parameters. We show the potential of integrating various shape priors to guide adaptation to plausible solutions, and validate our method in two challenging scenarios: MRI-to-CT adaptation of cardiac segmentation and cross-site adaptation of prostate segmentation. Our approach exhibits substantially better performances than the existing test-time adaptation methods. Even more surprisingly, it fares better than state-of-the-art domain adaptation methods, although it forgoes training on additional target data during adaptation. Our results question the usefulness of training on target data in segmentation adaptation, and points to the substantial effect of shape priors on test-time inference. Our framework can be readily used for integrating various priors and for adapting any segmentation network. The code is publicly available (https://github.com/mathilde-b/TTA).

Keywords: Test-time adaptation · Segmentation · Shape moments · Deep networks · Entropy minimization

1 Introduction

Deep neural networks have achieved state-of-the-art performances in various natural and medical-imaging problems [13]. However, they tend to under-perform when the test-image distribution is different from those seen during training. In medical imaging, this is due to, for instance, variations in imaging modalities and protocols, vendors, machines, clinical sites and subject populations. For semantic segmentation problems, labelling a large number of images for each different target distribution is impractical, time-consuming, and often impossible. To circumvent those impediments, methods learning robust representations with less supervision have triggered interest in medical imaging [5].

L. Wang et al. (Eds.): MICCAI 2022, LNCS 13434, pp. 736–745, 2022.
https://doi.org/10.1007/978-3-031-16440-8_70

This motivates *Domain Adaptation* (DA) methods: DA amounts to adapting a model trained on an annotated source domain to another target domain, with no or minimal new annotations for the latter. Popular strategies involve minimizing the discrepancy between source and target distributions in the feature or output spaces [18,19]; integrating a domain-specific module in the network [6]; translating images from one domain to the other [23]; or integrating a domain-discriminator module and penalizing its success in the loss function [19].

In medical applications, separating the source training and adaptation is critical for privacy and regulatory reasons, as the source and target data may come from different clinical sites. Therefore, it is crucial to develop adaptation methods, which neither assume access to the source data nor modify the pre-training stage. Standard DA methods, such as [6,18,19,23], do not comply with these restrictions. This has recently motivated *Source-Free Domain Adaptation* (SFDA) [3,9], a setting where the source data (neither the images nor the ground-truth masks) is unavailable during the training of the adaptation phase.

Evaluating SFDA methods consists in: (i) adapting on a dedicated training set Tr from the target domain; and (ii) measuring the generalization performance on an unseen test set Te in the target domain. However, emerging and recent *Test-Time Adaptation* (TTA) works, both in learning and vision [4,17,21] as well as in medical imaging [9,20], argue that this is not as useful as adapting directly to the test set Te. In various applications, access to the target distribution might not be possible. This is particularly common in medical image segmentation when only a single target-domain subject is available for test-time inference. In the context of image classification, the authors of [21] showed recently that simple adaptation of batch normalization's scale and bias parameters on a set of test-time samples can deal competitively with domain shifts.

With this context in mind, we propose a simple formulation for source-free and single-subject test-time adaptation of segmentation networks. During inference for a single testing subject, we optimize a loss integrating shape priors and the entropy of predictions with respect to the batch normalization's scale and bias parameters. Unlike the standard SFDA setting, we perform test-time adaptation on each subject separately, and forgo the use of target training set Tr during adaptation. Our setting is most similar to the image classification work in [21], which minimized a label-free entropy loss defined over test-time samples. Building on this entropy loss, we further guide segmentation adaptation with domain-invariant shape priors on the target regions, and show the substantial effect of such shape priors on TTA performances. We report comprehensive experiments and comparisons with state-of-the-art TTA, SFDA and DA methods, which show the effectiveness of our shape-guided entropy minimization in two different adaptation scenarios: cross-modality cardiac segmentation (from MRI to CT) and prostate segmentation in MRI across different sites. Our method exhibits substantially better performances than the existing TTA methods. Surprisingly, it also fares better than various state-of-the-art SFDA and DA methods, although it does not train on source and additional target data during adaptation, but just performs joint inference and adaptation on a single

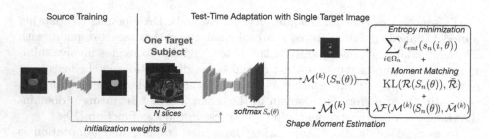

Fig. 1. Overview of our framework for Test-Time Adaptation with Shape Moments: we leverage entropy minimization and shape priors to adapt a segmentation network on a single subject at test-time.

3D data point in the target domain. Our results and ablation studies question the usefulness of training on target set Tr during adaptation and points to the surprising and substantial effect of embedding shape priors during inference on domain-shifted testing data. Our framework can be readily used for integrating various priors and adapting any segmentation network at test times.

2 Method

We consider a set of M source images $I_m : \Omega_s \subset \mathbb{R}^2 \to \mathbb{R}$, $m = 1, \ldots, M$, and denote their ground-truth K-class segmentation for each pixel $i \in \Omega_s$ as a K-simplex vector $\mathbf{y}_m(i) = \left(y_m^{(1)}(i), \ldots, y_m^{(K)}(i)\right) \in \{0, 1\}^K$. For each pixel i, its coordinates in the 2D space are represented by the tuple $\left(u_{(i)}, v_{(i)}\right) \in \mathbb{R}^2$.

Pre-training Phase. The network is first trained on the source domain only, by minimizing the cross-entropy loss with respect to network parameters θ:

$$\min_{\theta} \frac{1}{|\Omega_s|} \sum_{m=1}^{M} \ell\left(\mathbf{y}_m(i), \mathbf{s}_m(i, \theta)\right) \tag{1}$$

where $\mathbf{s}_m(i, \theta) = (s_m^{(1)}(i, \theta), \ldots, s_m^{(K)}(i, \theta)) \in [0, 1]^K$ denotes the predicted softmax probability for class $k \in \{1, \ldots, K\}$.

Shape Moments and Descriptors. Shape moments are well-known in classical computer vision [15], and were recently shown useful in the different context of supervised training [10]. Each moment is parametrized by its orders $p, q \in \mathbb{N}$, and each order represents a different characteristic of the shape. Denote $I_n : \Omega_t \subset \mathbb{R}^2 \to \mathbb{R}$, $n = 1, \ldots, N$ the 2D slices of a subject in the target domain. For a given $p, q \in \mathbb{N}$ and class k, the shape moments of the segmentation prediction of an image I_n can be computed as follows from the softmax matrix $S_n(\theta) = \left(s_n^{(k)}(\theta)\right)_{k=1\ldots K}$:

$$\mu_{p,q}\left(s_n^{(k)}(\theta)\right) = \sum_{i \in \Omega} s_n^{(k)}(i, \theta) u_{(i)}^p v_{(i)}^q$$

Central moments are derived from shape moments to guarantee translation invariance. They are computed as follows:

$$\bar{\mu}_{p,q}\left(\mathbf{s}_n^{(k)}(\theta)\right) = \sum_{i \in \Omega} s_n^k(i,\theta)\left(u_{(i)} - \bar{u}^{(k)}\right)^p \left(v_{(i)} - \bar{v}^{(k)}\right)^q.$$

where $\left(\frac{\mu_{1,0}(s_n^{(k)}(\theta))}{\mu_{0,0}(s_n^{(k)}(\theta))}, \frac{\mu_{0,1}(s_n^{(k)}(\theta))}{\mu_{0,0}(s_n^{(k)}(\theta))}\right)$ are the components of the centroid. We use the vectorized form onwards, e.g. $\mu_{p,q}\left(s_n(\theta)\right) = \left(\mu_{p,q}(s_n^{(1)}(\theta)), \ldots, \mu_{p,q}(s_n^{(K)}(\theta))\right)^\top$. Building from these definitions, we obtain 2D shape moments from the network predictions. We then derive the shape descriptors $\mathcal{R}, \mathcal{C}, \mathcal{D}$ defined in Table 1, which respectively inform on the size, position, and compactness of a shape.

Table 1. Examples of shape descriptors based on softmax predictions.

Shape Descriptor	Definition
Class-Ratio	$\mathcal{R}(s) := \frac{1}{|\Omega_t|}\mu_{0,0}(s)$
Centroid	$\mathcal{C}(s) := \left(\frac{\mu_{1,0}(s)}{\mu_{0,0}(s)}, \frac{\mu_{0,1}(s)}{\mu_{0,0}(s)}\right)$
Distance to Centroid	$\mathcal{D}(s) := \left(\sqrt[2]{\frac{\bar{\mu}_{2,0}(s)}{\mu_{0,0}(s)}}, \sqrt[2]{\frac{\bar{\mu}_{0,2}(s)}{\mu_{0,0}(s)}}\right)$

Test-Time Adaptation and Inference with Shape-Prior Constraints. Given a single new subject in the target domain composed of N 2D slices, $I_n : \Omega_t \subset \mathbb{R}^2 \to \mathbb{R}$, $n = 1, \ldots, N$, the first loss term in our adaptation phase is derived from [21], to encourage high confidence in the softmax predictions, by minimizing their weighted Shannon entropy: $\ell_{ent}(s_n(i,\theta)) = -\sum_k \nu_k s_n^k(i,\theta) \log s_n^k(i,\theta)$, where $\nu_k, k = 1 \ldots K$, are class weights added to mitigate imbalanced class-ratios.

Ideally, to guide adaptation, for each slice I_n, we would penalize the deviations between the shape descriptors of the softmax predictions $S_n(\theta)$ and those corresponding to the ground truth $\mathbf{y_n}$. As the ground-truth labels are unavailable, instead, we estimate the shape descriptors using the predictions from the whole subject $\{S_n(\theta), n = 1, \ldots, N\}$, which we denote respectively $\bar{\mathcal{C}}, \bar{\mathcal{D}}$.

The first shape moment we leverage is the simplest: a zero-order class-ratio $\mathcal{R}$. Seeing these class ratios as distributions, we integrate a KL divergence with the Shannon entropy:

$$\mathcal{L}_{TTAS}(\theta) = \sum_n \frac{1}{|\Omega_n|} \sum_{i \in \Omega_t} \ell_{ent}(s_n(i,\theta)) + \text{KL}(\mathcal{R}(S_n(\theta)), \bar{\mathcal{R}}). \tag{2}$$

It is worth noting that, unlike [2], which used a loss of the form in Eq. (2) for training on target data, here we use this term for inference on a test subject, as a part of our overall shape-based objective. Additionally, we integrate the centroid

$(\mathcal{M} = \mathcal{C})$ and the distance to centroid $(\mathcal{M} = \mathcal{D})$ to further guide adaptation to plausible solutions:

$$\min_{\theta} \quad \mathcal{L}_{TTAS}(\theta)$$
$$\text{s.t.} \quad \left| \mathcal{M}^{(k)}(S_n(\theta)) - \bar{\mathcal{M}}^{(k)} \right| \leq 0.1, \quad k = \{2, \ldots, K\}, n = \{1, \ldots, N\}. \tag{3}$$

Imposing such hard constraints is typically handled through the minimization of the Lagrangian dual in standard convex-optimization. As this is computationally intractable in deep networks, inequality constraints such as Eq. (3) are typically relaxed to soft penalties [7,8,11]. Therefore, we experiment with the integration of $\mathcal{C}$ and $\mathcal{D}$ through a quadratic penalty, leading to the following unconstrained objectives for joint test-time adaptation and inference:

$$\sum_n \frac{1}{|\Omega_t|} \sum_{i \in \Omega_n} \ell_{ent}(\mathbf{s}_n(i, \theta)) + \mathrm{KL}(\mathcal{R}(S_n(\theta)), \bar{\mathcal{R}}) + \lambda \mathcal{F}(\mathcal{M}(S_n(\theta)), \bar{\mathcal{M}}), \tag{4}$$

where $\mathcal{F}$ is a quadratic penalty function corresponding to the relaxation of Eq. (3): $\mathcal{F}(m_1, m_2) = [m_1 - 0.9m_2]_+^2 + [1.1m_2 - m_1]_+^2$ and $[m]_+ = \max(0, m)$, with λ denoting a weighting hyper-parameter. Following recent TTA methods [9,21], we only optimize for the scale and bias parameters of batch normalization layers while the rest of the network is frozen. Figure 1 shows the overview of the proposed framework.

3 Experiments

3.1 Test-time Adaptation with Shape Descriptors

Heart Application. We employ the 2017 Multi-Modality Whole Heart Segmentation (MMWHS) Challenge dataset for cardiac segmentation [24]. The dataset consists of 20 MRI (source domain) and 20 CT volumes (target domain) of non-overlapping subjects, with their manual annotations of four cardiac structures: the Ascending Aorta (AA), the Left Atrium (LA), the Left Ventricle (LV) and the Myocardium (MYO). We employ the pre-processed data provided by [6]. The scans were normalized as zero mean and unit variance, and data augmentation based on affine transformations was performed. For the domain adaptation benchmark methods (DA and SFDA), we use the data split in [6]: 14 subjects for training, 2 for validation, and 4 for testing. Each subject has $N = 256$ slices.

Prostate Application. We employ the dataset from the publicly available NCI-ISBI 2013 Challenge[1]. It is composed of manually annotated T2-weighted MRI from two different sites: 30 samples from Boston Medical Center (source domain), and 30 samples from Radboud University Medical Center (target domain). For the DA and SFDA benchmark methods, 19 scans were used for training, one

---

[1] https://wiki.cancerimagingarchive.net.

for validation, and 10 scans for testing. We used the pre-processed dataset from [14], who resized each sample to 384×384 in axial plane, and normalized it to zero mean and unit variance. We employed data augmentation based on affine transformations on the source domain. Each subject has $N \in [15, 24]$ slices.

Benchmark Methods. Our first model denoted $TTAS_{\mathcal{RC}}$ constrains the class-ratio $\mathcal{R}$ and the centroid $\mathcal{C}$ using Eq. (4); similarly, $TTAS_{\mathcal{RD}}$ constrains $\mathcal{R}$ and the distance-to-centroid $\mathcal{D}$. We compare to two TTA methods: the method in [9], denoted $TTDAE$, where an auxiliary branch is used to denoise segmentation, and $Tent$ [21], which is based on the following loss: $\min_\theta \sum_n \sum_{i \in \Omega_n} \ell_{ent}(\mathbf{s}_n(i, \theta))$. Note that $Tent$ corresponds to performing an ablation of both shape moments terms in our loss. As an additional ablation study, $TTAS_{\mathcal{R}}$ is trained with the class-ratio matching loss in Eq. (2) only. We also compared to two DA methods based on class-ratio matching, CDA [1], and $CurDA$ [22], and to the recent source-free domain adaptation ($SFDA$) method $AdaMI$ in [2]. A model trained on the source only, $NoAdap$, was used as a lower bound. A model trained on the target domain with the cross-entropy loss, $Oracle$, served as an upper bound.

Estimating the Shape Descriptors. For the estimation of the class-ratio $\bar{\mathcal{R}}$, we employed the coarse estimation in [1], which is derived from anatomical knowledge available in the clinical literature. For $\mathcal{M} \in \{\mathcal{C}, \mathcal{D}\}$, we estimate the target shape descriptor from the network prediction masks $\hat{\mathbf{y}}_\mathbf{n}$ after each epoch:
$$\bar{\mathcal{M}}^{(k)} = \frac{1}{|V^k|} \sum_{v \in V^k} v, \text{ with } V^k = \{\mathcal{M}^{(k)}(\hat{\mathbf{y}}_\mathbf{n}) \text{ if } \mathcal{R}^k(\hat{\mathbf{y}}_\mathbf{n}) > \epsilon^k, n = 1 \cdots N\}.$$
Note that, for a fair comparison, we used exactly the same class-ratio priors and weak supervision employed in the benchmarks methods in [1,2,22]. Weak supervision takes the form of simple image-level tags by setting $\bar{\mathcal{R}}^{(k)} = \mathbf{0}$ and $\lambda = 0$ for the target images that do not contain structure k.

Training and Implementation Details. For all methods, the segmentation network employed was UNet [16]. A model trained on the source data with Eq. (1) for 150 epochs was used as initialization. Then, for TTA models, adaptation is performed on each test subject independently, without target training. Our model was initialized with Eq. (2) for 150 epochs, after which the additional shape constraint was added using Eq. (4) for 200 epochs. As there is no learning and validation set in the target domain, the hyper-parameters are set following those in the source training, and are fixed across experiments: we trained with the Adam optimizer [12], a batch size of $min(N, 22)$, an initial learning rate of 5×10^{-4}, a learning rate decay of 0.9 every 20 epochs, and a weight decay of 10^{-4}. The weights ν_k are calculated as: $\nu_k = \frac{\bar{\mathcal{R}}_k^{-1}}{\sum_k \bar{\mathcal{R}}_k^{-1}}$. We set $\lambda = 1 \times 10^{-4}$.

Evaluation. The 3D Dice similarity coefficient (DSC) and the 3D Average Surface distance (ASD) were used as evaluation metrics in our experiments.

3.2   Results and Discussion

Table 2 and Table 3 report quantitative metrics for the heart and prostate respectively. Among DA methods, the source-free $AdaMI$ achieves the best DSC

Table 2. Test-time metrics on the cardiac dataset, for our method and various *Domain Adaptation* (DA), *Source Free Domain Adaptation* (SFDA) and *Test Time Adaptation* (TTA) methods.

Methods	DA	SFDA	TTA	DSC (%)					ASD (vox)				
				AA	LA	LV	Myo	Mean	AA	LA	LV	Myo	Mean
NoAdap (lower b.)				49.8	62.0	21.1	22.1	38.8	19.8	13.0	13.3	12.4	14.6
Oracle (upper b.)				91.9	88.3	91.0	85.8	89.2	3.1	3.4	3.6	2.2	3.0
CurDA [22]	✓	×	×	79.0	77.9	64.4	61.3	70.7	6.5	7.6	7.2	9.1	7.6
CDA [1]	✓	×	×	77.3	72.8	73.7	61.9	71.4	**4.1**	6.3	6.6	6.6	5.9
AdaMI [2]	×	✓	×	83.1	78.2	74.5	66.8	75.7	5.6	**4.2**	**5.7**	6.9	5.6
TTDAE [9]	×	×	✓	59.8	26.4	32.3	44.4	40.7	15.1	11.7	13.6	11.3	12.9
Tent [21]	×	×	✓	55.4	33.4	63.0	41.1	48.2	18.0	8.7	8.1	10.1	11.2
Proposed Method													
TTAS$_{\mathcal{R}e}$ (Ours)	×	×	✓	**85.1**	**82.6**	**79.3**	**73.2**	**80.0**	5.6	4.3	6.1	**5.3**	**5.3**
TTAS$_{\mathcal{R}\mathcal{D}}$ (Ours)	×	×	✓	82.3	78.9	76.1	68.4	76.5	4.0	5.8	6.1	5.7	5.4
Ablation study													
TTAS$_{\mathcal{R}}$	×	×	✓	78.9	77.7	74.8	65.3	74.2	5.2	4.9	7.0	7.6	6.2

improvement over the lower baseline *NoAdap*, with a mean DSC of 75.7% (cardiac) and 79.5% (prostate). Surprisingly though, in both applications, our method $TTAS_{\mathcal{R}\mathcal{D}}$ yields better scores: 76.5% DSC, 5.4 vox. ASD (cardiac) and 79.5% DSC, 3.9 vox. ASD (prostate); while $TTAS_{\mathcal{R}e}$ achieves the best DSC across methods: 80.0% DSC and 5.3 vox. ASD (cardiac), 80.2% DSC and 3.79 ASD vox. (prostate). Finally, comparing to the TTA methods, both $TTAS_{\mathcal{R}e}$ and $TTAS_{\mathcal{R}\mathcal{D}}$ widely outperform $TTADAE$, which yields 40.7% DSC, 12.9 vox. ASD (cardiac) and 73.2% DSC, 5.80 vox. ASD (prostate), and *Tent*, which

Table 3. Test-time metrics on the prostate dataset.

Methods	DA	SFDA	TTA	DSC (%)	ASD (vox)
NoAdap (lower bound)				67.2	10.60
Oracle (upper bound)				88.9	1.88
CurDA [22]	✓	×	×	76.3	3.93
CDA [1]	✓	×	×	77.9	**3.28**
AdaMI [2]	×	✓	×	79.5	3.92
TTDAE [9]	×	×	✓	73.2	5.80
Tent [21]	×	×	✓	68.7	5.87
Proposed Method					
TTAS$_{\mathcal{R}e}$ (Ours)	×	×	✓	**80.2**	3.79
TTAS$_{\mathcal{R}\mathcal{D}}$ (Ours)	×	×	✓	79.5	3.90
Ablation study					
TTAS$_{\mathcal{R}}$ (Ours)	×	×	✓	75.3	5.06

reaches 48.2% DSC, 11.2 vox. ASD (cardiac) and 68.7% DSC, 5.87 vox. ASD (prostate).

Qualitative segmentations are depicted in Fig. 2. These visuals results confirm that without adaptation, a model trained only on source data cannot properly segment the structures on the target images. The segmentation masks obtained using the TTA formulations $Tent$ [21], $TTADAE$ [9] only show little improvement. Both methods are unable to recover existing structures when the initialization $NoAdap$ fails to detect them (see fourth and fifth row, Fig. 2). On the contrary, those produced from our degraded model $TTAS_{\mathcal{R}}$ show more regular edges and is closer to the ground truth. However, the improvement over $TTAS_{\mathcal{R}}$ obtained by our two models $TTAS_{\mathcal{RC}}$, $TTAS_{\mathcal{RD}}$ is remarkable regarding the shape and position of each structures: the prediction masks show better centroid position (first row, Fig. 2, see LA and LV) and better compactness (third, fourth, fifth row, Fig. 2).

Image Ground Truth No Adap TTADAE [8] Tent [20] $TTAS_{\mathcal{R}}$ $TTAS_{\mathcal{RC}}$ $TTAS_{\mathcal{RD}}$
(ours_degraded) (ours) (ours)

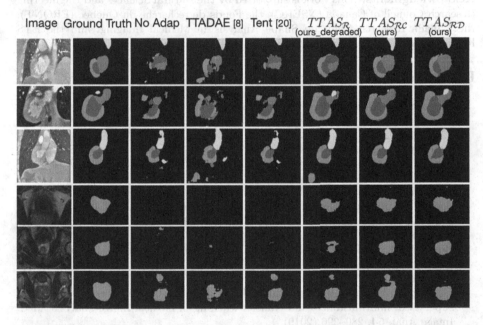

Fig. 2. Qualitative performance on cardiac images (top) and prostate images (bottom): examples of the segmentations achieved by our formulation ($TTAS_{\mathcal{RC}}, TTAS_{\mathcal{RD}}$), and benchmark TTA models. The cardiac structures of MYO, LA, LV and AA are depicted in blue, red, green and yellow respectively. (Color figure online)

4   Conclusion

In this paper, we proposed a simple formulation for *single-subject* test-time adaptation (TTA), which does not need access to the source data, nor the availability of a target training data. Our approach performs inference on a test subject by minimizing the entropy of predictions and a class-ratio prior over batchnorm parameters. To further guide adaptation, we integrate shape priors through penalty constraints. We validate our method on two challenging tasks, the MRI-to-CT adaptation of cardiac segmentation and the cross-site adaptation of prostate segmentation. Our formulation achieved better performances than state-of-the-art TTA methods, with a 31.8% (resp. 7.0%) DSC improvement on cardiac and prostate images respectively. Surprisingly, it also fares better than various state-of-the-art DA and SFDA methods. These results highlight the effectiveness of shape priors on test-time inference, and question the usefulness of training on target data in segmentation adaptation. Future work will involve the introduction of higher-order shape moments, as well as the integration of multiple shapes moments in the adaptation loss. Our test-time adaptation framework is straightforward to use with any segmentation network architecture.

Acknowledgments. This work is supported by the Natural Sciences and Engineering Research Council of Canada (NSERC), the Fonds de recherche du Quebec (FRQNT), the Canada Research Chair on Shape Analysis in Medical Imaging, and the ETS Research Chair on Artificial Intelligence in Medical Imaging.

References

1. Bateson, M., Dolz, J., Kervadec, H., Lombaert, H., Ben Ayed, I.: Constrained domain adaptation for image segmentation. IEEE Trans. Med. Imaging **40**(7), 326–334 (2021)
2. Bateson, M., Dolz, J., Kervadec, H., Lombaert, H., Ben Ayed, I.: Source-free domain adaptation for image segmentation (2021). https://arxiv.org/abs/2108. 03152
3. Bateson, M., Kervadec, H., Dolz, J., Lombaert, H., Ben Ayed, I.: Source-relaxed domain adaptation for image segmentation. In: Martel, A.L., et al. (eds.) MICCAI 2020. LNCS, vol. 12261, pp. 490–499. Springer, Cham (2020). https://doi.org/10. 1007/978-3-030-59710-8_48
4. Boudiaf, M., Mueller, R., Ben Ayed, I., Bertinetto, L.: Parameter-free online test-time adaptation. In: IEEE/CVF Conference on Computer Vision and Pattern Recognition (CVPR) (2022)
5. Cheplygina, V., de Bruijne, M., Pluim, J.P.W.: Not-so-supervised: a survey of semi-supervised, multi-instance, and transfer learning in medical image analysis. Med. Image Anal. **54**, 280–296 (2019)
6. Dou, Q., et al.: Pnp-adanet: plug-and-play adversarial domain adaptation network at unpaired cross-modality cardiac segmentation. IEEE Access **7**, 99065–99076 (2019)
7. He, F.S., Liu, Y., Schwing, A.G., Peng, J.: Learning to play in a day: faster deep reinforcement learning by optimality tightening. In: International Conference on Learning Representations (ICLR) (2017)
8. Jia, Z., Huang, X., Chang, E.I., Xu, Y.: Constrained deep weak supervision for histopathology image segmentation. IEEE Trans. Med. Imaging **36**(11), 2376–2388 (2017)
9. Karani, N., Erdil, E., Chaitanya, K., Konukoglu, E.: Test-time adaptable neural networks for robust medical image segmentation. Med. Image Anal. **68**, 101907 (2021)

10. Kervadec, H., Bahig, H., Létourneau-Guillon, L., Dolz, J., Ben Ayed, I.: Beyond pixel-wise supervision for segmentation: a few global shape descriptors might be surprisingly good! In: Medical Imaging with Deep Learning (MIDL) (2021)
11. Kervadec, H., Dolz, J., Tang, M., Granger, E., Boykov, Y., Ben Ayed, I.: Constrained-CNN losses for weakly supervised segmentation. Med. Image Anal. **54**, 88–99 (2019)
12. Kingma, D., Ba, J.: Adam: A method for stochastic optimization. In: International Conference on Learning Representations (ICLR) (2014)
13. Litjens, G., et al.: A survey on deep learning in medical image analysis. Med. Image Anal. **42**, 60–88 (2017)
14. Liu, Q., Dou, Q., Heng, P.-A.: Shape-aware meta-learning for generalizing prostate MRI segmentation to unseen domains. In: Martel, A.L., et al. (eds.) MICCAI 2020. LNCS, vol. 12262, pp. 475–485. Springer, Cham (2020). https://doi.org/10.1007/978-3-030-59713-9_46
15. Nosrati, M.S., Hamarneh, G.: Incorporating prior knowledge in medical image segmentation: a survey. arXiv preprint arXiv:1607.01092 (2016)
16. Ronneberger, O., Fischer, P., Brox, T.: U-Net: convolutional networks for biomedical image segmentation. In: Navab, N., Hornegger, J., Wells, W.M., Frangi, A.F. (eds.) MICCAI 2015. LNCS, vol. 9351, pp. 234–241. Springer, Cham (2015). https://doi.org/10.1007/978-3-319-24574-4_28
17. Sun, Y., Wang, X., Liu, Z., Miller, J., Efros, A., Hardt, M.: Test-time training with self-supervision for generalization under distribution shifts. In: International Conference on Machine Learning (ICML) (2020)
18. Tsai, Y.H., et al.: Learning to adapt structured output space for semantic segmentation. In: IEEE/CVF Conference on Computer Vision and Pattern Recognition (CVPR) (2018)
19. Tzeng, E., Hoffman, J., Saenko, K., Darrell, T.: Adversarial discriminative domain adaptation. In: IEEE/CVF Conference on Computer Vision and Pattern Recognition (CVPR) (2017)
20. Varsavsky, T., Orbes-Arteaga, M., Sudre, C.H., Graham, M.S., Nachev, P., Cardoso, M.J.: Test-time unsupervised domain adaptation. In: Martel, A.L., et al. (eds.) MICCAI 2020. LNCS, vol. 12261, pp. 428–436. Springer, Cham (2020). https://doi.org/10.1007/978-3-030-59710-8_42
21. Wang, D., Shelhamer, E., Liu, S., Olshausen, B., Darrell, T.: Tent: fully test-time adaptation by entropy minimization. In: International Conference on Learning Representations (ICLR) (2021)
22. Zhang, Y., David, P., Foroosh, H., Gong, B.: A curriculum domain adaptation approach to the semantic segmentation of urban scenes. IEEE Trans. Pattern Anal. Mach. Intell. **42**, 1823–1841 (2020)
23. Zhu, J., Park, T., Isola, P., Efros, A.A.: Unpaired image-to-image translation using cycle-consistent adversarial networks. In: IEEE/CVF Conference on Computer Vision (ICCV) (2017)
24. Zhuang, X., et al.: Evaluation of algorithms for multi-modality whole heart segmentation: an open-access grand challenge. Med. Image Anal. **58**, 101537 (2019)

Correction to: Pose-Based Tremor Classification for Parkinson's Disease Diagnosis from Video

Haozheng Zhang⬤, Edmond S. L. Ho⬤, Francis Xiatian Zhang⬤, and Hubert P. H. Shum⬤

Correction to:
Chapter 47 in: L. Wang et al. (Eds.): *Medical Image Computing and Computer Assisted Intervention – MICCAI 2022,* **LNCS 13434,**
https://doi.org/10.1007/978-3-031-16440-8_47

In an older version of this paper, the name of the third author was incorrect. It has now been updated.

The updated version of this chapter can be found at
https://doi.org/10.1007/978-3-031-16440-8_47

Author Index

Printed in the United States
by Baker & Taylor Publisher Services